HALSBURY'S
Laws of England

FOURTH EDITION
REISSUE

Volume 2

HALSBURY'S
Laws of England

FOURTH EDITION
REISSUE

LORD HAILSHAM OF ST. MARYLEBONE

Lord High Chancellor of Great Britain
1970–74 and 1979–87

Volume 2

BUTTERWORTHS

LONDON   1991

UNITED KINGDOM	Butterworth & Co (Publishers) Ltd 88 Kingsway, **London** WC2B 6AB and 4 Hill Street, **Edinburgh** EH2 3JZ
AUSTRALIA	Butterworths Pty Ltd, **Sydney, Melbourne, Brisbane, Adelaide, Perth, Canberra** and **Hobart**
CANADA	Butterworths Canada Ltd, **Toronto** and **Vancouver**
IRELAND	Butterworth (Ireland) Ltd, **Dublin**
MALAYSIA	Malayan Law Journal Sdn Bhd, **Kuala Lumpur**
NEW ZEALAND	Butterworths of New Zealand Ltd, **Wellington** and **Auckland**
PUERTO RICO	Equity de Puerto Rico, Inc, **Hato Rey**
SINGAPORE	Malayan Law Journal Pte Ltd, **Singapore**
USA	Butterworth Legal Publishers, **Austin**, Texas; **Boston**, Massachusetts; **Clearwater**, Florida (D & S Publishers); **Orford**, New Hampshire (Equity Publishing); **St Paul**, Minnesota; and **Seattle**, Washington

FIRST EDITION

Published in 31 volumes between 1907 and 1917 under the Editorship of the Rt. Hon. the Earl of Halsbury, Lord High Chancellor of Great Britain, 1885–86, 1886–92 and 1895–1905

SECOND EDITION

Published in 37 volumes between 1931 and 1942 under the Editorship of the Rt. Hon. the Viscount Hailsham, Lord High Chancellor of Great Britain, 1928–29 and 1935–38

THIRD EDITION

Published in 43 volumes between 1952 and 1964 under the Editorship of the Rt. Hon. the Viscount Simonds, Lord High Chancellor of Great Britain, 1951–54

FOURTH EDITION

Published in 56 volumes between 1973 and 1987 under the Editorship of the Rt. Hon. Lord Hailsham of St. Marylebone, Lord High Chancellor of Great Britain, 1970–74 and 1979–87

ISBN (complete set, standard binding) 0 406 03400 1
(this volume, standard binding) 0 406 03475 3

Typeset by Thomson Litho Ltd, East Kilbride, Scotland
Printed and bound in Great Britain by
The Bath Press, Avon

Editor in Chief

Editor

DAVID HAY, M.A., LL.M.
OF THE INNER TEMPLE, BARRISTER

Managing Editor (Commissioning)

DEBORAH SAUNDERS, B.A.
OF GRAY'S INN, BARRISTER

Senior Sub-Editor

SIMON HETHERINGTON, LL.B.

Sub-Editor

WILLIAM ENGLAND, LL.B.

Administrative Manager

SARAH L. HORNSBY, Dip.Pub.

Indexer

B. BURKE, B.Sc.

The Titles in Volume 2 have been contributed by the following:

ALLOTMENTS AND SMALLHOLDINGS	ANGELA SYDENHAM M.A., LL.B., a Solicitor of the Supreme Court; Chief Legal Adviser, Country Landowners Association
ANIMALS	T. G. FIELD-FISHER Esq., T.D., M.A., one of Her Majesty's Counsel, a Recorder
	J. J. G. SHARPE Esq., B.A., of the Inner Temple, Barrister
ARBITRATION	DAVID DONALDSON Esq., M.A., Dr.Jur., one of Her Majesty's Counsel
	ANDREW GREEN Esq., LL.B., of the Inner Temple, Barrister
	ADAM LEWIS Esq., B.A., of Gray's Inn, Barrister
	HUGO PAGE Esq., M.A., of the Inner Temple, Barrister
AUCTION	FRANKLIN MEISEL Esq., LL.B., of the Middle Temple, Barrister; Director of Training and Research, Eversheds
AVIATION	PETER MARTIN Esq., LL.B., F.R.Ae.S., a Solicitor of the Supreme Court; Partner in Frere Cholmeley; Visiting Professor in Aerospace Law, University College, London
	J. D. McCLEAN Esq., D.C.L., of Gray's Inn, Barrister; Pro-Vice-Chancellor and Professor of Law, University of Sheffield
	ELIZABETH DE MONTLAUR MARTIN, Avocat à la Cour d'Appel de Paris
BAILMENT	NORMAN PALMER Esq., B.C.L., M.A., of Gray's Inn, Barrister; Rowe and Maw Professor of Commercial Law, University College, London
	ALISON POWELL LL.B., of the Inner Temple, Barrister

The law stated in this volume is in general that in force on 3 June 1991.

TABLE OF CONTENTS

ARBITRATION

PAGE

AUCTION

AVIATION

BAILMENT

REFERENCES AND ABBREVIATIONS

ACT.	Australian Capital Territory
A-G	Attorney General
Adv-Gen	Advocate General
affd.	affirmed
Alta.	Alberta
App	Appendix
art	article
Aust	Australia
B.	Baron
BC	British Columbia
BFSP	British and Foreign State Papers
BS.	British Standard
Bk.	Book
C.	Command Paper (of a series published before 1900)
c	chapter number of an Act
CA	Court of Appeal
CAA.	Civil Aviation Authority
CA in Ch.	Court of Appeal in Chancery
CB	Chief Baron
CCA.	Court of Criminal Appeal
CC Fees Order 1982	County Court Fees Order 1982 (SI 1982/1706) as subsequently amended (see the current County Court Practice)
CCR.	County Court Rules 1981 (SI 1981/1687) as subsequently amended (see the current County Court Practice)
CCR.	Court for Crown Cases Reserved
CCT.	Common Customs Tariff
C-MAC.	Courts-Martial Appeal Court
Can.	Canada
Cd.	Command Paper (of the series published 1900–18)
Cf	compare
ch	chapter
cl.	clause
Cm	Command Paper (of the series published 1986 to date)
Cmd.	Command Paper (of the series published 1919–56)
Cmnd.	Command Paper (of the series published 1956–86)
Commons Journals	Journals of the House of Commons
Court Forms (2nd Edn).	Atkin's Encyclopaedia of Court Forms in Civil Proceedings, 2nd Edn. See note 2, p 17 post
Court Funds Rules 1987	Court Funds Rules 1987 (SI 1987/821) as subsequently amended (see the current Supreme Court Practice and County Court Practice)

DC	Divisional Court
Digest (Reissue)	The Digest Reissue Volumes (Green Band). Continuation Volume D includes cases reported 1971–75; Continuation Volume E includes cases reported 1976–79; Continuation Volume F includes cases reported 1980–83; Continuation Volume G includes cases reported 1984–85; Continuation Volume H includes cases reported 1986–90
EAT	Employment Appeal Tribunal
EC	European Communities
ECJ	Court of Justice of the European Communities
ECSC	European Coal and Steel Community
EEC	European Economic Community
ECt HR	European Court of Human Rights
Edn	Edition
EFTA	European Free Trade Association
Euratom	European Atomic Energy Community
Ex Ch	Court of Exchequer Chamber
FAI	Fédération Aéronautique Internationale
FC	Full Court
Fed	Federal
Forms & Precedents (5th Edn) . . .	Encyclopaedia of Forms and Precedents other than Court Forms, 5th Edn. See note 2, p 17 post
HC	High Court
HL	House of Lords
H of C	House of Commons
Halsbury's Statutes (4th Edn)	Halsbury's Statutes of England, 4th Edn. See note 2, p 17 post
IATA	International Air Transport Association
ICAO	International Civil Aviation Organisation
ILO	International Labour Organisation
IMF	International Monetary Fund
Ir	Ireland
J	Justice
JA	Judge of Appeal
LA	Lord Advocate
LC	Lord Chancellor
LCJ	Lord Chief Justice
LJ	Lord Justice of Appeal
LoN	League of Nations
MR	Master of the Rolls
Man	Manitoba
n	note
NB	New Brunswick
NI	Northern Ireland
NIRC	National Industrial Relations Court
NS	Nova Scotia
NSW	New South Wales
NZ	New Zealand
Nfld	Newfoundland
OJ	The Official Journal of the European Communities published by the Office for Official Publications of the European Communities

Ont.	Ontario
Ord.	Order
P	President
PC	Judicial Committee of the Privy Council
PEI	Prince Edward Island
Qld.	Queensland
Que	Quebec
r	rule
RPC	Restrictive Practices Court
RSC	Rules of the Supreme Court 1965 (SI 1965/1776) as subsequently amended (see the current Supreme Court Practice)
reg	regulation
Res	Resolution
revsd.	reversed
s	section
SA.	South Africa
S Aust.	South Australia
S&B AvR	Shawcross & Beaumont Aviation Reports
SC.	Supreme Court
SC Fees Order 1980	Supreme Court Fees Order 1980 (SI 1980/821) as subsequently amended (see the current Supreme Court Practice)
SI	Statutory Instruments published by authority
SR & O	Statutory Rules and Orders published by authority
SR & O Rev 1904.	Revised Edition comprising all Public and General Statutory Rules and Orders in force on 31 December 1903
SR & O Rev 1948.	Revised Edition comprising all Public and General Statutory Rules and Orders and Statutory Instruments in force on 31 December 1948
SRNI	Statutory Rules of Northern Ireland
Sask	Saskatchewan
Sch	Schedule
Sess.	Session
TS.	Treaty Series
Tas	Tasmania
ULFIS	Uniform Law on the International Sale of Goods
UN.	United Nations
V-C	Vice-Chancellor
Vict.	Victoria
W Aust.	Western Australia

NOTE 1. The abbreviations of law reports and other sources used in this work are listed in vol 1 (1) (Reissue) at p 15 et seq.

NOTE 2. Where references are made to other publications, the volume number precedes and the page number follows the name of the publication; eg the reference '12 Forms & Precedents (5th Edn) 44' refers to volume 12 of the Encyclopaedia of Forms and Precedents, page 44.

NOTE 3. An English statute is cited by short title or, where there is no short title, by regnal year and chapter number together with the name by which it is commonly known or a description of its subject matter and date. In the case of a foreign statute, the mode of citation generally follows the style of citation in use in the country concerned with the addition, where necessary, of the name of the country in parentheses.

NOTE 4. A statutory instrument is cited by short title, if any, followed by the year and number, or, if unnumbered, the date.

TABLE OF STATUTES

D

TABLE OF STATUTORY INSTRUMENTS

TABLE OF TREATIES, CONVENTIONS etc.

TABLE OF CASES

C

PARA

D

PARA

H

PARA

PARA

K

PARA

O

PARA

PARA

ALLOTMENTS AND SMALLHOLDINGS

4. COTTAGE HOLDINGS

1. INTRODUCTION

(1) ALLOTMENTS

1. Meaning of 'allotment'. The term 'allotment' is used in this title mainly as referring to lands which are held by local authorities under the Allotments Acts 1908 to 1950[1] for the purpose of providing persons resident in their areas with small plots of land for cultivation[2]. Whilst there is no comprehensive statutory definition of 'allotment' for the purposes of those Acts, a field garden[3] and an allotment garden[4] are generally allotments. There are no general statutory limits on the size of an allotment or requirements as to its use, though definitions for the purposes of particular enactments sometimes prescribe these; for example, 'allotment' in the Allotments Act 1925 means an allotment garden as defined below or any parcel of land not more than five acres in extent cultivated or intended to be cultivated as a garden or farm or partly as a garden and partly as a farm[5], and for the purpose of certain provisions relating to compensation on the termination of a tenancy[6] 'allotment' means any parcel of land, whether attached to a cottage or not, of not more than two acres in extent, held by a tenant under a landlord and cultivated as a farm or a garden or partly as a garden and partly as a farm[7].

'Allotment garden' means an allotment not exceeding one quarter of an acre[8] in extent which is wholly or mainly cultivated by the occupier for the production of vegetable or fruit crops for consumption by himself or his family[9].

1   These are the provisions relating to allotments in the Small Holdings and Allotments Act 1908 and in the Land Settlement (Facilities) Act 1919; the Allotments Act 1922; the Allotments Act 1925; the Small Holdings and Allotments Act 1926; the Agricultural Land (Utilisation) Act 1931 Pt II (the allotment provisions being ss 13–20: see s 20 (2)); and the Allotments Act 1950. The report of the Departmental Committee of Inquiry into Allotments 1969 (Cmnd 4166) recommended that existing legislation be repealed and a single new Act be passed (paras 661–669 of that report).

2   'Cultivation' includes horticulture and the use of land for any purpose of husbandry, including keeping or breeding livestock, poultry or bees, and growing fruit, vegetables and the like: Small Holdings and Allotments Act 1908 s 61 (1).

3   See ibid s 61 (1). For the meaning of 'field garden' see para 65 note 1 post.

4   See the Allotments Act 1925 s 1. For the meaning of 'allotment garden' see text to notes 8, 9 infra.

5   Ibid s 1. The definition is subject to any contrary requirement of the context.

6   See the Allotments Act 1922 s 3; and para 59 post.

7   Ibid s 3 (7): the definition is for the purposes of that section only. Such an allotment does not include a plot occupied by a seedsman for business purposes, but is a plot cultivated for food or pleasure: *Cooper v Pearse* [1896] 1 QB 562.

8   The original definition referred to 'forty poles'. The pole (30¼ square yards) is no longer recognised as a unit of area.

9   Allotments Act 1922 s 22 (1), applied by the Allotments Act 1925 s 1 and the Allotments Act 1950 s 14 (1); Agriculture Act 1947 s 109 (3) (amended by the Agriculture Act 1947 (Amendment) Regulations 1978, SI 1978/446, substituting '0.10 hectare'). Local authorities' obligations to provide allotments are now confined to providing allotment gardens: see para 8 post. The report of the Departmental Committee of Inquiry 1969 (Cmnd 4166) recommended that allotment gardens be termed 'leisure gardens' and suggested a definition (paras 672–681 of that report). For an account of the landscape and culture of the allotment garden see David Crouch and Colin Ward *The Allotment* (1988).

2. Parochial and other allotments. There are some allotments vested in bodies other than the local authorities which may be classed generally as parochial allotments, and which were provided mainly during the nineteenth century under certain Poor Law and Inclosure Acts[1].

In addition, a large acreage of land privately owned is let for use as allotments; these are quite free from any control by local authorities under the powers conferred by the Allotments Acts 1908 to 1950. Whilst the statutory provisions relating to the determination of tenancies and compensation[2] apply to such land it is otherwise governed by the general law relating to the letting of land, and is not further discussed in this title. It is nevertheless important to note that about one quarter of the allotment plots in England and Wales were privately owned in 1969[3].

1   See generally para 63 post. As to allotments for non-agricultural purposes see COMMONS.

2   See para 43 et seq post.

3   Report of Departmental Committee of Inquiry into Allotments 1969 (Cmnd 4166) para 320.

3. Application of other legislation. An allotment is agricultural land[1] for the purposes of the Agriculture Act 1947 if it comprises land used for agriculture[2], and is so used for the purposes of trade or business or is designated as agricultural land by the Minister of Agriculture, Fisheries and Food or, in Wales, the Secretary of State for Wales[3]. No such designation may extend to land used as allotment gardens[4].

An allotment is an agricultural holding[5] for the purposes of the Agricultural Holdings Act 1986 if it is agricultural land[6], and is comprised in a contract of tenancy[7] not being a contract under which the land is let to the tenant during his continuance in an office, appointment or employment held under the landlord[8]. An allotment garden is not, however, an agricultural holding, as, by definition[9], it cannot be land used for the purposes of trade or business.

Allotments, including allotment gardens, rank as agricultural land for the purposes of exemption from non-domestic rating[10].

1   For the meaning of 'agricultural land' in this context see the Agriculture Act 1947 s 109 (1); and AGRICULTURE vol I (2) (Reissue) para 602 note 2.
2   'Agriculture' includes horticulture, fruit growing, seed growing, dairy farming and livestock breeding and keeping, the use of land as grazing land, meadow land, osier land, market gardens and nursery grounds, and the use of land for woodlands where that use is ancillary to the farming of land for other agricultural purposes, 'agricultural' being construed accordingly, and 'livestock' includes any creature kept for the production of food, wool, skins or for, or for use in, the farming of land: Agriculture Act 1947 s 109 (3).
3   Ibid s 109 (1); Transfer of Functions (Wales) (No 1) Order 1978, SI 1978/272, art 2, Sch 1.
4   Agriculture Act 1947 s 109 (1) proviso (a).
5   For the meaning of 'agricultural holding' see the Agricultural Holdings Act 1986 s 1 (1); and AGRICULTURE vol I (2) (Reissue) para 301.
6   For the meaning of 'agricultural land' in this context see ibid s 1 (4); and AGRICULTURE vol I (2) (Reissue) para 302. This definition is similar to that referred to in note 1 supra.
7   For the meaning of 'contract of tenancy' see ibid s 1 (5); and AGRICULTURE vol I (2) (Reissue) para 303.
8   See *Stevens v Sedgman* [1951] 2 KB 434, [1951] 2 All ER 33, CA, where an allotment of under half an acre used by the tenant to produce vegetables was held to be an agricultural holding; and see the definition referred to in note 7 supra.
9   See para 1 text to notes 8, 9 ante.
10   Local Government Finance Act 1988 s 51, Sch 5 para 2 (d). As to this exemption see generally Sch 5; and RATING.

(2) SMALLHOLDINGS

4. Meaning of 'smallholding'. In general terms a smallholding may be said to be a unit of land let by a smallholdings authority[1] or the Minister of Agriculture, Fisheries and Food as a smallholding for cultivation by the occupier, with or without limited additional help. There is no definition of 'smallholding' in the Agriculture Act 1970, which reorganised the smallholdings system, but for the purposes of the Small Holdings and Allotments Acts 1908 to 1931[2] 'small holding' meant an agricultural holding exceeding 1 acre but either not exceeding 50 acres or, if exceeding 50 acres, at the date of sale or letting of an annual value for income tax purposes not exceeding £100[3].

For the purposes of the repealed smallholdings provisions of the Agriculture Act 1947[4] 'smallholding' meant a holding, other than a holding provided, or such as apart from that Act could be provided, under any enactment relating to the provision of cottage holdings[5], used or intended to be used for agriculture[6], being a holding exceeding 1 acre but not exceeding 50 acres[7]. As originally enacted this provision extended to include holdings of between 50 and 75 acres of which the annual full fair rent[8] did not exceed £150[9].

In the main statutory provisions relating to smallholdings, now embodied in Part III of the Agriculture Act 1970, 'existing smallholding' means a unit of land which, being held by a smallholdings authority[10] or, as the case may be, by the Minister of Agriculture, Fisheries and Food[11], for the purposes of smallholdings[12], is for the time being let[13] as a smallholding or, if it is not for the time being in use, was so let when it was last in use[14].

1 As to smallholdings authorities see para 117 post.

2 Ie in effect the Small Holdings and Allotments Act 1908, the Land Settlement (Facilities) Act 1919, the Small Holdings and Allotments Act 1926 and the Agricultural Land (Utilisation) Act 1931: see ibid s 25 (1). These Acts replaced various earlier Acts, but the position as regards smallholdings sold and leased under repealed Acts was preserved by s 66 of the 1908 Act, s 32 (2) of the 1919 Act, and the proviso to s 15 of the 1926 Act. The provisions of these Acts relating to smallholdings were almost wholly repealed by the Agriculture Act 1947 s 67 (2), with savings: see s 67 (2) proviso, Sch 8 Pt II, and the Agriculture Act 1970 s 64 (2), Sch 4.

3 Small Holdings and Allotments Act 1908 s 61 (1) (amended by the Small Holdings and Allotments Act 1926 s 16). Note that under those Acts 'small holding' was spelt as two words. 'Agriculture' in those Acts bears the same meaning as 'cultivation' (as to which see para 1 note 2 ante): Small Holdings and Allotments Act 1908 s 61 (1) (as amended: see supra).

4 See the Agriculture Act 1947 Pt IV (ss 47–67), largely repealed by the Agriculture Act 1970 (see s 113 (3), Sch 5 Pt III) and replaced by Pt III (ss 37–65) of the 1970 Act.

5 As to cottage holdings see paras 6, 129 post.

6 For the meaning of 'agriculture' see the Agriculture Act 1947 s 109 (3) and para 3 note 2 ante, applied for the purposes of the Agriculture Act 1970 by s 37 (4).

7 Agriculture Act 1947 s 66 (repealed); Agriculture (Miscellaneous Provisions) Act 1954 s 3 (1), Sch 3 (repealed).

8 Ie such rent as a tenant might reasonably be expected to pay for the holding if let as such on the terms, other than the terms as to rent, on which it was in fact let: Agriculture Act 1947 s 52 (2) (repealed).

9 This extended meaning operated until 4 June 1954, but any holding used or intended to be used for agriculture which before that date was provided as a smallholding for the purposes of the Small Holdings and Allotments Acts 1908 to 1931, or the Agriculture Act 1947 Pt IV, and any holding provided by virtue of the Agriculture (Miscellaneous Provisions) Act 1954 s 3 (2) (repealed), was to be treated as a smallholding for the purposes of Pt IV of the 1947 Act: s 3 (1) of the 1954 Act (repealed).

10 Any reference in the Agriculture Act 1970 Pt III to land so held must be construed as including a reference to any land in which an interest is so held by the authority, other than a right to take possession arising under the Small Holdings and Allotments Acts 1908 to 1931: Agriculture Act 1970 s 37 (2) (a).

11 As to land held by the minister see para 124 post.

12 'The purposes of smallholdings' includes the purposes which were the purposes of smallholdings in accordance with the Agriculture Act 1947 Pt IV: Agriculture Act 1970 s 37 (2) (c). Under the 1947 Act it was the duty of county councils, and certain county borough councils, to provide smallholdings for the purpose of affording to persons with agricultural experience an opportunity of becoming farmers on their own account: s 47 (1) (repealed). For the general aim of the 1970 Act see para 87 post.

13 Ie let under the Agriculture Act 1970 or under the previous enactments relating to smallholdings; as to which see note 2 supra.

14 Ibid s 37 (1).

5. The smallholdings system. Smallholdings, unlimited in size but, if above 50 acres, limited in value, could be provided under the Small Holdings and Allotments Acts 1908 to 1931, by county and county borough councils for persons desiring to buy or lease them and able themselves to cultivate them properly[1], the primary aim being to relieve unemployment and assist re-settling ex-servicemen.

The Agriculture Act 1947 repealed the smallholdings provisions of the earlier Acts and introduced a new smallholdings code[2], whereby county councils and certain county borough councils were under a duty to provide smallholdings, limited in size, to persons with agricultural experience seeking the opportunity of becoming farmers on their own account, to the extent that a demand existed for smallholdings, suitable land could be obtained for the purpose, and the smallholdings could be provided without detriment to the general interests of agriculture[3].

Provision was made by the Agriculture Act 1970, which repealed most of the Agriculture Act 1947, Part IV[4], for the reorganisation of smallholdings authorities'[5] smallholdings estates[6], having regard to the general interests of agriculture and of good estate management, with a view to providing opportunities for persons to be farmers on their own account by letting holdings to persons qualified, or likely shortly to become qualified, by reason of agricultural experience, to farm them on their own account[7], and a new smallholdings code[8] was introduced.

1 See the Small Holdings and Allotments Act 1926 s 1 (repealed in relation to smallholdings). See the Northfield Committee of Inquiry into the Acquisition and Occupancy of Agricultural Land (1979) (Cmnd 7599) for the history of smallholdings legislation.
2 See the Agriculture Act 1947 Pt IV (ss 47–67) (largely repealed).
3 See ibid s 47 (repealed).
4 For transitional provisions see the Agriculture Act 1970 s 64 (1), Sch 3.
5 As to smallholdings authorities see para 117 post.
6 See the Agriculture Act 1970 ss 40–43; and paras 89–93 post.
7 Ibid ss 39, 44; and paras 87, 100, 102, 103 post.
8 Ibid Pt III (ss 37–65).

(3) COTTAGE HOLDINGS

6. Meaning of 'cottage holding'. 'Cottage holding' means a holding comprising a dwelling house, together with not less than a quarter of an acre[1] and not more than one acre of agricultural land[2] which can be cultivated by the occupier of the dwelling house and his family[3].

1 The original definition referred to 'forty perches'. A perch, which is no longer officially recognised as a unit of area, was $30\frac{1}{4}$ square yards.
2 'Agriculture' has the same meaning as 'cultivation', as to which see para 1 note 2 ante: Small Holdings and Allotments Act 1908 s 61 (1). That Act is construed as one with the Agricultural Land (Utilisation) Act 1931: ibid s 20 (2).
3 Ibid s 20 (1).

7. Cottage holdings before and after 1970. Until 1 August 1970 cottage holdings might be acquired, bought, sold and let by county councils, county borough councils and the Greater London Council, and detailed statutory provisions governed their disposition, management and use. Whilst cottage holdings existing on that date continue to be subject to these provisions, a council[1] can no longer sell or let land as a cottage holding or acquire land for the purpose of being sold or let as a cottage holding[2].

The policy is therefore to allow existing cottage holdings, which are few in number, to run down and ultimately disappear, experience having shown that the cottage holding is no longer a viable agricultural unit and that in practice there has been a tendency for them to be confused, by local authorities as well as by occupiers, with smallholdings[3].

In this title the law relating to cottage holdings[4] is treated in detail only where it remains of importance[5].

1 By virtue of the Local Government Act 1972 s 272 (1), Sch 30 and the Local Government Act 1985 s 1, the reference to 'council' means a county council. The reference in the Agriculture Act 1970 s 60 (1) (a) to the Greater London Council has not, however, been removed, although that council was abolished by the Local Government Act 1985 s 1 as from 1 April 1986.
2 See the Agriculture Act 1970 s 60 (1) (amended by the Local Government Act 1972 s 272 (1), Sch 30); see para 131 post.
3 See First Report of Wise Committee of Inquiry into Statutory Smallholdings (Cmnd 2936) paras 132, 133, 481, 482.

4 The law relating to cottage holdings comprises in the main the smallholdings provisions of the Small Holdings and Allotments Act 1926 Pt I (ss 1–15), applied to cottage holdings by the Agricultural Land (Utilisation) Act 1931 s 12 (1) (and largely repealed, as regards smallholdings only, by the Agriculture Act 1947 s 67 (2), Sch 8 Pt II), and the Agriculture Act 1970 s 60.

5 See paras 129–142 post.

2. ALLOTMENTS

(1) PROVISION OF ALLOTMENTS

8. Councils' duty to provide allotments. A general duty is placed on the council of any district or parish[1], if it is of opinion that there is a demand for allotments[2] in its area, to provide a sufficient number of allotments, and to let them to persons resident[3] there and desiring to take the same[4]. In the case of an inner London borough the power is permissive not mandatory[5].

Representations in writing may be made to the local authority on the need for allotments by any six resident registered parliamentary electors or persons who are liable under the Local Government Finance Act 1988 to pay an amount in respect of any community charge[6].

Where the population of a district or parish, according to the last published census, is under 10,000, the council's duty is limited to the provision of allotment gardens[7]. Where the population is 10,000 or upwards, the council's obligation is limited to the provision of allotment gardens not exceeding one-eighth of an acre[8].

Any land which on 31 July 1953[9] was let by a council as an allotment garden under the Defence (General) Regulations 1939[10] or was appropriated for letting thereunder, may still be let for use by tenants as allotment gardens or to a society having as its object the cultivation of vacant land for the purpose of subletting for such use[11], but once any such land is returned to use as a park or open space or is otherwise appropriated for use for any purpose other than letting for allotment gardens it may not again be so let[12].

1 In rural parishes having no parish council the authority is the parish meeting: Small Holdings and Allotments Act 1908 s 61 (4). As to local authorities generally see para 79 post.

2 For the meaning of 'allotment' see para 1 ante.

3 For the meaning of 'resident' compare cases on the meaning of the word for the purposes of qualifying for the franchise: see ELECTIONS.

4 Small Holdings and Allotments Act 1908 s 23 (1) (amended by the Land Settlement (Facilities) Act 1919 s 25, Schs 2, 3). The Small Holdings and Allotments Act 1908 s 23 refers to borough and urban district councils. By virtue of the Local Government Act 1972 ss 1 (9), (10), 20 (6) both were abolished, and a reference to a borough no longer has any effect. Reference to an urban district is to be construed as a reference to a district established by ss 1 (1), (3), (4), 20 (1), (3), Sch 1 Pt I, Sch 4 Pt II: s 179 (1), (2). See LOCAL GOVERNMENT.

5 London Government Act 1963 s 55 (4) (a).

6 Small Holdings and Allotments Act 1908 s 23 (2) (amended by the Local Government Finance (Repeals, Savings and Consequential Amendments) Order 1990, SI 1990/776, art 8, Sch 3 para 2). This does not apply in the case of an inner London borough: London Government Act 1963 s 55 (4) (b). For a form of representation see 2 Forms & Precedents (5th Edn) 340, Form 9. See also note 4 supra regarding the effect of the Local Government Act 1972 on the Small Holdings and Allotments Act 1908 s 23.

7 Allotments Act 1950 s 9 (a). For the meaning of 'allotment garden' see para 1 ante.

8 Allotments Act 1950 s 9 (b). This referred to 'twenty poles'. A pole (30¼ square yards) is no longer recognised as a unit of measurement. References to 'borough' and 'urban district' in s 9 are affected by the Local Government Act 1972; see note 4 supra.

9 Ie the date of commencement of the Emergency Laws (Miscellaneous Provisions) Act 1953.
10 See the Defence (General) Regulations 1939, SR & O 1939/927, reg 62A (added by SR & O 1939/1838 and amended by SR & O 1940/1611, SR & O 1941/456) (revoked), which authorised a local authority to let, to tenants for use as an allotment garden or to an allotment society, land occupied by the authority, unoccupied land to the possession of which it was entitled, and land forming part of a park or open space under its management or control.
11 Emergency Laws (Miscellaneous Provisions) Act 1953 s 5 (1). A tenancy of land which, on 31 July 1953, was subsisting under the Defence (General) Regulations 1939 reg 62A, continues in force as if it had been granted under the Emergency Laws (Miscellaneous Provisions) Act 1953 s 5 (1): ibid s 5 (5).
12 Ibid s 5 (2).

9. Allotments and planning. Cultivation of an allotment involves agricultural use within the meaning of the term in the Town and Country Planning Act 1990[1]. Development permission is not required for the use of land for the purposes of agriculture[2], and so is not needed for the cultivation of allotments.

1 'Agriculture' includes, inter alia, horticulture: see the Town and Country Planning Act 1990 s 336 (1); and TOWN AND COUNTRY PLANNING. The definition is the same as in para 3 note 2 ante.
2 Ibid s 55 (2) (e).

(2) LAND FOR ALLOTMENTS

(i) Generally

10. Acquisition of land for allotments. The necessary land for allotments may be acquired by a local authority in the following ways, namely (1) by hiring by agreement[1], (2) by purchase by agreement[2], (3) by compulsory purchase[3], (4) by compulsory hiring by a district council on behalf of a parish council[4], and (5) by the appropriation of land held for other purposes[5].

District councils may enter on unoccupied land for the purpose of providing allotment gardens[6]. Local authorities may also acquire land by transfer from allotment wardens and trustees[7].

1 See paras 13–15 post.
2 See para 16 post.
3 See paras 17, 24–28 post.
4 See paras 18–28 post.
5 See paras 29, 30 post. As to local authorities see para 79 post.
6 See para 31 post. The consent of the Secretary of State for the Environment or, in Wales, the Secretary of State for Wales, is required for the exercise by a district council of its powers as to the purchase, hire, sale, mortgage or exchange of land: see the Small Holdings and Allotments Regulations 1919, SR & O 1919/1197, reg 1. As to the transfer of powers to the Secretaries of State see para 80 note 3 post. As to local authorities see para 79 post.
7 See para 67 post.

11. Acquisition of land for future allotments. A district council may acquire land for allotments, notwithstanding that it cannot immediately be let in allotments, if the Secretary of State for the Environment or, in Wales, the Secretary of State for Wales, is satisfied that there is a reasonable expectation that the land will eventually be required for allotments[1].

1 Allotments Act 1925 s 5. Reference to 'borough' and 'urban district' in s 5 is affected by the Local Government Act 1972; see para 8 note 4 ante. As to the transfer of functions to the Secretaries of State see para 80 note 4 post. As to local authorities see para 79 post.

12. Entry to ascertain suitability of land. A council, with a view to ascertaining whether any land is suitable to be acquired by it for allotments, may authorise in writing any person to enter and inspect the land specified in the authority, and any one who obstructs or impedes any person acting under such authority is liable on summary conviction to a fine not exceeding level 2 on the standard scale[1].

1 Land Settlement (Facilities) Act 1919 s 19 (amended by virtue of the Criminal Justice Act 1982 s 46).
  In any enactment contained in an Act passed either before or after the Criminal Justice Act 1982 'the standard scale' has the meaning given by s 37: s 75 (a). A standard scale of fines for summary offences was introduced by the Criminal Justice Act 1982 s 37 (1). Where any enactment contained in an Act passed either before or after that Act provides (1) that a person convicted of a summary offence is liable on conviction to a fine or a maximum fine by reference to a specified level on the standard scale, or (2) confers power by subordinate instrument to make a person liable on conviction of a summary offence, whether or not created by the instrument, to a fine or a maximum fine by reference to a specified level on the standard scale, it is to be construed as referring to the standard scale for which s 37 provides as that scale has effect from time to time by virtue either of that section or of an order under the Magistrates' Courts Act 1980 s 143: Criminal Justice Act 1982 s 37 (3). In relation to Acts passed before the Criminal Justice Act 1982, this provision applies where references to the standard scale are substituted by s 46 as read with s 38 or s 40. At the date at which this volume states the law, the standard scale is as follows, in relation to offences committed after 1 May 1984: level 1, £50; level 2, £100; level 3, £400; level 4, £1,000; level 5, £2,000: s 37 (2) (amended by the Criminal Penalties etc (Increase) Order 1984, SI 1984/447, art 2 (4), Sch 4). As from a day to be appointed, these sums are increased by the Criminal Justice Act 1991 s 17 (1) to £200, £500, £1,000, £2,500 and £5,000 respectively.

(ii) Acquisition by Agreement

13. Councils' power to take land on lease. The council of a district or parish may by agreement take on lease land, whether situated within or without its area, for the purpose of providing allotments[1].

1 Small Holdings and Allotments Act 1908 s 25 (1). Reference to 'borough' and 'urban district' in s 25 is affected by the Local Government Act 1972; see para 8 note 4 ante. For a form of lease see 2 Forms & Precedents (5th Edn) 362–364, Form 26. For the power of entry on land agreed to be hired see para 27 post. As to compensation for improvements at the determination of the tenancy see paras 61, 62 post. As to local authorities see para 79 post.

14. Leases by limited owners. A person who has power to lease land for agricultural purposes for a limited term[1] may lease land to a council for the purposes of allotments for a term not exceeding 35 years, either with or without such rights of renewal as are conferred in the case of land hired compulsorily[2]. A tenant for life may make a lease of settled land for any term of years absolute for a nominal rent, or for less than the best rent obtainable, or gratuitously, for the purposes of the Allotments Acts[3], but, except under a court order, not more than two acres in a district, or ten acres in a parish may be leased unless full consideration is paid or reserved for the excess[4].

1 Eg a mortgagor or mortgagee in possession: see the Law of Property Act 1925 s 99 (1), (2), (3) (i); see MORTGAGE.
2 Small Holdings and Allotments Act 1908 s 40 (1) (amended by the Agriculture Act 1970 s 113 (3), Sch 5 Pt III). As to the right of renewal see para 22 post.
3 Settled Land Act 1925 s 57 (2).
4 Ibid s 57 (2) proviso. Reference to 'urban district' in s 57 (2) proviso is affected by the Local Government Act 1972; see para 8 note 4 ante. Reference to 'rural district' no longer has any effect: ss 1 (10), 20 (6). Application for a court order is by originating summons in the Chancery Division of

the High Court (Settled Land Act 1925 s 113 (1); RSC Ord 5 r 3) or by originating application in a county court (County Courts Act 1984 s 24; CCR Ord 3 r 4).

15. Leases of Duchy of Cornwall land. The like powers of leasing as may be exercised by limited owners[1] may be exercised, in the case of land forming part of the possessions of the Duchy of Cornwall, by the Duke of Cornwall or other persons for the time being empowered to dispose of land belonging to that Duchy[2].

1 See para 14 ante.
2 Small Holdings and Allotments Act 1908 s 40 (2) (amended by the Crown Estate Act 1961 s 9 (4), Sch 3 Pt II and the Duchy of Lancaster Act 1988 s 1 (4), Schedule). Similar provisions relating to the Duchy of Lancaster and to glebe land have been repealed.

16. Purchase by agreement. The council of a district or parish may, for the purpose of providing allotments, by agreement purchase land whether situate within or without its area[1], and for this purpose the provisions of the Compulsory Purchase Act 1965[2] are applied, with certain exceptions[3]. Land in the Duchy of Lancaster may be sold for the purpose of allotments[4]. A tenant for life may make a grant in fee simple or absolutely of any part of the settled land for a nominal price, or for less than the best price obtainable, or gratuitously[5].

1 Small Holdings and Allotments Act 1908 s 25 (1). As to the power of entry on land agreed to be purchased see para 27 post. As to local authorities see para 79 post. See also para 13 ante.
2 See COMPULSORY ACQUISITION.
3 Small Holdings and Allotments Act 1908 s 38 (amended by the Compulsory Purchase Act 1965 s 38 (1), Sch 6). The provisions which do not apply are ss 4–8 (compulsory purchase), 10 (compensation for injurious affection), 23 (1)–(5) (conveyancing costs), and 31 (ecclesiastical property).
4 Local Government Act 1972 s 130. The Broads Authority which is established by the Norfolk and Suffolk Broads Act 1988 s 1, Sch 1, is to be classed as a local authority for the purposes of the Local Government Act 1972 s 130: s 265A (added by the Norfolk and Suffolk Broads Act 1988 s 21, Sch 6, para 10 (1)).
5 Settled Land Act 1925 s 57 (2). The amount which may be granted is restricted, as in the case of leases: see para 14 ante.

(iii) Compulsory Acquisition

A. COMPULSORY PURCHASE

17. Compulsory purchase generally. The council of a district or parish may purchase land, whether situated within or without its area, compulsorily for the purposes of providing allotments, provided it has been authorised to do so by the Secretary of State or, in Wales, the Secretary of State for Wales[1].

Any question of disputed compensation is determined by the Lands Tribunal[2]. In determining the amount of any disputed compensation no additional allowance may be made on account of the purchase being compulsory[3].

1 Small Holdings and Allotments Act 1908 ss 25 (1), 39 (1) (amended by the Acquisition of Land (Authorisation Procedure) Act 1946 s 6, Sch 4 and the Acquisition of Land Act 1981 s 34): the purchase must be in accordance with the provisions of the 1908 Act (see ss 39, 41–43, 45) and of the Acquisition of Land Act 1981, in that behalf. For the 1981 Act see COMPULSORY ACQUISITION. As to the transfer of functions to the Secretaries of State see para 80 note 3 post. As to local authorities see

para 79 post. Reference to 'borough' and 'urban district' in the Small Holdings and Allotments Act 1908 s 25 (1) is affected by the Local Government Act 1972; see para 8 note 4 ante.
2 Land Compensation Act 1961 s 1; see COMPULSORY ACQUISITION.
3 Small Holdings and Allotments Act 1908 s 39 (5). See further the Land Compensation Act 1961 s 5 (1); and COMPULSORY ACQUISITION.

B. COMPULSORY HIRING

18. Compulsory hiring generally. When a district council proposes to hire land compulsorily for the purpose of leasing it to a parish council[1] it may submit to the Secretary of State for the Environment or, in Wales, the Secretary of State for Wales, an order for the compulsory hiring of the land specified in the order for a period of not less than 14 and not more than 35 years[2].

The order[3] must incorporate any regulations made by the Secretary of State[4], must determine the terms and conditions of the hiring other than the rent, and, in particular, must provide for the insertion in the lease of covenants by the council to cultivate the land in a proper manner, and to pay to the landlord[5], at the determination of the tenancy on the council quitting the land, compensation for depreciation, and, unless otherwise agreed, to keep the buildings and premises in repair[6]. The order must not, except with the landlord's consent, confer on the council any right to fell or cut timber or trees, or any right to take, sell or carry away any minerals, gravel, sand or clay, except so far as may be necessary or convenient for the purpose of erecting buildings on the land or otherwise adapting the land for allotments, and except upon payment of compensation for minerals, gravel, sand or clay so used[7].

Where the land is glebe land or other land belonging to a Diocesan Board of Finance the order must provide that the rent or compensation for severance or other injury be paid to the Church Commissioners, to be applied as money paid to them on a sale under the Ecclesiastical Leasing Acts[8] of land belonging to a Diocesan Board[9].

The order may provide for the continuance or creation of easements over the land authorised to be acquired[10].

The order must be published and advertised by the council, and notice of it must be given to parties affected[11]. If an objection[12] to the order is lodged with the Secretary of State and persisted in, he must hold a public inquiry in the locality[13].

1 See para 28 post. The effect of the amendment to the Small Holdings and Allotments Act 1908 s 25 by the Acquisition of Land (Authorisation Procedure) Act 1946 and the Acquisition of Land Act 1981 is that a council no longer has any power of compulsory hiring for the purpose of allotments under the 1908 Act. The provisions as to compulsory hiring in the Small Holdings and Allotments Act 1908 apply only to district councils acquiring land for letting to parish councils for allotments under the Land Settlement (Facilities) Act 1919 s 17 (amended by the Local Government Act 1972 s 251, Sch 29 Pt II para 10).
2 Small Holdings and Allotments Act 1908 s 39 (2). As to the transfer of functions to the Secretaries of State see para 80 note 3 post.
3 The order must be in the form prescribed by the Small Holdings and Allotments (Compulsory Hiring) Regulations 1936, SR & O 1936/196, reg 1, Appendix (see 2 Forms & Precedents (5th Edn) 365–366, Form 28): Small Holdings and Allotments Act 1908 s 39 (2), Sch 1 Pt I para (1).
4 Ibid s 39 (2), Sch 1 Pt II para (1). These regulations are the Small Holdings and Allotments (Compulsory Hiring) Regulations 1936: see reg 28.
5 'Landlord' in relation to land compulsorily hired means the person for the time being entitled to receive the rent from the council: Small Holdings and Allotments Act 1908 s 61 (1).

6 Ibid Sch 1 Pt II para (2)(a). Where land is compulsorily hired the council must be allowed a reasonable time in which to remedy breaches of covenant: *Hopley v Tarvin Parish Council* (1910) 74 JP 209.

7 Small Holdings and Allotments Act 1908 Sch 1 Pt II para (2)(c).

8 See the Ecclesiastical Leasing Act 1858 s 2; and ECCLESIASTICAL LAW.

9 Small Holdings and Allotments Act 1908 Sch 1 Pt I para (8); Church Commissioners Measure 1947 ss 1, 2; Endowments and Glebe Measure 1976 ss 15, 20.

10 See para 25 post.

11 See the Small Holdings and Allotments Act 1908 Sch 1 Pt I para (2), the Small Holdings and Allotments (Compulsory Hiring) Regulations 1936 reg 2, and 2 Forms & Precedents (5th Edn) 367–368, Form 29.

12 Objections must be presented to the Secretary of State and, if required by the notice, a copy sent to the clerk to the council, within one calendar month from the date on which the notice was sent to the objector or, if no notice was sent to him, from the date of the latest advertisement: Small Holdings and Allotments (Compulsory Hiring) Regulations 1936 regs 2 (3), 4.

13 Small Holdings and Allotments Act 1908 Sch 1 Pt I paras (3), (4). As to inquiries see s 57; and para 86 post.

19. Compulsory hiring of pasture land. No order may be made authorising the compulsory hiring for the purpose of allotments of land which at the date of the order is pasture land, if it is proved to the satisfaction of the Secretary of State for the Environment or, in Wales, the Secretary of State for Wales, that arable land which is equally suitable is reasonably available for hiring by the council[1]. An order authorising the compulsory hiring of land for the provision of allotment gardens may authorise the breaking up of pasture[2], but in other cases the order may not authorise the breaking up of pasture unless the Secretary of State is satisfied that it can be broken up without depreciating the value of the land, or that the circumstances are such that allotments cannot otherwise be successfully cultivated[3].

1 Allotments Act 1922 s 8 (4). As to the transfer of functions to the Secretaries of State see para 80 note 4 post.

2 Allotments Act 1922 s 8 (5).

3 Small Holdings and Allotments Act 1908 s 39 (2), Sch 1 Pt II para (2)(b) (amended by the Land Settlement (Facilities) Act 1919 s 25(1), Sch 2). The meaning of 'successfully cultivated' was discussed in *Knowles v Salford Corpn* [1922] 1 Ch 328 at 344, CA, per Warrington LJ. For the meaning of 'cultivation' see para 1 note 2 ante.

20. Confirmation of compulsory hiring order. A compulsory hiring order is not effective unless and until it is confirmed by the Secretary of State for the Environment or, in Wales, the Secretary of State for Wales, who may confirm it with or without modifications[1]. Confirmation is conclusive evidence that the requirements of the Act have been complied with and that the order has been duly made and is within the powers of the Act[2].

Notice of confirmation of the order[3] must be given to each owner, occupier and lessee[4], and on the application of any person interested in the land the order must be so framed as to secure the interest of any party other than the owner or existing tenant in any compensation payable[5].

Where the land authorised to be compulsorily hired is subject to a mortgage, any lease made in pursuance of the order by the mortgagor or mortgagee in possession will have effect as if it were a lease authorised under the statutory power[6] to be made by the mortgagor or mortgagee in possession[7].

1 Small Holdings and Allotments Act 1908 s 39 (3) (amended by the Acquisition of Land (Authorisation Procedure) Act 1946 s 6, Sch 4, and the Statute Law (Repeals) Act 1986 Sch 1 Pt XII). As to the transfer of functions to the Secretaries of State see para 80 note 3 post.

2 Small Holdings and Allotments Act 1908 s 39 (3) (as amended: see note 1 supra). The validity of a
  confirmed order cannot be challenged: see *Ex p Ringer* (1909) 73 JP 436; but see *Minister of Health v R*,
  ex p Yaffe [1931] AC 494, HL, where it was held that a scheme unauthorised by the Housing Act 1925
  could not be made law by an order of the minister which, under that Act, was to have statutory
  effect. See also the general principle laid down in *Frewin v Lewis* (1838) 4 My & Cr 249 at 254 per
  Lord Cottenham LC. Where a council neglected to comply with the condition precedent of
  endeavouring to obtain suitable land by agreement before making an order (see the Compulsory
  Purchase Act 1965 s 5: notice to treat), an injunction restraining it from proceeding was refused
  while an inquiry was pending: *Reddaway v Lancashire County Council* (1925) 41 TLR 422.
3 See 2 Forms & Precedents (5th Edn) 368, Form 30.
4 Small Holdings and Allotments (Compulsory Hiring) Regulations 1936, SR & O 1936/196, reg
  5 (1).
5 Ibid reg 5 (2).
6 Ie under the Law of Property Act 1925 s 99: see MORTGAGE.
7 Small Holdings and Allotments Act 1908 s 39 (6).

21. Determination of compensation or rent payable on compulsory hiring. The amount of rent to be paid by a council for land compulsorily hired, the amount of any other compensation to be paid by a council to any person entitled to compensation in respect of the land or any interest in it or in respect of improvements executed on it or otherwise, and, where part only of a holding held for an unexpired term is hired, the rent to be paid for the residue of the holding during the remainder of the term, must, in default of agreement, be determined by a single valuer[1] appointed by the Secretary of State for the Environment or, in Wales, the Secretary of State for Wales[2], although a tenant in occupation may, by notice served on the council before the determination of his tenancy, require that any claim by him against the council be referred to arbitration under the Agricultural Holdings Act 1986[3] provided that Act applies[4]. Counsel and expert witnesses may not be heard in the assessing of compensation or rent unless the Secretary of State otherwise directs[5].

In fixing the rent to be paid by the council the valuer must take into consideration any rent at which the land has been let and the annual value of the land for the purposes of income tax or rating, any loss caused to the owner by severance, the terms of the hiring and all the other circumstances connected with the land, but he must not make any allowance in respect of any use to which the owner might otherwise have put the land, being a use in respect of which he might resume possession[6]. He must also take into consideration the interest of any existing tenant and the existence of any reservation, exception or easement affecting the land, which must be valued subject to such interest, reservation, exception or easement[7], and he must have regard not only to the value of the land but also to any damage to be sustained by the owner of the land by its severance from other land of his, or by reason of other land of his being otherwise injuriously affected[8].

Any compensation awarded to a tenant in respect of the depreciation of the value to him of the residue of his holding caused by the withdrawal from the holding of the hired land must so far as possible be provided for by taking that compensation into account in fixing the rent to be paid for the residue of the holding during the remainder of the term[9]. Every existing tenant is entitled to compensation from the council for the damage done to him in his tenancy by the severance of the hired land from unhired land held by him[10].

In assessing the value of the hired land the existence of mines and minerals[11] should be disregarded, and only the surface value should be taken into consideration[12].

Any person interested in the valuation must give the valuer all the assistance, information and explanations he requires and produce to him or give him access to relevant documents, at the council's expense[13].

1 The Acquisition of Land (Assessment of Compensation) Act 1919 s 7 (2) provided that any matter required by the Small Holdings and Allotments Act 1908 to be determined by such a valuer should be determined by an official arbitration under the 1919 Act. That provision was, however, repealed on 1 October 1949 on the coming into operation of the Agriculture Act 1947 Pt IV (ss 47–67) (see ss 110, 111, Sch 13, and the Agriculture Act 1947 (Commencement) Order 1949, SI 1949/1201), so that when the Lands Tribunal Act 1949 s 1 came into force on 1 January 1950 (see the Lands Tribunal Act (Appointed Day) Order 1949, SI 1949/2335) there was no provision in force requiring reference to an official arbitrator, and consequently the Lands Tribunal did not acquire jurisdiction under the Lands Tribunal Act 1949 s 1 (3) (a), although it has power to act as arbitrator with the parties' consent: see s 1 (5); and COMPULSORY ACQUISITION. Whilst the Land Compensation Act 1961 s 1 and the Compulsory Purchase Act 1965 s 6 give the Lands Tribunal general power to assess compensation, it is submitted that the detailed provisions in the text prevail.
2 Small Holdings and Allotments Act 1908 s 39 (2), Sch 1 Pt II para (3). As to the transfer of functions to the Secretaries of State see para 80 note 3 post.
3 See AGRICULTURE vol 1 (2) (Reissue) para 454.
4 Small Holdings and Allotments Act 1908 Sch 1 Pt II para (3) proviso (amended by the Agricultural Holdings Act 1986 s 100, Sch 14 para 3).
5 Small Holdings and Allotments Act 1908 s 39 (2), Sch 1 Pt I para (5); Allotments Act 1922 s 8 (3); Small Holdings and Allotments Act 1926 s 17 (3) (b); Lands Tribunal Act 1949 s 10 (4), Sch 2. In the Lands Tribunal counsel and one expert witness on each side may be heard as of right: see the Lands Tribunal Rules 1975, SI 1975/299, r 42; and COMPULSORY ACQUISITION.
6 Small Holdings and Allotments Act 1908 Sch 1 Pt II para (4). As to resuming possession see s 46 (1) (amended by the Land Settlement (Facilities) Act 1919 s 25, Sch 2); and para 23 post.
7 Small Holdings and Allotments (Compulsory Hiring) Regulations 1936, SR & O 1936/196, reg 13.
8 Ibid reg 14 (1).
9 Small Holdings and Allotments Act 1908 Sch 1 Pt II para (5).
10 Small Holdings and Allotments (Compulsory Hiring) Regulations 1936 reg 14 (2).
11 Subject to any provision in the compulsory hiring order mines and minerals are, unless the owner and council otherwise agree, reserved out of the lease: see ibid reg 22.
12 *Earl of Carlisle v Northumberland County Council* (1911) 105 LT 797.
13 See the Small Holdings and Allotments Act 1908 Sch 1 Pt II para (6) (amended by the Land Settlement (Facilities) Act 1919 s 25 (1), Sch 2).

22. Renewal of tenancy after compulsory hiring. Where land has been hired compulsorily, the council may, by giving notice in writing to the landlord[1], not more than two years nor less than one year before the expiration of the tenancy, renew the tenancy for such term, not being less than 14 nor more than 35 years, as may be specified in the notice, and at such rent as, in default of agreement, may be determined by valuation by a valuer[2] appointed by the Secretary of State for the Environment or, in Wales, the Secretary of State for Wales, but otherwise on the same terms and conditions as the original lease, and so from time to time[3]. If, on any such notice being given, the landlord proves to the Secretary of State's satisfaction that any land included in the tenancy is required for the amenity or convenience of any dwelling house, that land must be excluded from the renewed tenancy[4].

The notice to renew may be withdrawn[5] by the council at any time not less than three months before the expiration of the tenancy, if it appears to the council that the rent assessed is such as will involve loss to the council, but in any such case the landlord can obtain compensation for any consequential loss or expenses[6].

In assessing the rent to be paid under a renewal the valuer must not take into account any increase in the holding's value due to improvements by the council or to such possible user of the land as would entitle the landlord to resume possession[7], or to the establishment by the council or other allotments in the neighbourhood, or any depreciation in the value in respect of which the landlord would have been entitled to compensation if the council had quitted on the expiration of the tenancy[8].

1 See 2 Forms & Precedents (5th Edn) 376–377, Form 38. For the meaning of 'landlord' see para 18 note 5 ante.
2 See para 21 note 1 ante.
3 Small Holdings and Allotments Act 1908 s 44 (1). This power is saved by the Law of Property Act 1922 s 145, Sch 15 para 9, from the provisions of Sch 15 para 1, converting perpetually renewable leases into long terms. As to the transfer of functions to the Secretaries of State see para 80 note 3 post.
4 Small Holdings and Allotments Act 1908 s 44 (1) proviso.
5 See 2 Forms & Precedents (5th Edn) 377–378, Form 39.
6 Small Holdings and Allotments Act 1926 s 18 (1).
7 See para 23 post.
8 Small Holdings and Allotments Act 1908 s 44 (2).

23. Resumption of possession by landlord after compulsory hiring. Where land has been hired compulsorily, and the land or any part of it at any time during the tenancy is shown to the satisfaction of the Secretary of State for the Environment or, in Wales, the Secretary of State for Wales, to be required by the landlord to be used for building, mining, or other industrial purposes, or for roads necessary therefor, the landlord may resume possession of the land or part of it upon giving the council 12 months' previous notice[1] of his intention, or such shorter notice as may be required by the compulsory hiring order[2].

The notice will not be valid if given before the Secretary of State is satisfied as to the purpose for which the land is required, and where an applicant has failed to satisfy him that any land is required for such a purpose, no further application with a view to resuming possession of the same land or any part of it for the same purpose can be entertained within two years after the previous application[3].

1 See 2 Forms & Precedents (5th Edn) 378–379, Form 40.
2 Small Holdings and Allotments Act 1908 s 46 (1) (amended by the Land Settlement (Facilities) Act 1919 s 25 (1), Sch 2). For the council's right to compensation see para 62 post. As to the transfer of functions to the Secretaries of State see para 80 note 3 post.
3 Small Holdings and Allotments Act 1926 s 18 (2).

C. COMPULSORY ACQUISITION GENERALLY

24. General restrictions on compulsory acquisition. No land may be authorised by order to be acquired compulsorily for allotments, either by purchase[1] or hiring[2], which at the date of the order forms part of any park[3], garden, or pleasure ground, or forms part of the home farm attached to or usually occupied with a mansion house[4], or is otherwise required for the amenity or convenience of any dwelling house, or which is woodland not wholly surrounded by or adjacent to land acquired by a council[5], or which is part of the property of the National Trust[6]. Land forming part of any park or of any home farm attached to and usually occupied with a mansion house may, however, be compulsorily acquired if not required for the amenity or convenience of the mansion house[7].

An order may be made for the compulsory acquisition for the purpose of allotments of a holding of 50 acres or less in extent or any part of such a holding[8], but a holding of 50 acres or less in extent or of an annual value not exceeding £100 for the purposes of income tax must not be compulsorily acquired by a council, where it is shown to the council's satisfaction that the holding is the occupier's principal means of livelihood, except where the occupier is a tenant and consents to the acquisition[9].

A council in making, and the Secretary of State in confirming, an order, must have regard to the extent of land held or occupied in the locality by any owner or tenant, and to the convenience of other property belonging to or occupied by such persons, and must, so far as practicable, avoid taking an undue or inconvenient quantity of land from any one owner or tenant or displacing any considerable number of agricultural labourers or others employed on or about the land[10].

1 See para 17 ante.
2 See para 18 ante.
3 'Park' means an ordinary, not an ancient legal park: *Pease v Courtney* [1904] 2 Ch 503.
4 As to what is a mansion house cf the Settled Land Act 1925 s 65 (2); and SETTLEMENTS.
5 Small Holdings and Allotments Act 1908 s 41 (1) (amended by the Acquisition of Land (Authorisation Procedure) Act 1946 s 6, Sch 4).
6 Land Settlement (Facilities) Act 1919 s 28 (4). As to National Trust land see OPEN SPACES.
7 Ibid s 16 (1) (a).
8 Ibid s 16 (1) (b).
9 Ibid s 16 (2), (3) (amended by the Small Holdings and Allotments Act 1926 ss 21, 22, Schs 1, 2).
10 Small Holdings and Allotments Act 1908 s 41 (2). As to the transfer of functions to the Secretary of State see para 80 note 3 post.

25. Creation of easements. An order for the compulsory purchase[1] or hiring[2] of land for allotments may provide for the continuance of any existing easement or the creation of any new easement over the land[3]. If the owner of the land to be acquired so requires, every such order must provide for the creation of such new easements as are reasonably necessary to secure the continued use and enjoyment by the owner and his tenants of all means of access, water supply, and other similar conveniences used or enjoyed by them over the land to be acquired[3]. However, no new easement created by or in pursuance of the order over land hired by the council continues beyond the determination of the hiring[4].

1 See para 17 ante.
2 See para 18 ante.
3 Small Holdings and Allotments Act 1908 s 39 (4) (amended by the Acquisition of Land (Authorisation Procedure) Act 1946 s 6, Sch 4).
4 Small Holdings and Allotments Act 1908 s 39 (4) proviso.

26. Notice to treat. Unless notice to treat[1] is served within three calendar months after the date of the order, or the date of the confirmation of the order, for the compulsory acquisition of any land, whether by purchase[2] or hiring[3], the order will become null and void[4], and no further order authorising the compulsory acquisition of that land or any part of it, if made within three years after the expiration of those three calendar months, will be valid unless the Secretary of State for the Environment or, in Wales, the Secretary of State for Wales, is satisfied that there are special reasons justifying the failure to exercise the powers under the original order[5].

If, after the amount of the compensation (including, in the case of land compulsorily hired, the rent) to be paid has been determined, it appears to the council that the land cannot be let for allotments at an economic rent, the council may, within six weeks after the determination of the amount, by notice[6] withdraw the notice to treat subject to being liable to pay compensation[7] for loss or expenses caused by the notice to treat and the withdrawal[8], but where a council has entered on the land[9] it is not entitled to exercise this power of withdrawal[10].

1 See 2 Forms & Precedents (5th Edn) 368–369, Form 31.
2 See para 17 ante.
3 See para 18 ante.
4 Allotments Act 1922 s 12 (1).
5 Ibid s 12 (2). As to the transfer of powers to the Secretaries of State see para 80 note 4 post.
6 See 2 Forms & Precedents (5th Edn) 373–374, Form 36.
7 The Land Compensation Act 1961 does not apply to the determination of such compensation: see s 40 (2) (a), and the Small Holdings and Allotments Act 1926 s 17 (3) (a). The compensation is instead determined under the Agricultural Holdings Act 1986 (as to which see AGRICULTURE vol 1 (2) (Reissue) para 454): Small Holdings and Allotments Act 1908 ss 39 (8), 58 (1) (amended by the Agricultural Holdings Act 1986 s 100, Sch 14 para 2).
8 Small Holdings and Allotments Act 1908 s 39 (8).
9 Ie under the Compulsory Purchase Act 1965 s 11, modified by the Development of Rural Wales Act 1976 Sch 4 Pt II para 9 in relation to the acquisition of rights by the Development Board for Rural Wales: Development of Rural Wales Act 1976 s 6 (5) (amended by the Acquisition of Land Act 1981 s 34 (1), Sch 4 para 27). See COMPULSORY ACQUISITION.
10 Land Settlement (Facilities) Act 1919 s 2 (1) (amended by the Acquisition of Land (Authorisation Procedure) Act 1946 s 6, Sch 4 and the Acquisition of Land Act 1981 Sch 4 para 2).

27. Entry on land. Where the council has been authorised to purchase land compulsorily[1] or where an order for the compulsory hiring of land has been made and confirmed[2], the council may, at any time after a notice to treat[3] has been served, and on giving not less than 14 days' notice to each owner, lessee and occupier, enter on and take possession of the land or such part thereof as is specified in the notice without previous consent or determination and payment to the persons interested or into court of compensation for the interests in the land, but subject to the payment of that compensation[4] (including, in the case of compulsory hiring, compensation by way of rent or otherwise[5]) together with interest either (1) in the case of compulsory purchase, at the rate currently prescribed[6], or (2), in the case of compulsory hiring, on such part of the compensation as is not by way of rent at the rate of five per cent per annum from the time of entry as would have been payable if the council had at the date of entry hired the land and extinguished the interests of any existing tenants[7].

Where the council has agreed to purchase or hire land which is in the occupation of a yearly tenant the council may enter on and take possession of the land after giving not less than 14 days' notice to the person in possession, and the tenant is entitled to the compensation as if he had been required to quit before the expiration of his term or interest in the land in pursuance of an authorisation for compulsory purchase or a compulsory hiring order[8].

If the notice of entry relates to land on which there is a dwelling house, and the length of notice is less than three calendar months, the occupier of the dwelling house may within ten days after the service on him of the notice of entry appeal to an arbitrator[9] against the notice[10].

1 See para 17 ante.
2 See para 18 ante.
3 See para 26 ante.
4 Land Settlement (Facilities) Act 1919 s 2 (1) (as orginally enacted), (4); Small Holdings and Allotments (Compulsory Hiring) Regulations 1936, SR & O 1936/196, reg 25 (1) (hiring); Compulsory

Purchase Act 1965 s 11 (1), (4) (purchase) (modified by the Development of Rural Wales Act 1976; see para 26 note 9 ante).
5 Small Holdings and Allotments (Compulsory Hiring) Regulations 1936 reg 25 (2).
6 Land Compensation Act 1961 s 32 (1). The rate varies, and is from time to time prescribed by Acquisition of Land (Rate of Interest after Entry) Regulations. For the current regulations see COMPULSORY ACQUISITION.
7 Small Holdings and Allotments (Compulsory Hiring) Regulations 1936 reg 25 (2).
8 Land Settlement (Facilities) Act 1919 s 2 (2), (4); Small Holdings and Allotments (Compulsory Hiring) Regulations 1936 regs 8, 25 (1).
9 The arbitration is under the Agricultural Holdings Act 1986 (as to which see AGRICULTURE vol 1 (2) (Reissue) para 454): Land Settlement (Facilities) Act 1919 s 2 (3), (4) (sub-s 3 amended by the Acquisition of Land (Authorisation Procedure) Act 1946 s 6, Sch 4 and the Agricultural Holdings Act 1986 s 100, Sch 14).
10 Land Settlement (Facilities) Act 1919 s 2 (3), (4) (as amended: see note 9 supra); Small Holdings and Allotments (Compulsory Hiring) Regulations 1936 reg 25 (1).

28. Acquisition of land on behalf of parishes.

A parish council, including, in the case of a parish having no council, the parish meeting[1], which proposes to acquire land compulsorily, whether by purchase[2] or hiring[3], must make a representation to the district council, which may, on behalf of the parish council, exercise the statutory powers of compulsory acquisition. The order will be carried into effect by the district council, but the land acquired will be assured or demised to the parish council, which will pay all expenses[4]. If the district council refuses to proceed on the representation the parish council may petition the Secretary of State for the Environment or, in Wales, the Secretary of State for Wales, who may, after such inquiry as he thinks fit, make such an order as the district council might have made[5].

A district council may acquire land[6] for leasing to a parish council within the district by purchase by agreement or, if so authorised by the Secretary of State, compulsorily[7], or by leasing land by agreement or compulsorily[8], if the council is unable to acquire suitable land[9] for the purpose by agreement[10].

1 Small Holdings and Allotments Act 1908 s 61 (4). The reference to 'rural parish' in s 61 (4) is to be construed as respects England as a reference to a parish or as respects Wales as a reference to a community: Local Government Act 1972 ss 20 (6), 179 (1), (4).
2 See para 17 ante.
3 See para 18 ante.
4 Small Holdings and Allotments Act 1908 s 39 (7) (amended by the Local Government Act 1972 s 251, Sch 29 Pt II para 9 (4)).
5 Small Holdings and Allotments Act 1908 s 39 (7) proviso (as amended: see note 4 supra). As to the transfer of functions to the Secretaries of State see para 80 note 3 post.
6 The council no longer has power to acquire land in consideration of an annuity, nor can persons having power to sell land to the council sell for an annuity; the Land Settlement (Facilities) Act 1919 s 9 was repealed by the Rentcharges Act 1977 s 17 (2), Sch 2.
7 Compulsory purchase is authorised in accordance with the provisions of the Acquisition of Land Act 1981.
8 Ie in accordance with the compulsory hiring provisions of the Small Holdings and Allotments Act 1908, as to which see paras 18–23 ante.
9 The council is prima facie the judge as to what is suitable land for allotments, whether it can be obtained at a reasonable price, and the probable future financial success of the scheme: *Woodford Land and Building Co Ltd v Woodford UDC* (1921) 19 LGR 559.
10 Small Holdings and Allotments Act 1926 s 4 (amended by the Acquisition of Land (Authorisation Procedure) Act 1946 s 6, Sch 4 and the Local Government Act 1972 s 251, Sch 29 Pt II para 11), applied by the Land Settlement (Facilities) Act 1919 s 17 (amended by the Local Government Act 1972 Sch 29 Pt II para 10), by virtue of the Interpretation Act 1978 s 17 (2) (a), Sch 2 para 3, and the Small Holdings and Allotments Act 1926 s 15, and saved in its application to allotments by the Agriculture Act 1947 s 67 (2) (b).

(iv) Miscellaneous Powers of Acquisition

29. Appropriation of land for allotments or of allotment land. A district or parish council may appropriate for the purpose of allotments any land held by it for its other purposes[1], or may appropriate for its other purposes land acquired by it for allotments[2].

A local authority[3] may be authorised, by order made by it and confirmed by the Secretary of State, to appropriate for any purpose for which it can be authorised to acquire land, any land for the time being held by it which is or forms part of a common, open space or fuel or field garden allotment[4]. When so appropriated the land may be used in any manner[5] in accordance with planning permission notwithstanding anything in any enactment relating to land of that kind.

1 Land Settlement (Facilities) Act 1919 s 22 (1) (a) (amended by the Local Government, Planning and Land Act 1980 ss 1 (5), 194, Sch 5 para 3, Sch 34 Pt V). Reference to a borough and urban district in the Land Settlement (Facilities) Act 1919 s 22 (1) is affected by the Local Government Act 1972; see para 8 note 4 ante.
2 Land Settlement (Facilities) Act 1919 s 22 (1) (b) (as amended: see note 1 supra). There is no longer a requirement for the Secretary of State to consent to any appropriation of land under s 22. Consent is still required for an appropriation of land under s 12 (1) (c); see para 30 post.
3 Ie a local authority as defined by the Town and County Planning Act 1990 s 336 (1).
4 Ibid s 229 (1). By s 336 (1), 'fuel or field garden allotment' means any allotment set out as a fuel or field garden allotment under an Inclosure Act. See further paras 65, 69 post. Where the appropriation is under the Local Government Act 1972 ss 122, 126, the total amount of land appropriated in any particular common, fuel or field garden allotment must not exceed in aggregate 250 square yards (ss 122 (2) (a), 126 (4) (a) (amended by the Local Government, Planning and Land Act 1980 s 194, Sch 34 Pt XIII), notice of the proposed appropriation must be advertised and objections considered (Local Government Act 1972 ss 122 (2) (b), (2A) (added by the 1980 Act s 118, Sch 23 Pt V para 12 (2)), 126 (4) (b), (4A) (added by the 1980 Act Sch 23 Pt V para 17 (2)), and the appropriation will be subject to the rights of other persons in, over and in respect of the land (Local Government Act 1972 ss 122 (1), 126 (3)). See further ss 122, 126; and LOCAL GOVERNMENT.
5 Ie whether or not it involves the erection, construction or carrying out of any building or work, or the maintenance thereof: Town and Country Planning Act 1990 s 246 (3).
6 Ibid s 241 (1) (b).

30. Appropriation of commons and open spaces. Any land which forms part of a metropolitan common[1], or which is subject to regulations under an order or scheme made in pursuance of the Inclosure Acts 1845 to 1899[2], or under any local Act or otherwise, or which forms part of any town or village green, or is a public park, garden or pleasure ground, may not be appropriated for allotments[3].

Land acquired under the Small Holdings and Allotments Act 1908 can, with the consent of the Secretary of State, be appropriated by a district council[4]. If the land appropriated for the purpose of allotments forms part of any common, then the Secretary of State in giving or withholding consent must have regard to the same considerations[5] and hold the same inquiries[6] as are directed by the Commons Act 1876; any consent must be laid before Parliament, and if a motion is carried in either House within 21 days dissenting from the appropriation the order will be cancelled[7]. Where the consent provides for the giving of other land in exchange for the common or open space to be appropriated, an order made by the Secretary of State in relation to the consent may vest that other land in the persons in whom the common or open space was vested, subject to the same rights, trusts and incidents as attached to the common or open space, and will discharge the land appropriated from all rights, trusts and incidents to which it was previously subject[8].

1 Ie within the meaning of the Metropolitan Commons Act 1866 ss 3, 4: see COMMONS.
2 For these Acts see COMMONS.
3 Land Settlement (Facilities) Act 1919 s 28 (1); Acquisition of Land (Authorisation Procedure) Act 1946 s 6, Sch 4; Acquisition of Land Act 1981 s 19. See, however, the Town and Country Planning Act 1990 s 229 (1); and para 29 ante.
4 Land Settlement (Facilities) Act 1919 s 12 (1) (c).
5 See the Commons Act 1876 s 7, which requires the Secretary of State to consider whether the proposed inclosure will be for the benefit of the neighbourhood; and COMMONS.
6 See ibid ss 10, 11; and COMMONS.
7 Land Settlement (Facilities) Act 1919 s 28 (2); Acquisition of Land (Authorisation Procedure) Act 1946 s 6, Sch 4; Acquisition of Land Act 1981 s 19. As to the transfer of functions to the Secretaries of State see para 80 note 3 post.
8 Land Settlement (Facilities) Act 1919 s 28 (3); Acquisition of Land (Authorisation Procedure) Act 1946 s 6, Sch 4; Acquisition of Land Act 1981 s 19.

31. Entry on unoccupied land. A district council may enter on any land (not being agricultural land[1]), which is not the subject of a rateable occupation[2], for the purpose of providing allotment gardens[3]. The council may adapt the land for use for that purpose[4] and let it either to tenants or to any association for the purpose of sub-letting for such use[5], and on the termination of such occupation may remove any erection or work of adaptation, making good any injury to the land caused by the removal[6].

Before entry the council must give not less than 14 days' notice[7] to the owner[8] of the land[9].

These powers of entry do not apply to land which is the property of a local authority or which has been acquired by a corporation for a public undertaking, nor to any common, town or village green, public park or pleasure ground, nor to any part of the New Forest[10], nor to National Trust property[11].

The council's right of occupation may be terminated by the council on six months' notice[12] expiring on or before 6 April or on or after 29 September in any year[13], or by the owner on three months' notice[14] where the land is required for any purpose other than agriculture, sport or recreation, and on six months' notice expiring on the dates aforesaid where the land is required for use for sport or recreation[15]. The owner's notice must tell the council the purpose for which the resumption is required[16], and the council may, by counter-notice[17] served within 21 days of the receipt of that notice, demand that the question whether the resumption is required in good faith for the purpose specified be determined by arbitration[18]. Possession of the land may not be resumed until after the period for demanding arbitration has elapsed or, where arbitration is demanded, until after the arbitration[19].

Any person interested in any land entered upon who suffers any loss thereby will, on making a claim not later than one year after the termination of the right of occupation, be entitled to compensation by way of periodical payments or otherwise which in default of agreement will be determined by valuation made by a person appointed, in default of agreement, by the Secretary of State for the Environment or, in Wales, the Secretary of State for Wales[20]. Such periodical payment of compensation in the nature of rent must not exceed the rental value of the land[21].

1 Agricultural land as defined by the Local Government Finance Act 1988 s 51, Sch 5 para 2 (see RATING) is excepted by the Local Government Act 1929 s 132 (2), Sch 10 para 16.
2 'Rateable occupation' means occupation as would involve liability to payment of rates: Allotments Act 1922 s 10 (7); General Rate Act 1967 s 116 (1) (repealed). Domestic rates have been abolished and

replaced by a community charge by the Local Government Finance Act 1988. The Allotments Act 1922 s 10 (7) refers to the poor rate.

3 Ibid s 10 (1) (a), (6) (a). For the meaning of 'allotment garden' see para 1 ante.

4 Ibid s 10 (1) (b).

5 Ibid s 10 (1) (c). Any tenancy created must terminate when the council's right of occupation terminates: s 10 (1) (c).

6 Ibid s 10 (1) (d). References to borough and urban district in s 10 (1) are affected by the Local Government Act 1972; see para 8 note 4 ante. Reference to the Small Holdings and Allotments Act 1908 s 24 (2) no longer has effect by virtue of the repeal of s 24 by the Local Government Act 1972 s 272 (1), Sch 30.

7 See 2 Forms & Precedents (5th Edn) 379–380, Form 41.

8 'Owner' includes the person who, but for the council's occupation, would be entitled to possession of the land: Allotments Act 1922 s 10 (7).

9 Ibid s 10 (2). For the manner of giving notice see 10 (2), applying the Small Holdings and Allotments (Compulsory Hiring) Regulations 1936, SR & O 1936/196, reg 24.

10 Ie as defined in the New Forest Act 1877. The perambulations of the forest were altered by the New Forest Act 1964 s 1.

11 Allotments Act 1922 s 10 (6). As to National Trust property see OPEN SPACES.

12 See 2 Forms & Precedents (5th Edn) 380, Form 42.

13 Allotments Act 1922 s 10 (3) (a).

14 See 2 Forms & Precedents (5th Edn) 381, Form 43.

15 Allotments Act 1922 s 10 (3) (b) (substituted by the Allotments Act 1925 s 6).

16 Allotments Act 1922 s 11 (1).

17 See 2 Forms & Precedents (5th Edn) 381–382, Form 44.

18 Allotments Act 1922 s 11 (2) (amended by the Allotments Act 1925 s 9). Arbitration is under the Agricultural Holdings Act 1986, as to which see AGRICULTURE vol 1 (1) (Reissue) para 454: Allotments Act 1922 s 11 (2) (as so amended).

19 Ibid s 11 (3) (amended by the Allotments Act 1925 s 9).

20 Allotments Act 1922 s 10 (5). As to the transfer of functions to the Secretaries of State see para 80 note 3 post.

21 Ibid s 10 (5) proviso. 'Rental value' means the annual rent which a tenant might reasonably be expected to pay for the land if the land had continued in the same condition as at the date of entry or, as the case may be, as at the date when possession was first taken: s 10 (7).

32. Sale or lease of land for allotments. A county council may sell or let to a district or parish council for the purpose of allotments any land acquired by it for cottage holdings and a district or parish council may sell or let to the county council for the purpose of cottage holdings any land acquired by it for allotments[1].

A district council has power to sell or let any land acquired under the Small Holdings and Allotments Act 1908, subject in the case of a sale to the consent of the Secretary of State[2].

1 Small Holdings and Allotments Act 1908 ss 45, 61 (1) (amended by the Acquisition of Land (Authorisation Procedure) Act 1946 ss 6, 10, Schs 4, 6); Small Holdings and Allotments Regulations 1919, SR & O 1919/1197, reg 1 (1), (3). As to the application of the Acts of 1908 and 1919 to cottage holdings see para 129 text to note 9 post. As to the transfer of functions to the Secretaries of State see para 80 note 3 post.

2 Land Settlement (Facilities) Act 1919 s 12 (1) (b).

33. Common pasture and grazing rights. The powers of a council to acquire land for allotments include power to provide common pasture by means of a scheme prepared and effected by the council[1]; the rents must be sufficient to cover all the expenses incurred by the council, and rules may be made regulating the turning out of animals and fixing the charges to be made for each animal[2].

The council may also acquire land for the purpose of attaching grazing and other similar rights to allotments provided by it subject to such regulations as the council thinks expedient[3].

1 Small Holdings and Allotments Act 1908 s 34 (1) (amended by the Land Settlement (Facilities) Act 1919 s 33, Schs 2, 3 and the Local Government Act 1972 s 251, Sch 29 Pt II para 9 (2)).
2 Small Holdings and Allotments Act 1908 s 34 (2) (amended by the Local Government Act 1972 Sch 29 Pt II para 9 (3)).
3 Small Holdings and Allotments Act 1908 s 42 (amended by the Land Settlement (Facilities) Act 1919 s 25, Sch 2).

34. New Forest land. The Crown Estate Commissioners may let any land in the New Forest[1] to a local authority for use as allotment gardens[2]. If the land is used for any other purpose, the lease will become void[3]. While so let, the land is free from rights of common and similar rights except the right of the public to use any highway on the land[4].

1 Save in the case of New Forest land vested in Her Majesty which was being used for allotment gardens on 5 April 1922, the consent of the Secretary of State is required: Allotments Act 1922 s 21 (1). As to the transfer of functions to the Secretary of State see para 80 note 4 post. As to the New Forest see para 31 note 10 ante.
2 Ibid s 21 (1); Forestry (Title of Commissioners of Woods) Order 1924, SR & O 1924/1370; Crown Estate Act 1956 s 1 (repealed); Crown Estate Act 1961 s 1 (1).
3 Allotments Act 1922 s 21 (1) proviso.
4 Ibid s 21 (2). Rent received by the commissioners is divisible between them and the Verderers of the Forest in such proportions as may be agreed or, in default of agreement, determined by the arbitration of a single arbitrator: s 21 (3).

(3) MANAGEMENT OF ALLOTMENTS

(i) Improvement, Sale or Exchange

35. Improvement and adaptations of land. A district or parish council may improve any land acquired by it for allotments[1] and adapt it for letting by draining, fencing and making roads, and generally doing whatever is necessary for maintaining the allotments in a proper condition[2]. It may also adapt the land for allotments by erecting buildings and adapting existing buildings, but not more than one dwelling house may be erected for occupation with any one allotment, and no dwelling house may be erected for occupation with an allotment of less than one acre[3].

In general the provision of buildings or the making of any material change in the use of buildings on agricultural land requires planning permission under the town and country planning legislation[4]; but certain development is allowed without any application for permission being made[5].

1 As to the acquisition of land for allotments see para 10 ante. As to local authorities see para 79 post.
2 Small Holdings and Allotments Act 1908 s 26 (1). References to 'borough' and 'urban district' in s 26 (1) are affected by the Local Government Act 1972: see para 8 note 4 ante.
3 Small Holdings and Allotments Act 1908 s 26 (2). This building power is permissive, and the council may validly enter into restrictive covenants preventing its exercising the power: *Stourcliffe Estate Co Ltd v Bournemouth Corpn* [1910] 2 Ch 12, CA.
4 See the Town and Country Planning Act 1990 s 57; and TOWN AND COUNTRY PLANNING.
5 See the Town and Country Planning General Development Order 1988, SI 1988/1813, art 3 (1), Sch 2 Pt 2 (Minor Operations), Pt 4 (Temporary Buildings and Uses) (amended by SI 1989/603), Pt 6 (Agricultural Buildings and Operations) (amended by SI 1989/603): see TOWN AND COUNTRY PLANNING.

36. Sale or exchange of surplus land. Where land acquired by a district or parish council is no longer needed or is not suitable for allotments, the council may sell, let or exchange the land for more suitable land, and may pay or receive money for equality of exchange[1]. The proceeds must be applied in discharging the council's debts and liabilities in respect of land so acquired, or in acquiring, adapting or improving other land for allotments; any surplus may be applied for any purpose for which capital money may be applied, and interest and money received from the letting of land may be applied either in acquiring other land for allotments or in the same way as receipts from the allotments may be applied[2].

Where, however, a local authority has purchased or appropriated land for allotments, it must not sell, appropriate, use or dispose of the land for any purpose other than for allotments without the consent of the Secretary of State for the Environment or, in Wales, the Secretary of State for Wales, which may be given unconditionally or subject to such conditions as he thinks fit, but which must not be given unless he is satisfied that adequate provision will be made for the displaced allotment holders, or that such provision is unnecessary or not reasonably practicable[3].

1 Small Holdings and Allotments Act 1908 s 32 (1) (amended by the Local Government Act 1972 s 272 (1), Sch 30). References to 'borough' and 'urban district' in s 32 (1) are affected by the Local Government Act 1972: see para 8 note 4 ante.
2 Small Holdings and Allotments Act 1908 s 32 (2) (amended by the Local Government, Planning and Land Act 1980 ss 1 (5), 194, Sch 5 para 1 (b), Sch 34 Pt V). As to the transfer of functions to the Secretaries of State see para 80 note 5 post.
3 Allotments Act 1925 s 8 (amended by the Agricultural Land (Utilisation) Act 1931 s 17 (1), Sch 2). As to the transfer of functions to the Secretaries of State see para 80 notes 4, 7 post.

(ii) Terms and Conditions of Letting

37. Regulation of letting. A district or parish council may make such rules as appear to be necessary or proper for regulating the letting of allotments, for preventing any undue preference in such letting, and generally for giving effect to the Allotments Acts[1]. The rules[2] may define the persons eligible to be tenants[3], the notices to be given as to proposed lettings[4], the size of allotments, the conditions under which they are to be cultivated[5], and the rent[6] to be paid for them[7], and must provide for reasonable notice[8] to be given to determine the tenancy[9].

The rules are binding on all persons whatsoever, and the council must cause them to be made known and supply a copy free on demand to any inhabitants of the area[10].

Sub-letting of an allotment is forbidden, except with the consent of the council[11].

One or more allotments may be let to persons working on a co-operative system, or, with the consent of the Secretary of State for the Environment or, in Wales, the Secretary of State for Wales, be let or sold to an association formed for the purposes of creating or promoting the creation of allotments and so constituted that the division of profits among its members is prohibited or restricted[12].

1 Small Holdings and Allotments Act 1908 s 28 (1). Unless otherwise provided, the rules apply to an allotment held under a tenancy made before they come into operation: Land Settlement (Facilities) Act 1919 s 21 (3). As to local authorities see para 79 post.
2 The rules should be framed in accordance with the Model Rules formerly issued by the Secretary of State: for these rules, and for additional rules, see 2 Forms & Precedents (5th Edn) 325–329, Forms 1, 2.
3 They must be resident in the council's area: Small Holdings and Allotments Act 1908 s 23 (1) (amended by the Land Settlement (Facilities) Act 1919 ss 25 (1), 33, Sch 2). See the Model Rules r 2.

Where there are two or more eligible and suitable applicants preference should be given to one who does not already hold an allotment or agricultural land, other than a garden of one-eighth of an acre or less attached to his residence, but otherwise the land must be let to the applicant whose name is first on the list: r 5.

4 See ibid rr 4, 5.
5 See ibid r 7.
6 See ibid r 8.
7 Small Holdings and Allotments Act 1908 s 28 (2).
8 See the Model Rules r 10. For the length of notice in the case of an allotment which is an agricultural holding see the Agricultural Holdings Act 1986 s 25; and AGRICULTURE vol 1 (2) (Reissue) para 340; and, in the case of an allotment garden, see the Allotments Act 1922 s 1 (1) (a) (amended by the Allotments Act 1950 s 1) and para 44 post.
9 Small Holdings and Allotments Act 1908 s 28 (3) (amended by the Local Government, Planning and Land Act 1980 ss 1 (5), 194, Sch 5 para 1 (a), Sch 34 Pt V). The Model Rules also provide for the division of the land into plots shown on a plan (r 3), the form of the application and agreement (rr 5, 6, Schedule), inspection (r 9), exemptions (r 11) and the service of notices (r 12).
10 Small Holdings and Allotments Act 1908 s 28 (4).
11 Ibid s 27 (4) (amended by the Land Settlement (Facilities) Act 1919 s 25 (1), Sch 2).
12 Small Holdings and Allotments Act 1908 s 27 (6) (amended by the Land Settlement (Facilities) Act 1919 Sch 2); Small Holdings and Allotments Act 1926 s 3. As to letting land to an association see also the Allotments Act 1922 s 15. Generally as to allotment societies see para 82 post. As to the transfer of functions to the Secretaries of State see para 80 note 4 post. as to consent to lettings see the Small Holdings and Allotments Regulations 1919, SR & O 1919/1197, reg 1 (1), (3).

38. Rent. Land let by a council for use as an allotment must be let at such a rent as a tenant may reasonably be expected to pay for the land, taking into account the terms of the proposed letting[1], and not more than one quarter's rent may be required to be paid in advance[2], except where the yearly rent is £1.25 or less[3].

Land, however, may be let by a council to a person at a less rent if it is satisfied that there exist special circumstances affecting that person which render it proper for it to let the land to him at the less rent[4].

1 Allotments Act 1950 s 10 (1). 'Reasonable rent' was considered in *Harwood v Borough of Reigate and Banstead* (1982) 43 P & CR 336. The deputy judge held that the council should not discriminate between charges made for allotments and those made for other recreational activities provided by the council. The Departmental Committee of Inquiry into Allotments 1969 (Cmnd 4166) had recommended that 'allotment gardening should in future be considered primarily as a recreation'.
2 Allotments Act 1950 s 10 (2).
3 Ibid s 10 (2) proviso (amended by virtue of the Decimal Currency Act 1969 s 10 (1)).
4 Allotments Act 1950 s 10 (1) proviso.

39. Recovery of rent and possession. Rent, and the possession of any allotment after notice to quit or failure to deliver up possession as required by law, may be recovered by the council as landlords[1]. The court directing recovery of possession of an allotment from any tenant may stay delivery of possession until the payment of any compensation[2] due to the outgoing tenant has been made or secured to the court's satisfaction[3].

1 Small Holdings and Allotments Act 1908 s 30 (1). See also DISTRESS; LANDLORD AND TENANT.
2 As to compensation see para 46 et seq post.
3 Small Holdings and Allotments Act 1908 s 30 (3). The tenant of an agricultural holding is entitled to a charge on the holding in respect of compensation due from the landlord: see the Agricultural Holdings Act 1986 s 85 (2); and AGRICULTURE vol 1 (2) (Reissue) para 478.

40. Damage and theft. Any person who by any act done without lawful authority or by negligence causes damage to any allotment garden[1] or crops, fences or buildings thereon is liable, on summary conviction, to a penalty not exceeding level 1 on the standard scale, provided a notice to this effect is conspicuously displayed on or near the allotment garden[2].

It is an offence without lawful authority to destroy or damage any property belonging to another person either with intent to do so or recklessly as to whether the property be destroyed or damaged[3], or to steal anything[4].

1 For the meaning of 'allotment garden' see para 1 ante.
2 Allotments Act 1922 s 19(1) (amended by virtue of the Criminal Justice Act 1982 s 46). As to the standard scale see para 12 note 1 ante. At the date at which this volume states the law, level 1 on that scale is at £50.
3 See the Criminal Damage Act 1971 s 1 (1); and CRIMINAL LAW.
4 See the Theft Act 1968 s 1; and CRIMINAL LAW.

41. Keeping hens and rabbits. An occupier of land may keep hens or rabbits, otherwise than by way of trade or business, and erect and maintain structures reasonably necessary for that purpose, notwithstanding any provision of a lease or tenancy to the contrary or any covenant, contract or undertaking relating to the use of the land[1]. This provision does not authorise the keeping of hens or rabbits in a place or manner so as to be prejudicial to health or a nuisance, nor does it affect the operation of any enactment[2].

1 Allotments Act 1950 s 12(1).
2 Ibid s 12(1) proviso.

42. Unlet allotments. An allotment which cannot be let in accordance with the provisions of the Allotments Acts and the rules[1] may be let to any person whatever at the best annual rent which can be obtained, without premium or fine, and on such terms as may enable the council to resume possession within a period not exceeding 12 months if it should at any time be required for letting under the Acts[2].

1 As to the rules for letting allotments see para 37 ante.
2 Small Holdings and Allotments Act 1908 s 27(5).

(iii) Determination of Tenancies

43. Provisions applicable to determination of tenancy. The provisions applicable to the determination of the tenancy of an allotment differ according to whether the allotment concerned is an allotment garden or an agricultural holding, or is in neither of these categories. If the allotment is an allotment garden[1] it cannot also be an agricultural holding[2], and special provisions apply to the determination of its letting[3]. If the allotment is an agricultural holding[4] the tenancy may only be determined in accordance with the provisions of the Agricultural Holdings Act 1986[5]. If, however, the allotment falls within neither of these categories there are no statutory provisions specially applicable to the determination of a tenancy of it, except where it is let by a council, in which case, if the rent is in arrear for 40 days, or if it appears to the council that a tenant, not less than three months after the commencement of the tenancy, has not observed the rules affecting the allotment[6], or is resident more than a mile out of the district or parish, the council may give him one month's notice determining the tenancy[7]. Where the land comprised in a compulsory rights order under the Opencast Coal Act 1958 consists of land occupied under an allotment tenancy, the tenancy terminates on the date of entry under that order[8].

Where an allotment has been let to an unemployed person or a person not in full-time employment[9], his tenancy must not be terminated without his consent by reason only that he has ceased to be an unemployed person or a person not in full-time employment[10].

1 For the meaning of 'allotment garden' see para 1 ante.
2 See para 3 ante.
3 See infra.
4 Ie within the meaning of the Agricultural Holdings Act 1986 s 1 (1): see AGRICULTURE vol 1 (2) (Reissue) para 301.
5 See *Stevens v Sedgman* [1951] 2 KB 434, [1951] 2 All ER 33, CA. As to the determination of tenancies of agricultural holdings see AGRICULTURE vol 1 (2) (Reissue) paras 340 et seq, 405.
6 Ie rules made by or in pursuance of the Small Holdings and Allotments Act 1908: see para 37 ante.
7 Small Holdings and Allotments Act 1908 s 30 (2) (amended by the Allotments Act 1922 s 23 (2), Schedule). Notice is given by serving it on the tenant or, if he resides out of the council's area, by leaving it at his last known place of abode in the area, or by fixing it in some conspicuous manner on the allotment: Small Holdings and Allotments Act 1908 s 30 (2). As to local authorities see para 79 post. Reference to 'borough' in s 30 (2) is affected by the Local Government Act 1972; see para 8 note 4 ante.
8 Opencast Coal Act 1958 s 41 (1), Sch 8 para 2.
9 See the Agricultural Land (Utilisation) Act 1931 s 14.
10 Ibid s 15.

44. Determination of tenancy of allotment garden. Where land is let to a tenant for use as an allotment garden[1], or to any local authority or association for subletting for that use, the tenancy cannot be terminated by the landlord[2] by notice to quit or re-entry, notwithstanding any agreement to the contrary[3], except in one of the ways specified below[4]. For this purpose, unless the contrary is proved, land used by a tenant as an allotment garden is deemed to have been let as such[5], and land used by a subtenant as an allotment garden is deemed to have been let to the local authority or association which holds the land under a contract of tenancy, for subletting as such[6].

The tenancy may be determined by the landlord:

(1) by 12 months'[7] or longer notice to quit[8] expiring on or before 6 April or on or after 29 September[9]; or

(2) by re-entry after three months' previous written notice[10] to the tenant under a power of re-entry contained in or affecting the contract of tenancy, on account of the land being required for building, mining or other industrial purpose[11], or for roads or sewers necessary in connection with those purposes[12]; or

(3) by re-entry under a power contained in or affecting the contract of tenancy in the case of land let by a corporation or company being the owners or lessees of a railway, dock, canal, water or other public undertaking on account of the land being required for any non-agricultural[13] purpose for which the land was acquired or held by it or has been appropriated by it under statutory provision, but so that, except in a case of emergency, the tenant must be given three months' written notice of the intended re-entry[14]; or

(4) by re-entry under a power contained in or affecting the contract of tenancy in the case of land let by a local authority, being land which it acquired under the Housing Acts before 4 August 1922[15], on account of the land being

required for housing purposes, and, in the case of other land let by a local authority, after three months' previous written notice[16] to the tenant on account of the land being required for a non-agricultural[17] purpose for which it was acquired, or has been appropriated under any statutory provision[18]; or

(5) by re-entry for non-payment of rent, breach of covenant, bankruptcy of the tenant, the tenant compounding with creditors, or, in the case of an association, its liquidation[19].

These provisions, which do not apply to land attached to a cottage[20], apply to tenancies existing on 4 August 1922[21]. They do not apply to land held by the Secretary of State for Defence or by certain other Secretaries of State[22] and required for their purposes[23], or to land in the possession of a government department under enactments relating to the Defence of the Realm and regulations made thereunder, or to land forming part of a royal park, but otherwise they do apply to land vested in Her Majesty in right of the Crown or the Duchy of Cornwall and, except as before provided, to land vested in any government department for public purposes[24].

1 For the meaning of 'allotment garden' see para 1 ante.
2 'Landlord' means the person entitled to receive the rents and profits: Allotments Act 1922 s 22 (1); Allotments Act 1950 s 14 (1).
3 See *Wombwell UDC v Burke* [1966] 2 QB 149, [1966] 1 All ER 911, CA, where a notice expiring in accordance with the Act but not with the agreement was upheld.
4 Allotments Act 1922 s 1 (1). As to the determination by notice of an allotment tenancy by a council see para 43 ante.
5 Ibid s 22 (4) (a); Allotments Act 1950 s 7; Opencast Coal Act 1958 s 41 (1), Sch 8 para 1 (2).
6 Allotments Act 1922 s 22 (4) (b); Allotments Act 1950 s 7.
7 The period of six months originally prescribed by the Allotments Act 1922 s 1 (1) (a) still applies in the case of land let under the Defence (General) Regulations 1939, SR & O 1939/927, reg 62A (revoked), or the Emergency Laws (Miscellaneous Provisions) Act 1953 s 5: s 5 (3); Allotments Act 1950 s 6.
8 See 2 Forms & Precedents (5th Edn) 341–342, Forms 13, 14.
9 Allotments Act 1922 s 1 (1) (a) (amended by the Allotments Act 1950 s 1). Where under a contract made before 4 August 1922 the tenancy is determinable by the landlord on a date between 6 April and 29 September, any notice to quit must take effect on the latter date: Allotments Act 1922 s 1 (3).
10 See 2 Forms & Precedents (5th Edn) 342, Form 15.
11 'Industrial purpose' does not include use for agriculture or sport, and 'agriculture' includes forestry, horticulture or keeping and breeding livestock: Allotments Act 1922 s 22 (1).
12 Ibid s 1 (1) (b).
13 For the meaning of 'agriculture' see note 11 supra.
14 Allotments Act 1922 s 1 (1) (c).
15 Ie the date of the passing of the Allotments Act 1922.
16 See 2 Forms & Precedents (5th Edn) 342, Form 15.
17 For the meaning of 'agriculture' see note 11 supra.
18 Allotments Act 1922 s 1 (1) (d).
19 Ibid s 1 (1) (e). For notice determining the tenancy for non-payment of rent see 2 Forms & Precedents (5th Edn) 343, Form 16.
20 Allotments Act 1922 s 3 (1); Allotments Act 1950 s 6.
21 Allotments Act 1922 s 1 (2). They do not, however, affect notice to quit given, or proceedings begun, before that date (s 1 (2)), which is the date of the passing of the Allotments Act 1922.
22 Ie the Secretaries of State now exercising functions formerly performed by the Ministry of Supply, namely the Secretary of State for Education and Science, the Secretary of State for Trade and Industry and the Secretary of State for Wales: see the Transfer of Functions (Atomic Energy and Radioactive Substances) Order 1953, SI 1953/1673; the Transfer of Functions (Atomic Energy and Radioactive Substances) Order 1957, SI 1957/561; the Minister of Aviation Order 1959, SI 1959/1768; the Secretary of State for Education and Science Order 1964, SI 1964/490; the Minister of Technology Order 1964, SI 1964/2048; the Transfer of Functions (Civil Aviation) Order 1966, SI 1966/741; the Transfer of Functions (Civil Aviation) (No 2) Order 1966, SI 1966/1015; the Transfer of Functions (Wales) Order 1970, SI 1970/1536; the Secretary of State for Trade and Industry Order

1970, SI 1970/1537; the Ministry of Aviation Supply (Dissolution) Order 1971, SI 1971/719; the Secretary of State (New Departments) Order 1974, SI 1974/692; and the Transfer of Functions (Trade and Industry) Order 1983, SI 1983/1127.

23 Allotments Act 1922 s 1 (4) (amended by the Allotments Act 1950 s 8 and the Defence (Transfer of Functions) (No 1) Order 1964, SI 1964/488, art 2, Sch 1 Pt I).

24 Allotments Act 1922 s 7. As to compensation in the case of Crown or Duchy land see para 56 post.

45. Resumption of possession. Where land has been let to a local authority or an association for allotment gardens, or is occupied by a council under its power to enter unoccupied land[1], and the landlord[2], or the person who, but for such occupation, would be entitled to possession, proposes to resume possession for any particular purpose, written notice[3] of that purpose must be given to the local authority or association[4].

The local authority or association may, by counter-notice[5] served within 21 days after receipt of the notice on the person requiring possession, demand that the question whether possession is required in good faith for the specified purpose be determined by arbitration[6]. Possession must not be resumed until after the period of 21 days or the determination of the question[7].

1 See the Allotments Act 1922 s 10; and para 31 ante.
2 For the meaning of 'landlord' see para 44 note 2 ante.
3 See 2 Forms & Precedents (5th Edn) 365, 378–379, Forms 27, 40.
4 Allotments Act 1922 s 11 (1). This section does not apply where possession is required by a corporation or company as owners or lessees of a railway, dock, canal, water or other public undertaking: s 11 (4).
5 See 2 Forms & Precedents (5th Edn) 381–382, Form 44.
6 Allotments Act 1922 s 11 (2) (amended by the Allotments Act 1925 s 9). Arbitration is under the Agricultural Holdings Act 1986 (as to which see AGRICULTURE vol 1 (2) (Reissue) para 454): Allotments Act 1922 s 11 (2) (amended by the Agricultural Holdings Act 1986 s 100, Sch 14 para 10).
7 Allotments Act 1922 s 11 (3) (amended by the Allotments Act 1925 s 9).

(iv) Compensation at End of Tenancies

A. RIGHT TO COMPENSATION

46. Rights on expiration of tenancy. On the expiration of his tenancy of an allotment, a tenant may be entitled to compensation for improvements, for disturbance and other matters, and a landlord may be entitled to compensation for deterioration to the allotment. The tenant may alternatively have the right to remove fixtures, fruit trees and bushes and like matters. The rights of the landlord and tenant may arise under custom[1] or agreement, or under statute. The statutory provisions applicable differ, as in the case of determination of tenancies[2], according to whether the allotment is an allotment garden, an agricultural holding or an allotment not in either of these two groups. Further, where an allotment tenancy terminates on the date of entry in pursuance of a compulsory rights order under the Opencast Coal Act 1958[3], special rules as to compensation apply[4].

1 Customary rights are considered in relation to agricultural tenancies in AGRICULTURE vol 1 (2) (Reissue) paras 307–311.
2 See para 44 ante.
3 See para 43 ante.
4 See the Opencast Coal Act 1958 s 41, Sch 8; and MINES.

47. Presumption as to letting. Where land is used by the tenant as an allotment garden it is deemed[1], unless the contrary is proved, to have been let to him for such a use[2], and where the land so used has been sublet to him by a local authority or an association which holds the land under a contract of tenancy, the land is deemed[3], unless the contrary is proved, to have been let to the authority or association for the purpose of being sublet for use as an allotment garden[4].

1 Ie for the purposes of the Allotments Act 1922, the Allotments Act 1950 or the Opencast Coal Act 1958 Sch 8.
2 Allotments Act 1922 s 22 (4) (a); Allotments Act 1950 s 7; Opencast Coal Act 1958 s 41 (1), Sch 8 para 1 (2).
3 Ie for the purposes of the Allotments Act 1922.
4 Ibid s 22 (4) (b).

B. ALLOTMENT GARDENS

48. Compensation for improvements on quitting allotment gardens. The tenant of an allotment garden[1] which is not a parcel of land attached to a cottage[2], is entitled, notwithstanding any agreement to the contrary, on quitting the land or part of the land on the termination of the tenancy of the whole or that part of it, to obtain from the landlord[3] compensation[4] for ordinary growing crops[5] and for manure applied to the land[6] based on their value to an incoming tenant[7], but the compensation is recoverable only if the tenancy was terminated by the landlord by statutory re-entry[8] or by notice to quit[9]. A tenant whose tenancy is determined by the termination of his landlord's tenancy can recover compensation from his landlord as if notice to quit had been given by his landlord[10]. Compensation is similarly recoverable by a local authority or association where it has sublet land for allotment gardens[11]. Save as above or as provided by the contract of tenancy the tenant of an allotment garden is not entitled to compensation for improvements[12], although compensation for disturbance[13] may be recoverable[14].

1 For the meaning of 'allotment garden' see para 1 ante.
2 Allotments Act 1922 s 3 (1); Allotments Act 1950 s 6.
3 For the meaning of 'landlord' see para 44 note 2 ante.
4 Allotments Act 1922 s 2 (1), (7). As to compensation in respect of certain allotments see s 3; and para 59 post.
5 If the tenancy terminates between 29 September and 11 October, inclusive, by notice to quit or termination of the landlord's tenancy, the tenant is entitled to remove growing crops within 21 days after the tenancy terminates: ibid s 2 (9).
6 Ibid s 2 (3).
7 Ibid s 22 (3).
8 Ie under ibid s 1 (1) (b), (c) or (d): see para 44 ante.
9 Ibid s 2 (2) (substituted by the Allotments Act 1950 s 2 (1)). This provision applies also to land let under the Emergency Laws (Miscellaneous Provisions) Act 1953 s 5: s 5 (3).
10 Allotments Act 1922 s 2 (4).
11 See ibid s 2 (6); and para 61 post.
12 Ibid s 2 (8).
13 See para 49 post.
14 Allotments Act 1950 s 3 (3).

49. Compensation for disturbance of allotment garden. Where land is let for use by a tenant as an allotment garden[1] or to a local authority or association for the purpose of being sublet for such use and the tenancy is terminated, as to the whole or any part of the land, by statutory re-entry[2], by the termination of the landlord's[3] tenancy, or, where the landlord is a local authority which has let land previously unoccupied[4], by the termination of its right of occupation, the tenant is entitled, notwithstanding any agreement to the contrary, on quitting the land or that part of it, to recover from the landlord compensation for disturbance[5], in addition to any compensation to which a tenant may be entitled for growing crops and manure[6]. The amount of compensation for disturbance is one year's rent at the rate payable immediately before the termination of the tenancy where the whole tenancy is terminated[7] or, where the tenancy of only part of the land is terminated, an amount bearing to one year's rent the same proportion that the area of that part bears to the area of the whole[8].

1 For the meaning of 'allotment garden' see para 1 ante.
2 Ie under the Allotments Act 1922 s 1 (1) (b), (c) or (d): see para 44 ante.
3 For the meaning of 'landlord' see para 44 note 2 ante.
4 Ie under the Allotments Act 1922 s 10: see para 31 ante.
5 Allotments Act 1950 s 3 (1). This section applies whether the land was let before or after the passing of the Act on 26 October 1950 (s 3 (1)), but does not apply to any parcel of land attached to a cottage or let under the Defence (General) Regulations 1939, SR & O 1939/927, reg 62A (revoked) or under the Emergency Laws (Miscellaneous Provisions) Act 1953 s 5 (1950 Act s 6; 1953 Act s 5 (3)). As to the payment of compensation by government departments see para 78 post.
6 Allotments Act 1950 s 3 (3). As to such compensation see para 48 ante.
7 Ibid s 3 (2) (a).
8 Ibid s 3 (2) (b).

50. Compensation for deterioration. Where the tenant of land let to him for use as an allotment garden[1] quits the land on the termination of his tenancy, the landlord[2] is entitled, notwithstanding any agreement to the contrary, to recover from the tenant compensation in respect of any deterioration of the land caused by the tenant's failure to maintain it clean and in a good state of cultivation and fertility[3]. The amount of any such compensation is the cost, as at the date of the tenant's quitting the land, of making good the deterioration[4].

Where the tenant has remained on the land during two or more tenancies the landlord is not deprived of his right to compensation for deterioration by reason only that the tenancy during which part or all of the deterioration occurred was a tenancy other than that at the termination of which the tenant quitted the land[5].

1 For the meaning of 'allotment garden' see para 1 ante.
2 For the meaning of 'landlord' see para 44 note 2 ante.
3 Allotments Act 1950 s 4 (1). This section applies in the circumstances in which s 3 applies: see para 49 note 5 ante.
4 Ibid s 4 (2).
5 Ibid s 4 (3).

51. Compensation by mortgagee. Where the contract of tenancy in respect of an allotment[1] or allotment garden[2] is made with a mortgagor but is not binding on the mortgagee, the tenant is entitled, if deprived of possession by the mortgagee, to recover compensation[3], including compensation for disturbance[4], from him as if he were the landlord[5] and had terminated the tenancy, but subject to the deduction from the compensation of rent or other sums due from the tenant in respect of the land[6].

1 For the meaning of 'allotment' in this context see the Allotments Act 1922 s 3 (7); and para 1 ante.

2 For the meaning of 'allotment garden' see para 1 ante.
3 Ie under the Allotments Act 1922 ss 2, 3: see paras 48 ante, 59 post.
4 Ie under the Allotments Act 1950 s 3 (s 3 (4)): see para 49 ante.
5 For the meaning of 'landlord' see para 44 note 2 ante.
6 Allotments Act 1922 s 4 (2).

52. Compensation to outgoing tenant. A tenant of an allotment who has paid compensation to an outgoing tenant for fruit trees or bushes or other improvements, has the same rights as to compensation or removal as he would have had if the trees or bushes had been provided and planted or the improvement made by him and at his expense[1].

1 Allotments Act 1922 s 5.

53. Adjustment of compensation. Out of any money payable to the tenant of an allotment garden[1] by way of compensation for crops or manure or for disturbance[2], the landlord[3] is entitled to deduct any sum due to him from the tenant in respect of the tenancy, including compensation[4] for deterioration[5]. Similarly, out of any money due to the landlord in respect of the tenancy, including compensation for deterioration, the tenant is entitled to deduct any money due to him from the landlord by way of compensation for crops or manure or for disturbance[6].

1 For the meaning of 'allotment garden' see para 1 ante.
2 Ie under the Allotments Act 1922 s 2 (see para 50 ante) or the Allotments Act 1950 s 3 (see para 49 ante).
3 For the meaning of 'landlord' see para 44 note 2 ante.
4 Ie under the Allotments Act 1950 s 4: see para 50 ante.
5 Ibid s 5 (1).
6 Ibid s 5 (2).

54. Removal of improvements by tenant. Fruit trees and bushes provided and planted by a tenant of land held under a contract of tenancy of an allotment garden or certain allotments[1], and any erection, fencing or other improvement erected or made by him and at his expense or in respect of which he has paid compensation to an outgoing tenant may be removed by him before the expiration of the tenancy, provided he makes good any injury caused by the removal[2].

The tenant of an allotment may also, before the expiration of his tenancy, remove any fruit and other trees and bushes planted or acquired by him, and any tool-house, shed or greenhouse built or acquired by him, for which he has no claim for compensation[3].

1 Ie under the Allotments Act 1922 ss 1–3: see paras 44, 48 ante, 59 post.
2 Ibid ss 4 (1), 5.
3 Small Holdings and Allotments Act 1908 s 47 (4).

55. Assessment and recovery of compensation. In default of agreement, the compensation[1] must be assessed by the valuation of a person who, unless agreed upon by the landlord and tenant, must be appointed by the judge of the local county court[2]. If the amount agreed or determined is not paid within 14 days it may be recovered upon order made by the county court as money ordered to be paid by that court under its ordinary jurisdiction is recoverable[3].

The valuer's proper charges are borne by the landlord and tenant in such proportion as the valuer directs, but he may recover them from either party, and any amount paid by one party in excess of the amount the valuer directs to be borne by that party is recoverable from the other party or can be deducted from the compensation payable[4].

1 Ie compensation under the Allotments Act 1922 or under the Allotments Act 1950, and such further compensation, if any, as is recoverable under the contract of tenancy: Allotments Act 1922 s 6 (1); Allotments Act 1950 s 7.
2 Allotments Act 1922 s 6 (1); Allotments Act 1950 s 7.
3 Allotments Act 1922 s 6 (1); Allotments Act 1950 s 7. The order is made by the district judge on ex parte originating application filed in the court for the district where the person due to pay resides or carries on business, and the applicant must at the hearing produce the order or agreement (or a duplicate) under which the compensation is payable and file a copy of it together with an affidavit verifying the amount due : CCR Ord 25 r 12; Courts and Legal Services Act 1990 s 74 (1). As to the fee payable on an application for the recovery of an award under CCR Ord 25 r 12, see the County Court Fees Order 1982, SI 1982/1706, Sch 1 (amended by SI 1983/1681, SI 1985/574, SI 1985/1834, SI 1986/633, SI 1986/2143 and SI 1988/509). The High Court's jurisdiction is not excluded by this provision: *Horrell v Lord St John of Bletso* [1928] 2 KB 616.
4 Allotments Act 1922 s 6 (2); Allotments Act 1950 s 7.

56. Crown, Duchy, and government land. The foregoing provisions as to compensation[1] do not apply to land of which possession was taken on behalf of any government department under enactments relating to the Defence of the Realm or regulations thereunder, and possession of which has been continued by any enactment, or to land forming part of a royal park; otherwise, they apply to land vested in Her Majesty in right of the Crown or the Duchy of Lancaster, and to land forming part of the possessions of the Duchy of Cornwall, and, except as before provided, to land vested in any government department for public purposes[2].

1 Ie the Allotments Act 1922 ss 1–6 and the Allotments Act 1950 ss 1–6.
2 Allotments Act 1922 s 7; Allotments Act 1950 s 7.

57. Compensation to tenant at end of council's occupation. Unless the contract of tenancy otherwise provides, a tenant to whom land has been let by a council under its power in relation to unoccupied land[1] and whose tenancy is terminated by the termination of the council's right of occupation, is entitled to recover from the council such compensation, if any, as would have been recoverable if his tenancy had been terminated by notice to quit given by the council, and has the same right to remove his crops as if the tenancy had been so terminated[2]. If, however, the rent payable by the tenant exceeds 1 p per pole, the tenant is entitled to claim compensation notwithstanding any agreement in the contract of tenancy to the contrary[3]. Compensation for disturbance, also, may be claimed by the tenant notwithstanding any such agreement[4].

1 Ie under the Allotments Act 1922 s 10: see para 31 ante.
2 Ibid s 10 (4). As to compensation and the removal of crops see para 48 et seq ante.
3 Allotments Act 1925 s 7 (amended by virtue of the Decimal Currency Act 1969 s 10 (1)). A pole is 30¼ square yards. The rent referred to is an annual rent.
4 Allotments Act 1950 s 3 (1) (c): see para 49 ante.

C. OTHER ALLOTMENTS

58. Compensation for allotments which are agricultural holdings. Where an allotment is an agricultural holding[1] the tenant may claim compensation for improvements and tenant-right matters, for disturbance and for the continuous adoption of a special system of farming in accordance with the provisions of the Agricultural Holdings Act 1986 in that behalf[2], and has the rights of removing fixtures conferred on tenants of such holdings[3]. He is liable to pay compensation to his landlord for deterioration to the holding[4].

In the case of certain allotments of not more than two acres[5] which are also agricultural holdings, the tenant may alternatively claim compensation in accordance with the provisions of the Allotments Act 1922[6].

1 Ie within the meaning of the Agricultural Holdings Act 1986 s 1 (1): see AGRICULTURE vol 1 (2) (Reissue) para 301.
2 See AGRICULTURE vol 1 (2) (Reissue) para 383 et seq.
3 See AGRICULTURE vol 1 (2) (Reissue) para 323.
4 See AGRICULTURE vol 1 (2) (Reissue) paras 436–443.
5 Ie 'allotments' as defined in the Allotments Act 1922 s 3 (7): see para 59 post.
6 Ibid s 3 (5). As to these provisions see para 48 et seq ante. The tenant of an allotment let by a council may claim compensation for certain improvements as if the allotment were a market garden within the Agricultural Holdings Act 1986 s 79 or alternatively under the Allotments Act 1922 s 3, even if the allotment exceeds two acres: see the Small Holdings and Allotments Act 1908 s 47 (1), (3); and para 60 post. As to the 1986 Act s 79 see AGRICULTURE vol 1 (2) (Reissue) para 444.

59. Compensation for allotments not exceeding two acres. The tenant of an allotment of not more than two acres in extent, whether attached to a cottage or not, but not being an allotment garden[1], and which is cultivated as a farm or a garden, or partly as a garden and partly as a farm[2], is, on the termination of his tenancy by effluxion of time or from any other cause, entitled, notwithstanding any agreement to the contrary, to obtain from the landlord[3] compensation for:

(1) crops, including fruit, growing on the land in the ordinary course of cultivation, and for labour expended on and manure applied to the land; and

(2) fruit trees or bushes provided and planted by the tenant with the landlord's previous written consent, and drains, outbuildings, pigsties, fowlhouses or other structural improvements made or erected by the tenant and at his expense with such consent[4].

The compensation is based on the value to an incoming tenant of the crops and other subjects of compensation[5].

Any sum due to the landlord from the tenant in respect of rent, any breach of the contract of tenancy, or wilful or negligent damage committed or permitted by the tenant, must be deducted from the compensation[6], and, in default of agreement, the amount of compensation is determined and recovered as in the case of allotment gardens[7].

The tenant has the same right to remove fruit trees, bushes and fixtures, and to compensation where deprived of possession by a mortgagee or where he has paid compensation to an outgoing tenant, as has the tenant of an allotment garden[8].

Where the allotment is an agricultural holding[9] a claim for compensation may be made instead under the Agricultural Holdings Act 1986, but not under both provisions[10].

1 For the meaning of 'allotment garden' see para 1 ante.
2 Allotments Act 1922 s 3 (7).

3　For the meaning of 'landlord' see para 44 note 2 ante.
4　Allotments Act 1922 s 3 (2). Compensation under this provision in respect of allotments exceeding two acres and let by a council may also be claimed at the tenant's election under the Small Holdings and Allotments Act 1908 s 47 (3).
5　Allotments Act 1922 s 22 (3).
6　Ibid s 3 (3).
7　Ibid s 3 (4). As to compensation for allotment gardens see paras 48, 55 ante.
8　Ibid ss 4, 5: see paras 52, 54 ante.
9　Ie within the meaning of the Agricultural Holdings Act 1986 s 1 (1): see AGRICULTURE vol 1 (2) (Reissue) para 301.
10　See the Allotments Act 1922 s 3 (5), which provided for the substitution of the compensation provisions in s 3 for the corresponding provisions in the Agricultural Holdings Acts 1908 to 1921, which applied when the 1922 Act was passed. The Acts of 1908 to 1921 were repealed by the Agricultural Holdings Act 1923 and s 56 (2) similarly provided for the substitution of the provisions of the 1923 Act by those of the 1922 Act (ie s 6) in the case of agricultural holdings which also came within the text to note 2 supra. Section 56 (2) of the 1923 Act was repealed by the Agriculture Act 1947 ss 45, 110, Schs 7, 13, and not replaced by any corresponding provision in the Agricultural Holdings Act 1948, so it seems that on an application for compensation under the current Act of 1986 the whole of that Act, including the provisions as to the measure and recovery of compensation, will apply: see *Stevens v Sedgman* [1951] 2 KB 434 at 440, [1951] 2 All ER 33 at 35, CA, per Somervell LJ.

60. Compensation for allotments let by council. The tenant of an allotment let to him by a council has, as against the council, the same rights with respect to compensation for improvements effected by planting standard or other fruit trees or fruit bushes permanently set out, and planting strawberry plants and asparagus, rhubarb and other vegetable crops which continue productive for two or more years, as if it had been agreed in writing that the allotment should be let under the Agricultural Holdings Act 1986 as a market garden[1].

The tenant is not, however, entitled to compensation for such improvements if executed contrary to an express written prohibition by the council[2].

The tenant of an allotment provided by the council[3] may, if he so elects, claim compensation for improvements under the provisions applicable to allotments not exceeding two acres[4], instead of claiming as if the allotment were let as a market garden, notwithstanding that the allotment exceeds two acres[5].

1　Small Holdings and Allotments Act 1908 s 47 (1), Sch 2 Pt I; Agricultural Holdings Act 1986 s 79. As to compensation for market gardens see AGRICULTURE vol 1 (2) (Reissue) para 444.
2　Small Holdings and Allotments Act 1908 s 47 (1) proviso (amended by the Local Government, Planning and Land Act 1980 s 1 (5), Sch 5 para 1 (c), Sch 34 Pt VI).
3　Ie an allotment to which the Small Holdings and Allotments Act 1908 Pt II (ss 23–35) applies.
4　Ie an allotment as defined in the Allotments Act 1922 s 3 (7): see para 59 ante.
5　Small Holdings and Allotments Act 1908 s 47 (3).

D.　COMPENSATION TO COUNCILS OR ASSOCIATIONS AS TENANTS

61. Compensation for land let for allotment gardens. Where land is let to a local authority or association under a contract of tenancy made after 4 August 1922 for the purpose of being sublet for use by the tenants as allotment gardens[1], the authority or association may claim compensation for improvements in the same manner as may individual tenants of allotment gardens[2], notwithstanding that the crops have been grown and the manure applied by the subtenants[3]. The authority or association may also claim compensation for disturbance in respect of land let to it for subletting as allotment gardens[4].

1 For the meaning of 'allotment garden' see para 1 ante. For the presumption as to letting where land is
 used as allotment gardens see para 47 ante.
2 See para 48 ante.
3 Allotments Act 1922 s 2 (6).
4 See the Allotments Act 1950 s 3 (1); and para 49 ante.

62. Compensation for land let for allotments. Where land is let for the
provision of allotments, other than allotment gardens, to a council[1] or to an
association formed for the purpose of creating or promoting the creation of
allotments, the right of the council or association to claim compensation from the
landlord on the determination of the tenancy is subject to the terms of the contract
of tenancy, notwithstanding the provisions of any Act to the contrary[2].

On the determination of a tenancy of land hired by a council, whether compulsorily or by agreement, the council, on quitting the land, is entitled, subject to any
provision to the contrary in the agreement or order for hiring, to compensation
under the Agricultural Holdings Act 1986[3] for any improvement in respect of the
planting of standard or other fruit trees or fruit bushes permanently set out, or of
the planting of strawberry plants or of asparagus, rhubarb and other vegetable
crops which continue productive for two or more years[4], and in respect of any of
the following improvements which were necessary and proper to adapt the land for
allotments, namely erecting, altering or enlarging buildings; forming silos; laying
permanent pasture; making and planting osier beds; making water meadows or
works of irrigation; making gardens; making or improving roads or bridges;
making or improving watercourses, ponds, wells or reservoirs, or works for the
application of water power or for the supply of water for agricultural or domestic
purposes; making or removing permanent fences; planting hops; planting orchards
or fruit bushes; protecting young fruit trees; reclaiming waste land; warping or
weiring land; making embankments and sluices against floods; erecting wirework
in hop gardens; drainage; providing permanent sheep-dipping accommodation;
and, in the case of arable land, removing bracken, gorse, tree roots, boulders and
other like obstructions to cultivation[5]. In the case of land hired compulsorily the
compensation is such sum as fairly represents the increase, if any, in the value to the
landlord and his successors in title of the land due to such improvements[6].

1 Ie under the Small Holdings and Allotments Act 1908: see s 25; and para 13 ante.
2 Land Settlement (Facilities) Act 1919 s 23; Allotments Act 1922 s 2 (6). This provision does not
 prejudice or affect the tenant's right to claim compensation from the council on the determination of
 his tenancy (as to which see para 60 ante): Land Settlement (Facilities) Act 1919 s 23 proviso.
3 Compensation may be claimed under the Agricultural Holdings Act 1986 as if the land were a
 holding which it was agreed in writing under s 79 should be let as a market garden and as if the
 improvements specified in the text to note 5 infra were comprised in Schs 8, 10 to the 1986 Act: Small
 Holdings and Allotments Act 1908 s 47 (2) (amended by the Land Settlement (Facilities) Act 1919
 s 25, Sch 2 and the Agricultural Holdings Act 1986 s 100, Sch 14). As to compensation for market
 gardens see AGRICULTURE vol 1 (2) (Reissue) para 444.
4 Small Holdings and Allotments Act 1908 s 47 (2), Sch 2 Pt I (as amended: see note 3 supra).
5 Ibid s 47 (2), Sch 2 Pt II; Land Settlement (Facilities) Act 1919 s 25 (1), Sch 2; Small Holdings and
 Allotments Act 1926 s 21, Sch 1.
6 Small Holdings and Allotments Act 1908 s 47 (2) proviso.

(4) POOR, FIELD GARDEN AND FUEL ALLOTMENTS

63. Parochial and other allotments. During the nineteenth century allotments
were provided for cultivation by poor and industrious parishioners and as rec-

reation grounds for the parishioners[1] under certain Poor Law and Inclosure Acts and by appropriation of parochial charity lands for that purpose. The allotments here considered are poor allotments[2], field garden allotments[3], and allotments for fuel and certain other public purposes[4].

Allotments vested in the overseers[5], or churchwardens and overseers, of a rural parish were transferred to the parish council when that council came into being[6] or, where there was no parish council, the parish meeting[7]. Trustees holding any property for the purposes of allotments for the benefit of the inhabitants of a parish[8] having a parish council may, with the approval of the Charity Commissioners and with the consent of that council, transfer the property to the council or to persons appointed by it, to be held on the same trusts and subject to the same conditions as when it was held by the trustees[9]. The Local Government Board had power to confer on municipal, county borough and urban district councils the powers, duties and liabilities of parish councils[10], and in 1933 all remaining functions and liabilities of vestries and churchwardens not relating to the church or charities were transferred to the borough or urban district council[11].

Allotment wardens[12], who managed allotments and field gardens for the labouring poor, might by consent transfer the management to the borough, urban district or parish council[13], and the powers and duties of wardens, committees and managers of allotments in rural parishes were transferred to the parish council or, where there was no such council, persons appointed by the parish meeting[14].

Allotments held by overseers or churchwardens of urban parishes were transferred to county borough and urban district councils and are now vested in district councils[15].

Thus, with the exception of allotments which have not been transferred to the local authority by the trustees in whom they are vested, any such allotment, together with the powers and duties respecting it, is now vested in or under the control of the parish or district council, and is managed by it as one unit with lands acquired under the Allotments Acts[16].

1 As to allotments for recreation see COMMONS vol 6 (Reissue) para 530 et seq.
2 See para 64 post.
3 See paras 65–68, 73 post.
4 See paras 69–73 post.
5 Overseers were abolished and their functions transferred to rating authorities by the Rating and Valuation Act 1925 s 62 (1) (repealed), (3).
6 Local Government Act 1894 s 6 (1) (c) (iii).
7 Ibid s 19 (amended by the Statute Law Revision Act 1908, the Local Government Act 1933 ss 307, 308, Sch 11 Pt IV, the Charities Act 1960 s 48 (2), Sch 7 Pt I and the Local Authorities (Miscellaneous Provisions) Order 1979, SI 1979/1123); Overseers Order 1927, SR & O 1927/55, arts 4 (2), 7.
8 Charities Act 1960 s 37 (1) (amended by virtue of the Local Government Act 1972 s 179 (4) to reflect the abolition of rural parishes and their replacement by parishes; see para 28 note 1 ante).
9 Charities Act 1960 s 37 (1) (amended by the Local Government Act 1972 s 272, Sch 30; see also note 8 supra); see further CHARITIES. This provision replaced the Local Government Act 1894 s 14 (repealed).
10 Local Government Act 1894 s 33 (repealed).
11 Local Government Act 1933 s 269 (1) (repealed). The functions and liabilities are now vested in district councils: Local Government Act 1972 s 179; see para 8 note 4 ante.
12 See the Inclosure Act 1845 s 108.
13 Small Holdings and Allotments Act 1908 s 33 (1). See the Local Government Act 1972 s 179; and para 8 note 4 ante.
14 Small Holdings and Allotments Act 1908 s 33 (3); and see para 28 note 1 ante.
15 Overseers Order 1927 arts 4, 5. As to local authorities see paras 8 note 4 ante and 79 post.
16 Small Holdings and Allotments Act 1908 s 33 (4). As to local authorities see paras 8 note 4 ante and 79 post.

64. Poor allotments. Poor allotments are parish lands possessed or acquired by poor law authorities under the Poor Relief Act 1819, or by the inclosure of waste or common land under the Poor Relief Act 1831, or by the inclosure under the Crown Lands Allotments Act 1831 of forest or waste Crown land, for the employment of poor persons or for letting to poor persons for cultivation on their own account[1]. Land inclosed in the exercise of those powers or otherwise appropriated for the general benefit of the poor of any parish was subsequently authorised to be let to industrious cottagers living in or near the parish where the land was situated for the purpose of cultivation[2]. The rents derived from those lettings were to be applied, after the deduction of all proper charges, in aid of the poor rate[3] of the parish[4].

The powers under these statutes were exercisable by the overseers of the poor or the poor law guardians[5].

1 Poor Relief Act 1819 ss 12, 13; Poor Relief Act 1831 ss 1, 2; Crown Lands Allotments Act 1831. These Acts were repealed by the Poor Law Act 1927, itself repealed by the Poor Law Act 1930, repealed in turn by the National Assistance Act 1948 s 62, Sch 7 (repealed). Land held on 5 July 1948 for these purposes was deemed to have been appropriated for such of the purposes of the 1948 Act as the council determined: Sch 6 para 6; National Assistance Act (Appointed Day) Order 1948, SI 1948/1218. See now the Social Security Act 1988.
2 Allotments Act 1832 ss 1, 11.
3 This then became the general rate: General Rate Act 1967 s 116(1) (repealed). See now the Local Government Finance Act 1988, which abolished the domestic rate and introduced in its stead the community charge; see further RATING.
4 Poor Allotments Management Act 1873 s 14.
5 Union and Parish Property Act 1835 s 4 (repealed). As to the present authorities see para 63 ante.

65. Field garden allotments. Field gardens[1] are lands appropriated as allotments or field gardens for the labouring poor upon the inclosure of lands or the regulation of a common[2]. They were managed by allotment wardens consisting of the incumbent of the parish or ecclesiastical district or the officiating minister nominated by the incumbent, one of the churchwardens and two of the ratepayers of the parish, any two of whom could exercise the statutory powers[3].

1 'Field garden' means an allotment for the labouring poor: Commons Act 1876, preamble. The term 'allotment' in the Small Holdings and Allotments Act 1908 includes a field garden: s 61 (1). 'Field garden allotment' in the Acquisition of Land Act 1981 s 19 (4) and the Town and Country Planning Act 1990 s 336 means any allotment set out as a field garden allotment under an Inclosure Act.
2 Inclosure Act 1845 ss 31, 73 (s 31 amended by the Commons Act 1876 s 24); Inclosure Act 1846 s 4; Commons Act 1876 ss 21–23; Commonable Rights Compensation Act 1882 s 3; see generally COMMONS.
3 Inclosure Act 1845 s 108. As to the present authorities see para 63 ante.

66. Letting and management of field garden allotments. The allotment wardens or their successors[1] may let field garden allotments not exceeding one quarter of an acre to poor inhabitants of the parish for one year or on a tenancy from year to year at the full yearly agricultural value free of all rentcharge and other rates, but if any land cannot be let in quarter acre plots they can let field gardens not exceeding one acre in size at a fair agricultural rent sufficient to satisfy all rates, taxes, tithes and rentcharges[2]. Surplus rents are available for the maintenance and improvement of field gardens or of recreation grounds, and can also be used for drainage, fencing or the hiring or purchasing of additional land for field gardens or recreation grounds[3].

No building may be erected for or used as a dwelling house on a field garden allotment[4]. The tenancy can be determined by one month's notice in the event of the occupier being 40 days in arrears with his rent, or failing to observe the terms and conditions of his tenancy, or going to reside more than one mile outside the parish[5]. Possession, formerly recoverable in accordance with the Small Tenements Recovery Act 1838, can be recovered by county court proceedings, and rent can be recovered by distress or otherwise by the wardens or their successors as if the legal estate were vested in them[6].

1 See para 63 ante.
2 Inclosure Act 1845 s 109; Commons Act 1876 s 26. Tithe redemption annuities were extinguished by the Finance Act 1977, rentcharges by the Rentcharges Act 1977 and rates by the Local Government Finance Act 1988.
3 Commons Act 1876 s 27; Commons Act 1879 s 2; Commons Act 1899 s 16. Allotment wardens had to report on field gardens at intervals of not less than three nor more than five years to the Inclosure Commissioners (subsequently the Board of Agriculture and in due course the Minister of Agriculture, Fisheries and Food and now the Secretary of State for the Environment or, in Wales, the Secretary of State for Wales: see COMMONS vol 6 (Reissue) para 704 note 5).
4 Inclosure Act 1845 s 109.
5 Ibid s 110. The provision there made for the determination of field garden tenancies is similar to that made by the Small Holdings and Allotments Act 1908 s 30 (2), in respect of allotments let by councils, and the special statutory provisions applicable to the determination of tenancies of allotments which are allotment gardens or agricultural holdings (as to which see paras 43, 44 ante) apply equally to field gardens in either of those categories.
6 Inclosure Act 1845 ss 111, 112 (s 111 amended by the Rent Act 1965 s 51, Sch 6 para 1).

67. Sale, exchange, transfer and use of field garden allotments. The allotment wardens of a field garden or their successors[1] may, with the approval of the Secretary of State for the Environment or, in Wales, the Secretary of State for Wales[2], sell all or any part of it and purchase other suitable land for the same purpose[3], and the Secretary of State may also authorise the exchange of inconveniently placed or unsuitable field gardens for other land[4].

Allotment wardens may, by agreement with the council of the district or parish in which the field garden is wholly or partly situated, transfer the management of the land to the council upon such terms as may be agreed with the sanction, as regards the wardens, of the Secretary of State, and thereupon the land vests in the council[5].

Any land forming part of a field garden allotment[6] which has been compulsorily acquired[7] by a minister, local authority or statutory undertakers, or appropriated by a local authority for planning purposes, may, notwithstanding anything in any enactment relating to such allotments or by which the land is specially regulated, be used either, if acquired by a minister, in any manner for any purpose for which he acquired it or, in any other case, by any person in any manner in accordance with planning permission[8].

1 See para 63 ante.
2 As to the transfer of functions to the Secretaries of State see para 66 note 3 ante.
3 Commons Act 1876 s 27. Approval would not be given unless it was proved that more suitable land could and would be forthwith purchased: s 27.
4 Inclosure Act 1845 s 149.
5 Small Holdings and Allotments Act 1908 s 33 (1). As to the local authorities see paras 8 note 4, 28 note 1 ante, and 79 post.
6 For the meaning of 'field garden allotment' see para 65 note 1 ante.
7 As to compulsory acquisition see para 68 post.
8 Town and Country Planning Act 1990 s 241 (1). It was formerly unlawful to use any field garden for any purpose other than that declared by the Act and award under which it was set out, notwithstanding anything in any other Act: see the Commons Act 1876 s 19. See also para 29 ante. For schemes by the Charity Commissioners as to field gardens see para 73 post.

68. Acquisition of land for and appropriation of field garden allotments. The council of a district or parish may, for the purpose of providing field gardens, by agreement purchase or take on lease land, whether within or outside its area, or may purchase such land compulsorily in accordance with the provisions of the Small Holdings and Allotments Act 1908[1] and the Acquisition of Land Act 1981[2].

A county, London borough or district council may be authorised by the Secretary of State for the Environment to acquire compulsorily any land within its area which is required for development or other planning purposes[3], and may be authorised by an order made by it and confirmed by the Secretary of State to appropriate, for any purpose for which it can be authorised to acquire land under any enactment, any land held by it for other purposes, being land which is or forms part of a field garden allotment[4].

In so far as a compulsory purchase or appropriation order authorises the purchase or appropriation of land forming part of a field garden allotment[5] the order is subject to special parliamentary procedure[6] unless the Secretary of State or, in Wales, the Secretary of State for Wales, is satisfied that equivalent land has been or will be given in exchange, vested in the same persons and subject to the same rights, trusts and incidents, or that the land is required for the widening of an existing highway and that it is unnecessary to give other land in exchange, and certifies accordingly[7].

1 See the Small Holdings and Allotments Act 1908 ss 39, 41–43, 45; and paras 17, 24–26 ante.
2 Ibid ss 25 (1), 61 (1) (s 25 (1) amended by the Acquisition of Land (Authorisation Procedure) Act 1946 s 6, Sch 4 and the Acquisition of Land Act 1981 s 34, and by virtue of the Local Government Act 1972 s 179). As to local authorities see para 79 post.
3 Town and Country Planning Act 1990 s 226 (1), (3); see TOWN AND COUNTRY PLANNING.
4 Ibid s 229 (2).
5 For the meaning of 'field garden allotment' see para 65 note 1 ante.
6 See the Statutory Orders (Special Procedure) Act 1945; and PARLIAMENT.
7 Acquisition of Land Act 1981 s 19; Town and Country Planning Act 1990 s 229 (3); see COMMONS. As to the transfer of functions to the Secretaries of State see para 80 post.

69. Fuel allotments. In addition to the allotments for recreation grounds and field gardens, allotments for other public purposes may be resolved upon by the persons interested at the meeting held under the Inclosure Act 1845 for the appointment of the valuer or at some other meeting for the purpose, and may be embodied in his instructions[1]. The principal matters for which allotments may be made and continued in use under parochial or other management are allotments for the supply of fuel for the labouring poor, quarries for the supply of road materials, and allotments for public ponds or watering places[2].

Fuel allotments[3] were frequently set out both under private Inclosure Acts and in the early days of the Inclosure Commissioners in the north and other hilly regions where there were turbary rights, and peat or turf which could be used as fuel. They were often of considerable extent, and, coming as they did within the definition of land subject to be inclosed[4], when no longer suitable for the purposes for which they were set out or not required, were the subject of subsequent inclosure or regulation[5]. Because rights in fuel allotments are vested in a fluctuating body of people they cannot be registered as commons. In practice many areas of land formerly set aside as fuel allotments are now to all intents and purposes public open land.

Where fuel allotments provided under local Inclosure Acts before 1845 became useless and unproductive, the trustees, together with the churchwardens and overseers of the parish[6], were required to let them to industrious cottagers living in or near the parish for the purposes of cultivation[7], and the rents received from the lettings were to be applied for the purchase of fuel for distribution to poor parishioners[8].

1 See the Inclosure Act 1845 s 34; and COMMONS.
2 Ibid s 34.
3 'Fuel allotment' in the Acquisition of Land Act 1981 s 19 (4) and in the Town and Country Planning Act 1990 s 336 (1) means an allotment set out as a fuel allotment under an Inclosure Act. It is defined in the Charities Act 1960 Sch 4 para 1 (d), as land which by any enactment relating to inclosure or any instrument having effect thereunder is vested in trustees upon trust that the land or the rents and profits of it shall be used for the purpose of providing poor persons with fuel.
4 See the Inclosure Act 1845 s 11.
5 Eg the fuel allotment which was the subject of dispute in *A-G v Meyrick* [1893] AC 1, HL; and Harrow Weald Common, which was an old gravel allotment and was the subject of a scheme under the Metropolitan Commons Acts.
6 The Poor Allotments Management Act 1873 provided for the appointment of committees of management of allotments in certain cases. As to the transfer of churchwardens' and overseers' functions see para 63 ante.
7 Ie in accordance with the Allotments Act 1832.
8 Ibid s 8.

70. Allotments for other public purposes. Allotments may be made to highway authorities for obtaining stone, gravel and other materials for road repairs. The grass and herbage of such allotments may be awarded to other persons or let by the authority[1]. A highway authority may by ceasing to use such allotments and obtaining its materials elsewhere lose its right to extract such materials, and an adverse title may be acquired against the authority by other persons[2].

1 Inclosure Act 1845 s 72; Highways Act 1980 ss 179 (1), 340 (1). The terms of the 1845 Act and the award must be strictly adhered to. Where an allotment was made under the Inclosure Acts for obtaining stone, gravel and other materials for repairing highways and public and private roads for the use of the inhabitants of the parish, it was held that such allotments were for road repairs only, and that a user by inhabitants for private purposes was not authorised: *Rylatt v Marfleet* (1845) 14 M & W 233.
2 *Thew v Wingate* (1862) 10 B & S 714; *Smith v Stocks* (1869) 10 B & S 701 at 741.

71. Vesting of fuel and other allotments. Fuel allotments and other allotments for public purposes might be allotted to such persons and subject to such directions as the valuer with the approbation of the Secretary of State or his predecessors[1] should direct, or if the valuer, with such approbation, should not think it necessary or proper to direct it to be otherwise made, the allotment was to be made to the churchwardens and overseers of the parish[2].

They were frequently vested in the lord of the manor as trustee for the labouring poor of the parish or other persons entitled, or they may have been set out for this purpose, but not allotted to any specific persons by name or office. In such cases questions have arisen as to the ownership of the soil. Where the allotment was not made to any person by name or office, the lord's interest in the soil remained, if there was nothing in the Act or award to transfer it, and he consequently had power to refuse his consent to, and to prevent a subsequent inclosure[3]. If the allotment was made to the lord as trustee, and the trust as declared in the award did not exhaust the beneficial interest in the land, the lord was entitled to the unexhausted benefit[4].

Where, however, the allotment was made to the churchwardens and overseers for the purposes of a fuel allotment, the legal estate in the land was vested in them[5], and presumably the lord would be excluded from any benefit if he received an allotment in respect of his right and interest in the soil, and there was no reservation of rights from which a reservation of the soil of the fuel allotment might be implied[6].

  1 As to the transfer of functions to the Secretary of State see para 66 note 3 ante.
  2 Inclosure Act 1845 s 73. Overseers have been abolished, and fuel allotments are vested in parish or district councils: see para 63 ante.
  3 *R v Inclosure Comrs for England and Wales* (1871) 23 LT 778, where a large fuel allotment had been set out under an early inclosure on Chobham Common.
  4 *A-G v Meyrick* [1893] AC 1, HL.
  5 *Simcoe v Pethick* [1898] 2 QB 555, CA. See, however, note 2 supra.
  6 See *A-G v Meyrick* [1893] AC 1, HL.

72. Exchange, appropriation and change of use. The Secretary of State for the Environment or, in Wales, the Secretary of State for Wales[1], may, on the application of the trustees, or other persons interested, authorise the exchange of allotments held for the benefit of poor inhabitants or for any other public or parochial purpose for other more suitable lands[2]. A fuel allotment, notwithstanding the restriction on user otherwise than in accordance with the Act or award under which it was set out, may in certain circumstances be otherwise used[3] and may be the subject of compulsory acquisition and appropriation[4] in the same way as field garden allotments.

  1 As to the transfer of functions to the Secretary of State see para 66 note 3 ante.
  2 Inclosure Act 1845 s 149; see para 67 ante. Cf the Allotments Act 1832 s 9, and the Inclosure Act 1852 s 21.
  3 See the Town and Country Planning Act 1990 s 241 (1); and para 67 ante.
  4 See ibid ss 226 (3), (8), 229 (1)–(3); and para 68 ante.

73. Schemes by Charity Commissioners or court as to field garden and fuel allotments. The Charity Commissioners or the High Court may, notwithstanding the restriction on diverting fuel allotments[1] from the purposes declared by the Act authorising their inclosure[2], establish schemes for the administration of charitable fuel allotments[3], which may provide for the sale or letting of an allotment or any part of it, for the discharge of the land sold or let from restrictions on its use imposed by or under any enactment relating to inclosure, and for the application of the purchase money or rent received by the trustees[4], for the exchange of an allotment or part of it for other land and for the application of money payable to the trustees for equality of exchange[5], and for the use of an allotment or any part of it for any purposes specified in the scheme[6]. The scheme may modify or supersede in relation to the fuel allotment the provision made by the Inclosure Act or instrument thereunder setting up the allotment as if that provision had been made by a scheme[7].

Any provisions with respect to allotments for recreation grounds, field gardens or other public or parochial purposes contained in any Act relating to inclosure or in any award or order made under it, and any provisions as to the management of any such allotments contained in any such Act, award or order, may, on the application of any district or parish council interested in the allotment, be dealt with by a scheme of the Charity Commissioners in the exercise of their ordinary jurisdiction as if those provisions had been established by the founder in the case of a charity having a founder[8].

1 For the meaning of 'fuel allotment' in the Charities Act 1960 see para 69 note 3 ante.
2 See the Commons Act 1876 s 19; Charities (Fuel Allotments) Act 1939 s 1 (repealed).
3 Charities Act 1960 s 15 (3), Sch 4 para 2. As to the concurrent jurisdiction of the commissioners and the court see s 18. As to schemes generally see CHARITIES.
4 Ibid Sch 4 para 2 (a).
5 Ibid Sch 4 para 2 (b).
6 Ibid Sch 4 para 2 (c).
7 Ibid s 15 (3).
8 Commons Act 1899 s 18.

(5) FINANCE

74. Expenses on compulsory acquisition. The expenses of a district council incurred in respect of the compulsory acquisition of lands for allotments on behalf of a parish council must be paid by such parish council[1].

1 Small Holdings and Allotments Act 1908 s 39 (7) (amended by the Local Government Act 1972 s 251, Sch 29 Pt II para 9 (4)). References to a parish council, in the case of a parish not having a council, include references to the parish meeting: Small Holdings and Allotments Act 1908 s 61 (4).

75. Borrowing. County councils may borrow[1] for the purposes of making grants to co-operative societies[2]. Parish councils may borrow for the purposes of acquiring by agreement[3], or improving and adapting land for allotments[4]. A district council may borrow money for the purpose of acquiring, improving and adapting land for allotments or for the purpose of grants or advances to a co-operative society[5].

The Public Works Loan Commissioners may lend money to any local authority for any purpose for which the authority has power to borrow[6].

1 As to local authorities' borrowing powers generally see the Local Government and Housing Act 1989 Pt IV (ss 39–66). That Act applies for financial years beginning on or after 1 April 1990 in relation to the bodies mentioned therein, including county councils, district councils, London borough councils and the Common Council of the City of London, and other bodies to be specified by regulations: s 39 (1) (a)–(d), (k). Parish and community councils are among those bodies which may be specified by regulations: s 39 (3) (d); Local Government Finance Act 1988 s 144 (2). At the date at which this volume states the law, however, no regulations have been made in relation to such councils.
  Under the Local Government Act 1972 s 172, Sch 13 Pt I para 13, a local authority was empowered to make loans to another local authority for any purpose for which that latter authority was authorised to borrow money under any enactment. That provision has been repealed (except in relation to certain bodies, including parish and community councils: see note 4 infra) by the Local Government and Housing Act 1989 s 194 (2), Sch 12 Pt I; there is no provision in the 1989 Act as to whether a local authority is empowered to borrow money from another authority, or indeed as to whether an authority is empowered to lend money generally. It is consequently not clear whether the former power of a county council to borrow money for the purpose of lending to a parish council (see the 1972 Act Sch 13 Pt I para 1) has any current equivalent.
2 Small Holdings and Allotments Act 1908 s 52 (1) (amended by the Local Government Act 1929 s 137, Sch 12 Pt V and the Local Government Act 1933 s 307, Sch 11 Pt IV, and repealed in its application to Greater London by the London Government Order 1970, SI 1970/211, art 3 (8), Schedule). As to grants and advances to co-operative societies see para 83 post.

3 See the Small Holdings and Allotments Act 1908 ss 38, 39 (7); and paras 16, 28 ante.
4 Ibid s 53 (4) (amended by the Land Settlement (Facilities) Act 1919 s 25, Sch 2 and the London Government Order 1970 Schedule). As to a parish council's borrowing powers generally see the Local Government Act 1972 s 172, Sch 13 Pt I; s 172 is amended, and Sch 13 Pt I repealed, by the Local Government and Housing Act 1989 s 194 (2), Sch 12 Pt I, but that amendment and repeal do not apply in relation to bodies not listed in the 1989 Act s 39 (1) (a)–(j) and not prescribed by regulations under s 39 (3) (see note 1 supra): Local Government and Housing Act 1989 (Commencement No 5 and Transitional Provisions) Order 1990, SI 1990/431, Sch 1 para 1. Accordingly, until such time as regulations are made specifying parish and community councils, the borrowing powers of those councils continue to be governed by the 1972 Act. In addition, the power of a parish council to lend money to another authority (see Sch 13 Pt I para 13; and note 1 supra) is preserved for the same reason and until the same time.
5 Small Holdings and Allotments Act 1908 s 53 (4) (as amended: see note 4 supra, and as also amended by virtue of the Local Government Act 1972 s 179, effecting the removal of references to boroughs and urban districts).
6 National Loans Act 1968 s 3 (11), Sch 4 (s 3 (11) amended by the Finance Act 1984 ss 125 (2), 128 (6), Sch 23 Pt XIV; Sch 4 amended by the Housing (Consequential Provisions) Act 1985 s 4, Sch 2 para 15).

76. Provision of plants, fertilisers and implements. Where in the opinion of a district or parish council there are inadequate facilities for the purchase or hire from a society on a co-operative basis of fruit trees, seeds, plants, fertilisers or implements required for the purposes of allotments cultivated as gardens, whether provided by the council or otherwise, the council may purchase any of those articles and sell them to the cultivators or, in the case of implements, allow their use, at a price or charge sufficient to cover the cost of purchase[1].

The Secretary of State for the Environment or, in Wales, the Secretary of State for Wales, may, in accordance with regulations made by him with Treasury approval[2], make grants or advances to a county, district or parish council, or to an allotment society[3], for assisting the council or society in the provision of seeds, fertilisers and equipment for persons unemployed or not in full-time employment for whom allotments are provided, and, notwithstanding the foregoing[4], regulations may be made empowering the council, where necessary, to sell those articles and allow the use of equipment so purchased by the council at a price or charge less than sufficient to cover the purchase cost[5]. The Secretary of State may constitute a committee to advise him in the carrying out of these powers and duties, and the committee's expenses and the remuneration of any of his officers appointed to assist the committee are defrayed out of money provided by Parliament[6].

1 Land Settlement (Facilities) Act 1919 s 21 (1), (2). As to local authorities see para 79 post.
2 See the Agricultural Land (Utilisation) Act 1931 s 16 (1), (2). At the date at which this volume states the law no regulations are in force. As to the laying of regulations before Parliament see s 18.
3 As to societies see para 82 post.
4 See the text to note 1 supra.
5 Agricultural Land (Utilisation) Act 1931 s 16 (1) (amended by virtue of the Local Government Act 1972 s 179; see para 81 post). As to the transfer of functions to the Secretaries of State see para 80 note 4 post. As to local authorities see para 79 post.
6 Agricultural Land (Utilisation) Act 1931 s 16 (2).

77. Contributions to losses. Where it appears to a district or parish council that the provision of allotment gardens for resident persons who are unemployed or not in whole-time employment will entail a loss, it may submit proposals to the Secretary of State for the Environment or, in Wales, the Secretary of State for Wales, together with estimates of the expenses it is likely to incur and the sums it is likely to receive by way of rent or otherwise[2]. If the Secretary of State approves the proposals and estimates he may undertake to defray the loss likely to be incurred[3], but if the approved proposals are subsequently varied without his consent he will defray only such part of the loss as he thinks fit[4].

A council must keep separate accounts of transactions carried out under these provisions and give the Secretary of State any information which he may require[5]. The Secretary of State must, with the concurrence of the Treasury, make regulations for carrying these provisions into effect[6].

1 For the meaning of 'allotment garden' see para 1 ante.
2 Agricultural Land (Utilisation) Act 1931 s 14 (1) (amended by the Local Government Act 1972 s 272 (1), Sch 30, and by virtue of the 1972 Act s 179). As to the transfer of functions to the Secretary of State see para 80 note 4 post.
3 Agricultural Land (Utilisation) Act 1931 s 14 (2). Such approval may be with or without a requirement that modifications be made, and an undertaking by the Secretary of State to defray the loss may, with the approval of the Treasury, be subject to conditions as to records, certificates or audits, or other conditions: s 14 (2).
4 Ibid s 14 (4).
5 Ibid s 14 (6).
6 Ibid s 14 (7): see the Allotment Gardens (Contributions towards Losses) Regulations 1932, SR & O 1932/57, which apply only where proposals and estimates were submitted before 31 July 1931. As to the making of regulations see s 18 of the 1931 Act.

78. Compensation payments and receipts by ministers and government departments. Any expenses incurred by a minister of the Crown or by any government department, other than the Commissioners of Crown Lands, in paying compensation to a tenant of an allotment garden for disturbance[1] on his being required to quit the land are to be defrayed out of money provided by Parliament, and any sums received by a minister or government department as compensation for deterioration[2] are to be paid into the Exchequer[3].

1 Ie under the Allotments Act 1950 s 3; see para 48 ante.
2 Ie under ibid s 4; see para 50 ante.
3 Ibid s 13 (1).

(6) ADMINISTRATION

79. Allotments authorities. The local authorities primarily responsible for the provision and management of allotments are the councils of London boroughs, districts and parishes[1], although inner London boroughs are not obliged to provide allotments[2]. In the case of parishes not having parish councils the authority responsible is the parish meeting[3].

Where the council proposing to purchase land compulsorily for allotments is a parish council, the district council exercises the powers of compulsory acquisition on its behalf[4].

1 Small Holdings and Allotments Act 1908 s 23 (1) (amended by the Land Settlement (Facilities) Act 1919 s 25 (1), and by virtue of the Local Government Act 1972 ss 1 (9), (10), 20 (6), 179); and see the Allotments Act 1950 s 9. As to the extent of the obligation to provide allotments see para 8 ante. As to the district councils see paras 8 note 4, 14 note 4 ante. As to parish and community councils see para 28 note 1 ante.
2 London Government Act 1963 s 55 (4) (a), which operates so as to modify the Small Holdings and Allotments Act 1908 s 23 in respect of inner London boroughs.

3 Small Holdings and Allotments Act 1908 s 61 (4) (amended by virtue of the Local Government Act 1972 s 179 (4)).
4 Small Holdings and Allotments Act 1908 s 39 (7) (amended by the Local Government Act 1972 s 251, Sch 29 Pt II para 9 (4)).

80. Ministerial powers and functions. Ministerial powers and functions in respect of allotments are exercised primarily by the Secretary of State for the Environment or, in Wales, by the Secretary of State for Wales[1], as the successors to the several boards and ministers to whom those powers and functions were originally assigned, including the Inclosure Commissioners[2], the Board of Agriculture and Fisheries[3], the Minister of Agriculture and Fisheries[4], the Local Government Board[5], the Minister of Housing and Local Government[6] and the Minister of Health[7].

The Secretary of State may authorise a council to purchase land compulsorily for allotments[8]; he may defray losses incurred by a council in providing allotment gardens for unemployed persons[9] and make loans to allotment societies[10].

1 See the Secretary of State for Wales and Minister of Land and Natural Resources Order 1965, SI 1965/319, and the Ministry of Land and Natural Resources (Dissolution) Order 1967, SI 1967/156.
2 See para 66 note 3 ante.
3 The board originally exercised powers and functions under the Small Holdings and Allotments Act 1908 and the Land Settlement (Facilities) Act 1919. For the transfer of functions see the Ministry of Agriculture and Fisheries Act 1919 s 1 (1); the Transfer of Functions (Ministry of Food) Order 1955, SI 1955/554; the Minister of Land and Natural Resources Order 1965, SI 1965/143; the Ministry of Land and Natural Resources (Dissolution) Order 1967, SI 1967/156, and the Secretary of State for the Environment Order 1970, SI 1970/1681.
4 The minister originally exercised powers and functions under the Allotments Act 1922, the Allotments Act 1925, the Small Holdings and Allotments Act 1926, the Agricultural Land (Utilisation) Act 1931 and the Agriculture Act 1947. For the transfer of functions see the Transfer of Functions (Ministry of Food) Order 1955; the Minister of Land and Natural Resources Order 1965; the Ministry of Land and Natural Resources (Dissolution) Order 1967; and the Secretary of State for the Environment Order 1970.
5 See the Ministry of Health Act 1919 s 3 (1); the Transfer of Functions (Minister of Health and Minister of Local Government and Planning) (No 2) Order 1951, SI 1951/753; the Minister of Local Government and Planning (Change of Style and Title) Order 1951, SI 1951/1900; the Secretary of State for Wales and Minister of Land and Natural Resources Order 1965, SI 1965/319; and the Secretary of State for the Environment Order 1970.
6 See the Transfer of Functions (Minister of Health and Minister of Local Government and Planning) (No 1) Order 1951, SI 1951/142; the Minister of Local Government and Planning (Change of Style and Title) Order 1951; the Secretary of State for Wales and Minister of Land and Natural Resources Order 1965; and the Secretary of State for the Environment Order 1970.
7 See the Transfer of Functions (Minister of Health and Minister of Local Government and Planning) (No 1) Order 1951; the Transfer of Functions (Minister of Health and Minister of Local Government and Planning) (No 2) Order 1951; the Minister of Local Government and Planning (Change of Style and Title) Order 1951; the Secretary of State for Wales and Minister of Land and Natural Resources Order 1965; and the Secretary of State for the Environment Order 1970.
8 See the Small Holdings and Allotments Act 1908 s 39 (1) (amended by the Acquisition of Land (Authorisation Procedure) Act 1946 s 6, Sch 4, and the Transfer of Functions (Ministry of Food) Order 1955), and the Acquisition of Land Act 1981.
9 See the Agricultural Land (Utilisation) Act 1931 s 14 (amended by the Local Government Act 1972 s 272 (1), Sch 30, and by virtue of s 179 of the 1972 Act); and para 77 ante.
10 See the Small Holdings and Allotments Act 1908 s 39 (4) (as amended: see note 8 supra); and para 25 ante.

81. Allotment managers. The council of a district or parish may appoint and remove allotment managers of land acquired by it for allotments[1]. These managers must consist either partly of council members and partly of other persons who are residents and persons who are liable under the Local Government Finance Act 1988 to pay an amount in respect of any community charge, or wholly of such other persons[2], with such powers, including the power of incurring expenses, as the council determines[3].

1 Small Holdings and Allotments Act 1908 s 29 (1) (amended by virtue of the Local Government Act 1972 s 179). In a parish not having a parish council, allotment managers may be appointed by the parish meeting: Small Holdings and Allotments Act 1908 s 61 (4) (as so amended). As to local authorities see para 79 ante.

2 Small Holdings and Allotments Act 1908 s 29 (1). This subsection refers to persons 'contributory to the rate out of which the expenses of the council under [the 1908 Act] are paid'. Domestic rates were abolished by the Local Government Finance Act 1988 and replaced by the community charge. The Local Government and Housing Act 1989 s 149 empowers the Secretary of State to make regulations replacing references connected with rating with references to some other factor. At the date at which this volume states the law, no such regulations had been made with respect to the 1908 Act s 29, but it is suggested that the reference to rates is obsolete and should be replaced as indicated in the text.

3 Small Holdings and Allotments Act 1908 s 29 (2).

82. Promotion of allotments societies. A county or district council may promote the formation or extension of allotments societies[1].

Allotments societies[2] are societies on a co-operative basis having for their object, or one of their objects, the provision or profitable working of allotments, whether in relation to the purchase of requisites, the sale of produce, credit banking, insurance or otherwise[3].

1 Small Holdings and Allotments Act 1908 s 49 (1) (amended by the Land Settlement (Facilities) Act 1919 s 25 (1), Sch 2 and by virtue of the Local Government Act 1972 s 179); as to the repeal of the 1908 Act in relation to smallholdings see the Agriculture Act 1947 s 67 (2). Many of these societies are affiliated to the National Society of Allotment and Leisure Gardeners Ltd, 22 High Street, Flitwick, Bedford MK45 1DT, which gives them assistance in their formation. 'Society' includes any body of persons, whether incorporated or unincorporated: Agricultural Land (Utilisation) Act 1931 s 20 (1). As to local authorities see para 79 ante. As to the distribution of the proceeds of sale of land owned by an allotments society see *Re St Andrews' Allotment Association's Trusts, Sarjeant v Probert* [1969] 1 All ER 147, [1969] 1 WLR 229.

2 The term 'allotments society' is not a statutory term.

3 Small Holdings and Allotments Act 1908 s 49 (1).

83. Grants and allowances to allotments societies. District councils may assist allotments societies[1] financially by making grants or advances to a society or by guaranteeing advances made to a society, upon such terms and conditions as to rate of interest and repayment or otherwise, and on such security, as the council thinks fit[2]. For this purpose councils may borrow money[3] and the Public Works Loan Commissioners may lend it to them[4].

Councils may also let to a society accommodation for the sale or storage of goods[5], and may employ as their agent any other society having as one of its objects the promotion of co-operation in connection with the cultivation of allotments[6].

1 As to allotments societies see para 82 ante.

2 Small Holdings and Allotments Act 1908 s 49 (2) (amended by the Land Settlement (Facilities) Act 1919 s 25, Sch 2 and the Local Government, Planning and Land Act 1980 s 1 (5), Sch 5 para 1, and by virtue of the Local Government Act 1972 s 179). As to the councils which may be allotments authorities see para 79 ante.

3 Small Holdings and Allotments Act 1908 ss 52 (1), 53 (4) (amended by the Land Settlement (Facilities) Act 1919 Sch 2 and by virtue of the Local Government Act 1972 s 179).

4 National Loans Act 1968 s 3 (11), Sch 4 (s 3 (11) amended by the Finance Act 1984 s 125 (2); Sch 4 para 1 amended by the Local Government Finance (Repeals, Savings and Consequential Amendments) Order 1990, SI 1990/776, art 8, Sch 3). The ability of the Public Works Loans Commissioners to make such loans is restricted by reference to a maximum aggregate of outstanding commitments: National Loans Act 1968 s 4 (substituted by the Finance Act 1984 s 125 (1)). The permissible loans under the 1968 Act Sch 4 are loans to any local authority for any purpose for which the authority has power to borrow by virtue of any enactment or otherwise. 'Local authority' in this context means, in relation to England and Wales, a charging authority, a precepting authority, a combined police authority or a combined fire authority as defined in the Local Government Finance Act 1988 s 144, a levying body within the meaning of s 74 of that Act or a body as regards which s 75 of that Act (special levies) applies: 1968 Act Sch 4 para 1 (a) (substituted by the Local Government Finance (Repeals, Savings and Consequential Amendments) Order 1990 Sch 3 para 12).

5 Small Holdings and Allotments Act 1908 s 49 (2) (amended by the Small Holdings and Allotments Act 1926 s 21, Sch 1).

6 Small Holdings and Allotments Act 1908 s 49 (1), (4). With Treasury consent the Secretary of State may make grants to any other society out of money provided by Parliament: s 49 (4); Agriculture Act 1947 s 59 (abolition of Small Holdings Account). As to the Secretary of State see para 80 ante.

84. Sales or lettings to co-operative societies. A district or parish council may let one or more allotments to persons working on a co-operative system, and may, with the consent of the Secretary of State for the Environment or, in Wales, the Secretary of State for Wales, sell one or more allotments to any association formed for the purposes of creating or promoting the creation of allotments[1].

1 Small Holdings and Allotments Act 1908 s 27 (6) (amended by the Land Settlement (Facilities) Act 1919 s 25 (1), Sch 2). The terms of the 1908 Act s 27 (6) confer on councils the same powers of letting and selling as may be exercised in relation to smallholdings by a county council; as to these powers see the Small Holdings and Allotments Act 1926 s 3. For a council's power to sell or hire plants, fertilisers and implements to cultivators where facilities for purchase or hire from a society are inadequate see para 76 ante. The Secretary of State may, in accordance with regulations, make grants to help societies to provide seeds, fertilisers and equipment at a special rate to unemployed persons: see para 76 ante. For the transfer of functions to the Secretaries of State see para 80 note 3 ante. As to local authorities see para 79 ante.

85. Use of schoolroom. Any room in a county or voluntary primary or secondary school in respect of which a grant is made out of money provided by Parliament may, except while being used for educational purposes, be used free of charge for the purposes of the Allotments Acts or, with the consent of any two managers or, in the case of a county or voluntary secondary school, governors, be used for public meetings to discuss any question relating to allotments, subject to expenses and any damage being paid for by the council or persons calling the meeting[1].

Before any public meeting may be so held not less than six days' notice[2], signed by not less than six resident registered parliamentary electors or community charge payers, must be given to the clerk of the local education authority or, in the case of a voluntary school, to one of the managers or governors[3]. If the room is not then available the clerk, manager or governor must write to one of the signatories, naming some other day when the room will be available[4]. If the persons calling the meeting fail to obtain the use of the room they may appeal to the county council, which may make such other order respecting the use of the room as seems just[5].

1 Small Holdings and Allotments Act 1908 s 35 (1) (amended by the Local Government Act 1972 s 272 (1), Sch 30); Education Act 1944 ss 9, 120 (1) (a), (c) (s 9 amended by the Education Act 1980 s 38 (6), Sch 7 and the Education Act 1981 s 11; s 120 (1) (c) amended by the Education Act 1980 s 1 (3), Sch 1 para 14). As to such schools see EDUCATION. For the power in a parish, or a district or in

the council on which the powers of a parish council have been conferred, to use a schoolroom free of charge for certain public meetings, see the Local Government Act 1972 s 134 (amended by the Education Reform Act 1988 s 237 (1), Sch 12 Pt I para 13); and LOCAL GOVERNMENT.
2 See 2 Forms & Precedents (5th Edn) 340–341, Form 10.
3 Small Holdings and Allotments Act 1908 ss 23 (2), 35 (2) (a) (s 23 amended by the Land Settlement (Facilities) Act 1919 s 25, Sch 2 and by the Local Government Finance (Repeals, Savings and Consequential Amendments) Order 1990, SI 1990/776, art 8, Sch 3 para 2); Education Act 1944 ss 6, 120 (1) (c), Sch 1 (s 6 amended by the Local Government Act 1972 Sch 30; s 120 (1) (c) as amended: see note 1 supra; as to the 1944 Act Sch 1 see generally EDUCATION).
4 Small Holdings and Allotments Act 1908 s 35 (2) (b).
5 See ibid s 35 (3). This subsection provides for an appeal to 'the small holdings and allotments committee under this Act'. That committee, constituted under s 50 (repealed), was replaced by the smallholdings committee under the Agriculture Act 1947 s 61 (repealed). There are now no smallholdings committees, and the saving in the Agriculture Act 1970 s 64 (1), Sch 3 para 4 for allotments committees is inapt, and it is therefore submitted that the council which formerly constituted the committee with the approval of the Secretary of State may determine the appeal.

86. Local inquiries. The Secretary of State for the Environment and, in Wales, the Secretary of State for Wales, and their officers, have the same powers for the purposes of an inquiry under the Allotments Acts as they have for the purposes of an inquiry under the Public Health Acts[1]. Notices of the inquiries must be given and published in accordance with such general or special directions as the Secretary of State may give[2].

1 Small Holdings and Allotments Act 1908 s 57 (1) (amended by the Small Holdings and Allotments Act 1926 s 22 (1), Sch 2). As to inquiries under the Public Health Acts see PUBLIC HEALTH; LOCAL GOVERNMENT. As to the transfer of functions to the Secretary of State see para 80 ante.
2 Small Holdings and Allotments Act 1908 s 57 (2).

3. SMALLHOLDINGS

(1) PURPOSE OF SMALLHOLDINGS

87. General aim of statutory smallholdings. Smallholdings[1] authorities[2] must make it their general aim, having regard to the general interests of agriculture[3] and of good estate management, to provide opportunities for persons to be farmers on their own account by letting holdings limited in size so as to provide full-time employment for not more than the occupier and one other man[4], to persons satisfying certain requirements[5].

Smallholdings authorities were required to review their smallholdings estates, and to submit to the Minister of Agriculture, Fisheries and Food before 1 February 1972 their proposals for future management[6].

1 For a review of statutory smallholdings see the Northfield Committee of Inquiry into the Acquisition and Occupancy of Agricultural Land (1979) Pt VIII pp 189–203 (Cmnd 7599). The Committee recommended that statutory smallholdings should be renamed county holdings on the ground that holdings on some estates can be of quite substantial size. The Association of County Councils refer to their holdings as County Farms. Information on smallholdings is given in annual reports to Parliament.
2 As to smallholdings authorities see para 117 post.
3 For the meaning of 'agriculture' see para 3 note 2 ante.
4 See the Agriculture Act 1970 ss 39 (1), (2), 41 (4); and para 102 post.
5 Ibid s 39 (1). As to these requirements see ss 39 (2), 44 (6); and para 102 post.
6 See ibid ss 40–43; and para 89 post. As to the minister in relation to Wales see para 123 post.

88. Smallholdings and planning. The cultivation of smallholdings involves the use of land for the purposes of agriculture as defined in the Town and Country Planning Act 1990[1]. The position of smallholdings in relation to town planning legislation is similar to that of allotments used for agricultural purposes, which has been briefly mentioned earlier[2].

1 'Agriculture' is defined in the Town and Country Planning Act 1990 s 336 (1) in the same terms as in para 3 note 2 ante.
2 See para 9 ante.

(2) REORGANISATION OF SMALLHOLDINGS

89. Review and proposals for reorganisation of smallholdings estates. Every smallholdings authority[1] which immediately before 1 August 1970 held any land for the purposes of smallholdings[2] was required to review its smallholdings estate[3] and, unless otherwise directed[4], to submit to the Minister of Agriculture, Fisheries and Food, before 1 February 1972 or such extended date as the minister might in a particular case allow, proposals with respect to the future management of that estate[5]. The authority had, in particular, to consider to what extent, if any, with a view to giving effect to the general aim of statutory smallholdings[6] and having regard to the general interests of agriculture[7] and of good estate management, that estate should be reorganised:

(1) by enlarging existing smallholdings[8], or by amalgamating them or part of them with other land, with or without improvements[9];

(2) by improving existing smallholdings without any enlargement or amalgamation[10]; or

(3) by creating new smallholdings, with or without improvements[11].

The proposals had to comply with ministerial directions as to form and content[12].

1 As to smallholdings authorities see para 117 post.
2 As to land held by a smallholdings authority for the purposes of smallholdings see para 4 notes 10, 12 ante.
3 'Smallholdings estate' means the aggregate of the land for the time being held by a smallholdings authority for the purposes of smallholdings: Agriculture Act 1970 s 37 (1).
4 See ibid s 40 (4); and para 93 post.
5 Ibid s 40 (1); Agriculture Act 1970 (Commencement No 2) Order 1970, SI 1970/1048. As to the minister in relation to Wales see para 123 post. An authority could be permitted to submit its proposals in parts, each dealing with a different part of its smallholdings estate.
6 See para 87 ante.
7 For the meaning of 'agriculture' see para 3 note 2 ante.
8 For the meaning of 'existing smallholding' see para 4 ante.
9 Agriculture Act 1970 s 40 (2) (a). It is immaterial whether or not the other land is or forms part of an existing smallholding or is otherwise comprised in the authority's smallholdings estate (see note 3 supra): s 40 (2) (a).
10 Ibid s 40 (2) (b).
11 Ibid s 40 (2) (c). References in Pt III (ss 37–65) to the creation of a new smallholding must be construed as references to any letting of land by a smallholdings authority or by the minister where (1) the land is held by it or him for the purposes of smallholdings and the letting is a letting of the land as a smallholding; (2) immediately before the letting the land or part of it is being used (or, if not then in use, is land which was last used) otherwise than as land held and let as mentioned in (1); and (3) the land so let is not a holding resulting from an enlargement or amalgamation as in the text to notes 8 and 9 supra, or from a similar enlargement or amalgamation by the minister: s 37 (3).
12 Ibid s 40 (3).

90. Approval of proposals for reorganisation. The Minister of Agriculture, Fisheries and Food could either approve proposals for the reorganisation of a smallholdings estate submitted to him by a smallholdings authority[1], or reject them and direct the authority to submit new proposals within a time specified in the direction[2]. In determining whether to approve the proposals the minister had to have regard to the considerations to which the authority was required to have regard in making the proposals[3], and he might not approve proposals in so far as it appeared to him that any resulting smallholding would exceed the upper limit for a smallholding[4]. Nevertheless, he might approve proposals notwithstanding that any resulting smallholding would exceed this limit if certain conditions were satisfied[5].

Where the minister approved any proposals he could approve them either as submitted or with appropriate modifications, and could approve them, with or without modifications, either conditionally or unconditionally[6], and thereupon, until the proposals were amended or superseded, the smallholdings authority had a duty both to perform its statutory functions in such a way as to give effect to the proposals as so approved[7] and to comply with any conditions subject to which the approval was given[8].

1 See para 89 ante. As to the minister in relation to Wales see para 123 post.
2 Agriculture Act 1970 s 41 (1).
3 Ibid s 41 (5): see s 40 (2); and para 89 text and notes 7–11 ante.
4 Ibid s 41 (3). As to the upper limit for smallholdings see para 102 post.
5 See ibid s 41 (4); and para 102 post.
6 Ibid s 41 (2).
7 Ibid s 41 (6) (a).
8 Ibid s 41 (6) (b).

91. Subsequent reviews and proposals. At any time after the end of five years after approving proposals for the reorganisation of a smallholdings authority's smallholdings estate[1] the Minister of Agriculture, Fisheries and Food may direct the authority to carry out a further review of that estate and submit to him, within a specified period or such extended period as he may allow, proposals for its future management, indicating how far the authority's previous proposals are intended to remain unaltered and how far they are to be amended or superseded[2]. Where fresh proposals are approved[3] it is the authority's duty to perform its functions under Part III of the Agriculture Act 1970[4] in such a way as to give effect to the approved proposals for the time being in force[5] and to comply with any conditions subject to which the approval was given[6].

The minister may also direct subsequent reviews at intervals of not less than five years after the previous proposals have been approved[7].

1 See paras 89, 90 ante. Where different parts of proposals were approved on different dates the five years runs from the latest such date: Agriculture Act 1970 s 42 (7).
2 Ibid s 42 (1), (2). Sections 40 (2), (3), 41 (1)–(5) have effect, with the necessary modifications, in relation to the new proposals: s 42 (3). For those provisions see paras 89, 90 ante. As to the minister in relation to Wales see para 123 post.
3 As to approval see para 90 ante.
4 Ie the Agriculture Act 1970 ss 37–65.
5 Ibid s 42 (5) (a).
6 Ibid s 42 (5) (b).

7 Ibid s 42 (4). Where different parts of proposals were approved on different dates the five years runs from the latest such date: s 42 (7).

92. Other proposals. Where a smallholdings authority, other than an exempt smallholdings authority[1], proposes to enlarge, amalgamate or improve existing smallholdings or to create new smallholdings[2], it must submit its proposals to the Minister of Agriculture, Fisheries and Food if:

(1) the transaction would be inconsistent with any previously approved re-organisation proposals for the time being in force and has not been provided for by previously approved proposals not being the initial or review proposals[3], and

(2) the transaction is intended to be carried out at a time when no review of the smallholdings estate[4] is required by a direction of the minister to be carried out[5].

Such proposals must be submitted by way of amending the authority's previously approved proposals submitted on a review for the time being in force[6].

Where the proposals are approved[7] it is the authority's duty to perform its functions under Part III of the Agriculture Act 1970[8] in such a way as to give effect to the approved proposals for the time being in force, and to comply with any conditions subject to which the approval was given[9].

1 As to smallholdings authorities see para 117 post; as to exempt authorities see para 93 post.
2 Ie under the Agriculture Act 1970 s 40 (2) (a), (b) or (c): see para 89 ante.
3 See paras 89–91 ante.
4 For the meaning of 'smallholdings estate' see para 89 note 3 ante.
5 Agriculture Act 1970 s 43 (1). As to the minister in relation to Wales see para 123 post.
6 Ibid s 43 (2). Sections 40 (3), 41 (1)–(5) have effect, with the necessary modifications, in relation to the proposals: s 43 (5). For those provisions see paras 89, 90 ante.
7 As to the approval see para 90 ante.
8 Ie the Agriculture Act 1970 ss 37–65.
9 Ibid ss 42 (5), 43 (6).

93. Exemption from making proposals. A smallholdings authority could apply to the Minister of Agriculture, Fisheries and Food for a direction exempting it from the duty to submit reorganisation proposals in respect of its smallholdings estate[1], but had to satisfy him that its estate was not suitable to be reorganised[2].

Where an exempt authority[3] proposes to enlarge a smallholding or to amalgamate the whole or part of one or more existing smallholdings with other land or to create new smallholdings[4], and that transaction has not been included in previously approved proposals[5], it must submit to the minister proposals for carrying out that transaction[6]; if it proposes to improve an existing smallholding[7] it may, for the purpose of obtaining an increased capital grant[8], submit to the minister proposals for carrying out the improvement[9]. Where the proposals are approved[10] the authority has a duty both to perform its functions under Part III of the Agriculture Act 1970[11] in such a way as to give effect to the proposals as so approved and also to comply with any conditions subject to which the approval was given[12].

Any direction exempting an authority from making proposals may be revoked by the minister at any time after the end of five years from the date on which it was given, whereupon the authority must review its smallholdings estate and submit reorganisation proposals within 18 months from the date of revocation[13].

1 As to this duty see para 89 ante. As to the minister in relation to Wales see para 123 post.
2 Agriculture Act 1970 s 40 (4).
3 For the purposes of ibid s 43 (see text and notes infra) 'exempt authority' means one in respect of which a direction under s 40 (4) (see text and notes 1, 2 supra) has been made: s 43 (8).
4 Ie under ibid s 40 (2) (a) or (c): see para 89 ante.
5 Ie proposals under ibid s 43.
6 Ibid s 43 (3). Sections 40 (3), 41 (1)–(5) have effect, with the necessary modifications, in relation to the proposals: s 43 (5). For those provisions see paras 89, 90 ante.
7 Ie under ibid s 40 (2) (b): see para 89 ante.
8 See ibid s 51; and para 115 post.
9 Ibid s 43 (4). For provisions applied to the proposals see note 6 supra.
10 As to approval see para 90 ante.
11 Ie the Agriculture Act 1970 ss 37–65.
12 Ibid ss 41 (6), 43 (7).
13 Ibid ss 40 (1), 42 (6).

(3) LAND FOR SMALLHOLDINGS

94. Acquisition of land for smallholdings. A smallholdings authority[1] cannot acquire land compulsorily for the purposes of smallholdings[2]. Where such an authority proposes to acquire land outside its area for these purposes in the exercise of its power[3] to acquire land by agreement, it must consult the council of the county in whose area the land is situated[4].

The Minister of Agriculture, Fisheries and Food has power to acquire by agreement any land which in his opinion is required by him for the purposes of smallholdings[5], and may designate any land vested in him as being land held for those purposes[6].

1 As to smallholdings authorities see para 117 post.
2 Agriculture Act 1970 s 48 (2). For the meaning of 'the purposes of smallholdings' see para 4 note 12 ante. An authority was formerly able to acquire land by compulsory hiring or purchase: Agriculture Act 1947 s 48 (1) (repealed).
3 Ie under the Local Government Act 1972 ss 120, 124: see LOCAL GOVERNMENT.
4 Agriculture Act 1970 s 48 (1) (amended by the Local Government Act 1972 s 272 (1), Sch 30).
5 Agriculture Act 1970 s 55. This is part of his power under the Agriculture Act 1947 s 82 to acquire land by agreement: see AGRICULTURE. The power is exercised by the minister in both England and Wales: see para 123 post.
6 Agriculture Act 1970 s 54 (7).

95. Dealings with land held for smallholdings purposes. Without prejudice to its general power to appropriate[1] for some other approved purpose smallholdings land belonging to it and not required for that purpose, or to sell[2] such land which is not required for that purpose, or to exchange[3] such land for other land[4], a smallholdings authority[5] may let[6] land held by it for the purposes of smallholdings[7] which is not for the time being required for use for those purposes, for such period and for such purpose as it thinks fit, at the best rent which appears to it to be obtainable for it for that purpose, and on such other terms as it may determine[8].

Its general power to let land[9] does not enable a smallholdings authority to let land for the time being held by it for the purposes of smallholdings otherwise than in accordance with the above provision or in accordance with the specific provisions[10] as to the letting of smallholdings[11].

1 See the Local Government Act 1972 ss 122, 126 (both amended by the Local Government, Planning and Land Act 1980 ss 118, 194, Schs 23, 34, and by the Planning (Consequential Provisions) Act 1990 s 4, Sch 2); and LOCAL GOVERNMENT.

2 See the Local Government Act 1972 ss 123, 127 (s 123 amended by the Local Government, Planning and Land Act 1980 ss 118, 194, Schs 23, 34; s 127 amended by the 1980 Act s 118, Sch 23; both amended by the Planning (Consequential Provisions) Act 1990 s 4, Sch 2); and LOCAL GOVERNMENT.
3 See the Local Government Act 1972 ss 123, 127 (as amended: see note 2 supra); and LOCAL GOVERNMENT.
4 Agriculture Act 1970 s 49 (4).
5 As to smallholdings authorities see para 117 post.
6 For this purpose letting land includes granting, with the approval of the Minister of Agriculture, Fisheries and Food, a licence to a person to occupy the land for use as agricultural land, and granting a licence to a person to occupy the land where it is to be used only for grazing or mowing during a specified part of the year: Agriculture Act 1970 s 49 (2). For the meaning of 'agricultural land' see s 37 (4), applying the Agriculture Act 1947 s 109 (1); as to which see AGRICULTURE vol 1 (2) (Reissue) para 602. As to the minister in relation to Wales see para 123 post.
7 As to land held by a smallholdings authority for the purposes of smallholdings see para 4 notes 10, 12 ante.
8 Agriculture Act 1970 s 49 (1). The minister has the same power in respect of smallholdings land held by him: see para 96 post. As to the appropriation or disposal of land acquired or appropriated for planning purposes see the Town and Country Planning Act 1990 ss 232, 233; and TOWN AND COUNTRY PLANNING.
9 Ie under the Local Government Act 1972 ss 123, 127 (as amended: see note 2 supra); and see LOCAL GOVERNMENT.
10 See the Agriculture Act 1970 s 44; and para 100 post.
11 Ibid s 49 (3).

96. Letting of surplus land held by minister. In relation to land for the time being held by him for the purposes of smallholdings[1] the Minister of Agriculture, Fisheries and Food[2] has the same powers and duties with regard to the letting of surplus land[3] as have smallholdings authorities in relation to land held by them for those purposes[4].

1 As to such land see para 124 post.
2 The minister acts in both England and Wales: see para 123 post.
3 Ie under the Agriculture Act 1970 s 49 (1), (2): see para 95 ante.
4 Ibid s 54 (1), (2).

97. Leases and sales in special cases. Land forming part of the possessions of the Duchy of Cornwall[1] may be leased to a smallholdings authority or to the Minister of Agriculture, Fisheries and Food for the purposes of smallholdings[2] for a term not exceeding 35 years, with or without a right of renewal for a further similar term[3].

Where, in any other case, a person has statutory power[4] to lease land for agricultural purposes for a specified maximum term he may, without prejudice to that power, lease the land to a smallholdings authority or to the minister for the purposes of smallholdings for a term not exceeding 35 years, with or without a right of renewal for a further similar term[5].

1 The power of leasing is exercisable by the Duke of Cornwall or such other persons as for the time being have power to dispose of Duchy land: Agriculture Act 1970 s 61 (2) (b).
2 For the meaning of 'the purposes of smallholdings' see para 4 note 12 ante.
3 Agriculture Act 1970 s 61 (1) (amended by the Duchy of Lancaster Act 1988 s 1 (4), Schedule). The minister may acquire or hold land in both England and Wales: see para 123 post.
4 Ie by virtue of the Settled Land Act 1925, the Universities and College Estates Act 1925, or any other enactment.
5 Agriculture Act 1970 s 61 (6).

(4) MANAGEMENT OF SMALLHOLDINGS

(i) General Powers of Management

98. Managing smallholdings. The powers of a smallholdings authority[1] include, in general, all powers required by it for the management of land held by it for the purposes of smallholdings[2]. The powers given to smallholdings authorities which are considered in this paragraph relate only to their capacity as corporations[3]; nothing in these provisions may be construed as authorising any act or omission on the part of a smallholdings authority which, apart from these provisions, would be actionable at the suit of any persons on any grounds other than a limitation imposed by law on their capacity as corporations[4].

In particular, a smallholdings authority has the following powers:

(1) For the benefit of the occupiers of smallholdings provided by it, to further the formation of corporate or unincorporated bodies of persons having for their object or one of their objects the promotion of efficiency in the conduct of smallholdings through co-operative methods, including the co-operative purchase and hiring of requisites for, or the co-operative sale, marketing or preparation for marketing of the produce of, the smallholdings, and to assist the activities of such bodies[5].

(2) To assist or promote co-operative schemes for the conduct of smallholdings provided by the authority, by purchasing or hiring, and by selling or letting machinery and other equipment, live[6] or dead stock, seeds, fertilisers or other requisites, and by the provision of services[7].

(3) To carry out arrangements made by it for the disposal by it of the produce of smallholdings which it has provided[8].

(4) To provide, improve, maintain or repair fixed equipment or to carry out other improvements for the benefit of the land held by it for the purposes of smallholdings[9].

In general, the provision of buildings or the making of any material change in the use of buildings on land acquired for smallholdings requires planning permission, but certain development is permitted, as in the case of land used for allotments, without permission[10].

1 As to smallholdings authorities see para 117 post.
2 Agriculture Act 1970 s 47 (1). As to land held by smallholdings authorities for the purposes of smallholdings see para 4 notes 10, 12 ante. The minister has similar powers in relation to smallholdings land held by him: see para 99 post.
3 As to the capacity of corporations and the operation of the doctrine of ultra vires see CORPORATIONS.
4 Agriculture Act 1970 s 37 (5).
5 See ibid s 47 (2).
6 For the meaning of 'livestock' see para 3 note 2 ante.
7 See the Agriculture Act 1970 s 47 (3).
8 See ibid s 47 (4).
9 Ibid s 46 (1): see para 111 post.
10 See para 37 ante.

99. Managing smallholdings on land held by minister. In relation to land for the time being held by him for the purposes of smallholdings[1] the Minister of Agriculture, Fisheries and Food[2] has the same powers and duties with regard to managing smallholdings[3] as have smallholdings authorities in relation to land held by them for those purposes[4].

Where for the purpose of assisting the conduct of smallholdings on land held by him for the purposes of smallholdings the minister has purchased or hired machinery or other equipment, live[5] or dead stock, seeds, fertilisers or other requisites, or provides any services, his powers[6] to do so include powers to sell or let them to, or provide the services for, any persons, whether they are tenants or not[7], and where he has made arrangements[8] for the disposal of smallholdings produce and it appears that any facilities provided under the arrangements are not required to be reserved exclusively for that purpose he may extend the facilities to the disposal of the produce of other agricultural holdings[9].

1 As to such land see para 124 post.
2 The minister acts in both England and Wales: see para 123 post.
3 Ie under the Agriculture Act 1970 s 47: see para 98 ante.
4 Ibid s 54 (1), (2).
5 For the meaning of 'livestock' see para 3 note 2 ante.
6 Ie under the Agriculture Act 1970 s 47 (3), as applied by s 54 (2): see para 98 ante.
7 Ibid s 54 (3).
8 Ie under ibid s 47 (4), as applied by s 54 (2): see para 98 ante.
9 Ibid s 54 (4).

(ii) Letting as Smallholding

100. General provisions as to lettings. Any land held by a smallholdings authority for the purposes of smallholdings[1] may be let by it as a smallholding[2]. It may not, however, let a holding resulting from an enlargement or amalgamation of existing smallholdings[3] or create any new smallholding where the enlargement, amalgamation or creation is not in accordance with approved reorganisation proposals[4] for the time being in force[5], unless the letting or creation is effected with the written consent of the Minister of Agriculture, Fisheries and Food[6] given before reorganisation proposals[7] have been submitted to the minister or before proposals so submitted have been approved[8].

1 As to land held by a smallholdings authority for the purposes of smallholdings see para 4 notes 10, 12 ante; as to such authorities see para 117 post.
2 Agriculture Act 1970 s 44 (1). For the persons to whom the land may be let see para 103 post. The minister has the same power in relation to smallholdings land held by him: see para 105 post.
3 Ie under ibid s 40 (2) (a); see para 89 ante.
4 Ie under ibid ss 40–43; see paras 89–93 ante.
5 Ibid s 44 (4).
6 Ibid s 44 (5) (a). As to the minister in relation to Wales see para 123 post.
7 Ie under ibid s 40; see para 89 ante.
8 Ibid s 44 (5) (b). In general such proposals had to be submitted before 1 February 1972, but the minister might allow later submission, and such proposals may be made within 18 months after an exempt authority loses its exemption: see para 93 ante.

101. Advertisement of vacant holdings. Before letting land as a smallholding[1] every smallholdings authority[2] must, once in any year[3] during which any smallholding on its smallholdings estate[4] becomes available for letting, cause a notice to be published in at least one newspaper circulating substantially outside its area stating that it provides smallholdings for letting, describing the location and types of smallholdings on its estate or available for letting, and setting out the requirements to be fulfilled by tenants[5].

1 Ie under the Agriculture Act 1970 s 44: see para 100 ante.
2 As to smallholdings authorities see para 117 post.
3 'Year' means a 12 month period ending on 31 March: Smallholdings (Selection of Tenants) Regulations 1970, SI 1970/1049, reg 4 (2).
4 For the meaning of 'smallholdings estate' see para 89 note 3 ante.
5 Smallholdings (Selection of Tenants) Regulations 1970 reg 4 (1). As to the selection of tenants see para 103 post.

102. Extent of holdings. Holdings let by smallholdings authorities[1] must either fall within what is known as the upper limit for a smallholding, or must be let in accordance with the authority's reorganisation proposals[2], approved by the Minister of Agriculture, Fisheries and Food notwithstanding that it appears to him that in the case of one or more holdings the upper limit would be exceeded, if it is represented by the authority, and he is satisfied, that the holdings are to be let as smallholdings[3] and that, by reason of the nature or extent of fixed equipment[4] on the holding or holdings, or of the special qualities of the soil, or other exceptional circumstances, it is necessary or expedient for them to exceed that limit[5].

A holding is treated as falling within the upper limit for a smallholding if in the minister's opinion it is capable, when farmed under reasonably skilled management, of providing full-time employment for not more than two men, including the tenant, with or without additional part-time employment for another man[6]. The holding is treated as being so capable if its standard labour requirements are less than 900 standard man-days in aggregate in a year on average[7]. In any other case the holding is treated as exceeding the upper limit for a smallholding[8].

In estimating the number of men for whom the holding is capable of providing full-time employment it must be assumed that the system of husbandry suitable for the district is followed, and that the greater part of the feeding stuffs required by any livestock[9] kept on the holding is grown there[10]. In the case of an existing smallholding[11] the number of standard man-days is estimated by multiplying a prescribed number[12] per acre, based on the type of crop[13], or a prescribed manner[14] per head, based on the type of livestock[15], by the number of acres or average number of head of livestock shown to the minister's satisfaction to be comprised in the agricultural operations carried on on the holding in an average year, adding the crop and livestock results together, and increasing the total by 15 per cent[16]. In the case of a proposed smallholding[17] the number of standard man-days is estimated by making a similar calculation in respect of the acreage and average number of head of livestock shown to the minister's satisfaction to be capable of being comprised in the agricultural operations carried on on the holding when farmed under reasonably skilled management[18].

1 As to smallholdings authorities see para 117 post.
2 Ie under the Agriculture Act 1970 s 41: see para 89 ante.
3 Ie under ibid s 44: see para 100 ante.
4 'Fixed equipment' includes any building or structure affixed to land and any works on, in, over or under land, and anything grown on land for a purpose other than use after severance from the land, for consumption of the thing grown or of produce thereof, or for amenity; and 'produce' includes anything, whether live or dead, produced in the course of agriculture: Agriculture Act 1947 s 109 (3), applied by the Agriculture Act 1970 s 37 (4).
5 Ibid ss 39 (1), 41 (4). As to the minister in relation to Wales see para 123 post.

6 Ibid s 39 (2).
7 Smallholdings (Full-Time Employment) Regulations 1970, SI 1970/1050, reg 3 (2). These regulations were made under the Agriculture Act 1970 ss 39 (2), 63.
8 Ibid s 39 (2).
9 For the meaning of 'livestock' see para 3 note 2 ante.
10 Smallholdings (Full-Time Employment) Regulations 1970 reg 3 (1).
11 In this context 'existing smallholding' means a holding held by a smallholdings authority for the purposes of smallholdings and let as a smallholding at a time when the authority submits proposals to the minister under the Agriculture Act 1970 ss 40, 42 or 43, in which that holding is included (see paras 89–93 ante), or, if the holding is not at that time let as a smallholding and is not being used for any purpose, is a holding which, when last let, was let as a smallholding: Smallholdings (Full-Time Employment) Regulations 1970 reg 3 (1), Schedule.
12 See ibid Schedule, Table.
13 Where double cropping is practised the area of both crops is included: ibid Schedule para 3.
14 See ibid Schedule, Table.
15 Baby animals are not counted: see ibid Schedule para 6.
16 Ibid Schedule para 1.
17 'Proposed smallholding' means a holding which a smallholdings authority, in any proposals of the kind referred to in note 11 supra, submitted by it to the minister, proposes to form by enlarging or amalgamating existing smallholdings or by creating new smallholdings: see the Smallholdings (Full-Time Employment) Regulations 1970 Schedule.
18 Ibid Schedule para 2.

103. Selection of tenants. A smallholdings authority may not let land as a smallholding except to a person who is to farm the holding and who either is regarded by the authority as being qualified by reason of his agricultural experience to farm the holding on his own account[1] or is a person in respect of whom it is satisfied that within a reasonably short time he will become eligible to be so regarded[2].

Notwithstanding the foregoing a smallholdings authority may let land as a smallholding, or as part of a group of two or more smallholdings, to two or more persons proposing to farm the land together on a co-operative system if, having regard to their aggregate agricultural experience, the authority is satisfied that they are, or will within a reasonably short time become, qualified to farm the land together on such a system on their own account[3].

No person, other than the widow, residing on the smallholding, of the deceased tenant to whom the holding was let immediately before the letting which is under consideration[4], may be selected as a tenant unless he shows, to the authority's satisfaction, that for a period of not less than five years[5] he has been occupied in full-time practical farm work[6].

Where the smallholdings authority intends to re-let a smallholding after the death of a tenant it must first consider applications from eligible persons; namely the wife or husband, a brother or sister, or a child of the deceased tenant, or any child treated as a child of the family in relation to any marriage to which the deceased was a party[7].

1 Agriculture Act 1970 s 44 (2) (a).
2 Ibid s 44 (2) (b). The provisions apply also to smallholdings land held by the minister: see para 105 post.
3 Ibid s 44 (3).
4 Smallholdings (Selection of Tenants) Regulations 1970, SI 1970/1049, reg 3 (2). The regulations were made under the Agriculture Act 1970 s 44 (6).
5 The five years need not be continuous: Smallholdings (Selection of Tenants) Regulations 1970 reg 3 (1). Any period spent attending a full-time course in agriculture at a university, college or other further education establishment, up to a maximum of three years, ranks as a period of full-time practical farm work: reg 3 (1) proviso.

6 Ibid reg 3 (1).
7 Ibid reg 3 (3), (4) (added by SI 1976/2001).

104. Rent. In determining the rent at which it is to let land as a smallholding a smallholdings authority[1] must have regard to the rent which, in its opinion, might reasonably be expected to be determined to be the proper rent if the land were already let as an agricultural holding[2], if the terms of that letting, other than the terms as to rent, were those on which the authority proposes to let the land[3], and if the question what rent should be payable had been referred to arbitration[4], it being assumed that there would be no improvements[5], dilapidations, deterioration or damage of which special account, by way of reducing or increasing the rent, would fall to be taken in determining the rent payable[6].

These provisions, but without the assumption referred to above, also apply in relation to a revision by agreement of the rent at which land has been let by a smallholdings authority as a smallholding, including land so let under the previous enactments relating to smallholdings[7].

1 As to smallholdings authorities see para 117 post.
2 Agriculture Act 1970 s 45 (1) (a). As to the rent of agricultural holdings see AGRICULTURE vol 1 (2) (Reissue) para 325 et seq.
3 Ibid s 45 (1) (b).
4 Ibid s 45 (1) (c): the arbitration would be under the Agricultural Holdings Act 1986: see AGRICUL-TURE. As to arbitration on the rental of an agricultural holding see the 1986 Act s 12; and AGRICULTURE vol 1 (2) (Reissue) para 325 et seq.
5 This includes matters treated as equivalent to improvements. As to increases of rent for certain improvements to agricultural holdings see the Agricultural Holdings Act 1986 s 13; and AGRICUL-TURE.
6 Agriculture Act 1970 s 45 (2). These provisions apply also to smallholdings land held by the minister: see para 105 post.
7 Ibid s 45 (3). 'The previous enactments relating to smallholdings' means the Small Holdings and Allotments Acts 1908 to 1931 and the Agriculture Act 1947 Pt IV (ss 47–67) (largely repealed): Agriculture Act 1970 s 37 (1).

105. Letting of land held by minister. In relation to land for the time being held by him for the purposes of smallholdings[1] the Minister of Agriculture, Fisheries and Food[2] has the same powers and duties with regard to letting small-holdings[3] as have smallholdings authorities in relation to land held by them for those purposes[4].

1 As to such land see para 124 post.
2 The minister acts in both England and Wales: see para 123 post.
3 Ie under the Agriculture Act 1970 ss 44, 45; see paras 100, 103, 104 ante.
4 Ibid s 54 (1), (2).

106. Lettings and sales under earlier legislation. Where smallholdings were sold or let before 1 October 1949[1] the statutory provisions then applicable as to payments for sales by terminable annuities[2], as to the conditions affecting the holdings sold or let[3] and as to the recovery of possession on breach of those conditions[4] continue to apply subject to certain modifications[5].

Any land held by a smallholdings authority immediately before 1 August 1970[6] for the purposes of smallholdings[7] continues to be held by it for those purposes, subject to any power exercisable by it by virtue of any enactment to appropriate or dispose of the land for other purposes[8], and the repeal of the smallholdings provisions of earlier legislation[9] does not affect the validity of any letting effected before 1 August 1970[10].

1　Ie the date on which the Agriculture Act 1947 Pt IV (ss 47–67) came into operation: Agriculture Act 1947 (Commencement) Order 1949, SI 1949/1201.
2　See the Small Holdings and Allotments Act 1926 s 5. This section, with ss 6 and 7, continues to apply to cottage holdings without the modifications referred to in note 5 infra: see paras 132, 134, 135, 137 post.
3　See ibid s 6; and note 2 supra.
4　See ibid s 7; and note 2 supra.
5　Agriculture Act 1947 s 67 (2) (a), Sch 8 Pt II (amended by the Agriculture Act 1970 s 64 (2), Sch 4): the provisions referred to in notes 2–4 supra continue to apply except in so far as they provide for the sale or other disposition of smallholdings not authorised by the Agriculture Act 1970 Pt III (ss 37–65), and except in so far as the Small Holdings and Allotments Act 1926 s 6 (1) renders the minister's consent unnecessary where no contribution is payable by him, and the requirement of s 6 (1) (c) as to good husbandry must be construed as requiring the owner or occupier to fulfil his responsibilities to farm the holding in accordance with the rules of good husbandry, as to which see the Agriculture Act 1947 s 11; and AGRICULTURE.
6　Ie the date on which the Agriculture Act 1970 Pt III (ss 37–65) came into operation: Agriculture Act 1970 (Commencement No 2) Order 1970, SI 1970/1048.
7　As to land held by smallholdings authorities for the purposes of smallholdings see para 4 notes 10, 12 ante; as to smallholdings authorities see para 117 post.
8　Agriculture Act 1970 s 64 (1), Sch 3 para 2. As to such dealings see para 95 ante.
9　See ibid s 113 (3), Sch 5 Pt III, which repeals, inter alia, much of the Agriculture Act 1947 Pt IV (ss 47–67).
10　Agriculture Act 1970 s 64 (1), Sch 3 para 3; Agriculture Act 1970 (Commencement No 2) Order 1970.

107. Application of agricultural holdings legislation. A smallholding which is let under a contract of tenancy[1], not being a contract under which the land is let to the tenant during his continuance in office, appointment or employment held under the local authority, and which is used for the purposes of a trade or business, is an agricultural holding[2]. The statutory provisions affecting agricultural holdings, which are dealt with elsewhere, apply to such smallholdings[3]. Certain of those provisions which make express reference to smallholdings are set out in the following paragraphs.

1　Ie as defined in the Agricultural Holdings Act 1986 ss 1, 96: see AGRICULTURE vol 1 (2) (Reissue) para 303.
2　Ibid ss 1, 96.
3　See AGRICULTURE.

108. Freedom of cropping. The right given to the tenant of an agricultural holding to dispose of the produce of his holding and to practise any system of cropping arable land on the holding, notwithstanding any custom or provisions of the contract of tenancy or of any agreement to the contrary[1], does not apply to a tenancy of land let as a smallholding by a smallholdings authority or by the Minister of Agriculture, Fisheries and Food in pursuance of a scheme for the farming of smallholdings on a co-operative basis[2], or of a scheme which provides for the disposal of the produce of the holdings or provides other centralised services for the use of the tenants, the schemes in all cases being schemes approved[3] by the minister[4].

Where it appears to the minister that the provisions of any such approved scheme are not being satisfactorily carried out, he may serve notice on the persons respon-

sible for the management of the scheme withdrawing his approval and giving the
tenants concerned the statutory rights as regards disposal of produce and cropping
as from a specified date, not being earlier than one month after the service of the
notice[5]. The persons managing the scheme must be given an opportunity of
making representations to the minister[6]. If the minister does not withdraw that
notice before the date specified, the right to dispose of produce and to practise any
system of cropping thereupon applies to the tenancy[7].

1 Agricultural Holdings Act 1986 s 15 (1), (4).
2 Agriculture Act 1970 s 44 (3).
3 Ie for the purposes of the Agricultural Holdings Act 1986 s 82 (1).
4 Ibid s 82 (1).
5 Ibid s 82 (2), (3). In *Williams v Minister of Agriculture, Fisheries and Food* (1985) Times, 11 July, a
   scheme was terminated by the minister, not because there were defects in carrying out the scheme
   but because he considered the arrangements were no longer necessary or expedient.
6 Agricultural Holdings Act 1986 s 82 (2), (3); see AGRICULTURE vol 1 (2) (Reissue) para 331.
7 Ibid s 82 (3); and see AGRICULTURE vol 1 (2) (Reissue) para 331.

109. Notices to quit. A notice to quit an agricultural holding must relate to the
whole holding unless the contract provides otherwise, or the landlord's reversion
has been severed[1], or one of the statutory exceptions in the Agricultural Holdings
Act 1986 applies[2]. One such exception is where the notice to quit states that it is
given for the purpose of providing allotments, or the letting of land (with or
without other land) as a smallholding under Part III of the Agriculture Act 1970[3].

Generally, where a landlord serves a notice to quit an agricultural holding the
tenant is entitled to serve a counter notice[4]. He is not entitled to do so when the
holding has been let as a smallholding by a smallholdings authority or the minister
on or after 12 September 1984[5] and the notice to quit states that it is given under
Case A[6]. Certain conditions must be fulfilled: the tenant must have attained the age
of 65; and if the result of the notice to quit taking effect would be to deprive the
tenant of living accommodation occupied by him under the tenancy suitable
alternative accommodation[7] must be available for him by the time the notice takes
effect; and the instrument which granted the tenancy must contain an acknowledgment that the tenancy is subject to the provisions of Case A or its predecessor Case I
in the Agricultural Holdings (Notices to Quit) Act 1977. Basic but not additional
compensation is payable for disturbance[8].

A landlord can also serve an incontestable notice to quit where at the date when
he gives the notice his interest in the holding has been materially prejudiced by the
tenant's irremediable breach of covenant, provided that the covenant was not
inconsistent with the tenant's responsibilities to farm in accordance with the rules
of good husbandry. The notice to quit must state that it is given for this reason[9].
Where the landlord is a smallholdings authority or the minister (the holding being
land held by him for the purposes of smallholdings), then in considering whether
the interest of the landlord has been materially prejudiced regard has to be had to
the effect of the breach not only on the holding itself but also on the carrying out of
the arrangements made by the smallholdings authority or the minister for the
letting and conduct of smallholdings[10].

Where the consent of the Agricultural Land Tribunal is required to the operation
of a notice to quit (namely because it is not an incontestable notice) the tribunal
must give its consent if it is satisfied that the carrying out of the purpose for which
the smallholdings authority or minister proposes to terminate the tenancy is

desirable for the purpose of the enactments relating to smallholdings and it appears to them that a fair and reasonable landlord would insist on possession[11].

1 Law of Property Act 1925 s 140.
2 Agricultural Holdings Act 1986 s 31. See AGRICULTURE vol 1 (2) (Reissue) para 362.
3 Ibid s 31 (1) (b), (2) (c), (d).
4 Ibid s 26. See AGRICULTURE vol 1 (2) (Reissue) para 341 et seq.
5 The date when the Agricultural Holdings Act 1984 came into effect. The minister is, in relation to England, the Minister of Agriculture, Fisheries and Food, and in relation to Wales, the Secretary of State for Wales: Agricultural Holdings Act 1986 s 96 (1).
6 Ibid s 26, Sch 3 Pt I Case A.
7 As to suitable alternative accommodation see ibid Sch 3 Pt II paras 1–7; and AGRICULTURE vol 1 (2) (Reissue) para 344.
8 Ibid s 61 (2). As to compensation see AGRICULTURE vol 1 (2) (Reissue) para 383 et seq.
9 Ibid Sch 3 Pt I Case E, Pt II paras 11 (2), 9 (2). Provisions in the tenancy agreement for the conservation of flora or fauna or of geological or physiographical features of special interest; the protection of buildings or other objects of archaeological, architectural or historic interest; the conservation or enhancement of the natural beauty or amenity of the countryside or the promotion of its enjoyment by the public, are to be regarded as terms not inconsistent with good husbandry. As to Case E generally see AGRICULTURE vol 1 (2) (Reissue) para 348.
10 Ibid Sch 3 Pt II para 11 (1).
11 Ibid ss 26, 27 (1), (2); Smallholdings and Allotments Act 1908; Allotments Act 1922; Allotments Act 1950.

110. Succession on death. The succession provisions of the Agricultural Holdings Act 1986 do not apply to land held by a smallholdings authority or the minister[1] for the purposes of smallholdings within the meaning of Part III of the Agriculture Act 1970, whether the tenancy was granted before or after the commencement of Part III of the 1970 Act[2]. Smallholdings authorities are required, however, when reletting after the death of a tenant to consider certain near relatives of the deceased and to consider other applications only after applications from relatives have been refused[3].

1 As to 'the minister' see para 109 note 5 ante.
2 Agricultural Holdings Act 1986 s 38 (4), negating *Saul v Norfolk County Council* [1984] QB 559, [1984] 2 All ER 489, CA.
3 Smallholdings (Selection of Tenants) Regulations 1970, SI 1970/1049 (amended by SI 1976/2001); see para 103 ante.

(iii) Equipment

111. Equipment of smallholdings. A smallholdings authority[1] has power to provide, improve, maintain and repair fixed equipment[2] on land held by it for the purposes of smallholdings[3], and to carry out any other improvement on or for the benefit of any such land[4], and to enter into an agreement with a tenant of any such land for the provision, improvement, maintenance or repair by him of fixed equipment on the land[5], or the carrying out by him of other improvements on it or for its benefit[6], on terms specified in the agreement[7].

1 As to smallholdings authorities see para 117 post.
2 For the meaning of 'fixed equipment' see para 102 note 4 ante.
3 As to land held by a smallholdings authority for the purposes of smallholdings see para 4 notes 10, 12 ante.
4 Agriculture Act 1970 s 46 (1). The provisions of s 46 with respect to the powers of smallholdings authorities relate only to their capacity as corporations, and do not authorise any act or omission on

their part which, apart from those provisions, would be actionable at the suit of any person on any grounds other than a limitation on their capacity as corporations: s 37 (5).

5　Ibid s 46 (2) (a).
6　Ibid s 46 (2) (b).
7　Ibid s 46 (2). The minister has the same powers in respect of smallholdings land held by him: see para 112 post.

112. Equipping smallholdings on land held by minister. In relation to land for the time being held by him for the purposes of smallholdings[1] the Minister of Agriculture, Fisheries and Food[2] has the same powers and duties with regard to equipping smallholdings[3] as have smallholdings authorities in relation to land held by them for those purposes[4].

1　As to such land see para 124 post.
2　The minister acts in both England and Wales: see para 123 note 1 post.
3　Ie under the Agriculture Act 1970 s 46: see para 111 ante.
4　Ibid s 54 (1), (2).

(5) FINANCE

113. Loans and guarantees by smallholdings authorities. A smallholdings authority[1] may make loans for the purpose of providing working capital[2] for a tenant of a smallholding provided by it[3], or for an intending tenant, or may guarantee the repayment of and the payment of interest on any loan made for that purpose by another person[4], but no such loan or guarantee, or, if two or more loans are made or guaranteed, the aggregate amount of those loans, may exceed three-quarters of the aggregate working capital which, in the authority's opinion, is required for the proper working of the holding[5], and no loan may be made or guaranteed save under a written agreement specifying the maximum period of the loan or guarantee and the rate of interest[6].

1　As to smallholdings authorities see para 117 post.
2　'Working capital' includes any sum paid or payable by an incoming tenant, whether to the landlord or to the outgoing tenant, in respect of compensation paid or payable to an outgoing tenant: Agriculture Act 1970 s 37 (1).
3　'Smallholding provided by a smallholdings authority' means any land for the time being held by the authority for the purposes of smallholdings (as to which see para 4 notes 10, 12 ante) and let as a smallholding either under ibid Pt III (ss 37–65), or under the previous enactments relating to smallholdings (for the meaning of which see para 104 note 7 ante): s 37 (2) (b).
4　Ibid s 53 (1). The minister has a similar power in respect of smallholdings land held by him: see para 114 post.
5　Ibid s 53 (2).
6　Ibid s 53 (7). The loan must bear interest at one-half per cent above the rate which, on the date of the agreement, is the rate determined by the Treasury under the National Loans Act 1968 s 5 (substituted by the Finance Act 1982 s 153 (1) and subsequently amended by the Finance Act 1983 s 44), in respect of local loans then made on the security of local rates (as defined in the National Loans Act 1968 s 6 (2)) for the same period or, where two or more rates are so determined, such of those rates as the Treasury specifies for the purpose and publishes in the London Gazette: Agriculture Act 1970 s 53 (3)–(5), (8). The authority may not guarantee a loan which bears a higher rate of interest than would be chargeable had the authority made the loan: s 53 (6).

114. Loans by minister. The Minister of Agriculture, Fisheries and Food may, in accordance with arrangements made by him with Treasury approval, make loans to provide working capital[1] for a smallholdings tenant on land held by the minister for smallholdings purposes[2], or for an intending tenant[3], but the loan, or, if two or more loans are so made, the aggregate amount of the loans, must not exceed three-quarters of the aggregate working capital which in the minister's opinion is required for the proper working of the smallholding[4].

1 For the meaning of 'working capital' see para 113 note 2 ante.
2 As to such land see para 124 post.
3 Agriculture Act 1970 s 54 (5). The minister acts in both England and Wales: see para 123 note 1 post.
4 Ibid s 54 (6).

115. Increase of capital grants. Where a grant was made to a smallholdings authority[1] under a scheme made under the Agriculture Act 1970[2] in respect of expenditure incurred or to be incurred in respect of works or facilities, specified in the scheme by the Minister of Agriculture, Fisheries and Food for this purpose, which were in the minister's opinion required to give effect to approved reorganisation proposals[3], being expenditure qualified under the scheme for consideration for the grant within five years beginning with 1 January 1971, the date when the first such scheme[4] providing for grants to smallholdings authorities came into operation, the minister may increase the grant by one-tenth of the relevant expenditure[5]. No increase can, however, be granted if the land on which the works are to be carried out or the facilities provided is or forms part of a holding which, in the minister's opinion, would without those works or facilities be a commercial unit[6].

Application for an increase may be made at any time after the authority has submitted the relevant proposals[7] to the minister, and where the relevant proposals are comprised in reorganisation proposals submitted on an initial review[8] the increase may be granted when the minister has approved so much of those proposals as consist of the relevant proposals[9].

1 As to smallholdings authorities see para 117 post.
2 Eg a farm capital grant under the Agriculture Act 1970 s 29: see AGRICULTURE vol 1 (2) (Reissue) para 581 et seq.
3 Ie under ibid s 41 or 43: see paras 90, 92 ante.
4 Ie the Farm Capital Grant Scheme 1970 , SI 1970/1759 (amended by SI 1972/368) (revoked).
5 Agriculture Act 1970 s 51 (1). As to the minister in relation to Wales see para 123 post.
6 Ibid s 51 (1). For the meaning of 'commercial unit' see the Agriculture Act 1967 s 40 (2) (a); and AGRICULTURE.
7 Ie under the Agriculture Act 1970 s 40 or 43: see paras 89, 92 ante. 'Relevant proposals' means the proposals in connection with which the smallholdings authority claims that the works or facilities are required: s 51 (2) (a).
8 Ie under ibid s 40.
9 Ibid s 51 (2).

116. Contributions towards losses under previous enactments. Where a smallholdings authority formulated proposals for the provision, laying out, alteration or equipment of smallholdings, and it appeared that those proposals were likely to involve it in a loss, it could until 29 May 1970[1] submit estimates[2] to the Minister of Agriculture, Fisheries and Food and ask him to contribute to the loss[3]. If he approved the proposals and estimates[4] and the proposals were carried out he could contribute not more than three-quarters of the estimated loss[5]. He could also contribute not more than three-quarters of the expenses reasonably incurred in preparing proposals or in preparation for the acquisition of land for the purposes of the proposals, where the proposals were not carried out[6].

Under regulations[7] made by the minister[8] with Treasury approval[9], where any smallholdings land[10] is sold, exchanged, appropriated for other purposes or let otherwise than as a smallholding[11] by a smallholdings authority[12], the authority must forthwith after the completion of the transaction furnish particulars to the minister in a statement[13] signed by its treasurer, accountant or other authorised officer, and the minister may adjust[14], in such manner as he thinks appropriate, the amount of any contributions[15] payable to the authority where the land sold, exchanged, appropriated or let is land which has been or formed part of land in respect of which payments have been made[16] or contributions have been made or undertaken to be made[17] under earlier Acts[18]. The authority must furnish any other particulars the minister may require at any time to satisfy him that contributions should continue to be paid[19].

Application for the payment of contributions must be made to the minister annually not less than one month before the first instalment for the year[20] is due to be paid[21], signed by the authority's treasurer, accountant or other authorised officer[22]. Any person authorised by the minister in that behalf may at all reasonable times inspect the authority's books and other documents relating to transactions in connection with which contributions are payable[23].

Where a smallholdings authority does not comply with the statutory requirements[24] imposed on it in relation to land held by it for the purposes of smallholdings the minister may determine that contributions which would otherwise be payable to it shall be withheld or reduced[25].

1 Ie the date on which the Agriculture Act 1970 was passed.

2 For forms see the Smallholdings (Contributions Towards Losses) Regulations 1949, SI 1949/1815, reg 3, Sch 1.

3 Agriculture Act 1947 s 58 (1) (amended by the Agriculture Act 1970 ss 52 (1), 64 (2), Sch 4). The minister acts in both England and Wales: see para 123 post. He had a corresponding power to undertake to contribute towards losses incurred by local authorities providing smallholdings under the Small Holdings and Allotments Act 1926 s 2 (amended by the Agriculture Act 1970 s 113 (3), Sch 5 Pt III), and the Smallholdings (Contributions Towards Losses) Regulations 1970, SI 1970/1051 (amended by SI 1974/376). The 1926 Act s 2 is continued in operation in relation to proposals submitted before 1 October 1949, subject to those regulations: Agriculture Act 1947 s 67 (2), Sch 8 Pt II; Agriculture Act 1970 s 64 (2), Sch 4; Agriculture Act 1947 (Commencement) Order 1949, SI 1949/1201. Contributions undertaken by the minister to be paid under the 1947 Act s 58 or the 1926 Act s 2 may in some cases continue to be payable until the end of the present century. The minister also undertook under the Land Settlement (Facilities) Act 1919 s 27 (substituted by the Land Settlement (Facilities) Amendment Act 1925 s 1), to pay annual sums in respect of estimated losses suffered by smallholdings authorities in the acquisition of land for smallholdings under the Small Holdings and Allotments Act 1908. As to the commutation into a single payment of certain periodic smallholding payments under the 1919 Act s 27 see the Local Government Act 1988 s 36.

4 For the matters as to which the minister had to be satisfied see the Smallholdings (Contributions Towards Losses) Regulations 1949 reg 7.

5 Agriculture Act 1947 s 58 (2), (3). The contribution was annual, paid in two half-yearly instalments, and began in the first year in which, in the minister's opinion, the authority's proposals had been brought into full operation; years prior to the first year of full operation were treated as one accounting period for the purposes of contributions, the amount not to exceed three-quarters of the actual loss: see s 58 (4); Smallholdings (Contributions Towards Losses) Regulations 1949 regs 8–10; Smallholdings (Contributions Towards Losses) Regulations 1970 regs 4–6. As to the calculation of the expenditure on account of sinking fund charges see the 1947 Act s 58 (3) proviso, and the Agriculture (Miscellaneous Provisions) Act 1954 s 3 (3) (amended by the Agriculture Act 1970 Sch 5 Pt III and by the Transfer of Functions (Ministry of Food) Order 1955, SI 1955/554).

6 Agriculture Act 1947 s 58 (6); Smallholdings (Contributions Towards Losses) Regulations 1949 reg 15.

7 See the Smallholdings (Contributions Towards Losses) Regulations 1949 (amended by SI 1959/1426 and SI 1970/1051), made under the Agriculture Act 1947 s 58 (7) (amended by the Agriculture Act

1970 Sch 5 Pt III); and the Smallholdings (Contributions Towards Losses) Regulations 1970 (as amended: see note 3 supra), made under the Agriculture Act 1970 s 52 (2). The repeals effected by the 1970 Act Sch 5 Pt III do not affect the operation of the 1949 Regulations, nor of regulations made under the Small Holdings and Allotments Act 1926 s 2: Agriculture Act 1970 s 64 (1), Sch 3 para 8. The 1970 Regulations regs 4–8 do not apply to a smallholdings authority to which no contributions were payable in respect of smallholdings land (as defined in note 10 infra) on 1 August 1970, and cease to apply to it when contributions cease to be payable to it: reg 9 (a).

8   As to the minister in relation to Wales see para 123 post.
9   See the Agriculture Act 1970 s 52 (2).
10 'Smallholdings land' means land held by a smallholdings authority immediately before 1 August 1970 for the purposes of smallholdings: Smallholdings (Contributions Towards Losses) Regulations 1970 reg 2 (2) (as amended: see note 3 supra). As to land held by such authorities for those purposes see para 4 notes 10, 12 ante.
11 Ie otherwise than under the Agriculture Act 1970 s 44.
12 As to smallholdings authorities see para 117 post.
13 See the Smallholdings (Contributions Towards Losses) Regulations 1970 Sch 2.
14 The adjustments are made having regard to the amount realised by the sale, the rent received on a letting, or the value of land exchanged or appropriated, as certified by the district valuer: ibid reg 5. Where, by reason of such disposals and consequent adjustment of contribution payable to an authority, the aggregate amount of the contributions payable by him to the authority is reduced to nil, the minister does not require notification of further disposals of smallholdings land: reg 9.
15 'Contribution' means an annual contribution payable by the minister to a smallholdings authority towards its losses in respect of smallholdings land and, in relation to a contribution adjusted under ibid reg 5, means the contribution as so adjusted: reg 2 (2) (as amended: see note 3 supra).
16 Ie under the Land Settlement (Facilities) Act 1919 s 27 (as substituted: see note 3 supra). Until 1970 no adjustment could be made in respect of payments under the 1919 Act: see the Agriculture Act 1947 s 58 (7) (b) (repealed).
17 Ie under the Small Holdings and Allotments Act 1926 s 2 or the Agriculture Act 1947 s 58: see the text and note 3 supra.
18 Smallholdings (Contributions Towards Losses) Regulations 1970 reg 5 (1). The reference to adjustment is to be construed as including a reference to terminating any contribution: reg 5 (2).
19 Ibid reg 6.
20 The year begins on 1 April: ibid reg 4 (3).
21 Contributions are paid in two half-yearly instalments on such dates as the minister and the authority agree: ibid reg 4 (1).
22 Ibid reg 4 (2): the application must be in the form set out in Sch 1 or a form substantially to the like effect: reg 4 (2).
23 Ibid reg 8.
24 Ie under the Agriculture Act 1947 s 58, or the Agriculture Act 1970 Pt III (ss 37–65).
25 Smallholdings (Contributions Towards Losses) Regulations 1970 reg 7.

(6) ADMINISTRATION

(i) Smallholdings Authorities

117. Smallholdings authorities. County councils in England and Wales are the smallholdings authorities[1].

1   Agriculture Act 1970 s 38 (a) (amended by the Local Government Act 1972 s 272 (1), Sch 30 and the Local Government Act 1985 s 102 (2), Sch 17). Transitional provisions have been made relating to smallholdings authorities arising from the Local Government Act 1974; see the Local Authorities (Smallholdings) Order 1974, SI 1974/396.

118. Records and plans of smallholdings. Every smallholdings authority[1] must compile and keep, and, if so required by a person authorised by the Minister of Agriculture, Fisheries and Food, must produce to him, a record of all land which is or has at any time been held by the authority for the purposes of smallholdings[2], of the occupiers of such of the land as is let by it as smallholdings and of the rents, and of the purchasers of so much of the land as it has sold[3], and a map or plan showing the size, boundaries and situation of each smallholding it provides[4].

1 As to smallholdings authorities see para 117 ante.
2 As to land held by a smallholdings authority for the purposes of smallholdings see para 4 notes 10, 12 ante. As to the minister in relation to Wales see para 123 post.
3 Agriculture Act 1970 s 58 (2) (a).
4 Ibid s 58 (2) (b). As to smallholdings provided by a smallholdings authority see para 113 note 3 ante.

119. Annual reports of smallholdings authorities. Every smallholdings authority[1] must, before such date each year as the Minister of Agriculture, Fisheries and Food or, in Wales, the Secretary of State for Wales, directs, send him a report, relating to such matters as he directs, of its proceedings during the previous financial year[2]. Summaries of these reports are subsequently laid before Parliament[3].

1 As to smallholdings authorities see para 117 ante.
2 Agriculture Act 1970 ss 59 (1), 62 (1), (2) (a); Transfer of Functions (Wales) (No 1) Order 1978, SI 1978/272, art 2, Sch 1.
3 See para 128 post.

120. Accounts of smallholdings authorities. A smallholdings authority[1] must keep a separate account of its receipts and expenses, including capital receipts and expenses, with respect to smallholdings[2].

1 As to smallholdings authorities see para 117 ante.
2 Agriculture Act 1970 s 58 (1).

121. Promotion of smallholdings societies. For the benefit of the occupiers of smallholdings provided by it[1], a smallholdings authority[2] may further the formation of smallholdings societies, and assist their carrying on and the extension of their activities[3].

Smallholdings societies[4] are bodies of persons, whether corporate or unincorporate, having for their object or one of their objects the promotion of efficiency in the conduct of smallholdings through co-operative methods, and in particular through the co-operative purchase and hiring of requisites or the co-operative sale, marketing or preparation for marketing of produce[5].

1 As to smallholdings provided by an authority see para 113 note 3 ante.
2 As to smallholdings authorities see para 117 ante.
3 Agriculture Act 1970 s 47 (2).
4 The term 'smallholdings society' is not a statutory term.
5 Agriculture Act 1970 s 47 (2). For the meaning of 'produce' see the Agriculture Act 1947 s 109 (3): Agriculture Act 1970 s 37 (4); and AGRICULTURE vol 1 (2) (Reissue) para 602 note 4.

(ii) The Ministers

122. Ministerial powers and functions. Save in relation to Wales[1] the minister concerned with smallholdings is the Minister of Agriculture, Fisheries and Food[2].

He has power to approve reorganisation proposals[3], acquire smallholdings land[4], exercise control over the selection of tenants by making regulations[5], make loans in respect of smallholdings[6], increase the amount of certain capital grants[7], contribute towards losses of smallholdings authorities under previous enactments[8], let, equip and manage smallholdings on land held by him for smallholdings purposes[9], and act in default of smallholdings authorities[10], and he must lay an annual report before Parliament[11].

He or the Secretary of State for Wales[12] may by statutory instrument make regulations for any purpose for which regulations are authorised or required to be made relating to smallholdings[13].

1 As to Wales see para 123 post.
2 Agriculture Act 1970 s 37 (1).
3 See ibid ss 41–43; and paras 90–93 ante.
4 See ibid s 55; and para 94 ante. The minister exercises this power in relation to both England and Wales.
5 See ibid s 44 (6); and para 103 ante.
6 See ibid s 54 (5), (6); and para 114 ante.
7 See ibid s 51; and para 115 ante.
8 See ibid s 52; and para 116 ante. The minister exercises this power in relation to both England and Wales.
9 See ibid s 54; and para 124 post.
10 See ibid s 56; and para 125 post.
11 See ibid s 59 (2); and para 128 post.
12 See ibid s 37; and the Transfer of Functions (Wales) (No 1) Order 1978, SI 1978/272; see also para 123 post.
13 Agriculture Act 1970 s 63 (1), (2). Any such statutory instrument is subject to annulment in pursuance of a resolution of either House of Parliament: s 63 (2).

123. Wales. Where under many of the provisions relating to smallholdings[1] anything is authorised or required to be done by the minister in relation to a county council in Wales, including Monmouthshire[2], or by such a council in relation to the minister, whether or not the council falls within the provision in its capacity as a smallholdings authority, the reference to the minister must be construed as a reference to the Secretary of State for Wales[3].

1 Ie the Agriculture Act 1970 Pt III (ss 37–65), except ss 37, 52 (1), 54, 55, 56 (2), (4), 59 (2), 61, Sch 3 (s 62 (2) (a)); the Small Holdings and Allotments Act 1926 ss 2 (7), 6 (1) proviso, in so far as they have effect in relation to matters in existence before 1 October 1949 (Agriculture Act 1970 s 62 (2) (b): see para 134 post); and the provisions of the Small Holdings and Allotments Acts 1908 to 1926 (other than s 2 (2) of the Act of 1926) as applied to cottage holdings by the Agricultural Land (Utilisation) Act 1931 (Agriculture Act 1970 s 62 (2) (c)). As to local authorities see para 117 ante. As to cottage holdings generally see para 129 et seq post.
2 Agriculture Act 1970 s 62 (3).
3 Ibid ss 37 (1), 62 (1); Transfer of Functions (Wales) (No 1) Order 1978, SI 1978/272, art 2, Sch 1.

124. Smallholdings land held by minister. The Minister of Agriculture, Fisheries and Food may designate any land vested in him as being land held for the purposes of smallholdings, and may at any time revoke such designation[1].

In relation to land for the time being held by him for those purposes the minister has the same powers and duties with regard to letting[2], equipping[3] and managing[4] smallholdings and the letting of surplus land[5] as smallholdings authorities have in relation to land held by them for those purposes[6].

1 Agriculture Act 1970 s 54 (7). The minister acts in both England and Wales: see para 123 ante. For the meaning of 'the purpose of smallholdings' see para 4 note 12 ante.

2 See paras 100, 103–105 ante.
3 See paras 111, 112 ante.
4 See paras 98, 99 ante.
5 See paras 95, 96 ante.
6 Agriculture Act 1970 s 54 (1), (2).

125. Default powers. Where the Minister of Agriculture, Fisheries and Food or, in Wales, the Secretary of State for Wales, is satisfied that a smallholdings authority[1] is not satisfactorily exercising its functions he may (1) without prejudice to any other power to give directions, direct the authority to exercise its functions in such manner as is specified in the direction[2]; or (2) by order transfer all or any of its functions to the minister[3], but before making such an order the minister or Secretary of State must give the authority an opportunity of making representations[4] to him, which he must consider, and if it so requires must afford it the opportunity of being heard by a person appointed by him for the purpose[5]. The performance by the minister of functions so transferred has effect as if he were the authority's duly authorised agent[6].

An order varying or revoking an order transferring functions to the minister[7] may contain such provisions as appear expedient to the minister or the Secretary of State with respect to the transfer, vesting and discharge of property or liabilities acquired or incurred by him in the exercise of those functions[8]. Before he comes to a decision on an application by a smallholdings authority to revoke an order transferring its functions, being an application made not earlier than 12 months after the making of the order or of any previous application, he must give a similar opportunity to make representations and be heard as he must give before making the order[9].

1 As to smallholdings authorities see para 117 ante. As to the Secretary of State for Wales see the Transfer of Functions (Wales) (No 1) Order 1978, SI 1978/272, art 2, Sch 1.
2 Agriculture Act 1970 ss 56 (1) (a), (6), 62 (1), (2) (a).
3 Ibid ss 56 (1) (b), (2), 62 (1), (2) (a). Functions so transferred are transferred only to the minister, not to the Secretary of State for Wales: s 62 (2) (a), which excepts s 56 (2) from the provisions of s 62 (1).
4 As to representations see the Agriculture Act 1947 s 104, applied by the Agriculture Act 1970 s 56 (7); and AGRICULTURE vol 1 (2) (Reissue) para 969.
5 Ibid ss 56 (3), 62 (1), (2) (a).
6 Ibid ss 56 (4), 62 (1), (2) (a); and see note 3 supra. As to the expenses of transferred functions see para 126 post.
7 Power to make such an order may be inferred from ibid s 56 (5); the Act contains no such explicit power as was given by the Agriculture Act 1947 s 108 (3).
8 Agriculture Act 1970 ss 56 (5), 62 (1), (2) (a).
9 Ibid ss 56 (3) (b), 62 (1), (2) (a).

126. Minister's expenses on acting in default. Where the Minister of Agriculture, Fisheries and Food exercises his default powers upon being satisfied that the functions of a smallholdings authority are not being performed satisfactorily, and those functions are by order transferred to him[1], he must defray the expenses he incurs in the first instance[2], and, in relation to such successive periods as he may determine, must certify in relation to each such period the amount of those expenses and the amount of his receipts from the performance of those functions; the difference between these amounts being recoverable by him from the authority or, as the case may require, payable by him to the authority[3].

1 See the Agriculture Act 1970 s 56 (1), (2); and para 125 ante.

2 Ibid s 56 (4) (a).
3 Ibid s 56 (4) (b).

127. Ministers' expenses and receipts generally. Any expenses incurred by
the Minister of Agriculture, Fisheries and Food or the Secretary of State for Wales
under the Agriculture Act 1970, and any increase attributable to that Act in the
sums payable out of money provided by Parliament under any other enactment is
payable out of money provided by Parliament[1], and all receipts by the minister or
Secretary of State under that Act must be paid into the Consolidated Fund[2].

1 Agriculture Act 1970 s 111 (1).
2 Ibid s 111 (2).

128. Ministers' annual reports. The Minister of Agriculture, Fisheries and
Food in relation to England, and the Secretary of State for Wales[1] must each lay
before Parliament each financial year a report summarising the annual reports
submitted by smallholdings authorities[2] and his own proceedings in relation to
smallholdings[3].

1 The Agriculture Act 1970 s 59 (2) imposes this duty on 'the Ministers'; see s 37 (1); as to the transfer
   of functions where the ministers were formerly required to act jointly see the Transfer of Functions
   (Wales) (No 1) Order 1978, SI 1978/272.
2 As to these annual reports see para 119 ante.
3 Agriculture Act 1970 ss 59 (2), 62 (1), (2) (a). Section 59 (2) originally referred to 'proceedings of the
   Minister, and of the Ministers acting jointly'. See note 1 supra.

4. COTTAGE HOLDINGS

(1) PROVISION OF COTTAGE HOLDINGS

129. Provision of cottage holdings. The council of a county[1] or county
borough[2], or the Greater London Council[3], as cottage holding authorities[4], had
power until 1 August 1970[4] to provide cottage holdings[5] for sale or letting to any
person who in its opinion was suitable and who satisfied the council that he would
reside permanently in the dwelling house comprised in the holding, and that he had
the intention, knowledge and capital to cultivate satisfactorily the land forming
part of the holding[6]. The provisions of the Small Holdings and Allotments Act
1908 to 1931[7] applicable to smallholdings before 1 October 1949[8] apply to cottage
holdings, with the further provision that the owner or occupier should reside in the
dwelling house[9]. The council could make advances towards the purchase price, as
in the case of smallholdings[10].

1 A county council has power to delegate its powers in respect of cottage holdings to a district council:
   Small Holdings and Allotments Act 1926 s 9 (amended by the Local Government Act 1972 s 272 (1),
   Sch 30); as to county councils see the 1972 Act s 179; and LOCAL GOVERNMENT.
2 Small Holdings and Allotments Act 1908 s 61 (1) (amended by the Agricultural Land (Utilisation)
   Act 1931, to effect the inclusion of county boroughs in the definition of 'county council', and by the
   Local Government Act 1972 Sch 30, to reflect the abolition of county boroughs by s 1 of the 1972
   Act).
3 London Government Act 1963 s 55 (2) (repealed). The Greater London Council was abolished by the
   Local Government Act 1985 s 1.

4 Ie the date on which the Agriculture Act 1970 Pt III (ss 37–65) came into force: Agriculture Act 1970 (Commencement No 2) Order 1970, SI 1970/1048; see the Agriculture Act 1970 s 60 (1); and para 131 post.
5 For the meaning of 'cottage holding' see para 6 ante.
6 Small Holdings and Allotments Act 1926 s 1; Agricultural Land (Utilisation) Act 1931 s 12 (1) (amended by the Agriculture Act 1970 s 64 (2), Sch 4). The Agricultural Land (Utilisation) Act 1931 s 12 is subject to the Agriculture Act 1970 s 60 (see para 131 post): Agricultural Land (Utilisation) Act 1931 s 12 (1) proviso (as so amended). For certain default powers of the Minister of Agriculture, Fisheries and Food see s 9 (repealed). As to the consideration on sale see para 132 post.
7 See para 4 note 2 ante.
8 Ie the date on which the Agriculture Act 1947 Pt IV (ss 47–67) came into force: Agriculture Act 1947 (Commencement) Order 1949, SI 1949/1201. That Part, largely repealed by the Agriculture Act 1970, governed the position with regard to smallholdings provided after that date, but did not apply to cottage holdings (1947 Act s 66 (1) (repealed)).
9 Agricultural Land (Utilisation) Act 1931 s 12 (1) (as amended: see note 6 supra), which has effect subject to the Agriculture Act 1970 s 60 (see para 131 post): 1931 Act s 12 (1) (as so amended).
10 Small Holdings and Allotments Act 1926 s 13 (1), (4) (s 13 (1) amended by the Agricultural Land (Utilisation) Act 1931 s 17, Sch 2).

130. Acquisition of land. Although a council might formerly acquire land for the purpose of providing cottage holdings[1], no land may be acquired by a council after 1 August 1970, whether by purchase or lease, for the purpose of being sold or let as a cottage holding[2].

1 See the Small Holdings and Allotments Act 1926 s 4 (amended by the Acquisition of Land (Authorisation Procedure) Act 1947 s 6, Sch 4 and the Local Government Act 1972 s 259, Sch 29 Pt II para 11), applied to cottage holdings by the Agricultural Land (Utilisation) Act 1931 s 12 (1) (amended by the Agriculture Act 1970 s 64 (2), Sch 4 as so to render it subject to s 60 of the 1970 Act: see text and note 2 infra).
2 Agriculture Act 1970 s 60 (1) (c); Agriculture Act 1970 (Commencement No 2) Order 1970, SI 1970/1048.

(2) MANAGEMENT OF COTTAGE HOLDINGS

131. Sale of cottage holding land. After 1 August 1970 no land may be sold by a county council as a cottage holding[1]. This does not mean that cottage holding land cannot be sold; any such sale must, however, be for some purpose other than the use of the land for cottage holdings.

Where any cottage holdings land[2] is sold, exchanged or appropriated for other purposes by a council[3] to which contributions[4] are payable in respect of cottage holdings land[5], the council must forthwith after completion of the sale, exchange or appropriation furnish particulars thereof to the appropriate minister[6] in a prescribed form of statement[7] signed by the treasurer, accountant or other authorised council officer, and the appropriate minister may adjust, in such manner as he thinks fit having regard to any such particulars, the amount or aggregate amount of any contributions payable to the council in relation to cottage holdings land in a case where the land sold, exchanged or appropriated is land which has been, or formed part of, land in respect of which contributions have been made or undertaken to be made[8] in connection with proposals and estimates relating to that land[9]. The council must also furnish any other particulars which the appropriate minister may require at any time for the purpose of satisfying him that contributions payable to it should continue to be paid[10].

If such a council does not comply with the statutory requirements[11] in relation to land held by it for the purpose of cottage holdings the appropriate minister may determine that contributions which would otherwise be payable to it shall be withheld or reduced, whereupon he must withhold or reduce them accordingly[12].

Any person authorised by the appropriate minister may at all reasonable times inspect the council's books and other documents relating to transactions in connection with which any contributions are payable to the council[13].

1 Agriculture Act 1970 s 60 (1) (a) (amended by the Local Government Act 1972 s 272 (1), Sch 30); Agriculture Act 1970 (Commencement No 2) Order 1970, SI 1970/1048. No repealing provision having been made, the 1970 Act s 60 (1) still technically refers to the Greater London Council, though following the abolition of that body by the Local Government Act 1985 s 1, that reference must be regarded as redundant.
2 'Cottage holdings land' means land held by a council immediately before 1 August 1970 for the purposes of cottage holdings: Smallholdings (Contributions Towards Losses) Regulations 1970, SI 1970/1051, reg 2 (2) (amended by the Local Authorities (Smallholdings) Order 1974, SI 1974/396); Agriculture Act 1970 (Commencement No 2) Order 1970.
3 As to this power see the Local Government Act 1972 ss 122, 126 (both amended by the Local Government, Planning and Land Act 1980 ss 118, 194, Sch 23 Pt V, Sch 34 Pt XIII, and by the Planning (Consequential Provisions) Act 1990 s 4, Sch 2 para 28 (1)).
4 See text and note 8 infra.
5 The Smallholdings (Contributions Towards Losses) Regulations 1970 regs 4–8 do not apply to a council to which no contributions are payable in respect of cottage holdings land, and cease to apply to it when contributions cease to be payable to it: reg 9.
6 'Appropriate minister' means, in relation to England, the Minister of Agriculture, Fisheries and Food, and in relation to Wales and Monmouthshire, the Secretary of State for Wales: ibid reg 2 (2); Transfer of Functions (Wales) (No 1) Order 1978, SI 1978/272, arts 2, 11, Sch 1.
7 See the Smallholdings (Contributions Towards Losses) Regulations 1970 reg 5, Sch 2; and see note 5 supra.
8 Ie under the Small Holdings and Allotments Act 1926 s 2, as applied to cottage holdings by s 12 (repealed) or by the Agricultural Land (Utilisation) Act 1931 s 12: Smallholdings (Contributions Towards Losses) Regulations 1970 regs 3 (2), 5 (2) (b). As to these contributions see para 140 post. See also note 5 supra.
9 Ibid reg 5 (1); and see note 5 supra.
10 Ibid reg 6; and see note 5 supra.
11 Ie the requirements of the Agriculture Act 1970 Pt III (ss 37–65), under which the Smallholdings (Contributions Towards Losses) Regulations 1970 were made.
12 Ibid reg 7; and see note 5 supra.
13 Ibid reg 8; and see note 5 supra.

132. Consideration for sale of cottage holdings. Where a council sold a cottage holding the consideration had to be a terminable annuity equal to the full fair rent[1] of the holding for 60 years or, at the purchaser's option, a terminable annuity for a less period of an equivalent capital value[2]. The annuity is paid in equal half-yearly instalments, secured by a charge on the holding[3]. The council may postpone payment of all or part of the annuity for up to five years on account of capital expenditure by the purchaser which in its opinion increases the holding's value, but must do so on such terms as will, in its opinion, prevent the council from incurring any loss or increased loss[4].

1 Questions as to what is a full fair rent or as to the amount of the annuity were to be determined by the council: Small Holdings and Allotments Act 1926 s 5 (5). As to the application of this Act to cottage holdings see para 7 note 4 ante.
2 Small Holdings and Allotments Act 1926 s 5 (1). The Rentcharges Act 1977 ss 8–10, relating to the redemption of rentcharges, would apply to a terminable annuity under this section when charged on the holding.
3 Small Holdings and Allotments Act 1926 s 5 (2).
4 Ibid s 5 (3).

133. Advances for cottage holdings. A council had power to make advances to the prospective purchaser of a cottage holding, corresponding with its power to make such advances in respect of a smallholding[1].

The council may advance money to owners of cottage holdings provided by it or purchased with its assistance, for the purpose of constructing, altering or adapting houses or farm buildings on the holding, and may guarantee advances, including interest, made for these purposes by a building, industrial or provident society to owners who are members of that society[2]. The council must be satisfied that the houses will be in all respects fit for human habitation, and that the houses and buildings will be necessary for the requirements of the cottage holdings[3]. The advance, which must be made after a valuation[4], must be secured by a mortgage not exceeding 90 per cent of the mortgagor's interest, and must provide for repayment by instalments or by an annuity, or, in the event of non-compliance with conditions, on demand[5]. It may be made by instalments during construction of up to 50 per cent of the value of the work done[6].

1 See the Small Holdings and Allotments Act 1926 s 13 (1), (3), (4) (s 13 (1) amended by the Agricultural Land (Utilisation) Act 1931 s 17, Sch 2), applied by the Agricultural Land (Utilisation) Act 1931 s 12 (1) (amended by the Agriculture Act 1970 s 64 (2), Sch 4). A cottage holding can no longer be purchased: see para 131 ante. This provision continues to apply to smallholdings in respect of advances made before 1 October 1949: Agriculture Act 1947 s 67 (2) proviso (a), Sch 8 Pt II (amended by the Agriculture Act 1970 s 113 (3), Sch 5 Pt III); Agriculture Act 1947 (Commencement) Order 1949, SI 1949/1201.
2 Small Holdings and Allotments Act 1926 s 14 (1) (as amended and applied: see note 1 supra). These provisions continue to apply to smallholdings in respect of advances made before 1 October 1949: see note 1 supra. The making of advances and the fulfilling of guarantees (except of interest) are purposes for which the council may borrow: s 14 (4) (amended by the Local Government Act 1933 s 307, Sch 11 Pt IV (repealed), and the London Government Order 1970, SI 1970/211, art 3 (8), Schedule).
3 Small Holdings and Allotments Act 1926 s 14 (2).
4 Ibid s 14 (3) (c).
5 Ibid s 14 (3) (a).
6 Ibid s 14 (3) (b).

134. Conditions affecting cottage holdings sold by council. Land sold by a council for cottage holdings was required to be sold, except where the Minister of Agriculture, Fisheries and Food or his predecessor otherwise directed, subject to a reservation of all minerals vested in the council[1], and any cottage holding so sold must have been held for a term of 40 years from the date of the sale and for so long thereafter as the holding remained charged with the terminable annuity, and must have been so held subject to the following conditions[2]:

(1) Periodical payments under the annuity must be duly made[3];
(2) The holding might not be divided[4], sold, assigned, let or sublet without the council's consent[5];
(3) It must be cultivated by the owner or occupier in accordance with the rules of good husbandry[6] and used for the purpose of agriculture only[7];
(4) The owner or occupier must reside in the dwelling house[8];
(5) Any dwelling house erected on it must comply with council requirements as to health and overcrowding[9];
(6) Any dwelling house or other building on it must be kept in repair and insured against fire[10];

(7) No dwelling house or building on it may be used for the sale of intoxicating liquors[11].

The council may relax or dispense with any of these conditions[12]. If any condition is broken the council may, after giving an opportunity of remedying the breach, take possession or order the sale of the holding without taking possession[13].

1 Land Settlement (Facilities) Act 1919 s 11 (1) (amended by the Small Holdings and Allotments Act 1926 s 22 (1), Sch 2; see also the Ministry of Agriculture and Fisheries Act 1919 s 1 and the Transfer of Functions (Ministry of Food) Order 1955, SI 1955/554). As to the application of these provisions to cottage holdings see para 129 text and note 9 ante.
2 Small Holdings and Allotments Act 1926 s 6 (1); Agricultural Land (Utilisation) Act 1931 s 12 (1) (amended by the Agriculture Act 1970 s 64 (2), Sch 4). In addition to these conditions two further conditions applied to smallholdings: (1) not more than one dwelling house might be erected unless the council considered additional accommodation necessary (1926 Act s 6 (1) (d)), (2) no dwelling house might be erected without the consent of the council on a holding on which in its opinion a dwelling house might not be erected (s 6 (1) (h)). These conditions continue to apply to smallholdings sold or let before 1 October 1949: see para 106 ante.
3 Ibid s 6 (1) (a).
4 If the holding, while subject to these conditions, would on the owner's decease become subdivided by reason of any devise, bequest, intestacy or otherwise, the council may require it to be sold within 12 months of the decease to some one person, and if default is made in so selling it, may either take posession, or order a sale without taking possession: ibid s 6 (3).
5 Ibid s 6 (1) (b).
6 Ie as defined in the Agricultural Holdings Act 1923 s 57 (repealed); see now the Agriculture Act 1947 s 11; and AGRICULTURE vol 1 (2) (Reissue) para 603.
7 Small Holdings and Allotments Act 1926 s 6 (1) (c).
8 Agricultural Land (Utilisation) Act 1931 s 12 (1). This condition never applied to smallholdings.
9 Small Holdings and Allotments Act 1926 s 6 (1) (e).
10 Ibid s 6 (1) (f). Premium receipts must be produced to the council when required: s 6 (1) (f).
11 Ibid s 6 (1) (g).
12 Ibid s 6 (1) proviso. Where a contribution is payable by the minister he must consent to any relaxation or dispensation and, in giving consent, may impose terms as to the consideration to be charged and its application in satisfaction of his contributions: s 6 (1) proviso; Agriculture Act 1970 ss 37 (1), 62 (1), (2) (b). As to such contributions see para 140 post. In the continued application of these conditions to smallholdings sold or let before 1 October 1949 (as to which see para 106 ante) ministerial consent is always necessary, even though no contribution is payable: Agriculture Act 1947 s 67 (2), Sch 8 Pt II.
13 Small Holdings and Allotments Act 1926 s 6 (2). As to sales without taking possession see para 138 post.

135. Letting of cottage holdings. No land could be let by a county council, county borough council or the Greater London Council as a cottage holding by a letting effected after 1 August 1970, whether the land was previously so let or not[1]. Because a cottage holding let by a council is generally held subject to the same conditions under which it would be held if it were sold[2], and because these conditions are consistent only with the use of the land as a cottage holding, this means in effect that land used for cottage holdings cannot be let for any purpose. A council may, however, appropriate the land for some purpose other than cottage holdings[3], and then let the land.

Land let by a council as a cottage holding before 1 August 1970 continues to be so let.

1 Agriculture Act 1970 s 60 (1) (b) (subsequently amended by the Local Government Act 1972 s 272 (1), Sch 30, to reflect the abolition of county boroughs by that Act; see also para 129 notes 2, 3 ante as to the abolition of the Greater London Council); Agriculture Act 1970 (Commencement No 2) Order 1970, SI 1970/1048.

2 Small Holdings and Allotments Act 1926 s 6 (4). As to these conditions see s 6 (1): and para 134 ante.
3 Local Government Act 1972 ss 122, 126 (both amended by the Local Government, Planning and Land Act 1980 ss 118, 194, Sch 23 Pt V, Sch 34 Pt XIII, and by the Planning (Consequential Provisions) Act 1990 s 4, Sch 2 para 28 (1)).

136. Assistance to cottage holdings. Councils providing cottage holdings[1] have all the powers of promoting and assisting co-operative associations that they formerly possessed in respect of smallholdings[2]. These powers are the same as those exercisable in relation to allotments[3].

1 See para 129 ante.
2 See the Small Holdings and Allotments Act 1908 s 49 (amended by the Land Settlement (Facilities) Act 1919 ss 25, 33, Schs 2, 3, the Small Holdings and Allotments Act 1926 s 21, Sch 1 and the Local Government, Planning and Land Act 1980 s 1 (5), Sch 5 para 1), and the Agricultural Land (Utilisation) Act 1931 s 12 (1) (amended by the Agriculture Act 1970 s 64 (2), Sch 4).
3 See paras 82, 83 ante.

137. Council taking possession. Where a council, either on breach of any condition[1] or on the decease of an owner[2], takes possession of a cottage holding, it vests in the council[3], which may take action to recover possession[4], and may either retain it under the council's own management or sell[5] or otherwise dispose of it[6]. However, where it takes possession, the council must pay the owner an agreed sum, or the value[7] of the interest in the holding less the redemption value[8] of the annuity and any arrears of annuity then due[9]. The costs incidental to taking possession or disposing of the holding[10] are deducted from the sum payable to the owners[11]. If the value of the holding, ascertained as mentioned above, proves to be less than the redemption value together with any arrears of the annuity, the council may recover the deficiency summarily from the owner as a civil debt[12].

1 See para 134 text to note 13 ante.
2 See para 134 note 4 ante.
3 Small Holdings and Allotments Act 1926 s 7 (1). As to the application of this Act to cottage holdings see para 7 note 4 ante.
4 Ibid s 7 (5) (amended by the Rent Act 1965 s 52 (1), Sch 7 Pt II). The procedure is as if the council were a landlord and the owner of the holding a tenant, and possession may be recovered, whatever the value of the holding, by county court action under the County Courts Act 1984 ss 21 (1), 137. As to such actions see LANDLORD AND TENANT.
5 As to the procedure on sale without taking possession see para 138 post; as to sales generally see para 131 ante.
6 Small Holdings and Allotments Act 1926 s 7 (1).
7 In the absence of sale and in default of agreement the value must be settled by an arbitrator under the Agricultural Holdings Act 1986 ss 83, 84, Sch 11 para 1 (see AGRICULTURE vol 1 (2) (Reissue) para 449 et seq): Small Holdings and Allotments Act 1926 s 7 (2) (b); Interpretation Act 1978 s 17 (2).
8 Ie the amount at which the annuity may be redeemed under the Law of Property Act 1925 s 191 (repealed: see now the Rentcharges Act 1977 ss 8–10): Small Holdings and Allotments Act 1926 s 7 (2) (b).
9 Ibid s 7 (2).
10 These include the costs of any arbitration: see note 7 supra; and AGRICULTURE vol 1 (2) (Reissue) para 449 et seq.
11 Small Holdings and Allotments Act 1926 s 7 (4). The sum payable carries interest at five per cent per annum from the date of taking possession if not paid within three months after that date: s 7 (3).
12 Ibid s 7 (6). As to the recovery of civil debts see the Magistrates' Courts Act 1980 s 58; and MAGISTRATES.

138. Council ordering sale without taking possession. Where a council orders the sale of a cottage holding[1] without taking possession, it must cause the holding to be put up for auction[2]. The sale by auction may be made either subject to the charge in respect of the terminable annuity[3], or free, wholly or partly, from that charge; in either case, the purchase money to be paid by the purchaser on the auction is subject to the same provisions as purchase money payable on the first sale of a holding[4]. The council must retain out of the proceeds of sale a sum equal to the redemption value of any annuity charged on the holding, unless the holding is sold subject to the terminable annuity, together with any arrears of the annuity and all costs, the balance being paid to the owner[5]. If, however, the council is unable to sell the holding for such sum as will reimburse it the aforementioned amounts, it may take possession without being liable to pay the owner anything, and with the right to recover summarily from him, as a civil debt, the amount of the deficiency[6].

1 The council cannot sell the land as a cottage holding (Agriculture Act 1970 s 60 (1) (a)); it must therefore be sold for other purposes.
2 Small Holdings and Allotments Act 1926 s 8 (1). For the application of this Act to cottage holdings see para 129 text to note 9 ante. As to sales see further para 131 ante.
3 As to the terminable annuity see para 132 ante.
4 Small Holdings and Allotments Act 1926 s 8 (3). As to the provisions referred to see para 132 ante.
5 Ibid s 8 (1).
6 Ibid s 8 (2). As to the recovery of civil debts see the Magistrates' Courts Act 1980 s 58; and MAGISTRATES.

139. Compensation for improvements; right of removal. A tenant to whom a cottage holding has been let has against the council the same right to compensation for specified improvements[1] as he would have had if the holding had been a market garden[2]. He is not, however, entitled to compensation for improvements executed contrary to an express written prohibition by the council[3]. If the tenant feels aggrieved by such a prohibition he may appeal to the Minister of Agriculture, Fisheries and Food, who may confirm, vary or annul the prohibition. In this respect the minister's decision is final[4].

A tenant may, before the expiration of his tenancy, remove any fruit and other trees and bushes planted or acquired by him for which he has no claim for compensation, and may remove any toolshed, greenhouse, fowlhouse or pigsty built or acquired by him for which he has no such claim[5].

If the cottage holding is an agricultural holding[6] he may claim compensation for improvements and remove buildings and fixtures in accordance with the Agricultural Holdings Act 1986[7].

1 Ie the planting of (1) standard or other fruit trees permanently set out, (2) fruit bushes permanently set out, (3) strawberry plants, and (4) asparagus, rhubarb and other vegetable crops which continue productive for two or more years: Small Holdings and Allotments Act 1908 s 47, Sch 2 Pt I.
2 Ibid s 47 (1). For a market garden tenant's right to compensation for improvements see AGRICULTURE vol 1 (2) (Reissue) para 444.
3 Ibid s 47 (1) proviso (amended by the Local Government, Planning and Land Act 1980 s 1 (5), Sch 5 para 1 (c)).
4 Agricultural Land (Utilisation) Act 1931 s 12 (1A) (added by the Local Government, Planning and Land Act 1980 s 193, Sch 33 para 2).
5 Small Holdings and Allotments Act 1908 s 47 (4).
6 Ie within the meaning of the Agricultural Holdings Act 1986 (as to which see AGRICULTURE vol 1 (2) (Reissue) para 301). By virtue of the Interpretation Act 1978 s 17, the definition of 'agricultural holding' is substituted for the definitions contained successively in the Agricultural Holdings Acts of 1908, 1923 and 1948 (all repealed).
7 See AGRICULTURE vol 1 (2) (Reissue) para 383 et seq.

140. Contribution by minister towards losses. Where it appeared to a council that the provision of any cottage holdings would entail a loss, it had to submit proposals, with estimates of expenditure and income, to the Minister of Agriculture, Fisheries and Food or the Secretary of State for Wales[1], and he, after approval with or without modification, might thereupon make contributions up to, but not exceeding, 75 per cent of the estimated annual loss[2]. If the proposals, after approval by the minister, are varied by the council, the minister may reduce his contribution or, if the variation was made with his consent, vary his contribution by either increasing or decreasing it[3]. He might also contribute towards the expenses of preparing proposals, even if they were not submitted or, if submitted, not approved[4]. Where land was acquired without ministerial consent these provisions apply only to expenses likely to be incurred in equipping the land and adapting it for cottage holdings[5].

Payment of contributions to a council is made by the minister on agreed dates in two half-yearly instalments[6] on application signed by the council's treasurer, accountant or other authorised officer and made to the minister annually not less than a month before the first instalment for the year is due to be paid[7].

1 Small Holdings and Allotments Act 1926 s 2 (1) (amended by the Transfer of Functions (Ministry of Food) Order 1955, SI 1955/554). As to the application of this Act to cottage holdings see para 129 text to note 9 ante. The function of receiving proposals so submitted, but not that of approving them or making contributions towards losses, is transferred, in relation to Wales, to the Secretary of State for Wales by virtue of the Agriculture Act 1970 ss 37 (1), 62 (2) (c), and the Transfer of Functions (Wales) (No 1) Order 1978, SI 1978/272.
2 Small Holdings and Allotments Act 1926 s 2 (2) (amended by the Agricultural Land (Utilisation) Act 1931 s 17 (1), Sch 2); Agriculture Act 1947 s 59. This power is exercised in both England and Wales by the Minister of Agriculture, Fisheries and Food; see note 1 supra. In considering the estimates the minister must satisfy himself that they are made on the basis of the full fair rent being charged for each holding: Small Holdings and Allotments Act 1926 s 2 (2) proviso. 'Full fair rent' means the rent which a tenant might reasonably be expected to pay for the holding if it were let as such and the landlord undertook to bear the cost of structural repairs: s 2 (6). The minister's approval may be subject to such conditions as to records, certificates, audit or otherwise as he may, with Treasury approval, determine: s 2 (2). These provisions continue in operation in their application to small-holdings with modifications in relation to proposals submitted before 1 October 1949: see the Agriculture Act 1947 s 67 (2), Sch 8 Pt II; and para 116 ante.
3 Small Holdings and Allotments Act 1926 s 2 (3).
4 Ibid s 2 (8) (added by the Agricultural Land (Utilisation) Act 1931 Sch 2).
5 Small Holdings and Allotments Act 1926 s 2 (5).
6 Smallholdings (Contributions Towards Losses) Regulations 1970, SI 1970/1051, reg 4 (1). For this purpose the year ends on 31 March: reg 4 (3).
7 Ibid reg 4 (2). For the form of application see Sch 1. As to the duty to furnish particulars of transactions affecting contributions see para 131 ante.

141. Delegation of powers. A county council may make arrangements with the council of any district in the county for the exercise, as agents for the county council, of any of its powers for the adaptation and management of cottage holdings for the district, and the district council may undertake to pay the whole or any part of the loss, if any, incurred in connection with such cottage holdings; any sum so payable must be defrayed as part of the general expenses of the district council[1].

1 Small Holdings and Allotments Act 1926 s 9 (amended by the Local Government Act 1972 s 272 (1), Sch 30); Agricultural Land (Utilisation) Act 1931 s 12 (1). These arrangements do not authorise the

exercise on behalf of a county council of the power of submitting to the minister or Secretary of State proposals and estimates for the purpose of obtaining contributions (as to which see para 140 ante): Small Holdings and Allotments Act 1926 s 9.

142–200. Lists, plans and reports. The council must keep a list of owners and occupiers of cottage holdings, sold or let by it, and a map or plan showing the size, boundaries and situation of each holding[1].

1 Small Holdings and Allotments Act 1926 s 10; Agricultural Land (Utilisation) Act 1931 s 12. For the application of these provisions to cottage holdings see para 129 text to note 9 ante.

ANCIENT MONUMENTS

See OPEN SPACES AND HISTORIC BUILDINGS; TOWN AND COUNTRY PLANNING

ANIMALS

3. PROTECTION OF WILD ANIMALS

4. DOGS AND HORSES

9. VETERINARY SURGEONS AND THE PRACTICE OF VETERINARY SURGERY

1. ANIMALS AS THE SUBJECT OF PROPERTY

(1) OWNERSHIP

(i) Domestic Animals

201. Classification. In law the term 'animals' includes all creatures of the animal world not belonging to the human race, and is so used throughout this title except where a specially restricted meaning is appropriate[1]. In law animals are divided into two classes, domestic and wild, and this classification affects the rights of property in them and also liability for their behaviour[2].

1 'Animals' is specifically defined for the purposes of certain statutes, eg the Protection of Animals Acts 1911 to 1964 (see para 405 note 9 post) and the Animal Health Act 1981 (see para 483 post).
2 3 Co Inst 109; 1 Hall PC 512. See *Nye v Niblett* [1918] 1 KB 23. The Animals Act 1971 effected a major change in the law of strict liability for the acts of wild animals: by ss 1, 2, 6 (1), (2), such liability only exists in the case of animals of a 'dangerous species', defined, inter alia, as a species not commonly domesticated in the British Islands. See para 467 post. For definitions of 'domestic' and 'wild' animals see paras 202, 204 post respectively. As to the British Islands see para 380 note 1 post.

202. Meaning of 'domestic animals'. The term 'domestic animals' includes all those domestic or tame animals as by habit or training live in association with man[1]. An animal which does not exist in a wild state anywhere in the world is in law a domestic animal[2]. It is a question of law, not fact, whether an animal is within the class of domestic animals or wild animals[3].

1 3 Co Inst 109; 1 Hall PC 512. See *Nye v Niblett* [1918] 1 KB 23. Such animals are referred to as *domitae* or *mansuetae naturae*.
2 *McQuaker v Goddard* [1940] 1 KB 687 at 696, [1940] 1 All ER 471 at 475, CA, per Scott LJ (camel at Chessington Zoo). Judicial notice will be taken of the ordinary course of nature in regard to the position of animals: *McQuaker v Goddard* supra at 700, 478 per Clauson LJ. A domestic animal which reverts to a wild state is in law no longer domestic but wild: *Falkland Islands Co v R* (1864) 2 Moo PCCNS 266.
3 *McQuaker v Goddard* [1940] 1 KB 687, [1940] 1 All ER 471, CA.

203. Absolute property in domestic animals. Domestic animals, like other personal and movable chattels, are the subject of absolute property. The owner can maintain an action for their detention or conversion, or for trespass to goods in respect of them, and retains his property in them if they stray or are lost[1].

As a general rule the property in the young of domestic animals is in the owner of the mother[2], but in the case of a lease of livestock the progeny belong to the lessee in the absence of express stipulation to the contrary[3], and the ownership of cygnets is divided between the owners of the cock and hen swans[4].

1 *Putt v Roster* (1682) 2 Mod Rep 318. The owner of a lost dog may maintain an action in trover, and the finder has no right to detain it until he is paid for its keep: *Binstead v Buck* (1777) 2 Wm Bl 1117. Merely keeping and feeding an animal does not, apart from contract, confer any right of lien: see BAILMENT.

2 Brooke's Abridgment, 'Propertie', para 29; cf 2 Bl Com (14th Edn) 389–399. The common law follows the maxim of the civil law: *partus sequitur ventrem*.

3 *Wood v Ash and Foster* (1586) Owen 139; *Tucker v Farm and General Investment Trust Ltd* [1966] 2 QB 421, [1966] 2 All ER 508, CA.

4 *Case of Swans* (1592) 7 Co Rep 15b.

(ii) Wild Animals

A. PROPERTY IN LIVING WILD ANIMALS

204. Meaning of 'wild animals'. The term 'wild' (ferae naturae) applied to animals includes not only those animals which are savage by nature but also those of a more mild or timid nature which cannot be classed as domestic or tame animals[1].

1 As to animals which, though originally wild, or ferae naturae, have been tamed and are actually in a state of subjection, see para 206 post. Domestic animals which have reverted to a wild state are ferae naturae: see *Falkland Islands Co v R* (1864) 2 Moo PCCNS 266.

205. No absolute property in wild animals. There is no absolute property in wild animals while living, and they are not goods or chattels[1]. There may, however, be what is known as a qualified property in them, either (1) *per industriam*[2], (2) *ratione impotentiae et loci*[3], or (3) *ratione soli* and *ratione privilegii*[4]. This qualified property is defeasible, for if the animal has no intention to return, but resumes its wildness and is at large again and not under pursuit, it is free and may be taken by another person[5]. Thus the special right of property, called qualified property, if conferred *ratione impotentiae et loci, ratione soli* or *ratione privilegii*, is in substance an exclusive right to reduce the wild animal into possession[6], but if acquired *per industriam* it is an exclusive right to the possession of the wild animal which, in the case of a living animal, will continue while it has the intention to return[7].

1 *Case of Swans* (1592) 7 Co Rep 15b at 17b.

2 See para 206 post.

3 See para 207 post.

4 See para 208 post.

5 2 Bl Com (14th Edn) 393, cited with approval in *Hamps v Darby* [1948] 2 KB 311 at 321, [1948] 2 All ER 474 at 477, CA; *Case of Swans* (1592) 7 Co Rep 15b at 17b.

6 *Blades v Higgs* (1865) 11 HL Cas 621 at 631 per Lord Westbury LC and at 638 per Lord Chelmsford; *Keble v Hickringill* (1706) as reported in 11 Mod Rep 73 at 75 per Powell J. Cf *Young v Hichens* (1843) 6 QB 606 (fishery; fish not completely reduced into possession: no property); *Aberdeen Arctic Co v Sutter* (1862) 4 Macq 355, HL (custom of Greenland whale fishery; property only in a whale held fast by a line).

7 See 2 Bl Com (14th Edn) 391–392, cited with approval in *Hamps v Darby* [1948] 2 KB 311 at 320–321, [1948] 2 All ER 474 at 477, CA; *Purcell v Minister for Finance* [1939] IR 115 at 122.

206. Qualified property per industriam. A qualified property in living animals ferae naturae obtained *per industriam* arises by lawfully taking, taming, or reclaiming them[1]. Animals ferae naturae become the property of any person who takes, tames, or reclaims them, until they regain their natural liberty[2]. Animals such as deer, swans, and doves are the subjects of this qualified property, which is lost if they regain their natural liberty, and have not the intention to return[3].

Thus an action for trespass or conversion will lie for taking a captive thrush, singing bird, muskrat, parrot or ape, because, although they are ferae naturae, they have been held to be merchandise and valuable when in a state of capitivity[4]; and for taking doves out of a dovehouse[5], hares, pheasants, or partridges in a warren or inclosure[6], deer in a park[7], a hawk if tame[8], fish in a stew pond[9], rabbits in a warren[10], swans marked or in private waters[11], or bees in a hive.

Bees are ferae naturae, and there is thus no property in them except by reclamation. So if a swarm settles on a man's tree, no property passes until the bees are hived; when hived, they become the property of the hiver; and if a swarm leaves the hive this property continues in the hiver so long as they can be seen and followed[12].

1 *Case of Swans* (1592) 7 Co Rep 15b at 17b; *Blades v Higgs* (1865) 11 HL Cas 621 at 638 per Lord Chelmsford. In many instances the taking, etc, of wild animals is unlawful: see paras 320–351 post.
2 Bracton, lib ii, cap i.
3 *Case of Swans* (1592) 7 Co Rep 15b at 17b; Bracton, lib ii, cap i. See also *Hamps v Darby* [1948] 2 KB 311, [1948] 2 All ER 474, CA (pigeons).
4 Brooke's Abridgment, 'Trespas', para 407; *Grymes v Shack* (1610) Cro Jac 262. Live wild birds and their eggs cannot, however, now be lawfully sold: see the Wildlife and Countryside Act 1981 s 6; and para 344 post.
5 Com Dig Trespass (A 1); Fitz Nat Brev 211.
6 Fitz Nat Brev 208. As to wild duck see *Lord Fitzhardinge v Purcell* [1908] 2 Ch 139.
7 *Mallock v Eastly* (1685) 3 Lev 227.
8 *Fines v Spender* (1572) 3 Dyer 306b.
9 *Pollexfen and Ashford v Crispin* (1671) 1 Vent 122.
10 Fitz Nat Brev 208.
11 *Case of Swans* (1592) 7 Co Rep 15b at 17b. There is much learning in this case relating to swans; see further CONSTITUTIONAL LAW.
12 Bracton, lib ii, cap 1; 2 Bl Com (14th Edn) 392–393; *Quantrill v Spragge* (1907) 71 JP Jo 425; *Kearry v Pattinson* [1939] 1 KB 471, [1939] 1 All ER 65, CA; cf *Hannam v Mockett* (1824) 2 B & C 934 at 944. But the hiver has no right to follow the swarm on to another person's land without permission: *Kearry v Pattinson* supra. The animus revertendi appears to be inferred from the following.

207. Qualified property ratione impotentiae et loci. The owner of land has a qualified property *ratione impotentiae et loci* in the young of animals ferae naturae born on the land until they can fly or run away[1], as where hawks, herons or rabbits make their nests or burrows on the land and have young; and an action of trespass[2] will lie for taking young animals so born[3].

1 *Case of Swans* (1592) 7 Co Rep 15b at 17b. Coke treats the young of wild animals while powerless to escape as the subject of 'possessory property' in the owner of the land, and although this falls short of absolute property, which cannot apply to animals ferae naturae, yet an action for trespass would lie.
2 *Case of Swans* (1592) 7 Co Rep 15b at 17b; Fitz Nat Brev 207, 213.
3 *Blades v Higgs* (1865) 11 HL Cas 621; *Ewart v Graham* (1859) 7 HL Cas 331 at 344 per Lord Campbell.

208. Qualified property ratione soli and ratione privilegii. The owner of land who has retained the exclusive right to hunt, take and kill animals ferae naturae on his own land has a qualified property *ratione soli* in them for the time being while they are there[1], but if he grants to another the right to hunt, take and kill animals ferae naturae on his land, by licence or grant of shooting or sporting rights[2], the grantee has a qualified property *ratione privilegii*[3]. Such a grant is an incorporeal hereditament and an interest in realty, and amounts to a licence of a profit à prendre which can only be validly granted or demised by deed[4].

1 *Blades v Higgs* (1865) 11 HL Cas 621.
2 As to game rights see para 248 et seq post; and FISHERIES; LANDLORD AND TENANT.
3 *Blades v Higgs* (1865) 11 HL Cas 621; *Keble v Hickringill* (1706) 11 Mod Rep 74 at 75 per Powell J. Cf *Gott v Measures* [1948] 1 KB 234, [1947] 2 All ER 609, DC, where it was said that sporting rights confer no property in wild game; 'property' in the context of the judgment of Lord Goddard CJ in this case must mean absolute property. The effect of this decision has been overruled by the Criminal Damage Act 1971 s 5 (3): see para 236 post. As to a tenant's right under the Ground Game Acts to take and kill hares and rabbits see para 257 post.
4 *Ewart v Graham* (1859) 7 HL Cas 331 at 344–345 per Lord Campbell LC; Law of Property Act 1925 ss 52, 205 (1) (ix); see EASEMENTS.

B. PROPERTY IN DEAD WILD ANIMALS

209. Absolute property in dead wild animals. Although there is only a qualified property in animals ferae naturae while they are alive, yet if they are killed, or die, there is an absolute property in the dead animal, which vests in the owner or occupier of the land or the grantee or licensee of the shooting or sporting rights, as the case may be, who may maintain an action against anyone infringing his rights therein[1].

1 *Fitzgerald v Firbank* [1897] 2 Ch 96, CA; cf *Lowe v Adams* [1901] 2 Ch 598. See, however, the Theft Act 1968 s 4 (4); and para 230 post. Thus a person who kills and carries away a wild animal is not guilty of theft; this is so even if he carries it away after having temporarily abandoned it, provided no one else is in course of reducing it into possession: see the Theft Act 1968 s 4 (4). For the cases in which a person may be guilty of theft of a dead wild animal see para 230 post.

210. Wild animals killed by trespasser. The absolute property which the owner or occupier of land, or the grantee of the privilege, has in dead animals ferae naturae is not confined to animals killed by him or his agents, and if the animals are killed by a trespasser, the trespasser has no property in them[1], and an action for conversion will lie against him[2]. Thus where poachers take rabbits, sell them, and send them away by rail, the servants of the owner of the land are justified in following them up and taking possession of them from the purchaser[3].

If a trespasser starts an animal ferae naturae in the ground of one person, and hunts it into the ground of another and there kills it, the property has been held to be in the killer[4], who, however, is liable to an action of trespass for hunting in either ground. This view of the law has been adversely criticised[5], but it has been received for so long that it is not now likely to be altered by judicial decision.

1 *Sutton v Moody* (1697) 1 Ld Raym 250; and see *Blades v Higgs* (1865) 11 HL Cas 621 at 632–633 per Lord Westbury.
2 *Earl of Lonsdale v Rigg* (1856) 11 Exch 654; affd (1857) 1 H & N 923, Ex Ch. The position as to theft, however, is governed by the Theft Act 1968 s 4 (4): see para 230 post.
3 *Blades v Higgs* (1864) 11 HL Cas 621.
4 *Churchward v Studdy* (1811) 14 East 249, where a huntsman maintained trespass for a dead hare against the owner of the land upon which the animal was killed by hounds.

5 See *Blades v Higgs* (1865) 11 HL Cas 621 at 640 per Lord Chelmsford; and cf *Gundry v Feltham* (1786) 1
   Term Rep 334; *Paul v Summerhayes* (1878) 4 QBD 9, DC (foxhunting); and see para 265 post.

(iii) Game

211. Meaning of 'game'. There is no comprehensive statutory definition of the
term 'game'[1], but it has been variously defined for the purposes of particular Acts.
Thus in the Game Act 1831, 'game' is deemed to include hares, pheasants, partridges, grouse, heath or moor game and black game[2]. This definition appears also
in the Night Poaching Act 1828, but with the addition of bustards[3]. The Poaching
Prevention Act 1862, however, omits bustards and adds rabbits, woodcock, snipe,
and the eggs of pheasants, partridges, grouse and black or moor game[4]. In the
Game Licences Act 1860, deer, as well as rabbits, woodcock and snipe, are added to
the game in respect of which a licence to take or kill is required[5].

The term 'ground game' was introduced by the Ground Game Act 1880, and
means hares and rabbits[6].

The meaning of the word 'game' in a deed is a matter of the construction of the
document[7].

1 See *Jeffryes v Evans* (1865) 19 CBNS 246 at 265. As to the meaning of 'game' in agreements in leases
   reserving the right to kill game, and as to the reservation of shooting and sporting rights generally,
   see para 251 post. As to deer see para 320 et seq post.
2 Game Act 1831 s 2 (amended by the Protection of Birds Act 1954 s 15 (2), Sch 6 (repealed)). Game,
   whether dead or alive, or wild or tame, is within the definition (*Loome v Baily* (1860) 3 E & E 444;
   Harnett v Miles (1884) 48 JP 455, DC; *Cook v Trevener* [1911] 1 KB 9, DC), but the Game Act 1831
   does not apply to game killed abroad (*Guyer v R* (1889) 23 QBD 100, DC). Some provisions of that
   Act are expressly extended to include other creatures: see eg s 31 (amended by the Protection of Birds
   Act 1954 Sch 6 (repealed)) (extended to include woodcock, snipe and rabbits); and para 272 post.
3 Night Poaching Act 1828 s 13.
4 Poaching Prevention Act 1862 s 1.
5 Game Licences Act 1860 ss 2, 4 (amended by the Protection of Birds Act 1954 Sch 6 (repealed)). The
   game in respect of which a dealer requires an excise licence is game within the meaning of the Game
   Act 1831 s 2: Game Licences Act 1860 ss 13, 14: see para 319 post.
6 Ground Game Act 1880 s 8.
7 See *Inglewood Investment Co Ltd v Forestry Commission* [1989] 1 All ER 1, [1988] 1 WLR 1278, CA,
   where on the construction of a particular deed containing a reservation of sporting rights deer were
   excluded from the definition of 'game'. See para 251 post.

212. Rights over game. There is no absolute property in game, which belongs
to the class of wild animals, but the qualified property *ratione soli* which an owner or
occupier of land has in such animals[1] is recognised by the law intervening to protect
private interests in game by limiting the right over it to certain classes of persons[2].
This qualified property becomes absolute when the game is killed[3] or otherwise
reduced into possession[4], whether this is done by the owner of the land, someone
claiming under him, or someone acting without his authority[5]. A possible exception arises where the game is pursued from elsewhere and killed and taken by the
hunter on land in different occupation from that where it was started, in which case
it has been held that it belongs to the hunter[6].

1 See para 208 ante.
2 See *Blades v Higgs* (1865) 11 HL Cas 621 at 631; and *Cattell v Ireson* (1858) EB & E 91 at 99. As to game
   rights generally see para 248 et seq post.
3 *Case of Swans* (1592) 7 Co Rep 15b; *Blades v Higgs* (1865) 11 HL Cas 621 at 631 per Lord Westbury
   LC.

4 Ie by being tamed or made captive. As to the theft of such animals see para 230 post.

5 *Blades v Higgs* (1865) 11 HL Cas 621; and see *Rigg v Earl of Lonsdale* (1857) 1 H & N 923, ExCh.

6 *Sutton v Moody* (1697) 1 Ld Raym 250. The decision was doubted by Lord Chelmsford in *Blades v Higgs* (1865) 11 HL Cas 621, but it has not been overruled. The hunter will, of course, be liable to proceedings for trespassing in search of game; see para 210 ante.

213. Right of property in eggs of game birds. The right of property in the eggs of game birds rather curiously follows the principle of the right over game in general, instead of that of the right over young or captive game[1], that is to say, the property in them is qualified, not absolute.

In order that the property may become absolute, the eggs must first have been collected from the nests or otherwise reduced into possession[2]. The taking of eggs from the nests of wild birds does not amount to theft[3], but, as in the case of game generally, the qualified right of property receives recognition and support from provisions of the game laws which create special offences in the case of taking or destroying the eggs of certain birds, and thereby protect them against trespassers[4].

1 See para 207 ante.

2 *R v Stride and Millard* [1908] 1 KB 617, CCR.

3 *R v Stride and Millard* [1908] 1 KB 617 at 627, CCR, per Lord Alverstone CJ. In this case the words 'one thousand pheasants' eggs of the goods and chattels of and of and belonging to W G' were held to be a sufficient averment that the eggs were the subject of larceny, although the indictment contained no allegation that the eggs had been reduced into possession: see para 287 post. Taking eggs of game birds that are tame or in captivity would no doubt amount to theft, but it would be necessary in the absence of an averment of reduction into possession to state in the indictment that they were the eggs of a tame or captive bird: *R v Stride and Millard* supra at 626 per Lord Alverstone CJ; *R v Gallears* (1849) 1 Den 501 at 502, CCR. See also the Theft Act 1968 s 4 (4); and para 287 post.

4 The Game Act 1831 s 24 provides penalties for destroying or taking the eggs of 'game' (see para 211 text to note 2 ante), swan, wild duck, teal or widgeon: see para 340 post. The Poaching Prevention Act 1862 s 1 includes within its protection as 'game' the eggs of pheasants, partridges, grouse and black game or moor game. As to the protection afforded to the eggs of other wild birds under the Wildlife and Countryside Act 1981 see para 341 post.

(2) AGISTMENT AND OTHER CONTRACTS

(i) Agistment

214. Nature of contract of agistment. A contract of agistment[1] arises where one man, the agister, takes another man's cattle, horses or other animals to graze on his land for reward, usually at a certain rate per week, on the implied term that he will redeliver them to the owner on demand[2]. Agistment is in the nature of a contract of bailment[3]; it confers no interest in the land and therefore does not require to be in writing[4].

1 The term agistment is said to be derived from the French *gyser*, to lie, because the beasts are there levant and couchant: see 4 Co Inst 293.

2 2 Bl Com (14th Edn) 452; *R v Croft (Inhabitants)* (1819) 3 B & Ald 171 at 177 per Best J. Agistment would apparently not amount to a breach of a covenant not to permit another person to use or occupy land: *Richards v Davies* [1921] 1 Ch 90. *Corbett v Packington* (1827) 6 B & C 268 was decided on a point of pleading, namely, that a claim for breach of contract to deliver must be in assumpsit.

3 See BAILMENT.
4 Ie under the Law of Property (Miscellaneous Provisions) Act 1989 s 2; see *Jones v Flint* (1839) 10 Ad & El 753.

215. Liability of agister. The agister is not an insurer of the beasts taken in by him, but he must take reasonable and proper care of them, and is liable for injury caused to them by negligence or by neglect of such reasonable and proper care[1]. If the animals are stolen without the default of the agister and it is proved that he did not use reasonable diligence to recover them, the onus is on the agister to prove that his failure to use such diligence made no difference to the result[2]. Where the owner is aware of the dangerous state of a field in which the animals are to be pastured, the agister will not be liable for injury occurring thereby[3].

1 *Smith v Cook* (1875) 1 QBD 79; *Broadwater v Blot* (1817) Holt NP 547. Thus he must make good the loss in case of injury if he puts a horse in a field with heifers, knowing that a bull is kept on adjoining land separated only by a shallow ditch, and has several times been found in the field, although he does not know it is vicious (*Smith v Cook* supra); or if he puts a horse in a field where there is a barbed wire fence concealed by long grass (*Turner v Stallibrass* [1898] 1 QB 56, CA); or leaves a gate open so that the agisted animal strays out and is lost (*Broadwater v Blot* supra) or injured (*Halestrap v Gregory* [1895] 1 QB 561, where an agisted horse escaped owing to the negligence of the defendant's servant in leaving a field gate open, and when the occupiers of the adjoining land endeavoured to drive the horse back through the gate it fell over a fence and was injured: held, the injury was the natural consequence of the gate's being left open); or if the agister puts agisted animals on pasture that is dangerous because there are wells, pits or shafts on it (*Rooth v Wilson* (1817) 1 B & Ald 59 at 61 per Lord Ellenborough CJ).
2 *Coldman v Hill* [1919] 1 KB 443, CA. See further BAILMENT.
3 *Reid v Calderwood* (1911) 45 ILT 139.

216. Rights of agister. In the absence of special agreement[1], the agister has no lien upon the animals he agists, for he expends no skill upon them; he merely takes care of them and supplies them with food, and his remedy is to bring an action for the price of grazing[2]. He has, however, a sufficient possessory property in them to entitle him to sue in trespass or conversion[3].

The custom of agistment is notorious, and agisted animals are not in the order and disposition of the agister so as to fall within the property divisible amongst his creditors on his bankruptcy[4].

1 *Richards v Symons* (1845) 8 QB 90.
2 *Chapman v Allen* (1631) Cro Car 271; *Jackson v Cummins* (1839) 5 M & W 342; *Judson v Etheridge* (1833) 1 Cr & M 743; *Hobby v Ruell* (1845) 1 Car & Kir 716.
3 Cf *Sutton v Buck* (1810) 2 Taunt 302 at 309 and *Rooth v Wilson* (1817) 1 B & Ald 59. See also *Worthington v Tipperary County Council* [1920] 2 IR 233, CA. In an indictment concerning the agisted animals, the property in them may be laid in the agister: *R v Woodward* (1796) 2 East PC 653. See also the Theft Act 1968 s 5 (1); and CRIMINAL LAW.
4 See the Insolvency Act 1986 s 283; *Re Woodward, ex p Huggins* (1886) 54 LT 683; *Re James, ex p Swansea Mercantile Bank Ltd* (1907) 24 TLR 15, CA. Where, however, the agistment agreement is a sham and the purported agister is in fact the true owner of the animals, the animals are assets in his bankruptcy: *Re Capon, ex p Trustee in Bankruptcy v R C Knight & Sons, ex p Trustee in Bankruptcy v Woodward and Woodward* [1940] Ch 442, [1940] 2 All ER 135, CA. See generally BANKRUPTCY AND INSOLVENCY.

(ii) Contractual Restrictions

217. Restrictions on keeping of animals. Contractual restrictions on the keeping of animals or poultry on premises let are sometimes inserted in leases or tenancy agreements and, in general, will be enforceable in accordance with the ordinary law of landlord and tenant[1]. Notwithstanding any such restriction, or any restrictive provision to the like effect contained in any covenant, contract or undertaking relating to the use to be made of land, an occupier of any land may keep, otherwise than by way of trade or business, hens or rabbits in any place thereon and may erect and maintain such structures on the land as are reasonably necessary for that purpose[2], provided this is not done in a manner so as to be prejudicial to health or a nuisance or contrary to the provisions of any enactment[3].

1 As to the obligation to observe negative covenants in leases see LANDLORD AND TENANT.
2 Allotments Act 1950 s 12 (1).
3 Ibid s 12 (1) proviso.

(3) SALE

(i) Caveat Emptor; Warranty

218. No implied guarantee of quality. Domestic animals are goods and chattels, and the ordinary law as to the sale of goods applies to them[1]. The purchase of an animal is essentially a purchase of an unknown quantity, for no prudence can guard against all latent defects[2]; and although upon the sale of any animal there is an implied condition that the vendor has the right to sell[3], and although if an animal is sold for a particular purpose made known to the seller, expressly or by implication, so as to show that the buyer is relying on the seller's skill and judgment and if the seller is in the way of business of selling such animals, there is an implied condition that it is reasonably fit for that purpose[4], yet there is no implied condition or warranty[5] as to the quality of the animal[6] and the rule caveat emptor applies[7]. It is, therefore, usual, and certainly advisable, for the buyer to protect himself by requiring an express guarantee with the animal of any quality or virtue he may require[8].

A statement by the vendor on the sale that the animal is sound will prima facie amount merely to a warranty, but if the vendor undertakes to take the animal back if it proves not to be as stated, the statement will be converted from a warranty to a condition[9].

1 *Edwards v Pearson* (1890) 6 TLR 220; see SALE OF GOODS. There being no property in wild animals while living, they cannot be the subject of sale: *Case of Swans* (1592) 7 Co Rep 15b; see generally para 205 ante. For restrictions upon the exposing for sale of animals in a street or public place in the metropolitan police district or city of London to the annoyance of inhabitants or passengers see ROAD TRAFFIC. See also para 465 post.
2 Cf *Jones v Bright* (1829) 5 Bing 533 at 544 per Best CJ.
3 Sale of Goods Act 1979 s 12 (1).
4 Ibid s 14 (3); *Chanter v Hopkins* (1838) 8 LJ Ex 14 per Parke B.
5 As to the classification of contractual terms into conditions, warranties and 'intermediate' terms, and as to the effect of breach of a contractual term, see generally CONTRACT. Cf the meaning of 'warranty' as a guarantee or representation; see para 219 note 1 post.
6 Sale of Goods Act 1979 s 14 (1).
7 As to liability for selling diseased animals see para 219 post.
8 See paras 224–226 post.
9 *Harling v Eddy* [1951] 2 KB 739 at 742, [1951] 2 All ER 212 at 215, CA, per Evershed MR. This case must be read in the light of subsequent developments in the law which introduced the concept of 'intermediate' or 'innominate' terms of a contract; see eg *Cehave NV v Bremer Handelsgesellschaft mbH, The Hansa Nord* [1976] QB 44, [1975] 3 All ER 739, CA. It is submitted, however, that the ratio of *Harling v Eddy* supra remains good law. See note 5 supra.

219. Liability for selling diseased animals. On the sale of an animal, whether suffering from an infectious or contagious disease or not, the maxim caveat emptor applies; thus where a person sent diseased pigs to market and refused to give any warranty[1], but stated that the animals must be taken 'with all faults', it was decided that he was not liable for the damage caused thereby, even if he knew that the pigs were diseased, unless he was guilty of fraud[2].

1 'Warranty' here and in paras 220–226 post is generally used, as in the cases cited, in its older sense of guarantee, promise or representation, and not to denote a contractual term distinct from a condition; see *Oscar Chess Ltd v Williams* [1957] 1 All ER 325 at 327–328, [1957] 1 WLR 370 at 374, CA, per Denning LJ; and 4 Words and Phrases (3rd Edn) 413. Such guarantees, promises or representations may, depending on all the circumstances, become terms of the contract, and breach of such terms may entitle a party to damages or to rescission of the contract; see generally CONTRACT vol 9 paras 542–544.
2 *Ward v Hobbs* (1878) 4 App Cas 13, HL. Lord Cairns LC refrained in this case from criticising the proposition of Blackburn J in *Bodger v Nicholls* (1873) 28 LT 441 at 445 that 'the defendant by taking the cow to a public market to be sold, though he does not warrant her to be sound, yet thereby furnishes evidence of a representation that, so far as his knowledge goes, the animal is not suffering from any infectious disease', beyond saying that no such representation could be implied where there was a clear statement that the buyer must take his purchase with all faults (*Ward v Hobbs* supra at 23). The question is not affected by the fact that taking diseased animals to market is a breach of a statutory duty (*Ward v Hobbs* supra; and see reports of that case in the courts below, 2 QBD 331; 3 QBD 150). As to the remedy for breach of such statutory duty see *Gorris v Scott* (1874) LR 9 Exch 125; and STATUTES vol 44 para 941 et seq. See generally MISREPRESENTATION; SALE OF GOODS.

220. No liability under warranty for patent defects. A warranty[1] is not intended to guard against defects which are obvious to the senses[2]. It has been said that if a man guarantees that a horse has two eyes he is not liable if it has not, for the buyer could have an examination before he bought[3]; but it is otherwise if the eye had some defect which is congenital, or which could not be ascertained by an ordinary man[4]. Whether a defect is patent or not, or the purchaser has used ordinary care, are questions of fact. A splint may or may not cause lameness, and a warranty of soundness will be taken as meaning that a splint which was plainly visible and pointed out to the buyer was not at that time such a splint as would cause future lameness, and the warranty is broken if lameness arises from it[5]. If the buyer is not present at the time of the treaty for sale, then the warranty will cover patent defects[6], or if the seller warrants the animal with the intention of preventing the buyer examining it and so discovering a patent defect, or uses any other artifice to conceal such a defect, then also the warranty will cover it[7]. If a person purchases a horse, knowing it to be blind, he cannot sue the seller on a general warranty of soundness[8].

1 See para 219 note 1 ante.
2 Cf *Anon* (1471) YB 11 Edw 4, fo 6, pl 10 per Fairfax J.
3 *Anon* (1471) YB 11 Edw 4, fo 6, pl 10 per Brian J. 'To warrant a thing that may be perceived by sight is not good': *Baily v Merrell* (1616) 3 Bulst 95 per Haughton J.
4 *Holliday v Morgan* (1858) 1 E & E 1; *Southerne v Howe* (1617) 2 Roll Rep 5.
5 *Margetson v Wright* (1831) 7 Bing 603; on rehearing (1832) 8 Bing 454; *Weston v Potter* (1846) 8 LTOS 137; *Smith v O'Bryan* (1864) 11 LT 346.
6 *Drewe v E* (1412) YB 13 Hen 4, fol 1 B per Thirning J.
7 *Dorrington v Edwards* (1621) 2 Roll Rep 188; *Kenner v Harding* (1877) 85 Ill 264 (US); 28 Am R 615.
8 *Margetson v Wright* (1831) 7 Bing 603 at 605 per Tindall CJ.

221. Warranty given by agent. An agent to sell is not always an agent to warrant[1], but when a groom or servant is sent to sell a horse, slight evidence is sufficient to prove an agency to warrant[2]. A distinction has generally been made between the servant of a private seller and that of a horse-dealer[3]; if the servant or agent of a private individual takes upon himself to warrant, in the absence of authority to do so, the master is not bound, unless the sale be made at a fair or other public market, in which case the servant or agent is more in the position of the servant of a horse-dealer, and has an implied authority to warrant[4]; if the servant or assistant of a horse-dealer gives a warranty the principal is bound, even though the servant was expressly forbidden to warrant[5].

Any person dealing with an agent or assistant of a horse-dealer has a right to assume an authority to warrant, and evidence of a custom amongst horse-dealers not to warrant is inadmissible[6]. A horse-dealer is not bound by the action of his servant who is sent merely to deliver a horse already sold, and who signs a receipt containing a warranty[7], or who warrants such an incidental matter as that a horse may safely be placed with others in a stable, because the warranty is not given in the course of the transaction of sale[8].

On the other hand, a buyer who sends a servant to accept a horse with a warranty is not bound if the servant accepts it without a warranty, and may return the horse[9].

A minor, not being able to contract except for necessaries, is not liable for breach of warranty of a horse[10].

1 See para 219 note 1 ante.
2 *Miller v Lawton* (1864) 15 CBNS 834. A warranty by one of two horse-dealing partners binds the other, even though between them there is an agreement not to warrant: *Sandilands v Marsh* (1819) 2 B & Ald 673.
3 *Brady v Todd* (1861) 9 CBNS 592; *Bank of Scotland v Watson* (1813) 1 Dow 40 at 45; cf *Helyear v Hawke* (1803) 5 Esp 72.
4 *Alexander v Gibson* (1811) 2 Camp 555; *Brooks v Hassall* (1883) 49 LT 569.
5 *Howard v Sheward* (1866) LR 2 CP 148 at 152 per Byles J; *Pickering v Busk* (1812) 15 East 38 at 45. Cf *Coleman v Riches* (1855) 24 LJCP 125 at 128. Generally, as to the authority of an agent, see AGENCY vol 1 (2) (Reissue) para 44 et seq.
6 *Howard v Sheward* (1866) LR 2 CP 148 at 151 per Willes J.
7 *Woodin v Burford* (1834) 2 Cr & M 391. Cf *Strode v Dyson* (1804) 1 Smith KB 400; and see *Cornfoot v Fowke* (1839) 9 LJ Ex 297.
8 *Baldry v Bates* (1885) 1 TLR 558.
9 *Jordon v Norton* (1838) 4 M & W 155.
10 See INFANTS, CHILDREN AND YOUNG PERSONS.

(ii) Express Warranty

222. Nature and extent of express warranty. By a warranty[1] the seller undertakes absolutely that the animal possesses the virtues attributed to it in the warranty, and is at the time of the sale free from the defects warranted against, whether they are known to him or not[2]. Special words may, however, limit the warranty to defects within the seller's knowledge[3].

It is not uncommon to insert the warranty given in the receipt for the price; and such insertion was held not to make the receipt liable to stamp duty as an agreement[4]. No particular form of words is necessary to constitute a warranty[5]. Any statement of fact made at the time of the sale and before it is completed, and intended to be a warranty, is a warranty in law[6]. The questions of the intention of the statement, and whether the statement was part of the contract of sale, are questions of fact[7]. Thus, a statement 'You may depend upon it that the horse is perfectly quiet and free from vice' is a sufficient warranty, although the word 'warrant' is not used[8].

If the word 'warrant' is used, the warranty extends only to so much as is governed by that word[9]. If the word 'warranted' is used alone, it is taken to refer to soundness only, and not to a preceding description[10]. The warranty may be limited in any way[11], but if a horse is warranted 'sound and quiet in all respects', that is general, and includes being quiet in harness[12]. A horse is most commonly warranted as to soundness and freedom from vice, but any quality may be warranted[13].

The fact that a sound price, that is a good or fair price for a sound animal, is given for the animal does not amount to a warranty that the animal is sound[14].

Distinct statements of fact printed in an auctioneer's catalogue, if such as to confer additional value on the animal sold, amount to warranties[15]. They are not generally difficult to interpret, because they are usually printed and explained in the conditions of sale[16]. An oral statement at the sale by a vendor, even if it amounts merely to a warranty, may override the written terms of sale[17].

1   See para 219 note 1 ante.
2   Cf *Stuart v Wilkins* (1778) 1 Doug KB 18; *Williamson v Allison* (1802) 2 East 446.
3   *Wood v Smith* (1829) 5 Man & Ry KB 124. Cf *Dunlop v Waugh* (1792) Peake 123; *Pinder v Button* (1862) 7 LT 269.
4   *Skrine v Elmore* (1810) 2 Camp 407. An agreement under hand only for or relating to the sale of goods is exempt from stamp duty: Stamp Act 1891 Sch 1.
5   *Gee v Lucas* (1867) 16 LT 357.
6   *Pasley v Freeman* (1789) 3 Term Rep 51; *Hopkins v Tanqueray* (1854) 15 CB 130. If made after the sale there must be a new consideration to support the warranty: *Roscorla v Thomas* (1842) 3 QB 234. Cf *Cave v Coleman* (1828) 3 Man & Ry KB 2 at 3 per Bayley J.
7   *Salmon v Ward* (1825) 2 C & P 211; *Hopkins v Tanqueray* (1854) 15 CB 130; *Wood v Smith* (1829) 5 Man & Ry KB 124; *Percival v Oldacre* (1865) 18 CBNS 398; *Schawel v Reade* (1912) 46 ILT 281, HL. A statement that a cow has been served or is in calf has been held to be a description and not a warranty: *Thomas v Griffths* (1956) 167 Estates Gazette 448.
8   *Cave v Coleman* (1828) 3 Man & Ry KB 2 per Lord Tenterden CJ.
9   Thus, 'a black horse rising five years, quiet to ride and drive and warranted sound' is not a warranty that the horse is quiet to drive and ride: *Anthony v Halstead* (1877) 37 LT 433; *Budd v Fairmaner* (1831) 8 Bing 48.
10   Eg where a horse was described as 'a black gelding, five years old, has been constantly driven in the plough, warranted': *Richardson v Brown* (1823) 1 Bing 344.
11   *Jones v Cowley* (1825) 4 B & C 445; *Hemming v Parry* (1834) 6 C & P 580.
12   *Smith v Parsons* (1837) 8 C & P 199.
13   Eg its age (*Buchanan v Parnshaw* (1788) 2 Term Rep 745), or that it has been hunted with a certain pack (*Head v Tattersall* (1871) LR 7 Exch 7), or that a mare is in foal to a certain horse (*Gee v Lucas* (1867) 16 LT 357).
14   *Parkinson v Lee* (1802) 2 East 314 at 322.
15   *Gee v Lucas* (1867) 16 LT 357 at 358 per Kelly CB. As to sales by auction generally see AUCTION.
16   A sale 'with all faults' and without a warranty relieves the seller from all liability in respect of any disease or defect: *Ward v Hobbs* (1878) 4 App Cas 13, HL.
17   *Couchman v Hill* [1947] KB 554, [1947] 1 All ER 103, CA; *Harling v Eddy* [1951] 2 KB 739, [1951] 2 All ER 212, CA, following *Couchman v Hill* supra and distinguishing *Hopkins v Tanqueray* (1854) 15 CB 130.

223. What amounts to unsoundness. If at the time of sale a horse has any disease or defect which actually diminishes, or in its ordinary progress will diminish, its natural usefulness, it is not sound[1]. A congenital defect, such as convexity of the cornea of the eye, which causes short-sightedness and induces the habit of shying, is unsoundness[2]. The slightness of the disease, or the ease with which it is cured, may affect the amount of damages, but does not affect the principle, unless it is of so trifling a character as not to amount to unsoundness at all[3]. A cough[4], and temporary lameness[5], have, therefore, both been held to be unsoundness. The question of soundness or unsoundness is one of fact[6].

1 See *Coates v Stephens* (1838) 2 Mood & R 157 per Parke B. Cf *Kiddell v Burnard* (1842) 9 M & W 668.
2 *Holliday v Morgan* (1858) 1 E & E 1.
3 Cf *Kiddell v Burnard* (1842) 9 M & W 668 at 670–671 per Parke B.
4 *Coates v Stephens* (1838) 2 Mood & R 157; *Shillitoe v Claridge* (1816) 2 Chit 425.
5 *Elton v Brogden* (1815) 4 Camp 281.
6 *Lewis v Peake* (1816) 7 Taunt 153. For the various diseases, defects, and bad habits which have been held to amount to unsoundness or vice see Oliphant on Horses (6th Edn) 67–115. 'Vice' means either a defect in the temper of the horse which makes it dangerous or diminishes its usefulness, or a bad habit which is injurious to its health: *Scholefield v Robb* (1839) 2 Mood & R 210.

224. Warranty relating to future. Unless otherwise expressly stated, a warranty[1] only relates to facts as they are at the time of sale[2]. It may, however, expressly relate to the future, as where the seller undertakes to deliver horses sound at the end of a fortnight[3]; but 'warranted sound for one month' has been held to mean not that the horse was warranted to continue sound for a month, but that the duration of the warranty was limited to one month, and that complaint of unsoundness must be made within one month of sale[4].

1 See para 219 note 1 ante.
2 *Liddard v Kain* (1824) 2 Bing 183; and see *Anon* (1471) YB 11 Edw 4, fo 6, pl 10 per Choke J.
3 *Liddard v Kain* (1824) 2 Bing 183; *Eden v Parkison* (1781) 2 Doug KB 732; *Kyle v Sim* 1925 SC 425.
4 *Chapman v Gwyther* (1866) LR 1 QB 463. Cf *Buchanan v Parnshaw* (1788) 2 Term Rep 745.

(iii) Breach of Warranty

225. Notice to seller of breach. The buyer should give notice to the seller as soon as possible of any alleged breach of warranty[1], although this is not absolutely necessary[2]. If there is no time limit in the contract within which complaint must be made, the buyer is not prejudiced by anything done by him before he discovers the defects[3].

1 See para 219 note 1 ante.
2 See *Fielder v Starkin* (1788) 1 Hy Bl 17; *Patteshall v Tranter* (1835) 3 Ad & El 103.
3 *Best v Osborn* (1825) 2 C & P 74.

226. Return of animal. If the buyer has reserved a right to return the animal within a specified time, he may return it at any time within that period, and is not bound to do so the moment he discovers the defects; so that if injury happens to the animal while in his possession, and without his fault, he is not liable for it and may still return the animal within the period[1]; and if the animal under such circumstances becomes injured so that it cannot be returned within the specified time, the non-return by the buyer within the period stipulated will not bar an action for breach of warranty[2].

If the animal is sold upon a condition that it may be returned within a specified period in case of unsuitability or for any other reason, and it dies within the specified period without any default of the buyer, the loss falls on the seller, there being no completed sale in the proper sense until the buyer has given approval expressly or by implication from his keeping the animal beyond that period[3].

It is a usual stipulation in warranties or conditions, especially at sales by auction, that complaint be made or the animal returned within a specified time; if this stipulation is not complied with no action can be brought[4]. A stipulation that a warranty of soundness shall remain in force until noon of the day after the sale, when it will be deemed to have been performed and the seller's responsibility will terminate, unless in the meantime a notice to the contrary and a certificate of any alleged unsoundness be given, is reasonable[5], and, if brought to the buyer's notice, is binding upon him[6].

1 *Head v Tattersall* (1871) LR 7 Exch 7.
2 *Chapman v Withers* (1888) 20 QBD 824; and see also *Taylor v Caldwell* (1863) 3 B & S 826.
3 *Elphick v Barnes* (1880) 5 CPD 321.
4 *Hinchcliffe v Barwick* (1880) 5 Ex D 177; *Smart v Hyde* (1841) 8 M & W 723; *Mesard v Aldridge* (1801) 3 Esp 271; *Head v Tattersall* (1871) LR 7 Exch 7.
5 *Smart v Hyde* (1841) 8 M & W 723.
6 *Bywater v Richardson* (1834) 1 Ad & El 508.

(iv) Misrepresentation and Fraud

227. Effect of innocent misrepresentation. Where a misrepresentation[1] innocently made has induced a person to enter into a contract in relation to an animal, he may be entitled to rescind it, the court having a discretion to order rescission or damages[2]. Further, a person guilty of an innocent misrepresentation is liable in damages for any loss resulting if he would have been so liable had he acted fraudulently, unless he proves that he had reasonable grounds for believing, and did believe, up to the time of the making of the contract, that the facts represented were true[3].

1 As to misrepresentation generally see MISREPRESENTATION.
2 See the Misrepresentation Act 1967 s 2 (2).
3 Ibid s 2 (1).

228. Effect of fraud. Fraud[1] renders a contract voidable at the option of the party defrauded. On discovery of the fraud the buyer may either return the animal and bring an action for return of the price paid[2], or keep the animal and claim damages. This is so even where the fraud concerns something outside an express warranty; thus proof of fraud at the time of the sale, for example, as to a horse's age, would vitiate the sale although the warranty was only as to soundness and freedom from vice[3].

1 As to fraud generally see MISREPRESENTATION.
2 Cf *Kennedy v Panama, etc, Mail Co* (1867) LR 2 QB 580 at 587.
3 *Steward v Coesvelt* (1823) 1 C & P 23. As to criminal proceedings see *R v Sanders* [1919] 1 KB 550, CCA. So far as animal dealers are concerned see also the Trade Descriptions Act 1968 ss 1, 2.

(4) THEFT

229. Domestic animals as subjects of theft. At common law, domestic and tame animals, such as horses, cattle, oxen, sheep, poultry, peacocks, and all animals which are fit for human food, and their young and eggs, were the subject of larceny[1]. Dogs of all kinds, cats and animals of base nature were exceptions[2].

By statute, however, all animals which have value and are the property of any person can be the subject of theft[3], which is punishable on indictment by imprisonment for a term not exceeding ten years[4]. Domestic animals are to be regarded as belonging to any person having possession or control of them or having any proprietary right or interest in them, other than a mere equitable interest arising from an agreement to transfer or to grant an interest[5].

1   1 Hawk PC (8th Edn) 149–150; 1 Hale PC 510.
2   3 Co Inst 109; 1 Hale PC 511; *Case of Swans* (1592) 7 Co Rep 15b at 18a, citing YB 12 Hen 8, fo 3 and 18 Hen 8, fo 2, where it is said that bloodhounds or mastiffs are of 'so base a nature that no felony can be committed of them and no man shall lose life or member for them'. The skin of a dog when dead was always the subject of larceny: see *R v Halloway* (1823) 1 C & P 127 note (b).
3   See the Theft Act 1968 ss 1–6. It follows that they may also be the subject of the offence of handling stolen goods (ss 22 (1), 34 (2) (b)), punishable by imprisonment not exceeding 14 years (s 22 (2)). As to theft and other offences of dishonesty generally see CRIMINAL LAW. As to the offence in a dealer in rags and old clothes of selling or delivering any animal, fish, bird or other living thing to a person under the age of 14 see the Public Health (Control of Disease) Act 1984 s 55; and PUBLIC HEALTH.
4   Theft Act 1968 s 7.
5   Ibid s 5 (1).

230. Wild animals as subjects of theft. Although a wild animal, whether tamed or untamed, is to be regarded as property by statute, neither it nor its carcase can be the subject of theft if the animal is not tamed or ordinarily kept in captivity[1] unless either it has been reduced into possession by or on behalf of someone other than the taker, and possession of it has not since been lost or abandoned, or it is in course of being reduced into possession by another person[2]. Thus, a person who kills and carries away a wild animal is not guilty of theft even if he temporarily abandons possession of it.

1   At common law living wild animals were not the subject of larceny unless reclaimed and fit for human food; nor were those animals ferae naturae kept merely for pleasure the subject of larceny: 2 East PC 607, 614. The following authorities under the law obtaining before the Theft Act 1968 may still be useful in considering the questions of taming and keeping in captivity: *Case of Swans* (1592) 7 Co Rep 15b; *R v Cory* (1864) 10 Cox CC 23 (young pheasants hatched under hen in field); *R v Shickle* (1868) LR 1 CCR 158 (young pheasants and partridges hatched under hen in coop); *R v Brooks* (1829) 4 C & P 131; *R v Cheafor* (1851) 21 LJMC 43; and *Hamps v Darby* [1948] 2 KB 311, [1948] 2 All ER 474, CA (tame pigeons in dovecote); 1 Hawk PC (8th Edn) 149; 2 Bl Com (14th Edn) 394; 1 Hale PC 511 (reclaimed hawks or falcons).
2   Theft Act 1968 s 4 (4). As to property in wild animals generally see para 205 ante; as to theft and other offences of dishonesty see CRIMINAL LAW.

231. Animals as subjects of obtaining by deception. Since, for the purposes of the Theft Act 1968, animals, both domestic and wild, are to be regarded as property, it follows that they may be subjects of the offence of obtaining property by deception, punishable on indictment by imprisonment for a term not exceeding ten years[1].

1   Theft Act 1968 ss 15, 34 (1); see CRIMINAL LAW.

232. Advertising rewards for return of animals. To advertise publicly a reward for the return of any animal stolen or lost, using any words to the effect that no questions will be asked, or that the person producing the animal will be safe from apprehension or inquiry, or that any money paid for its purchase or advanced by way of loan on it will be repaid, is an offence for which the advertiser, printer and publisher is liable on summary conviction to a fine not exceeding level 3 on the standard scale[1].

1 Theft Act 1968 ss 23, 34 (2) (b) (amended by virtue of the Criminal Justice Act 1982 ss 38, 46). In any enactment contained in an Act passed either before or after the Criminal Justice Act 1982 'the standard scale' has the meaning given by s 37: s 75 (a). A standard scale of fines for summary offences was introduced by the Criminal Justice Act 1982 s 37 (1), to avoid the need, in times of high inflation, for frequent amendment of primary legislation. Where any enactment contained in an Act passed either before or after that Act provides (1) that a person convicted of a summary offence is liable on conviction to a fine or a maximum fine by reference to a specified level on the standard scale, or (2) confers power by subordinate instrument to make a person liable on conviction of a summary offence, whether or not created by the instrument, to a fine or a maximum fine by reference to a specified level on the standard scale, it is to be construed as referring to the standard scale for which s 37 provides as that scale has effect from time to time by virtue either of that section or of an order under the Magistrates' Courts Act 1980 s 143: Criminal Justice Act 1982 s 37 (3). In relation to Acts passed before the Criminal Justice Act 1982, this provision applies where references to the standard scale are substituted by s 46 as read with s 38 or s 40. At the date at which this volume states the law, the standard scale is as follows, in relation to offences committed after 1 May 1984: level 1, £50; level 2, £100; level 3, £400; level 4, £1,000; level 5, £2,000: s 37 (2) (amended by the Criminal Penalties etc (Increase) Order 1984, SI 1984/447, art 2 (4), Sch 4). As from a day to be appointed, the levels are increased by the Criminal Justice Act 1991 s 17 (1), to £200, £500, £1,000, £2,500 and £5,000 respectively.

233. Offences triable summarily. Those offences under the Theft Act 1968 already referred to which are triable on indictment[1] may be dealt with summarily if the accused, when informed of his right to trial by jury, so consents[2], in which event the maximum punishment is imprisonment for six months or a fine not exceeding the prescribed sum[3] or both[4].

1 See paras 229, 231 ante.
2 Magistrates' Courts Act 1980 s 17, Sch 1 para 28.
3 The 'prescribed sum' means £2,000 or such sum as is for the time being substituted therefor by an order in force under ibid s 143 (1) (substituted by the Criminal Justice Act 1982 s 48 (1)): Magistrates' Courts Act 1980 s 32 (9) (amended by the Criminal Penalties etc (Increase) Order 1984, SI 1984/447, art 2 (1), Sch 1). As from a day to be appointed, the prescribed sum is increased to £5,000 by the Criminal Justice Act 1991 s 17 (2).
4 Magistrates' Courts Act 1980 s 32.

(5) INJURY TO ANIMALS; TRESPASS AND CONVERSION

234. Killing or injuring animals. Domestic animals are 'property' within the definition in the Criminal Damage Act 1971, as are wild animals which have been tamed or are ordinarily kept in captivity[1], and other wild animals or their carcases if, but only if, they have been reduced into possession which has not been lost or abandoned or are in the course of being reduced into possession[2].

A person who without lawful excuse[3] destroys or damages any animal as above belonging to another, either intending to destroy or damage the property of another, or being reckless as to whether the property of another will be destroyed or damaged, commits an offence[4] punishable on indictment by imprisonment for a term not exceeding ten years[5]. The offence is triable summarily with the defendant's consent, in which case the maximum punishment is six months' imprisonment or a fine of the prescribed sum[6] or both[7].

The necessary mental element in the offence is accordingly that of intention or recklessness[8]. It should be noted that the offence is limited to destroying or damaging animals belonging to other persons, but destroying or damaging one's own animals may amount to an offence under the Protection of Animals Act 1911[9].

For the purposes of the offence an animal is to be taken as belonging to someone if that person (1) has the custody or control of it; (2) has any proprietary right or interest in it, not being an equitable interest arising only from an agreement to transfer or grant an interest; or (3) has a charge on it[10].

1   As to animals in captivity see para 230 note 1 ante.
2   Criminal Damage Act 1971 s 10 (1) (a). For offences of damage to property generally see CRIMINAL LAW vol 11 (1) (Reissue) para 593 et seq.
3   See para 236 post.
4   Criminal Damage Act 1971 s 1 (1). It would not be necessary to prove that the injury was inflicted with an instrument: *R v Bullock* (1868) 11 Cox CC 125. It is an additional offence to have anything in one's custody or under one's control intending without lawful excuse to use it to destroy or damage property: Criminal Damage Act 1971 s 3.
5   Ibid s 4 (2). If the offence is committed with the aggravating factor of intention to endanger life or recklessness in that respect, whether the animal belongs to the offender or someone else, it carries a maximum punishment of life imprisonment: ss 1 (2), 4 (1).
6   As to the prescribed sum see para 233 note 3 ante.
7   Magistrates' Courts Act 1980 ss 17, 32, Sch 1 para 29. This does not apply to a conviction under the Criminal Damage Act 1971 s 1 (2).
8   For the purposes of the Criminal Damage Act 1971 a person is reckless if he does an act which in fact involves a serious risk, obvious to an ordinary prudent individual, of causing injury or damage and either (1) he fails to give any thought to the possibility of there being any such risk, or (2) having recognised that there is some risk involved he nevertheless goes on to take that risk: *Metropolitan Police Comr v Caldwell* [1982] AC 341 at 354, [1981] 1 All ER 961 at 967, 73 Cr App Rep 13 at 20, HL, per Lord Diplock.
9   See para 405 et seq post; and see *Armstrong v Mitchell* (1903) 88 LT 870; and *Barnard v Evans* [1925] 2 KB 794, DC. As to the protection of wild birds and their nests see para 332 et seq post.
10 Criminal Damage Act 1971 s 10 (2).

235. Threats to kill or injure animals. Any person who without lawful excuse[1] makes to another a threat, intending that the other would fear it would be carried out, to destroy or damage any animal[2] belonging to that other person commits an offence[3] punishable on indictment by imprisonment for a term not exceeding ten years[4] or, if tried summarily with the defendant's consent, by imprisonment for a term not exceeding six months or a fine not exceeding the prescribed sum or both[5].

1   See para 236 post.
2   As to the animals included see para 234 text to notes 1, 2 ante.
3   Criminal Damage Act 1971 s 2 (a).
4   Ibid s 4 (2).
5   Magistrates' Courts Act 1980 ss 17, 32, Sch 1 para 29. As to the prescribed sum see para 233 note 3 ante.

236. Lawful excuse. The Criminal Damage Act 1971 provides specific excuses for what would otherwise be offences under the Act[1]. Thus, a defendant is excused if at the time of the alleged offence he believed[2] that the person whom he believed[2] to be entitled to consent to the destruction of or damage to the animal in question had so consented or would have so consented if he had known of it and its circumstances[3]; or if the defendant acted as he did in order to protect property belonging to himself or another or a right or interest, including sporting rights[4], in it which he, or that other person, either possessed or he believed[5] possessed, and at the time of the offence he also believed[5] (1) that the property, right or interest was in immediate need of protection and (2) that the means of protection adopted or proposed were or would be reasonable having regard to all the circumstances[6].

1 See the Criminal Damage Act 1971 s 5. These excuses are in addition to any recognised defences: s 5 (5). An honest, even if unreasonable, belief that the animal belonged to the defendant would be a good defence: see *R v Smith* [1974] QB 354, [1974] 1 All ER 632. Belief that the animal was wild and not reduced into possession (see para 205 ante) would not be a good defence: *Horton v Gwynne* [1921] 2 KB 661, DC; *Cotterill v Penn* [1936] 1 KB 53, DC. If the act is done in self-defence the defendant is entitled to be acquitted: *Hanway v Boultbee* (1830) 4 C & P 350.
2 It is immaterial whether a belief is justified or not, provided that it is honestly held: Criminal Damage Act 1971 s 5 (3).
3 Ibid s 5 (2) (a).
4 'Right or interest in property' includes any right or privilege in or over land, whether created by grant, licence or otherwise: ibid s 5 (4).
5 See note 2 supra.
6 Criminal Damage Act 1971 s 5 (2) (b). The court must first decide what the defendant believed, then decide as a matter of law whether the defendant's actions on the facts believed by him could constitute protection of property: *R v Hill, R v Hall* (1989) 89 Cr App Rep 74, CA.

237. Compensation for killing or damaging animal. The general power of a court by or before which a person is convicted of an offence to make a compensation order[1] applies in relation to the offence of destroying or damaging property, including an animal[2]. Where the person is convicted of such an offence, the court, instead of or in addition to dealing with him in any other way, may, on application or otherwise[3], make a compensation order requiring him to pay compensation for any loss or damage resulting from that offence or from any other offence which is taken into account by the court in determining sentence[4]. Compensation must be of such amount as the court considers appropriate, having regard to any evidence and to any representations that are made by or on behalf of the accused or the prosecutor[5]. The maximum amount which a magistrates' court may order by way of compensation is £2,000 for each offence of which the offender is convicted[6].

1 Ie under the Powers of Criminal Courts Act 1973 s 35; see generally CRIMINAL LAW vol 11 (2) para 1238 et seq.
2 Ie under the Criminal Damage Act 1971 s 1; see para 234 ante.
3 It should be noted that the court may act of its own motion.
4 Powers of Criminal Courts Act 1973 s 35 (1) (substituted by the Criminal Justice Act 1982 s 67).
5 Powers of Criminal Courts Act 1973 s 35 (1A) (added by the Criminal Justice Act 1982 s 67).
6 Magistrates' Courts Act 1980 s 40 (amended by the Criminal Penalties etc (Increase) Order 1984, SI 1984/447, art 2 (1), Sch 1).

238. Civil liability for shooting domestic animals. The shooting of a tame or domestic animal renders the shooter liable to a civil action for its value unless he can show that he had no other means of protecting his property[1]. Where no such justification exists, shooting at and injuring an animal may amount to an offence of cruelty[2].

1 *Cresswell v Sirl* [1948] 1 KB 241, [1947] 2 All ER 730, CA; *Hamps v Darby* [1948] 2 KB 311, [1948] 2 All ER 474, CA.
2 Ie under the Protection of Animals Act 1911 s 1: see para 405 et seq post. See *Barnard v Evans* [1925] 2 KB 794, DC.

239. Mitigating nuisance by doves, pigeons etc. Subject to certain safe-guards[1], a local authority may seize, destroy, sell or otherwise dispose of[2] any house doves or pigeons which in its belief have no owner[3] and which constitute a nuisance or annoyance or are causing damage[4]; an authority may also take steps for the purpose of abating or mitigating any nuisance, annoyance or damage caused by starlings or sparrows[4].

1 The authority must act humanely and must not contravene the provisions of the Wildlife and Countryside Act 1981 Pt I (ss 1–27): Public Health Act 1961 s 74 (3), (4) (amended by the Wildlife and Countryside Act 1981 s 72 (6)).
2 This power is not negated by the Theft Act 1968 s 4 (4) (wild animals as the subject of property): Public Health Act 1961 s 74 (2). The Theft Act 1968 s 4 (4) replaces the Larceny Act 1861 s 23, which is referred to in the 1961 Act s 74 (2).
3 Public Health Act 1961 s 74 (1), (2).
4 Ibid s 74 (1); see PUBLIC HEALTH.

240. Killing or taking animals in course of trespass. To go on to the land of another and there take or kill any wild animal not reduced into the possession of that other person, although not theft[1], is a trespass for which the injured party has a right of action[2]. If the animal taken or killed, or the objective of the trespass, was game, the trespasser is liable to statutory penalties and the occupier of the land may prosecute him[3].

1 As to theft of wild animals see para 230 ante. As to restrictions on the possession of firearms see CRIMINAL LAW vol 11 (1) (Reissue) para 197 et seq.
2 See generally TRESPASS.
3 See para 248 et seq post.

(6) IMPORT AND EXPORT

241. Restrictions on import and export of endangered species. The import-ation and the exportation of animals[1], whether alive or dead[2], that are considered to be endangered species, and the importation and exportation of products derived from certain such species[3], are prohibited, except when carried out under a licence[4] issued by the Secretary of State and in accordance with its terms[5]. Provision for the enforcement of this prohibition, and for the control of such importation as is licensed, has been made, and several offences have been created[6]. Where such an offence is committed by a body corporate, but it is proved that the offence was committed with the consent or connivance of, or was attributable to any neglect on the part of, a director, manager, secretary or other similar officer of the body corporate (or any person who was purporting to act in any such capacity) he, as well as the body corporate, is guilty of the offence and is liable to be proceeded against and punished accordingly[7].

1 Ie all kinds of mammals, birds, reptiles and amphibians, except the kinds specified in the Endangered Species (Import and Export) Act 1976 s 1, Sch 1 Pt I (substituted by the Endangered Species (Import and Export) Act 1976 (Modification) Order 1982, SI 1982/1230), and also the kinds of fish, insects, molluscs and black corals that are specified in the Endangered Species (Import and Export) Act 1976

Sch 1 Pt II (as so substituted). It is impracticable to summarise the Schedules to the Act here: reference should be made to the text of the Act when considering specific species. The Secretary of State may, after consulting any scientific authority or authorities (as to which see para 242 note 2 post), make such modifications in the Schedules as he considers necessary or desirable for certain specified purposes: s 3.

2 Reference to a dead animal includes reference to the body of an animal which is frozen, dried or preserved by chemicals, or to a body which, although not complete (having been, eg, stuffed), is substantially complete and externally substantially resembles a complete body: ibid s 12 (2).

3 See ibid Sch 3 (substituted by the Endangered Species (Import and Export) Act 1976 (Modification) Order 1982 and amended by SI 1983/1609 and SI 1985/1502); see also note 1 supra as to the content of the Schedule.

4 See para 242 post.

5 Endangered Species (Import and Export) Act 1976 s 1 (1), (2). Any person authorised in writing by the Secretary of State may enter premises where animals of any of the kinds to which Sch 1 applies are kept, in order to ascertain whether any of the animals kept there have been imported unlawfully, and any person who wilfully obstructs such a person is liable on summary conviction to a maximum fine of level 3 on the standard scale (as to which see para 232 note 1 ante): s 1 (10), (11) (added by the Wildlife and Countryside Act 1981 s 15 (1), Sch 10 Pt I para 3 and amended by virtue of the Criminal Justice Act 1982 ss 38, 46). At the date at which this volume states the law, level 3 on the standard scale is at £400.

6 See paras 242–246 post.

7 Endangered Species (Import and Export) Act 1976 s 8.

242. Licences for import or export. Applications for a licence should be addressed to the Secretary of State, who must[1] submit any such application to the scientific authority[2] he considers is the best able to advise him as to whether a licence should be issued, and as to its terms[3]. Having allowed the authority a reasonable time in which to advise him, he may then issue or decline to issue a licence[4]. Such a licence may be, to any degree, general or specific, may be issued to all persons, to persons of a class or to a particular person, may be subject to compliance with any specified conditions, and may be modified or revoked at any time by the Secretary of State[5]. Any person who for the purposes of obtaining the issue of a licence, whether for himself or for another, makes a statement or representation, or furnishes a document or information, which he knows to be false in a material particular, or who recklessly[6] makes a statement or representation or furnishes a document or information which is false in a material particular, commits an offence[7]; furthermore, when such an offence is committed the relevant licence is void[8].

1 Unless the scientific authority concerned has already advised the Secretary of State as to whether licences should be issued in pursuance of applications of that description and, if so, their terms: Endangered Species (Import and Export) Act 1976 s 1 (3A) (added by the Wildlife and Countryside Act 1981 s 15 (1), Sch 10 Pt I para 1 (1)).

2 Ie a body whose duty it is to advise the Secretary of State on any question which he may refer to it, and on any question on which it considers it should offer its advice, in connection with the administration of the Act and generally in connection with the import and export of animals of kinds which appear to the Secretary of State or to the body to be, or to be likely to become, endangered as a result of international trade, and items derived wholly or partly from such animals: Endangered Species (Import and Export) Act 1976 s 2 (4). The Secretary of State must establish at least one such body, consisting of such members as he may from time to time appoint, or assign the above-mentioned duties to at least one other body: s 2 (1), (2).

3 Ibid s 1 (3).

4 Ibid s 1 (2), (3). The Secretary of State may charge such sum as is for the time being prescribed by his order for the issue of a licence: s 1 (5).

5 Ibid s 1 (4) (amended by the Wildlife and Countryside Act 1981 Sch 10 Pt I para 1 (3)).

6 See para 234 note 8 ante; the definition is equally applicable to the 1976 Act.

7 Endangered Species (Import and Export) Act 1976 s 1 (6); the maximum penalty on summary conviction is a fine of the prescribed sum (as to which see para 233 note 3 ante), or on conviction on indictment two years' imprisonment, a fine, or both: s 1 (6) (amended by virtue of the Magistrates' Courts Act 1980 s 32 (2)). At the date at which this volume states the law, the prescribed sum is £2,000.
8 Endangered Species (Import and Export) Act 1976 s 1 (7).

243. Power to restrict places of importation. If it appears to the Secretary of State desirable to do so for the purpose of assisting the discovery of the unlawful[1] importation of any live animal, he may make an order, relating to any kind of animal[2]. Such an order may provide that (subject to such exceptions as may be specified in the order) it is prohibited to import any live animal of a specified kind, or to import any such animal except at a specified port, airport or place[3].

1 Ie under the Endangered Species (Import and Export) Act 1976 s 1; see para 241 ante.
2 Ibid s 5 (1).
3 Ibid s 5 (2).

244. Power to restrict movement of animals after importation. Where a licence[1] has been issued or applied for and, after consulting one or more of the scientific authorities[2], the Secretary of State considers that it is desirable to do so, he may give a direction in relation to the animal in respect of which the licence was applied for[3]. If he does so, then for as long as the direction is not revoked by the Secretary of State the animal must be taken to and kept at specified premises[4] immediately after the relevant event[5] occurs, until such time as the Secretary of State requires or permits the animal to be moved to other specified premises or until he revokes the direction[6]. When such a direction is in force, at any time after the relevant event a person commits an offence if he knows (or ought to know) of the direction and he knowingly takes the animal, or knowingly permits it to be taken, to premises which he knows (or ought to know) are not at the time of the taking the specified premises; or if he knowingly moves the animal, or knowingly permits it to be moved, when the move is made from premises which he knows (or ought to know) are specified premises, and he knows (or ought to know) that the removal is made without the Secretary of State's requirement or permission[7]; or if he knowingly keeps the animal at premises which he occupies and which he knows (or ought to know) are not specified premises[8].

1 Ie a licence under the Endangered Species (Import and Export) Act 1976 s 1 (2); see para 241 ante.
2 See para 242 note 2 ante.
3 Endangered Species (Import and Export) Act 1976 s 6 (1).
4 'Specified premises' means such premises as are for the time being, and in whatever manner, specified in relation to the animal by the Secretary of State: ibid s 6 (5). Before specifying any premises he must consult one or more of the scientific authorities (s 7 (1)), and he must not specify any premises unless in his opinion the animal in question may suitably be kept there (s 7 (2)). Any person duly authorised by the Secretary of State may enter premises which are for the time being specified in order to enable the Secretary of State to decide whether the premises remain such that, in his opinion, the animal may suitably be kept there, and/or to ascertain whether the animal is being kept there: s 7 (3). Anyone who wilfully obstructs such a person is liable on summary conviction to a maximum fine of level 5 on the standard scale: s 7 (4) (amended by virtue of the Criminal Justice Act 1982 ss 38, 46). As to the standard scale see para 232 note 1 ante. At the date at which this volume states the law, level 5 on that scale is at £2,000.

5 'Relevant event' means either the completion by the animal of a period of quarantine or other detention connected with its importation, or the animal's departure from any premises connected with its importation, whichever occurs later: Endangered Species (Import and Export) Act 1976 s 6 (4).

6 Ibid s 6 (2). Before revoking a direction the Secretary of State must consult one or more of the scientific authorities (as to which see para 242 note 2 ante): s 7 (1).

7 Ie such a requirement or permission as is referred to in the text to note 6 supra: ibid s 6 (3) (b) (ii).

8 Ibid s 6 (3). The maximum penalty on summary conviction is a fine of level 5 on the standard scale: s 6 (3) (amended by virtue of the Criminal Justice Act 1982 ss 38, 46). As to the standard scale see para 232 note 1 ante. At the date at which this volume states the law, level 5 on that scale is at £2,000. Proceedings for the offence may be brought within six months of evidence sufficient (in a prosecutor's opinion) to warrant proceedings coming to his knowledge; however, no proceedings may be brought more than three years after the commission of the offence: Endangered Species (Import and Export) Act 1976 s 6 (6). A certificate signed by or on behalf of the prosecutor and stating the date on which such evidence came to his knowledge is conclusive evidence of the fact; and a certificate stating that matter and purporting to be so signed is deemed to be so signed unless the contrary is proved: s 6 (7).

245. Powers of Customs and Excise Commissioners. Where any live or dead animal is in the process of being imported or exported, a person commissioned or authorised by the Commissioners of Customs and Excise may require proof that the animal's import or export is not unlawful[1], on pain of forfeiture of the animal[2].

1 Ie under the Endangered Species (Import and Export) Act 1976 s 1: see para 241 ante.

2 Ibid s 1 (8). Where, in the case of a live animal which is condemned or deemed to be condemned as forfeited, the Commissioners of Customs and Excise incur any expenses in connection with or with a view to its return to the wild or its being kept at suitable premises, those expenses may be recovered as a debt due to the Crown from the importer or intending exporter of the animal, or from any person possessing or having control of it at the time of its seizure: s 1 (9) (added by the Wildlife Countryside Act 1981 s 15 (1), Sch 10 Pt I para 2).

246. Sale, etc, of endangered species or things made from them. Any person who sells[1], offers or exposes for sale, has in his possession or transports for the purpose of sale, or displays to the public[2], anything unlawfully[3] imported or anything which is made wholly or partly from such thing and which, at the time of the sale or other dealing, constitutes an item the sale of which is restricted, is guilty of an offence[4]. Any person who deals in a similar way with an animal (alive or dead) the sale of which is restricted[5], or an egg or other immature stage of such an animal, or any part of or anything which derives from, or is made wholly or partly from, such an animal, egg or other immature stage, also commits an offence[6]. These offences do not, however, apply to anything done under, and in accordance with the terms of, a licence issued by the Secretary of State[7]. Nor is a person guilty of either offence if he proves that at the time when the restricted article[8] first came into his possession he made such enquiries (if any) as were reasonable in the circumstances[9] in order to ascertain whether it was a restricted article, and that at the time the alleged offence was committed he had no reason to believe it was a restricted article[10]. A person guilty of either offence is liable on summary conviction to a maximum fine of the prescribed sum or on conviction on indictment to imprisonment for a term not exceeding two years, a fine, or both[11].

1 Reference to sale includes references to hire, barter and exchange: Endangered Species (Import and Export) Act 1976 s 4 (6) (amended by the Wildlife and Countryside Act 1981 s 15 (1), Sch 10 para 5).

2 This includes display to the public generally or to any section of it, and (in either case) whether in return for money or otherwise: Endangered Species (Import and Export) Act 1976 s 4 (7).
3 Ie in contravention of ibid s 1; see para 241 ante.
4 Ibid s 4 (1) (as amended: see note 1 supra).
5 Ie an animal listed in ibid Sch 4 (added by the Wildlife and Countryside Act 1981 s 15 (1), Sch 10 Pt I para 5 (6), Pt II). The Schedule covers a wide range of mammals, birds, reptiles, amphibians, fish and molluscs, and reference should be made to the full text of the Act when considering specific species.
6 Endangered Species (Import and Export) Act 1976 s 4 (1A) (added by the Wildlife and Countryside Act 1981 Sch 10 Pt I para 5). This offence is not committed if the thing dealt with is covered by the Endangered Species (Import and Export) Act 1976 s 4 (1) (ie the offence described at text to note 2 supra), nor if the thing was imported, or is a part of or derives from or is made wholly or partly from anything which has been imported, before 30 October 1981: s 4 (1A) (as so added).
7 Ibid s 4 (1B) (as added: see note 6 supra). The Secretary of State need not consult any scientific authority before granting or refusing such a licence, but in other respects the criteria for such a licence are as described in para 242 ante: s 4 (1B).
8 Ie any thing covered by the above-mentioned offences: ibid s 4 (1C) (as added: see note 6 supra).
9 Without prejudice to the generality of this provision, a person is to be taken to have made the necessary enquiries if he produces to the court a certificate furnished by the supplier of the restricted article, which is signed by the supplier (or a person authorised by him) and which states that the supplier made enquiries at the time the restricted article came into his possession in order to ascertain whether it was a restricted article, and that he had no reason to believe at the time he relinquished possession of the restricted article to the accused that the article was at that time a restricted article: ibid s 4 (3). Anyone who furnishes for the above-mentioned purposes a certificate which he knows to be false in a material particular, or who recklessly furnishes for those purposes a certificate which is false in a material particular, commits an offence: s 4 (4). The penalty for this offence is the same as is described in the text to note 11 infra: s 4 (5) (amended by virtue of the Magistrates' Courts Act 1980 s 32 (1)).
10 Endangered Species (Import and Export) Act 1976 s 4 (2) (as amended: see note 1 supra).
11 Ibid s 4 (5) (as amended: see note 9 supra). As to the prescribed sum see para 233 note 3 ante. At the date at which this volume states the law, that sum is at £2,000.

247. Restrictions on import and export of other animals. In addition to the statutory control over the import of rare animals[1], there are various other statutory restrictions on both the import and export of other animals, both domestic and wild, whose details fall to be considered elsewhere in this work but to which brief reference may usefully be made here.

Thus there are comprehensive regulations made under the Animal Health Act 1981 as to the import and export of animals with the purpose of controlling, eradicating and preventing disease[2]. 'Animals' under that Act means cattle, sheep and goats and all other ruminating animals and swine[3], but the ministers[4], who administer the Act, have power to extend the definition to other creatures[5]. Poultry are also dealt with under the Act[6].

The import of dogs, cats and other mammals is subject to special provisions[7], and there are certain classes of destructive non-indigenous wild animals whose import or keeping is either prohibited or controlled by licence[8].

1 See para 241 et seq ante.
2 See paras 502–506 post.
3 Animal Health Act 1981 s 87 (1).
4 Ie the Minister of Agriculture, Fisheries and Food, the Secretary of State for Scotland and the Secretary of State for Wales, acting jointly: ibid s 86 (1) (c).
5 Ibid s 87 (2), (3); see para 483 post.
6 Ibid s 87 (4), (5); see para 523 post.
7 See para 492 post.
8 See AGRICULTURE vol 1 (2) (Reissue) para 660 et seq.

2. GAME RIGHTS

(1) OWNERS' AND TENANTS' RIGHTS

(i) Owners' Rights

248. Rights of owner-occupier. Where an owner-occupier of land reserves to himself the rights over the game[1] on the land, then subject to the general protective provisions of the law in the interests of wildlife[2] and to the possession of a game licence[3] he may kill and take such game whenever and however he pleases.

Where an owner-occupier grants the game rights over his land to another, the latter may exercise those rights in the same manner and to the same extent as the owner, save that he has no right to kill hares without a licence[4]. The owner-occupier, however, has a concurrent right to kill ground game[5].

1 For the meaning of 'game' see para 211 ante.
2 See para 406 post.
3 See para 306 et seq post.
4 A right to kill hares is confined to persons in actual occupation and owners with the right of killing the game and persons authorised by them in writing: Hares Act 1848 s 1; Game Licences Act 1860 s 5, Exemption 4. See also para 308 post.
5 Ground Game Act 1880 s 1. 'Ground game' means hares and rabbits: s 8.

249. Rights of non-occupying owner. If the owner does not occupy his own land, but lets it to a tenant, the rights over game may or may not be reserved. Where they are not reserved, they pass in every case, with the possession of the land, to the tenant[1].

1 *Pochin v Smith* (1887) 52 JP 4, DC; *Anderson v Vicary* [1900] 2 QB 287, CA. As to the occupier's rights in respect of ground game see para 257 post. This is in accordance with the common law doctrine as to rights arising out of the land. The rule was finally established as to existing leases by the Game Act 1831 s 7, which expressly reserved to the landlord all rights over game in the case of all such leases except where the rights were specifically granted to the tenant or where the lease was for more than 21 years. All future leases, however, were left to be governed, except where the game was specifically reserved (see para 250 note 2 post), by the general law of trespass. A contrary principle obtains in Scotland, where the right over the game is considered a right personal to the owner of the land: *Saunders v Pitfield* (1888) 58 LT 108, DC.

250. Reservation by lessor of game rights. The power to reserve a right of entry on the land to the owner or any other person is expressly saved by statute[1]. The reservation may be effected either by a covenant in the lease or by a separate contract[2], and the terms of the agreement may enable the right to be exercised by persons not parties to the instrument reserving the right[3]. The reservation need not be made by deed; a verbal reservation is sufficient[4].

A reservation to the lessor of exclusive sporting rights is void in so far as it applies to ground game[5], but such a reservation is severable, and in so far as it applies to any other than ground game it is valid[6]. The right to the game being regarded as a right arising out of the land, such a covenant for reservation of the sporting rights may be sued on by an assignee of the reversion[7].

The reserved right is defended by statutory provisions which make it an offence for the tenant in such a case to kill or take the game other than ground game or to permit anyone else to do so[8]. In the case, however, of a tenancy created since 1880, the landlord cannot by any reservation of the sporting rights deprive the tenant of the right to kill ground game[9].

1 Game Act 1831 s 8.
2 The usual method is to insert a covenant in the lease creating the tenancy, but the right of entry may be contained in any deed, grant, lease or any written or parol demise or contract. As to leases generally see LANDLORD AND TENANT.
3 *Wickham v Hawker* (1840) 7 M & W 63; *Gardiner v Colyer* (1864) 10 LT 715.
4 *Jones v Williams and Roberts* (1877) 46 LJMC 270, DC; and see *R v Thurlstone (Inhabitants)* (1859) 1 E & E 502; *Coleman v Bathurst* (1871) LR 6 QB 366.
5 Ground Game Act 1880 s 3. 'Ground game' means hares and rabbits: s 8.
6 *Stanton v Brown* [1900] 1 QB 671, DC. The tenant may recover damages from the shooting tenant in respect of injury caused to his crops by the land being overstocked with game: see *Farrer v Nelson* (1885) 15 QBD 258. The overstocking must, however, be due to the defendant's extraordinary, non-natural or unreasonable action: see *Seligman v Docker* [1949] Ch 53, [1948] 2 All ER 887, where the increase of pheasants was found to be due to weather conditions; *Peech v Best* [1931] 1 KB 1 at 14, CA, per Scrutton LJ.
7 *Hooper v Clark* (1867) LR 2 QB 200. A condition of re-entry, if the tenant is guilty of an offence against the game laws, does not go with the reversion, as that is not a covenant arising out of the land: *Stevens v Copp* (1868) LR 4 Exch 20.
8 Game Act 1831 s 12; Ground Game Act 1880 s 1; see para 276 post.
9 Ground Game Act 1880 s 3. The tenant's right, however, is subject to the restrictions contained in s 6; see para 252 post.

251. Effect of reservation of game rights. When the game rights are reserved, the owner, or any person to whom he may grant them, may exercise the rights to the same extent and precisely as if he were the occupier of the land, subject to:

(1) such rights over the ground game as are given to the tenant by the Ground Game Acts[1], and

(2) such claim as the tenant may have in respect of damage caused by game[2].

A reservation of sporting rights by the owner operates by way of regrant by the tenant to the owner, and the parties' rights must be ascertained on that footing[3]. The tenant is entitled to use the land and to destroy gorse and underwood in the ordinary way[4] or to carry out any reasonable and normal operations which might be deemed advisable for the purpose of dealing with the land to the best advantage[5], but he must not designedly drive the game away[6]. On the other hand the owner, or his tenant of shooting rights, must not trample fields of standing crops at a time when it is not usual or reasonable to do so[7], and if the owner or that tenant causes game to increase to an unreasonable extent, the tenant of the land can recover damages for the injury to his crops[8]. The owner is, however, entitled to be indemnified by the shooting tenant against compensation claims[9], but not if the grant to the shooting tenant does not enable him to shoot on the part of the land adversely affected[10].

A reservation must be construed strictly against the person claiming under it[11]. The meaning of the word 'game' in a deed reserving sporting rights is a matter of the construction of the document[12]. The more usual agreement reserving the shooting or sporting rights has the effect of reserving the right to kill all things which are usually the object of sport[13].

A covenant that the tenant shall not destroy the game does not have the effect of reserving the right of killing it to a landlord who does not reserve the right of entry for that purpose[14].

1 See para 257 post.

2 See para 250 note 6 ante and the text to note 8 infra; and see AGRICULTURE vol 1 (2) (Reissue) paras 393–395.
3 See *Mason v Clarke* [1954] 1 QB 460, [1954] 1 All ER 189, CA; revsd on other grounds [1955] AC 778, [1955] 1 All ER 914, HL, but see at 786 and 915–916 respectively per Viscount Simonds.
4 *Jeffryes v Evans* (1865) 19 CBNS 246.
5 *Peech v Best* [1931] 1 KB 1 at 18, CA, per Greer LJ; cf *Mason v Clarke* [1955] AC 778 at 796, [1955] 1 All ER 914 at 921, HL, per Viscount Simonds; and as to reservations generally see DEEDS.
6 *Jeffryes v Evans* (1865) 19 CBNS 246; and see *Mason v Clarke* [1955] AC 778, [1955] 1 All ER 914, HL.
7 *Hilton v Green* (1862) 2 F & F 821.
8 *Hilton v Green* (1862) 2 F & F 821; *Birkbeck v Paget* (1862) 31 Beav 403; *Farrer v Nelson* (1885) 15 QBD 258. See also para 246 note 6 ante; and AGRICULTURE vol 1 (2) (Reissue) para 383.
9 Agricultural Holdings Act 1986 s 20 (5); see AGRICULTURE vol 1 (2) (Reissue) para 395.
10 See *Cornewall v Dawson* (1871) 24 LT 664.
11 See DEEDS. See also *Moore v Earl of Plymouth* (1817) 7 Taunt 614 at 627 (liberty of 'hunting' does not include shooting feathered game); *Wickham v Hawker* (1840) 7 M & W 63 (conveyance of land by A and B to D, excepting and reserving sporting rights to A, B and C, is not a reservation but a new grant by D); *Brown v Marquis of Sligo* (1859) 10 I Ch R 1 (agreement giving tenant exclusive shooting and coursing rights but not fishing, held to reserve fishing rights to landlord); *Jeffryes v Evans* (1865) 19 CBNS 246 (reservation of right of 'shooting and sporting' is not limited to game strictly so called); *Houston v Marquis of Sligo* (1886) 55 LT 614, HL (exception of shooting 'by way of grant and not of reservation' is a regrant by tenant to landlord). See also the text to note 14 infra.
12 See para 211 ante.
13 *Jeffryes v Evans* (1865) 19 CBNS 246; *Moore v Earl of Plymouth* (1817) 7 Taunt 614 at 627. While a tenant who infringes reserved rights of killing game, strictly defined, commits an offence (see para 276 text and note 5 post), a tenant who kills other birds, the right to which may have been reserved, is only liable to an action for breach of the covenant or agreement.
14 *Coleman v Bathurst* (1871) LR 6 QB 366.

(ii) Tenants' Rights

A. GENERAL

252. Shooting ground game at night. An occupier of land other than the owner, although entitled to kill hares and rabbits by virtue of the Ground Game Act 1880[1], or because the owner has not reserved sporting rights[2], is liable to a penalty not exceeding level 1 on the standard scale[3] if in the exercise of this right he uses firearms between the expiration of the first hour after sunset and the commencement of the last hour before sunrise, unless he does so with the written authorisation of a person authorised to take and kill ground game on the land[4].

1 As to the rights conferred by this Act see para 257 post.
2 *Saunders v Pitfield* (1888) 58 LT 108, DC; *Waters v Phillips* [1910] 2 KB 465, DC.
3 As to the standard scale see para 232 note 1 ante. At the date at which this volume states the law, level 1 on that scale is at £50.
4 Ground Game Act 1880 s 6 (amended by the Prevention of Damage by Rabbits Act 1939 ss 5 (2), 6 (3) and by virtue of the Criminal Justice Act 1982 s 46). The prohibition does not extend to the owner of the land, whether or not he is in occupation (*Smith v Hunt* (1885) 54 LT 422, DC), or to any person not in occupation who is entitled by grant or licence from the owner to kill hares and rabbits (*May v Waters* [1910] 1 KB 431, DC; *Leworthy v Rees* (1913) 109 LT 244, DC). Additionally, notwithstanding this provision, the occupier of any land himself, or one other person authorised by him under the Ground Game Act 1880 s 1 (see para 260 post), may use firearms for killing ground game thereon during the prohibited period if (except where he has the exclusive right) the occupier has the written authority of the other person or one of the other persons entitled to kill and take the ground game: Wildlife and Countryside Act 1981 s 12, Sch para 1.

253. Shooting tenant's rights. The shooting tenant may have obtained his rights over game either:

(1) from the owner–occupier, or

(2) from an owner who has let his land but reserved his shooting rights, or

(3) from an occupying tenant where the rights have not been reserved.

In all these cases the shooting tenant may have either the right to shoot the game or else general shooting and sporting rights[1]. Subject to this he takes, in cases (1) and (2), precisely those rights which the owner himself would have had. In case (1), however, the owner retains his occupier's rights under the Ground Game Act 1880[2]. An owner–occupier or tenant who infringes his shooting tenant's rights by pursuing, killing or taking the game commits an offence for which he may be prosecuted[3], but an owner not in occupation who does so is merely liable to a civil claim for breach of contract. The grantee of exclusive sporting rights has a right of action against anyone whose acts interfere with his enjoyment of them[4].

The right to kill and carry away game is not a mere licence, but a profit à prendre[5], and, being an incorporeal hereditament, should be granted by deed[6], though on a verbal letting of lands the owner can reserve the game to himself[7]. An agreement for the enjoyment of such a right should be in writing[8], but in the absence of writing it may be enforceable on the ground of part performance[9]. If there has been actual enjoyment under a parol grant of a right of shooting[10] the rent can be recovered in an action for use and occupation, and the tenant is liable under the stipulations in the grant[11]. Where the lease is by deed, the benefit of a covenant by the tenant, such as a covenant to leave the land as well stocked with game as at the time of the demise, runs with the reversion[12]. A yearly tenancy of sporting rights may be created by payment of rent, but the tenant is only entitled to a reasonable notice to quit, and not to the customary six months' notice[13].

1 See para 250 text to note 5, ante.

2 *Anderson v Vicary* [1900] 2 QB 287, CA. As to these rights see para 248 ante.

3 Game Act 1831 s 12. A shooting tenant who prosecutes must prove his right to the game strictly by producing the deed granting it to him: *Barker v Davis* (1865) 34 LJMC 140.

4 *Fitzgerald v Firbank* [1897] 2 Ch 96, CA; *Nicholls v Ely Beet Sugar Factory* [1931] 2 Ch 84.

5 *Wickham v Hawker* (1840) 7 M & W 63; *Ewart v Graham* (1859) 7 HL Cas 331; *Webber v Lee* (1882) 9 QBD 315, CA; *Lowe v Adams* [1901] 2 Ch 598. As to profits à prendre see EASEMENTS.

6 Law of Property Act 1925 ss 52 (1), 205 (1) (ix); *Bird v Higginson* (1837) 6 Ad & El 824; *Brigstocke v Rayner* (1875) 40 JP 245. As to the conveyance of incorporeal hereditaments by deed see DEEDS. An invalid lease capable of specific enforcement may, however, operate as an agreement for a lease under the doctrine of *Walsh v Lonsdale* (1882) 21 ChD 9, CA; see LANDLORD AND TENANT. A lessee who has had the benefit of a lease which is not made by deed cannot set up the want of a deed as a defence to an action on the covenants: *Adams v Clutterbuck* (1883) 10 QBD 403; cf *Thomas v Fredericks* (1847) 10 QB 775. Where there is an agreement not made by deed letting shooting rights a landlord may be restrained from interfering with the exercise of those rights pending the execution of a lease: *Frogley v Earl of Lovelace* (1859) John 333.

7 *Jones v Williams and Roberts* (1877) 46 LJMC 270.

8 *Webber v Lee* (1882) 9 QBD 315, CA.

9 See *McManus v Cooke* (1887) 35 Ch D 681 and *Mason v Clarke* [1955] AC 778, [1955] 1 All ER 914, HL.

10 *Tomlinson v Day* (1821) 2 Brod & Bing 680; *Dawes v Dowling* (1874) 31 LT 65.

11 See *Adams v Clutterbuck* (1883) 10 QBD 403.

12 *Hooper v Clark* (1867) LR 2 QB 200.

13 *Lowe v Adams* [1901] 2 Ch 598, where a month's notice determining a shooting tenancy, given at the end of the season, was held to be sufficient.

254. Alterations to land affecting shooting rights. In the absence of any special covenants, the grantor of shooting rights is not precluded from using the land in the ordinary and accustomed way, having regard to its character at the date of the grant[1]. Thus, in the case of farming land, he cannot be prevented from altering the course of husbandry[2], cutting down timber or underwood, or doing any other act falling within the ordinary course of estate management[3]. But any act done with the intention of injuring the rights granted[4], or any user of the land which does not fall within the ordinary course of its management, or which works a substantial change in its character is, if it substantially injures the rights granted, a derogation from the grant and a breach of the usual covenant for quiet enjoyment[5].

Where an accident, such as a fire, threatens damage to his shooting rights, the shooting tenant is entitled to adopt such means for the preservation of his rights as are reasonably necessary[6].

1 *Jeffryes v Evans* (1865) 19 CBNS 246; *Gearns v Baker* (1875) 10 Ch App 355; *Peech v Best* [1931] 1 KB 1 at 18, CA.
2 *Jeffryes v Evans* (1865) 19 CBNS 246.
3 *Gearns v Baker* (1875) 10 Ch App 355.
4 *Jeffryes v Evans* (1865) 19 CBNS 246; *Bird v Great Eastern Rly Co* (1865) 19 CBNS 268; *Gearns v Baker* (1875) 10 Ch App 355.
5 *Dick v Norton* (1916) 85 LJ Ch 623, where, although an interlocutory injunction to restrain the grantor from cutting down all the timber for commercial purposes was refused, damages were recovered at the trial; *Peech v Best* [1931] 1 KB 1, CA, where a substantial portion of the land was sold for the purpose of erecting racing stables. See also *Wenner v Morris* (1935) 79 Sol Jo 252 (use of land for gliding flights). The decision of Jessel MR in *Pattison v Gilford* (1874) LR 18 Eq 259 was apparently distinguished on the basis that there the land was sold expressly subject to shooting rights, that no immediate building activity was threatened and, possibly, by the application of the de minimis rule: *Peech v Best* supra at 12–14, 23.
6 *Cope v Sharpe (No 2)* [1912] 1 KB 496, CA. As to trespass by dogs see para 369 post.

B. AGRICULTURAL TENANTS' RIGHTS

255. Agricultural tenant's rights generally. An agricultural tenant in occupation of land on which the sporting rights are not reserved has the same rights over game as an owner-occupier[1], save that with one exception he may not kill ground game at night with a gun[2]. This restriction does not, however, apply where the right to kill and take rabbits has been expressly conferred on him[3]. He may grant his rights, including the right to take and kill the ground game, to a shooting tenant[4], but such grant will not preclude him from exercising his concurrent right to kill ground game himself[5].

1 See para 248 ante.
2 Ground Game Act 1880 s 6. 'Ground game' means hares and rabbits: s 8. For the exception see the Wildlife and Countryside Act 1981 s 12, Sch 7; and para 252 ante.
3 *May v Waters* [1910] 1 KB 431, DC; *Leworthy v Rees* (1913) 109 LT 244, DC.
4 *Morgan v Jackson* [1895] 1 QB 885, DC.
5 *Morgan v Jackson* [1895] 1 QB 885 at 887, DC, per Wright J.

256. Agricultural tenant's rights where sporting rights reserved. An agricultural tenant in occupation of land on which the sporting rights have been reserved has certain statutory rights in regard to game in the interests of good husbandry and for the better security of the capital and labour invested by him in the cultivation of the soil[1]. They comprise direct rights in the case of ground game, and indirect rights in the case of game generally. The rights are conferred in the one case by the Ground Game Acts[2], and in the other by the Agricultural Holdings Act 1986[3].

1 See the preamble to the Ground Game Act 1880.
2 See para 257 note 1 post.
3 See AGRICULTURE vol 1 (2) (Reissue) paras 393–395.

257. Rights over ground game. The occupier's right under the Ground Game Acts[1] is to kill and take ground game[2] on the land in his occupation, whether or not any other person is entitled also to kill and take ground game on the same land[3]. The right is incident to and inseparable from his occupation, so that he cannot be divested of it in any way[4]. Any agreement, condition or arrangement is void[5] which purports to alienate it from him or which gives him an advantage in consideration of his forbearing to exercise it or imposes any disadvantage on him in consequence of his exercising it[6].

A person with a mere right of common is not an occupier within the Ground Game Acts[7].

1 Ie the Ground Game Act 1880 and the Ground Game (Amendment) Act 1906.
2 'Ground game' means hares and rabbits: Ground Game Act 1880 s 8.
3 Ibid s 1. However, an occupier of land (other than the owner) is liable on summary conviction to a fine not exceeding level 1 on the standard scale if in the exercise of this right he uses firearms between the expiration of the first hour after sunset and the commencement of the last hour before sunrise: s 6 (amended by the Pests Act 1954 s 15 (2), Schedule (repealed) and by virtue of the Criminal Justice Act 1982 s 46). As to the standard scale see para 232 note 1 ante. At the date at which this volume states the law, level 1 on that scale is at £50. See also para 252 ante.
4 Ground Game Act 1880 ss 1, 3, 7.
5 See *Sherrard v Gascoigne* [1900] 2 QB 279, DC, where the tenant was induced to leave ground game unshot by the landlord's promise to compensate him for damage done by it; it was held that the agreement was void and the tenant could not recover compensation under it.
6 Ground Game Act 1880 s 3. Though clauses in an agreement are void as contravening this provision the rest of the agreement may be good: see *Beardmore v Meakin* (1884) 20 LJNC 8; *Stanton v Brown* [1900] 1 QB 671, DC. In *Morgan v Jackson* [1895] 1 QB 885, DC, it was held that this provision was directed only against occupiers of land depriving themselves, in collusion with their landlords, of their statutory right to kill game.
7 Ground Game Act 1880 s 1 proviso (2). Cf the Game Act 1831 s 10; and *Cooper v Marshall* (1757) 1 Burr 259.

258. Sublessee's rights. The right to kill and take ground game is granted expressly to occupiers as such. Hence, if a tenant sublets his land, he parts with the ground and the sublessee acquires it for the duration of the sublease. The right to kill ground game on land is withheld from anyone who merely has a right of common over it[1], and from anyone who is in occupation for the purpose of grazing or pasturage of sheep, cattle or horses for a period of nine months or less[2].

1 Ground Game Act 1880 s 1 proviso (2); cf the Game Act 1831 s 10; and *Cooper v Marshall* (1757) 1 Burr 259.
2 Ground Game Act 1880 s 1 proviso (2). The precise language of this exception leaves in some doubt the question whether it covers occupation for the purpose of grazing other animals, eg goats or pigs.

259. Occupier's rights over moorland. In the case of moorland and uninclosed non-arable land, except detached portions of either which are less than 25 acres in extent and adjoin arable lands, the time at which the occupier's right to kill ground game may be exercised is limited: between 11 December of one year and 31 March of the next year, inclusive, the right may be exercised and ground game may be killed in any legal way[1]; between 1 April and 31 August, inclusive, the right is suspended altogether; but between 1 September and 10 December, inclusive, the right may be exercised otherwise than by the use of firearms[2], and as between those latter dates a valid agreement may be made between the occupier and the owner or shooting tenant for the joint exercise of the right or for its exercise for their joint benefit[3].

Moreover, occupiers of lands on which the right to take and kill ground game is vested by lease, contract of tenancy or other contract bona fide made for valuable consideration before 7 September 1880[4] in some other person, are not entitled to exercise their right until the determination of that contract, and in places where before that date any person other than the landlord, lessor or occupier became entitled by virtue of any charter or Act to a special right of killing or taking ground game, the occupier is precluded from any action that might affect that special right[5].

1 Ground Game Act 1880 s 1 proviso (3).
2 Ground Game (Amendment) Act 1906 s 2. As to trapping and other methods of destruction see para 428 post.
3 Ground Game (Amendment) Act 1906 s 3.
4 Ie the date of the passing of the Ground Game Act 1880.
5 Ibid s 5. When a tenant held land under a tenancy from year to year, but there was an agreement made before 7 September 1880 for a 14 years' lease to be granted at the expiration of the tenancy, and that lease contained a covenant reserving rights over ground game to the landlord, it was held that the rights to the ground game remained vested in the landlord until the expiration of that year's lease: *Allhusen v Brooking* (1884) 26 ChD 559; cf *Hassard v Clark* (1884) 13 LR Ir 391.

260. Who may exercise right. In all places the exercise of the right[1] is confined to the occupier and to persons duly authorised by him in writing[2]. Where there are joint tenants, each of them is at liberty to exercise the right[3], but if they authorise other persons, presumably they must do so jointly.

The written authority need not be in any prescribed form, and no provision requires it to be either signed or dated, but obviously it should state the name of the person authorised and indicate the place in regard to which the authority is given. Every person so authorised by the occupier may be required by any person having a concurrent right to take and kill the ground game on the land, or by any person authorised by the latter in writing, to produce the authority, and if he fails to do so he will not be deemed to be an authorised person[4].

The only persons who may be authorised to kill ground game are:

(1) members of the occupier's household[5] resident[6] on the land in his occupation[7];
(2) persons in his ordinary service on such land[8]; and
(3) any one other person bona fide employed by him for reward[9] in the taking and destruction of ground game[10].

Only one other person besides the occupier himself may be authorised by him to exercise his rights by killing the ground game with firearms[11].

1 See para 257 text to note 3 ante.
2 Ground Game Act 1880 s 1 proviso (1). A person who kills ground game on the occupier's verbal instruction only is a trespasser: cf *Richardson v Maitland* (1897) 34 SLR 426.
3 Cf *Assessed Tax Appeal Case (No 1473)* (1840) 6 JP 186; *Morrison v Anderson* 1913 JC 114.
4 Ground Game Act 1880 s 1 proviso (1) (c).
5 The household will include household servants, namely, those who live and board at his house but presumably not such as live in other houses on the farm: cf *Re Drax, Savile v Yeatman* (1887) 57 LT 475; *Ogle v Morgan* (1852) 1 De GM & G 359.

6 A man's residence has been described as the place where he eats, drinks and sleeps, or where his family or servants eat, drink and sleep: *R v North Curry (Inhabitants)* (1825) 4 B & C 953 at 959 per Bayley J. The question is one of fact in each case, but a person invited to stay for a week and shoot rabbits was held by a Scottish court to satisfy the condition: *Stuart v Murray* (1884) 12 R 9, Ct of Sess. It is not necessary that the occupier should reside there himself: cf *R v North Curry (Inhabitants)* supra.

7 This would seem to limit the authority given to this class of person to the farm on which they were resident, so that if a tenant held two or more farms the household resident on each could take and kill the ground game on that farm, but not on the others.

8 'Ordinary service' presumably means regular service, so that casual labour taken on for a week or two, as for harvest, would be excluded, Moreover, servants who, however regularly employed, do not find their customary work on the land would also be excluded. There is otherwise no limit to the number of persons who might be included in this class.

9 'Employed' includes an employment, direct or indirect: *Mason v Clarke* [1954] 1 QB 460 at 468, [1954] 1 All ER 189 at 192, CA, per Denning LJ; revsd without reference to this point [1955] AC 778, [1955] 1 All ER 914, HL. This introduction of a stranger on to the land is dissociated from any idea of sport to be had out of killing the ground game. It must be a business transaction (eg a person employed as a professional rabbit-catcher). It is no doubt possible that a friend or servant might be employed if he were definitely paid for it, but whereas in the case of the rabbit-catcher the fact of his being allowed to keep all or some of the rabbits taken would probably be considered bona fide employment for reward (cf *Bruce v Prosser* (1898) 35 SLR 433, commented on in (1898) 62 JP 466, where it was so decided by the Scottish courts), a similar gift to a friend asked to come and shoot could hardly be so construed. Definite employment for the purpose is required; verbal instructions are insufficient; see note 2 supra.

10 Ground Game Act 1880 s 1 proviso (1) (b). As to the power of the Minister of Agriculture, Fisheries and Food to authorise other persons to kill ground game under the Pests Act 1954 s 1 (4) see AGRICULTURE vol 1 (2) (Reissue) para 657.

11 Ground Game Act 1880 s 1 proviso (1) (a).

261. Compensation for damage by game. In addition to the protection from damage by hares and rabbits which is given to an agricultural tenant by the right to shoot them under the Ground Game Act 1880[1], he is entitled to compensation from his landlord in certain cases for damage done to his crops by deer, pheasants, partridges, grouse and black game[2]. Any agreement to the contrary or in limitation of this compensation is void[3]. Where the right to kill and take game is vested in some person other than the landlord, the landlord is entitled to an indemnity from that person against all claims by the tenant for compensation for damage by such game[4].

1 See para 257 ante.
2 This compensation and the circumstances in which it is payable are provided for under the Agricultural Holdings Act 1986 s 20: see AGRICULTURE vol 1 (2) (Reissue) para 395.
3 See AGRICULTURE vol 1 (2) (Reissue) para 393.
4 See AGRICULTURE vol 1 (2) (Reissue) para 395.

(iii) Rights Ratione Privilegii

262. Nature of right. In certain cases the right to kill or take game may be claimed *ratione privilegii* without reference to the occupation of the land on which the game is found.

The ancient right of franchise to kill or take game without reference to the occupation of the land whereon the game is found, whose origin was a grant by the Crown in the exercise of the royal prerogative or by prescription supposing such a grant, no longer exists[1]. In so far as the game rights of the lord of the manor were founded in free warren, which was a franchise of this nature, they also are now abolished[2]. There still remains, however, the manorial right to shoot and take game *ratione privilegii*[3].

1 Wild Creatures and Forest Laws Act 1971 s 1 (1) (b). The principal franchises of this nature were those of forest or chase and free warren.
2 Ibid s 1 (1) (b).
3 See para 263 post.

263. Lord of the manor. The right of the lord of the manor to shoot or take game on the uninclosed waste land of the manor is a right which belongs to him by virtue of his ownership of the soil[1]. He may accordingly grant the right as a profit à prendre to another separately from the ownership of the soil[2]. Where, however, waste lands have been inclosed[3] and have been allotted to the commoners as their freehold, prima facie the right of sporting belongs to them as incident to their property in the soil[4].

1 As to the lord of the manor's game rights see COMMONS vol 6 (Reissue) para 642. Rights to take game, fish and fowl were preserved by the Law of Property Act 1922 s 128 (2), Sch 12 para (5), notwithstanding the enfranchisement of copyhold land by s 128; see COPYHOLDS vol 9 para 788.
2 *Ewart v Graham* (1859) 7 HL Cas 331; *Wickham v Hawker* (1840) 7 M & W 63, adopted in *Musgrave v Forster* (1871) LR 6 QB 590 at 592. The Game Act 1831 gives no interest in game to the owners of cattlegates or rights of common and does not prejudice the rights of lords of the manor, who are to have the game on the wastes: s 10. A person with a mere right of common is not an occupier entitled to kill ground game under the Ground Game Act 1880: s 1 proviso (2).
3 As to inclosure see COMMONS vol 6 (Reissue) para 704 et seq.
4 As to the effect of inclosure on sporting rights see COMMONS vol 6 (Reissue) paras 742, 743.

(2) CIVIL REMEDIES FOR INFRINGEMENT OF RIGHTS

(i) Remedies at Law

264. Nature of private rights over game. Private rights over game, whatever their origin, are essentially local in character, and the principle upon which their security depends is that of the law of trespass[1]. Trespass is committed by any person who enters the land of another without authority to do so[2]. Such an act requires no motive, such as the search for or pursuit of game, to supply a ground of action to the injured party; but while the right of action is open to any occupier whose ground is trespassed on, it is of special importance to the holder of rights over game, as it is the means whereby the game on land in his occupation is protected from disturbance[3].

1 See para 212 ante; and the Game Act 1831 s 6.
2 Ie *quare clausum fregit*: *Cubitt v Porter* (1828) 8 B & C 257; see generally TRESPASS.
3 Ie if he is an occupier. A shooting tenant not in occupation cannot bring such an action unless the occupier is joined as plaintiff, but he has the right to take criminal proceedings: see para 272 et seq post.

265. Remedies for trespass. The ordinary remedy for trespass is an action by the aggrieved party, who can claim (1) an injunction to restrain the alleged trespasser from committing any further acts of trespass; (2) a declaration of the plaintiff's rights; and (3) damages[1]. Entry on land by any unauthorised person renders him liable to such an action. If, therefore, a person standing on his own ground shoots game which falls upon his neighbour's land, he cannot enter that neighbour's land to gather it without committing an act of trespass[2]; again, if a person while hunting enters the land of another without his consent, he commits an act of trespass[3].

Further, the entry need not be personal in order to be actionable. A man who does not himself enter, but invites or authorises others to do so, is liable for trespass[4]. The mere firing of a gun into the land of another[5], or the sending of a dog on to such land in pursuit of game[6], is also ground for an action for trespass.

1 Damages are as a rule only awarded to the extent to which the aggrieved party has actually suffered loss, but where the trespass is aggravated by wilful annoyance or other special circumstances, they may be given on a more generous scale; see *Merest v Harvey* (1814) 5 Taunt 442, where damages of £500 were awarded, not in consequence of the damage done, but expressly on account of the attendant circumstances, the defendant having persisted in joining a shooting party unasked. As to aggravation of damage, and for the distinction between aggravated and exemplary damages, see DAMAGES. As to injunctions to restrain trespass see INJUNCTIONS.

2 See *Tanton v Jervis* (1879) 43 JP 784. As to whether other proceedings can be taken see para 272 et seq post.

3 *Paul v Summerhayes* (1878) 4 QBD 9, DC; cf, however, *Gundry v Feltham* (1786) 1 Term Rep 334, where it was said that entry could be justified if no more was done than was necessary to kill the fox.

4 *Robinson v Vaughton* (1838) 8 C & P 252; *Baker v Berkeley* (1827) 3 C & P 32, where a master of hounds was held liable for trespass committed by members of the hunt, unless he distinctly desired them not to enter the land. One member of the hunt, not holding an official position, cannot, however, be held liable for the trespass of other members: *Paget v Birkbeck* (1863) 3 F & F 683. For a full review of the authorities relative to the responsibilities of the master of a hunt see *League against Cruel Sports Ltd v Scott* [1986] QB 240, [1985] 2 All ER 489.

5 See *Pickering v Rudd* (1815) 4 Camp 219 at 220. Quaere, as to the firing of a gun over the land of another, *Pickering v Rudd* supra at 220.

6 *R v Pratt* (1855) 4 E & B 860 at 868 per Crompton J. The fact of allowing a dog, known to be addicted to chasing, to be at large near the lands of another would render the owner liable to an action for trespass if the dog in fact entered the land: *Read v Edwards* (1864) 17 CBNS 245: cf *Dimmock v Allenby* (1810) cited in 2 Marsh at 582; *Brown v Giles* (1823) 1 C & P 118. As to unauthorised entry by dogs generally see para 369 note 1 post.

266. Trespass on the highway.

The right of the public over a highway is limited to its use for the purpose of passing and repassing on it, so that a trespass may be committed if the highway is used for the purpose of interfering with sporting rights[1]. Consequently the owner of land adjoining the highway who is also owner of the soil of the highway may employ all the means at his disposal for resisting a trespass there that he might use in the case of any land in his occupation[2].

1 *Harrison v Duke of Rutland* [1893] 1 QB 142, CA; followed in *Hickman v Maisey* [1900] 1 QB 752, CA; and approving *R v Pratt* (1855) 4 E & B 860. As to the criminal offence see para 273 text to note 13 post. As to rights over highways generally see HIGHWAYS.

2 *Harrison v Duke of Rutland* [1893] 1 QB 142, CA.

267. Injury to game rights without entry on land.

It is possible, without entering upon the land of another, to injure that other's right to the game on that land, but in order to succeed in an action the injured party must prove that the act was wrongful and was done with the wilful intention of injuring his rights[1]. It is not actionable to entice game away from the land of another, but it is actionable deliberately to scare them away from it[2].

1 *Ibottson v Peat* (1865) 3 H & C 644. A man may also be injured in his trade if he owns a decoy for wild duck, and the birds are wilfully scared by another with intent to injure him: *Keeble v Hickeringill*

(1706) 11 East 574n. The intent to injure may be inferred from the circumstances in which the gun, etc, was fired: *Carrington v Taylor* (1809) 11 East 571.
2 *Ibottson v Peat* (1865) 3 H & C 644.

268. Right to remove trespasser. In addition to his right of action, an aggrieved party has the right to remove a trespasser who declines to leave his land, provided that he does not use more force than is necessary[1].

1 See generally TRESPASS; and *Harrison v Duke of Rutland* [1893] 1 QB 142, CA.

(ii) Physical Protection against Infringement of Rights

269. Killing or injuring dogs. The law permits a person, in clearly defined circumstances, to kill or injure a dog in order to protect livestock[1], and it is a defence to a charge of destroying or damaging a dog[2] to establish the lawful excuse that it was chasing game and that the defendant reasonably believed that his action was necessary to protect his interest in the game[3].

But, it seems, a person acting in such a way in protecting game or other animals ferae naturae which have not been either reclaimed or reduced into possession by killing cannot justify what is otherwise an actionable wrong[4]. The old remedy of distress damage feasant, abolished in relation to animals by the Animals Act 1971[5], was held to apply to dogs[6], but since the new remedy of detention and sale of trespassing livestock[7] does not by definition extend to dogs[8] it is clear that this class of remedy is no longer available in any form applicable to dogs.

1 See the Animals Act 1971 s 9; and para 387 post.
2 Ie under the Criminal Damage Act 1971 s 1; see CRIMINAL LAW.
3 See the Criminal Damage Act 1971 s 5 (1)–(3), overruling *Gott v Measures* [1948] 1 KB 234, [1947] 2 All ER 609, DC.
4 *Vere v Lord Cawdor* (1809) 11 East 568 at 570 per Le Blanc J. Cf *Taylor v Newman* (1863) 4 B & S 89 at 91 per Blackburn J, commenting on *Vere v Lord Cawdor* supra. Two county court decisions, however, have taken the same line as Le Blanc J: see 45 JP 83, and *Brown v Belfast Water Comrs* (1912) 47 ILT 153; and in view of the express omission from the Animals Act 1971 ss 9, 11 of any reference to game it is submitted that this is correct.
5 Ibid s 7 (1).
6 *Bunch v Kennington* (1841) 1 QB 679.
7 See the Animals Act 1971 s 7; and paras 478, 479 post.
8 Animals Act 1971 s 11.

270. Dog spears, traps and spring guns. The limitation placed by the law on the killing or injuring of dogs[1] does not extend to prevent the occupier of land from taking measures to protect his game in his absence. He may set dog spears in his woods, and if a dog trespasses, and is injured thereby, he need not prove that his methods were necessary in order to protect his rights to the game, as he was acting within his rights on his own soil[2]. But he must not so use his land as to tempt the dogs of others to destruction; thus if he sets traps baited with strong-smelling meat so near his neighbour's yard, or so near a highway where dogs may lawfully pass, that dogs are irresistibly drawn to the traps, he is liable in damages[3].

1 See para 269 ante.
2 *Deane v Clayton* (1817) 7 Taunt 489; *Jordin v Crump* (1841) 8 M & W 782.

3 *Townsend v Wathen* (1808) 9 East 277. He would probably now also be liable to prosecution under the Protection of Animals Act 1911 or the Criminal Damage Act 1971: see para 405 et seq post. As to the protection of animals from poison see para 415 post; for restrictions on the use of protective devices calculated to destroy or harm humans see para 288 post.

271. Barbed wire. An occupier of land may make use of barbed wire on his land, but if the barbed wire is so placed on land adjoining a highway that it is likely to be injurious to persons or animals lawfully using the highway, it is a nuisance which the local authority may by notice call upon the occupier to remove[1].

1 Highways Act 1980 s 164. If he fails to comply with the notice a magistrates' court may, on the local authority's complaint, require him to abate the nuisance: s 164 (1); see HIGHWAYS.

(3) CRIMINAL OFFENCES BY INFRINGING GAME RIGHTS

(i) Poaching and Trespass in Pursuit of Game

A. GENERAL

272. Criminal proceedings for poaching by day. The occupier of land and any person having the right to the game, and the gamekeeper and servants of either, and any person authorised by either, may request a trespasser in the daytime[1] in search or pursuit of game[2], woodcock, snipe or rabbits to quit the land and to give his Christian name and surname and place of abode with a view to a summons being issued against him, and if he wilfully continues or returns upon the land, or refuses to tell his real name and address, or gives such a general description of his place of abode as to be illusory for the purpose of discovery, they may arrest him[3]. If the offender cannot be brought before a justice within 12 hours from the time of his arrest he must be released, but may subsequently be proceeded against by summons or warrant[4].

A police constable may, similarly, request a trespasser to quit the land and to give his Christian name, surname and place of abode[5]; and if he has reasonable grounds for suspecting that a person is committing an offence of poaching[6] on any land[7] he may enter on that land for the purpose of exercising this power, or for the purpose of arresting him[8].

In addition to the occupier's right to bring a civil action[9], a right to prosecute is given to the occupier, the owner of the soil not in occupation, and the person having the right to the game[10], and to any informer[11].

Where, however, a prosecution has been instituted for trespass in pursuit of game by day, no civil action for trespass may be brought against the offender for the same act of trespass by anyone at whose instance or with whose concurrence or assent the prosecution was instituted[12].

1 Daytime runs from the beginning of the last hour before sunrise to the expiration of the first hour after sunset: Game Act 1831 s 34; see also para 278 note 4 post and TIME vol 45 paras 1113–1116.
2 For the meaning of 'game' see para 211 ante.
3 Game Act 1831 s 31 (amended by the Protection of Birds Act 1954 s 15 (2), Sch 6 and the Wild Creatures and Forest Laws Act 1971 s 1 (4), Schedule). The penalty for refusal to give name and address, for giving an illusory description of place of abode or for wilfully continuing or returning

upon the land, is a fine not exceeding level 1 on the standard scale: Game Act 1831 s 31 (amended by virtue of the Criminal Justice Act 1982 s 46). As to the standard scale see para 232 note 1 ante. At the date at which this volume states the law, level 1 on that scale is at £50. The better view seems to be that it is not necessary in order to justify arrest that the trespasser should have been required both to give his real name and address and to quit the land: cf *R v Prestney* (1849) 3 Cox CC 505 per Parke B, with *R v Long* (1836) 7 C & P 314 per Williams J. It is, however, necessary that the trespasser, before being arrested under these provisions, should be asked both for his name and for his address: *R v Wilson* [1955] 1 All ER 744, [1955] 1 WLR 493, CCA. Though a person unlawfully arrested under these provisions cannot be convicted under the Offences against the Person Act 1861 s 38 of assault with intent to resist arrest (see CRIMINAL LAW vol 11 (1) (Reissue) para 321), he may be convicted of common assault if the jury is of opinion that he used more force than necessary to avoid the unlawful arrest: see *R v Wilson* supra and cf *R v Day and Cox* (1870) 22 LT 452, CCR. Generally as to conviction for an offence other than that charged see CRIMINAL LAW.
4 Game Act 1831 s 31 proviso. The reason for his not being brought before the justice must be the justice's absence, the distance of the justice's residence, or some other reasonable cause: s 31 proviso.
5 Ibid s 31A (added by the Police and Criminal Evidence Act 1984 s 119 (1), Sch 6 para 1).
6 Ie under the Game Act 1831 s 30; see para 273 post.
7 'Land' includes land belonging to Her Majesty in right of the Crown or Duchy of Lancaster or in her private capacity, land belonging to the Duchy of Cornwall, and land belonging to a government department or held in trust for Her Majesty for the purposes of such a department: Game Laws (Amendment) Act 1960 s 2 (2). The power of entry is not, however, exercisable in relation to land occupied or managed for the purposes of defence, aviation or atomic energy, by the service authorities of a visiting force as defined by the Visiting Forces Act 1952 s 12 (1), or by any headquarters or organisation designated for the purposes of the International Headquarters and Defence Organisations Act 1964: Game Laws (Amendment) Act 1960 s 2 (3) (amended by the Visiting Forces and International Headquarters (Application of Law) Order 1965, SI 1965/1536, art 12 (2), Sch 3).
8 In accordance with the Police and Criminal Evidence Act 1984: Game Laws (Amendment) Act 1960 s 2 (1) (a), (b) (amended by the Police and Criminal Evidence Act 1984 Sch 6 para 10).
9 See para 265 ante.
10 Game Act 1831 s 30.
11 *Midelton v Gale* (1838) 8 Ad & El 155; *Morden v Porter* (1860) 7 CBNS 641; see para 284 post.
12 Game Act 1831 s 46. To bar an action it is not necessary that the prosecution be successful: *Robinson v Vaughton* (1838) 8 C & P 252. There is no corresponding provision in the Night Poaching Acts of 1828 or 1844, so it would appear that a prosecution for night poaching is no bar to an action.

273. Offence of poaching by day. It is an offence for any trespasser to enter or be upon land[1] in the daytime[2] in search or pursuit of game or woodcock, snipe or rabbits, and an offender is liable upon conviction before one or more justices of the peace to a penalty not exceeding level 1 on the standard scale[3].

It is not neccessary to prove that the search or pursuit was in order to kill game at the time[4]. There must, however, be an actual entry by some person on the land[5]. To discharge a gun into or over the land of a neighbour does not therefore in itself constitute the offence described[6]. Where, however, an entry is made for the purpose of gathering a bird or beast named above which, before being shot, is on or rises from that land, an offence is committed[7].

If a bird rises on the shooter's own ground and is shot at by him while in the air, either over his own or his neighbour's land, and the shooter attempts to gather it on his neighbour's land, then if the bird is dead or unable to escape, so that no fresh effort is required to gather it, no criminal offence is committed[8], but it is otherwise if the bird is merely wounded[9]. The same position would result in the case of ground game started on the shooter's own land and shot at by him before it crossed the boundary, and probably even if shot at after it crossed[10].

A shooter who stands upon his neighbour's land to shoot game that is being beaten out of a boundary hedge by a person on the shooter's own land commits an offence within this provision[11].

No offence is committed by any person hunting or coursing upon any lands with hounds or greyhounds in fresh pursuit of any deer, hare or fox already started on any other land, nor by any lord or steward of the Crown of any manor, lordship or royalty, or reputed manor, lordship or royalty, or by any gamekeeper appointed by him within its limits[12]. But a person who uses a highway, the soil of which is the property of another, to shoot at birds flushed on that other ground, commits an offence[13], and where one person from a highway assists another who is trespassing in pursuit of game, both commit an offence[14].

1 To enter and be upon any land constitutes one offence: *R v Mellor* (1833) 2 Dowl 173.
2 For the meaning of 'daytime' see para 272 note 1 ante.
3 Game Act 1831 s 30 (amended by the Protection of Birds Act 1954 s 15 (2), Sch 6, the Game Laws (Amendment) Act 1960 s 5 (1), and by virtue of the Criminal Justice Act 1982 ss 38, 46). As to the standard scale see para 232 note 1 ante. At the date at which this volume states the law, level 1 on that scale is at £50. If the offender is tried before one justice only, the maximum penalty is £1: Magistrates' Courts Act 1980 s 121 (5). As to trial before justices generally see MAGISTRATES. As to penalties for refusing to provide a game licence or to give one's name and address when called upon by a gamekeeper, etc see para 311 post. As to search of a person and forfeiture of game, guns, traps, etc see para 282 post.
4 *Stiff v Billington* (1901) 84 LT 467, DC; *Burrows v Gillingham* (1893) 57 JP 423.
5 *R v Alsopp* (1691) 1 Show 339; *R v Pratt* (1855) 4 E & B 860; *Mayhew v Wardley* (1863) 14 CBNS 550; and cf *Horn v Raine* (1898) 67 LJQB 533; *Pratt v Martin* [1911] 2 KB 90.
6 Cf para 265 ante, which relates to civil remedies.
7 *Osbond v Meadows* (1862) 26 JP 439. This is so even if the attempt to gather the bird were made some hours after it had been shot, and it had in fact already been gathered by another: *Horne v Raine* (1898) 67 LJQB 533, where the shooting and the attempt to gather the bird were held to be one continuous act. It is possible that, if the game were shot by day and not gathered until night, no offence would be committed, for this offence is trespassing by day, and in this case there would be no entry in the daytime, while as the game is dead there would be no offence under the Night Poaching Acts 1828 and 1844, and if there was always in the poacher's mind the intention to gather there could be no theft: *R v Townley* (1871) LR 1 CCR 315.
8 *Kenyon v Hart* (1865) 6 B & S 249. This is so even if the bird were killed some days before: *Tanton v Jervis* (1879) 43 JP 784. Cf *Nicoll v Strachan* (1912) 50 SLR 120.
9 In this case the bird is in no sense reduced into possession, and it therefore becomes the potential property of the person on whose land it alighted: see para 212 ante.
10 *Kenyon v Hart* (1865) 6 B & S 249 at 255 per Blackburn J; cf *Sutton v Moody* (1697) 1 Ld Raym 250.
11 *Philpot v Bugler* (1890) 54 JP 646, DC.
12 Game Act 1831 s 35 (amended by the Statute Law Revision (No 2) Act 1888 and the Wild Creatures and Forest Laws Act 1971 s 1 (4), Schedule). Permission given verbally by the landlord or person entitled to the game justifies fresh pursuit on an adjoining field: *Jones v Williams and Roberts* (1877) 46 LJMC 270, DC.
13 *R v Pratt* (1855) 4 E & B 860.
14 *Stacey v Whitehurst* (1865) 18 CBNS 344; and see *R v Passey* (1836) 7 C & P 282; and *R v Whittaker* (1848) 2 Car & Kir 636, CCR.

274. Poaching by day in company. Where five or more persons trespass in the daytime[1] in pursuit of game, woodcock, snipe or rabbits, each of them is liable to a penalty not exceeding level 3 on the standard scale[2].

If any of the number is armed with a gun, and he or any of the others by violence, intimidation or menace prevents or endeavours to prevent the approach of any person authorised[3] in that behalf for the purpose of requiring them to quit the land or declare their names and addresses, each person preventing or endeavouring to prevent such approach, and every person aiding or abetting him or them, is liable upon conviction before two or more justices to a penalty not exceeding level 4 on the standard scale[4] in addition to any other penalty which he or they may have incurred[5].

1 For the meaning of 'daytime' see para 272 note 1 ante.
2 Game Act 1831 s 30 (amended by the Protection of Birds Act 1954 s 15 (2), Sch 6 and the Game Laws (Amendment) Act 1960 s 5 (1), and by virtue of the Criminal Justice Act 1982 ss 38, 46). As to the standard scale see para 232 note 1 ante. At the date at which this volume states the law, level 3 on that scale is at £400. As to search of persons and forfeiture of game, guns, traps, etc see para 282 post.
3 As to who is authorised see para 272 ante.
4 The maximum penalty was formerly level 1 on the standard scale (Game Act 1831 s 32 (amended by virtue of the Criminal Justice Act 1982 ss 38, 46)) and was increased to level 4 by the Criminal Justice Act 1988 s 64. As to the standard scale see para 232 note 1 ante. At the date at which this volume states the law, level 4 on that scale is at £1,000.
5 Game Act 1831 s 32 (amended by the Wild Creatures and Forest Laws Act 1971 s 1 (4), Schedule, and as described in note 4 supra). They may be charged together or separately: *R v Littlechild* (1871) LR 6 QB 293. A defendant may be charged with aiding or abetting only: *Stacey v Whitehurst* (1865) 18 CBNS 344.

275. Defences. A person charged with the statutory offence of trespassing in the daytime in search or pursuit of game or woodcock, snipe or rabbits[1] may prove by way of defence any matter which would have been a defence to an action for the trespass[2], but the onus of proof is on him[3].

1 Ie the offence under the Game Act 1831 s 30; see paras 273, 274 ante.
2 Ibid s 30 proviso. For specific defences, see paras 276, 277 post.
3 Ibid s 42 (amended by the Statute Law Revision (No 2) Act 1888). Cf *Gleeson v Hurley* [1916] 2 IR 180.

276. Leave and licence. The leave and licence of the occupier of the land is a valid defence to a charge of trespassing in the daytime in search or pursuit of game, woodcock, snipe or rabbits[1] when the occupier is the person having the right to the game[2], but the act must be strictly within the terms of the leave or licence[3].

When, however, the right to the game has been reserved, the holder of that right is the legal occupier for the purpose of granting leave or licence to enter in search or pursuit of game, woodcock, snipe or rabbits, and the actual occupier's leave or licence provides no defence[4], since the tenant himself has no such right and can himself be convicted of trespassing in pursuit of game[5]. In the case of wastes or commons within a manor, lordship or royalty, or reputed manor, lordship or royalty, the lord or steward of the Crown of the manor, lordship or royalty is the legal occupier for this purpose[6].

1 Ie the offence under the Game Act 1831 s 30: see paras 273, 274 ante.
2 Ibid s 30. See *Pochin v Smith* (1887) 52 JP 4, DC. Leave or licence given after the fact would not condone the offence: *Morden v Porter* (1860) 7 CBNS 641 at 647 per Williams J.
3 If, therefore, a man obtains leave or licence from the occupier's wife to hunt rabbits and proceeds to course a hare, he is not within the provision: *Taylor v Jackson* (1898) 78 LT 555. Quaere, whether in any case the wife's leave is a valid defence: *Taylor v Jackson* supra.
4 Game Act 1831 s 30; *Pryce v Davies* (1872) 36 JP 214; *Morden v Porter* (1860) 7 CBNS 641. If the person to whom leave is granted by the actual occupier kills, takes or is in pursuit of game (but not woodcock, snipe or rabbits), the actual occupier himself is liable to a penalty for the pursuit and for every head of game killed or taken: Game Act 1831 s 12; see para 250 ante. When, as for instance on a parol lease of land, there is a dispute as to whether the right to game is reserved, it seems that the question is one of fact for the magistrates to decide: *R v Critchlow* (1878) 26 WR 681, DC. Where under an agreement not validly executed a person has taken the right to shoot, he cannot give valid leave to another to do so, as he has no legal right himself: *Brigstocke v Rayner* (1875) 40 JP 245.
5 *Liversedge v Whiteoak* (1893) 57 JP 692, DC. He cannot, however, be convicted for trespassing in pursuit of rabbits, since 'game' is to be understood in the strict sense of the definition of the Game Act 1831 s 2 (see para 211 ante): *Spicer v Barnard* (1859) 1 E & E 874 at 878–880. Neither the tenant nor

anyone acting under his direction is, in such case, liable to be prosecuted under the Game Act 1831 s 30 for trespass (*Spicer v Barnard* supra), so that the animals and birds mentioned in that section which are not 'game' can be killed by the tenant without risk of prosecution: *Spicer v Barnard* supra; *Padwick v King* (1859) 7 CBNS 88. For the tenant's statutory right to kill and take ground game, see para 257 ante.

6 Game Act 1831 s 30.

277. Claim of right. A person charged with trespassing in the daytime in search or pursuit of game or woodcock, snipe or rabbits[1] may also set up such a claim of right as will oust the justices' jurisdiction[2]. To have this effect the claim must be to a right relating to the land[3] made bona fide[4] and upon reasonable grounds[5]. If the claim is a bona fide claim, it is not for the justices to inquire into all the circumstances to see if it is impossible. When it is not on the face of it impossible, the justices' jurisdiction is at an end[6], but their jurisdiction is not ousted by a bona fide claim of a right which cannot exist in law, nor by a bona fide but mistaken belief on the part of the defendant that he has a right to kill the game[7].

1 Ie the offence under the Game Act 1831 s 30: see paras 273, 274 ante.
2 *R v Cridland* (1857) 7 E & B 853; cf *Cole v Miles* (1888) 57 LJMC 132; and *Morrison v Anderson* 1913 JC 114.
3 In order to succeed, the defendant must set up a title to the land in himself or in some other through whose licence or authority he was acting: *Leatt v Vine* (1861) 30 LJMC 207; *Cornwell v Sanders* (1862) 3 B & S 206. Where a boundary hedge was being beaten and the defendant was standing on land to which he had no title, he could not set up a claim of right: *Philpot v Bugler* (1890) 54 JP 646, DC. When in the course of the hearing of a summons for assault defendant gamekeepers claimed the right to take from the prosecutor a bag, the prosecutor's property, on the ground that it contained rabbits belonging to the landlord, this was not such a claim of right as would oust the justices' jurisdiction, as it did not relate to an interest in land: *White v Fox* (1880) 49 LJMC 60, DC. See also *Legg v Pardoe* (1860) 9 CBNS 289. Cf the dicta in *Andrews v Carlton* (1928) 93 JP 65, DC.
4 *White v Feast* (1872) LR 7 QB 353; *Lovesy v Stallard* (1874) 30 LT 792; *Penwarden v Palmer* (1894) 10 TLR 362, DC; *Adams v Masters* (1871) 24 LT 502.
5 The absence of mens rea is not of itself a complete defence: *Kiddle v Kayley* (1864) 10 LT 339; *Watkins v Major* (1875) LR 10 CP 662; *Birnie v Marshall* (1876) 41 JP 22, DC; and see *Morden v Porter* (1860) 7 CBNS 641; *Newcombe v Fewins* (1876) 41 JP 581, DC; *Mann v Nurse* (1901) 17 TLR 569, DC; *Dickinson v Ead* (1914) 30 TLR 496, DC.
6 *Pochin v Smith* (1887) 52 JP 4, DC; *Scott v Baring* (1895) 64 LJMC 200 at 202, DC, per Kennedy J; cf *Watkins v Smith* (1878) 38 LT 525, DC.
7 *Mussett v Burch* (1876) 35 LT 486, DC; *Hudson v MacRae* (1863) 4 B & S 585; *Leatt v Vine* (1861) 30 LJMC 207.

B. NIGHT POACHING

278. Offence of poaching by night. It is an offence, punishable on summary conviction by a fine not exceeding level 3 on the standard scale[1], to take[2] or destroy any game[3] or rabbits unlawfully by night[4] upon any land, whether open or inclosed[5], or upon any public road, highway or path, or the sides thereof, or at the openings, outlets or gates from any such land into a public road, highway or path[6], or unlawfully to enter or be upon any land, whether open or inclosed, by night with a gun, net, engine or other instrument for the purpose of taking or destroying game[7].

1 As to the standard scale see para 232 note 1 ante. At the date at which this volume states the law, level 3 on that scale is at £400.
2 'To take' means to catch, not, as in the case of theft, to take away: *R v Glover* (1814) Russ & Ry 269, CCR; *Bevan v Hopkinson* (1876) 34 LT 142, DC.

3 'Game' here includes hares, pheasants, partridges, grouse, heath or moor game, black game and bustards: Night Poaching Act 1828 s 13. It means live game the property in which is not absolute. It is not an offence under this provision to enter for the purpose of taking young pheasants from a coop: *R v Garnham* (1861) 2 F & F 347.

4 'Night' is considered to commence at the expiration of the first hour of sunset and to conclude at the beginning of the last hour before sunrise: Night Poaching Act 1828 s 12. 'Sunset' means the actual hour at which the sun sets in the particular place: *Curtis v March* (1858) 3 H & N 866; cf *Gordon v Cann* (1899) 68 LJQB 434, DC. See further, for the meanings of 'night' and 'sunset', TIME vol 45 paras 1113–1116.

5 Night Poaching Act 1828 s 1 (amended by the Criminal Law Act 1977 ss 15, 30, Sch 1, and by virtue of the Criminal Justice Act 1982 s 46). This offence and the offence of unlawfully entering or being on land (see the text to note 7 infra) are two separate offences and cannot be charged in the alternative in one count: see *R v Disney* [1933] 2 KB 138, CCA; and CRIMINAL LAW.

6 Night Poaching Act 1844 s 1.

7 Night Poaching Act 1828 s 1 (as amended: see note 5 supra). Rabbits are not here included. Waste land at the side of a highway is not 'open land' in the sense intended: *Veysey v Hoskins, Harris v Hoskins* (1865) 34 LJMC 145. In order to prove that a person is unlawfully on land at night it is not necessary to prove that he did not have leave or licence to be there: *R v Wood* (1856) Dears & B 1, CCR. As to the search of a person and the forfeiture of game, guns, traps, etc see para 282 post.

279. Arrest of night poacher. Where any person is found on any land committing an offence of night poaching[1], the owner or occupier of the land, or the lord of the manor or reputed manor in which the land is situate, and any gamekeeper or servant of any such person or any person assisting such gamekeeper or servant may seize and apprehend the offender on the land or, in case of pursuit being made, in any place to which he may have escaped from the land, and must deliver him as soon as may be into the custody of a police officer so that he may be taken before the justices[2]. A person committing an offence of night poaching on a public road, highway or path[3] may similarly be apprehended by the owner or occupier of any land adjoining either side of that part of the road, highway or path where the offender may be, or by his gamekeeper or servant or any person assisting such gamekeeper or servant[4].

A police constable who has reasonable grounds for suspecting that a person is committing an offence of night poaching on any land[5] may enter on the land for the purpose of arresting him[6].

1 Ie under the Night Poaching Act 1828 s 1: see para 278 ante.
2 Ibid s 2 (amended by the Wild Creatures and Forest Laws Act 1971 s 1 (4), Schedule): see further para 301 post.
3 Ie under the Night Poaching Act 1844 s 1: see para 278 ante.
4 Ibid s 1.
5 For the meaning of 'land', and for exceptions, see para 272 note 7 ante.
6 In accordance with the Police and Criminal Evidence Act 1984 s 25: Game Laws (Amendment) Act 1960 s 2 (1) (amended by the Police and Criminal Evidence Act 1984 s 119 (1), Sch 6 para 10).

280. Assault by night poacher. A person found poaching by night[1] who assaults or offers any violence with an offensive weapon[2] towards any person authorised to arrest him[3] is liable on summary conviction to imprisonment for up to six months or a fine not exceeding level 4 on the standard scale or both[4]. When an assault is committed by one of a party of poachers, a member of the party who did not take any part in the assault cannot be convicted of the assault unless there was a common purpose not merely to poach but also to use violence[5].

If three or more persons by night[6] unlawfully enter or are upon any land, whether open or inclosed, for the purpose of taking or destroying game or rabbits, and any of them is armed[7] with a gun, cross-bow, firearms, bludgeon or any other offensive weapon[8], each of them is liable on summary conviction to imprisonment for up to six months or a fine not exceeding level 4 on the standard scale, or both[9]. It is not essential that all the persons should actually enter the land; if all are associated for a common purpose and some enter while others remain near enough to assist, all of them may be convicted[10]. It is not necessary that all of them should be on land in the same ownership[11], but they must have a plan in common[12]. They may be convicted even though they have abandoned their arms before being arrested[13].

1 Ie an offender under the Night Poaching Act 1828 s 1, or the Night Poaching Act 1844 s 1: see para 278 ante.
2 The weapons specifically mentioned in the Night Poaching Act 1828 s 2 are those mentioned in the text to note 8 infra, and also a stick and a club.
3 As to arrest see para 279 ante.
4 Night Poaching Act 1828 s 2 (amended by the Criminal Law Act 1977 ss 15 (4) (a), 30 (3), 65, Sch 12, and by virtue of the Criminal Justice Act 1982 s 46). As to the standard scale see para 232 note 1 ante. At the date at which this volume states the law, level 4 on that scale is at £1,000. A person charged first with a count for assault under this provision, and secondly with a count for common assault, could not be convicted of a common assault on the first count after the second count had been abandoned: see *R v Day and Cox* (1870) 22 LT 452, CCR; and cf *R v Wilson* [1955] 1 All ER 744, [1955] 1 WLR 493, CCA, cited in para 272 note 3 ante.
5 *R v Pearce* (1929) 21 Cr App Rep 79, CCA. As to seizure of game see para 282 post. If, however, the trespasser assaults a person at a time or in a place (eg a highway) when or where that person is not attempting to arrest him, he is not guilty of an assault under this provision: *R v Doddridge* (1860) 8 Cox CC 335.
6 For the meaning of 'night' see para 278 note 4 ante.
7 If one of the party is armed all are deemed to be so: *R v Goodfellow* (1845) 1 Car & Kir 724, CCR; *R v Smith* (1818) Russ & Ry 368, CCR; and see *R v Andrews* (1837) 2 Mood & R 37; *R v Southern* (1821) Russ & Ry 444, CCR.
8 Large stones have been held to be offensive weapons: *R v Grice* (1837) 7 C & P 803. A stick is not necessarily an offensive weapon; whether it is so depends on the object with which it is taken out: *R v Fry and Webb* (1837) 2 Mood & R 42; cf *R v Palmer* (1831) 1 Mood & R 70; *R v Williams* (1878) 14 Cox CC 59. This may perhaps be the case even if it is in fact used offensively: *R v Merry* (1847) 2 Cox CC 240; but see *R v Sutton* (1877) 13 Cox CC 648. For the meaning of 'offensive weapon' under the Prevention of Crime Act 1953 s 1 (4), see CRIMINAL LAW vol 11 (1) (Resissue) para 167 note 6.
9 Night Poaching Act 1828 s 9 (amended by the Criminal Justice Administration Act 1962 (repealed) s 20 (2), Sch 5 Pt II, and the Criminal Law Act 1977 ss 30 (3), 65, Sch 12, and by virtue of the Criminal Justice Act 1982 s 46). As to the standard scale see para 232 note 1 ante. At the date at which this volume states the law, level 4 on that scale is at £1,000.
10 *R v Whittaker* (1848) 2 Car & Kir 636, CCR; *R v Passey* (1836) 7 C & P 282; *R v Scotton* (1844) 5 QB 493; *R v Andrews* (1837) 2 Mood & R 37. Sending in a dog to drive hares into a net set in the fence is not an entering of the land within the statute: *R v Nickless* (1839) 8 C & P 757.
11 *R v Uezzell, Eaton and Parkins* (1851) 2 Den 274, CCR.
12 *R v Nickless* (1839) 8 C & P 757. If one is in a wood separated by a high road from the land where the others are, there may not be sufficient evidence of a common plan: *R v Dowsell* (1834) 6 C & P 398.
13 *R v Nash and Weller* (1819) Russ & Ry 386.

C. PREVENTION OF POACHING: POWERS OF ARREST, SEARCH AND SEIZURE

281. Powers of arrest. Powers of arrest are given to owners and occupiers of land and their gamekeepers and servants, and to police constables, to arrest persons found poaching on land whether by day[1] or night[2].

1 See para 272 ante.
2 See para 279 ante.

282. Powers of search and seizure. A police constable may, in any highway, street or public place[1], search any person whom he has good cause to suspect of coming from land where he has been unlawfully in search or pursuit of game[2], or any person aiding or abetting him, and of having in his possession any gun, part of a gun, cartridges or other ammunition, or any nets, traps, snares or other devices of a kind used for the taking of game[3]. This right of search extends to stopping and searching any cart or other conveyance in or on which the constable suspects any such game or article is being carried[4]. He may seize and detain any such game or article found, whereupon he must issue a summons against the person concerned who, upon conviction, is liable to a fine not exceeding level 3 on the standard scale[5]. Actual search is not necessary where the presence of the incriminating thing is evident[6]. There is no right of arrest under this provision[7].

When any person is found poaching on any land, whether by day or night, any person having the right to kill game on the land, or the occupier, or the gamekeeper or servant of either of them, or any person acting by order in aid of any of those persons, may demand and, if refused, may seize any recently-killed game[8] in that person's possession for the benefit of the person entitled to the game on the land[9].

Further, when a person is apprehended by a police constable[10] for poaching offences[11], a police constable by or in whose presence he was apprehended may search him and may seize and detain any game[12] or rabbits, or any gun, part of a gun or other article[13] of a kind used for killing or taking of game or rabbits, which are found in his possession[14].

The disposal of seized articles is a matter for the court[15].

1 A public place would seem for this purpose to be any place in which the police would be in the ordinary execution of their duty: *Clarke v Crowder* (1869) LR 4 CP 638 at 641 per Bovil CJ. See also *Re Freestone* (1856) 1 H & N 93; and for the meaning of 'public place' in other statutes see CRIMINAL LAW vol 11 (1) (Reissue) paras 100, 167.

2 'Game' in this context means hares, pheasants and partridges and their eggs, woodcock, snipe, rabbits, grouse, black or moor game, and the eggs of grouse and black or moor game: Poaching Prevention Act 1862 s 1.

3 Ibid s 2 (amended by the Game Laws (Amendment) Act 1960 s 3 (2)).

4 Poaching Prevention Act 1862 s 2. See also the Code of Practice for the Exercise by Police Officers of Statutory Powers of Stop and Search, 1991, HM Stationery Office.

5 Poaching Prevention Act 1862 s 2 (amended by the Game Laws (Amendment) Act 1960 ss 3 (3), 5 (3), and by virtue of the Criminal Justice Act 1982 ss 38, 46). As to the standard scale see para 232 note 1 ante. At the date at which this volume states the law, level 3 on that scale is at £400. There are two offences with which a suspect may be charged: (1) having obtained game by having been unlawfully on land (see *Evans v Botterill* (1863) 3 B & S 787; *Brown v Turner* (1863) 13 CBNS 485; and *Fuller v Newland* (1863) 27 JP 406) in pursuit of game; and (2) having used a gun or net, etc for unlawfully taking game (whether or not it was used successfully: see *Jenkin v King* (1872) LR 7 QB 478; *Gray v Hawthorn* 1961 JC 13). Unless a person is charged with one or other of these offences or with being an accessory no offence is disclosed: *Lundy v Botham* (1877) 41 JP 774, DC; *Garman v Plaice* [1969] 1 All ER 62, [1969] 1 WLR 19, DC). The summons must be for an offence against the Poaching Prevention Act 1862 s 2, and no other: *Stowe v Benstead* [1909] 2 KB 415, DC.

6 *Hall v Knox* (1863) 4 B & S 515; *Ex p Hurst* (1863) 27 JP 824; *Lloyd v Lloyd* (1885) 14 QBD 725, DC.

7 *R v Spencer* (1863) 3 F & F 854, 857.

8 For the meaning of 'game' in this context see para 211 text to note 2 ante.

9 Game Act 1831 s 36 (amended by the Wild Creatures and Forest Laws Act 1971 s 1 (4), Schedule). See also para 286 post.

10 In accordance with the Police and Criminal Evidence Act 1984 s 25: Game Laws (Amendment) Act 1960 s 4 (1) (amended by the Police and Criminal Evidence Act 1984 s 119 (1), Sch 6 para 11).

11 Ie under the Night Poaching Act 1828 ss 1, 9, and the Game Act 1831 s 30; see paras 273, 274, 278, 280 ante.

12 'Game' in this context includes hares, pheasants, grouse, heath or moor game, black game, bustards, woodcock and snipe: Game Laws (Amendment) Act 1960 s 4 (5).

13 Ie articles as enumerated in the text to note 3 supra.

14 Game Laws (Amendment) Act 1960 s 4 (1) (as amended: see note 10 supra). This is without prejudice to any other power a police constable has to search an arrested person and to detain things found in his possession, and to the powers of gamekeepers and others to seize game from trespassers under the Game Act 1831 s 36 (see supra): Game Laws (Amendment) Act 1960 s 4 (3). No search under that Act may be an intimate search, nor a search of a person in police detention at a police station: Police and Criminal Evidence Act 1984 s 53 (1).

15 See para 286 post.

D. PROCEEDINGS; PENALTIES

283. Regulation of proceedings. The proceedings both before and at the hearing before the justices are regulated by the Magistrates' Courts Act 1980[1].

Proceedings under the Game Act 1831 must be commenced within three calendar months after the commission of the offence[2].

1 *Ryland v Wynn* (1900) 64 JP 522. See also the Magistrates' Courts Rules 1981, SI 1981/552 (as amended); and MAGISTRATES.

2 Game Act 1831 s 41. The three months must be calculated so as to exclude the day of the offence, but to include that on which the information is laid: *Radcliffe v Bartholomew* [1892] 1 QB 161. The exact date need not be specified so long as it is stated to be within the required three months' limit: cf *Onley v Gee* (1861) 7 Jur NS 570.

284. Persons to lay information. Information may be laid by anyone, whether he is interested in the land trespassed on or not[1]. Though usually made in writing it need not be so[2], but unless it is in writing and substantiated on oath a justice may not issue a warrant for arrest[3]; nor should a warrant be issued where a summons will effect the purpose[4], but if a summons is ineffectual in obtaining the defendant's presence at the hearing a warrant may be issued[5].

One information is sufficient where more than one offender is a party to the same offence[6] and the justices have a discretion as to whether the offenders shall be tried together or not; but in any case there should be a separate conviction of each of them[7]. The information must charge one offence only[8], and the conviction, if any, must be for that offence[9].

1 *Midelton v Gale* (1838) 8 Ad & El 155; *Morden v Porter* (1860) 7 CBNS 641.
2 *R v Hughes* (1879) 4 QBD 614, CCR; and see MAGISTRATES.
3 Magistrates' Courts Act 1980 s 1 (3); see MAGISTRATES.
4 *O'Brien v Brabner* (1885) 49 JP Jo 227, DC.
5 Magistrates' Courts Act 1980 s 13; see MAGISTRATES.
6 *R v Cridland* (1857) 7 E & B 853; *R v Littlechild* (1871) LR 6 QB 293; *R v Staffordshire Justices* (1858) 32 LTOS 105. This is the case whether all are principals or some principals and some aiders or abettors.
7 *R v Littlechild* (1871) LR 6 QB 293.
8 Magistrates' Courts Rules 1981, SI 1981/552, r 12; and see *R v Cridland* (1857) 7 E & B 853.
9 Cf *Martin v Pridgeon* (1859) 1 E & E 778; *R v Brickhill* (1864) 4 New Rep 166; and see MAGISTRATES.

285. Irregularity in information or summons. An irregularity in the information or summons is cured by the defendant's appearance to answer the charge[1]. Where more than one defendant is charged with the same offence under one of the Acts in respect of which a penalty is imposed on every person offending against the statute, each of them is liable to the full penalty if convicted[2]. A defendant who is

convicted may appeal to the Crown Court[3], or he may require the justices to state a
case for the opinion of the High Court upon a point of law[4].

1 *R v Hughes* (1879) 4 QBD 614. When the defendant has once appeared it may be possible to prefer
   another charge against him: *R v Hughes* supra.
2 *R v Littlechild* (1871) LR 6 QB 293.
3 Magistrates' Courts Act 1980 s 108 (1): see COURTS.
4 Ibid s 111; RSC Ord 56 rr 5, 6: see MAGISTRATES.

286. Forfeiture and disposal of seized game, guns and other articles. Where
a person is convicted of an offence relating to obtaining game by unlawfully going
on land, or using a gun or other article for unlawfully killing or taking game[1], the
court convicting him may, if it thinks fit, direct that any game, gun or other article
duly seized from that person[2] which was in his possession or which was being
carried by him in any cart or other conveyance be forfeited, whether or not the
offence of which he was convicted concerned that game, gun or article[3].

Further, where a person apprehended by a police constable[4] for a poaching
offence[5] is convicted of such an offence, the court may if it thinks fit direct that any
game[6] or rabbit, or any gun or other article, duly seized[7] on his apprehension and
which was in his possession, be forfeited, whether or not the offence of which he
was convicted concerned that game, rabbit, gun or other article[8].

Anything forfeited must be sold or otherwise disposed of in such manner as the
court may direct, the proceeds of sale being applied as if they were a fine[9].

If the person charged is not convicted the game or other thing seized, or its value,
must be restored to him[10].

A person who sells seized game under a justice's written direction is not liable to
any penalty for the sale[11].

1 Ie an offence under the Poaching Prevention Act 1862 s 2: see para 282 ante. For the meaning of
   'game' see para 282 note 2 ante, the definition being applied by the Game Laws (Amendment) Act
   1960 s 3 (5).
2 See para 282 ante.
3 Game Laws (Amendment) Act 1960 s 3 (3).
4 In accordance with the Police and Criminal Evidence Act 1984 s 25: Game Laws (Amendment) Act
   1960 s 4 (1) (amended by the Police and Criminal Evidence Act 1984 s 119 (1), Sch 6 para 11); see para
   282 ante.
5 Ie under the Night Poaching Act 1828 ss 1, 9, and the Game Act 1831 s 30.
6 For the meaning of 'game' in this context see para 282 note 12 ante.
7 Ie under the Game Laws (Amendment) Act 1960 s 4 (1) (as amended: see note 4 supra): see para 282
   ante.
8 Ibid s 4 (2).
9 Magistrates' Courts Act 1980 s 140.
10 Game Laws (Amendment) Act 1960 ss 3 (4), 4 (4). Where a conviction is quashed, the value of the
   goods to be restored is their value at the time the conviction is quashed: *Stowe v Benstead* [1909] 2 KB
   415, DC. Where a seizure of eggs which might properly have been made under the Poaching
   Prevention Act 1862 is wrongly made with a view to prosecution under the Game Act 1831, an
   action for conversion is maintainable against the person who seized the eggs: see *Stowe v Benstead*
   supra.
11 Game Laws (Amendment) Act 1960 ss 3 (4), 4 (4). See also para 314 post.

(ii) Other Criminal Offences

287. Theft of game and eggs. Animals which constitute game in its various
statutory definitions can be the subject of theft once they are reduced into pos-

session, in the same way as wild creatures generally[1]. The same rules apply to young birds unable to fly[2] and to the eggs of game birds[3]. A poacher who kills game and takes it away is not guilty of theft[4].

1 See the Theft Act 1968 s 4 (4). Generally as to theft see paras 229, 230 ante.
2 It is submitted that the statutory provisions have not altered the situation under the common law in this regard; see *R v Shickle* (1868) LR 1 CCR 158.
3 See note 2 supra; and *R v Stride and Millard* [1908] 1 KB 617, CCR. As to the protection of wild birds and their eggs see para 332 et seq post.
4 See the Theft Act 1968 s 4 (4).

288. Use of spring guns and man traps. An owner of rights over game is not entitled to set or place, or cause to be set or placed, any spring gun, man trap or other engine[1] calculated to destroy human life or inflict grievous bodily harm, with intent that it shall, or whereby it may, destroy or inflict grievous bodily harm upon a trespasser or other person who may come in contact with it[2]; and if he knowingly and wilfully permits any such engine which may have been set or placed in any place in his possession or occupation by some other person to continue to be so set or placed, he is deemed to have set or placed it with the above-mentioned intent[3].

1 This does not include a pair of electrified wires: see *R v Munks* [1964] 1 QB 304, [1963] 3 All ER 757, CCA.
2 Offences against the Person Act 1861 s 31. To do so is an offence punishable with imprisonment for not more than five years: s 31 (amended by virtue of the Penal Servitude Act 1891 s 1 and the Criminal Justice Act 1948 s 1 (1), (2)).
3 Offences against the Person Act 1861 s 31. An action for damages will lie at the suit of anyone injured by such devices: *Bird v Holbrook* (1828) 4 Bing 628. Aliter where the plaintiff was a trespasser and knew of their existence: *Ilott v Wilkes* (1820) 3 B & Ald 304.

(4) CLOSE DAYS AND SEASONS FOR GAME

289. Sundays and Christmas Day. It is an offence to kill or take any game[1] on a Sunday or Christmas Day, or to use for that purpose any dog, gun, net or other engine or instrument[2]. It is not an essential ingredient of the offence that the instrument should be set on a Sunday or Christmas Day; a person setting an instrument for the purpose of killing or taking game is using it for that purpose so long as it remains set[3]. The offender is liable on conviction before two justices of the peace to a penalty not exceeding level 1 on the standard scale[4] for every such offence[5].

1 Ie game under the Game Act 1831: see para 211 ante.
2 Ibid s 3. The term engine (derived from *ingenium*) includes a snare, which is a device or contrivance (an engine) for killing game: *Allen v Thompson* (1870) LR 5 QB 336 at 339 per Blackburn J. The offence may be committed by two or more persons who may be out together, and though only one gun was employed they may be separately convicted of the offence: *R v Littlechild* (1871) LR 6 QB 293.
3 *Allen v Thompson* (1870) LR 5 QB 336.
4 As to the standard scale see para 232 note 1 ante. At the date at which this volume states the law, level 1 on that scale is at £50.
5 Game Act 1831 s 3 (amended by virtue of the Criminal Justice Act 1982 ss 38, 46 and by the Statute Law (Repeals) Act 1989 Sch 1 Pt I).

290. Close season. The close season, namely, that part of the year during which the killing or taking[1] of game is forbidden, varies in different cases.

Thus, grouse or red game may not be killed or taken between 10 December and 12 August; black game between 10 December and 20 August or, in Somerset, Devon and the New Forest, 1 September; partridges between 1 February and 1 September; and pheasants between 1 February and 1 October[2]. The penalty for killing or taking any of these kinds of game in the prohibited period is a fine not exceeding level 1 on the standard scale[3] for every head of game killed or taken[4]. These restrictions do not, however, operate in cases where the Minister of Agriculture, Fisheries and Food has imposed a requirement that game be killed or destroyed for the purpose of preventing damage to crops, pasture, foodstuffs, livestock, trees, hedges, banks or any works on land[5].

1 'Taking' means catching, as eg in a snare, with a view to keeping or killing: *R v Glover* (1814) Russ & Ry 269, CCR; *Watkins v Price* (1877) 47 LJMC 1, DC. As to the computation of periods of time within which certain acts may or may not be done see TIME vol 45 para 1127 et seq.
2 Game Act 1831 s 3. The days mentioned in each case are not within the prohibited period, and it is therefore not unlawful to kill or take game on either the first or the last day of the period. The section also provides that bustard may not be killed or taken between 1 March and 1 September, but they are now covered by the Wildlife and Countryside Act 1981 s 1 (1): see para 332 post.
3 As to the standard scale see para 232 note 1 ante. At the date at which this volume states the law, level 1 on the that scale is at £50.
4 Game Act 1831 s 3 (amended by the Game Act 1970 s 1 (1) (a) and the Statute Law (Repeals) Act 1989 Sch 1 Pt I, and by virtue of the Criminal Justice Act 1982 ss 38, 46).
5 See the Agriculture Act 1947 s 98 (1), (2), the Transfer of Functions (Ministry of Food) Order 1955, SI 1955/554; and AGRICULTURE vol 1 (2) (Reissue) para 654.

291. Restrictions on purchase and sale. The protection afforded by the foregoing restrictions on killing or taking[1] is supplemented by further restrictions upon the purchase or sale of game birds during close seasons, restrictions which differ according to whether the person concerned is or is not the holder of a dealer's licence granted by the local authority.

The holder of a dealer's licence[2] may not after the expiration of ten days[3] from the day on which it became unlawful to kill such a bird buy or sell any bird of game[4], whether dead or alive[5], wild or tame[6], other than foreign game imported dead[7] or live birds for rearing or exhibition purposes or for sale alive[8]. Exactly the same restrictions apply to any person not holding a dealer's licence, including the permitted exception in respect of live birds, save that he cannot lawfully sell them to a licensed dealer unless he is in possession of a game licence[9].

A contravention of these provisions renders the offender liable on conviction before two justices to a fine not exceeding level 1 on the standard scale[10] for every head of game the subject of the offence[11].

1 See paras 289, 290 ante.
2 See paras 313–319 post.
3 The ten days must be calculated by including either the last day of the open season or the day of purchase or sale, but not both: Game Act 1831 s 4.
4 This expression is used so as to exclude hares, for which there is no close season: see para 292 post.
5 *Loome v Baily* (1860) 3 E & E 444; *Cook v Trevener* [1911] 1 KB 9, DC.
6 *Harnett v Miles* (1844) 48 JP 455, DC; *Cook v Trevener* [1911] 1 KB 9, DC.
7 *Guyer v R* (1889) 23 QBD 100, DC.
8 Game Act 1831 s 4 (amended by the Game Act 1970 s 1 (1) (c), (d)).
9 Game Act 1831 ss 4, 17 (s 4 as amended: see note 8 supra); Game Licences Act 1860 s 13 proviso. As to game licences see paras 306–312 post.
10 As to the standard scale see para 232 note 1 ante. At the date at which this volume states the law, level 1 on the standard scale is at £50.
11 Game Act 1831 s 4 (amended by the Game Act 1970 s 1 (1) (b) and the Statute Law (Repeals) Act 1989 Sch 1 Pt I, and by virtue of the Criminal Justice Act 1982 ss 38, 46).

292. Close season for hares and rabbits. There is no general close season for killing or taking hares, but during the months of March, April, May, June and July the sale or exposure for sale of hares (other than foreign hares imported into this country) and of leverets is prohibited and is punishable on summary conviction with a penalty of level 1 on the standard scale including the costs of the conviction[1]; and the right of killing and taking hares and rabbits conferred by the Ground Game Acts[2] does not, in the case of the occupier of moorlands and uninclosed non-arable lands (other than detached portions of such lands, less than 25 acres in extent, adjoining arable lands), and of persons authorised by him, extend to (1) killing or taking them between 1 April and 31 August (both inclusive)[3], or (2) killing them by the use of firearms between 1 September and 10 December (both inclusive)[4]. Save as aforesaid there is no close season for rabbits.

1 Hares Preservation Act 1892 ss 2–4 (amended by virtue of the Criminal Justice Act 1982 s 46). The sale of game birds during close season is also prohibited: see para 291 ante. As to close seasons in respect of deer see para 323 post. As to the standard scale see para 232 note 1 ante. At the date at which this volume states the law, level 1 on that scale is at £50.
2 Ie the Ground Game Act 1880 and the Ground Game (Amendment) Act 1906; see para 257 ante.
3 Ground Game Act 1880 ss 1 (3), 8.
4 Ground Game (Amendment) Act 1906 s 2.

(5) GAMEKEEPERS

(i) Appointment

293. Appointment of gamekeepers. Gamekeepers are engaged in the same manner and on the same terms as to notice and the like by ordinary employers as any other servants[1].

1 If the gamekeeper occupies a cottage as such, he may be required to leave the cottage at the time he leaves his employer's service without further notice: *Bertie v Beaumont* (1812) 16 East 33; *White v Bayley* (1861) 10 CBNS 227; and see LANDLORD AND TENANT, where the distinction between a lease and a mere licence to occupy premises is discussed. As to the general relations of master and servant see EMPLOYMENT.

294. Gamekeepers in manors. In a manor, lordship or royalty, or reputed manor, lordship or royalty[1], the lord or, in the case of a manor, lordship or royalty belonging to the Crown, the steward thereof, may by deed or, in the case of a body corporate, by writing under its seal, appoint[2] one or more persons to act as gamekeeper[3] to preserve or kill the game[4] within its limits for the use of the lord or steward[5], with authority to seize for such use dogs, nets and other engines and instruments for killing or taking game[6] used by unlicensed persons within its limits.

Moreover, the lord or steward may appoint and depute any person, whether or not acting as gamekeeper to any other person or retained and paid for as the male servant of any other person, to be a gamekeeper for the manor, lordship or royalty or for such division or district thereof as he may think fit, and may authorise him to kill game for the use of the gamekeeper or of any other person specified in the appointment or deputation and to exercise all the powers of a gamekeeper of a manor[7]. A gamekeeper so authorised to kill game for the use of any person other than the lord or steward must not be entered or paid for as the gamekeeper or male servant of the lord or steward[8].

1 A wapentake or hundred, the lord of which cannot 'appoint', is not included: *Earl of Ailesbury v Pattison* (1778) 1 Doug KB 28. Reputed manors are manors the existence of which can be proved only by evidence of reputation: see COPYHOLDS. The general statutory enfranchisement of copyhold land did not affect the rights of the lord of manor in respect of taking game: see COPYHOLDS.
2 The right of appointment is inseparable from the lordship of the manor, so that it cannot be granted to another: *Calcraft v Gibbs* (1792) 5 Term Rep 19. Where the manor is part of a trust estate, the trustee may appoint a gamekeeper for the purpose of preserving the game in the interest of the estate, but not in his own interest: *Webb v Earl of Shaftesbury, Earl of Shaftesbury v Arrowsmith* (1802) 7 Ves 480 at 488.
3 If the gamekeeper's right is challenged it is sufficient for him to prove that the lord has a colourable title to the manor (*Hunt v Andrews* (1820) 3 B & Ald 341), but in the absence or disproof of even a colourable title mere good faith on the part of the gamekeeper is insufficient to protect him (*Calcraft v Gibbs* (1792) 5 Term Rep 19).
4 For the meaning of 'game' see para 211 ante.
5 Unless the contrary is proved it will be assumed that the game killed by the gamekeeper is for the use of the lord: *Spurrier v Vale* (1809) 10 East 413.
6 Game Act 1831 s 13; Law of Property (Miscellaneous Provisions) Act 1989 s 1.
7 Game Act 1831 s 14.
8 Ibid s 14.

295. Gamekeepers in Wales. In Wales an owner of land of the clear annual value of £500 which is not within the bounds of any manor, lordship or royalty, or which, if within such bounds, has been enfranchised or alienated therefrom, is entitled, by deed, to appoint a gamekeeper or gamekeepers to preserve or kill game on his lands[1]. He may also, with the written permission of any other owner of similar lands in Wales, extend the authority of his gamekeeper to preserve or kill the game on those lands[2].

1 Game Act 1831 s 15; Law of Property (Miscellaneous Provisions) Act 1989 s 1.
2 Game Act 1831 s 15. The £500 limit is not expressed by s 15 to apply to such lands.

296. Registration. Appointments and deputations of gamekeepers are not valid until registered with the clerk of the county council wherein the manors, lordships or royalties to which they relate are situated[1]. After registration the appointment or deputation continues in force until the date named therein for its expiration or until revocation by dismissal or otherwise[2].

1 Game Act 1831 s 16 (amended by virtue of the Courts Act 1971 s 56 (1), Sch 8 Pt I para 1 (1) (b), (2), (4) and the Local Government Act 1922 s 1 (10)): see *Rushworth v Craven* (1825) M'Cle & Yo 417; *Bush v Green* (1837) 4 Bing NC 41. Stamp duty on appointments or deputations of gamekeepers was abolished by the Finance Act 1949 s 35 (1), Sch 8 Pt I.
2 Game Act 1831 s 16. 'Otherwise' includes the death of the grantor, after which a new appointment or deputation must be made by his successor. Where, however, a gamekeeper, after the death of the person appointing him, continued to be employed by that person's successors, employment of a watcher by him has been considered sufficient authority to the watcher to arrest night poachers: *R v Fielding and Corbett* (1848) 2 Car & Kir 621.

(ii) Powers of Gamekeepers

297. Need to hold game licence. A gamekeeper who is required to kill game[1] must either take out a game licence himself or his employer must take one out for him[2]. Without a game licence a gamekeeper may assist his employer in killing game if his employer has a game licence[3].

In manors or royalties the lord who grants the gamekeeper his appointment or deputation[4] may take out a licence for him[5]. Elsewhere the employer, who must, however, be a person having the right to kill game on lands in England, Wales or Scotland, may do so[6].

Such a licence may be obtained by the lord or employer in the same manner as he would obtain a game licence for himself[7], and he must make a declaration in the approved form to the issuing officer[8]. It is an annual licence expiring on 31 July, and the duty payable is £4[9]. Should the employee in respect of whom it was taken out leave his employer's service before the date the licence expires it is available for his successor up to that date without payment of further duty[10].

This licence, however, is strictly local in its character, and it does not entitle the gamekeeper to kill game on any land on which his employer has no right to do so[11].

1 'Game' includes woodcock, snipe, rabbits and deer: see para 211 ante.
2 Game Licences Act 1860 ss 2, 4 (amended by the Finance Act 1937 s 5, Sch 2 (which Act repealed the male servants' licence duty) and the Protection of Birds Act 1954 s 15 (2), Sch 6).
3 Game Licences Act 1860 s 5 Exemption 3. As to game licences see paras 306–312 post.
4 See para 294 ante.
5 Game Licences Act 1860 s 7 (amended by the Finance Act 1937 Sch 2).
6 Game Licences Act 1860 s 2 proviso (amended by the Finance Act 1937 Sch 2); Wales and Berwick Act 1746 (repealed) s 3. Note, however, that a reference to England in any Act passed since the Welsh Language Act 1967 (27 July 1967) does not include a reference to Wales: Interpretation Act 1978 s 22, Sch 2 Pt I.
7 As to the grant, issue and form of game licences see para 309 post.
8 Game Licences Act 1860 s 2; Finance Act 1937 s 5 (2), Sch 2.
9 Game Licences Act 1860 ss 2 proviso, 7; Customs and Inland Revenue Act 1883 s 4; Fees for Game and Other Licences (Variation) Order 1968, SI 1968/120.
10 Game Licences Act 1860 s 8 (amended by the Finance Act 1937 Sch 2). The issuing authority must indorse on the licence the name and address of the successor and declare the licence to be a renewed licence free of duty: Game Licences Act 1860 s 8.
11 Ibid s 9. Elsewhere he may only assist his employer to kill game if his employer has a game licence: s 5 Exemption 3. If he kills or takes game (within the meaning of the Game Act 1831: see para 211 ante) or uses a gun, dog, net or other engine or instrument for that purpose elsewhere, he is liable to the same penalty to which he would have been liable had he no licence at all (Game Act 1831 s 6), namely level 1 on the standard scale: s 23 (amended by the Statute Law (Repeals) Act 1989 Sch 1 Pt I and by virtue of the Criminal Justice Act 1982 s 46). As to the standard scale see para 232 note 1 ante. At the date at which this volume states the law, level 1 on that scale is at £50. This penalty is in addition to the revenue penalty of £20 (Game Licences Act 1860 s 4): see para 306 post. Should he kill or take elsewhere not game within the meaning of the 1831 Act, but woodcock, snipe, rabbits or deer (which are not game within that meaning), he is liable to the revenue penalty only.

298. Power to sell game. A game licence does not enable the gamekeeper to sell game except on the account and with the written authority of his employer[1]. In order to be able to sell game without these restrictions the gamekeeper must hold an annual licence to kill game, the duty payable on which is £6[2].

1 See the Game Act 1831 s 17 proviso. Game for the purposes of this Act includes only hares, pheasants, partridges, grouse, heath or moor game and black game: see para 211 ante. Thus the gamekeeper does not require a licence to enable him to sell eg woodcock or rabbits.
2 Game Licences Act 1860 ss 6, 13 (amended by the Fees for Game and Other Licences (Variation) Order 1968, SI 1968/120): see para 309 post.

299. Power to demand licence. A gamekeeper who has a licence to kill game[1] has the right to call upon any person whom he may find anywhere doing an act for which such a licence is required to produce his licence to be read and, if required, copied[2], but if a gamekeeper himself has no such licence his right to call upon any other person to produce one is confined to such persons as he may find doing an act for which a licence is required upon the lands on which his employer has the right to the game[3].

1 For the meaning of 'game' see para 211 ante.
2 Game Licences Act 1860 s 10. As to what acts require a game licence see para 306 post. If the licence is not produced on demand the gamekeeper may call for the trespasser's name and address and the place the licence was issued; a refusal to give these or to allow the licence to be read and copied renders the offender liable to a penalty: see para 311 post.
3 Game Licences Act 1860 s 10.

300. Powers as to daytime poaching. If a gamekeeper, whether or not he is himself licensed, finds anyone trespassing in the daytime[1] upon land on which his employer has the right to the game in search or pursuit of game[2] or woodcock, snipe or rabbits, he may require the trespasser forthwith to quit the land and also to state his Christian name, surname and place of abode[3]. Should the trespasser refuse to state his real name or place of abode, or give such a general description of the latter as to be illusory for the purpose of discovery, or wilfully continue or return upon the land, the gamekeeper, or anyone acting by his order and in his aid, may apprehend him and convey him or cause him to be conveyed as soon as conveniently may be before a justice of the peace[4].

If the gamekeeper finds five or more persons so trespassing together, one or more of them being armed with a gun, and any of them by violence, intimidation or menace prevent or endeavour to prevent his approach for the purpose of ordering them to quit or to state their names or places of abode, those so offending are liable to an additional penalty[5].

1 For the meaning of 'daytime' see para 272 note 1 ante.
2 For the meaning of 'game' in this context see para 211 ante.
3 Game Act 1831 s 31 (amended by the Protection of Birds Act 1954 s 15 (2), Sch 6 and the Wild Creatures and Forest Laws Act 1971 s 1 (4), Schedule). For acts which cannot be challenged see the Game Act 1831 s 35; and para 273 ante. As to powers in the case of manors, etc see para 304 post. The employer's other servants have the same powers as his gamekeeper: Game Act 1831 s 31; see para 272 ante.
4 Ibid s 31 (amended by the Wild Creatures and Forest Laws Act 1971 s 1 (4), Schedule); see further para 272 note 3 ante.
5 Game Act 1831 s 32 (amended by the Wild Creatures and Forest Laws Act 1971 s 1 (4), Schedule); see para 274 ante.

301. Powers as to night poaching. A gamekeeper has the following powers of arrest at night[1], but only on land of which his employer is either lord of the manor, owner, or occupier[2].

If he or any of his assistants finds upon such land, whether open or inclosed, or upon any part of any public road, highway, or path or the sides thereof, or at the openings, outlets, or gates from the land into any such road, highway, or path, any person unlawfully taking or destroying game[3] or rabbits, he may seize and arrest him there, or in case of pursuit in any place to which he may have escaped therefrom, and deliver him as soon as may be to a policeman, with a view to his being brought before two justices of the peace[4].

A gamekeeper has the same right of arrest on the spot or after pursuit if he finds anyone either actually on or entering on such land with a gun, net, engine or other instrument for the purpose of taking or destroying game[5]. Rabbits are not here comprised in the term 'game', but the gamekeeper or his assistants may arrest offenders actually on or entering on such land, whether with or without nets, engines or other instruments, for the purpose of destroying game or rabbits, if the offenders are three or more in number and any one of them is armed with an offensive weapon[6].

Gamekeepers whose employers are neither owners nor occupiers, but merely have shooting rights, have no such right of arrest[7].

1 For the meaning of 'night' see para 278 note 4 ante.
2 Night Poaching Act 1828 s 2 (amended by the Wild Creatures and Forest Laws Act 1971 s 1 (4), Schedule); Night Poaching Act 1844 s 1. Any other servant of the employer has the same rights: Night Poaching Act 1828 s 2 (as so amended); Night Poaching Act 1844 s 1. A gamekeeper who is appointed by an agent who was himself appointed by the lord of the manor has sufficient authority from the lord to arrest night poachers: *R v King* (1884) 48 JP 149.
3 For the meaning of 'game' see para 278 note 3 ante.
4 Night Poaching Act 1828 ss 1, 2 (as amended: see note 2 supra); Night Poaching Act 1844 s 1. The keeper must not wait on the highway for poachers to emerge thereon from his employer's lands on which they have been poaching, although he may pursue them from the land and then arrest them anywhere: *R v Meadham and Haines* (1848) 2 Car & Kir 633. Notice that he intends to arrest the offenders is not required, nor is the employer's written authority: *R v Payne, Russell and Everett* (1833) 1 Mood CC 378; *R v Price* (1835) 7 C & P 178.
5 Night Poaching Act 1828 ss 1, 2 (as amended: see note 2 supra). Snares and nets etc are ejusdem generis: *Allen v Thompson* (1870) LR 5 QB 336.
6 Being or entering on land in these circumstances is an offence under the Night Poaching Act 1828 s 9. Though no power of arrest is expressly mentioned in that section it is to be implied, as the offence is merely an aggravation of that under s 1: *R v Ball* (1832) 1 Mood CC 330. As to what is an offensive weapon see para 280 note 8 ante.
7 *R v Addis* (1834) 6 C & P 388; *R v Price* (1951) 15 JP 149; and see *R v Wood* (1859) 1 F & F 470.

302. Other powers of arrest. Except in the cases and within the limits dealt with in the preceding paragraphs[1] a gamekeeper has no special powers of arrest. Outside the limits of his employer's ground a gamekeeper may arrest only with the authority of the owner or gamekeeper of the land on which the offender is found, unless he has pursued the offender from his own employer's ground[2], but he has the right, in common with everyone else, of arresting anyone who is in the act of committing an arrestable offence[3] (or anyone whom he has reasonable grounds for suspecting to be committing such an offence), and anyone who is guilty of the offence (or anyone whom he has reasonable grounds for suspecting to be guilty of it) where an arrestable offence has been committed[4]. Additionally a gamekeeper (again, like everyone else) may arrest a person for a breach of the peace committed in his presence, or where he reasonably believes such a breach will be committed in the immediate future, or where a breach has been committed and it is reasonably believed a renewal is threatened[5].

1 See paras 300, 301 ante.
2 *R v Davis* (1837) 7 C & P 785.
3 'Arrestable offence' is defined in the Police and Criminal Evidence Act 1984 s 24 (1); see CRIMINAL LAW vol 11 (1) (Reissue) para 703.
4 Ibid s 24.
5 *Lavin v Albert* [1982] AC 546, [1981] 3 All ER 878, HL; *R v Howell* [1982] QB 416, [1981] 3 All ER 383; Police and Criminal Evidence Act 1984 s 25 (6).

303. Right to protect employer's property. A gamekeeper is entitled to take such steps as are necessary to protect his employer's property, and to this end, when that property is threatened by a real and imminent danger, may take reasonable steps to protect it, even if it transpires that in the event those steps were not necessary[1].

1 See *Cope v Sharpe (No 2)* [1912] 1 KB 496, CA, where a gamekeeper employed by a shooting tenant was held justified in burning strips of heather on the landlord's land to arrest a fire threatening game to which the tenant was entitled. The fire was put out before it reached the burnt strip.

304. Power to seize instruments. Gamekeepers appointed[1] by a lord or steward of a manor, and expressly authorised by him to do so, may seize for the use of the lord or steward any dogs, nets and other engines[2] and instruments for the taking or killing of game[3] which are being used within the limits of the manor by a person who has no licence to kill game[4].

1 As to the persons who may appoint a gamekeeper see paras 294, 295 ante.
2 'Other engines' includes snares (*Allen v Thompson* (1870) LR 5 QB 336), but not guns, which are purposely omitted (*Daddle v Hickton* (1868) 17 LT 549). Cf the Game Act 1831 s 3, where 'gun' appears between 'dog' and 'net'.
3 'Game' here includes only those within the definition in the Game Act 1831 (see para 211 ante), and not those other animals and birds for the taking or killing of which a licence is required.
4 Game Act 1831 s 13. The dog, net, etc must be in actual use at the time: *Wingfield v Stratford and Osman* (1752) 1 Wils 315; *Robers v Carter* (1768) 2 Wils 387; *R v Gardner* (1738) 2 Stra 1098. As to the seizing of guns by a constable under the Poaching Prevention Act 1862 see para 282 ante: cf *Protheroe v Mathews* (1833) 5 C & P 581. The articles seized may be kept, and if a dog is seized it may perhaps be killed (*Kingsnorth v Bretton* (1814) 5 Taunt 416; and see *Roy v Duke of Beaufort* (1741) 2 Atk 190), but this measure should not be resorted to unless it is necessary for the preservation of game then being pursued (*Vere v Earl Cawdor and King* (1809) 11 East 568). The dog of the keeper of a neighbouring manor cannot be seized: *Rogers v Carter* supra. These powers given to gamekeepers on a manor must be exercised, if not by themselves, by someone acting immediately on a particular order: *Bird v Dale* (1817) 7 Taunt 560. As to the recovery by force of a wrongfully-seized instrument see *Whatford v Carty* (1960) Times, 29 October, DC.

305. Killing of gamekeepers. The principles relating to the offence committed where officers of justice are killed as the result of intentional forcible opposition to them in the discharge of their duties apply where gamekeepers are killed in the discharge of their statutory powers of arrest[1].

1 For the principles referred to see CRIMINAL LAW. See also the following cases concerning the unlawful killing of gamekeepers: *R v Whithorne* (1828) 3 C & P 394; *R v Ball* (1832) 1 Mood CC 330; *R v Warner* (1833) 1 Mood CC 380; *R v Wesley* (1859) 1 F & F 528.

(6) GAME LICENCES

(i) Need for, and Grant of, Licences

306. Game licences. As a general rule[1], a person must hold a game licence[2] before he can take or kill game, whether by shooting or in any other manner. The obligation is created by the Game Act 1831 and the Game Licences Act 1860. The two statutes differ in their scope and in the penalties for their contravention. The same act may constitute an offence under both statutes, and subject the offender to the two separate penalties provided thereby[3].

Under the Game Act 1831 the offence consists in taking[4] or killing any game as therein defined[5], or using any dog, gun, net or other engine or instrument for the purpose of searching for or killing or taking such game without a licence[6]. It is punishable upon conviction before two justices of the peace by a fine not exceeding level 1 on the standard scale[7]. The information may be laid by anyone[8], but must be laid within three calendar months of the commission of the offence[9]; and it may be laid before, and the summons may be issued by, one justice[10].

The Game Licences Act 1860 prohibits the taking, killing or pursuing[11], or aiding or assisting in any manner in the taking, killing or pursuing, by any means whatever, or using any dog, gun, net or other engine for the purpose of taking, killing or pursuing, either game as defined in the Game Act 1831[12], or any woodcock, snipe, rabbit or deer, without a licence[13]. The sanction is an excise penalty of level 2 on the standard scale[14] recoverable summarily[15].

1 For exceptions and exemptions see para 308 post.
2 The term 'game certificate' in the Hares Act 1848 and the Game Act 1831 is to be construed as meaning the game licence (ie licence to kill game) required under the Game Licences Act 1860: s 6. The obtaining of a firearm certificate under the Firearms Act 1968 does not relieve a person of the obligation to take out a game licence: s 58 (5). As to that Act see CRIMINAL LAW; POLICE.
3 See the Game Act 1831 s 23 and the Game Licences Act 1860 s 4, and cf *Clark v Westaway* [1927] 2 KB 597, DC.
4 The taking of game out of a trap in which it has been accidentally caught with a view to killing or keeping it is a taking for which a licence must be held: *Watkins v Price* (1877) 47 LJMC 1, DC.
5 Ie hares, pheasants, partridges, grouse, heath or moor game and black game: see para 211 ante.
6 Game Act 1831 s 23. A person may be convicted under this section although he has already been acquitted, for lack of corroboration, on a charge of trespass in pursuit of game: *Bollard v Spring* (1887) 51 JP 501. To kill and take and to use a dog, gun, etc are separate offences, but an offender who kills game with a gun cannot be convicted of more than one of the offences on the same occasion (cf *Laxton v Jeffries* (1893) 58 JP 318, DC), although proof of either act involves liability to the penalty imposed for killing game without a licence: *Hebden v Henty* (1819) 1 Chit 607; *Hunter v Clark* (1902) 66 JP 247, DC). It seems that the killing of game with a gun more than once on the same day does not amount to more than one offence: *R v Mathews* (1711) 10 Mod Rep 26; *R v Lovet* (1797) 7 Term Rep 152; but quaere if a different means of killing or taking were employed or the game were killed in different places. If an unlicensed person kills game by accident he is liable to the penalty if he carries it away: *Molton v Cheeseley* (1788) 1 Esp 123. If a man courses a hare with greyhounds, though not at a recognised meeting, and picks it up, he does not incur the penalty: *Dolby v Halmshaw* [1937] 1 KB 196, [1936] 3 All ER 229, DC.
7 Game Act 1831 s 23 (amended by virtue of the Criminal Justice Act 1982 s 46 and by the Statute Law (Repeals) Act 1989 Sch 1 Pt I). As to the standard scale see para 232 note 1 ante. At the date at which this volume states the law, level 1 on that scale is at £50.
8 *Midelton v Gale* (1838) 8 Ad & El 155; *Morden v Porter* (1860) 7 CBNS 641.
9 Game Act 1831 s 41.
10 Magistrates' Court Act 1980 s 1 (1). As to the procedure before justices see MAGISTRATES.
11 To take, kill and pursue constitutes one offence: *Laxton v Jeffries* (1893) 58 JP 318, DC; see note 6 supra.
12 See note 5 supra.
13 Game Licences Act 1860 s 4 (amended by the Protection of Birds Act 1954 s 15 (2), Sch 6).
14 As to the standard scale see para 232 note 1 ante. At the date at which this volume states the law, level 2 on that scale is at £100.
15 Game Licences Act 1860 ss 3, 4 (amended by the Customs and Excise Act 1952 s 320, Sch 12 (repealed) and by virtue of the Criminal Justice Act 1982 s 46). As to the exercise of customs and excise functions see paras 305, 315 post; the Customs and Excise Management Act 1979 (and s 176 thereof as to the exclusion of functions); and CUSTOMS AND EXCISE.

307. Effect of Game Acts. The effect of the two enactments[1] is therefore to make it a punishable offence to take or kill or attempt[2] to take or kill any of the animals named in them either with or without a dog, gun, net or other engine without a licence; but while the penalties sanctioned by either or both of these Acts may be enforced against an offender in the case of game as defined in the Game Act

1831[3], only those contained in the Game Licences Act 1860 can be enforced against an offender in the case of woodcock, snipe, rabbits or deer[4]. The latter Act requires a licence to be taken out by any person aiding or assisting in any manner in the taking, killing or pursuing by any means whatever of the birds or animals therein mentioned[5], but this provision is subject to certain specified exemptions[6].

1 See para 306 note 3 ante.
2 To walk about with a dog or gun on land where there is game, or to point a gun at game, is evidence of commission of an offence: *R v Davis* (1795) 6 Term Rep 177; *Hebden v Hentey* (1819) 1 Chit 607; cf *Assessed Tax Appeal Cases (No 2189) (1850), (No 2292) (1852), (Nos 2505–2507) (1857), (No 2523) (1859), (No 2561) (1860)*. Where several persons, none of whom has a licence to kill game, fire at the same bird, all commit an offence, although it is impossible to identify the person who killed the bird: *Hunter v Clark* (1902) 66 JP 247, DC.
3 See para 211 ante.
4 See para 306 text and note 13 ante.
5 Game Licences Act 1860 s 4 (amended by the Protection of Birds Act 1954 s 15 (2), Sch 6): see para 306 ante.
6 See para 308 post.

308. Exemptions. Members of the royal family, and gamekeepers appointed on behalf of the Crown by the Crown Estate Commissioners[1] under the authority of any Act of Parliament relating to the land revenues of the Crown, do not require a game licence in any case[2].

The following persons do not require a game licence for the limited purpose specified in each case:

(1) persons merely aiding or assisting in the taking or killing of any game, woodcock, snipe, rabbit or deer, when in the company or presence and for the use of another duly licensed person who is by virtue of that licence then and there using his own dog, gun, net or other engine for the purpose, and who is not acting therein by virtue of any deputation or appointment[3];

(2) persons authorised under the Hares Act 1848 to kill hares upon land to which such authority extends[4];

(3) the occupier and persons duly authorised by him for the purpose of killing hares and rabbits on land in his occupation[5];

(4) the proprietor of any warren or of any inclosed ground whatever, or the tenant of lands or persons directed or permitted by him to take and destroy rabbits thereon[6];

(5) the owner or occupier of inclosed lands and persons directed or permitted by him to take and kill deer thereon[7];

(6) persons taking woodcock and snipe with nets or springes[8], or pursuing and killing hares, whether by coursing with greyhounds or by hunting with beagles or other hounds[9], or pursuing and killing deer by hunting with hounds[10].

1 For the transfer of functions from the Commissioners of Woods, see the Forestry (Title of Commissioner of Woods) Order 1924, SR & O 1924/1370, the Crown Estate Act 1956 s 1 (repealed), and the Crown Estate Act 1961 s 1 (1).
2 Game Licences Act 1860 s 5, Exemptions 1, 2.
3 Ibid s 5, Exemption 3 (amended by the Protection of Birds Act 1954 s 15 (2), Sch 6), the effect of which is to exempt beaters, loaders and other assistants from the necessity of being licensed, provided they do not assist a gamekeeper who holds his position by deputation or appointment; nor must they use or lend their own dogs, carry or use their own guns or fire their employers' guns: cf *Ex p Sylvester* (1829) 9 B & C 61.
4 Game Licences Act 1860 s 5, Exemption 4. The persons authorised are any person in actual occupation of any inclosed lands, any owner thereof with the right to kill game thereon, or any

person directed or authorised by such occupier or owner in writing: Hares Act 1848 s 1, Schedule. Such authority must not be given to more than one person at a time; the authority, or a copy, must be delivered to the magistrates' clerk, who must register it and give notice if it is revoked; unless revoked it remains good until after 1 February in the year following that in which it was granted: s 2, which is in practice obsolete in view of the Ground Game Acts.

5 Ground Game Act 1880 s 4 (amended by the Local Government Act 1966 s 43 (2) (a), Sch 6 Pt I).

6 Game Licences Act 1860 s 5, Exception 2. A warren, unlike a forest or chase, is an incorporeal hereditament, and rights over it may be held by one who is not the owner of the soil. A shooting tenant who has rented the warren may thus claim to be entitled by this provision to shoot without a licence: cf *Assessed Tax Appeal Case (No 257) (1828)*; *Earl of Beauchamp v Winn* (1873) LR 6 HL 223. The wording of the exception takes the form: 'the taking . . . of conies [ie rabbits] . . . by the proprietor . . . or by the tenant . . ., either by himself or by his direction or permission': it is perhaps doubtful whether the last phrase means persons directed or permitted (1) either by the proprietor or the tenant, or (2) by the tenant only; because the phrase is in close conjunction with the term 'tenant' the probability is that it means persons directed or permitted by the tenant only.

7 Game Licences Act 1860 s 5, Exception 5. Here the persons directed or permitted to take and kill are those directed or permitted by the owner or occupier, to whichever of the two the right to take or kill the deer on the inclosed land may belong.

8 Ibid s 5, Exception 1. A springe is a snare for catching small game.

9 Ibid s 5, Exception 3. Coursing is not confined to organised coursing: *Dolby v Halmshaw* [1937] 1 KB 196, [1936] 3 All ER 229; not following *R v Clarke* [1930] NI 174.

10 Game Licences Act 1860 s 5, Exception 4.

309. Grant, issue and form of game licences. Game licences are granted by district councils, London borough councils and the Common Council of the City of London[1]. They are normally issued by the Post Office on the council's request to it to act as its agent, in which event the Secretary of State for Trade and Industry may direct the Post Office to comply[2].

A game licence and an excise licence to deal in game must denote the amount of duty charged on it[3]; it must contain the proper Christian name and surname and place of residence of the person to whom it is granted, together with any other particulars which the Commissioners of Customs and Excise may direct to be inserted, and it must be dated on the day on which it is actually issued[4]. A game licence is in force on the day of issue and from the time of issue[5], so that an offence committed on the day of issue but before the time of issue is not condoned by the issue of the licence on that day[6].

A game licence continues in force until the close of the day on which it is stated to expire[7]. A game licence taken out in Northern Ireland is available in Great Britain[8].

The licence will be forfeited if the holder is convicted of trespassing in the daytime upon lands in search of game in England, Wales or Scotland[9].

1 Licences for killing game, as well as licences to deal in game (see para 313 post), were among the excise licences the proceeds of the duties on which, as local taxation licences, were made receivable by the councils mentioned by the Local Government Act 1888 ss 20 (3), 32 (repealed), Sch 1, and the London Government Act 1963 s 83 (1), Sch 17 para 2. The power of levying the duties on these and other local taxation licences was transferred to the councils mentioned by the Local Government Act 1972 s 213. The transfer vests in the councils mentioned, within their respective areas, the powers, duties and liabilities of the Commissioners of Inland Revenue relating to those duties with the exception of the Crown's special privileges as respects legal proceedings (s 20 (3), (4) (iii) of the Act of 1888), and the power to prescribe and print licence forms and to issue licences (Order in Council dated 19 October 1908, SR & O 1908/844, arts II–IV): see generally LOCAL GOVERNMENT. For the provisions of the Customs and Excise Management Act 1979 applied in relation to licences, see para 319 note 12 post.

2 Post Office Act 1969 ss 12 (1), (2), (4), 134 (s 12 amended by the Ministry of Posts and Telecommunications (Dissolution) Order 1974, SI 1974/691, arts 2, 3 (3)). As to the Post Office's remuneration for issuing licences see the Post Office Act 1969 s 135. Councils are under a duty to enable

persons to obtain licences near their residences: Local Government Act 1888 s 20 (5) (a); see also the
Order in Council dated 19 October 1908 art IV.

3 Game Licences Act 1860 s 16. The power to prescribe forms rests with the Treasury: Order in
Council dated 19 October 1908 art II. They are printed and provided by the Commissioners of
Inland Revenue: art III. The rates at which duty is charged for a game licence are: (1) for a licence
issued after 31 July and before 1 November, £6 if it expires on the following 31 July and £4 if it
expires on 31 October in the year of issue: Game Licences Act 1860 s 2 (amended by the Customs and
Inland Revenue Act 1883 s 4 and the Fees for Game and Other Licences (Variation) Order 1968, SI
1968/120 (made under the Local Government Act 1966 s 35 (2), Sch 3 Pt II)); (2) for a licence issued
on or after 1 November to expire on the following 31 July, £4: Game Licences Act 1860 s 2 (as so
amended); and (3) for an occasional licence for a continuous period of 14 days specified on the
licence, £2: Customs and Inland Revenue Act 1883 s 5 (amended by the Fees for Game and Other
Licences (Variation) Order 1968). As to gamekeepers' licences see para 293 ante; as to licences to deal
in game see para 316 et seq post.

4 Game Licences Act 1860 s 16 (amended by virtue of the Customs and Excise Management Act 1979
s 177 (1), Sch 4 para 1).

5 Game Licences Act 1860 s 16. The time at which it is issued is stated on the face of the licence.

6 Campbell v Strangeways (1877) 3 CPD 105.

7 Game Licences Act 1860 s 16. No regard is paid to fractions of a day: see eg Lester v Garland (1805) 15
Ves 248 at 257 and TIME.

8 Finance Act 1924 s 17 (1). No further duty is payable (s 17 (1)) unless the duty on game licences in
Great Britain is higher than that in Northern Ireland, in which case the difference must be paid
(s 17 (1) proviso). 'Great Britain' means England, Wales and Scotland: Union with Scotland Act
1706, preamble, art 1; Wales and Berwick Act 1746 s 3; see para 297 note 6 ante. Northern Ireland,
the Channel Islands and the Isle of Man are not included.

9 Game Licences Act 1860 s 11; Game Act 1831 s 30 (see para 269 ante); Game (Scotland) Act 1832.

310. Licence register. The clerk to each council granting game licences[1] must
keep a register of the names and residences of the several persons to or for whom
licences to kill game have been granted in its area, distinguishing the persons acting
under any deputation, appointment or authority from others, and the manors,
royalties, or lands for which deputations, appointments or authorities have been
granted, and also distinguishing the rate of duty paid for such licences[2].

1 As to these councils see para 309 text and note 1 ante.
2 Game Licences Act 1860 s 15; London Government Act 1963 s 83 (1), Sch 17 para 2; Order in Council
dated 19 October 1908, SR & O 1908/844, arts XIV, XVII. The Game Licences Act 1860 s 12 authorises
publication in the newspapers, but this method of publication has fallen out of use. In practice the
lists are published in post offices or on the doors of the churches of the places where the licences are
issued. A list will also be supplied to any person requiring it by the local supervisor of excise.

(ii) Production and Contravention

311. Production of game licence. If any person is discovered doing any act
whatever in Great Britain[1] for which a licence to kill game is required by the Game
Licences Act 1860, he may be called upon by any of the persons mentioned
hereafter to produce his licence[2]. The demand must be made upon the land where
the person on whom it is made was discovered or so soon after he has left the land
that the whole incident forms part of the same transaction[3].

Should he fail to produce his licence the person calling upon him to do so may
next require him forthwith to declare his Christian name and surname and place of
residence, and the place where he took out his licence[4]. Any person who when so
called upon wilfully refuses to produce his licence or give the required information,
or who produces or gives a false or fictitious licence, name or place, or who refuses

to permit the licence he produces to be read or copied, is liable to an excise penalty of level 2 on the standard scale[5].

The persons entitled to demand production of the licence and such information are any officer of the local authority concerned[6] to whom the duty of executing the Act has been delegated[7], or any person who has duly taken out a game licence, or any lord or gamekeeper of the manor, royalty or land where the person to whom the demand is made is discovered committing an act which requires a licence, or the owner, landlord, lessee or occupier thereof[8].

1 For the meaning of 'Great Britain' see para 309 note 8 ante.
2 Game Licences Act 1860 s 10. He must permit the person demanding it to read the licence and take a copy of it or part of it: s 10.
3 *Scarth v Gardener* (1831) 5 C & P 38.
4 Game Licences Act 1860 s 10.
5 Ibid ss 3, 10 (amended by virtue of the Criminal Justice Act 1982 s 46). As to the standard scale see para 232 note 1 ante. At the date of which this volume states the law, level 2 on that scale is at £100. No offence is committed by refusing to produce a licence if there is no refusal of the further particulars: *Molton v Rogers* (1802) 4 Esp 215. If the person refuses to give his name the offence is complete, even if the further question as to where the licence was taken out is not asked: *Scarth v Gardener* (1831) 5 C & P 38.
6 See para 309 text and note 1 ante.
7 See para 312 text and note 2 post.
8 Game Licences Act 1860 s 10. A shooting tenant not in occupation of the land is not so entitled unless he himself holds a licence, and a gamekeeper, except on a manor, etc, is in the same position (see para 299 ante). A duly licensed person making such a demand is not obliged to produce his own licence: *Scarth v Gardener* (1831) 5 C & P 38. If the person discovered does not have a licence proceedings can be taken only by an officer of the local authority (see para 312 post), unless he has also committed an offence against the Game Act 1831, when proceedings may be instituted for that offence (but not for the failure to take out a licence) by anyone: see para 306 ante.

312. Proceedings. The power of taking proceedings for a contravention of the Game Licences Act 1860 is now vested in the local authorities concerned[1]. Every authority may delegate to such of its officers as it may select the powers and duties formerly belonging to officers of the Inland Revenue and any officer so selected is subject to the same liabilities as an officer of the Inland Revenue[2]. No proceedings can be instituted by such officers without the specific authority of the local authority[3]. Any information must be laid within six months of the commission of the offence charged[4]. The local authority concerned may stay or compound proceedings for any offence and, after judgment, may remit or mitigate any penalty[5].

1 See para 309 text and note 1 ante. The transfer of the powers of the Commissioners of Inland Revenue to local authorities does not extend to any special privilege of the Crown as respects any legal proceedings: Local Government Act 1888 s 20 (4) (iii); Finance Act 1908 s 6 (2).
2 Order in Council dated 19 October 1908, SR & O 1908/844, art IX. A person subject to liability for failure to comply with a demand formerly made by an Inland Revenue officer, or for obstructing, molesting or hindering him, is subject to the same liability on failure to comply with a similar demand made by a selected local authority officer, or for obstructing, molesting or hindering him: art X.
3 Inland Revenue Regulation Act 1890 s 21 (1); Customs and Excise Management Act 1979 ss 145, 154 (1) (a), (c); Order in Council dated 19 October 1908 art 1; Transferred Excise Duties (Application of Enactments) Order 1952, SI 1952/2205, art 1, Schedule; *Jones v Wilson* [1918] 2 KB 36, DC. See also para 315 note 12 post. See also *Dyer v Tulley* [1894] 2 QB 794, DC; *Hargreaves v Hilliam* (1894) 58 JP 655, DC.

4 Magistrates' Courts Act 1980 s 127. Cf *M'Lean v Johnston* 1913 JC 1.
5 Finance Act 1908; s 6 (1); Order in Council dated 19 October 1908 Customs and Excise Management Act 1979 s 152; applied by the Transferred Excise Duties (Application of Enactments) Order 1952 art 1, Schedule.

(7) LICENCES TO DEAL IN GAME

(i) Introduction

313. Licences to deal in game. In order to deal in game[1], that is, to sell game wholesale or retail to anyone, a person must hold two licences: (1) a 'local' licence granted by the local authority[2]; (2) an excise licence[3].

1 Ie hares, pheasants, partridges, grouse, heath or moor game and black game: see para 211 ante.
2 See para 316 post.
3 Game Licences Act 1860 s 14. As to excise licences see para 319 post.

314. Who may sell game. Apart from the holder of a local authority's licence[1] no one may sell game[2] except:
  (1) the holder of a £6 game licence[3], and he only to the holder of a local licence[4];
  (2) an innkeeper or tavern keeper, and he only game procured from the holder of a local licence for consumption in his own house[5];
  (3) a person directed in writing by a justice of the peace to sell game[6] seized[7] as having been unlawfully taken[8];
  (4) in the case of hares killed in pursuance of the rights conferred by the Ground Game Act 1880[9], the occupier of the land on which they were killed[10].
Any contravention of these provisions renders the offender liable on conviction before two justices to a fine not exceeding level 1 on the standard scale[11] for each head of game sold[12].

No one except the holder of a local licence may buy game from anyone except the holder of a local licence or bona fide from a person purporting by the exhibition of the prescribed board[13] to be the holder of a local licence[14]. A contravention of this provision renders the offender liable on conviction before two justices to a fine not exceeding level 1 on the standard scale for each head of game the subject of the offence[15].

1 Game Act 1831 s 25: see para 316 post.
2 For the meaning of 'game' see para 313 note 1 ante.
3 See paras 306, 309 ante.
4 Game Act 1831 ss 17, 25; Game Licences Act 1860 s 13.
5 Game Act 1831 s 26: see para 316 post.
6 For the meaning of 'game' in this context see para 282 notes 2, 12 ante.
7 Ie under the Poaching Prevention Act 1862 s 2, or the Game Laws (Amendment) Act 1960 s 4 (1): see para 282 ante.
8 Game Laws (Amendment) Act 1960 ss 3 (4), 4 (4). See para 286 ante.
9 See para 256 ante.
10 Ground Game Act 1880 s 4 (amended by the Local Government Act 1966 s 43 (2) (a), Sch 6 Pt I).
11 As to the standard scale see para 232 note 1 ante. At the date at which this volume states the law, level 1 on that scale is at £50.
12 Game Act 1831 s 25 (amended by virtue of the Criminal Justice Act 1982 s 46 and by the Statute Law (Repeals) Act 1989 Sch 1 Pt I).
13 See para 317 post.
14 Game Act 1831 s 27 (amended by virtue of the Criminal Justice Act 1982 s 46 and by the Statute Law (Repeals) Act 1989 Sch 1 Pt I).
15 Game Act 1831 s 27 (as amended: see note 14 supra). As to the standard scale see note 11 supra.

315. No dealing without excise licence. The holder of a local licence[1] may not deal in game until he has obtained an excise licence, and if he does so he incurs an excise penalty of level 2 on the standard scale[2].

1 See para 316 post.
2 Game Licences Act 1860 s 14 (amended by virtue of the Criminal Justice Act 1982 s 46). As to the standard scale see para 232 note 1 ante. At the date at which this volume states the law, level 2 on that scale is at £100. Proceedings for recovery of the penalty may only be taken by order of the local authority concerned (see para 319 post) and in the name of its selected officer (Order in Council dated 19 October 1908, SR & O 1908/844, arts 1, IX), but this provision does not prevent proceedings being instituted by order or in the name of a law officer of the Crown in any case in which he thinks it proper, and where a person is arrested for an offence any court before whom he is brought may deal with the case although proceedings have not been commenced by order of the local authority or in the name of its officer (Customs and Excise Management Act 1979 s 145 (5), (6) (amended by the Police and Criminal Evidence Act 1984 s 114 (1)), applied by the Transferred Excise Duties (Application of Enactments) Order 1952, SI 1952/2205, art 1, Schedule).

(ii) Local Authority's Licence

316. Local authority's licence. The local authority[1] may grant a licence[2] to any person not falling within certain classes specially excepted who is a householder or keeps a shop or stall within its area[3]. Its jurisdiction is discretionary[4], and mandamus will not issue for the purpose of reviewing its decision[5]. The excepted classes are innkeepers[6], victuallers, persons licenced to sell beer by retail[7], owners, guards or drivers of any mail coach or other vehicle employed in the conveyance of mails, or any stage coach or waggon, van or other public conveyance, carriers, higglers[8], and persons in the employment of members of such classes[9]. Persons trading in partnership at one house, shop or stall need not take out more than one licence for that house, shop or stall[10].

The licence is an annual licence, but at whatever date it may be granted it expires on 1 July next ensuing[11].

If the holder of a local licence is convicted of any offence under the Game Act 1831, the licence is thereby rendered null and void[12].

Any person falsely assuming or pretending to be the holder of a local licence is liable on conviction before two justices to a fine not exceeding level 1 on the standard scale[13].

1 Ie the council of the district or London borough in which the business is carried on or, in the City of London, the Common Council: Game Act 1831 s 18; Local Government Act 1894 ss 21 (3), 27 (1) (c), 32; London Government (Public General Acts) Order 1965, SI 1965/602, art 3; Local Government Act 1972 s 179. The jurisdiction was originally that of the justices.
2 The form of licence prescribed by the Game Act 1831 s 18, Sch A, requires adaptation as a result of the transfer of jurisdiction from the justices; for a modern form see 2 Forms & Precedents (5th Edn) 466–467, Form 34. It is to be noted that, although many local authorities charge for issuing such a licence, they do so without statutory authority.
3 Game Act 1831 s 18.
4 Ibid s 18. This discretion is conferred in terms of an authority's being authorised, if it thinks fit, to grant such a licence: s 18. The provisions contained in this section as to the meeting of justices, etc, are inapplicable to the local authorities to whom the justices' jurisdiction has been transferred: see note 1 supra.
5 As to judicial review by way of mandamus in respect of discretionary acts, and against local authorities, see ADMINISTRATIVE LAW vol 1 (1) (Reissue) para 152.

6 Innkeepers and tavern keepers may, without a licence, sell game for consumption in their own houses provided they procured it from a licence holder: Game Act 1831 s 26.
7 A shopkeeper holding a grocer's licence for the sale of beer not to be drunk on the premises was within this exception: *Shoolbred & Co v St Pancras Justices* (1890) 24 QBD 346.
8 A higgler is an itinerant dealer who buys farm produce in exchange for petty commodities from the shops in town: Oxford English Dictionary.
9 Game Act 1831 s 18.
10 Ibid s 21.
11 Ibid s 18 (amended by 2 & 3 Vict c 35 (1839) s 4). The amending provision, though repealed by the Revenue Act 1869, is kept alive in so far as it deals with licences to deal in game by the Game Licences Act 1860 s 13
12 Game Act 1831 s 22.
13 Ibid s 28 (amended by virtue of the Criminal Justice Act 1982 s 46 and by the Statue Law (Repeals) Act 1989 Sch 1 Pt I). As to the standard scale see para 232 note 1 ante. At the date at which this volume states the law, level 1 on that scale is at £50.

317. Extent of authorisation of local licence. A local licence empowers the holder, and any person employed on his behalf and acting in the usual course of his employment, to buy game anywhere from any person who may lawfully sell game[1], and to sell it, whether on his own account or on account of some other holder of a local licence, at one house, shop or stall only, kept by him[2], subject to his affixing and keeping affixed on the outside of the front thereof a board having upon it in clear and legible characters his Christian name and surname and the words 'Licensed to deal in game'[3].

1 See para 314 ante.
2 Game Act 1831 ss 18, 29.
3 Ibid s 18 proviso. For offences see para 318 post.

318. Contraventions and penalties. A holder of a local licence who buys or obtains game from anyone except the holder of a game licence[1] or another holder of a local licence is liable on conviction before two justices to a fine of level 1 on the standard scale[2]. A holder of a local licence who sells game or offers it for sale without having the prescribed board[3] affixed to the outside of his house, shop or stall, or sells game at any place other than the house, shop or stall to which the board is affixed, or affixes a board to more than one house, shop or stall, is liable on conviction before two justices to a fine of level 1 on the standard scale[4].

A holder of a local licence who, after the expiration of ten days, one inclusive and the other exclusive, from the day on which it became unlawful to kill such a bird[5], buys or sells any bird of game, whether dead or alive or wild or tame[6] other than foreign game imported dead[7], or live birds for rearing or exhibition purposes or for sale alive, is liable on conviction before two justices to a fine not exceeding level 1 on the standard scale[8] for every head of game so bought or sold[9].

1 See para 306 et seq ante.
2 Game Act 1831 s 28 (amended by virtue of the Criminal Justice Act 1982 s 46 and by the Statue Law (Repeals) Act 1989 Sch 1 Pt I). As to the standard scale see para 232 note 1 ante. At the date at which this volume states the law, level 1 on that scale is at £50.
3 See para 317 ante.
4 Game Act 1831 s 28 (as amended: see note 2 supra).
5 As to close seasons for game birds see para 290 ante.
6 See para 291 notes 5, 6 ante.
7 See para 291 note 7 ante.
8 As to the standard scale see para 232 note 1 ante. At the date at which this volume states the law, level 1 on that scale is at £50.

9 Game Act 1831 s 4 (amended by the Game Act 1989 Sch 1 Pt I, and by virtue of the Criminal Justice Act 1982 s 46).

(iii) Excise Licence

319. Excise licence to deal in game. An excise licence costing £4[1], granted by a district council, a London borough council or the Common Council of the City of London[2], and normally issued by the Post Office as agent of the local authority[3], is required for dealing in hares, pheasants, partridges, grouse, heath or moor game and black game[4]. It is immaterial whether the game dealt with is British or foreign[5], wild or tame[6], dead or alive[7].

The licence is an annual licence[8]. It is dated on the day on which it is issued[9], has effect from the actual time of issue[10], and expires on the day mentioned in it for its termination[11].

Certain general provisions of the Customs and Excise Management Act 1979 relating to excise licences for the carrying on of a trade apply to local authorities in respect of excise licences granted by them[12]. These provisions include requirements as to the grant of a licence on payment of the duty[13] and in respect of the premises to which a licence extends[14], and govern the renewal of the licence[15] and its continuance on the death of the holder or his removal to other premises[16].

A local authority may authorise police prosecutions for offences connected with excise duties arising out of licences granted by it[17].

1 Game Licences Act 1860 s 2 (amended by the Game and Other Licences (Variation) Order 1968, SI 1968/120). As to the form of the licence see para 309 ante.
2 Local Government Act 1888 s 20 (3), Sch 1, applied by the London Government Act 1963 s 83 (1), Sch 17 para 2; Local Government 1972 s 213; see para 309 text and note 1 ante.
3 Post Office Act 1969 ss 12 (1), (2), (4), 134; Order in Council dated 19 October 1908, SR & O 1908/844, art IV: see para 309 text and note 2 ante.
4 Game Act 1831 s 2 (amended by the Protection of Birds Act 1954 s 15 (2), Sch 6); Game Licences Act 1860 ss 13, 14.
5 Customs and Inland Revenue Act 1893 s 2.
6 *Loome v Baily* (1860) 3 E & E 444; *Cook v Trevener* [1911] 1 KB 9, DC.
7 *Harnett v Miles* (1884) 48 JP 455, DC; *Cook v Trevener* [1911] 1 KB 9, DC.
8 Game Licences Act 1860 s 14.
9 Ibid s 16.
10 Cf *Campbell v Strangeways* (1877) 3 CPD 105; see also TIME.
11 Game Licences Act 1860 s 16.
12 See the Transferred Excise Duties (Application of Enactments) Order 1952, SI 1952/2205, art 1, Schedule, which takes effect under the Customs and Excise Management Act 1979 s 176. In addition to the provisions referred to in the text and notes following, the following sections of the 1979 Act are applied by that order in relation to the local authorities and their officers to which power to levy excise duties has been transferred with respect to those duties and licences on which they are imposed, subject to modifications: ss 11 (assistance to be rendered by police etc; but only so far as it relates to a constable), 16 (obstruction of officers), 145 (institution of proceedings), 146 (service of process); 147 (2), (4) (punishment and appeal), 148 (place of trial), 150 (incidental provisions as to proceedings), 151 (application of penalties; but not so as to prejudice the operation of the Justices of the Peace Act 1979 ss 59, 61)), 152 (a)–(c) (mitigation of penalties), 154 (1) (a), (c), (d) (proof of certain matters), 171 (1), (3) (general provisions as to offences and penalties). See further, as to excise duties and penalties, CUSTOMS AND EXCISE.
13 See the Customs and Excise Management Act 1979 s 102.
14 See ibid s 102.
15 See ibid s 103.

16 See ibid s 104.
17 Ibid s 176: see CUSTOMS AND EXCISE.

3. PROTECTION OF WILD ANIMALS

(1) PROTECTION OF DEER

(i) General

320. Meaning of 'deer'. For the purposes of the Deer Act 1991 'deer' means deer of any species and includes the carcase of any deer or any part thereof[1]. Different close seasons are set by the Act for different species of deer[2]. With this exception there is no statutory definition of deer, and in those Acts which mention deer the term therefore applies to every species of deer of either sex and of all ages[3].

1 Deer Act 1991 s 16.
2 See ibid s 2, Sch 1; and para 323 post.
3 *R v Strange* (1843) 1 Cox CC 58.

321. Tame deer. Tame deer are personal property, and accordingly can be the subject of theft[1].

1 Theft Act 1968 ss 4 (1), (4).

322. Wild deer. Although wild deer are to be regarded as property, they cannot be the subject of theft[1], but they are otherwise protected by statute[2].

1 Theft Act 1968 s 4 (4).
2 Ie by the Deer Act 1991: see para 325 post.

323. Close seasons and times for deer. It is an offence[1] to take or intentionally kill[2] deer of any species and description specified in the Deer Act 1991 during the close season thereby prescribed[3]. This offence, however, is not committed when (1) farmed deer are killed during the close season by their keeper or his servants or agents[4], or (2) one of a specified class of persons[5] takes or kills any deer by shooting it, or in an attempt to do so injures any deer, on any cultivated land, pasture or enclosed woodland[6].

It is also an offence to take or intentionally kill any deer[7] between the end of the first hour after sunset and the beginning of the last hour before sunrise[8].

Neither of the above offences is committed if the act is done to prevent the suffering of an injured or diseased deer[9], or if the act is done in pursuance of a requirement of the Minister of Agriculture, Fisheries and Food[10] relating to the prevention of damage by pests[11]. There is a further exception in the case of taking deer at any time where the act is done under a licence granted by the Nature Conservancy Council for England or the Countryside Council for Wales[12].

1 For powers of search and seizure by a constable see para 325 post; for penalties see para 331 post.

2 'To take' means to catch: *R v Glover* (1814) Russ & Ry 269, CCR; *Watkins v Price* (1877) 42 JP 21, DC. The killing must be deliberate and intentional, not by accident or inadvertence, and the mind of the person who does the act must go with it: see *R v Senior* [1899] 1 QB 283 at 290, CCR, per Lord Russell of Killowen; *R v Walker* (1934) 24 Cr App Rep 117, CCA; and *Eaton v Cobb* [1950] 1 All ER 1016. See also para 415 note 2 post.

3 Deer Act 1991 s 2 (1). The close seasons, species and descriptions specified by s 2 (1), (2), Sch 1 are: 1 March to 31 October inclusive for Red deer (*Cervus elaphus*) hinds, Fallow deer (*Dama dama*) doe, Roe deer (*Capreolus capreolus*) doe, and Sika deer (*Cervus nippon nippon*) hinds; 1 November to 31 March inclusive for Roe deer buck; and 1 May to 31 July inclusive for Red deer stags, Fallow deer buck and Sika deer stags. After consultation with any organisations representative of interested persons the Secretary of State may by statutory instrument add close seasons for further species, or vary or delete any such addition: Deer Act 1991 ss 2 (4), (5), 15 (1), (2). At the date at which this volume states the law no such instrument had been made.

4 Ibid s 2 (3). The deer must be kept by a person by way of business, on land surrounded by a deer-proof barrier, for the production of meat, other foodstuffs, skins or other by-products, or as breeding stock: s 2 (3) (a). The deer must be conspicuously marked in such a way as to identify them as kept by that person: s 2 (3) (b).

5 The specified persons are: the occupier of the land on which the action is taken; any member of his household normally resident on the land, or any person in his ordinary service on the land, acting with his written authority; or any person having the right to take or kill deer on the land, or any person acting with the written authority of a person having that right: ibid s 7 (4). Such a person may not rely on this defence as respects anything done in relation to any deer on any land unless he shows that he had reasonable grounds for believing that deer of the same species were causing, or had caused, damage to crops, vegetables, fruit, growing timber or any other property on the land; that it was likely further damage would be so caused and any such damage was likely to be serious; and that his action was necessary for the purpose of preventing any such damage: s 7 (3).

6 Ibid s 7 (1).

7 'Deer' here means any species of deer whatever: ibid s 16.

8 Ibid s 3. Cf para 278 note 3 ante.

9 Ibid s 6 (2).

10 Ie under the Agriculture Act 1947 s 98; see AGRICULTURE.

11 Deer Act 1991 s 6 (1).

12 Ibid s 8. A licence granted under this provision may exempt the grantee and any person acting with his written authority from the provisions of the Act in respect of certain acts done for the purpose of removing deer to another area or taking them alive for scientific or educational purposes: s 8.

324. Game licences for deer. Although deer are not game within the Game Act 1831[1], a game licence is required for taking or killing them[2]. This does not, however, apply to the pursuing and killing of deer by hunting with hounds[3], or to the taking and killing of deer in inclosed land by or by the direction or permission of the owner or occupier of the land[4].

1 See para 211 ante.

2 Game Licences Act 1860 s 2. Any person assisting the taking or killing requires a licence, unless he is assisting a duly licensed person: s 5, Exemption 3; see para 308 ante. As to obtaining a licence and penalties for acting without one see paras 309, 312 ante. No licence is required for dealing in deer. As to fence months, and other restrictions for the benefit of deer on rights of common in forest, see COMMONS vol 6 (Reissue) para 514.

3 Game Licences Act 1860 s 5, Exception 4.

4 Ibid s 5, Exception 5.

(ii) Unlawful Taking, Driving or Killing of Deer

325. Poaching of deer. Any person who enters any land without the consent of the owner or occupier, or without other lawful authority[1], in search or pursuit of any deer with the intention of taking, killing or injuring it commits an offence[2]. So too does any person who while on any land intentionally takes, kills or injures any deer, or attempts to do so, or searches for or pursues any deer with the intention of doing so, or removes the carcase of any deer, without such consent or other lawful authority[3]. Any authorised person[4] who suspects with reasonable cause that any person is committing or has committed either of the above offences on any land may require that person to give his full name and address and to quit that land forthwith; failure to comply with any such requirement is also an offence[5].

1 A person who does anything in the belief that he would have the consent of the owner or occupier of the land if the owner or occupier knew of his doing it and the circumstances of it, or that he has other lawful authority to do it, does not commit the offence: Deer Act 1991 s 1 (3).
2 Ibid s 1 (1). For penalties see para 331 post.
3 Ibid s 1 (2). The defence available under s 1 (3) also applies to this offence; see note 1 supra. For penalties see para 331 post.
4 'Authorised person' means the owner or occupier of the land or any person authorised by the owner or occupier, and includes any person having the right to take or kill deer on the land: ibid s 1 (5).
5 Ibid s 1 (4). For penalties see para 331 post.

326. Prohibited weapons and other articles. It is an offence[1] to set in position any article which is a trap, snare or poisoned or stupefying bait, and is of such a nature and so placed as to be calculated to cause bodily injury to any deer[2] coming in contact with it[3]; or to use for the purpose of killing or taking any deer any such trap, snare or bait, or any net[4], or to use for the purpose of injuring, killing or taking any deer any firearm or ammunition of a specified kind[5], any arrow, spear or similar missile[6], or any missile, however discharged, carrying or containing any poison, stupefying drug or muscle-relaxing agent[7]. It is also an offence to have in one's possession[8] for the purpose of committing an offence against the Deer Act 1991 any of the above prohibited articles or any firearm or ammunition[9].

There are exceptions where a trap or net is set in position or used for the purpose of preventing suffering by an injured or diseased deer[10]; where an act is done under a licence granted by the Nature Conservancy Council for England or the Countryside Council for Wales[11]; where a person uses a smooth-bore gun to kill a deer if he shows that the deer had been so seriously injured (otherwise than by his unlawful act) or was in such a condition that to kill it was an act of mercy[12]; and where a person uses a gun and ammunition of specified size[13] as a slaughtering instrument[14]. Specified persons[15] are not guilty of an offence of using a prohibited firearm or ammunition[16] by reason of the use of any smooth-bore gun which meets certain specifications as to the gauge and size of cartridge[17].

1 For penalties see para 331 post.
2 'Deer' means deer of any species: Deer Act 1991 s 16.
3 Ibid s 4 (1) (a).
4 Ibid s 4 (1) (b).
5 Ibid s 4 (2) (a). The firearms prohibited are smooth-bore guns, any rifle having a calibre of less than .240 inches or a muzzle-energy of less than 2,305 joules (1,700 foot pounds), and any air gun, air rifle or air pistol; the ammunition prohibited is any cartridge for use in a smooth-bore gun and any bullet for use in a rifle other than a soft-nosed or hollow-nosed bullet: s 4 (2) (a), Sch 2. The Secretary of State may by statutory instrument amend the schedule: ss 4 (3), 15.
6 Ibid s 4 (2) (b).
7 Ibid s 4 (2) (c).
8 'Possession' means possession in the popular sense: see *Webb v Baker* [1916] 2 KB 753, DC; *Oliver v Goodger* [1944] 2 All ER 481, DC; and *Towers & Co Ltd v Gray* [1961] 2 QB 351, [1961] 2 All ER 68, DC.

9 Deer Act 1991 s 5 (2). The offences referred to are those against ss 2–4. See para 323 ante and text and notes 1–7 supra. 'Firearm' and 'ammunition' have the same meanings as in the Firearms Act 1968 s 57 (1), (2) (see CRIMINAL LAW vol 11 (1) (Reissue) para 197 et seq): Deer Act 1991 s 16.

10 Ibid s 6 (3); this exception applies to an offence under s 4 (1) (a) or (b) (see text and notes 3, 4 supra).

11 Ibid s 8; see para 323 note 10 ante.

12 Ibid s 6 (4). This exception applies to an offence under s 4 (2) (a).

13 In order to come within this exception, which applies to offences under ibid s 4 (2) (a), the gun must be smooth-bore and of a gauge not less than 12 bore, must have a barrel less than 24 inches (609.6 millimetres) in length, and must be loaded with a cartridge purporting to contain shot none of which is less than .203 inches (5.16 millimetres) in diameter (ie size AAA or larger): s 6 (5) (a)–(c).

14 Ibid s 6 (5).

15 As to such persons and the circumstances in which the defence is not available see para 323 note 5 ante.

16 Ie an offence under the Deer Act 1991 s 4 (2) (a); see text and note 5 supra.

17 Ibid s 7 (2). The specifications which must be satisfied are as follows: (1) the gun must be smooth-bore and of a gauge not less than 12 bore; and (2) it must be loaded with either (a) a cartridge containing a single, non-spherical projectile weighing not less than 350 grains (22.68 grammes), or (b) a cartridge purporting to contain shot each of which is .203 inches (5.16 millimetres) in diameter (ie size AAA): s 7 (2) (a), (b). The Secretary of State and the Minister of Agriculture, Fisheries and Food may by order made by statutory instrument repeal this exception or make any amendment or addition to the conditions and specifications contained therein: s 7 (5)–(7). At the date at which this volume states the law, no such order had been made.

327. Prohibition on use of vehicles. It is an offence[1] to discharge a firearm[2] or project a missile at a deer[3] from a mechanically propelled vehicle[4], or to use such a vehicle for the purpose of driving deer[5], except in the case of anything done by or with the written authority of the owner of any enclosed land where deer are usually kept, in relation to deer on that land[6].

1 For penalties see para 331 post.

2 'Firearm' has the same meaning as in the Firearms Act 1968 s 57 (1) (see CRIMINAL LAW vol 11 (1) (Reissue) para 197 et seq): Deer Act 1991 s 16.

3 'Deer' means deer of any species: ibid s 16.

4 Ibid s 4 (4) (a). 'Vehicle' includes an aircraft, hovercraft or boat: s 16.

5 Ibid s 4 (4) (b).

6 Ibid s 4 (5).

(iii) Regulation of Dealing in Venison

328. Dealing in venison. No one except a licensed game dealer[1] may (1) at any time during the 'prohibited period'[2] sell[3] or offer or expose for sale or have in his possession for sale any venison[4], nor (2) at any time sell or offer or expose for sale any venison otherwise than to a licensed game dealer. To do so is an offence punishable on summary conviction with a fine not exceeding level 3 on the standard scale[5].

Any person who sells or offers or exposes for sale or has in his possession for sale, or purchases or offers to purchase or receives, any venison which he knows or has reason to believe comes from a deer which has been unlawfully taken or killed[6], commits an offence punishable on summary conviction with a fine not exceeding level 4 on the standard scale[7], imprisonment for up to three months, or both[8].

Every licensed game dealer[9] who sells[10], offers, exposes for sale or has in his possession for sale any venison must keep a record book in prescribed form[11] and enter in that book forthwith full particulars of all his purchases and receipts of venison[12]. Authorised officers of the local authority and constables may inspect such record books, any venison in the dealer's possession or under his control or on premises or in vehicles under his control, and invoices, consignment notes, receipts and other documents relating to entries in the record book[13]. Any dealer who without reasonable excuse fails to comply with these provisions commits an offence[14], as does any person who wilfully obstructs any authorised officer or constable making an inspection or who knowingly or recklessly makes or causes to be made in a record book any entry which is false or misleading in a material particular[15]. The penalty on summary conviction for either offence is a fine not exceeding level 2 on the standard scale[16].

1 Ie a person licensed to deal in game under the Game Act 1831 and the Game Licences Act 1860, or a servant of such a person: Deer Act 1991 s 10 (5); see paras 313–319 ante.
2 Ie, in relation to any venison which comes from deer for which a close season has been prescribed (under ibid s 2, Sch 1), the period beginning with the expiry of the tenth day, and ending with the expiry of the last day, of that season: s 10 (2). For details of the prescribed close seasons see para 323 note 3 ante.
3 'Sale' includes barter and exchange, and 'sell' and 'purchase' are to be construed accordingly: ibid s 10 (5).
4 'Venison' includes imported venison, and means any carcase of a deer, or any edible part thereof, which has not been cooked or canned: ibid s 16.
5 Ibid s 10 (1). As to the standard scale see para 232 note 1 ante. At the date at which this volume states the law, level 3 on that scale is at £400.
6 Ie contrary to the provisions of ibid ss 1–9: see paras 323, 325, 326 ante.
7 As to the standard scale see para 232 note 1 ante. At the date at which this volume states the law, level 4 on that scale is at £1,000.
8 Deer Act 1991 s 10 (3), (4).
9 See note 1 supra.
10 See note 3 supra.
11 Ie in the form set out in the Deer Act 1991 Sch 3, or a form substantially to the like effect: s 11 (1) (a). These requirements may be altered by statutory instrument: s 11 (2). Record books must be kept for three years following the last entry in the book, and supporting documentation must be kept for three years: s 11 (4) (c), (5).
12 Ibid s 11 (1) (b). The particulars required are implied by the prescribed form, and include the date of purchase or receipt, species of deer, the means by which it was killed, the number, gender and weight of carcases, and the number, description and weight of parts of carcases, purchased or received, particulars of the seller, and the registration number of the vehicle delivering the venison: Sch 3, Form. Where, however, a licensed game dealer purchases or receives venison from another licensed dealer, or from a venison dealer registered or licensed in Scotland, it is sufficient for him to record that the venison was so purchased or received, the name and address of the other dealer, the date of the purchase or receipt, and the total weight of the venison: s 11 (3).
13 Ibid s 11 (4).
14 Ibid s 11 (6).
15 Ibid s 11 (7).
16 Ibid s 11 (8). As to the standard scale see para 232 note 1 ante. At the date at which this volume states the law, level 2 on that scale is at £100.

(iv) Legal Proceedings

329. Attempts to commit offences. Any person who attempts[1] to commit an offence of taking or killing deer in close season or at night, or of using prohibited weapons or other articles[2] is guilty of an offence against the Deer Act 1991 and is punishable in like manner as for the offence itself[3].

1 A person is guilty of attempting to commit an offence if he does an act which is more than merely preparatory to the commission of the offence: Criminal Attempts Act 1981 s 1 (1); see generally CRIMINAL LAW vol 11 (1) (Reissue) para 71 et seq.

2 Ie an offence under the Deer Act 1991 ss 2–4; see paras 323, 326, 327 ante.
3 Ibid s 5 (1). As to punishment under the Act see para 331 post.

330. Powers of search and seizure. If a constable suspects with reasonable cause[1] that a person is committing or has committed any offence under the Deer Act 1991[2], he may without warrant stop and search that person and search or examine any vehicle, animal, weapon or other thing which that person may then be using (if he suspects with reasonable cause that evidence of the commission of the offence is to be found on the person or on the vehicle, etc)[3].

A constable may also seize and detain for the purposes of proceedings under the Act anything which is evidence of the commission of the offence and any deer, vehicle, animal, weapon or other thing which is liable to be forfeited[4]. For the purposes of exercising these powers, or for arresting a person in accordance with his general powers of arrest[5] for an offence under the Act, he may enter any land other than a dwelling house[6]. He may sell any deer or venison[7] seized, and the net proceeds of the sale are then liable to be detained and forfeited in the same manner as the deer sold; but he is not liable if he neglects or fails to exercise this power[8].

1 These words require, it is submitted, that the constable has reasonable grounds for suspicion and also that he does actually suspect: see *R v Banks* [1916] 2 KB 621; *Nakkuda Ali v Jayaratne* [1951] AC 66, PC. The existence of reasonable grounds for suspicion, and of the actual suspicion, are questions of fact for the court to decide: see *McArdle v Egan* (1933) 150 LT 412, CCA; *Nakkuda Ali v Jayaratne* supra. Cf *Liversidge v Anderson* [1942] AC 206, [1941] 3 All ER 338, HL.
2 See paras 323, 325–329 ante.
3 Deer Act 1991 s 12 (1) (a), (b).
4 Ibid s 12 (1) (c). As to forfeiture see para 331 post.
5 Under the Police and Criminal Evidence Act 1984 s 25 (as to which see CRIMINAL LAW).
6 Deer Act 1991 s 12 (2).
7 For the meaning of 'venison' see para 328 note 4 ante.
8 Deer Act 1991 s 12 (3).

331. Proceedings, penalties and forfeiture. In general, offences under the Deer Act 1991 are punishable on summary conviction by a fine not exceeding level 4 on the standard scale[1], imprisonment for a term not exceeding three months, or both[2]. Where such an offence under the Act is committed in respect of more than one deer the maximum fine is determined as if the person convicted had been convicted of a separate offence in respect of each deer[3]. The convicting court may also order the forfeiture of any deer or venison in respect of which the offence was committed or which was found in the defendant's possession, and of any vehicle, animal, weapon or other thing which was used to commit the offence or which was capable of being used to take, kill or injure deer and was found in the defendant's possession[4].

Where a person is convicted of an offence relating to poaching, selling or dealing in game or the keeping of records by licensed game dealers[5], the court may additionally disqualify that person from holding or obtaining a licence to deal in game for such period as the court thinks fit, and it may cancel any firearm or shotgun certificate held by him[6]. When such an offence which has been committed by a body corporate is proved to have been committed with the consent or connivance of, or to be attributable to any neglect on the part of, any director, manager, secretary or other similar officer of the body corporate or any person who was purporting to act in any such capacity, he as well as the body corporate is guilty of the offence and is liable to be proceeded against and punished accordingly[7].

1 As to the standard scale see para 232 note 1 ante. At the date at which this volume states the law, level 4 on that scale is at £1,000.
2 Deer Act 1991 s 9 (1). The exceptions are noted in para 328 ante.
3 Ibid s 9 (2).
4 Ibid s 13 (1). Note that there is no power of sale.
5 Ie an offence under ibid ss 1, 10, 11; see paras 325, 328 ante.
6 Ibid s 13 (2). Where the court cancels a certificate, it must notify in writing the chief officer of police by whom the certificate was granted, and the chief officer must by notice in writing require the holder of the certificate to surrender it. If he fails to do so within 21 days of the date of that requirement he commits an offence and is liable on summary conviction to a maximum fine of level 2 on the standard scale: s 13 (3). As to the standard scale see para 232 note 1 ante. At the date at which this volume states the law, level 2 on that scale is at £100.
7 Ibid s 14 (1).

(2) PROTECTION OF BIRDS

(i) Protection of Wild Birds, Nests and Eggs

332. Protection of wild birds generally. Wild birds[1] are specially protected by the Wildlife and Countryside Act 1981.

It is an offence[2] intentionally to kill, injure or take any wild bird, or to take, damage or destroy the nest of any wild bird while the nest is in use or being built, or to take or destroy an egg of any wild bird[3].

It is also an offence to have in one's possession or control any live or dead wild bird or any part of, or anything derived from, such a bird, or any egg or part of an egg of a wild bird[4].

If the offences stated above are committed in respect of any wild bird listed in Schedule 1 to the Act, the offender is liable to a special penalty[5]. Similarly, the act of intentionally disturbing any wild bird listed in Schedule 1 while it is building a nest or is in, on or near a nest containing eggs or young, or of intentionally disturbing the dependent young of such a bird, is an offence carrying a special penalty[6].

The term 'wild bird' does not include any bird which is shown to have been bred in captivity[7].

Licences to permit certain prohibited activities may be granted[8].

1 'Wild bird' means generally under the Wildlife and Countryside Act 1981 any bird of a kind which is ordinarily resident in or is a visitor to Great Britain in a wild state, but does not include poultry (ie domestic fowls, geese, ducks, guinea fowls, pigeons and quails, and turkeys) or any game bird (ie pheasant, partridge, grouse or moor game, black or heath game, or ptarmigan): s 27 (1).
2 As to the punishment for such offences see para 348 post.
3 Wildlife and Countryside Act 1981 s 1 (1). The use of the word 'intentionally' avoids the interpretation of the word 'wilfully' used in the Protection of Birds Acts 1954 to 1967 (repealed). An attempt to commit an offence relating to the protection of wild birds is also an offence, punishable in like manner: Wildlife and Countryside Act 1981 s 18; and see para 348 post. To destroy an egg includes doing anything to it which is calculated to prevent it from hatching: s 27 (1).
4 Ibid s 1 (2). The offence is one of strict liability: *Kirkland v Robinson* (1986) 151 JP 377, DC. It is a defence to show that the bird or egg had not been killed or taken, or had been killed or taken otherwise than in contravention of the statute; or that the bird, egg or other thing in the person's possession or control had been sold, whether to him or any other person, otherwise than in contravention of the statute: Wildlife and Countryside Act 1981 s 1 (3). The onus lies on the defendant.
5 Ibid s 1 (4). For penalties see para 348 post.

6 Ibid s 1 (5).
7 Ibid s 1 (6).
8 Ibid s 16; see para 343 post.

333. Close seasons. Subject to the Secretary of State's power by order made by statutory instrument to extend the periods[1], the close season for capercaillie and woodcock is from 1 February to 30 September; for snipe from 1 February to 11 August; for wild duck and wild geese in or over an area below the ordinary spring tide high water mark, from 21 February to 31 August; and for other birds from 1 February to 31 August[2].

1 Ie under the Wildlife and Countryside Act 1981 s 2 (5). At the date at which this volume states the law no such order was in force.
2 Ibid s 2 (4).

334. Exceptions to general prohibition. It is no offence[1] for an authorised person[2] to kill or take or attempt to kill or take, or to injure during an attempt to kill, any wild bird listed in Part II of Schedule 2 to the Wildlife and Countryside Act 1981[3]; nor, except in a prescribed area[4] on Sundays, is it an offence for any person to kill or take or attempt to kill or take, or to injure during an attempt to kill, a wild bird listed in Part I of Schedule 2 to that Act[5] outside the appropriate close season[6].

It is no offence[7] for an authorised person[8] to take, damage or destroy a nest in use by a wild bird listed in Part II of Schedule 2 to the Act[9], or for such a person to take or destroy an egg of such a bird[10].

1 Ie under the Wildlife and Countryside Act 1981 s 1; see para 332 ante.
2 'Authorised person' means the owner or occupier of any land on which the action takes place, or any person authorised by him, anyone authorised in writing by the local authority, the Nature Conservancy Council or certain other statutory authorities or bodies, or anyone authorised in writing by the National Rivers Authority, a water undertaker or a sewerage undertaker: ibid s 27 (1) (amended by the Water Act 1989 s 190 (1), (3), Sch 25 para 66 (1), Sch 27 Pt I). 'Occupier', in relation to any land except the foreshore, includes anyone having any right of hunting, shooting, fishing or taking game or fish: Wildlife and Countryside Act 1981 s 27 (1). As to a person authorised by an authorised person see *R v Gilham* (1884) 52 LT 326.
3 Wildlife and Countryside Act 1981 ss 2 (2), 18 (1). As to Sch 2 Pt II see para 341 note 5 post.
4 'Prescribed area' means any administrative area of England and Wales prescribed by order by the Secretary of State for the purpose: ibid s 2 (3). The Secretary of State is the Secretary of State for the Environment as respects England, or, as respects Wales the Secretary of State for Wales. The areas of the following administrative areas (constituted before the coming into force of the Local Government Act 1972) were prescribed by orders made under the Protection of Birds Act 1954 s 2 (2), (5) (repealed) which it is thought now have effect as if made under the Wildlife and Countryside Act 1981 s 2 (3): the counties of Caernarvon, Carmarthen, Devon, the Isle of Ely, Montgomery, Norfolk, Pembroke and York (North and West Ridings), and the county boroughs of Doncaster, Great Yarmouth and Leeds (Wild Birds (Sundays) Order 1955, SI 1955/1286); the counties of Brecknock, Cardigan, Denbigh and Merioneth (Wild Birds (Sundays) Order 1956, SI 1956/1310); the counties of Cornwall, Glamorgan and Somerset (Wild Birds (Sundays) Order 1957, SI 1957/429); and the county of Anglesey (Wild Birds (Sunday in Anglesey) Order 1963, SI 1963/1700).
5 As to the Wildlife and Countryside Act 1981 Sch 2 Pt I see para 341 note 4 post.
6 Ibid ss 2 (1), (3), 18 (1). As to close seasons see para 333 ante. 'Close season' here includes any period of special protection specified by order made by the Secretary of State: s 2 (6). As to such orders see para 337 post.
7 Ie under ibid s 1; see para 332 ante.

8 See note 2 supra.
9 As to the Wildlife and Countryside Act 1981 Sch 2 Pt II see para 341 note 5 post.
10 Ibid s 2 (2).

335. Creation of areas of special protection. The Secretary of State¹ may by order provide in respect of any area specified in the order, or any part so specified, at any time or period specified, that any person who intentionally kills, injures or takes any wild bird or any specified wild bird; or takes, damages or destroys the nest of such a bird while it is in use or being built; or takes or destroys an egg of such a bird; or disturbs such an bird while it is building a nest or is in, or near a nest containing eggs or young, or disturbs its dependent young; is guilty of an offence².

Such an order may also provide that any person who, except as may be provided in the order, enters any specified area or any specified part of it either at any time or during any specified period, commits an offence and is liable to a special penalty³.

An authorised person⁴ commits no offence in relation to the matters mentioned above in respect of any bird included in Part II of Schedule 2 to the Wildlife and Countryside Act 1981⁵.

The Secretary of State is obliged, before making any such order, to give particulars either by notice in writing to every owner or occupier within the area or, if this is in his opinion impracticable, by way of newspaper advertisement⁶. No order may be made unless all such persons have consented or raised no objections within three months or have withdrawn any such objections made⁷.

1 See para 334 note 4 ante.
2 Wildlife and Countryside Act 1981 s 3 (1) (a).
3 Ibid s 3 (1) (b), (c). As to the special penalty see para 348 post. Such order does not affect any right vested in any owner, lessee or occupier: s 3 (3).
4 For the meaning of 'authorised person' see para 334 note 2 ante.
5 Wildlife and Countryside Act 1981 s 3 (2).
6 Ibid s 3 (4).
7 Ibid s 3 (5).

336. Defences. Anything done in pursuance of a requirement of the Minister of Agriculture, Fisheries and Food or the Secretary of State for Wales in relation to the prevention of damage by pests¹, or anything done under or in pursuance of an order made under section 21 or 22 of the Animal Health Act 1981², or except in the case of a wild bird included in Schedule 1 to the Wildlife and Countryside Act 1981³ or its nest or eggs, anything done in or in pursuance of an order made under any other provision of the Animal Health Act 1981⁴, is not an offence against the general provisions for the protection of wild birds, their nests and eggs⁵, nor against any order⁶ establishing an area of special protection⁷.

It is a defence for an authorised person to any charge of killing, injuring or attempting to kill a wild bird other than a bird listed in Schedule 1 to the Wildlife and Countryside Act 1981⁸ to show⁹ that the action was necessary to preserve public health or public or air safety; or to prevent the spread of disease; or to prevent serious damage to livestock or foodstuffs for livestock, crops, vegetables, fruit, growing timber or fisheries¹⁰. It is a defence to any charge of taking or attempting to take any wild bird to show that the bird had been disabled otherwise than by the defendant's act, and that it was taken or to be taken solely to tend it and release it when no longer disabled¹¹. On a charge of killing any wild bird it is a defence to show that the bird had been so seriously disabled otherwise than by the defendant's act that there was no reasonable chance of its recovering[12], and on a charge relating to any act made unlawful by the provisions referred to above[13] to show that the act was the incidental result of a lawful operation and could not reasonably have been avoided[14].

1 Ie under the Agriculture Act 1947 s 98; see also the Pests Act 1954 ss 1 (6), 2–4; and AGRICULTURE vol 1 (2) paras 654, 658.
2 See para 507 post.
3 See para 341 note 1 post.
4 See para 482 et seq post. See also para 514 post.
5 Ie under the Wildlife and Countryside Act 1981 s 1; see para 332 ante.
6 Ie under ibid s 3; see para 335 ante.
7 Ibid s 4 (1).
8 See para 341 note 1 post.
9 Being on the defendant, the onus is discharged on a balance of probability: see *R v Carr-Briant* [1943] KB 607, [1943] 2 All ER 156, CCA; and *R v Dunbar* [1958] 1 QB 1, [1957] 2 All ER 737, CCA.
10 Wildlife and Countryside Act 1981 s 4 (3). For the meaning of 'authorised person' see para 334 note 2 ante. See *Robinson v Whittle* [1980] 3 All ER 459, [1980] 1 WLR 1476, DC.
11 Wildlife and Countryside Act 1981 s 4 (2) (a).
12 Ibid s 4 (2) (b).
13 See the text to notes 5–6 supra.
14 Wildlife and Countryside Act 1981 s 4 (2) (c).

337. Special protection outside close seasons. If it apears to the Secretary of State expedient that any wild birds included in Part II of Schedule 1 or Part I of Schedule 2 to the Wildlife and Countryside Act 1981[1] should be protected outside the close season for those birds, he may by order with respect to the whole or any specified part of Great Britain declare any period not exceeding 14 days as a period of special protection for them[2].

Before making any such order, the Secretary of State must consult a person appearing to him to be a representative of those interested in the shooting of birds proposed to be so protected[3].

1 See para 341 post.
2 Wildlife and Countryside Act 1981 s 2 (6). The effect is to make any such period a part of the close season for the birds in question: s 2 (6). Such orders, being of a temporary nature, are not recorded in this work.
3 Ibid s 2 (7).

338. Prohibited methods of killing or taking wild birds. Except under a licence granted under the Wildlife and Countryside Act 1981[1], it is an offence against that Act carrying a special penalty[2] to set in position any of the following articles, being of such a nature and so placed as to be calculated to cause bodily injury to any wild bird coming into contact with it: namely, any springe, trap, gin, snare, hook and line, any electrical device for killing, stunning or frightening, or any poisonous, poisoned or stupefying substance[3].

It is similarly an offence to use, for the purpose of killing or taking any wild bird, any of those articles, whether or not of such a nature and so placed, or any net, baited board, bird-lime or similar substance[4]. The use for the purpose of killing or taking any wild bird of any bow or crossbow; any explosive other than ammunition for a firearm; any automatic or semi-automatic weapon not including one whose magazine is incapable of holding more than two rounds[5]; any shotgun with internal muzzle diameter exceeding one and three-quarter inches; any target illuminating or sighting device for night shooting; any form of artificial lighting or mirror or dazzling device; any gas or smoke not already listed; or any chemical wetting agent, is an offence rendering the offender liable to a special penalty[6]. So also is the use of certain decoys and methods of decoy and of mechanical propelled vehicles in immediate pursuit of a wild bird[7].

It is an offence carrying a special penalty knowingly to cause or permit to be done any of the acts described above which is not within the exceptions laid down by statute[8].

The Secretary of State may by order, either generally or in relation to any specified kind of wild bird, amend the provisions stated above by adding any method of killing or taking wild birds or by omitting any such method as is mentioned[9]. This power must not be exercised, except for the purpose of complying with an international obligation, in relation to any method of killing or taking wild birds which involves the use of a firearm[10].

1 Ie under the Wildlife and Countryside Act 1981 s 16 (1); see para 343 post.
2 As to special penalties see para 348 post.
3 Wildlife and Countryside Act 1981 s 5 (1) (a). It is a good defence to such a charge that the article was so set by the accused for the purpose of killing or taking, in the interests of public health, agriculture, forestry, fisheries or nature conservation, any wild animals which could be lawfully killed or taken by those means and that he took all reasonable precautions to prevent injury to wild birds: s 5 (4). It is also a defence to a charge under s 5 (1) (a) in respect of poison to show that the act alleged to constitute the offence was done for the purpose of destroying grey squirrels or coypus in compliance with an order permitting the use of a specific poison against those animals: Agriculture (Miscellaneous Provisions) Act 1972 s 19 (1), (2); Interpretation Act 1978 s 17 (2) (a). As to such orders see para 425 post. See also note 8 infra.
4 Wildlife and Countryside Act 1981 s 5 (1) (b).
5 Ibid s 27 (1).
6 Ibid s 5 (1) (c).
7 Ibid s 5 (1) (d), (e). As to the special penalty see para 348 post. As to the use of decoys in cruel circumstances see para 457 post. As to immediate pursuit see *Hawthorn v Cramb* 1960 JC 97.
8 Wildlife and Countryside Act 1981 s 5 (1) (f) (added by the Wildlife and Countryside (Amendment) Act 1991 s 1 (3)). As to the statutory exceptions and the special penalty see paras 339, 348 post. In any proceedings under that provision relating to an act mentioned in the Wildlife and Countryside Act 1981 s 5 (1) (a) (see text and note 3 supra) it is a defence to show that the article was set for the purpose of killing or taking wild animals which could be lawfully killed or taken by those means, in the interests of agriculture, public health, forestry, fisheries or nature conservation, and that he took or caused to be taken all reasonable precautions to prevent injury to wild birds: s 5 (4A) (added by the Wildlife and Countryside (Amendment) Act 1991 s 1 (4)).
9 Wildlife and Countryside Act 1981 s 5 (2). At the date at which this volume states the law, no such order had been made.
10 Ibid s 5 (3).

339. Exceptions to unlawful methods of killing or taking wild birds. None of the offences relating to unlawful methods of killing or taking wild birds[1] is committed by an authorised person[2] who uses a cage-trap or net for the purpose of taking a wild bird listed in Part II of Schedule 2 to the Wildlife and Countryside Act 1981[3]; nor by any person who uses nets for the purpose of taking wild duck in a duck decoy which is shown[4] to have been in use immediately before 4 June 1954[5]; nor by any person who uses a cage-trap or net for the purpose of taking any game bird if it is shown[6] that the taking of the bird is solely for the purpose of breeding[7].

Nothing in the above exceptions authorises the use of any net for taking birds in flight, or the use for taking birds on the ground of any net which is projected or propelled otherwise than by hand[8].

1 See para 338 ante.

2 For the meaning of 'authorised person' see para 334 note 2 ante.
3 See para 341 post.
4 The onus of proof is on the defendant; see para 336 note 9 ante.
5 Ie the date of the passing of the Protection of Birds Act 1954 (repealed).
6 See note 4 supra.
7 Wildlife and Countryside Act 1981 s 5 (5).
8 Ibid s 5 (5) proviso.

340. Possession of eggs of game. Any person, whether a licensed dealer[1] or not, who knowingly has in his house, shop, possession or control at any time of the year the eggs of any bird of game[2], swan, wild duck, teal or widgeon which have been wilfully taken out of or destroyed on the nest on any land by anyone who has not the right of killing the game thereon, nor the permission of the owner of such right, is guilty of an offence[3], and is liable upon conviction before two justices to a fine not exceeding level 1 on the standard scale for every egg found in his house, shop, possession or control[4], and if he is a licensed dealer the licence granted to him to deal in game is thereby forfeited[5].

1 As to licences to deal in game see paras 313–319 ante.
2 Ie pheasants, partridges, grouse, heath or moor game or black game: Game Act 1831 s 2.
3 Ibid s 24. It is also an offence, similarly punishable, for any person not having the right of killing game on any land, nor having permission from the person having that right, wilfully to take out of the nest or destroy in the nest the eggs of any of the birds mentioned: s 24. As to game rights generally see para 248 et seq ante.
4 Ibid s 24 (amended by virtue of the Criminal Justice Act 1982 s 46 and by the Statute Law (Repeals) Act 1989 Sch 1 Pt I). As to the standard scale see para 232 note 1 ante. At the date at which this volume states the law, level 1 on that scale is at £50. There is no power, however, to seize the eggs: *Stowe v Benstead* [1909] 2 KB 415, DC. A constable cannot seize eggs in the possession of a carrier under powers given by the Poaching Prevention Act 1862 s 2 (see para 282 ante), and then proceed under the Game Act 1831 against the carrier and any person alleged to have induced him to steal the eggs: *Stowe v Benstead* supra.
5 Game Act 1831 s 22.

341. The scheduled wild birds. The general effect of the Schedules to the Wildlife and Countryside Act 1981 is as follows: those wild birds listed in Schedule 1[1], and their eggs, are protected by special penalties, either at all times (Part I) or only during the appropriate close season[2] (Part II)[3]; those wild birds listed in Schedule 2 may either be killed or taken outside the close season (Part I)[4] or, at any time, only by authorised persons (Part II)[5]; and those wild birds listed in Part I of Schedule 3 may not be sold alive unless ringed and bred in captivity[6].

The Secretary of State may, by order made by statutory instrument, and made either generally or with respect to any specified provisions of the Act, areas of Great Britain[7] or times of the year, add any wild bird to or remove any wild bird from any of or any part of Schedules 1 to 3[8], and any such order adding any bird to Part II of Schedule 1 or to Part I of Schedule 2 may prescribe a close season for that bird, which must commence on a date not later than 21 February and end on a date not earlier than 31 August[9].

1 Wildlife and Countryside Act 1981 Sch 1. The birds included in Part I of that Schedule (birds which are protected by special penalties at all times) are: Avocet (*Recurvirostra avosetta*); Bee-eater (*Merops apiaster*); Bittern (*Botaurus stellaris*); Little Bittern (*Ixobrychus minutus*); Bluethroat (*Luscinia svecica*); Brambling (*Fringilla montifringilla*); Cirl Bunting (*Emberiza cirlus*); Lapland Bunting (*Calcarius lapponicus*); Snow Bunting (*Plectrophenax nivalis*); Honey Buzzard (*Pernis apivorus*); Chough (*Pyrrhocorax pyrrhocorax*); Corncrake (*Crex crex*); Spotted Crake (*Porzana porzana*); all species of Cross-

bills (*Loxia*); Stone Curlew (*Burhinus oedicnemus*); all species of Divers (*Gavia*); Dotterel (*Charadrius morinellus*); Long-tailed Duck (*Clangula hyemalis*); Golden Eagle (*Aquila chrysaetos*); White-tailed Eagle (*Haliaetus albicilla*); Gyr Falcon (*Falco Rusticolus*); Fieldfare (*Turdus pilaris*); Firecrest (*Regulus ignicapillus*); Garganey (*Anas querquedula*); Black-tailed Godwit (*Limosa limosa*); Goshawk (*Accipiter gentilis*); Black-necked Grebe (*Podiceps nigricollis*); Slavonian Grebe (*Podiceps auritus*); Greenshank (*Tringa nebularia*); Little Gull (*Larus minutus*); Mediterranean Gull (*Larus Melanocephalus*); all species of Harriers (*Circus*); Purple Heron (*Ardea purpurea*); Hobby (*Falco subbuteo*); Hoopoe (*Upupa epops*); Kingfisher (*Alcedo atthis*); Red Kite (*Milvus milvus*); Merlin (*Falco columbarius*); Golden Oriole (*Oriolus oriolus*); Osprey (*Pandion haliaetus*); Barn Owl (*Tyto alba*); Snowy Owl (*Nyctea scandiaca*); Peregrine (*Falco peregrinus*); Leach's Petrel (*Oceanodroma leucorhoa*); Red-necked Phalarope (*Phalaropus lobatus*); Kentish Plover (*Charadrius alexandrinus*); Little ringed Plover (*Charadrius dubius*); Common Quail (*Coturnix coturnix*); Black Redstart (*Phoenicurus ochruros*); Redwing (*Turdus iliacus*); Scarlet Rosefinch (*Carpodacus erythrinus*); Ruff (*Philomachus pugnax*); Green Sandpiper (*Tringa ochropus*); Purple Sandpiper (*Calidris maritima*); Wood Sandpiper (*Tringa glareola*); Scaup (*Aythya marila*); Common Scoter (*Melanitta nigra*); Velvet Scoter (*Melanitta fusca*); Serin (*Serinus serinus*); Shorelark (*Eremophila alpestris*); Red-backed Shrike (*Lanius collurio*); Spoonbill (*Platalea leucorodia*); Black-winged Stilt (*Himantopus himantopus*); Temminck's Stint (*Calidris temminckii*); Bewick's Swan (*Cygnus bewickii*); Whooper Swan (*Cygnus cygnus*); Black Tern (*Chlidonias niger*); Little Tern (*Sterna albifrons*); Roseate Tern (*Sterna dougallii*); Bearded Tit (*Panurus biarmicus*); Crested Tit (*Parus cristatus*); Short-toed Treecreeper (*Certhia brachydactyla*); Cetti's Warbler (*Cettia cetti*); Dartford Warbler (*Sylvia undata*); Marsh Warbler (*Acrocephalus palustris*); Savi's Warbler (*Locustella luscinioides*); Whimbrel (*Numenius phaeopus*); Woodlark (*Lullula arborea*); Wryneck (*Jynx torquilla*).

The birds included in Pt II of that Schedule (birds which are protected by special penalties during the close season) are: Goldeneye (*Bucephala clangula*); Greylag Goose (*Anser anser*), only in the Outer Hebrides, Caithness, Sutherland and Wester Ross; Pintail (*Anas acuta*).

2 As to close seasons see para 333 ante.

3 Wildlife and Countryside Act 1981 ss 1, 4, 6, 19, 22.

4 Ibid Sch 2 Pt I lists the following wild birds, which may be killed or taken outside the close season: Capercaillie (*Tetrao urogallus*); Coot (*Fulica atra*); Tufted Duck (*Aythya fuligula*); Gadwall (*Anas strepera*); Goldeneye (*Bucephala clangula*); Canada Goose (*Branta canadensis*); Greylag Goose (*Anser anser*); Pink-footed Goose (*Anser brachyrhynchus*); White-fronted Goose (*Anser albifrons*), only in England and Wales; Mallard (*Anas platyrhynchos*); Moorhen (*Gallinula chloropus*); Pintail (*Anas acuta*); Golden Plover (*Pluvialis apricaria*); Pochard (*Aythya ferina*); Shoveler (*Anas clypeata*); Common Snipe (*Gallinago gallinago*); Teal (*Anas crecca*); Wigeon (*Anas penelope*); Woodcock (*Scolopax rusticola*).

5 Ibid ss 2, 3, 22. For the meaning of 'authorised person' see para 334 note 3 ante. The wild birds listed in Sch 2 Pt II, which may be killed by authorised persons at any time are: Crow (*corvus corone*); Collared Dove (*Streptopelia decaocto*); Great Black-backed Gull (*Larus marinus*); Lesser Black-backed Gull (*Larus fuscus*); Herring Gull (*Larus argentatus*); Jackdaw (*Corvus monedula*); Jay (*Garrulus glandarius*); Magpie (*Pica pica*); Feral Pigeon (*Columba livia*); Rook (*Corvus frugilegus*); House Sparrow (*Passer domesticus*); Starling (*Sturnus vulgaris*); Woodpigeon (*Columba palumbus*).

6 Ibid s 6. The following wild birds which may not be sold alive unless ringed and bred in captivity are listed in Sch 3 Pt I: Blackbird (*Turdus merula*); Brambling (*Fringilla montifringilla*); Bullfinch (*Pyrrhula pyrrhula*); Reed Bunting (*Emberiza schoeniclus*); Chaffinch (*Fringilla coelebs*); Dunnock (*Prunella modularis*); Goldfinch (*Carduelis carduelis*); Greenfinch (*Carduelis chloris*); Jackdaw (*Corvus monedula*); Jay (*Garrulus glandarius*); Linnet (*Carduelis cannabina*); Magpie (*Pica pica*); Barn Owl (*Tyto alba*); Redpoll (*Carduelis flammea*); Siskin (*Carduelis spinus*); Starling (*Sturnus vulgaris*); Song Thrush (*Turdus philomelos*); Twite (*Carduelis flavirostris*); Yellowhammer (*Emberiza citrinella*).

As to the sale of live or dead wild birds see para 344 post.

7 For the meaning of 'Great Britain' see para 309 note 9 ante.

8 Wildlife and Countryside Act 1981 s 22 (1).

9 Ibid s 22 (2).

342. Trapping of wild birds. Unless authorised by licence[1], it is an offence for any person to employ certain methods of killing or trapping wild birds including pheasants, partridges, grouse (or moor game), or black (or heath) game[2], which involve an element of cruelty[3]. An offender is liable on summary conviction to a fine not exceeding level 5 on the standard scale[4].

1 Wildlife and Countryside Act 1981 s 16; see para 343 post.

2 Ibid s 27 (1).
3 Ibid s 5; see para 338 ante.
4 Ibid s 21 (1) (a) (amended by virtue of the Criminal Justice Act 1982 s 46). As to the standard scale see
  para 232 note 1 ante. At the date at which this volume states the law, level 5 on that scale is at £2,000.

(ii) Licences; Sale

343. Power to grant licences. Licences may be granted by specified appropriate
authorities[1] to permit acts which would otherwise contravene one or more of the
provisions of the Wildlife and Countryside Act 1981 concerning the protection of
wild birds, their nests and eggs, if done for certain specified purposes[2].

The specified purposes are (1) scientific or educational; (2) ringing or marking,
or examining any ring or mark on, wild birds; (3) conserving wild birds; (4)
protecting any collection of wild birds; (5) falconry or aviculture; (6) any public
exhibition or competition; (7) taxidermy; (8) photography; (9) preserving public
health or public or air safety; (10) preventing the spread of disease; (11) preventing
serious damage to livestock, foodstuffs for livestock, crops, vegetables, fruit,
growing timber or fisheries[3].

Certain specified provisions of the Act do not apply to anything done under and
in accordance with the terms of a licence granted by the appropriate authority[4].

Licences under the Act may be, to any degree, general or specific; may be
granted either to persons of a class or to a particular person; may be subject to any
specified conditions and subject to modification or revocation at any time; and are
valid for the period stated in the licence[5].

The making of false statements or representations to obtain the grant of a licence
is an offence[6].

The appropriate authority depends upon the nature of the licence involved and
may be the Secretary of State for the Environment or for Wales, the Minister of
Agriculture, Fisheries and Food or the Nature Conservancy Council[7].

1 As to the appropriate authorities see text and note 7 infra.
2 Wildlife and Countryside Act 1981 s 16 (1). The provisions concerned are s 1 (see para 332 ante); s 5
  (see paras 338, 339 ante); s 6 (3) (see para 344 post); s 7 (see para 346 post); s 8 (see para 345 post); and
  orders made under s 3 (see para 335 ante).
3 Ibid s 16 (1).
4 Ibid s 16 (4) (a). The specified provisions are contained in s 6 (1), (2); see para 344 post.
5 Ibid s 16 (5). The authority may charge such reasonable sum as it may determine: s 16 (5).
6 Ibid s 17. As to punishment see s 21 (3), (5), (6) (amended by virtue of the Criminal Justice Act 1982
  s 46); see para 348 post.
7 See the Wildlife and Countryside Act 1981 ss 16 (9) (which sets out the appropriate authority in
  respect of licences covering the various provisions of the Act) and 27 (1). Provision is included for
  consultation involving advisory bodies such as the Nature Conservancy Council; see eg s 16 (9) (a),
  (b), (10).

344. Sale of live or dead wild birds and their eggs. Except when authorised
under a licence granted by the appropriate authority[1], it is an offence for any person
(1) to sell, offer or expose for sale or have in his possession, or transport for the
purpose of sale, any live wild bird other than a bird included in Part I of Schedule 3

to the Wildlife and Countryside Act 1981[2], or an egg of a wild bird or any part of such an egg; or (2) to publish or cause to be published any advertisement likely to be understood as conveying that he buys or sells, or intends to buy or sell, any of those things[3].

Except when authorised by licence, it is an offence for any person not for the time being registered in accordance with regulations made by the Secretary of State[4], similarly (a) to sell, offer or expose for sale or have in his possession, or transport for the purpose of sale, any dead wild bird other than a bird included in Part II or III of Schedule 3 to the Act[5], or any part of, or anything derived from, such a wild bird; or (b) to publish or cause to be published any advertisement likely to be understood as conveying that he buys or sells, or intends to buy or sell, any of those things[6].

Except when authorised by licence, it is an offence for any person to show, or cause or permit to be shown, for the purposes of any competition or in any premises where a competition is being held (i) any live wild bird other than one included in Part I of Schedule 3 to the Act[7] or (ii) any live bird one of whose parents was such a wild bird[8].

Any person convicted of any of the offences mentioned above in respect of a bird included in Schedule 1 to the Act[9] or in respect of any part of, or anything derived from, such a bird, or an egg of such bird or any part of such an egg, is liable to a special penalty[10].

Any person authorised in writing by the Secretary of State may at any reasonable time and, if required to do so, upon producing evidence that he is authorised, enter and inspect any premises where a registered person keeps any wild birds, for the purpose of ascertaining whether an offence under these provisions is being, or has been, committed on the premises[11]. The intentional obstruction of such a person exercising such a power is an offence[12].

1 See para 343 text and note 7 ante.
2 See para 341 ante. A reference in the Wildlife and Countryside Act 1981 s 6 to a bird included in Sch 3 Pt I is a reference to any bird in that Part which was bred in captivity and has been ringed or marked in accordance with regulations made by the Secretary of State: s 6 (5); see the Wildlife and Country-side (Ringing of Certain Birds) Regulations 1982, SI 1982/1220. A bird is not to be treated as bred in captivity unless its parents were lawfully in captivity when the egg was laid: Wildlife and Country-side Act 1981 s 27 (2).
3 Ibid s 6 (1). 'Advertisement' includes a catalogue, a circular and a price list: s 27 (1). For penalties see para 348 post.
4 A person who, for the purposes of obtaining such a registration, whether for himself or another, knowingly or recklessly makes a statement or representation, or furnishes a document or infor-mation, which is false in a material particular, is guilty of an offence: ibid s 17. For penalties see para 348 post.
5 The birds included in the Wildlife and Countryside Act 1981 Sch 3 Pt II (birds which may be sold dead at all times) are: Feral Pigeon (*Columba livia*); Woodpigeon (*Columba palumbus*).
    The birds included in Sch 3 Pt III (birds which may be sold dead from 1 September to 28 February) are: Capercaillie (*Tetrao urogallus*); Coot (*Fulica atra*); Tufted Duck (*Aythya fuligula*); Mallard (*Anas platyrhynchos*); Pintail (*Anas acuta*); Golden Plover (*Pluvialis apricaria*); Pochard (*Aythya ferina*); Shoveler (*Anas clypeata*); Common Snipe (*Gallinago gallinago*); Teal (*Anas crecca*); Wigeon (*Anas penelope*); Woodcock (*Scolopax rusticola*).
    Any reference in s 6 to any bird included in Sch 3 Pt II or III is a reference to any bird included in Pt II and, between 1 September and 28 February following, any bird included in Pt III: s 6 (6).
6 Ibid s 6 (2). For penalties see para 348 post. See the Wildlife and Countryside (Registration to Sell, etc, Certain Dead Wild Birds) Regulations 1982, SI 1982/1219.
7 See para 341 ante and note 2 supra.
8 Wildlife and Countryside Act 1981 s 6 (3). For penalties see para 348 post.
9 See para 341 ante.

10 Wildlife and Countryside Act 1981 s 6 (4). For special penalties see para 348 post.
11 Ibid s 6 (9). See also s 19 (3); para 347 post.
12 Ibid s 6 (10). For penalties see para 348 post.

(iii) Captive Birds

345. Protection of captive birds. Any person who keeps or confines any bird in any cage or other receptacle which is not sufficient in height, length and breadth to permit it to stretch its wings freely is guilty of an offence under the Wildlife and Countryside Act 1981 and liable to a special penalty[1].

This provision does not apply to poultry, nor to the keeping and confining of any bird while it is in the course of conveyance by whatever means, or while it is being shown for exhibition or competition purposes for a period not exceeding 72 hours, or while it is undergoing veterinary treatment[2].

Any person who promotes, arranges, conducts, assists in, receives money for or takes part in any event at or during which captive birds are liberated by hand or other means for the purpose of thereupon being shot, or who, as the owner or occupier of land, permits it to be used for such an event, is guilty of an offence and liable to a special penalty[3].

1 Wildlife and Countryside Act 1981 s 8 (1). For penalties see para 348 post. It is suggested that 'keeping' clearly encompasses a wider class of person than the owner. Cf 'keeping an animal' for the purposes of the Animals Act 1971 s 2 (1); see para 467 post. As to the protection of captive birds from cruelty see para 457 post.
2 Wildlife and Countryside Act 1981 s 8 (2).
3 Ibid s 8 (3). For special penalties see para 348 post. For the meaning of 'occupier' and 'poultry' see s 27 (1); and, in relation to poultry, para 332 ante.

346. Registration of captive birds. If any person keeps or has in his possession or under his control any bird included in Schedule 4 to the Wildlife and Countryside Act 1981[1] which has not been registered and ringed or marked in accordance with regulations[2] made by the Secretary of State, he is guilty of an offence and liable to a special penalty[3].

If any person keeps or has in his possession or under his control any bird included in Schedule 4 to the Act either within five years of having been convicted of an offence under Part I of the Act for which a special penalty is provided, or within three years of having been convicted of any other offence under Part I relating to the protection of birds or other animals, or any offence involving their ill-treatment, he is guilty of an offence[4].

If any person knowingly disposes of or offers to dispose of any bird included in Schedule 4 to any person within the periods detailed above after that person's conviction for either of the above offences, he is guilty of an offence[5].

Any person authorised in writing by the Secretary of State may at any reasonable time and, if required to do so, upon producing evidence that he is authorised, enter and inspect any premises where any birds included in Schedule 4 are kept, for the purpose of ascertaining whether an offence under these provisions is being, or has been, committed on the premises[6]. The intentional obstruction of such a person exercising such a power is an offence[7].

The above-mentioned provisions do not apply to anything done for certain purposes under licence[8].

1 The birds included in the Wildlife and Countryside Act 1981 Sch 4 are: Avocet (*Recurvirostra avosetta*); Bee-eater (*Merops apiaster*); Bittern (*Botaurus stellaris*); Little Bittern (*Ixobrychus minutus*); Bluethroat (*Luscinia svecica*); Cirl Bunting (*Emberiza cirlus*); Lapland Bunting (*Calcarius lapponicus*); Snow Bunting (*Plectrophenax nivalis*); Chough (*Pyrrhocorax pyrrhocorax*); Corncrake (Crex crex); Spotted Crake (*Porzana porzana*); all species of Crossbills (*Loxia*); Stone Curlew (*Burhinus oedicnemus*); all species of Divers (*Gavia*); Dotterel (*Charadrius morinellus*); Long-tailed Duck (*Clangula hyemalis*); all species of Falcons (*Falconidae*); Fieldfare (*Turdus pilaris*); Firecrest (*Regulus ignicapillus*); Black-tailed Godwit (*Limosa limosa*); Black-necked Grebe (*Podiceps nigricollis*); Slavonian Grebe (*Podiceps auritus*); Greenshank (*Tringa nebularia*); True Hawks, except Buzzards, Eagles, Harriers, Hawks and Kites (*Accipitridae*, except the genera *Aegypius, Gypaetus, Gypohierax, Gyps, Neophron, Sarcogyps* and *Trigonoceps*); Hoopoe (*Upupa epops*); Kingfisher (*Alcedo atthis*); Golden Oriole (*Oriolus oriolus*); Osprey (*Pandion haliaetus*); Leach's Petrel (*Oceanodroma leucorhoa*); Red-necked Phalarope (*Phalaropus lobatus*); Kentish Plover (*Charadrius alexandrinus*); Little ringed Plover (*Charadrius dubius*); Common Quail (*Coturnix coturnix*); Black Redstart (*Phoenicurus ochruros*); Redwing (*Turdus iliacus*); Scarlet Rosefinch (*Carpodacus erythrinus*); Ruff (*Philomachus pugnax*); Green Sandpiper (*Tringa ochropus*); Purple Sandpiper (*Calidris maritima*); Wood Sandpiper (*Tringa glareola*); Common Scoter (*Melanitta nigra*); Velvet Scoter (*Melanitta fusca*); Serin (*Serinus serinus*); Shorelark (*Eremophila alpestris*); Red-backed Shrike (*Lanius collurio*); Spoonbill (*Platalea leucorodia*); Black-winged Stilt (*Himantopus himantopus*); Temminck's Stint (*Calidris temminckii*); Black Tern (*Chlidonias niger*); Little Tern (*Sterna albifrons*); Roseate Tern (*Sterna dougallii*); Bearded Tit (*Panurus biarmicus*); Crested Tit (*Parus cristatus*); Short-toed Treecreeper (*Certhia brachydactyla*); Cetti's Warbler (*Cettia cetti*); Dartford Warbler (*Sylvia undata*); Marsh Warbler (*Acrocephalus palustris*); Savi's Warbler (*Locustella luscinioides*); Whimbrel (*Numenius phaeopus*); Woodlark (*Lullula arborea*); Wryneck (*Jynx torquilla*).
2 See the Wildlife and Countryside (Registration and Ringing of Certain Captive Birds) Regulations 1982, SI 1982/1221 (amended by SI 1991/478), made under the Wildlife and Countryside Act 1981 s 7 (2). The obtaining of a registration by means of knowingly or recklessly making false statements or representations is an offence: s 17. For penalties see para 348 post.
3 Ibid s 7 (1). For special penalty see para 348 post.
4 Ibid s 7 (3). No account is to be taken for these purposes of any conviction which has become spent for the purposes of the Rehabilitation of Offenders Act 1974 (as to which see CRIMINAL LAW vol 11 (2) (Reissue) para 1566 et seq): Wildlife and Countryside Act 1981 s 7 (5). For penalties see para 348 post.
5 Ibid s 7 (4). See also note 4 supra.
6 Ibid s 7 (6).
7 Ibid s 7 (7). For penalties see para 348 post.
8 Ibid s 16 (1); see para 343 ante.

(iv) Legal Proceedings

347. Search and arrest. If a constable suspects with reasonable cause that any person is committing or has committed an offence under Part I of the Wildlife and Countryside Act 1981, he has power without warrant to stop and search that person, search or examine any thing he is using and seize and detain any thing which may be evidence of the commission of the offence, and for the purpose of exercising such powers or of arresting a person for such offence, he may enter any land other than a dwelling house[1].

Any authorised person[2] may enter and inspect premises to ascertain whether an offence in respect of the sale of wild birds, their eggs or any part of such birds or eggs is being or has been committed[3]. In addition, if a justice of the peace is satisfied on information on oath that there are reasonable grounds for suspecting that an offence under Part I of the Act in respect of which a special penalty is provided[4], or an offence as above, has been committed and that evidence of the offence may be found on any premises, he may grant a warrant to any constable, with or without other persons, to enter and search those premises[5].

1 Wildlife and Countryside Act 1981 s 19 (1), (2) (amended by the Police and Criminal Evidence Act 1984 ss 26 (1), 119 (1), Sch 6 Pt I para 25, Sch 7 Pt I). See also the Police and Criminal Evidence Act 1984 ss 25, 53 (1); and CRIMINAL LAW vol 11 (1) (Reissue) paras 660 et seq, 707.

2 For the meaning of 'authorised person' see the Police and Criminal Evidence Act 1984 s 25 (1); and paras 343, 344 ante.
3 Ie under the Wildlife and Countryside Act 1981 s 6 (see para 344 ante): s 6 (9).
4 Ie under ibid ss 1, 3, 5, 7, 8.
5 Ibid s 19 (3).

348. Proceedings and penalties. Summary proceedings for offences under Part I of the Wildlife and Countryside Act 1981 involving the killing, taking, etc of any wild bird or the taking of an egg of such a bird[1], or the infringement of the protection afforded to wild birds specified in areas of special protection[2], may be brought within six months from the date on which evidence sufficient in the prosecutor's opinion to warrant the proceedings came to his notice[3]. A certificate signed by or on his behalf stating the relevant date is conclusive[4].

A local authority[5] may institute proceedings for any offence under Part I of the Act or any order made under it which is committed within its area[6]. For the purpose of jurisdiction, an offence is deemed to have been committed in any place where the offender is found or to which he is first brought after the commission of the offence[7].

A person found guilty on summary conviction of an offence under Part I of the Act or any order made under it which carries a special penalty[8] is liable to a fine not exceeding level 5 on the standard scale; a summary conviction for obtaining a licence by a false statement or representation[9] is punishable by a fine not exceeding level 4 on the standard scale, and a summary conviction for any other offence by a fine not exceeding level 3 on that scale[10]. Where an offence was committed in respect of more than one bird, nest, egg or other thing, the maximum fine is to be determined as if the person convicted had been convicted of a separate offence in respect of each bird, nest, egg or thing[11]. On conviction, the court must order the forfeiture of any bird, nest, egg or other thing in respect of which the offence was committed, and may order the forfeiture of any vehicle, animal, weapon or other thing which was used to commit the offence[12].

1 Ie under the Wildlife and Countryside Act 1981 s 1; see para 332 ante. Part I of the Act comprises ss 1–27.
2 Ie under ibid s 3 (1); see para 335 ante.
3 Ibid s 20 (1), (2). No such proceedings may be brought more than two years after the commission of the offence: s 20 (2).
4 Ibid s 20 (3).
5 'Local authority' means a county, district or London borough council or the Common Council of the City of London: ibid ss 27 (1), 71 (amended by the Local Government Act 1985 s 102 (2), Sch 17).
6 Wildlife and Countryside Act 1981 s 25 (2).
7 Ibid s 21 (7).
8 Ie under ibid ss 1, 3, 5, 6, 7 or 8.
9 Ie under ibid s 17; see para 343 text and note 6 ante.
10 Ibid s 21 (1), (3) (amended by virtue of the Criminal Justice Act 1982 s 46). As to the standard scale see para 232 note 1 ante. At the date at which this volume states the law, level 3 on that scale is at £400, level 4 at £1,000 and level 5 at £2,000.
11 Wildlife and Countryside Act 1981 s 21 (5).
12 Ibid s 21 (6).

(v) Administration

349. Secretary of State's power to make orders. The powers of the Secretary of State to make orders under the various provisions of the Wildlife and Countryside Act 1981 have been noted specifically in the appropriate paragraphs throughout[1]. He is assisted in administering the Act generally and in assessing the different questions arising in the protection of animals by such advisory body or bodies as he may establish, consisting of such members as he may from time to time appoint, and to which he may assign the duty to advise him on any question he may refer to them, or upon which they consider that they should offer their advice[2]. He must consult with whichever of the advisory bodies he considers is best able to advise him as to the making of the particular order[3].

Orders are made by statutory instrument and in certain cases[4] are subject to annulment in pursuance of a resolution of either House of Parliament[5]. Notice of the making of orders must be published in the London Gazette[6].

Every local authority[7] must take such steps as it considers expedient for bringing to the attention of the public and of schoolchildren in particular the effect of the provisions of Part I of the Act and of any order made thereunder affecting the whole or any part of its area[8].

1 The powers are: (1) to vary the close seasons for all or part of Great Britain (Wildlife and Countryside Act 1981 s 2 (5); see para 333 ante); (2) to create areas of special protection by restricting the killing, etc, of birds therein (s 3 (1); see para 335 ante); (3) to vary the birds listed in the Schedules to the Act, by species, areas or times of year (s 22 (1), (2); see para 341 ante); (4) to make special protective orders for periods outside the close seasons (s 2 (6); see para 337 ante).
2 Ibid s 23.
3 Ibid s 26 (4) (b). He may also give the appropriate local authorities, and any other person affected, the opportunity to submit objections or representations, and he may, if he thinks fit, hold a public inquiry: s 26 (4) (a), (c). He must consider any proposals for orders with respect to any area made to him by the local authority for that area: s 26 (6).
4 Ie in the present context those made under ibid s 2 (5) (varying the close seasons) or s 22 (varying the Schedules): s 26 (2).
5 Ibid s 26 (1).
6 Ibid s 26 (5).
7 For the meaning of 'local authority' see para 348 note 5 ante.
8 Wildlife and Countryside Act 1981 s 25 (1). Part I of the Act comprises ss 1–27.

(3) PROTECTION OF ANTARCTIC FAUNA

350. General conservation provisions. The Antarctic Treaty Act 1967 gives effect to measures agreed upon for the conservation of Antarctic fauna and flora by the parties to the Antarctic Treaty[1] signed at Washington on 1 December 1959. The Act has been extended by Order in Council to the Isle of Man[2] and to the Channel Islands[3], and can be so extended to any colony[4].

In general, except under the authority of a permit issued by the Secretary of State[5] or by or on behalf of another contracting party[6], no person to whom the provision applies[7] may, when he is in any part of Antarctica[8], wilfully[9] kill, injure, molest or take any native mammal or native bird[10]; gather any native plant within a specially protected area[11] or drive any vehicle within such an area[12]; or bring into Antarctica any mammal or bird of a species not indigenous to Antarctica[13]. Exempted from this are observers and exchanged scientists and their staffs designated by one of the contracting parties[14].

1 For the Treaty see the Antarctic Treaty Act 1967 Sch 1.
2 Antarctic Treaty Act 1967 (Isle of Man) Order 1970, SI 1970/1436 (amended by SI 1990/1198).
3 Antarctic Treaty Act 1967 (Channel Islands) Order 1974, SI 1974/1109.
4 Antarctic Treaty Act 1967 s 9.

5 Ibid s 2 (1) (a). He may delegate his powers to certain persons: see s 3 (2). The permit may be subject to conditions and limitations: s 3 (3). Failure to comply with its requirements in an offence carrying on summary conviction a fine not exceeding level 3 on the standard scale; a similar penalty applies where any false statement is made knowingly or recklessly in any report called for by the Secretary of State under s 3 (4) when granting a permit: s 4 (4) (amended by virtue of the Criminal Justice Act 1982 ss 38, 46). As to the standard scale see para 232 note 1 ante. At the date at which this volume states the law, level 3 on that scale is at £400.

6 Antarctic Treaty Act 1967 s 2 (1) (b). 'Contracting party' means a party to the Antarctic Treaty: s 10 (5).

7 Ie any British citizen, British Dependent Territories citizen or British Overseas citizen; any person who under the British Nationality Act 1981 is a British subject or a British protected person; any other person owning or crewing a British ship registered in the United Kingdom; and British Nationals (Overseas): Antarctic Treaty Act 1967 s 1 (3) (amended by the British Nationality Act 1981 s 52 (6), Sch 7 and the Hong Kong (British Nationality) Order 1986, SI 1986/948, art 8, Schedule). The list may be extended by Order in Council to other persons: Antarctic Treaty Act 1967 s 7 (4).

8 'Antarctica' means the area south of the 60th parallel of south latitude, and the high seas including ice shelves: ibid ss 7 (3), 10 (5); Conservation of Antarctic Mammals and Birds (High Seas) Order 1973, SI 1973/1755.

9 For the meaning of 'wilfully' see para 415 note 2 post.

10 Antarctic Treaty Act 1967 s 1 (1) (a). 'Native mammal' and 'native bird' mean any mammal or bird at any stage of its life cycle (including eggs) indigenous to the Antarctic or occurring there through natural agencies of dispersal (but not whales): s 10 (5), Sch 2 art II (a), (b).

11 Ie an area designated under the Antarctic Treaty Act 1967: ss 7 (2) (b), 10 (5). Such areas have been designated under Sch 2 Annex B and (by orders made under s 7 (2) (b)) by the Antarctic Treaty (Specially Protected Areas) Orders 1968, SI 1968/888 (amended by SI 1977/1235 and SI 1988/587); 1971, SI 1971/1236; 1977, SI 1977/1235; and 1988, SI 1988/587.

12 Antarctic Treaty Act 1967 s 1 (1) (b).

13 Ibid s 1 (2).

14 Ibid s 1 (4). As to observers and exchanged scientists see s 10 (5), Sch 1 arts III (1) (b), VII (1).

351. Offences and penalties. Any act done or attempted in contravention of the provisions for general conservation[1] is an offence[2], but it is a defence to prove that the act was done or attempted in extreme emergency involving possible loss of human life or the safety of a ship or aircraft[3]. Summary conviction carries a maximum penalty of level 3 on the standard scale[4], but the wilful killing or taking of any seal by the owner or master of a British ship registered in the United Kingdom, or by any member of its crew, is punishable summarily by imprisonment for a term not exceeding three months or a fine not exceeding the prescribed sum[5] or both, or on indictment by imprisonment for a term not exceeding two years or a fine or both[6].

1 See para 350 ante.

2 Antarctic Treaty Act 1967 s 1 (5).

3 Ibid s 2 (3). The onus of proof is on the defendant; see para 336 note 9 ante.

4 Ibid s 4 (2), (3) (amended by virtue of the Criminal Justice Act 1982 ss 38, 46). As to the standard scale see para 232 note 1 ante. At the date at which this volume states the law, level 3 on that scale is at £400.

5 As to the prescribed sum see para 233 note 3 ante. At the date at which this volume states the law, the prescribed sum is £2,000.

6 Antarctic Treaty Act 1967 s 4 (1) (amended by virtue of the Magistrates' Courts Act 1980 s 32 (2)). As to the protection of seals generally see the Conservation of Seals Act 1970; and FISHERIES vol 18 para 936 et seq.

(4) PROTECTION OF BADGERS

352. Taking, injuring or killing badgers or interfering with badger setts. The Badgers Act 1973 gives special protection to badgers.

It is an offence[1] wilfully[2] to kill, injure or take a badger[3], or to attempt to do so[4]; or to dig for any badger[5]. It is also an offence[6] to use in the course of killing or taking any badger (or attempting to do so) any badger tongs[7]; or to use for the purpose of killing or taking any badger certain firearms[8].

As from 25 October 1991 it is also an offence[9] for a person, intentionally or recklessly as to whether his actions will have the prohibited consequences, to interfere with a badger sett[10] by (1) damaging a sett or any part of it, (2) destroying a sett, (3) obstructing access to or any entrance of a sett, (4) causing a dog to enter a sett, or (5) disturbing a badger when it is occupying a sett[11].

1 For general exceptions see para 356 post; as to enforcement, proceedings and penalties see para 357 post.
2 For the meaning of 'wilfully' see para 415 note 2 post.
3 'Badger' means any member of the species *Meles meles*: Badgers Act 1973 s 11. Badgers are also given protection by the Wildlife and Countryside Act 1981 Pt I (ss 1–27) (see para 348 et seq post).
4 Badgers Act 1973 s 1 (1). As to where a dog is present or used in the commission of this offence see para 357 post. A person is not guilty of this offence by reason of the killing or taking or the attempted killing or taking of any badger, or the injuring of any badger in the course of taking it or attempting to kill or take it, if he shows that his action was necessary for the purpose of preventing serious damage to land, crops, poultry or any other form of property. However, this defence does not apply if it had become apparent, before the action was taken, that the action would prove necessary for the purposes mentioned and either a licence authorising the action had not been applied for as soon as was reasonably practicable thereafter, or an application for such a licence had been determined: s 8 (1A) (a), (b), (1B) (added by the Wildlife and Countryside Act 1981 s 12, Sch 7 para 10 (1)). As to licences see para 356 post. A person found committing this offence on any land may be required by the owner or occupier of the land, any servant of his, or any constable, to quit the land forthwith and also to give his name and address. If that person wilfully remains on the land, or refuses to give his full name or address, he commits an offence punishable on summary conviction with a maximum fine of level 3 on the standard scale: Badgers Act 1973 ss 5, 10 (2) (a) (amended by virtue of the Criminal Justice Act 1982 s 46; as from a day to be appointed s 10 (2) is amended by the Criminal Justice Act 1991 s 26 (3) and the relevant provision becomes s 10 (2) (c)). As to the standard scale see para 232 note 1 ante. At the date at which this volume states the law, level 3 on that scale is at £400.
5 Badgers Act 1973 s 2 (1) (c) (amended by the Wildlife and Countryside Act 1981 Sch 7 para 9 (2) and the Wildlife and Countryside (Amendment) Act 1985 s 1 (2)). As to where a dog is present at or used in the commission of this offence see para 357 post.
6 See note 1 supra.
7 Badgers Act 1973 s 2 (1) (b) (amended by the Wildlife and Countryside (Amendment) Act 1985 s 1 (2)). See also note 5 supra.
8 Badgers Act 1973 s 2 (1) (d) (amended by the Wildlife and Countryside (Amendment) Act 1985 s 1 (2)). See also note 5 supra. The firearms permitted are a smooth bore weapon of not less than 20 bore and a rifle using ammunition having a muzzle energy of not less than 160 footpounds and a bullet weighing not less than 38 grains: Badgers Act 1973 s 2 (1) (d). 'Firearm' and 'ammunition' have the same meaning as in the Firearms Act 1968 s 57 (as to which see CRIMINAL LAW vol 11 (1) (Reissue) paras 197, 200): Badgers Act 1973 s 11.
9 See note 1 supra.
10 'Badger sett' means any structure or place which displays signs indicating current use by a badger: Badgers Act 1973 s 11 (definition added by the Badgers Act 1991 s 5).
11 Badgers Act 1973 s 2 (3) (added by the Badgers Act 1991 s 1). A person is not guilty of this offence if he shows that his action was necessary for the purpose of preventing serious damage to land, crops, poultry or any other form of property: Badgers Act 1973 s 8 (1A) (c) (added by the Badgers Act 1991 s 2 (1)). As to when this defence does not apply see the 1973 Act s 8 (1B) (as added: see note 4 supra). A person is not guilty of an offence of damaging a sett or obstructing access to or an entrance of a sett, or of disturbing a badger in occupation, if he shows that his action was the incidental result of a lawful operation and could not reasonably have been avoided, or in certain circumstances relating to

foxhunting with hounds where his only action is to obstruct entrances with specified materials in a specified manner, or where the offence would be committed by virtue of his hounds marking at a badger sett provided the hounds are withdrawn as soon as reasonably practicable: Badgers Act 1973 s 8 (4)–(6) (added by the Badgers Act 1991 ss 2 (2), 3).

353. Possession of badgers. It is an offence[1] for any person to have in his possession or under his control any dead badger or any part of, or anything derived from, a dead badger[2]; and for any person to sell[3], offer for sale or have in his possession or under his control any live badger[4].

1 For exceptions see para 356 post; as to enforcement, proceedings and penalties see para 357 post.
2 Badgers Act 1973 s 1 (2) (substituted by the Wildlife and Countryside Act 1981 s 12, Sch 7 para 8). A person has a defence if he shows that the badger had not been killed, or was not killed in contravention of the provisions of the Badgers Act 1973; or if he shows that the thing in question had been sold (whether to him or to any other person) and, at the time of the purchase, the purchaser had had no reason to believe that the badger had been killed in contravention of the Act: s 1 (3) (as so substituted). The offender may be required to quit land and give his name and address, as for an offence under s 1 (1): see s 5; and para 352 note 4 ante.
3 'Sale' includes hire, barter and exchange, and cognate expressions are to be construed accordingly: ibid s 11 (amended by the Wildlife and Countryside Act 1981 Sch 7 para 12).
4 Badgers Act 1973 s 3. This offence is not committed if a person has a live badger in his possession or under his control and either it has been kept in captivity by that person for a continuous period beginning before the passing of the Act (ie before 25 July 1973); or it is in that person's possession or under his control in the course of his business as a carrier; or it has been taken when it had been already disabled, it was taken solely for the purpose of tending it, and it is necessary for that purpose for it to remain in that person's possession or under his control: s 8 (2) (amended by the Wildlife and Countryside Act 1981 ss 12, 73, Sch 7 para 9 (4), Sch 17 Pt II).

354. Cruelty to badgers. It is an offence[1] for any person cruelly to ill-treat any badger[2].

1 For exceptions see para 356 post; as to enforcement, proceedings and penalties see para 357 post.
2 Badgers Act 1973 s 2 (1) (a) (amended by the Wildlife and Countryside (Amendment) Act 1985 s 1 (2)). The offences under the Badgers Act 1973 s 2 (1) (b)–(d), described in para 352 ante, are also described in the sidenote to the section as offences of cruelty. As to where a dog is present at or used in the commission of this offence see para 357 post.

355. Marking and ringing. It is an offence[1] for any person to mark, or attach any ring, tag or other marking device to, any badger[2].

1 For exceptions see para 356 post; as to enforcement, proceedings and penalties see para 357 post.
2 Badgers Act 1973 s 4.

356. Exceptions; licences. A person is not guilty of an offence[1] by reason only of the following: the taking or attempted taking of any badger which had been disabled otherwise than by his act and was so taken or to be taken solely for the purpose of tending it; the killing or attempted killing of any badger which appeared to be so seriously injured or in such a condition that to kill it would be an act of mercy; or the unavoidable killing or injuring of any badger as an incidental result of a lawful action[2]. Nor is a person guilty by reason only of doing anything which is authorised under the Animals (Scientific Procedures) Act 1986[3].

Additionally, a licence may be granted to any person by the Nature Conservancy Council authorising that person to kill, take, sell, have in his possession, or mark badgers or interfere with setts in certain limited circumstances[4]. The Minister of Agriculture, Fisheries and Food or, in Wales, the Secretary of State for Wales[5], may also grant a licence to any person, authorising him to kill or take badgers or interfere with setts within an area specified in the licence, by any means so specified for the purpose of preventing the spread of disease[6] or for the purpose of preventing serious damage to land, crops, poultry or any other form of property, or to interfere with any badger sett for the purpose of any agricultural or forestry operation or any work to maintain or improve watercourses, or any drainage works including works for defence against sea or tidal water[7]. The relevant minister of the Nature Conservancy Council for England (or the Countryside Council for Wales) may grant a licence to interfere with a badger sett for the purpose of controlling foxes in order to protect livestock, game or wildlife[8]. A licence may be revoked at any time by the authority that granted it[9]. The licence may be granted subject to compliance with any conditions specified in it[10]. Any person who contravenes or fails to comply with any condition imposed on the grant of a licence commits an offence, and this is without prejudice to any other liability to a penalty which he may have incurred under the Badgers Act 1973 or any other Act[11].

A licence under these provisions must not be unreasonably withheld or revoked[12].

1 Ie under the Badgers Act 1973: see paras 352–355 ante.
2 Ibid s 8 (1).
3 Ibid s 8 (3); see para 429 et seq post.
4 Ibid s 9 (1) (a)–(c), (2) (a) (amended by the Nature Conservancy Council Act 1973 s 1, Sch 1 para 12, and by the Badgers Act 1991 s 4 (e)). Licences may be granted authorising the taking or killing (by specified means), sale, or possession of a specified number of badgers for scientific or educational purposes, or for the conservation of badgers (Badgers Act 1973 s 9 (1) (a)); authorising the taking (by specified means), sale, or possession of a specified number of badgers for the purpose of any zoological gardens or collection specified in the licence (s 9 (1) (b)); and authorising the marking of badgers, or the attaching to them of any ring, tag or other marking device as specified in the licence, for the purpose of ringing and marking (s 9 (1) (c)); and authorising the interference with any sett for the purpose of a development under the Town and Country Planning Act 1990 s 55 (1), of investigating any offence in connection with proceedings before any court, or of investigating or preserving a monument under the Ancient Monuments and Archaeological Areas Act 1979 s 1: Badgers Act 1973 s 9 (1) (f), (i), (j) (added by the Badgers Act 1991 s 4 (d)). The licence will specify the area in which the activity is authorised: see the Badgers Act 1973 s 9 (1) (a)–(c), (f), (i), (j).
5 See the Transfer of Functions (Wales) (No 1) Order 1978, SI 1978/272, art 2, Sch 1.
6 If the use of poison is sanctioned by the licence for this purpose, it is a defence in proceedings under the Protection of Animals Act 1911 s 8 (b) (as to which see para 425 post) to show that the act alleged to constitute the offence was done under the authority of such a licence and that any conditions specified in the licence were complied with: Badgers Act 1973 s 9 (4) (added by the Conservation of Wild Creatures and Wild Plants Act 1975 s 16, and saved by the Wildlife and Countryside Act 1981 s 73 (4)).
7 Badgers Act 1973 s 9 (1) (d), (e), (g), (h), (2) (b) (amended by the Wildlife and Countryside Act 1981 s 12, Sch 7 para 10 (2), (3); s 9 (1) (g), (h) added by the Badgers Act 1991 s 4 (d); s 9 (2) (b) amended by the 1991 Act s 4 (f)). The minister must consult from time to time with the Nature Conservancy Council as to the issue of licences for the purpose of preventing serious damage to property or in relation to agricultural, forestry or drainage works, and may not grant a licence of any description unless he has been advised by the Council as to the circumstances in which, in the Council's opinion, licences of that description should be granted: Badgers Act 1973 s 9 (5) (added by the Wildlife and Countryside Act 1981 Sch 7 para 10 (3), and renumbered (in consequence of a previous drafting error) and amended by the Badgers Act 1991 s 4 (h)).
8 Badgers Act 1973 s 9 (1) (k), (2) (c) (added by the Badgers Act 1991 s 4 (d), (g) respectively).
9 Badgers Act 1973 s 9 (3).
10 See ibid s 9 (1).

11 Ibid s 9 (3). As to enforcement, proceedings and penalties see para 357 post. The exceptions described in the text to notes 1–3 supra apply equally to this offence: see s 8.

12 Ibid s 9 (6) (added by the Badgers Act 1991 s 4 (i)).

357. Enforcement, proceedings and penalties. A constable who has reasonable grounds for suspecting that any person is committing an offence under the Badgers Act 1973, or that he has committed such an offence and evidence of the commission of the offence is to be found on him or any vehicle or article he has with him, may without warrant stop and search him and search any vehicle or article he has with him[1]; and he may seize and detain for the purposes of proceedings anything which may be evidence of the commission of the offence, or may be liable to be forfeited[2]. The court before which any person is convicted of such an offence must order the forfeiture of any badger or badger's skin in respect of which the offence was committed, and may, if it thinks fit, order the forfeiture of any weapon or article in respect of or by means of which the offence was committed[3].

In any proceedings for an offence consisting of attempting to kill, injure or take a badger[4], if there is evidence from which it could be reasonably concluded that at the material time the accused was attempting to kill, injure or take a badger, he is presumed to have been attempting to do so unless the contrary is shown[5]. Similarly, in any proceedings for an offence of digging for a badger[6], if there is evidence from which it could reasonably be concluded that at the material time the accused was digging for a badger, he is presumed to have been doing so unless the contrary is shown[7].

All but one of the offences[8] under the Badgers Act 1973 are punishable on summary conviction by a fine not exceeding level 5 on the standard scale[9]; if, however, the offence was committed in respect of more than one badger the maximum fine is to be determined as if the person convicted has been convicted of a separate offence in respect of each badger[10].

Where a dog has been used in or was present at the commission of an offence relating to the taking, injuring or killing of badgers or to cruelty to badgers[11], the court may, on convicting the offender, in addition to or substitution for any other sentence, order the destruction[12] or disposal of the dog or disqualify[13] the offender from having custody of a dog for such period as it thinks fit[14]. Where an order is made for destruction or disposal, the court may appoint a person to undertake such destruction or disposal, and require any person having custody of the dog to give it up for that purpose[15]. The offender may be ordered to pay the expenses of destruction or disposal and of the keeping of the dog before destruction or disposal[16].

1 Badgers Act 1973 s 10 (1) (a).

2 Ibid s 10 (1) (c). As to forfeiture see the text to note 3 infra.

3 Ibid s 10 (3).

4 Ie under ibid s 1 (1): see para 352 ante.

5 Ibid s 1 (1A) (added by the Wildlife and Countryside (Amendment) Act 1985 s 1 (1)). The onus of proof is therefore on the defendant to show the contrary. It is submitted that, in accordance with general principles, the standard of proof is the balance of probabilities. See para 336 note 9 ante.

6 Ie under the Badgers Act 1973 s 2 (1) (c): see para 352 ante.

7 Ibid s 2 (2) (added by the Wildlife and Countryside (Amendment) Act 1985 s 1 (2)); see note 5 supra.

8 Except for the offence created by the Badgers Act 1973 s 5, as to which see para 352 note 4 ante.

9 Ibid s 10 (2) (b) (amended by virtue of the Criminal Justice Act 1982 s 46 and, as from a day to be appointed, by the Criminal Justice Act 1991 s 26 (3), when the relevant provisions become s 10 (2) (a), (b)). As to the standard scale see para 232 note 1 ante. At the date at which this volume states the law, level 5 on that scale is at £2,000.

10 Badgers Act 1973 s 10 (2) proviso.
11 Ie an offence under ibid ss 1 (1), 2; see para 352 ante.
12 Where the offender is not the owner of the dog, the owner may appeal to the Crown Court: Badgers (Further Protection) Act 1991 s 1 (3).
13 A person so disqualified may apply after one year for a direction terminating the disqualification: ibid s 1 (5). On such application regard must be had to the applicant's character, conduct since disqualification and other circumstances of the case: s 1 (6) (a). The applicant may be ordered to pay all or part of the costs of the application: s 1 (6) (b). If an application is refused no further application may be made for a further period of one year: s 1 (6). Any person who has custody of a dog in contravention of a disqualification order is guilty of an offence and liable on summary conviction to a fine not exceeding level 5 on the standard scale: s 1 (7) (a). As to the standard scale see note 9 supra.
14 Ibid s 1 (1).
15 Ibid s 1 (2) (a). Failure to comply with such a requirement is an offence punishable on summary conviction by a fine not exceeding level 5 on the standard scale: s 1 (7) (b). As to the standard scale see note 9 supra.
16 Ibid s 1 (2) (b). Any sum ordered to be so paid is recoverable summarily as a civil debt: s 1 (8).

(5) PROTECTION OF OTHER WILD ANIMALS

358. Protection of certain wild animals. The Wildlife and Countryside Act 1981 protects certain wild animals[1] by creating a number of offences[2]. Any person who intentionally[3] kills, injures or takes such an animal commits an offence[4], as does any person who has in his possession or control any such animal, whether alive or dead, or any part of, or anything derived from, such an animal[5]. Anyone who intentionally damages or destroys, or obstructs access to, any structure or place which such an animal uses for shelter or protection, or who disturbs any such animal while it is occupying a structure or place which it uses for that purpose, also commits an offence[6]. So, too, does any person who sells, offers or exposes for sale, or has in his possession or transports for the purpose of sale, any such animal (alive or dead), or any part of, or anything derived from, such an animal[7]; or who publishes or causes to be published any advertisement likely to be understood as conveying that he buys or sells, or intends to buy or sell, any of those things[8].

1 Ie a wild animal included in the Wildlife and Countryside Act 1981 s 9, Sch 5 (amended by the Wildlife and Countryside Act 1981 (Variation of Schedules) Orders 1988, 1989 and 1991, SI 1988/288, SI 1989/906 and SI 1991/367). The Wildlife and Countryside Act 1981 Sch 5 as amended now includes the following animals: certain sea anemones; apuses; horseshoe bats; typical bats; violet click and rainbow leaf beetles; burbots; most types of butterfly; wild cats; New Forest cicadas; crickets; dolphins; dormice; Norfolk Aeshna dragonflies; wart-biter grasshoppers; medicinal leeches; sand lizards; most types of moth; freshwater pearl mussels; great crested newts; common otters; pine martens; trembling sea mats; harbour porpoises; lagoon sandworms; allis shads; fairy and lagoon sand shrimps; certain snails; certain snakes; Fen Raft and ladybird spiders; red squirrels; natterjack toads; marine turtles (all species); vendaces; walruses; whales (all species); and whitefish. Reference should be made to the up-to-date Schedule when considering any particular animal. It should be noted that the Schedule lists animals' scientific, ie Linnaean, names. The common names are included by way of guidance only: Sch 5 Note. For powers to vary Sch 5 see para 364 post.
2 In relation to these offences, for exceptions see para 359 post; as to licences see para 361 post; as to enforcement, proceedings and penalties see para 363 post. Nothing described in this paragraph makes unlawful anything done in pursuance of a requirement by the Minister of Agriculture, Fisheries and Food or the Secretary of State for Wales under the Agriculture Act 1947 s 98 (as to which see AGRICULTURE vol 1 (2) (Reissue) para 654), nor anything done under, or in pursuance of an order made under, the Animal Health Act 1981 (as to which see para 482 et seq post): Wildlife and Countryside Act 1981 s 10 (1).
3 For the meaning of 'intentionally' see CRIMINAL LAW vol 11 (1) (Reissue) para 11.
4 Wildlife and Countryside Act 1981 s 9 (1).
5 Ibid s 9 (2). A person is not guilty of this offence if he shows that the animal had not been killed or taken, or had been killed or taken otherwise than in contravention of Part I of the 1981 Act (ss 1–27)

or the Conservation of Wild Creatures and Wild Plants Act 1975 (repealed), or if he shows that the animal or other thing in question had been sold (whether to him or any other person) otherwise than in contravention of those provisions: Wildlife and Countryside Act 1981 s 9 (3).

6 Ibid s 9 (4). This does not apply to anything done within a dwelling house (s 10 (2)); however, a person cannot rely on this defence as respects anything done in relation to a bat (except in the living area of a dwelling house) unless he had notified the Nature Conservancy Council of the proposed action or operation and allowed them a reasonable time to advise him as to whether it should be carried out and, if so, the method to be used (s 10 (5)).

7 Ibid s 9 (5) (a).

8 Ibid s 9 (5) (b).

359. Exceptions. A person is not guilty of the above offences[1] by reason of the taking of any wild animal if he shows that the animal had been disabled otherwise than by his unlawful act and was taken solely for the purpose of tending it and releasing it when no longer disabled[2]; by reason of the killing of any wild animal if he shows that the animal had been so seriously disabled otherwise than by his unlawful act that there was no reasonable chance of its recovering[3]; nor if he shows that the unlawful act was the incidental result of a lawful operation and could not reasonably have been avoided[4].

An authorised person[5] is not guilty of the above offences[6] by reason of the killing or injuring of certain wild animals[7] if he shows that his action was necessary for the purpose of preventing serious damage to livestock, foodstuffs for livestock, crops, vegetables, fruit, growing timber or any other form of property, or to fisheries[8].

1 Ie offences under the Wildlife and Countryside Act 1981 s 9: see para 358 ante.

2 Ibid s 10 (3) (a).

3 Ibid s 10 (3) (b).

4 Ibid s 10 (3) (c).

5 For the meaning of 'authorised person' see para 334 note 2 ante.

6 See note 1 supra.

7 Ie those wild animals included in the Wildlife and Countryside Act 1981 Sch 5 (amended by SI 1988/288 and SI 1989/906): see para 358 note 3 ante.

8 Wildlife and Countryside Act 1981 s 10 (4). However, he is not entitled to rely on this defence if it had become apparent, before the action was taken, that the action would prove necessary for the purposes mentioned and either a licence authorising the action (as to which see para 361 post) had not been applied for as soon as was reasonably practicable thereafter, or an application for such a licence had been determined: s 10 (6).

360. Prohibition of certain methods of killing or taking. The Wildlife and Countryside Act 1981 additionally creates offences[1] relating to certain methods of killing or taking any wild animals, and other offences relating to methods of killing or taking a particular group of animals.

Any person commits an offence if he sets in position a self-locking snare which is of such a nature and so placed as to be calculated to cause bodily injury to any wild animal coming into contact with it[2]; or if he uses for the purpose of killing or taking any wild animal any self-locking snare (whether or not of such a nature, or so placed, as stated above)[3]; or if he uses for that purpose any bow or crossbow, or any explosive other than ammunition for a firearm[4]; or if he uses for that purpose any live mammal or bird whatever as a decoy[5].

It is also an offence to set in position any trap or snare, any electrical device for killing or stunning, or any poisonous, poisoned or stupefying substance, that is of such a nature and is so placed as to be calculated to cause bodily injury to certain wild animals[6] which come into contact with it[7]; to use any such article (whether or not of such a nature, or so placed, as stated above, or any net, for the purpose of killing or taking any such animal[8]; to use for that purpose any automatic or semi-automatic weapon, any device for illuminating a target or sighting device for night shooting, any form of artificial light or any mirror or other dazzling device, or any gas or smoke[9]; to use any sound recording as a decoy for that purpose[10]; and to use any mechanically propelled vehicle[11] in immediate pursuit of such an animal for the purpose of driving, killing or taking that animal[12].

It is an offence knowingly to cause or permit to be done any of the acts described above[13].

1 The exceptions described in para 359 ante do not apply to these offences: cf the Wildlife and Countryside Act 1981 s 10. As to licences see para 361 post; as to enforcement, proceedings and penalties see para 363 post. The Secretary of State for the Environment may amend these provisions by statutory instrument in order to comply with an international obligation: Wildlife and Countryside Act 1981 ss 11 (4), 26 (1). For other offences relating to poisoning animals see para 425 post; for other offences relating to traps see paras 427, 428 post.

2 Ibid s 11 (1) (a).

3 Ibid s 11 (1) (b).

4 'Firearm' has the same meaning as in the Firearms Act 1968 s 57 (as to which see CRIMINAL LAW vol 11 (1) (Reissue) para 197): Wildlife and Countryside Act 1981 s 27.

5 Ibid s 11 (1) (c).

6 Ie a wild animal included in ibid Sch 6. The following animals are included: badgers; horseshoe bats (all species); typical bats (all species); wild cats; bottle-nosed and common dolphins; dormice (all species); hedgehogs; pine martens; common otters; polecats; harbour porpoises; shrews (all species); red squirrels: Sch 6. Reference should be made to the up-to-date Schedule when considering any particular animal. It should be noted that the Schedule lists animals' scientific, ie Linnaean, names. The common names are included by way of guidance only: Sch 6 Note. For powers to vary Sch 6 see para 364 post.

7 Ibid s 11 (2) (a). It is a defence to show that the article was set in position by the accused for the purpose of killing or taking, in the interests of public health, agriculture, forestry, fisheries or nature conservation, any wild animals which could be lawfully killed or taken by those means and that he took all reasonable precautions to prevent injury thereby to any wild animals included in Sch 6 (see note 6 supra): s 11 (6).

8 Ibid s 11 (2) (b).

9 Ibid s 11 (2) (c).

10 Ibid s 11 (2) (d).

11 'Vehicle' includes aircraft, hovercraft and boat: ibid s 27 (1).

12 Ibid s 11 (2) (e).

13 Ibid s 11 (1) (d), (2) (f) (added by the Wildlife and Countryside (Amendment) Act 1991 s 2 (1), (2) (b), (3) (b) respectively). In any proceedings for an offence under the 1981 Act s 11 (2) (f) (as so added) relating to an act mentioned in s 11 (2) (a) (see text and note 7 supra), a defence similar to that described in note 7 supra is available: s 11 (7) (added by the 1991 Act s 2 (6)).

361. Licences. The offences described above[1] do not apply to anything done under and in accordance with the terms of a licence[2] granted by the appropriate authority[3] for, generally[4], certain specified purposes[5].

A person who in order to obtain a licence makes a statement or representation, or furnishes a document or information, which he knows to be false in a material particular, or who recklessly[6] makes a statement or representation, or furnishes a document or information, which is false in a material particular, commits an offence[7].

1 See paras 358, 360 ante.

2 Such a licence may be, to any degree, general or specific; may be granted either to persons of a class or to a particular person; may be subject to compliance with any specified conditions; and may be modified or revoked at any time by the appropriate authority (as to which see note 3 infra): Wildlife and Countryside Act 1981 s 16 (5). A fee may be charged: s 16 (5). A licence authorising the killing of

wild animals must specify the area within which, and the methods by which, the animals may be killed, and it must not be valid for more than two years: s 16 (6). If the use of poison is sanctioned by the licence, it is a defence in proceedings under the Protection of Animals Act 1911 s 8 (b) (as to which see para 425 post) to show that the act alleged to constitute the offence was done under the authority of such a licence and that any conditions specified in the licence were complied with: Wildlife and Countryside Act 1981 s 16 (7).

3 Ibid s 16 (3), (4). The 'appropriate authority' is as follows: for heads (a) to (e) in note 5 infra, the Nature Conservancy Council; for heads (f) to (h), the Minister of Agriculture, Fisheries and Food or, in relation to Wales, the Secretary of State for Wales (who must from time to time consult with the Nature Conservancy Council as to the exercise of this function, and may not grant a licence unless he has been advised by the Council as to the circumstances in which, in their opinion, such licences should be granted: s 16 (10)); for the activities otherwise prohibited by s 9 (5) (see note 2 supra), the Secretary of State for the Environment, after consulting with an advisory body: see s 16 (9). As to advisory bodies see para 349 ante.

4 A purpose need not be specified in a licence making lawful what would otherwise be an offence under ibid s 9 (5) (see para 358 text and notes 7, 8 ante): s 16 (4).

5 These are: (a) scientific or educational purposes; (b) ringing or marking, or examining any ring or mark on, wild animals; (c) conserving wild animals or introducing them to particular areas; (d) protecting any zoological or botanical collection; (e) photography; (f) preserving public health or public safety; (g) preventing the spread of disease; and (h) preventing serious damage to livestock, foodstuffs for livestock, crops, vegetables, fruit, growing timber or any other form of property, or to fisheries: ibid s 16 (3).

6 As to recklessness see para 234 note 8 ante; and CRIMINAL LAW.

7 Wildlife and Countryside Act 1981 s 17. As to enforcement, proceedings and penalties see para 363 post.

362. Snares.
It is an offence to set in position, or knowingly cause or permit to be set in position, any snare which is of such a nature and so placed as to be calculated to cause bodily injury to any wild animal coming into contact with it, and while the snare remains in position to fail, without reasonable excuse, to inspect it or cause it to be inspected at least once every day[1].

1 Wildlife and Countryside Act 1981 s 11 (3) (amended by the Wildlife and Countryside (Amendment) Act 1991 s 2 (1), (4)). Licences are not available: cf the Wildlife and Countryside Act 1981 s 16. As to enforcement, proceedings and penalties see para 363 post. See also para 360 ante for other offences connected with snares.

363. Enforcement, proceedings and penalties.
A constable who suspects with reasonable cause that any person is committing or has committed an offence[1] may without warrant stop and search that person and search or examine any thing he may then be using or have in his possession[2]. He may seize and detain for the purpose of proceedings anything which may be evidence of the commission of the offence, or which may be liable to be forfeited[3]. He may enter any land other than a dwelling house in order to exercise these powers, or in order to arrest a person[4].

A justice of the peace may grant a warrant to any constable to enter and search premises if he is satisfied by information on oath that an offence[5] has been committed and evidence of the offence may be found on those premises[6].

In proceedings for certain offences[7], the animal in question is presumed to have been a wild animal unless the contrary is shown[8].

Any person who attempts to commit an offence[9] is guilty of an offence and is liable to be punished in like manner as for the offence attempted[10]; so too is any person who for the purposes of committing such an offence has in his possession anything capable of being used for committing the offence[11].

Proceedings for an offence involving the killing or taking of a wild animal[12] may be brought within six months from the date on which evidence sufficient in the prosecutor's opinion to warrant the proceedings came to his knowledge[13]. Any offence[14] is deemed to have been committed in any place where the offender is found, or to which he is first brought after the offence has been committed[15]. A local authority[16] may institute proceedings for any offence committed within its area[17].

The maximum penalty on summary conviction of the offences under section 9[18] or section 11 (1) or 11 (2)[19] of the Wildlife and Countryside Act 1981 is a fine of level 5 on the standard scale; for the offences under section 11 (3)[20] or section 17[21] of the Act it is a fine of level 4 on the standard scale[22]. If, however, any of these offences is committed in respect of more than one animal or other thing the maximum fine is to be determined as if the person convicted has been convicted of a separate offence in respect of each animal, etc[23]. The convicting court must order the forfeiture of any animal, etc, in respect of which the offence was committed, and may, if it thinks fit, order the forfeiture of any vehicle[24], animal, weapon or other thing which was used to commit the offence[25].

1   Ie under the Wildlife and Countryside Act 1981 Pt I (ss 1–27): see para 358 et seq ante.
2   Ibid s 19 (1) (a), (b). He must suspect with reasonable cause that evidence of the offence is to be found on the person or the thing, as the case may be: s 19 (1) (a), (b).
3   Ibid s 19 (1) (d).
4   Ibid s 19 (1), (2) (amended by the Police and Criminal Evidence Act 1984 ss 26 (1), 119 (1), Sch 6 Pt I para 25, Sch 7 Pt I). He must suspect with reasonable cause that a person is committing an offence under Part I of the Act: Wildlife and Countryside Act 1981 s 19 (1), (2). The power of arrest is that given by the Police and Criminal Evidence Act 1984 s 25: Wildlife and Countryside Act 1981 s 19 (1), (2) (as amended: see supra).
5   The offences are those described in paras 358, 360 ante.
6   Wildlife and Countryside Act 1981 s 19 (3).
7   Ie under ibid ss 9 (1), (2), (5) (a), 11 (1) (b), (c), (2) (b)–(e); or proceedings for an offence under s 11 (1) (d) or (2) (f) (both added by the Wildlife and Countryside (Amendment) Act 1991 s 2), relating to an act mentioned in the 1981 Act s 11 (1) (b), (c), (2) (b)–(e): see paras 358, 360 ante.
8   Wildlife and Countryside Act 1981 ss 9 (6), 11 (5) (amended by the Wildlife and Countryside (Amendment) Act 1991 s 2 (1), (5)).
9   See note 1 supra.
10 Wildlife and Countryside Act 1981 s 18 (1).
11 Ibid s 18 (2).
12 Under ibid s 9 (1): see para 358 ante.
13 Ibid s 20 (1) (b), (2). A certificate signed by or on behalf of the prosecutor stating the relevant date is conclusive: s 20 (3). No proceedings may be brought more than two years after the commission of the offence: s 20 (2).
14 See note 1 supra.
15 Wildlife and Countryside Act 1981 s 21 (7).
16 Ie a county, district or London borough council or the Common Council of the City of London: ibid ss 27 (1), 71.
17 Ibid s 25 (2).
18 See para 358 ante.
19 See para 360 ante.
20 See para 352 ante.
21 See para 351 ante.
22 Wildlife and Countryside Act 1981 s 21 (2), (3) (amended by virtue of the Criminal Justice Act 1982 s 46). As to the standard scale see para 232 note 1 ante. At the date at which this volume states the law, levels 4 and 5 on that scale are at £1,000 and £2,000 respectively.
23 Wildlife and Countryside Act 1981 s 21 (5).
24 'Vehicle' includes aircraft, hovercraft and boat: ibid s 27 (1).

25 Ibid s 21 (6).

364. Power to make orders. The Secretary of State for the Environment may by statutory instrument vary the list of animals protected by the Wildlife and Countryside Act 1981[1].

1 He may vary the Wildlife and Countryside Act 1981 Sch 5 on representations being made to him by the Nature Conservancy Council or for the purpose of complying with an international obligation, having (in the latter case) consulted an appropriate advisory body (as to which see para 349 ante), and having (in either case) given affected parties an opportunity to submit objections or representations: see ss 22 (3), (4), 23, 26 (1), (4); and see para 349 ante for further details of the consultation required. The Nature Conservancy Council may at any time, and must on every fifth anniversary of the passing of the Act (30 October 1981), review Sch 5 and advise the Secretary of State accordingly: see s 24. The Secretary of State may also vary the list of animals included in Sch 6, but only in order to comply with an international obligation and after similar consultation: see ss 22 (4), 23, 26 (1), (4). Orders have been made varying Sch 5: Wildlife and Countryside Act 1981 (Variation of Schedules) Orders 1988, 1989 and 1991, SI 1988/288, SI 1989/906 and SI 1991/367.

365. Duties of local authorities. Every local authority[1] must take such steps as it considers expedient for bringing to the attention of the public, and of school-children in particular, the effect of the provisions of Part I of the Wildlife and Countryside Act 1981 and of any order made thereunder affecting the whole or part of its area[2].

1 For the meaning of 'local authority' see para 363 note 16 ante.
2 Wildlife and Countryside Act 1981 s 25 (1). Part I of the Act comprises ss 1–27.

4. DOGS AND HORSES

(1) DOGS

(i) Dog Registration Scheme; Licences

366. Dog registration scheme. The Secretary of State may by regulations make provision for the establishment and administration of a dog registration scheme by local authorities or by such other organisations as he may, after consulting with them, designate[1].

1 Local Government Act 1988 s 37. At the date at which this volume states the law, no such regulations had been made. Dog licences were abolished by ss 38 (1), (4), 41, Sch 7 Pt V.

367. Game licence. Every person[1], before he uses any dog for taking, killing or pursuing any game[2], woodcock, snipe, rabbit or deer, must take out a game licence[3] under a penalty of level 2 on the standard scale[4]. No such licence is, however, necessary for pursuing and killing hares by coursing with greyhounds or by hunting with beagles or other hounds[5]; or for pursuing and killing deer by hunting with hounds[6].

1 Subject to certain exemptions: see para 308 ante.

2 Ie hares, pheasants, partridges, grouse, heath or moor game and black game: Game Act 1831 s 2.
3 As to game licences see para 306 ante.
4 Game Licences Act 1860 s 4 (amended by the Protection of Birds Act 1954 s 15 (2), Sch 6 (repealed) and by virtue of the Criminal Justice Act 1982 s 46). As to the standard scale see para 232 note 1 ante. At the date at which this volume states the law, level 2 on that scale is at £100.
5 Game Licences Act 1860 s 5, Exception 3.
6 Ibid s 5, Exception 4.

368. Disqualification from keeping dog. On the conviction of a person under the Protection of Animals Act 1911[1] of an offence of cruelty to a dog, the court may order him to be disqualified from having the custody of any animal, or any animal of a specified kind, for such period as it thinks fit[2]. Disqualification may also be ordered where a person has been convicted of an offence under the Badgers Act 1973, where a dog was present at or used in the commission of the offence[3].

1 See para 412 et seq post.
2 Protection of Animals Act 1911 s 1; Protection of Animals (Amendment) Act 1954 s 1 (1) (amended by the Protection of Animals (Amendment) Act 1988 s 1 (1)). This power applies to offences of cruelty to any animal, not only dogs. See further para 462 post.
3 See the Badgers (Further Protection) Act 1991 s 1; and para 357 ante.

(ii) Trespass; Control of Dogs

369. Trespass by dog. The owner of a dog is not answerable in trespass for its unauthorised entry into the land of another, often described as an unprovoked trespass[1], but a man is liable in trespass if he wilfully sends a dog on another's land in pursuit of game, although he did not himself go on the land[2], or if he allows a dog to roam at large, knowing it to be addicted to destroying game[3].

Where a trespassing dog causes damage by killing or injuring livestock, any person who is a keeper of the dog is liable for the damage caused[4]. For this purpose the dog's keeper is the person who either owns the dog or has it in his possession or is the head of a household of which a member under 16 owns the dog or has it in his possession[5].

1 *Mitten v Faudrye* (1626) Poph 161, where the defendant chased sheep off his land with a little dog, which continued chasing them when on the plaintiff's land; the defendant, it was said, was entitled to chase the sheep off his own land, and if a trespass at all, it would be an involuntary trespass, as he called the dog back. This case is distinguished in *Beckwith v Shordike* (1767) 4 Burr 2092, where a defendant was held liable in trespass for his dog killing a deer, on the ground that the owner took the dog with him and was really the trespasser. See also *Mason v Keeling* (1700) 1 Ld Raym 606 at 608 per Holt CJ: 'The law does not oblige the owner to keep the dog in his house; for if a dog break a neighbour's close, the owner will not be subject to an action for it', quoting *Mitten v Faudrye* supra. Cf per Willes J in *Read v Edwards* (1864) 17 CBNS 245 at 261, and in *Cox v Burbidge* (1863) 13 CBNS 430 at 440–441; but the point did not really arise in *Read v Edwards* supra, as it was there held that the chasing of game was a mischievous propensity, and scienter was proved. See also *Brown v Giles* (1823) 1 C & P 118; *Sanders v Teape and Swan* (1884) 51 LT 263, where a big dog jumped over a garden wall and alighted on the plaintiff, who was digging a well; and *Hines v Tousley* (1926) 95 LJKB 773, CA (uncontrolled dog causing injury on common staircase). As to cats see para 472 post.
2 *R v Pratt* (1855) 4 E & B 860; *Dimmock v Allenby* (1810) cited 2 Marsh at 582.
3 *Read v Edwards* (1864) 17 CBNS 245.

4 See paras 381, 382 post. As to liability for damage caused by animals generally see para 467 et seq post.

5 Animals Act 1971 s 6 (3).

370. Orders for regulation and control of dogs. The ministers[1] have extensive powers to make orders for the regulation and control of dogs in a wide variety of circumstances[2]. These powers and any orders made in the exercise of them are dealt with in the following paragraphs and under their appropriate headings later in this title[3].

1 'The ministers' means the Minister of Agriculture, Fisheries and Food, the Secretary of State for Scotland and the Secretary of State for Wales, acting jointly: Animal Health Act 1981 s 86 (1) (c). The Minister of Agriculture, Fisheries and Food may also make certain orders on his own behalf: see eg s 13.

2 See ibid ss 1, 13. Orders made under Acts repealed by the 1981 Act continue in force and have effect as though made under that Act: see s 95; and the Interpretation Act 1978 s 17 (2) (b).

3 The principal orders now in force relating to dogs are the Control of Dogs Order of 1930, SR & O 1930/399 (amended by SR & O 1939/683, SR & O 1931/80 and SI 1976/919) (see para 371 post); the Rabies (Importation of Dogs, Cats and Other Mammals) Order 1974, SI 1974/2211 (amended by SI 1977/361, SI 1984/1182 and SI 1986/2062) (see para 492 post); and the Rabies (Control) Order 1974, SI 1974/2212 (see para 493 post). Dogs are also 'animals' for the purposes of the Animals (Miscellaneous Provisions) Order of 1927, SR & O 1927/290 (amended by SR & O 1938/197 and SI 1976/919) (see para 488 note 1 post), and the Anthrax Order of 1938, SR & O 1938/204 (amended by SI 1972/971) (see para 440 note 5 post).

371. Wearing of collars. Every dog while in a highway or place of public resort[1] must wear a collar with the name and address of the owner inscribed on it, or on a plate or badge attached thereto, but this requirement does not apply to any pack of hounds[2], or to any dog while being used for sporting purposes, for the capture or destruction of vermin, or for the driving or tending of cattle or sheep[3].

If a dog is found in a highway or place of public resort without the prescribed collar it may be seized and treated as a stray dog[4], and the owner of the dog, any person in charge of it, and any person allowing the dog to be in the highway or place of public resort are each guilty of an offence and liable on summary conviction to a fine not exceeding level 5 on the standard scale or, if the offence is committed in relation to more than ten dogs, not exceeding level 3 on the standard scale for each dog[5]. The power of seizing an offending dog and of prosecuting an offender is vested in the police and in inspectors[6].

1 A 'place of public resort' has been said to mean a place to which the public goes as a matter of fact as distinct from a matter of right: see *Kitson v Ashe* [1899] 1 QB 425 at 429, DC (a case on construction of a byelaw). A place may be a place of public resort notwithstanding that a charge is made for admission: *Glynn v Simmonds* [1952] 2 All ER 47 DC (a decision under the Vagrancy Act 1824 s 4); *Russell v Thompson* [1953] NI 51, CA (dance hall to which admission obtained by buying a ticket held to be place of public resort).

2 As to the exemption of a hound puppy out at walk see *Burton v Atkinson* (1908) 98 LT 748; *Rasdall v Coleman* (1909) 100 LT 934.

3 Control of Dogs Order of 1930, SR & O 1930/399, art 1. The provisions of the order are to be executed and enforced by local authorities: art 7.

4 Ibid art 4; see para 385 post.

5 Control of Dogs Order of 1930 art 6 (amended by SR & O 1930/683); Animal Health Act 1981 s 75 (1) (a), (b) (amended by virtue of the Criminal Justice Act 1982 ss 38, 46), which has replaced corresponding provisions in the Acts referred to in that article. As to the standard scale see para 232 note 1 ante. At the date at which this volume states the law, levels 3 and 5 on that scale are at £400 and £2,000 respectively.

6 Control of Dogs Order 1930 art 5, which makes dogs 'animals' for the purposes of the Animal Health Act 1981 ss 60, 63, which relate to the powers of police and of inspectors appointed for the purpose of that Act by the minister or by local authorities: see further paras 511, 512 post; and see also s 66.

372. Worrying of cattle and sheep. With a view to the prevention of worrying of cattle[1], a local authority may make regulations requiring that dogs or any class of dogs shall, during all or any of the hours between sunset and sunrise, be kept under control in the manner prescribed by the regulations[2]. Where a dog is proved to have injured cattle or poultry or chased sheep it may be dealt with as a dangerous dog[3].

Any person committing, or aiding, abetting, counselling or procuring the commission of, any breach of the regulations is liable on summary conviction to a fine not exceeding level 5 on the standard scale or, if the offence is committed with respect to more than ten animals, to a fine not exceeding level 3 on the standard scale for each animal[4].

1 'Cattle' in this context includes horses, mules, asses, sheep, goats and swine: Control of Dogs Order of 1930, SR & O 1930/399, art 2 (2).
2 Ibid art 2 (1). A copy of the regulations, signed and certified by the clerk of the local authority, is prima facie proof of the regulations: art 2 (4) (amended by SR & O 1931/80 and SI 1976/919).
3 Dogs Act 1906 s 1 (4) (amended by the Dogs (Amendment) Act 1928 s 1 (1)); see para 373 post.
4 Control of Dogs Order of 1930 art 6; Animal Health Act 1981 s 75 (1) (a), (b) (amended by virtue of the Criminal Justice Act 1982 ss 38, 46). As to the standard scale see para 232 note 1 ante. At the date at which this volume states the law, levels 3 and 5 on that scale are at £400 and £2,000 respectively. For a dog owner's criminal responsibility for the worrying of livestock on agricultural land under the Dogs (Protection of Livestock) Act 1953 see para 384 post.

(iii) Dangerous Dogs

A. DANGEROUS DOGS GENERALLY

373. Dangerous dogs not under control. On complaint made to a court of summary jurisdiction, the court may order that a dog which appears to it to be dangerous[1] and not kept under proper control[2] be kept by the owner[3] under proper control[4] or destroyed, under penalty of a fine for every day during which the non-compliance continues[5]. Alternatively, if the dog is male and it appears to the court on such a complaint that the dog would be less dangerous if neutered, the court may order it to be neutered[6]. Notice of the penalty must be given to the owner[7]. Where a destruction order is made, the court may also appoint a person to undertake the destruction and require any person having custody of the dog to deliver it up for that purpose, and, if it thinks fit, make an order disqualifying the owner from having a dog for a specified period[8].

A person who fails to comply with a destruction order or to deliver a dog up for destruction as ordered is guilty of an offence and on conviction, in addition to being liable to a fine, may be disqualified from having custody of a dog for a specified period[9].

An order to destroy a dog may be made without giving the owner the option of keeping it under proper control[10]. An order for destruction may be made although the dog has been moved out of the jurisdiction of the court after the offence, unless there has been a bona fide disposal of the dog by its owner[11], in which case an order may be made against the new owner[12]. If the owner fails to comply with an order to keep a dog under proper control, a fresh complaint may be made that it is dangerous or not under proper control and the court may order its destruction, but it cannot order destruction on a mere summons for non-compliance with the original order[13].

An appeal lies to the Crown Court against any such order specified above[14]. Unless the owner of a dog which is ordered to be delivered up and destroyed gives notice to the court that he does not intend to appeal, the dog must not be destroyed pursuant to the order (1) until the end of the period within which notice of appeal can be given and (2) if such notice is given within that period, until the appeal is determined or withdrawn[15].

It is inadvisable for proceedings under the Dogs Act 1871 and any proceedings under the Dogs (Protection of Livestock) Act 1953[16] to be heard together, the better practice being to dispose first of the criminal proceedings[17].

1 'Dangerous' includes dangerous to animals: *Henderson v M'Kenzie* (1876) 3 R 623; *Williams v Richards* [1907] 2 KB 88. A dog may be dangerous under this provision even though it has been held under the Metropolitan Police Act 1839 s 54 (see para 374 post) not to be ferocious: *Keddle v Payn* [1964] 1 All ER 189, [1964] 1 WLR 262, DC. It is unnecessary to prove the owner's knowledge that the dog is dangerous before making an order: *Parker v Walsh* (1885) 1 TLR 583. Where a dog bit a child in circumstances consistent with the bite being accidental or, at least provoked, it was held that the isolated bite did not warrant an order under this provision (*Macdonald v Munro* 1951 JC 8); but it is open to the court to find that a dog is dangerous from a single and not particularly violent incident (*Lamb v Gorham* (1971) 115 Sol Jo 831). See also note 5 infra. As to dogs bred for fighting see para 374 post.

2 This is not confined to a public place but extends to the owner's private property where other people have the right of access: *Philp v Wright* 1940 JC 9. Whether a dog is under control or not is a question of fact, not of law: *Wren v Pocock* (1876) 40 JP 646; *R v Huntingdon Justices* (1879) 4 QBD 522; cf *Re Application for Mandamus, ex p Hay* (1866) 3 TLR 24.

3 There is no reason to suppose that 'owner' here includes 'keeper'. Cf the extended meaning under the Animals Act 1971 s 6 (3); see para 467 post.

4 The court may specify the method of control: see the Dangerous Dogs Act 1991 s 3 (5) (b); note 5 infra.

5 Dogs Act 1871 s 2. The fine will not exceed level 3 on the standard scale: Dangerous Dogs Act 1989 s 1 (3). As to the standard scale see para 232 note 1 ante. At the date at which this volume states the law, level 3 on that scale is at £400. An order may be made whether or not the dog is shown to have injured any person and may specify the measures to be taken for keeping the dog under proper control, whether by muzzling, keeping on a lead, excluding it from specified places or otherwise: Dangerous Dogs Act 1991 s 3 (5). Where a dog is proved to have injured cattle or poultry or chased sheep it may be dealt with under the Dogs Act 1871 s 2 as a dangerous dog: Dogs Act 1906 s 1 (4) (amended by the Dogs (Amendment) Act 1928 s 1). As to muzzling and keeping on a lead see para 374 post.

6 Dangerous Dogs Act 1991 s 3 (6), which provides for such an order to be made under the Dogs Act 1871 s 2.

7 *Haldane v Allan* 1956 JC 41.

8 Dangerous Dogs Act 1989 s 1 (1).

9 Ibid s 1 (3). This includes any other order made by virtue of the Dogs Act 1871 s 2, but not in relation to an order made thereunder by virtue of the Dangerous Dogs Act 1991 s 3 (6) (see note 6 supra), where the matters arose before s 3 (6) came into force (ie 12 August 1991): s 3 (7). The fine will not exceed level 3 on the standard scale. As to the standard scale see note 5 supra.

10 *Pickering v Marsh* (1874) 43 LJMC 143; *R v Dymock, R v Moger* (1901) 17 TLR 593.

11 *Lockett v Withey* (1908) 99 LT 838; *R v Jones, ex p Daunton* [1963] 1 All ER 368, [1963] 1 WLR 270, DC.

12 *R v Leicester Justices, ex p Workman* [1964] 2 All ER 346, [1964] 1 WLR 707, DC.

13 *Rhodes v Heritage* [1951] 1 All ER 904, DC.

14 Ie any order made under the Dogs Act 1871 s 2 or under the Dangerous Dogs Act 1989 s 1 (1): see the 1989 Act s 1 (2).

15 Ibid s 1 (2)

16 See para 384 post.
17 *R v Dunmow Justices, ex p Anderson* [1964] 2 All ER 943, [1964] 1 WLR 1039, DC.

374. Ferocious dog at large; fighting dogs. It is an offence to suffer to be at large[1] any unmuzzled ferocious[2] dog, or to set on or urge any dog or other animal to attack, worry or put in fear any person, horse or other animal in any thoroughfare or public place in the metropolitan police district[3], or in any street in a town to which the Town Police Clauses Act 1847 applies[4]; on summary conviction the punishment is, in relation to the metropolitan police district, a fine not exceeding level 2 on the standard scale[5], and elsewhere a fine not exceeding level 3 on the standard scale[6].

It is prohibited to breed or breed from, give, sell, exchange, or offer, advertise[7] or expose for sale, exchange or gift, any pit bull terrier, Japanese tosa or other dog of a type which is bred for fighting or which has the characteristics of a dog so bred[8]. It is also an offence for a person to allow such a dog of which he is owner[9] or for the time being in charge to be in a public place[10] without being muzzled and kept on a lead[11], or to abandon it or allow it to stray[12]. As from 30 November 1991[13] it is an offence for a person to have such a dog in his possession or custody, except under a power of seizure or in accordance with an order for its destruction[14], or in accordance with exemptions permitted by the Secretary of State[15]. A scheme has been made for payments to be made to owners who destroy the dogs or arrange to have them destroyed before that date[16]. Contravention of these provisions is an offence punishable on summary conviction by a fine not exceeding level 5 on the standard scale, or imprisonment for up to six months, or both[17]. The Secretary of State may by order made by statutory instrument make provision corresponding to any or all of the above provisions relating to muzzles, leads, abandonment and allowing to stray, with modifications, to other types of dog which he considers present a serious danger to the public[18].

The owner[19] or, if different, the person for the time being in charge[20] of a dog which is dangerously out of control[21] in a public place is guilty of an offence; if the dog injures any person while it is out of control, the owner or person in charge is guilty of an aggravated offence[22]. If the owner or person for the time being in charge of a dog allows it to enter a place which is not a public place but where it is not permitted to be, and while there it injures any person or there are reasonable grounds for apprehension that it will do so, the owner or person in charge is guilty of an offence, and, if the dog injures any person, of an aggravated offence[23].

Where a person is convicted of an offence relating to prohibited fighting dogs, other specified dangerous dogs or dogs dangerously out of control[24], the court may, and in certain circumstances must, order the destruction of the dog[25]. The offender may be disqualified, for such period as the court thinks fit, for having custody of a dog[26]. A constable or an officer of the local authority authorised for these purposes may seize any prohibited fighting dog or other designated specially dangerous dog in respect of which an offence[27] is being committed, or any dog in a public place which appears to him to be dangerously out of control[28]. A constable may, with a warrant, enter and search premises and seize any dog or other thing which is evidence of an offence against these provisions[29]. In certain circumstances[30] a dog which has been seized may or must[31] be destroyed[32].

1 A dog on a lead is not 'at large': *Ross v Evans* [1959] 2 QB 79, [1959] 2 All ER 222, DC.
2 There is a distinction between a dangerous dog and a ferocious one: *Keddle v Payn* [1964] 1 All ER 189, [1964] 1 WLR 262, DC; and see para 373 note 1 ante.

3 As to this district see the London Government Act 1963 s 76; and LONDON.

4 Ie any street, road, square, court, alley, thoroughfare or public passage within the limits of any special Act for the improvement or regulation of a town or district, being an Act with which the Town Police Clauses Act 1847 is incorporated: ss 2, 3.

5 Metropolitan Police Act 1839 s 54 para 2 (amended by virtue of the Criminal Justice Act 1982 s 46). As to the standard scale see para 232 note 1 ante. At the date at which this volume states the law, level 2 on that scale is at £100.

6 Town Police Clauses Act 1847 s 28 (amended by the Criminal Justice Act 1982 ss 39, 46, Sch 3). As to the standard scale see para 232 note 1 ante. At the date at which this volume states the law, level 3 on that scale is at £400.

7 As to advertisements see note 17 infra.

8 Dangerous Dogs Act 1991 s 1 (1), (2) (a)–(c). Dogs in the third category are designated by the Secretary of State (ie the Home Secretary): s 1 (1) (c), (8). See the Dangerous Dogs (Designated Types) Order 1991, SI 1991/1743, which specifies dogs of the types Dogo Argentino and Fila Braziliero. The prohibition as to sale, exchange etc does not render unlawful anything done with a view to removing the dog from the United Kingdom: Dangerous Dogs Act 1991 s 1 (4).

  If in any proceedings it is alleged by the prosecution that the dog is one to which s 1 applies, it is presumed that it is such a dog unless the contrary is shown by the accused, having given the prosecution at least 14 days' notice of the evidence he intends to adduce in that regard: s 5 (5).

9 Where a dog is owned by a person who is less than 16 years old, the reference to 'owner' includes a reference to the head of the household, if any, of which that person is a member: ibid s 6.

10 'Public place' means any street, road or other place, enclosed or not, to which the public have access for payment or otherwise and includes the common parts of a building containing two or more separate dwellings: ibid s 10 (2).

11 'Muzzled' means securely fitted with a muzzle sufficient to prevent the dog biting any person: ibid s 7 (1) (a). 'Kept on a lead' means securely held in that manner by a person who is not less than 16 years old: s 7 (1) (b). The Secretary of State may by order made by statutory instrument prescribe kinds of muzzle or lead, in which case a reference to 'muzzle' or 'lead' is to the muzzle or lead so prescribed: s 7 (2), (3). At the date at which this volume states the law, no such order had been made.

12 Ibid s 1 (2) (d), (e).

13 See the Dangerous Dogs Act 1991 (Commencement and Appointed Day) Order 1991, SI 1991/1742, art 2.

14 Dangerous Dogs Act 1991 s 1 (3) (a), (b).

15 Ibid s 1 (5). See the Dangerous Dogs Compensation and Exemption Schemes Order 1991, SI 1991/1744, arts 3–10. Under the scheme comprised in those provisions, possession or custody of a dog is not prohibited in relation to dogs born before 30 November 1991 (see arts 3, 1 (2) (c); and the Dangerous Dogs Act 1991 (Commencement and Appointed Day) Order 1991 art 2), where certain conditions are complied with. Those conditions relate to: (1) reporting to the police (Dangerous Dogs Compensation and Exemption Schemes Order 1991 art 6); (2) neutering and identification (art 7); (3) third party insurance (art 8); and (4) the certificate of exemption (arts 9, 10). The conditions vary slightly according to whether the dog is an adult dog (art 4) or a puppy (art 5). The administration of the scheme, and of that referred to in text and note 16 infra, is conducted by an agency for the time being designated by the Secretary of State: arts 1 (2) (b), 11; Dangerous Dogs Act 1991 s 1 (6).

16 Ibid s 1 (3). See the Dangerous Dogs Compensation and Exemption Schemes Order 1991 art 2, which sets down the amounts payable, and the procedure to obtain compensation. See also note 15 supra.

17 Dangerous Dogs Act 1991 s 1 (7). However, a person who publishes an advertisement (see text and notes 9, 10 supra) is not liable to imprisonment if he shows that he did so to the order of someone else and did not himself devise it, and is not liable to conviction if he additionally shows that he neither knew nor reasonably suspected that it related to a restricted dog: s 1 (7). 'Advertisement' includes any means of bringing a matter to the attention of the public; 'advertise' must be construed accordingly: s 10 (2).

  As to the standard scale see para 232 note 1 ante. At the date at which this volume states the law, level 5 on that scale is at £2,000.

18 Ibid s 2 (1), (5). Such orders may contain exceptions and may create summary offences punishable as described in text and note 17 supra: s 2 (2), (3). Before making such an order the Secretary of State must consult persons and bodies having relevant knowledge or experience, including bodies concerned respectively with animal welfare, veterinary science and practice and breeds of dogs: s 2 (4).

  If in any proceedings it is alleged by the prosecution that the dog is one to which an order under s 2 applies it is presumed to be such a dog unless the contrary is shown by the accused, having given the prosecution at least 14 days' notice of the evidence he intends to adduce in that regard: s 5 (5).

19 See ibid s 6; and note 9 supra.

20 It is a defence for an owner to show that the dog was in the charge of a person whom he reasonably believed to be a fit and proper person: ibid s 3 (2).

21 A dog is regarded as dangerously out of control on any occasion on which there are grounds for reasonable apprehension that it will cause injury to any person, whether or not it does so, except where the dog is being used for a lawful purpose by a constable or person in the service of the Crown: ibid s 10 (3). Cf para 373 ante.

22 Ibid s 3 (1). A person guilty of the offence is liable on summary conviction to a fine not exceeding level 5 on the standard scale or imprisonment for up to six months, or both; the aggravated offence is punishable on summary conviction by a fine not exceeding the statutory maximum or imprison- ment for up to six months, or both, and on conviction on indictment, by a fine or imprisonment for up to two years, or both: s 3 (4). As to the standard scale see para 232 note 1 ante. At the date at which this volume states the law, level 5 on that scale is at £2,000. As to the statutory maximum see para 233 note 3 ante. At the date at which this volume states the law, that sum is at £2,000.

23 Ibid s 3 (3). The offence and aggravated offence are punishable as described in note 22 supra. See also note 9 supra.

24 Ie an offence under ibid ss 1, 3 (1) or (3), or under an order made by virtue of s 2: see text and notes 7–22 supra.

25 Ibid s 4 (1) (a). The court must make such an order where the offence is under s 1 or is an aggravated offence under s 3 (1) or (3): s 4 (1) (a). Unless the order is compulsory, the owner, if he is not the offender, may appeal against it to the Crown Court: s 4 (2). Destruction must not take place until after any appeal against the conviction or order is determined, or the time for appealing has elapsed, or the owner or offender has given notice that there will be no appeal: s 4 (3). The court may appoint a person to undertake the destruction of the dog and require that the dog be given up to that person, and may order the offender to pay the expenses of destroying the dog and keeping it before destruction (s 4 (4)); such sum is treated as if it were a fine imposed on conviction (s 4 (5)). Failure to comply with an order to give up the dog for destruction is an offence punishable on summary conviction with a fine not exceeding level 5 on the standard scale: s 4 (8) (b). As to the standard scale see para 232 note 1 ante. At the date at which this volume states the law, level 5 on that scale is at £2,000.

26 Ibid s 4 (1) (b). Custody of a dog in contravention of a disqualification order is an offence punishable on summary conviction with a fine not exceeding level 5 on the standard scale: s 4 (8). As to the standard scale see para 232 note 1 ante. At the date at which this volume states the law, level 5 on that scale is at £2,000. A person may apply after at least one year for the termination of the disqualifi- cation, whereupon the court may grant or refuse the application, having regard to the applicant's character and conduct and other circumstances since the disqualification; if the application is refused, no further application may be made within one year after that refusal: s 4 (6), (7).

27 Ie an offence against ibid ss 1, 2; see text and notes 7–18 supra.

28 Ibid s 5 (1).

29 Ibid s 5 (2).

30 Ie where no prosecution is to be brought because, for instance, the owner cannot be found: ibid s 5 (4).

31 Destruction is compulsory where the dog is one to which ibid s 1 applies: s 5 (4). See text and notes 8, 24 supra.

32 Ibid s 5 (4).

B. GUARD DOGS

375. Control of guard dogs. A person must not use or permit the use of a guard dog[1] at any premises[2] unless a handler capable of controlling it is present on the premises and the dog is under his control at all times while it is being so used, except while it is secured so that it is not at liberty to go freely about the premises[3].

The handler of a guard dog must keep it under his control at all times while it is being used as a guard dog at any premises except while another handler has control of it or while it is secured as defined above[4]. The use of a guard dog at any premises is unlawful unless a notice that a guard dog is present is clearly exhibited at each entrance to the premises[5].

1 Ie a dog which is being used to protect (1) premises, (2) property kept on the premises or (3) a person guarding such premises or property: Guard Dogs Act 1975 s 7.
2 Ie land other than agricultural land and land within the curtilage of a dwelling house, and buildings, including parts of buildings, other than dwelling houses: ibid s 7.
3 Ibid s 1 (1). See *Hobson v Gledhill* [1978] 1 All ER 945, [1978] 1 WLR 215, DC.
4 Guard Dogs Act 1975 s 1 (2).
5 Ibid s 1 (3).

376. Licence to keep a guard dog. A person must not keep a dog at guard dog kennels[1] unless he holds a licence[2] in respect of the kennels, and must not use or permit the use at any premises[3] of a guard dog[4] if he knows or has reasonable cause to suspect that, when not being used as a guard dog, it is normally kept at guard dog kennels in breach of this provision[5]. These provisions are not yet in force[6].

1 Ie a place where a person in the course of business keeps a dog which, notwithstanding that it is used for other purposes, is used as a guard dog elsewhere, other than a dog used as a guard dog only at premises belonging to its owner: Guard Dogs Act 1975 s 7.
2 Ie a licence under ibid s 3; see para 377 post.
3 For the meaning of 'premises' see para 375 note 2 ante.
4 For the meaning of 'guard dog' see para 375 note 1 ante.
5 Guard Dogs Act 1975 s 2 (2).
6 The Guard Dogs Act 1975 (Commencement No 1) Order 1975, SI 1975/1767, did not bring this section into force.

377. Guard dog kennel licences. A local authority may[1], on the application[2] of a person who runs or intends to run guard dog kennels[3] at premises within its area, grant that person a licence in respect of those kennels[4]. A licence must be subject to conditions prescribed by regulations and to such other conditions as the local authority thinks fit[5]. It remains in force for 12 months unless cancelled by a court in certain circumstances[6]. Regulations may be made enabling a local authority to revoke a licence and, on application by the holder, to vary certain of its conditions[7]. They may also provide for the continuance or transfer of a licence where an appeal is made and on the death of the holder[8]. These provisions are not yet in force[9].

1 Ie a district council, a London borough council or the Common Council of the City of London: Guard Dogs Act 1975 s 7.
2 Application must be in the prescribed form and accompanied by the prescribed fee: ibid s 3 (1). Regulations may require payment of a prescribed fee on inspection by the local authority of premises the subject of an application: s 6 (1) (b).
3 As to guard dog kennels see para 376 note 1 ante.
4 Guard Dogs Act 1975 s 3 (1).
5 Ibid s 3 (2).
6 Ibid s 3 (3). Cancellation may follow a conviction under the Guard Dogs Act 1975, the Protection of Animals Act 1911, the Pet Animals Act 1951, the Animal Boarding Establishments Act 1963 or the Breeding of Dogs Act 1973: Guard Dogs Act 1975 s 3 (4). The court may suspend the cancellation pending an appeal: s 3 (5).
7 Ibid s 6 (1) (a). Conditions which may be varied are those other than conditions prescribed by the regulations.
8 Ibid s 6 (1) (c). As to appeals see para 378 post.
9 See para 376 note 6 ante.

378. Appeals. An appeal will lie to a magistrates' court against the refusal by a local authority[1] to grant a licence; against certain conditions[2] to which a licence is subject; against the authority's refusal to vary the conditions; and against the revocation of a licence[3]. On appeal, the court may, if it thinks fit, give directions to the local authority with respect to the licence or to the conditions, and the local authority must comply[4]. These provisions are not yet in force[5].

1 For the meaning of 'local authority' see para 377 note 1 ante.
2 Ie conditions other than the prescribed conditions: Guard Dogs Act 1975 s 4 (1) (b). As to the prescribed conditions see s 3.
3 Ibid s 4 (1).
4 Ibid s 4 (2).
5 See para 376 note 6 ante.

379. Offences, penalties and civil liability. A person who contravenes the provisions of the Guard Dogs Act 1975 relating to the control of guard dogs[1] or restricting their keeping without a licence[2] is guilty of an offence[3].

Contravention of the Act or of regulations made under it or of the terms or conditions of a licence does not give rise to civil liability, nor does it derogate from it[4].

These provisions are in force except in so far as they relate to the licensing scheme[5].

1 Ie the Guard Dogs Act 1975 s 1; see para 375 ante.
2 Ie ibid s 2; see para 376 ante.
3 Ibid s 5 (1). The penalty on summary conviction is a fine not exceeding level 5 on the standard scale: s 5 (1) (amended by virtue of the Criminal Justice Act 1982 ss 38, 46). As to the standard scale see para 232 note 1 ante. At the date at which this volume states the law, level 5 on that scale is at £2,000.
4 Guard Dogs Act 1975 s 5 (2).
5 See para 376 note 6 ante.

(iv) Injury to Mankind

380. Civil liability for injuries to mankind. Dogs belong to a non-dangerous species for the purpose of deciding questions of liability for any injuries to human beings caused by them, since they are domesticated in the British Islands[1]. The same tests and considerations for determining such questions apply to dogs as to other non-dangerous species of animals, and accordingly the general principles involved are dealt with later in this title[2].

1 Animals Act 1971 ss 2 (2), 6 (2). 'British Islands' means the United Kingdom, the Channel Islands, the Isle of Man and the Republic of Ireland; the United Kingdom means Great Britain (ie England, Scotland and Wales) and Northern Ireland: see the Interpretation Act 1978 ss 5, 22, Sch 1.
2 See para 467 et seq post.

(v) Injury to Livestock

381. Civil liability for injury to livestock. Any person who keeps a dog[1] which causes damage by killing or injuring[2] livestock[3] is absolutely liable for the damage, subject to certain specified statutory defences[4]. In law a person is the keeper of an animal if he either owns it or has it in his possession, or is the head of a household of which a member under 16 owns the animal or has it in his possession[5]. Moreover, a person remains in law the keeper of an animal until someone else fulfilling these qualifications succeeds him[6], but a person who takes possession of an animal to prevent it causing damage or to restore it to its owner does not, by virtue only of that possession, become its keeper[7].

1 Where damage is caused by two or more dogs acting together, each dog in law occasions the whole of the damage and consequently the keeper of each will be responsible for the whole: *Arneil v Paterson* [1931] AC 560, HL, commenting on *Piper v Winnifrith and Leppard* [1917] WN 358.
2 As to injury see *Campbell v Wilkinson* (1909) 43 ILT 237 (dog barking at foals which injured themselves); and *Ives v Brewer* (1951) 95 Sol Jo 286 (poultry ceasing laying as a result of shock).
3 'Livestock' for this purpose means cattle, horses, asses, mules, hinnies, sheep, pigs, goats, poultry, deer not in a wild state, and also, while in captivity, pheasants, partridges and grouse; 'poultry' means the domestic varieties of fowls, turkeys, geese, ducks, guinea-fowls, pigeons, peacocks and quails: Animals Act 1971 s 11.
4 Ibid s 3. For these defences see para 382 post. As to the offence of worrying livestock on agricultural land see para 384 post.
5 Animals Act 1971 s 6 (3).
6 Ibid s 6 (3).
7 Ibid s 6 (4). Eg the position of rescue societies and homes.

382. Exceptions to liability. A person deemed in law to be the keeper[1] of a dog will not be liable for any damage it causes to livestock[2] if such damage is due wholly to the fault of the person whose livestock it is[3]; or if the livestock was killed or injured on land on to which it has strayed and either the dog belonged to the occupier of that land or its presence on that land was authorised by him[4].

1 For the meaning of 'keeper' see para 381 ante.
2 For the meaning of 'livestock' see para 381 note 3 ante.
3 Animals Act 1971 s 5 (1).
4 Ibid s 5 (4). The 'belonging' or the presence of the dog clearly covers the various possibilities included in the meaning of 'keeper' in s 6 (3).

383. Unburied carcases of cattle. Any person who knowingly[1] and without reasonable excuse permits the carcase of any head of cattle belonging to him or under his control to remain unburied in a field or other place to which dogs can gain access, is liable on summary conviction to a fine not exceeding level 1 on the standard scale[2].

1 As to 'knowingly' see para 395 note 7 post.
2 Dogs Act 1906 s 6 (amended by the Dogs (Amendment) Act 1928 s 3, the Criminal Justice Act 1967 s 92 (1), Sch 3 Pt I; and by virtue of the Criminal Justice Act 1982 ss 38, 46). As to the standard scale see para 232 note 1 ante. At the date at which this volume states the law, level 1 on the scale is at £50. The object of this provision is to prevent the owners of cattle, who have a remedy for injury done to their cattle by dogs (see para 381 ante), from encouraging in dogs the propensity to trespass, by leaving carcases in places which are accessible to dogs.

384. Worrying livestock on agricultural land. Subject to certain exceptions, if a dog worries livestock[1] on any agricultural land[2], the owner of the dog and, if it is in the charge of anyone other than its owner, that person also, is guilty of an offence[3] punishable on summary conviction by a fine not exceeding level 3 on the standard scale[4]. 'Worrying livestock' means being at large, that is not on a leash or under close control, in a field or enclosure where there are sheep and either attacking livestock or chasing it[5] in such a way as may be reasonably expected to cause it injury[6] or suffering, or, in the case of females, abortion or loss of or diminution in their produce[7].

The owner of a dog is not to be convicted of this offence if he proves[8] that at the material time the dog was in the charge of some other person whom he reasonably believed to be a fit and proper person to be in charge of the dog[9]. Nor is a person guilty of the offence if at the material time the livestock were trespassing[10] on the land in question and the dog was owned by, or in the charge of, the occupier of that land or a person authorised by him, except in a case where the said person causes[11] the dog to attack the livestock[12].

Proceedings in respect of such an offence cannot be brought except by or with the consent of the chief officer of police for the area where the land is situated, or by the occupier of the land or the owner of any of the livestock[13]. Where a police officer reasonably believes[14] that a dog found on any land has been worrying livestock there and the land appears to him to be agricultural land, and no person is present who admits to being the owner of the dog or in charge of it, then, in order to ascertain its owner, the officer may seize the dog and detain it until the owner has claimed it and paid all expenses incurred by it detention[15].

Further, a justice of the peace may issue a warrant authorising the entry and search of premises if satisfied upon application by a constable that there are reasonable grounds for believing that an offence under the Dogs (Protection of Livestock) Act 1953 has been committed and that the dog involved is on those premises[16].

1 'Livestock' for this purpose means cattle, sheep, goats, swine, horses or poultry; 'cattle' means bulls, cows, oxen, heifers or calves; 'horses' includes asses and mules; and 'poultry' means domestic fowls, turkeys, geese or ducks (Dogs (Protection of Livestock) Act 1953 s 3 (1). This is not quite such a wide definition as that under the Animals Act 1971 s 11 (see para 381 note 3 ante). Rabbits are not included, even if kept commercially: see *Tallents v Bell and Goddard* [1944] 2 All ER 474, CA.

2 'Agricultural land' means land used as arable, meadow or grazing land, or for the purpose of poultry or pig farming, market gardens, allotments, nursery grounds or orchards: Dogs (Protection of Livestock) Act 1953 s 3 (1). In *Williams v Richards* (1970) 144 Sol Jo 864, a cricket field on which sheep were grazing was held to be agricultural land. The Minister of Agriculture, Fisheries and Food may by order made by statutory instrument exempt land consisting wholly or mainly of mountain, hill, moor, heath or down land: Dogs (Protection of Livestock) Act 1953 ss 1 (5), 3 (2), (3); Transfer of Functions (Ministry of Food) Order 1955, SI 1955/554. At the date at which this volume states the law no such instrument was in force.

3 Dogs (Protection of Livestock) Act 1953 s 1 (1).

4 Ibid s 1 (6) (amended by the Criminal Justice Act 1967 s 92 (1), Sch 3 Pt I and by virtue of the Criminal Justice Act 1982 ss 35, 46). As to the standard scale see para 232 note 1 ante. At the date at which this volume states the law, level 3 on that scale is at £400.

5 Actual pursuit need not be proved; it is sufficient for the dog to run among the livestock so as to alarm them: *Stephen v Milne* 1960 SLT 276.

6 As to injury see para 381 note 2 ante.

7 Dogs (Protection of Livestock) Act 1953 s 1 (2). Exceptions include a dog owned by or in charge of the owner of the field or of the sheep, or a person authorised by them; a police dog, guide dog, trained sheepdog, working gundog or hounds: s 1 (2); Animal Health Act 1981 s 12, Sch 7.

8 The onus being on the defendant, he discharges it upon a balance of probabilities: *R v Carr-Briant* [1943] KB 607, [1943] 2 All ER 156, CCA; *R v Dunbar* [1958] 1 QB 1, [1957] 2 All ER 737, CCA.

9 Dogs (Protection of Livestock) Act 1953 s 1 (4).

10 It is sufficient to constitute a trespass if part of the body of an animal intrudes on the land: cf *Ellis v Loftus Iron Co* (1874) LR 10 CP 10. See also *Wormald v Cole* [1954] 1 QB 614, [1954] 1 All ER 683, CA; and *Singleton v Williamson* (1861) 7 H & N 410.

11 Possibly a person may 'cause' a dog to attack although he acts at the instigation of another: cf *R v Wilson* (1856) Dears & B 127, CCR. But a person who stands back and lets another act cannot, in

general, be said to 'cause': cf *Kelly's Directories Ltd v Gavin and Lloyds* [1902] 1 Ch 631, CA; see also *Swallow v LCC* [1916] 1 KB 224; aliter, perhaps, where he has a legal duty to prevent the other from acting: cf *Baker v Ellison* [1914] 2 KB 762, DC.

12 Dogs (Protection of Livestock) Act 1953 s 1 (3).

13 Ibid s 2 (1). As to the procedure where proceedings are also brought under the Dogs Act 1871 s 2 see para 373 text and notes 15, 16 ante.

14 It seems that the officer must not only have reasonable cause to believe but must also actually believe: see *R v Banks* [1916] 2 KB 621, CCA; *R v Harrison* [1938] 3 All ER 134, CCA; and *Nakkuda Ali v M F de S Jayaratne* [1951] AC 66, PC. Whether or not he had reasonable cause to believe is for the court to decide: see *McArdle v Egan* (1933) 150 LT 412, CA; *Nakkuda Ali v M F de S Jayaratne* supra; *Liversidge v Anderson* [1942] AC 206, [1941] 2 All ER 338, HL.

15 Dogs (Protection of Livestock) Act 1953 s 2 (2). The dog is then treated as though seized as a stray under the Dogs Act 1906 s 3 (4)–(10) (see para 385 post): Dogs (Protection of Livestock) Act 1953 s 2 (3).

16 Ibid s 2A (added by the Police and Criminal Evidence Act 1984 s 119 (1), Sch 6 Pt I para 7).

(vi) Stray Dogs

385. Seizure and detention of stray dogs. A police officer or a duly authorised officer of a local authority may seize any dog found in a highway or place of public resort[1] which he has reason to believe[2] is a stray dog and detain it until the owner has claimed it and paid all expenses incurred by its detention[3]. This power extends to privately owned land with the consent of the owner or occupier of the land[4]. If the dog wears a collar[5] with an address on or attached to it, or the owner of the dog is known, the police or local authority officer must serve on the person whose address is given, or on the owner, written notice stating that the dog has been seized, and is liable to be sold or destroyed if not claimed within seven clear days after the service[6]. The police officer or other person having charge of any dog detained must cause it to be properly fed and maintained[7].

Where a dog has been detained for seven clear days after being seized or, if such notice has been served, after service, and the owner has not claimed the dog and paid all expenses, the dog may be sold or destroyed in a manner to cause as little pain as possible[8], but no dog so seized may be given or sold for the purposes of vivisection[9].

The police and the local authority must keep a register of all dogs so seized which are not transferred to an establishment for the reception of stray dogs[10], and dogs must not be transferred to such an establishment unless a similar register is kept there[11]. The register must contain a brief description of the dog, the date of seizure, and particulars as to the manner in which it is disposed of, and is open to public inspection at all reasonable times on payment of 5p[12].

All expenses incurred by the police in connection with stray dogs are defrayed out of, and any money received by them on that account must be paid to, the police fund[13].

Local authorities have power to designate roads upon which dogs must be held on a lead[14].

1 For the meaning of 'place of public resort' see para 371 note 1 ante.

2 As to 'reason to believe' see para 384 note 14 ante.

3 Dogs Act 1906 s 3 (1) (amended by the Local Government Act 1988 s 39 (1)–(3), (6), (7). 'Local authority' means a district council, a London borough council, the Common Council of the City of London or the Council of the Isles of Scilly: Dogs Act 1906 s 3 (9A) (added by the Local Government Act 1988 s 39 (2) (e)). A police officer may also seize a dog worrying livestock on agricultural land; see para 384 ante.

4 Dogs Act 1906 s 3 (1), (1A) (amended and added respectively by the Local Government Act 1988 s 39 (3)).
5 As to the necessity for a collar see para 371 ante.
6 Dogs Act 1906 s 3 (2) (amended by the Local Government Act 1988 s 39 (2)). The notice may be served by delivering it to the person to be served, or by leaving it at or posting it to his usual or last-known place of abode or the address on the collar: Dogs Act 1906 s 3 (3).
7 Ibid s 3 (8).
8 Ibid s 3 (4) (as amended: see note 6 supra).
9 Ibid s 3 (5).
10 Ibid s 3 (6) (as amended: see note 6 supra).
11 Ibid s 3 (7) (as amended: see note 6 supra).
12 Ibid s 3 (6), (7) (amended by virtue of the Decimal Currency Act 1969 s 10 (1)).
13 Dogs Act 1906 s 3 (9).
14 See the Road Traffic Act 1988 s 27; and ROAD TRAFFIC.

386. Duty of finder of stray dog. Any person[1] who finds and takes possession of a stray dog must forthwith either return it to its owner or take the dog to the nearest police station and inform the police where it was found[2].

If the finder desires to keep the dog, he may, after taking it to the police station, remove it on giving his name and address, when he will receive from the police a certificate describing the dog and stating where it was found, when it was taken to the police and the finder's name and address[3]. He must, however, keep the dog for not less than one month[4]. If he does not desire to keep the dog, the police must treat it as if it were a stray dog seized by a police officer[5].

Failure to comply with any of these provisions renders the finder liable to a fine not exceeding level 1 on the standard scale[6].

1 Except a duly authorised officer of a local authority (as to which, see para 385 ante): Dogs Act 1906 s 4 (1) (amended by the Local Government Act 1988 s 39 (1), (4)).
2 Dogs Act 1906 s 4 (1) (substituted by the Dogs (Amendment) Act 1928 s 2).
3 Dogs Act 1906 s 4 (2) (a) (as substituted: see note 2 supra). For the certificate, which is prescribed by the Secretary of State, see the Order dated 4 August 1928, SR & O 1928/612. The police will then act as in the case of any stray found in a public place (see para 376 ante), and if the owner claims the dog within the prescribed time he will be entitled to it; otherwise the finder will be entitled to keep it.
4 Dogs Act 1906 s 4 (2) (a) (as substituted: see note 2 supra).
5 Ibid s 4 (2) (b) (as substituted: see note 2 supra). As to strays see para 385 ante.
6 Ibid s 4 (3) (as substituted: see note 2 supra; and amended by virtue of the Criminal Justice Act 1982 s 46). As to the standard scale see para 232 note 1 ante. At the date at which this volume states the laws level 1 on that scale is at £50.

(vii) Killing or Injuring Dogs

387. Killing or injuring another's dog. To kill, shoot or injure another man's dog without legal justification is a wrong actionable at common law[1]. Such legal justification arises from the statutory provisions relating to the protection of livestock[2] from dogs.

In any civil proceedings for the killing or injuring of a dog it is a defence to prove[3] that the defendant acted for the protection of any livestock and was a person entitled so to act[4], and that within 48 hours of the killing or injury the defendant gave notice of it to the officer in charge of a police station[5]. A person is entitled to act for the protection of any livestock if, and only if, (1) the livestock or the land on which it is belongs to him[6] or to any person under whose express or implied authority he is acting[7], and (2) the livestock was not killed or injured on land on to which it had strayed and either the dog belonged to the occupier or its presence there was authorised by him[8].

A person so acting is deemed to be acting for the protection of any livestock if, and only if, either (1) the dog is worrying[9] or is about to worry the livestock and there are no other reasonable means of ending or preventing the worrying[10], or (2) the dog has been worrying livestock, has not left the vicinity, is not under the control of any person, and there are no practicable means of ascertaining to whom it belongs[11]. A belief on reasonable grounds by the defendant that either of these conditions was satisfied is sufficient[12].

A dog attacking a human being may be shot in self-defence[13], but the shooting even of a ferocious dog is not justified after the animal has ceased its attacks[14], in marked contrast to the right to kill after an attack upon livestock in the circumstances set out above.

1 See *Vere v Earl Cawdor* (1809) 11 East 568; *Moore v Clarke* (1898) 62 JP 522; *Barnard v Evans* [1925] 2 KB 794, DC. A notice that trespassing dogs will be shot is no defence: *Corner v Champneys* (1814) cited in 2 Marsh at 584.
2 For the meaning of 'livestock' in this context see para 381 note 3 ante.
3 The onus is on the defendant, discharged on a balance of probabilities; see para 384 note 8 ante.
4 Animals Act 1971 s 9 (1) (a).
5 Ibid s 9 (1) (b).
6 For this purpose an animal belongs to any person who owns it or has it in his possession, and land belongs to any person who is the occupier of it: ibid s 9 (5).
7 Ibid s 9 (2) (a).
8 Ibid ss 5 (4), 9 (2) (b).
9 There is no definition of 'worrying' in the Animals Act 1971; for the definition in the Dogs (Protection of Livestock) Act 1953 s 1 (2) see para 384 ante.
10 Animals Act 1971 s 9 (3) (a).
11 Ibid s 9 (3) (b).
12 Ibid s 9 (4).
13 *Morris v Nugent* (1836) 7 C & P 572 per Lord Denman CJ. In *Clark v Webster* (1823) 1 C & P 104 an allegation that a dog was accustomed to attack and bite mankind was treated as material. Killing otherwise than by shooting must clearly also be justified.
14 *Morris v Nugent* (1836) 7 C & P 572, where the dog was shot while running away after the attack. This case must, however, be looked at with care in the light of the principles established in *Cresswell v Sirl* [1948] 1 KB 241, [1947] 2 All ER 730, CA, which principles formed the basis of the statutory provisions of the Animals Act 1971 s 9, set out in the text supra.

388. Protection of property other than livestock. A person who kills or injures another's dog which is attacking property of any kind other than livestock[1], whether his own or another person's, commits no offence if he acts to protect that property or a right or interest, provided that (1) he honestly believes at the time that the property is in immediate need of protection, and (2) the means used are reasonable having regard to all the circumstances[2]. The principles of civil liability for his action are, however, different.

Thus to kill or injure a dog in protection of game and other wild animals not reclaimed is still probably an actionable wrong[3]. No doubt the same would apply when property other than animals is attacked. Where animals other than livestock[4] are attacked by a dog, liability for the killing or injuring by shooting of the dog will depend upon whether the defendant can prove (1) that at the material time the dog was either actually attacking the animals or, if left at large, would renew the attack so that the animals would be left in real and imminent danger unless renewal was prevented; and (2) that either there was in fact no practicable means other than shooting of stopping the present attack or such renewals, or that, having regard to all the circumstances in which he found himself, he acted reasonably in regarding the shooting as necessary[5].

1 For the meaning of 'livestock' for the purposes of the Animals Act 1971 s 9 see s 11; and para 381 note 3 ante.
2 See the Criminal Damage Act 1971 s 5 (2) (b); and para 236 ante.
3 *Vere v Earl Cawdor* (1809) 11 East 568 at 570 per Le Blanc J, followed in two county court decisions, one reported at (1881) 45 JP Jo 83, and *Brown v Belfast Water Comrs* (1912) 47 ILT 153. There is, however, an obiter dictum of Blackburn J to the contrary effect in *Taylor v Newman* (1863) 4 B & S 89 at 91, commenting on *Vere v Earl Cawdor* supra. If to shoot a dog in pursuit of game was actionable the position was unaffected by *Cresswell v Sirl* [1948] 1 KB 241, [1947] 2 All ER 730, CA, or the Animals Act 1971.
4 See note 1 supra.
5 *Cresswell v Sirl* [1948] 1 KB 241 at 249, [1947] 2 All ER 730 at 733, CA. No doubt, in killing or injuring by means other than shooting, the same would apply.

389. Baiting or trapping dogs. Although in certain circumstances a man may justifiably act to protect his property from attack by dogs, even by shooting if necessary[1], he must not so use his land as to tempt other people's dogs to destruction; thus if he sets traps baited with strong-smelling meat so near his neighbour's yard, or so near a highway where dogs may lawfully pass, that dogs are irresistibly drawn to the traps, he is liable in damages[2].

1 See para 387 ante.
2 *Townsend v Wathen* (1808) 9 East 277. He would probably now also be liable to prosecution under the Criminal Damage Act 1971 s 3, for possessing articles with intent to damage or destroy (see CRIMINAL LAW); or the Protection of Animals Act 1911 (see para 405 post).

(2) HORSES

390. General. Legal provisions expressly affecting horses will be found throughout this title under their appropriate headings. These include the regulation of riding establishments[1], the transport of horses[2], the use of anaesthetics[3], the prohibition of docking and nicking[4], the regulation of farriery[5], matters relating to diseases[6], the export of horses and ponies[7], and artificial insemination[8].

1 See paras 393–395 post.
2 See para 413 post.
3 See para 417 post.
4 See para 422 post.
5 See para 423 post.
6 See para 482 et seq post.
7 See para 506 post.
8 See AGRICULTURE vol 1 (2) (Reissue) para 819.

5. ANIMAL ESTABLISHMENTS, DANGEROUS WILD ANIMALS AND ZOOS

(1) ANIMAL BOARDING AND BREEDING ESTABLISHMENTS

391. Boarding dogs and cats. No one may keep a boarding establishment for animals[1] without a licence granted by the appropriate local authority[2]. Persons who are disqualified from keeping such an establishment[3], from keeping a pet shop[4], or from having the custody of animals[5], cannot be granted a licence[6].

In determining whether to grant a licence the local authority, without prejudice to its discretion to withhold a licence on other grounds, must have regard in particular to the need to secure that the animals will be suitably accommodated, fed, exercised and protected from disease and fire and that a proper register of animals with dates of arrival and departure and owners' names and addresses is kept[7]. Any licence granted must contain such conditions as will ensure the attainment of these objectives[8]. Such fee as may be determined by the local authority may be charged for the licence[9].

An appeal lies to a magistrates' court by any person aggrieved[10] against the refusal of a licence or against any condition imposed, and the court may give such directions as to the issue of a licence, or as regards the conditions to be imposed, as it thinks proper[11].

Keeping a boarding establishment without a licence or failing to comply with any condition of a licence is an offence punishable on summary conviction by imprisonment for up to three months or a fine not exceeding level 2 on the standard scale or both[12]. On convicting a person of any offence under the Animal Boarding Establishments Act 1963, the Protection of Animals Act 1911, the Protection of Animals (Scotland) Act 1912 or the Pet Animals Act 1951 the court may cancel the offender's licence to keep a boarding establishment and, whether or not he holds such a licence, may disqualify him from holding such a licence for such period as it thinks fit[13].

A local authority may authorise in writing any of its officers or any veterinary surgeon or veterinary practitioner[14] to inspect premises so licensed, and any such person has powers of entry and inspection at reasonable times[15]. Wilful obstruction[16] of or delay to any such person is an offence punishable on summary conviction by a fine not exceeding level 2 on the standard scale[17].

1　This is defined as carrying on at any premises (including a private dwelling) a business of providing accommodation for other people's cats and dogs: Animal Boarding Establishments Act 1963 s 5 (1), (2). A person is not deemed to be carring on such a business if he provides such accommodation in connection with a business of which the provision of such accommodation is not the main activity: s 5 (1) proviso (a). This eg excludes veterinary surgeons or practitioners who may provide accommodation as a sideline to their practices. Nothing in the Act affects the keeping of an animal at premises in pursuance of a requirement under the Animal Health Act 1981: Animal Boarding Establishments Act 1963 s 5 (1) proviso (b).

2　Ibid s 1 (1), (2). 'Local authority' means a district council, London borough council or the Common Council of the City of London: s 5 (2) (amended by the Local Government Act 1972 ss 179 (1), (3), 272 (1), Sch 30).

3　See text to note 13 infra.

4　Ie under the Pet Animals Act 1951 s 5 (3): see para 466 post.

5　Ie under the Protection of Animals (Amendment) Act 1954 s 1: see para 462 post.

6　Animal Boarding Establishments Act 1963 s 1 (2) (amended by the Protection of Animals (Amendment) Act 1988 s 3 (2), (3), Schedule).

7　Animal Boarding Establishments Act 1963 s 1 (3).

8　Ibid s 1 (3). The licence relates to the year it was granted or the next following year: see s 1 (5).

9　Ibid s 1 (2) (amended by the Local Government Act 1974 ss 35, 42 (2), Sch 6 para 17, Sch 8).

10　For the meaning of 'person aggrieved' see ADMINISTRATIVE LAW vol 1 (1) (Reissue) para 56.

11　Animal Boarding Establishments Act 1963 s 1 (4).

12　Ibid s 1 (8), 3 (1) (amended by virtue of the Criminal Justice Act 1982 ss 38, 46). As to the standard scale see para 232 note 1 ante. At the date at which this volume states the law, level 2 on that scale is at £100.

13　Animal Boarding Establishments Act 1963 s 3 (3).

14 Ie one registered under the Veterinary Surgeons Act 1966 s 2 and s 8 respectively: see paras 547, 548 post.
15 Animal Boarding Establishments Act 1963 s 2 (1).
16 The phrase 'wilful obstruction' is used in many statutes but has normally been judicially interpreted in the context of the Police Act 1964 s 51 (3). In *Lewis v Cox* [1985] QB 509, [1984] 3 All ER 672, DC, the authorities were reviewed and it was held that a person 'wilfully obstructs' a police officer in the execution of his duty if his conduct actually prevents the police from carrying out their duty or makes it more difficult for them to do so and if he intentionally does the act realising that it would have an obstructive effect, regardless of his underlying motives. It is submitted that a similar interpretation (mutatis mutandis) should be given to the same words in the Animal Boarding Establishments Act 1963.
17 Ibid ss 2 (2), 3 (2) (amended by virtue of the Criminal Justice Act 1982 ss 38, 46). As to the standard scale see para 232 note 1 ante and note 12 supra.

392. Breeding of dogs. No one may keep a breeding establishment for dogs[1] without a licence granted by the appropriate local authority[2]. Persons who are disqualified from keeping such an establishment, or a pet shop[3], or from having the custody of animals[4], or from the boarding of animals[5], cannot be granted a licence[6].

In determining whether to grant a licence the local authority, without prejudice to its discretion to withhold a licence on other grounds, must have regard in particular to the need to secure that the dogs will be suitably accommodated, fed, exercised and protected from disease and fire and that appropriate steps will be taken to secure that the dogs will be provided with suitable food, drink and bedding and adequately exercised when being transported to or from the breeding establishment[7]. Any licence granted must contain such conditions as will ensure the attainment of these objectives[8].

An appeal lies to a magistrates' court by any person aggrieved[9] against the refusal of a licence or against any condition imposed, and the court may give such directions as to the issue of a licence, or as regards the conditions to be imposed, as it thinks proper[10].

Keeping a breeding establishment without a licence or failing to comply with any condition of a licence is an offence punishable on summary conviction by a fine not exceeding level 4 on the standard scale[11]. On convicting a person of any offence under the Breeding of Dogs Act 1973, the Protection of Animals Act 1911, the Protection of Animals (Scotland) Act 1912, the Pet Animals Act 1951 or the Animal Boarding Establishments Act 1963 the court may cancel the offender's licence to keep a breeding establishment and, whether or not he holds such a licence, may disqualify him from keeping such an establishment for such period as it thinks fit[12].

A local authority may authorise in writing any of its officers or any veterinary surgeon or veterinary practitioner[13] to inspect premises so licensed, and any such person has power to enter and inspect at reasonable times[14]. Wilful obstruction of or delay to any such person is an offence punishable on summary conviction by a fine not exceeding level 3 on the standard scale[15].

The foregoing provisions[16] do not apply to the breeding of dogs for use in regulated procedures[17], if they are bred at a designated[18] breeding establishment[19].

Where there are reasonable grounds for suspecting that an unlicensed breeding establishment for dogs is being or has been kept on any premises in the area of a local authority[20], a warrant[21] may be issued empowering an officer of the local authority, a veterinary surgeon or veterinary practitioner[22], authorised in writing by the local authority for the purpose, to enter[23] and inspect the premises and any animal or thing found therein[24]. Precautions may be specified to prevent the spread of infectious or contagious diseases, and must be complied with if so specified[25]. The obstruction or delaying of any person in the exercise of such powers of entry and inspection is an offence punishable on summary conviction by a fine not exceeding level 3 on the standard scale[26]. A person convicted of such offence may be disqualified from keeping a breeding establishment for such period as the court thinks fit, and no licence to do so may be granted to him during that period[27].

1 This is defined as carrying on at any premises (including a private dwelling) a business of breeding dogs with a view to their being sold in the course of such business whether by the keeper or any other person: Breeding of Dogs Act 1973 s 5 (1). A breeding establishment is any premises (including a private dwelling) where more than two bitches are kept for the purpose of breeding for sale: s 5 (2). Nothing in the Act affects the keeping of a dog at premises in pursuance of a requirement under the Animal Health Act 1981: Breeding of Dogs Act 1973 s 5 (1) proviso; Interpretation Act 1978 s 17 (2) (b).

2 Breeding of Dogs Act 1973 s 1 (1). 'Local authority' means the council of a London borough or of a district, or the Common Council of the City of London: s 5 (2) (amended by the Local Government Act 1974 ss 42 (1), 43 (2), Sch 7 para 15 (2)).

3 Ie under the Pet Animals Act 1951 s 5 (3): see para 466 post.

4 Ie under the Protection of Animals (Amendment) Act 1954 s 1: see para 462 post.

5 Ie under the Animal Boarding Establishments Act 1963 s 3 (3): see para 391 ante.

6 Breeding of Dogs Act 1973 s 1 (2) (amended by the Protection of Animals (Amendment) Act 1988 s 3 (2), (3), Schedule).

7 Breeding of Dogs Act 1973 s 1 (4).

8 Ibid s 1 (4). The fee for the licence is £2 or such reasonable sum as the authority may determine: s 1 (2) (amended by the Local Government, Planning and Land Act 1980 s 1 (6), Sch 6 para 15 (1)). The licence relates to the year it was granted or the following year: Breeding of Dogs Act 1973 s 1 (6).

9 For the meaning of 'person aggrieved' see ADMINISTRATIVE LAW vol 1 (1) (Reissue) para 56.

10 Breeding of Dogs Act 1973 s 1 (5).

11 Ibid s 1 (9), 3 (1) (amended by virtue of the Criminal Justice Act 1982 ss 38, 46). As to the standard scale see para 232 note 1 ante. At the date at which this volume states the law, level 4 on that scale is at £1,000.

12 Breeding of Dogs Act 1973 s 3 (3).

13 Ie one registered under the Veterinary Surgeons Act 1966 s 2 and s 8 respectively: see the Breeding of Dogs Act 1973 s 5 (2). See also paras 547, 548 post.

14 Ibid s 2 (1).

15 Ibid ss 2 (2), 3 (2) (amended by virtue of the Criminal Justice Act 1982 ss 38, 46). As to the standard scale see para 232 note 1 ante. At the date at which this volume states the law, level 3 on that scale is at £400.

16 Ie the Breeding of Dogs Act 1973.

17 For the meaning of 'regulated procedures' see the Animals (Scientific Procedures) Act 1986 s 2; para 430 post.

18 Ie designated by a certificate issued under ibid s 7; see para 435 post.

19 Ibid s 27 (3).

20 Ie that an offence has been or is being committed against the Breeding of Dogs Act 1973 s 1 (1); see text and notes 1, 2 supra.

21 The warrant continues in force for one month: Breeding of Dogs Act 1991 s 1 (4) (b). It must be produced if required: s 1 (5) (a).

22 Persons may be authorised to accompany the person executing the warrant: ibid s 1 (4) (a). 'Local authority', 'veterinary surgeon' and 'veterinary practitioner' have the same meanings as in the Breeding of Dogs Act 1973 (see notes 2, 13 supra): Breeding of Dogs Act 1991 s 1 (7).

23 The power of entry may be exercised at all reasonable times: ibid s 1 (5). Such entry may, if necessary, be effected by reasonable force: s 1 (1).

24 Ibid s 1 (1). No warrant, however, may be issued authorising entry to premises used for the time being as a private dwelling: s 1 (2). 'Private dwelling' does not include any garage, outhouse or other structure, whether or not part of the same building, belonging to or usually enjoyed with the premises: s 1 (3).

25 Ibid s 1 (5) (b). As to animal health generally see Pt 8 (paras 482–540) of this title post.

26 Ibid s 2 (1). As to the standard scale see para 232 note 1 ante. At the date at which this volume states the law, level 3 on that scale is at £400.

27 Ibid s 2 (2). Licences are granted under the Breeding of Dogs Act 1973 s 1; see text and note 3 supra.

(2) RIDING ESTABLISHMENTS

393. Licensing of riding establishments. No person may keep a riding establishment, that is to say, carry on the business of keeping horses[1] either for letting out on hire for riding or for providing riding instruction in return for payment, or both[2], except under the authority of a licence granted by the appropriate local authority[3]. No one who is disqualified from keeping a riding establishment[4], from keeping a pet shop[5], from having the custody of animals[6], or from keeping an animal boarding establishment[7], or who is under 18, can obtain such a licence, which must specify the premises at which the business is to be carried on and may include conditions as to its operation[8].

The local authority must not decide whether to grant a licence until it has received and considered a report by its inspecting veterinary surgeon or veterinary practitioner[9] of the result of an inspection of the relevant premises[10] within the 12 months prior to the receipt by the authority of the application or thereafter[11], and it must have regard, in considering whether to grant a licence, to the suitability of the applicant or his manager, the suitability of the accommodation and pasturage, the adequacy of the provisions for the horses' health, welfare and exercise, the precautions against fire and disease, and the suitability of the horses for the purposes for which they are kept[12].

An appeal lies to a magistrates' court against the refusal of a licence or against any condition included in it[13], and the court may give such directions as to the issue of a licence and its conditions as it thinks proper[14].

1 'Horse' means any mare, gelding, pony, foal, colt, filly or stallion, and any ass, mule or jennet: Riding Establishments Act 1964 s 6 (4).
2 Ibid s 6 (1). Such a business is exempt if the premises (including land) where the horses are kept are occupied by or under the management of the Secretary of State for Defence, or if it is carried on solely for police purposes or by the Zoological Society of London (s 6 (1), (4)), or if the horses are kept by a university for the instruction of students undergoing an approved course leading to a veterinary degree (s 6 (2)). A person keeping a riding establishment is taken to keep it at the premises where the horses are kept: s 6 (3).
3 Ibid s 1 (1), (2). 'Local authority' means the council of a district or London borough or the Common Council of the City of London: s 6 (4) (amended by the Local Government Act 1972 ss 251 (2), 272 (1), Sch 29 Pt II para 42, Sch 30). A provisional licence for three months, renewable once, may be issued where the local authority is not satisfied that a permanent licence may be granted: Riding Establishments Act 1970 s 1 (1), (2). A licence is granted on payment of such fee as may be determined by the local authority: Riding Establishments Act 1964 s 1 (2) (amended by the Local Government Act 1974 s 35, Sch 6 para 18). The licence relates to the year in which it was granted or the following year: see the Riding Establishments Act 1964 s 1 (6).
4 A court convicting a person of any offence under the Protection of Animals Act 1911, the Pet Animals Act 1951, the Animal Boarding Establishments Act 1963 or the Riding Establishments Act 1964 may disqualify him from keeping a riding establishment for such time as it thinks fit: ibid s 4 (3).
5 Ie under the Pet Animals Act 1951 s 5 (3); see para 466 post.
6 Ie under the Protection of Animals (Amendment) Act 1954 s 1 (1); see para 462 post.
7 Ie under the Animal Boarding Establishments Act 1963 s 3 (3); see para 391 ante.
8 Riding Establishments Act 1964 s 1 (2) (amended by the Protection of Animals (Amendment) Act 1988 s 3 (2), (3), Schedule. As to the conditions see the Riding Establishments Act 1964 s 1 (4) (substituted by the Riding Establishments Act 1970 s 2 (1) (ii)). In addition, every licence is subject to conditions, whether specified in the licence or not, as to not using horses found on inspection to need veterinary attention until certified fit, the provision of proper supervision for riders needing it, the business not being left in the charge of a person under 16, the holding of proper insurances and the

keeping of a register of horses aged three years and under: Riding Establishments Act 1964 s 1 (4A) (added by the Riding Establishments Act 1970 s 2 (1) (ii)).
9 See para 394 post.
10 'Premises' includes land: Riding Establishments Act 1964 s 6 (4).
11 Ibid s 1 (3).
12 Ibid s 1 (4) (as substituted: see note 8 supra).
13 No appeal lies against a condition set out in ibid s 1 (4A) (as added: see note 8 supra).
14 Ibid s 1 (5) (amended by the Riding Establishments Act 1970 s 2 (2)).

394. Inspection of premises. A local authority[1] may authorise a person to inspect premises[2] in its area where it has reason to believe a person is keeping a riding establishment or as respects which a licence is in force or has been applied for[3]. A person so authorised, who may be an officer of the authority, an officer of another local authority, a veterinary surgeon or a veterinary practitioner[4], may enter the premises and inspect horses and things found there for the purpose of making a report[5] or ascertaining whether an offence has been or is being committed against the Riding Establishments Act 1964[6].

1 For the meaning of 'local authority' see para 393 note 3 ante.
2 'Premises' includes land: Riding Establishments Act 1964 s 6 (4).
3 Ibid s 2 (1).
4 Ibid s 2 (1). As to professional inspectors see s 2 (3). As to veterinary surgeons and practitioners see paras 547, 548 post.
5 See the Riding Establishments Act 1964 s 1 (3); and para 393 ante.
6 Ibid s 2 (2). As to obstructing or delaying an inspector see para 395 post.

395. Offences, penalties and disqualification. It is an offence to keep a riding establishment without a licence, and the grantee of a licence is guilty of an offence if he contravenes or does not comply with any condition[1] of the licence[2].

A person commits an offence who:

(1) lets out a horse on hire, or uses it for providing riding instruction in return for payment or for demonstration riding, when it is in such a condition that riding it would be likely to cause it suffering[3], or when it is aged three years or under, or is a mare heavy with foal or within three months after foaling[4]; or

(2) supplies, for a horse which is let out on hire by him for riding, equipment which is used in the course of the hiring and which when supplied suffers from a defect apparent on inspection and likely to cause suffering to the horse or an accident to the rider[5]; or

(3) fails to provide suitable curative care for a sick or injured horse kept by him with a view to its being let out on hire or used as mentioned in (1) above[6]; or

(4) in keeping a riding establishment, knowingly[7] permits any person disqualified from keeping one[8] to have control or management[9]; or

(5) conceals or causes to be concealed any horse maintained by the riding establishment with intent to avoid inspection[10]; or

(6) for the purpose of obtaining a licence gives information he knows to be false in a material particular or makes a statement he knows to be so false, or recklessly gives any information which is so false or makes a statement which is so false[11]; or

(7) wilfully obstructs[12] or delays any person in the exercise of his powers of entry or inspection[13].

A local authority[14] may prosecute for any offence committed in its area[15]. Only a local authority may institute proceedings for contravention of or failure to comply with conditions in a licence, and it must first consider a report by an inspecting veterinary surgeon or veterinary practitioner[16].

Any of the above offences, other than under (7), is punishable on summary conviction with a fine not exceeding level 3 on the standard scale or imprisonment for a term not exceeding three months or both[17]. The summary punishment for an offence under (7) is a fine not exceeding level 2 on the standard scale[18]. A court convicting a person of any of these offences or of an offence under certain other Acts relating to animals[19] may cancel his licence to keep a riding establishment and, whether or not he is so licensed, disqualify him from keeping a riding establishment for such period as the court thinks fit[20].

1   This includes a condition of the kind referred to in para 393 note 8 ante.
2   Riding Establishments Act 1964 s 1 (9) (amended by the Riding Establishments Act 1970 s 2 (2)).
3   Riding Establishments Act 1964 s 3 (1) (a).
4   Ibid s 3 (1) (aa) (added by the Riding Establishments Act 1970 s 3).
5   Riding Establishments Act 1964 s 3 (1) (b).
6   Ibid s 3 (1) (c).
7   Knowledge must be proved by the prosecution: see *Gaumont British Distributors Ltd v Henry* [1939] 2 KB 711, [1939] 2 All ER 808, DC; *R v Hallam* [1957] 1 QB 569, [1957] 1 All ER 665, CCA. To refrain deliberately from making inquiries may amount to actual knowledge of the facts: see *Knox v Boyd* 1941 JC 82 at 86; *Taylor's Central Garages (Exeter) Ltd v Roper* (1951) 115 JP 445 at 449, DC, per Devlin J; *Mallon v Allon* [1964] 1 QB 385, [1963] 3 All ER 843, DC; *Wallworth v Balmer* [1965] 3 All ER 721, [1966] 1 WLR 16, DC.
8   See para 393 ante.
9   Riding Establishments Act 1964 s 3 (1) (d).
10   Ibid s 3 (1) (e).
11   Ibid s 3 (2).
12   For the meaning of 'wilfully obstructs' see para 382 note 16 ante.
13   Riding Establishments Act 1964 s 2 (4). As to these powers see para 394 ante. For the meaning of 'wilfully obstructs' see para 391 note 16 ante.
14   For the meaning of 'local authority' see para 393 note 3 ante.
15   Riding Establishments Act 1964 s 5 (1).
16   Ibid s 5 (2).
17   Ibid s 4 (1) (amended by virtue of the Criminal Justice Act 1982 ss 38, 46). As to the standard scale see para 232 note 1 ante. At the date at which this volume states the law, level 3 on that scale is at £400.
18   Riding Establishments Act 1964 s 4 (2) (amended by virtue of the Criminal Justice Act 1982 ss 38, 46). As to the standard scale see para 232 note 1 ante. At the date at which this volume states the law, level 2 on that scale is at £100.
19   See para 393 note 4 ante.
20   Riding Establishments Act 1964 s 4 (3). The court may suspend the operation of the order pending an appeal: s 4 (4).

(3) KEEPING DANGEROUS WILD ANIMALS

396. Keeping dangerous wild animals: general. Generally[1], no person may keep any dangerous wild animal[2], except under the authority of a licence granted by a local authority[3]. The authority may authorise a veterinary surgeon or veterinary practitioner to inspect any premises where any such animal is being held or where it is proposed to hold any such animal[4]. A licence must not be granted unless such an inspection has been made and a report on the premises considered by the authority[5]. Where any such animal is being kept without a licence, or where any condition of a licence is contravened or not complied with, the authority may seize the animal and retain it, destroy it or otherwise dispose of it, and is not liable to pay compensation[6]. Any person who keeps a dangerous wild animal without a licence, and any person who wilfully obstructs or delays any person entering or inspecting premises[7], commits an offence[8]; if any condition of a licence is contravened or not complied with, so do both the person to whom the licence is granted and any other person who is entitled to keep any animal under the authority of the licence and who was primarily responsible for the contravention or failure to comply[9].

1 Exceptions apply to licensed zoos (see para 398 post), circuses, licensed pet shops (see para 465 post), and designated establishments under the Animals (Scientific Procedures) Act 1986 (see para 434 post): Dangerous Wild Animals Act 1976 s 5 (amended by the Zoo Licensing Act 1981 s 22 (1) (a) and the Animals (Scientific Procedures) Act 1986 s 27 (2), Sch 3 para 10).

2 Ie any animal of a kind for the time being specified in the Dangerous Wild Animals Act 1976 Schedule: s 7 (4). The kinds of animal so specified include most species of non-domesticated cattle, goats and sheep, wild dogs and horses, marsupials, monkeys, lemurs and apes, sloths, armadillos, anteaters, porcupines, pandas, badgers, raccoons, civets, walruses, seals and sealions, aardvarks, antelopes, wild cats and members of the cat family, gazelles, camels, monkeys, crocodiles and alligators, dangerous snakes, dangerous spiders, giraffes, hippopotami, hyaenas, elephants, rhinoceri, ostriches, tapirs, emus, bears, cassowaries and pronghorns: see Schedule (substituted by the Dangerous Wild Animals Act 1976 (Modifications) Order 1984, SI 1984/1111). Reference to the Schedule should be made for the status of any specific species. The Schedule to the Dangerous Wild Animals Act 1976 classifies species by their scientific, ie Linnaean, names, and their common names are included by way of explanation only: see s 7 (5). The Schedule may be modified by the Home Secretary by way of statutory instrument: s 8.

3 Ibid s 1 (1). 'Local authority' means a district council, London borough council or the Common Council of the City of London: s 7 (4). As to the criteria for granting such licences see para 397 post.

4 Ibid s 3 (1). As to veterinary surgeons and veterinary practitioners see paras 547, 548 post.

5 Ibid s 1 (5).

6 Ibid s 4.

7 Ie those authorised by the local authority to inspect: see text to note 4 supra.

8 Ibid ss 2 (5), 3 (4). Persons guilty of any offence under this Act are liable on summary conviction to a maximum fine of level 5 on the standard scale: s 6 (1) (amended by virtue of the Criminal Justice Act 1982 ss 38, 46). As to the standard scale see para 232 note 1 ante. At the date at which this volume states the law, level 5 on that scale is at £2,000. Further, where a person is convicted of, inter alia, any offence under the Dangerous Wild Animals Act 1976 the convicting court may cancel any licence held by him under the Act and may also disqualify him from keeping any dangerous wild animal for such period as the court thinks fit: s 6 (2).

9 Ibid s 2 (6). It is a defence for the person charged under this sub-section to prove that he took all reasonable precautions and exercised all due diligence to avoid the commission of the offence: s 2 (7). For the court's powers on conviction see note 8 supra.

397. Licences for keeping dangerous wild animals. An application for a licence for keeping dangerous wild animals must specify the species of animal and the number of animals of each species proposed to be kept and the premises where they are to be held[1]. The applicant must normally be the person who both owns and possesses the animal or animals, or who proposes to do so[2]. No-one under 18, nor anyone disqualified from keeping a dangerous wild animal, may apply for a licence[3]. The local authority must not grant a licence unless it is satisfied that it is not contrary to the public interest to do so, that the applicant is a suitable person to hold a licence, that any animal concerned will be kept in secure and suitable accommodation, supplied with adequate and suitable food, drink and bedding, and visited at suitable intervals, that the animal will have room to exercise, that appropriate steps will be taken for the protection of the animal in case of fire or other emergency, and that all reasonable precautions will be taken to prevent and control the spread of infectious diseases[4]. Subject to these qualifications, the local authority may grant or refuse a licence as it thinks fit[5]. If it grants a licence it must specify certain conditions[6] and may specify such other conditions as it thinks fit[7];

these conditions may be subsequently varied or (except where compulsory) revoked[8]. Where a person is aggrieved by the refusal of a local authority to grant a licence, by a condition on a granted licence, or by the variation or revocation of a condition, he may appeal to a magistrates' court[9].

1 Dangerous Wild Animals Act 1976 s 1 (2). The application must be accompanied by such fee as the authority may stipulate: s 1 (2).
2 Ibid s 1 (4).
3 Ibid s 1 (2) (d).
4 Ibid s 1 (3).
5 Ibid s 1 (6).
6 Ibid s 1 (6).
7 Ibid s 1 (7).
8 Ibid s 1 (9).
9 Ibid s 2 (1).

(4) LICENSING AND REGULATION OF ZOOS

398. Licences. It is unlawful to operate a zoo[1] except under the authority of a licence issued by the local authority[2] for the area within which the whole or major part of the zoo is situated[3]. An application for a licence will not be considered unless written notice of it has been given at least two months beforehand, notice of the intended application has been published in one local and one national newspaper and a copy exhibited at the site[4]. The notice must contain certain specified information[5].

When considering the application the local authority must take into account representations made by or on behalf of certain specified persons including the applicant[6], and must consider inspectors' reports or consult persons nominated by the Secretary of State[7].

The local authority must refuse a licence if it is satisfied that the zoo would injuriously affect the health or safety of persons living in the neighbourhood or seriously affect the preservation of law and order[8]. It may refuse a licence if not satisfied as to the adequacy of the accommodation, staffing or management of the zoo, or if the applicant, an officer of or a keeper in the zoo has been convicted of certain offences involving ill-treatment of animals[9].

An original licence is for four years, and a fresh licence granted to an existing licence holder is for six years from the expiry of the existing one[10]. A licence may be made subject to certain conditions[11] and may be transferred to another person or surrendered[12]. A copy must be displayed at every public entrance to the zoo[13].

1 'Zoo' means an establishment where wild animals are kept for exhibition to the public otherwise than for purposes of a circus and otherwise than in a pet shop; the Act applies to any zoo to which members of the public have access, with or without charge for admission, on more than 7 days in any 12 consecutive months: Zoo Licensing Act 1981 s 1 (2).
   The animals covered by the Act are of the classes Mammalia, Aves, Reptilia, Amphibia, Pisces and Insecta and any other multi-cellular organism that is not a plant or fungus, and 'wild animals' means animals not normally domesticated in Great Britian: s 21 (1).
   'Circus' means a place where animals are kept or introduced wholly or mainly for the purposes of performing tricks or manoeuvres in that place; and 'pet shop' means premises for whose keeping a pet shop licence is in force or required under the Pet Animals Act 1951: Zoo Licensing Act 1981 s 21 (1).
2 Local authorities for the purpose are district councils, London borough councils and the Common Council of the City of London: ibid s 1 (3).
3 Ibid s 1 (1). As to offences see para 404 post.

4 Ibid s 2 (1). The local authority must keep the notice available for inspection by the public until the application is disposed of: s 2 (3).
5 Ibid s 2 (2).
6 Ibid s 3.
7 Ibid s 4 (1). As to those nominated see s 8; and para 399 post.
8 Ibid s 4 (2).
9 Ibid s 4 (3)–(5). A licence may also be refused if planning permission has not been granted: s 4 (6) (amended by the Planning (Consequential Provisions) Act 1990 s 4, Sch 2 para 49). The grounds of refusal must be sent by post to the applicant: Zoo Licensing Act 1981 s 4 (7).
10 Ibid s 5 (1), (2). There are provisions for charging fees for the grant, renewal or transfer of a licence and for applications for the same and for expenses of inspectors: s 15.
11 Ibid s 5 (3). In considering attaching conditions, the local authority must have regard to any standards specified by the Secretary of State under s 9 (see para 399 post) and sent by him to the authority: s 5 (4). The licence must contain any condition which he directs the authority to attach: s 5 (5). As to restrictions on conditions imposed by the authority see s 5 (6), (7).
12 Ibid s 7. As to extension of licences pending renewal see s 6.
13 Ibid s 4 (8).

399. Secretary of State's power to specify standards. The Secretary of State must compile a list of veterinary surgeons and practitioners who have experience of zoo animals, and also of persons who are competent to inspect animals in zoos and advise on their welfare and on the management of zoos[1].

After consulting persons on the list and such other persons as he thinks fit, the Secretary of State may specify standards with respect to the management of zoos and the animals in them[2].

1 Zoo Licensing Act 1981 s 8 (1)–(3). The Secretary of State must first consult with the presidents of the British Veterinary Association, the National Federation of Zoological Gardens and the National Zoological Association, and with such other persons as he thinks fit: s 8 (1). As to veterinary surgeons and veterinary practitioners see paras 547, 548 post.
2 Ibid s 9.

400. Inspections. The local authority concerned must carry out periodical inspections of any licensed zoo[1]. These must be made during the first year of an original licence and then not later than six months before the end of the fourth year, and in the case of a renewed or fresh licence, during the third year and not later than six months before the end of the sixth year[2].

Provision is made for the conduct of inspections, including the number of inspectors and the right of objection by the zoo operator to any inspector, the presence of representatives of the operator, the production of the zoo records and the contents of the inspector's report[3].

The local authority may at any time carry out a special inspection of a licensed zoo if it thinks it appropriate in view of certain specified circumstances[4]. Such an inspection must be carried out by authorised persons who appear to the authority to be competent for the purpose[5]. Both the appointed inspectors and the zoo operator must be informed of the purpose of the inspection[6].

The local authority must make arrangements for a licensed zoo to be informally inspected once in each year in which no formal inspection[7] is made[8].

1 Zoo Licensing Act 1981 s 10 (1). The local authority must give the zoo's operator at least 28 days' notice of the proposed date of inspection: s 10 (2).
2 Ibid s 10 (3).
3 Ibid s 10 (4), (5).
4 Ibid s 11 (1).

5 Ibid s 11 (2).
6 Ibid s 11 (4).
7 Ie under s 10 or s 11.
8 Ibid s 12.

401. Exemptions and special cases. The Secretary of State may exempt a zoo from the whole or part of the Zoo Licensing Act 1981 if a local authority informs him that in its opinion such a dispensation should be made because of the small size of the zoo or the small number of the kinds of animal kept there[1].

On information from the operator that for the above reasons the number of inspectors provided for by the requirement as to periodical inspections is too large, the Secretary of State may also exempt a zoo from such requirement[2].

When a local authority is the owner of a zoo, it must, as soon as practicable after the grant of a licence, its extension or the receipt of an inspectors' report, send a copy of those documents to the Secretary of State. The latter, and not the authority, has the power to revoke the licence[3].

1 Zoo Licensing Act 1981 s 14 (1).
2 Ibid s 14 (2).
3 Ibid s 13 (1), (2), (4).

402. Alteration and revocation of licences. The local authority may alter a licence at any time after its grant if it considers it necessary or desirable for ensuring the proper conduct of the zoo during the period of the licence[1]. Such alteration may be by varying, cancelling or attaching conditions or by a combination of those methods[2]. The licence holder must be given an opportunity to make representations[3].

If the Secretary of State directs a local authority to alter a licence, the authority must give effect to such direction within a reasonable time[4].

The local authority may revoke a licence on certain specified grounds concerning the conduct of the zoo or the conviction of any officer or keeper[5], but no licence may be revoked on grounds involving the care or treatment of animals unless the authority first consults persons nominated by the Secretary of State[6].

1 Zoo Licensing Act 1981 s 16 (1).
2 Ibid s 16 (4). No such condition must be inconsistent with the terms of a condition attached or varied
   in pursuance of a direction by the Secretary of State: s 16 (5).
3 Ibid s 16 (2).
4 Ibid s 16 (3).
5 Ibid s 17 (1). The licence holder must be given an opportunity to be heard: s 17 (1).
6 Ibid s 17 (2).

403. Appeals. There is a right of appeal to a magistrates' court for the area concerned against a refusal to grant a licence, or against any condition attached thereto or any variation or cancellation of a condition, or against the revocation of a licence[1]. An appeal must be brought within 21 days from receipt of written notification of the authority's decision, and will lie whether or not the authority's decision was made pursuant to a direction by the Secretary of State[2].

On an appeal, the court may confirm, vary or reverse the local authority's decision and may give such directions as it thinks proper[3].

When a licence is revoked[4], it continues in force until six months after the time for appeal has expired, or until the determination or abandonment of an appeal[5]. If on appeal the court confirms a revocation, the licence continues for six months commencing with the date of confirmation[6].

Where the attachment or variation of a condition requires the carrying out of works, the condition or variation will have no effect during the 21 day appeal period, nor, where an appeal is brought, before it is determined or abandoned[7].

1 Zoo Licensing Act 1981 s 18 (1). The appeal is by way of complaint and the Magistrates' Courts Act 1980 applies to the proceedings: Zoo Licensing Act 1981 s 18 (5).
2 Ibid s 18 (2).
3 Ibid s 18 (3).
4 Ie under ibid s 17; see para 402 ante.
5 Ibid s 18 (8).
6 Ibid s 18 (9).
7 Ibid s 18 (7).

404. Offences and penalties. A person who operates a zoo without a licence in contravention of the Zoo Licensing Act 1981[1], or who fails without reasonable excuse to comply with any condition attached to a zoo's licence[2], is guilty of an offence[3]. A person who intentionally obstructs an inspector acting under the Act[4] is guilty of an offence[5].

Where an offence committed by a body corporate is proved to have been committed with the consent or connivance of, or to have been attributed to any neglect on the part of, any director, manager, secretary or any other similar officer of the body corporate, or any person purporting to act in any such capacity, he is also guilty of the offence and liable to be proceeded against[6].

1 Zoo Licensing Act 1981 s 1; see para 398 ante.
2 Ie under ibid s 5 or s 16.
3 Ibid s 19 (1), (2). The penalty on summary conviction is a fine not exceeding level 4 on the standard scale: s 19 (4) (amended by virtue of the Criminal Justice Act 1982 s 46). As to the standard scale see para 232 note 1 ante. At the date at which this volume states the law, level 4 on that scale is at £1,000.
4 As to inspectors see para 400 ante.
5 Zoo Licensing Act 1981 s 19 (3). The penalty on summary conviction is a fine not exceeding level 3 on the standard scale: s 19 (4) (as amended: see note 3 supra). As to the standard scale see para 232 note 1 ante. At the date at which this volume states the law, level 3 on that scale is at £400.
6 Ibid s 19 (5).

6. PROTECTION OF ANIMALS FROM CRUELTY

(1) GENERAL

405. Cruelty to animals generally. It is provided by statute[1] that a number of offences against animals are offences of cruelty, upon conviction of which the offender is liable to a fine or imprisonment or both[2], and, as a result of such conviction, orders may be made by a magistrates' court in respect of compensation and deprivation of ownership or destruction of the animal[3]. Upon conviction of certain offences the court may cancel a licence to keep a pet shop, and disqualify the offender from keeping a pet shop[5]. Likewise it may cancel a licence to keep, or disqualify a person for keeping, an animal boarding establishment[6] or a riding establishment[7]. The court may also order disqualification from having custody of any animal, or any animal of a specified kind[8].

These provisions of the Acts apply to all domestic and captive animals, as defined therein[9], and decisions under the earlier Acts by which it was held that wild animals, even though reclaimed or in captivity, were not protected are not now applicable. Wild animals are not within the Acts, however, unless in captivity or confinement[10].

A person may be charged and convicted on one summons with having cruelly ill-treated a number of animals, for instance five cows, on a certain date. An information should not contain more than one offence[11], but it is not necessary to have a separate summons in respect of each animal where the offences in respect of all arise out of substantially one act[12]; in such case there cannot be a separate conviction in respect of each animal[13]. One summons may be issued against the same person in respect of several informations[14].

1 See the Protection of Animals Act 1911, which consolidated with amendments and extensions the enactments previously in force. This Act has been amended by the Protection of Animals Act (1911) Amendment Act 1921, the Protection of Animals (Amendment) Act 1927, the Protection of Animals (Amendment) Act 1954, the Protection of Animals (Penalties) Act 1987, the Protection of Animals (Amendment) Act 1988 and the Protection against Cruel Tethering Act 1988; and it has been supplemented by the Protection of Animals Act 1934 (public exhibition: see para 455 post), the Protection of Animals (Anaesthetics) Act 1954 and the Protection of Animals (Anaesthetics) Act 1964 (see para 417 post), the Abandonment of Animals Act 1960 (see para 416 post), and the Animals (Cruel Poisons) Act 1962 (see para 425 note 3 post). The foregoing Acts may be cited as the Protection of Animals Acts 1911 to 1964: 1964 Act s 2 (1) (a).

   Other Acts dealing with cruelty to animals are the Performing Animals (Regulation) Act 1925 (see para 454 post), the Cinematograph Films (Animals) Act 1937 (see para 456 post), the Docking and Nicking of Horses Act 1949 (see para 422 post), the Pet Animals Act 1951 (see paras 465, 466 post), the Cockfighting Act 1952 (see para 458 post), the Pests Act 1954 s 12 (myxomatosis: see para 426 post), the Animal Boarding Establishments Act 1963 (see para 391 ante), the Riding Establishments Act 1964 (see paras 393–395 ante), the Badgers Act 1973 (see para 352 et seq ante), the Farriers (Registration) Act 1975 (see para 423 post), the Wildlife and Countryside Act 1981 (see para 332 et seq ante) and the Animals (Scientific Procedures) Act 1986 (vivisection: see para 429 et seq post). For provisions governing the slaughter of animals, see FOOD; and para 411 post.

2 See para 461 post.
3 See paras 461–463 post.
4 See para 368 ante.
5 Pet Animals Act 1951 s 5 (3): see para 466 post.
6 Animal Boarding Establishments Act 1963 s 3 (3): see para 391 ante.
7 Riding Establishments Act 1964 s 4 (3): see para 395 ante.
8 Protection of Animals (Amendment) Act 1954 s 1 (1): see para 462 post.
9 In the Protection of Animals Act 1911 (save in s 11, where 'animal' means any horse, mule, ass, bull, sheep, goat or pig: see para 410 post), 'animal' means any domestic or captive animal; 'domestic animal' means any horse (defined as including any mare, gelding, pony, foal, colt, filly or stallion), ass, mule, bull (defined as including any cow, bullock, heifer, calf, steer or ox), sheep (defined as including any lamb, ewe or ram), pig (defined as including any boar, hog or sow), goat (defined as including a kid), dog (defined as including any bitch, sapling or puppy), cat (defined as including a kitten), or fowl (defined as including any cock, hen, chicken, capon, turkey, goose, gander, duck, drake, guineafowl, peacock, peahen, swan or pigeon), or any other animal of whatsoever kind or species, whether a quadruped or not, which is tame or which has been or is being sufficiently tamed to serve some purpose for man's use; and 'captive animal' means any non-domestic animal of whatsoever kind or species, whether a quadruped or not, including any bird, fish or reptile, which is in captivity or confinement or is maimed, pinioned or subjected to any appliance or contrivance for hindering or preventing its escape: s 15 (a)–(d). This definition is applied by the Cinematograph Films (Animals) Act 1937 s 1 (4) (b), the Protection of Animals (Amendment) Act 1954 s 4 (1) (a), and the Abandonment of Animals Act 1960 s 2. It is also applied by the Protection of Animals

(Anaesthetics) Act 1954 s 1 (4), save that 'animal' does not include a fowl or other bird, fish or reptile, and the above definitions of 'horse' and 'bull' are applied by the Protection of Animals Act 1934 s 1 (3).

In the Protection of Animals (Anaesthetics) Act 1964 'cattle' is defined in the same terms as 'bull' above (s 1 (5)). In the Performing Animals (Regulation) Act 1925 'animal' does not include invertebrates (s 5 (1)). In the Docking and Nicking of Horses Act 1949 'horse' means stallion, gelding, colt, mare, filly, pony, mule and hinny (s 3), and in the Riding Establishments Act 1964 'horse' has the same meaning, excluding hinny and adding foal, ass and jennet (s 6 (4)). In the Pet Animals Act 1951 'animal' includes any description of vertebrate (s 7 (3)); in the Animals (Cruel Poisons) Act 1962 it means any mammal (s 3); and in the Animal Boarding Establishments Act 1963 it means any dog or cat (s 5 (2)).

10 *Crown Prosecution Service v Barry* (1989) 153 JP 557, sub nom *DPP v Barry* [1989] Crim LR 645. A whale temporarily stranded without the agency of man and surrounded by people was held not to be in captivity or close confinement in *Steele v Rogers* (1912) 106 LT 79. A stag hunted and captured and then killed was held not to have become, at the time of the killing, in a state of captivity: *Rowley v Murphy* [1964] 2 QB 43, [1964] 1 All ER 50, DC. See also *Budge v Parsons* (1863) 3 B & S 382 (fighting cocks), and *Colam v Pagett* (1883) 12 QBD 66 (linnets kept as decoys), decisions made under the previous legislation, holding that the subjects in each case were domestic animals. See, however, para 406 post.
11 *Edwards v Jones* [1947] KB 659, [1947] 1 All ER 830, DC.
12 *R v Cable, ex p O'Shea* [1906] 1 KB 719.
13 *R v Rawson* [1909] 2 KB 748.
14 Magistrates' Courts Rules 1981, SI 1981/552, r 98 (3).

406. Protection of animal and bird life generally. The provisions for the protection of birds and other wild animals[1], of badgers[2] and of game[3] have been discussed earlier in this title. These provisions give a large measure of protection to animal and bird life generally, including protecting it from acts of cruelty.

Certain other provisions also protect animal and bird life generally. Thus under the Pests Act 1954 the use and sale of spring traps for the killing or taking of animals are prohibited unless the traps are of a type approved by the Minister of Agriculture, Fisheries and Food[4]; and further protection is enjoyed by virtue of the National Parks and Access to the Countryside Act 1949, under which living creatures of any description in nature reserves may be protected by byelaws of the Nature Conservancy Council, and those byelaws may also prohibit or restrict the shooting of any birds within an area surrounding or adjoining a nature reserve which appears to the council requisite for the protection of the reserve[5].

1 Ie under the Wildlife and Countryside Act 1981 Pt I (ss 1–27); see as to birds para 332 et seq ante and as to other wild animals para 358 et seq ante.
2 Ie under the Badgers Act 1973; see para 352 et seq ante.
3 See para 248 et seq ante.
4 See the Pests Act 1954 s 8. For orders made by the minister approving various traps, and as to trapping generally, see para 427 post.
5 National Parks and Access to the Countryside Act 1949 s 20 (2) (b), (c) (amended by the Nature Conservancy Council Act 1973 s 1 (1) (b), (7), Sch 1 para 1); see OPEN SPACES.

407. Intention and cruelty. Except in one instance[1] the Protection of Animals Act 1911 does not expressly refer to wilfulness or intention in the mind of the offender, and the offences which it creates consist in the doing of forbidden acts, or causing or procuring or permitting[2] them to be done with, in certain cases, the qualification that they are offences if done cruelly[3]. Thus, in general, an intention to commit cruelty need not be proved[4]; the questions, in those cases where the enactment specifies that the offence is doing an act cruelly, are whether pain or suffering was inflicted and, if so, whether it was inflicted without good reason[5]. On the other hand, if the charge is of causing or procuring an act to be done, guilty knowledge must be shown, or the causation or procuring will not be proved[6].

It must be borne in mind that the climate of public opinion changes considerably over the years, and older authorities where cruelty was not found to have been committed might well not be even persuasive today.

It is important to ascertain as nearly as possible what is meant here by 'cruelty'. The mere infliction of pain, even if extreme pain, is not by itself sufficient to constitute the offence. Pain is constantly inflicted upon the brute creation under various sanctions, such as surgery, or war, or where it is reasonably necessary. The mere whim or convenience or, as a rule, the profit of man will not constitute reasonable necessity; though an operation without which an animal does not attain its full development, or is not so serviceable, or is dangerous, may be justified as necessary if properly done. No doubt suffering is caused by the breaking in or the castration of horses, but such acts may usually be justified on the principles above stated, if fairly and reasonably done[7].

A terse and satisfactory definition of the cruelty aimed at is 'the unnecessary abuse of the animal'[8]. Branding lambs on the nose with a hot iron was once held to be not necessarily cruelly ill-treating them, since it might be reasonably necessary for their identification[9]. In accordance with the principles above stated, however, the very painful operation of dishorning cattle by sawing off their horns close to their heads for the purpose of slightly increasing their value, and for convenience in feeding and packing, has been held to be unjustifiable and unnecessary, and to be cruelty[10]. Nor can dubbing or cutting off the combs of cocks, which causes them pain, be justified for the purpose of exhibiting them or for cockfighting[11]. On the other hand, the spaying of sows, which was said to make them more useful for food, was held—in 1887—not to be within the Act merely because it caused pain[12].

1   Ie the offence of wilfully causing poisonous or injurious substances to be taken by an animal; see the Protection of Animals Act 1911 s 1 (1) (d); and para 415 post. Cf *Dee v Yorke* (1914) 78 JP 359, where drugs were administered, but no unnecessary suffering was caused, the charge being, it seems, under the Protection of Animals Act 1911 s 1 (1) (a).

2   See para 420 post.

3   See the Protection of Animals Act 1911 s 1 (1) (a); and para 412 post.

4   *Duncan v Pope* (1899) 80 LT 120. See also the Scottish case of *Easton v Anderson* 1949 JC 1.

5   See *Ford v Wiley* (1889) 23 QBD 203 at 218 per Hawkins J; *Waters v Braithwaite* (1913) 30 TLR 107 at 108.

6   See para 408 post. As to 'permitting' see particularly para 420 post.

7   See *Ford v Wiley* (1889) 23 QBD 203 at 209 per Lord Coleridge CJ, and at 219 per Hawkins J.

8   *Budge v Parsons* (1863) 3 B & S 382 at 385 per Wightman J. See also *Barnard v Evans* [1925] 2 KB 794, DC, where it was said that the expression 'cruelly ill-treat' applies to a case where a person wilfully causes pain to an animal without justification for so doing (at 797 per Avory J), and that cruelty means 'causing unnecessary suffering' (at 798 per Shearman J).

9   *Bowyer v Morgan* (1906) 95 LT 27.

10 *Ford v Wiley* (1889) 23 QBD 203. The Court of Justiciary in Scotland and the Queen's Bench Division in Ireland refused to follow this case, holding that dishorning cattle when performed with skill and in the usual manner for the purpose of preventing injury is not an offence: see *Renton v Wilson* (1888) 15 R 84, followed in *Todrick v Wilson* (1891) 18 R 41; *Callaghan v Society for the Prevention of Cruelty to Animals* (1885) 16 LR Ir 325, and *R v McDonagh* (1891) 28 LR Ir 204, but, contra, *Brady v McArdle* (1884) 14 LR Ir 174; and see *Donaghy v Walsh* [1914] 2 IR 261 at 273. *Ford v Wiley* supra is, however, binding on justices in England and Wales. For statutory provisions as to the use of anaesthetics for dishorning operations see para 417 text to note 13 post.

11 *Murphy v Manning* (1877) 2 ExD 307. As to cockfighting see paras 414, 458 post.

12 *Lewis v Fermor* (1887) 18 QBD 532, distinguished in *Ford v Wiley* (1889) 23 QBD 203.

408. Causing or procuring cruelty. Guilty knowledge must be proved if the charge is of causing or procuring the cruelty[1]. It is not sufficient to show that a defendant would have known of the suffering of the animal had he properly performed his duties[2]. The mere fact that it is the duty of a man in the position of a manager to see that horses are fit to be worked does not render him liable to be convicted when they are worked in an unfit state, without proof of his knowledge of the actual cruelty[3]. Where the defendant visited cattle and failed to loosen their head-ropes after disembarkation, and one was found suffering from a bad wound, the conviction was quashed in the absence of proof of his knowledge of the animal's suffering[4]. Where a veterinary surgeon certified a mare as fit for work, and was subsequently summoned for cruelly ill-treating the mare by causing it to be worked in an unfit state, the magistrate found that he knowingly counselled the owner to cause the act of cruelty to be perpetrated, but that he did not himself cause it to be perpetrated, and acquitted him; the Divisional Court remitted the case for conviction on the ground that under what is now the Magistrates' Courts Act 1980[5] the veterinary surgeon, having counselled an act of cruelty to be committed, was liable to be proceeded against as if he were a principal offender[6].

1 A lion tamer was convicted where a pony was attacked by one of the performing lions, but the court was careful not to lay down a general rule that it is an offence to put a domestic animal with a tamed beast; there must be some evidence of mens rea: *Thielbar v Craigen* (1905) 69 JP 421.
2 As to causing unnecessary suffering see para 412 post.
3 *Small v Warr* (1882) 47 JP 20. Cf *Greenwood v Backhouse* (1902) 86 LT 566; *Hughes v Mooney* (1909) 43 ILT 127 (non-liability of company secretary).
4 *Elliott v Osborn* (1891) 65 LT 378.
5 See the Magistrates' Courts Act 1980 s 44; and MAGISTRATES.
6 *Benford v Sims* [1898] 2 QB 641. This decision proceeded upon the very special findings in the case, and is not an authority for holding that every veterinary surgeon who gives a wrong opinion is liable to be convicted if cruelty in fact results: *Benford v Sims* [1898] 2 QB at 646 per Channell J.

409. Omission to alleviate suffering. It is an offence wantonly or unreasonably to do or omit to do any act, or to cause or procure the omission or commission of any act, whereby unnecessary suffering is caused to any animal[1].

Turning a mare into a field where its grazing must involve torture, instead of tending it in a stable, has been held to be cruelty[2]. Causing cows to be overstocked with milk[3] and, in Scotland, allowing a horse to remain in a cab exposed and hungry[4], have been held to be offences. If a man begins to kill an animal he must kill it outright; to allow it to linger in pain is cruelty[5].

It is an offence to fail to provide an impounded animal[6] with a sufficient quantity of wholesome and suitable food and water, and any person who has impounded or confined it or caused this to be done who so fails is liable upon summary conviction to a fine not exceeding level 1 on the standard scale[7].

1 Protection of Animals Act 1911 s 1 (1) (a). Decisions prior to the passing of this Act must be read in the light of the wording of the Act: see *Powell v Knight* (1878) 38 LT 607; *Hooker v Gray* (1907) 96 LT 706; *Potter v Challans* (1910) 102 LT 325; but see *Green v Cross* (1910) 103 LT 279 (omission to release dog caught in a trap). There was no corresponding offence involving omission under the previous legislation.
2 *Everitt v Davies* (1878) 38 LT 360.
3 *R v Cable, ex p O'Shea* [1906] 1 KB 719; *Waters v Braithwaite* (1913) 110 LT 266, where exposing cows for sale in this condition was held to be cruelty, although in accordance with an old-established custom in the district.

4 *Anderson v Wood* (1881) 9 R 6, Ct of Sess.
5 *Adcock v Murrell* (1890) 54 JP 776; *Duncan v Pope* (1899) 80 LT 120.
6 As to detaining and impounding animals generally see paras 478–481 post.
7 Protection of Animals Act 1911 s 7 (1) (amended by virtue of the Criminal Justice Act 1982 s 46). As to the standard scale see para 232 note 1 ante. At the date at which this volume states the law, level 1 on that scale is at £50.

410. Destruction of diseased or injured animals. If a police constable finds any horse, mule, ass, bull, sheep, goat or pig so diseased or so severely injured or in such a physical condition that, in his opinion, having regard to the means available for the removal of the animal, there is no possibility of removing it without cruelty, he must, if the owner is absent or refuses to consent to the destruction of the animal, at once summon a duly registered veterinary surgeon[1], if one resides within a reasonable distance; and, if it appears by the latter's certificate that the animal is mortally injured, or so severely injured, or so diseased, or in such a physical condition, that it is cruel to keep it alive, the constable may, without the owner's consent, slaughter the animal or cause or procure it to be slaughtered, with such instruments or appliances, and with such precautions, and in such manner, as to inflict as little suffering as practicable, and, if on any public highway, may remove the carcase or cause or procure it to be removed[2]. If the veterinary surgeon certifies that the injured animal can without cruelty be removed, it is the duty of the person in charge of the animal to cause it forthwith to be removed with as little suffering as possible, and, if he fails so to do, the constable may cause the animal forthwith to be so removed[3].

Reasonable expenses incurred in carrying out these provisions, including the veterinary surgeon's fee, may be recovered from the owner as a civil debt[4], and, subject thereto, are defrayed out of police funds[5].

1 Ie one registered under the Veterinary Surgeons Act 1966 ss 2, 6: see paras 547, 548 post.
2 Protection of Animals Act 1911 s 11 (1), (4).
3 Ibid s 11 (2).
4 Ie under the Magistrates' Courts Act 1980 s 38: see MAGISTRATES.
5 Protection of Animals Act 1911 s 11 (3).

411. Slaughterhouses and knackers' yards. The law relating to slaughterhouses and knackers' yards in general is dealt with elsewhere in this work[1]; it includes special provisions applicable to the trades there carried on, in the interests of the welfare of the animals concerned, designed to reduce suffering and possible ill-treatment. For the purposes of this title it is sufficient to indicate that no such specialised legislation prevents the general application of the provisions of the Protection of Animals Acts 1911 to 1964 to acts of cruelty in such circumstances.

For the purposes of the provisions of the Protection of Animals Act 1911 relating to offences of cruelty[2] a knacker[3] is deemed to be the owner of an animal delivered to him[4]: that is, delivered either to himself or to any person on his behalf or at his yard[5].

For the purpose of examining whether there is or has been any contravention of or non-compliance with that Act a constable has the right of entry to a knacker's yard at any time of day or whenever business is, or is apparently, in progress or is usually carried on, and obstruction or the refusal of entry is an offence punishable on summary conviction by a fine not exceeding level 1 on the standard scale[6].

1 See FOOD vol 18 para 1314 et seq.

2 Ie the Protection of Animals Act 1911 s 1: see para 405 et seq ante and para 412 et seq post.

3 'Knacker' means a person whose trade or business it is to kill any cattle not killed for butcher's meat, and 'cattle' includes any horse, ass, mule, bull, sheep, goat or pig as defined in para 405 note 8 ante: ibid s 15 (e).

4 Ibid s 5 (3).

5 Ibid s 5 (4). 'Knacker's yard' means any building or place used for the purpose, or partly for the purpose, of a knacker's trade or business: s 15 (e).

6 Ibid s 5 (2) (amended by virtue of the Criminal Justice Act 1982 s 46). As to the standard scale see para 232 note 1 ante. At the date at which this volume states the law, level 1 on that scale is at £50.

(2) PARTICULAR OFFENCES

(i) Miscellaneous

412. Ill-treatment of animals amounting to cruelty. It is an offence of cruelty[1] cruelly[2] to beat, kick, ill-treat[3], over-ride, over-drive, over-load, torture, infuriate or terrify any animal[4], or to cause or procure it to be so used, or by wantonly or unreasonably doing or omitting to do any act, or causing or procuring the commission or omission of any act, to cause any unnecessary suffering to any animal[5]. An owner[6] who permits such usage or suffering is guilty of a similar offence[7].

In addition to these general provisions a number of other offences of cruelty are specifically provided against[8].

1 As to punishment of offences of cruelty see para 461 post.

2 'Cruelly' governs what follows, but each alternative word amounts to a separate offence: *Johnson v Needham* [1909] 1 KB 626. Several animals may be covered by one summons (*R v Cable, ex p O'Shea* [1906] 1 KB 719), but in such case there should not be a conviction in respect of each animal: *R v Rawson* [1909] 2 KB 748. Absence of intention to be cruel is immaterial if there was cruelty in fact: *Duncan v Pope* (1899) 80 LT 120.

3 A person cruelly ill-treats an animal where he wilfully causes pain to it without justification: *Barnard v Evans* [1925] 2 KB 794 at 797 per Avory J.

4 For the meaning of 'animal' see para 405 note 9 ante.

5 Protection of Animals Act 1911 s 1 (1) (a). This section does not render illegal lawful experiments on animals or apply to the killing of animals for food without unnecessary suffering or, subject to certain exceptions, to the coursing or hunting of captive animals: s 1 (3); see further paras 419, 429 et seq post.

6 As to when a knacker is deemed to be an owner see para 411 ante.

7 Protection of Animals Act 1911 s 1 (1) (a). As to owners permitting cruelty see para 420 post.

8 For other offences under ibid s 1 (1) see paras 413–418 post.

413. Carriage of animals. It is an offence of cruelty[1] to convey or carry or cause or procure to be conveyed or carried any animal[2] in such manner or position as to cause that animal any unnecessary suffering, and an owner who permits an animal to be so conveyed or carried is equally guilty[3].

1 As to punishment of offences of cruelty see para 461 post.

2 For the meaning of 'animal' see para 405 note 9 ante.

3 Protection of Animals Act 1911 s 1 (1) (b). As to owners permitting cruelty see para 420 post. See also para 501 post for regulations made under the Animal Health Act 1981 as to the conditions in which animals may be carried.

414. Fighting or baiting of animals. It is an offence of cruelty[1] to cause, procure or assist at the fighting[2] or baiting[3] of any animal[4]; or to keep, use, manage or act or assist in the management of any premises or place for the purpose, or partly for the purpose, of fighting or baiting any animal; or to permit any premises or place to be so kept, managed or used; or to receive, or cause or procure any person to receive, money for the admission of any person to such premises or place[5].

It is also an offence, punishable by a penalty of not more than level 4 on the standard scale or imprisonment for not more than one month, to keep or use or act in the management of any house, room, pit or other place for the purpose of fighting or baiting any animal[6]. Persons found without lawful excuse on any premises so kept or used may be fined not more than level 4 on the standard scale[7].

A person commits an offence if, without reasonable excuse[8], he is present when animals are placed together for the purpose of their fighting each other[9]. So too does a person who publishes or causes to be published an advertisement for a fight between animals knowing that it is such an advertisement[10]. Both these offences are punishable on summary conviction by a fine not exceeding level 4 on the standard scale[11].

Proceedings may be taken for any of the offences mentioned above under their respective statutes, depending on the circumstances, but an offender cannot be punished twice for the same offence[12].

1 As to punishment of offences of cruelty see para 461 post.
2 See also the Cockfighting Act 1952 s 1; and para 458 post.
3 *Pitts v Millar* (1874) LR 9 QB 380, which held that turning out rabbits into an inclosed space before dogs was not 'baiting', was nullified by the amendment to the Protection of Animals Act 1911 s 1 (3) (b) by the Protection of Animals Act (1911) Amendment Act 1921 s 1: see para 419 post.
4 For the meaning of 'animal' see para 405 note 9 ante.
5 Protection of Animals Act 1911 s 1 (1) (c).
6 Metropolitan Police Act 1839 s 47 (amended by the Protection of Animals (Amendment) Act 1988 s 2 (1), (4)); Town Police Clauses Act 1847 s 36 (amended by the Protection of Animals (Amendment) Act 1988 s 2 (1), (4)); Public Health Act 1875 s 171 (extended by the Local Government Act 1972 s 180, Sch 14 para 23). As to the standard scale see para 232 note 1 ante. At the date at which this volume states the law, level 4 on that scale is at £1,000. The 1839 Act refers to 'lions, bears, badgers, cocks, dogs, or other animals'; the 1847 Act refers simply to 'any animals'. A conviction does not exempt the owner, keeper or manager of any such place from any penalty or penal consequence to which he may be liable for the nuisance thereby occasioned: see the Metropolitan Police Act 1839 s 47 and the Town Police Clauses Act 1847 s 36. Although not specifically mentioned in the statutes, it can be inferred that the offences are summary offences from the penalties and from references in the provisions to the justices' discretion.
7 Metropolitan Police Act 1839 s 47 (as amended: see note 6 supra); Town Police Clauses Act 1847 s 36 (as amended: see note 6 supra).
8 What is 'reasonable excuse' is largely a question of fact: cf *Leck v Epsom RDC* [1922] 1 KB 383.
9 Protection of Animals Act 1911 s 5A (added by the Protection of Animals (Amendment) Act 1988 s 2 (2)).
10 Protection of Animals Act 1911 s 5B (as added: see note 9 supra).
11 Ibid ss 5A, 5B (as added: see note 9 supra). As to the standard scale see para 232 note 1 ante. At the date at which this volume states the law, level 4 on that scale is at £1,000.
12 Interpretation Act 1978 s 18, Sch 2 para 1; see CRIMINAL LAW.

415. Administering poisonous or injurious drugs. It is an offence of cruelty[1] wilfully[2], without any reasonable cause or excuse, to administer or cause or procure to be administered to, or to cause to be taken by, any animal[3] any poisonous or injurious drug or substance, and an owner who permits the administration is equally guilty[4].

1 As to punishment of offences of cruelty see para 461 post.

2 'Wilfully' means that the act is done deliberately and intentionally, not by accident or inadvertence, but so that the mind of the person who does the act goes with it': *R v Senior* [1899] 1 QB 283 at 290–291 per Lord Russell of Killowen CJ; '. . . deliberately—for that is what 'wilfully' means . . .': *Hall v Jordan* [1947] 1 All ER 826 at 827 per Lord Goddard CJ. Cf, in the context of wilful neglect as opposed to a wilful act, *R v Sheppard* [1981] AC 394 at 404, [1980] 3 All ER 899 at 904, HL, per Lord Diplock.

3 For the meaning of 'animal' see para 405 note 9 ante.

4 Protection of Animals Act 1911 s 1 (1) (d). As to the use of poisons on animals see also para 425 post. As to owners permitting cruelty see para 420 post.

416. Abandonment of animals. Any person, being the owner or having charge or control of any animal[1], who without reasonable cause or excuse abandons it, whether permanently or not, in circumstances likely to cause it any unnecessary suffering, is guilty of an offence of cruelty[2]. Equally, to cause or procure such abandonment or, being the owner, to permit it, is an offence of cruelty[3].

1 For the meaning of 'animal' see para 405 note 9 ante.

2 Abandonment of Animals Act 1960 s 1. The offence is an offence of cruelty within the meaning of the Protection of Animals Act 1911 s 1 (1): Abandonment of Animals Act 1960 s 1. As to punishment of offences of cruelty see para 461 post.

3 Abandonment of Animals Act 1960 s 1. As to owners permitting cruelty see para 420 post.

417. Operations on animals. Any person who subjects any animal[1] to an operation which is performed without due care and humanity is guilty of an offence of cruelty[2], as is anyone who causes or procures such an operation or, being the owner of the animal, permits it[3].

Subject to certain statutory exceptions all operations on animals[4], with or without instruments, involving interference with its sensitive tissues or bone structure, without the use of anaesthetics so administered as to prevent any pain during the operation, are deemed to be operations performed without due care and humanity[5]. The exceptions are:

(1) the making of injections or extractions by means of a hollow needle[6];

(2) any procedure duly authorised under the Animals (Scientific Procedures) Act 1986[7];

(3) the rendering in emergency of first aid for the purpose of saving life or relieving pain[8];

(4) the docking of a dog's tail, or the amputation of its dew claws, before its eyes are open[9];

(5) the castration of a sheep under the age of three months, or of a bull, goat or pig under the age of two months, except by the use of a rubber ring or other device to constrict the flow of blood to the scrotum, unless applied within the first week of life[10]; and

(6) any minor operation performed by a veterinary surgeon or veterinary practitioner[11] which by reason of its quickness or painlessness is customarily performed without an anaesthetic, or any minor operation, whether performed by such a surgeon or practitioner or by some other person, which is not customarily performed only by such a surgeon or practitioner[12]; these exceptions do not, however, permit castration, de-horning or dis-budding except by chemical cauterisation within the first week of life, the docking of lambs' tails by the use of a rubber ring unless applied in the first week of life[13], the docking of the tails of pigs more than seven days old[14], nor the removal of antlers in velvet[15].

The Minister of Agriculture, Fisheries and Food, the Secretary of State for Wales and the Secretary of State for Scotland, acting jointly, may, after consultation with the Royal College of Veterinary Surgeons and such other persons appearing to the ministers to represent agricultural interests as they consider appropriate, by order made by statutory instrument amend any of the ages specified in (5) above[16], or extend the classes of operations in which anaesthetics must be used so as to include other operations[17].

1 For the meaning of 'animal' see para 405 note 9 ante. See, however, note 4 infra.
2 As to punishment of offences of cruelty see para 461 post.
3 Protection of Animals Act 1911 s 1 (1) (e). As to owners permitting cruelty see para 420 post.
4 In this context 'animal' does not include a fowl or other bird, fish or reptile, but otherwise it has the meaning given in para 405 note 9 ante: Protection of Animals (Anaesthetics) Act 1954 s 1 (4).
5 Ibid s 1 (1), (2).
6 Ibid s 1 (2) (a).
7 Ibid s 1 (2) (b), Sch 1 para 1 (amended by the Animals (Scientific Procedures) Act 1986 s 27 (2), Sch 3 para 3). As to such experiments, which are by way of vivisection, see para 429 et seq post.
8 Protection of Animals (Anaesthetics) Act 1954 Sch 1 para 2.
9 Ibid Sch 1 paras 3, 4.
10 Ibid Sch 1 paras 6, 6A (substituted by the Protection of Animals (Anaesthetics) Act 1964 s 1 (1), (3) and amended by the Protection of Animals (Anaesthetics) Act 1954 (Amendment) Order 1982, SI 1982/1626).
11 For the meaning of 'veterinary surgeon' and 'veterinary practitioner' see paras 547, 548 post.
12 Protection of Animals (Anaesthetics) Act 1954 Sch 1 paras 7, 8.
13 Protection of Animals (Anaesthetics) Act 1964 s 1 (1), (4).
14 Agriculture (Miscellaneous Provisions) Act 1968 ss 5, 51 (1); Docking of Pigs (Use of Anaesthetics) Order 1974, SI 1974/798.
15 Agriculture (Miscellaneous Provisions) Act 1968 ss 5, 51 (1); Removal of Antlers in Velvet (Anaesthetics) Order 1980, SI 1980/685.
16 Protection of Animals (Anaesthetics) Act 1954 s 1 (3); Transfer of Functions (Ministry of Food) Order 1955, SI 1955/554; Transfer of Functions (Wales) (No 1) Order 1978, SI 1978/272, art 11, Sch 5.
17 Agriculture (Miscellaneous Provisions) Act 1968 ss 5, 51 (1).

418. Cruel tethering. It is an offence of cruelty[1] to tether any horse, ass or mule under such conditions or in such manner as to cause that animal unnecessary suffering[2].

1 As to punishment of offences of cruelty see para 461 post.
2 Protection of Animals Act 1911 s 1 (1) (f) (added by the Protection against Cruel Tethering Act 1988 s 1).

419. Exceptions not constituting cruelty. The foregoing provisions relating to cruelty[1] do not apply to any act lawfully done under the Animals (Scientific Procedures) Act 1986[2], nor to the commission or omission of any act in the course of the destruction or preparation for destruction of any animal as food for mankind, unless the destruction or preparation was accompanied by the infliction of unnecessary suffering[3]; nor to the coursing or hunting of any captive animal[4] unless that animal is liberated in an injured, mutilated, or exhausted condition[5]. A captive animal is not, however, deemed to be coursed or hunted before it is liberated for that purpose, or after it has been recaptured, or if it is under control[6], nor where it is coursed or hunted in an inclosed space from which it has no reasonable chance of escape[7].

1 See paras 412–418 ante.

2 Protection of Animals Act 1911 s 1 (3) (amended by the Animals (Scientific Procedures) Act 1986 s 27 (2), Sch 3 para 1). The 1986 Act deals with experiments upon animals: see paras 429–452 post.
3 Protection of Animals Act 1911 s 1 (3) (a).
4 A mere temporary inability to escape is not a state of captivity: *Rowley v Murphy* [1964] 2 QB 43, [1964] 1 All ER 50, DC. See also *Steele v Rogers* (1912) 106 LT 79.
5 Protection of Animals Act 1911 s 1 (3) (b).
6 Ibid s 1 (3) (b).
7 Ibid s 1 (3) (b) (amended by the Protection of Animals Act (1911) Amendment Act 1921 s 1, in consequence of the decision in *Waters v Meakin* [1916] 2 KB 111). See also *Rodgers v Pickersgill* (1910) 103 LT 33 (alleged cruelty to hunted hind); *Jenkins v Ash* (1929) 93 JP 229 (rabbit dangled in sight of dogs and released; not within the protection of the subsection because liberated in 'exhausted condition' and ill-treatment occurred before liberation for coursing); *White v Fox and Dawes* (1932) 48 TLR 641 (carted hind; in the circumstances not a domestic animal, but a captive animal and hunting permitted).

420. Owner of animal permitting cruelty. In relation to all the foregoing offences of cruelty[1] the owner of an animal[2] is deemed to have permitted cruelty if he has failed to exercise reasonable care and supervision in respect of the protection of the animal from cruelty[3], the onus of proving such care and supervision being upon him[4]. Where, however, the owner is convicted of cruelty to an animal by reason only of his having failed to exercise such care and supervision he is not liable to imprisonment without the option of a fine[5].

1 See paras 412–418 ante.
2 As to knackers as owners see para 411 ante.
3 Protection of Animals Act 1911 s 1 (2).
4 *Whiting v Ivens* (1915) 85 LJKB 1878. As to this onus see para 384 note 8 ante.
5 Protection of Animals Act 1911 s 1 (2) proviso.

421. Use of dogs for haulage. Any person who uses a dog, or causes or procures or, being the owner, permits it to be used, on any public highway for the purpose of drawing or helping to draw any cart, carriage, truck or barrow, is liable on summary conviction to a fine not exceeding level 1 on the standard scale[1].

1 Protection of Animals Act 1911 s 9 (amended by virtue of the Criminal Justice Act 1982 ss 38, 46). As to the standard scale see para 232 note 1 ante. At the date at which this volume states the law, level 1 on that scale is at £50.

422. Docking and nicking of horses. The docking[1] or nicking[2] of horses[3] is prohibited[4], except in a case where a member of the Royal College of Veterinary Surgeons, after examination of the horse, has certified in writing that the operation is in his opinion necessary for its health because of disease or injury to the tail[5]. Any person who performs such an operation in contravention of this provision or who causes or permits such an operation to be so performed is punishable on summary conviction by a fine not exceeding level 3 on the standard scale or imprisonment for a term not exceeding three months or both[6].

1 'Docking' means the deliberate removal of any bone or part of a bone from the tail: Docking and Nicking of Horses Act 1949 s 3.
2 'Nicking' means the deliberate severing of any tendon or muscle in the tail: ibid s 3.
3 'Horse' includes stallion, gelding, colt, mare, filly, pony, mule and hinny: ibid s 3.
4 Ibid s 1 (1).
5 Ibid s 1 (2). As to veterinary surgeons see para 547 post.

6 Ibid s 1 (3) (amended by virtue of the Criminal Justice Act 1982 s 46). As to importing docked horses see para 504 post. As to the standard scale see para 232 note 1 ante. At the date at which this volume states the law, level 3 on that scale is at £400.

423. Farriery. The practice of farriery[1] has been regulated in order, inter alia, to prevent and avoid suffering by and cruelty to horses arising from the shoeing of horses by unskilled persons[2]. A Farriers Registration Council has been established[3]. The council is charged with keeping and maintaining a register of farriers[4]. Only those who satisfy the council that they have gained adequate experience and expertise in farriery may be included in the register[5]. A person who is judged[6] to be guilty of serious misconduct in any professional respect, a person who was not in fact qualified for registration at the time he was registered, and a person convicted of an offence involving cruelty to animals may be removed from the register, or his registration may be suspended for a specified period[7].

It is an offence (subject to certain exceptions[8]) for a person who is not registered[9] to carry out any farriery[10], and it is also an offence for such a person to use or adopt the style, title or description 'farrier' or 'shoeing smith' or any other style, title or description which is likely to cause any other person to believe that he is so registered[11]. Additionally, it is an offence for any person wilfully[12] to procure or attempt to procure the entry of his name in the register by making or producing or causing to be made or produced any false or fraudulent representation or declaration[13]. Each of these offences is punishable on summary conviction with a fine not exceeding level 3 on the standard scale[14].

Detailed provision has been made for determining the constitution and powers of the council and for regulating its proceedings[15]. The council is empowered to make rules with respect to the register[16].

1 'Farriery' here means any work in connection with the preparation or treatment of the foot of a horse for the immediate reception of a shoe thereon, the fitting by nailing or otherwise of a shoe to the foot or the finishing off of such work to the foot: Farriers (Registration) Act 1975 s 18. This definition appears not to cover filing, rasping or trimming a horse's hoof in order to keep it in good condition, at least not when a shoe is not immediately thereafter fitted, even though these are operations commonly and properly entrusted to farriers.
2 See the Farriers (Registration) Act 1975, long title.
3 By ibid s 2.
4 Ibid s 3 (1).
5 See ibid s 7 (substituted by the Farriers (Registration) (Amendment) Act 1977 s 1 (1), Schedule). Subject to s 15 of the 1975 Act (see text and notes 6, 7 infra), a person is entitled to be registered (in Part I of the register) if he satisfies the council that he is appropriately qualified and if he pays the fees prescribed under s 4. Registration is open to those who on 1 January 1976 were registered in the Register of Farriers kept by the Worshipful Company of Farriers; those who have satisfied such conditions as to apprenticeship or training or both as the council may prescribe, those who have completed a course of training as a farrier in Her Majesty's Army, and those who have been registered in Parts II or IV of the register, and who (in each case) have passed a prescribed examination; and those who hold an approved qualification that was granted outside the United Kingdom and who have since obtaining that qualification been regularly and gainfully employed in the shoeing of horses for two years: see s 7 (1) (as so substituted). Registration in Parts II, III or IV of the register was formerly available for those not meeting the requirements for registration in Part I, but applications for registration in these Parts were required to be made before a date prescribed by the council and such date was prescribed as 1 July 1980; see ss 4 (1), 7 (2)–(4) (as substituted), 18. In any case, however, in which it appears to the council that a person for sufficient reason failed to make application for registration in Parts II–IV before the prescribed date, the council may direct that he nevertheless shall be entitled to apply within such period as may be specified in that direction: s 7 (5) (as substituted). Registration in Part II was available for those with, in general, two years' post-apprenticeship experience of shoeing horses in a farrier's business or in a smithy; in Part III for those

with two years' experience in shoeing their own horses or shoeing others' horses gratis; and in Part IV (a) for those with, in general, two years' post-apprenticeship work shoeing horses, and (b) for those who completed apprenticeship or training as prescribed under Part I, and such additional apprenticeship or training as the council might require, but who had not passed a prescribed examination: see s 7 (2)–(4) (as substituted).

6 By the council's Disciplinary Committee, as to which see ibid s 14, Sch 3; and note 15 infra.

7 Ibid s 15. The names of deceased persons and those who have applied for their names to be removed must also be removed from the register: s 6.

8 The offence is not committed when farriery is carried out by apprentices while serving under approved articles of apprenticeship, by trainees at an approved institution, by veterinary surgeons or veterinary practitioners, by trainee veterinary surgeons (when supervised), or by those rendering first-aid in an emergency: see ibid s 16 proviso.

9 Except for a person whose name has been removed from the register but who has not been notified of this, and for a person who has applied for registration and not had his application finally determined: ibid ss 15A (1) proviso, 16 (2) (s 15A added by the Farriers (Registration) (Amendment) Act 1977 ss 1 (1), 2 (3), Schedule).

10 Farriers (Registration) Act 1975 s 16 (1) (a), (2) (b). It is also an offence for a person registered in Part III of the register (see note 5 supra) to carry out any farriery by way of trade or for reward: s 16 (1) (b).

11 Ibid s 15A (1) (as added: see note 9 supra).

12 As to the meaning of 'wilfully' see para 415 note 2 ante.

13 Farriers (Registration) Act 1975 s 5.

14 Ibid ss 5, 15A (2) (as added: see note 9 supra), 16 (3) (all amended by virtue of the Criminal Justice Act 1982 ss 38, 46). As to the standard scale see para 232 note 1 ante. At the date at which this volume states the law, level 3 on that scale is at £400.

15 See the Farriers (Registration) Act 1975 s 2, Sch 1 (constitution, powers and proceedings of the council); s 3 (maintenance of register); s 6 (removal of names from register); s 10 (issue of certificates or acknowledgments of registration); s 11 (approval of courses, qualifications and institutions); s 12 (supervision of approved institutions and examinations); s 13 (establishment of Investigating Committee for preliminary investigation of disciplinary cases); s 14 (establishment of Disciplinary Committee for hearing of appeals from registrar's decisions and for consideration and determination of disciplinary cases); s 15 (power to remove names for disciplinary cases, etc, and provisions as to appeal).

16 Ibid s 4. References in the Act to 'prescribed' mean prescribed by rules drawn up by the council: s 18.

424. Cruelty to livestock. Any person[1] who causes unnecessary pain or distress to livestock[2] on agricultural land[3] and under his control or who permits such livestock to suffer unnecessary pain or distress of which he knows or may reasonably be expected to know, is guilty of an offence[4].

After consultation with such persons appearing to them to represent interests concerned as they consider appropriate, the Minister of Agriculture, Fisheries and Food, the Secretary of State for Scotland and the Secretary of State for Wales[5] may make such provision by regulation[6] or codes of recommendation[7] with respect to the welfare of livestock situated on agricultural land as they see fit, and may incur, with Treasury approval, such expenditure on the giving of free advice on the welfare of livestock as may seem fit[8].

For the purposes of ascertaining whether an offence[9] has been committed, a person authorised in writing by the Minister of Agriculture, Fisheries and Food or, in relation to Wales, the Secretary of State for Wales (or, in the case of a breach of a regulation relating to the food and diet of livestock, by a local authority) may enter upon land, other than premises used wholly or mainly as a dwelling[10], and may take samples for analysis[11]. The occupier or his servant must, if he can, comply with any request to indicate the places where livestock or food for livestock are kept and facilitate the access of the authorised person to those places[12]. Failure to do so, or wilful obstruction, is an offence[13].

The offences of causing unnecessary pain or distress and of contravening regulations are punishable on summary conviction by imprisonment for a term not exceeding three months or a fine not exceeding level 4 on the standard scale, or both[14].

1 This includes an officer or servant of the Crown: Agriculture (Miscellaneous Provisions) Act 1968 s 8 (3).
2 'Livestock' means any creature kept for the production of food, wool, skin or fur or for use in the farming of land or for such purpose as the Minister of Agriculture, Fisheries and Food may by order specify: ibid ss 8 (1), 50 (1). No other purposes had been so specified at the date at which this volume states the law.
3 'Agricultural land' means land used for agriculture within the meaning of the Agriculture Act 1947 s 109 (3), which is so used for the purposes of a trade or business: Agriculture (Miscellaneous Provisions) Act 1968 s 8 (1).
4 Ibid s 1 (1). The subsection does not apply to any act lawfully done under the Animals (Scientific Procedures) Act 1986 or under a licence for scientific research: Agriculture (Miscellaneous Provisions) Act 1968 s 1 (2) (amended by the Animals (Scientific Procedures) Act 1986 s 27 (2), Sch 3 para 7).
5 The ministers may act jointly in relation to Great Britain, the Minister of Agriculture, Fisheries and Food may act separately in relation to England and the Secretary of State for Wales in relation to Wales: see the Agriculture (Miscellaneous Provisions) Act 1968 ss 2 (1), 8 (4), 50 (1) and the Transfer of Functions (Wales) (No 1) Order 1978, SI 1978/272, art 2, Sch 1.
6 Agriculture (Miscellaneous Provisions) Act 1968 s 2 (1). The regulations may also provide for any breach of them to be an offence, for exemptions and other matters: s 2 (2). The following regulations have been made: Welfare of Livestock (Intensive Units) Regulations 1978, SI 1978/1800 (disapplied to battery hens by SI 1987/2020); Welfare of Livestock (Deer) Order 1980, SI 1980/593; Welfare of Livestock (Prohibited Operations) Regulations 1982, SI 1982/1884 (amended by SI 1987/114); Welfare of Battery Hens Regulations 1987, SI 1987/2020; Welfare of Calves Regulations 1987, SI 1987/2021; Welfare of Pigs Regulations 1991, SI 1991/1477.
7 Agriculture (Miscellaneous Provisions) Act 1968 s 3 (1). Failure to comply with a code of recommendation does not of itself involve any liability to proceedings but may be relied upon in a prosecution for causing unnecessary pain or distress: s 3 (4). Cf the relevance of the Highway Code in the case of road traffic offences: see ROAD TRAFFIC vol 40 para 13. At the date at which this volume states the law no code was in force.
8 Agriculture (Miscellaneous Provisions) Act 1968 ss 4, 50 (1). This power is without prejudice to the minister's other powers relating to diseases of animals under the Animal Health Act 1981 ss 5 (1), 86 (1), 87 (1). The ministers may, after consultation, by order extend the classes of operation in which anaesthetics must be used: see para 417 ante.
9 Ie under the Argiculture (Miscellaneous Provisions) Act 1968 Pt I (ss 1–8).
10 Ibid s 6 (1), (2).
11 Ibid s 6 (4).
12 Ibid s 6 (6).
13 Ibid s 6 (7). As to the meaning of 'wilful obstruction' see para 391 note 16 ante. The penalty on summary conviction is a fine not exceeding level 3 on the standard scale: s 7 (2) (amended by the Criminal Justice Act 1982 ss 39 (2), 46, Sch 3). As to the standard scale see para 232 note 1 ante. At the date at which this volume states the law, level 3 on that scale is at £400. Local authorities have power to prosecute for contraventions in their areas of regulations relating to the food and diet of livestock: Agriculture (Miscellaneous Provisions) Act 1968 s 7 (3).
14 Ibid s 7 (1) (amended by virtue of the Criminal Justice Act 1982 ss 35, 46). As to the standard scale see para 232 note 1 ante. At the date at which this volume states the law, level 4 on that scale is at £1,000.

425. Poisoned grain and bait. It is an offence to sell or offer or expose for sale or give away, or cause or procure or knowingly be a party to such sale, offer or exposure for sale or giving away, any grain or seed which has been rendered poisonous except for bona fide use in agriculture[1].

It is a further offence knowingly to put or place, or cause or procure or knowingly be a party to the putting or placing in or upon any land or building any poison, or any fluid or edible matter (not being sown seed or grain) which has been rendered poisonous[2]. Subject to any regulations made by the Secretary of State to prohibit or restrict the use of any cruel poison to destroy any mammal or any mammal of a particular description[3], it is in this latter case a defence that the poison was placed by the accused for the purpose of destroying insects and other invertebrates, rats, mice or other small ground vermin, where such is found to be necessary in the interests of public health, agriculture, or the preservation of other animals, domestic or wild, or for the purpose of manuring the land, provided that he took all reasonable precautions to prevent injury to dogs, cats, fowls or other domestic animals and wild birds[4]. It is also a defence to show that the act was done under the authority of a licence and that any conditions specified in the licence were complied with[5].

A person is not guilty of any of these offences by reason only that he uses poisonous gas in any hole, burrow or earth for the purpose of killing rabbits, hares and other rodents, deer, foxes or moles, or places there a substance which, by evaporation or in contact with moisture, generates poisonous gas[6].

The penalty on summary conviction for any of the above offences is a fine not exceeding level 4 on the standard scale[7].

There is nothing to prevent the use of non-poisonous substances as the bait for traps for animals. Should the bait be of such a nature and so near a boundary as to attract animals which would not otherwise be likely to have entered the land, the occupier, or whoever set the bait or caused it to be set, may be liable to an action for the value of the animals destroyed[8], and it is probable that even if he has acted merely in defence of his property he may be liable to criminal prosecution for possessing articles with intent to damage or destroy[9].

It is an offence to put or cause to be put at any time any poison or poisonous ingredient on ground, whether open or inclosed, where game usually resort, or in any highway, with intent to destroy or injure game[10], and an offender is liable on conviction before two justices to a penalty not exceeding level 1 on the standard scale[11].

The relevant minister[12] may by order [13], applying either to the whole of Great Britain[14] or to any specified area, specify a poison for use for the purpose of destroying grey squirrels or coypus and the manner of its use for that purpose, and the use of that poison in compliance with such an order does not render the user liable to prosecution under the provisions protecting animals[15] and birds[16] from the use of poisons[17]. An order has been made permitting, in certain circumstances, the use of warfarin against grey squirrels[18].

1 Protection of Animals Act 1911 s 8 (a). The use of poisoned, poisonous or stupefying substances for certain defined purposes may, however, be licensed under the Wildlife and Countryside Act 1981 s 16 and the Badgers Act 1973 s 9: see text and note 5 infra.

2 Protection of Animals Act 1911 s 8 (b). It is a defence to show that the act was done for the purpose of destroying grey squirrels or coypus in compliance with an order permitting the use of a specified poison against those animals: Agriculture (Miscellaneous Provisions) Act 1972 s 19 (1), (2). As to such orders see text and notes 12–18 infra. For other offences relating to poisoning etc see para 360 ante.

3 The regulations are made by statutory instrument under the Animals (Cruel Poisons) Act 1962 s 2, where the Secretary of State is satisfied that a poison cannot be used for destroying animals (defined by s 3 as mammals) or animals of any description without causing undue suffering and that other suitable methods of destroying them exist and are or would in certain circumstances be adequate. Contravention of the regulations is punishable on summary conviction by a fine not exceeding level 3 on the standard scale or imprisonment for a term not exceeding three months, or both: s 1 (b) (amended by virtue of the Criminal Justice Act 1982 s 46); Protection of Animals Act 1911 s 8 (b). As to the standard scale see para 232 note 1 ante. At the date at which this volume states the law, level 3

on that scale is at £400. The Animals (Cruel Poisons) Regulations 1963, SI 1963/1278, made under this power, bans such use of yellow phosphorous and red squill in all cases, and such use of strychnine except for destroying moles.

4 Protection of Animals Act 1911 s 8 proviso (substituted by the Protection of Animals (Amendment) Act 1927 s 1).

5 Badgers Act 1973 s 9 (4) (in respect of a licence granted under s 9 (1) (d) to kill or take badgers within a specified area and by specified means in order to prevent the spread of disease); Wildlife and Countryside Act 1981 s 16 (7) (in respect of a licence granted under s 16 (1) or (3) for the purposes therein mentioned): see paras 343, 356, 361 ante.

6 Prevention of Damage by Rabbits Act 1939 s 4; Agriculture Act 1947 s 98 (3): see AGRICULTURE vol 1 (2) (Reissue) para 658. As to rabbit holes see para 428 note 3 post.

7 Protection of Animals Act 1911 s 8 (amended by the Criminal Justice Act 1982 ss 39 (2), 46, Sch 3). As to the standard scale see para 232 note 1 ante. At the date at which this volume states the law, level 4 on that scale is at £1,000.

8 See *Townsend v Wathen* (1808) 9 East 277.

9 Ie under the Criminal Damage Act 1971 s 3: see CRIMINAL LAW. In view of the strictly limited rights to damage or destroy in defence of property set out in the Act of 1971 the decisions under the Malicious Damage Act 1861 s 41 of *Daniel v Janes* (1877) 2 CPD 351, and *Bryan v Eaton* (1875) 40 JP 213, do not seem in point.

10 This provision applies only to game as defined in the Game Act 1831 s 2 (see para 211 ante), and not to rabbits.

11 Game Act 1831 s 3 (amended by virtue of the Criminal Justice Act 1982 ss 38, 46, and by the Statute Law (Repeals) Act 1989, Sch 1 Pt I). As to the standard scale see para 232 note 1 ante. At the date at which this volume states the law, level 1 on that scale is at £50.

12 Ie in the case of an order applying in England, the Minister of Agriculture, Fisheries and Food and in the case of an order applying in Wales and Monmouthshire, the Secretary of State for Wales: Agriculture (Miscellaneous Provisions) Act 1972 ss 19 (5), 26 (1); Transfer of Functions (Wales) (No 1) Order 1978, SI 1978/272, art 2 (2).

13 Such an order may make different provisions in relation to grey squirrels and in relation to coypus: Agriculture (Miscellaneous Provisions) Act 1972 s 19 (4). Before an order is made the minister must consult with such organisations as appear to him to represent the interests concerned, and a draft of the order must be laid before and approved by a resolution of each House of Parliament: s 19 (3).

14 For the meaning of 'Great Britain' see para 309 note 8 ante.

15 See the Protection of Animals Act 1911 s 8 (b); and text and note 2 supra.

16 See the Wildlife and Countryside Act 1981 s 5 (1) (a); and para 338 text and note 3 ante.

17 Agriculture (Miscellaneous Provisions) Act 1972 s 19 (1).

18 Grey Squirrels (Warfarin) Order 1973, SI 1973/744.

426. Spreading of myxomatosis. Any person who knowingly[1] uses or permits the use of a rabbit infected with myxomatosis to spread the disease among uninfected rabbits is guilty of an offence and on summary conviction is liable to a fine not exceeding level 3 on the standard scale[2]. This provision does not render unlawful any procedure duly authorised under the Animals (Scientific Procedures) Act 1986[3].

1 As to 'knowingly' see para 395 note 7 ante.

2 Pests Act 1954 s 12 (amended by virtue of the Criminal Justice Act 1982 s 46). As to the standard scale see para 232 note 1 ante. At the date at which this volume states the law, level 3 on that scale is at £400.

3 Pests Act 1954 s 12 proviso (amended by the Animals (Scientific Procedures) Act 1986 s 27 (2), Sch 3 para 4). As to such experiments see paras 429–452 post.

(ii) Traps for Rabbits, Hares and Other Animals

427. Restriction on types of spring trap; inspection. It is an offence for the purpose of killing or taking animals[1] to use or knowingly[2] permit the use of any spring trap other than an approved trap[3], or to use or knowingly permit the use of an approved trap in circumstances for which it is not approved[4]. It is also an offence to sell or expose or offer for sale any spring trap other than an approved trap with a view to its being used unlawfully as above[5], or to have any spring trap in one's possession for such an unlawful purpose[6]. On summary conviction these offences carry a punishment of a fine not exceeding level 3 on the standard scale[7].

Failure to inspect or to cause some competent person to inspect, at least once every day between sunrise and sunset, any spring trap set, or caused or procured to be set, for the purpose of catching any hare or rabbit, or placed so as to be likely to catch any hare or rabbit, is an offence punishable on summary conviction by a fine not exceeding level 1 on the standard scale[8].

1 'Animals' is not defined. Cf para 405 note 9 ante and para 483 post.
2 As to 'knowingly' see para 395 note 7 ante.
3 Ie a trap approved by the Minister of Agriculture, Fisheries and Food by order made by statutory instrument, either generally or for certain animals or for use in certain circumstances: Pests Act 1954 s 1 (3), (8) (amended by the Transfer of Functions (Ministry of Food) Order 1955, SI 1955/554). The Spring Traps Approval Order 1975, SI 1975/1647 (amended by SI 1982/53 and SI 1988/2111) has been made under this power. The Pests Act 1954 s 1 does not apply to traps of any description specified by order of the minister, made by statutory instrument, as being solely for the destruction of rats, mice or other small ground vermin: s 1 (5) (as amended: see supra). The Small Ground Vermin Traps Order 1958, SI 1958/24, has been made under this power.
4 Pests Act 1954 s 8 (1) (a). This prohibition does not extend to the experimental use of a spring trap under licence or the authority of the minister: s 8 (4) (amended by SI 1955/554). See also, as to snares and other methods of trapping, paras 360, 362 ante.
5 Pests Act 1954 s 8 (1) (b).
6 Ibid s 8 (1) (c).
7 Ibid s 8 (2) (amended by virtue of the Criminal Justice Act 1982 ss 35, 46). As to the standard scale see para 232 note 1 ante. At the date at which this volume states the law, level 3 on that scale is at £400.
8 Protection of Animals Act 1911 s 10 (amended by virtue of the Criminal Justice Act 1982 s 46). Traps of this nature are prohibited, except in rabbit holes, by the Pests Act 1954 s 9: see para 428 post. As to the standard scale see para 232 note 1 ante. At the date at which this volume states the law, level 1 on that scale is at £50. For a similar offence see para 362 ante.

428. Open trapping of hares and rabbits. A person who for the purpose of killing or taking hares or rabbits uses or knowingly[1] permits the use of a spring trap[2] elsewhere than in a rabbit hole[3] is guilty of an offence[4] unless the trap is used in circumstances and subject to conditions prescribed by regulations made by statutory instrument by the Minister of Agriculture, Fisheries and Food or under and in accordance with a licence granted by him[5]. An offender is liable on summary conviction to a fine not exceeding level 3 on the standard scale[6].

1 As to 'knowingly' see para 395 note 7 ante.
2 See para 427 ante.
3 Ie that part of the burrow which is inside the ground and covered by a roof and not the ground which is scraped away outside: *Brown v Thompson* (1882) 9 R 1183. It does not mean a hole scooped out under a wire fence with no roof of soil: *Fraser v Lawson* (1882) 10 R 396.
4 Pests Act 1954 s 9 (1).
5 Ibid s 9 (3), (4) (amended by the Transfer of Functions (Ministry of Food) Order 1955, SI 1955/554).
6 Pests Act 1954 s 9 (2) (amended by virtue of the Criminal Justice Act 1982 ss 35, 46). As to the standard scale see para 232 note 1 ante. At the date at which this volume states the law, level 3 on that scale is at £400.

(iii) Experiments on Living Animals

A. SCIENTIFIC PROCEDURES

429. Protection of living animals. Authority for, and the conduct and regulation of, experiments or other scientific procedures on living animals is provided by the Animals (Scientific Procedures) Act 1986. A protected animal under that Act is any living[1] vertebrate[2] other than man[3], but such protection extends to any such vertebrate in its foetal, larval or embryonic form from the stage of its development when (1) in the case of a mammal, bird or reptile, half the gestation or incubation period for its species has elapsed, and (2) in any other case, it becomes capable of independent feeding[4].

1 An animal is regarded as continuing to live until the permanent cessation of circulation or the destruction of its brain: Animals (Scientific Procedures) Act 1986 s 1 (4).
2 'Vertebrate' means any animal of the Sub-phylum Vertebrata of the Phylum Chordata, and 'invertebrate' means any animal not of that Sub-phylum: ibid s 1 (5).
3 Ibid s 1 (1). The Secretary of State for the Home Department may by order extend the definition so as to include invertebrates of any description: s 1 (3) (a).
4 Ibid s 1 (2). The Secretary of State may by order alter the stage of development so specified: s 1 (3) (b). He may also make provision in lieu of s 1 (2) as respects any animal which becomes a protected animal by virtue of an order under s 1 (3) (a) (see note 3 supra): s 1 (3) (c).

430. Regulated procedures. A regulated procedure is any experimental or other scientific procedure applied to a protected animal[1] which may have the effect of causing it pain, suffering, distress or lasting harm[2]. The definition does not cover anything done in accordance with any recognised veterinary, agricultural or animal husbandry practice[3]. It does, however, apply where what is done is part of a series or combination of such procedures, whether the same or different, applied to the same animal and the series or combination may have the same effect, and the animal is a protected animal throughout or it attains the status of a protected animal in its development in the course of the series or combination of procedures[4].

Anything done for the purpose of, or liable to result in, the birth or hatching of a protected animal is also a regulated procedure if it may cause the animal pain, suffering, distress or lasting harm[5].

Also excluded from the definition of regulated procedure is the ringing, tagging or marking of an animal or the application of any other humane procedure for the sole purpose of enabling it to be identified if it causes only momentary pain or distress and no lasting harm[6]. Nor is the killing of an animal within the definition unless it is killed for experimental or other scientific use in a designated establishment[7] and the method used is not appropriate to the animal[8].

The administration of any substance or article to an animal for the purposes of a medical test of the substance or article in accordance with the Medicines Act 1968 is not within the definition[9].

1 For the meaning of 'protected animal' see para 429 ante.
2 Animals (Scientific Procedures) Act 1986 s 2 (1). In determining whether pain, suffering, distress or lasting harm may be caused, the use of anaesthetics, analgesics, decerebration and any other method of rendering an animal insentient must be disregarded: s 2 (4). A use of such means for the purposes of any experimental or other scientific procedure is itself a regulated procedure: s 2 (4).
3 Ibid s 2 (8).
4 Ibid s 2 (4).
5 Ibid s 2 (3).

6 Ibid s 2 (5). Such exception would clearly apply to the method of identification by implantation of a microchip.
7 As to designated establishments see ibid ss 6, 7; and para 434 post.
8 Ibid s 2 (7). 'Appropriate' means appropriate under Sch 1, which prescribes standard methods of humane killing for (1) animals other than foetal, larval and embryonic forms, and (2) foetal, larval and embryonic forms.
9 Ibid s 2 (6); ie a test within the meaning of the Medicines Act 1968 s 32 (6); see MEDICINE vol 30 para 674 et seq.

431. Prohibition of unlicensed procedures. No person may apply a regulated procedure[1] to an animal unless (1) he holds a personal licence[2] qualifying him to apply a regulated procedure of that description to an animal of that description; (2) the procedure is applied as part of a programme of work specified in a project licence[3] authorising the application, as part of that programme, of a regulated procedure of that description to an animal of that description; and (3) the place where the procedure is carried out is a place[4] specified in both the personal licence and the project licence[5].

Contravention of these provisions is an offence, punishable on conviction on indictment by imprisonment for a term not exceeding two years or a fine or both, and on summary conviction by imprisonment for a term not exceeding six months or a fine not exceeding the statutory maximum or both[6].

1 For the meaning of 'regulated procedure' see para 430 ante.
2 For the meaning of 'personal licence' see para 432 post.
3 For the meaning of 'project licence' see para 433 post.
4 For the meaning of 'place' see para 432 note 2 post.
5 Animals (Scientific Procedures) Act 1986 s 3. A person is not guilty of an offence under s 3 of acting without the authority of a project licence if he shows that he reasonably believed, after making due enquiry, that he had such authority: s 22 (4). Nor, if the conditions of his licence permit him to use assistants to perform, under his direction, tasks not requiring technical knowledge, is anything done by an assistant in accordance with such a condition an offence: s 10 (4).
6 Ibid s 22 (1). 'Statutory maximum' means the sum prescribed by the Magistrates' Courts Act 1980 s 32: Criminal Justice Act 1982 s 74 (1); see para 233 note 3 ante. At the date at which this volume states the law, the prescribed sum is £2,000.

432. Personal licences. A personal licence is one granted by the Secretary of State qualifying the holder to apply specified regulated procedures[1] to animals of specified descriptions at a specified place[2] or places[3].

Applications for personal licences must be made to the Secretary of State in such form and supported by such information as he may reasonably require[4]. Except where he dispenses with such requirements, any such application must be endorsed by a person who is himself the holder of a personal licence or a licence treated under the Animals (Scientific Procedures) Act 1986 as such a licence[5] and who has knowledge of the biological or other relevant qualifications and the training, experience and character of the applicant[6]. The person endorsing such an application should, if practicable, be a person occupying a position of authority at a place where the applicant is to be authorised by the licence to carry out the specified procedures[7]. No one under the age of 18 may be granted a licence[8].

A personal licence continues in force until revoked, but the Secretary of State must review each such licence at intervals not exceeding five years and may for that purpose reasonably require information from the holder[9].

Provision has been made for the appropriate conditions to be contained in a personal licence and for the variation, revocation and suspension of the licence[10].

1 For the meaning of 'regulated procedure' see para 430 ante.
2 'Place' includes any place within the seaward limits of the territorial waters of the United Kingdom, including any vessel other than a ship which is not a British ship: Animals (Scientific Procedures) Act 1986 s 30 (2).
3 Ibid s 4 (1).
4 Ibid s 4 (2). As to false or misleading statements in an application as an offence see s 23 (1); para 449 post.
5 Ie under the transitional procedures of ibid s 27 (4), Sch 4.
6 Ibid s 4 (3).
7 Ibid s 4 (3).
8 Ibid s 4 (4).
9 Ibid s 4 (5).
10 See ibid ss 9–13; and paras 437–441 post.

433. Project licences. A project licence is a licence granted by the Secretary of State specifying a programme of work and authorising the application, as part of that programme, of specified regulated procedures[1] to animals of specified descriptions at a specified place[2] or places[3]. Such a licence must only be granted to a person who undertakes overall responsibility for the programme[4]. It must not be granted unless the Secretary of State is satisfied that the programme is undertaken for one or more of the following purposes: (1) the prevention (whether by the testing of any product or otherwise) or the diagnosis or treatment of disease, ill-health or abnormality, or their effects, in man, animals or plants; (2) the assessment, detection, regulation or modification of physiological conditions in man, animals or plants; (3) the protection of the natural environment in the interests of the health or welfare of man or animals; (4) the advancement of knowledge in biological or behavioural sciences; (5) education or training otherwise than in primary or secondary schools; (6) forensic enquiries; (7) the breeding of animals for experimental or other scientific use[5].

In determining whether and on what terms to grant a project licence, the Secretary of State must weigh the likely adverse effect on the animals concerned against the benefit likely to accrue from the specified programme[6]. Nor must he grant a licence unless he is satisfied that the applicant has given adequate consideration to the feasibility of achieving the purpose of the programme by means not involving the use of protected animals[7].

Furthermore, the Secretary of State may not grant a project licence authorising the use of cats, dogs, primates or equidae unless he is satisfied that animals of no other species are suitable for the purposes of the programme or that it is not practicable to obtain animals of any other suitable species[8].

There are provisions relating to the conditions to be contained in a project licence and to its variation, revocation and suspension[9].

Unless revoked, a licence continues in force for the period specified in it, and it may be renewed for further periods, up to a maximum of five years since its grant, without prejudice to the grant of a new licence in respect of the programme in question[10]. A licence terminates on the death of the holder[11].

Any holder of a project licence who (a) procures or knowingly permits a person under his control to carry out a regulated procedure other than as part of the programme specified, or (b) procures or knowingly permits such a person to carry out a regulated procedure other than in accordance with that person's personal licence[12], is guilty of an offence[13].

1 For the meaning of 'regulated procedure' see para 430 ante.

2 For the meaning of 'place' see para 432 note 2 ante.
3 Animals (Scientific Procedures) Act 1986 s 5 (1). As to false or misleading statements in an application as an offence see s 23 (1); para 449 post.
4 Ibid s 5 (2).
5 Ibid s 5 (3).
6 Ibid s 5 (4).
7 Ibid s 5 (5).
8 Ibid s 5 (6).
9 See ibid ss 9–13; and paras 437–441 post.
10 Ibid s 5 (7).
11 Ibid s 5 (8). There are transitional provisions for a programme to continue for up to 28 days after notification of death: s 5 (8).
12 As to personal licences see para 432 ante.
13 Ibid s 22 (2). The penalties are prescribed by s 22 (1); see para 431 ante.

434. Scientific procedure establishments. For the purpose of a project licence[1] no place[2] may be specified unless it is designated by the Secretary of State as a scientific procedure establishment[3]. Application for a certificate to that effect is made to him in such form and supported by such information as he may reasonably require[4].

The certificate must not be issued except to a person in a position of authority at the establishment, nor unless the application nominates both a suitable person or persons to be specified in the certificate to be responsible for the day-to-day care of the protected animals[5] kept there for experimental or other purposes, and a veterinary surgeon or other suitably qualified person to provide advice on their health and welfare[6].

If it appears to any person so specified in a certificate that the health or welfare of any protected animal gives rise to concern, he must notify the holder of the personal licence[7] in charge of the animal or, if there is no such person or it is not practicable to notify him, take steps to ensure that the animal is cared for and, if such is necessary, that it is killed by an appropriate[8] or approved method[9].

The certificate remains in force until revoked and there is a prescribed annual fee[10]. There are provisions relating to the conditions to be contained in a certificate and to its variation, revocation and suspension[11].

1 As to project licences see para 433 ante.
2 For the meaning of 'place' see para 432 note 2 ante.
3 Animals (Scientific Procedures) Act 1986 s 6 (1). A person convicted of an offence of cruelty under the Protection of Animals Act 1911 s 1 (see para 412 et seq ante) in respect of an animal at a designated establishment is liable to the penalties prescribed by the Animals (Scientific Procedures) Act 1986 s 22 (1); see para 431 ante.
4 Ibid s 6 (3). As to false or misleading statements in an application as an offence see s 23 (1); para 449 post.
5 For the meaning of 'protected animal' see para 429 ante.
6 Animals (Scientific Procedures) Act 1986 s 6 (4), (5). If the Secretary of State thinks fit, the same person may be specified under both requirements: s 6 (5). As to veterinary surgeons and practitioners see paras 547, 548 post.
7 As to personal licences see para 432 ante.
8 Ie appropriate under the Animals (Scientific Procedures) Act 1986 Sch 1; see para 430 ante.
9 Ibid s 6 (6). Notification in such event may be given to the person specified in the certificate under either heading (if different) or to one of the inspectors appointed under s 18 (see para 446 post): s 6 (7). 'Approved' means approved by the Secretary of State: s 6 (6).
10 Ibid ss 6 (8), 8. See the Animals (Scientific Procedures) Act (Fees) Order 1989, SI 1989/2302.
11 See the Animals (Scientific Procedures) Act 1986 ss 9–13; and paras 437–441 post.

435. Breeding and supplying establishments. A person must not at any place[1] breed for use in regulated procedures[2] (whether there or elsewhere) protected animals[3] of a specified description[4] unless that place is designated by the Secretary of State as a breeding establishment[5].

A person must not keep at any place any such protected animals which have not been bred there but are to be supplied for use elsewhere in regulated procedures, unless that place is designated by the Secretary of State as a supplying establishment[6].

Application for such certificates of designation is made to the Secretary of State in such form and supported by such information as he may reasonably require[7]. The certificate must not be issued unless the application nominates both a suitable person or persons to be specified in the certificate to be responsible for the day-to-day care of the animals bred or kept there for breeding or, as the case may be, for the purposes of being supplied for use in regulated procedures, and a veterinary surgeon or other suitably qualified person to provide advice on their health and welfare[8].

If it appears to any person specified in a certificate that the health or welfare of any protected animal gives rise to concern, he must take steps to ensure that it is cared for and, if such is necessary, that it is killed by an appropriate[9] or approved method[10].

The certificate remains in force until revoked and there is a prescribed annual fee[11]. There are provisions relating to the conditions to be contained in a certificate and to its variation, revocation and suspension[12].

1 For the meaning of 'place' see para 432 note 2 ante.
2 For the meaning of 'regulated procedure' see para 430 ante.
3 For the meaning of 'protected animal' see para 429 ante.
4 The Animals (Scientific Procedures) Act 1986 s 7(1), Sch 2 specifies mice, rats, guinea-pigs, hamsters, rabbits, dogs, cats and primates. The Secretary of State has power to amend Sch 2 by order: s 7 (9).
5 Ibid s 7 (1). As to punishment on conviction of an offence see note 6 infra. The Breeding of Dogs Act 1973 (see para 392 ante) does not apply to the breeding of dogs for use in regulated procedures if they are bred at a designated breeding establishment: Animals (Scientific Procedures) Act 1986 s 27 (3).
6 Ibid s 7 (2). Contravention of s 7 (1) or (2) is an offence punishable on summary conviction by imprisonment for a term not exceeding three months or a fine not exceeding level 4 on the standard scale or both: s 22 (3). As to the standard scale see para 232 note 1 ante. At the date at which this volume states the law, level 4 on that scale is at £1,000.
7 Ibid s 7 (3). As to false or misleading statements in an application as an offence see s 23 (1); para 449 post.
8 Ibid s 7 (4), (5). If the Secretary of State thinks fit, the same person may be specified under both requirements: s 7 (5). As to veterinary surgeons and practitioners see paras 547, 548 post.
9 Ie appropriate under ibid Sch 1; see para 430 ante.
10 Ibid s 7 (6). Notification in such event may be given to the person specified in the certificate under either heading (if different) or to one of the inspectors appointed under s 18 (see para 446 post): s 7 (7). 'Approved' means approved by the Secretary of State: s 7 (6).
11 Ibid ss 7 (8), 8. See the Animals (Scientific Procedures) Act (Fees) Order 1989, SI 1989/2302.
12 See the Animals (Scientific Procedures) Act 1986 ss 9–13; and paras 437–441 post.

436. Consultation. Before granting a licence or issuing a certificate under the Animals (Scientific Procedures) Act 1986, the Secretary of State must consult one of the inspectors appointed under the Act[1] and may also consult an independent assessor[2] or the Animals Procedure Committee established under the Act[3].

1 Ie under the Animals (Scientific Procedures) Act 1986 s 18; see para 446 post.

2 Where he proposes to consult an independent assessor the Secretary of State must notify the applicant, and in selecting the assessor he must have regard to any representations made by the applicant: ibid s 9 (2).

3 Ibid s 9 (1). As to the Animals Procedure Committee see s 19; para 447 post.

437. Conditions of licences. Subject to certain compulsory conditions referred to below, the Secretary of State may impose such conditions in licences and certificates as he thinks fit[1].

A personal licence[2] must include (1) a condition to the effect that the holder must take precautions to prevent or reduce to the minimum consistent with the purposes of the authorised procedures[3] any pain, distress or discomfort to the animals to which those procedures may be applied; and (2) an inviolable termination condition, that is one specifying circumstances in which a protected animal[4] which is being or has been subjected to a regulated procedure must in every case be immediately killed by a method appropriate to the animal[5] or by such other method as may be authorised by the licence[6].

Unless the Secretary of State considers that an exception is justified, a project licence[7] must include conditions to the effect that (a) no cat or dog may be used under the licence unless it has been bred at and obtained from a designated breeding establishment[8], and (b) no other protected animal of a specified[9] description may be used under the licence unless it has been bred at a designated breeding establishment or obtained from a designated supplying establishment[10].

Breach of a condition in a licence does not invalidate it but is a ground for variation or revocation[11].

1 Animals (Scientific Procedures) Act 1986 s 10 (1).
2 As to personal licences see para 432 ante.
3 Ie authorised regulated procedures; see para 430 ante.
4 For the meaning of 'protected animal' see para 429 ante.
5 Ie appropriate under the Animals (Scientific Procedures) Act 1986 Sch 1; see para 430 ante.
6 Ibid s 10 (2).
7 As to project licences see para 433 ante.
8 For the meaning of 'designated breeding establishment' see para 435 ante.
9 Ie specified in the Animals (Scientific Procedures) Act 1986 Sch 2: s 10 (3); see para 435 note 4 ante.
10 Ibid s 10 (3). No exception may be made as to a dog or cat unless the Secretary of State is satisfied that no animal suitable for the purpose of the programme specified in the licence can be obtained within the condition: s 10 (3). As to supplying establishments see s 7 (2); and para 435 ante.
11 Ibid s 10 (7).

438. Conditions of designation certificates. A certificate designating a scientific procedure establishment[1] must include a condition prohibiting the killing other than by an appropriate method or one approved by the Secretary of State of any protected animal[2] kept at the establishment for experimental or other scientific purposes but not subjected to a regulated procedure[3] or required[4] to be killed[5].

A certificate designating a breeding or supplying establishment[6] must include a condition prohibiting the killing other than by an appropriate method or one approved by the Secretary of State[7] of any animal of a specified description[8] bred or kept for breeding at the establishment, or for the purposes of being supplied for use in regulated procedures but not used, or supplied for use, for that purpose[9].

Both a certificate designating a scientific procedure establishment and one designating a breeding or supplying establishment must include conditions to secure the availability thereat of a person competent to kill animals in accordance with the appropriate or approved methods[10] and for the keeping of records as respects the source and disposal of animals kept at the establishment[11].

Breach of a condition in a certificate does not invalidate it but is a ground for variation or revocation[12].

1 For the meaning of 'scientific procedure establishment' see para 434 ante.
2 For the meaning of 'protected animal' see para 429 ante.
3 For the meaning of 'regulated procedure' see para 430 ante.
4 Ie under the Animals (Scientific Procedures) Act 1986 s 15; see para 443 post.
5 Ibid s 10 (5).
6 For the meaning of 'breeding or supplying establishment' see para 435 ante.
7 Ie appropriate under the Animals (Scientific Procedures) Act 1986 Sch 1.
8 Ie designated under ibid s 7, Sch 2.
9 Ibid s 10 (5).
10 See note 6 supra.
11 Animals (Scientific Procedures) Act 1986 s 10 (6).
12 Ibid s 10 (7).

439. Variation and revocation of licences and certificates. A licence or certificate may be varied or revoked by the Secretary of State either on the ground[1] of breach of a condition or in any other case in which it appears to him appropriate to do so, or at the request of the holder[2].

1 Ie the ground mentioned in the Animals (Scientific Procedures) Act 1986 s 10 (7); see paras 437, 438 ante.
2 Ibid s 11.

440. Right to make representations. Where the Secretary of State proposes to refuse a licence or certificate or to vary or revoke it other than at the request of the holder, he must serve on the holder a notice of his intention to do so[1]. The notice must state the reasons for which he proposes to act and give particulars of the right of the person concerned to make representations[2]. Written or oral representations may be made to a person appointed by the Secretary of State[3]. The holder of a licence or certificate who is dissatisfied with any condition contained in it may likewise make written or oral representations to such person[4], who must, after considering them, make a report to the Secretary of State[5]. The latter must furnish a copy of the report to the person making the representations and take it into account in making his decision to refuse or vary or revoke the licence or certificate[6]. The credentials of a person appointed to receive representations are laid down[7].

1 Animals (Scientific Procedures) Act 1986 s 12 (1). The notice may be served either personally or by post: s 12 (8).
2 Ibid s 12 (2).
3 Ibid s 12 (3). Notice of the wish to make such representations must be given to the Secretary of State before such date as is specified in the notice of refusal, not being less than 28 days after the date of service: s 12 (3). See the Animals (Scientific Procedures) (Procedures for Representation) Rules 1986, SI 1986/1911.
4 Animals (Scientific Procedures) Act 1986 s 12 (4). Representations do not affect the operation of any condition unless and until it is varied under s 11: s 12 (4); see para 439 ante.
5 Ibid s 12 (6).
6 Ibid s 12 (6).
7 Ibid s 12 (5).

441. Suspension in cases of urgency. If it appears to the Secretary of State to be urgently necessary for the welfare of any protected animals[1] that a licence or certificate should cease to have effect forthwith, he may by notice served on the holder suspend its operation for a period not exceeding three months[2]. If during that period a notice of proposed variation or revocation of the licence or certificate is served[3], but at the end of that period (1) the time for notifying[4] the Secretary of State of a wish to make representations has not expired; or (2) representations are to be or are being made; or (3) representations have been made but the Secretary of State has not received or not completed consideration of the report of the person to whom they were made, he may by notice served on the holder further suspend the licence or certificate until he is able to decide whether to vary or revoke it[5]. Such further suspension cannot be for longer than three months at a time[6].

1 For the meaning of 'protected animals' see para 429 ante.
2 Animals (Scientific Procedures) Act 1986 s 13 (1). The notice may be served personally or by post: s 13 (3).
3 Ie under ibid s 12; see para 440 ante.
4 Ie under ibid s 12 (3).
5 Ibid s 13 (2).
6 Ibid s 13 (2).

442. Re-use of protected animals. No protected animal[1] which has been subjected to a series of regulated procedures[2] for any purpose and which has been given a general anaesthetic for any of those procedures and allowed to recover consciousness may be used for any further regulated procedures[3].

Where any protected animal has not been given a general anaesthetic in such circumstances, it may not be used for any further regulated procedure without the consent of the Secretary of State[4].

A person who contravenes these provisions is guilty of an offence and on summary conviction is liable to imprisonment for a term not exceeding three months or to a fine not exceeding level 4 on the standard scale or to both[5].

1 For the meaning of 'protected animal' see para 429 ante.
2 For the meaning of 'regulated procedures' see para 430 ante.
3 Animals (Scientific Procedures) Act 1986 s 14 (1). This does not preclude the use of an animal with the consent of the Secretary of State if (1) the procedure, or each procedure, for which the anaesthetic was given consisted only of surgical preparation essential for a subsequent procedure, or (2) the anaesthetic was administered solely to immobilise the animal, or (3) the animal is under general anaesthesia throughout the further procedures and not allowed to recover consciousness: s 14 (2). Consent may relate to a specified animal or to animals used in specified procedures or circumstances: s 14 (4).
4 Ibid s 14 (3). As to consent see note 3 supra.
5 Ibid s 22 (3). As to the standard scale see para 232 note 1 ante. At the date at which this volume states the law, level 4 on that scale is at £1,000. These provisions apply to offences under the Animals (Scientific Procedures) Act 1986 ss 14–17, 18 (3); see paras 443–446 post.

443. Killing animals at conclusion of regulated procedures. Where a protected animal[1] has been subjected to a series of regulated procedures[2] for a particular purpose and at the conclusion of the series is suffering or likely to suffer adverse effects, the person who applied those procedures, or the last of them, must cause the animal to be killed immediately by an appropriate method[3] or by such other method as may be authorised by the personal licence[4] of the person by whom it is killed[5].

A person who contravenes this provision is guilty of an offence[6].

1 For the meaning of 'protected animal' see para 429 ante.

2 For the meaning of 'regulated procedures' see para 430 ante.
3 Ie appropriate under the Animals (Scientific Procedures) Act 1986 Sch 1; see para 430 ante.
4 As to personal licences see para 432 ante. This clearly involves killing by the person applying the procedures or someone 'caused' by him to do the killing.
5 Animals (Scientific Procedures) Act 1986 s 15 (1). This is without prejudice to any condition in a project licence (see para 437 ante) requiring an animal to be killed at the conclusion of a regulated procedure in circumstances other than those mentioned above: s 15 (2).
6 Ibid s 22 (3). For penalties see para 442 text and note 5 ante.

444. Prohibition of public displays. No person may carry out any regulated procedure[1] as an exhibition to the general public or carry out any such procedure which is shown live on television for general reception[2]. No person may publish a notice or advertisement announcing the carrying out of any regulated procedure in a manner which would contravene the above provision[3].

A person who contravenes these provisions is guilty of an offence[4].

1 For the meaning of 'regulated procedure' see para 430 ante.
2 Animals (Scientific Procedures) Act 1986 s 16 (1).
3 Ibid s 16 (2).
4 Ibid s 22 (3). For penalties see para 442 text and note 5 ante.

445. Use of neuromuscular blocking agents. No person may in the course of a regulated procedure[1] use any neuromuscular blocking agent unless expressly authorised to do so by the personal and project licences[2] under which the procedure is carried out, or use any such agent instead of an anaesthetic[3].

A person who contravenes these provisions is guilty of an offence[4].

1 For the meaning of 'regulated procedure' see para 430 ante.
2 As to personal and project licences see paras 432, 433 ante respectively.
3 Animals (Scientific Procedures) Act 1986 s 17.
4 Ibid s 22 (3). For penalties see para 442 text and note 5 ante.

446. Inspectors. The Secretary of State has power to appoint inspectors for the purposes of the Animals (Scientific Procedures) Act 1986 having such medical or veterinary qualifications as he thinks requisite[1].

An inspector's duties include advising the Secretary of State on applications for personal and project licences[2] and requests for their variation, revocation or periodical review; likewise on applications for certificates[3] and requests for variation or revocation; and also visiting (1) places[4] where regulated procedures[5] are carried out to determine whether those procedures are authorised by the requisite licences and whether the conditions of those licences are being complied with, and (2) designated establishments[6] to determine whether the conditions of their certificates are being complied with[7].

In addition, an inspector must report to the Secretary of State any case in which any provision of the Animals (Scientific Procedures) Act 1986 or any condition of a licence or certificate under the Act has not been or is not being complied with, and to advise him on the appropriate action to be taken[8].

If an inspector considers that a protected animal[9] is undergoing excessive suffering he may require it to be killed immediately by an appropriate method[10] or one which may be authorised by the personal licence of any person to whom he addresses the requirement[11].

1 Animals (Scientific Procedures) Act 1986 s 18 (1).
2 As to personal and project licences see paras 432, 433 ante respectively.
3 As to such certificates see para 434, 435 ante.
4 For the meaning of 'place' see para 432 note 2 ante.
5 For the meaning of 'regulated procedure' see para 430 ante.
6 Ie designated by a certificate under the Animals (Scientific Procedures) Act 1986 s 6 or s 7; see paras 434, 435 ante.
7 Ibid s 18 (2) (a)–(d).
8 Ibid s 18 (2) (e).
9 For the meaning of 'protected animal' see para 429 ante.
10 Ie appropriate under the Animals (Scientific Procedures) Act 1986 Sch 1; see para 430 ante.
11 Ibid s 18 (3). Failure to comply with such a requirement is an offence: s 22 (3). For penalties see para 442 text and note 5 ante.

447. The Animal Procedures Committee. The Animals (Scientific Procedures) Act 1986 makes provision for the appointment of an Animal Procedures Committee[1] with the duty of advising the Secretary of State on such matters concerned with the Act and his functions under it as the committee may determine, or as may be referred to it by the Secretary of State[2].

In its consideration of any matter the committee must have regard to the legitimate requirements of science and industry and the protection of animals against avoidable suffering and unnecessary use in scientific procedures[3].

It may promote research relevant to its functions and may obtain advice or assistance from other persons with knowledge or experience appearing to the committee to be relevant[4]. It may perform any of its functions by sub-committees[5].

1 Animals (Scientific Procedures) Act 1986 s 19 (1). As to the composition of the committee, qualifications, appointment, remuneration and expenses see s 19 (2)–(9). It must report each year: s 20 (5).
2 Ibid s 20 (1).
3 Ibid s 20 (2).
4 Ibid s 20 (4).
5 Ibid s 20 (3).

448. Guidance and codes of practice. The Secretary of State must publish information as guidance to the manner in which he proposes to exercise his power to grant licences[1] and certificates[2] under the Animals (Scientific Procedures) Act 1986 and in regard to proposed conditions to be included in them[3]. He must issue codes of practice as to the care of protected animals[4] and their use for regulated procedures[5], and may approve such codes issued by other persons[6], but he must consult the Animal Procedures Committee before issuing, approving, altering or approving any alteration in any such codes[7].

The Secretary of State must publish and lay before Parliament each year such information as he considers appropriate with respect to the use of protected animals in the previous year for experimental or other purposes[8].

1 As to licences under the Animals (Scientific Procedures) Act 1986 see paras 432, 433 ante.
2 As to certificates under the Animals (Scientific Procedures) Act 1986 see paras 434, 435 ante.
3 Ibid s 21 (1). The Secretary of State must consult the Animal Procedures Committee (see para 447 ante) before publishing or altering any such information: s 21 (3). Guidance has been issued under reference number HC 182.
4 For the meaning of 'protected animals' see para 429 ante.
5 For the meaning of 'regulated procedures' see para 430 ante.
6 Animals (Scientific Procedures) Act 1986 s 21 (2). As to the effect of breach of any provision of a code upon criminal or civil proceedings see para 452 post.

7 Ibid s 21 (3).
8 Ibid s 21 (7).

449. False statements to obtain licences or certificates. A person is guilty of an offence if, for the purpose of obtaining or assisting another to obtain a licence[1] or certificate[2], he furnishes information which he knows to be false or misleading in a material particular or recklessly furnishes such information[3].

1 As to licences see paras 432, 433 ante.
2 As to certificates see paras 434, 435 ante.
3 Animals (Scientific Procedures) Act 1986 s 23 (1). On summary conviction the penalty is imprisonment for a term not exceeding three months or a fine not exceeding level 4 on the standard scale, or both: s 23 (2). As to the standard scale see para 232 note 1 ante. At the date at which this volume states the law, level 4 on that scale is at £1,000.

450. Protection of confidential information. A person is guilty of an offence if, other than for the purpose of discharging his functions under the Animals (Scientific Procedures) Act 1986, he discloses any information which has been obtained by him in the exercise of those functions and which he knows or has reasonable grounds for believing to have been given in confidence[1].

1 Animals (Scientific Procedures) Act 1986 s 24 (1). Punishment on conviction on indictment is a term of imprisonment not exceeding two years or a fine, or both; on summary conviction, a term not exceeding six months or a fine not exceeding the statutory maximum, or both: s 24 (2). As to the statutory maximum see para 233 note 3 ante. At the date at which this volume states the law, the statutory maximum is £2,000.

451. Powers of search and prosecutions. If satisfied by information on oath that there are reasonable grounds for believing that an offence under the Animals (Scientific Procedures) Act 1986 has been or is being committed at any place[1], a justice of the peace may issue a warrant authorising a constable to enter it, if need be by such force as is reasonably necessary, to search it and require any person found there to give his name and address[2]. A warrant may authorise a constable to be accompanied by an inspector[3] appointed under the 1986 Act and it must require it if the place in question is a designated establishment[4].

Any intentional obstruction of a constable or inspector in these circumstances or refusal to give a correct or any name and address is an offence[5].

Prosecutions either under the 1986 Act or for an offence of cruelty under the Protection of Animals Act 1911, if the allegation concerns an animal at a designated establishment, may not be brought in England and Wales except by or with the consent of the Director of Public Prosecutions[6].

Summary proceedings for an offence under the 1986 Act may be taken against any person at any place at which he is for the time being[7]. An information triable summarily in England and Wales may be so tried if laid at any time within three years after the offence and within six months after the date on which evidence sufficient in the opinion of the Director of Public Prosecutions to justify proceedings comes to his knowledge[8].

1 For the meaning of 'place' see para 432 note 2 ante.
2 Animals (Scientific Procedures) Act 1986 s 25 (1).
3 As to the appointment of inspectors see para 446 ante.

4 Animals (Scientific Procedures) Act 1986 s 25 (2). As to designated establishments see paras 434, 435 ante.

5 Ibid s 25 (3). Punishment on summary conviction is imprisonment for a term not exceeding three months or a fine not exceeding level 4 on the standard scale, or both: s 25 (3). As to the standard scale see para 232 note 1 ante. At the date at which this volume states the law, level 4 on that scale is at £1,000.

6 Ibid s 26 (1). See the Protection of Animals Act 1911; para 412 et seq ante.

7 Animals (Scientific Procedures) Act 1986 s 26 (2).

8 Ibid s 26 (3), notwithstanding anything in the Magistrates' Courts Act 1980 s 127 (1). A certificate by the Director of Public Prosecutions as to the date is conclusive evidence of the fact: s 26 (5).

452. Effect of evidence of failure to comply with code. A failure by any person to comply with any provision of a code issued by the Secretary of State or approved by him under the provisions of the Animals (Scientific Procedures) Act 1986[1] does not of itself render that person liable to criminal or civil proceedings; however, any such code is admissible in evidence in any such proceedings and, if any of its provisions appears to the court to be relevant to any question arising in those proceedings, it must be taken into account in determining that question[2].

1 As to such codes see para 448 ante.
2 Animals (Scientific Procedures) Act 1986 s 21 (4).

B. MEDICINAL TESTS

453. Medicinal tests on animals. The law relating generally to medicinal products is dealt with elsewhere in this work, and the legislation applicable to that subject contains special provisions dealing with clinical trials and medicinal tests carried out on animals, which include restrictions on the disposal of such animals[1]. No such specialised provisions, however, unless so expressed, derogate from the general provisions of the law relating to cruelty to animals[2].

1 See the Medicines Act 1968 ss 31–39; and MEDICINE vol 30 para 674 et seq.
2 As to cruelty generally see para 405 et seq ante.

(3) PERFORMANCES AND PUBLIC EXHIBITIONS

454. Performing animals. A person who exhibits[1] or trains[2] any performing animal[3] must be registered with a local authority[4]. These provisions do not apply to the training of animals for bona fide military, police, agricultural or sporting purposes, or the exhibition of any animals so trained[5]. A non-registered person who exhibits or trains a performing animal[6] or who applies to be registered when disqualified[7], a registered person who exhibits or trains a performing animal with respect to which or in a manner with respect to which he is not registered[8], or who without reasonable excuse fails to produce his certificate of registration on demand[9], or a person who in any part of Great Britain contravenes or fails to comply with an order made by a magistrates' court under the Performing Animals (Regulation) Act 1925[10], or who obstructs or wilfully delays any constable or local authority officer in the execution of his powers of entry or inspection under the Act[11], or who conceals any animal with a view to avoiding such inspection[12], commits an offence punishable on summary conviction by a fine not exceeding level 3 on the standard scale[13].

Proceedings in respect of contravention of the Performing Animals (Regulation) Act 1925 can only be taken by a constable or local authority officer[14], who are empowered to enter any premises at all reasonable times where performing animals are being trained, exhibited or kept, to inspect the premises and the animals, and to require any trainer or exhibitor to produce his certificate of registration[15]. They are not, however, entitled to go on or behind the stage during a public performance of performing animals[16].

Upon conviction of any offence against the 1925 Act or the Protection of Animals Act 1911[17], a person may, if registered, have his name removed from the register, and in any case be either permanently or for a specified time disqualified for being registered[18]. Where it is proved to the satisfaction of a magistrates' court that the training or exhibition of a performing animal has been accompanied by cruelty and should be prohibited or allowed only subject to conditions, an order may be made prohibiting the training or exhibition or allowing it only upon conditions[19]. The court must send a copy of any order to the local authority and to the Secretary of State, and particulars of it must be indorsed on any certificate of registration[20].

A person aggrieved[21] by the making or refusal of any order may appeal to the Crown Court[22]. Any order made does not come into force until seven days after it is made, or until any appeal has been determined[23].

1 To 'exhibit' means to exhibit at any entertainment to which the public are admitted, whether on payment of money or otherwise: Performing Animals (Regulation) Act 1925 s 5 (1).

2 To 'train' means to train for the purpose of any exhibition at any entertainment to which the public are admitted, whether on payment of money or otherwise: ibid s 5 (1).

3 'Animal' for this purpose does not include invertebrates: ibid s 5 (1). As to vertebrates see para 429 note 2 ante.

4 Ibid s 1 (1). Application for registration, containing prescribed particulars of the animals and the performances, must be made to the local authority for the district where the applicant resides or, if he has no fixed residence in Great Britain, to such one as he may choose of certain prescribed authorities, paying a registration fee: ss 1 (2), (3), 5 (3) (amended by the Local Government Act 1974 ss 35, 42 (1), Sch 6 para 2 (2), Sch 8); Performing Animals Rules 1925, SR & O 1925/1219, rr 1, 2, 9 (amended by SI 1968/1464), Sch 1, made by the Secretary of State under the Performing Animals (Regulation) Act 1925 s 5 (2). A certificate of registration is issued and a copy sent by the local authority to the Home Office: s 1 (4), (7); Performing Animals Rules 1925 rr 5, 8, Sch 3. The registers are open to inspection, for which a fee may be charged: Performing Animals (Regulation) Act 1925 s 1 (5), (7), (8) (amended by the Local Government Act 1974 s 35, Sch 6 para 2 (1)); Performing Animals Rules 1925 rr 3, 4, 8, Sch 2. 'Local authority' means the Common Council in the City of London, the London borough council in a London borough, and elsewhere the county council: Performing Animals (Regulation) Act 1925 s 5 (1); London Government Act 1963 s 4 (2) (b). The expenses of a county council are defrayed out of the county fund: Performing Animals (Regulation) Act 1925 s 5 (3) (amended by the Local Government Order 1966, SI 1966/1305, art 2 (15), Sch 1).

5 Performing Animals (Regulation) Act 1925 s 7.

6 Ibid s 4 (1) (a).

7 Ibid s 4 (1) (g); see text and notes 17, 18 infra.

8 Ibid s 4 (1) (b).

9 Ibid s 4 (1) (f).

10 Ibid s 4 (1) (c). As to orders see s 2; text and notes 19–23 infra.

11 Ibid s 4 (1) (d). As to powers of entry see s 3; text and notes 14–16 infra. As to 'obstructing' and 'wilfully' see para 391 note 16 ante.

12 Ibid s 4 (1) (e).

13 Ibid s 4 (1) (amended by virtue of the Criminal Justice Act 1982 ss 38, 46). As to the standard scale see para 232 note 1 ante. At the date at which this volume states the law, level 3 on that scale is at £400.

14 Performing Animals (Regulation) Act 1925 ss 2 (1), 4 (1).

15 Ibid s 3 (1).

16 Ibid s 3 (2).

17 As to the Protection of Animals Act 1911 see paras 412–418 ante.
18 Performing Animals (Regulation) Act 1925 s 4 (2).
19 Ibid s 2 (1).
20 Ibid ss 2 (4), 4 (2).
21 For the meaning of 'person aggrieved' see ADMINISTRATIVE LAW vol 1 (1) (Reissue) para 56.
22 Performing Animals (Regulation) Act 1925 ss 2 (2), 4 (2) (s 2 (2) amended by the Courts Act 1971 s 56 (2), Sch 9 Pt I); see COURTS.
23 Performing Animals (Regulation) Act 1925 ss 2 (3), 4 (2).

455. Public exhibition. Any person who promotes, causes or knowingly[1] permits to take place or takes part in any public performance (other than a cinematograph performance[2]) which includes any episode consisting of or involving throwing or casting, with ropes or other appliances, any unbroken horse[3] or untrained bull[3], or wrestling, fighting or struggling with any untrained bull[4], or riding or attempting to ride any horse or bull which, by the use of any appliance or treatment involving cruelty, is or has been stimulated with the intention of making it buck during the performance[5] is guilty of an offence, and is liable on summary conviction to a fine not exceeding level 4 on the standard scale or imprisonment for a term not exceeding three months, or both[6].

1 For the meaning of 'knowingly' see para 395 note 7 ante.
2 Protection of Animals Act 1934 s 1 (3). As to films see para 456 post.
3 'Horse' and 'bull' have the same meanings as in the Protection of Animals Act 1911 s 15 (d) (see para 405 note 9 ante): Protection of Animals Act 1934 s 1 (3).
4 Ibid s 1 (1) (a), (b). If the animal appears or is represented to spectators to be unbroken or untrained, it lies on the defendant to prove that it is in fact broken or trained: s 1 (2). As to a defendant's burden of proof see para 336 note 12 ante.
5 Protection of Animals Act 1934 s 1 (1) (c). Where the animal is a horse it is a defence for the defendant to prove that he did not know and could not reasonably be expected to know that the appliance or treatment was to be or was used: s 1 (2). As to the burden of proof see para 336 note 9 ante.
6 Ibid ss 1 (1), 2 (amended by virtue of the Criminal Justice Act 1982 s 46). As to the standard scale see para 232 note 1 ante. At the date at which this volume states the law, level 4 on that scale is at £1,000.

456. Films involving animal cruelty. No person may exhibit to the public[1] or supply to any person for public exhibition[1], whether by himself or another person, any cinematograph film, whether produced in Great Britain or elsewhere, if in connection with its production any scene represented in it was organised or directed in such a way as to involve the cruel infliction of pain or terror on any animal[2] or the cruel goading of any animal to fury[3]. Any person contravening this provision is liable on summary conviction to a fine not exceeding level 3 on the standard scale or to imprisonment for a term not exceeding three months, or both[4]. In any proceedings the court may, without prejudice to any other mode of proof, infer from the film as exhibited or supplied for exhibition that a scene represented was organised or directed in such a way but, whether it draws such an inference or not, it is a defence for the defendant to prove that he believed and had reasonable cause to believe that no scene represented was so organised or directed[5].

1 A film is deemed to be exhibited to the public when, and only when, it is exhibited in a place to which for the time being members of the general public as such have access, whether on payment of money or otherwise, and 'public exhibition' is construed accordingly: Cinematograph Films (Animals) Act 1937 s 1 (4) (a).
2 'Animal' has the same meaning as in the Protection of Animals Act 1911 s 15 (see para 405 note 9 ante): Cinematograph Films (Animals) Act 1937 s 1 (4) (b).
3 Ibid s 1 (1).

4 Ibid s 1 (3) (amended by virtue of the Criminal Justice Act 1982 s 46). As to the standard scale see para 232 note 1 ante. At the date at which this volume states the law, level 3 on that scale is at £400.
5 Cinematograph Films (Animals) Act 1937 s 1 (2). As to the burden of proof see para 336 note 9 ante.

457. Captive birds; decoys. It is an offence to promote, arrange, conduct, assist in, receive money for, or take part in, any event whatever at or in the course of which captive birds are liberated by hand or by any other means for the purpose of being shot immediately after their liberation[1]. The penalty is a fine not exceeding level 5 on the standard scale[2]. Where an offence is committed in respect of more than one bird the maximum fine is determined as if the offender had been convicted separately in respect of each bird[3].

The owner or occupier[4] of any land who permits it to be used for such a purpose is similarly punishable[5].

A person is guilty of an offence, similarly punishable, if, for the purpose of killing or taking any wild bird, he uses as a decoy any sound recording, or any live bird or other animal whatever which is tethered or is secured by means of braces or other similar appliances, or which is blind, maimed or injured, or knowingly causes or permits such an act, being unlawful, to be done[6]. The court may also order the decoy to be forfeited[7].

There are other statutory provisions prohibiting and restricting the methods of killing or taking wild birds[8].

1 Wildlife and Countryside Act 1981 s 8 (3).
2 Ibid s 21 (1) (a) (amended by virtue of the Criminal Justice Act 1982 s 46). As to the standard scale see para 232 note 1 ante. At the date at which this volume states the law, level 5 on that scale is at £2,000.
3 Wildlife and Countryside Act 1981 s 21 (5).
4 'Occupier' includes, except in relation to the foreshore, anyone with any right of hunting, shooting, fishing or taking game or fish: ibid s 27 (1).
5 Ibid s 8 (3).
6 Ibid s 5 (1) (d), (f) (s 5 (1) (f) added by the Wildlife and Countryside (Amendment) Act 1991 s 1 (1), (3)); see para 338 ante.
7 Wildlife and Countryside Act 1981 s 21 (6).
8 See generally, as to the protection of birds, para 332 et seq ante.

458. Possession of cockfighting instruments. The possession of any instruments or appliance designed or adapted for use in connection with the fighting of any domestic fowl for the purpose of so using it or permitting its use is an offence carrying a punishment on summary conviction of imprisonment for a term not exceeding three months or a fine not exceeding level 3 on the standard scale, or both[1]. Upon conviction the court may order the instrument or appliance to be destroyed or otherwise dealt with[2].

1 Cockfighting Act 1952 s 1 (1) (amended by virtue of the Criminal Justice Act 1982 s 46). As to the standard scale see para 232 note 1 ante. At the date at which this volume states the law, level 3 on that scale is at £400. For other offences relating to cockfighting see para 414 ante.
2 Cockfighting Act 1952 s 1 (2). The order does not take effect until the expiration of the 14 days allowed for appealing, or until the determination of any appeal: s 1 (2) proviso.

(4) LEGAL PROCEEDINGS

459. Arrest. A constable may arrest without warrant any person who he has reason to believe is guilty of an offence under the Protection of Animals Act 1911 which is punishable by imprisonment without the option of a fine[1], whether upon his own view of it or upon the complaint and information of any other person, who must declare his name and place of abode to the constable[2]. On the arrest of a person in charge of a vehicle or animal[3], the police may take charge of the vehicle or animal and deposit it in a place of safe custody until the termination of the proceedings, or until the court directs its delivery to the person charged or the owner[4]. The reasonable costs of the detention (including, where necessary, veterinary treatment) are, in the event of a conviction, recoverable from the owner as a civil debt, or, where the owner himself is convicted, become part of the costs of the case[5].

1 Ie for an offence of cruelty under the Protection of Animals Act 1911 s 1 (1), other than an offence by the owner of permitting cruelty within s 1 (2): see para 461 post.
2 Ibid s 12 (1). This power has been specifically preserved by the Police and Criminal Evidence Act 1984 s 26 (2), Sch 2: see CRIMINAL LAW. The power does not give an officer of the RSPCA a right to give offenders into custody; he should complain to a constable: cf *Line v Royal Society for Prevention of Cruelty to Animals and Marsh* (1902) 18 TLR 634. As to proof of appointment when proceedings are taken on the complaint of a local authority inspector see *Ross v Helm* [1913] 3 KB 462, DC.
3 For the meaning of 'animal' see para 405 note 9 ante.
4 Protection of Animals Act 1911 s 12 (2).
5 Ibid s 12 (2). As to the recovery of civil debts see the Magistrates' Courts Act 1980 ss 58, 96; and MAGISTRATES.

460. Production of drivers or animals. Where proceedings are instituted under the Protection of Animals Act 1911 against the driver or conductor of a vehicle, the court may issue a summons directed to his employer requiring him to produce the driver or conductor at the hearing of the case[1]. In any proceedings under the Act the court may issue a summons directed to the owner of the animal[2] requiring him to produce it at or before the hearing, for the inspection of the court, if such production is possible without cruelty[3].

On failure to comply with any such summons without satisfactory excuse the employer or owner is liable on summary conviction to a fine not exceeding level 1 on the standard scale, and may be required to pay the costs of any adjournment rendered necessary by his failure[4].

1 Protection of Animals Act 1911 s 13 (1).
2 For the meaning of 'animals' see para 405 note 9 ante.
3 Protection of Animals Act 1911 s 13 (2).
4 Ibid s 13 (3) (amended by virtue of the Criminal Justice Act 1982 ss 38, 46). As to the standard scale see para 232 note 1 ante. At the date at which this volume states the law, level 1 on that scale is at £50.

461. Punishment. The penalty on summary conviction for any offence of cruelty inder the Protection of Animals Act 1911 is a fine not exceeding level 5 on the standard scale, or imprisonment for a term not exceeding six months, or both[1], except that where an owner is convicted of permitting cruelty by reason only of his having failed to exercise reasonable care and supervision in respect of the protection of the animal[2] therefrom, he is not liable to imprisonment without the option of a fine[3].

1 Protection of Animals Act 1911 s 1 (1) (amended by the Protection of Animals (Penalties) Act 1987 s 1 (1)). A person guilty of an offence under the Protection of Animals Act 1911 s 1 in respect of an animal at a 'designated establishment' under the Animals (Scientific Procedures) Act 1986 s 6 or s 7 (see paras 434, 435 ante) is liable to the penalties specified in s 22 (1) of the 1986 Act (as to which see

para 431 ante): s 22 (5). As to the standard scale see para 232 note 1 ante. At the date at which this volume states the law, level 5 on that scale is at £2,000.
2 For the meaning of 'animal' see para 405 note 9 ante.
3 Protection of Animals Act 1911 s 1 (2) proviso.

462. Deprivation of ownership; disqualification. If the owner of an animal[1] is convicted of an offence of cruelty under the Protection of Animals Act 1911, the court may, if it thinks fit, in addition to any other punishment, deprive him of the ownership of the animal, and may make such order as to its disposal as it thinks fit[2]. Such order, however, may not be made unless it is shown by evidence as to a previous conviction, or as to the character of the owner, or otherwise, that the animal, if left with the owner, is likely to be exposed to further cruelty[3].

Upon the conviction of an offender for an offence of cruelty the court may cancel any licence he holds to keep a pet shop, animal boarding establishment or riding establishment and disqualify him from keeping such a shop or establishment[4], may order the removal of any registration he has in respect of performing animals and disqualify him from being registered[5], and may disqualify him from keeping a dangerous wild animal[6]. The court may also, if it thinks fit, in addition to or in substitution for any other punishment[7], order him to be disqualified, for such period as it thinks fit, from having the custody of any animal or any animal of a specified kind[8]. The court may suspend the operation of the order as may be necessary to make arrangements for custody, or pending an appeal[9]. A person so disqualified may apply to the same court after 12 months for the removal of the disqualification, and the court may either remove or vary the order or refuse the application[10]. If it varies the order or refuses the application no further application can be made until another 12 months have elapsed[11]. Breach of any such disqualification order is punishable on summary conviction by a fine not exceeding level 3 on the standard scale or imprisonment for a term not exceeding three months, or both[12].

1 For the meaning of 'animal' see para 405 note 9 ante.
2 Protection of Animals Act 1911 s 3.
3 Ibid s 3 proviso. As to proof of previous convictions see the Magistrates' Courts Rules 1981, SI 1981/552, r 72; and MAGISTRATES.
4 Pet Animals Act 1951 s 5 (3) (see para 466 post); Animal Boarding Establishments Act 1963 s 3 (3) (see para 391 ante); Riding Establishments Act 1964 s 4 (3) (see para 395 ante).
5 Performing Animals (Regulation) Act 1925 s 4 (2); see para 411 ante.
6 Dangerous Wild Animals Act 1976 s 6 (2); see para 396 ante.
7 See para 461 ante.
8 Protection of Animals (Amendment) Act 1954 s 1 (1) (amended by the Protection of Animals (Amendment) Act 1988 s 1 (1)). Note that the order can only disqualify from having *custody*, and not from ownership. A disqualification from having custody of 'cattle' extends to sheep: *Wastie v Phillips* [1972] 3 All ER 302, [1972] 1 WLR 1293, DC.
9 Protection of Animals (Amendment) Act 1954 s 1 (2).
10 Ibid s 1 (3).
11 Ibid s 1 (3) proviso.
12 Ibid s 2 (amended by virtue of the Criminal Justice Act 1982 ss 38, 46). As to the standard scale see para 232 note 1 ante. At the date at which this volume states this law, level 3 on that scale is at £400.

463. Destruction of animals. Where the owner of an animal[1] is convicted of an offence of cruelty under the Protection of Animals Act 1911 the court may, if satisfied that it would be cruel to keep the animal alive, direct that it be destroyed[2] and assign it to any suitable person, who must as soon as possible destroy it or have it destroyed in his presence without unnecessary suffering[3]. Any reasonable expenses incurred in destroying it may be ordered by the court to be paid by the owner, and may be recovered summarily as a civil debt[4]. Unless the owner assents, however, no order may be made except upon the evidence of a duly registered veterinary surgeon[5].

1 For the meaning of 'animal' see para 405 note 9 ante.
2 No appeal lies from an order to destroy an animal: Protection of Animals Act 1911 s 14 (1).
3 Ibid s 2.
4 Ibid s 2. As to the recovery of civil debts see the Magistrates' Court Act 1980 ss 58, 96; and MAGISTRATES.
5 Protection of Animals Act 1911 s 2 proviso. As to the registration of veterinary surgeons see the Veterinary Surgeons Act 1966 ss 2, 6; and paras 547, 548 post.

464. Appeal. Appeal lies to the Crown Court from any conviction or order, other than an order for the destruction of an animal[1], by a court of summary jurisdiction under the Protection of Animals Acts 1911 to 1964[2] or under the Animals (Scientific Procedures) Act 1986[3].

Where there is an appeal by the owner of an animal under the Acts of 1911 to 1964 the court may order him not to sell or part with the animal until the appeal is determined or abandoned, and to produce it on the hearing of the appeal if such production is possible without cruelty; failure to comply with such an order without satisfactory excuse is punishable on summary conviction with a fine not exceeding level 1 on the standard scale[4].

1 See para 463 ante.
2 Protection of Animals Act 1911 s 14 (1) (amended by the Courts Act 1971 s 56 (2), Sch 9 Pt I). For the Acts concerned see para 405 note 1 ante.
3 See the Magistrates' Courts Act 1980 s 108.
4 Protection of Animals Act 1911 s 14 (2) (amended by the Criminal Justice Act 1948 ss 79, 82, Sch 9 and by virtue of the Criminal Justice Act 1982 s 46). As to the standard scale see para 232 note 1 ante. At the date at which this volume states the law, level 1 on that scale is at £50.

(5) PET SHOPS; SALE OF PET ANIMALS

465. Licensing and sale. No person may keep a pet shop[1] unless he is licensed so to do by the local authority[2]. In deciding whether to grant a licence the authority must have regard in particular to the need for securing that animals will be kept in suitable accommodation; that they will be adequately supplied with food and drink and, so far as necessary, visited; that, if mammals, they will not be sold at too early an age; and that reasonable precautions will be taken to prevent the spread of infectious diseases and to guard against fire or other emergency; and the authority must specify in any licences granted such conditions as appear to it necessary or expedient to secure these objects[3]. An appeal lies to a magistrates' court against the refusal of a licence, or against any condition subject to which it is proposed to be granted[4].

Carrying on a business of selling animals as pets[5] in any street or public place, including a market, is an offence[6]. An animal may not be sold as a pet[7] to any person whom the seller has reasonable cause to believe to be under the age of 12 years[8].

1 The keeping of a pet shop means the carrying on at premises of any nature, including a private dwelling, of a business of selling animals as pets, and the keeping of animals in any such premises with a view to their being sold in the course of such a business, whether by the keeper or any other person: Pet Animals Act 1951 s 7 (1). A person is not, however, deemed to keep a pet shop by reason only of his keeping or selling pedigree animals bred by him or the offspring of an animal kept by him as a pet; and a local authority may direct that a particular breeder shall not be deemed to keep a pet shop merely because he sells as pets animals which he acquired for breeding or show purposes but found not to be suitable or required for such use: s 7 (1) proviso. 'Animal' includes any description of vertebrate, and 'pedigree animal' means any animal which is by its breeding eligible for registration with a recognised club or society keeping a register of that description of animal: s 7 (3). As to what are vertebrates see para 429 note 2 ante. As to local authorities see note 2 infra.
2 Pet Animals Act 1951 s 1 (1), (2). A fee is charged for a licence and the licence is granted subject to conditions specified in it: s 1 (2) (amended by the Local Government Act 1974 s 35 (1), (2), 42 (2), Sch 6 para 8, Sch 8). A licence may be granted either for the current year, in which case it comes into force on the day when it is granted, or for the next following year; in either case it comes into force on the day when it is granted, or for the next following year; in either case it expires at the end of the year in question: Pet Animals Act 1951 s 1 (5), (6). 'Local authority' means the council of any district or London borough, or the Common Council of the City of London: s 7 (3) (amended by the Local Government Act 1972 s 272 (1), Sch 30).
3 Pet Animals Act 1951 s 1 (3).
4 Ibid s 1 (4).
5 Selling an animal as a pet includes, as respects a dog or cat, selling it wholly or mainly for domestic purposes, and as respects any animal, selling it for ornamental purposes: ibid s 7 (2).
6 Ibid s 2 (amended by the Pet Animals Act 1951 (Amendment) Act 1983 s 1).
7 See note 5 supra.
8 Pet Animals Act 1951 s 3. Having 'reasonable cause to believe' means having such cause and in fact so believing: *R v Banks* [1916] 2 KB 621, CCA; *R v Harrison* [1938] 3 All ER 134, CCA.

466. Offences. Contravention of any provisions relating to pet animals or of a condition of a licence[1] is punishable on summary conviction with a fine not exceeding level 2 on the standard scale or imprisonment for a term not exceeding three months, or both[2].

A local authority[3] may authorise any of its officers or a veterinary surgeon or veterinary practitioner[4] to inspect a pet shop, and the wilful obstruction of such an inspector is punishable with a fine not exceeding level 2 on the standard scale[5].

On conviction for any of these offences or of any offence under the Protection of Animals Act 1911 a licence may be cancelled, and the holder, whether or not he holds a licence, may be disqualified from keeping a pet shop for such period as the court thinks fit[6].

1 See para 465 ante.
2 Pet Animal Act 1951 ss 1 (7), 5 (1) (amended by virtue of the Criminal Justice Act 1982 ss 38, 46). As to the standard scale see para 232 note 1 ante. At the date at which this volume states the law, level 2 on that scale is at £100.
3 For the meaning of 'local authority' see para 465 note 2 ante.
4 For the meaning of 'veterinary surgeon' and 'veterinary practitioner' see paras 547, 548 post.
5 Pet Animals Act 1951 ss 4, 5 (2) (amended by virtue of the Criminal Justice Act 1982 ss 38, 46). For the meaning of 'wilful obstruction' see para 391 note 16 ante. As to the standard scale see note 2 supra.
6 Pet Animals Act 1951 s 5 (3). The cancellation or disqualification may be suspended pending an appeal: s 5 (4).

7. LIABILITY OF OWNERS AND KEEPERS OF ANIMALS

(1) INJURIES CAUSED BY ANIMALS

467. Strict liability for damage. Where any damage[1] is caused by an animal belonging to a dangerous species[2], any person who is its keeper[3] is strictly liable for the damage, subject to certain exceptions[4].

A dangerous species is one which is not commonly domesticated in the British Islands, and whose fully-grown animals normally have such characteristics that they are likely, unless restrained, to cause severe damage, or that any damage they may cause is likely to be severe[5].

A person is a keeper of an animal if he either owns it or has it in his possession, or if he is the head of a household of which a member under the age of 16 owns the animal or has it in his possession, and if at any time such ownership or possession ceases, then the person who immediately before that time qualified as being the animal's keeper continues as such until replaced by another person[6]. A person does not, however, become a keeper of an animal for this purpose merely by reason of his taking it and keeping it in his possession to prevent its causing damage or to restore it to its owner[7].

1 'Damage' includes the death of, or injury to, any person, including any disease and any impairment of physical or mental condition: Animals Act 1971 s 11.
2 'Species' includes sub-species and variety: ibid s 11.
3 It seems clear from the wording that more than one person may qualify as an animal's keeper. See also text and notes 5–7 infra.
4 Animals Act 1971 s 2 (1). This provision replaces the former common law rules based on the principle of ferae naturae: s 1 (1) (a). For exceptions from liability see para 469 post.
5 Ibid s 6 (1), (2). For the meaning of 'British Islands' see para 344 note 7 ante. Whether an animal is domesticated or not appears to be a question of law (*McQuaker v Goddard* [1940] 1 KB 687 at 696, [1940] 1 All ER 471 at 475, CA, per Scott LJ), but it is submitted that the Act now draws a distinction between domesticated (see *McQuaker v Goddard* supra) and domesticated in these islands. Clearly an animal may be dangerous under the Act because of its sheer size or its unpredictability (as by becoming frightened and stampeding), regardless of any sort of viciousness in it: cf *Behrens v Bertram Mills Circus Ltd* [1957] 2 QB 1, [1957] 1 All ER 583. Bees appear to be domesticated: see *O'Gorman v O'Gorman* [1903] 2 IR 573 (negligence expressly found).
6 Animals Act 1971 s 6 (3). This follows the common law rule that responsibility for an animal's acts depended upon ownership or possession and control: see *M'Kone v Wood* (1831) 5 C & P 1; *Knott v LCC* [1934] 1 KB 126 at 141, CA, per Lord Wright. However, it is submitted that *Smith v Great Eastern Rly Co* (1866) LR 2 CP 4 (stray dog on premises but nothing done to encourage it or exercise control over it: no liability) would still be good law.
7 Animals Act 1971 s 6 (4).

468. Necessity for knowledge. Where damage[1] is caused by an animal which does not belong to a dangerous species[2] its keeper[3] is strictly liable for the damage, subject to certain exceptions discussed in the next paragraph[4], if:

(1) the damage is of a kind which the animal, unless restrained, was likely to cause or which, if caused by the animal, was likely to be severe[5]; and

(2) such likelihood was due to characteristics of the animal not normally found in animals of the same species[6] or, if so found, only at particular times or in particular circumstances[7]; and

(3) those characteristics were known to that keeper, or were at any time known to a person who at that time had charge of the animal as that keeper's servant or, if the keeper is the head of a household, if they were known to any other

member of the household under the age of 16 who is also deemed to be a keeper of the animal[8].

Thus liability for a harmless animal's acts only arises if it has an abnormal dangerous characteristic, which must be known to its keeper, and in the absence of these circumstances liability will depend upon the ordinary law of negligence[9]. The fact that an animal of a non–dangerous species such as a dog is of a particular breed is no justification for excepting it from the ordinary category of dogs[10]. The tendency of untended sheep to endanger vehicles on a highway would not amount to a dangerous characteristic[11].

1   For the meaning of 'damage' see para 467 note 1 ante.
2   For the meaning of 'dangerous species' see para 467 ante.
3   For the meaning of 'keeper' see para 467 ante.
4   See para 469 post.
5   Animals Act 1971 s 2 (2) (a). See *Cummings v Grainger* [1977] QB 397, [1977] 1 All ER 104, CA.
6   For the meaning of 'species' see para 467 note 2 ante.
7   Animals Act 1971 s 2 (2) (b). The words 'characteristics . . . not normally found in animals of the same species' are to be given their ordinary and natural meaning: *Wallace v Newton* [1982] 2 All ER 106, [1982] 1 WLR 375; *Smith v Ainger* (1990) Times, 5 June. See eg *Howard v Bergin, O'Connor & Co* [1925] 2 IR 110 (tendency of bullocks to become wild on unloading from the railway); *Barnes v Lucille Ltd* (1907) 96 LT 680 (bitch only fierce when with pups); *Curtis v Betts* [1990] 1 All ER 769, [1990] 1 WLR 459 (tendency of dog to defend its territory). Comparison should be made with the appropriate breed characteristics where one existed, since 'species' is defined as including sub-species and variety in the Animals Act 1971 s 11: *Hunt v Wallis* (1991) Times, 10 May.
8   Animals Act 1971 s 2 (2) (c). The knowledge must clearly be of the precise characteristic displayed: see *Osborne v Choqueel* [1896] 2 QB 109 (dog's tendency to attack and bite other animals not relevant to attack on plaintiff); *Glanville v Sutton & Co Ltd* [1928] 1 KB 571 (horse's tendency to bite other horses not relevant to attack on plaintiff); *Worth v Gilling* (1866) LR 2 CP 1; *Jones v Perry* (1796) 2 Esp 482; *Curtis v Mills* (1833) 5 C & P 489; *Beck v Dyson* (1815) 4 Camp 198. In *Knapp v Harvey* [1911] 2 KB 725, CA, where the plaintiff had been ordered to give particulars of specific occasions on which the defendant's dog had bitten persons, interrogatories to ascertain the names of the persons bitten were disallowed. A caution not to go near a dog has been held to be evidence of knowledge (see *Judge v Cox* (1816) 1 Stark 285; *Hartley v Harriman* (1818) 1 B & Ald 620 at 624 per Abbot J); likewise a statement that a particular bull would run at anything red (*Hudson v Roberts* (1851) 6 Exch 697); but an offer of compensation ought not to be so regarded (*Beck v Dyson* (1815) 4 Camp 198; *Thomas v Morgan* (1835) 2 Cr M & R 496; *Sanders v Teape and Swan* (1884) 51 LT 263).
9   See *Draper v Hodder* [1972] 2 QB 556, [1972] 2 All ER 210, CA; *Fardon v Harcourt-Rivington* (1932) 146 LT 391, HL; cf *Fitzgerald v E D and A D Cooke Bourne (Farms) Ltd* [1964] 1 QB 249, [1963] 3 All ER 36, CA.
10 *Tallents v Bell and Goddard* [1944] 2 All ER 474, CA. The number of dogs involved in an attack may, however, be an important factor: see *Draper v Hodder* [1972] 2 QB 556, [1972] 2 All ER 210, CA.
11 *Heath's Garage Ltd v Hodges* [1916] 2 KB 370, CA.

469. Exceptions from liability. A person is not liable for any damage[1] caused which would otherwise be the subject of strict liability[2] if it is due wholly to the fault[3] of the person suffering it[4], nor for any damage suffered by a person who has voluntarily accepted the risk of its happening[5]. However, a person employed as a servant by a keeper of an animal who incurs a risk incidental to his employment is not to be treated as accepting it voluntarily[6].

Where a trespasser on any premises or structure suffers damage caused by any animal kept thereon, there will be no strict liability if it is proved either that the animal was not kept there for the protection of persons or property[7] or, if it was so kept, that keeping it there for that purpose was not unreasonable[8]. It seems likely, however, that despite the Animals Act 1971, where a person enters under a claim of right, even if that right is contested, he could maintain an action[9].

1 For the meaning of 'damage' see para 467 note 1 ante.
2 Ie liability either for animals of a dangerous species (see para 467 ante), or for animals of a non-dangerous species with abnormal dangerous characteristics coupled with knowledge of the same (see para 468 ante).
3 'Fault' means negligence, breach of statutory duty or other act or omission which gives rise to a liability or would, apart from the Law Reform (Contributory Negligence) Act 1945, give rise to the defence of contributory negligence: s 4; Animals Act 1971 s 11; see NEGLIGENCE vol 34 para 68 et seq. A person who pats a dog which springs at and bites him is not guilty of contributory negligence: *Gordon v Mackenzie* 1913 SC 109.
4 Animals Act 1971 s 5 (1); see *Marlor v Ball* (1900) 16 TLR 239, CA.
5 Animals Act 1971 s 5 (2). See *Cummings v Grainger* [1977] QB 397, [1977] 1 All ER 104, CA. As to the defence of volenti generally see NEGLIGENCE vol 34 para 62 et seq.
6 Animals Act 1971 s 6 (5). Thus it appears that an employee whose duty is to tend a dangerous animal can now recover for any injury he sustains unless he has been entirely to blame; cf *Rands v McNeil* [1955] 1 QB 253, [1954] 3 All ER 593, CA (now overruled by the Animals Act 1971 s 6 (5)); *James v Wellington City* [1972] NZLR 70 (NZ SC).
7 Animals Act 1971 s 5 (3) (a). Thus a trespasser in a properly fenced field who is gored by a savage bull has no remedy: *Brock v Copeland* (1794) 1 Esp 203, cited in *Bird v Holbrook* (1828) 4 Bing 628 at 638; see also *Marlor v Ball* (1900) 16 TLR 239, CA; *Sylvester v Chapman Ltd* (1935) 79 Sol Jo 777; *Lee v Walkers* (1939) 162 LT 89. Contrast *Mansfield v Baddeley* (1876) 34 LT 696; *Gould v McAuliffe* [1941] 2 All ER 527, CA; *Pearson v Coleman Bros* [1948] 2 KB 359, [1948] 2 All ER 274, CA (person in search of lavatory).
8 Animals Act 1971 s 5 (3) (b). Whether it was reasonable or not must be a question of fact in each case according to the circumstances prevailing; thus the keeper of a fierce dog kept to protect his property would not be excused it he put it in the way of access to the house so that innocent visitors on lawful business might be injured: *Sarch v Blackburn* (1830) 4 C & P 297 at 300 per Tindal CJ; and see *Smillie v Boyd* (1886) 14 R 150; *Cummings v Grainger* [1977] QB 397 [1977] 1 All ER 104, CA; *Kavanagh v Stokes* [1942] IR 596.
9 *Brock v Copeland* (1794) 1 Esp 203, cited in *Bird v Holbrook* (1828) 4 Bing 628 at 638.

470. Negligence. The owner of a domestic and harmless animal may be liable on the ground of negligence for damage caused by it to third parties[1].

A person who brings an animal on to the highway must use all reasonable care to prevent it doing damage to other persons there[2]. In general, the driving of animals along the highway without having them under sufficient control amounts to negligence which will entail a liability for resulting damage or injury[3]. The bolting of a horse which has been left unattended in a public street is prima facie evidence of negligence on the part of the owner[4], and in certain circumstances the owner of a runaway horse may be liable to a person who tries to stop it[5].

1 See eg *Draper v Hodder* [1972] 2 QB 556, [1972] 2 All ER 210, CA (child attacked by pack of Jack Russell terriers allowed to roam free; dogs previously harmless: owner liable); *Jones v Owen* (1871) 24 LT 587 (two dogs leashed together rushed against a passer-by, threw him down and broke his leg: owner held liable on ground of negligence in having two big dogs coupled together on highway at night and not keeping them in hand). Cf *Fardon v Harcourt-Rivington* (1932) 146 LT 391, HL (dog left in motor car). The owner may be liable where he leaves a dog in such a position and in such circumstances as to render it likely that the dog will cause damage to persons lawfully passing along the highway: *Sycamore v Ley* (1932) 147 LT 342 at 345, CA. A dog with a long loose lead on the streets is a nuisance, and also prima facie evidence of negligence: *Pitcher v Martin* [1937] 3 All ER 918. See also *Toogood v Wright* [1940] 2 All ER 306, CA (racing greyhounds; no special control required). As to the liability of the owner of an animal to a trespasser see para 469 ante.
2 *Deen v Davis* [1935] 2 KB 282, CA (improper tethering); *Gomberg v Smith* [1963] 1 QB 25, [1962] 1 All ER 725, CA. As to straying on the highway see para 474 post.
3 *Turner v Coates* [1917] 1 KB 670 (unbroken colt driven without halter in the dark); *Harpers v Great North of Scotland Rly Co* (1886) 13 R 1139; *Pinn v Rew* (1916) 32 TLR 451; *Turnbull v Wieland* (1916) 33 TLR 143 (insufficient control of cows); *Rose v G H Collier Ltd* [1939] WN 19, CA (mare of known nervous disposition left unattended on tow-path: owner liable for injury by kicking); *Lathall v A Joyce & Son* [1939] 3 All ER 854 (escape of bull through negligence; attack on human being unusual:

no liability); *Aldham v United Dairies (London) Ltd* [1940] 1 KB 507, [1939] 4 All ER 522, CA (horse known to be restive left unattended on highway: owner liable for injury to passer-by directly caused therefrom); *Wright v Callwood* [1950] 2 KB 515, CA (animal driven from highway into yard escaped into highway and injured cyclist: owner not liable); *Bativala v West* [1970] 1 QB 716, [1970] 1 All ER 332 (pony escaping from gymkhana on to highway), where former ordinary rules in respect of escape on to highway (see para 474 post) not applied. Cf *Walker v Crabb* (1916) 33 TLR 119. In *Catchpole v Minster* (1913) 109 LT 953 it was held that a person driving a flock of sheep along a highway at night is under no duty to carry a light, but changed traffic conditions since this decision may well throw doubt on it. The Highway Code para 152 enjoins persons herding animals to carry lights after sunset. As to the effect of failure to observe the code see the Road Traffic Act 1988 s 38 (7); and ROAD TRAFFIC vol 40 para 13. As to the liability of market owners see *Brackenborough v Spalding UDC* [1942] AC 310, [1942] 1 All ER 34, HL; and see MARKETS AND FAIRS.

4 *Gayler and Pope Ltd v B Davies & Son Ltd* [1924] 2 KB 75.

5 *Haynes v Harwood* [1935] 1 KB 146, CA, criticising dicta of Scrutton LJ in *Cutler v United Dairies (London) Ltd* [1933] 2 KB 297 at 303, CA. As to civil liability for accidents arising from the negligent driving or riding of horses see NEGLIGENCE. As to criminal liability in respect of the riding or driving of horses on the highway see ROAD TRAFFIC.

471. Damage caused by infected animals. The common law affecting diseases of animals concerned itself primarily with liability to third parties for damage arising out of their condition. Thus the owner or possessor of animals having an infectious or contagious disease is liable for the damage caused by their infected state in the following cases:

(1) if, knowing them to be suffering from an infectious or contagious disease, he allows them to mingle with the animals of another person[1];

(2) if, knowing that they are diseased and infectious to persons handling them, he employs a person to handle their carcases who is ignorant of their state, and that person becomes infected[2];

(3) if, knowing of their diseased state, he gratuitously bails them (and a fortiori if the bailment is for reward), knowing that the bailee probably will or may place them with other animals which are healthy, without warning the bailee of their diseased state[3];

(4) if he sells them with a warranty that they are free from infectious or contagious disease, whether he knows of their diseased state or not[4];

(5) if he is guilty of fraud or actual concealment in the sale[5];

(6) if, knowing them to be diseased, and that they may be put in with healthy animals, he sells them at a public market or fair, or at a public auction; and possibly even if he sells them privately[6].

It is an indictable public nuisance to keep animals or fowls to the annoyance of the public through the unwholesomeness of their kennels or coops, or to take a horse diseased with glanders into a public place with the danger of infecting persons[7].

1 *Cooke v Waring* (1836) 2 H & C 332; *Earp v Faulkner* (1875) 34 LT 284 (knowledge of servant); *Theyer v Purnell* [1918] 2 KB 333; but see *Weller & Co v Foot and Mouth Disease Research Institute* [1966] 1 QB 569, [1965] 3 All ER 560, where the defendants were held to have no duty to the plaintiff cattle auctioneers, whose business suffered through the closure of markets owing to the escape of a cattle virus imported by the defendants for experimental purposes; aliter had the plaintiffs been owners of cattle infected.

2 *Davies v England and Curtis* (1864) 33 LJQB 321.

3 *Penton v Murduck* (1870) 22 LT 371, where the declaration (now the statement of claim) alleging that the defendant knowingly delivered an infected horse to the plaintiff to be put with his horse without telling him it was infected was held good without any allegation of concealment, fraud or breach of

warranty. The case was distinguished from *Hill v Balls* (1857) 2 H & N 299 on the ground that the latter was a case of buyer and seller and that there was no question of the diseased horse being put near another, but that case would now seem to be of very doubtful authority.

4 *Ward v Hobbs* (1878) 4 App Cas 13, HL. As to warranties on sales of animals see para 218 et seq ante; and generally see SALE OF GOODS.

5 *Mullett v Mason* (1866) LR 1 CP 559; *Clarke v Army and Navy Co-operative Society Ltd* [1903] 1 KB 155, CA.

6 *Bodger v Nicholls* (1873) 28 LT 441. As to markets and fairs generally see MARKETS AND FAIRS.

7 *R v Henson* (1852) Dears CC 24.

(2) TRESPASS BY ANIMALS

(i) Liability for Trespass

472. Involuntary trespass. So far as those domestic animals are concerned which are comprised in the term 'livestock' as therein defined[1], the Animals Act 1971 makes the person to whom they belong strictly liable for damage caused by their trespassing on another's land[2], and this and the remedies open to the sufferer are dealt with later.

Cats are not within the statute, and nor were they at common law the subject of strict liability for damage while trespassing[3]. Strict liability for damage by trespassing dogs is restricted under the statute to dogs killing or injuring livestock[4].

For trespass to take place, it is sufficient if any part of the animal crosses the boundary of the properties, for example, if it passes through the fence[5] or stretches its neck over a ditch[6]. A mere trespass to the person or to goods such as horses or cattle does not generally render the owner of the trespassing animal liable where there is no trespass to land[7].

Leave and licence of the plaintiff, if established, is a good defence[8].

1 See para 475 note 1 post.

2 See the Animals Act 1971 s 4; and para 475 post.

3 *Buckle v Holmes* [1926] 2 KB 125, CA.

4 Ie under the Animals Act 1971 s 3, which replaces the Dogs Act 1906 s 1 (1)–(3). See, as to dogs generally, para 369 et seq ante. In view of the comprehensive nature of the definition of livestock in s 11 of the Act of 1971, it is doubtful if liability for domestic animals outside the definition other than dogs and cats in such circumstances is a practical problem, but it is submitted that in so far as it might arise the former rule would still apply, ie that their owner will be liable, if they escape and commit a trespass, for such damage as it is in their nature ordinarily to commit: *Cox v Burbidge* (1863) 13 CBNS 430 at 436 per Erle LJ. It is noted that the statutory rules under the Animals Act 1971 s 4 replace the rules of the common law *cattle* trespass principle: s 1 (1) (c). For a full review of the authorities relative to the responsibilities of a master of foxhounds see *League Against Cruel Sports Ltd v Scott* [1986] QB 240; [1985] 2 All ER 489.

5 See *Ellis v Loftus Iron Co* (1874) LR 10 CP 10.

6 *Ponting v Noakes* [1894] 2 QB 281.

7 *Manton v Brocklebank* [1923] 2 KB 212, CA (mare kicked horse in field).

8 As to what must be proved when this defence is relied upon see *Wellaway v Courtier* [1918] 1 KB 200 at 203 per Lawrence J; *Park v J Jobson & Son* [1945] 1 All ER 222, CA.

473. Damage by reclaimed animals. If a man reclaims wild animals and puts them on his land, he is liable, if they trespass, for any damage caused by them which it is in their ordinary nature to commit. Thus where pigeons from a dovecot fly on to neighbouring land and eat the corn, their owner is liable in an action for the loss of the corn[1]. Whether it is in the ordinary nature of hived bees to sting men or cattle[2] seems doubtful on the authorities, though it is difficult to resist the fact that everyone knows that they often do so. An interesting question still open is for how long the owner of a reclaimed animal is liable after its escape. It is presumably a question of fact as to whether the animal has reverted to the wild state or not[3].

1 *Dewell v Sanders* (1618) Cro Jac 490, where it was said that a dovecot is not a common nuisance, but that the court may take cognisance of it. Dicta in that case concerning a landowner's right to kill pigeons coming on his land were criticised, and the accuracy of the report of the case was doubted, in *Hamps v Darby* [1948] 2 KB 311, [1948] 2 All ER 474, CA.
2 See para 467 note 5 ante.
3 See *Brady v Warren* [1900] 2 IR 632, where the defendant was held liable for damage done by park deer which had escaped some six years previously, and had wandered about uncontrolled ever since. Cf *Mitchil v Alestree* (1677) 1 Vent 295 per Twisden J.

474. Trespass and straying on highway. The owner of the soil of a highway may bring an action for trespass if cattle depasture his herbage otherwise than in the lawful exercise of grazing rights[1]. If cattle are being lawfully driven along the highway and they crop the roadside herbage, the trespass may be justified as involuntary[2].

The former common law principle whereby, because there was no general obligation on an owner or occupier of land adjoining a highway to fence his land or to keep his domestic animals off the highway, he was not liable for injury inflicted on a user of the highway save in certain exceptional circumstances when his animals escaped on to it, has been abolished by statute, and accordingly the ordinary principles of negligence now apply to such a situation[3].

Where damage is caused by animals straying from unfenced land on to a highway, the person who placed them on the land is not to be regarded as being negligent in so doing if the land is either common land[4], or is situated in an area where fencing is not customary[5], or is a town or village green[6], and if he had a right to place them where he did[7].

Where animals are brought on to a highway a different principle applies[8].

If any horse[9], cattle, sheep, goats or swine are found straying or lying[10] on or at the side of any highway[11], except on such part of it as passes over any common or waste or uninclosed ground[12], the keeper of the animals[13] is liable to a maximum fine on summary conviction of level 3 on the standard scale[14], together with the reasonable expenses, recoverable summarily as a civil debt, of removing the animals to his premises or the common pound or other place provided, and any proper charges of the pound-keeper[15]. This provision does not prejudice or affect any right of pasture which may exist on the side of a highway[16], but a keeper exercising his right must keep his animals from straying, except temporarily, or lying on the actual road[17]. These penalties are provided for the protection of the public, and do not render the keeper liable to an action at law[18]. The release, without lawful authority or excuse, of any animal so impounded or seized for the purpose of being so impounded, or the damaging of any place where it is impounded, is an offence punishable by a maximum fine on summary conviction of level 2 on the standard scale[19].

Cattle[20] found at large in any street[21] in a district to which the Town Police Clauses Act 1847[22] applies, without any person having charge of them, may be impounded, by any constable or resident, in any common pound within the district[23] or in such other place as the local authority may appoint for the purpose; and may be detained until the owner pays the authority a penalty not exceeding £2 and the reasonable expenses of impounding and keeping them[24]. Provision is made for the sale of impounded cattle if the money is not paid within three days[25], and for punishing persons guilty of pound-breach[26].

1 *Stevens v Whistler* (1809) 11 East 51; *Cox v Burbidge* (1863) 13 CBNS 430 at 435 per Erle CJ; *Higgins v Searle* (1909) 100 LT 280, CA, per Cozens-Hardy MR and Buckley LJ; *Heath's Garage Ltd v Hodges* [1916] 2 KB 370 at 377, CA, per Cozens-Hardy MR. See also *Durrant v Child* (1611) 1 Bulst 157; *Haigh v West* [1893] 2 QB 19, CA; and *A-G and Spalding RDC v Garner* [1907] 2 KB 480. As to the rights of the owner of the soil of a highway see further HIGHWAYS.

2 Rolle Abr Trespass K.

3 Animals Act 1971 s 8 (1), which reversed the rule in *Searle v Wallbank* [1947] AC 341, [1947] 1 All ER 12, HL.

4 'Common land' means land subject to rights of common (which includes cattlegates or beastgates and rights of sole or several vesture or herbage or of sole or several pasture, but not rights held for a term of years or from year to year), whether those rights are exercisable at all times or only during limited periods, and waste land of a manor not subject to rights of common, but does not include a town or village green (as to which see note 6 infra) or any land forming part of a highway: Commons Registration Act 1965 s 22 (1); Animals Act 1971 s 11. See COMMONS.

5 'Fencing' includes the construction of any obstacle designed to prevent animals from straying: ibid s 11. It would thus include any ditch or cattle-grid designed for that purpose. Note that no definition is attempted of areas where fencing is not customary, which must remain a question of fact, presumably decided on evidence of local knowledge.

6 'Town or village green' means land which has been allotted by or under any Act for the exercise or recreation of the inhabitants of any locality or on which such inhabitants have a customary right to indulge in lawful sports or pastimes or on which they have indulged in such sports and pastimes as of right for not less than 20 years: Commons Registration Act 1965 s 22 (1); Animals Act 1971 s 11. See COMMONS.

7 Ibid s 8 (2). A person with a right to graze cattle on common land can licence another to graze his cattle, thereby enjoying his protection: *Davies v Davies* [1975] QB 172, [1974] 3 All ER 817, CA. An owner is liable once the animal strays beyond the area of co-existing common land and highway: *Rees v Morgan* (1976) 120 Sol Jo 148.

8 See para 461 ante.

9 'Horse' includes pony, ass and mule: Highways Act 1980 s 329 (1).

10 The offences of allowing to 'stray' and allowing to 'lie' are distinct: *Lawrence v King* (1868) LR 3 QB 345. Animals are not 'straying' if they are under the control of an attendant: *Lawrence v King* supra; *Morris v Jeffries* (1866) LR 1 QB 261; *Sherborn v Wells* (1863) 3 B & S 784; *Golding v Stocking* (1869) LR 4 QB 516; *Horwood v Goodall, Horwood v Hill* (1872) 36 JP 486. If they are 'lying' on or at the side of a highway the presence of a keeper is not in itself an excuse but apparently animals on a journey may be allowed to rest for a reasonable time: *Lawrence v King* supra; *Horwood v Goodall* supra.

11 'Highway' means the whole or part of a highway other than a ferry or waterway, and includes a bridge over or tunnel through which the highway passes: Highways Act 1980 s 328.

12 Ibid s 155 (1). This exception applies only to pieces of land of some considerable size: see *Bothamley v Danby* (1871) 24 LT 656; *Golding v Stocking* (1869) LR 4 QB 516; *Plumbley v Lock* (1902) 67 JP 237, DC. As to rights of pasture see COMMONS.

13 'Keeper' means the person in whose possession the animals are: Highways Act 1980 s 155 (1).

14 Highways Act 1980 ss 155, 310 (s 155 amended by virtue of the Criminal Justice Act 1982 ss 35, 38, 46). As to the standard scale see para 232 note 1 ante. At the date at which this volume states the law, level 3 on that scale is at £400.

15 Highways Act 1980 s 155 (3). As to the recovery of civil debts see the Magistrates' Courts Act 1980 s 58; and MAGISTRATES. Any person lawfully using the highway may remove the animals to the pound, but if he does so he must feed and water them (see the Protection of Animals Act 1911 s 7; and para 472 note 1 post). As to his other duties see *Bignell v Clarke* (1860) 5 H & N 485; *Wilder v Speer* (1838) 8 Ad & El 547.

16 Highways Act 1980 s 155 (5).

17 *Bothamley v Danby* (1871) 24 LT 656; *Golding v Stocking* (1869) LR 4 QB 516.

18 *Heath's Garage Ltd v Hodges* [1916] 2 KB 370, CA. See further *Catchpole v Minster* (1913) 109 LT 953; *Turner v Coates* [1917] 1 KB 670; *Gill v Carson and Nield* [1917] 2 KB 674, DC.

19 Highways Act 1980 ss 155 (4), 310 (and see note 14 supra).

20 'Cattle' in this context includes horses, asses, mules, sheep, goats and swine: Town Police Clauses Act 1847 s 3.

21 For the meaning of 'street' see ibid s 3; and para 374 note 4 ante.
22 Originally the Town Police Clauses Act 1847 applied only to towns where it was incorporated in a local Act (s 1), but the provisions here referred to (ss 24–27) were applied to all boroughs and urban districts by the Public Health Act 1875 s 171, which now extends them throughout England and Wales, except in Greater London (Local Government Act 1972 s 180, Sch 14 Pt II paras 23, 26 (a)). See further LOCAL GOVERNMENT.
23 The local authority may provide and maintain a pound: Town Police Clauses Act 1847 s 27.
24 Ibid s 24. Quaere whether the £2 penalty is per head of cattle or in total.
25 Ibid s 25.
26 Ibid s 26. As to the offence of pound-breach see para 481 post.

475. Liability for trespassing livestock. Where livestock[1] belonging to any person[2] strays on to land in the ownership or occupation of another person and there causes damage[3] to the land or any property on it in that person's ownership or possession, the person to whom the livestock belongs is liable for that damage[4], and also for any expenses reasonably incurred by that other person in keeping the livestock while it cannot be restored to the person to whom it belongs, or while the right of detention is being exercised over it[5], or while it is being ascertained to whom it belongs[6].

Thus the old common law rule of strict liability for cattle trespass irrespective of negligence has been preserved by statute[7], and the aggrieved person has a right of action in trespass.

There is, however, no liability for damage caused by livestock trespassing on another's land where the livestock strayed from a highway and its presence there was a lawful use of the highway[8], nor where the damage is due wholly to the fault[9] of the person suffering it[10]. A person is not to be considered as being at fault in regard to any damage suffered by him by reason only that he could have prevented it by fencing[11], but no one is to be liable for such damage where it is proved that the straying of the livestock on to the land would not have occurred but for a breach by any other person, being someone with an interest in the land, of a duty to fence[12].

Although the Animals Act 1971 binds the Crown, no proceedings under the Act may be brought against the Sovereign in her private capacity[13].

1 'Livestock' means cattle, horses, asses, mules, hinnies, sheep, pigs, goats and poultry, and also deer not in the wild state; and 'poultry' means the domestic varieties of fowls, turkey, geese, ducks, guinea-fowls, pigeons, peacocks and quails: Animals Act 1971 s 11. Dogs (see para 472 ante) and cats (see *Buckle v Holmes* [1926] 2 KB 125, CA) have never created this liability at common law.
2 For this purpose livestock belongs to the person in whose possession it is: Animals Act 1971 s 4 (2).
3 Despite the definition of 'damage' in ibid s 11 as including death or personal injury, it is submitted that the wording of s 4 makes clear that any damage to land and property is included. Moreover, though mere treading down of herbage, or even encumbering the land, may be a sufficient damage (*Ambergate Rly Co v Midland Rly Co* (1853) 2 E & B 793), it seems that damage to game or other animals ferae naturae is not, since they are the subject of only potential, not actual, property (see para 205 ante). Quaere whether damage by infection is included: see *Theyer v Purnell* [1918] 2 KB 333. Thus *Wormald v Cole* [1954] 1 QB 614, [1954] 1 All ER 683, CA, is overruled by the Animals Act 1971 s 1. Damage for which liability exists in any person is to be treated as his fault for the purposes of the Fatal Accidents Act 1976, the Law Reform (Contributory Negligence) Act 1945 and the Limitation Act 1980: Animals Act 1971 s 10; Interpretation Act 1978 s 17 (2) (a): see NEGLIGENCE. For the meaning of 'fault' in this context see the Law Reform (Contributory Negligence) Act 1945 s 4, the Animals Act 1971 s 11; and para 469 note 3 ante.
4 Animals Act 1971 s 4 (1) (a).
5 For the right to detain trespassing livestock see ibid s 7 (2), (3); and para 478 post.
6 Ibid s 4 (1) (b).
7 See *Ellis v Loftus Iron Co* (1874) LR 10 CP 10 at 13 per Brett J; *Tillett v Ward* (1882) 10 QBD 17 at 19 per Lord Coleridge CJ; and *Read v J Lyons & Co Ltd* [1947] AC 156 at 166, [1946] 2 All ER 471 at 474,

HL, per Viscount Simon LC. Presumably the defence of act of God would still be a defence: see *Powell v Salisbury* (1828) 2 Y & J 391.

8 Animals Act 1971 s 5 (5): see further para 476 post.

9 For the meaning of 'fault' see the Law Reform (Contributory Negligence) Act 1945 s 4, the Animals Act 1971 s 11; and para 469 note 3 ante.

10 Animals Act 1971 s 5 (1).

11 For the meaning of 'fencing' see para 474 note 5 ante.

12 Animals Act 1971 s 5 (6). This is designed to overcome the difficulty caused by the decision and the circumstances prevailing in *Crow v Wood* [1971] 1 QB 77, [1970] 3 All ER 425, CA.

13 Animals Act 1971 s 12 (1).

476. Trespass from the highway. An exception to the rule of strict liability for damage done by trespassing livestock[1] exists where the livestock strays from the highway, and its presence there was a lawful use of the highway[2]. In such cases it is necessary to prove negligence, and in the absence of negligence the person to whom the livestock belongs is not liable for damage[3]. It is a risk a man takes who has property adjoining the highway, and the loss falls upon him if he does not take precautions by fencing or otherwise to protect it[4]. Where, therefore, an ox being driven through a street went through an open shop door without any negligence on the drover's part, and did damage before it could be driven out, the owner was not liable[5].

It is submitted, however, that this exception must be modified in the event of an animal straying from a highway on to adjoining land and a wholly unreasonable delay occurring before it is removed[6].

1 See para 475 ante.

2 Animals Act 1971 s 5 (5), which restates the common law position which enabled animals which were trespassing on the highway (eg using it for grazing or for any purpose other than passing or repassing) and which strayed on to adjoining land, to be distrained damage feasant at once: *Dovaston v Payne* (1795) 2 Hy Bl 527.

3 *Tillett v Ward* (1882) 10 QBD 17 at 20 per Lord Coleridge CJ; *Gayler and Pope Ltd v B Davies & Son Ltd* [1924] 2 KB 75; cf *Gilligan v Robb* 1910 SC 856.

4 *Goodwyn v Cheveley* (1859) 4 H & N 631; cf *Fletcher v Rylands* (1866) LR 1 Exch 265 at 286 per Blackburn J; affd sub nom *Rylands and Horrocks v Fletcher* (1868) LR 3 HL 330. On the other hand, a railway company was held not bound to fence against straying and trespassing cattle under the Railways Clauses Consolidation Act 1845 s 68; *Luscombe v Great Western Rly Co* [1899] 2 QB 313.

5 *Tillett v Ward* (1882) 10 QBD 17. It is hardly necessary to support this decision by reference to this exception, for there is no liability for an involuntary trespass, which seems a much shorter ground for the decision. Indeed it is the precise case mentioned in *Mitten v Faudrye* (1626) Poph 161 at 162, of a man driving 'goods' through a town, one of which goes into another man's house, as an instance of an involuntary trespass. The decision did not turn on the fact that the door was open: see *Gayler and Pope Ltd v B Davies & Son Ltd* [1924] 2 KB 75 at 83.

6 See *Goodwyn v Cheveley* (1859) 4 H & N 631.

477. No trespass by wild animals. No action will lie for the trespass of animals ferae naturae on the land of another, for the owner has only a qualified property in them while they are alive, and they go with and belong to the soil; as soon as they have crossed from the land of one man to that of another, the latter, though not the owner, has the right to kill them and reduce them into possession[1]. An owner of land, therefore, is not liable for the damage done by rabbits or other wild animals that come from his land (for his neighbour may kill them as soon as they come on his land[2]) unless he brings on to his land a greater quantity of game or wild animals than can reasonably and properly be kept on it, in which case he is liable for damage done by them on the principle that one must so use one's own property as not to injure that of another[3].

It is apprehended that an action will not lie unless the defendant has actually brought the animals on to the land; a mere failure to keep the existing stock within reasonable limits would not, apart from express agreement to do so, be sufficient; and the fact that rabbits have become a nuisance owing to their numbers does not justify entering upon the land of another and digging up the burrows to abate the nuisance[4].

1 See paras 205, 208 ante.
2 Cf *Boulston's Case* (1597) 5 Co Rep 104b; *Stearn v Prentice Bros Ltd* [1919] 1 KB 394 (rats escaping from defendants' premises and damaging plaintiff's corn); *Brady v Warren* [1900] 2 IR 632.
3 *Farrer v Nelson* (1885) 15 QBD 258 at 260 per Pollock B (shooting tenant brought on to the land in coops 450 pheasants which had been reared elsewhere: held liable for damage); *Seligman v Docker* [1949] Ch 53, [1948] 2 All ER 887. Cf *Boulston's Case* (1597) 5 Co Rep 104b, where the making of the rabbit burrows was an active interference with the existing state of things on the land; *Hilton v Green* (1862) 2 F & F 821; *Birkbeck v Paget* (1862) 31 Beav 403. Where the tenant of an agricultural holding has sustained damage to his crops from game which he has not the right to kill, he is entitled to statutory compensation against his landlord and, where the right to kill the game is vested in some person other than the landlord, the landlord is entitled to be indemnified by that other person; see the Agricultural Holdings Act 1986 s 20; and AGRICULTURE vol 1 (2) (Reissue) para 395. As to the duty imposed on occupiers to clear and free the land of rabbits see AGRICULTURE vol 1(2) (Reissue) paras 657, 658.
4 *Cooper v Marshall* (1757) 1 Burr 259.

(ii) Remedies for Trespass; Distress

478. Right to detain trespassing livestock. Where livestock[1] strays on to any land, the occupier of the land has not only a right of action against the person to whom the livestock belongs for any damage it may there cause[2], but also an immediate right to detain the livestock, provided that at the time it is not under anyone's control[3].

The right of detention ceases either:

(1) at the end of a period of 48 hours, unless within that period notice of the detention has been given to the officer in charge of a police station and also, if the person exercising the right of detention knows to whom the livestock belongs, to that person[4]; or

(2) when sufficient money is tendered to satisfy any claim for damage caused by the livestock on the land and any expenses reasonably incurred in keeping it[5]; or

(3) if no such claim exists[6], when the livestock is claimed by a person entitled to its possession[7]; or

(4) when a court orders the return of the livestock[8].

Any person exercising this power of detention is liable for any damage caused to the detained livestock by a failure to treat it with reasonable care and to supply it with adequate food and water[9].

The above right of detention and its corollary, the right of sale after detention[10], replaces the old common law remedy of distress damage feasant[11], which had become virtually obsolete. The old right to distrain carried no right of pursuit[12], and it seems that this would apply equally to its successor.

1 For the meaning of 'livestock' see para 475 note 1 ante.
2 As to this right of action see para 475 ante.
3 Animals Act 1971 s 7 (2). Presumably one reason for the inclusion of the provision about the livestock being under anyone's control is to avoid a possible breach of the peace.

4 Ibid s 7 (3) (a).
5 Ibid s 7 (3) (b). As to such a claim and expenses see s 4 (1); and para 475 ante.
6 Ie no claim under ibid s 4. No claim can exist where there has been no damage to land or property by the trespassing livestock or any expenses in keeping it. Moreover, no claim can lie for this purpose in respect of damage done by or expenses incurred in connection with the livestock before the particular straying which led to the detention: s 7 (7).
7 Ibid s 7 (3) (c). This person obviously need not be the owner, or even someone on his behalf but, whatever right to possession the claimant may have, he must clearly establish it to the reasonable satisfaction of the person detaining the livestock.
8 Ibid s 7 (2).
9 Ibid s 7 (6). There is also an obligation under the Protection of Animals Act 1911 s 7 to feed and water any impounded livestock, and failure to do so is an offence; see para 481 note 1 post.
10 See para 479 post.
11 Animals Act 1971 s 7 (1). It is submitted that since the statutory right is similar, in that it is a mere right of detention, albeit linked with a later right of sale, the person detaining the livestock would similarly have no right to use it in any way, 'for he hath it by law only for a gage' (*Bagshawe v Goward* (1607) Cro Jac 147); such a user entitled the owner to interfere and recover his beast, the distrainor by his action becoming a trespasser ab initio: see *Smith v Wright* (1861) 6 H & N 821.
12 *Vaspor v Edwards* (1701) 12 Mod Rep 658; cf *Clement v Milner* (1800) 3 Esp 95.

479. Right to sell detained livestock. Where livestock[1] has been lawfully detained[2] for a period of not less than 14 days after straying on to land other than that of the person to whom it belongs[3], the detainer may sell it, either at a market or by public auction, unless proceedings are then pending for the return of the livestock or for any claim[4] by the detainer for damage done by the livestock or for expenses in keeping it[5].

Where such a sale takes place and the proceeds of sale, less the costs of and incidental to it, exceed the amount of any claim which the vendor had in respect of such damage and expenses, then the excess is recoverable from him by the person who would be entitled to the possession of the livestock but for the sale[6].

1 For the meaning of 'livestock' see para 475 note 1 ante.
2 As to detention see para 478 ante.
3 For this purpose livestock belongs to the person in whose possession it is: Animals Act 1971 s 4 (2).
4 Ie under ibid s 4; see para 475 ante.
5 Ibid s 7 (4). As to markets generally see MARKETS AND FAIRS.
6 Ibid s 7 (5).

480. Distress on agisted animals. Agisted animals[1] are not, at common law, privileged from distress for rent[2] any more than cattle that have escaped on to the land[3], except in the case of a temporary agistment on the road to or at a fair or market[4], which is a consequence arising out of the necessity for their refreshment, and is an instance of a privilege arising as accessory to another privilege[5].

In the case of an agricultural holding[6] there is a statutory exemption: livestock taken in by the tenant of such a holding to be fed at a fair price[7] may not be distrained by the landlord for rent where there is other sufficient distress to be found and, if they are distrained by reason of there being no other sufficient distress, the landlord can only recover by such distress rent up to the price of the feeding which remains unpaid[8], subject to the owner's right to redeem the livestock by paying that price to the distrainor[9]. So long as any portion of the livestock remains on the holding the right to distrain extends to the full extent of the unpaid price of feeding the whole of the livestock[10].

1 As to agistment generally see paras 214–216 ante.

2 Bac Abr, Distress B; Rolle Abr 669. But it is perhaps open to argument that an exemption from liability to be distrained may be claimed on the ground that agisted animals are delivered to the agister in the regular way of his trade: *Miles v Furber* (1873) LR 8 QB 77 at 83 per Mellor J.
3 Co Litt 47a.
4 2 Saund 290 n 7; *Nugent v Kirwan* (1838) 1 Jebb & S 97.
5 Per Alderson B in *Muspratt v Gregory* (1836) 1 M & W 633 at 647.
6 For the meaning of 'agricultural holding' see AGRICULTURE vol 1 (2) (Reissue) para 301.
7 The 'fair price' need not necessarily be money. Cows agisted on the terms of 'milk for meat' (a very common form of contract by which the farmer takes the milk of the cows, instead of a money payment, in return for their feed) are 'taken in to be fed at a fair price' within the meaning of this provision, and are entitled to the partial exemption (*London and Yorkshire Bank v Belton* (1885) 15 QBD 457), but livestock taken in under a contract for the letting of the herbage or grazing of land are not protected by this provision: *Masters v Green* (1888) 20 QBD 807. Cf *Burt v Moore* (1793) 5 Term Rep 329.
8 Agricultural Holdings Act 1986 s 18 (1), (2). 'Livestock' includes any animal capable of being distrained: s 18 (5).
9 Ibid s 18 (3).
10 Ibid s 18 (4).

481. Unlawful release of impounded animals.

At common law pound-breach is an indictable offence, though it may perhaps be regarded as virtually obsolete. It consists in the forcible release of cattle or other animals lawfully placed in a proper pound[1], or in forcibly damaging or destroying the pound with that object[2].

There is also a summary procedure before justices whereby any person who releases or attempts to release from a pound any horse, ass, sheep, swine or other beast or cattle, including cows and heifers[3], lawfully seized for the purpose of being impounded in consequence of having been found wandering, straying, lying or being depastured on any inclosed land without the consent of the owner or occupier, or damages or destroys any part of the pound, commits an offence for which he is liable to a maximum fine on conviction of level 1 on the standard scale, together with reasonable expenses, and imprisonment in default of payment[4]. This jurisdiction is, however, ousted if any question arises as to title to lands, bankruptcy, execution under legal process, or any obligation to maintain walls or fences[5]. In places to which the Town Police Clauses Act 1847 applies[6], a similar offence is punishable on summary conviction by imprisonment for a term not exceeding three months[7].

Now that the right of distress damage feasant has been abolished in relation to animals[8], the only remaining relevance of pounds would seem to be in connection with distress for rent[9], or after removal of any animal from the highway under the Highways Act 1980[10].

1 Animals impounded or confined in a pound (which includes any receptacle of a like nature: Protection of Animals Act 1911 s 15 (f)) must be properly fed and watered; failure to do so on the part of the person impounding them is summarily punishable by a maximum fine of level 1 on the standard scale: s 7 (1) (amended by virtue of the Criminal Law Act 1977 s 31 and by virtue of the Criminal Justice Act 1982 s 46). As to the standard scale see para 232 note 1 ante. At the date at which this volume states the law, level 1 on that scale is at £50. The duty to feed and water is not the pound keeper's: *Dargan v Davies* (1877) 2 QBD 118. If impounded animals are without sufficient suitable food and water for six successive hours any person may enter the pound to feed and water them: Protection of Animals Act 1911 s 7 (2). The reasonable cost of food and water supplied is recoverable summarily as a civil debt: s 7 (3); see the Magistrates' Courts Act 1980 s 58; and MAGISTRATES.
2 See *R v Bradshaw* (1835) 7 C & P 233; *Green v Duckett* (1883) 11 QBD 275; and *R v Butterfield* (1893) 17 Cox CC 598. See further CRIMINAL LAW.
3 *R v Gee* (1885) 49 JP 212.
4 Pound-breach Act 1843 s 1 (amended by virtue of the Criminal Justice Act 1982 ss 38, 46). As to the standard scale see note 1 supra.

5 Pound-breach Act 1843 s 2.
6 As to the application of this Act see para 474 note 22 ante.
7 Town Police Clauses Act 1847 s 26.
8 Animals Act 1971 s 7 (1).
9 As to distress on agisted animals see para 480 ante; as to distress generally see DISTRESS.
10 See para 474 ante.

8. ANIMAL HEALTH

(1) INTRODUCTION

482. Statutory provisions. The common law position with its accent on liability to third parties[1] has been greatly added to in modern times by legislation aimed at the eradication and prevention of disease in animals, and for these purposes statutory controls have been established over the whole field of animal movement, treatment and slaughter. The principal provisions are to be found in the Animal Health Act 1981 and in regulations made thereunder[2].

Wide powers are conferred by the Act on the ministers[3] and upon local authorities[4], upon whom further powers may be conferred by the ministers[5].

Measures have also been taken by the European Communities to improve the health of livestock[6].

1 See para 471 ante.
2 The Animal Health Act 1981 consolidates the Diseases of Animals Acts 1935, 1950 and 1975, the Ponies Act 1969, the Rabies Act 1974 and certain related enactments: see the Animal Health Act 1981, long title. Importation orders made under the Diseases of Animals Act 1950 ss 24–33 (substituted and amended by the Diseases of Animals Act 1975 (repealed) ss 1, 4 (3), Sch 2) continue in force as if s 1 of the 1975 Act had not come into operation, except that they may be varied or revoked as if made under the Animal Health Act 1981 s 10: s 95 (1), (2). Other orders made under the Acts repealed by the 1981 Act have effect by virtue of the Interpretation Act 1978 s 17 (2) (b).
3 'The ministers' means, in relation to the whole of Great Britain, the Minister of Agriculture, Fisheries and Food, the Secretary of State for Scotland and the Secretary of State for Wales, acting jointly: ibid s 86 (1) (c).
4 For the meaning of 'local authority' see para 536 post.
5 See para 530 post.
6 See EC Council Directive 78/52, which established national plans for the eradication of brucellosis, tuberculosis and enzootic leukosis in cattle. As to European Community control over animal health see AGRICULTURE vol 1 (2) (Reissue) para 1028 et seq.

483. Meaning of 'animals'. Unless the context otherwise requires, the word 'animals' in the Animal Health Act 1981 generally means cattle[1], sheep and goats, and all other ruminating animals and swine[2]. The ministers[3] may, however, by order[4] extend this definition to include, for any purpose of the Act, any kind of mammal except man, and any kind of four-footed beast which is not a mammal[5], and to include for any purpose of the Act (except so far as it relates to disease) fish, reptiles, crustaceans or other cold-blooded creatures of any species[6]. Additionally, under certain provisions of the Act the meaning given above does not apply[7].

1 'Cattle' means bulls, cows, steers, heifers and calves: Animal Health Act 1981 s 89 (1).

2　Ibid s 87 (1). The Act generally has effect in relation to poultry as it does in relation to animals: ibid s 87 (4). For the meaning of 'poultry' see para 517 post.

3　As to the ministers see para 482 note 3 ante.

4　This power has been frequently exercised. See in particular the Diseases of Animals (Extension of Definitions) Order 1952, SI 1952/1236, art 2, which extends the definition to include horses, asses, mules and jennets. See also the Control of Dogs Order of 1930, SR & O 1930/399 (amended by SR & O 1930/683, SR & O 1931/80 and SI 1976/919); the Anthrax Order of 1938, SR & O 1938/204 (amended by SI 1972/971); the Diseases of Animals (Ascertainment of Compensation) Order 1959, SI 1959/1335 (amended by SI 1964/1150 and SI 1964/1152); the Hares (Control of Importation) Order 1965, SI 1965/2040 (amended by SI 1990/2371); the Transit of Animals (General) Order 1973, SI 1973/1377 (amended by SI 1975/1024, SI 1988/815 and SI 1988/851); the Rabies (Importation of Dogs, Cats and Other Mammals) Order 1974, SI 1974/2211 (amended by SI 1977/361, SI 1984/1182, SI 1986/2062 and SI 1990/2371); the Importation of Processed Animal Protein Order 1981, SI 1981/677 (amended by SI 1982/459 and SI 1990/2371); the Aujeszky's Disease Order 1983, SI 1983/344; the Diseases of Animals (Ascertainment of Disease) Order 1985, SI 1985/1765; the Infectious Diseases of Horses Order 1987, SI 1987/790; the Bovine Spongiform Encephalopathy (No 2) Order 1988, SI 1988/2299 (amended by SI 1990/1930); the Zoonoses Order 1989, SI 1989/285; the Processed Animal Protein Order 1989, SI 1989/661; the Movement of Animals (Restrictions) Order 1990, SI 1990/760 (amended by SI 1991/1155 and SI 1991/1251); the Specified Diseases (Notification) Order 1991, SI 1991/1155.

　　As to the exercise of the power in relation to the definition of poultry see para 517 post.

5　Animal Health Act 1981 s 87 (2).

6　Ibid s 87 (3). This latter power may only be exercised in respect of creatures not covered by the power available under s 87 (2) (see text and note 4 supra): s 87 (3).

7　See eg ibid s 10 (4) and Sch 2.

484. Meaning of 'disease'. Unless the context otherwise requires, and except in relation to poultry[1], the word 'disease' in the Animal Health Act 1981 means cattle plague or rinderpest[2], contagious pleuro-pneumonia of cattle, foot-and-mouth disease, sheep-pox, sheep scab or swine fever[3]. The ministers[4] may, however, by order[5] extend this definition to include, for any purpose of the Act, any other disease of animals[6]. Additionally, under certain provisions of the Act the meaning given above does not apply[7].

1　As to which see the Animal Health Act 1981 s 88 (3); and para 517 post.

2　See ibid s 89 (1).

3　Ibid ss 88 (1), 89 (1). 'Swine-fever' means typhoid fever of swine, soldier purples, red disease, hog cholera or swine-plague: s 89 (1).

4　See para 483 note 3 ante.

5　See the Anthrax Order of 1938, SR & O 1938/204 (amended by SI 1972/971); the Brucellosis Melitensis Order of 1940, SR & O 1940/1251 (amended by SR & O 1942/143 and SI 1977/945); the Diseases of Animals (Extension of Definitions) Order 1952, SI 1952/1236; the Hares (Control of Importation) Order 1965, SI 1965/2040 (amended by SI 1990/2371); the Diseases of Animals (Extension of Definitions) Order 1971, SI 1971/531; the Swine Vesicular Disease Order 1972, SI 1972/1980 (amended by SI 1973/101 and SI 1977/944); the Teschen Disease Order 1974, SI 1974/1185; the Rabies (Control) Order 1974, SI 1974/2212; the Importation of Equine Animals Order 1979, SI 1979/1701 (amended by SI 1990/2371); the Enzootic Bovine Leukosis Order 1980, SI 1980/79; the African Swine Fever Order 1980, SI 1980/145; the Warble Fly (England and Wales) Order 1982, SI 1982/234 (amended by SI 1985/328, SI 1987/1601 and SI 1989/244); the Aujeszky's Disease Order 1983, SI 1983/344; the Tuberculosis (England and Wales) Order 1984, SI 1984/1943 (amended by SI 1990/1869); the Diseases of Animals (Ascertainment of Disease) Order 1985, SI 1985/1765; the Warble Fly (Ascertainment of Infestation) (England and Wales) Order 1985, SI 1985/1766; the Zoonoses Order 1988, SI 1988/2264 (amended by SI 1988/2299); the Bovine Spongiform Encephalopathy (No 2) Order 1988, SI 1988/2299 (amended by SI 1990/1930); the Blue Eared Pig Disease Order 1991, SI 1991/1381.

　　As to the diseases applicable to poultry see para 517 post.

6　Animal Health Act 1981 s 88 (2).

7　See eg ibid ss 3 (1), 5 (1), 10 (4), Sch 2.

(2) ERADICATION AND PREVENTION OF DISEASE

(i) General

485. Eradication of disease. Power is given to the ministers[1] to expend such sums, with Treasury approval, as they think fit, with the object of eradicating as far as practicable diseases of animals in Great Britain[2]. For the purpose of obtaining information required for these purposes, the ministers may authorise in writing any veterinary inspector or other ministry officer to inspect animals, and any person so authorised may at reasonable times on producing his authority if demanded enter on any land or premises and apply such tests and take such samples as he considers necessary[3]. In this connection 'animals' include horses and poultry and 'disease' is not restricted by its definition in the Animal Health Act 1981[4]. The ministers may make orders declaring eradication areas for cattle for any particular disease when they are satisfied that a substantial majority of the cattle therein are free from the disease[5], and declaring attested areas when they are satisfied that the disease is for practical purposes non-existent[6]. They may also make orders prohibiting and regulating the movement of cattle into, out of or within such areas or, if the area is an eradication or attested area for brucellosis, imposing necessary restrictions there for the purpose of eradicating that disease[7].

The appropriate minister[8] also has power to draw up a scheme, with Treasury consent, for the purpose of eradicating brucellosis in cattle[9].

The ministers[10] have power, with Treasury approval, to afford veterinary services, including diagnostic services, to persons who carry on livestock businesses and who participate in approved arrangements for keeping their stock so far as practicable free from disease and in good health[11].

1 See para 482 note 3 ante. As to European Community provision for eradication and control see AGRICULTURE vol 1 (2) (Reissue) para 1030.
2 Animal Health Act 1981 s 3 (1). The Pig Industry Levy Act 1983 imposes a levy on the pig industry to cover the costs of eradicating Aujeszky's disease: see AGRICULTURE vol 1 (2) (Reissue) para 810.
3 Animal Health Act 1981 s 3 (2), (3). See the Processed Animal Protein Order 1989, SI 1989/661.
4 Animal Health Act 1981 ss 3 (1), 87 (4). For the meaning of 'disease' under the 1981 Act in relation to animals see para 484 ante, and, in relation to poultry para 517 post.
5 Ibid s 6 (a).
6 Ibid s 6 (b). The whole of England and Wales, subject to certain exceptions, is now an attested area for purposes connected with the control of tuberculosis: see the Tuberculosis (England and Wales) Attested Area) Order 1960, SI 1960/1708.
7 Animal Health Act 1981 s 6 (c). See the Brucellosis (England and Wales) Order 1981, SI 1981/1455 (amended by SI 1986/2295).
8 For these purposes 'appropriate minister' means the Minister of Agriculture, Fisheries and Food or, in relation to Scotland the Secretary of State: Agriculture Act 1970 s 106 (9).
9 Agriculture Act 1970 s 106 (1): see AGRICULTURE vol 1 (2) (Reissue) para 609. See the Brucellosis Incentive Payments Scheme 1977, SI 1977/1303 (amended by SI 1978/594). It is an offence to offer for sale otherwise than for slaughter any animal known to be a reactor to brucella abortus: Agriculture Act 1970 s 106 (4) (amended by virtue of the Criminal Justice Act 1982 ss 38, 46); see para 515 post.
10 See note 1 supra.
11 Animal Health Act 1981 s 5 (1). 'Disease' is not restricted by its definition in the 1981 Act: s 5 (1). As to the regulation of the manufacture of and other matters connected with veterinary therapeutic substances see ibid s 5 (2), Sch 1; and MEDICINE vol 30 para 621.

486. Control of zoonoses. With a view to reducing the risk to human health from any disease[1] of, or organism carried in, animals[2] the ministers[3] may by order designate any such disease or organism which in their opinion constitutes such a risk[4], may modify in relation to a designated disease the effect of any provision of the Animal Health Act 1981 which has effect in relation to the disease[5], and may, subject to any such modification, apply any provision of that Act in relation to the presence of a designated organism in an animal as if the presence of the organism were a disease to which that Act applied[6].

The ministers may by order require a person who, in specified circumstances, knows or has reason to suspect that an animal of a specified description is or was affected with a designated disease or is or was a carrier of a designated organism to furnish information to a specified person in a specified form and time[7], and, if it appears to the appropriate minister[8] that a person may have information relating to such an animal, he may by written notice require him to furnish it to a specified person in a specified form and time[9].

A veterinary inspector[10] who has reason to believe that such an animal is or has been on any land may, on producing if required evidence of his authority, enter on the land and make tests and take samples there, and may require the owner or person having charge of any animals there to take specified steps to collect or restrain them so as to facilitate the making of tests and taking of samples[11].

A person who fails to comply with any requirement imposed on him by these provisions or who, being required to furnish information, knowingly or recklessly furnishes information which is false in a material particular[12], is guilty of an offence[13].

1 'Disease' is not here restricted by its definition in the Animal Health Act 1981: ss 29 (1), 30 (1).
2 'Animals' for this purpose includes poultry: ibid s 87 (4). A zoonose is a disease which can be communicated from one kind of animal to another or to a human being: Oxford English Dictionary.
3 See para 482 note 3 ante.
4 Animal Health Act 1981 s 29 (1). Bovine spongiform encephalopathy, salmonella and brucella have been so designated: Zoonoses Order 1988, SI 1988/2264 (amended by SI 1988/2299); Zoonoses Order 1989, SI 1989/285.
5 Animal Health Act 1981 s 29 (2) (a).
6 Ibid s 29 (2) (b). For diseases to which the 1981 Act applies see para 441 ante.
7 Ibid s 29 (3). As to designated diseases and organisms see note 4 supra.
8 'The appropriate minister' means the Minister of Agriculture, Fisheries and Food in relation to England and the Secretary of State in relation to Scotland and Wales: ibid s 86 (1) (b).
9 Ibid s 30 (1).
10 As to veterinary inspectors see para 535 post.
11 Animal Health Act 1981 s 30 (2).
12 As to the meaning of 'false in a material particular' see para 504 note 7 post.
13 Animal Health Act 1981 s 30 (3). For penalties see para 514 post.

(ii) Notice of Disease; Separation and Treatment

487. Notice of disease. Every person having in his possession or under his charge an animal affected with disease[1] must with all practicable speed give notice[2] that the animal is affected to a local police constable[3], who must forthwith give information thereof to such person or authority as the ministers[4] by order direct[5]. Orders have been made[6], additionally, containing requirements as to the notices to be given to or by various persons and authorities in the case of particular diseases[7]. In general, these orders require anyone with a diseased animal in his possession or under his charge, and any veterinary surgeon who examines such an animal in the course of his duties, to give notice of the fact forthwith to the local veterinary inspector[8].

Where a local authority receives notice of disease in a carcase of an animal[9] that has died or been slaughtered in the district of another local authority, it must forthwith inform that other authority[10].

Where there is ground for suspecting that any of certain diseases exists or has within a prescribed period existed on any premises, a veterinary inspector must make inquiries and examine the animals and any carcases on the premises concerned, for which purpose he has a power of entry and persons concerned must afford him the necessary facilities[11]. If satisfied that there are reasonable grounds for suspecting an animal or carcase to be affected with certain diseases he must certify accordingly to the ministry and notify prescribed authorities, such as the police, local authorities and the nearest railway station[12].

In the case of certain diseases restrictions come into force immediately the veterinary inspector certifies that the disease exists, and for a limited period it is unlawful to move any animal out of an area within five miles of the place of the outbreak or along or across any road there, although the inspector may licence any necessary movement, and the period and area may be extended[13].

1 For the meaning of 'animal' and 'disease' see paras 483, 484 ante.
2 The burden of proof is on the accused to show that he gave the notice, not on the prosecution to show that he did not: *Huggins v Ward* (1873) LR 8 QB 521. That burden is discharged on a balance of probabilities: see *R v Carr-Briant* [1943] KB 607, [1943] 2 All ER 156, CCA, and *R v Dunbar* [1958] 1 QB 1, [1957] 2 All ER 737, CCA. The accused must know the animal was diseased (*Nichols v Hall* (1873) LR 8 CP 322; and cf *Carroll v Ewers* (1873) IR 7 CL 226); but knowledge is presumed unless he shows to the court's satisfaction that he had no knowledge and could not with reasonable diligence have obtained it: Animal Health Act 1981 s 79 (2). See also *Maclean v Laidlaw* 1909 SC 68; *Wilson v Yates* (1927) 91 JP 188, 44 TLR 25.
3 Animal Health Act 1981 s 15 (1) (b).
4 See para 482 note 3 ante.
5 Animal Health Act 1981 s 15 (3).
6 See the Animals (Miscellaneous Provisions) Order of 1927, SR & O 1927/290, art 12; Animals (Miscellaneous Provisions) Order of 1938, SR & O 1938/197, art 3; Cattle Plague Order of 1928, SR & O 1928/206, art 1 (substituted by SR & O 1938/194); Pleuro-Pneumonia Order of 1928, SR & O 1928/205, art 1 (substituted by SR & O 1938/195); Sheep-Pox Order of 1938, SR & O 1938/229, art 1; Anthrax Order of 1938, SR & O 1938/204, art 1; Swine Fever Order 1963, SI 1963/286, art 3; Teschen Disease Order 1974, SI 1974/1185, art 4; Rabies (Control) Order 1974, SI 1974/2212, art 4 (see para 493 post); Enzootic Bovine Leukosis Order 1980, SI 1980/79, art 4; Warble Fly (England and Wales) Order 1982, SI 1982/234, art 4 (amended by SI 1985/328); Aujeszky's Disease Order 1983, SI 1983/344, art 5; Foot-and-Mouth Disease Order 1983, SI 1983/1950, art 4; Tuberculosis (England and Wales) Order 1984, SI 1984/1943, arts 5, 6; Sheep Scab Order 1986, SI 1986/862, art 3; Infectious Diseases of Horses Order 1987, SI 1987/790, art 4; Bovine Spongiform Encephalopathy (No 2) Order 1988, SI 1988/2299, art 4 (amended by SI 1990/1930); Tuberculosis (Deer) Order 1989, SI 1989/878, art 4; Blue Eared Pig Disease Order 1991, SI 1991/1381, art 4. See also the Specified Diseases (Notification) Order 1991, SI 1991/1155, which sets out notification requirements in relation to: lumpy skin disease (cattle); blue tongue and Rift valley fever (cattle and sheep); vesicular stomatitis (horses, zebras, cattle, pigs); peste des petits ruminants (ungulates); goat pox (goats); and viral haemorrhagic disease (rabbits).
7 See the Animal Health Act 1981 s 15 (4).
8 As to veterinary inspectors see para 535 post. For the exact requirements as to notification see the orders listed in note 6 supra. If a veterinary surgeon or veterinary practitioner notifies a local authority of disease in pursuance of an order under the Act requiring such notification, he is to be paid the fee (not exceeding 12p) prescribed in the order: ibid s 15 (6). As to veterinary surgeons and practitioners see paras 547, 548 post.

9 'Animal' in this context includes cattle, sheep, goats and all other ruminating animals, and swine, horses, asses, mules, dogs and cats: Animals (Miscellaneous Provisions) Order of 1938, SR & O 1938/197, art 3.
10 Ibid art 3.
11 See the Anthrax Order of 1938 art 4; Cattle Plague Order of 1928 art 4 (amended by SR & O 1938/194); Pleuro-Pneumonia Order of 1928 art 4 (amended by SR & O 1938/195); Sheep-Pox Order of 1938 arts 3, 4; Swine Fever Order 1963 art 5; Teschen Disease Order 1974 art 6; Rabies (Control) Order 1974 art 6; Enzootic Bovine Leukosis Order 1980 art 6; Warble Fly (England and Wales) Order 1982 art 5 (amended by SI 1987/1601, SI 1989/244); Aujeszky's Disease Order 1983 art 8; Foot-and-Mouth Disease Order 1983 art 6; Tuberculosis (England and Wales) Order 1984 art 7; Sheep Scab Order 1986 art 6; Infectious Diseases of Horses Order 1987 art 6; Bovine Spongiform Encephalopathy (No 2) Order 1988 art 6; Tuberculosis (Deer) Order 1989 art 6; Blue Eared Pig Disease Order 1991 art 6. See also the Movement of Animals (Restrictions) Order 1990, SI 1990/760 (amended by SI 1991/1155 and SI 1991/1251), art 5, which, additionally, gives the veterinary inspector power to mark animals. The obliteration of that mark is an offence against the Animal Health Act 1981: Movement of Animals (Restrictions) Order 1990 art 8 (a). As to penalties for offences against that Act see para 513 post.
12 See the Cattle Plague Order of 1928 art 5; Sheep-Pox Order of 1938 art 4.
13 See the Cattle Plague Order of 1928 art 6; Sheep-Pox Order of 1938 art 5. For similar restrictions see also Foot-and-Mouth Disease Order 1983 art 8.

488. Information as to diseased animals. Every person who has or has had in his possession or under his charge any animal[1] affected with or suspected of disease[2], or any animal which has been in any way in contact with such an animal, or who, being an auctioneer, has sold or offered for sale any such animal, must, if required in writing by the Ministry of Agriculture, Fisheries and Food, the local authority[3] or an inspector, give all information in his possession as to the animal and its movements and the persons through or into whose hands it has passed[4]. Refusal to give information or the giving of false information is an offence under the Animal Health Act 1981[5].

1 'Animal' in this context means cattle, sheep, goats, all other ruminating animals, swine, horses, asses, mules, dogs and other canine animals: Animals (Miscellaneous Provisions) Order of 1927, SR & O 1927/290, art 1.
2 'Disease' includes any disease which is by order declared to be a disease for the purposes of the Animal Health Act 1981 (see para 484 ante): Animals (Miscellaneous Provisions) Order of 1927 art 12 (2).
3 As to local authorities see para 536 post.
4 Animals (Miscellaneous Provisions) Order of 1927 art 12 (1). See also para 486 text and notes 7, 9 ante.
5 Ibid art 12 (1). As to such offences see paras 514, 515 post.

489. Separation and treatment. Every person having in his possession or under his charge an animal affected with disease[1] must as far as practicable keep it separate from animals not so affected[2].

For the purpose of preventing the spread of disease the ministers[3] may cause to be treated with serum or vaccine or both any animal or bird which has been in contact with a diseased animal or bird or which appears to the ministers to be or to have been exposed to the infection of disease, or which is in an infected area[4]. These powers extend to the taking of any action necessary for enabling the appropriate treatment to be administered or which is otherwise required in connection with such treatment, and for the purpose of exercising them any officer of the minister may, subject to producing his authority on demand, enter any land or premises, taking with him any other necessary persons[5].

1 For the meanings of 'animal' and 'disease' see paras 483, 484 ante.
2 Animal Health Act 1981 s 15 (1) (a). See also para 500 post.
3 See para 482 note 3 ante.
4 Animal Health Act 1981 s 16 (1). As to infected areas see para 496 post. See the Foot-and-Mouth Disease (Infected Areas) (Vaccination) Order 1972, SI 1972/1509.
5 Animal Health Act 1981 s 16 (2). 'Minister' means in relation to the whole of Great Britain, the Minister of Agriculture, Fisheries and Food: s 86 (1) (a).

490. Cleansing and disinfection. The ministers[1] may make such orders[2] as they think fit for: (1) prescribing and regulating the cleansing and disinfection of places used for the holding of markets, fairs, exhibitions or sales of animals, or for lairage of animals, and yards, sheds, stables and other places used for animals[3]; (2) prescribing and regulating the cleansing and disinfection of vessels, aircraft, vehicles and pens and other places, used for the carrying of animals for hire or connected purposes[4]; (3) prescribing and regulating the disinfection of the clothes of persons coming in contact with or employed about diseased or suspected animals and the use of precautions against the spreading of disease by such persons[5]; and (4) prescribing modes of cleansing and disinfection[6]. In particular disinfectants have been approved in respect of the orders relating to foot-and-mouth disease, swine vesicular disease, fowl pest and tuberculosis, and in respect of general orders in which there is a requirement for disinfection[7].

If a person is charged with an offence against the Animal Health Act 1981 in not having duly cleansed or disinfected any place, vessel, aircraft vehicle or thing of his or in his charge, and a presumption is raised against him by the prosecution, it is for him to prove that the cleansing and disinfection was carried out[8].

1 See para 482 note 3 ante.
2 The orders made or having effect wholly or partly under the provisions described in this paragraph are: the Markets, Sales and Lairs Orders of 1925, SR & O 1925/1349 (amended by SR & O 1926/546 and SR & O 1927/982); the Transit of Animals Order of 1927, SR & O 1927/289 (amended by SR & O 1927/399, SR & O 1939/501, SI 1975/1024 and SI 1977/944); the Animals (Miscellaneous Provisions) Order of 1927, SR & O 1927/290 (amended by SR & O 1936/1297, SR & O 1938/197, SI 1953/37, SI 1953/38, SI 1959/1335, SI 1974/1185, SI 1975/888 (revoked) and SI 1976/919); the Pleuro-Pneumonia Order of 1928, SR & O 1928/205 (amended by SR & O and SI 1977/944); the Cattle Plague Order of 1928, SR & O 1928/206 (amended by SR & O 1938/194 and SI 1977/944); the Anthrax Order of 1938, SR & O 1938/204; the Sheep-Pox Order of 1938, SR & O 1938/229 (amended by SI 1977/944); the Brucellosis Melitensis Order of 1940, SR & O 1940/1251 (amended by SR & O 1942/143 and SI 1977/945); the Horses (Sea Transport) Order 1952, SI 1952/1291 (amended by SI 1958/1272); the Psittacosis or Ornithosis Order 1953, SI 1953/38; the Fowl Pest (Infected Areas Restrictions) Order 1956, SI 1956/1611 (amended by SI 1958/1442 and SI 1983/941) (see para 478 post); the Swine Fever Order 1963, SI 1963/286 (amended by SI 1976/919, SI 1990/2487, SI 1991/1030); the Export of Horses (Protection) Order 1969, SI 1969/1784; The Teschen Disease Order 1974, SI 1974/1185; the Movement and Sale of Pigs Order 1975, SI 1975/203 (amended by SI 1975/346, SI 1977/944 and SI 1987/233); the Transit of Animals (Road and Rail) Order 1975, SI 1975/1024 (amended by SI 1979/1013 and SI 1988/815); the Importation of Animals Order 1977, SI 1977/944; the Diseases of Animals (Approved Disinfectants) Order 1978, SI 1978/32 (amended by SI 1991/631 and SI 1991/1770); the Importation of Birds, Poultry and Hatching Eggs Order 1979, SI 1979/1702; the Enzootic Bovine Leukosis Order 1980, SI 1980/79; the Export of Animals (Protection) Order 1981, SI 1981/1051; the Brucellosis (England and Wales) Order 1981, SI 1981/1455 (amended by SI 1986/2295); the Aujeszky's Disease Order 1983, SI 1983/344; the Foot-and-Mouth Disease Order 1983, SI 1983/1950; the Tuberculosis Order 1984, SI 1984/1943 (amended by SI 1990/1869); the Sheep Scab Order 1986, SI 1986/862 (amended by SI 1987/836); the Infectious Diseases of Poultry Order 1986, SI 1986/1755; the Infectious Diseases of Horses Order 1987, SI 1987/790; the Zoonoses Order 1988, SI 1988/2264 (amended by SI 1988/2299); the Bovine Spongiform Encephalopathy (No 2) Order 1988, SI 1988/2299 (amended by SI 1990/1930); the Zoonoses Order 1989, SI 1989/285; the Tuberculosis (Deer) Order 1989, SI 1989/878; the Blue Eared Pig Disease Order 1991, SI 1991/1381.

3 Animal Health Act 1981 s 7 (1) (a).
4 Ibid s 7 (1) (b). 'Vessel' includes hovercraft: see s 90 and the Hovercraft (Application of Enactments)
   Order 1972, SI 1972/971.
5 Animal Health Act 1981 s 7 (1) (c).
6 Ibid s 7 (1) (d). As to the power of a veterinary inspector in certain circumstances to require the
   cleansing and disinfection of premises see the Movement of Animals (Restrictions) Order 1990, SI
   1990/760 (amended by SI 1991/1155 and SI 1991/1251), art 6.
7 See the Diseases of Animals (Approved Disinfectants) Order 1978 (as amended: see note 2 supra).
8 Animal Health Act 1981 s 79 (3). See also text to note 4 supra.

491. Dipping against sheep scab. The ministers[1] may make orders[2] for prescribing, regulating and securing the periodical treatment of all sheep by effective
dipping[3] or by the use of some other remedy for sheep scab[4]. Inspectors of the
minister[5] and, if so authorised[6], local authority[7] inspectors may, for the purposes
of any such order, enter any premises and examine sheep there[8], and the owner and
person in charge of the sheep must comply with the inspector's reasonable requirements as to the collection and penning of the sheep and afford all other reasonable
facilities for their examination[9].

Local authorities may provide, fit up, and maintain portable dipping tanks or
dipping places, and charge for their use[10]. But no such dipping place may be used if
the water in any stream, reservoir or other place constructed or used for the supply
of water for drinking or other domestic purposes would thereby be injuriously
affected[11].

1 See para 482 note 3 ante.
2 See the Sheep Scab Order 1986, SI 1986/862 (amended by SI 1987/836), and the Sheep Scab
   (National Dip) Order 1990, SI 1990/1557.
3 Where an order makes it an offence to fail to dip sheep in an approved sheep dip within a certain
   period, a conviction for not dipping sheep in an approved dip on a particular day in that period is bad
   as disclosing no offence: *Bingley v Quest* (1907) 97 LT 394.
4 Animal Health Act 1981 s 14 (1).
5 Ie the Minister for Agriculture, Fisheries and Food: ibid s 86 (1) (a).
6 Orders giving such authorisations are not statutory instruments: ibid s 91 (5).
7 As to the local authorities and their power to make regulations see paras 536, 538 post.
8 Animal Health Act 1981 s 14 (2).
9 Ibid s 14 (3).
10 Ibid s 56 (1).
11 Ibid s 56 (3).

(iii) Rabies

492. Rabies: importation and quarantine. The ministers[1] may by orders make
such provision as they think fit for the purpose of preventing the introduction of
rabies into Great Britain, and such orders may include provision for the destruction
by prescribed persons of affected animals[2]. They may also make orders requiring
mammals which may be carriers of rabies to be kept in quarantine in such cases, for
such periods and under such conditions as they may prescribe[3], and prohibiting or
regulating the importation of rabies virus in any form[4]. Under those powers, an
order has been made[5] controlling the landing from abroad[6] of any animal belonging to certain orders of mammals[7].

A licence[8] from the Minister of Agriculture, Fisheries and Food is required
before such an animal may be landed[9] in Great Britain[10]. Similarly, a licence is
required for the landing of an animal from a place other than a country outside

Great Britain[11], if while outside Great Britain that animal has been or may have been in contact with an animal for the landing of which a licence would be required[12]. Except where otherwise provided, the provisions are to be executed and enforced by the local authority[13].

Only specified ports and airports[14] may be used for the landing of animals, although in exceptional circumstances the licence, and in emergencies an inspector[15], may permit landing at another port or airport[16]. Any terms or conditions subject to which the licence was granted must be complied with[17], and immediately after being landed the animal must be detained and isolated[18] in quarantine at its owner's expense at such premises and subject to such conditions as may be specified in the licence[19]. Only premises authorised by a licence granted by the minister and under the supervision of a veterinary surgeon (or, in the case of research premises only, a registered medical practitioner) authorised in writing by the minister may be used for detention and isolation in quarantine[20]. During the quarantine period every dog or cat must be vaccinated against rabies at its owner's expense, unless the minister is satisfied that a dog or cat has been brought to Great Britain for use at research premises in connection with scientific research and that vaccination might interfere with the research[21].

Upon landing, the person in charge of the animal must ensure that it is either (1) handed over to the authorised carrying agent[22], who must forthwith remove it to the quarantine premises specified in the licence[23], or (2) immediately removed by an authorised carrying agent to premises within or in the vicinity of the port or airport approved for the temporary accommodation of animals for quarantine[24]. Whilst in quarantine an animal may not be moved from the authorised quarantine premises except to other such premises, except for the purposes of treatment of a kind which cannot be administered at such premises[25].

The requirements of a licence and quarantine do not apply where satisfactory arrangements have previously been made for the exportation, within 48 hours of its landing, of an animal from the port or airport at which it was landed, or where the minister has granted a licence (which may be general or specific) for the landing of an animal and its subsequent transit through Great Britain to a port or airport for exportation[26].

If an animal which is required to be detained and isolated in quarantine is not so detained and isolated, or there is reason to believe that an animal has been landed in Great Britain in contravention of these provisions or of a licence, an inspector may by written or oral notice served on the person appearing to him to be in charge of the animal, require that person immediately to detain and isolate the animal and, within the time specified in the notice, to ensure that it is moved to a vessel, vehicle or aircraft for exportation or to authorised quarantine premises[27]. On failure to comply with such a notice, an inspector or a constable may seize or cause to be seized the animal to which the notice relates and arrange for the notice to be complied with[28]. If the inspector reasonably believes that such an animal does not have an owner, or he is unable, after reasonable enquiry, to trace the owner or any person otherwise having charge of it, or he reasonably believes that the service of a notice would result in unreasonable delay in dealing with the animal, he may seize the animal or cause it to be seized, and arrange for its exportation or detention and isolation[29]. An inspector or constable may seize or cause to be seized, and thereafter destroy or cause to be destroyed, any animal landed in Great Britain in contravention of these provisions or of a licence, or any animal in respect of which, after it has been landed, there is a contravention of a licence[30].

Any person landing or attempting to land in Great Britain an animal the landing of which is prohibited, or causing or permitting such landing or attempted landing, or contravening or failing to comply with the provisions of the Rabies (Importation of Dogs, Cats and Other Mammals) Order 1974, a licence or a notice, or causing or permitting such contravention or non-compliance, is guilty of an offence punishable on summary conviction by a fine not exceeding level 5 on the standard scale or, if the offence is committed in respect of more than ten animals, not exceeding level 3 on the standard scale for each[31]. A person who knowingly and with intent to evade any provision of the order or of a licence (1) lands or attempts to land an animal in Great Britain the landing of which is prohibited or causes or permits the landing or attempted landing of any such animal, or (2) lands or attempts to land an animal in Great Britain in contravention of the order or of a licence or fails to comply with any such provision, or causes or permits any such contravention or non-compliance, or (3) with respect to an animal which has been landed in Great Britain, does or omits to do anything in relation to the detention and isolation in quarantine of the animal in contravention of any provision of the 1974 Order or of a licence, commits an offence against the Animal Health Act 1981 and is liable to prosecution on indictment and on conviction to a fine or imprisonment for a term not exceeding 12 months, or to both[32].

A person who lands or attempts to land an animal in Great Britain in contravention of the 1974 Order or of a licence is also liable to be dealt with under the Customs and Excise Management Act 1979 for improperly importing or attempting to import goods, and the animal may be seized or detained as liable to forfeiture[33].

1 See para 482 note 3 ante.
2 Animal Health Act 1981 s 10 (1), (5).
3 Ibid ss 1, 24 (a). The Rabies (Importation of Dogs, Cats and Other Mammals) Order 1974, SI 1974/2211 (amended by SI 1977/361, SI 1984/1182, SI 1986/2062 and SI 1990/2371) has effect partly under these sections and partly under the Animal Health Act 1981 s 10, by virtue of the Interpretation Act 1978 s 17 (2) (b).
4 Animal Health Act 1981 ss 1, 24 (b). The importation of rabies virus except under licence is prohibited by the Rabies Virus Order 1979, SI 1979/135, which takes effect under the 1981 Act.
5 Ie the Rabies (Importation of Dogs, Cats and Other Mammals) Order 1974 (as amended: see note 3 supra).
6 A licence is not required in respect of an animal brought from a place in Northern Ireland, the Republic of Ireland, the Channel Islands or the Isle of Man: ibid art 4 (2); but, where the animal has been brought to that place from a place outside those countries (other than a place in Great Britain), the prohibition on landing does apply unless the animal has been detained and isolated in quarantine for a period of at least six calendar months before being landed in Great Britain: art 4 (2) proviso. As to the meaning of licence see note 8 infra.
7 Ten classes are specified, namely: *carnivora, chiroptera, dermoptera, edentata, hyracoidea, insectivora, lagomorpha, marsupialia, primates* and *rodentia*; man is excluded. The definition of 'animals' in the Animal Health Act 1981 (see para 440 ante) is accordingly extended: Rabies (Importation of Dogs, Cats and Other Mammals) Order 1974 art 3, Sch 1 Pt II.
8 'Licence' includes any permit, approval or other form of authorisation: ibid art 2 (1).
9 An animal is deemed to have been landed immediately it is unloaded or taken out of or in any other manner leaves or escapes from, a vessel, vehicle or aircraft, or immediately it crosses the frontier through the Channel Tunnel: ibid art 2 (2) (amended by the Channel Tunnel (Amendment of Agriculture, Fisheries and Food Import Legislation) Order 1990, SI 1990/2371). See also note 27 infra.
10 Rabies (Importation of Dogs, Cats and Other Mammals) Order 1974 art 4 (1), (3).
11 Eg an oil rig not forming part of any country.
12 Rabies (Importation of Dogs, Cats and Other Mammals) Order 1974 art 4 (9) (added by SI 1984/1182); this does not, however, apply to a dog belonging to the police, Her Majesty's Customs and Excise or Her Majesty's Forces which is kept under the control of a trained handler while outside

Great Britain: Rabies (Importation of Dogs, Cats and Other Mammals) Order 1974 art 4 (10) (as so added).

13 Ibid art 18. For the meaning of 'local authority' see the Animal Health Act 1981 s 50; and para 536 post.

14 The ports so specified are: (1) Dover, Eastern Docks; (2) Harwich, Parkeston Quay; (3) Hull; (4) Portsmouth; and (5) Southampton. The airports so specified are: (i) Birmingham; (ii) Edinburgh; (iii) Gatwick; (iv) Glasgow; (v) Heathrow; (vi) Leeds; (vii) Manchester; (viii) Norwich; and (ix) Prestwick: Rabies (Importation of Dogs, Cats and Other Mammals) Order 1974 art 4 (4), Sch 2 (Sch 2 Pt I substituted by SI 1984/1182; Pts I, II subsequently amended by SI 1986/2062).

15 Ie an inspector appointed by the minister or a local authority for the purposes of the Animal Health Act 1981, including, in the former case, a veterinary inspector: Rabies (Importation of Dogs, Cats and Other Mammals) Order 1974 art 2 (1).

16 Ibid art 4 (4), (5).

17 Ibid art 4 (3).

18 The minister may by licence permit two or more animals to be kept together in quarantine, in which case the period of six months (see note 20 infra) is computed, for all the animals so kept, from the latest date of landing of any of the animals: ibid art 5 (3).

19 Ibid art 5 (1), (2). In most cases the period of quarantine is six months: art 5 (2), Sch 1 Pt II. In the case of vampire bats (*desmontidae*, of the order *chiroptera*) the period is the life of the animal: art 5 (1), Sch 1 Pt I. If there is an outbreak of rabies at the premises or if the minister has reason to suspect that an animal detained or previously detained there may be or may have been affected by rabies, he may extend the period in relation to those premises: art 5 (5).

20 Ibid art 9 (1), (2). The person in charge of authorised quarantine premises must adopt such system for the identification of animals, and keep records as to the receipt, treatment and subsequent release or death of animals, as the minister may require: see art 11. As to charges for the use of quarantine stations see para 539 post.

21 Ibid art 6 (1), (2). 'Dog' means an animal of the species *Canis familiaris*, and 'cat' means an animal of the species *Felis catus*, both of the order of mammals *Carnivora*: art 2 (1).

22 The minister may in writing authorise any person to be an authorised carrying agent: see ibid art 10. If the animal is landed at a port or airport other than that specified in the licence, a person other than an authorised carrying agent may be authorised for the purpose of moving the animal: art 7 (5).

23 Ibid art 7 (1) (a).

24 Ibid art 7 (1) (b). Where an animal is taken to such approved premises, it must be removed without undue delay, and in any case within 48 hours, to the authorised quarantine premises specified in the licence: art 7 (2).

Where the authorised carrying agent acts on behalf of the person who was in charge of the animal at the time of landing, the latter is the person required to ensure the removal of the animal to an approved temporary quarantine station: *City of London Corpn v British Caledonian Airways Ltd* [1980] 2 All ER 297.

25 Rabies (Importation of Dogs, Cats and Other Mammals) Order 1974 art 7 (3), (4).

26 See ibid art 8 (amended by SI 1977/361 and SI 1984/1182).

27 Rabies (Importation of Dogs, Cats and Other Mammals) Order 1974 art 13 (1) (amended by SI 1990/2371; see note 9 supra). References to 'vessel', 'boat' or 'ship' etc, include hovercraft: see the Animal Health Act 1981 s 90 and the Hovercraft (Application of Enactments) Order 1972, SI 1972/971.

28 Rabies (Importation of Dogs, Cats and Other Mammals) Order 1974 art 13 (2) (amended by SI 1977/361). The person on whom the notice was served, the owner of the animal and any other person having charge of the animal must render all reasonable assistance to the inspector or constable. The reasonable expenses of the inspector or constable are recoverable on demand by the minister, the local authority or the police authority as a civil debt from the owner or the person on whom the notice was served: Rabies (Importation of Dogs, Cats and Other Mammals) Order 1974 art 13 (2) (as so amended).

29 Ibid art 13 (4) (as amended: see note 28 supra). Where the identity of the owner is or subsequently becomes known to him, he must inform the owner in writing as soon as practicable: art 13 (4) proviso.

30 Ibid art 14 (amended by SI 1977/361). The reasonable expenses incurred in the exercise of this power are recoverable on demand by the minister or the local or police authority as a civil debt from the owner: Rabies (Importation of Dogs, Cats and Other Mammals) Order 1974 art 14 (as so amended).

31 Ibid art 16. Animal Health Act 1981 s 75 (amended by virtue of the Criminal Justice Act 1982 ss 35, 38, 46). As to the standard scale see para 232 note 1 ante. At the date at which this volume states the law, levels 3 and 5 on that scale are at £400 and £2,000 respectively.

32 Rabies (Importation of Dogs, Cats and Other Mammals) Order 1974 art 17; Animal Health Act 1981 s 76 (1), (2) (b).
33 Rabies (Importation of Dogs, Cats and Other Mammals) Order 1974; Customs and Excise Management Act 1979 ss 49, 50, 139–144; Animal Health Act 1981 s 74.

493. Rabies: control. An order has been made[1] laying down a comprehensive procedure for the control of possible rabies[2] outbreaks in Great Britain. The order covers virtually all animals which live on land[3], irrespective of whether they are domesticated or wild, or living in captivity or not[4].

Any person who knows that an animal to which the order applies is suffering from rabies, or has died from that disease, must with all practicable speed report that fact to an inspector[5] or to a police constable, unless he reasonably believes that another person has already done so[6]. A person who knows or suspects that an animal in his possession or under his charge is, or was at the time of its death, affected with rabies must, as far as practicable, keep the animal or carcase separate from any other animal[7].

Where an inspector receives information regarding an animal affected with or suspected of being affected with rabies at any premises, or the death of any such animal at any such premises, or through any other cause he reasonably suspects that rabies exists or has existed at such premises within the preceding 56 days, or that there is an animal which has been or may have been exposed to infection, he may by notice declare the premises to be an infected place[8]. Such a notice remains in force until cancelled or varied by further written notice[9], and copies of any notice must be sent to the Ministry[10].

Where a Ministry veterinary inspector has grounds for suspecting the existence of rabies[11], he must carry out an enquiry to establish whether rabies exists, and for this purpose he is given power to enter land, remove animals and carcases for investigation and take diagnostic samples. The occupier of the infected place and anyone who may have been connected with animals at the premises are required to assist at the enquiry and to supply any relevant information[12]. The opinion of the Ministry veterinary inspector is subject to confirmation by or on behalf of the Chief Veterinary Officer[13]. Where the Minister for Agriculture, Fisheries and Food believes or suspects that rabies exists or has existed in an area within the preceding six months, he may by order declare the area, together with adjoining areas into which he considers that there is a possibility of the disease spreading, an infected area[14]. He may arrange for the destruction of foxes[15] and the erection of warning notices[16] in an infected area and a Ministry veterinary inspector may prohibit by notice any sporting or recreational activity on land in the area[17]. Contravention of the order is an offence[18].

Any animal in an infected place which is affected or suspected of being affected with rabies, or any animal which has been in contact with such animal, must be detained and isolated in an approved part of the infected place[19]. No person, except an inspector, the owner or his representative or a veterinary surgeon employed by him, or a person tending the animal, may have access to an animal so detained and isolated except by authority of a licence[20]. No animal or carcase may be moved into or out of an infected place except under licence, and a carcase must be disposed of in a manner specified by a veterinary inspector[21]. An animal may be slaughtered by the owner after notice has been given to a veterinary inspector; steps must be taken to ensure that the head and neck are not damaged and the carcase must, if required, be made available to a veterinary inspector for investigation[22]. Notice of the death of an animal in the infected place must be given with all practicable speed to a veterinary inspector by the owner or person in charge of the animal or by the occupier of the infected place[23]. Nothing coming from or used in connection with an infected or suspected animal or an animal which has been in contact therewith may be removed from the infected place except under licence[24]. The occupier must disinfect every part of an infected place where any such animal has been in a manner approved by a Ministry inspector, and must prominently display warning notices approved by an inspector[25].

Any constable of the metropolitan police force may destroy any dog or other animal reasonably suspected of being in a rabid state or of having been bitten by any dog or other animal in a rabid state[26].

Compensation is payable on the slaughter of an animal under the provisions described above. In the case of an animal affected with rabies at the time of its slaughter, compensation is 50 per cent of the full market value immediately before it contracted the disease; in any other case compensation is the full market value of the animal at the time of the slaughter[27].

1 The Rabies (Control) Order 1974, SI 1974/2212. This now has effect under the Animal Health Act 1981: see para 482 ante.
2 Rabies is made a disease for the purposes of what is now the Animal Health Act 1981: Rabies (Control) Order 1974 art 3; see para 441 ante. Accordingly, the minister is empowered to slaughter animals suspected of the disease: see para 507 post. As to compensation payable upon such slaughter see text and note 27 infra.
3 Specifically, the provisions of the Rabies (Control) Order 1974 apply to the following orders of animals: artiodactyla; carnivora; chiroptera; dermoptera; edentata; hyracoidea; insectivora; lagamorpha; marsupialia; monotremata; perissodactyla; pholidota; primates (except hominidae (man)); proboscidea; rodentia; and tubulidentata: art 2 (1), Sch 1.
4 Ibid arts 2 (1), 4 (1).
5 Ie an inspector appointed for the purposes of the Animal Health Act 1981 by the Minister of Agriculture, Fisheries and Food or by a local authority, including, in relation to a Ministry inspector, a veterinary inspector; a veterinary inspector is an inspector appointed by the ministry: Rabies (Control) Order 1974 art 2 (1).
6 Ibid art 4 (1). This does not apply in relation to an animal infected with rabies virus under the authority of a licence and in accordance with the conditions of that licence: art 4 (4); Rabies Virus Order 1979, SI 1979/135, art 10. See also the Animal Health Act 1981 s 15 under which the 1974 Order partially takes effect.
Where notice is given under this provision to a police constable or a local authority inspector, he must transmit the information by the most expeditious means (1) in the case of a police constable, to the Divisional Veterinary Officer and to a local authority inspector, and (2) in the case of a local authority inspector, to the Divisional Veterinary Officer: Rabies (Control) Order 1974 art 4 (3). The Divisional Veterinary Officer is the person appointed for the time being by the minister to receive information regarding animals and carcases in relation to specified diseases in the particular area: art 2 (1).
7 Ibid art 4 (2). The exemption described in note 6 supra applies also to this requirement: Rabies Virus Order 1979 art 10.
8 Rabies (Control) Order 1974 art 5 (1). The form of the notice is prescribed in Sch 2. As to the rules which apply to an infected place under the 1974 Order see arts 5 (2), 7; text and notes 19–25 infra. A Ministry veterinary inspector may direct the alteration of the limits of the infected place specified in the notice, and may direct that any of the standard rules is not to apply in a particular case, or that additional rules are to apply: art 5 (3).
9 Ibid art 5 (4).
10 Ibid art 5 (5).
11 See text and note 8 supra.
12 Rabies (Control) Order 1974 art 6.
13 Ibid art 6 (1).
14 Ibid art 9 (1). Such an order may provide for the division of an infected area into zones, and may specify for the application of provisions of Sch 3 to each such zone: art 9 (2). Those provisions relate to: (1) the restriction of movement into and out of a zone of animals prescribed in the order; (2) the

control of dogs and cats; (3) the control of other animals prescribed by the order; (4) the seizure, detention and disposal (including destruction) of animals not under control; (5) the compulsory vaccination of animals of prescribed species; (6) the prohibition of prescribed kinds of events at which animals or prescribed species of animals are gathered together; the prohibition of (i) hunting (including hunting and stalking deer) and cubbing, (ii) racing or coursing, or training therefor, of hounds or dogs, (iii) point-to-point meetings, and (iv) shooting of game or other wildlife; and (7) the notification of deaths of animals. See also the Animal Health Act 1981 s 20.

15 Ibid s 19; Rabies (Control) Order 1974 art 10.
16 Ibid art 12.
17 Ibid art 11.
18 Ibid art 13; and see para 514 post. An increased maximum fine is provided for offences under this order by the Animal Health Act 1981 s 75 (3), but this provision has been made redundant by the increase in the maximum fine available for all offences under the Act (see s 75 (1) as amended).
19 Rabies (Control) Order 1974 art 7 (1) r 1.
20 Ibid art 7 (1) r 2.
21 Ibid art 7 (1) rr 3, 4.
22 Ibid art 7 (1) r 5.
23 Ibid art 7 (1) r 6.
24 Ibid art 7 (1) r 7.
25 Ibid art 7 (1) rr 8, 9. If the occupier of the infected place fails to comply with either of these requirements, the local authority may enter the infected place and carry out the work required, recovering their reasonable expenses from the occupier as a civil debt: art 7 (2).
26 Metropolitan Police Act 1839 s 61. The owner of such an animal who permits it to go at large commits an offence punishable on summary conviction by a maximum fine of level 1 on the standard scale: s 61. As to the standard scale see para 232 note 1 ante. At the date at which this volume states the law, level 1 on that scale is at £50.
27 Rabies Compensation Order 1976, SI 1976/2195. See para 508 post.

494. Keeping and introduction of rabies virus. The importation[1], keeping[2] or deliberate introduction into animals[3] of any rabies virus[4] are prohibited except under the authority of and in accordance with the conditions of a licence issued by the appropriate minister[5]. Where an inspector[6] reasonably suspects the importation, keeping or deliberate introduction into animals of rabies virus in contravention of these provisions or of a licence, he may serve on the owner or person in charge of the virus or animal written notice requiring the detention of the virus or animal, or may at any time seize it or cause it to be seized; a veterinary inspector may then destroy it or cause it to be destroyed without compensation[7].

A veterinary inspector may by written notice require the occupier of any premises or place or the owner or person in charge of any vehicle[8] in which rabies virus is or has been present in contravention of these provisions or of a licence, to cleanse and disinfect the place, premises or vehicle in the manner specified in the notice, at his own expense[9]. Where the requirements of a notice have not been carried out, the veterinary inspector may carry out or cause to be carried out the cleaning and disinfecting and for this purpose may enter, with other persons, the place, premises or vehicle[10]. The veterinary inspector's expenses in relation to such a notice are recoverable by the minister as a civil debt from the person on whom the notice was served[11].

A person acting under the authority of a licence must produce it on demand by an officer of Customs and Excise, a veterinary inspector, an officer of the minister, an inspector of a local authority or a constable[12].

Contravention of any of the above provisions, or of a licence issued or a notice served under these provisions, is an offence[13].

1 'Importation' includes the importation of rabies virus in combination or admixture with any other material or in any living creature (including eggs) being used as a carrier of the virus for the purpose

of importation: Rabies Virus Order 1979, SI 1979/135, art 2. See the Animal Health Act 1981 s 24 (b) under which the 1979 Order partially takes effect.

2 'Keeping' includes the keeping of rabies virus in combination or admixture with any other material or in any living creature (including eggs) but does not include the presence of rabies virus resulting from natural or accidental infection with that virus: ibid art 2.

3 'Animals' has the same meaning as in the Animal Health Act 1981 s 87 as extended by the Rabies (Importation of Dogs, Cats and Other Mammals) Order 1974, SI 1974/2211 (see paras 483, 492 ante): Rabies Virus Order 1979 art 2; the 1979 Order takes effect under the Animal Health Act 1981 by virtue of the Interpretation Act 1978 s 17.

4 'Rabies virus' means virus of the genus lyssavirus of the family Rhabdoviridae including whole virus, attenuated or otherwise genetically altered virus and any fraction thereof: Rabies Virus Order 1979 art 2.

5 Ibid art 3 (1). This prohibition does not apply in relation to any rabies virus contained in a medicinal product which may be imported, kept or introduced into animals under the Medicines Act 1968 ss 7, 32 (see MEDICINE): Rabies Virus Order 1979 art 4.
  The 'appropriate minister' is the Minister of Agriculture, Fisheries and Food or the Secretary of State for Wales: art 2. The appropriate minister may, by written notice, vary, revoke or suspend a licence: art 3 (2).

6 'Inspector' means a person appointed to be an inspector by the minister or by a local authority, and when used in relation to an officer of the ministry, includes a veterinary inspector, and 'veterinary inspector' means an inspector appointed by the ministry: Animal Health Act 1981 s 89 (1). See also note 3 supra.

7 Rabies Virus Order 1979 art 5 (1). The powers of the inspector in relation to the virus extend to any material or living creature (including eggs) being used as a carrier of the virus: art 5 (2). Where the inspector requires the detention of the virus or animal, such detention must be in such manner, for such period and at such place as he may specify in the notice: art 5 (1).

8 'Vehicle' includes any vessel, boat, hovercraft, aircraft and any other description of vehicle or any part thereof: ibid art 2.

9 Ibid art 5 (3). Where a vehicle is required to be disinfected and cleansed, the veterinary inspector may detain the vehicle until the notice has been complied with: art 5 (4).

10 Ibid art 5 (5).

11 Ibid art 5 (6).

12 Ibid art 6.

13 See ibid arts 7–9. As to penalties for such offences see the Animal Health Act 1981 ss 75, 76; and para 513 et seq post.

495. Arrest, entry and search in respect of rabies. A constable is empowered to arrest without warrant any person whom he reasonably suspects to be committing or to have committed any of the following offences: (1) landing or attempting to land, or importing or attempting to import through the Channel Tunnel, any animal in contravention of an order expressed to be for the purpose of preventing the introduction of rabies into Great Britain[1]; (2) failure by any person having the charge or control of any vessel or boat to discharge any obligation imposed on him by such an order[2]; or (3) the movement of any animal into or out of any place[3] or area[4] declared to be infected with rabies, in contravention of any order governing such a place or area[5]. For the purpose of making such an arrest a constable may enter, by force if necessary, any vessel, boat, aircraft or vehicle of any other description in which the person is or in which the constable reasonably suspects him to be[6].

Where a power to seize an animal or cause it to be seized is conferred on a constable by an order expressed to be for the purpose of preventing the introduction of rabies into Great Britain[7], the constable may enter, by force if necessary, and search any vessel, boat, aircraft or vehicle of any other description in which there is, or in which he reasonably suspects there to be, an animal in respect of which the power of seizure applies[8].

These powers are in addition to the general powers of arrest under the Animal Health Act 1981[9], but, unlike those general powers, are not exercisable by an inspector[10].

1 See the Rabies (Importation of Dogs, Cats and Other Mammals) Order 1974, SI 1974/2211 (amended by SI 1977/361, SI 1984/1182, SI 1986/1062 and SI 1990/2371); para 492 ante.
2 See the Rabies (Importation of Dogs, Cats and Other Mammals) Order 1974 art 12 (substituted by SI 1977/361). The general duty of such a person is to ensure that any animal which has been outside Great Britain, Northern Ireland, the Republic of Ireland, the Channel Islands and the Isle of Man within the preceding six months, and which is on board a vessel, (1) is restrained and confined, (2) does not come into contact with any animal except one which has been transported with it, and (3) is in no circumstances permitted to land (except under licence or under controlled transportation arrangements): Rabies (Importation of Dogs, Cats and Other Mammals) Order 1974 art 12 (1)–(3) (as so substituted). In addition that person is under a duty to give notice of the loss of such an animal and the person in charge of the animal must give notice of any incident whereby rabies virus could be transmitted to a human or to another animal: art 12 (4), (5) (as so substituted). References to 'vessel', 'boat' or 'ship' etc, include hovercraft: see the Animal Health Act 1981 s 90 and the Hovercraft (Application of Enactments) Order 1972, SI 1972/971.
3 As to the provisions applying in infected places see para 493 text and note 8 ante.
4 As to the meaning of 'infected area', and as to provisions which may be applied in infected areas, see para 493 text and note 14 ante.
5 Animal Health Act 1981 s 61 (amended by the Channel Tunnel (Amendment of Agriculture, Fisheries and Food Import Legislation) Order 1990, SI 1990/2371). This power of arrest without warrant is expressly preserved by the Police and Criminal Evidence Act 1984 s 26 (2), Sch 2.
6 Animal Health Act 1981 s 62 (1). See also note 2 supra.
7 See note 1 supra.
8 Animal Health Act 1981 s 62 (2). See also note 2 supra.
9 See ibid s 60 (amended by the Police and Criminal Evidence Act 1984 ss 26, 119, Schs 6, 7). As to the powers of the police generally see POLICE.
10 Animal Health Act 1981 s 63 (1). As to the meaning of inspector see para 494 note 6 ante.

(iv) Infected Places and Areas

496. Infected places and areas generally. The ministers[1] may make orders[2] prescribing the cases in which places and areas are to be declared infected with a disease[3], and the authority, mode and conditions by, in and on which such declarations are to be made, their effect, consequences, duration and discontinuance, and other relevant matters[4].

Whilst the provisions vary for different diseases, the general position is that 'infected places'[5] are premises declared to be infected places by local authority inspectors, whilst 'infected areas'[6] surrounding infected places, with defined boundaries situated a certain number of miles distant from the infected places, are declared by special order of the ministers. In addition, in the case of foot-and-mouth disease, the ministers may by special order declare an area surrounding an infected area to be a 'controlled area'[7].

The owner or person in charge of animals in an infected place or area may affix a notice there forbidding persons who have by law no right of entry or way to enter without permission[8].

The ministers may make orders[9] prescribing and regulating the publication by placards, handbills or otherwise, in the immediate neighbourhood of an infected place or area, of the fact of the declaration; prohibiting or regulating the movement of animals and persons into, within or out of an infected place or area[10]; regulating the isolation and separation of animals there; prohibiting or regulating the removal of carcases, fodder, litter[11], utensils, pens, hurdles, dung or other things into, within or out of an infected place or area, and regulating their destruction, burial, disposal or treatment; and regulating the cleansing and disinfection of infected places and areas and of the clothes of persons in infected places, and the use of precautions against the spreading of disease by such persons[12].

1 See para 482 note 3 ante.
2 Cattle Plague Order of 1928, SR & O 1928/206, art 3 (amended by SR & O 1938/194); Pleuro-Pneumonia Order of 1928, SR & O 1928/205, art 3 (amended by SR & O 1938/195); Anthrax Order of 1938, SR & O 1938/204, art 3; Sheep-Pox Order of 1938, SR & O 1938/229, art 2; Fowl Pest (Infected Areas Restrictions) Order 1956, SI 1956/1611, art 3 (amended by SI 1958/1442); Swine Fever (Infected Areas Restrictions) Order 1956, SI 1956/1750, art 3 (amended by SI 1958/1284); Swine Fever Order 1963, SI 1963/286, art 4; Teschen Disease Order 1974, SI 1974/1185, art 5; Rabies (Control) Order 1974, SI 1974/2212, arts 5, 9 (see para 448 post); Aujeszky's Disease Order 1983, SI 1983/344, arts 7, 15; Warble Fly (England and Wales) (Infected Areas) Order 1985, SI 1985/1542, art 3; Foot-and-Mouth Disease Order 1983, SI 1983/1950, art 5; Sheep Scab Order 1986, SI 1986/862, arts 5, 14; Infectious Diseases of Horses Order 1987, SI 1987/790, art 5; Infectious Diseases of Poultry Order 1986, SI 1986/1755, art 6; Zoonoses Order 1989, SI 1989/285, art 6; Blue Eared Pig Disease Order 1991, SI 1991/1381, arts 5, 11. See also the Movement of Animals (Restrictions) Order 1990, SI 1990/760, art 4A (added by SI 1991/1251), which applies to diseases specified in the Specified Diseases (Notification) Order 1991, SI 1991/1155 (see para 487 note 6 ante), but not to any disease the existence of which could be discovered under the provision of any other order: Movement of Animals (Restrictions) Order 1990 art 3 (3) (substituted by SI 1991/1155).
3 For the meaning of 'disease' see para 484 ante.
4 Animal Health Act 1981 s 17 (1). Upon such a declaration being made the place or area becomes an infected place or area: s 17 (2). The Minister of Agriculture, Fisheries and Food may, on inquiry and after consulting the local authority, cancel the declaration (s 18(1)), whereupon, or if the place or area is declared free of disease, it ceases to be an infected place or area: s 18 (2). Orders of the minister or a local authority under these provisions, and notices served under directions of the minister or a local authority by virtue of an order of the minister, are conclusive evidence of the matters whereon the orders or notices proceeded: ss 17 (3), 18 (3).
5 See para 497 post.
6 See para 498 post.
7 See para 498 post.
8 Animal Health Act 1981 s 27. Disobedience is an offence under s 72 (b): see para 514 post.
9 Cattle Plague Order of 1928 arts 7, 8; Pleuro-Pneumonia Order of 1928 arts 5, 6; Anthrax Order of 1938 art 7; Sheep-Pox Order of 1938 arts 6, 8; Fowl Pest (Infected Areas Restrictions) Order 1956 (amended by SI 1958/1442, SI 1983/941); Swine Fever (Infected Areas Restrictions) Order 1956 (amended by SI 1958/1284, SI 1977/944); Swine Fever Order 1963 arts 6, 9; Teschen Disease Order 1974 arts 7, 8; Rabies (Control) Order 1974 arts 7, 12; Warble Fly (England and Wales) Order 1982, SI 1982/234, art 4; Aujeszky's Disease Order 1983 arts 9, 16; Warble Fly (England and Wales) (Infected Areas) Order 1985 arts 4, 5; Foot-and-Mouth Disease Order 1983 arts 9, 10, 11, 18; Sheep Scab Order 1986 arts 7, 15; Infectious Diseases of Poultry Order 1986 art 8; Infectious Diseases of Horses Order 1987 art 7; Zoonoses Order 1989 art 7; Blue Eared Pig Disease Order 1991 arts 5, 12, Sch 1 r 1; Movement of Animals (Restrictions) Order 1990 art 4B (as added: see note 2 supra).
10 The offence is complete as soon as an animal is moved in contravention of the order: see *R v Williams* (1866) 15 LT 290. As to the justices' jurisdiction see also *Midland Rly Co v Freeman* (1884) 12 QBD 629, and, generally, MAGISTRATES.
11 'Carcase' means the carcase of an animal (as defined in para 483 ante) and includes part of a carcase, and the meat, bones, hide, skin, hooves, offal or other part of an animal, separately or otherwise, or any portion thereof; 'fodder' means hay or other substance commonly used for food of animals; and 'litter' means straw or other substance commonly used for bedding or otherwise for or about animals: Animal Health Act 1981 s 89 (1).
12 Ibid s 23. Where anything destroyed, buried or disposed of under such an order could have been seized under s 35 (1) (amended by the Animal Health and Welfare Act 1984 s 1 (1), (2)), compensation is payable as if it had been so seized: Animal Health Act 1981 s 36 (4); see para 504 post.

497. Infected places. A local authority inspector notified of the existence of certain diseases, or who suspects that such a disease exists or has within a prescribed period existed on any premises, must give notice to the veterinary inspector unless this has already been done, and serve notice on the occupier of the premises, whereupon the premises become an infected place until the notice is withdrawn[1].

Movement and activity in infected places are governed by rules, which vary according to the disease. For example, they may prohibit the movement of animals save under licence[2]; the removal of carcases, fodder, litter, dung or other things save under licence or with permission[3]; the removal of milk[4]; the removal of fleeces without permission[5]; and the tending, without permission, of unaffected animals by a person who has tended diseased or affected animals[6]; may require persons leaving infected places to disinfect their clothing in disinfectant provided and to wash their hands[7]; and may require liquid manure to be disinfected before being drained away[8].

Places in which animals affected with disease have been kept must or may be required to be disinfected and cleansed in a prescribed manner[9].

1 See the orders cited in para 496 note 2 ante.
2 See the Cattle Plague Order of 1928, SR & O 1928/206, art 7 (1) r 1; Pleuro-Pneumonia Order of 1928, SR & O 1928/205, art 5 (1) r 1; Sheep-Pox Order of 1938, SR & O 1938/229, art 6 (1) r 1; Teschen Disease Order 1974, SI 1974/1185, art 7 r 1; Rabies (Control) Order 1974, SI 1974/2212, art 7 r 3; Aujeszky's Disease Order 1983, SI 1983/344, art 9 (1) r 1; Foot-and-Mouth Disease Order 1983, SI 1983/1950, art 9 r 1; Sheep Scab Order 1986, SI 1986/862, art 7 r 1; Infectious Diseases of Horses Order 1987, SI 1987/790, art 7 r 2; Zoonoses Order 1989, SI 1989/285, art 6 (2) (a); Blue Eared Pig Disease Order 1991, SI 1991/1381, art 12, Sch 1 r 2.
3 See the Cattle Plague Order of 1928 art 7 (1) r 2; Pleuro-Pneumonia Order of 1928 art 5 (1) rr 2, 3, art 6; Sheep Pox Order of 1938 art 6 (1) rr 2, 8; Anthrax Order of 1938, SR & O 1938/204, art 7 r 6; Swine Fever Order 1963, SI 1963/286, art 6 rr 4, 6; Teschen Disease Order 1974 art 7 rr 3, 4; Rabies (Control) Order 1974 art 7 r 4, 7; Aujeszky's Disease Order 1983 art 9 r 1; Foot-and-Mouth Disease Order 1983 art 9 r 1; Sheep Scab Order 1986 art 7 (1) r 2; Infectious Diseases of Horses Order 1987 art 7 (1) rr 2, 3; Zoonoses Order 1989 art 6 (2) r 2 (a), (b); Blue Eared Pig Disease Order 1991 Sch 1 r 2.
4 See the Foot-and-Mouth Disease Order 1983 art 9 r 1.
5 See the Sheep-Pox Order of 1938 art 6 (1) r 3; Sheep Scab Order 1986 art 7 (1) r 2.
6 See the Sheep-Pox Order of 1938 art 6 (1) r 6.
7 See the Cattle Plague Order of 1928 art 7 r 4; Sheep-Pox Order of 1938 art 6 (1) r 5; Swine Fever Order 1963 art 6 r 8; Teschen Disease Order 1974 art 7 r 7; Aujeszky's Disease Order 1983 art 9 (1) r 5; Foot-and-Mouth Disease Order 1983 art 9 r 4; Infectious Diseases of Horses Order 1987 art 7 (1) r 4.
8 See the Cattle Plague Order of 1928 art 7 (1) r 5; Blue Eared Pig Disease Order 1991 Sch 1 rr 5, 6.
9 See the Cattle Plague Order of 1928 art 9; Pleuro-Pneumonia Order of 1928 art 7; Sheep-Pox Order of 1938 art 9; Anthrax Order of 1938 art 9; Swine Fever Order 1963 art 16; Teschen Disease Order 1974 art 10; Rabies (Control) Order 1974 art 7 (1) r 8; Aujeszky's Disease Order 1983 art 13; Foot-and-Mouth Disease Order 1983 art 11; Sheep Scab Order 1986 art 9; Infectious Diseases of Horses Order 1987 art 11; Zoonoses Order 1989 art 9. See also the Blue Eared Pig Disease Order 1991 Sch 1 rr 8, 9. The use of disinfectants is regulated by the Diseases of Animals (Approved Disinfectants) Order 1978, SI 1978/32 (amended by SI 1991/631 and SI 1991/1770); see para 490 ante.

498. Infected and controlled areas. The movement of animals[1] and activities connected therewith in relation to infected areas or (in relation to foot-and-mouth disease) controlled areas are governed by rules[2] which vary according to the disease. The following are matters for which provision has been made in relation to infected areas:

(1) the prohibition, except under licence, on the movement of animals out of[3], into[4] or within[5] infected areas;
(2) the control of movement through infected areas[6];
(3) control of animals during and after movement[7];

(4) provisions concerning the grant and revocation of licences[8];

(5) restrictions on the holding of markets, sales, gatherings or exhibitions of animals in infected areas[9];

(6) the requirement to treat cattle for warble fly or to dip sheep, and to give notice and make a declaration regarding such treatment or dipping[10];

(7) exemption from such treatment or dipping[11];

(8) the restriction of movement of untreated cattle or undipped sheep[12];

(9) approved holding premises[13];

(10) the grazing or keeping of cattle on common land in an infected area[14];

(11) the receipt of untreated cattle at markets outside infected areas[15];

(12) restrictions on the public sale of sheep on farms and on the movement of sheep from local authority pounds[16];

(13) the control of slaughterhouse and knackery products, and of milk produced in an infected area, and the disposal of manure, slurry and litter[17];

(14) the control of dogs and poultry in infected areas, and the prevention of animals from straying into an infected area[18];

(15) precautions to be taken by persons clipping or dipping sheep[19];

(16) the restriction on the movement of embryos, ova and semen[20];

(17) the power to close footpaths and prevent entry on to premises, and the prohibition of certain sporting and recreational activities[21];

(18) the cleansing and disinfection of certain premises and vehicles[22].

Separate provisions, broadly similar to some of those mentioned above[23], apply to controlled areas[24]; additionally, hunting and stalking deer may be prohibited[25].

1 'Animals' means cattle, sheep, goats, all other ruminating animals, swine and elephants: Foot-and-Mouth Disease Order 1983, SI 1983/1950, Pt I art 3. A slightly different definition is given by the Aujeszky's Disease Order 1983 art 2 (1), namely: cattle, sheep, goats, swine, deer, horses, dogs and cats.

2 The provisions currently governing restrictions in infected areas are: the Swine Fever (Infected Areas Restrictions) Order 1956, SI 1956/ 1750 (amended by SI 1955/1284 and SI 1977/944); the Aujeszky's Disease Order 1983, SI 1983/344; the Foot-and-Mouth Disease Order 1983; the Warble Fly (England and Wales) (Infected Areas) Order 1985, SI 1985/1542; the Sheep Scab Order 1986, SI 1986/862 (amended by SI 1987/836); the Blue Eared Pig Disease Order 1991, SI 1991/1381; and the Movement of Animals (Restrictions) Order 1990, SI 1990/760 (amended by SI 1991/1155 and SI 1991/1251), which relates to the diseases specified in the Specified Diseases (Notification) Order 1991, SI 1991/1155 (see para 487 note 6 ante), but not to any disease the existence of which could be discovered under the provisions of any other order. See the orders cited in para 496 note 2 ante. All these orders were made or partially made, or take effect or partial effect, under the Animal Health Act 1981 s 17; also made or taking effect under that section are the Rabies Control Order 1974, SI 1974/2212, as to which see para 448 ante, and the Fowl Pest (Infected Areas Restrictions) Order 1956, SI 1956/1611 (amended by SI 1958/1442 and SI 1983/941), as to which see para 521 post.

3 Swine Fever (Infected Areas Restrictions) Order 1956 arts 5, 7; Aujeszky's Disease Order 1983 art 16; Foot-and-Mouth Disease Order 1983 art 18; Warble Fly (England and Wales) (Infected Areas) Order 1985 art 4; Sheep Scab Order 1986 art 15; Blue Eared Pig Disease Order 1991 art 12; Movement of Animals (Restrictions) Order 1990 art 4B (1) (added by SI 1991/1251).

4 Swine Fever (Infected Areas Restrictions) Order 1956 arts 5, 6; Foot-and-Mouth Disease Order 1983 art 18.

5 Swine Fever (Infected Areas Restrictions) Order 1956 arts 5, 7; Foot-and-Mouth Disease Order 1983 art 18; Sheep Scab Order 1986 art 16; Movement of Animals (Restrictions) Order 1990 art 5B (3) (as added: see note 3 supra).

6 Swine Fever (Infected Areas Restrictions) Order 1956 arts 5, 7A; Aujeszky's Disease Order 1983 art 16; Foot-and-Mouth Disease Order 1983 art 18; Warble Fly (England and Wales) (Infected Areas) Order 1985 art 4; Sheep Scab Order 1986 art 15; Blue Eared Pig Disease Order 1991 art 12.

7 Swine Fever (Infected Areas Restrictions) Order 1956 art 8.

8 Swine Fever (Infected Areas Restrictions) Order 1956 arts 9, 9A; Aujeszky's Disease Order 1983 art 18; Foot-and-Mouth Disease Order 1983 arts 41, 42; Warble Fly (England and Wales) (Infected

Areas) Order 1985 art 16; Sheep Scab Order 1986 arts 38, 39; Blue Eared Pig Disease Order 1991 art 13.

9 Swine Fever (Infected Areas Restrictions) Order 1956 art 4; Foot-and-Mouth Disease Order 1983 art 19; Warble Fly (England and Wales) (Infected Areas) Order 1985 art 10; Sheep Scab Order 1986 art 17.

10 Warble Fly (England and Wales) (Infected Areas) Order 1985 arts 5, 7, 8; Sheep Scab Order 1986 arts 20–22.

11 Warble Fly (England and Wales) (Infected Areas) Order 1985 art 14; Sheep Scab Order 1986 art 20.

12 Warble Fly (England and Wales) (Infected Areas) Order 1985 art 6; Sheep Scab Order 1986 art 23.

13 Warble Fly (England and Wales) (Infected Areas) Order 1985 art 12; Sheep Scab Order 1986 arts 24, 25.

14 Warble Fly (England and Wales) (Infected Areas) Order 1985 art 9.

15 Ibid art 11.

16 Sheep Scab Order 1986 arts 18, 19.

17 Foot-and-Mouth Disease Order 1983 arts 20–22.

18 Ibid arts 23, 24.

19 Ibid art 25.

20 Ibid art 26.

21 Ibid arts 27, 29.

22 Ibid art 28.

23 Ie those mentioned in heads (1), (2), (5), (13), (14) (in relation to straying animals), and (18).

24 Ie infected areas to which the Foot-and-Mouth Disease Order 1983 Pt IV (arts 30–37) apply: art 30 (1).

25 Ibid art 37.

(v) Regulation of Movement

499. Diseased animals at market, in transit or on open land. The Minister of Agriculture, Fisheries and Food may make orders[1] respecting animals[2] affected with pleuro-pneumonia or foot-and-mouth disease while exposed for sale or exhibited in a market, fair, sale-yard, place of exhibition or other place; or while placed in a lair or other place before exposure for sale; or while in transit or in course of being moved by land, air or water; or while in a slaughterhouse or place where animals are slaughtered or are kept with a view to slaughter; or while on common or uninclosed land[3]; or generally while in a place not in the possession or occupation or under the control of the owner of the animals[4].

Such an animal found to be affected, or suspected of being affected, with either of these diseases, or with certain other diseases, must be seized, together with other animals in the same place, by a local authority inspector, who must at once notify the ministry and the veterinary inspector; the animals must be detained and isolated where they are or moved to some convenient isolated place for detention, and may not then be moved save under ministry direction or licence[5].

1 See the Pleuro-Pneumonia Order of 1928, SR & O 1928/205, art 11 (amended by SR & O 1938/195 and SI 1977/944); and the Foot-and-Mouth Disease Order 1983, SI 1983/1950, art 16.

2 For the meaning of 'animal' see para 483 ante.

3 In *Jemmison v Priddle* [1972] 1 QB 489, [1972] 1 All ER 539, DC, it was held that 'inclosed land' under the Game Licences Act 1860 s 5, meant farmland as opposed to moorland.

4 Animal Health Act 1981 s 26 (1).

5 See the orders cited in note 1 supra, the Cattle Plague Order of 1928, SR & O 1928/206, art 14 (amended by SR & O 1938/194), the Sheep-Pox Order of 1938, SR & O 1938/229, art 13. No animal seized under the order relating to foot-and-mouth disease may be moved at all except by direction of a ministry inspector: Foot-and-Mouth Disease Order 1983 art 16 (5). See also the Tuberculosis (England and Wales) Order 1984, SI 1984/1943, art 14, under which an inspector may require an affected or suspected animal to be removed from a market.

500. Movement of animals generally. As regards all diseases[1] the ministers[2] may make orders[3] prohibiting or regulating the exposure of diseased or suspected animals[4] in markets, fairs, sale-yards or other public or private places where animals are commonly exposed for sale, and the placing thereof in lairs or other places adjacent to or connected with markets or fairs, or where animals are commonly placed before exposure for sale[5]; or the sending or carrying of such animals, or of dung[6] or other things likely to spread disease, or the causing the same to be sent or carried, on railways, canals, rivers or inland navigation, or in coasting vessels, or in an aircraft, or otherwise[7]; or the carrying, leading or driving of such animals, or the causing them to be carried, led or driven, on highways or thoroughfares or elsewhere[8]; or the placing or keeping them on commons or uninclosed lands, or in fields or other places insufficiently fenced, or on the sides of highways[9].

They may by order[10] prescribe and regulate the marking of animals, prohibit or regulate the movement of animals, and the removal of carcases, fodder, litter[11], dung and other things, and regulate the isolation of animals newly purchased[12] and the issue and production of licences[13] respecting movement and removal of animals and things[14]. They may also by order[15] prohibit absolutely or conditionally the use, for the carrying of animals, of any vessel, vehicle, aircraft or pen or other place in respect of the use of which a penalty has previously been recovered, and prohibit or regulate the holding of markets, fairs, exhibitions, and sales[16] of animals[17].

Furthermore, they may by order[18] make provision for protecting animals from unnecessary suffering during inland transit[19] or while exposed for sale or awaiting removal after being so exposed[20]. Orders may also be made for ensuring that animals carried by sea or by air are given proper ventilation and are protected from unnecessary suffering during the passage and on landing[21].

Thus, for example, an inspector may serve on the owner or person in charge of an animal a notice prohibiting any person to move that animal, to move any animal to or from the same place, or to permit any animal to which the notice relates to stray out of that place or to come into contact with any other animal[22], and if a ministry inspector has reasonable grounds for believing that the movement of any person, animal or thing may carry a risk of spreading any of certain diseases he may prohibit or restrict the movement[23].

It is unlawful for a person to expose an animal affected or suspected of being affected with any of certain diseases in a market or other place where animals are commonly exposed for sale or exhibited, to move it by road, rail or water, to place it or allow it to stray on common, uninclosed or insufficiently fenced land, or to graze it on roadside verges[24].

1 For the meaning of 'disease' see para 484 ante.
2 See para 482 note 3 ante.
3 See the Pleuro-Pneumonia Order of 1928, SR & O 1928/205 (amended by SR & O 1938/195, SI 1977/944); Cattle Plague Order of 1928, SR & O 1928/206 (amended by SR & O 1938/194, SI 1977/944); Anthrax Order of 1938, SR & O 1938/204; Sheep-Pox Order of 1938, SR & O 1938/229 (amended by SI 1977/944); Swine Fever Order 1963, SI 1963/286 (amended by SI 1976/919, SI 1990/2487, SI 1991/1030); Teschen Disease Order 1974, SI 1974/1185; Transit of Animals (Road and Rail) Order 1975, SI 1975/1024 (amended by SI 1979/1013, SI 1988/815); Enzootic Bovine Leukosis Order 1980, SI 1980/79; Warble Fly (England and Wales) Order 1982, SI 1982/234 (amended by SI 1985/328, SI 1987/1601, SI 1989/244); Aujeszky's Disease Order 1983, SI 1983/344; Foot-and-Mouth Disease Order 1983, SI 1983/1950; Tuberculosis (England and Wales) Order 1984, SI 1984/1943 (amended by SI 1990/1869); Warble Fly (England and Wales) (Infected Areas) Order

1985, SI 1985/1542; Sheep Scab Order 1986, SI 1986/862 (amended by SI 1987/836); Tuberculosis
(Deer) Order 1989, SI 1989/878; Blue Eared Pig Disease Order 1991, SI 1991/1381.
4 For the meaning of 'animal' see para 483 ante.
5 Animal Health Act 1981 s 25 (a).
6 Cf *Youngman v Morris* (1866) 15 LT 276.
7 Animal Health Act 1981 s 25 (b). The reference to aircraft applies where an aircraft is engaged in a
flight or a part of a flight beginning and ending in Great Britain: s 25 (b).
8 Ibid s 25 (c).
9 Ibid s 25 (d).
10 See the Markets, Sales and Lairs Order of 1925, SR & O 1925/1349 (amended by SR & O 1926/545,
SR & O 1927/982); Pleuro-Pneumonia Order of 1928 (as amended: see note 3 supra); Cattle Plague
Order of 1928 (as amended: see note 3 supra); Anthrax Order of 1938; Sheep-Pox Order of 1938 (as
amended: see note 3 supra); Horses (Sea Transport) Order 1952, SI 1952/1291 (amended by SI
1972/971); Swine Fever (Infected Areas Restrictions) Order 1956, SI 1956/1750 (amended by SI
1958/1284, SI 1977/944); Swine Fever Order 1963 (as amended: see note 3 supra); Transit of Animals
(General) Order 1973, SI 1973/1377 (amended by SI 1975/1024, SI 1988/815); Diseases of Animals
(Waste Food) Order 1973, SI 1973/1936 (amended by SI 1987/232); Teschen Disease Order 1974;
Movement and Sale of Pigs Order 1975, SI 1975/203 (amended by SI 1975/346, SI 1977/944, SI
1987/233); Transit of Animals (Road and Rail) Order 1975, SI 1975/1024 (amended by SI 1979/1013,
SI 1988/815); Enzootic Bovine Leukosis Order 1980; Export of Animals (Protection) Order 1981, SI
1981/1051; Brucellosis (England and Wales) Order 1981, SI 1981/1455 (amended by SI 1986/2295);
Warble Fly (England and Wales) Order 1982 (as amended: see note 3 supra); Aujeszky's Disease
Order 1983; Foot-and-Mouth Disease Order 1983; Tuberculosis (England and Wales) Order 1984
(as amended: see note 3 supra); Warble Fly (England and Wales) (Infected Areas) Order 1985;
Diseases of Animals (Ascertainment of Disease) Order 1985, SI 1985/1765; Warble Fly (Ascertainment of Infestation) (England and Wales) Order 1985, SI 1985/1766; Sheep Scab Order 1986 (as
amended: see note 3 supra); Infectious Diseases of Horses Order 1987, SI 1987/790; Zoonoses Order
1988, SI 1988/2264 (amended by 1988/2299); Bovine Spongiform Encephalopathy (No 2) Order
1988/2299 (amended by SI 1990/1930); Tuberculosis (Deer) Order 1989; Tuberculosis (Deer) Notice
of Intended Slaughter and Compensation Order 1989, SI 1989/1316; Movement of Animals
(Restrictions) Order 1990, SI 1990/760 (amended by SI 1991/1155 and SI 1991/1251); Sheep Scab
(National Dip) Order 1990, SI 1990/1557; Bovine Animals (Identification, Marking and Breeding
Records) Order 1990, SI 1990/1867; Blue Eared Pig Disease Order 1991.
11 For the meanings of 'carcase', 'fodder' and 'litter' see para 496 note 11 ante.
12 Animal Health Act 1981 s 8 (1) (a), (b).
13 If a licence is produced the justices cannot inquire into the sufficiency of the evidence on which it was
granted: *Stanhope v Thorsby* (1866) LR 1 CP 423.
14 Animal Health Act 1981 s 8 (1) (c). The British Railways Board may be convicted of moving
animals, or causing, directing or permitting them to be moved, in contravention of an order relating
to the movement of animals, even though it is not a party to the consignment contract, if it conveys
them into a prohibited district (*Midland Rly Co v Freeman* (1884) 12 QBD 629), but it is entitled to
refuse to carry them at all where the requirements of the order are not strictly complied with
(*Williams v Great Western Rly Co* (1885) 52 LT 250).
15 See note 10 supra.
16 Hawking pigs is not holding a sale: *McClean v Monk* (1898) 77 LT 663.
17 Animal Health Act 1981 s 8 (1) (d), (e).
18 See para 501 notes 6–14 post.
19 The reference to inland transit includes transit by air on a flight beginning and ending in Great
Britain: Animal Health Act 1981 s 37 (1) (a).
20 Ibid s 37 (1).
21 Ibid s 37 (2). See also para 501 notes 6–14 post.
22 Cf Cattle Plague Order of 1928 art 10; Pleuro-Pneumonia Order of 1928 art 8 (amended by SR & O
1938/195); Sheep-Pox Order of 1938 art 10; Swine Fever Order 1963 art 7; Teschen Disease Order
1974 art 9; Aujeszky's Disease Order 1983 art 10; Sheep Scab Order 1986 art 10; Blue Eared Pig
Disease Order 1991 art 7.
23 See the Cattle Plague Order of 1928 art 19; Sheep-Pox Order of 1938 art 18; Teschen Disease Order
1974 art 11; Swine Fever Order 1963 art 19; Aujeszky's Disease Order 1983 art 11; Bovine Spongiform Encephalopathy (No 2) Order 1988 art 7; Blue Eared Pig Disease Order 1991 art 8.
24 See the Cattle Plague Order of 1928 art 13; Pleuro-Pneumonia Order of 1928 art 10; Sheep-Pox
Order of 1938 art 12; Swine Fever Order 1963 art 11. As to the controls over movement between
member states of bovine animals and swine see AGRICULTURE vol 1 (2) (Reissue) para 1029.

501. Transport of animals and prevention of suffering. The ministers[1] may make orders prohibiting the conveyance of animals by any specified vessel or aircraft to or from any port or aerodrome[2] in the United Kingdom[3]. They may also make orders to protect animals from unnecessary suffering during inland transit, or while exposed for sale or while awaiting removal after being exposed for sale[4], and to ensure proper ventilation for animals carried by sea or by air, and to protect them from unnecessary suffering during the passage and on landing[5].

Under these powers an order has been made regulating the carriage by road and rail of farm animals and horses throughout Great Britain[6]. Provision is made as to the protection of animals during loading and unloading, their movement within a vehicle or receptacle and their accommodation and protection during carriage[7], including specific provision as to overcrowding and the separation of animals (including which animals may be carried together in the same undivided vehicle, crate, box or pen)[8], and the tethering of animals[9]. General principles are laid down designed to ensure that those concerned will have proper regard to the welfare of the animals with which they are dealing, and certain specific requirements are also laid down. Provision is also made as to feeding and watering during carriage, carrying unfit animals or animals likely to give birth during the carriage, cleansing and disinfection, the prohibition of carrying carcases and live animals together, facilities to be provided by British Railways Board and other railway companies, and the keeping of records[10]. The order also lays down detailed requirements for the construction and maintenance of vehicles, crates and boxes used for transporting animals[11].

Further orders have been made covering practically all animals[12], and most birds[13], in relation to the carriage of animals that is not otherwise controlled[14]. The orders cover animals transported within Great Britain and those carried on a vessel or aircraft to or from a port or airport in Great Britain, whether or not they are unloaded[15]. Carriers and other persons in charge of animals during their carriage are placed under a general duty to ensure that the statutory provisions are applied to those animals[16], and a further duty is imposed on those concerned with the loading, unloading and carriage of animals to ensure that these operations are carried out in such a way as will ensure that the animals are not caused injury or unnecessary suffering[17]. Such persons are also required to ensure the safety of the animals in a number of particulars[18]. Other provisions of the orders deal with the feeding, watering and general care of animals during carriage[19], and with their accommodation in vessels, aircraft or vehicles[20], and there are special requirements with regard to the carriage of animals in crates or boxes[21], animals injured during carriage[22], and the carriage of cold-blooded animals[23]. Loading or carrying unfit, infirm, ill, injured or fatigued animals, or animals likely to give birth during carriage, is prohibited except where permitted by a veterinary inspector of the Ministry of Agriculture, Fisheries and Food[24]. Inspectors of the Ministry, and of the local authority, may prohibit the carriage of animals if they have grounds for believing that such carriage is likely to cause injury or unnecessary suffering, or that the animals are unfit, infirm, ill, injured or fatigued, or likely to give birth during carriage[25].

A person contravening any provision of such an order is guilty of an offence under the Animal Health Act 1981[26].

The British Railways Board and every railway company[27] must ensure that animals[28] are properly supplied with water and food at such railway stations as the minister directs[29], and must supply water or food on the request[30] of the consignor or the person in charge[31] of the animals[32]. The consignor or person in charge is guilty of an offence if he fails to request water, and in consequence the animal goes without water for 24[33] hours[34]. The consignor and consignee may be charged for the expense of supplying water and food[35].

1 See para 482 note 3 ante.

2 'Aerodrome' means any area of land or water designed, equipped, set apart or commonly used for affording facilities for the landing and departure of aircraft: Animal Health Act 1981 s 89 (1).

3 Ibid s 9. Such orders are not noted in this work. References to 'vessel', 'boat' or 'ship' etc, include hovercraft: see s 90 and the Hovercraft (Application of Enactments) Order 1972, SI 1972/971.

4 Animal Health Act 1981 s 37 (1) (a); this includes inland air transit.

5 Ibid s 37 (2).

6 Transit of Animals (Road and Rail) Order 1975, SI 1975/1024 (amended by SI 1979/1013 and SI 1988/815).

7 Transit of Animals (Road and Rail) Order 1975 arts 4, 5, 6, 8 (arts 4, 6, 8 amended by SI 1988/815).

8 Transit of Animals (Road and Rail) Order 1975 arts 7, 9, Sch 2 (Sch 2 amended by SI 1979/1013).

9 Transit of Animals (Road and Rail) Order 1975 art 9A (added by SI 1988/815).

10 Transit of Animals (Road and Rail) Order 1975 arts 10–17, Schs 3, 4 (arts 15, 17 amended by SI 1979/1013).

11 See the Transit of Animals (Road and Rail) Order 1975 art 3, Sch 1.

12 The definition of 'animals' in the Animal Health Act 1981 (see para 483 ante) is extended to include all mammals other than man and any kind of four-footed beast which is not a mammal, together with all fish, reptiles, crustaceans and other cold-blooded creatures: Transit of Animals (General) Order 1973, SI 1973/1377, art 2.

13 The definition of 'poultry' in the Animal Health Act 1981 (see para 517 post) is extended to cover birds of any species other than domestic fowls, turkeys, geese, ducks, guinea fowls, pheasants, partridges and quails: Transit of Animals (General) Order 1973 (amended by the Welfare of Poultry (Transport) Order 1988, SI 1988/851).

14 Transit of Animals (General) Order 1973; Welfare of Poultry (Transport) Order 1988. As to other legislation see the 1973 Order, art 4, and see text and notes 6–11 supra as to farm animals and horses being transported by road or rail. See also the Animals (Sea Transport) Order 1930, SR & O 1930/923 (amended by SR & O 1932/248 and partially revoked by SI 1977/944); the Transit of Animals Order 1927, SR & O 1927/289 (amended by SI 1977/944); the Export of Animals (Protection) Order 1981, SI 1981/1051; the Export of Horses (Protection) Order 1969, SI 1969/1784; and the Horses (Sea Transport) Order 1952, SI 1952/1291 (amended by SI 1958/1272).

15 The 1973 Order does not, however, apply to acts done by a foreign national in foreign territory: *Air India v Wiggins* [1980] 2 All ER 593, [1980] 1 WLR 815, HL. See also note 3 supra.

16 See *British Airways Board v Wiggins* [1977] 3 All ER 1068, [1977] 1 WLR 1150, DC.

17 Transit of Animals (General) Order 1973 art 5 (1), (2).

18 Ibid art 5 (3) (substituted by SI 1988/815).

19 Transit of Animals (General) Order 1973 art 6 (amended by SI 1988/815).

20 Transit of Animals (General) Order 1973 art 9 (amended by SI 1988/815). See also note 3 supra.

21 Transit of Animals (General) Order 1973 art 8 (substituted by SI 1988/815); and see *British Airways Board v Wiggins* [1977] 3 All ER 1068, [1977] 1 WLR 1150, DC.

22 Transit of Animals (General) Order 1973 art 10.

23 Ibid art 5A (added by SI 1988/815).

24 See the Transit of Animals (General) Order 1973 art 7; as to poultry see the Welfare of Poultry (Transport) Order 1988.

25 Transit of Animals (General) Order 1973 arts 5 (5), 7 (3).

26 Ibid art 11; Transit of Animals (Road and Rail) Order 1975 art 20. For the offence see the Animal Health Act 1981 s 72. A carrier who knowingly permits the carriage of animals which by reason of their unfitness were likely to be subjected to unnecessary suffering during transportation is guilty of causing unnecessary suffering, contrary to s 72 and the Transit of Animals (Road and Rail) Order 1975 art 11 (1): *Cheshire County Council v Helliwell & Sons (Bolton) Ltd (in liquidation)* (1990) Times, 6 December, DC. As to the penalties for offences against the Animal Health Act 1981 see s 75; para 513 et seq post.

27 'Railway company' includes a company or person working a railway under lease or otherwise: Animal Health Act 1981 s 38 (2) (ii).

28 For the meaning of 'animal' in this context see para 483 ante.

29 Animal Health Act 1981 s 38 (2). The 'appropriate minister' is the Minister of Agriculture, Fisheries and Food or the Secretary of State for Wales: s 86 (1) (b).
30 Even when no such request is made, it will be implied if it becomes reasonably necessary that the animals should be fed during transit, and it is the duty of the carrier to supply such food: *Great Southern and Western Rly Co v Hourigan* (1910) 44 ILT 86.
31 Cf *North Staffordshire Rly Co v Waters* (1913) 110 LT 237, DC.
32 Animal Health Act 1981 s 38 (2), Sch 4 para 1.
33 Ibid Sch 4 para 3 gives power to vary the period, but not so as to make it less than 12 hours.
34 Ibid Sch 4 para 2. The penalty for this offence is prescribed by s 75; see para 513 et seq post.
35 See ibid paras 4–6.

(vi) Import and Export

A. IMPORT

502. Import of animals: general powers. The ministers[1] may make by order[2] such provision as they think fit for preventing the introduction or spreading of disease[3] into or within Great Britain through the importation[4] of animals[5], carcases, eggs, and any other things (animate or inanimate) by or by means of which it appears to them that any disease might be carried or transmitted[6].

In particular, they may prohibit or regulate the import of any of the things specified above[7]. They may provide as to persons, animals and other things which have been or may have been in contact with imports[8]. They may provide as to conditions or licences (which may be specific or general and conditional or unconditional) for importation; the prohibition of importation save at designated ports or airports, the landing, quarantine, seizure, detention, treatment, marking, testing, use and slaughter of animals, and the destruction of other things; the movement of persons, animals or other things; cleansing, disinfection and inspection; costs; and compensation[9]. Orders may make different provision for different cases[10]. An order that is expressed to be for the purpose of preventing the introduction of rabies into Great Britain may include provision for the destruction of animals in respect of which the order, or a licence granted under it, is contravened[11]. Imported animals must be landed in accordance with the requirements of the Commissioners of Customs and Excise[12].

1 As to the ministers see para 482 note 3 ante.
2 See the Importation of Animals Order 1977, SI 1977/944 (amended by SI 1990/2371); para 503 post. See also the Hares (Control of Importation) Order 1965, SI 1965/2040 (amended by SI 1990/2371); the Importation of Equine Animals Order 1979, SI 1979/1701 (amended by SI 1990/2371); the Importation of Birds, Poultry and Hatching Eggs Order 1979, SI 1979/1702 (amended by SI 1990/2371); the Importation of Hay and Straw Order 1979, SI 1979/1703 (amended by SI 1990/2371); the Importation of Embryos, Ova and Semen Order 1980, SI 1980/12 (amended by SI 1990/2371); the Importation of Animal Products and Poultry Products Order 1980, SI 1980/14 (amended by SI 1980/1934, SI 1981/1238, SI 1982/948 and SI 1990/2371); the Enzootic Bovine Leukosis Order 1980, SI 1980/79; the Importation of Animal Pathogens Order 1980, SI 1980/1212; the Importation of Processed Animal Protein Order 1981, SI 1981/677 (amended by SI 1982/459 and SI 1990/2371); the Exportation of Pigeons Order 1983, SI 1983/872; the Tuberculosis (England and Wales) Order 1984, SI 1984/1943 (amended by SI 1990/1869); the Importation of Salmonid Viscera Order 1986, SI 1986/2265; and the Bovine Animals (Identification, Marking and Breeding Records) Order 1990, SI 1990/1867. Orders must be laid before both Houses of Parliament: Animal Health Act 1981 s 10 (6).
3 'Disease' is not here restricted by its definition in the Animal Health Act 1981: s 10 (4).
4 The time of importation by sea or air is taken to be: (1) in the case of goods brought by sea, the time when the carrying ship comes within the limits of a port; and (2) in the case of goods brought by air,

the time when the carrying aircraft lands in the United Kingdom or when the goods are unloaded in the United Kingdom, whichever is the earlier: Customs and Excise Management Act 1979 s 5 (2) (a), (b), applied by the Animal Health Act 1981 s 10 (7).

In relation to anything brought through the Channel Tunnel, the time of importation is taken to be: (i) in the case of goods brought through the tunnel before the date specified as the date on which the English section meets the French section, the time when the goods enter the English section; (ii) otherwise, the time when the goods cross the frontier: Channel Tunnel (Customs and Excise) Order 1990, SI 1990/2167, art 5 (1)–(4), applied by the Animal Health Act 1981 s 10 (7) (as amended by the Channel Tunnel (Amendment of Agriculture, Fisheries and Food Import Legislation) Order 1990, SI 1990/2371). As to the meaning of 'English section' and 'French section', and as to the Channel Tunnel generally, see the Channel Tunnel Act 1987.

5 'Animals' here includes any kind of mammal, except man, any kind of four-footed beast which is not a mammal, and other fish, reptiles, crustaceans and other cold-blooded creatures: Animal Health Act 1981 s 10 (4); and the powers described have effect in relation to poultry: see s 87 (4).

6 Ibid s 10 (1). See the Importation of Animals Order 1977 and the orders cited in note 2 supra. As to European Community provisions relating to import of bovine animals and swine see AGRICULTURE vol 1 (2) (Reissue) para 1029.

7 Animal Health Act 1981 s 10 (2) (a). See the Importation of Animals Order 1977 and the orders cited in note 2 supra.

8 Animal Health Act 1981 s 10 (2) (b). See eg the Enzootic Bovine Leukosis Order 1980.

9 Animal Health Act 1981 s 10 (2) (d), Sch 2. See the Importation of Animals Order 1977; the Hares (Control of Importation) Order 1965; the Importation of Equine Animals Order 1979; the Importation of Hay and Straw Order 1979; the Importation of Animal Products and Poultry Products Order 1980; the Importation of Animal Pathogens Order 1980; the Importation of Processed Animal Protein Order 1981; the Tuberculosis (England and Wales) Order 1984; the Importation of Salmonid Viscera Order 1986; and the Bovine Animals (Identification, Marking and Breeding Records) Order 1990.

10 Animal Health Act 1981 s 10 (2) (c).

11 Ibid s 10 (5); see para 492 ante.

12 Ibid s 10 (8). As to the requirements of the Customs and Excise Commissioners see CUSTOMS AND EXCISE.

503. Controls on import of ruminating animals and swine. The importation of cattle, sheep, goats and all other ruminating animals[1] and swine is regulated by order[2]. The landing[3] of any such animal is prohibited except under a licence (general or specific) granted by the Minister of Agriculture, Fisheries and Food, which may contain conditions designed to prevent disease and protect animals from unnecessary suffering[4]. A licence is also required for animals on board a vessel which enters a harbour even if the animals are not landed[5]. However, in exceptional circumstances, imported animals not licensed to be landed, or ships not licensed to enter a harbour, may do so under the supervision of a veterinary inspector[6]. The other main provisions of the order concern (1) the carriage of imported animals into Great Britain; the cleansing and disinfection of vessels carrying or which have carried imported animals[7]; (2) the carriage of injured or diseased animals or animals which die during carriage[8]; (3) the unloading of animals and carcases[9]; (4) the movement of animals after unloading[10]; (5) the control of animals intended for re-export[11]; (6) the approval and regulation of premises for reception and quarantine[12]; and (7) the action to be taken in the case of injury or disease among animals (which may include the slaughter of animals without payment of compensation)[13]. Local authorities are made responsible for enforcing the order[14]. Any landing of an animal in Great Britain without an import licence, or which contravenes such a licence, or any contravention of the statutory provisions or of the provisions of a licence, may result in the detention, re-export or slaughter of the animal[15].

Certain offences involving intent to evade the provisions of this order may be prosecuted on indictment[16].

1 In this context, 'ruminating animals' includes llamas, guanacos, alpacas, vicunas, Bactrian camels and Arabian camels: Importation of Animals Order 1977, SI 1977/944, art 2 (1).

2 Importation of Animals Order 1977 (amended by SI 1990/2371), made under the powers described in para 502 ante.

3 In this context an animal is deemed to have been landed: (1) if it has been carried by sea, immediately it is put or otherwise arrives on land in Great Britain; (2) if it has been carried by air, immediately the aircraft touches down in Great Britain; (3) if it has been carried by a vehicle or otherwise arrives through the Channel Tunnel, immediately it crosses the frontier (see further the Channel Tunnel Act 1987 and the Channel Tunnel (Customs and Excise) Order 1990, SI 1990/2167): Importation of Animals Order 1977 art 2 (3) (amended by SI 1990/2371).

4 Importation of Animals Order 1977 art 3 (1)–(3). A licence must designate the ports and airports at which animals may be landed, and must specify approved premises to which animals are authorised to be moved after landing: art 3 (5). A licence must be produced on demand made by a Customs and Excise officer, a veterinary inspector or an officer of the minister, or an inspector of the local authority or a constable, who may take copies or extracts: art 20.

5 Ibid art 16. References to 'vessel', 'boat' or 'ship' etc, include hovercraft: see the Animal Health Act 1981 s 90 and the Hovercraft (Application of Enactments) Order 1972, SI 1972/971.

6 Importation of Animals Order 1977 art 17. See also note 5 supra.

7 Ibid arts 4 (1), 6. In default of the owner, master or operator carrying out a cleansing and disinfection as required, the local authority, veterinary inspector or other person acting for the minister may do so, and recover the expenses as a civil debt: art 18.
   The cleansing and disinfection of a vessel not carrying animals, but which has previously carried or come into contact with animals, and which may thus give rise to the risk of introducing or spreading disease in Great Britain, may also be ordered, with similar consequences for default: arts 15, 19 (2). See also note 5 supra.

8 Ibid art 4 (2)–(8). In general it is prohibited to unload such an animal without the written consent of a veterinary inspector: art 4 (2).

9 Ibid art 5.

10 Ibid art 8.

11 If such animals are in fact exported within the time specified by the import licence for re-export, and while in Great Britain are dealt with according to the terms of the licence, they do not have to be detained at approved premises: ibid art 9.

12 Ibid arts 10, 11. A reception centre must be at or near the port or airport in question, and quarantine premises must be at the port or airport and located so that there is no significant risk of the spread of disease through the movement of animals thereto: art 10 (2).

13 Ibid arts 12, 13, 19 (1).

14 Ibid art 22.

15 Ibid art 14.

16 See ibid art 21 (1). As to offences under the 1977 Order not triable on indictment see art 21 (2); and para 513 et seq post.

504. Landing of docked horses. No docked[1] horse[2] coming from outside the United Kingdom may be landed from a ship, aircraft or hovercraft unless permitted to do so by a customs officer, who must be satisfied that it will be exported as soon as practicable, or under licence granted by the Minister of Agriculture, Fisheries and Food, who must be satisfied that it is to be used for breeding purposes[3].

An offence, punishable on summary conviction by a customs penalty[4] or, as the case may be, a fine, not exceeding level 3 on the standard scale[5] or by imprisonment for a term not exceeding three months, or both, is committed by any person who lands a horse or causes or permits a horse to be landed in contravention of this provision or who, for the purpose of obtaining permission from a customs officer or a licence from the minister, makes any statement that he knows to be false[6] in a material particular[7] or recklessly makes any statement that is false in a material particular[8].

1 For the meaning of 'docked' see para 422 note 1 ante.
2 For the meaning of 'horse' see para 422 note 3 ante.
3 Docking and Nicking of Horses Act 1949 s 2 (1), (2) (s 2 (1) amended by the Transfer of Functions (Ministry of Food) Order 1955, SI 1955/554); Hovercraft Act 1968 s 3, Sch 1 para 1 (e).
4 For the recovery of customs penalties see CUSTOMS.
5 As to the standard scale see para 232 note 1 ante. At the date at which this volume states the law, level 3 on that scale is at £400: Criminal Justice Act 1982 s 37 (2) (amended by the Criminal Penalties, etc (Increase) Order 1984, SI 1984/447, art 2 (4), Sch 4).
6 See *R v Lord Kylsant* [1932] 1 KB 442, CCA; *R v Bishirgian* [1936] 1 All ER 586, CCA; *Jones v Meatyard* [1939] 1 All ER 140; and *Stevens and Steeds Ltd and Evans v King* [1943] 1 All ER 314. See further CRIMINAL LAW.
7 A particular may be material on the mere ground that it renders something else more credible: *R v Tyson* (1867) LR 1 CCR 107, a case under the Perjury Act 1911 s 1. As to materiality under that section see further CRIMINAL LAW.
8 Docking and Nicking of Horses Act 1949 s 2 (3), (4) (amended by the Criminal Justice Act 1982 s 46 and the Transfer of Functions (Ministry of Food) Order 1955, SI 1955/554).

B. EXPORT

505. Regulation of exports. For the purpose of preventing the conveyance of disease[1] by animals exported from Great Britain, the appropriate minister[2] may, with Treasury consent, provide facilities for the examination of animals[3] intended for export and provide or approve export quarantine stations for their reception, isolation and examination[4]. No compensation is payable in respect of any animal intended for export which, by reason of its having been diseased or suspected, or of its having been exposed to the infection of any disease, is slaughtered in an export quarantine station[5].

In the interests of animal or human health the Minister for Agriculture, Fisheries and Food may by order[6] make provision for regulating the export from Great Britain to a state which is a member of the European Communities of animals or poultry or their carcases, and in particular for prohibiting exports without a prescribed certificate or licence, and as to the circumstances in which and the conditions on which a certificate or licence may be obtained[7].

Additionally, the ministers[8] may by order provide in the interests of animal welfare for regulating the export of animals from Great Britain to any country; in particular, they may provide for exportation to be prohibited without a prescribed certificate or licence, and for requiring persons proposing to export animals to furnish information about the animals' intended ultimate destination and the arrangements for conveying them there, and any other matters that may be specified[9].

1 For the meaning of 'disease' see para 484 ante.
2 See para 486 note 8 ante.
3 For the meaning of 'animals' see para 483 ante.
4 Animal Health Act 1981 s 12 (1). See the Export Quarantine Stations (Regulation) Order 1973, SI 1973/824 for provisions regulating export quarantine stations.
5 Animal Health Act 1981 s 12 (2).
6 See the Exportation of Pigeons Order 1983, SI 1983/872; Diseases of Animals (Export Health Certificates) Order 1985, SI 1985/217; Export of Sheep (Prohibition) (No 2) Order 1987, SI 1987/1808 (amended by SI 1989/1767 and SI 1990/1936).

7 Animal Health Act 1981 s 11. See also AGRICULTURE vol 1 (2) (Reissue) para 1029 et seq.
8 See para 482 note 3 ante.
9 Animal Health Act 1981 s 39. See the Export of Animals (Protection) Order 1981, SI 1981/1051, which implements EC Council Directive 77/489 and which, inter alia, provides that in granting or refusing an export licence the minister must have regard to all matters connected with the welfare of the animals intended for export and in particular must not grant a licence unless he is satisfied that the arrangements for transporting the animals to their final destination are such as to protect them from unnecessary suffering: Export of Animals (Protection) Order 1981 art 3 (2). As to the extent of the minister's duty under art 3 (2) see *R v Minister of Agriculture, Fisheries and Food, ex p Roberts; R v Minister of Agriculture, Fisheries and Food, ex p RSPCA* (1990) Times, 19 November.

506. Horses, asses, mules and ponies. The shipment or attempted shipment by sea or air, except in such cases as the ministers[1] may by order[2] prescribe, of any horse[3] in any vessel or aircraft from any port or aerodrome[4] in Great Britain to any port or aerodrome in Europe other than in the Republic of Ireland outside the United Kingdom, the Channel Islands and the Isle of Man, is unlawful unless immediately before shipment the horse has been examined by a veterinary inspector appointed by the minister and has been certified in writing[5] by him to be capable of being conveyed to such port or aerodrome and disembarked or landed without cruelty, and to be capable of being worked without suffering[6].

Where the inspector is satisfied that the animal is a heavy draft horse, a vanner, mule or jennet (or hinny), or an ass, shipment is unlawful unless in the inspector's opinion the animal is not more than eight years of age and is of not less than a certain value[7]. These further conditions do not apply in the case of a horse intended to be used as a performing animal, or a horse, or foal at foot accompanying a horse, which is registered in the stud book of a recognised society for the encouragement of horse-breeding and which is intended to be used for breeding or exhibition purposes[8].

The shipment of any pony[9] in any vessel or aircraft from any port or aerodrome in Great Britain to any port or aerodrome outside the United Kingdom, the Channel Islands and the Isle of Man is similarly unlawful unless the minister is satisfied that the pony is intended for breeding, riding or exhibition, and is of not less than a certain value[10], and immediately before shipment it has been individually inspected by a veterinary inspector and certified in writing[11] to be capable of being conveyed to its destination and disembarked or landed without unnecessary suffering[12].

If any horse or pony is found on examination or inspection to be in such a physical condition that it is cruel to keep it alive, or to be permanently incapable of being worked without suffering, the inspector must forthwith slaughter it or cause it to be slaughtered with a suitable mechanically operated instrument, and no compensation is payable to its owner[13]. The veterinary inspector may mark a horse certified by him in the prescribed manner, and it is an offence for any person with a view to evading the above provisions to mark a horse with the prescribed mark or any mark so nearly resembling it as to be calculated to deceive[14].

If a horse shipped from any port in Great Britain to any port outside the United Kingdom, Channel Islands and the Isle of Man has a limb broken or is otherwise seriously injured so as to be incapable of being disembarked without cruelty, the master of the vessel must forthwith cause it to be slaughtered[15]. It is the duty of the owner and master to see that the vessel is provided with a proper killing instrument[16].

None of the above provisions[17] applies in the case of a thoroughbred horse certified in writing[18] by a steward or the secretary of the Jockey Club to have arrived in Great Britain not more than one month before the date of shipment for the purpose of being run in a race, or to be shipped for the purpose of being run in a race, or to be shipped in order to be used for breeding purposes[19].

The shipment of a registered pony[20] is unlawful unless there has first been obtained from the secretary of a society in whose stud book the pony is registered a certificate[21] that the pony is registered with that society[22].

Inspectors of the minister and of local authorities may enter vessels and aircraft to ascertain whether these provisions[23] are being complied with[24]. It is the duty of local authorities to enforce the provisions in so far as the minister by order directs[25], and any person infringing them is guilty of an offence against the Animal Health Act 1981[26].

Orders have been made supplementing these provisions[27].

1 See para 482 note 3 ante.
2 See the Export of Horses (Excepted Cases) Order 1969, SI 1969/1742 (amended by SI 1972/971), which, by art 3, exempts from these provisions any horse shipped to any port or aerodrome which is in the Republic of Ireland or which is not in Europe, or which the minister is satisfied is intended for exhibition, breeding, racing, jumping, riding or polo, or a foal travelling with its dam if the dam is any such horse.
3 'Horse' includes an ass or mule: Animal Health Act 1981 s 89 (1). Hinnies or jennets are not mentioned. As to ponies see the text to notes 9–12 infra. As to thoroughbreds see the text to notes 18, 19 infra.
4 'Aerodrome' means any area of land or water designed, equipped, set apart or commonly used for affording facilities for the landing and departure of aircraft: ibid s 89 (1).
5 The certificate must be delivered at the time of shipment to the master of the vessel or pilot of the aircraft on which the animal is shipped, and he must on demand produce it to and allow it to be copied by any constable or inspector or other officer of the appropriate minister or local authority: ibid s 48. The appropriate minister is the Minister of Agriculture, Fisheries and Food or the Secretary of State for Wales: s 86 (1) (b).
6 Ibid s 40 (1), (2); Export of Horses (Excepted Cases) Order 1969, SI 1969/1742, art 3 (a). As to the inspection of horses which are exempted from these provisions, other than horses shipped from Great Britain to any place outside Europe, see the Export of Horses (Protection) Order 1969, SI 1969/1784, art 7.
7 Animal Health Act 1981 s 40 (3). The values are: heavy draft horse, £715; vanner, mule or jennet, £495; ass, £220: s 40 (3).
8 Ibid s 40 (4).
9 'Pony' means a horse not more than 147 centimetres in height, except a foal travelling with its dam if the dam is over 147 centimetres: ibid s 89 (1).
10 Ie £300; or in the case of a pony not exceeding 122 centimetres in height (other than a Shetland pony not exceeding 107 centimetres in height), £220; or in the case of such a Shetland pony, £145: ibid s 41 (1) (a).
11 See note 5 supra.
12 Animal Health Act 1981 s 41 (1) (b). A pony may not be so certified if, being a mare, it is, in the inspector's opinion, heavy in foal, showing fullness of udder or too old to travel or, being a foal, if it is in his opinion too young to travel: s 41 (2).
13 Ibid s 44.
14 Ibid s 45.
15 Ibid s 46 (1). Note that there is no corresponding duty in respect of the pilot of an aircraft; hovercraft however, are included: see s 90.
16 Ibid s 46 (2).
17 Ie ibid s 40, 41 and 46.
18 See note 5 supra.
19 Animal Health Act 1981 s 47.
20 'Registered pony' means a pony registered in the stud book of the Arab Horse Society, National Pony Society, British Palomino Society, British Spotted Horse and Pony Society or the breed

society for English Connemara, Dales, Dartmoor, Exmoor, Fell, Highland, New Forest, Shetland or Welsh ponies: ibid s 42.

21 See note 5 supra.
22 Animal Health Act 1981 s 42.
23 Ie the provisions of ibid ss 40–42 and 44–48, and any order made under the Act relating to the exportation or shipment of horses: s 49 (1).
24 Ibid s 49 (1).
25 Ibid s 49 (2).
26 Ibid s 49 (3). See para 513 et seq post.
27 See the Export of Horses (Veterinary Examination) Order 1966, SI 1966/507; Export of Horses (Excepted Cases) Order 1969; Export of Horses (Protection) Order 1969.

(vii) Slaughter of Animals; Compensation

507. Slaughter of animals. The Minister of Agriculture, Fisheries and Food must cause to be slaughtered[1] all animals[2] affected with cattle plague[3] and all cattle[4] affected with pleuro-pneumonia[5]. A local authority must cause to be slaughtered every animal within its district which is affected with or suspected of rabies or which is shown to the satisfaction of an inspector to have been bitten by an animal so affected[6].

The minister may cause to be slaughtered:

(1) any animal affected with brucellosis melitensis or foot-and-mouth disease, any bovine animal[7] affected with brucellosis or tuberculosis or which has reacted to a tuberculin test, any sheep affected with sheep-pox, any swine affected with swine fever, and any animal[8] affected with any disease[9] to which the provisions are by order applied;

(2) any animal suspected of cattle plague or foot-and-mouth disease, any cattle suspected of pleuro-pneumonia, any sheep suspected of sheep-pox, any swine suspected of swine fever, any bovine animal suspected of brucellosis and any animal[10] suspected of any disease[11] to which the provisions are by order applied;

(3) any animals in a place infected with cattle plague or in such parts of an area so infected as are not comprised in a place so infected, but in the latter case subject to such regulations as the Treasury by statutory instrument think fit to make[12];

(4) any cattle, animals, sheep or swine which are or have been in the same field, shed, sty or other place, or in the same herd or flock or otherwise in contact with cattle affected with pleuro-pneumonia or, as the case may be, animals affected with cattle plague[13] or foot-and-mouth disease, or sheep affected with sheep-pox, or swine affected with swine fever, or which appear to him to have been in any way exposed to the infection of that disease, and any animal which has been exposed to the infection of brucellosis melitensis, any bovine animal which has been exposed to the infection of brucellosis or tuberculosis, and any animal[14] exposed to the infection of any disease[15] to which the provisions are by order applied[16].

The minister may also by order provide for the destruction of wild members of one or more species in any area, if he is satisfied that in that area there exists in the wild members of the species a disease[17] (other than rabies) which is being or has been transmitted from members of the species to animals of any kind in the area, and destruction of members of the species is necessary to eliminate or substantially to reduce the incidence of that disease in animals of any kind in the area[18]. Where an authorised officer[19] reasonably suspects that a disease[20] exists among the wild members of any species in an area he may enter any land in the area and take samples of the wild members of the species and of things with which they may have been in contact, and carry out other necessary investigations with a view to determining whether a destruction order should be made[21]. An authorised officer may also enter land to carry out destruction under such an order[22], or to determine whether the species in question is recolonising the area[23], but he is not empowered to enter a dwelling-house[24]. In exercising any such power of entry, the authorised officer must, if required by the owner or occupier or person in charge of the land, produce proof of his authority and state in writing his reasons for entering[25].

Notwithstanding the above provisions the minister may reserve for observation and treatment any animal liable to be slaughtered, subject to the payment of compensation as in the case of actual slaughter[26]. When the minister has decided that any head of cattle is to be slaughtered on account of pleuro-pneumonia he must, if the owner by notice so requires, cause them to be slaughtered within 21 days[27].

1 As to the disposal of carcases after slaughter see generally para 510 post.
2 For the meaning of 'animal' see para 440 ante. As to the slaughter of poultry see para 522 post.
3 Animal Health Act 1981 s 31, Sch 3 para 1 (1).
4 For the meaning of 'cattle' see para 483 ante.
5 Animal Health Act 1981 Sch 3 para 2 (1). 'Pleuro-pneumonia' means contagious pleuro-pneumonia of cattle: s 89 (1).
6 See the Rabies Control Order 1974, SI 1974/2212, and para 493 ante.
7 'Bovine animal' means bull, cow, steer, heifer or calf: Tuberculosis (England and Wales) Order 1984, SI 1984/1943, art 2 (1); or bull, cow, heifer or calf: Brucellosis (England and Wales) Order 1981, SI 1981/1455, art 2 (1).
8 'Animal' in this context includes horses: Animal Health Act 1981 s 32 (4) (a).
9 'Disease' in this context is not confined to the statutory definition: ibid s 32 (4) (b).
10 See note 7 supra.
11 See note 8 supra.
12 As to infected places and areas see para 496 ante. At the date at which this volume states the law no such instrument was in force.
13 In the case of cattle plague the minister must be satisfied that the slaughter is necessary for preventing the spread of the disease: Animal Health Act 1981 Sch 3 para 1 (2).
14 See note 7 supra.
15 See note 8 supra.
16 Animal Health Act 1981 ss 31, 32 (1), (2), Sch 3 paras 1–4. The provisions have been applied by the following orders: the Sheep-Pox Order of 1938, SR & O 1938/229 (amended by SI 1977/944); the Brucellosis Melitensis Order of 1940, SR & O 1940/1251 (amended by SR & O 1942/143 and SI 1977/945); the Swine Vesicular Disease Order 1972, SI 1972/1980 (amended by SI 1973/101 and SI 1977/944); the Enzootic Bovine Leukosis Order 1980, SI 1980/79; the Brucellosis (England and Wales) Order 1981, SI 1981/1455 (amended by SI 1986/2295); the Aujeszky's Disease Order 1983, SI 1983/344; the Tuberculosis (England and Wales) Order 1984, SI 1984/1943 (amended by SI 1990/1869); the Bovine Spongiform Encephalopathy (No 2) Order 1988, SI 1988/2299 (amended by SI 1990/1930); and the Tuberculosis (Deer) Notice of Intended Slaughter and Compensation Order 1989/1316.
17 Ie a disease for the purposes of the Animal Health Act 1981; see para 484 ante.
18 Ibid s 21 (1), (2). The minister must consult with the Nature Conservancy Council before making such an order: s 21 (3). At the date at which this volume states the law, no such order is in force. However, for an example of an order previously having effect under these provisions, see the Badgers (Control Areas) Order 1977, SI 1977/1721 (revoked by SI 1986/2061). As to the details which may be contained in such an order, particularly with regard to methods of destruction and the power to prevent the movement of living creatures into an area to which an order applies, see the Animal Health Act 1981 s 21 (4)–(10).
19 Ie an officer of the appropriate minister (the Minister of Agriculture, Fisheries and Food or the Secretary of State for Wales), a veterinary inspector or some other person authorised for the purpose by the appropriate minister: ibid s 22 (1).

20 See note 17 supra.
21 Animal Health Act 1981 s 22 (2).
22 Ibid s 22 (3) (a). He is authorised to enter land to see if destruction has been effectively carried out: s 22 (3) (c).
23 Ibid s 22 (4).
24 Ibid s 22 (5).
25 Ibid s 22 (6). An officer cannot demand entry to land forming part of a nature reserve (see OPEN SPACES) unless he has given seven days' notice; in the exercise of his functions on such land he must do so in such manner as to minimise damage to certain flora, fauna and physiographical or geological features: s 22 (7).
26 Ibid s 34 (1).
27 Ibid Sch 3 para 2 (4).

508. Compensation for slaughter. Compensation is payable to persons whose animals are slaughtered for the common good. The rate varies according to the disease for the prevention of which the animal was slaughtered, and according to whether the animal was actually affected with disease or not[1]. If the sum received by the Minister of Agriculture, Fisheries and Food on sale of a carcase exceeds the amount paid for compensation to the owner of the slaughtered animal, the minister must pay that excess to the owner after deducting reasonable expenses[2].

When insurance is payable upon animals thus slaughtered, the insurers may deduct the amount of compensation received by the owner before they make the payment[3].

Unless some other method of ascertaining the value of any animal or bird the subject of compensation is prescribed[4], the minister must, as soon as practicable, give a written statement of value to the owner and if the owner does not within 14 days serve a written counter-notice disputing the valuation, that sum becomes the compensation; if such a counter-notice is served, the compensation is settled by the arbitration of a single arbitrator[5].

The minister may, if he thinks fit, withhold compensation, either wholly or partially, in the case of an imported animal which was, in his judgment, diseased at the time of its landing or, before or while being brought from a state which is a member of the European Communities, exposed to the infection of disease[6]. Compensation is not payable in respect of any animal intended for export that is slaughtered in an export quarantine station by reason of its having been diseased, suspected of disease, or exposed to infection[7].

1 Compensation in relation to certain diseases is provided for in the Animal Health Act 1981; see s 31, Sch 3. The position, broadly speaking, is that if the animal was affected with the disease compensation is its value immediately before it became affected (foot-and-mouth disease), or half that value (swine fever or, with a maximum of £20, cattle plague), or of three-quarters that value with a maximum of £30 (pleuro-pneumonia); if the animal was not affected with the disease compensation is its value immediately before it was slaughtered (foot-and-mouth disease, swine fever) with a maximum of £40 (cattle plague, pleuro-pneumonia); Sch 3 paras 1 (4), 2 (3), 3 (2), 4 (2). In relation to other diseases compensation is provided for by orders made under s 32 (3); see the Sheep-Pox Order of 1938, SR & O 1938/229 (amended by SI 1977/944); the Brucellosis Melitensis Order of 1940, SR & O 1940/1251 (amended by SR & O 1942/143 and SI 1977/945); the Swine Vesicular Disease (Compensation) Order 1972, SI 1972/2014; the Rabies (Compensation) Order 1976, SI 1976/2195 (see para 493 ante); the Brucellosis and Tuberculosis (England and Wales) Compensation Order 1978, SI 1978/1483 (amended by SI 1981/1412); the Enzootic Bovine Leukosis (Compensation) Order 1980, SI 1980/80; the Aujeszky's Disease (Compensation for Swine) Order 1983, SI 1983/345; the Tuberculosis (Deer) Notice of Intended Slaughter and Compensation Order 1989, SI 1989/1316; and the Bovine Spongiform Encephalopathy Compensation Order 1990, SI 1990/222.
2 Animal Health Act 1981 s 34 (3). As to the disposal of carcases of animals slaughtered at the direction of the minister see para 507 text and notes 20, 21.

3 Ibid s 34 (5). As to income tax in relation to compensation see INCOME TAXATION vol 23 (Reissue) para 313.
4 Ie under ibid s 34 (7); see eg the Brucellosis Melitensis Order of 1940 (value to be agreed in writing between the minister and the owner or, in the case of dispute, ascertained as in the text to note 5 infra).
5 Diseases of Animals (Ascertainment of Compensa. tion) Order 1959, SI 1959/1335, art 3 (i)–(iii). Arbitration is conducted under the Arbitration Act 1950, as to which see ARBITRATION. An arbitrator may be appointed by agreement between the owner and the minister: art 3 (iv). If no such agreement is reached within 14 days after service of the counter-notice, either party may apply to the President of the Chartered Auctioneers' and Estate Agents' Institute to appoint an arbitrator: art 3 (v).
6 Animal Health Act 1981 s 34 (6).
7 Ibid s 12 (2). An 'export quarantine station' is a quarantine station provided or approved for the reception, isolation and examination of animals intended for export: s 12 (1).

509. Seizure of things likely to spread disease. The ministers[1] may by order[2] make such provision for the seizure of anything (except an animal, but including animal products and carcases) by or by means of which they consider certain diseases[3] might be carried or transmitted, and for the destruction, burial, disposal or treatment of anything so seized, as they think expedient for preventing the spread of any such disease[4].

The Minister of Agriculture, Fisheries and Food[5] must pay compensation for anything seized under any such order for the purpose of preventing foot-and-mouth disease, and for anything so seized for the purpose of preventing the spread of any other disease except the carcase of, or anything obtained from or produced by, any animal or bird affected with the disease[6], although the ministers[7] may by order provide for the payment of compensation for such carcases or things in respect of diseases other than foot-and-mouth disease or fowl pest[8]. Compensation is based on the value of the thing at the time of the seizure[9]. Where anything destroyed, buried or disposed of under an order made for the regulation thereof in respect of infected places or areas[10] could have been seized under the present provisions, the compensation is payable as if it had been so seized at the time of the destruction, burial or disposal[11]. The ministers may make such orders as they think fit for prescribing how the value of anything seized is to be ascertained, for arranging the method of payment, and for regulating the destruction, burial or disposal of anything seized[12].

1 Ie the Minister of Agriculture, Fisheries and Food and the Secretaries of State for Scotland and for Wales, acting jointly: Animal Health Act 1981 s 86 (1) (c).
2 See the Diseases of Animals (Seizure of Carcases, etc) Order 1964, SI 1964/1255 (amended by SI 1972/2041 and SI 1983/346), which applies to certain animals and birds affected by foot-and-mouth disease, swine vesicular disease, swine fever, fowl pest and Aujeszky's disease: see art 3, Schedule (Schedule amended by the instruments noted above).
3 These powers are exercisable in relation to the diseases in respect of which powers of slaughter are exercisable under the Animal Health Act 1981, namely, cattle plague, pleuro-pneumonia, foot-and-mouth disease and swine fever, and any disease to which s 32 applies (see para 507 note 15 ante); and any disease as defined in relation to poultry by or under s 88 (see para 517 post): s 35 (2).
4 Ibid s 35 (1), (1A) (s 35 (1) amended, and s 35 (1A) added, by the Animal Health and Welfare Act 1984 s 1).
5 See the Animal Health Act 1981 s 86 (1) (a).
6 Ibid s 36 (1) (amended by the Animal Health and Welfare Act 1984 s 1 (3)).
7 See note 1 supra.
8 Animal Health Act 1981 s 36 (2) (amended by the Animal Health and Welfare Act 1984 s 1 (3)). Compensation is not payable under the Diseases of Animals (Seizure of Carcases, etc) Order 1964 in respect of carcases affected with any disease other than foot-and-mouth disease: art 4 (3) (amended by SI 1972/2041).
9 Animal Health Act 1981 s 36 (3).

10 Ie an order made under ibid s 23 (e). See generally para 496 et seq ante.
11 Ibid s 36 (4).
12 Ibid s 36 (5). See the Diseases of Animals (Seizure of Carcases, etc) Order 1964 arts 3, 4 (art 4 amended by SI 1972/2041).

510. Disposal of carcases. When an animal has been slaughtered at the direction of the Minister of Agriculture, Fisheries and Food, the carcase[1] belongs to him and must be disposed of by him or as he directs, as the condition of the animal or carcase and other circumstances require or admit[2]. The minister may use for the burial of the carcase any suitable land in the possession or occupation of the animal's owner or any common or uninclosed land[3]. The ministers[4] may make orders[5] regulating the destruction, burial, disposal or treatment of the carcases of animals slaughtered at their direction[6], or of animals dying while diseased or suspected[7].

It is unlawful for any person, except under a licence from the ministers, to dig up, or cause to be dug up, the buried carcase of any animal[8].

1 For the meaning of 'carcase' see para 496 note 7 ante.
2 Animal Health Act 1981 s 34 (2). As to the seizure of carcases see para 509 ante.
3 Ibid s 34 (4). As to uninclosed land see para 499 note 3 ante.
4 Ie the Minister of Agriculture, Fisheries and Food and the Secretaries of State for Scotland and Wales, acting jointly: ibid s 86 (1) (c).
5 See the Anthrax Order of 1938, SR & O 1938/204; the Swine Fever Order 1963, SI 1963/286 (amended by SI 1976/919); and the Brucellosis (England and Wales) Order 1981, SI 1981/1455 (amended by SI 1986/2295).
6 Animal Health Act 1981 s 34 (7).
7 Ibid s 35 (3) (a). See the Brucellosis (England and Wales) Order 1981 (as amended: see note 5 supra). As to rabies see para 493 ante.
8 See the Animal Health Act 1981 s 35 (3) (c); the Animals (Miscellaneous Provisions) Order of 1927, SR & O 1927/290, art 16. For the meaning of 'animals' in this context see para 488 note 1 ante.

(viii) Enforcement and Offences

511. Functions of police. It is the duty of the police force of each police area to execute and enforce the Animal Health Act 1981 and orders made by the Minister of Agriculture, Fisheries and Food under that Act[1]. A constable[2] may, without warrant, stop and detain a person who is seen or found committing, or is reasonably suspected[3] of being engaged in committing, an offence against the Act[4]. In addition the constable may stop, detain and examine any animal, vehicle, boat or thing to which the suspected offence relates, and require it to be taken back to any place from which it was unlawfully removed[5].

If a person obstructs, impedes or assists in obstructing or impeding an officer other than a constable in the execution of the Act, of an order of the Minister of Agriculture, Fisheries and Food, or of a regulation of a local authority, the officer may without warrant apprehend him[6].

A person apprehended under any of the provisions described above must be taken with all practicable speed before a justice, and may not be detained longer than is necessary for that purpose[7].

In any case in which a constable stops any person, animal, vehicle, boat or other thing the constable must make a written report to his superior officer, including an account of his proceedings in consequence[8].

Additional powers are conferred on constables in relation to the prevention of the introduction or spread of rabies in Great Britain[9].

1 Animal Health Act 1981 s 60 (1). For the meaning of 'police force' and 'police area' see the Police Act 1964 s 62 (a), (c); and POLICE.
2 These provisions extend to a person called by a constable to his assistance: Animal Health Act 1981 s 60 (8). As to the exercise of constables' powers by inspectors see para 512 post.
3 It seems that this means not only that there was reasonable cause to suspect but there was actually such suspicion: *R v Harrison* [1938] 3 All ER 134, CCA; *Nakkuda Ali v M F De Jayaratne* [1951] AC 66, PC.
4 Animal Health Act 1981 s 60 (2). There is no specific power of arrest under the Act, save for officers other than constables (see s 60 (5) (amended by the Police and Criminal Evidence Act 1984 s 119 (1), Sch 6 Pt I para 24); text and note 6 infra), and save for the powers as to rabies (see para 495 ante). As to police powers of arrest generally see the Police and Criminal Evidence Act 1984 ss 24, 25; and POLICE.
5 Animal Health Act 1981 s 60 (4) (amended by the Police and Criminal Evidence Act 1984 s 119, Sch 7). References to 'vessel', 'boat' or 'ship' etc, include hovercraft: see the Animal Health Act 1981 s 90 and the Hovercraft (Application of Enactments) Order 1972, SI 1972/971.
6 Animal Health Act 1981 s 60 (5) (amended by the Police and Criminal Evidence Act 1984 Schs 6, 7).
7 Animal Health Act 1981 s 60 (6).
8 Ibid s 60 (9).
9 See para 495 ante.

512. Functions of inspectors. Inspectors[1] appointed by local authorities[2] and the veterinary[3] or other inspectors appointed by the Minister of Agriculture, Fisheries and Food are entrusted with various functions under the Animal Health Act 1981 and orders made under the Act. The powers conferred upon a local authority inspector are normally exercisable only in relation to the district for which he is appointed[4], whereas a ministry inspector has all the powers of an inspector throughout England and Wales or that part for which he is appointed[5], and where an order gives any power to a local authority inspector, that power may be exercised by the ministry inspector[6]. Both ministry and local authority inspectors have, for the purposes of the Act, certain of the powers of constables[7]. Additionally, they may enter any land or shed to which the Act applies, any building or place where they have reasonable grounds for supposing that disease exists or has within 56 days existed, that the carcase of a diseased animal has been kept or disposed of, that there is to be found any pen, place, vehicle or thing in respect of which there has been non-compliance with the Act or an order or local authority regulation, or that the Act or an order or regulation has not been complied with[8], and any pen, vehicle, vessel, boat or aircraft in which or in respect of which he has reasonable grounds for supposing that the Act or an order or regulation has not been complied with[9]. An inspector must, if required by the owner or occupier, state in writing his reasons for entering[10].

An inspector may also enter vessels, boats, aircraft or other vehicles that are within port limits or within an airport, or vessels, boats or aircraft that he reasonably supposes have been recently brought into Great Britain, in order to ascertain whether any order made to prevent disease being introduced into Great Britain through the importation of animals, carcases, eggs or other things[11], or a licence issued under such an order, is being complied with[12]. He may enter land, buildings or other places, and vessels, boats, aircraft or other vehicles (wherever they may be) when he reasonably supposes an animal or other thing whose importation is prohibited or regulated by such an order is or has been kept there[13].

A Ministry inspector who is satisfied that the Act, an order of the Minister of Agriculture, Fisheries and Food, or a local authority regulation is not being complied with or has not been complied with on board a vessel in port may so state in writing, whereupon the vessel may be detained until the Minister directs otherwise[14].

The certificate of a ministry veterinary inspector is conclusive evidence in all courts that an animal is or was affected with a disease specified therein[15].

Local authority inspectors are directly responsible to the minister for sending and giving such notices, reports, returns and information as he requires[16].

If inspectors act negligently in executing the minister's orders the local authority is not answerable[17].

1 'Inspector' means a person appointed to be an inspector for the purposes of the Animal Health Act 1981 by the Minister of Agriculture, Fisheries and Food or by a local authority and, when used in relation to an officer of the ministry, includes a veterinary inspector: s 89 (1).
2 As to the appointment of local authority inspectors see para 537 post.
3 As to the appointment of inspectors generally see para 535 post.
4 See the Animal Health Act 1981 s 51.
5 Ibid s 63 (8).
6 Animals (Miscellaneous Provisions) Order of 1927, SR & O 1927/290, art 3.
7 They have the powers outlined in para 511 text and note 4 ante; but not certain powers which relate to rabies (described in para 495 ante): Animal Health Act 1981 s 63 (1).
8 Ibid s 63 (2).
9 Ibid s 63 (3) (amended by the Animal Health and Welfare Act 1984 s 16 (1), Sch 1 para 4). For the power to enter premises to examine sheep see para 447 ante. References to 'vessel', 'boat' or 'ship' etc, include hovercraft: see the Animal Health Act 1981 s 90 and the Hovercraft (Application of Enactments) Order 1972, SI 1972/971.
10 Animal Health Act 1981 s 63 (4).
11 Ie an order made under ibid s 10; see para 502 ante.
12 Ibid s 63 (5). See also note 9 supra.
13 Ibid s 63 (6). See also note 9 supra.
14 Ibid s 65 (1). A copy of the inspector's representations must be delivered to the master of the vessel: s 65 (2). By virtue of s 65 (4), this power may be extended by order to aircraft. At the date at which this volume states the law, no such order had been made. See also s 65 (3); the Merchant Shipping Act 1894 s 692; and SHIPPING.
15 See the Animal Health Act 1981 s 63 (7). See *Harris v Smith* (1879) 44 JP 361; *Jameson v Dow* (1898) 2 F 24, Ct of Sess; *Henderson v Wardrope* 1932 JC 18.
16 Animal Health Act 1981 s 81.
17 *Stanbury v Exeter Corpn* [1905] 2 KB 838. See also *Ministry of Housing and Local Government v Sharp* [1970] 2 QB 223 at 268, [1970] 1 All ER 1009 at 1015, CA, per Lord Denning MR.

513. Offences, proceedings and penalties: general. Landing, shipping or bringing through the Channel Tunnel an animal or thing, or attempting to do so, in contravention of the Animal Health Act 1981 or a Minister's order renders a person liable under the customs and excise Acts[1] to the penalties imposed on persons importing or exporting or attempting to import or export prohibited goods; and this is without prejudice to any proceedings under the Animal Health Act 1981[2]. Goods improperly imported are liable to forfeiture[3]. Importing, unshipping or landing an animal with intent to evade the statutory restrictions is an offence punishable on summary conviction by a penalty of the prescribed sum[4], or three times the value of the goods, whichever is the greater, or imprisonment for up to six months, or both, and on conviction on indictment by a penalty of any amount or imprisonment for up to seven years, or both[5]. Similar penalties are available for offences of exporting prohibited goods[6].

An offence against the Animal Health Act 1981 which is declared to be such by an order expressed to be made for the purpose of preventing the introduction of rabies into Great Britain[7] may be tried either summarily or on indictment[8]. So too may offences of contravening, or failing to comply with, any such order, or failing to observe a condition of a licence issued under such an order, when the order declares that the offence is so triable[9]. A person guilty of such an offence is liable on summary conviction to a fine not exceeding the statutory maximum[10], and on conviction on indictment to a fine or to imprisonment for up to 12 months, or to both[11].

Other offences under the Act, discussed in the following paragraphs, are summary offences[12]. Any person aggrieved by the decision of a magistrates' court under the Act may appeal to the Crown Court[13].

The right to lay informations for offences under the Animal Health Act 1981 is not restricted to local authorities, but prosecutions may be instituted by a private prosecutor[14].

In any proceedings under the Animal Health Act 1981 no proof is required of the appointment or handwriting of an inspector or officer of the minister, or of the clerk, inspector or other officer of a local authority[15]. Where a person is charged with an offence against the Act in relation to a disease, he is presumed to have had knowledge of the existence of the disease unless he shows that he did not have such knowledge, and could not with reasonable diligence have obtained it[16].

1 'Customs and Excise Acts' means the Customs and Excise Management Act 1979, the Customs and Excise Duties (General Relief) Act 1979, the Alcoholic Liquor Duties Act 1979, the Hydrocarbon Oil Duties Act 1979, the Matches and Mechanical Lighters Duties Act 1979, the Tobacco Products Duty Act 1979 and any other enactment for the time being in force relating to customs and excise: Customs and Excise Management Act 1979 s 1 (1), applied by the Animal Health Act 1981 s 89 (1).
2 Ibid s 74 (amended by the Channel Tunnel (Amendment of Agriculture, Fisheries and Food Import Legislation) Order 1990, SI 1990/2371). For the provisions as to prohibiting or regulating the importation or exportation of animals see para 502 et seq ante. References to 'vessel', 'boat' or 'ship' etc, include hovercraft: see the Animal Health Act 1981 s 90 and the Hovercraft (Application of Enactments) Order 1972, SI 1972/971.
3 Customs and Excise Management Act 1979 s 49 (modified as respects the Channel Tunnel by the Channel Tunnel (Customs and Excise) Order 1990, SI 1990/2167).
4 As to the prescribed sum see para 233 note 3 ante. At the date at which this volume states the law, that sum is at £2,000.
5 Customs and Excise Management Act 1979 s 50 (1) (a), (2)–(4) (s 50 (2), (3) amended by the Police and Criminal Evidence Act 1984 s 114 (1); s 50 (4) amended by the Forgery and Counterfeiting Act 1981 s 23 (1) and by the Finance Act 1988 s 12 (1) (a)). That provision is modified as respects the Channel Tunnel: see note 3 supra.
6 See the Customs and Excise Management Act 1979 s 68 (amended by virtue of the Criminal Justice Act 1982 ss 38, 46, and by the Forgery and Counterfeiting Act 1981 s 23 (2) and the Finance Act 1988 s 12 (1) (a)). That provision is modified as respects the Channel Tunnel: see note 3 supra.
7 Ie an order made under the Animal Health Act 1981 s 10. See the Rabies (Importation of Dogs, Cats and Other Mammals) Order 1974, SI 1974/2211, art 17 (para 492 ante), and the Rabies (Virus) Order 1979, SI 1979/135, art 8 (para 494 ante).
8 Animal Health Act 1981 s 76 (1).
9 Ibid s 76 (3).
10 Ie the prescribed sum within the meaning of the Magistrates' Courts Act 1980 s 32: Animal Health Act 1981 s 76 (4) (a). As to the prescribed sum see para 233 note 3 ante. At the date at which this volume states the law, that sum is at £2,000.
11 Ibid s 76 (2).
12 See paras 514, 515 post. Every offence against the Act is deemed to have been committed, and every cause of complaint or matter for summary proceeding under the Act, order or regulation is deemed to have arisen either where it actually was committed or arose, or where the defendant happens to be at the time of the institution of the charge, complaint or proceeding: ibid s 79 (4).
13 Ibid s 78.
14 *R v Stewart* [1896] 1 QB 300; cf *Tranton v Astor* (1917) 33 TLR 383.
15 Animal Health Act 1981 s 79 (1).
16 Ibid s 79 (2). As to the raising of a presumption in cases relating to cleansing and disinfection see s 79 (3); and para 490 ante.

514. Specific offences. A person is guilty of an offence against the Animal Health Act 1981 if he:

(1) acts without a licence or with an expired licence, where a licence is required, with intent to evade the Act or an order of the minister[1] or a regulation of a local authority[2];

(2) uses, offers or attempts to use an incomplete or false licence, makes a declaration or statement false in a material particular for the purpose of obtaining a licence, certificate or instrument, obtains or endeavours to obtain one by false pretences, or grants or issues one false in a material particular, unless he shows to the court's satisfaction that he did not know of the incompleteness, untruth or falsity, and could not with reasonable diligence have known of it[3];

(3) grants or issues a document either knowing that he has no authority to do so, or in blank[4];

(4) uses or offers or attempts to use a blank instrument unless he shows to the court's satisfaction that he did not know it was issued in blank and could not with reasonable diligence have known[5];

(5) digs up or causes to be dug up without lawful authority or excuse, proof of which lies on him, a carcase[6] buried under the direction of the minister, a local authority or a receiver of wreck[7]; or

(6) does anything without lawful authority, proof of which lies on him, which the minister has prohibited relating to the use of a vessel, aircraft, vehicle or place for the carrying of animals or for any purpose connected therewith[8].

On conviction he is liable to a fine not exceeding level 5 on the standard scale or, if the offence is committed with respect to more than ten animals, a fine not exceeding level 3 on the standard scale for each animal or, if the offence is committed in relation to carcases, fodder, litter[9], dung or other things, a fine not exceeding level 3 on the standard scale for every 508 kilogrammes after the first 508 kilogrammes, in addition to the first fine not exceeding level 5 on the standard scale[10]; alternatively he may be imprisoned for a term not exceeding two months[11].

A person is also guilty of an offence against the Act if, without lawful authority or excuse, proof of which lies on him, he:

(a) does anything contravening the Act, an order of the minister or a local authority regulation[12];

(b) fails to keep an animal apart or give notice of disease when required by the Act or an order to do so[13];

(c) fails to give, produce, observe or do any notice, licence, rule or thing as required by the Act or by an order or regulation[14];

(d) does anything which the Act or an order makes or declares to be not lawful[15];

(e) does or omits anything the doing or omission of which is declared by the Act or an order to be an offence by him against the Act[16];

(f) refuses admission to an inspector or officer with a power of entry or examination, or obstructs or impedes him[17]; or

(g) throws or places, or causes or suffers to be thrown or placed, into any river, stream, canal, navigation or other water, or into the sea within 4.8 kilometres of the shore, the carcase of an animal which has died of disease or been slaughtered as diseased or suspected[18].

On conviction he is liable to the fines specified above[19]. On a further conviction for a second or subsequent similar offence he may alternatively be imprisoned for a term not exceeding one month[20].

1 'An order of the minister' means an order of: (1) the Minister of Agriculture, Fisheries and Food; (2) that minister and the Secretaries of State for Scotland and for Wales, acting jointly; or (3) any of those persons: Animal Health Act 1981 ss 86 (1), 89 (1).
2 Ibid s 71 (a), (b).
3 Ibid ss 67 (a), 69, 71 (c). As to the meaning of 'false in a material particular' see para 504 note 6 ante. As to false pretences see CRIMINAL LAW.
4 Ibid ss 67 (b), 68 (a).
5 Ibid s 68 (b).
6 For the meaning of 'carcase' see para 496 note 11 ante.
7 Animal Health Act 1981 s 35 (4) (b).
8 Ibid s 8 (2).
9 For the meanings of 'carcase', 'fodder' and 'litter' see para 496 note 11 ante.
10 Animal Health Act 1981 s 75 (1) (amended by virtue of the Criminal Justice Act 1982 ss 38, 46). As to the standard scale see para 232 note 1 ante. At the date at which this volume states the law, levels 3 and 5 on that scale are at £400 and £2,000 respectively.
11 Animal Health Act 1981 s 75 (5).
12 Ibid s 73 (a). As to an 'order of the minister' see note 1 supra.
13 Ibid s 15 (7).
14 Ibid s 73 (b).
15 Ibid s 72 (b).
16 Ibid s 72 (a).
17 Ibid s 66.
18 Ibid s 35 (4) (a).
19 See ibid s 75; text and note 10 supra.
20 Ibid s 75 (4). Quaere whether the Criminal Justice Act 1982 s 35 gives magistrates a discretion to impose a term of imprisonment on any conviction for these offences.

515. Other offences. Other offences against the Animal Health Act 1981 include contraventions of the provisions relating to the export of horses[1], and refusal to give or the giving of false information as to diseased animals[2]. Obtaining compensation for slaughtered animals by deception is an indictable offence punishable by imprisonment for a term not exceeding ten years[3].

Knowingly or recklessly making a false statement for the purpose of obtaining any sum payable for the eradication of bovine tuberculosis, brucellosis or other diseases of animals may be punished on summary conviction with a fine of level 3 on the standard scale or imprisonment for three months, or both[4]. Obstruction of any person duly authorised to make an inspection for the purpose of such eradication is punishable with a fine of level 3 on the standard scale or imprisonment for one month, or both[5]. Any person who offers for sale, otherwise than for slaughter, any animal known to him to be a reactor to brucella abortus is liable on summary conviction to a fine not exceeding level 5 on the standard scale or, if the offence is committed with respect to more than ten animals, to a fine not exceeding level 3 on the standard scale for each animal[6].

1 See the Animal Health Act 1981 ss 45 (2), 49 (3); and para 506 ante.
2 See the Animals (Miscellaneous Provisions) Order of 1927, SR & O 1927/290, art 12 (1); and para 488 ante.
3 See the Theft Act 1968 s 15 (1); and CRIMINAL LAW.
4 Animal Health Act 1981 s 4 (1) (amended by virtue of the Criminal Justice Act 1982 ss 38, 46). As to the standard scale see para 232 note 1 ante. At the date at which this volume states the law, level 3 on that scale is at £400.
5 Animal Health Act 1981 s 4 (2) (as amended: see note 4 supra). See para 485 ante. As to the standard scale see note 4 supra.

6 Agriculture Act 1970 s 106 (4) (amended by virtue of the Criminal Justice Act 1982 ss 38, 46). As to the standard scale see para 232 note 1 ante. At the date at which this volume states the law, level 5 on that scale is at £2,000.

(3) POULTRY

516. Application of Animal Health Act 1981 to poultry. Subject to the provisions referred to in the following paragraphs the Animal Health Act 1981 has effect in relation to poultry[1] as it has effect in relation to animals[2].

1 For the meaning of 'poultry' see para 517 post.
2 Animal Health Act 1981 s 87 (4). As to European Community provisions see AGRICULTURE vol 1 (2) (Reissue) para 1034.

517. Meaning of 'poultry' and 'disease'. 'Poultry' in the Animal Health Act 1981 means domestic fowls, turkeys, geese, ducks, guinea-fowls, pigeons, pheasants and partridges[1], but the ministers[2] may by order[3] extend the definition to include, for any purpose of the Animal Health Act 1981, any other species of bird, or restrict it to exclude pheasants or partridges[4].

In the application of the Act to poultry, 'disease' means fowl pest in any of its forms (including Newcastle disease and fowl plague), fowl cholera, infectious bronchitis, infectious laryngotracheitis, pullorum disease, fowl typhoid, fowl pox and fowl paralysis[5]; but the ministers[6] may by order[7] extend the definition to include other bird diseases or restrict it so as to exclude any of the foregoing diseases except fowl pest in any of its forms[8].

1 Animal Health Act 1981 s 87 (4).
2 See para 482 note 3 ante.
3 The definition has been extended by the following orders: Diseases of Animals (Extension of Definition of Poultry) Order 1953, SI 1953/37; Transit of Animals (General) Order 1973, SI 1973/1377 (amended by SI 1975/1024, SI 1988/815, 1988/851); Importation of Birds, Poultry and Hatching Eggs Order 1979, SI 1979/1702 (amended by SI 1990/2371); Importation of Embryos, Ova and Semen Order 1980, SI 1980/12 (amended by SI 1984/1326, SI 1990/2371); Importation of Animal Products and Poultry Products Order 1980, SI 1980/14 (amended by SI 1980/1238, SI 1982/948, SI 1990/2371); Importation of Animal Pathogens Order 1980, SI 1980/1212; Foot-and-Mouth Disease Order 1983, SI 1983/1950; Fowl Pest Orders (Amendment) Order 1983, SI 1983/941 (amended by SI 1986/1755); Infectious Diseases of Poultry Order 1986, SI 1986/1755; Welfare of Poultry (Transport) Order 1988, SI 1988/851 (amended by SI 1989/52); Zoonoses Order 1989, SI 1989/285; Processed Animal Protein Order 1989, SI 1989/661. See also para 521 notes 1–5 post.
4 Animal Health Act 1981 s 87 (5).
5 Ibid s 88 (3).
6 See note 2 supra.
7 The definition has been extended by the following orders: Psittacosis or Ornithosis Order 1953, SI 1953/38; Importation of Birds, Poultry and Hatching Eggs Order 1979 (as amended: see note 3 supra); Importation of Animal Products and Poultry Products Order 1980 (as amended: see note 3 supra); Infectious Diseases of Poultry Order 1986; Marek's Disease (Restriction on Vaccination) Order 1987, SI 1987/905.
8 Animal Health Act 1981 s 88 (4).

518. Eradication; zoonoses. Subject to Treasury approval, the ministers[1] have identical powers in relation to expending money as they think fit upon the eradication of poultry diseases as they have in relation to diseases of other animals[2]. The provisions relating to the control of zoonoses[3] apply to poultry as they apply to other animals[4].

1 See para 482 note 3 ante.
2 Animal Health Act 1981 s 3 (1). See para 485 ante.
3 See para 486 ante. For the meaning of 'zoonoses' see para 486 note 2 ante.
4 Animal Health Act 1981 s 87 (4). As to the testing of poultry flocks for salmonella see para 519 post.

519. Laying flocks, breeding flocks and hatcheries. An owner or person in charge of a laying flock[1] must ensure that samples are taken in respect of the flock and are submitted to a laboratory for testing for salmonella[2]. No person may treat or tamper with any such sample[3].

A person in charge of a laboratory to which a sample has been submitted must ensure that the test is carried out in a prescribed manner[4] and the result reported to the person who submitted it[5].

Records must be kept of the dates on which samples are taken, the results of tests and the movements of poultry on or off the premises[6]. Records must be retained for a year and produced on demand to an inspector or officer of the minister[7].

Effective measures must be taken to keep poultry houses and buildings used to store eggs free from vermin[8]; poultry houses where poultry are housed permanently throughout their laying period must not be accessible to other birds[9]. Eggs must be collected and handled in the prescribed manner[10].

Breach of the above provisions is an offence against the Animal Health Act 1981[11].

Samples must be taken from breeding flocks[12] and hatcheries[13], and tested for salmonella in a prescribed manner[14]. The results must be reported to the person who submitted the sample[15]. No person may treat or tamper with any such sample[16]. Records must be kept of the samples taken, the results of any tests on such samples and the movement on or off the premises on which the breeding flock is kept or which are used as a hatchery, of poultry, eggs or chicks[17]. Records must be retained for a year and produced on demand to an inspector or officer of the minister[18]. No person may, except under licence, vaccinate poultry with any vaccine likely to affect the result of any test carried out on a sample taken from a breeding flock or a hatchery[19]. Contravention of these provisions or of a licence issued thereunder is an offence against the Animal Health Act 1981[20].

1 'Laying flock' means any flock of poultry consisting of not less than 25 birds which are kept for the production of eggs for human consumption (including birds which are being reared for that purpose), or less than 25 birds any of the eggs of which are sold for human consumption: Poultry Laying Flocks (Testing and Registration etc) Order 1989, SI 1989/1964, art 2 (1).
2 Ibid art 3, Sch 1. Salmonella has been designated a form of zoonose: see the Zoonoses Order 1989, SI 1989/285; and paras 486, 518 ante. As to the taking of samples see the Poultry Laying Flocks (Testing and Registration etc) Order 1989 art 3 (a), Sch 1 Pt I. As to the notification by a registered person of the results of tests see para 526 post.
3 Ibid art 7 (1). 'Treating' a sample is doing anything likely to affect the result of the test required under the order: art 7 (2).
4 As to the methods prescribed for testing see ibid art 4 (1) (a), Sch 1 Pt II.
5 Ibid art 4 (1). If the person who submitted the sample is not the owner or person in charge of the flock, he must pass the report to the owner or person in charge: art 4 (2). See also para 526 post.
6 Ibid art 8 (a), Sch 3.
7 Ibid art 8 (b), (c).
8 'Vermin' means rats, flies, mice and cockroaches: ibid art 2 (1).
9 Ibid art 6.
10 Ibid art 5, Sch 2 (amended by SI 1990/348). The requirements relate to the washing of hands, regular collection of eggs, separation and removal of damaged eggs, cleanliness of equipment, trays and storage and packing units and storage in condensation-free areas.
11 Poultry Laying Flocks (Testing and Registration etc) Order 1989 art 13. As to penalties for offences against the Animal Health Act 1981 see para 513 ante.

12 'Breeding flock' means any flock of poultry consisting of not less than 25 birds kept (or being reared) for the production of hatching eggs or birds for sale or supply for breeding purposes or the production of eggs or meat: Poultry Breeding Flocks and Hatcheries (Registration and Testing) Order 1989, SI 1989/1963, art 2 (1).

13 'Hatchery' means any premises, with a total incubator capacity of not less than 1,000 eggs, on which the eggs of poultry are incubated or hatched and from which chicks are sold or supplied: ibid art 2 (1).

14 Ibid arts 6, 8, 9. As to the manner of taking samples see arts 6 (a), 8 (a), Sch 3 Pts I, II (amended by SI 1990/347; as to the prescribed methods of testing see the Poultry Breeding Flocks and Hatcheries (Registration and Testing) Order 1989 arts 6 (c), 8 (c), Sch 3 Pt III. The minister may issue a certificate of exemption from these provisions: art 13.

Blood samples must be taken from a breeding flock which contains domestic fowl; the samples must be tested for the presence of *Salmonella pullorum:* art 7, Sch 4.

15 Ibid art 9 (1) (b). If the person who submitted the sample is not the person registered in the Breeding Flocks Register or the Hatcheries Register (see para 526 post) he must pass the report to the person so registered: art 9 (2).

16 Ibid art 10 (1). 'Treating' a sample is doing anything likely to affect the result of the test required under the order: art 10 (2).

17 Ibid art 11 (a)–(e), Sch 5.

18 Ibid art 11 (f), (g).

19 Ibid art 12.

20 Ibid art 17. As to penalties for offences against the Animal Health Act 1981 see para 513 ante.

520. Notice of disease; separation. The ministers[1] may by order[2] regulate the separation of diseased poultry from poultry not affected with disease, and the notification of disease in, or illness of, poultry[3].

1 See para 482 note 3 ante.

2 See the Infectious Diseases of Poultry Order 1986, SI 1986/1755, art 4 (person in possession of diseased poultry must with all practicable speed notify the fact to a constable of the police force for the area or to a veterinary inspector).

3 Animal Health Act 1981 s 15 (5).

521. Infected places and areas. Where an inspector has reasonable grounds for supposing the existence of disease[1] he may declare the premises concerned to be an infected place, whereupon rules come into force prohibiting the movement of poultry[2] into or out of that place save under licence, and governing the removal of carcases, eggs and other things, the entry and disinfection of persons and other related matters[3].

The Minister of Agriculture, Fisheries and Food may by order declare to be an infected area any area in which he is satisfied that fowl pest is prevalent, and may vary or revoke the order by subsequent order[4]. No poultry[5] may be moved out of an infected area except under licence issued by a veterinary inspector or other officer of the ministry if satisfied that the poultry are to be used for special breeding purposes[6]; no poultry may be moved into an infected area except to a licensed slaughterhouse (where they must be slaughtered) or, under licence, to other premises (where they must be detained for 28 days)[7]; and no poultry may be moved within the area except under licence issued by a local authority inspector if satisfied that they are intended for immediate slaughter or by a veterinary inspector or other officer of the ministry if satisfied that they are store poultry or are for use for special breeding purposes[8].

The sale within an infected area of poultry or day-old chicks[9] is prohibited save under licence or where the birds are not on the premises, and poultry exhibitions within the area are prohibited[10]. Inspectors may prohibit entry to footpaths, fields, sheds and other places save with permission or under licence[11]; operators of egg packing stations and persons sexing day-old chicks or using vehicles to carry poultry must take special disinfection precautions[12]; the disposal of slaughterhouse manure and refuse is regulated[13]; and an inspector may require the occupier of any premises in the area on which poultry are kept or detained to keep them under specified control[14].

1 'Disease' in this context means Newcastle disease, fowl plague or paramyxovirus infection of pigeons: Infectious Diseases of Poultry Order 1986, SI 1986/1755, art 3 (1).
2 'Poultry' in this context means any live domestic fowl, turkeys, geese, quails, ducks and guinea fowl, and partridges, pheasants and pigeons: ibid art 3 (1) (b).
3 Ibid arts 6, 8. The licence is issued by an inspector of the ministry: art 8 (1).
4 Fowl Pest (Infected Areas Restrictions) Order 1956, SI 1956/1611, art 3 (1) (amended by SI 1958/1442).
5 'Poultry' in this context means domestic fowls, turkeys, geese, ducks and guinea fowls, other than day-old chicks of those species, and pigeons, pheasants, partridges and quails: Fowl Pest (Infected Areas Restrictions) Order 1956 art 2 (1) (amended by SI 1983/941). 'Day-old chick' means a live bird of one of the following species, that is to say, domestic fowls, turkeys, geese, ducks and guinea-fowls, during the first 72 hours of its life or while it has not been fed, whichever is the shorter period: Fowl Pest (Infected Areas Restrictions) Order 1956 art 2 (1) (as amended).
6 Ibid art 4 (amended by SI 1958/1442).
7 Fowl Pest (Infected Areas Restrictions) Order 1956 art 5 (amended by SI 1958/1442).
8 Fowl Pest (Infected Areas Restrictions) Order 1956 art 6 (amended by SI 1958/1442). Poultry may, however, be moved directly by rail through an infected area: Fowl Pest (Infected Areas Restrictions) Order 1956 art 7.
9 See note 5 supra.
10 Fowl Pest (Infected Areas Restrictions) Order 1956 arts 8, 9 (art 8 substituted by SI 1958/1442).
11 Fowl Pest (Infected Areas Restrictions) Order 1956 art 10.
12 See ibid arts 12, 13, 15.
13 See ibid art 14.
14 Ibid art 11.

522. Slaughter. The Minister of Agriculture, Fisheries and Food may if he thinks fit cause to be slaughtered any diseased or suspected poultry, or any poultry which have been in the same field, pen, shed or other place as, or otherwise in contact with, diseased poultry or which appear to him to have been exposed to infection[1].

For poultry, other than diseased poultry, so slaughtered the minister must pay as compensation the value of the bird immediately before it was slaughtered[2]. For diseased poultry so slaughtered he may by order prescribe the payment of compensation in accordance with a scale approved by the Treasury, except in the case of poultry affected with fowl pest in any of its forms, including Newcastle disease and fowl plague[3].

The minister may also by order[4] provide for the seizure of carcases, fodder, litter[5], eggs and fertilisers and the destruction, disposal or treatment of anything so seized as he may think expedient for preventing the spread of any poultry disease[6]. Provisions for compensation at the value at the time of seizure are similar to those outlined in respect of slaughter[7].

Slaughter of poultry other than under the above powers is governed by legislation treated elsewhere in this work[8].

1 Animal Health Act 1981 s 31 (e), Sch 3 para 5 (1). Ibid s 32 (slaughter of animals: see para 507 ante) does not apply to poultry: s 32 (4).
2 Ibid Sch 3 para 5 (2).
3 Ibid Sch 3 para 5 (3). At the date this volume states the law no order has been made.
4 See the Diseases of Animals (Seizure of Carcases, etc) Order 1964, SI 1964/255 (amended by SI 1972/2041, SI 1983/346); Poultry (Seizure of Hatching Eggs) Order 1990, SI 1990/232.

5 For the meaning of 'carcase', 'fodder' and 'litter' see para 496 note 11 ante.
6 Animal Health Act 1981 s 35 (1) (amended by the Animal Health and Welfare Act 1984 s 1).
7 See the Animal Health Act 1981 s 36 (amended by the Animal Health and Welfare Act 1984 s 1 (3)).
8 See FOOD, DAIRIES AND SLAUGHTERHOUSES vol 18 para 1352.

523. Import and export of poultry and eggs. The ministers[1] may make orders[2] prohibiting or regulating the import into Great Britain[3] of poultry or poultry carcases, and eggs[4]. The Minister of Agriculture, Fisheries and Food may also make orders[5] regulating the export of poultry or poultry carcases from Great Britain to states which are members of the European Communities[6].

1 See para 482 note 3 ante.
2 See the Importation of Birds, Poultry and Hatching Eggs Order 1979, SI 1979/1702; Importation of Embryos, Ova and Semen Order 1980, SI 1980/12 (amended by SI 1984/1326); Importation of Animal Products and Poultry Products Order 1980, SI 1980/14 (amended by SI 1980/1934, SI 1981/1238, SI 1982/948).
3 For the meaning of 'Great Britain' see para 309 ante.
4 Animal Health Act 1981 s 10. See also Case 40/82 *EC Commission v United Kingdom* [1984] ECR 283, ECJ (provisions amount to quantitative restriction on imports contrary to EEC Treaty, art 30).
5 See the Exportation of Pigeons Order 1983, SI 1983/872.
6 Animal Health Act 1981 s 11.

524. Cleansing, disinfection and protection. The ministers[1] may make orders[2] regulating the cleansing and disinfection of receptacles or vehicles used for the conveyance or exposure for sale of poultry[3] and protecting poultry from unnecessary suffering in connection with their exposure for sale and disposal after sale[4].

1 See para 482 note 3 ante.
2 See the Poultry Pens, Fittings and Receptacles (Disinfection) Order 1952, SI 1952/437 (amended by SI 1963/1956, SI 1972/971); Poultry Premises and Vehicles (Disinfection) Order 1956, SI 1956/11; Welfare of Poultry (Transport) Order 1988, SI 1988/851 (amended by SI 1989/52 and SI 1990/2628).
3 Animal Health Act 1981 s 7 (2).
4 Ibid s 37 (1). As to cleansing and disinfection generally see para 490 ante; as to protection from suffering see para 501 ante.

525. Functions of inspectors. For the purpose of enforcing an order for protecting poultry from unnecessary suffering[1] an inspector[2] may examine poultry to which the order relates and any receptacle or vehicle used for their conveyance or exposure for sale, and may enter any premises, vessel or aircraft in which he has reasonable grounds for supposing that there are poultry exposed for sale, in course of conveyance or packed for conveyance or exposure for sale[3].

A ministry inspector and, if so authorised by order of the Minister of Agriculture, Fisheries and Food, a local authority inspector, may enter any pen, shed, land or other place in which he has reasonable grounds for supposing that poultry are or have been kept, for the purpose of ascertaining whether disease exists or has existed therein[4].

1 See paras 501, 524 ante.
2 For the meaning of 'inspector' see para 512 note 1 ante.
3 Animal Health Act 1981 s 64 (2).
4 Ibid s 64 (1).

526. Registration of laying flocks, breeding flocks and hatcheries. A person is prohibited from keeping a laying flock[1] on any premises unless his name is entered in the Laying Flocks Register in respect of those premises[2]. The minister[3] must enter the name of an applicant in the register[4] unless the application does not specify the prescribed particulars[5].

The registration remains in force for an unlimited period, except that the appropriate minister[6] is required to revoke it if he has been notified by the registered person, within 28 days of any anniversary of the date of registration, that the number of birds kept by that person on the premises is less than 100 and such person has not informed the appropriate minister that he anticipates that the number of birds will increase to 100 or more during the 12 months following the date of that anniversary[7].

It is the duty of a registered person to notify the appropriate minister of the results of tests carried out for salmonella[8] which have been reported to him[9]. Such notification must be given at intervals of 12 weeks starting with the date of the first such report, and must contain prescribed particulars[10].

Contravention of the above provisions is an offence against the Animal Health Act 1981[11].

A person may not keep a breeding flock[12] on any premises unless he is registered in the Breeding Flocks Register in respect of those premises[13]. The minister[14] must enter the name of an applicant in the register[15] unless the application does not contain the prescribed particulars[16], or the minister is satisfied on inspection[17] that certain requirements as to the cleanliness of the premises are not complied with and could not be complied with by the intended date of registration[18]. Registration lasts for one year and may be renewed on further application provided that the requirements mentioned above are complied with[19].

No person may use any premises as a hatchery[20] unless he is registered in the Hatcheries Register in respect of those premises[21].

It is the duty of the person registered in the Breeding Flocks Register or the Hatcheries Register to keep the records which are required to be kept of the taking and testing of samples for salmonella[22].

Contravention of the above provisions is an offence against the Animal Health Act 1981[23].

1 For these purposes 'laying flock' means a flock of poultry consisting of not less than 100 birds which are kept for the production of eggs for human consumption (excluding birds which are being reared for that purpose): Poultry Laying Flocks (Testing and Registration etc) Order 1989, SI 1989/1964, art 2 (1).

2 Ibid art 9 (1), (2). The register is kept by the appropriate minister, namely the Minister of Agriculture, Fisheries and Food in relation to England, and in relation to Scotland and Wales the Secretary of State: art 2 (1).

   The requirement for registration does not apply where the name of the person keeping the laying flock is entered in the Breeding Flocks Register (as to which see text and notes 12–19 infra: art 9 (7).

3 As to the appropriate minister see note 2 supra.

4 Poultry Laying Flocks (Testing and Registration etc) Order 1989 art 9 (3).

5 Ibid art 9 (4). The prescribed particulars arc: (1) the name, address and telephone number both of the applicant and of the premises where the flock is to be kept; (2) the name of the person (if not the applicant) in charge of the premises; (3) the approximate number of birds in the flock; (4) in the case of birds which are to be housed continuously, the number of houses which will be maintained for those birds; and (5) in the case of birds which are to have free access to more than one house, the number of groups of houses which will be maintained for those birds: art 9 (4), Sch 4.

   The person who is registered must notify the minister of any change in the particulars within 28 days of each anniversary of the registration.

6 See note 2 supra.

7 Poultry Laying Flocks (Testing and Registration etc) Order 1989 art 9 (6).

8 As to these tests see ibid arts 3, 4; and para 519 ante.

9 Ibid art 10 (1).

10 Ibid art 10 (2). The particulars prescribed are: (1) the name and address of the registered person giving the notification; (2) a description of the type of sample tested; (3) the date on which the sample was taken and the address of the premises and identification of the house or group of houses from which it was taken; (4) the result of the test; and (5) the name and address of the testing laboratory: art 10 (2), Sch 5.

11 Ibid art 13. As to penalties for offences against the Animal Health Act 1981 see para 513 ante.

12 For the meaning of 'breeding flock' see para 519 note 12 ante.

13 Poultry Breeding Flocks and Hatcheries (Registration and Testing) Order 1989, SI 1989/1963, art 3 (1), (2).

The requirement for registration does not apply in the case of a breeding flock consisting of birds kept solely for the production of hatching eggs or chicks for use in the manufacture of vaccines or research or other scientific purposes: art 3 (9).

14 The 'appropriate minister' is the Minister of Agriculture, Fisheries and Food in relation to England, and in relation to Scotland and Wales the Secretary of State: ibid art 2 (1).

15 Ibid art 3 (3).

16 Ibid art 3 (4). The prescribed particulars are: (1) the name, address and telephone number both of the applicant and of the premises where the flock is to be kept; (2) the name of the person (if not the applicant) in charge of the premises; (3) the species of birds in the flock; and (4) the approximate number of birds in the flock: art 3 (4), Sch 1 Pt I.

17 As to the power to carry out such inspections see ibid art 14.

18 Ibid art 3 (5), Sch 2 Pt I.

19 Ibid art 3 (6)–(8).

20 For the meaning of 'hatchery' see para 519 note 13 ante.

21 Poultry Breeding Flocks and Hatcheries (Registration and Testing) Order 1989 art 4 (1), (2). The conditions for registration in the Hatcheries Register are similar to those in relation to the Breeding Flocks Register (see text and notes 12–19 supra), save that the required particulars must include the incubator capacity of the premises and the species of birds to be hatched there: see arts 4 (3)–(5), 14, Sch 1 Pt II, Sch 2 Pt II. Registration is for a renewable period of one year: art 4 (6)–(8).

The requirement for registration does not apply in the case of premises used solely for the incubation or hatching of eggs from which chicks are sold or supplied for use in the manufacture of vaccines or research or other scientific purposes: art 4 (9).

22 Ibid art 11. As to these tests see para 519 ante.

23 Ibid art 17. As to penalties for offences against the Animal Health Act 1981 see para 513 ante.

(4) BEES

527. Bees; general powers. Orders may be made[1] for preventing the introduction into, or spreading within, Great Britain of pests or diseases affecting bees[2]. Such an order may, inter alia[3], prohibit or regulate the importation into or movement within Great Britain of bees and combs, bee products (for instance honey or beeswax), hives, containers, other appliances used in connection with keeping or transporting bees, and any other thing which has or may have been exposed to infection[4]; and it may make provision as to: (1) the conditions to be observed on importation of bees; (2) licences for importation; (3) the securing of information relevant to determining whether any bees or other things subject to control have been exposed to infection; (4) the circumstances in which and the time at which bees and other things are to be regarded as imported; (5) the treatment of infected bees; (6) cleansing and disinfection; (7) the marking of hives and other containers; (8) the recovery of costs; and (9) the payment of compensation[5]. A person authorised by the Minister of Agriculture, Fisheries and Food[6] may examine bees or other things controlled by an order, and take samples of them[7], and destroy any that are found to be infected or to have been exposed to infection[8]. Anyone importing bees or other things into, or moving them within, Great Britain, or otherwise contravening or failing to comply with an order or the terms of a licence issued under such an order commits an offence, punishable on summary conviction with a fine not exceeding level 5 on the standard scale[9]. Authorised persons have power to enter any premises or other place, and any vessel, boat, hovercraft, aircraft or other vehicle, where they reasonably suppose[10] that there are or have been controlled bees or other things[11], and anyone intentionally obstructing[12] a person acting in exercise of this power is liable on summary conviction to a fine not exceeding level 3 on the standard scale[13].

1 See the Importation of Bees Order 1980, SI 1980/792 (amended by SI 1987/867) (para 528 post), and the Bee Diseases Control Order 1982, SI 1982/107 (para 529 post).
2 Bees Act 1980 s 1 (1). The orders are made by the Minister of Agriculture, Fisheries and Food, the Secretary of State for Scotland and the Secretary of State for Wales, acting jointly: s 1 (1). The term 'bees' includes bees in any stage of their life cycle: s 3.
3 The ministers are empowered to make such orders as they think fit: ibid s 1 (1).
4 Ibid s 1 (2) (a).
5 Ibid s 1 (2) (b), Schedule.
6 See ibid s 3.
7 Ibid s 1 (3).
8 Ibid s 1 (4). They may be destroyed if imported into Great Britain in contravention of an order with or without an opportunity being first allowed for them to be re-exported: s 1 (5). No compensation is payable in respect of the exercise of any of these powers: s 1 (6).
9 Ibid s 1 (7) (amended by virtue of the Criminal Justice Act 1982 s 46). As to the standard scale see para 232 note 1 ante. At the date at which this volume states the law, level 5 on that scale is at £2,000.
10 See para 511 note 3 ante.
11 Bees Act 1980 s 2 (1). The authorised person must produce evidence of his authority if so required: s 2 (2).
12 See para 391 ante.
13 Bees Act 1980 s 2 (3). As to the standard scale see para 232 note 1 ante. At the date at which this volume states the law, level 3 on that scale is at £400.

528. Importation of bees. The importation of bees[1] or bee pests[2] into Great Britain is in general prohibited[3]. However, the responsible minister[4] may grant licences, which may be general or specific, exempting importation from such prohibition[5]. A general licence, which authorises importation from any country named therein, must be published in a manner decided by the minister, and may be issued subject to conditions[6]. A specific licence authorises a named person to import a specific consignment or specific consignments, and may be issued subject to conditions[7]. The conditions of either a general or a specific licence may be varied, or the licence revoked, at any time[8].

1 'Bees' means any members of the genus Apis and includes bees in any stage of their life cycle: Importation of Bees Order 1980, SI 1980/792, art 2. The contravention of this prohibition, or of the provisions of a licence (see text and notes 4–7 infra), is an offence: Bees Act 1980 s 1 (7); see para 527 text and note 9 ante.
2 'Bee pests' means any organisms or pathogens which are injurious to bees or any cultures of any such organisms or pathogens: ibid art 2 (definition added by SI 1987/867).
3 Importation of Bees Order 1980 art 3 (amended by SI 1987/867).
4 Ie the Minister of Agriculture, Fisheries and Food or the Secretary of State for Wales: Importation of Bees Order 1980 art 2.
5 Ibid arts 4 (1), 5 (1) (both as amended: see note 3 supra).
6 Ibid art 4 (2) (a)–(c) (as amended: see note 3 supra).
7 Ibid art 5 (2) (a)–(c) (as amended: see note 3 supra).
8 Ibid arts 4 (2) (c), (d), 5 (2) (c), (d) (both as amended: see note 3 supra).

529. Control of bee diseases. If an owner or person in charge of any hive[1] knows or reasonably supposes that any bees from it are infected with American foul brood[2], European foul brood[3] or Varroasis[4], he must with all practicable speed give notice to the responsible minister[5]. He must not remove or permit to be removed any hive, bees, combs, quilts[6], bee products[7] or appliances[8] until (1) an authorised person confirms that he is satisfied that the disease is not present, (2) notification is given of a report on a sample confirming the absence of the disease[9], or (3) the statutory prohibition on removal is replaced by a notice of prohibition[10] served on that owner or person in charge[11]. An owner or person in charge may submit samples of any combs to an approved laboratory[12] to see if they are free from infection[13]. An authorised person may take samples of bees, combs or hive debris and submit them to an approved laboratory, and may mark any hive or applicance for identification[14].

Where an authorised person reasonably supposes disease to be present, or he is refused entry to premises or any place where he reasonably supposes bees or things connected with them to be, he may serve a notice prohibiting the removal of the bees or such things except under licence[15].

A report on a sample must be sent by the person in charge of the approved laboratory to the responsible minister, who must send a copy to the owner or person in charge of the hive; if the report does not confirm the presence of disease the minister must serve on that owner or person a notice withdrawing any notice of prohibition of removal[16].

Beekeepers are further required to provide reasonable facilities and information to an authorised person[17], and unless licensed, not to treat their bees with certain drugs that disguise the presence of disease[18]. Where any person fails to take any action required of him by a notice under this order, an authorised person may take the action himself and recover the expenses of so doing from the person in default as a civil debt[19].

Particular steps are prescribed which may be taken on the discovery of the presence of each of the three diseases mentioned above, including, in certain circumstances, the isolation, treatment or destruction of bees or the declaration of an area to be an infected area[20].

Contravention of any of the above provisions or of the provisions of any licence granted or notice served thereunder is an offence[21].

1 'Hive' means any receptacle which contains or has at any time contained a colony of bees: Bee Diseases Control Order 1982, SI 1982/107, art 2. 'Bees' includes bees at any stage in their life cycle: art 2.
2 'American foul brood' means the disease caused by the organism *Bacillus larvae*: ibid art 2.
3 'European foul brood' means the disease caused by the organism *Streptococcus pluton*: ibid art 2.
4 'Varroasis' means infestation of bees by the mite *Varroa Jacobsoni*: ibid art 2.
5 Ibid art 3 (1). The 'responsible minister' is the Minister of Agriculture, Fisheries and Food or the Secretary of State for Wales: art 2.
6 'Quilt' means any form of cloth material used to cover a bee colony in a hive: ibid art 2.
7 'Bee product' means any natural product of the activities of bees (eg honey or beeswax) in its natural state: ibid art 2.
8 'Appliances' means containers and other appliances and apparatus used in connection with keeping or transporting bees: ibid art 2.
9 Ie a report under ibid art 5; see text and note 16 infra.
10 Ie a notice served under ibid art 4 (2) (see text and note 15 infra). A notice is deemed to be properly served if delivered personally to, or left at or posted to the last known place of abode or business of, the person on whom it is required to be served: art 11 (1).
11 Ibid art 3 (1) (a)–(c). An 'authorised person' is a person generally or specially authorised in writing by the responsible minister: art 2.
12 An 'approved laboratory' means a laboratory generally or specially approved by the responsible minister: ibid art 2.

13 Ibid art 3 (2). Such samples must be packed so as to prevent the risk of spread of infection during transit: art 3 (2). In the case of Varroasis samples of bees or hive debris may also be submitted: art 3 (2).
14 Ibid art 4 (1). It is prohibited to interfere with such identifying mark: art 9 (1).
15 Ibid art 4 (2). Licences may be general or specific, and may be subject to variation, revocation or suspension: art 13.
　　Persons concerned or connected with research into, or courses of training relating to, bees and bee diseases may be exempted by licence from the provisions of the 1982 Order: art 12.
16 Ibid art 5. As to service of notices see note 10 supra.
17 Ibid art 9 (2).
18 Ibid art 9 (3).
19 Ibid art 10.
20 Ibid arts 6–8, 11 (2), Schedule.
21 Bees Act 1980 s 1 (7); see para 527 text and note 9 ante.

(5) ADMINISTRATION

(i) Central Administration

530. Orders of the ministers. Subject and according to the provisions of the Animal Health Act 1981, the ministers[1] are empowered to make orders generally for the better execution of the Act, or for the purpose of in any manner preventing the spreading of disease, and in particular for the various purposes set out in the Act[2]. Thus orders may be made providing for modes of cleansing and disinfection[3]; the marking of animals[4]; the seizure, detention and disposal of diseased or suspected animals exposed, carried, kept or otherwise dealt with in contravention of an order[5]; the supply of water and food to animals during detention[6]; the disposal of carcases and the digging up of buried carcases[7]; the disinfection of the clothes of persons coming into contact with diseased or suspected animals and the use of precautions against the spreading of disease by such persons[8]; and the payment and recovery of expenses in respect of animals[9].

Orders made under Acts repealed by the Animal Health Act 1981 have effect, mutatis mutandis, as if made under that Act[10]. Orders made under the Act are, with some exceptions[11], statutory instruments[12]. Some of these,such as those declaring controlled or infected areas for foot-and-mouth disease[13], are classified as local, and are not printed in the annual volumes of statutory instruments, but in almost every case the minister or ministers, as the case may be, must publish notice of the order in the London Gazette[14].

When so authorised by order of the ministers[15], local authorities may make regulations for the purposes of the Act, or of orders of the ministers[16].

Where any power to make provisions by an order under the Animal Health Act 1981 does not include power to provide for its operation in or over territorial waters of the United Kingdom adjacent to Great Britain, it is to be treated as including such power unless the context otherwise requires[17].

1 See para 482 note 3 ante.
2 Animal Health Act 1981 s 1 (a). Orders made or having effect under the Act are referred to in the appropriate places in this part of the title. See also notes 3–17 infra.
3 Ibid s 7 (1) (d).
4 Ibid s 8 (1) (a).
5 Ibid ss 28, 35.
6 Ibid s 38.
7 Ibid s 35 (3).

8 Ibid s 7 (1) (c).
9 Ibid ss 1 (b), 34, 36.
10 See the Interpretation Act 1978 s 17 (2) (b).
11 Ie orders under the Animal Health Act 1981 ss 14 (2), 59 (1).
12 Ibid s 91 (5).
13 See para 496 ante.
14 Animal Health Act 1981 s 91 (1).
15 See note 1 supra.
16 Animal Health Act 1981 s 2. As to 'orders of the minister' see para 514 note 1 ante. As to local
	authority regulations see para 538 post.
17 See the Animal Health and Welfare Act 1984 s 3.

531. Licences. Wherever by any order of the Minister of Agriculture, Fisheries and Food anything is prohibited either absolutely or conditionally, or is required to be done by any person, the minister may by licence from him, or signed by an inspector or other officer of the ministry, authorise or exempt such person from such requirement with or without conditions[1].

1 See the Animals (Miscellaneous Provisions) Order of 1927 SR & O 1927/290, art 2.

532. Revocation of orders. Revocation of any order does not revive anything no longer in force; nor does it affect the previous operation of anything already duly done; nor does it affect any rights or liabilities already accrued, or any penalty, forfeiture or punishment already incurred, and legal proceedings may still be instituted after such revocation in respect of any offence against any such order prior to its revocation[1].

1 Animals (Miscellaneous Provisions) Order of 1927, SR & O 1927/290, art 5 (2). Cf the Interpretation
	Act 1978 s 16 (1), Sch 2 para 3; and STATUTES.

533. Stamp duty. No stamp duty is payable on any appointment, certificate, declaration, licence or thing under the Animal Health Act 1981, or an order of the minister or regulation of a local authority[1].

1 Animal Health Act 1981 s 85. As to 'an order of the minister' see para 514 note 1 ante. As to the
	construction of exemptions from stamp duty see STAMP DUTIES.

534. Fees. The ministers[1] may by order made with Treasury approval prescribe fees payable with respect to any business under the Animal Health Act 1981 as may be specified in the order[2].

1 See para 482 note 3 ante.
2 Animal Health Act 1981 s 84 (1). See the Diseases of Animals (Waste Food) (Fees for Licences) Order
	1987, SI 1987/361; Processed Animal Protein Order 1989, SI 1989/661; Poultry Flocks, Hatching
	and Processed Animal Protein (Fees) Order 1990, SI 1990/530; Diseases of Animals (Fees for the
	Testing of Disinfectants) Order 1991, SI 1991/1168.

535. Appointment of inspectors. The Minister of Agriculture, Fisheries and Food appoints inspectors and veterinary inspectors for the purposes of the Animal Health Act 1981 under his general power of appointment of staff[1].

1 Board of Agriculture Act 1889 s 5 (1); Board of Agriculture and Fisheries Act 1903 s 1 (1); Ministry of
   Agriculture and Fisheries Act 1919 s 1; Transfer of Functions (Ministry of Food) Order 1955, SI
   1955/554. As to the functions of inspectors see paras 486, 512, 525 ante.

(ii) Local Administration

536. Responsible local authorities. The local authorities responsible for executing and enforcing the Animal Health Act 1981 and every order of the minister so
far as the same are to be executed and enforced by the local authorities are: (1) in
London boroughs, the borough councils; (2) in the City of London (and for the
purpose of the statutory provisions relating to imported animals[1], Greater London), the Common Council of the City of London; (3) in counties, the county
councils[2]. Where the district of a local authority comprises part of a port or
aerodrome[3] the appropriate minister may by order make a body other than that
local authority the local authority for the purpose of the statutory provisions
relating to imported animals[4].

Normally the powers given by the Act to local authorities or their inspectors or
officers are exercisable only within and in relation to their districts[5]. Local authorities, their inspectors and officers must give the appropriate minister such notices,
reports, returns and information as he requires[6].

Where a local authority fails to execute or enforce any provision of the Act or
order of the Minister of Agriculture, Fisheries and Food, the appropriate minister[7]
may by order[8] empower a named person to act instead[9], without prejudice to the
power or right of the appropriate minister or any other authority or any person to
take any other proceedings for requiring the defaulting local authority to act[10].

1 See para 502 et seq ante.
2 Animal Health Act 1981 s 50 (1), (2), (5). 'Greater London' means the London boroughs, the City of
   London and the Inner and Middle Temples: see the London Government Act 1963 s 2 (1). As to
   'order of the minister' see para 514 note 1 ante.
3 For the meaning of 'aerodrome' see para 501 note 2 ante.
4 Animal Health Act 1981 s 50 (4); see note 7 infra. See the Designation of Local Authority (Heathrow
   Airport—London) Order 1976, SI 1976/2101 (Corporation of London designated local authority);
   Designation of Local Authority (Southampton Port Health District) Order 1978, SI 1978/163
   (Southamton Port Health Authority designated local authority). See also the Isles of Scilly (Importation of Animals Regulations) Order 1949, SI 1949/2012, art 2 (i).
5 Animal Health Act 1981 s 51.
6 Ibid s 81.
7 As to the meaning of 'appropriate minister' see para 506 note 5 ante.
8 Such orders are not statutory instruments: Animal Health Act 1981 s 91 (5).
9 Ibid s 59 (1). The expenses of such persons must be paid by the defaulting local authority: see s 59 (2),
   (3).
10 Ibid s 59 (4).

537. Appointment of local authority inspectors. Every local authority must
appoint as many inspectors[1] and other officers as it thinks necessary for the
execution and enforcement of the Animal Health Act 1981, and must assign to
them such duties and may delegate to them such authority and discretion as it
thinks fit[2]. Wherever an inspector is so appointed, or ceases to be an inspector, and
whenever there is any change in an inspector's name, address or district, the
authority must forthwith report the fact to the Ministry of Agriculture, Fisheries
and Food[3].

1 As to inspector's functions see paras 512, 525 ante.
2 Animal Health Act 1981 s 52. It is usual for chief officers of police to be appointed for their districts. It has been held that a local authority is not liable for damages or to an order of mandamus if it fails to appoint an inspector and disease breaks out: see *Mulcahy v Kilmacthomas Union Guardians* (1886) 18 LR Ir 200. It is, however, doubted whether this would be followed today. As to the default of local authorities see the Animal Health Act 1981 s 59; and para 536 ante.
3 Animals (Miscellaneous Provisions) Order of 1927, SR & O 1927/290, art 10 (amended by SR & O 1938/197).

538. Local authority regulations. The ministers[1] may make orders[2] authorising local authorities to make regulations for any of the purposes of the Animal Health Act 1981[3].

A local authority making any such regulations must publish them in a newspaper circulating in its district or in such other manner as it considers best fitted to ensure publicity[4]. It must send two copies to the ministry and, where the regulations affect animal movement, to the British Railways Board[5]. A local authority regulation may be proved by producing a newspaper purporting to contain the regulation or a copy of the regulation purporting to be certified as a true copy by the authority's clerk[6], and a regulation so proved is taken to have been duly made unless and until the contrary is proved[7].

1 See para 482 note 3 ante.
2 See the Control of Dogs Order of 1930, SR & O 1930/399, art 2 (amended by SR & O 1931/80, SI 1976/919); Isles of Scilly (Importation of Animals Regulations) Order 1949, SI 1949/2012, art 2; Swine Fever Order 1963, SI 1963/286, art 21 (amended by SI 1976/919).
3 Animal Health Act 1981 s 2. As to the validity of regulations see *Scott v Glasgow Corpn* [1899] AC 470, HL; and LOCAL GOVERNMENT.
4 Animals (Miscellaneous Provisions) Order of 1927, SR & O 1927/290, art 8 (1).
5 Ibid art 8 (3); Transport Act 1962 s 31; Railway Clearing House Scheme Order 1954, SI 1954/139.
6 Animal Health Act 1981 s 58 (1).
7 Ibid s 58 (2).

539. Provision of wharves and other places; acquisition of land. A local authority may provide wharves, stations, lairs, sheds and other places for landing, reception, keeping, selling, slaughtering or disposing of imported and other animals, or carcases, fodder, litter[1], dung or other things[2]. Such places are 'markets' within the Markets and Fairs Clauses Act 1847, the provisions of which relating to building, maintaining and holding markets, erecting and managing slaughterhouses, weighing goods, levying tolls, making byelaws, and accounts[3], are incorporated with the Animal Health Act 1981[4].

A local authority may charge for the use of such a wharf or other place provided by them[5]. Periodical returns of expenditure and receipts must be made to the appropriate minister[6].

A local authority may buy or rent by agreement, or buy compulsorily if so authorised by the minister[7], land within or without its district on which to build wharves or other places, and also for the burial of carcases[8].

1 For the meaning of 'carcase', 'fodder' and 'litter' see para 496 note 11 ante.
2 Animal Health Act 1981 s 54 (1).
3 See the Markets and Fairs Clauses Act 1847 ss 10–50; and MARKETS AND FAIRS.
4 Animal Health Act 1981 s 54 (2), (3). In *Scott v Glasgow Corpn* [1899] AC 470, HL, it was held that a byelaw prohibiting the use of rings at a public market for private sales was not ultra vires.
5 Animal Health Act 1981 s 54 (4). Sums charged for the use of such a place must be carried to a separate account and applied in payment of interest and repayment of principal on money borrowed

and, subject thereto, to discharge of expenses: s 54 (5). For the meaning of 'use' in this context see *City of London Corpn v British Caledonian Airways Ltd* [1980] 2 All ER 297, affd (1981) Times, 21 May, CA.

6 Animal Health Act 1981 s 54 (6). As to the meaning of 'appropriate minister' see para 506 note 5.
7 For the procedure on compulsory acquisition, see the Acquisition of Land Act 1981; and COMPUL-SORY PURCHASE.
8 Animal Health Act 1981 s 55.

540. Carcases washed ashore. Local authorities must pay the expenses of the burial or destruction of carcases[1] washed ashore, when such burial or destruction is carried out under the direction of a receiver of wreck with authority from the Secretary of State[2], but may recover the expenses from the owner of the vessel from which the carcase was thrown or washed[3].

1 For the meaning of 'carcase' see para 496 note 11 ante. This provision is not restricted to diseased carcases or the carcases of animals shipped alive; it applies to a cargo of frozen meat: *The Suevic* [1908] P 292.
2 Animal Health Act 1981 s 57 (1). In this instance the Secretary of State referred to is the Secretary of State for Transport.
3 Ibid s 57 (3).

9. VETERINARY SURGEONS AND THE PRACTICE OF VETERINARY SURGERY

(1) THE LEGISLATION AND REGULATION OF THE PROFESSION

541. Introduction. 'Veterinary surgery' means the art and science of veterinary surgery and medicine, and is taken to include (1) the diagnosis of diseases in and injuries to animals[1], including tests performed on animals for diagnostic purposes; (2) the giving of advice based upon such diagnosis; (3) medical or surgical treatment of animals; and (4) the performance of surgical operations on animals[2]. The profession of veterinary surgery is regulated by the charters[3] from time to time granted to the Royal College of Veterinary Surgeons and by the Veterinary Surgeons Act 1966. Some of the provisions regulating the registration[4] and practice[5] of, and disciplinary powers over [6], veterinary surgeons are to be found in subordinate legislation. Powers to make orders have been conferred on the Privy Council and on the Minister of Agriculture, Fisheries and Food, the Secretary of State and the Minister of Agriculture for Northern Ireland[7], and must be exercised by statutory instrument[8]. Any power conferred[9] on the Privy Council may be exercised by any two or more of its members[10].

The law forbids the practice of veterinary surgery except by persons registered in the register of veterinary surgeons[11] or in the supplementary veterinary register[12], but for this purpose 'veterinary surgery' has been given a limited meaning to exclude certain minor operations which certain unqualified persons may perform[13].

A registered veterinary surgeon or practitioner who is actually practising his profession is excusable as of right from jury service[14].

1 'Animals' includes birds and reptiles: Veterinary Surgeons Act 1966 s 27 (1).

2 Ibid s 27 (1).
3 As to these charters see para 561 post.
4 As to registration see para 547 et seq post.
5 As to practice see para 544 et seq post. For other statutory provisions relevant to the practice of veterinary surgery see MEDICINE vol 30 para 10. As to the direct effect of the EEC Treaty, art 57, see EUROPEAN COMMUNITIES vol 51 para 6.74, vol 52 paras 16.112, 16.126, 16.127.
6 As to discipline see para 571 et seq post.
7 Under the Northern Ireland Act 1974 s 1 (3), Sch 1 para 2 (1) (b), interim provision is made whereby the Department of Agriculture for Northern Ireland discharges the functions of the Minister of Agriculture for Northern Ireland.
8 Veterinary Surgeons Act 1966 s 25 (3). Any statutory instrument made in the exercise of any power conferred by s 1 (4), s 3, s 19 (4) or s 21 is subject to annulment by resolution of either House of Parliament: s 25 (5). The draft of an order under s 19 (5) must be approved by both Houses of Parliament: s 25 (4). See further STATUTES.
9 Ie conferred by the Veterinary Surgeons Act 1966.
10 Ibid s 23 (1). Any document purporting to be an instrument of appointment or approval made by the Privy Council under the Veterinary Surgeons Act 1966 or any other instrument so made, and purporting to be signed by the Clerk of the Privy Council or other authorised person, is evidence of the fact that the instrument was so made and of its terms: s 23 (2).
11 As to this register see para 547 post.
12 As to this register see para 548 post.
13 See the Veterinary Surgeons Act 1966 s 19 (3), (4), Sch 3 (s 19 (4) amended by the Animals (Scientific Procedures) Act 1986 s 27, Sch 3 para 5; 1966 Act Sch 3 substituted by the Veterinary Surgeons Act 1966 (Schedule 3 Amendment) Order 1988, SI 1988/526, and amended by the Education Reform Act 1988 s 237, Sch 12 para 66); and para 544 post.
14 Juries Act 1974 s 9 (1), Sch 1 Pt III. See further JURIES vol 26 para 607.

542. Membership and functions of the Royal College of Veterinary Surgeons.

Any person who has obtained a university degree in veterinary surgery at certain recognised universities in the United Kingdom and the Republic of Ireland or who has passed examinations in veterinary surgery held by the Royal College of Veterinary Surgeons at other universities in the United Kingdom[1], or who holds Commonwealth or foreign qualifications[2] in veterinary surgery and has satisfied the council of the college by examination or otherwise, that he has the requisite knowledge and skill to fit him for practising veterinary surgery in the United Kingdom[3], is entitled to be registered in the register of veterinary surgeons[4] and on being so registered becomes a member of the college[5]. The management of the college is in the hands of its council[6], which appoints the officers of the college[7], controls the arrangements for registration and the annual fees payable by persons on the registers[8], has supervisory functions over the courses of study in veterinary surgery in the United Kingdom and the Republic of Ireland and holds examinations at some universities[9]. Through its disciplinary committee it exercises certain powers relating to the removal or suspension of names from the registers[10].

1 See paras 550, 551 post.
2 'Qualification' means any diploma, degree, fellowship, membership, licence, authority to practise, letters testimonial, certificate or other status or document granted by any university, corporation, college or other body or by any department of, or persons acting under the authority of, the government of any country or place: Veterinary Surgeons Act 1966 s 27 (1). 'Commonwealth qualification' means a qualification granted in a place outside the United Kingdom which is within the Commonwealth, and 'foreign qualification' means a qualification granted in any other place outside the Commonwealth and the Republic of Ireland: ss 6 (6), 27 (1). See further para 552 post.
3 See para 552 post.
4 See para 547 post.
5 See paras 550, 552 post.
6 See para 563 post.
7 See paras 566, 567 post.

8 See paras 556, 560 post.
9 See para 569 post.
10 See para 571 et seq post.

543. Functions relating to cruelty to animals and similar matters. Enact-ments relating to the protection of animals from suffering, disease and cruelty restrict and control the manner of performance of operations on animals, and impose duties on veterinary surgeons. These enactments, which are discussed elsewhere in this work[1], prohibit the docking and nicking of horses except where certified as necessary by a veterinary surgeon[2], require certain operations upon horses, dogs, cats, cattle and other specified animals to be performed under anaesthetics[3] and regulate the protection of all living vertebrate animals used for experimental or other scientific purposes[4].

The Minister of Agriculture, Fisheries and Food may appoint veterinary inspec-tors to inspect dairy cattle[5]. A local authority may authorise a veterinary surgeon to enter and inspect premises used as riding establishments, examine horses found on them, and make a report[6], and may authorise its officers or a veterinary surgeon or veterinary practitioner to inspect pet shops[7], animal boarding establishments[8] and premises licensed for the breeding of dogs[9].

A veterinary surgeon who, in the course of his practice, finds an animal or a carcase of an animal that is diseased[10], and a veterinary surgeon who examines an animal or its carcase affected with or suspected of rabies[11], must notify the police.

1 For provisions as to cruelty to animals, and as to diseases of animals, see paras 405 et seq, 482 et seq ante.
2 See para 422 ante.
3 See para 417 ante.
4 See para 429 et seq ante.
5 See FOOD vol 18 para 1213.
6 See paras 393, 394 ante.
7 See para 466 ante.
8 See para 391 ante.
9 See the Breeding of Dogs Act 1973 s 2 (1); and para 392 ante.
10 See para 484 ante for the meaning of 'disease' and para 487 ante as to the notification.
11 See para 493 ante.

544. Restriction on practice by unqualified persons. Any person who is not a registered veterinary surgeon[1] or a registered veterinary practitioner[2] and who practises or holds himself out as practising or as being prepared to practise veterin-ary surgery[3], is liable on summary conviction to a fine not exceeding the prescribed sum[4] and on conviction on indictment to a fine[5]. This provision does not, how-ever, operate to prohibit (1) the carrying out of any experiment duly authorised under the Animals (Scientific Procedures) Act 1986[6]; (2) any treatment given to an animal[7] by its owner or another member of his household or by a person in the employment of the owner or any other member of such a household[8]; (3) anything (except a laparotomy) done otherwise than for reward to an animal used in agriculture, as defined in the Agriculture Act 1947[9], by the owner of the animal or by a person engaged or employed in caring for such animals[10]; (4) emergency first aid for saving life or relieving pain[11]; (5) subject to certain exceptions[12], the performance by persons of or over the age of 18 of operations of castration or caponising, whether by chemical means or otherwise; the tailing of a lamb; the docking of a dog's tail or amputation of its dew claws before its eyes are open[13]; (6) the performance of castration or caponising, or docking a lamb's tail, by any person of the age of 17 undergoing instruction in animal husbandry if certain conditions[14] are fulfilled[15]; (7) the disbudding of a calf by a person undergoing instruction, if those same conditions are fulfilled[16]; (8) the performance by a registered medical practitioner[17] of an operation on an animal for the purpose of removing an organ or tissue for use in the treatment of human beings[18]; (9) the carrying out or performance of any treatment, test or operation by a registered medical practitioner or a registered dentist[19] at the request of a registered veterinary surgeon or a registered veterinary practitioner[20]; (10) the carrying out or perform-ance of any minor treatment, test or operation specified in an order made by the ministers[21] after consultation with the Council of the Royal College of Veterinary Surgeons, so long as any conditions so specified are complied with[22]; (11) the carrying out or performance, under regulations made by the council, of any prescribed veterinary treatment, test or operation, subject to compliance with certain prescribed conditions, by specified classes of students of veterinary sur-gery[23].

There is power to amend the exemptions contained in heads (2) to (5) and head (10)[24].

1 As to registration see para 547 et seq post.
2 As to veterinary practitioners see para 548 post.
3 For the meaning of 'veterinary surgery' see para 541 ante.
4 Veterinary Surgeons Act 1966 s 19 (1) (a) (amended by virtue of the Magistrates' Courts Act 1980 s 32 (2)). As to the prescribed sum see para 233 note 3 ante. At the date at which this volume states the law, that sum is at £2,000.
5 Veterinary Surgeons Act 1966 s 19 (1) (b).
6 Ibid s 19 (4) (a) (amended by the Animals (Scientific Procedures) Act 1986 s 27, Sch 3 para 5). As to experiments authorised by the 1986 Act see para 429 et seq ante.
7 For the meaning of 'animals' see para 541 ante.
8 Veterinary Surgeons Act 1966 s 19 (4) (b), Sch 3 Pt I para 1 (substituted by the Veterinary Surgeons Act 1966 (Schedule 3 Amendment) Order 1988, SI 1988/526). Membership of a household is a question of fact and degree: see *Simmons v Pizzey* [1979] AC 37 at 59, [1977] 2 All ER 432 at 441, HL, per Lord Hailsham of St Marylebone; applied in *Hackney London Borough v Ezidiuma* [1981] 3 All ER 438; it may not lapse by temporary separation: *Santos v Santos* [1972] Fam 247 at 262, [1972] 2 All ER 246 at 255, CA.
9 See AGRICULTURE.
10 Veterinary Surgeons Act 1966 Sch 3 Pt I para 2 (as substituted: see note 8 supra).
11 Ibid Sch 3 Pt I para 3 (as substituted: see note 8 supra).
12 The exceptions are as follows: (1) the castration of (a) a horse, pony, ass or mule; (b) a bull, boar or goat which has reached two months; (c) a ram which has reached three months; (d) a cat or dog; (2) the spaying of a cat or dog; (3) the removal of any part of a deer's antlers before the velvet is frayed and the greater part of it has been shed; (4) the desnooding of a turkey which has reached 21 days; (5) the removal of the combs of any poultry which has reached 72 hours; (6) the cutting of the toes of a domestic fowl or turkey which has reached 72 hours; (7) the performance of a vasectomy or electro-ejaculation on any animal or bird kept for food, wool, skin or fur or for use in farming; (8) the removal of the supernumerary teats of a calf which has reached three months; or (9) the dehorning or disbudding of a sheep or goat, except the trimming of the insensitive tip of an ingrowing horn which could cause pain or distress if untreated: ibid Sch 3 Pt II (as substituted: see note 8 supra).
13 Ibid Sch 3 Pt I para 4 (as substituted: see note 8 supra).
14 Ie the instruction in animal husbandry is given by a registered veterinary surgeon or a registered veterinary practitioner and the operation is performed under his direct personal supervision; or the instruction is given at a recognised institution and the operation performed under the direct personal supervision of a person appointed to give instruction there: ibid Sch 3 Pt I para 5 (a), (b) (as substituted: see note 8 supra). 'Recognised institution' means (i) an institution maintained or assisted by a local education authority; (ii) any other institution providing higher or further education for which a grant is paid by the Secretary of State; or (iii) an institution recognised for the present

purpose by the Secretary of State: Sch 3 Pt I para 5 (as so substituted, and as amended by the Education Reform Act 1988 s 237, Sch 12 para 66).
15 Veterinary Surgeons Act 1966 Sch 3 Pt I para 5 (as substituted and amended: see notes 8, 14 supra).
16 Ibid Sch 3 Pt I para 5 (as substituted and amended: see notes 8, 14 supra).
17 As to registered medical practitioners see MEDICINE.
18 Veterinary Surgeons Act 1966 s 19 (4) (c).
19 As to registered dentists see MEDICINE.
20 Veterinary Surgeons Act 1966 s 19 (4) (d).
21 'The ministers' means the Minister of Agriculture, Fisheries and Food, the Secretary of State for Scotland, the Secretary of State for Wales and the Minister of Agriculture for Northern Ireland, acting jointly: ibid s 27 (1); Transfer of Functions (Wales) (No 1) Order 1978, SI 1978/272, art 4 (2), Sch 2. As to Northern Ireland see para 541 note 7 ante.
22 Veterinary Surgeons Act 1966 s 19 (4) (e). See also para 541 note 8 ante. Exemption has been given to certain treatments of animals by physiotherapy given in certain circumstances, and some tests and minor operations on certain fowls and turkeys (Veterinary Surgery (Exemptions) Order 1962, SI 1962/2557 (amended by SI 1973/308, SI 1982/1627 and SI 1983/6)); to the vaccination of poultry with any licensed vaccine (Veterinary Surgery (Exemptions) Order 1973 SI 1973/308) and to the taking of blood samples from farm animals and poultry for use for prescribed purposes: Veterinary Surgery (Blood Sampling) Order 1983, SI 1983/6 (amended by SI 1988/1090).
23 Veterinary Surgeons Act 1966 s 19 (3). The Veterinary Surgeons (Practice by Students) Regulations 1981 (contained in the Veterinary Surgeons (Practice by Students) Regulations Order of Council 1981, SI 1981/988, Schedule), have been made under this provision. By these regulations students of veterinary surgery who have attained the age of 18 years, are attending full-time university or veterinary school courses in the United Kingdom or elsewhere leading to a veterinary qualification (see para 297 post), and have entered upon that part of the curriculum which deals with clinical studies may examine animals and carry out tests, treatment and surgical operations under varying degrees of supervision.
24 These exemptions are contained in the Veterinary Surgeons Act 1966 s 19 (4) (b), (e), Sch 3 (as substituted: see note 8 supra). After consultation with the council and with persons appearing to the ministers to represent interests so appearing to be substantially affected, the ministers may by order amend the provisions of Sch 3: s 19 (5). See also para 541 note 8 ante. Any order under s 19 (4) (e), (5), may be varied or revoked by a subsequent order similarly made: s 19 (6). For such orders under s 19 (4) (e), see note 22 supra.

(2) THE PRACTICE OF VETERINARY SURGERY

545. Use of descriptions as to professional status. A person is guilty of an offence for which he is liable on summary conviction to a fine not exceeding the prescribed sum[1] or on conviction on indictment to a fine[2] if, not being registered in the register of veterinary surgeons[3], he takes or uses[4] the title 'veterinary surgeon' or any name, title, addition or description implying that he is so registered[5]; or if, not being registered in that register or in the supplementary veterinary register[6], he takes or uses the title 'veterinary practitioner' or any name, title, addition or description implying that he is a practitioner of or qualified to practise[7] veterinary surgery[8]. Without prejudice to these provisions, a person is guilty of an offence for which he is similarly liable[9] if he uses, in connection with any business carried on by him or at any premises at which such a business is carried on, a description implying that he or any person acting for the purposes of the business possesses any veterinary qualifications which he does not in fact possess[10].

Where either of these offences by a body corporate is proved to have been committed with the consent or connivance of or to be attributable to neglect on the part of any officer of the body corporate or person purporting to act as such, he, as well as the body corporate, is deemed to be guilty of the offence and may be proceeded against and punished accordingly[11].

1 Veterinary Surgeons Act 1966 s 20 (4) (a) (amended by virtue of the Magistrates' Courts Act 1980 s 32). As to the prescribed sum see para 233 note 3 ante. At the date at which this volume states the law, that sum is at £2,000.
2 Veterinary Surgeons Act 1966 s 20 (4) (b).
3 As to the register see para 547 post.
4 For the meaning of 'takes or uses' see *Brown v Whitlock* (1903) 67 JP 451, DC; *Robertson v Hawkins* [1913] 1 KB 57, DC; *Blair v King* [1918] 2 KB 30, DC.
5 Veterinary Surgeons Act 1966 s 20 (1).
6 As to this register see para 548 post.
7 Ie to any greater extent than is authorised by or under the Veterinary Surgeons Act 1966 s 19 (3) (as to which see para 544 ante): s 20 (2).
8 Ibid s 20 (4). For the meaning of 'veterinary surgery' see para 541 ante. The Veterinary Surgeons Act 1881 s 17 (repealed), had made it an offence inter alia for any unregistered person to take or use the title 'veterinary surgeon' or 'veterinary practitioner' or any name, title, addition or description stating that he was a veterinary surgeon or a practitioner of veterinary surgery or of any branch of it, or was specially qualified to practise it. It was held that a shoeing smith who described his premises as a 'veterinary forge' had taken a description stating that he was specially qualified to practise a branch of veterinary surgery: *Royal College of Veterinary Surgeons v Robinson* [1892] 1 QB 557. The authority of this decision was recognised somewhat reluctantly in *Royal College of Veterinary Surgeons v Collinson* [1908] 2 KB 248, where the use by an unregistered person of the words 'canine specialist' was held to infringe the prohibition. Cases in which it was held that there was no infringement are *Veterinary College v Groves* (1893) 57 JP 505 ('pharmaceutical and veterinary chemist'), and *Royal College of Veterinary Surgeons v Kennard* [1914] 1 KB 92 ('canine surgery'); but see now the Veterinary Surgeons Act 1966 s 20 (3): text to note 10 infra.
9 See text and notes 1, 2 supra.
10 Veterinary Surgeons Act 1966 s 20 (3). For the meaning of 'qualification' see para 542 note 2 ante. Where a limited company used the description 'Churchill's Veterinary Sanatorium Ltd', and inscribed on its shop window the words 'James Churchill, Managing Director, MD, USA, Specialist, Dogs and Cats Boarded. Advice Gratis', it was held that there was a representation that James Churchill, the managing director, was specially qualified to practise a branch of veterinary surgery: *A-G v Churchill's Veterinary Sanatorium Ltd* [1910] 2 Ch 401.
11 Veterinary Surgeons Act 1966 s 20 (5).

546. Liability for negligence and breach of warranty. A veterinary surgeon or practitioner, like other professional men, is liable for any damage caused by his negligence[1]. In addition, where he supplies or administers for regard a substance such as a serum or toxoid, he impliedly warrants that the substance is reasonably fit for the purpose for which it is required, namely, for administration to animals[2].

1 For the cases on medical negligence see MEDICINE vol 30 para 34 et seq. In *Chute Farms Ltd v Curtis* (1961) Times, 10 October, Elwes J held that a veterinary surgeon was vicariously liable for the negligence of his assistant who failed to inject a thoroughbred yearling colt with anti-tetanus serum after it had injured its foot.
2 *Dodd and Dodd v Wilson and McWilliam* [1946] 2 All ER 691.

(3) REGISTRATION AND QUALIFICATIONS

(i) The Registers

547. The register of veterinary surgeons. The register of veterinary surgeons contains the names, addresses and qualifications[1] of all persons entitled to be registered under the provisions of the Veterinary Surgeons Act 1966[2]. In consists of four lists: (1) 'the general list', which is of persons entitled to be registered as holders of veterinary degrees of, or on passing appropriate examinations held by the Royal College of Veterinary Surgeons in, universities in the United Kingdom[3];

(2) 'the Commonwealth list', which is of persons entitled to be registered as holding some Commonwealth qualification[4]; (3) 'the foreign list' which is of persons so registered as holding some foreign qualification[5]; and (4) 'the temporary list' which is of persons whom the Council of the Royal College of Veterinary Surgeons permits to practise on a temporary basis[6].

Persons holding recognised qualifications from member states of the European Communities are entitled to be registered if certain conditions are met[7].

1 For the meaning of 'qualification', see para 542 note 2 ante.
2 Veterinary Surgeons Act 1966 s 2 (1). The register was originally made and maintained under the Supplemental Royal Charter of 1876 and continued by the Veterinary Surgeons Act 1881 s 3 (1) (repealed), and is further continued by the 1966 Act s 2 (1).
3 Ibid s 2 (2) (a) (amended by the Veterinary Surgeons Qualifications (EEC Recognition) Order 1980, SI 1980/1951, art 3 (1)). As to qualifications for persons on the general list see the Veterinary Surgeons Act 1966 ss 3, 4, 5A (added by SI 1980/1951 and subsequently amended by SI 1982/1076); and paras 550, 553 post.
4 Veterinary Surgeons Act 1966 s 2 (2) (b). For the meaning of 'Commonwealth qualification' see para 542 note 2 ante. As to qualification for registration as a Commonwealth practitioner see para 552 post.
5 Ibid s 2 (2) (c). For the meaning of 'foreign qualification' see para 542 note 2 ante. As to qualification for registration as a foreign practitioner see para 552 post.
6 Ibid s 2 (2) (d). As to the council's power to permit persons to practise on a temporary basis see s 7; and para 554 post.
7 See para 553 post.

548. The supplementary veterinary register. The supplementary veterinary register[1] contains the names and addresses of the following persons (who are known as 'veterinary practitioners'): (1) persons registered in this register immediately before the commencement of the Veterinary Surgeons Act 1966[2]; (2) persons at some previous time registered in this register who were not so registered immediately before the commencement of the 1966 Act, but whose names have been restored to the register on a direction of the disciplinary committee of the Royal College of Veterinary Surgeons[3]; and (3) persons who for an aggregate of not less than seven out of the ten years immediately preceding 2 December 1965 held a licence under the provision of the Veterinary Surgeons Act 1948[4] permitting the licensing of employees of certain societies and institutions providing free treatment for animals[5].

1 See the Veterinary Surgeons Act 1966 s 8.
2 Ibid s 8 (1) (a). The 1966 Act was, for present purposes, fully in force by 15 November 1967. The register under the Veterinary Surgeons Act 1948 contained the names of certain persons of good personal character who, for a period of not less than seven out of the ten years preceding 30 July 1949, had been, as their principal means of livelihood, diagnosing diseases of animals and giving medical and surgical treatment to animals: s 6 (2) (repealed).
3 Veterinary Surgeons Act 1966 s 8 (1) (b). As to restoration to the register see s 18: and para 589 post.
4 Ie under the Veterinary Surgeons Act 1948 s 7 (repealed). Licences were granted under s 7 by the Minister of Agriculture, Fisheries and Food to employees of certain societies and institutions wholly supported by voluntary contributions or endowments or both, and providing free medical or surgical treatment for animals, where the minister was satisfied that the society or institution could not obtain the services of an adequate number of veterinary surgeons. A person holding such a licence may not, however, practise veterinary surgery otherwise than as an employee of any such society or institution (Veterinary Surgeons Act 1966 s 8 (2) (a)) or with permission granted by the Council of the Royal College of Veterinary Surgeons and subject to such restrictions as the council may impose (s 8 (2) (b)). A certificate purporting to be a certificate of the Minister of Agriculture, Fisheries and Food stating that any person held, or did not hold, a licence under the Veterinary Surgeons Act 1948 s 7, for a period specified in the certificate is, for the purposes of registration, conclusive of the matters stated in it: Veterinary Surgeons Act 1966 s 8 (5).

5 Ibid s 8 (1) (c), (2). The entry in the supplementary register against the name of such a person must state whether he is the employee of any such society or institution (s 8 (3) (a)), whether he has been granted permission to practise veterinary surgery (s 8 (3) (b)) and any restrictions subject to which he may practise it (s 8 (3) (c)). For the meaning of 'veterinary surgery' see para 541 ante. If he fails to comply with any restrictions subject to which he is so registered, the council may cause his name to be removed from the register: s 8 (4).

549. Publication of the registers. The register of veterinary surgeons[1] and the supplementary veterinary register[2] are kept by the registrar of the Royal College of Veterinary Surgeons[3]. The Council of the Royal College of Veterinary Surgeons[4] must cause the registers to be printed and published as often as it thinks fit[5]. Copies of the registers purporting to be printed and published by the council, as altered by any alterations purporting to be printed and published by the council, are evidence that the persons specified in the registers are registered in them and that persons not named in them are not registered[6]. If a name does not appear in a copy of the register as altered, a certified copy under the hand of the registrar of the entry relating to that person in the register concerned is, however, evidence that the name is on that register[7].

1 See para 547 ante.
2 See para 548 ante.
3 Veterinary Surgeons Act 1966 s 9 (1), (8). As to the registrar see para 567 post. The registrar must from time to time insert in the registers any alteration in the name or address of any registered person which may come to his knowledge: s 9 (7), (8). The registrar must perform such other duties in connection with the registers as the council directs, and must act on such evidence as in each case appears sufficient: s 9 (2), (8).
4 As to the Royal College of Veterinary Surgeons see para 561 post, and as to the council see para 563 post.
5 Veterinary Surgeons Act 1966 s 9 (3), (8). If in any year either register is not published, the council must cause any alterations in the entries in that register which have been made since its last publication to be printed and published within that year: s 9 (4), (8).
6 Ibid s 9 (5), (8).
7 Ibid s 9 (6), (8).

(ii) Qualifications for the Register of Veterinary Surgeons

550. Qualifications for the register. Where a university in the United Kingdom[1] provides courses of study and examinations leading to a veterinary degree[2] which appear to the Privy Council, after consultation with the Council of the Royal College of Veterinary Surgeons[3], sufficiently to guarantee that holders of the degree will have acquired the knowledge and skill needed for the efficient practice of veterinary surgery[4], the Privy Council may by order (known as 'a recognition order') direct that any person on whom the degree is conferred after attending those courses at that university is entitled to be registered in the register of veterinary surgeons and thereby becomes a member of the college[5].

On representations by the council of the college that the courses no longer justify the continuance of such an order[6], the Privy Council may, if it thinks fit, after considering[7] any objections and observations made by the university concerned, revoke or suspend the order by subsequent order[8].

On the application of any university in the United Kingdom for which no recognition order is in force the Privy Council, after consultation with the Council of the Royal College of Veterinary Surgeons, may direct the college to hold examinations in veterinary surgery for the students of veterinary surgery attending at that university[9]. Any such student passing the examination is entitled to be registered in the register of veterinary surgeons and on being so registered becomes a member of the Royal College of Veterinary Surgeons[10].

1 Ie the United Kingdon of Great Britain and Northern Ireland: Interpretation Act 1978 s 5, Sch 1.
2 Veterinary Surgeons Act 1966 s 3 (1) (a).
3 As to the council see para 563 et seq post.
4 Veterinary Surgeons Act 1966 s 3 (1) (b). For the meaning of 'veterinary surgery' see para 541 ante.
5 Ibid s 3 (1). See also para 541 note 8 ante. The Privy Council has approved the following degrees at the universities named in the orders cited:
   Bachelor of Veterinary Science: Veterinary Surgeons (University Degrees) (Liverpool) Order of Council 1950, SI 1950/1110; Veterinary Surgeons (University Degrees) (Bristol) Order of Council 1950, SI 1950/1301;
   Bachelor of Veterinary Medicine and Surgery: Veterinary Surgeons (University Degrees) (Glasgow) Order of Council 1951, SI 1951/571; Veterinary Surgeons (University Degrees) (Edinburgh) Order of Council 1952, SI 1952/1602;
   Bachelor of Veterinary Medicine: Veterinary Surgeons (University Degrees) (London) Order of Council 1952, SI 1952/959; Veterinary Surgeons (University Degrees) (Cambridge) Order of Council 1953, SI 1953/404; Veterinary Surgeons (Republic of Ireland University Degrees) (National University) Order of Council 1973, SI 1973/1420 (see para 551 post);
   Bachelor in Veterinary Medicine: Veterinary Surgeons (Republic of Ireland University Degrees) (Dublin) Order of Council 1973, SI 1973/1419 (see para 551 post).
   It should be noted that persons who have been awarded certain Irish qualifications thereby hold a 'recognised European qualification' for the purposes of registration as members of the college: see paras 551, 553 post.
6 The Council of the Royal College of Veterinary Surgeons may make such representations if it appears to it, while a recognition order is in force, that the courses of study and degree examinations no longer justify the order: Veterinary Surgeons Act 1966 s 3 (2). As to the council's power to supervise courses and examinations see s 5 and para 569 post. The Privy Council must notify the university in question that such representations have been made, giving such particulars as may be requisite to enable the university to formulate its observations on or objections to the representations: s 3 (3).
7 Such consideration must take place within such time, being not less than two months, after the giving of notice under ibid s 3 (3) (see note 6 supra), as the Privy Council may determine: s 3 (4).
8 Ibid s 3 (4). An order suspending a recognition order may be revoked by a subsequent order if it appears to the Privy Council expedient in consequence of representations by the Council of the Royal College of Veterinary Surgeons or the university in question that the recognition order should be revived: s 3 (5).
9 Ibid s 4 (1). Such a direction ceases to have effect if a recognition order for that university comes into force or is revived, or may be revoked by a subsequent direction of the Privy Council made after consultation with the university and the council of the college: s 4 (2).
10 Ibid s 4 (1).

551. Holders of Irish veterinary degrees. To give effect to any agreement with Respect to veterinary surgeons made between Her Majesty's government in the United Kingdom and the government of the Republic of Ireland[1], the Privy Council may, on the recommendation of the Council of the Royal College of Veterinary Surgeons[2], by order[3] direct that the holder of any university veterinary degree of the Republic of Ireland[4] is entitled, subject to any exception so specified and on compliance with any conditions so specified, to be registered in the register of veterinary surgeons and on being so registered thereby becomes a member of the college[5].

Persons who are members of the college by virtue of these provisions[6] are not required to pay a fee in respect of membership in any year[7]. Persons who hold certain Irish qualifications are entitled to be registered by virtue of such qualifications being recognised European qualifications[8].

1 See the Agreement with Respect to Veterinary Surgeons (London, 11 April 1988), confirmed and brought into force by the Veterinary Surgeons (Agreement with the Republic of Ireland) Order 1988, SI 1988/784, the Schedule to which contains the text of the agreement. This Order in Council was made under the Veterinary Surgeons Act 1966 s 21 (1). As to the contents of such orders see s 21 (1) (a)–(d), (2). Such an order may be varied or revoked by a subsequent order under s 21: s 21 (3).

2 As to the council see para 563 et seq post.

3 As to the making of orders see para 541 note 8 ante.

4 This provision has been applied to the Irish degrees mentioned in para 550 note 5 ante, and in respect of diploma membership of the Royal College of Veterinary Surgeons awarded as a result of an examination following full time study at either of the universities named therein or at the Veterinary College of Ireland: 1988 Agreement art 3 (1) (see note 1 supra).

5 Veterinary Surgeons Act 1966 s 21 (1) (b) (i). Any order so made may be suspended or revoked: s 21 (1) (b) (ii).

6 See note 4 supra.

7 See the 1988 Agreement art 3; and note 1 supra. A fee must be paid, however, if the person wishes to participate in the election of members to the council: see para 563 post.

8 Veterinary Surgeons Act 1966 s 5A (added by the Veterinary Surgeons Qualifications (EEC Recognition) Order 1980, SI 1980/1951); see para 553 post.

552. Commonwealth and foreign practitioners. A person who shows to the satisfaction of the registrar of the Royal College of Veterinary Surgeons[1] that he is of good character[2], that he holds a Commmonwealth or foreign qualification[3] in veterinary surgery[4] and that he has satisfied the council of the college that he has the requisite knowledge and skill to fit him for practising veterinary surgery in the United Kingdom[5] is entitled to be registered in the register of veterinary surgeons[6], and on being so registered he becomes a member of the college[7]. For the purpose of satisfying itself that a person has the requisite knowledge and skill, the council must require that person to sit for examinations[8] unless the Commonwealth or foreign qualification held by him is of a kind accepted for the time being by the council as constituting, in itself, satisfactory proof that that person possesses the requisite knowledge and skill[9].

1 As to the registrar see para 567 post.

2 Veterinary Surgeons Act 1966 s 6 (1) (a).

3 For the meaning of 'Commonwealth qualification' and 'foreign qualification' see para 542 note 2 ante.

4 Veterinary Surgeons Act 1966 s 6 (1) (b). For the meaning of 'veterinary surgery' see para 541 ante. The council may direct that a particular person who has passed the examinations required to obtain such a qualification is to be treated for this purpose as a person holding such a qualification: s 6 (5). As to the continued registration of persons registered by virtue of qualifications granted in territories whose status has changed see the Bangladesh Act 1973 s 1 (3), Schedule para 14; Zimbabwe Act 1979 s 6 (1), Sch 2 para 6 (b).

5 Veterinary Surgeons Act 1966 s 6 (1) (c).

6 As to the register see para 547 ante.

7 Veterinary Surgeons Act 1966 s 6 (1).

8 Ibid s 6 (2). The examinations are held for the purposes of s 6 by or under arrangements made by the college: s 6 (2). The council may make regulations as to such examinations: s 6 (4); see the Veterinary Surgeons (Examination of Commonwealth and Foreign Candidates) Regulations 1967 (contained in the Veterinary Surgeons (Examination of Commonwealth and Foreign Candidates) Regulations Order of Council 1967, SI 1967/599, Schedule (amended by SI 1971/749, SI 1976/1168, SI 1980/999 and SI 1984/1072)), which prescribe the content and standard of the examinations, the conditions for entry and the fees payable.

9 Veterinary Surgeons Act 1966 s 6 (3).

553. Holders of recognised European qualifications. A person who is a national of a member state of the European Communities and holds a recognised

European qualification[1] in veterinary surgery[2] is entitled to be registered in the general list, and, on being so registered, becomes a member of the Royal College of Veterinary Surgeons[3]. A person who holds a scheduled European qualification[4] granted in a member state before that state implemented the Training Directive[5] is not thereby entitled to be registered unless he produces to the registrar[6] a certificate of the competent authority of that state to the effect that the qualification meets the standards laid down by the Training Directive, or that the person has been lawfully practising veterinary surgery for at least three consecutive years of the five years immediately preceding the date of the certificate[7]. A person holding a recognised European qualification which is not a scheduled qualification[8] is not entitled to be registered unless he produces to the registrar a certificate to the effect that he has been lawfully practising veterinary surgery for at least three consecutive years of the five years immediately preceding the date of the certificate[9].

Registration of a person under the provisions described above disentitles such a person to registration as a foreign or Commonwealth practitioner[10].

Detailed provision has been made by the Council of the European Communities for the implementation of the Communities' policy on (1) the mutual recognition of qualifications awarded by authorities of the different member states, (2) the minimum standards member states should adopt for allowing persons to practise, and (3) the authorisation of drugs for veterinary use[11].

1 A 'recognised European qualification' is any European qualification specified by the Veterinary Surgeons Act 1966 s 5A (5), Sch 1A (both added by the Veterinary Surgeons Qualifications (EEC Recognition) Order 1980, SI 1980/1951; the 1966 Act Sch 1A subsequently amended by SI 1981/205 and SI 1987/447), granted in a member state on or after the date on which that state implemented the Training Directive (see infra); or any European qualification in veterinary surgery granted in a member state before that date or after it where the training of which the qualification is evidence commenced before that date: Veterinary Surgeons Act 1966 s 5A (1) (a), (b) (as added: see supra; and s 5A (1) (b) subsequently amended by the Medical, Nursing, Dental and Veterinary Qualifications (EEC Recognition) Order 1982, SI 1982/1076). The 'Training Directive' means EC Council Directive 78/1027 concerning the co-ordination of provisions in respect of the activities of veterinary surgeons: 1966 Act s 5A (5) (as added: see supra). For these purposes a state is deemed to have implemented the Training Directive on the date which it notifies the European Communities Commission as that on which it did so: s 5A (4) (as so added).
2 As to the meaning of 'veterinary surgery' see para 541 ante.
3 Veterinary Surgeons Act 1966 s 5A (1) (as added: see note 1 supra). As to the general list see para 547 ante.
4 Ie a qualification specified in ibid Sch 1A (as added: see note 1 supra).
5 For the meaning of 'the Training Directive' see note 1 supra.
6 As to the registrar see para 567 post.
7 Veterinary Surgeons Act 1966 s 5A (2) (as added: see note 1 supra).
8 Ie a qualification within ibid s 5A (1) (b) (as added and amended: see note 1 supra).
9 Ibid s 5A (3) (as added: see note 1 supra; and subsequently amended by the Medical, Nursing, Dental and Veterinary Qualifications (EEC Recognition) Order 1982.
10 Veterinary Surgeons Act 1966 s 6 (6) (amended by the Veterinary Surgeons Qualifications (EEC Recognition) Order 1980. As to registration as a foreign or Commonwealth practitioner see para 552 ante.
11 See EUROPEAN COMMUNITIES vol 51 para 6.74, vol 52 paras 16.112, 16.126 et seq. Much of the provisions made by the EC Council has been enacted by the United Kingdom Parliament to form the provisions described above.

554. Temporary registration. The Council of the Royal College of Veterinary Surgeons, with a view to permitting a person who satisfies it that he has attended a course of study, and has passed the examinations, leading to a degree to which a recognition order[1] relates[2], and a person holding a Commonwealth or foreign qualification[3] in veterinary surgery[4], to practise veterinary surgery temporarily or otherwise subject to restrictions, may direct that he be registered subject to such restrictions as the council may specify with respect to the period for which, the place or places at which and the circumstances in which he may practise[5]. Any person with respect to whom such a direction is given is entitled to be registered subject to the entry against his name of the restrictions so specified[6].

1 As to recognition orders see para 550 ante.
2 Veterinary Surgeons Act 1966 s 7 (1) (a).
3 For the meaning of 'Commonwealth qualification' and 'foreign qualification' see para 542 note 2 ante and as to such qualifications see para 552 ante.
4 Veterinary Surgeons Act 1966 s 7 (1) (b). For the meaning of 'veterinary surgery' see para 541 ante. The council may direct that a particular person who has passed the examinations required to obtain such a qualification is to be treated for this purpose as a person holding such a qualification: s 7 (4).
5 Ibid s 7 (1).
6 Ibid s 7 (1). Registration under s 7 does not make it lawful for a person to practise veterinary surgery otherwise than subject to the restrictions: s 7 (2). If a person so registered fails to comply with any restriction the council may cause his name to be removed from the register: s 7 (3).

(iii) Entry of Names and Qualifications

555. Procedure for registration. Any right to registration[1] in the register of the Royal College of Veterinary Surgeons or the supplementary register is conditional on the making of an application supported by the requisite evidence[2]. A person applying to be registered must produce or send to the registrar[3] the document conferring or evidencing his qualification for registration, together with a statement of his name and address and the other particulars, if any, required for registration[4].

1 As to registration see paras 547, 548 ante.
2 Veterinary Surgeons Act 1966 s 10 (1).
3 As to the registrar see para 567 post.
4 Veterinary Surgeons Act 1966 s 10 (2). As to the regulations for registration see the Veterinary Surgeons and Veterinary Practitioners Registration Regulations 1967 (contained in the Schedule to the Veterinary Surgeons and Veterinary Practitioners (Registration Regulations) Order of Council 1967, SI 1967/395); and para 556 note 1 post. As to offences in respect of procuring or attempting to procure registration by making or producing false declarations, certificates or representations see CRIMINAL LAW.

556. Regulations with respect to the register. The Council of the Royal College of Veterinary Surgeons may make regulations[1] with respect to the form and keeping of the registers[2], the making of entries in them, and the removal of entries from them[3], including, in particular, regulations (1) prescribing a fee to be charged on the entry of a name in either register or on the restoration of any entry to either register[4], or in respect of the retention of the name of a person in any year subsequent to the year in which he was first registered[5]; and (2) authorising the registrar, notwithstanding anything in the Veterinary Surgeons Act 1966, to refuse to make in, or restore to, either register any entry until a prescribed fee has been paid[6], and authorising him to remove the name of any person from either register if after prescribed notices and warnings he fails to pay the fee prescribed for the retention of his name in that register[7]. The council may give directions authorising any additional qualifications[8] specified in the directions to be entered in either register on the application of registered veterinary surgeons who hold them[9].

1 The current regulations are the Veterinary Surgeons and Veterinary Practitioners Registration Regulations 1967, approved by the Privy Council and brought into force by the Veterinary Surgeons and Veterinary Practitioners (Registration Regulations) Order of Council 1967, SI 1967/395, and contained in the Schedule thereto (amended by SI 1975/70, SI 1988/2099 and SI 1989/2431).
2 As to the registers see paras 547, 548 ante. Although the provisions of the Veterinary Surgeons Act 1966 s 11 (1)–(5), apply to both the veterinary surgeons register and the supplementary veterinary register, regulations may make different provision in relation to them: s 11 (6).
3 Ibid s 11 (1), (6).
4 Ibid s 11 (1) (a), (6). Different fees may be chargeable in different cases, and fees may be excused in prescribed cases: s 11 (4).
5 Ibid s 11 (1) (b), (6). See also note 4 supra.
6 Ibid s 11 (1) (c), (6).
7 Ibid s 11 (2), (6). If within a prescribed period a person whose name has been removed pays the due fee and any additional prescribed sum, his name is to be restored: s 11 (3).
8 For the meaning of 'qualification', see para 542 note 2 ante.
9 Veterinary Surgeons Act 1966 s 11 (5).

557. Abbreviations of qualifications granted abroad. Where a person's name is entered in the Commonwealth list or the foreign list[1], or an additional qualification[2] granted in a place outside the United Kingdom is entered against a person's name in any part of the register of veterinary surgeons, the registrar must enter the qualification by virtue of which that person is registered or the additional qualification, in such abbreviated form as the registrar, after consultation with the Council of the Royal College of Veterinary Surgeons, may select as being convenient[3].

1 As to these lists see para 547 ante.
2 For the meaning of 'qualification' see para 542 note 2 ante.
3 Veterinary Surgeons Act 1966 s 12.

558. Removal of name on death or cesser from practice. The registrar of the Royal College of Veterinary Surgeons must remove from the registers[1] the name of every deceased person; and a registrar of births and deaths[2], on registering the death of a registered veterinary surgeon, must, without charge, send forthwith by post to the registrar of the college a copy certified under his hand of the entry in the register of deaths relating to the death[3].

If a registered veterinary surgeon has ceased to practise, the registrar of the college may at his request or with his consent remove his name from the register[4]. The registrar may send by post to a registered veterinary surgeon a notice inquiring whether he has ceased to practise or has changed his residence and, if no answer is received to the inquiry within six months from the posting of the notice, he may remove the veterinary surgeon's name from the register[5]. In such a case, or where the person's name was removed at his request or with his consent on his ceasing to practise, the person's name may be restored to the register on his application unless the original entry was incorrectly or fraudulently made[6].

1 The provisions discussed in this paragraph apply to both the veterinary surgeons register and the supplementary veterinary register: see the Veterinary Surgeons Act 1966 s 13 (5). As to the registers see paras 547, 548 ante.
2 As to such registrars see REGISTRATION.
3 Veterinary Surgeons Act 1966 s 13 (1).
4 Ibid s 13 (2).
5 Ibid s 13 (3).
6 Ibid s 13 (4). The Council of the Royal College of Veterinary Surgeons may restore the name on receipt of an application form, a restoration fee and a retention fee for the financial year in which the

application is made: Veterinary Surgeons and Veterinary Practitioners Registration Regulations 1967, reg 15 (a). As to these regulations see para 556 note 1 ante; the fees are prescribed by regs 22 and 20 respectively (amended by SI 1989/2431). In the case of an applicant who has not been included in either register during any of the five years immediately preceding the date of application, the application must be accompanied by evidence establishing to the council's satisfaction the applicant's identity and good character: 1967 Regulations reg 15 (b).

559. Incorrect and fraudulent entries. It is the duty of the Council of the Royal College of Veterinary Surgeons to refer to the disciplinary committee[1] any case in which it appears to it that an entry in the register of veterinary surgeons or the supplementary veterinary register[2] has been fraudulently made. It is also its duty to remove from the registers any other entry which has been incorrectly made[3].

1 As to the disciplinary committee see para 573 post. For the procedure see para 588 post.
2 As to these registers see paras 547, 548 ante.
3 Veterinary Surgeons Act 1966 s 14.

560. Fees. A person must pay a registration fee for the entry of his name in the general list, the Commonwealth list or the foreign list[1]. This fee covers the insertion in the list of the appropriate particulars[2] and entitles the veterinary surgeon[3] to the retention of his name in the list until the end of the financial year[4] next following that in which the entry was made[5]. He must then pay a retention fee[6] for the retention of his name in the list for each further financial year[7].

No fee is charged for the entry of a name in the supplementary veterinary register[8], but a veterinary practitioner[9] must pay a retention fee[10] for the retention of his name in that register for each financial year following that in which his name is first entered in it[11].

Where the registrar of the Royal College of Veterinary Surgeons has not received by 1 June of any year from a veterinary surgeon or veterinary practitioner resident in the United Kingdom a retention fee due on the preceding 31 March he must send a warning that failure to pay the fee will result in the removal from the appropriate register of the name in relation to which the fee is due, and if the fee is not received within one month of the issue of the warning, he must remove the name from the register[12]. The registrar must restore the name to the relevant register if (1) within a period of two months from the removal the veterinary surgeon or veterinary practitioner pays the retention fee due plus a restoration fee[13]; or (2) after the expiry of a period of two months from the removal, the veterinary surgeon pays the prescribed fee for entry in the general, Commonwealth or foreign list[14]; or (3) after the expiry of a period of two months from the removal, the veterinary practitioner pays the retention fee due from him in default of payment of which his name was removed from the supplementary veterinary register together with any retention fee which may then become due[15] and the fee prescribed for restoration to that register[16].

1 See the Veterinary Surgeons and Veterinary Practitioners Registration Regulations 1967 reg 16 (amended by SI 1975/70 and SI 1989/2431). As to these regulations see para 556 note 1 ante. As to the lists see para 547 ante.
2 Veterinary Surgeons and Veterinary Practitioners Registration Regulations 1967 (as to which see para 556 note 1 ante) reg 17 (a). For the particulars see reg 4 (1).
3 'Veterinary surgeon' means a person registered in the register: ibid reg 2.
4 'Financial year' means the financial year of the Royal College of Veterinary Surgeons running from 1 April to 31 March: ibid reg 2.

5 Ibid reg 17 (b).
6 See ibid reg 20 (a)–(c), proviso (substituted by SI 1975/70, and amended by SI 1989/2431).
7 Veterinary Surgeons and Veterinary Practitioners Registration Regulations 1967 (as to which see para 556 note 1 ante) reg 19 (a). An application form for retention, a notice of fees payable and a warning that failure to pay fees entails removal from the register is sent out not later than 14 March each year: see reg 8.
8 Ibid reg 18. As to this register see para 548 ante.
9 'Veterinary practitioner' means a person registered in the supplementary veterinary register: ibid reg 2.
10 See ibid reg 20 (d), (e) (as substituted and amended: see note 6 supra).
11 Ibid reg 19 (b). See also reg 8; and note 7 supra.
12 Ibid reg 9. In the case of a person resident outside the United Kingdom, if the fee has not been paid within three months after the issue of a warning letter the council must decide what further action, if any, is to be taken before the name is removed: reg 9.
13 Ibid reg 14 (a) (substituted by SI 1975/70). For the restoration fee see the 1967 Regulations reg 22 (as so substituted and amended by SI 1989/2431).
14 Veterinary Surgeons and Veterinary Practitioners Registration Regulations 1967 (as to which see para 556 note 1 ante) reg 14 (b) (as substituted: see note 13 supra). The payment of this fee entitles the veterinary surgeon to the retention of his name in the appropriate list only until the end of the financial year in which such fee is paid: reg 14 (b) (as so substituted).
15 Ie in respect of the financial year during which he makes application for restoration: ibid reg 14 (c) (as substituted: see note 13 supra).
16 Ibid reg 14 (c) (as substituted: see note 13 supra).

(4) THE ROYAL COLLEGE OF VETERINARY SURGEONS

(i) The College

561. Incorporation. The Royal College of Veterinary Surgeons was incorporated in 1844 by royal charter, and this charter, and two supplemental charters granted in 1876 and 1879, were confirmed by statute[1]. Further charters have been granted to the college from time to time[2], the most recent one being in 1967, which revoked all previous supplemental charters together with a substantial portion of the charter of 1844. It restates and consolidates provisions of the previous charters relating to the administration of the college which are not covered by the Veterinary Surgeons Act 1966. The college has perpetual succession and a common seal[3].

1 Veterinary Surgeons Act 1881 ss 2, 14 (repealed). The original charter recites that the veterinary art was not recognised as a profession (see also *Sewell v Corp* (1824) 1 C & P 392), declared that it should be so recognised, and provided that members of the college should be known and distinguished by the name or title of 'veterinary surgeons'. As to incorporation by charter generally see CORPORATIONS vol 9 para 1233 et seq.
2 Ie in 1883, 1892, 1914, 1923, 1932, 1961, 1963, 1965 and 1967.
3 As to the corporate seal see CORPORATIONS vol 9 para 1217 et seq.

562. Constitution. The Royal College of Veterinary Surgeons consists of fellows, members and honorary associates.

A fellow of the college is a member who is elected to this position or has presented a thesis, passed an examination, or made a meritorious contribution to learning[1].

Persons holding veterinary degrees of universities to which recognition orders relate[2], students of other universities in the United Kingdom who have passed examinations held by the college[3], Commonwealth or foreign practitioners[4], and holders of recognised European qualifications in veterinary surgery[5], on being registered in the register of veterinary surgeons, become members of the college[6].

Honorary associates are persons elected to this position by the council of the college[7].

1 Byelaws of the college prescribe conditions for the diploma of fellowship and relating to the award of the diploma of veterinary anaesthesia and veterinary radiology.
2 As to recognition orders see para 550 ante.
3 As to college examinations see para 550 ante.
4 As to Commonwealth and foreign practitioners see para 552 ante.
5 See para 553 ante.
6 See paras 550, 552, 553 ante.
7 Honorary associates are persons of special eminence or who have rendered special services to veterinary science or the veterinary profession.

(ii) The Council of the College

A. CONSTITUTION, MEMBERS AND OFFICERS

563. Constitution of the council. The government of the Royal College of Veterinary Surgeons is vested in a council, consisting of: 24 members of the college elected from among themselves[1] by members of the college[2]; four persons appointed by the Privy Council[3]; two persons, at least one of whom must be a member of the college, appointed by each university in the United Kingdom for which a recognition order is in force[4]; and such additional persons as are elected or appointed in accordance with the terms of any agreement between Her Majesty's government in the United Kingdom and the government of the Republic of Ireland[5]. Where the Privy Council makes an order[6] relating to the recognition of a university which results in a change in the number of members appointed by universities, it may after consultation with the council by order make such alteration in the number of elected members as may secure that there is a majority of elected members over all other members of the council[7], and make such consequential provision as to the term of office of the elected members as appears necessary or expedient in consequence of the change in the total number of elected members[8].

1 Elections of elected members must be conducted in accordance with a scheme made by the council of the college and approved by the Privy Council (Veterinary Surgeons Act 1966 s 1 (3), Sch 1 para 9), and must be held before the annual general meeting of the college at which the relevant vacancy occurs (Sch 1 para 6 (1)). Such a scheme may be amended by the council but no amendment has effect unless approved by the Privy Council: Sch 1 para 10. Members of the college who are not required to pay a fee for membership by reason of an agreement between the governments of the United Kingdom and Ireland (see para 551 ante) may nonetheless not participate in elections, whether proposing, standing or voting, unless they have paid a prescribed fee: s 1 (1A) (added by the Veterinary Surgeons (Agreement with the Republic of Ireland) Order 1988, SI 1988/784, art 4. See also the 1988 Agreement art 3 (3).
2 Veterinary Surgeons Act 1966 s 1 (1) (a).
3 Ibid s 1 (1) (b).
4 Ibid s 1 (1) (c). As to recognition orders see para 550 ante.
5 See ibid s 21 (1) (a); and para 551 ante. The 1988 Agreement provided that the representative appointed by the Irish Minister of Agriculture, Fisheries and Food and two Irish elected members should cease to hold office on 31 May 1988: art 2. The previous Agreement (1972 Agreement art 2 (2) (b), (3) (a)) provided for the two Irish universities each to appoint one representative, whose term of office would be four years, and who would then be eligible for re-appointment. Although

the 1988 Agreement does not expressly terminate the tenure of these office holders, it does revoke the 1972 Agreement and does not make new provisions as to such representatives. It should be noted that veterinary surgeons or practitioners with recognised European qualifications (which would include those awarded by Irish universities) are eligible for membership of the college, and therefore for membership of the council: see para 553 ante.

6 Ie under the Veterinary Surgeons Act 1966 s 3: see para 550 ante.
7 Ibid s 1 (4) (a). See also para 541 note 8 ante.
8 Ibid s 1 (4) (b). Such an order may include provision modifying Sch 1: s 1 (4) (b). See also para 541 note 8 ante.

564. Terms of office and vacancies for membership of the council. The term of office of any member of the Council of the Royal College of Veterinary Surgeons is, as near as may be, four years, and the day on which he ordinarily retires is the day of the annual general meeting of the college in the year in which he retires[1]. Each year the six elected members of the council who have been such members for the longest time without re-election must retire[2]. A person ceasing to be a member of the council is eligible to be re-elected[3]. A member of the council may at any time resign his office as member by notice in writing addressed to the registrar[4]. An elected member of the council, or a member of the council appointed by a university as being a member of the college, ceases to hold office if he ceases to be a member of the college[5].

1 Veterinary Surgeons Act 1966 s 1 (3), Sch 1 para 1 (1). If on the coming into force of a recognition order for any university a member of the council is appointed by that university between two annual general meetings of the college, then his term of office does not expire until the fourth annual general meeting after it began: Sch 1 para 1 (3). If a recognition order ceases to be in force for any university, any member appointed to the council by that university thereupon ceases to hold office: Sch 1 para 5. As to recognition orders see para 550 ante.
2 Ibid Sch 1 para 1 (2).
3 Ibid Sch 1 para 8.
4 Ibid Sch 1 para 3.
5 Ibid Sch 1 para 4.

565. Filling casual vacancies. Where a casual vacancy occurs among the elected members of the Council of the Royal College of Veterinary Surgeons, the vacancy is filled by the unsuccessful candidate who at the last previous ordinary election received most votes and has not since become a member[1], or, if two or more such candidates received equal votes, by the candidate registered longest on the register[2], or, if there were no unsuccessful candidates at that election, by a person appointed by the council[3]. A person filling a casual vacancy among elected members holds office until the date on which the person whose vacancy he fills would have regularly retired[4].

Where a casual vacancy occurs among members of the council appointed by the Privy Council or a university, the appointing body fills the vacancy[5].

1 Veterinary Surgeons Act 1966 s 1 (3), Sch 1 para 7 (1) (a).
2 Ibid Sch 1 para 7 (1) (b). If two or more such candidates have been registered longer than any other but for the same period as each other, the vacancy is filled by one of them chosen by lot: Sch 1 para 7 (1) (b).
3 Ibid Sch 1 para 7 (1) (c).
4 Ibid Sch 1 para 7 (4).
5 Ibid Sch 1 para 7 (2).

566. President and vice-presidents. The Royal College of Veterinary Surgeons has a president and two vice-presidents who must be elected from among themselves by members of the council of the college[1]. The term of office of the president or a vice-president is, as near as may be, one year, and he must retire at the next meeting of the council after the annual general meeting[2]. He may at any time by notice in writing addressed to the registrar resign his office[3].

Elections to fill an ordinary vacancy in the office of president or vice-president are held at the meeting of the council at which the vacancy occurs[4]. Where a casual vacancy occurs in such an office, the vacancy is filled by an election held at the first meeting of the council after the vacancy occurs[5], and the person filling the casual vacancy holds office until the date on which the person whose vacancy he fills would have regularly retired[6].

1 Veterinary Surgeons Act 1966 s 1 (2).
2 Ibid s 1 (3), Sch 1 para 2. He holds office until that next meeting notwithstanding that he has ceased to be a member of the council, unless he resigns his office or ceases to be a member of the council by resignation or because he ceases to be a member of the college, or a recognition order for a university by which he has been appointed ceases to be in force: Sch 1 para 2. A person ceasing to be president or vice-president is eligible to be re-elected: Sch 1 para 8.
3 Ibid Sch 1 para 3.
4 Ibid Sch 1 para 6 (2).
5 Ibid Sch 1 para 7 (3).
6 Ibid Sch 1 para 7 (4).

567. Registrar and assistant registrar. The registrar of the Royal College of Veterinary Surgeons is appointed by the council of the college[1]. He must keep the registers[2] and perform such other duties in connection with them as the council directs; and in the execution of his duties he must act on such evidence as in each case appears sufficient[3]. The council may appoint an assistant registrar who is entitled to perform all the functions of the registrar[4].

1 Veterinary Surgeons Act 1966 s 9 (1).
2 Ibid s 9 (1), (8). These are the register of veterinary surgeons and the supplementary veterinary register: see paras 547, 548 ante.
3 Ibid s 9 (2), (8).
4 Ibid s 27 (2).

B. FUNCTIONS

568. Management of the college. The Council of the Royal College of Veterinary Surgeons has entire management of the college and exercises the various powers and duties of the college relating to the examination and registration of veterinary surgeons. It has certain powers to make rules and regulations[1] which do not take effect unless approved by order of the Privy Council[2].

The powers of the council and of its committees may be exercised notwithstanding any vacancy, and no proceedings of the council or of its committees are invalidated by any defect in the election or appointment of a member[3].

1 See the Veterinary Surgeons Act 1966 s 6 (4) (see para 552 note 8 ante), s 11 (1) (see para 556 ante), s 19 (3) (see para 544 text and note 23 ante), and Sch 2 Pt II para 5 (see para 574 post).
2 Ibid s 25 (1). Such an order, which must be made by statutory instrument (s 25 (3)), may be revoked by a subsequent order of the Privy Council (s 25 (2)).
3 Ibid s 1 (3), Sch 1 para 11.

569. Supervision of courses of study and examinations. The Council of the Royal College of Veterinary Surgeons has powers to secure that courses of study followed by students training to be veterinary surgeons, and the standard of proficiency required for registration in the register of veterinary surgeons[1], are such as sufficiently to guarantee that persons registered in the register will have acquired the knowledge and skill needed for the efficient practice of veterinary surgery[2]; and the council has a duty to exercise the following powers for this purpose[3].

It may appoint persons to visit the universities for which recognition orders[4] are in force or are proposed to be made, and any other universities which for the time being provide or propose to provide courses leading to examination by the college, and to report on the courses of study, staffing, accommodation and equipment available for training, and the other arrangements and facilities for such training[5]. It may appoint persons to attend at examinations in any aspect of veterinary surgery at universities for which recognition orders are in force or are proposed to be made, and to report to it as to the sufficiency of the examinations and such other matters relating to them as it may require[6]. A copy of any report must be sent by the council to the university concerned[7], which may within two months of receiving it make to the council observations on the report or objections to it[8]. As soon as practicable after the period has expired a copy of the report and any observations and objections which have been made, together with the council's comments, must be sent to the Privy Council[9].

Every university for which a recognition order is in force must, on written request, furnish the council of the college with any information specified in the request as to the courses of study and examinations leading to the degree to which the recognition order relates, and a university for whose students of veterinary surgery examinations are held by the college[10] must, on being so requested, furnish the council with any information specified in the request as to the courses of study preparing students for those examinations[11].

1 As to the register see para 547 ante.
2 For the meaning of 'veterinary surgery' see para 541 ante.
3 Veterinary Surgeons Act 1966 s 5 (1).
4 As to recognition orders see para 550 ante.
5 Veterinary Surgeons Act 1966 s 5 (2).
6 Ibid s 5 (3). This provision does not, however, authorise a person so appointed to interfere with the conduct of any examination: s 5 (3) proviso.
7 Ibid s 5 (4) (a).
8 Ibid s 5 (4) (b).
9 Ibid s 5 (4) (c).
10 Ie under ibid s 4: see para 550 ante.
11 Ibid s 5 (5).

570. Control by the Privy Council. If it appears to the Privy Council that the Council of the Royal College of Veterinary Surgeons has failed, but ought, to discharge any of its functions under the Veterinary Surgeons Act 1966, the Privy Council may notify its opinion to the council and may direct it to discharge that function in such a manner and within such a period as may be specified in the direction[1]. If the council of the college fails to comply with such a direction, the Privy Council may itself discharge the function in question[2].

1 Veterinary Surgeons Act 1966 s 22 (1).
2 Ibid s 22 (2). As to the performance of the functions of the Privy Council see para 541 ante.

(5) DISCIPLINE

571. Grounds for removal from the registers or suspension. The disciplinary committee[1] of the Council of the Royal College of Veterinary Surgeons may exercise its disciplinary powers if (1) a registered veterinary surgeon or a registered veterinary practitioner is convicted in the United Kingdom or elsewhere of a criminal offence which, in the committee's opinion renders him unfit to practise veterinary surgery[2]; or (2) any such person is judged by the committee to have been guilty of disgraceful conduct in any professional respect[3]; or (3) the committee is satisfied that the name of any such person has been fraudulently entered in the register of veterinary surgeons or the supplementary veterinary register[4]. In these circumstances the committee may, if it thinks fit, direct that the person's name be removed from the appropriate register or, except in the case of fraudulent entry, that his registration be suspended[5]. Where any such direction is made, the registrar of the council must serve notice of the direction on the person concerned[6].

1 As to the disciplinary committee see para 573 post.
2 Veterinary Surgeons Act 1966 s 16 (1) (a), (3). For the meaning of 'veterinary surgery' see para 541 ante. As to the principles underlying this jurisdiction see MEDICINE vol 30 para 124.
3 Ibid s 16 (1) (b), (3). See *Re Hans* (1960) Times, 12 October, DC. 'Conduct disgraceful in a professional respect' is not limited either to conduct involving moral turpitude or to a veterinary surgeon's conduct in pursuit of his profession, but may extend to conduct which, although reprehensible in anyone, is, in the case of a professional man, so much more reprehensible as to be disgraceful, in the sense that it tends to bring disgrace to the profession which he practises: *Marten v Disciplinary Committee of Royal College of Veterinary Surgeons* [1966] 1 QB 1, [1965] 1 All ER 949, DC. Driving under the influence of drugs and dangerous driving was held not to be such conduct as to justify removal from the register: *Re Hans* supra, where the court substituted suspension for removal. See also MEDICINE vol 30 para 125.
4 Veterinary Surgeons Act 1966 s 16 (1) (c), (3).
5 Ibid s 16 (1), (3). These directions must be carried out by the registrar: Veterinary Surgeons and Veterinary Practitioners Registration Regulations 1967 reg 13. As to these regulations see para 556 note 1 ante. Suspension results in the registration having no effect during the period specified in the direction: Veterinary Surgeons Act 1966 s 16 (1). As to the removal of names from the register in other than disciplinary cases see paras 558, 559 ante.
　　Where a person is registered both in the register and in its Irish equivalent, and alleged misconduct has occurred within the jurisdiction of the Irish Council, the Irish Council is empowered to exercise its disciplinary functions against that person as if he were registered only in the Irish register: see the 1988 Agreement between the United Kingdom and Republic of Ireland governments (para 551 note 1 ante), art 4.
6 Veterinary Surgeons Act 1966 s 16 (2).

572. The preliminary investigation committee. It is the duty of a committee of the Council of the Royal College of Veterinary Surgeons known as 'the preliminary investigation committee' to conduct a preliminary investigation into every disciplinary case[1] and to decide whether the case should be referred to the disciplinary committee[2]. The preliminary investigation committee is set up by the council[3] and consists of the president and vice-president of the college and three other members of the council elected by the council[4].

1 'Disciplinary case' means a case in which it is alleged that a person is liable to have his name removed from the register or to have his registration suspended under the Veterinary Surgeons Act 1966 s 16 (see para 571 ante): ss 15 (1), 27 (1).

2 Ibid s 15 (1). As to the disciplinary committee see para 573 post.
3 Ibid s 15 (1).
4 Ibid s 15 (3), Sch 2 Pt I para 1 (1). Three members, of whom at least one must be the president or a vice-president of the college, form a quorum: Sch 2 Pt I para 1 (3). The members hold office for such term as the council may determine from time to time: Sch 2 Pt I para 3. As to elections see Sch 2 Pt I para 1 (2).

573. The disciplinary committee. The disciplinary committee of the Council of the Royal College of Veterinary Surgeons has the duty of considering and determining any disciplinary case[1] referred to it by the preliminary investigation committee[2] and any case[3] for the restoration of a name to the register or the removal of a suspension of registration[4]. The disciplinary committee consists of a chairman elected by the council and of eleven other members so elected[5]. Members of the disciplinary committee must be members of the council[6], not less than six of them being elected members and not less than one of them being a member appointed to the council by the Privy Council[7]. No person who acted as a member of the preliminary investigation committee in any case may act as a member of the disciplinary committee with respect to that case[8]. The members of the disciplinary committee hold office for such term as may be determined from time to time by the council[9].

At any meeting of the disciplinary committee the chairman of the committee, or in his absence a committee member chosen by the committee, presides[10]. All its acts are decided by a majority of its members present[11]. The quorum is five, of whom at least one must be an elected member of the council[12].

1 For the meaning of 'disciplinary case' see para 572 note 1 ante.
2 Veterinary Surgeons Act 1966 s 15 (2) (a). As to this committee see para 572 ante.
3 Ie any case of which the disciplinary committee has cognisance under ibid s 18: see para 589 post.
4 Ibid s 15 (2) (b).
5 Ibid s 15 (3), Sch 2 Pt I para 2 (1). In the case of proceedings relating to the supplementary veterinary register there must be added to the committee four persons registered in that register appointed by the ministers (defined in para 544 note 21 ante): Sch 2 Pt I para 2 (4).
6 Ibid Sch 2 Pt I para 2 (2).
7 Ibid Sch 2 Pt I para 2 (3).
8 Ibid Sch 2 Pt I para 2 (5).
9 Ibid Sch 2 Pt I para 3.
10 Disciplinary Committee (Procedure and Evidence) Rules 1967 r 3. As to these rules see para 574 note 1 post.
11 Ibid r 17 (1).
12 Veterinary Surgeons Act 1966 Sch 2 Pt I para 2 (6). In the case of a disciplinary case against a person registered in the supplementary veterinary register, the quorum is seven, of whom at least one must be an elected member of the council and at least two must be persons registered in the supplementary veterinary register: Sch 2 Pt I para 2 (6).

574. Disciplinary rules. Provision is made by rules[1] made by the Council of the Royal College of Veterinary Surgeons as to the procedure to be followed and the rules of evidence to be observed in disciplinary cases[2] before the disciplinary committee[3]. Such rules do not come into force until approved by order of the Privy Council[4].

For any aspect of the conduct of proceedings for which specific provision is not made by such rules, the procedure is determined by the chairman[5].

1 See the Disciplinary Committee (Procedure and Evidence) Rules 1967, approved by the Privy Council and brought into force by the Veterinary Surgeons and Veterinary Practitioners (Disciplin-

ary Committee) (Procedure and Evidence) Rules Order of Council 1967, SI 1967/659. The rules are set out in the Schedule to the order, and are amended by rules approved by SI 1990/1959.

2 For the meaning of 'disciplinary case' see para 572 note 1 ante.

3 Veterinary Surgeons Act 1966 s 15 (3), Sch 2 Pt II para 5. The committee may waive any procedural requirement of the rules with the consent of the parties or in any case where the interests of justice so demand: Disciplinary Committee (Procedure and Evidence) Rules 1967, r 16 (5). See also text and note 5 infra.

4 Veterinary Surgeons Act 1966 s 25 (1): see para 568 ante. See note 1 supra for the approval of the current rules.

5 Disciplinary Committee (Procedure and Evidence) Rules 1967 r 19 (4) (added by SI 1990/1959).

575. Legal assessor. In all proceedings before the disciplinary committee in disciplinary cases[1] there must be an assessor to the committee for the purpose of advising it on questions of law arising in such cases[2]. The assessor must be a person who has a ten year general qualfication[3]. The power of appointing an assessor is exercisable by the council, but if no assessor appointed by the council is available to act in any particular proceedings, the committee may itself appoint an assessor so qualified for those proceedings[4]. An assessor may be appointed either generally or for any particular proceedings or class of proceedings, and holds and vacates office in accordance with the terms of the instrument under which he is appointed[5]. Any remuneration paid by the council to persons appointed to act as assessors must be at such rates as the council, with the consent of the Lord Chancellor, determines[6].

It is the assessor's duty to be present at all proceedings before the disciplinary committee relating to the removal of a person's name from the register or the restoration of a person's name to the register, and to advise the committee on any questions of law and the admission of evidence arising which may be referred to him by the committee[7]. He must inform the committee forthwith of any irregularity in the conduct of the proceedings which comes to his knowledge, and advise the committee of his own motion where it appears to him that, but for such advice, there is a possibility of a mistake of law being made[8].

His advice must be tendered to the committee in the presence of every party[9], or person representing a party, to the proceedings who appears at them[10]; if, however, a question is referred by the committee to the assessor while the committee is deliberating in private, and the committee considers that it would be prejudicial to the discharge of its duties for the advice to be tendered in the presence of the parties or their representatives, it may be tendered in their absence, but the assessor must, as soon as may be, inform them, or see that they are informed, of the question put to him by the committee and of his advice on it, and his advice must subsequently be put in writing and a copy of it made available to every party or representative[11].

If on any occasion the committee does not accept the assessor's advice, a record must be made of the question referred to him, of the advice given and of the refusal to accept it, together with the reasons for the refusal, and a copy of the record must be given to every party, or person representing a party, to the proceedings who appears[12].

1 For the meaning of 'disciplinary case' see para 572 note 1 ante.

2 Veterinary Surgeons Act 1966 s 15 (3), Sch 2 Pt II para 6 (1).

3 Ibid Sch 2 Pt II para 6 (1) (amended by the Courts and Legal Services Act 1990 s 71 (2), Sch 10 para 28). A 'general qualification' is a right of audience in any class of proceedings in any part of the Supreme Court, or all proceedings in county courts or magistrates' courts: Courts and Legal Services Act 1990 s 71 (3) (c). An advocate or solicitor in Scotland of at least ten years' standing, or a

member of the Bar of Northern Ireland or a solicitor of the Supreme Court of Northern Ireland of at
least ten years' standing, is also eligible for appointment: Veterinary Surgeons Act 1966 Sch 2 Pt II
para 6 (as so amended).
4 Ibid Sch 2 Pt II para 6 (2).
5 Ibid Sch 2 Pt II para 6 (4).
6 Ibid Sch 2 Pt II para 6 (5).
7 Veterinary Surgeons (Disciplinary Proceedings) Legal Assessor Rules 1967, SI 1967/684, r 3. These
rules were made by the Lord Chancellor under the Veterinary Surgeons Act 1966 Sch 2 Pt II
para 6 (3). See generally MEDICINE vol 30 para 122.
8 Veterinary Surgeons (Disciplinary Proceedings) Legal Assessor Rules 1967 r 4.
9 'Party' means (1) in any case the respondent; and (2) in any case relating to fraudulent entry, any
person who is alleged to have been a party to the alleged fraud: Disciplinary Committee (Procedure
and Evidence) Rules 1967 r 2 (1). 'Respondent' means (a) in a case relating to conduct or to
conviction, the person against whom the allegation is made; or (b) in a case relating to fraudulent
entry, the person whose name it is alleged is fraudulently entered in the register: r 2 (1). As to these
rules see para 574 note 1 ante.
10 Veterinary Surgeons (Disciplinary Proceedings) Legal Assessor Rules 1967 r 5.
11 Ibid r 5 proviso. Copies of written advice must be available on application to every party to the
proceedings who does not appear: r 7.
12 Ibid r 6. As to copies of written advice see note 11 supra.

576. Notice of inquiry. In a case relating to conduct or to conviction, as soon as
may be after the case has been referred to the disciplinary committee, the registrar
must serve[1] on the respondent[2] a notice of inquiry[3], specifying the matters alleged
against him in the form of a charge or charges and stating the day[4], time and place at
which the committee will hold an inquiry into these matters, together with a copy
of the rules[5]. If any disciplinary case has been referred to the committee by the
preliminary investigation committee[6] as a result of a complaint received from a
member of the public, the registrar must send that person a copy of the notice and
of the rules[7]. The committee may not hold an inquiry unless a notice of inquiry has
been served on the respondent[8].

Where, before the inquiry opens, it appears to the chairman, or where at any
stage of the proceedings it appears to the disciplinary committee, that a notice of
inquiry is defective, the chairman or the committee must cause the notice to be
amended unless it appears that the required amendment cannot be made without
injustice, or, if he or it considers that the circumstances in which an amendment is
made require it, he or it may direct that the amended notice be served on the
respondent, and that the inquiry be postponed[9].

1 Service is by letter addressed to the respondent in accordance with the Veterinary Surgeons Act 1966
s 26 (2): Disciplinary Committee (Procedure and Evidence) Rules 1967 r 4 (1). As to these rules see
para 574 note 1 ante. Any notice or other document authorised or required to be served under the
Veterinary Surgeons Act 1966 on a registered veterinary surgeon or veterinary practitioner may,
without prejudice to any other method of service, be served on him by post in a letter addressed to
him at his address in the relevant register or, if different, at his last known address if it appears to the
registrar that such service will be more effective: s 26 (2).
2 For the meaning of 'respondent' see para 575 note 9 ante.
3 The notice must be as nearly as may be in the form set out in the Disciplinary Committee (Procedure
and Evidence) Rules 1967, Appendix: r 4 (1).
4 Except with the respondent's agreement, the inquiry must not be held earlier than 28 days after the
date of posting of the notice of inquiry: ibid r 4 (4).
5 Ibid r 4 (1). As to the rules see para 574 ante.
6 As to the preliminary investigation committee see para 572 ante.
7 Disciplinary Committee (Procedure and Evidence) Rules 1967 r 4 (3). As to the rules see para 574
note 1 ante.
8 Ibid r 4 (2).

9 Ibid r 5 (2). Notice of the postponement, and of the date of the hearing, must be sent by the registrar, as soon as may be, to all parties to whom a notice of inquiry was sent: r 5 (3).

577. Access to documents.

Upon application by any party[1] to an inquiry relating to conduct or to conviction and on payment of proper charges, the solicitor[2] must send him copies of any statutory declaration, explanation, answer, admission or other statement or communication sent to the Royal College of Veterinary Surgeons by any party to the inquiry[3].

1 For the meaning of 'party' see para 575 note 9 ante.
2 'The solicitor' means the solicitor nominated by the Royal College of Veterinary Surgeons to act as its solicitor for the purpose of the Disciplinary Committee (Procedure and Evidence) Rules 1967, and in relation to proceedings before the disciplinary committee it includes counsel instructed by that solicitor: r 2 (1). As to these rules see para 574 note 1 ante.
3 Ibid r 6.

578. Legal representation.

Any party[1] who is an individual may appear either in person or by counsel or solicitor[2], and any party which is a body corporate or an unincorporated body of persons may appear by its secretary or other officer duly appointed for the purpose or by counsel or solicitor[3].

1 For the meaning of 'party' see para 575 note 9 ante.
2 Disciplinary Committee (Procedure and Evidence) Rules 1967 r 19 (1). As to these rules see para 574 note 1 ante.
3 Ibid r 19 (2).

579. The hearing.

In general all proceedings before the disciplinary committee must take place in the presence of all the parties[1] to the proceedings who appear and must be held in public[2]. However, subject to certain exceptions[3], the committee may at any time and for any purpose during or after the hearing of any proceedings deliberate in camera with or without the legal assessor[4]. In addition, where in the interests of justice it appears to the committee that the public should be excluded from any proceedings or part of them, the committee may direct that the public is to be excluded; but such a direction does not apply to the announcement of a determination of the committee[5]. The committee may adjourn its proceedings from time to time as it thinks fit[6].

The chairman of the disciplinary committee, of his own motion or upon the application of any party to the inquiry, may postpone the hearing for any period not exceeding three months[7].

In the absence of specific provision, the procedure for any aspect of the hearing is determined by the chairman[8].

1 For the meaning of 'party' see para 575 note 9 ante.
2 Disciplinary Committee (Procedure and Evidence) Rules 1967 r 15 (2). As to these rules see para 574 note 1 ante.
3 Ie subject to the provisions of the Veterinary Surgeons Act 1966 Sch 2 Pt II para 6 (3), and of any rules made under it (legal assessor: see para 575 ante): Disciplinary Committee (Procedure and Evidence) Rules 1967 r 15 (1).
4 Ibid r 15 (1). As to the legal assessor see para 575 ante.
5 Ibid r 15 (3).
6 Ibid r 15 (4).
7 Ibid r 5 (1). The registrar must, as soon as may be, give to all parties to whom notice of inquiry was sent notification of the decision to postpone and of the date fixed for the hearing: r 5 (3).
8 See para 574 text and note 5 ante.

580. The case against the respondent. In a disciplinary case[1] the charge is read in the presence of the respondent[2], when he may, if he so desires, object to the charge, or any part of it, in point of law[3]. The solicitor[4] may answer any such objection, and the respondent has the right of final reply. If the objection is upheld no further proceedings may be taken on that charge or that part of the charge to which the objection relates[5].

Where the case arises out of an allegation that the respondent has been convicted in the United Kingdom or elsewhere of a criminal offence rendering him unfit to practise veterinary surgery, the registrar then, if the respondent appears, asks him whether he admits each conviction alleged in the charge or charges[6]; and the solicitor then, if the respondent has not appeared or has not admitted every conviction alleged, adduces evidence of any conviction not admitted[7]. Where the case arises out of an allegation that the respondent has been guilty of disgraceful conduct in a professional respect, the registrar asks the respondent, if he appears, whether he admits each fact alleged in the charge or charges[8]; and the solicitor then, if the respondent has not appeared or has not admitted each fact alleged in the charge or charges, adduces evidence of the facts not admitted[9]. In either case, whether the conviction or the facts alleged are admitted or not, the solicitor addresses the disciplinary committee at this stage[10].

1 For the meaning of 'disciplinary case' see para 572 note 1 ante. Where the charges against the respondent (defined in para 575 note 9 ante) relate to both convictions and conduct, the disciplinary committee must proceed upon the charge or charges of each kind separately under the Disciplinary Committee (Procedure and Evidence) Rules 1967 r 8, where the charge relates to a conviction, or under r 9 where it relates to conduct, and must then proceed under so much of r 10 (see para 586 post) as may be applicable either upon the charge or charges of each kind separately or upon the charges of all kinds concurrently, as the circumstances may require: r 11. As to the rules see para 574 note 1 ante.
2 Ibid r 7 (1). If the respondent does not appear but the committee nevertheless decides that the inquiry is to proceed, the charge must be read in his absence: r 7 (1) proviso. If there are two or more respondents, the procedure here expounded applies with the necessary adaptations and subject to any directions given to the committee as to the order in which the proceedings are to be taken, so, however, that any right ensured to a respondent under the rules is to be exercised separately by each respondent who desires to invoke it: r 18.
3 Ibid r 7 (2).
4 For the meaning of 'the solicitor' see para 577 note 2 ante.
5 Disciplinary Committee (Procedure and Evidence) Rules 1967 r 7 (2).
6 Ibid r 8 (1) (a).
7 Ibid r 8 (1) (b) (i). If no evidence is adduced concerning any particular conviction which has not been admitted by the respondent, the chairman of the disciplinary committee must thereupon announce that it has not been proved: r 8 (1) (c).
8 Ibid r 9 (1) (a).
9 Ibid r 9 (1) (b) (i). If no evidence is adduced concerning any particular charge on which there has been no admission of fact by the respondent, the committee must make a finding on this charge in favour of the respondent, and the chairman must announce its findings in the appropriate terms: r 9 (1) (c).
10 Ibid rr 8 (1) (b) (ii), 9 (1) (b) (ii). In cases relating to conviction, he may adduce evidence with regard to the nature and circumstances of the offence to show that, if the convictions alleged are proved or admitted, they are such as to render the respondent unfit to practise veterinary surgery: r 8 (1) (b) (ii). In cases relating to conduct he addresses the committee to show that if such facts are proved the respondent is by reason of those facts guilty of disgraceful conduct in a professional respect: r 9 (1) (b) (ii).

581. The case for the respondent and the right of reply. Where the respondent[1] appears in a case relating to conviction, he may adduce evidence concerning any conviction which he has not admitted on the question whether he was convicted as alleged, and may address the disciplinary committee on that question[2]. He may also address the committee and adduce evidence with regard to the nature and circumstances of the offence to show that he is not unfit by reason thereof to practise veterinary surgery[3]. If the respondent adduces evidence, the solicitor[4] may adduce evidence in rebuttal[5].

Where the respondent appears in a case relating to conduct he may, at the close of the case against him, submit either that no sufficient evidence has been adduced to enable the committee to find the facts alleged against him proved[6], or that the facts alleged do not constitute disgraceful conduct in any professional respect[7], or he may make both these submissions. Where any such submission is made, the solicitor may answer the submission, and the respondent has the right of final reply[8]. The committee must then consider the submission and determine whether it is to be upheld, and must record, and the chairman must announce, its findings in appropriate terms[9]. The respondent may adduce evidence in answer to any charge concerning which evidence has been adduced and, whether he adduces evidence or not, may address the committee[10]. The solicitor may address the committee by way of reply to the respondent's case in certain circumstances[11], in which event the respondent has a right of final reply[12].

1 For the meaning of 'respondent' see para 575 note 9 ante.
2 Disciplinary Committee (Procedure and Evidence) Rules 1967 r 8 (2) (a). As to these rules see para 574 note 1 ante.
3 Ibid r 8 (2) (b).
4 For the meaning of 'the solicitor' see para 577 note 2 ante.
5 Disciplinary Committee (Procedure and Evidence) Rules 1967 r 8 (2) (c).
6 Ibid r 9 (2) (a) (i).
7 Ibid r 9 (2) (a) (ii).
8 Ibid r 9 (2) (a).
9 Ibid r 9 (2) (b).
10 Ibid r 9 (2) (c). At the close of the respondent's case, the solicitor, with the leave of the committee, may adduce evidence in rebuttal, but if he does so, the respondent may make a further address limited to the rebutting evidence: r 9 (2) (d).
11 The circumstances are (1) if oral evidence (not being evidence as to character) other than that of the respondent himself has been given on his behalf (ibid r 9 (2) (e) (i)); or (2) with the leave of the committee, where no such evidence has been given (r 9 (2) (e) (ii)); or (3) if the respondent has made a submission on a point of law, in which case the solicitor's right of reply is limited to that submission and the respondent has the right of final reply (r 9 (2) (g)).
12 Ibid r 9 (2) (f).

582. Witnesses and evidence. The disciplinary committee may administer oaths for the purpose of any proceedings before it, and any party[1] to the proceedings may sue out writs of subpœna ad testificandum and duces tecum, but no person can be compelled under any such writ to produce any document which he could not be compelled to produce on the trial of an action[2].

The committee may receive oral, documentary or other evidence of any fact which appears to it relevant to the inquiry into the case before it[3]; but where a fact which it is sought to prove or the form in which any evidence is tendered would not be admissible in criminal proceedings in an English court, the committee may not receive evidence of that fact or in that form unless, after consultation with the legal assessor, the committee is satisfied that it is desirable in the interests of justice to receive it having regard to the difficulty and expense of obtaining evidence which would be admissible[4]. The committee may cause any person to be called as a witness in any proceedings before it whether or not the parties consent. Questions may be put to any witness by the committee through the chairman or by the legal assessor with the leave of the chairman[5].

Where any respondent[6] or applicant[7] has supplied to the committee or to the registrar on its behalf the name of any person to whom reference may be made confidentially as to his character or conduct, the committee may consider any information received from such person in consequence of the reference without disclosing it to the respondent or applicant[8].

1 For the meaning of 'party' see para 575 note 9 ante.
2 Veterinary Surgeons Act 1966 s 15 (3), Sch 2 Pt II para 4 (1). The Supreme Court Act 1981 s 36 (see EVIDENCE vol 17 para 248), applies to compel the attendance of witnesses who are out of the jurisdiction but who are within the United Kingdom: Veterinary Surgeons Act 1966 Sch 2 Pt II para 4 (2).
3 Disciplinary Committee (Procedure and Evidence) Rules 1967 r 16 (2). As to these rules see para 574 note 1 ante. If satisfied that the interests of justice will not thereby be prejudiced, the committee may admit in evidence without strict proof copies of documents which are themselves admissible, maps, plans, photographs, certificates of conviction and sentence, certificates of birth and marriage and death, the records (including the registers) of the Royal College of Veterinary Surgeons, the notes of proceedings before the committee and other tribunals and the records of such tribunals; and it may also take note of the professional qualifications, the registration, the address and identity of the respondent and of any other veterinary surgeons or veterinary practitioners: r 16 (3). The committee may also accept admissions made by any party and may in such case dispense with proof of the matters admitted: r 16 (4). It may waive any rule of evidence with the consent of the parties: r 16 (5).
4 Ibid r 16 (2) proviso. For the meaning of 'party' see para 575 note 9 ante.
5 Ibid r 16 (6).
6 For the meaning of 'respondent' see para 575 note 9 ante.
7 Ie any applicant for restoration to the register or removal of suspension under the Disciplinary Committee (Procedure and Evidence) Rules 1967 r 14: see para 589 post.
8 Ibid r 16 (1).

583. Shorthand note. A shorthand writer must be appointed by the disciplinary committee to take shorthand notes of its proceedings, and any party[1] to the proceedings must, on application to the solicitor[2] and on payment of the proper charges, be furnished by the solicitor with a transcript of the shorthand notes of any part of the proceedings at which the parties were entitled to be present[3].

1 For the meaning of 'party' see para 575 note 9 ante.
2 For the meaning of 'the solicitor' see para 577 note 2 ante.
3 Disciplinary Committee (Procedure and Evidence) Rules 1967 r 19 (3). As to these rules see para 574 note 1 ante.

584. Determination of the committee. At the conclusion of the proceedings the disciplinary committee must consider, in cases relating to conviction, whether the facts alleged in the charge or charges have been proved, and must determine whether the respondent[1] has been convicted of an offence which, in its opinion, renders him unfit to practise veterinary surgery[2]. The chairman must then announce the findings of the committee[3].

In cases relating to conduct, the committee must at this stage consider and determine as respects each charge which remains outstanding whether the facts alleged in the charge have been proved to its satisfaction[4]. The chairman must announce its findings in the appropriate terms[5].

1 For the meaning of 'respondent' see para 575 note 9 ante.

2 Disciplinary Committee (Procedure and Evidence) Rules 1967 r 8 (3). As to these rules see para 574 note 1 ante. This provision refers to an offence to which the Veterinary Surgeons Act 1966 s 16 (1) (a), applies: see para 571 ante. See generally MEDICINE vol 30 paras 124, 125.

3 Disciplinary Committee (Procedure and Evidence) Rules 1967 r 8 (3).

4 As to the standard of proof see MEDICINE vol 30 para 125.

5 Disciplinary Committee (Procedure and Evidence) Rules 1967 r 9 (3). The appropriate terms of the record of the committee and the finding of the chairman are that in respect of the matters to which the charge relates the respondent is (or is not) guilty of disgraceful conduct in a (or any) professional respect: r 9 (4), (5).

585. Voting. Acts of the disciplinary committee are decided by a majority of the members present[1]. Any questions put to the vote must be put in the form of a motion, upon which members vote by show of hands, the chairman declaring the apparent result[2]. If the voting is equal, the chairman does not have a casting vote, but the question is deemed to have been resolved in favour of the respondent[3] or applicant[4], as the case may be[5].

1 Disciplinary Committee (Procedure and Evidence) Rules 1967 r 17 (1). As to these rules see para 574 note 1 ante.

2 Ibid r 17 (2). The chairman himself may vote for or against the motion: r 17 (2); but see text and notes 4, 5 infra.

3 For the meaning of 'respondent' see para 575 note 9 ante.

4 Ie the applicant for restoration to the register or removal of suspension under the Disciplinary Committee (Procedure and Evidence) Rules 1967 r 14: see para 589 post.

5 Ibid r 17 (3). For this purpose a decision to postpone judgment must be taken to be in favour of the respondent or applicant unless he has indicated to the committee that he is opposed to postponement: r 17 (3). As to the postponement of judgment see paras 586, 587 post.

586. Procedure on proof of facts alleged. Where the disciplinary committee in a case relating to conviction has found that the facts alleged in a charge have been proved, or in a case relating to conduct has recorded a finding against the respondent[1], the chairman invites the solicitor[2] to address the committee and to adduce evidence as to the respondent's character and previous history[3]. The chairman must then invite the respondent to address the committee by way of mitigation and to adduce evidence on the same subject[4].

The committee then considers its judgment, which may be postponed or delivered forthwith[5]. If the committee determines to postpone judgment, the judgment stands postponed for a period not exceeding two years, and the chairman announces its determination in such terms as the committee may approve[6]. If the committee determines not to postpone judgment, it must determine whether, by reason of its findings against the respondent, the registrar of the Royal College of Veterinary Surgeons should be directed to remove the name of the respondent from the register or that his registration should be suspended for a specified period, or whether it is sufficient to warn him as to his future conduct, and the chairman must announce its determination in such terms as the committee may approve[7].

1 For the meaning of 'respondent' see para 575 note 9 ante.

2 For the meaning of 'the solicitor' see para 577 note 2 ante.

3 Disciplinary Committee (Procedure and Evidence) Rules 1967 r 10 (1). As to these rules see para 574 note 1 ante.

4 Ibid r 10 (1).

5 Ibid r 10 (2).

6 Ibid r 10 (3). For the procedure on postponement see para 587 post.

7 Ibid r 10 (4).

587. Procedure on postponement of judgment. Where the judgment of the disciplinary committee in any case stands postponed, the registrar of the Royal College of Veterinary Surgeons must send to the respondent[1], not later than six weeks before the day fixed for the resumption of the proceedings, a notice specifying the day, time and place at which the proceedings are to be resumed and inviting him to appear[2]; unless the chairman otherwise directs, the respondent must be invited to furnish the registrar with the names and addresses of persons to whom reference may be made confidentially or otherwise concerning his character and conduct[3], and to send to the solicitor[4], not less than three weeks before the day fixed for the resumption of proceedings, a copy of any statement or statutory declaration, whether made by the respondent or not, relating to his conduct or other matters since the hearing of his case or setting out any material facts which have arisen since that hearing[5].

At the meeting at which the proceedings are resumed the chairman first invites the solicitor to recall, for the information of the committee, the position in which the case stands[6]. The committee may then receive further oral or documentary evidence in relation to the case, or to the respondent's conduct since the hearing, and hears any party to the proceedings who desires to be heard[7].

The committee then considers and determines whether it should further postpone its judgment on the charges on which its judgment was previously postponed; and if it determines further to postpone judgment, its judgment stands further postponed for a period not exceeding two years; the chairman announces its determination in such terms as it may approve[8].

If the committee determines that judgment should not be further postponed, the chairman then announces its judgment in the usual way[9].

1 For the meaning of 'respondent' see para 575 note 9 ante.
2 Disciplinary Committee (Procedure and Evidence) Rules 1967 r 12 (1) (a) (i). As to these rules see para 574 note 1 ante.
3 Ibid r 12 (1) (a) (ii).
4 For the meaning of 'the solicitor' see para 577 note 2 ante.
5 Disciplinary Committee (Procedure and Evidence) Rules 1967 r 12 (1) (a) (iii).
6 Ibid r 12 (1) (b).
7 Ibid r 12 (1) (b). At any resumed proceedings any new charge alleged against the respondent is first dealt with in accordance with rr 8–10, as applicable (see paras 580, 581, 584, 586 ante), and if the committee determines not to postpone judgment in respect of any such new charge it may give judgment simultaneously on the new charge and on the original charge: r 12 (2). The validity of any proceedings resumed upon a postponed judgment cannot be called in question by reason only of the fact that the committee is differently constituted: r 12 (4). At any resumed hearing the committee may receive evidence of any conviction recorded against the respondent which has not been made the subject of a disciplinary charge: r 12 (3). For the meaning of 'party' see para 575 note 9 ante.
8 Ibid r 12 (1) (c).
9 Ibid r 12 (1) (d). As to the announcement of judgment see para 586 ante.

588. Procedure in cases of fraudulent registration. Where any question whether an entry in the register is fraudulent is referred[1] to the disciplinary committee, the solicitor[2] must send to the respondent[3] a notice of inquiry[4], and must send a copy of the notice to each party[5] in the case and to such other persons, if any, as the chairman directs[6]. The procedure at the inquiry is similar to that at an inquiry relating to disgraceful conduct[7]. If the committee determines that the entry has been proved to its satisfaction to have been made fraudulently it must order[8] that the entry be removed from the register[9].

1 As to such references see para 559 ante.

2 For the meaning of 'the solicitor' see para 577 note 2 ante.

3 For the meaning of 'respondent' see para 575 note 9 ante.

4 Disciplinary Committee (Procedure and Evidence) Rules 1967 r 13 (1). As to these rules see para 574 note 1 ante. The notice must specify the nature of the fraud alleged and state the date, time and place at which the committee will hold an inquiry into the question and invite the respondent's attendance at the inquiry; it must also contain such further information as the nature of the case requires: r 13 (1). The provisions of r 4 (see para 576 ante) apply to the notice: r 13 (1).

5 For the meaning of 'party' see para 575 note 9 ante.

6 Disciplinary Committee (Procedure and Evidence) Rules 1967 r 13 (2).

7 Ibid r 13 (3). Thus r 9 (see paras 580, 581, 584 ante) applies to the inquiry so far as may be: r 13 (3).

8 The order must be in writing under the hand of the chairman: ibid r 13 (4).

9 Ibid r 13 (4).

589. Restoration to the registers. Where the name of a person has been removed from the register of veterinary surgeons or the supplementary veterinary register[1] in pursuance of a direction[2] by the disciplinary committee of the Council of the Royal College of Veterinary Surgeons, the name of that person must not again be entered in the appropriate register unless application is made to the committee for restoration and it directs restoration[3]. Similarly where a person's registration in either register is suspended in pursuance of such a direction, his name must not be entered in the register so long as the suspension has effect unless such application for restoration is made and the committee directs restoration[4]. Application may not be made within ten months of the date of removal or suspension[5] or of a previous application[6].

The committee may determine its own procedure on the hearing of the application[7], except that it must afford the applicant an opportunity of being heard and of adducing evidence[8]. The committee may require such other evidence as it thinks necessary concerning the applicant's identity and character or conduct since his name was removed from the register or since his registration was suspended, and for this purpose it may receive written or oral evidence[9].

1 As to these registers see paras 547, 548 ante.

2 Ie under the Veterinary Surgeons Act 1966 s 16 (see para 571 ante): s 18 (1).

3 Ibid s 18 (1).

4 Ibid s 18 (2).

5 Ibid s 18 (3) (a).

6 Ibid s 18 (3) (b).

7 Disciplinary Committee (Procedure and Evidence) Rules 1967 r 14 (2). As to these rules see para 574 note 1 ante.

8 Ibid r 14 (1) (a).

9 Ibid r 14 (1) (b).

590. Appeals. A person whose name the disciplinary committee of the Council of the Royal College of Veterinary Surgeons has directed to be removed from the register or a person whose registration it has directed to be suspended[1] may appeal against the direction to the Judicial Committee of the Privy Council within 28 days of the service of notice of the direction[2]. The appeal is brought by entering an appearance in the Privy Council registry and at the same time lodging a petition of appeal there[3]. The council of the college may appear as respondent and is deemed to be a party on any such appeal for the purpose of enabling directions to be given as to the costs of the appeal whether it appears or not[4]. It must deliver to the appellant a certified typewritten record of the proceedings before the disciplinary committee and, if it wishes to appear, must enter an appearance forthwith in the registry[5].

When each side has lodged its case in the appeal[6] the appeal may be set down for hearing[7].

Certain of the general rules of procedure applicable to the exercise of the appellate jurisdiction of the Judicial Committee of the Privy Council apply with necessary modifications to appeals from determinations of the disciplinary committee[8].

1 As to such directions see para 571 ante, and as to the registers see paras 547, 548 ante.
2 Veterinary Surgeons Act 1966 s 17 (1). The Judicial Committee Act 1833 applies in relation to appeals from the disciplinary committee as it applies in relation to such courts as are mentioned in s 3 thereof: Veterinary Surgeons Act 1966 s 17 (1). As to the Judicial Committee see COURTS vol 10 para 767 et seq. Where a person desiring to appeal *in forma pauperis* proves by affidavit to the satisfaction of the Privy Council registrar that he is not worth £100 in the world, excepting his wearing apparel, and that he is unable to provide sureties, and lodges a certificate of counsel that he has reasonable grounds of appeal, the appeal must proceed *in forma pauperis* and the appellant will not be required to pay any council office fees: Judicial Committee (Veterinary Surgeons Rules) Order 1967, SI 1967/1150, Schedule rr 1, 16. As to council office fees see Schedule r 14, Schedule of Fees. This order was made under the Veterinary Surgeons Act 1966 s 17 (1).
3 Judicial Committee (Veterinary Surgeons Rules) Order 1967 Schedule rr 1, 2. The petition of appeal must recite succinctly the principal steps in the proceedings leading up to the appeal but must not contain argumentative material or travel into the merits of the case: Schedule r 3. A copy of the petition must be served on the council of the college: r 2.
4 Veterinary Surgeons Act 1966 s 17 (2).
5 Judicial Committee (Veterinary Surgeons Rules) Order 1967 Schedule r 4. The record must be delivered to the appellant with all convenient speed after the receipt of the copy of the petition: Schedule r 4. Within 21 days of the receipt of the record the appellant must lodge it, together with eight copies, in the registry, and transmit three copies to the council of the college: Schedule r 5. For the form of copies see Schedule rr 1, 6.
6 Within 28 days of the lodging of the record the appellant must lodge eight copies of his or its case in the appeal, such copies being signed by a least one of the counsel who attends the hearing or the appeal or by the party himself if he conducts his appeal in person: ibid Schedule r 7. The council of the college must within 28 days of the transmission to it of the three copies of the record lodge eight copies of its case in the appeal signed by at least one of the counsel who attends the hearing: Schedule r 8. The cases must consist of numbered paragraphs stating as concisely as possible the circumstances out of which the appeal arises, the contentions to be urged by the parties, and the reasons of appeal: Schedule r 9. Where the appellant, having lodged a petition of appeal, does not proceed on it in time, the council of the college may petition Her Majesty in Council praying that the appeal be dismissed for non-prosecution: Schedule r 13. The appellant may withdraw his appeal on a petition to Her Majesty in Council: Schedule r 12.
7 Ibid Schedule r 10. If the council of the college does not appear or lodge its case in time the appeal may be set down ex parte if the appellant's case has been lodged: Schedule r 11. Upon the setting down of the appeal each side must send three copies of its case to the other: Schedule r 10.
8 See the Judicial Committee Rules 1982, SI 1982/1676, rr 42, 60, 71, 72, 74, 77–81, 83, 84–86, as applied to appeals under the Judicial Committee (Veterinary Surgeons Rules) Order 1967 Schedule rr 15, 17, 18 (all amended by the 1982 Rules r 4, Sch 1); otherwise those rules do not apply: Schedule r 18. All bills of costs under any order of the Judicial Committee made on appeal stand referred to the Privy Council registrar or such other person as the Judicial Committee may appoint, for taxation, which is regulated by the Schedule of Fees: Schedule r 14.

591–600. When directions of disciplinary committee take effect. Where an appeal is brought against a direction[1] of the disciplinary committee of the Council of the Royal College of Veterinary Surgeons as regards the removal of a person's name from the register or his suspension from registration, the direction takes effect if and when the appeal is dismissed and not otherwise[2]. Where no appeal is brought within the time limited for the appeal or it is brought but then withdrawn or struck out for want of prosecution, the direction takes effect on the expiration of that time[3] or, as the case may be, on the withdrawal or striking out of the appeal[4].

1 As to such directions see para 571 ante.
2 Veterinary Surgeons Act 1966 s 17 (3) (c).
3 Ibid s 17 (3) (a).
4 Ibid s 17 (3) (b).

ANNUITIES

See RENTCHARGES AND ANNUITIES

APPEAL

See COUNTY COURTS; COURTS; CRIMINAL LAW; MAGISTRATES; PARLIAMENT; PRACTICE AND PROCEDURE

APPEARANCE
(ACKNOWLEDGMENT OF SERVICE)

See PRACTICE AND PROCEDURE

APPOINTMENT, POWERS OF

See PERPETUITIES AND ACCUMULATIONS; POWERS

ARBITRATION

1. REFERENCE TO ARBITRATION

(1) ARBITRATION

601. Definition and scope. Arbitration is the process by which a dispute or difference between two or more parties as to their mutual legal rights and liabilities is referred to and determined judicially and with binding effect by the application of law by one or more persons (the arbitral tribunal) instead of by a court of law[1]. The decision of the arbitral tribunal is usually called an award. The reference to arbitration may arise from the agreement of the parties (private arbitration) or from statute: this title deals solely with private arbitration[2]. The agreement of the parties is in practice almost invariably in writing and therefore subject to the Arbitration Acts[3].

1 Because of the judicial nature of their functions, arbitrators enjoy immunity from actions for negligence in the performance of their functions: see *Pappa v Rose* (1871) LR 7 CP 32; *Tharsis Sulphur and Copper Co v Loftus* (1872) LR 8 CP 1; *Stevenson v Watson* (1879) 4 CPD 148; *Chambers v Goldthorpe* [1901] 1 KB 624, CA. It is now established, contrary to earlier authority, that a similar immunity is not enjoyed by a 'quasi-arbitrator' such as an expert valuer or certifier: *Arenson v Casson Beckman Rutley & Co* [1977] AC 405, [1975] 3 All ER 901, sub nom *Arenson v Arenson* [1976] 1 Lloyd's Rep 179, HL. See also *Sutcliffe v Thackrah* [1974] AC 727, [1974] 1 All ER 859, [1974] 1 Lloyd's Rep 319, HL. The provisions of the Supply of Goods and Services Act 1982 s 13 that in certain contracts for the supply of a service there is an implied term that the service will be carried out with reasonable care and skill do not apply to the services rendered by an arbitrator or umpire in his capacity as such: Supply of Goods and Services (Exclusion of Implied Terms) Order 1985, SI 1985/1.
2 Numerous statutes provide for the settlement of disputed questions by arbitration. In some cases arbitration is compulsory: in others it is optional at the instance of one or both parties. With the exception of ss 2 (1), 3, 5, 18 (3), 24, 25, 27 and 29, the provisions of the Arbitration Act 1950 Pt I (ss 1–34) apply to a statutory arbitration except in so far as they are inconsistent with the Act giving rise to the arbitration or any rules of procedures authorised or recognised thereby: s 31 (amended by the Arbitration Act 1975 s 8 (2)). The particular Act may further exclude the application of the Arbitration Act 1950 in whole or in part: see eg the Registered Homes Act 1984 s 43 (3), the Agricultural Holdings Act 1986 s 84 (1) and the Channel Tunnel Act 1987 s 15.
    The title also covers arbitration in foreign investment disputes under the Arbitration (International Investment Disputes) Act 1966: see para 719 et seq post.
3 Arbitration Act 1950 s 32. The Acts in question are the Arbitration Act 1950, the Arbitration Act 1975 and the Arbitration Act 1979. An oral agreement is valid as a matter of common law, but is rarely encountered and has serious disadvantages compared with the position under the Arbitration Acts (see para 608 post).

602. Dispute or difference. Arbitration is concerned with the determination of matters in issue between the parties. Accordingly, in the absence of a dispute or difference a court will not order the stay of court proceedings raising a claim covered by the arbitration agreement[1], for example when one party admits liability but fails to pay[2], or where the court considers that the suggested defence advanced by the defendant is unarguable[3].

1 See para 622 post.
2 *London and North Western Rly Co v Jones* [1915] 2 KB 35, DC.
3 *Nova (Jersey) Knit Ltd v Kammgarn Spinnerei GmbH* [1977] 2 All ER 463, [1977] 1 WLR 713, [1977] 1 Lloyd's Rep 463, HL.

603. Mutual legal rights and liabilities. The dispute or difference must relate to a matter capable of being decided in civil proceedings between the parties and being compromised by accord and satisfaction[1]. It therefore does not extend to a criminal charge[2]. Nor can arbitration cover proceedings seeking a change in status, such as a divorce[3], or an action in rem against a vessel[4].

1 Bac Abr, Arbitrament and Award A.
2 *Horton v Benson* (1675) Freem KB 204; *R v Coombs, R v Rant* (1797), cited in Kyd on Awards 64; *R v Blakemore* (1850) 14 QB 544; *R v Hardey* (1850) 14 QB 529. But the mere fact that the party injured

has been injured in a manner amounting to an indictable offence does not prevent him referring his claim to arbitration, provided that in addition he has a cause of action which may legitimately be compromised: *Keir v Leeman* (1846) 9 QB 371; *Re Metropolitan Saloon Omnibus Co* (1860) 1 LT 294; *Baker v Townsend* (1817) 1 Moore CP 120 at 124; *R v Bardell* (1836) 5 Ad & El 619; *R v Corbishley* (1824) 2 LJOSKB 150.

3 A husband and wife may, however, refer to arbitration the terms on which they shall separate, because they can make a valid agreement between themselves on that matter: see *Soilleux v Herbst* (1801) 2 Bos & P 444; *Bateman v Ross* (1813) 1 Dow 235; *Hooper v Hooper* (1860) Sea & Sm 156; and see *Wilson v Wilson* (1848) 1 HL Cas 538; *Besant v Wood* (1879) 12 ChD 605; *Hart v Hart* (1881) 18 ChD 670; *Cahill v Cahill* (1883) 8 App Cas 420, HL.

4 *The Sylph* (1867) LR 2 A & E 24.

604. Determined by one or more persons. The arbitral tribunal may consist of one or more arbitrators, in practice normally one or three. In some cases, two arbitrators are appointed, one by each party: in the event of disagreement by the arbitrators the dispute is decided by an umpire. The composition of the tribunal is determined by the parties or a third person in accordance with the procedure in the arbitration agreement or by the court[1]. The arbitral process may include an appellate tier. Though arbitration involves the determination of a legal dispute otherwise than by a court of law, a judge of the Commercial Court or an official referee may accept appointment as a sole arbitrator or umpire[2].

1 See para 655 et seq post.
2 See para 655 note 3 post.

605. Determined judicially. The arbitral tribunal must be impartial. It must also decide the dispute on the basis of such evidence and submissions as the parties seek to make to it, where the nature of the dispute does not render this inappropriate[1].

1 *Arenson v Casson Beckman Rutley & Co* [1977] AC 405 at 428, [1975] 3 All ER 901 at 915–916, sub nom *Arenson v Arenson* [1976] 1 Lloyd's Rep 179 at 190–191, HL, per Lord Wheatley; *Re Carus-Wilson and Greene* (1886) 18 QBD 7, CA. An arbitrator is in this respect in a different position from a valuer or certifier appointed as expert.

606. The application of law. The arbitral tribunal is required to determine the dispute by the application of law[1]. An agreement by the parties to contrary effect is not a valid arbitration agreement[2].

1 This refers to substantive as opposed to procedural law: see eg *Tehno-Impex v Gebr Van Weelde-Scheepvaartkantoor BV* [1981] QB 648, [1981] 2 All ER 669, [1981] 1 Lloyd's Rep 587, CA. The law to be applied by the arbitral tribunal may be English law, or such other system or systems of law as may be designated by the rules of private international law or as the parties agree shall be applicable: see paras 717, 718 post.
2 *Home and Overseas Insurance Co Ltd v Mentor Insurance Co (UK) Ltd (in liquidation)* [1989] 3 All ER 74, [1990] 1 WLR 153, [1989] 1 Lloyd's Rep 473, CA. To avoid invalidity on this ground the courts have endeavoured to treat so-called 'equity' or 'honourable engagement' clauses found frequently in reinsurance contracts as merely confirming the power of the arbitrators to adopt a business-like as opposed to a literal interpretation of the contract: *Eagle Star Insurance Co Ltd v Yuval Insurance Co Ltd* [1978] 1 Lloyd's Rep 357, CA; *Home Insurance Co and St Paul Fire and Marine Insurance Co v Administratia Asigurarilor de Stat* [1983] 2 Lloyd's Rep 674; *Home and Overseas Insurance Co Ltd v Mentor Insurance Co (UK) Ltd* supra.

607. Binding effect. It is of the nature of arbitration that the decision of the arbitral tribunal shall be legally binding and enforceable as between the parties. In accordance with this principle, the award of the arbitral tribunal is legally enforceable[1] and gives rise to defences of *res judicata* in subsequent proceedings[2].

1 See para 712 post.
2 See para 684 post.

(2) ARBITRATION AGREEMENTS

(i) Parties to Arbitration Agreement

608. Oral arbitration agreements: common law. Arbitrations based on an oral agreement to arbitrate, rarely encountered in practice, are governed by common law and not subject to the Arbitration Acts, which apply only to arbitration based on written agreements[1]. An oral agreement is valid only if it relates to an existing dispute and incomplete until the appointment of the arbitrator[2], and the arbitrator's authority to conduct the arbitration can be revoked at any time before publication of the award[3]. The numerous powers conferred on arbitrators and the court by the Arbitration Acts[4] have no application to arbitrations based on an oral agreement.

1 *Imperial Metal Industries (Kynoch) Ltd v Amalgamated Union of Engineering Workers* [1979] 1 All ER 847, [1979] ICR 23, CA; Arbitration Act 1950 s 32; Arbitration Act 1975 s 7 (1).
2 Bac Abr, Arbitrament and Award; Com Dig, Arbitrament; *Livingstone v Ralli* (1855) 5 E & B 132; *Ex p Glaysher* (1864) 3 H & C 442.
3 Cf Bac Abr, Arbitrament and Award (B); *Re Rouse & Co and Meier & Co* (1871) LR 6 CP 212 per Willes J; *Lord v Lee* (1868) LR 3 QB 404 at 407 per Blackburn J; *Fleming v J S Doig (Grimsby) Ltd* (1921) 38 RPC 57.
4 See eg paras 673–680 post.

609. Written arbitration agreements. In practice, arbitrations are almost invariably based on a written agreement to arbitrate. Such arbitrations are accordingly governed by the Arbitration Acts, which apply to any 'written agreement to subject present or future differences to arbitration whether an arbitrator is named or not'[1]. The agreement may confer the right to require arbitration on only one party[2].

The requirement of writing is satisfied where there is a document which recognizes, incorporates, or confirms the existence of an agreement to arbitrate[3]. The document need not be signed by either party, and the assent of the parties to the arbitration term may be given orally or by conduct[4]. In the case of an agreement conferring an option to elect for arbitration, the statutory requirement of a written agreement is satisfied when both the option agreement and the exercise of the option are in writing[5]. The written document may itself contain the arbitration clause, or it may incorporate the arbitration clause by reference[6], if the words of reference make clear the intention of the parties to incorporate the clause[7].

1 Arbitration Act 1950 s 32. See also the Arbitration Act 1975 s 7.
2 *Pittalis v Sherefettin* [1986] QB 868, [1986] 2 All ER 227, CA; *Woolf v Collis Removal Service* [1948] 1 KB 11, [1947] 2 All ER 260, CA.
3 *Excomm Ltd v Bamaodah, The St Raphael* [1985] 1 Lloyd's Rep 403, CA.

4 *Baker v Yorkshire Fire and Life Assurance Co* [1892] 1 QB 144; *Hickman v Kent or Romney Marsh Sheep-breeders Association* [1915] 1 Ch 881; *Beattie v E & F Beattie Ltd* [1938] Ch 708, [1938] 3 All ER 214, CA; *London Sack and Bag Co Ltd v Dixon & Lugton Ltd* [1943] 2 All ER 763, CA; *Excomm Ltd v Bamaodah, The St Raphael* [1985] 1 Lloyd's Rep 403, CA (buyer bound by arbitration clause printed on reverse of seller's quotation); *Zambia Steel and Building Supplies Ltd v James Clark and Eaton Ltd* [1986] 2 Lloyd's Rep 225, CA, applying *The St Raphael* supra (buyer bound by arbitration clause in standard form of commodity contract referred to in broker's note sent to buyer).

5 *Westfal-Larsen and Co A/S v Ikerigi Compania Naviera SA, The Messiniaki Bergen* [1983] 1 All ER 382, [1983] 1 Lloyd's Rep 423.

6 The reference may be to a standard form of contract which includes an arbitration clause, without specific reference to the clause itself: see eg *Excomm Ltd v Bamaodah, The St Raphael* [1985] 1 Lloyd's Rep 403, CA.

7 The incorporation in a bill of lading of all the 'conditions' or 'terms and conditions' of a charterparty does not extend to the arbitration clause in the charterparty: *T W Thomas & Co Ltd v Portsea SS Co Ltd* [1912] AC 1, HL; *The Njegos* [1936] P 90; *The Annefield, Annefield (Owners) v Annefield (Cargo Owners)* [1971] P 168, [1971] 1 All ER 394, [1971] 1 Lloyd's Rep 1, CA; *Skips A/S Nordheim v Syrian Petroleum Co Ltd, The Varenna* [1984] QB 599, [1983] 3 All ER 645, [1983] 2 Lloyd's Rep 592, CA; *Federal Bulk Carriers Inc v C Itoh & Co Ltd, The Federal Bulker* [1989] 1 Lloyd's Rep 103, CA. Contrast the exceptional case where the arbitration clause was expressed to apply to disputes under both the charterparty and any bill of lading: *The Merak, Merak (Cargo Owners) v Merak (Owners)* [1965] P 223, [1965] 3 All ER 638, [1964] 2 Lloyd's Rep 527, CA.

610. Persons bound by arbitration agreement.

An arbitration agreement is binding on the parties thereto and on persons claiming through or under them[1]. Such derivative parties include an assignee[2], a successor by operation of law, for example a personal representative[3], a trustee in bankruptcy who adopts the contract containing the arbitration agreement[4], and a statutory transferee of rights against insurers[5]. The derivative party is obliged and entitled to arbitrate any claim, and can take advantage of any claim already advanced in pending arbitration proceedings by the original party so as to defeat any time bar arising before assignment or transfer[6].

1 Arbitration Act 1950 ss 4, 16; Arbitration Act 1975 s 1; and see para 616 et seq post. See, however, the Consumer Arbitration Agreements Act 1988 (para 615 post) as to the circumstances in which an arbitration agreement cannot be enforced against a person entering into a contract as a consumer.

2 *Shayler v Woolf* [1946] Ch 320, [1946] 2 All ER 54, CA; *Montedipe SpA v JTP-RO Jugotanker, The Jordan Nicolov* [1990] 2 Lloyd's Rep 11. The assignment may be limited to a particular right or claim arising under the contract: *Rumput (Panama) SA v Islamic Republic of Iran Shipping Lines, The Leage* [1984] 2 Lloyd's Rep 259. See also *Baytur SA v Finegro Holdings SA* (1991) Times, 21 June, CA (before an equitable assignee of a cause of action can become party to an arbitration relating to it but commencing before the assignment, he must at least serve notice on the other side and submit to the jurisdiction of the arbitrator).

3 Arbitration Act 1950 s 2 (1). This provision does not apply in the case of a statutory arbitration: s 31; see para 601 note 2 ante.

4 Arbitration Act 1950 s 3 (1). Where the trustee in bankruptcy does not adopt the contract, the court having jurisdiction in the proceedings may, on the application of any other party to the agreement or (with the consent of the creditors' committee established under the Insolvency Act 1986 s 301) the trustee in bankruptcy, order that any matter to which the arbitration agreement applied shall be referred to arbitration: Arbitration Act 1950 s 3 (2) (amended by the Insolvency Act 1986 s 439 (2), Sch 14). These provisions do not apply in the case of a statutory arbitration: Arbitration Act 1950 s 31 (2).

5 *Socony Mobil Oil Co Inc v West of England Ship Owners Mutual Insurance Association (London) Ltd, The Padre Island* [1984] 2 Lloyd's Rep 408. The factual ground for the decision of Leggatt J in this case was 'agreed to have been erroneous' in later proceedings between the parties: see *Firma C-Trade SA v Newcastle Protection and Indemnity Association, The Fanti, Socony Mobil Oil Co Inc v West of England Ship Owners Mutual Insurance Association (London) Ltd (No 2), The Padre Island* [1991] 2 AC 1 at 24, [1990] 2 All ER 705 at 709, [1990] 2 Lloyd's Rep 191 at 195, HL, per Lord Brandon of Oakbrook.

6 *Montedipe SpA v JTP-RO Jugotanker, The Jordan Nicolov* [1990] 2 Lloyd's Rep 11; see also *London Steamship Owners Mutual Insurance Association Ltd v Bombay Trading Co Ltd, The Felicie* [1990] 2 Lloyd's Rep 21n at 27 (though opposed to the reasoning in *The Jordan Nicolov* supra).

611. The Crown. All the provisions of Part I of the Arbitration Act 1950[1] and of the Arbitration Act 1979 apply to the Crown[2], but not the provisions of Part II of the Arbitration Act 1950[3] or the Arbitration Act 1975[4].

1 Ie the Arbitration Act 1950 ss 1–34 (general provisions as to arbitration).
2 Arbitration Act 1950 s 30 (amended by the Arbitration Act 1975 s 8 (2)); Arbitration Act 1979 s 7 (1) (c).
3 Ie the Arbitration Act 1950 ss 35–43 (concerning the effect of certain foreign awards).
4 In consequence the mandatory stay of court proceedings in respect of matters falling within a non–domestic arbitration agreement under the Arbitration Act 1975 s 1 (see para 616 post) does not apply to the Crown. Nor is the Crown bound by ss 3–6 concerning the enforcement of awards covered by the New York Convention on the Recognition and Enforcement of Foreign Arbitral Awards (see para 715 post).

(ii) Scope of Arbitration Agreement

612. Nature of dispute. A dispute as to whether there has ever been a binding contract between the parties is not within the scope of an arbitration agreement, and so an arbitrator does not have jurisdiction to make a binding award on the reference of such a dispute[1]. This is the only inherent limitation on the type of dispute that can be referred to arbitration[2]. The following types of dispute have been considered capable of falling within the scope of a suitably drafted arbitration agreement[3]: whether there has been a repudiation of the contract by one party and, if so, whether that repudiation has been accepted by the other party[4]; whether the contract has been frustrated[5]; whether the making of the contract was induced by misrepresentation[6]; whether the contract is voidable on the ground of non–disclosure[7]; whether the contract is binding on the parties despite the failure of a condition precedent to the contract[8]; whether one party is able to escape liability under the contract by relying on a termination provision in the contract[9]; whether the parties entered into the contract under a mistake giving rise to a claim for rectification of the contract[10]; whether the contract is unenforceable for illegality[11]; whether the contract is voidable on the ground of fraud[12]; whether the contract has been varied or replaced by a new contract[13]; a claim as to the existence of a trade custom affecting the rights and obligations of the parties to the contract[14]; a claim that the contract contained an implied term or that there was a collateral contract[15]; a claim for damages for breach of the arbitration agreement itself[16]; a claim for a general average contribution[17]; a claim in tort where the tortious claim has a sufficiently close connection with the contractual claim[18].

1 *Heyman v Darwins Ltd* [1942] AC 356 at 366, 370–371, 384, [1942] 1 All ER 337 at 343, 345, 353, HL, per Viscount Simon LC and Lords Macmillan and Wright; *Ashville Investments Ltd v Elmer Contractors Ltd* [1989] QB 488 at 494, 506, [1988] 2 All ER 577 at 582, 591, CA, per May and Bingham LJJ; *Toller v Law Accident Insurance Society* [1936] 2 All ER 952, CA; *H E Daniels Ltd v Carmel Exporters and Importers Ltd* [1953] 2 QB 242, [1953] 2 All ER 401; *Golodely v Schrier* (1947) 80 Ll L Rep 647; *Christopher Brown Ltd v Genossenschaft Oesterreichischer Waldbesitzer Holzwirtschaftsbetriebe Registrierte GmbH* [1954] 1 QB 8 at 10, [1953] 2 All ER 1039 at 1040–1041; *Willcock v Pickfords Removals Ltd* [1979] 1 Lloyd's Rep 244.
  Consequently, the following disputes do not fall within the scope of an arbitration agreement: a dispute as to whether the contract was void ab initio for illegality (*Heyman v Darwins Ltd* supra at 366, 343 per Viscount Simon LC; *Mackender v Feldia AG* [1967] 2 QB 590, [1966] 3 All ER 847, CA; *Prodexport State Company for Foreign Trade v E D and F Man Ltd* [1973] QB 389, [1973] 1 All ER 355, [1972] 2 Lloyd's Rep 375; see also *Dalmia Dairy Industries Ltd v National Bank of Pakistan* [1978] 2 Lloyd's Rep 223, CA); a dispute as to whether there was consideration for the contract (*Goldsack v Shore* [1950] 1 KB 708, [1950] 1 All ER 276; *S A Hersent v United Towing Co Ltd and White, The*

Tradesman [1961] 3 All ER 661, [1962] 1 WLR 61, [1961] 2 Lloyd's Rep 183); a dispute as to whether the contract was void for uncertainty (*Payne and Routh v Hugh Baird & Sons* (1921) 9 Ll L Rep 167); a dispute as to whether the parties have agreed to treat the contract as if it had never existed (*Heyman v Darwins Ltd* supra at 371, 345 per Lord Macmillan); a dispute as to whether a subsequent contract was an accord and satisfaction substituting wholly new rights and obligations for those under the original contract (*Kianta Osakeyhtio v Britain and Overseas Trading Co Ltd* [1954] 1 Lloyd's Rep 247, CA. See also *Taylor v Warden Insurance Co* (1935) 45 Ll L Rep 218, CA). See *Mackender v Feldia AG* supra at 598, 849 per Lord Denning MR, obiter in relation to *non est factum*.

2 *Ashville Investments Ltd v Elmer Contractors Ltd* [1989] QB 488 at 506, [1988] 2 All ER 577 at 591, CA, per Bingham LJ. It is, however, an aspect of this limitation that an arbitrator cannot make a binding award as to the existence of facts which found his jurisdiction.

3 See para 613 post for the appropriate forms of words.

4 *Heyman v Darwins Ltd* [1942] AC 356, [1942] 1 All ER 337, HL. A repudiation by one party which is accepted by the other party does not put the contract out of existence but rather it survives for the purpose of measuring the claims arising out of the breach: *Heyman v Darwins Ltd* supra at 374, 346–347 per Lord Macmillan.

5 *Heyman v Darwins Ltd* [1942] AC 356 at 366–367, 383, 400–401, [1942] 1 All ER 337 at 343–344, 352, 361–362, HL, per Viscount Simon LC and Lords Wright and Porter; *Kruse v Questier & Co Ltd* [1953] 1 QB 669, [1953] 1 All ER 954 (applying the dicta in *Heyman v Darwins Ltd* supra, and not following *Hirji Mulji v Cheong Yue SS Co* [1926] AC 497, PC); *Gunter Henck v Andre & Cie SA* [1970] 1 Lloyd's Rep 235. It is immaterial whether the contract is partly executed or wholly executory; *Kruse v Questier & Co Ltd* supra. If the contract has been frustrated the arbitrator has power to grant relief in respect of quasi-contractual claims for a quantum meruit or claims for compensation under the Law Reform (Frustrated Contracts) Act 1943 s 1: *Government of Gibraltar v Kenney* [1956] 2 QB 410, [1956] 3 All ER 22.

6 *Golding v London and Edinburgh Insurance Co Ltd* (1932) 43 Ll L Rep 487, CA; *Stevens & Sons v Timber and General Mutual Accident Insurance Association Ltd* (1933) 102 LJKB 337, CA; *Ashville Investments Ltd v Elmer Contractors Ltd* [1989] QB 488, [1988] 2 All ER 577, CA, not following *Monro v Bognor UDC* [1915] 3 KB 167, CA. An arbitrator can rescind the contract or award damages in lieu of rescission under the Misrepresentation Act 1967 s 2 (2).

7 *Mackender v Feldia AG* [1967] 2 QB 590, [1966] 3 All ER 847, CA. Where a contract is avoided on the ground of non-disclosure, it is not avoided from the beginning but only from the moment of avoidance: *Mackender v Feldia AG* supra at 598, 849–850 per Lord Denning MR.

8 *De La Garde v Worsnop & Co* [1928] Ch 17.

9 *Stebbing v Liverpool and London and Globe Insurance Co Ltd* [1917] 2 KB 433; *Woodall v Pearl Assurance Co Ltd* [1919] 1 KB 593; *Stevens & Sons v Timber and General Mutual Accident Insurance Association Co Ltd* (1933) 102 LJKB 337.

10 *Ashville Investments Ltd v Elmer Contractors Ltd* [1989] QB 488, [1988] 2 All ER 577, CA (not following *Printing Machinery Co Ltd v Linotype and Machinery Ltd* [1912] 1 Ch 566; *Crane v Hegeman-Harris Co Inc* [1939] 4 All ER 68, CA); *Overseas Union Insurance Ltd v AA Mutual International Insurance Co Ltd* [1988] 2 Lloyd's Rep 63. But see *Heyman v Darwins Ltd* [1942] AC 356 at 371, 384, [1942] 1 All ER 337 at 346, 353, HL, per Lords MacMillan and Wright for the view that a dispute as to mistake is not within the scope of an arbitration agreement.

11 *Mackender v Feldia AG* [1967] 2 QB 590, [1966] 3 All ER 847, CA (drawing a distinction between a contract void ab initio for illegality (see note 1 supra), which cannot fall within the scope of an arbitration agreement, and a contract which is unenforceable for supervening illegality, which can be within a suitably drafted arbitration agreement); *Prodexport State Co for Foreign Trade v E D and F Man Ltd* [1973] QB 389, [1973] 1 All ER 355, [1972] 2 Lloyd's Rep 375; *Joe Lee Ltd v Lord Dalmeny* [1927] 1 Ch 300; *Smith, Coney and Barrett v Becker, Gray & Co* [1916] 2 Ch 86. See also *Dalmia Dairy Industries Ltd v National Bank of Pakistan* [1978] 2 Lloyd's Rep 223, CA.

12 *Heyman v Darwins Ltd* [1942] AC 356 at 378, 384 and 392, [1942] 1 All ER 337 at 350, 353 and 357, HL, per Lords Wright and Porter; *Trainor v Phoenix Fire Assurance Co* (1891) 65 LT 825; *Kenworthy v Queen Insurance Co* (1892) 8 TLR 211.

13 *Hattersley v Hatton* (1862) 3 F & F 116; *Wade-Gery v Morrison* (1887) 37 LT 270; *Morgan v William Harrison Ltd* [1907] 2 Ch 137, CA; *Taylor v Warden Insurance Co Ltd* (1933) 45 Ll L Rep 218, CA; *Kianta Osakeyhtio v Britain and Overseas Trading Co Ltd* [1954] 1 Lloyd's Rep 247, CA; *Union of India v E B Aaby's Rederi A/S* [1975] AC 797, [1974] 2 All ER 874, sub nom *E B Aaby's Rederi A/S v Union of India, The Evje* [1974] 2 Lloyd's Rep 57, HL; *Faghirzadeh v Rudolf Woolf (SA) (Pty) Ltd* [1977] 1 Lloyd's Rep 630; *Compania Maritima Zorroza SA v Maritime Bulk Carriers Corpn, The Marques de Bolarque* [1980] 2 Lloyd's Rep 186.

14 *Produce Brokers Co Ltd v Olympia Oil and Cake Co Ltd* [1916] 1 AC 314, HL.

15 *Overseas Union Insurance Ltd v AA Mutual International Insurance Ltd* [1988] 2 Lloyd's Rep 63.
16 *Mantovani v Carapelli SpA* [1980] 1 Lloyd's Rep 375, CA.
17 *Union of India v E B Aaby's Rederi A/S* [1975] AC 797, [1974] 2 All ER 874, sub nom *E B Aaby's Rederi A/S v Union of India, The Evje* [1974] 2 Lloyd's Rep 57, HL; *Alma Shipping Corpn v Union of India, The Astraea* [1971] 2 Lloyd's Rep 494; *Astro Vencedor Compania Naviera SA of Panama v Mabanaft GmbH, The Damianos* [1971] 2 QB 588, [1971] 2 All ER 1301, [1971] 1 Lloyd's Rep 502, CA.
18 *Woolf v Collis Removal Service* [1948] 1 KB 11, [1947] 2 All ER 260, CA (a claim in negligence had a sufficiently close connection with the alternative claim under the contract as the contractual claim was founded on the obligation of diligence in the contract and the tortious claim was founded on the non-contractual obligation); *Empresa Exportadora de Azucarv Industria Azucarera Nacional SA, The Playa Larga and The Marble Islands* [1983] 2 Lloyd's Rep 171, CA (a claim for conversion had a sufficiently close connection with the claims under the contract); *Ashville Investments Ltd v Elmer Contractors Ltd* [1989] QB 488, [1988] 2 All ER 577, CA (a claim for damages for negligent misstatement was within the scope of the arbitration agreement); *Astro Vencedor Compania Naviera SA of Panama v Mabanaft GmbH, The Damianos* [1971] 2 QB 588, [1971] 2 All ER 1301, [1971] 1 Lloyd's Rep 502, CA (a claim for wrongful arrest of a ship was within the scope of the arbitration agreement). See also *Re Polemis and Furniss, Withy & Co Ltd* [1921] 3 KB 560; *Lonrho Ltd v Shell Petroleum Co Ltd* (1978) Times, 1 February.

613. Form of words. Whether a particular dispute falls within the scope of an arbitration agreement is a question of construction of the form of words of the arbitration clause, giving the words their natural and proper meaning in all the circumstances of the case[1]. The court is not bound by the doctrine of precedent to construe a particular form of words in an arbitration clause in one contract in the same way as that form of words has been construed in an earlier case involving another contract[2]. Nevertheless, a decision as to the meaning of a particular form of words may be of persuasive authority in a later case involving the construction of the same form of words[3].

An arbitration agreement which provides for the reference of disputes 'arising out of' the contract is widely drafted[4] and has been said to cover every dispute except a dispute as to whether there was ever a binding contract[5]. This form of words has been held to cover disputes as to mistake[6], frustration[7], construction[8], non-disclosure[9], the variation or replacement of the contract[10], the existence of a trade custom affecting the rights and obligations of the parties to the contract[11], damages for breach of the arbitration agreement itself[12], general average contribution[13] and conversion[14]. An arbitration agreement in these terms is wider in its scope than one which provides for the reference of disputes 'arising under' the contract[15]. Disputes as to repudiation[16], frustration[17], non-disclosure[18], illegality rendering the contract unenforceable[19] and general average contribution[20] are all disputes 'arising under' the contract. However, a tortious claim is not a dispute 'arising under' the contract[21].

An arbitration agreement which provides for the reference of disputes 'in connection with' the contract has been held to cover disputes as to misrepresentation[22], negligent mis-statement[23] and mistake giving rise to a claim for rectification[24].

The words 'in respect of' are capable of covering disputes as to repudiation[25], frustration[26], rectification[27] and claims that the contract contained an implied term or that there was a collateral contract[28]. The words 'with regard to' have been considered capable of covering disputes as to repudiation and frustration[29].

1 *Ashville Investments Ltd v Elmer Contractors Ltd* [1989] QB 488 at 495, [1988] 2 All ER 577 at 582, CA, per May LJ; *Overseas Union Insurance Ltd v AA Mutual International Insurance Co Ltd* [1988] 2 Lloyd's Rep 63 at 66 per Evans J.
2 *Ashville Investments Ltd v Elmer Contractors Ltd* [1989] QB 488 at 495, [1988] 2 All ER 577 at 582, CA, per May LJ.

3 *Ashville Investments Ltd v Elmer Contractors Ltd* [1989] QB 488 at 495, [1988] 2 All ER 577 at 582, CA, per May LJ. The extent to which an earlier decision may be persuasive will depend upon the similarity between the contracts and the surrounding circumstances in the two cases; *Ashville Investments Ltd v Elmer Contractors Ltd* supra at 495, 582 per May LJ.

4 *Government of Gibraltar v Kenney* [1956] 2 QB 410 at 421, [1956] 3 All ER 22 at 25, CA, per Sellers J; *Gunter Henck v Andre & Cie SA* [1970] 1 Lloyd's Rep 235; *Mantovani v Carapelli SpA* [1980] 1 Lloyd's Rep 375 at 381, CA, per Lawton LJ.

5 *H E Daniels Ltd v Carmel Exporters and Importers Ltd* [1953] 2 QB 242, [1953] 2 All ER 401, [1953] 2 Lloyd's Rep 103; *Ethiopian Oilseeds and Pulses Export Corpn v Rio del Mar Foods Inc* [1990] 1 Lloyd's Rep 86 at 97 per Hirst J.

6 *Ethiopian Oilseeds and Pulses Export Corpn v Rio del Mar Foods Inc* [1990] 1 Lloyd's Rep 86.

7 *Kruse v Questier & Co Ltd* [1953] 1 QB 669, [1953] 1 All ER 954; *Government of Gibraltar v Kenney* [1956] 2 QB 410, [1956] 3 All ER 22; *Gunter Henck v Andre & Cie SA* [1970] 1 Lloyd's Rep 235.

8 *Thorburn v Barnes* (1867) LR 2 CP 384.

9 *Stebbing v Liverpool and London and Globe Insurance Co Ltd* [1917] 2 KB 433.

10 *Faghirzadeh v Rudolf Woolf (SA) (Pty) Ltd* [1977] 1 Lloyd's Rep 630.

11 *Produce Brokers Co Ltd v Olympia Oil and Cake Co Ltd* [1916] 1 AC 314, HL.

12 *Mantovani v Carapelli SpA* [1980] 1 Lloyd's Rep 375, CA.

13 *Union of India v E B Aaby's Rederi A/S* [1975] AC 797, [1974] 2 All ER 874, sub nom *E B Aaby's Rederi A/S v Union of India, The Evje* [1974] 2 Lloyd's Rep 57, HL.

14 *Empresa Exportadora de Azucar v Industria Azucarera Nacional SA, The Playa Larga and The Marble Islands* [1983] 2 Lloyd's Rep 171, CA; *Ulysses Compania Naviera SA v Huntingdon Petroleum Service Ltd, The Ermoupolis* [1990] 1 Lloyd's Rep 160.

15 *Heyman v Darwins Ltd* [1942] AC 356 at 383, 395, [1942] 2 All ER 377 at 352, 358, HL, per Lords Wright and Porter; *Government of Gibraltar v Kenney* [1956] 2 QB 410 at 421, [1956] 3 All ER 22 at 25 CA, per Sellers J; *Gunter Henck v Andre & Cie SA* [1970] 1 Lloyd's Rep 235 at 240 per Mocatta J; *Ethiopian Oilseeds and Pulses Export Corpn v Rio del Mar Foods Inc* [1990] 1 Lloyd's Rep 86 at 97 per Hirst J. See *Samick Lines Co Ltd v Owners of the Ship Antonis P Lemos, The Antonis P Lemos* [1985] AC 711 at 727, [1985] 1 All ER 695 at 700, [1985] 1 Lloyd's Rep 283 at 287, HL, per Lord Brandon of Oakbrook. But see *Union of India v E B Aaby's Rederi A/S* [1975] AC 797 at 814, 817, [1974] 2 All ER 874 at 885, 886–887, sub nom *E B Aaby's Rederi A/S v Union of India, The Evje* [1974] 2 Lloyd's Rep 57 at 66, 67, HL, where Viscount Dilhorne and Lord Salmon expressed difficulty in understanding the difference between the two forms of wording.

16 *Heyman v Darwins Ltd* [1942] AC 356 at 366, [1942] 1 All ER 337 at 343, per Viscount Simon LC.

17 *Heyman v Darwins Ltd* [1942] AC 356 at 366, 383, [1942] 1 All ER 337 at 343, 352–353, HL, per Viscount Simon LC and Lord Wright.

18 *Mackender v Feldia AG* [1967] 2 QB 590 at 598, [1967] 3 All ER 847 at 849–850, CA, per Lord Denning MR.

19 *Mackender v Feldia AG* [1967] 2 QB 590, [1966] 3 All ER 847, CA.

20 *Alma Shipping Corpn v Union of India, The Astraea* [1971] 2 Lloyd's Rep 494; *Union of India v E B Aaby's Rederi A/S* [1975] AC 797, [1974] 2 All ER 874, sub nom *E B Aaby's Rederi A/S v Union of India, The Evje* [1974] 2 Lloyd's Rep 57, HL.

21 *Ashville Investments Ltd v Elmer Contractors Ltd* [1989] QB 488 at 508, [1988] 2 All ER 577 at 593, CA, per Bingham LJ, also leaving open the question whether this form of words covers quasi-contractual or restitutionary claims, or claims for rectification. See also *Woolf v Collis Removal Services* [1948] 1 KB 11 at 18, [1947] 2 All ER 260 at 263, CA, per Asquith LJ.

22 *Ashville Investments Ltd v Elmer Contractors Ltd* [1989] QB 488, [1988] 2 All ER 577, CA, not following *Monro v Bognor UDC* [1915] 3 KB 167 and *Blue Circle Industries plc v Holland Dredging Co (UK) Ltd* (1987) 37 BLR 40, CA, per Purchas LJ.

23 *Ashville Investments Ltd v Elmer Contractors Ltd* [1989] QB 488, [1988] 2 All ER 577, CA, not following *Blue Circle Industries plc v Holland Dredging Co (UK) Ltd* (1987) 37 BLR 40, CA, per Purchas LJ.

24 *Ashville Investments Ltd v Elmer Contractors Ltd* [1989] QB 488, [1988] 2 All ER 577, CA, not following *Crane v Hegeman-Harris Co Inc* [1939] 4 All ER 68, CA.

25 *Heyman v Darwins Ltd* [1942] AC 356 at 360, 362, 366, [1942] 1 All ER 337 at 339–340, 341, 343, HL, per Viscount Simon LC.

26 *Heyman v Darwins Ltd* [1942] AC 356 at 366, [1942] 1 All ER 337 at 343, HL, per Viscount Simon LC.

27 *Overseas Union Insurance Ltd v AA Mutual International Insurance Co Ltd* [1988] 2 Lloyd's Rep 63.

28 *Overseas Union Insurance Ltd v AA Mutual International Insurance Co Ltd* [1988] 2 Lloyd's Rep 63.

29 *Heyman v Darwins Ltd* [1942] AC 356 at 366, [1942] 1 All ER 337 at 343, HL, per Viscount Simon LC.

(iii) Dispute or Difference

614. Dispute or difference. Arbitration agreements generally make it a precondition of the right to arbitrate that there be a dispute or difference[1] between the parties about a matter covered by the arbitration agreement[2]. A dispute or difference arises where there is disagreement about central issues: no claim need be formulated, and the cause of action need not be fully constituted[3]. However, the mere making of a claim does not necessarily constitute a dispute or difference[4]. There is no dispute or difference if one party's claim has been expressly or impliedly admitted[5], or if the other party demonstrably has no defence[6]. There is a dispute or difference if the amount of damages remains in issue although liability is not contested[7].

1 Most arbitration agreements provide for the reference to arbitration of 'disputes or differences', or one of them. For practical purposes, a 'dispute' and a 'difference' are the same, although 'difference' has been held to have a wider meaning: *F & G Sykes (Wessex) Ltd v Fine Fare Ltd* [1967] 1 Lloyd's Rep 53 at 60.
2 As to what matters are covered by particular forms of words in arbitration agreements see para 613 ante.
3 *J F Robertson & Co v A T James & Co* (1923) 16 Ll L Rep 34 at 36; *Ramac Construction Co Ltd v J E Lesser (Properties) Ltd* [1975] 2 Lloyd's Rep 430. Cf *Brightside Kilpatrick Engineering Services Ltd v Mitchell Construction (1973) Ltd* [1975] 2 Lloyd's Rep 493, CA; *The American Sioux* [1980] 2 Lloyd's Rep 224, CA; *Union of India v E B Aaby's Rederi A/S* [1975] AC 797, [1974] 2 All ER 874, sub nom *E B Aaby's Rederi A/S v Union of India, The Evje* [1974] 2 Lloyd's Rep 57, HL.
4 See *Union of India v E B Aaby's Rederi A/S* [1975] AC 797 at 807, [1974] 2 All ER 874 at 879, sub nom *E B Aaby's Rederi A/S v Union of India, The Evje* [1974] 2 Lloyd's Rep 57 at 61, HL.
5 See the cases cited in para 631 note 2 post.
6 In practical terms, the question whether a party demonstrably has no defence arises upon the other party's application for summary judgment, which is met by a cross-application for a stay. As to the determination of whether there is a dispute or difference in this context see para 631 note 3 post.
7 See the cases cited in para 631 note 4 post.

(iv) Consumer Arbitration Agreements

615. Consumer arbitration agreements. Where a person enters into a contract as a consumer[1], an agreement that any future differences arising between parties to the contract are to be referred to arbitration cannot be enforced against that person in respect of specified causes of action[2] unless: (1) he gives his written consent after the differences have arisen; (2) he has submitted to arbitration in pursuance of the agreement, whether in relation to the differences in question or any other differences; or (3) the court[3] orders that these provisions are not to apply to the particular cause of action[4]. In relation to specified causes of action[5], the court may make such an order as is mentioned above[6] where it is satisfied that referring the difference to arbitration in pursuance of the agreement is not detrimental to the interests of the consumer[7]. In determining whether a reference to arbitration is detrimental the court must have regard to all relevant factors, including in particular the availability of legal aid and the relative expense to the consumer of arbitration and proceedings before the court[8]. A stay of proceedings cannot be obtained in respect of an arbitration agreement to which the provisions described above apply[9].

1 For these purposes, a person enters into a contract as a consumer where he neither makes the contract in the course of a business nor holds himself out as so doing, the other party does make the contract in the course of a business, and any goods passing are of a type ordinarily supplied for private use or

consumption: Consumer Arbitration Agreements Act 1988 s 3 (1). On a sale by auction or competitive tender the buyer is never to be regarded as a consumer: s 3 (1). It is for the party claiming that a person entered a contract otherwise than as a consumer to show that he did so: s 3 (3).

2 These provisions apply to a cause of action if proceedings on it would be within the jurisdiction of a county court, or if it meets other conditions which may be specified in an order made for the purpose: ibid ss 1 (2), 5; as to the jurisdiction of the county court see COUNTY COURTS. They do not apply to a non-domestic arbitration agreement (see the Arbitration Act 1975 s 1; and para 617 post), or to a contract which by virtue of the Unfair Contract Terms Act 1977 s 1 (2), Sch 1 falls outside the operation of ss 2, 3, 4, 7 of that Act (terms purporting to exclude or limit liability): Consumer Arbitration Agreements Act 1988 s 2.

    At the date at which this volume states the law, no order had been made under the 1988 Act s 5.

3 Ie the High Court or a county court: ibid s 4 (1).

4 Ibid ss 1 (1), 4 (1).

5 Ie any cause of action in respect of which proceedings would be within the jurisdiction of the county court and would not fall within the small claims limit, or which meets any additional conditions prescribed for the purpose (see note 2 supra): ibid s 4 (4). The small claims limit is £500: see s 4 (5); the County Courts Act 1984 s 64; and CCR Ord 19 r 2.

6 See text and note 4 supra.

7 Consumer Arbitration Agreements Act 1988 s 4 (2).

8 Ibid s 4 (3).

9 Ibid s 1 (3), which excludes the operation of the Arbitration Act 1950 s 4 (1); see paras 616, 625 post.

2. STAY OF COURT PROCEEDINGS

(1) JURISDICTION AND PROCEDURE

616. Statutory jurisdiction to stay proceedings. If any party[1] to an arbitration agreement[2], or any person claiming through or under him[3], commences any legal proceedings in any court[4] against any other party to the agreement, or any person claiming through or under him[5], in respect of any matter agreed to be referred[6], any party to those legal proceedings[7] may at any time after acknowledgment of service[8], but before serving any pleadings or taking any other steps in the proceedings[9], apply to that court to stay the proceedings. For the purposes of obtaining a stay, an arbitration agreement is either domestic or non-domestic[10]. If the arbitration agreement is a domestic arbitration agreement, the court has a discretion to make an order[11] staying the proceedings[12], if it is satisfied that there is no sufficient reason[13] why the matter should not be referred in accordance with the agreement, and that the applicant was, at the time when the proceedings were commenced, and still remains, ready and willing to do all things necessary to the proper conduct of the arbitration[14]. If the arbitration agreement is a non-domestic arbitration agreement, the court must grant a mandatory stay[15], unless it is satisfied either that the arbitration agreement is null and void, inoperative or incapable of being performed[16], or that there is not in fact any dispute between the parties with regard to the matter agreed to be referred[17].

1 See para 625 post.

2 See para 622 post.

3 See para 625 post.

4 See para 623 post. The jurisdiction to stay is conferred on the court in which the proceedings are commenced. This includes the county court: *Morriston Tinplate Co v Brooker, Dore & Co* [1908] 1 KB 403.

5 See para 626 post.

6 See para 624 post.

7 The Arbitration Act 1950 s 4 refers to 'appearance', but following the changes made by the Rules of the Supreme Court (Writ and Appearance) 1979, SI 1979/1716, 'appearance' has become 'acknowledgment of service' in the High Court and Court of Appeal.
8 See para 626 post.
9 See para 627 post.
10 See the Arbitration Act 1975 s 1 (4); and para 617 post.
11 See para 632 et seq post.
12 Under the Arbitration Act 1950 s 4 (1). As to the grant of an injunction restraining arbitration proceedings see para 642 post. However, under certain circumstances the application of s 4 (1) is excluded by the Consumer Arbitration Agreements Act 1988: see paras 615 ante, 625 post.
13 See para 628 post.
14 See para 629 post.
15 Under the Arbitration Act 1975 s 1 (1).
16 See para 630 post.
17 See para 631 post.

617. Domestic and non-domestic. A domestic arbitration agreement is one which does not provide[1], expressly or by implication, for arbitration in a state other than the United Kingdom[2], and to which neither (1) an individual who is a national[3] of, or habitually resident[4] in, any state other than the United Kingdom, nor (2) a body corporate which is incorporated in, or whose central management and control is exercised in, any state other than the United Kingdom, is a party at the time the proceedings were commenced[5]. A non-domestic arbitration agreement is an arbitration agreement in respect of which one or more of these requirements is not met.

1 The question of what the arbitration agreement provides is governed by its proper law. See para 717 post.
2 Ie the United Kingdom of Great Britain and Northern Ireland: Interpretation Act 1978 s 5, Sch 1.
3 The question of who are nationals of a foreign state is governed by the law of the state in question: *Stoeck v Public Trustee* [1921] 2 Ch 67 at 82.
4 The word 'habitual' denotes a regular physical presence enduring for some time. Habitual residence is not the same as ordinary residence, and is equivalent to the level of residence necessary to establish domicile but without the element of intention: *Cruse v Chittum (formerly Cruse)* [1974] 2 All ER 940. A person resides where he lives. A temporary absence is immaterial provided that there is an intention to return and an address to which to return: *R v St Leonard's Shoreditch Inhabitants* (1865) LR 1 QB 21; *R v Glossop Union* (1866) LR 1 QB 227. The word 'reside' implies a degree of permanence: *Levene v IRC* [1928] AC 217 at 222–223, HL; *Fox v Stirkand Bristol Electoral Registration Officer* [1970] 2 QB 463 at 477, [1970] 3 All ER 7 at 13, CA. A person may be resident in more than one place at a time: *Levene v IRC* supra at 223; *Langford Property Co Ltd v Tureman* [1949] 1 KB 29 at 33, sub nom *Langford Property Co Ltd v Athanassoglu* [1948] 2 All ER 722 at 724, CA; and contrast *Beck v Scholz* [1953] 1 QB 570, [1953] 1 All ER 814, CA.
5 Arbitration Act 1975 s 1 (4). The 1975 Act was passed in order to give effect to the New York Convention on the Recognition and Enforcement of Foreign Arbitral Awards.
  As to the application of this provision to the determination of disputes by the arbitral tribunal in connection with the Channel Tunnel see the Channel Tunnel Act 1987 s 15; as to the meaning of the 'arbitral tribunal' see s 2 (10).

618. Stay under the inherent jurisdiction. The general power of the court to order a stay of proceedings[1] is in principle available in a matter relating to arbitration[2], but the courts will only exercise that jurisdiction to deal with cases not contemplated by the statutory provisions[3].

1 See the Supreme Court Act 1981 s 49.
2 See *Roussel-Uclaf v G D Searle & Co Ltd* [1978] 1 Lloyd's Rep 225 at 230; *O T M Ltd v Hydranautics* [1981] 2 Lloyd's Rep 211.

3 *Etri Fans Ltd v N M B (UK) Ltd* [1987] 2 All ER 763 at 767, [1987] 1 WLR 1110 at 1114, [1987] 2 Lloyd's Rep 565 at 568, CA.

619. Procedure. Where the proceedings have been commenced in the Queen's Bench Division, the application to stay is by summons[1] to a master or district judge[2]. In the Chancery Division and the Admiralty Court, the application may be made either by summons, respectively to a master or the Admiralty Registrar, or by motion[3] on notice to the plaintiff. In the Chancery Division a simpler procedure is available if the parties consent to the stay[4]. Appeal from the master, district judge or Admiralty Registrar lies to the judge in chambers[5], and from the judge in chambers to the Court of Appeal with the leave of the judge or the Court of Appeal[6]. In the county court the application is made by notice of application[7]. The application must be supported by an affidavit[8].

1 For a summons and supporting affidavit see 6 Court Forms (2nd Edn) (1989 Issue) 117–118, Forms 35, 36. Where a summons for a stay of proceedings under the Arbitration Act 1975 s 1 is issued by mistake, including a mistake by the defendant or his advisers as to the law, and where no prejudice has been caused to the plaintiff by the issue of the summons, the court has discretion to allow the summons to be withdrawn: *Finnish Marine Insurance Co Ltd v Protective National Insurance Co* [1990] 1 QB 1078, [1989] 2 All ER 929, [1989] 2 Lloyd's Rep 99.
2 RSC Ord 73 r 3 (1). The office of district judge replaces that of district registrar: Courts and Legal Services Act 1990 s 74.
3 RSC Ord 73 r 3 (1). For a notice of motion and supporting affidavit see 6 Court Forms (2nd Edn) (1989 Issue) 117–118, Forms 35, 36. In practice almost all applications for a stay in the Chancery Division and the Admiralty Court are made by motion, although they should be made by summons unless there is a sufficient degree of urgency or other good reason which justifies proceeding by motion: *Practice Direction* [1984] 1 All ER 720, [1984] 1 WLR 447.
4 If the proceedings in the Chancery Division have not been set down, and if all parties are represented by solicitors, they may lodge, personally or by post, an application for a consent order discontinuing or staying the proceedings, in the form of minutes signed by the solicitors. If the proceedings have been set down, the parties must apply in person to the clerk to the appropriate judge to take the case out of the list and sign a note to the effect that this has been done. The master will then make the appropriate order on production of this note: *Practice Direction* [1971] 1 All ER 64, [1971] 1 WLR 78.
5 RSC Ord 58 r 1; and see note 2 supra.
6 RSC Ord 58 r 6 (1); Supreme Court Act 1981 s 18 (1) (h).
7 CCR Ord 13 r 1. For a notice of application see 6 Court Forms (2nd Edn) (1989 Issue) 120, Form 40.
8 The party seeking a stay is under an obligation to be candid with the court as to what the issues in the proceedings are going to be. It is not enough to say that outline details of such issues have already been given to the plaintiff: *Turner v Fenton* [1982] 1 All ER 8, [1982] 1 WLR 52.

620. Costs of application for stay. The court may make any order as to costs that it thinks just[1]. The usual order if a stay is granted is that the defendant be awarded the costs of the action and of the application to stay. Courts have on occasion directed that the costs of the application for a stay should be reserved to the discretion of the arbitrator[2]. It is, however, unlikely that a court would make such a direction, or that it would be valid, if either party were to object to it. If no direction as to costs is made in the order to stay, costs do not automatically follow the event under the Rules of the Supreme Court[3], because the relevant provision does not apply to arbitrations[4].

1 Arbitration Act 1950 s 28.

2 *Belfield v Bourne* [1894] 1 Ch 521 at 528.
3 Ie under RSC Ord 62 r 3 (3). See PRACTICE AND PROCEDURE.
4 See *Warburg & Co v McKerrow & Co* (1904) 90 LT 644.

(2) CONDITIONS OF OBTAINING A STAY

621. Burden of proof. If a defendant to English proceedings is to obtain a discretionary stay on the basis of a domestic arbitration agreement, or a mandatory stay on the basis of a non-domestic arbitration agreement, he must establish that certain conditions[1] are fulfilled[2]. If the application is for a discretionary stay, the defendant must also establish that certain additional conditions[3] are fulfilled[4]. The court will then consider how to exercise its discretion, and the burden is on the plaintiff to persuade the court that it is proper to refuse a stay[5]. If the application is for a mandatory stay, the court will grant a stay unless the plaintiff can show that either the condition as to the operation of the agreement or the condition as to the existence of a dispute[6] is not fulfilled[7].

1 Ie the conditions set out in paras 622–627 post.
2 Arbitration Act 1950 s 4 (1); Arbitration Act 1975 s 1 (1); and see para 616 ante.
3 Ie the conditions set out in paras 628, 629 post.
4 Arbitration Act 1950 s 4 (1); and see para 616 ante. It is, however, arguable that the burden of establishing that the condition set out in para 628 post has not been met in fact rests on the plaintiff.
5 As to the exercise of the discretion and the burden of proof in that context see para 632 et seq post.
6 Ie the conditions set out in paras 630, 631 post.
7 Arbitration Act 1975 s 1 (1); and see para 616 ante.

622. Arbitration agreement. The applicant for either a discretionary or a mandatory stay must prove the existence of a written[1] arbitration agreement[2]. The agreement may be in respect of present or future disputes or differences[3], and it may have been made after the proceedings sought to be stayed have been commenced[4]. The applicant for a discretionary stay must not only prove that a purported agreement exists, but also that it is capable of being enforced[5]. It appears, however, that in order to satisfy this condition the applicant for a mandatory stay need show only the existence of the proposed agreement, and the plaintiff then has the burden of showing that it is null and void, inoperative or incapable of being performed[6]. Where an applicant relies on an arbitration agreement contained in a clause in a substantive contract, that applicant cannot deny the existence ab initio of the substantive contract[7], but he can contend that it has come to an end[8]. If the plaintiff denies the existence ab initio of the substantive contract, or that the clause was incorporated in it, the court must decide that issue at an interlocutory stage[9].

1 An oral agreement is insufficient: *Fleming v J S Doig (Grimsby) Ltd* (1921) 38 RPC 57. As to the requirement for writing see also *Zambia Steel and Building Supplies Ltd v James Clark and Eaton Ltd* [1986] 2 Lloyd's Rep 225, CA.
2 Arbitration Act 1950 s 4 (1); Arbitration Act 1975 s 1 (1); and see para 616 ante. Under the 1950 Act s 32 the term 'arbitration agreement' is defined as 'a written agreement to submit present or future disputes to arbitration'; under the 1975 Act s 7 it is defined as 'an agreement in writing (including an agreement contained in an exchange of letters or telegrams) to submit to arbitration present or future differences capable of settlement by arbitration'; cf para 609 ante. As to 'disputes' and 'differences capable of settlement by arbitration' see paras 612–614 ante.
3 Arbitration Act 1950 s 32; Arbitration Act 1975 s 7.

4 *The Tuyuti* [1984] QB 838 at 852, [1984] 2 All ER 545 at 555, [1984] 2 Lloyd's Rep 51 at 64–65, CA, per Robert Goff LJ.

5 *Moffat v Cornelius* (1878) 39 LT 102, CA; *Deutsche Springstoff AG v Briscoe* (1888) 20 QBD 177; *Randell, Saunders & Co Ltd v Thompson* (1876) 1 QBD 748 at 756, CA.

6 *Overseas Union Insurance Ltd v AA Mutual International Insurance Co Ltd* [1988] 2 Lloyd's Rep 63 at 70; see para 630 post.

7 A stay would not be granted if such a denial formed part of the applicant's case: *Republic of Liberia v Gulf Oceanic Inc* [1985] 1 Lloyd's Rep 539, CA; *Metal Scrap Trade Corpn Ltd v Kate Shipping Co Ltd, The Gladys* [1990] 1 All ER 397, [1990] 1 WLR 115, [1990] 1 Lloyd's Rep 297, HL.

8 Owing to, for example, an accepted repudiation. Under such circumstances the arbitration agreement would still be effective, and a stay may be granted: *Heyman v Darwins Ltd* [1942] AC 356, [1942] 1 All ER 337, HL.

9 Because the arbitrator cannot make a binding award on a matter which affects his own jurisdiction: *Modern Buildings Wales Ltd v Limmer* [1975] 2 All ER 549, [1975] 1 WLR 1281, [1975] 2 Lloyd's Rep 318, CA. But see *Willcock v Pickfords Removals Ltd* [1979] 1 Lloyd's Rep 244, CA; *O T M Ltd v Hydranautics* [1981] 2 Lloyd's Rep 211.

623. Legal proceedings commenced in any court. For the purposes of obtaining a stay, the commencement of legal proceedings in any court includes proceedings commenced by writ, by originating summons, by counterclaim[1], by third party notice or by contribution notice, in the last two cases notwithstanding that the prior parties to the action are not bound by the arbitration agreement, and that the prior proceedings will therefore continue despite the stay[2]. For these purposes 'any court' means any English court[3].

1 *Chappell v North* [1891] 2 QB 252. A stay is not, however, available to prevent a defendant relying on a matter covered by the arbitration agreement by way of a pure defence: *Bulk Oil (Zug) AG v Trans-Asiatic Oil Ltd SA* [1973] 1 Lloyd's Rep 129 at 135. Where a plaintiff commences an action seeking a declaration that he is not a party to a contract containing an arbitration clause, and the defendant serves a counterclaim claiming a declaration that the plaintiff is a party and damages for breach, the plaintiff cannot rely on the arbitration clause as entitling him to stay of the counterclaim: *Republic of Liberia v Gulf Oceanic Inc* [1985] 1 Lloyd's Rep 539, CA. A claimant who commences arbitration proceedings in England, claiming that a contract negotiated abroad has been concluded and that it includes an English arbitration clause, and claiming damages for breach of contract, is entitled to bring a counterclaim for the same claims in the other party's action for a declaration that there is no such contract or clause, even though the claimant may thereby found jurisdiction for the claims, which, apart from the disputed clause, have no connection with England, and for which leave may not be obtained to bring an action in an English court: *Metal Scrap Trade Corpn Ltd v Kate Shipping Co Ltd, The Gladys* [1990] 1 All ER 397, [1990] 1 WLR 115, [1990] 1 Lloyd's Rep 297, HL.

2 *W Bruce Ltd v Strong* [1951] 2 KB 447, [1951] 1 All ER 1021, [1951] 2 Lloyd's Rep 5, CA; *The Jemrix* [1981] 2 Lloyd's Rep 544.

3 It may, however, be possible to obtain an injunction restraining proceedings in a foreign court in breach of an arbitration agreement: *Tracomin SA v Sudan Oil Seeds Co Ltd (No 2)* [1983] 3 All ER 140, [1983] 1 WLR 1026, [1983] 2 Lloyd's Rep 624, CA; *Marazura Navegacion SA v Oceanus Mutual Underwriting Association (Bermuda) Ltd* [1977] 1 Lloyd's Rep 283; *Pena Copper Mines Ltd v Rio Tinto Co Ltd* (1911) 105 LT 846, CA; *World Pride Shipping Ltd v Daiichi Chuo Kisen Kaisha, The Golden Anne* [1984] 2 Lloyd's Rep 489; *Mike Trading and Transport Ltd v R Pagnan & Flli, The Lisboa* [1980] 2 Lloyd's Rep 546, CA; *Gorthon Invest AB v Ford Motor Co Ltd, The Maria Gorthon* [1976] 2 Lloyd's Rep 720.

624. Any matter agreed to be referred. The matter in question in the legal proceedings sought to be stayed must be within the scope of the arbitration agreement[1]. If nothing is in dispute[2], then where the arbitration clause is limited to disputes or differences, there is no matter agreed to be referred to arbitration[3].

1 See the Arbitration Act 1950 s 4 (1) and the Arbitration Act 1975 s 1 (1). As to the scope of the arbitration agreement see paras 612, 613 ante.

2 As to when there is nothing in dispute see para 631 post, where the specific requirement under the Arbitration Act 1975 s 1 (1) that there be a dispute is discussed. Of the cases there cited some were decisions on applications under the Arbitration Act 1950 and most are relevant to applications under the 1950 Act as well as under the 1975 Act.

3 If the clause extends for example to 'claims', there may be a matter agreed to be referred even in the absence of a dispute, but (a) a stay would probably be refused in the case of a domestic agreement as a matter of discretion under the Arbitration Act 1950 s 4 (1), and (b) a stay would be refused in the case of a non-domestic agreement on the ground that 'there is not in fact any dispute between the parties with regard to the matter agreed to be referred': Arbitration Act 1975 s 1 (1). See para 631 post.

625. The plaintiff. The applicant must show that the plaintiff who has commenced the legal proceedings was a party to the arbitration agreement, or that he is a person[1] who claims through or under such a party to the arbitration agreement[2]. The original party may have assigned his rights to the plaintiff[3], or they may have been otherwise transferred[4]. The plaintiff may be able to rely on the fact that he entered into the contract including the arbitration agreement as a consumer, as preventing the applicant enforcing the arbitration agreement[5].

1 'Person' includes any body of persons corporate or unincorporate: see the Interpretation Act 1978 s 5, Sch 1.

2 Arbitration Act 1950 s 4 (1); Arbitration Act 1975 s 1 (1); and see para 616 ante.

3 *Aspell v Seymour* [1929] WN 152, CA; *Roussel-Uclaf v G D Searle & Co Ltd* [1978] 1 Lloyd's Rep 225; *Rumput (Panama) SA v Islamic Republic of Iran Shipping Lines, The Leage* [1984] 2 Lloyd's Rep 259.

4 Eg by death (Arbitration Act 1950 s 2) or bankruptcy (Arbitration Act 1950 s 3). See para 610 ante.

5 The Consumer Arbitration Agreements Act 1988 restricts the availability of a stay against certain plaintiffs. A stay in respect of a domestic arbitration agreement cannot be obtained against a plaintiff who entered into the contract including the arbitration agreement as a consumer if certain conditions are met: see para 615 ante.

626. The applicant. The applicant must be a party to the legal proceedings and a party to the arbitration agreement, or a person[1] claiming through or under such a party to the arbitration agreement[2]. An applicant who applies to be joined in the proceedings simply to seek a stay is not a party to the legal proceedings for these purposes[3]. It is sufficient for one party to the arbitration agreement to make the application, even if other parties to it concur with the plaintiff in wishing that the matter should be litigated in court rather than referred to arbitration[4].

1 For the meaning of 'person' see para 625 note 1 ante.

2 Arbitration Act 1950 s 4 (1); Arbitration Act 1975 s 1 (1); and see para 616 ante. See also para 625 ante.

3 *Etri Fans Ltd v N M B (UK) Ltd* [1987] 2 All ER 763, [1987] 1 WLR 1110, [1987] 2 Lloyd's Rep 565, CA.

4 *Willesford v Watson* (1873) 8 Ch App 473.

627. Acknowledgment of service and step in the proceedings. The applicant must have taken[1] no step in the proceedings after acknowledgment of service[2]. A step in the proceedings is an act which both invokes the jurisdiction of the court[3] and which demonstrates the applicant's election to allow the action to proceed[4]. An applicant may take what would otherwise be a step if he makes it clear that that act is done without prejudice to his right to apply for a stay[5]. Steps in the proceedings have been held to include: the filing of an affidavit in opposition to a summons for summary judgment[6], service of a defence[7], and an application to the court for leave to serve interrogatories[8], or for a stay pending the giving of security for costs[9], or for an extension of time for serving a defence[10], or for an order for discovery[11], or for an order for further and better particulars[12]. The following have been held not to be steps: acts preliminary to the issue of proceedings, a request in correspondence for an extension of time for serving a defence[13], the filing of affidavits in answer to an application by the plaintiff for the appointment of a receiver[14], transferring a summons into counsel's list[15], applying to strike out a defective statement of claim[16], resisting an application for an interlocutory injunction by putting in evidence and appearing in court[17], and applying for a stay on grounds other than that the dispute was subject to an arbitration agreement[18].

1 The statute contemplates some positive act by way of offence on the part of the applicant rather than merely parrying a blow by the plaintiff: *Roussel-Uclaf v G D Searle & Co Ltd* [1978] 1 Lloyd's Rep 225. It is, however, sufficient if the applicant appears to resist or concur in an application made to the court by the plaintiff: *Turner and Goudy v McConnell* [1985] 2 All ER 34, [1985] 1 WLR 898, CA; *Parker, Gaines & Co Ltd v Turpin* [1918] 1 KB 358; *County Theatres and Hotels Ltd v Knowles* [1902] 1 KB 480, CA; *Richardson v Le Maitre* [1903] 2 Ch 222; *Ochs v Ochs Bros* [1909] 2 Ch 121; and cf *Metropolitan Tunnel and Public Works Ltd v London Electric Rly Co* [1926] Ch 371 at 384, CA. It is probably not sufficient if the applicant merely invites the plaintiff to take a step, eg by serving a statement of claim: *Ives and Barker v Willans* [1894] 2 Ch 478, CA. An applicant should nevertheless state that such an invitation is made without prejudice.

2 Arbitration Act 1950 s 4 (1); Arbitration Act 1975 s 1 (1); and see para 616 ante. 'Appearance', referred to in the statutes, now means acknowledgment of service: see para 616 note 7 ante; and RSC Ord 12 r 10. However, ticking the appropriate boxes in the form of acknowledgment of service of the writ in order to apply for a transfer of the proceedings from a district registry to London, or to another district registry, does not constitute a step in the action, but is to be construed merely as acknowledging service: *Skopos Design Group Ltd (trading as Anker Contract Carpets) v Homelife Nursing Ltd* (1988) Times, 24 March, CA.

3 Any act which does not involve the court does not invoke its jurisdiction: see text and notes 13–15 infra. As a general rule any application to the court, or filing of pleadings or documents, does invoke its jurisdiction and does amount to a step in the proceedings: see text and notes 6–12 infra. Under certain circumstances however, such actions may not amount to steps. See text and notes 16–18 infra.

4 *Eagle Star Insurance Co Ltd v Yuval Insurance Co Ltd* [1978] 1 Lloyd's Rep 357, CA; *Metropolitan Tunnel and Public Works Ltd v London Electric Rly Co* [1926] Ch 371 at 384, CA; *Ives and Barker v Willans* [1894] 2 Ch 478 at 484, 490, 494, CA; *Ford's Hotel Co Ltd v Bartlett* [1896] AC 1, HL. But per contra, it was held in *Parker, Gaines & Co Ltd v Turpin* [1918] 1 KB 358 that a step is taken in proceedings by a party notwithstanding his ignorance at the time of the existence of the arbitration clause.

5 By stating that this is the case, or by simultaneously issuing a summons to stay: *Metropolitan Tunnel and Public Works Ltd v London Electric Rly Co* [1926] Ch 371, CA; *London Sack and Bag Co Ltd v Dixon and Lugton Ltd* [1943] 2 All ER 763 at 767, CA; *Pitchers Ltd v Plaza (Queensbury) Ltd* [1940] 1 All ER 151, CA; *Richardson v Le Maitre* [1903] 2 Ch 222 at 225. See also *Brighton Marine Palace and Pier Ltd v Woodhouse* [1893] 2 Ch 486.

6 Unless an application for a stay is made before or at the same time: *Pitchers Ltd v Plaza (Queensbury) Ltd* [1940] 1 All ER 151, CA; *Rumput (Panama) SA v Islamic Republic of Iran Shipping Lines, The Leage* [1984] 2 Lloyd's Rep 259; *Turner and Goudy v McConnell* [1985] 2 All ER 34, [1985] 1 WLR 898, CA.

7 *West London Dairy Society Ltd v Abbott* (1881) 44 LT 376.

8 *Chappell v North* [1891] 2 QB 252.

9 *Adams v Catley* (1892) 66 LT 687.

10 *Ford's Hotel Co Ltd v Bartlett* [1896] AC 1, HL; see also *Smith & Co v British Marine Mutual Insurance Association* [1883] WN 176.

11 *Parker, Gaines & Co Ltd v Turpin* [1918] 1 KB 358.

12 *Chappell v North* [1891] 2 QB 252.

13 *Ives and Barker v Willans* [1894] 2 Ch 478, CA; *Brighton Marine Palace and Pier Ltd v Woodhouse* [1893] 2 Ch 486.

14 *Zalinoff v Hammond* [1898] 2 Ch 92; *Cie du Sénégal et de la Côte Occidentale d'Afrique v Smith & Co and Woods & Co* (1883) 53 LJ Ch 166 at 169.

15 *Lane v Herman* [1939] 3 All ER 353, CA.

16 *Eagle Star Insurance Co Ltd v Yuval Insurance Co Ltd* [1978] 1 Lloyd's Rep 357.

17 *Roussel-Uclaf v G D Searle & Co Ltd* [1978] 1 Lloyd's Rep 225.

18 *R G E (Group Services) Ltd v Cleveland Offshore Ltd* (1986) 11 Con LR 77.

628. Domestic agreements: no sufficient reason. Before it grants a stay of proceedings in relation to domestic arbitration agreements, the court must be satisfied that there is no sufficient reason why the matter should not be referred to arbitration in accordance with the agreement[1].

> 1 Arbitration Act 1950 s 4 (1). Even if so satisfied, the court has a discretion to refuse a stay: *Taunton-Collins v Cromie* [1964] 2 All ER 332, [1964] 1 WLR 633, CA.

629. Domestic agreements: ready and willing to do all things necessary. The applicant for a discretionary stay must satisfy the court not only that he is, but also that he was at the commencement of the proceedings, ready and willing[1] to do everything necessary for the proper conduct of the arbitration[2]. The affidavit in support of the application for a stay must state that this is the case[3]. A party may be 'ready and willing' within the meaning of this condition notwithstanding his contention that he has a perfect defence, such as that the time limit for reference to arbitration in the arbitration agreement has expired[4].

> 1 An applicant is only ready and willing if he does not intend to use the arbitration to postpone resolution of the dispute, or to block the progress by refusing to appoint an arbitrator: *Manchester Ship Canal Co Ltd v S Pearson & Son Ltd* [1900] 2 QB 606, CA. Great delay by an applicant may imply that he is not ready and willing, but mere delay is insufficient: *Hodson v Railway Passengers' Assurance Co* [1904] 2 KB 833 at 841, CA. The applicant must be prepared to refer the whole dispute: see *Davis v Starr* (1889) 41 ChD 242, CA, as explained in *Renshaw v Queen Anne Residential Mansions and Hotel Co Ltd* [1897] 1 QB 662, CA.
> 2 Arbitration Act 1950 s 4 (1); see para 616 ante.
> 3 *Piercy v Young* (1879) 14 ChD 200 at 209, CA.
> 4 *W Bruce Ltd v Strong* [1951] 2 KB 447, [1951] 1 All ER 1021, [1951] 2 Lloyd's Rep 5, CA. See also *Eastern Counties Farmers Ltd v J & J Cunningham Ltd* [1962] 1 Lloyd's Rep 261 at 263, CA.

630. Non-domestic agreements: null and void, inoperative or incapable of being performed. The plaintiff can prevent the grant of a mandatory stay if he can show that the arbitration agreement is null and void, inoperative or incapable of being performed[1]. An arbitration agreement is null and void if it is void ab initio[2]. An arbitration agreement may be inoperative either by reason of some subsequent agreement between the parties[3], or by reason of an order of an English court[4], or possibly in certain circumstances by reason of the doctrines of frustration or discharge by breach[5]. An arbitration agreement is only incapable of performance if the circumstances are such that it could no longer be performed even if both parties were ready, willing and able to perform it[6]. It is not incapable of being performed merely because the claim is time-barred[7], or the applicant does not have the means to satisfy any award made against him[8], or the applicant does not have the means to contest the arbitration[9].

> 1 Arbitration Act 1975 s 1 (1). Once the applicant has proved the existence of what appears to be a relevant arbitration agreement, the burden shifts to the plaintiff to prove that the agreement is in fact null and void, inoperative or incapable of being performed. See *Overseas Union Insurance Ltd v AA Mutual International Insurance Co Ltd* [1988] 2 Lloyd's Rep 63 at 70. See generally *Ethiopian Oilseeds and Pulses Export Corpn v Rio del Mar Foods Inc* [1990] 1 Lloyd's Rep 86.
> 2 'Null and void' does not include a merely voidable agreement: *The Tradesman, SA Hersent v United Towing Co Ltd* [1961] 3 All ER 661, [1962] 1 WLR 61, [1961] 2 Lloyd's Rep 183, following *Heyman v Darwins Ltd* [1942] AC 356, [1942] 1 All ER 337, HL.

3 *H Kruidenier (London) Ltd v Egyptian Navigation Co, The El Amria (No 2)* [1980] 2 Lloyd's Rep 166.
4 See paras 633, 636, 660 et seq post. Overlap in the issues in the arbitration and issues in proceedings between parties not bound by the arbitration agreement, and the possibility of inconsistent findings, do not make it inoperative: *Lonrho Ltd v Shell Petroleum Co Ltd* (1978) Times, 1 February. Nor should the court be led by such overlap to make any order that would make it inoperative: *City Centre Properties (I T C Pensions) Ltd v Tersons Ltd* [1969] 2 All ER 1121, sub nom *City Centre Properties (I T C Pensions) Ltd v Matthew Hall & Co Ltd* [1969] 1 WLR 772, CA.
5 See paras 612, 613 ante . However, it was held in *Radio Publicity (Universal) Ltd v Cie Luxembourgeoise de Radiodifusion* [1936] 2 All ER 721 at 728 that an arbitration agreement is operative until all matters in dispute under the agreement have been settled, notwithstanding that the relations between the parties had been discontinued.
6 *Paczy v Haendler and Natermann GmbH* [1981] 1 Lloyd's Rep 302 at 307, CA; eg where the named arbitrator is unable or refuses to act, and the court has no power to alter the situation.
7 *The Merak, Merak (Cargo Owners) v Merak (Owners)* [1965] P 223 at 239–240, [1964] 3 All ER 638 at 649–650, [1964] 2 Lloyd's Rep 283 at 295; on appeal [1965] P 223 at 241, [1965] 1 All ER 230, [1964] 2 Lloyd's Rep 527, CA. The arbitration could validly proceed, even if it would inevitably end in dismissal of the claim. See also *W Bruce Ltd v Strong* [1951] 2 KB 447, [1951] 1 All ER 1021, [1951] 2 Lloyd's Rep 5, CA.
8 *The Rena K* [1979] QB 377, [1979] 1 All ER 397, [1978] 1 Lloyd's Rep 545; *The Tuyuti* [1984] QB 838, [1984] 2 All ER 545, [1984] 2 Lloyd's Rep 51, CA.
9 *Paczy v Haendler and Natermann GmbH* [1981] 1 Lloyd's Rep 302, CA.

631. Non-domestic agreements: not in fact any dispute. The plaintiff can prevent the grant of a mandatory stay if he can show that there is not in fact any dispute between the parties with regard to the matter to be referred under a non–domestic arbitration agreement[1]. There is no dispute if the plaintiff's claim has been expressly or impliedly admitted[2], or if the applicant demonstrably has no defence[3]. There is a dispute if the amount of damages remains in issue although liability is not contested[4].

1 Arbitration Act 1975 s 1 (1); and see para 616 ante .
2 *London and North Western and Great Western Joint Rly Cos v J H Billington Ltd* [1899] AC 79, HL (difference must arise before submission to arbitration); *Tradax Internacional SA v Cerrahogullari TAS, The M Eregli* [1981] 3 All ER 344, [1981] 2 Lloyd's Rep 169 (claim said to be indisputable). However, it appears that where the applicant has never replied to the plaintiff's demands, there is a dispute because the applicant has never agreed that it is under any obligation: *Ellerine Bros (Pty) Ltd v Klinger* [1982] 2 All ER 737, [1982] 1 WLR 1375, CA. It also appears that a mere denial can constitute a dispute. There is a dispute until the applicant admits that a sum is due and payable: *Tradax Internacional SA v Cerrahogullari TAS, The M Eregli* supra.
3 *First Steamship Co Ltd v C T S Commodity Transport Shipping Schiffahrtsgesellschaft mbH, The Ever Splendor* [1988] 1 Lloyd's Rep 245. The words 'not in fact any dispute' do not extend to the situation where there is a dispute but only just: *Afia Worldwide Insurance Co v Deutsche Ruck Versicherungs AG* (1983) 133 NLJ 621. See also *Hayter v Nelson and Home Insurance Co* [1990] 2 Lloyd's Rep 265. The test is probably the same as for an application for summary judgment under RSC Ord 14: *Associated Bulk Carriers Ltd v Koch Shipping Inc, The Fuohsan Maru* [1978] 2 All ER 254, [1978] 1 Lloyd's Rep 24, CA; *SL Sethia Liners v State Trading Corpn of India Ltd* [1986] 2 All ER 395, [1985] 1 WLR 1398, [1986] 1 Lloyd's Rep 31, CA. If the plaintiff has applied for summary judgment and the applicant has cross-applied for a stay, the court will grant judgment and dismiss the application for a stay if the applicant's defence is based solely on a point of law on which the plaintiff is clearly right, because there is no dispute. Thus no stay will be granted of an action on a bill of exchange where the only suggested defence is a mere cross-claim not capable of set-off against such a claim: *Nova (Jersey) Knit Ltd v Kammgam Spinnerei GmbH* [1977] 2 All ER 463, [1977] 1 WLR 713, [1977] 1 Lloyd's Rep 463, HL. Similarly a claim for freight ought not to be stayed on the basis of a mere cross-claim for breach of charter not capable of set-off: *Cleobulos Shipping Co Ltd v Intertanker Ltd, The Cleon* [1983] 1 Lloyd's Rep 586, CA. However, if it is not immediately obvious that the plaintiff is right, the court should grant a stay without deciding the point of law: *Home and Overseas Insurance Co Ltd v Mentor Insurance Co (UK) Ltd (in liquidation)* [1989] 3 All ER 74, [1990] 1 WLR 153, [1989] 1 Lloyd's Rep 473, CA; *SL Sethia Liners v State Trading Corpn of India Ltd* supra. See also *Comdel Commodities Ltd v Siporex Trade SA* [1987] 1 Lloyd's Rep 325; *Imodco v Wimpey Major Projects Ltd and Taylor Woodrow*

International Ltd (1987) 40 BLR 1; *John Mowlem & Co plc v Carlton Gate Development Co Ltd* (1990) 6 Const LJ 298.

4 *Associated Bulk Carriers Ltd v Koch Shipping Inc, The Fuohsan Maru* [1978] 2 All ER 254, [1978] 1 Lloyd's Rep 24, CA; but there may be a stay as to quantum only, with liability being decided upon an application for summary judgment: *Texaco Ltd v Eurogulf Shipping Co Ltd* [1987] 2 Lloyd's Rep 541.

(3) DOMESTIC AGREEMENTS: THE EXERCISE OF THE DISCRETION

632. The general approach. In the case of domestic arbitration agreements[1], if the court is satisfied that the conditions are fulfilled, it has a discretion to grant a stay[2]. The burden is on the plaintiff to show good reason why he should not be required to abide by the agreement to arbitrate[3]. The grounds for refusal of a stay cannot be defined, but a number of factors[4] have been considered.

1 See para 617 ante.
2 See para 621 et seq ante.
3 The courts have a prima facie duty to act upon such an agreement: *Willesford v Watson* (1873) 8 Ch App 473 at 479–480. See also *Ford v Clarksons Holidays Ltd* [1971] 3 All ER 454, [1971] 1 WLR 1412, CA.
4 See paras 633–637 post.

633. The arbitrator. If the arbitrator is identifiable, the court will consider whether the arbitrator is able to conduct the arbitration in a proper and impartial manner[1]. In the case of an agreement to refer future disputes, the court may give leave to revoke the authority of the arbitrator and refuse a stay notwithstanding that the plaintiff knew or ought to have known that the arbitrator might not be capable of impartiality[2].

1 The test is whether there are grounds on which a reasonable man knowing all the relevant facts would think that the arbitrator could not or would not fairly determine the issue: *Bremer Handelsgesellschaft mbH v E T S Soules et Cie* [1985] 1 Lloyd's Rep 160; affd [1985] 2 Lloyd's Rep 199, CA; *Tracomin SA v Gibbs Nathaniel (Canada) Ltd and George Jacob Bridge* [1985] 1 Lloyd's Rep 586; *Cook International Inc v BV Handelmaatschappij Jean Delvaux* [1985] 2 Lloyd's Rep 225; and see also *Eckersley v Mersey Docks and Harbour Board* [1894] 2 QB 667, CA; *Ives and Barker v Willans* [1894] 2 Ch 478 at 488, CA. Cf *Beddow v Beddow* (1878) 9 ChD 89; *Malmesbury Rly Co v Budd* (1876) 2 ChD 113; *Jackson v Barry Rly Co* [1893] 1 Ch 238, CA; *Re Haigh and London and North-Western and Great Western Rly Cos* [1896] 1 QB 649. Where a contract provides for the submission of disputes to the arbitration of the engineer of one of the parties, it is not enough merely to allege that the arbitrator is not an independent person (*Bristol Corpn v John Aird & Co* [1913] AC 241 at 260, HL); but an application to stay will be refused if one of the questions between the parties is whether the local authority's engineer appointed as arbitrator under the contract has acted unreasonably in the discharge of his duties as engineer (*G Freeman & Sons v Chester RDC* [1911] 1 KB 783, CA), or if the arbitrator without any fault of his own is bound to be in the position of judge and witness (*Bristol Corpn v John Aird & Co* supra at 258–259, where the principles that should actuate the courts in dealing with applications to stay are laid down by Lord Moulton).
2 Arbitration Act 1950 s 24 (1), (3).

634. The parties to the agreement. The inability of the plaintiff to afford the extra expense of an arbitration or to obtain legal aid in respect of it, is not a ground for refusing a stay[1], unless the plaintiff's impecuniosity was a direct result of the applicant's breach of contract[2]. The fact that arbitration might be more expensive than litigation is not a ground for refusing a stay[3]. A stay has been refused where all the parties expected to join in the reference had not done so[4]. Unmeritorious conduct by the applicant is a material factor[5].

1 *Smith v Pearl Assurance Co Ltd* [1939] 1 All ER 95, (1939) 63 Ll L Rep 1, CA; *Ford v Clarksons Holidays Ltd* [1971] 3 All ER 454 at 457–458, 459, [1971] 1 WLR 1412 at 1416, 1418, CA. Cf *Goodman v Winchester and Alton Rly plc* [1984] 3 All ER 594, [1985] 1 WLR 141, CA (impecuniosity 'a relevant but not a decisive factor'). See also *Paczy v Haendler and Natermann GmbH* [1981] 1 Lloyd's Rep 302, CA (impecuniosity does not render a non-domestic arbitration agreement 'incapable of being performed' within the meaning of the Arbitration Act 1975 s 1 (1)).

2 *Fakes v Taylor Woodrow Construction Ltd* [1973] QB 436, [1973] 1 All ER 670, CA. Even then, it is to be balanced against the applicant's position: *Goodman v Winchester and Alton Rly plc* [1984] 3 All ER 594, [1985] 1 WLR 141, CA.

3 *Ford v Clarksons Holidays Ltd* [1971] 3 All ER 454, [1971] 1 WLR 1412, CA. But contrast *Halifax Overseas Freighters Ltd v Rasno Export, The Pine Hill* [1958] 2 Lloyd's Rep 146 at 152, where expense was regarded as material.

4 *Mason v Haddan* (1859) 6 CBNS 526 at 534. But it is not always necessary that all parties to an arbitration agreement should join in the reference; see para 626 ante.

5 *Croudace Ltd v Lambeth Borough Council* (1986) 33 BLR 20, CA.

635. The content of the arbitration agreement. If the arbitration agreement includes a Scott v Avery clause[1], there will be no purpose in refusing a stay, since the action would automatically fail[2]. If the dispute raises issues of law, a clause in the arbitration agreement excluding the parties' right to legal representation may be a ground for refusing a stay[3]. The fact that the terms of the arbitration agreement are oppressive in providing that each party should pay half the costs of the arbitration, whatever the result, is not a ground for refusing a stay[4].

1 See *Scott v Avery* (1856) 5 HL Cas 811: this is a clause which makes it a condition precedent of any right of action under the substantive contract that an arbitral award has been obtained. See para 646 post.

2 Because the condition precedent of obtaining an award would not have been fulfilled: *Smith, Coney and Barrett v Becker, Gray & Co* [1916] 2 Ch 86, CA; *City Centre Properties (I T C Pensions) Ltd v Tersons Ltd* [1969] 2 All ER 1121, sub nom *City Centre Properties (I T C Pensions) Ltd v Matthew Hall & Co Ltd* [1969] 1 WLR 772, CA; *Dennehy v Bellamy* [1938] 2 All ER 262, 60 Ll L Rep 269, CA. The stay will be granted even if the plaintiff is out of time to commence an arbitration: *W Bruce Ltd v Strong* [1951] 2 KB 447, [1951] 1 All ER 1021, [1951] 2 Lloyd's Rep 5, CA. However, a stay would not be refused where the applicant has waived his right to rely on the clause (see para 646 text and note 9 post), or the court has exercised its power under the Arbitration Act 1950 s 25 (4) to order that the clause has no effect (see para 647 post). If the application is for an injunction restraining foreign proceedings rather than a stay of English proceedings, the presence of a Scott v Avery clause is not conclusive, but may support the making of an injunction: *Tracomin SA v Sudan Oil Seeds Co Ltd (No 2)* [1983] 3 All ER 140, [1983] 1 WLR 1026, [1983] 2 Lloyd's Rep 624, CA.

3 *Perez v John Mercer & Sons* (1921) 7 Ll L Rep 1 at 2.

4 *Clough v County Live Stock Insurance Association Ltd* (1916) 85 LJKB 1185.

636. The subject matter of the dispute. The fact that points of law are in issue is relevant to the exercise of the discretion, but is not a ground in itself for refusing a stay[1]. If the point of law cannot be decided without ascertaining a number of facts, a stay will be ordered[2]. Some questions of law may be peculiarly suitable for determination by a court, and a stay may be refused[3]. A stay may also be refused where a question can only be decided effectively by the court, as where a plaintiff's claim is based on a statute which gives a particular discretion only to the court[4], or where an arbitrator cannot give the relief claimed[5]. The fact that the matter in dispute involves a charge of fraud[6] against one of the parties may lead to a stay where the arbitration agreement is for the reference of future disputes, and perhaps in certain other cases[7].

1 *Randegger v Holmes* (1866) LR 1 CP 679; *Willesford v Watson* (1873) 8 Ch App 473 at 480; *Valle-Jones v Liverpool and London and Global Insurance Co Ltd* (1933) 46 Ll L Rep 313, CA; *Hyams v Docker* [1969] 1 Lloyd's Rep 341; *Green Star Shipping Co v London Assurance* (1928) 31 Ll L Rep 4 at 6–7, CA. A stay may be more likely to be refused if the dispute consists entirely of questions of law: *Rowe Bros & Co Ltd v Crossley Bros Ltd* (1912) 108 LT 11, CA. But cf *John Mowlem & Co plc v Carlton Gate Development Co Ltd* (1990) 6 Const LJ 298 at 303, where the court took the view that the appointment of a legally qualified arbitrator was desirable to deal with complex issues of constuction law, and made it a condition of the stay that such an arbitrator be appointed.

2 *Home and Overseas Insurance Co Ltd v Mentor Insurance Co (UK) Ltd (in liquidation)* [1989] 3 All ER 74, [1990] 1 WLR 153, [1989] 1 Lloyd's Rep 473, CA; *Rowe Bros & Co Ltd v Crossley Bros Ltd* (1912) 108 LT 11, CA; *Metropolitan Tunnel and Public Works Ltd v London Electric Rly Co* [1926] Ch 371, CA.

3 *Halifax Overseas Freighters Ltd v Rasno Export, The Pine Hill* [1958] 2 Lloyd's Rep 146; *Hyams v Docker* [1969] 1 Lloyd's Rep 341 (construction question); but cf *John Mowlem & Co plc v Carlton Gate Development Co Ltd* (1990) 6 Const LJ 298; *Barnes v Youngs* [1898] 1 Ch 414 (expulsion of a partner); but cf *Re Phoenix Timber Co Ltd's Application* [1958] 2 QB 1, [1958] 1 All ER 815, [1958] 1 Lloyd's Rep 305, CA (dispute 'eminently suitable' for trial by court, yet interpleader issue still referred to arbitration).

4 *Olver v Hillier* [1959] 2 All ER 220, [1959] 1 WLR 551; see eg the Partnership Act 1890 s 35 (f). See also *Phoenix v Pope* [1974] 1 All ER 512, [1974] 1 WLR 719.

5 *Melgrave and Melgrave v Finer* (1959) Times, 18 February; affd sub nom *Finer v Melgrave* (1959) Times, 4 June, CA.

6 *Vawdrey v Simpson* [1896] 1 Ch 166 at 169; *Radford v Hair* [1971] Ch 758, [1971] 2 All ER 1089 ('actual dishonesty'). It is probable that professional misconduct suffices, but not negligence: *Charles Osenton & Co v Johnston* [1942] AC 130, [1941] 2 All ER 245, HL. Where a professional man's reputation will be at stake in an arbitration, the court may allow an action commenced by him in respect of a matter covered by the arbitration agreement to proceed: *Turner v Fenton* [1982] 1 All ER 8, [1982] 1 WLR 52.

7 When fraud is alleged and the person against whom the allegation is made wishes to be heard in court, a stay will generally be refused, but where the party against whom the allegation is made wants a stay, an allegation of fraud by itself is insufficient reason to stay: *Camilla Cotton Oil Co v Granadex SA* [1976] 2 Lloyd's Rep 10, HL; *Cunningham-Reid v Buchanan-Jardine* [1988] 2 All ER 438, [1988] 1 WLR 678, CA. See also para 662 post. See also *Russell v Russell* (1880) 14 ChD 471; *Barnes v Youngs* [1898] 1 Ch 414 at 419; *Radford v Hair* [1971] Ch 758, [1971] 2 All ER 1089, following *Charles Osenton & Co v Johnston* [1942] AC 130, [1941] 2 All ER 245, HL. The court may also order that the arbitration agreement shall cease to have effect, or give leave to revoke the authority of the arbitrator or arbitrators under the Arbitration Act 1950 s 24 (2), (3).

637. The balance of convenience.

An applicant who has failed to apply promptly may be refused a stay[1]. If the matter is urgent, the court may deal with it itself rather than refer it to the slower process of arbitration[2]. It is not material that, if a stay is granted, the plaintiff will be out of time to commence an arbitration[3]. A stay may be refused if the result of its being granted would be that identical or connected issues would be tried in more than one forum[4]. This might arise because the arbitration agreement covers only part of the matters in dispute[5], or because the arbitrator could not grant part of the relief claimed[6], or because the same or connected issues are being or will be tried in another action between different parties[7]. However, where a defendant in an action brings in a third party the latter may be granted a stay if there is an arbitration clause in the contract between him and the defendant, even though the same subject matter would be under consideration in both the action and the arbitration[8].

1 *World Pride Shipping v Daiichi Chuo Kisen Kaisha, The Golden Anne* [1984] 2 Lloyd's Rep 489; *The Christos* [1977] 1 Lloyd's Rep 109; *The Elizabeth H* [1962] 1 Lloyd's Rep 172; *Doleman & Sons v Ossett Corpn* [1912] 3 KB 257 at 268, CA; *Minifie v Railway Passengers' Assurance Co* (1881) 44 LT 552 at 554; *Pitchers Ltd v Plaza (Queensbury) Ltd* [1940] 1 All ER 151 at 156, CA; *Permavox Ltd v Royal Exchange Assurance* (1939) 64 Ll L Rep 145. Detriment in reliance upon a delay will make it more likely that a stay will be refused.

2 *Gilbert-Ash (Northern) Ltd v Modern Engineering (Bristol) Ltd* [1974] AC 689 at 726, [1973] 3 All ER 195 at 223, HL; or vice versa if arbitration would be achieved more rapidly: *The Tradesman, SA Hersent v United Towing Co Ltd* [1961] 3 All ER 661 at 667, [1962] 1 WLR 61 at 69–70, [1961] 2 Lloyd's Rep 183 at 189–190.

3 *W Bruce Ltd v Strong* [1951] 2 KB 447, [1951] 1 All ER 1021, [1951] 2 Lloyd's Rep 5, CA; *The Jemrix* [1981] 2 Lloyd's Rep 544.

4 *Halifax Overseas Freighters Ltd v Rasno Export, The Pine Hill* [1958] 2 Lloyd's Rep 146; *Eastern Counties Farmers Ltd v J & J Cunningham Ltd* [1962] 1 Lloyd's Rep 261 at 266, CA; *Taunton-Collins v Cromie* [1964] 2 All ER 332, [1964] 1 WLR 633, CA; *Brazendale & Co Ltd v Saint Frères SA* [1970] 2 Lloyd's Rep 34 at 38; *The Jade, The Eschersheim* [1976] 1 All ER 441 at 452, sub nom *The Eschersheim, The Jade* [1976] 1 WLR 339 at 352, sub nom *The Eschersheim* [1976] 1 Lloyd's Rep 81, CA; affd [1976] 1 All ER 920, [1976] 1 WLR 430, [1976] 2 Lloyd's Rep 1, HL. But see also *Bulk Oil (Zug) AG v Trans-Asiatic Oil Ltd SA* [1973] 1 Lloyd's Rep 129 at 138–140; *Northern Regional Health Authority v Derek Crouch Construction Co Ltd* [1984] 1 QB 644, [1984] 2 All ER 175, CA (no rule of law that an arbitrator must decide all the matters in dispute between the parties); *Green Star Shipping Co v London Assurance* (1928) 31 Ll L Rep 4; *Frota Nacional de Petroleiros v Skibsaktieselskapet Thorsholm* [1957] 1 Lloyd's Rep 1 at 5, CA.

5 *Turnock v Sartoris* (1889) 43 ChD 150, CA; *Young v Buckett* (1882) 51 LJ Ch 504; but cf *Ives and Barker v Willans* [1894] 2 Ch 478, CA (a stay will not be granted where the matters outside the scope of the arbitration agreement are insignificant); *Bristol Corpn v John Aird & Co* [1913] AC 241 at 250, 255, 261, HL; and *Hyams v Docker* [1969] 1 Lloyd's Rep 341. In *Radio Publicity (Universal) Ltd v Cie Luxembourgeoise de Radiodifusion* [1936] 2 All ER 721, a claim for damages for conspiracy was excluded from a stay as being outside the arbitration agreement.

6 As in *Willesford v Watson* (1873) 8 Ch App 473, where a stay was nevertheless granted. See also *Law v Garrett* (1878) 8 ChD 26 at 37, CA (if a sufficient case were shown for granting relief that an arbitrator could not grant, in this instance an injunction and the appointment of a receiver, then a stay would not be ordered). And cf *Cie du Sénégal et de la Côte d'Afrique v Smith & Co and Woods & Co* (1883) 53 LJ Ch 166 (where the court stayed the action except to the extent necessary to appoint a receiver, which only the court could do).

7 *Navarino Salvors Ltd v Navarino Recovery Ltd* (1925) 23 Ll L Rep 36; *City Centre Properties (I T C Pensions) Ltd v Tersons Ltd* [1969] 2 All ER 1121, sub nom *City Centre Properties (I T C Pensions) Ltd v Matthew Hall & Co Ltd* [1969] 1 WLR 772, CA.

8 *W Bruce Ltd v Strong* [1951] 2 KB 447, [1951] 1 All ER 1021, [1951] 2 Lloyd's Rep 5, CA.

(4) THE EFFECT AND TERMS OF A STAY

638. Effect, variation and discharge of stay. The court probably has power to vary or discharge a discretionary stay, though it is prudent to provide for this by the inclusion in the order of liberty to apply[1]. Similarly the refusal of a discretionary stay does not preclude the subsequent referral of issues to arbitration after the court has decided points of law[2]. However, where proceedings have been brought but no application for a stay has been made, or a stay has been refused, the arbitrator may not be able to proceed, against the plaintiff's will, with an arbitration in respect of the same matter, and any award made by him would be ineffective[3]. A mandatory stay can only be discharged if the statutory requirements[4] cease to be satisfied. An application for a mandatory stay is a denial of the jurisdiction of the court to decide the dispute, and does not amount to a voluntary submission to the jurisdiction[5]. The existence of a non-domestic arbitration agreement which would, if invoked, lead to a mandatory stay is not a bar to an ex parte application for leave to serve proceedings out of the jurisdiction[6], because the defendant might prefer to have the dispute decided in the English courts. If, however, the defendant does invoke the clause, and seeks to set aside the order made ex parte, then in clear cases it will be set aside without a formal application for a stay[7].

1 See *Cie du Sénégal et de la Côte Occidentale d'Afrique v Smith & Co and Woods & Co* (1883) 53 LJ Ch 166 at 169. This enables the court not only to remove the stay but also to amend the terms on which the stay is granted, and to grant ancillary relief.

2 *Printing Machinery Co Ltd v Linotype and Machinery Ltd* [1912] 1 Ch 566 at 574; *Re Carlisle, Clegg v Clegg* (1890) 44 ChD 200.

3 *Doleman & Sons v Ossett Corpn* [1912] 3 KB 257, CA; but cf *Lloyd v Wright, Dawson v Wright* [1983] QB 1065 at 1071–1072, 1074, 1075 and 1075–1076, [1983] 2 All ER 969 at 971, 972, 974 and 975, CA.

4 Ie the requirements of the Arbitration Act 1975 s 1 (1); see para 616 et seq ante.

5 *Finnish Marine Insurance Co Ltd v Protective National Insurance Co Ltd* [1990] 1 QB 1078, [1989] 2 All ER 929, [1989] 2 Lloyd's Rep 99.

6 Ie under RSC Ord 11.

7 *A and B v C and D* [1982] 1 Lloyd's Rep 166; cf *Qatar Petroleum Producing Authority v Shell Internationale Petroleum Maatschappij BV* [1983] 2 Lloyd's Rep 35, CA.

639. Terms of the stay. The court has no power to impose terms as a condition of the grant of a mandatory stay under the Arbitration Act 1975[1]. Under the Arbitration Act 1950 on the other hand, the court has a discretion as to the terms on which a stay is granted. It may for example require the applicant to give security for costs[2], to permit a change in the composition of the tribunal, to consent to an appeal on a question of law arising out of the award, to proceed with dispatch or according to a specified timetable, or to abandon a particular claim or argument. The court may require that the arbitrator to be appointed should be a person who is legally qualified and who has knowledge of the particular subject matter[3]. The court may grant a discretionary stay in respect of only part of the action, so that some issues are decided by the court and others by the arbitrator[4]. The court may grant a stay to allow just the question of quantum to go to arbitration, and may grant it subject to any appropriate conditions, including the making of an interim payment[5].

1 *The Rena K* [1979] QB 377 at 401, [1979] 1 All ER 397 at 412–413, [1978] 1 Lloyd's Rep 545 at 557; *The World Star* [1986] 2 Lloyd's Rep 274 at 275.

2 *Hitachi Shipbuilding and Engineering Co Ltd v Viafel Compania Naviera SA* [1981] 2 Lloyd's Rep 498, CA; *Flender Werft AG v Aegean Maritime Ltd* [1990] 2 Lloyd's Rep 27; *Fal Bunkering of Sharjah v Grecale Inc of Panama* [1990] 1 Lloyd's Rep 369.

3 *John Mowlem & Co plc v Carlton Gate Development Co Ltd* (1990) 6 Const LJ 298 at 303–304.

4 *Bristol Corpn v John Aird & Co* [1913] AC 241 at 261, HL. For example if part of the relief claimed is outside the jurisdiction of the arbitrator: *Radio Publicity (Universal) Ltd v Cie Luxembourgeoise de Radiodifusion* [1936] 2 All ER 721; or if the court wishes to split issues of fact and law: *Hyams v Docker* [1969] 1 Lloyd's Rep 341. Where part of a claim is established beyond reasonable doubt the court may give summary judgment for that part and refer the balance to arbitration: *Ellis Mechanical Services Ltd v Wates Construction Ltd* [1978] 1 Lloyd's Rep 33 at 37, CA.

5 *Texaco Ltd v Eurogulf Shipping Co Ltd* [1987] 2 Lloyd's Rep 541.

640. Ancillary relief. When granting a mandatory or a discretionary stay[1] or at any time thereafter[2] the court may grant any relief which would not be obtainable from the arbitrator, such as the appointment of a receiver[3] or an injunction[4], including a Mareva injunction[5]. The court may in addition refuse to release a vessel from arrest even where the action has been the subject of a mandatory stay[6].

1 For the form of order see 6 Court Forms (2nd Edn) (1989 Issue) 119–120, Forms 38, 39.

2 *Zalinoff v Hammond* [1898] 2 Ch 92 at 95.

3 *Law v Garrett* (1878) 8 ChD 26, CA; *Pini v Roncoroni* [1892] 1 Ch 633; *Cie du Sénégal et de la Côte Occidentale d'Afrique v Smith & Co and Woods & Co* (1883) 53 LJ Ch 166.

4 *Brighton Marine Palace and Pier Ltd v Woodhouse* [1893] 2 Ch 486; *Willesford v Watson* (1873) 8 Ch App 473; *Re Phoenix Timber Co Ltd's Application* [1958] 2 QB 1, [1958] 1 All ER 815, [1958] 1 Lloyd's Rep 305, CA. See also para 642 et seq post.

5 *Hitachi Shipbuilding and Engineering Co Ltd v Viafel Compania Naviera SA* [1981] 2 Lloyd's Rep 498, CA. See also para 677 post. As to Mareva injunctions see INJUNCTIONS.

6 See para 673 post; and *The Rena K* [1979] QB 377, [1979] 1 All ER 397, [1978] 1 Lloyd's Rep 545, distinguishing *The Golden Trader* [1975] QB 348, [1974] 2 All ER 686; *The Tuyuti* [1984] QB 838, [1984] 2 All ER 545, [1984] 2 Lloyd's Rep 51, CA; *The Silver Athens (No 2)* [1986] 2 Lloyd's Rep 583; *The World Star* [1986] 2 Lloyd's Rep 274.

(5) INTERPLEADER

641. Interpleader. Where interpleader relief[1] is granted and it appears to the High Court that the claims in question are matters to which an arbitration agreement, to which the claimants are parties, applies, the High Court[2] may direct the issue between the claimants to be determined in accordance with the agreement[3]. The court's jurisdiction is discretionary, but the discretion should be exercised in the same way as the discretion to order a stay of court proceedings[4].

1 See generally INTERPLEADER vol 25 para 1001 et seq.

2 The jurisdiction conferred on the High Court by the Arbitration Act 1950 s 5 may be exercised in the Queen's Bench Division by a judge in chambers, a master or the Admiralty Registrar (RSC Ord 73 r 3 (1); see also RSC Ord 73 r 6, which provides that matters to be heard by a judge should be heard by a commercial judge). For the mode of making the application see RSC Ord 73 r 3 (3). An appeal lies to a judge in chambers from a decision of a master or the Admiralty Registrar (RSC Ord 58 r 1 (1); see also RSC Ord r 1 (2)–(4)) and an appeal lies to the Court of Appeal from the decision of a judge in chambers (RSC Ord 58 r 6 (1)). The Arbitration Act 1950 s 5 does not require an application to be made for the court to exercise the jurisdiction: it can do so of its own motion. For the relevant forms see 6 Court Forms (2nd Edn) (1989 Issue) 121–122, Forms 41, 42.

3 Arbitration Act 1950 s 5.

4 Under ibid s 4: see para 616 et seq ante. See *Re Phoenix Timber Co Ltd's Application* [1958] 2 QB 1, [1958] 1 All ER 815, CA, where the fact that the dispute was eminently suitable to be tried by the court was not a sufficient ground for refusing to direct the issue to be determined in accordance with the agreement.

3. INJUNCTION AND DECLARATION

642. Injunction restraining arbitration proceedings. The court[1] has an inherent jurisdiction to restrain arbitration proceedings by injunction, where it is necessary in order to protect a legal or equitable right[2]. Arbitration proceedings have been restrained in the following circumstances:

(1) where the contract containing the arbitration agreement is invalid or where there is a challenge to its validity[3];

(2) where the point at issue between the parties is so clear that there could not properly be said to be a dispute[4];

(3) where the reference has been terminated by agreement, express or implied[5];
(4) where the arbitration agreement refers to a specific arbitrator, and he is
     disqualified by reason of corruption or bias[6].

An injunction may also be available in cases where the arbitration agreement is
rendered unenforceable by the operation of the Consumer Arbitration Agreements
Act 1988[7].

An injunction will not be granted restraining arbitration proceedings where the
underlying contract, though valid, is terminated by repudiation[8] or where supervening illegality prevents performance[9]. Nor is there, apparently, jurisdiction to
grant an injunction where it appears that the arbitrator is about to exceed his
jurisdiction[10], though in these circumstances declaratory relief is available[11].

Though there is jurisdiction to restrain foreign arbitration proceedings, the court
will exercise caution in doing so, and will apply the same principles as apply to
injunctions restraining foreign court proceedings[12].

  1 In the case of a judge-arbitrator (see paras 604 ante, 655, 661 post), the power to grant an injunction
     can only be exercised by the Court of Appeal: Administration of Justice Act 1970 s 4 (5). As to
     injunctions generally see INJUNCTIONS.
  2 *Malmesbury Rly Co v Budd* (1876) 2 ChD 113; *North London Rly Co v Great Northern Rly Co* (1883) 11
     QBD 30, CA, approved in *Siskina (Cargo Owners) v Distos Compania Naviera SA* [1979] AC 210,
     [1977] 3 All ER 803, sub nom *Ibrahim Shanker & Co v Distos Compania Naviera SA, The Siskina* [1978]
     1 Lloyd's Rep 1, HL; *Bremer Vulkan Schiffbau und Maschinenfabrik v South India Shipping Corpn Ltd*
     [1981] AC 909, [1981] 1 All ER 289, [1981] 2 Lloyd's Rep 253, HL.
  3 *Kitts v Moore* [1895] 1 QB 253, CA; *Mylne v Dickinson* (1815) Coop G 195, DC; *Maunsell v Midland
     Great Western (Ireland) Rly Co* (1863) 1 Hem & M 130; *Ben & Co Ltd v Pakistan Edible Oils Corpn Ltd*
     (1978) Times, 13 July, CA. But contrast *Turk Gemi Kurtama v Ithaka (Owners), The Ithaka* [1939] 3
     All ER 630, CA, and *Industrie Chimiche Italia Centrale v Alexander G Tsavliris and Sons Maritime Co,
     The Choko Star* [1987] 1 Lloyd's Rep 508, CA, in which one of the parties had released the security of
     a salvaged vessel in reliance upon their right to a salvage arbitration; *M'Harg v Universal Stock
     Exchange* [1895] 2 QB 81, CA.
  4 *Sissons v Oates* (1894) 10 TLR 392; but contrast the cases cited in note 9 infra.
  5 See para 643 post.
  6 *Malmesbury Rly Co v Budd* (1876) 2 ChD 113; *Beddow v Beddow* (1878) 9 ChD 89.
  7 See para 615 ante.
  8 *Heyman v Darwins Ltd* [1942] AC 356, [1942] 1 All ER 337, HL.
  9 *Edward Grey & Co v Tolme and Runge* (1914) 31 TLR 137, CA; *Smith, Coney and Barrett v Becker, Gray
     & Co* [1916] 2 Ch 86, CA; *Scott & Sons Ltd v R & N Del Sel* 1923 SC (HL) 37, 14 Ll L Rep 65.
 10 *North London Rly Co v Great Northern Rly Co* (1883) 11 QBD 30, CA; *Den of Airlie SS Co Ltd v Mitsui
     & Co Ltd and British Oil and Cake Mills Ltd* (1912) 106 LT 451, CA. See also *Farrar v Cooper* (1890) 44
     ChD 323.
 11 See para 643 post.
 12 *Black Clawson International Ltd v Papierwerke Waldhof-Aschaffenburg AG* [1981] 2 Lloyd's Rep 446.

643. Injunction after termination of the reference by agreement. An arbitration agreement may be terminated by agreement, express or implied. Though a
reference cannot be repudiated or frustrated merely by inordinate delay in prosecution of the proceedings[1], a long period of inactivity by both parties may give
rise to an implied agreement to terminate the reference[2]. Such termination will
only be inferred where:
  (1) the clear inference to be drawn from the claimant's inactivity was that he did
       not wish to proceed provided that the respondent also agreed not to proceed;
  (2) the clear inference to be drawn from the respondent's inactivity was that he
       consented to the abandonment;

(3) these inferences did not conflict with the respondent's actual understanding of the position³.

On an application for an injunction restraining the arbitration proceedings in such a case, the court will consider the termination issue on its merits, and will grant an injunction if it finds that the reference has been terminated⁴.

1 *Bremer Vulkan Schiffbau und Maschinenfabrik v South India Shipping Corpn Ltd* [1981] AC 909, [1981] 1 All ER 289, [1981] 2 Lloyd's Rep 253, HL; *Paal Wilson & Co A/S v Partenreederei Hannah Blumenthal, The Hannah Blumenthal* [1983] 1 AC 854, [1983] 1 All ER 34, [1983] 1 Lloyd's Rep 103, HL.
2 The inference was drawn in *Andre et Cie SA v Marine Transocean Ltd, The Splendid Sun* [1981] QB 694, [1981] 2 All ER 993, [1981] 2 Lloyd's Rep 29, CA (eight year delay during which one of the arbitrators died and was not replaced), approved in *Paal Wilson & Co A/S v Partenreederei Hannah Blumenthal, The Hannah Blumenthal* [1983] 1 AC 854, [1983] 1 All ER 34, [1983] 1 Lloyd's Rep 103, HL; *Excomm Ltd v Guan Guan Shipping (Pte) Ltd, The Golden Bear* [1987] 1 Lloyd's Rep 330 (eight year delay); *Tankrederei Ahrenkeil GmbH v Frahuil SA, The Multitank Holsatia* [1988] 2 Lloyd's Rep 486 (six year delay, doubtful claim); and *The Torm Herdis* (1990, unreported) (three year delay). Cf *Allied Marine Transport Ltd v Vale do Rio Doce Navegacao SA, The Leonidas D* [1985] 2 All ER 796, [1985] 1 WLR 925, [1985] 2 Lloyd's Rep 18, CA; *Gebr van Weelde Scheepvaartkantor BV v Compania Naviera Sea Orient SA, The Agrabele* [1987] 2 Lloyd's Rep 233, CA; *Food Corpn of India v Antclizo Shipping Corpn, The Antclizo* [1988] 2 All ER 513, [1988] 1 WLR 603, [1988] 2 Lloyd's Rep 93 HL; *The Achillet* (8 September 1989, unreported); and *Thai-Europe Tapioca Service Ltd v Seine Navigation Co Inc, The Maritime Winner* [1989] 2 Lloyd's Rep 506. See also *Unisys International Services Ltd v Eastern Counties Newspapers Ltd* [1991] 1 Lloyd's Rep 538.
3 *Tankrederei Ahrenkeil GmbH v Frahuil SA, The Multitank Holsatia* [1988] 2 Lloyd's Rep 486; *Thai-Europe Tapioca Service Ltd v Seine Navigation Co Inc, The Maritime Winner* [1989] 2 Lloyd's Rep 506.
4 See the cases referred to in note 2 supra.

644. Declaration. The court¹ has, owing to its general power to make declarations, the power to declare that an arbitrator has no jurisdiction to hear or determine any claim in question², or that a reference has been terminated by agreement³. Where one party applies to the court for a declaration as to the jurisdiction of the arbitrator, the other party may found the court's jurisdiction to try the underlying dispute by counterclaiming in the same proceedings⁴. The counterclaim may then be stayed pending the outcome of the declaration proceedings⁵.

1 In the case of a judge-arbitrator (see paras 604 ante, 655, 661 post), the power to make a declaration can be exercised only by the Court of Appeal: Administration of Justice Act 1970 s 4 (5).
2 *Government of Gibraltar v Kenney* [1956] 2 QB 410, [1956] 3 All ER 22; *Atlas Levante-Linie Aktiengesellschaft v Gesellschaft fuer Getreidehandel AG, The Phönizien* [1966] 1 Lloyd's Rep 150; *Metal Scrap Trade Corpn Ltd v Kate Shipping Co Ltd, The Gladys* [1990] 1 All ER 397, [1990] 1 WLR 115, [1990] 1 Lloyd's Rep 297, HL.
3 *Excomm Ltd v Guan Guan Shipping (Pte) Ltd, The Golden Bear* [1987] 1 Lloyd's Rep 330; *Tankrederei Ahrenkeil GmbH v Frahuil SA, The Multitank Holsatia* [1988] 2 Lloyd's Rep 486.
4 *Metal Scrap Trade Corpn Ltd v Kate Shipping Co Ltd, The Gladys* [1990] 1 All ER 397, [1990] 1 WLR 115, [1990] 1 Lloyd's Rep 297, HL.
5 *Metal Scrap Trade Corpn Ltd v Kate Shipping Co Ltd, The Gladys* [1990] 1 All ER 397, [1990] 1 WLR 115, [1990] 1 Lloyd's Rep 297, HL.

4. OUSTER OF THE COURT'S JURISDICTION;
SCOTT v AVERY CLAUSES

645. The court's residual jurisdiction. The parties to an arbitration agreement cannot oust the court's jurisdiction, and any agreement which purports to do so is illegal and void as being contrary to public policy[1]. In consequence the existence of an arbitration agreement[2] is not a bar or defence to court proceedings brought in respect of a dispute agreed to be referred[3]. The party seeking to rely upon the arbitration agreement must apply for a stay of the court proceedings, and any grant of a stay may be revoked. The stay is granted to give effect to the arbitration agreement, and does not preclude the court making orders ancillary to the arbitration[4].

1 The principle was established in *Thompson v Charnock* (1799) 8 Term Rep 139. See also *Scott v Avery* (1856) 5 HL Cas 811. An arbitration agreement not expressly purporting to oust the jurisdiction is not to be read as doing so. The standard phrase that an arbitrator's award shall be 'final and binding' does not oust the court's jurisdiction, and prefacing the words 'accepted by all parties as' adds nothing: *Ford v Clarksons Holidays Ltd* [1971] 3 All ER 454, [1971] 1 WLR 1412, CA. See also para 646 post. As to agreements excluding the right to appeal to the High Court on questions of law or to apply for the determination of a preliminary issue, see the Arbitration Act 1979 ss 3, 4; and para 706 et seq post.

2 Where the wording of the arbitration agreement makes the obtaining of an award a condition precedent to the existence of a cause of action, or to the right to enforce it, then there is a defence: *Scott v Avery* (1856) 5 HL Cas 811; see para 646 post. Provided that the arbitration has not proceeded to the making of a valid award, the fact that an arbitration is actually in progress when the court proceedings are commenced does not mean that there is a defence or a bar to those proceedings: *Pena Copper Mines Ltd v Rio Tinto Co Ltd* (1911) 105 LT 846 at 851, CA; *Doleman & Sons v Ossett Corpn* [1912] 3 KB 257 at 262–263, CA.

3 If a party institutes court proceedings then, in the absence of an application for a stay, they will proceed in exactly the same way as if the arbitration agreement did not exist, and any award made by the arbitrator is ineffective: *Doleman & Sons v Ossett Corpn* [1912] 3 KB 257, CA. The principle only applies if the proceedings are in an English court: *World Pride Shipping Ltd v Daiichi Chuo Kisen Kaisha, The Golden Anne* [1984] 2 Lloyd's Rep 489.

4 See para 640 ante.

646. Scott v Avery clauses. A provision in an arbitration agreement, known as a 'Scott v Avery clause'[1], whereby the making of an arbitral award is expressed to be a condition precedent[2] to any right of action in respect of any of the matters agreed to be referred, does not oust the jurisdiction of the court[3]. Such a clause constitutes a defence[4] to any proceedings[5] brought before the making of the award, and the plaintiff can only enforce his rights by going to arbitration. It does not however operate to postpone the running of any period of limitation[6]. Reliance on a Scott v Avery clause amounts to an affirmation of the jurisdiction of the arbitrator, and a party who relies on the clause cannot subsequently resist enforcement of the award on the basis that the arbitrator had no jurisdiction to determine a particular question[7]. Where an award has been made, the successful party's subsequent rights are based on the award, and not on the original cause of action[8]. A party may by his conduct waive his ability to rely upon a Scott v Avery clause[9].

1 This clause takes its name from *Scott v Avery* (1856) 5 HL Cas 811.

2 The condition need not be the making of the award. A similar effect is achieved by a clause which provides that the only obligation of the defendant is to pay the amount set out in an arbitral award: *Scott v Liverpool Corpn* (1858) 3 De G & J 334; *Braunstein v Accidental Death Insurance Co* (1861) 1 B & S 782; *Elliott v Royal Exchange Assurance Co* (1867) LR 2 Exch 237.

3 *Czarnikow v Roth, Schmidt & Co* [1922] 2 KB 478 at 485, CA; *Scott v Avery* (1853) 8 Exch 487 at 502;
   Freshwater v Western Australian Assurance Co Ltd [1933] 1 KB 515 at 523; *Central Electricity Generating
   Board v Halifax Corpn* [1963] AC 785 at 801, 806, [1962] 3 All ER 915 at 920, 923, HL (this case is no
   longer good law as to when the limitation period runs from when there is a Scott v Avery clause: see
   note 5 infra).
4 *Scott v Avery* (1856) 5 HL Cas 811; *Tredwen v Holman* (1862) 1 H & C 72; *Braunstein v Accidental Death
   Insurance Co* (1861) 1 B & S 782; *Elliott v Royal Exchange Assurance Co* (1867) LR 2 Exch 237; *Viney v
   Bignold* (1887) 20 QBD 172; *Trainor v Phoenix Fire Assurance Co* (1891) 65 LT 825; *Scott v Mercantile
   Accident and Guarantee Insurance Co Ltd* (1892) 66 LT 811, CA; *Caledonian Insurance Co v Gilmour*
   [1893] AC 85, HL; *Spurrier v La Cloche* [1902] AC 446, PC; *Sharpington v Fulham Guardians* [1904] 2
   Ch 449; *King v Phoenix Assurance Co* [1910] 2 KB 666, CA (award condition precedent to right to
   take proceedings for recovery of workmen's compensation); *Hallen v Spaeth* [1923] AC 684, PC;
   Board of Trade v Cayzer, Irvine & Co Ltd [1927] AC 610, HL; *Monmouthshire County Council v Costelloe
   and Kemple Ltd* (1965) 63 LGR 429, CA. Cf *Collins v Locke* (1879) 4 App Cas 674, PC, and *Dawson v
   Fitzgerald* (1876) 1 ExD 257, CA (in which cases it was held that an action was maintainable although
   there had been no reference to arbitration). Consequently an application for a stay of English
   proceedings would be very likely to succeed: see para 634 ante.
5 A Scott v Avery clause is only a defence to proceedings if on the proper construction of the clause the
   issue to be determined and/or the relief sought in the proceedings would have been within the
   jurisdiction of the arbitrators: *Cie Européene de Cereals SA v Tradax Export SA* [1986] 2 Lloyd's Rep
   301. A Scott v Avery clause only amounts to a defence to proceedings brought in an English court,
   although other jurisdictions may have a similar doctrine. If an application is made in an English court
   for an injunction restraining proceedings in a foreign court in breach of an arbitration agreement, the
   existence of a Scott v Avery clause is not conclusive, but merely supportive of the application: see
   Tracomin SA v Sudan Oil Seeds Co Ltd (No 2) [1983] 3 All ER 140, [1983] 1 WLR 1026, [1983] 2
   Lloyd's Rep 624, CA; and para 623 ante.
6 Limitation Act 1980 s 34 (2), and see para 649 et seq post. Cf *Central Electricity Generating Board v
   Halifax Corpn* [1963] AC 785 at 801, 806, [1962] 3 All ER 915 at 920, 923, HL, a case reflective of the
   earlier position.
7 *South British Insurance Co Ltd v Gauci Bros & Co* [1928] AC 352, PC.
8 *Woodall v Pearl Assurance Co Ltd* [1919] 1 KB 593 at 608, CA.
9 Waiver may take the form of action inconsistent with reliance upon the clause, or of conduct
   preventing the defendant fulfilling the condition required of it: *Toronto Rly Co v National British and
   Irish Millers Insurance Co Ltd* (1914) 111 LT 555, CA; *Hardwick Game Farm v Suffolk Agricultural and
   Poultry Producers' Association* [1964] 2 Lloyd's Rep 227; *Hickman & Co v Roberts* [1913] AC 229, HL;
   Edwards v Aberayron Mutual Ship Insurance Society Ltd (1876) 1 QBD 563. Cf *Woodall v Pearl Assurance
   Co Ltd* [1919] 1 KB 593, CA.

647. Court's power to set aside condition. Where the court orders[1] that an
arbitration agreement subject to a provision making an award a condition precedent should cease to have effect with regard to any particular dispute, it may
further order that the provision making an award a condition precedent shall also
cease to have effect as regards that dispute[2].

1 Either under the Arbitration Act 1950 s 25 (2) (amended by the Administration of Justice Act 1970 s 4
   (4), Sch 3 para 11) or under 'any other enactment' (see the Arbitration Act 1950 s 25 (4) (as so
   amended)). Under s 25 (2) (as so amended) the High Court or the Court of Appeal may make such an
   order where the authority of an arbitrator or arbitrators or umpire is revoked by leave of the High
   Court or the Court of Appeal, or where the High Court or the Court of Appeal has removed a sole
   arbitrator or all the arbitrators or an umpire who has entered on the reference. Under s 24 (2), which
   probably falls within 'any other enactment', a similar order can be made by the High Court where
   the dispute involves the question whether a party has been guilty of fraud.
2 Ibid s 25 (4). See *Getreide-Import GmbH v Contimar SA Compania Industrial Comercial Y-Maritima*
   [1953] 1 All ER 257, [1953] 1 WLR 207, affd on different grounds [1953] 2 All ER 223, [1953] 1 WLR
   793, CA. As to the situation where a claim is brought under the Third Parties (Rights Against
   Insurers) Act 1930 see *Socony Mobil Oil Co Inc v West of England Ship Owners Mutual Insurance
   Association (London) Ltd, The Padre Island* [1984] 2 Lloyd's Rep 408; *Firma C-Trade v Newcastle
   Protection and Indemnity Association, The Fanti* [1987] 2 Lloyd's Rep 299; *Socony Mobil Oil Co Inc v
   West of England Ship Owners Mutual Insurance Association (London) Ltd, The Padre Island (No 2)* [1987]

2 Lloyd's Rep 529; the appeals of the two cases last cited were taken together: see [1989] 1 Lloyd's Rep 239, CA; [1991] 2 AC 1, [1990] 2 All ER 705, [1990] 2 Lloyd's Rep 191, HL. See also *London Steamship Owners Mutual Insurance Association v Bombay Trading Co Ltd, The Felicie* [1990] 2 Lloyd's Rep 21.

648. Atlantic Shipping clauses. A provision in an arbitration agreement known as an 'Atlantic Shipping clause'[1] barring all claims unless a claim is made in writing and an arbitrator appointed within a limited period has been held binding[2], and does not oust the jurisdiction of the court. There is, however, statutory power to extend time so as to avoid undue hardship and to achieve justice[3].

1 See para 652 et seq post. This clause takes its name from *Atlantic Shipping and Trading Co Ltd v L Dreyfus & Co* [1922] 2 AC 250, HL. The most common form is now the 'Centrocon' arbitration clause: see para 652 note 1 post.
2 *Atlantic Shipping and Trading Co Ltd v L Dreyfus & Co* [1922] 2 AC 250, HL; *Williams and Mordey v W H Muller & Co (London) Ltd* (1924) 18 Ll L Rep 50; *Union of India v E B Aaby's Rederi A/S* [1975] AC 797, [1974] 2 All ER 874, sub nom *E B Aaby's Rederi A/S v Union of India, The Evje* [1974] 2 Lloyd's Rep 57, HL. Cf *H Ford & Co Ltd v Cie Furness (France)* [1922] 2 KB 797.
3 Under the Arbitration Act 1950 s 27; see para 654 post. That section is to be read in its ordinary meaning as conferring on the High Court jurisdiction to extend time whenever an arbitration agreement imposes a time limit for commencement of arbitration, whether or not a discretion to extend time has been conferred on the arbitrator under the terms of the agreement: *Comdel Commodities Ltd v Siporex Trade SA (No 2)* [1991] 1 AC 148, [1990] 2 Lloyd's Rep 207, sub nom *Comdel Commodities Ltd v Siporex Trade SA* [1990] 2 All ER 552, HL.

5. LIMITATION OF CLAIMS

(1) LIMITATION BY STATUTE

649. Applicability of statutes to arbitrations. A time limit in a statute which applies to arbitrations is a defence to a claim if the time limit has expired[1]. The Limitation Act 1980[2] and the Foreign Limitation Periods Act 1984[3] both apply to arbitrations. When the limitation period begins is a matter of construction of the statute[4]. When an action is brought on an award, the limitation period runs from the failure to honour the award[5]. However, where there is a clause in an arbitration agreement to the effect that no cause of action shall accrue in respect of any matter required to be referred until an award is made under the agreement, known as a Scott v Avery clause[6], for the purposes of the Limitation Act 1980 and of any other enactment relating to the limitation of actions (whether in their application to arbitrations or to other proceedings), the cause of action is deemed to have accrued, in respect of any matter agreed to be referred, at the time when it would have accrued but for that term in the agreement[7].

1 *Re Astley and Tyldesley Coal and Salt Co and Tyldesley Coal Co* (1889) 68 LJQB 252; *Board of Trade v Cayzer, Irvine & Co Ltd* [1927] AC 610 at 614, HL. Whether a particular statute applies to arbitrations is a matter for construction of the statute. In general, most statutory time limits will be construed as applying to arbitrations, so as to prevent parties contracting out of statutory limitations: *Denny Mott and Dickson Ltd v Lynn Shipping Co Ltd* [1963] 1 Lloyd's Rep 339. Where a statutory and a contractual time limit conflict, it is a question of construction which prevails: *Unicoopjapan and Marubeni-Iida Co Ltd v Ion Shipping Co, The Ion* [1971] 1 Lloyd's Rep 541; *Sabah Flour and Feedmills v Comfez Ltd* [1987] 2 Lloyd's Rep 647; affd [1988] 2 Lloyd's Rep 18, CA.

2 Limitation Act 1980 s 34 (1); and see LIMITATION OF ACTIONS. Arbitrations for these purposes include statutory arbitrations: see the Limitation Act 1980 s 34 (6). In applying the Act to a statutory arbitration a right to proceed to arbitration is to be treated in the same way as a cause of action would be treated if the proceedings were before a court: *Pegler v Railway Executive* [1948] AC 332, [1948] 1 All ER 559, HL.

3 Foreign Limitation Periods Act 1984 s 5.

4 Under the Limitation Act 1980 time begins to run when the complete cause of action has accrued. Under the Carriage of Goods by Sea Act 1971, for example, the period begins to run when the cargo was or ought to have been delivered.

5 An award gives rise to a new cause of action: see para 712 et seq post.

6 See para 646 ante.

7 Limitation Act 1980 s 34 (2), (7).

650. Commencement of the arbitration. For the purposes of statutory limitation, an arbitration is deemed to be commenced, and time ceases to run[1], when one party properly serves on the other a notice requiring the other to appoint an arbitrator or to agree to the appointment of an arbitrator, or, where the arbitration agreement[2] provides that the reference shall be to a person named or designated in the agreement, requiring the other to submit the dispute to the person so named or designated[3]. The nature of the dispute must be communicated to the other party[4]. Proper service may be achieved by[5]: (1) delivering the notice to the party to be served[6]; or (2) leaving the notice at the usual or last known place of abode in England and Wales of that party[7]; or (3) sending it by post in a registered letter or by recorded delivery service addressed to that party at his usual or last known place of abode in England and Wales[8]; or (4) serving it in any other manner stipulated in the arbitration agreement[9].

1 See the Limitation Act 1980 s 34.

2 In relation to a statutory arbitration, references to an arbitration agreement must be read as references to such of the provisions of the Act or of any order, scheme, rules, regulations or byelaws made thereunder as relate to arbitration: Limitation Act 1980 s 34 (6). As to the determination of the commencement of causes of arbitration arising under statute see *Pegler v Railway Executive* [1948] AC 332, [1948] 1 All ER 559, HL; *Layen v London Passenger Transport Board* [1944] 1 All ER 432 (claims for statutory compensation to officers).

3 Limitation Act 1980 s 34 (3). See *Nea Agrex SA v Baltic Shipping Co Ltd and Intershipping Charter Co, The Agios Lazaros* [1976] QB 933, [1976] 2 All ER 842, [1976] 2 Lloyd's Rep 47, CA; *Surrendra Overseas Ltd v Government of Sri Lanka* [1977] 2 All ER 481, [1977] 1 WLR 565, [1977] 1 Lloyd's Rep 653; *NV Stoomv Maats 'De Maas' v Nippon Yusen Kaisha, The Pendrecht* [1980] 2 Lloyd's Rep 56.

4 *Interbulk Ltd v Ponte dei Sospiri Shipping Co, The Standard Ardour* [1988] 2 Lloyd's Rep 159.

5 Under the Limitation Act 1980 s 34 (4). The four methods specified are not, however, exclusive: *NV Stoomv Maats 'De Maas' v Nippon Yusen Kaisha, The Pendrecht* [1980] 2 Lloyd's Rep 56 at 64; *Stylo Shoes Ltd v Prices Tailors Ltd* [1960] Ch 396, [1959] 3 All ER 901. But see *Nea Agrex SA v Baltic Shipping Co Ltd and Intershipping Charter Co, The Agios Lazaros* [1976] QB 933, [1976] 2 All ER 842, [1976] 2 Lloyd's Rep 47, CA. In *Peter Cremer GmbH & Co v Sugat Food Industries Ltd, The Rimon* [1981] 2 Lloyd's Rep 640, it was held that it was sufficient that the sellers sent a telex to the buyers requesting them to appoint an arbitrator. As to notice by telex see also *The Pendrecht* supra at 66.

6 Limitation Act 1980 s 34 (4) (a). As to delivery to agents see *Minerals and Metals Trading Corpn of India Ltd v Encounter Bay Shipping Co Ltd, The Samos Glory* [1986] 2 Lloyd's Rep 603. The 1980 Act s 34 (4) (a) does not apply to corporations: *NV Stoomv Maats 'De Maas' v Nippon Yusen Kaisha, The Pendrecht* [1980] 2 Lloyd's Rep 56 at 66.

7 Limitation Act 1980 s 34 (4) (b). As to the place of abode of corporations see COMPANIES.

8 Ibid s 34 (4) (c); Recorded Delivery Service Act 1962 s 1 (1). It is thought that, since the Limitation Act 1980 consolidated the Limitation Act 1939 (to which the provisions of the Recorded Delivery Service Act 1962 applied) without changing the law, the recorded delivery service may be used in the present context as an alternative to registered post notwithstanding that the 1980 Act s 34 (4) (c) does not mention recorded delivery, or that the 1962 Act does not apply to the 1980 Act (see the 1962 Act s 2). As to registered post and recorded delivery generally see POST OFFICE vol 36 para 716 et seq.

Where a notice is posted under the Limitation Act 1980 s 34 (4) (c), service is deemed to have been effected, unless the contrary is proved, at the time at which the letter would have been delivered in the ordinary course of post.

9 Ibid s 34 (4).

651. Extension of time in certain circumstances. Where the High Court orders that an award be set aside, or, after the commencement of an arbitration, orders that the arbitration agreement[1] shall cease to have effect[2] with respect to the dispute referred[3], the court may further order that the period between the commencement of the arbitration[4] and the date of the court order is to be excluded in computing the time prescribed by the limitation enactment for the commencement of proceedings, including arbitration, with respect to the dispute referred[5]. The relevant limitation enactment may also provide for the extension of time in certain circumstances[6].

1 See the Limitation Act 1980 s 34 (5).
2 Under the Arbitration Act 1950 ss 24, 25. See paras 633, 636, 647, 648 ante, 660 et seq post.
3 See paras 660, 692 post.
4 As to the commencement of the arbitration see para 650 ante.
5 Limitation Act 1980 s 34 (5).
6 See generally LIMITATION OF ACTIONS.

(2) LIMITATION BY CONTRACT

652. Types of contractual time-bar. Arbitration agreements may contain a clause[1] which requires a certain act[2] to be completed within a specified[3] period[4], and which provides that if that act is not done, either the claim[5] or the ability to commence an arbitration[6] will be barred[7].

1 Such clauses are sometimes known as 'Atlantic Shipping' clauses, after *Atlantic Shipping and Trading Co Ltd v L Dreyfus & Co* [1922] 2 AC 250, HL, in which it was held that a clause barring all claims unless a claim was made in writing and an arbitrator appointed within a specified period, was binding and did not oust the jurisdiction of the court. A common modern clause in this form is the 'Centrocon' clause, which provides: 'Any claim must be made in writing and claimant's arbitrator appointed within [nine] months of final discharge, and where this provision is not complied with the claim shall be deemed to be waived and absolutely barred.' A party in fundamental breach cannot rely on an exemption clause, and for this purpose Atlantic Shipping clauses are to be treated as exemption clauses: *Smeaton Hanscomb & Co Ltd v Sassoon I Setty, Son & Co* [1953] 2 All ER 1471 at 1473, [1953] 1 WLR 1468 at 1470, [1953] 2 Lloyd's Rep 580 at 583–584, although in that case there was no fundamental breach. See further para 648 ante.
2 The most common specified acts are the notification of a claim and the appointment of an arbitrator. As to when those acts are regarded as having been completed see para 653 post.
3 The date from which time may start to run may be fixed in any manner agreed by the parties, but common dates are (1) when a dispute arises, and (2) when an event, such as the discharge of a ship, takes place. As to (1), such clauses are in effect construed contra proferentem with regard to the scope of the disputes to which they relate (*Minister of Materials v Steel Bros & Co Ltd* [1952] 1 All ER 522, [1952] 1 Lloyd's Rep 87, CA; *Hardwick Game Farm v Suffolk Agricultural and Poultry Producers' Association Ltd* [1964] 2 Lloyd's Rep 227 at 273; affd in part on other matters [1966] 1 All ER 309, [1966] 1 WLR 287, [1966] 1 Lloyd's Rep 197, CA), and with regard to the events which can be considered to constitute disputes (*Monmouthshire County Council v Costelloe and Kemple Ltd* (1965) 63 LGR 429, CA). As to (2), such clauses will be inapplicable if the stipulated event never takes place (*Denny, Mott and Dickson Ltd v Lynn Shipping Co Ltd* [1963] 1 Lloyd's Rep 339). But the mere circumstance that the facts necessary to enable a party to make a claim could not have been known in time will not make such clauses inapplicable: *A/S Det Dansk-Franske Dampskibsselskab v Cie Financière D'Investissements Transatlantiques SA (Compafina), The Himmerland* [1965] 2 Lloyd's Rep 353 at 360.
4 Depending on the nature and circumstances of the contract, the specified period may be very short. See *Atlantic Shipping and Trading Co Ltd v L Dreyfus & Co* [1922] 2 AC 250, HL (three months);

Ayscough v Sheed, Thomson & Co (1924) 93 LJKB 94, 19 Ll L Rep 104, HL (three days); *Smeaton Hanscomb v Sassoon I Setty Son & Co* [1953] 2 All ER 1471, [1953] 1 WLR 1468, [1953] 2 Lloyd's Rep 580 (14 days); *W J Alan & Co Ltd v El Nasr Export and Import Co* [1971] 1 Lloyd's Rep 401 (7, 14 and 30 days). An unreasonably short period might be invalid under the Unfair Contract Terms Act 1977. See also *Isbirligi ve Ticeret AS v Uzunoglu* (1984) Times, 8 December (whether a party can rely on a limitation provision in an arbitration agreement depends upon the application of that provision in the context of the contract as a whole, having regard to the nature and circumstances of the alleged breach and taking into consideration the significance of the breach in the context of the contract as a whole).

5 'Claim-barring clauses', which bar the claim, operate in the same way as a statutory time-bar. If the act required by the clause is not done, the claimant cannot succeed on his substantive claim. He could still commence an arbitration, but the award would necessarily be against him. A High Court action would fail in the same way that a claim barred by statute would fail.

6 'Remedy-barring clauses' which bar the ability to commence an arbitration, do not have the effect of barring the substantive claim. The claimant may still pursue that claim through other avenues, such as the High Court, but may not commence an arbitration.

7 The effect of the particular clause is a matter of construction. Some clauses may be both claim-barring and remedy-barring. As to the difference between the two types of clauses see *Metalimpex Foreign Trade Corpn v Eugenie Maritime Co Ltd* [1962] 1 Lloyd's Rep 378 and *Pinnock Bros v Lewis and Peat Ltd* [1923] 1 KB 690. Examples of claim-barring clauses are the Centrocon clause, and the clauses in *Panchaud Frères SA v Etablissements General Grain Co* [1970] 1 Lloyd's Rep 53, CA; *Alma Shipping Corpn v Union of India, The Astraea* [1971] 2 Lloyd's Rep 494; *Ayscough v Sheed, Thomson & Co* (1924) 93 LJKB 94, 19 Ll L Rep 104; and *Smeaton Hanscomb v Sassoon I Setty Son & Co* [1953] 2 All ER 1471, [1953] 1 WLR 1468, [1953] 2 Lloyd's Rep 580. An example of a remedy-barring clause is that in *Hardwick Game Farm v Suffolk Agricultural and Poultry Producers' Association* [1964] 2 Lloyd's Rep 227 at 274; see also note 3 supra. As to whether rectification of the contract affects the application of contractual limitation clauses see *Metalimpex Foreign Trade Corpn v Eugenie Maritime Co Ltd* supra; and as to whether an out of time amendment of a timeous claim is permissible in the presence of such clauses see *Panchaud Frères SA v Etablissements General Grain Co* supra, following *A/S Rendal v Arcos Ltd* [1937] 3 All ER 577, 58 Ll L Rep 287, HL.

653. Completion of the specified act.

In order to amount to notice of a claim for these purposes, the claimant's notification must make it clear[1] that a claim is being made, not merely that the claimant is considering making a claim, and must be in sufficient detail[2] to allow the other party to know what is claimed against him and to prepare its response. The notice must actually be communicated to the other party, unless the contract provides for some other form of notice[3]. If the clause requires notice in writing, it must be given in writing[4]. An arbitrator is appointed for these purposes when the claimant has communicated to him his authority to act, he has accepted it and has so informed the claimant, and the other party has been informed that these things have happened[5].

1 *A/S Rendal v Arcos Ltd* [1937] 3 All ER 577 at 580, 58 Ll L Rep 287 at 293, HL.

2 A notice will be good if in the context of other correspondence adequate information had been supplied and it is clear to the recipient to what claim the notice refers: *Court Line Ltd v Aktiebolaget Gtaverken, The Halcyon the Great* [1984] 1 Lloyd's Rep 283. As to the extent of the information to be given see *A/S Rendal v Arcos Ltd* (1936) 54 Ll L Rep 309, CA; on appeal [1937] 3 All ER 577, 58 Ll L Rep 287, HL. As to whether a subsequent out of time claim is a 'new claim' or a claim within the arbitrators' jurisdiction in respect of the original dispute see *Mosvolds Rederi A/S v Food Corpn of India, The Arras and The Hoegh Rover* [1989] 1 Lloyd's Rep 131.

3 *A/S Rendal v Arcos Ltd* [1937] 3 All ER 577, 58 Ll L Rep 287, HL.

4 The requirement may be waived by the recipient: *Lickiss v Milestone Motor Policies at Lloyd's* [1966] 2 All ER 972, [1966] 1 WLR 1334.

5 *Tradax Export SA v Volkswagenwerk AG* [1970] 1 QB 537, [1970] 1 All ER 420, [1970] 1 Lloyd's Rep 62, CA; *Edm J M Mertens & Co PVBA v Veevoeder Import Export Vimex BV* [1979] 2 Lloyd's Rep 372; *Union of India v E B Aaby's Rederi A/S* [1975] AC 797, [1974] 2 All ER 874, sub nom *E B Aaby's Rederi*

A/S v Union of India, The Evje [1974] 2 Lloyd's Rep 57, HL; *Carras Shipping Co Ltd v Food Corpn of India, The Delian Leto and The Delian Spirit* [1978] 2 Lloyd's Rep 433; on appeal [1979] 2 Lloyd's Rep 179, CA.

654. Avoidance of contractual time-bars. The consequences of the expiry of a contractual limitation period before the completion of the specified act may however be avoided in the following circumstances: (1) if the court, pursuant to the Arbitration Act 1950[1], exercises its discretion[2] to extend the period[3] to avoid 'undue hardship'[4]; (2) if the arbitration clause confers a discretion on the arbitrator to extend the period and he exercises it[5]; (3) if the conduct of the other party precludes his relying on the time bar against the claimant[6].

1 See the Arbitration Act 1950 s 27, which provides that: 'Where the terms of an agreement to refer future disputes to arbitration provide that any claims to which the agreement applies shall be barred unless notice to appoint an arbitrator is given or an arbitrator is appointed or some other step to commence arbitration proceedings is taken within a time fixed by the agreement, and a dispute arises to which the agreement applies, the High Court, if it is of opinion that in the circumstances of the case undue hardship would otherwise be caused, and notwithstanding that the time so fixed has expired, may, on such terms, if any, as the justice of the case may require, but without prejudice to the provisions of any enactment limiting the time for the commencement of arbitration proceedings, extend the time for such period as it thinks proper'. The application may be made in chambers to a judge or master (RSC Ord 73 r 3 (1)), by originating summons or, if there are pending proceedings, by summons in those proceedings, supported in either case by affidavit. In Admiralty, applications are, in practice, made by motion. For an affidavit see 6 Court Forms (2nd Edn) (1989 Issue) 123–124, Form 44. The 1950 Act s 27 does not apply to statutory arbitrations: s 31.
2 The court may conclude that undue hardship exists, yet in the exercise of its discretion still refuse to grant an extension. The claimant must therefore take all reasonable steps to get his application for an extension before the court as soon as possible, and cannot deliberately delay: *First Steamship Co Ltd v C T S Commodity Transport Shipping Schiffahrtsgesellschaft mbH, The Ever Splendor* [1988] 1 Lloyd's Rep 245; *A/S Det Dansk-Franske Dampskibsselskab v Cie Financière D'Investissements Transatlantiques SA (Compafina), The Himmerland* [1965] 2 Lloyd's Rep 353 at 361; *Timmerman's Graan-en Maalhandel en Maalderij BV v Sachs* [1980] 1 Lloyd's Rep 194 at 209; *Richmond Shipping Ltd v Agro Co of Canada Ltd, The Simonburn (No 2)* [1973] 2 Lloyd's Rep 145 at 150. Although the power to grant an extension is discretionary, the Court of Appeal will overturn a decision made on an incorrect legal basis or if material factors were not taken into account or if immaterial factors were taken into account: *Liberian Shipping Corpn 'Pegasus' v A King & Sons Ltd* [1967] 2 QB 86 at 99, [1967] 1 All ER 934 at 938, [1967] 1 Lloyd's Rep 302 at 307, CA, per Lord Denning MR *Libra Shipping and Trading Corpn Ltd v Northern Sales Ltd, The Aspen Trader* [1981] 1 Lloyd's Rep 273 at 281–282, CA.
3 The Arbitration Act 1950 s 27 applies to clauses which are remedy-barring as well as to clauses which are claim-barring: *Consolidated Investment and Contracting Co v Saponaria Shipping Co Ltd, The Virgo* [1978] 3 All ER 988 at 992, 994, [1978] 1 WLR 986 at 990, 993, [1978] 2 Lloyd's Rep 167 at 169, 171, CA. It does not, however, apply when the giving of notice of a claim required by the arbitration clause operates other than as a step to commence arbitration: *Babanaft International Co SA v Avant Petroleum Inc, The Oltenia* [1982] 3 All ER 344, [1982] 1 WLR 871, [1982] 2 Lloyd's Rep 99, CA; as to what qualifies as a step to commence arbitration see *Tradax Export SA v Italcarbo Societa di Navigazione SpA, The Sandalion* [1983] 1 Lloyd's Rep 514 at 519; *Jedranska Slobodna Plovidba v Oleagine SA, The Luka Botic* [1984] 1 Lloyd's Rep 145; *Mariana Islands Steamship Corpn v Marimpex Mineraloel-Handelsgesellschaft mbH & Co KG, The Medusa* [1986] 2 Lloyd's Rep 328, CA; *Pittalis v Sherefettin* [1986] QB 868, [1986] 2 All ER 227, CA. The section cannot be used to defeat a statutory time limit, unless the statutory time limit is one which is applicable only because the parties agreed that it should be: *Nea Agrex SA v Baltic Shipping Co Ltd and Intershipping Charter Co, The Agios Lazaros* [1976] QB 933, [1976] 2 All ER 842, [1976] 2 Lloyd's Rep 47, CA; but cf *Kenya Railways v Antares Co Pte Ltd, The Antares* [1987] 1 Lloyd's Rep 424, CA. A claimant can have resort to the Arbitration Act 1950 s 27 even if the arbitration agreement purports to confer an absolute discretion to extend time on the arbitrator and he has refused to do so: *Comdel Commodities Ltd v Siporex Trade SA* [1990] 1 All ER 216, sub nom *Comdel Commodities Ltd v Siporex Trade SA (No 2)* [1989] 2 Lloyd's Rep 13, CA; affd sub nom *Comdel Commodities Ltd v Siporex Trade SA (No 2)* [1991] 1 AC 148, [1990] 2 Lloyd's Rep 207, sub nom *Comdel Commodities Ltd v Siporex Trade SA* [1990] 2 All ER 552, HL. The word 'claims' in the 1950 Act s 27 is not to be construed as meaning 'causes of action', but should

be given a wide and liberal interpretation and it will thus extend to any claim to have determined by arbitration a matter in issue between the parties, including for example a claim for an arbitration to assess the proper amount of a salvage award: *Sioux Inc v China Salvage Co, Kwangchow Branch* [1980] 3 All ER 154, [1980] 1 WLR 996, CA.

4 If there is no reasonable claim, then there will be no hardship. The court will not, however, look beyond the prima facie position into the substance of the claim: *The Cunard Carrier, Eleranta and Martha* [1977] 2 Lloyd's Rep 261; *Mediterranea Raffineria Siciliana Petroli SpA v Kuwait Oil Tanker Co SAK, The Al Faiha* [1981] 2 Lloyd's Rep 99 at 105; *Salenrederierna SA v Blue Star Line Ltd, The New York Star* [1982] 1 Lloyd's Rep 78. Undue hardship does not involve any concept of law: *Richmond Shipping Ltd v Agro Co of Canada Ltd, The Simonburn (No 2)* [1973] 2 Lloyd's Rep 145 at 150. As to what factors influence the court in deciding whether 'undue' hardship would be caused if an extension were refused see *Liberian Shipping Corpn 'Pegasus' v A King & Sons* [1967] 2 QB 86, [1967] 1 All ER 934, [1967] 1 Lloyd's Rep 302, CA (factors indicating that an extension should be given include excusable mistake by the claimant, disproportionate loss likely to be suffered by the claimant in comparison to the degree of its fault in allowing the claim to become time-barred and the extent to which the claimant was late in carrying out the necessary steps, claimant's mistake shared by or contributed to by the other party, parties negotiating during period, the fact that another claim which is not time-barred depends on the same facts as the claim that is); *Moscow v/o Exportkhleb v Helmville Ltd, The Jocelyne* [1977] 2 Lloyd's Rep 121 (factors indicating that an extension should not be given include that the other party would face difficulties in amassing evidence or in claiming an indemnity from a third party); *Graham H Davies (UK) Ltd v Marc Rich & Co Ltd* [1985] 2 Lloyd's Rep 423 at 426, CA (an extension of time always prejudices the other party in that it loses the benefit of an accrued limitation defence, but unless the other party can point to an additional detriment as a result of the extension, for example by reason of the delay in commencing the arbitration, there is no reason weighing against giving an extension); *Libra Shipping and Trading Corpn Ltd v Northern Sales Ltd, The Aspen Trader* [1981] 1 Lloyd's Rep 273, CA (general considerations); *Etablissements Soules & Cie v International Trade Development Co Ltd* [1979] 2 Lloyd's Rep 122 at 138 (that the possibility of a claim was not apparent until after expiry of period is a factor which indicates that an extension should be given); *Tradax Internacional SA v Cerrahogullari TAS, The M Eregli* [1981] 3 All ER 344, [1981] 2 Lloyd's Rep 169 (that the claim is admitted or is almost certain to succeed is a factor which indicates that an extension should be given); *The Cunard Carrier, Eleranta and Martha* supra (that the claimant can pursue a claim against another party is a factor indicating that an extension should not be given); *European Grain and Shipping Ltd v Dansk Landbrugs Grovvareslskab* [1986] 1 Lloyd's Rep 163 (that the arbitrator has rejected an invitation to exercise a discretion to extend conferred on him by the arbitration agreement is a factor indicating that an extension should not be given by the court, but the existence of the discretion in the arbitrator, and even his refusal to extend, does not mean that the court cannot give an extension if it feels that it is appropriate to do so; see also *European Grain and Shipping Ltd v R & H Hall plc* [1990] 2 Lloyd's Rep 139); *Tote Bookmakers Ltd v Development and Property Holding Co Ltd* [1985] Ch 261, [1985] 2 All ER 555 ('hardship' is caused when a justiciable claim is barred: 'undue hardship' is caused when such hardship is not warranted by the circumstances). See also *The Baiona* (1991) Financial Times, 1 March; *Navigazione Alta Italia SpA v Concordia Maritime Chartering, The Stena Pacifica* [1990] 2 Lloyd's Rep 234; *Mitsubishi Corpn v Castletown Navigation Ltd, The Castle Alpha* [1989] 2 Lloyd's Rep 383; *Garrick Shipping Co v Euro-Frachtkontor GmbH, The World Agamemnon* [1989] 2 Lloyd's Rep 316; *Sparta Navigation v Transocean America Inc, The Stephanos* [1989] 1 Lloyd's Rep 506; *Transpetrol Ltd v Ekali Shipping, The Aghia Marina* [1989] 1 Lloyd's Rep 62; *Irish Agricultural Wholesale Society Ltd v Partenreederei: M S Eurotrader, The Eurotrader* [1987] 1 Lloyd's Rep 418, CA; *Casillo Grani v Napier Shipping Co, The World Ares* [1984] 2 Lloyd's Rep 481; *Federal Commerce and Navigation Ltd v Xcan Grain (Europe) Ltd, The Ratna Vandana* [1982] 1 Lloyd's Rep 499; *The Al Faiha* supra; *The Aspen Trader* supra; *H Kruidenier (London) Ltd v Egyptian Navigation Co, The El Amria (No 2)* [1980] 2 Lloyd's Rep 166; *Cast Shipping Ltd v Tradax Export SA, The Hellas in Eternity* [1979] 2 Lloyd's Rep 280, CA; *Sanko SS Co Ltd v Tradax Export SA* [1979] 2 Lloyd's Rep 273, CA; *Atlantic Shipping Co SA v Tradax Internacional SA, The Bratislava* [1977] 2 Lloyd's Rep 269; *Intermare Transport GmbH v Naves Transoceanicas Armadora SA, The Aristokratis* [1976] 1 Lloyd's Rep 552; *International Tank and Pipe SAK v Kuwait Aviation Fuelling Co KSC* [1975] QB 224, [1975] 1 All ER 242, [1975] 1 Lloyd's Rep 8.

5 The clause must expressly confer the discretion on the arbitrator: *Amalgamated Metal Corpn v Khoon Seng Co Ltd* [1977] 2 Lloyd's Rep 310. For examples of clauses conferring such a discretion see *Panchaud Frères SA v Etablissements General Grain Co* [1969] 2 Lloyd's Rep 109; on appeal [1970] 1 Lloyd's Rep 53, CA; *Provimi Hellas AE v Warinco AG* [1978] 1 Lloyd's Rep 373, CA; *Bunge SA v Kruse* [1979] 1 Lloyd's Rep 279; on appeal [1980] 2 Lloyd's Rep 142, CA; *Edm J M Mertens & Co PVBA v Veevoeder Import Export Vimex BV* [1979] 2 Lloyd's Rep 372; and *Timmerman's Graan-en*

Maalhandel en Maalderij BV v Sachs [1980] 1 Lloyd's Rep 194. Whether or not the discretion exists is ultimately a matter for the court: *Cie Europeene de Cereals SA v Tradax Export SA* [1986] 2 Lloyd's Rep 301. The fact that an application to the court under the Arbitration Act 1950 s 27 has been made and has failed does not preclude reliance on the arbitrator's discretion: *The Cunard Carrier, Eleranta and Martha* [1977] 2 Lloyd's Rep 261. The way in which the arbitrator exercises his discretion is a matter for him, and the court will only review his exercise of the discretion if he has acted mala fide or has taken into account obviously irrelevant considerations: *Cook Industries v BV Handelmaatschappij Jean Delvaux* [1985] 1 Lloyd's Rep 120, CA.

6 The other party's conduct may amount to a waiver of his right to rely on the time bar, or may give rise to an estoppel. See generally *Nippon Yusen Kaisha v Pacifica Navegacion, The Ion* [1980] 2 Lloyd's Rep 245; *Alma Shipping Corpn v Union of India, The Astraea* [1971] 2 Lloyd's Rep 494 at 502.

6. APPOINTMENT AND COMPOSITION OF THE TRIBUNAL

(1) APPOINTMENT UNDER ARBITRATION AGREEMENT

655. Appointment of tribunal under arbitration agreement. It is open to the parties to an arbitration agreement to agree to whatever form of tribunal, and to appoint[1] whomever they want, to arbitrate on any dispute. The parties may agree[2] to a tribunal consisting of a single arbitrator[3], or two arbitrators and an umpire in reserve, or three arbitrators, or a larger number of persons such as the committee of a trade association[4]. Where the parties have agreed that the arbitration shall be before a person or persons having special qualifications (for example, by being members of a trade association), the award of non-qualified persons will be void[5] unless the party impeaching the award is estopped from disputing their lack of qualifications[6]. Parties may refer disputes to a foreign court[7], but reference to a foreign court, rather than a foreign arbitral tribunal, is not a reference to arbitration[8]. It is generally speaking the parties' own affair if they choose an incompetent or unfit person as arbitrator, unless he does not have the qualifications required by the agreement[9], and under certain circumstances unless he is or may be incapable of impartiality[10].

The arbitration agreement itself may name the arbitrator or arbitrators, or it may without naming them direct how they are to be selected, or it may simply provide for a reference to arbitration without either specifying the mode of reference, or naming the arbitrators or directing how they are to be selected. A person who is appointed arbitrator or umpire does not by acceptance of the office become bound to make an award[11], but he may bind himself to do so[12].

1 For forms of appointment see 3 Forms & Precedents (5th Edn) 117–122, Forms 2–12. As to the court's power to extend the time for appointment see paras 646, 647 ante.

2 As to the terms implied in an arbitration agreement see para 659 post and para 601 et seq ante.

3 Where an arbitration agreement provides that reference shall be to an official referee or a circuit judge discharging the functions of an official referee, any such official referee or circuit judge to whom application is made may, if in all the circumstances he thinks fit and if the Lord Chief Justice has given him permission, hear and determine the matters agreed to be referred: Arbitration Act 1950 s 11 (substituted by the Courts and Legal Services Act 1990 s 99); Supreme Court Act 1981 s 68 (1) (a), (7) (amended by the Administration of Justice Act 1982 s 59); RSC Ord 36 rr 5 (2), (3), 7. An official referee or circuit judge so appointed has all the powers of an arbitrator: *Northern Regional Health Authority v Derek Crouch Construction Co Ltd* [1984] QB 644, [1984] 2 All ER 175, CA. By the Administration of Justice Act 1970 s 4 (1), and subject to the Lord Chief Justice's permission being

given under s 4 (2) (amended by the Courts Act 1971 s 56, Sch 8), a judge of the Commercial Court constituted under the Supreme Court Act 1981 s 6 may, if in all the circumstances he thinks fit, accept appointment as a sole arbitrator, or as umpire, by or by virtue of an arbitration agreement within the meaning of the 1950 Act. As to the way in which provisions of the 1950 Act are modified for such 'judge-arbitrators' see the Administration of Justice Act 1970 s 4 (4), (5), Sch 3, and the Arbitration Act 1979 s 5 (3).

4 *Re Keighley, Maxsted & Co and Durant & Co* [1893] 1 QB 405, CA, where the committee was an appeal tribunal.
5 *Jungheim, Hopkins & Co v Foukelmann* [1909] 2 KB 948; *Rahcassi Shipping Co SA v Blue Star Line Ltd* [1969] 1 QB 173, [1967] 3 All ER 301 (agreement stipulated umpire to be a commercial man not a lawyer; award of lawyer umpire void); *Pando Compania Naviera SA v Filmo SAS* [1975] QB 742, [1975] 2 All ER 515, [1975] 1 Lloyd's Rep 560 (full-time maritime arbitrator and non-executive director of shipping companies held to be a commercial man).
6 *Oakland Metal Co Ltd v D Benaim & Co Ltd* [1953] 2 QB 261, [1953] 2 All ER 650 (party putting forward arbitrator cannot contend after the award that he is not qualified).
7 *Law v Garrett* (1878) 8 ChD 26, CA; *Austrian Lloyd SS Co v Gresham Life Assurance Society Ltd* [1903] 1 KB 249, CA; *Kirchner & Co v Gruban* [1909] 1 Ch 413; *The Cap Blanco* [1913] P 130.
8 *Racecourse Betting Control Board v Secretary for Air* [1944] Ch 114 at 125–126, [1944] 1 All ER 60 at 65, CA; *The Fehmarn* [1958] 1 All ER 333, [1958] 1 WLR 159, CA. But see para 617 ante.
9 *Re Shaw and Sims* (1851) 17 LTOS 160.
10 A party to an arbitration agreement for future differences can apply for an arbitrator's authority to be revoked notwithstanding the party's knowledge of facts which indicated that the arbitrator was or might be incapable of impartiality: Arbitration Act 1950 s 24; see para 661 et seq post. Where the arbitrator is appointed by a party in ignorance of the fact that the arbitrator is disqualified from acting on the ground of interest and the award is set aside on that ground, the party who objected to the award is not entitled to recover the costs incurred in the abortive arbitration: *Sellar v Highland Rly Co* 1919 SC (HL) 19.
11 *Lewin v Holbrook* (1843) 11 M & W 110; *Crawshay v Collins* (1818) 1 Swan 40.
12 *Pappa v Rose* (1872) LR 7 CP 525 at 527.

656. Reference to a single arbitrator. An arbitration agreement will require reference to a single arbitrator, either if it expressly so provides or if it is silent as to the composition of the tribunal[1]. If the arbitration agreement is silent as to the method of appointment of the single arbitrator, both parties must reach agreement[2], and obtain the consent of the person[3] so chosen. The arbitration agreement may require a third party to appoint the single arbitrator[4]. Where on a reference to two arbitrators, one to be nominated by each party, one party fails to appoint, the other party may in certain circumstances have the dispute determined by his nominee as a single arbitrator[5].

1 Arbitration Act 1950 s 6: 'Unless a contrary intention is expressed therein, every arbitration agreement shall, if no other mode of reference is provided, be deemed to include a provision that the reference shall be to a single arbitrator'. As to the expression of a contrary intention see *Scrimaglio v Thornett and Fehr* (1924) 131 LT 174, CA; *Bright & Bros v Gibson & Co* (1916) 32 TLR 533; *Naumann v Edward Nathaniel & Co Ltd* (1930) 36 Ll L Rep 268; *Palmer & Co Ltd v Pilot Trading Co Ltd* (1929) 45 TLR 214; *Re Eyre and Leicester Corpn* [1892] 1 QB 136, CA; *Smeaton Hanscomb & Co Ltd v Sassoon I Setty Son & Co (No 2)* [1953] 2 All ER 1588, [1953] 1 WLR 1481, [1953] 2 Lloyd's Rep 580.
2 In practice, one party provides the other with a name or a list of names, and if the other agrees to one of the names, both parties will invite that person to act as arbitrator. If the parties are unable to agree, it will be necessary to make an application to the court: see para 660 post .
3 By the Administration of Justice Act 1970 s 4, the parties may agree to appoint a judge of the Commercial Court as a sole arbitrator; see para 655 note 3 ante.
4 Such as the president of a particular professional association. In *Davies, Middleton and Davies v Cardiff Corpn* (1964) 62 LGR 134, CA, it was held that where an arbitration agreement for future differences left blank the space where a single arbitrator's name was to be entered, and provided 'in the event of his death or unwillingness or inability to act', that the President of the Royal Institute of British Architects should nominate an arbitrator, the President could do so notwithstanding the parties' failure to enter a name in the space. If the third party fails to appoint a single arbitrator, it will be

necessary to make an application to the court: see para 660 post. If the third party chooses a single arbitrator but that arbitrator refuses to act, the claimant should invite the third party to choose another: *Re Wilson & Son and Eastern Counties Navigation and Transport Co* [1892] 1 QB 81 at 84.
5 See para 657 post.

657. Reference to two arbitrators.

Where an arbitration agreement provides for the appointment of two arbitrators, one by each of the parties[1], three separate conditions must be fulfilled before any appointment is valid: (1) the arbitrator must be notified of the appointment; (2) he must consent to act; and (3) his name and the fact of his appointment must be communicated to the other party[2]. If the agreement requires an arbitrator to be appointed within a specified time, it is necessary for all three conditions to be fulfilled within the time limited[3], or within the time extended by the court[4] or by agreement[5].

Where the reference is to two arbitrators, they may appoint an umpire at any time after they themselves are appointed, and must do so forthwith if they cannot agree[6]. Where the arbitration agreement provides for such a reference it is deemed that it also includes an implied provision enabling the umpire to enter upon the reference instead of the arbitrators in the event of their disagreeing[7].

Where an arbitration agreement provides that the reference shall be to two arbitrators, one to be appointed by each party, then, unless a contrary intention is expressed therein[8], if either of the arbitrators so appointed refuses to act[9], or is incapable of acting, or dies, the party who appointed him may appoint a new arbitrator in his place[10]. Further, if on such a reference one party fails to appoint an arbitrator, either originally or by way of substitution as provided above, for seven clear days after the other party, having appointed his arbitrator, has served the party making default with notice to make the appointment[11], then the party who has appointed the arbitrator may appoint that arbitrator[12] to act as sole arbitrator in the reference[13], unless the agreement provides that something else should happen[14]. If the party does so, the award of the arbitrator so appointed is binding on both parties as if he had been appointed by consent[15]. The High Court or a judge thereof[16] may, however, set aside an appointment made under these provisions[17], save in the case of a judge-arbitrator[18].

1 The agreement may provide that both arbitrators are to be appointed by a third party. If the third party fails to appoint, it will be necessary to make an application to the court: see para 660 post. If the third party chooses arbitrators but one or both of them refuse to act, the claimant should invite the third party to choose another or others: *Re Wilson & Son and Eastern Counties Navigation and Transport Co* [1892] 1 QB 81. As to where both parties appoint both arbitrators by agreement see *Itex Shipping Pte Ltd v China Ocean Shipping Co, The Jing Hong Hai* [1989] 2 Lloyd's Rep 522.
2 *Tew v Harris* (1847) 11 QB 7; *Thomas v Fredericks* (1847) 10 QB 775; *Tradax SA v Volkswagenwerk AG* [1969] 2 QB 599, [1969] 2 All ER 144, [1969] 1 Lloyd's Rep 494; affd [1970] 1 QB 537, [1970] 1 All ER 420, [1970] 1 Lloyd's Rep 62, CA. As to the circumstances under which a party will be estopped from denying that an arbitrator has been validly appointed see *Legumbres S A C I F I A v Central de Cooperativas de Productores do Rio Grande do Sul Ltda* [1986] 1 Lloyd's Rep 401 at 403, CA. As to waiver of the right to appoint an arbitrator, and when the right revives, see *World Pride Shipping v Dauchi Chuo Kisen Kaisha, The Golden Anne* [1984] 2 Lloyd's Rep 489.
3 *Tradax SA v Volkswagenwerk AG* [1969] 2 QB 599, [1969] 2 All ER 144, [1969] 1 Lloyd's Rep 494; affd [1970] 1 QB 537, [1970] 1 All ER 420, [1970] 1 Lloyd's Rep 62, CA; *European Grain and Shipping Ltd v Dansk Landbrugs Grovvareslskab* [1986] 1 Lloyd's Rep 163.
4 See the Arbitration Act 1950 s 27: para 654 ante.
5 The term of the arbitrators' appointment having expired whilst they were in disagreement, the umpire, in the presence of the parties and of the arbitrators, dictated the document appointing him umpire pursuant to a pre-executed submission. It was held that the arbitrators were reappointed and the umpire's appointment was valid: *Albeck v A B Y-Cecil Manufacturing Co Pty Ltd* [1965] VR 342 (Vict FC).

6 Arbitration Act 1950 s 8 (1) (amended by the Arbitration Act 1979 s 6 (1)); see para 659 post. The arbitrators must act carefully and reasonably in choosing a sensible person to act as umpire: *Pescod v Pescod* (1887) 58 LT 76. If they do not appoint an umpire the court may exercise its powers of appointment under the Arbitration Act 1950 s 10 (1) (c) (now amended by the Arbitration Act 1979 s 6): *Iossifoglu v Coumantaros* [1941] 1 KB 396, CA: see para 660 post.

7 See para 659 post

8 As to the expression of a contrary intention see para 656 note 1 ante.

9 The refusal to act must be an actual refusal to act as arbitrator and not merely a refusal to act in a particular manner: *Burkett Sharp & Co v Eastcheap Dried Fruit Co and Perera* [1962] 1 Lloyd's Rep 267 at 276, CA.

10 Arbitration Act 1950 s 7 (a). The section only applies where the reference is to a tribunal of two arbitrators, one to be appointed by each party: *Marinos and Frangos Ltd v Dulien Steel Products Inc of Washington* [1961] 2 Lloyd's Rep 192. The arbitration agreement may provide for such a reference either expressly or impliedly by custom: *Laertis Shipping Corpn v Exportadora Espanola de Cementos Portland SA, The Laertis* [1982] 1 Lloyd's Rep 613. An agreement which provides that a majority decision of two out of three arbitrators is binding is not an agreement providing for such a reference: *Marinos and Frangos Ltd v Dulien Steel Products Inc of Washington* supra (which applied to the position before the substitution of the Arbitration Act 1950 s 9 by the Arbitration Act 1979 s 6 (2): see para 658 post).

11 See 3 Forms & Precedents (5th Edn) 148–149, Forms 56, 57. As to notices to appoint see *Nea Agrex SA v Baltic Shipping Co Ltd and Intershipping Charter Co, The Agios Lazaros* [1976] QB 933, [1976] 2 All ER 842, [1976] 2 Lloyd's Rep 47, CA; and *Peter Cremer GmbH & Co v Sugat Food Industries Ltd, The Rimon* [1981] 2 Lloyd's Rep 640.

12 The appointment cannot be made before default is made. Thus where a party appointed his arbitrator and served a notice on the other party requiring him to name his arbitrator within seven days, and concluded 'failing which the said dispute and differences will stand referred to the said RGW alone as sole arbitrator', it was held that this was not a valid exercise of the right to appoint: *Drummond v Hamer* [1942] 1 KB 352, [1942] 1 All ER 398. The statutory timetable must be strictly adhered to: *Rubin v W Smith & Co (Grimsby) Ltd* (1939) 64 Ll L Rep 7; *Ministry of Food, Government of Bangladesh v Bengal Liner Ltd, The Bengal Pride* [1986] 1 Lloyd's Rep 167; *Kyril Mischeff v British Doughnut Co* [1954] 1 Lloyd's Rep 237.

13 Arbitration Act 1950 s 7 (b). The section only applies where the reference is to a tribunal of two arbitrators, one to be appointed by each party: *Marinos and Frangos v Dulien Steel Products* [1961] 2 Lloyd's Rep 192.

14 The agreement may make provision for what happens if a party fails to appoint an arbitrator. If it does the agreed consequences take place rather than those contained in the statute: *Vigers Bros Ltd v Montague L Meyer Ltd* (1938) 62 Ll L Rep 35 at 39.

15 Arbitration Act 1950 s 7 (b).

16 This includes a master: RSC Ord 73 r 3 (1).

17 Arbitration Act 1950 s 7 proviso. As to when the discretion should be exercised see *Burkett Sharp and Co v Eastcheap Dried Fruit Co and Perera* [1962] 1 Lloyd's Rep 267, CA.

18 Administration of Justice Act 1970 s 4 (4), Sch 3 para 3. The statutory provision is plain enough but, it seems, it is otiose, for the Arbitration Act 1950 s 7 deals exclusively with references to two arbitrators, whilst the Administration of Justice Act 1970 s 4 (1) empowers a judge-arbitrator to accept appointment only as sole arbitrator or umpire. Whilst a reference to two arbitrators may result in a hearing by only one, a judge-arbitrator cannot be expected to foresee this when considering whether or not he is free to accept an appointment.

658. Reference to three arbitrators. Unless the contrary intention is expressed in the arbitration agreement, in any case where there is a reference to three arbitrators, however they are to be appointed[1], the award of any two of them is binding[2]. Unless the arbitration agreement provides to the contrary, where there is a reference to three arbitrators, the tribunal must be fully constituted by the appointment of the third arbitrator before any valid award can be made[3].

1 It is no longer the case that, where an arbitration agreement provides that the reference shall be to three arbitrators, one to be appointed by each party and the third by the two so appointed, the agreement has effect as if it provided instead for the appointment of an umpire by the two arbitrators appointed by the parties. The position was changed by the substitution of the Arbitration Act 1950

s 9 by the Arbitration Act 1979 s 6 (2). For the court's power to fill a vacancy where the reference is to three arbitrators, see s 10 (1) (d), (3)–(3D) (substituted by the Courts and Legal Services Act 1990 s 101); and para 660 post.

2 Arbitration Act 1950 s 9 (as substituted: see note 1 supra); *European Grain and Shipping Ltd v Johnston* [1983] QB 520, [1982] 3 All ER 989, [1982] 2 Lloyd's Rep 550, CA.

3 *Poliakoff v Brown Products Ltd* (1921) 8 Ll L Rep 501; cf *British Metal Corpn Ltd v Ludlow Bros (1913) Ltd* [1938] 1 All ER 135 (where the arbitration agreement did provide to the contrary).

659. Appointment of umpire under arbitration agreement. Umpires are rarely appointed under arbitration agreements other than ones which provide for reference to two arbitrators[1]. Where the reference is to two arbitrators, the arbitrators may at any time after their own appointment appoint an umpire[2], unless a contrary intention is expressed[3] in the arbitration agreement. They must do so forthwith if they cannot agree[4]. Every arbitration agreement is deemed to include a provision, where such a provision is applicable to the reference and unless a contrary intention is expressed[5] in the arbitration agreement, that if the arbitrators have delivered to any party to the arbitration agreement, or to the umpire, a written notice stating that they cannot agree[6], the umpire may forthwith enter on the reference[7] in lieu of the arbitrators[8].

The appointment of an umpire by the arbitrators is a judicial act; they must therefore exercise the power together[9]. They owe a duty to the parties to select a fit and proper person as umpire; they must not, therefore, leave the selection to chance[10] but it is possible that, as between several persons whom they both consider fit and proper persons to discharge the duty of umpire, arbitrators may be able to select by lot which person they will appoint[11].

At any time after the appointment of an umpire, however appointed, the High Court[12] may, on the application[13] of any party to the reference and notwithstanding anything to the contrary in the arbitration agreement, order that the umpire shall enter upon the reference in lieu of the arbitrators and as if he were sole arbitrator[14]. This power does not apply to a judge-umpire; but a judge-umpire may, on the application of any party to the reference and notwithstanding anything to the contrary in the arbitration agreement, enter on the reference in lieu of the arbitrators and as if he were the sole arbitrator[15].

1 An umpire has been defined as a person appointed to settle differences arising between two or more arbitrators: *Re Eyre and Leicester Corpn* [1892] 1 QB 136 at 139–140. A committee can act as an umpire: *Re Keighley, Maxsted & Co and Durant & Co* [1893] 1 QB 405 at 408.

2 Arbitration Act 1950 s 8 (1) (amended by the Arbitration Act 1979 s 6 (1)).

3 As to the expression of a contrary intention see para 656 note 1 ante. As to express requirements in the arbitration agreement that an umpire be appointed forthwith and not merely upon disagreement, and the effect of failure to so appoint, see *Royal Commission on Sugar Supply v Trading Society Kwik Hoo Tong* (1922) 11 Ll L Rep 163; *Tarmarea SRL v Rederiaktiebolaget Sally, The Dalny* [1979] 2 All ER 989, [1979] 1 WLR 1320, [1979] 2 Lloyd's Rep 439.

4 Arbitration Act 1950 s 8 (1) (as amended: see note 2 supra). Whether it is desirable to appoint an umpire before disagreement depends upon all the circumstances of the arbitration and the likelihood of the arbitrators being able to reach an agreed award. See *The Myron, Myron (Owners) v Tradax Export SA Panama City RP* [1970] 1 QB 527 at 533, [1969] 2 All ER 1263 at 1265, [1969] 1 Lloyd's Rep 411 at 415.

5 As to the expression of a contrary intention see para 656 note 1 ante.

6 The disagreement may be as to either procedural or substantive matters: *Cudliff v Walters* (1839) 2 Mood & R 232 (where the disagreement concerned the production of evidence); *Iossifoglu v Coumantaros* supra (where two arbitrators failed to agree on the place and time of meetings). The disagreement may occur during the interlocutory stages of the reference: *Iossifoglu v Coumantaros* supra. The disagreement may relate to one or more of a number of issues which arise: *Winteringham v Robertson* (1858) 27 LJ Ex 301 (where the arbitrators held different opinions at the conclusion of the

evidence); *Sinclair v Fraser* (1884) 11 R 1139; *Lang v Brown* (1855) 25 LTOS 297; *Wicks v Cox* (1847) 11 Jur 542 (where the disagreement was solely as to costs); *Cerrito v North Eastern Timber Importers Ltd* [1952] 1 Lloyd's Rep 330; see also *Smailes v Wright* (1815) 3 M & S 559 (where the disagreement was a refusal by the arbitrators to proceed with the arbitration).

7 As to the court's power to order the umpire to enter upon the reference see the Arbitration Act 1950 s 8 (3); and notes 12–15 infra.

8 Ibid s 8 (2).

9 *Re Hopper* (1867) LR 2 QB 367 at 376; *Re Lord and Lord* (1855) 5 E & B 404. However, the mere signing of the appointment is not a judicial act, and the arbitrators need not sign it together: *Re Hopper* supra; cf *European Grain and Shipping Ltd v Johnston* [1983] QB 520, [1982] 3 All ER 989, [1982] 2 Lloyd's Rep 550, CA (in which it was held per curiam that arbitrators need not meet to sign the award, and *Re Lord and Lord* supra was not followed). For forms see 3 Forms & Precedents (5th Edn) 151, Forms 60, 61. If they do not meet to appoint the umpire, the court may exercise its powers of appointment under the Arbitration Act 1950 s 10 (1) (c) (amended by the Arbitration Act 1979 s 6 (3)): *Iossifoglu v Coumantaros* [1941] 1 KB 396, CA; see para 660 post.

10 *Pescod v Pescod* (1887) 58 LT 76; *Re Greenwood and Titterington* (1839) 9 Ad & El 699 (parties not informed that choice was by Act; no acquiescence by parties).

11 *Neale v Ledger* (1812) 16 East 51. But cf *European and American Steam Shipping Co Ltd v Crosskey* (1860) 8 CBNS 397, and *Re Cassell* (1829) 9 B & C 624.

12 This includes a judge in chambers or a master: RSC Ord 73 r 3 (1). In Admiralty, applications are, in practice, made by motion.

13 In the Queen's Bench Division the application is usually made to a master by originating summons supported by affidavit. For forms see 6 Court Forms (2nd Edn) (1989 Issue) 109–111, Forms 23–25.

14 Arbitration Act 1950 s 8 (3).

15 Administration of Justice Act 1970 s 4 (4), Sch 3 para 4. The application is made to the judge-umpire himself.

(2) APPOINTMENT BY HIGH COURT

660. Appointment of arbitrator or umpire by High Court. The court has no inherent jurisdiction to appoint an arbitrator or umpire or to compel any party to the agreement or reference to do so[1]. In the following cases the High Court[2] has a limited statutory jurisdiction to appoint either arbitrators or an umpire:

(1) where an arbitration agreement provides, or is deemed[3] to provide, that the reference should be to a single arbitrator, and all the parties do not, after differences have arisen, concur in the appointment of an arbitrator[4];

(2) if an appointed arbitrator refuses to act, or is incapable of acting[5], or dies, and the arbitration agreement does not show that it was intended that the vacancy should not be filled, and the parties do not fill the vacancy themselves[6];

(3) where the parties or two arbitrators are required or are at liberty to appoint an umpire or third arbitrator and do not appoint him[7];

(4) where an appointed umpire or third arbitrator refuses to act, or is incapable of acting[8], or dies, and the arbitration agreement does not show that it was intended that the vacancy should not be filled, and the parties or arbitrators do not fill the vacancy themselves[9];

(5) where an arbitration agreement provides for the appointment of an arbitrator or an umpire by a person who is neither one of the parties nor an existing arbitrator (whether the provision applies directly or in default of agreement by the parties or otherwise) and that person refuses to make the appointment or does not make it within the time specified in the agreement, or if no time is specified, within a reasonable time[10];

(6) where an arbitration agreement provides for a reference to three arbitrators, one to be appointed by each party and the third to be appointed by the two appointed by the parties or in some other manner specified in the agreement, and one of the parties ('the party in default') refuses to appoint an arbitrator or does not do so within the time specified in the agreement, or if no time is specified, within a reasonable time[11].

In these cases any party may serve the other parties or the arbitrators, as the case may be, with written notice[12] to appoint, or concur in appointing[13], an arbitrator, umpire or third arbitrator; and if the appointment is not made within seven clear days[14] after service of the notice, the High Court or a judge thereof may, on application[15] by the party[16] who gave the notice, appoint an arbitrator, umpire or third arbitrator[17], who will then have the like powers to act in the reference and make an award as if he had been appointed by consent of all parties[18].

In addition to the cases mentioned above, there are two other cases in which the High Court possesses powers of appointment. These are as follows:

(7) On the application of a party to the arbitration agreement, the High Court may appoint a person or persons to act as arbitrator or arbitrators or umpire in place of an arbitrator (not being a sole arbitrator), or two or more arbitrators (not being all the arbitrators), or an umpire who has not entered on the reference, who has or have been removed by the High Court[19]. In the case of a judge-umpire[20] who has been removed by the Court of Appeal, the application for an order appointing a replacement must be made to the Court of Appeal[21].

(8) Where the authority of an arbitrator or arbitrators or umpire is revoked by leave of the High Court[22], or a sole arbitrator or all the arbitrators or an umpire who has entered on the reference is or are removed by the High Court[23], the High Court may, on the application of a party to the arbitration agreement, either appoint a person to act as sole arbitrator in place of the person or persons removed[24], or order that the arbitration agreement cease to have effect with respect to the dispute referred[25]. In the case of a sole judge-arbitrator or a judge-umpire whose authority has been revoked by the Court of Appeal, the application for an order appointing a sole arbitrator or for an order that the arbitration agreement cease to have effect must be made to the Court of Appeal[26].

A person appointed under either of the last two preceding provisions has all the powers he would have had if appointed under the arbitration agreement[27].

1 *Re Smith and Service and Nelson & Sons* (1890) 25 QBD 545, CA; and see *Re Wilson & Son and Eastern Counties Navigation and Transport Co* [1892] 1 QB 81; on appeal (1892) 8 TLR 264, CA; and *Re Percival* (1885) 2 TLR 150.
2 This includes a judge or master: see the Arbitration Act 1950 s 10; and RSC Ord 73 r 3 (1). In Admiralty, applications are, in practice, made by motion.
3 Under the Arbitration Act 1950 s 6. See *Laertis Shipping Corpn v Exportadora Espanola de Cementos Portland SA, The Laertis* [1982] 1 Lloyd's Rep 613; and para 656 ante.
4 Arbitration Act 1950 s 10 (1) (a). The court can only intervene under s 10 (1) (a) once 'differences have arisen': it was held in *Mayer Newman & Co Ltd v A I Ferro Commodities Corpn SA* (1990) Times, 9 April, CA, that a difference permitting an appointment under the Arbitration Act 1950 s 10 (1) (a) must be assumed to require the existence between the parties of a 'genuinely disputable issue', and that accordingly the party seeking the appointment by the court must assert more than the existence of a claim against the other party. The 1950 Act s 10 (1) (a) does not extend to cases where the agreement provides for the appointment of a single arbitrator by a third party, unless there is also an express or implied agreement that if the third party fails to appoint, the parties themselves will agree

on an arbitrator, and they then fail to do so: *National Enterprises Ltd v Racal Communications Ltd* [1974] Ch 251, [1974] 1 All ER 1118, [1974] 2 Lloyd's Rep 21; affd [1975] Ch 397, [1974] 3 All ER 1010, [1975] 1 Lloyd's Rep 225, CA. Where a third party fails to appoint a single arbitrator, the court can intervene under the 1950 Act s 10 (2) (added by the Arbitration Act 1979 s 6 (4)).

5   As to what amounts to a refusal to act, and as to the position where the parties intended any vacancy to be filled by somebody else, see *Re Wilson & Son and Eastern Counties Navigation and Transport Co* [1892] 1 QB 81. The refusal of the arbitrator appointed by one of the parties to act in the reference does not render the party appointing him liable to an action at the suit of the other party: *Cooper v Shuttleworth* (1856) 25 LJ Ex 114. The arbitrator is only incapable of acting if the disability is serious enough to put him out of action altogether so far as the arbitration is concerned: *Succula Ltd and Pomona Shipping Co Ltd v Harland and Wolff Ltd* [1980] 2 Lloyd's Rep 381 at 388.

6   Arbitration Act 1950 s 10 (1) (b).

7   Ibid s 10 (1) (c) (amended by the Arbitration Act 1979 s 6 (3)). This power may be exercised even if it is shown that the arbitrators have failed to agree on the time and place of a preliminary meeting, for they have entered upon the reference as soon as they have accepted their appointment and communicated with one another about the reference: *Iossifoglu v Coumantaros* [1941] 1 KB 396, CA. The court has power to bring the arbitrators before it to ascertain their views before making an appointment, and to make an order for the appointment of an umpire and as to the costs of the arbitrators, on the application of one party, although the other party has not been made a respondent to the application: *Taylor v Denny, Mott and Dickson Ltd* [1912] AC 666 at 671, HL.

8   See note 5 supra.

9   Arbitration Act 1950 s 10 (1) (d). The considerations are broadly the same as where an application is made under s 10 (1) (b).

10 Ibid s 10 (2) (as added: see note 4 supra). Where anything is to be done within a 'reasonable time', the question of what is a reasonable time depends on all the circumstances of the case and is therefore a question of fact: *Hick v Raymond and Reid* [1893] AC 22 at 29, HL.

11 Arbitration Act 1950 s 10 (3) (added by the Administration of Justice Act 1985 s 58, and subsequently substituted by the Courts and Legal Services Act 1990 s 101). The sub-section as originally added applies to arbitration agreements whether they were entered into before or after the section came into force on 30 December 1985, so long as they were entered into before 1 April 1991 (ie the date on which the 1990 Act s 101 came into force: see the Courts and Legal Services Act 1990 (Commencement No 3) Order 1991, SI 1991/608). Under the 1950 Act s 10 (3) in its substituted form, which applies to arbitration agreements entered into after 1 April 1991, a power of appointment is conferred on the giver of a notice under s 10 in the alternative to the court's power of appointment in the same context: see note 18 infra. As to 'reasonable time' see note 10 supra.

12 See 6 Court Forms (2nd Edn) (1989 Issue) 99–100, Forms 6–8. Expressions referring to writing are, unless the contrary appears, to be construed as including references to other modes of reproducing words in a visible form: Interpretation Act 1978 s 5, Sch 1.

13 A notice to 'concur in the appointment' of an arbitrator is good and no arbitrator need be named: *Re Eyre and Leicester Corpn* [1892] 1 QB 136.

14 The general rule in cases where an act is to be done within a specified time is that the day from which the time runs is not to be counted: *Goldsmith's Co v West Metropolitan Rly* [1904] 1 KB 1, CA; *Stewart v Chapman* [1951] 2 KB 792.

15 The application is made by originating summons, expedited form (RSC Ord 73 r 3 (3); see 6 Court Forms (2nd Edn) (1989 Issue) 100–101, Form 9), and should be supported by affidavit (see eg 6 Court Forms (2nd Edn) (1989 Issue) 101–105, Forms 10–14). In the Queen's Bench Division the application may be, and usually is, made to a master, from whose decision appeal lies to a judge in chambers, and thence to the Court of Appeal: *Simbro Trading Co v Posograph (Parent) Corpn* [1929] 2 KB 266, CA; RSC Ord 58 r 6 (1). Service out of the jurisdiction of (a) any originating summons or notice of originating motion under the Arbitration Act 1950 or the Arbitration Act 1979, or (b) any order made on such a summons or motion, is permissible with the leave of the court provided that the arbitration to which the summons, motion or order relates is governed by English law or has been, is being or is to be held within the jurisdiction: RSC Ord 73 r 7 (1). However, service out of the jurisdiction of an originating summons for leave to enforce an award is permissible with the leave of the court whether or not the arbitration is governed by English law: RSC Ord 73 r 7 (1A). As to the consequences of failing to serve parties out of the jurisdiction, see *Denny Mott and Dickson v Standard Export Lumber* [1912] 2 KB 542, CA; affd sub nom *Taylor v Denny Mott and Dickson* [1912] AC 666, HL.

16 The application can be made only by a party to the arbitration agreement: *Re Franklin and Swathling's Arbitration* [1929] 1 Ch 238.

17 Arbitration Act 1950 s 10 (1), (2), (3), (3C) (s 10 (2) added by the Arbitration Act 1979 s 6 (4); s 10 (3), (3C) substituted by the Courts and Legal Services Act 1990 s 101 (1)). Where these steps have been taken the court will, as a general rule, tend to make an appointment. However, relief under the 1950 Act s 10 is discretionary, and on occasion the court will refuse to appoint an arbitrator, eg where the applicant is a foreigner resident outside the jurisdiction, unless as in *Re Bjornstad and Ouse Shipping Co Ltd* [1924] 2 KB 673, CA, the foreign applicant provides security for costs, or where, the dispute being as to whether a party was liable at all on a contract, the appointment of an arbitrator would force that party to arbitrate on the footing that he was so liable (*Miller, Gibb & Co v Smith and Tyrer Ltd* [1916] 1 KB 419 at 424). See also *Re Eyre and Leicester Corpn* [1892] 1 QB 136, CA, which was distinguished in *Re Bjornstad and Ouse Shipping Co Ltd* supra. As to the exercise of the discretion see also *Abu Dhabi Gas Liquefaction Co Ltd v Eastern Bechtel Corpn* [1982] 2 Lloyd's Rep 425 at 427, CA (court has power under the section to appoint one arbitrator to hear two separate arbitrations arising out of the same facts); *Tritonia Shipping Inc v South Nelson Forest Products Corpn* [1966] 1 Lloyd's Rep 114.

18 Arbitration Act 1950 s 10. Subsection (3B) (added by the Courts and Legal Services Act 1990 s 101 (1)) confers a power of appointment on the giver of the notice, in the alternative to the powers of the court, where there is a vacancy in a tribunal of three arbitrators. The party who gave the notice must specify whether it is given under the 1950 Act s 10 (3C) (as so added), in which case the court has its normal powers, or under s 10 (3B) (as so added), in which case, unless a contrary intention is expressed in the agreement, the party who gave the notice may, if the appointment required in the notice is not made within seven clear days, appoint his arbitrator to act as sole arbitrator, and his award is binding on both parties as if he had been appointed by consent: s 10 (3A) (as so added). An appointment made under s 10 (3B) may be set aside by the court: s 10 (3D) (as so added). The court's powers under s 10 generally have been held to exist only so long as the parties do not express a contrary intention in the arbitration agreement, although with the exception of sub-s (3B), s 10 does not so limit itself: *Medor Lines SPA v Traelandsfos A/S* [1969] 2 Lloyd's Rep 225 at 227. There must be an arbitration agreement in existence within the meaning of the Arbitration Act 1950 s 32 before the powers can be exercised: *Westfal-Larsen & Co A/S v Ikerigi Compania Naviera SA, The Messsiniaki Bergen* [1983] 1 All ER 382, [1983] 1 Lloyd's Rep 424.

19 Arbitration Act 1950 s 25 (1) (amended by the Administration of Justice Act 1970 s 4 (4), Sch 3 para 11).

20 This cannot apply to a judge-arbitrator, as such an arbitrator is bound to be a sole arbitrator: see the Administration of Justice Act 1970 s 4 (1); and para 655 ante.

21 Arbitration Act 1950 s 25 (1) (as amended: see note 19 supra). The application is by summons: RSC Ord 59 r 14 (1).

22 Under the Arbitration Act 1950 s 1 or s 24 (1).

23 Under ibid s 13 (3) or s 23 (1). It is not clear whether an arbitrator whose appointment has been set aside under the proviso to s 7 has been removed within the meaning of s 25 (2).

24 Ibid s 25 (2) (a).

25 Ibid s 25 (2) (b). See *Stockport Metropolitan Borough Council v O'Reilly* [1983] 2 Lloyd's Rep 70.

26 Arbitration Act 1950 s 25 (2) (amended by the Administration of Justice Act 1970 Sch 3 para 11). The application is by summons: RSC Ord 59 r 14 (1).

27 Arbitration Act 1950 s 25 (3) (amended by the Administration of Justice Act 1970 Sch 3 para 11).

(3) REMOVAL AND REVOCATION OF AUTHORITY OF ARBITRATOR

661. Revocation of authority of an arbitrator. The authority of an arbitrator or umpire appointed by or by virtue of a written arbitration agreement is, unless a contrary intention is expressed in the agreement, irrevocable except by leave of the High Court[1]. In the case of a judge-arbitrator or judge-umpire, the leave must be that of the Court of Appeal[2]. However, a party to an oral arbitration agreement may revoke the authority of an arbitrator appointed by him at will and without leave, though he might as a result be liable in damages for breach of contract[3].

1 Arbitration Act 1950 ss 1, 32.
2 Administration of Justice Act 1970 s 4 (4), Sch 3 para 2.

3 The reason is that, apart from statute, the courts will not specifically enforce an arbitration agreement: *Doleman & Sons v Ossett Corpn* [1912] 3 KB 257 at 268, CA; *Pena Copper Mines Ltd v Rio Tinto Co Ltd* (1911) 105 LT 846; *Bankers and Shippers Insurance Co of New York v Liverpool Marine and General Insurance Co Ltd* (1925) 21 Ll L Rep 86.

662. Circumstances in which leave may be given.

Revocation of the authority of an umpire deprives one party of his contractual rights. Leave to revoke the authority of an arbitrator is therefore treated by the court as an extreme remedy, which is used sparingly, and only in unusual cases[1]. Leave may be given in the following circumstances: (1) serious and irreparable misconduct[2]; (2) actual or potential bias[3]; (3) deficiencies in capability or performance for which the Arbitration Acts provide no other remedy[4]; (4) where justice requires that the proceedings should be halted, temporarily or permanently, and no other method of doing so is available to the court[5].

1 *City Centre Properties (I T C Pensions) Ltd v Tersons Ltd* [1969] 2 All ER 1121, sub nom *City Centre Properties (I T C Pensions) Ltd v Matthew Hall & Co Ltd* [1969] 1 WLR 772, CA; *Scott v Van Sandau* (1841) 1 QB 102; *Den of Airlie SS Co Ltd v Mitsui & Co Ltd and British Oil and Cake Mills Ltd* (1912) 106 LT 451, CA; See also *Belcher v Roedean School Site and Buildings Ltd* (1901) 85 LT 468, CA; *Succula Ltd and Pomona Shipping Co Ltd v Harland and Wolff Ltd* [1980] 2 Lloyd's Rep 381; *Stockport Metropolitan Borough Council v O'Reilly* [1983] 2 Lloyd's Rep 70.
2 *City Centre Properties (I T C Pensions) Ltd v Tersons Ltd* [1969] 2 All ER 1121, sub nom *City Centre Properties (I T C Pensions) Ltd v Matthew Hall & Co Ltd* [1969] 1 WLR 772, CA, per Lord Denning MR. See also para 697 post.
3 See the Arbitration Act 1950 s 24 (1). It is no answer to such an application that the agreement refers to a named arbitrator and that the applicant, at the time when he made the agreement, knew, or ought to have known, that the arbitrator, by reason of his relation towards any other party to the agreement or of his connection with the subject referred, might not be capable of impartiality. The test for bias is whether a reasonably intelligent man, fully appraised of all the circumstances, would feel a serious apprehension of bias: *R v Moore, ex p Brooks* [1969] 2 OR 677, 684, 6 DLR (3d) 465.
4 *Burkett Sharp & Co v Eastcheap Dried Fruit Co and Perera* [1962] 1 Lloyd's Rep 267, CA.
5 *Stockport Metropolitan Borough Council v O'Reilly* [1983] 2 Lloyd's Rep 70 at 78–80.

663. Practice and effect.

The application for leave to revoke the authority of an arbitrator is made by originating summons to a Commercial judge in chambers, a master or the Admiralty Registrar[1]. In the case of a judge-arbitrator or judge-umpire, the application is to the Court of Appeal[2].

Where the court also exercises its power to order that the arbitration agreement shall cease to have effect[3], the whole tribunal is divested of any authority. In other cases the court has power to appoint a sole arbitrator to replace the tribunal[4]. Where this power is not exercised, the party responsible for appointing the arbitrator whose authority has been revoked must make a fresh appointment[5].

1 RSC Ord 73 rr 3, 6 (1).
2 Arbitration Act 1950 s 1; Administration of Justice Act 1970 s 4 (4), Sch 3 para 2.
3 Ie under the Arbitration Act 1950 s 25 (2) (b); see para 660 ante.
4 Presumably only where the authority of the whole tribunal has been revoked: see ibid s 25 (2) (a) (amended by the Administration of Justice Act 1970 Sch 3 para 11).
5 Otherwise the court may exercise its default powers under the Arbitration Act 1950 ss 7, 10 (see paras 657, 660 ante).

664. Removal of arbitrator for misconduct or delay.

The High Court has a statutory jurisdiction to remove an arbitrator or umpire[1] where he has misconducted himself or the proceedings[2], including where he has continued to take part in the proceedings having given an appearance of bias[3]. Further, the High Court[4] may, on the application of a party to the reference, remove an arbitrator or umpire who fails to use all reasonable dispatch in entering on and proceeding with the reference[5] and making an award[6]. An arbitrator or umpire who is removed for such failure is not entitled to receive any remuneration for his services[7]. Where an arbitrator or umpire is removed by the High Court[8], the court may appoint a person or persons to act as arbitrators or umpire in place of the person or persons so removed[9].

1 An application for removal is made by originating notice of motion to a commercial judge: RSC Ord 73 rr 2 (1) (b), 6 (1). For forms see 6 Court Forms (2nd Edn) (1989 Issue) 111–114, Forms 26–28. In the case of a judge-arbitrator or judge-umpire the jurisdiction to remove for misconduct is exercised, on application by summons, by the Court of Appeal: Administration of Justice Act 1970 s 4, Sch 3 para 9 (1) (amended by the Aribtration Act 1979 s 8 (3)); RSC Ord 59 r 14 (1).

2 Arbitration Act 1950 s 23 (1). As to what constitutes misconduct for this purpose see para 694 post, and the cases cited in the notes thereto. See also *Re Enoch and Zaretzky, Bock & Co* [1910] 1 KB 327, CA (where an arbitrator who had called witnesses to fact without the consent of the parties was removed); *Modern Engineering (Bristol) Ltd v C Miskin & Son Ltd* [1981] 1 Lloyd's Rep 135, CA; *Pratt v Swanmore Builders Ltd and Baker* [1980] 2 Lloyd's Rep 504.

3 *Catalina (Owners) v Norma (Owners)* (1938) 61 Ll L Rep 360, 82 Sol Jo 698, DC (where an arbitrator who had shown bias by his remarks at the hearing was removed); *Veritas Shipping Corpn v Anglo-Canadian Cement Ltd* [1966] 1 Lloyd's Rep 76; see also *Schofield v Allen* (1904) 48 Sol Jo 176, CA. The test is whether there exist grounds from which a reasonable person would think that there was a real likelihood of bias: *Tracomin SA v Gibbs Nathaniel (Canada) Ltd and George Jacob Bridge* [1985] 1 Lloyd's Rep 586. See also *Metropolitan Properties Co (FGC) Ltd v Lannon* [1969] 1 QB 577, [1968] 3 All ER 304, CA; *Hannam v Bradford Corpn* [1970] 2 All ER 690, [1970] 1 WLR 937, CA; *R v Liverpool City Justices, ex p Topping* [1983] 1 All ER 490, [1983] 1 WLR 937, DC; *Ardahalian v Unifert International SA, The Elissar* [1984] 2 Lloyd's Rep 84, CA.

4 The jurisdiction may be exercised by a judge in chambers or a master: RSC Ord 73 r 3 (1). In Admiralty, applications are, in practice, made by motion. The proceedings should be served on the arbitrator: *Succula Ltd and Pomona Shipping Co Ltd v Harland and Wolff Ltd* [1980] 2 Lloyd's Rep 381; *Pratt v Swanmore Builders Ltd and Baker* [1980] 2 Lloyd's Rep 504.

5 For this purpose 'proceeding with a reference' includes, in a case where two arbitrators are unable to agree, giving notice of that fact to the parties and to the umpire: Arbitration Act 1950 s 13 (3).

6 Ibid s 13 (3). See also *Lewis Emanuel & Son Ltd v Sammut* [1959] 2 Lloyd's Rep 629. This provision does not apply to a judge-arbitrator or judge-umpire, who may enlarge any time limited for making his award (whether under the Arbitration Act 1950 or otherwise) whether that time has expired or not: Administration of Justice Act 1970 Sch 3 para 6.

7 Arbitration Act 1950 s 13 (3). As to the remuneration of arbitrators generally see para 665 et seq post.

8 Or, in the case of a judge-arbitrator or judge-umpire, the Court of Appeal.

9 Arbitration Act 1950 s 25 (1) (amended by the Administration of Justice Act 1970 s 4 (4), Sch 3 para 11). Where the arbitrator removed is the sole arbitrator, or where the court removes all the arbitrators or an umpire who has entered on the reference, the court may either appoint a sole arbitrator or order that the arbitration agreement cease to have effect with respect to the dispute referred: Arbitration Act 1950 s 25 (2) (as so amended).

7. REMUNERATION OF ARBITRATOR OR UMPIRE

665. Fixing remuneration. The parties may agree the remuneration of the arbitrator or umpire with him expressly in advance, and he will be entitled to be paid the agreed amount if he completes the reference and makes a valid award. If they do not agree the remuneration in advance, a lay arbitrator or umpire is ordinarily entitled to reasonable remuneration[1]. If the reference is completed and a valid award is made[2], then in the absence of a contrary intention in the arbitration agreement, the arbitrator or umpire may himself assess the amount of his remuneration, and tax it in his award[3], or may instead elect not to tax it in the award, but to leave the taxation to the High Court[4]. The fees of a judge-arbitrator of the Commercial Court acting as such are fixed by law and are taken in the High Court[5]. In appropriate circumstances, arbitrators may ask for security for their fees, or for the payment in advance of a non-refundable 'commitment fee', to protect themselves against the possibility of the arbitration not taking place[6].

Where the reference is to two arbitrators and an umpire, and the arbitrators fail to agree, so that the duty of making the award devolves on the umpire, the umpire may include the fees of the arbitrators with his own charges as part of the costs of the award[7]. If he does so, he should distinguish between his own charges and the arbitrators' remuneration[8].

Umpires and arbitrators assessing their own fees, and umpires assessing arbitrators' fees, must take into account the interests of those who will have to pay them. This assessment involves the application of an independent mind and judgment, and it is desirable that the basis on which the fee is calculated should be stated[9].

If the arbitrator or umpire does not include his remuneration in the award, the party liable to pay his charges may, as between himself and the other party to the reference, have the charges taxed[10].

1 *Crampton and Holt v Ridley & Co* (1887) 20 QBD 48; *Willis v Wakeley Bros* (1891) 7 TLR 604; *Brown v Llandovery Terra Cotta Co Ltd* (1909) 25 TLR 625. As to the distinction, if any, between lay and legal arbitrators, see para 669 post. As to what criteria are relevant in the assessment of a reasonable fee see *S N Kurkjian (Commodity Brokers) Ltd v Marketing Exchange for Africa Ltd (No 2)* [1986] 2 Lloyd's Rep 618. See also *Government of Ceylon v Chandris* [1963] 2 QB 327, [1963] 2 All ER 1, [1963] 1 Lloyd's Rep 214. As to disentitlement to remuneration for failure to use all reasonable dispatch see para 676 post.

2 It is not clear what the arbitrator's or umpire's entitlement to remuneration is where the reference does not proceed to an award, either as a result of the parties' actions or as a result of the arbitrator's or umpire's, or where the award is for some reason invalid.

3 As part of 'the costs of the reference and award' under the Arbitration Act 1950 s 18 (1); para 689 post; *Re Prebble and Robinson* [1892] 2 QB 602; and *Re Stephens, Smith & Co and Liverpool and London and Globe Insurance* (1892) 36 Sol Jo 464. As to the difficulties in assessing remuneration generally see *Rolimpex Centrala Handlu Zagranicznego v Haji E Dossa & Sons Ltd* [1971] 1 Lloyd's Rep 380 at 384. As to enforcement of the arbitrator's direction with regard to the payment of his remuneration see *Hicks v Richardson* (1797) 1 Bos & P 93.

4 Under the Arbitration Act 1950 s 18 (2), or if the arbitrator's lien has been exercised, under s 19 (1). See *Government of Ceylon v Chandris* [1963] 2 QB 327, [1963] 2 All ER 1, [1963] 1 Lloyd's Rep 214; and para 667 post.

5 Administration of Justice Act 1970 s 4 (3); Arbitration Act 1950 s 11 (3) (substituted by the Courts and Legal Services Act 1990 s 99). The fees are £500 on appointment (refundable if the arbitration does not proceed) and £500 for every day or part thereof (after the first day): Supreme Court Fees Order 1980, SI 1980/821, art 5 (2), Fee 25.

6 *K/S Norjal A/S v Hyundai Heavy Industries Co Ltd* [1991] 3 All ER 211, [1991] 1 Lloyd's Rep 524, CA. The parties appointed arbitrators and asked them to reserve a 12 week period two years in the future for the hearing. The arbitrators accepted the appointment but stipulated that they should receive a proportion of their costs in advance as a 'commitment fee'. One of the parties refused to contribute to such a fee, and applied to the court for the removal of the arbitrators for their misconduct in asking for it. The other party cross-applied for a declaration that it could pay the entire commitment fee itself without giving rise to any imputation of bias against the arbitrators. At first instance the court dismissed both applications: it had not been improper for the arbitrators to ask for the commitment fee in the circumstances of the case, but it would not have been appropriate for the fee to have been paid by one party alone. In order to avoid similar problems, the court stressed that all fee negotiation should take place before appointment and that arbitrators should only accept an appointment if it was absolutely clear that all the parties were aware of and agreed the basis of remuneration. The Court of Appeal dismissed both parties' appeals, holding first that an arbitrator is entitled to

negotiate before appointment a commencement fee, but not to insist upon such a fee after he has been appointed, and secondly that an arbitrator acts properly if he declines to agree a fee with one party to which the other objects.

7 *Ellison v Ackroyd* (1850) 1 LM & P 806; Arbitration Act 1950 s 18 (1); and see *Threlfall v Fanshawe* (1850) 1 LM & P 340, where the reference was under a court order; and *Appleton v Norwich Union Fire Insurance Society Ltd* (1922) 13 Ll L Rep 345.

8 Where the umpire had included his own and the arbitrators' remuneration in the award without specifying how much was in respect of his own charges and how much in respect of those of the arbitrators, the court remitted the award with a direction that he should state those amounts: *Re Gilbert and Wright* (1904) 68 JP 143.

9 *Government of Ceylon v Chandris* [1963] 2 QB 327, [1963] 2 All ER 1, [1963] 1 Lloyd's Rep 214. Where the umpire fixes the charges of advocate-umpires, he should distinguish between the part of their fees attributable to their role as arbitrators and the part attributable to their role as advocates.

10 *Re Prebble and Robinson* [1892] 2 QB 602; *Re James & Sons* [1903] WN 99 (where the umpire had fixed a scale fee depending on the amount of the award and this was disallowed on taxation, despite the party's preparedness to pay on that basis); and see *Roberts v Eberhardt* (1857) 3 CBNS 482 at 508. Where the charges fixed by the arbitrator or umpire include a sum paid by him to his solicitors for preparing his award, the party liable to pay those charges is entitled to tax the solicitor's bill under the Solicitors Act 1974 s 71: see *Re Collyer-Bristow & Co* [1901] 2 KB 839, CA; and cf *Galloway v Keyworth* (1854) 15 CB 228, where the arbitrator was not allowed to add his solicitor's bill to his own fees.

666. Lien on award. An arbitrator or umpire has a lien on the arbitration agreement and award for the amount of his charges[1]. The ordinary practice is for him to notify to the parties the amount of his charges as soon as the award is ready, and to retain possession of the award until the charges have been paid[2]. The lien does not extend to documents handed to the arbitrator in the course of the reference[3].

1 *R v South Devon Rly Co* (1850) 15 QB 1043; *Government of Ceylon v Chandris* [1963] 2 QB 327, [1963] 2 All ER 1, [1963] 1 Lloyd's Rep 214.

2 In most cases in which a tribunal taxes and settles its own fees, it will exercise a lien upon the award to compel payment. In such cases there is sometimes an effective appeal under the Arbitration Act 1950 s 19 (see para 667 post). This right is rendered ineffective where the application of the dissatisfied party is forestalled by the other party taking up and paying for the award. But following *Government of Ceylon v Chandris* [1963] 2 QB 327, [1963] 2 All ER 1, [1963] 1 Lloyd's Rep 214, many awards of costs have been unspecific and have not stated the amount of the arbitrators' remuneration (thus enabling either party to apply for a taxation under the Arbitration Act 1950 s 18 (2) : see para 689 post) but have been accompanied by an intimation that the parties could take up the award on payment to the arbitrators of a specified sum. This preserved the lien, and if neither party would take up the award on those terms, s 19 could be invoked. But in *Rolimpex Centrala Handlu Zagranicznego v Haji E Dossa & Sons Ltd* [1971] 1 Lloyd's Rep 380 the arbitral tribunal took advantage of a rule which required the party seeking a special case to pay a large deposit by way of security for the costs of the award. Previously this could be treated as a refusal to state a case and the provisions of the Arbitration Act 1950 s 21 could be relied on (s 21 has been repealed, and the statement of case procedure replaced by appeal to the High Court: see the Arbitration Act 1979 ss 1 (1), 8 (3); and para 706 et seq post; now the tribunal might require security before giving reasons for its award, and this might be treated as a refusal to give reasons contrary to the 1979 Act s 1). But the real problem was created by the fact that by reason of the exercise of the power, no lien was exercised on the award, and the party at risk as to costs was deprived of the opportunity of challenging the reasonableness of the charges in a taxation under s 19. If, as in *Rolimpex Centrala Handlu Zagranicznego v Haji E Dossa & Sons Ltd* supra, the charges had been settled and taxed in the award, then the party at risk was also deprived of the opportunity of challenging their reasonableness under the 1950 Act s 18. The problem was resolved as follows: there being a motion to set the award aside, it was adjourned by consent in order that all parties might apply to the chief taxing master for a taxation by consent under s 18 (2). An alternative approach would have been to have remitted the award by consent to enable the tribunal to delete the reference to taxation and settlement.

3 *Ponsford v Swaine* (1861) 1 John & H 433.

667. Taxation of remuneration by High Court. If the remuneration of an arbitrator or umpire has not been agreed in advance and has not been taxed in the award, but simply demanded and the lien not exercised, then the party liable can cause a taxation by the High Court[1]. If the arbitrator or umpire (not being a judge-arbitrator or judge-umpire) exercises his lien and refuses to deliver his award[2] except on payment of fees demanded by him, the High Court may, on an application for the purpose, order the arbitrator or umpire to deliver the award to the applicant on payment into court by him of the fees demanded, and further order that the fees demanded be taxed by the taxing officer and that out of the money paid into court there be paid out to the arbitrator or umpire by way of fees such sum as may be found reasonable on taxation, and that the balance of the money, if any, be paid out to the applicant[3]. The application[4] may be made by any party to the reference unless the fees demanded have been fixed by a written agreement between him and the arbitrator or umpire[5]. A taxation under this provision is subject to review in the same manner as a taxation of costs[6]. The arbitrator or umpire is entitled to appear and be heard on any such taxation or review[7].

In the case of a judge-arbitrator or judge-umpire the court has no power to order that the award be delivered on payment into court of the appropriate fees[8], but a judge-umpire may withhold his award until the fees payable to the arbitrator have been paid into the High Court[9], and unless those fees have been fixed by written agreement between a party and the arbitrator that party can apply for taxation before payment out[10]. The taxation may be reviewed in the same manner as a taxation of the costs of an award[11]. On such taxation or review an arbitrator is entitled to appear and be heard[12].

Except under the above provisions there is no means of taxing or otherwise disputing the amount of fees fixed by the arbitrator or umpire[13], unless the amount is so unreasonable that the court would hold the arbitrator or umpire guilty of misconduct and so set aside or remit the award[14].

1 Under the Arbitration Act 1950 s 18 (2). An arbitrator or umpire will rarely fail to exercise the lien.
2 Including an interim award: see ibid s 14.
3 Ibid s 19 (1). The section is probably applicable whether or not the arbitrator or umpire included a taxation in the award: see *Rolimpex Centrala Handlu Zagranicznego v Haji E Dossa & Sons Ltd* [1971] 1 Lloyd's Rep 380.
4 Application is made by originating summons or, if there are pending proceedings, by ordinary summons, to a judge in chambers or (normally, in the Queen's Bench Division) a master: RSC Ord 73 r 3 (1). In Admiralty, applications are, in practice, made by motion. For forms see 6 Court Forms (2nd Edn) (1989 Issue) 137–138, Forms 66–68.
5 Arbitration Act 1950 s 19 (2).
6 Ibid s 19 (3); see PRACTICE AND PROCEDURE.
7 Ibid s 19 (4).
8 Administration of Justice Act 1970 s 4 (4), Sch 3 para 8 (1).
9 Ibid Sch 3 para 8 (2).
10 Ibid Sch 3 para 8 (3).
11 Ibid Sch 3 para 8 (4).
12 Ibid Sch 3 para 8 (5).
13 Eg if the arbitrator or umpire taxes the fees in the award and does not exercise the lien, or if the party who takes up the award is not the party who complains of the excess: see *Rolimpex Centrala Handlu Zagranicznego v Haji E Dossa & Sons Ltd* [1971] 1 Lloyd's Rep 380; and para 666 note 2 ante. See also *Re Stephens, Smith & Co and London, Liverpool and Globe Insurance Co* (1892) 36 Sol Jo 464.
14 *Re Prebble and Robinson* [1892] 2 QB 602 at 604; *Appleton v Norwich Union Fire Insurance Society Ltd* (1922) 13 Ll L Rep 345; *Government of Ceylon v Chandris* [1963] 2 QB 327, [1963] 2 All ER 1, [1963] 1 Lloyd's Rep 214; *S N Kurkjian (CommodityBrokers) Ltd v Marketing Exchange for Africa Ltd (No 2)* [1986] 2 Lloyd's Rep 618. See also para 668 post.

668. Recovery of excessive remuneration. If the arbitrator or umpire fixes his remuneration at an unreasonable and excessive amount, a party who has paid such amount in order to take up the award can bring an action to recover back the sum by which such charges exceed what is fair and reasonable unless the amount is included in the award itself, in which case his only remedy is to move to set aside the award or so much of it as relates to the arbitrator's remuneration[1]. The court will not intervene unless the fees are extravagant or the arbitrator or umpire has seriously misunderstood his duty with regard to the assessment of his fees[2].

1 *Llandrindod Wells Water Co v Hawksley* (1904) 68 JP 242, CA; *Fernley v Branson* (1851) 20 LJQB 178 (the action was specified as being in money had and received); *Barnes v Braithwaite and Nixon* (1857) 2 H & N 569; *Barnes v Hayward* (1857) 1 H & N 742 at 743; *Re Coombs and Freshfield and Fernley* (1850) 4 Exch 839 at 841; and cf *Dossett v Gingell* (1841) 2 Man & G 870. As to the factors relevant in assessing what amount is reasonable see *S N Kurkjian (CommodityBrokers) Ltd v Marketing Exchange for Africa Ltd (No 2)* [1986] 2 Lloyd's Rep 618.
2 *Government of Ceylon v Chandris* [1963] 2 QB 327, [1963] 2 All ER 1, [1963] 1 Lloyd's Rep 214. Such a misunderstanding may be inferred, in the absence of adequate information, where the fees appear to be out of proportion to the work involved: *Government of Ceylon v Chandris* supra.

669. Action by arbitrator or umpire to obtain payment of remuneration. Where there is an express agreement by the parties that they will pay him, the arbitrator or umpire can maintain an action to recover reasonable remuneration[1]. It was formerly held that there was no implied promise by the parties to a submission that they would pay the arbitrator or umpire for his services[2], but this appears to be no longer the law where the reference is to lay arbitrators[3]; and if a lay arbitrator may bring an action on an implied promise by the parties that they would pay him reasonable remuneration for his services, there would seem to be no sound reason why a legal arbitrator should not also be entitled to do so.

1 *Hoggins v Gordon* (1842) 3 QB 466.
2 *Virany v Warne* (1801) 4 Esp 47; *Burroughes v Clarke* (1831) 1 Dowl 48.
3 *Willis v Wakeley Bros* (1891) 7 TLR 604; *Crampton and Holt v Ridley & Co* (1887) 20 QBD 48; *Re Coombs and Freshfield and Fernley* (1850) 4 Exch 839 at 841; *Tuckett v Isle of Thanet Electric Tramways and Lighting Co Ltd* (1902) 46 Sol Jo 158; *Swinford v Byrne* (1818) Gow 5 at 8; *Brown v Llandovery Terra Cotta Co Ltd* (1909) 25 TLR 625. See also *Marsack v Webber* (1860) 6 H & N 1, where it was held that where one party pays the arbitrator's fees in order to take up the award and neither party is entitled to costs, the party who has paid the fees can recover half from the other; cf *Bates v Townley* (1848) 2 Exch 152.

8. CONDUCT OF THE ARBITRATION

(1) GENERAL

670. General. An arbitration is, in the absence of an agreement to the contrary, conducted in accordance with legal principles[1].

This has a number of important consequences as regards the conduct of the arbitration. First, unless the parties agree to the contrary[2], an arbitration is conducted by way of an oral hearing[3]. Secondly, unless the parties agree to the contrary[4], each party must be notified of the hearing[5]. Thirdly, unless the parties agree to the contrary[6] each party must be given a reasonable opportunity to attend the hearing[7]. Where a party fails to attend the hearing having been given due notice and having had a reasonable opportunity to attend, the arbitrator can proceed with the hearing[8]. Fourthly, each party must be given a reasonable opportunity to adduce evidence[9] and to argue his case[10].

1   *Ritchie v W Jacks & Co* (1922) 10 Ll L Rep 519 at 520, CA, per Lord Sterndale MR.
2   *Ritchie v W Jacks & Co* (1922) 10 Ll L Rep 519, CA; *Star International Hong Kong (UK) Ltd v Bergbau-Handel, GmbH* [1966] 2 Lloyd's Rep 16; *The Myron, Myron (Owners) v Tradax Export SA Panama City RP* [1970] 1 QB 527 at 532–533, [1969] 2 All ER 1263 at 1265, [1969] 1 Lloyd's Rep 411 at 415 per Donaldson J. See also *Henry Bath & Son Ltd v Birgby Products* [1962] 1 Lloyd's Rep 389.
3   *Altco Ltd v Sutherland* [1971] 2 Lloyd's Rep 515; *Ritchie v W Jacks & Co* (1922) 10 Ll L Rep 519 at 520, CA, per Lord Sterndale MR.
4   *Russian Oil Products Ltd v Caucasian Oil Co Ltd* (1928) 31 Ll L Rep 109; *French Government v Tsurushima Maru (Owners)* (1921) 37 TLR 961 at 962, CA, per Atkin LJ; *Oakland Metal Co Ltd v D Benaim & Co Ltd* [1953] 2 Lloyd's Rep 192 at 199 per Parker J.
5   *Oswald v Earl Grey* (1855) 24 LJQB 69; *The Warwick* (1890) 15 PD 189; *French Government v Tsurushima Maru* (1921) 37 TLR 961 at 962, CA, per Atkin LJ; *Golodetz v Schrier* (1947) 80 Ll L Rep 647 at 651 per Lord Goddard LCJ. If a meeting takes place before the oral hearing of the reference and one party is not given notice of the meeting and so fails to attend, the award will not be invalidated provided that nothing was done at the meeting: *Re Morphett* (1845) 2 Dowl 967. As to waiver of irregularities see *Bignall v Gale* (1841) 9 Dowl 631; *Hamilton v Bankin* (1850) 3 De G & SM 782.
6   *A A Amram Ltd v Bremar Co Ltd* [1966] 1 Lloyd's Rep 494.
7   This is independent of the requirement that the parties must be notified of the hearing, since a party may be notified of the hearing but unable to attend because of the time and place fixed for the hearing. The arbitrator will generally consult the convenience of the parties as to the time and place of the hearing and will, as far as possible, accommodate their wishes; however, the fixing of the hearing is a matter within the arbitrator's discretion and the courts are reluctant to interfere with this discretion provided that the arbitrator has acted reasonably in fixing the hearing: see *Fetherstone v Cooper* (1803) 9 Ves 67; *Ginder v Curtis* (1863) 14 CBNS 723; *Nares v Drury* (1864) 10 LT 305; *Re Whitwam's Trustees, etc and Wrexham, Mold and Connah's Quay Rly Co* (1895) 39 Sol Jo 692.
8   *Waller v King* (1723) 9 Mod Rep 63; *Fetherstone v Cooper* (1803) 9 Ves 67; *Wood v Leake* (1806) 12 Ves 412; *Harcourt v Ramsbottom* (1820) 1 Jac & W 505 at 512; *Scott v Van Sandau* (1844) 6 QB 237; *Tryer v Shaw* (1858) 27 LJ Ex 320; *Angus v Smythies, Smythies v Angus* (1861) 2 F & F 381; *Re Hewitt and Portsmouth Waterworks Co* (1862) 10 WR 780; *Baroness Wenlock v River Dee Co* (1883) 53 LJQB 208; *Golodetz v Schrier* (1947) 80 Ll L Rep 647. If a reasonable excuse for a party's failure to attend is shown, an award made pursuant to such a hearing will be set aside: *Gladwin v Chilcote* (1841) 9 Dowl 550.
9   *Carey and Brown v Henderson and Liddell* (1920) 2 Ll L Rep 479 at 480, CA, per Atkin LJ; *Oakland Metal Co Ltd v D Benaim & Co Ltd* [1953] 2 Lloyd's Rep 192 at 199 per Parker J; *Montrose Canned Foods Ltd v Eric Wells (Merchants) Ltd* [1965] 1 Lloyd's Rep 597; *A A Amram Ltd v Bremar Co Ltd* [1966] 1 Lloyd's Rep 494 at 499 per Megaw J; *Altco Ltd v Sutherland* [1971] 2 Lloyd's Rep 515; *Modern Engineering (Bristol) Ltd v C Miskin & Sons Ltd* [1981] 1 Lloyd's Rep 135.
10   *Ritchie v W Jacks & Co* (1922) 10 Ll L Rep 519 at 521, CA, per Lord Sterndale MR; *A A Amram Ltd v Bremar Co Ltd* [1966] 1 Lloyd's Rep 494 at 499 per Megaw J; *Oakland Metal Co Ltd v D Benaim & Co Ltd* [1953] 2 Lloyd's Rep 192 at 199 per Parker J. See also *Star International Hong Kong (UK) Ltd v Bergbau-Handel GmbH* [1966] 2 Lloyd's Rep 16; *Henry Bath & Son Ltd v Birgby Products* [1962] 1 Lloyd's Rep 389 at 398–399 per McNair J.

(2) PROCEDURE AND EVIDENCE

671. Procedure. The parties to an arbitration agreement may expressly agree the procedure to be followed at the reference[1]. However, the parties rarely expressly agree a complete code of procedure, in which case the procedure to be followed must be implied from the language of the arbitration agreement, the surrounding circumstances of the reference and any custom or trade practice which is incorporated into the arbitration agreement[2]. An award made by the arbitrator in breach of the agreed procedure may be set aside on the basis that the parties have not agreed to be bound by an award made by the procedure in fact adopted[3].

1 Such an agreement will be enforced unless it is so contrary to fundamental principles that it is treated as contrary to public policy: *Naumann v Edward Nathan & Co Ltd* (1930) 37 Ll L Rep 249 at 252, CA, per Scrutton LJ; *London Export Corpn Ltd v Jubilee Coffee Roasting Co Ltd* [1958] 1 All ER 494 at 497–498, [1958] 1 WLR 271 at 277–278 per Diplock J; affd [1958] 2 All ER 411, [1958] 1 WLR 661, CA.
2 *London Export Corpn Ltd v Jubilee Coffee Roasting Co Ltd* [1958] 1 All ER 494 at 498, [1958] 1 WLR 271 at 278 per Diplock J.
3 *London Export Corpn Ltd v Jubilee Coffee Roasting Co Ltd* [1958] 1 All ER 494 at 497, [1958] 1 WLR 271 at 277 per Diplock J.

672. Evidence. As a general rule, the arbitrator is bound by the rules of evidence of English law regarding the admissibility of evidence[1]. The arbitrator must not, therefore, admit and act upon evidence which is inadmissible and which goes to the root of an issue which he has to determine[2]. If he does so, the award may be set aside on the grounds of misconduct[3]. However, the parties may agree, either expressly[4] or impliedly[5], that the strict rules regarding the admissibility of evidence need not be followed by the arbitrator. The parties may also waive a possible objection to the admissibility of particular evidence[6].

1 *A-G v Davison* (1825) M'Cle & Yo 160; *East and West India Dock Co v Kirk and Randall* (1887) 12 App Cas 738, HL; *Re Enoch and Zaretzky, Bock & Co* [1910] 1 KB 327, CA, explaining *Re Keighley Maxsted & Co and Bryan Durant & Co* [1893] 1 QB 405, CA.
  The admissibility of hearsay evidence in civil proceedings is governed by the Civil Evidence Act 1968; see generally EVIDENCE vol 17 para 53 et seq. The Act applies to arbitrations other than those in relation to which the strict rules of evidence do not apply: s 18 (1) (b). The rules of court made pursuant to the Civil Evidence Act 1968 s 8 (RSC Ord 38 Pt III (rr 20–34)) apply to such arbitrations, unless excluded by agreement, subject to such modifications as may be appropriate: Civil Evidence Act 1968 s 10 (3). If any question arises as to what modifications are appropriate, that question is to be determined by the arbitrator or umpire in default of agreement: s 10 (4).
  The admissibility of expert evidence, both oral and written, and evidence of foreign law in civil proceedings is governed by the Civil Evidence Act 1972; see generally EVIDENCE vol 17 para 83 et seq. The Act applies to arbitrations other than those in relation to which the strict rules of evidence do not apply: s 5 (1), adopting the meanings assigned by the Civil Evidence Act 1968 s 18 (1), (2). By the Civil Evidence Act 1972 s 5 (2), the Civil Evidence Act 1968 s 10 (3), (4) apply for the purposes of ss 2 and 4 of the 1972 Act.
  As a general rule, an arbitrator should not rely on his knowledge of facts relating to issues in dispute unless he informs the parties and provides them with opportunity to comment on or to challenge it: *Louis Dreyfus & Co v Produce Brokers' New Co (1924) Ltd* (1936) 54 Ll L Rep 60; *Owen v Nicholl* [1948] 1 All ER 707, CA; *Grand Trunk Rly Co of Canada v R* [1923] AC 150, PC; *Youroveta Home and Foreign Trade Co Inc v Coopman* (1920) 3 Ll L Rep 242, DC. However, an arbitrator is frequently appointed because of his knowledge and experience in a particular area. Consequently, in certain circumstances, it has been held that an arbitrator may make use of his knowledge and experience to determine issues in dispute without hearing expert evidence. For example, in a quality dispute, an arbitrator appointed because of his knowledge and experience can decide questions of both quality and damage without hearing expert evidence: *Mediterranean and Eastern Export Co v Fortress Fabrics (Manchester) Ltd* [1948] 2 All ER 186; *Eads v Williams* (1854) 4 De G M & G 674; *Wright v Hawson* (1888) 4 TLR 386; *Jordenson & Co v Stora Kopparbergs Bergslags Aktiebolag* (1931) 41 Ll L Rep 201. See also *British Oil and Cake Mills Ltd v Horace Battin & Co Ltd* (1922) 13 Ll L Rep 443.
  Where expert evidence is adduced at the hearing, an arbitrator should use his knowledge and experience to understand and evaluate that expert evidence: *James Longley v South West Thames Regional Health Authority* (1983) 25 BLR 56 at 63; *Top Shop Estates Ltd v Danino* [1985] 1 EGLR 9 at 11. An arbitrator should not use his knowledge and experience to refute the expert evidence adduced by one party unless he gives that party an opportunity to challenge his preferred view: *Fox v P G Wellfair Ltd* [1981] 2 Lloyd's Rep 514, CA.

An arbitrator may for his own guidance consult a third party with expert knowledge on an issue in the arbitration, although he must form his own judgment on every issue referred to him: *Emery v Wase* (1801) 5 Ves 846; affd (1803) 8 Ves 505 at 517; *Hopcraft v Hickman* (1824) 2 Sim & St 130; *Anderson v Wallace* (1835) 3 Cl & Fin 26; *Caledonian Rly Co v Lockhart* (1860) 3 Macq 808; *Gray v Wilson* (1865) LR 1 CP 50; *Re Hare, Milne and Haswell* (1839) 6 Bing NC 158 at 162; *Johnson v Latham* (1850) 19 LJQB 329. An arbitrator may obtain legal assistance in framing his award: *Fetherstone v Cooper* (1803) 9 Ves 67; *Baker v Cotterill* (1849) 7 Dow & L 20; *Behren v Bremer* (1854) 3 CLR 40; *Rolland v Cassidy* (1888) 13 App Cas 770 at 776–777, PC; *Threlfall v Fanshawe* (1850) 1 LM & P 340; *Galloway v Keyworth* (1854) 15 CB 228; *Re Underwood and Bedford and Cambridge Rly Co* (1861) 11 CBNS 442; *Giacomo Costa Fu Andrea v British Italian Trading Co Ltd* [1961] 2 Lloyd's Rep 392; affd [1963] 1 QB 201, [1962] 2 All ER 53, [1962] 1 Lloyd's Rep 151, CA.

2 *Walford, Baker & Co v Macfie & Sons* (1915) 84 LJKB 2221; *Agroexport Entreprise d'Etat pour le Commerce Exterieur v NV Goorden Import Co SA* [1956] 1 Lloyd's Rep 319.

3 *Walford, Baker & Co v Macfie & Sons* (1915) 84 LJKB 2221; *Agroexport Entreprise d'Etat pour le Commerce Exterieur v N V Goorden Import Co SA* [1956] 1 Lloyd's Rep 319. An award will probably not be set aside merely on account of a supposed mistake of the arbitrator as to the admissibility of evidence: *Re M'Clean & Co and Marcus* (1890) 6 TLR 355 at 356 per Lord Coleridge LCJ. Nor will a court be willing to set aside an award where inadmissible evidence was admitted unless this resulted in a substantial injustice: *Re Enoch and Zaretzky, Bock & Co* [1910] 1 KB 327 at 336, CA, per Farwell LJ. Nor will an award be set aside where an arbitrator, acting honestly and judicially, erroneously admitted inadmissible evidence: *Wm Adolph & Co v Keene Co* (1921) 7 Ll L Rep 142; *Agroexport Entreprise d'Etat pour le Commerce Exterieur v N V Goorden Import Co SA supra*. See also *Grand Trunk Rly Co of Canada v R* [1923] AC 150, PC.

4 *Macpherson Train & Co Ltd v J Milhem & Sons* [1955] 2 Lloyd's Rep 59, CA; *Henry Bath & Son Ltd v Birgby Products* [1962] 1 Lloyd's Rep 389 at 399 per McNair J. See also *French Government v Tsurushima Maru (Owners)* (1921) 37 TLR 961, CA; *F E Hookway & Co Ltd v Alfred Isaacs & Sons* [1954] 1 Lloyd's Rep 491 at 500.

5 *Henry Bath & Son Ltd v Birgby Products* [1962] 1 Lloyd's Rep 389 at 399 per McNair J. An implied agreement will arise where the parties agree to a form of arbitration in which the strict rules of evidence are not generally followed: *Henry Bath & Son Ltd v Birgby Products supra*.

6 *Re Enoch and Zaretsky, Bock & Co* [1910] 1 KB 327 at 336, CA, per Farwell LJ; *Macpherson Train & Co Ltd v J Milhem & Sons* [1955] 1 Lloyd's Rep 597 at 600 per McNair J; affd [1955] 2 Lloyd's Rep 591, CA. See also *London Dock Co v Shadwell Parish* (1862) 7 LT 381.

(3) POWERS OF THE ARBITRATOR OR UMPIRE

673. General. By the arbitration agreement, the parties empower the arbitrator to make an award on the disputes or differences referred to arbitration. The parties may also confer on the arbitrator such other incidental powers as they consider appropriate[1], although they cannot confer on the arbitrator powers of a kind which only a judge can exercise[2].

As an arbitrator (and subsequently an umpire) obtains his jurisdiction from the arbitration agreement, he can neither reject any part of that agreement[3] nor disregard any limitations placed on his authority[4]. However, an arbitrator is entitled to consider whether or not he has jurisdiction to act, so as to satisfy himself that it is worth while to proceed[5]. An umpire, when substituted for the arbitrators, has the same powers as they had[6]. The umpire must adjudicate on the whole of the dispute which is referred to him[7], although it is possible for the two arbitrators to make an award on some matters in dispute and to refer to the umpire other matters on which they are not in agreement[8].

1 Powers which are expressly conferred on the arbitrator cannot be exercised against persons who are not parties to the arbitration agreement.

2 *Kursell v Timber Operators and Contractors Ltd* [1923] 2 KB 202 at 206 per Salter J. Examples of powers which only a judge can exercise are the power to commit for contempt (*Re Unione Stearinerie Lanza and Weiner* [1917] 2 KB 558) and the power to order the issue of a writ of habeas corpus ad testificandum (*Kursell v Timber Operators and Contractors Ltd supra* at 206 per Salter J).

3 Where arbitrators were appointed to arbitrate in a dispute which had arisen 'under contract and addendum', it was held not to be open to the arbitrators (or the umpire) to hold that a provision of the addendum did not apply to the agreement; *Cie Algerienne de Meunerie v Kyprianou* [1960] 1 Lloyd's Rep 366; affd [1961] 2 Lloyd's Rep 113, CA.

4 Eg a limitation on his right to appoint an umpire: *Rahcassi Shipping Co SA v Blue Star Line* [1969] 1 QB 173, [1967] 3 All ER 301.

5 An award which expressly or impliedly refers to such a finding is not thereby invalidated: *Christopher Brown Ltd v Genossenschaft Oesterreichischer Waldbesitzer Holzwirtschaftsbetriebe Registrierte GmbH* [1954] 1 QB 8, [1953] 2 All ER 1039; *Luanda Exportadora SARL and Colprogeca-Sociedade Geral De Fibras, Cafes E Produtos Coloniais Lda v Wahbe Tamari & Sons Ltd and Jaffa Trading Co* [1967] 2 Lloyd's Rep 353 at 364 per Roskill J; *Golodetz v Schrier* (1947) 80 Ll L Rep 647 at 650 per Lord Goddard.

6 See the Arbitration Act 1950 ss 8, 10. See also *Taylor v Dutton* (1823) 1 LJOSKB 158. The umpire may also receive assistance from the arbitrators acting in a non-judicial capacity: see para 675 post. However, the umpire usually sits with the arbitrators from the commencement of the reference as the parties would otherwise have to repeat the evidence: see *Re Salkeld and Slater and Harrison* (1840) 12 Ad & El 767. Furthermore, the parties often expressly agree that the umpire is empowered to make all procedural rulings during the course of the reference.

7 *Cerrito v North Eastern Timber Importers Ltd* [1952] 1 Lloyd's Rep 330. See also *Orion Compania Espanola de Seguros v Belfort Maatschappij Voor Algemene Verzekgringeen* [1962] 2 Lloyd's Rep 257.

8 See *Lang v Brown* (1855) 25 LTOS 297, HL.

674. Statutorily implied powers. Unless a contrary intention is expressed therein, every arbitration agreement is deemed to contain a provision that the parties to the reference, and all persons claiming through them respectively, shall, subject to any legal objection[1], submit to be examined by the arbitrator or umpire, on oath or affirmation, in relation to the matters in dispute, and shall, subject as aforesaid, produce before the arbitrator or umpire all documents within their possession or power respectively which may be required or called for[2], and do all other things[3] which during the proceedings on the reference the arbitrator or umpire may require[4]. Unless a contrary intention is expressed therein, every arbitration agreement is deemed to contain a provision that the witnesses on the reference shall, if the arbitrator or umpire thinks fit, be examined on oath or affirmation[5].

An arbitrator or umpire has, unless a contrary intention is expressed in the arbitration agreement, the power to administer oaths to, or take the affirmations of, the parties to and witnesses on a reference under the agreement[6].

1 These words apply to all the subsequent provisions of the section (ie the Arbitration Act 1950 s 12): *Re Société Les Affréteurs Réunis and the Shipping Controller* [1921] 3 KB 1. They enable a party to refuse compliance with an order which he could not be compelled to obey if made by the High Court, such as an order for the disclosure of documents protected by Crown privilege: *Re Société les Affréteurs Réunis and the Shipping Controller* supra.

2 See para 672 ante; and EVIDENCE. These words enable an arbitrator to order the production and inspection of named documents, but they probably do not give him the power to order general discovery: *Kursell v Timber Operators and Contractors Ltd* [1923] 2 KB 202. These words are subject to the usual rules as to privilege, ie Crown privilege (*Re Société les Affréteurs Réunis and the Shipping Controller* [1921] 3 KB 1) and 'without prejudice' correspondence (*Finney Lockseeds Ltd v George Mitchell (Chesterhall) Ltd* [1979] 2 Lloyd's Rep 301).

As arbitration proceedings are private, the only test for disclosure of documents is relevance, and confidentiality is not material: *Mitchell Construction Kinnear Moodie Group v East Anglia Regional Hospital Board* [1971] CLY 375.

3 These words empower an arbitrator to do anything which he may require for determining facts or law in order that he may decide the reference: *Re Unione Stearinerie Lanza and Wiener* [1917] 2 KB 558 at 562 per Viscount Reading CJ. They do not, however, give the arbitrator all the powers of the court: *Vasso (Owners) v Vasso (Cargo owners), The Vasso* [1983] 3 All ER 211 at 216, [1983] 1 WLR 838 at 844, [1983] 2 Lloyd's Rep 346 at 350 per Lloyd J.

An arbitrator may direct delivery of points of claim and of defence, and may exercise his discretion as to allowing or disallowing amendments of the same: *Edward Lloyd Ltd v Sturgeon Falls Pulp Co Ltd* (1901) 85 LT 162; *Re Crighton and Law, Car and General Insurance Corpn Ltd* [1910] 2 KB 738.

An arbitrator may order either party to make discovery of documents or to answer interrogatories on oath: *Kursell v Timber Operators and Contractors Ltd* [1923] 2 KB 202.

An arbitrator may order the inspection of property which is the subject matter of the reference: *The Vasso* supra.

An arbitrator has no power, without the consent of the parties, to order concurrent hearings in two different references, involving different parties, both of which have been referred to him: *Oxford Shipping Co Ltd v Nippon Yusen Kaisha, The Eastern Saga* [1984] 3 All ER 835, [1984] 2 Lloyd's Rep 373.

An arbitrator has no common law power to strike out arbitration proceedings and to dismiss a claim for want of prosecution on the ground of inordinate and inexcusable delay: *Crawford v A E A Prowting Ltd* [1973] QB 1, [1972] 1 All ER 1119. However, it has been suggested that if an arbitrator were to give a peremptory direction requiring the claimant to give proper particulars of the claim within a limited time and the claimant failed to tender such particulars, the arbitrator could proceed to a hearing at which the claimant would be debarred from tendering evidence of any claim of which he had not given the required particulars, and the arbitrator would have jurisdiction to dismiss the claim: *Crawford v A E A Prowting Ltd* supra at 8, 1204 per Bridge J; *Bremer Vulkan Schiffbau und Maschinenfabrik v South India Shipping Corpn Ltd* [1981] AC 909 at 986–987, [1981] 1 All ER 289 at 302, [1981] 1 Lloyd's Rep 253 at 263, HL, per Lord Diplock. But see the Arbitration Act 1950 s 13A (added by the Courts and Legal Services Act 1990 s 102; in force as from a day to be appointed under s 124 (3)).

An arbitrator has no power to make an order for security for costs unless such a power is conferred by the arbitration agreement, as the object of an application for security for costs has nothing to do with the arbitrator ascertaining the true position between the parties in order to assist him in arriving at a determination of the dispute: *Re Unione Stearinerie Lanza and Wiener* [1917] 2 KB 558; *Mavani v Ralli Bros Ltd* [1973] 1 All ER 555 at 559, [1973] 1 WLR 468 at 472 per Kerr J.

4 Arbitration Act 1950 s 12 (1). When the question arises of an arbitrator exercising powers under s 12 (1) or (2), he must proceed on the basis of deciding whether or not in his judgment the exercise of any of the powers is necessary for the proper determination of the disputes referred to him: *Kirkawa Corpn v Gatoil Overseas Inc, The Peter Kirk* [1990] 1 Lloyd's Rep 154.

5 Arbitration Act 1950 s 12 (2). See note 3 supra.

6 Ibid s 12 (3).

675. Power of joint arbitrators to act in non-judicial capacity.

Where the reference is made to two arbitrators with power to appoint an umpire in the event of a disagreement, and the umpire enters on the reference when the arbitrators disagree, the arbitrators are functus officio as arbitrators[1]. In such circumstances, the arbitrators may be empowered by the parties[2] to continue to participate in the reference in a non-judicial capacity. The arbitrators may, for example, give the umpire evidence of fact[3] or expert evidence[4] or appear before the umpire as advocates for the parties by whom they were appointed[5]. Where the arbitrators become the advocates of the parties by whom they were appointed, they are the agents of the respective parties so as to enable them to waive procedural irregularities[6]. The arbitrators can also enlarge the umpire's powers provided they have the authorisation of the parties by whom they were appointed[7].

1 See Arbitration Act 1950 s 8 (2). See para 656 ante.

2 This continued involvement of the arbitrators may be expressly or impliedly agreed by the parties to the reference. The parties may, for example, impliedly agree by consenting to a 'commercial' arbitration where the practice is known to operate.

3 *Bourgeois v Weddell & Co* [1924] 1 KB 539.

4 *Cerrito v North Eastern Timber Importers Ltd* [1952] 1 Lloyd's Rep 330.

5 *Re Enoch and Zaretzky, Bock & Co* [1910] 1 KB 327 at 334, CA, per Farwell LJ; *French Government v Tsurushima Maru SS (Owners)* (1921) 37 TLR 961, CA; *Ritchie v W Jacks & Co* (1922) 10 Ll L Rep 519; *Russian Oil Products Ltd v Caucasian Oil Co Ltd* (1928) 31 Ll L Rep 109; *Wessanen's Koninklijke Fabrieken NV v Isaac Modiano Brother & Sons Ltd* [1960] 3 All ER 617, [1960] 1 WLR 1243, [1960] 2 Lloyd's Rep 257; *Kawasaki Kisen Kaisha Ltd v Government of Ceylon* [1962] 1 Lloyd's Rep 424;

Rahcassi Shipping Co SA v Blue Star Line Ltd [1969] 1 QB 173, [1967] 3 All ER 301; *Westminster Chemical and Produce Ltd v Eichholz and Loeser* [1954] 1 Lloyd's Rep 99.
6 *Ritchie v Jacks & Co* (1922) 10 Ll L Rep 519; *Wessanen's Koninklijke Fabrieken NV v Isaac Modiano Brother & Sons Ltd* [1960] 3 All ER 617, [1960] 1 WLR 1243, [1960] 2 Lloyd's Rep 257; *Kawasaki Kisen Kaisha v Government of Ceylon* [1962] 1 Lloyd's Rep 424 at 429 per McNair J; *Government of Ceylon v Chandris* [1963] 2 QB 327, [1963] 2 All ER 1, [1963] 1 Lloyd's Rep 214; *Rahcassi Shipping Co SA v Blue Star Line Ltd* [1969] 1 QB 173, [1967] 3 All ER 301; *Hill Court Shipping Co SA v Cie Continentale (France) SA, The Yperagia* [1977] 1 Lloyd's Rep 29 at 36 per Mocatta J. See also *French Government v Tsurushima Maru SS (Owners)* (1921) 37 TLR 961, CA.
7 *Kawasaki Kisen Kaisha Ltd v Government of Ceylon* [1962] 1 Lloyd's Rep 424 at 429 per McNair J. See *Westminster Chemical and Produce Ltd v Eichholz and Loeser* [1954] 1 Lloyd's Rep 99 at 106 per Devlin J for consideration of what constitutes authorisation.

676. Time for making award. Except where an award is remitted by the court[1], in which case the arbitrator must make his award within three months after the date of the order remitting the award, unless the order otherwise directs[2], and subject to anything to the contrary in the arbitration agreement, an arbitrator or umpire has power to make an award at any time[3].

Even where the time for making an award is limited[4], the High Court or a judge thereof may enlarge the time so limited whether or not it has expired[5]. However, an arbitrator or umpire must use all reasonable dispatch in making his award or he may be removed by the High Court with the result that he loses his entitlement to receive any remuneration in respect of his services[6].

1 Under either the Arbitration Act 1950 s 22 or the Arbitration Act 1979 s 1. As to remission under these sections see para 690 et seq post.
2 Arbitration Act 1950 s 22 (2); Arbitration Act 1979 s 1 (2).
3 Arbitration Act 1950 s 13 (1).
4 Whether under the Arbitration Act 1950 or otherwise.
5 Ibid s 13 (2). Although s 13 (2) does not apply to a reference to a judge-arbitrator or judge-umpire, a judge-arbitrator or judge-umpire may enlarge any time limited for making his award, whether under the Arbitration Act 1950 or otherwise, whether that time has expired or not: Administration of Justice Act 1970 s 4 (4), Sch 3 para 6.
6 See the Arbitration Act 1950 s 13 (3). This provision does not apply to a reference to a judge-arbitrator or judge-umpire: see the Administration of Justice Act 1970 Sch 3 para 6.

(4) POWERS OF THE HIGH COURT

677. Interlocutory powers. The High Court has no inherent jurisdiction to supervise the conduct of the reference and of the arbitrator[1]. However, the High Court possesses various powers which may be invoked during the course of the reference[2]. Without prejudice to the powers which may be vested in the arbitrator or umpire in these matters, the High Court[3] has, for the purpose of and in relation to a reference, the same power of making orders as it has for the purpose of and in relation to an action or matter in the High Court in respect of the following: (1) security for costs[4]; (2) the giving of evidence by affidavit[5]; (3) the examination on oath of any witness before an officer of the High Court or any other person, and the issue of a commission or request for the examination of a witness out of the jurisdiction[6]; (4) the preservation, interim custody or sale of any goods which are the subject matter of the reference[7]; (5) securing the amount in dispute in the reference[8]; (6) the detention, preservation or inspection of any property or thing which is the subject of the reference or as to which any question may arise therein, and authorising for any of the purposes aforesaid any persons to enter upon or into any land or building in the possession of any party to the reference, or authorising any samples to be taken or any observation to be made or experiment to be tried which may be necessary or expedient for the purpose of obtaining full information or evidence[9]; and (7) interim injunctions or the appointment of a receiver[10].

In the case of a judge-arbitrator or judge-umpire these powers are exercisable as in the case of any other reference to arbitration, but are exercisable also by the judge-arbitrator or judge-umpire himself[11], and anything he does in the exercise of these powers is done by him in his capacity as a judge of the High Court and has effect as if done by that court; this is without prejudice, however, to any power vested in the arbitrator or umpire in his capacity as such[12].

1 *Exormisis Shipping SA v Oonsoo, the Democratic Peoples Republic of Korea and the Korean Foreign Transportation Corpn* [1975] 1 Lloyd's Rep 402 at 434 per Donaldson J; *Bremer Vulkan Schiffbau und Maschinenfabrik v South India Shipping Corpn Ltd* [1981] AC 909, [1981] 1 All ER 289, [1981] 1 Lloyd's Rep 253, HL; *K/S A/S Bill Biakh v Hyundai Corpn* [1988] 1 Lloyd's Rep 187 at 189 per Steyn J. But see *Japan Line Ltd v Aggeliki Charis Compania Maritima SA, The Angelic Grace* [1980] 1 Lloyd's Rep 288 at 292 per Lord Denning MR (expressly disapproved by the House of Lords in *Bremer Vulkan Schiffbau und Maschinenfabrik v South India Shipping Corpn Ltd* supra).

2 See the Supreme Court Act 1981 s 43A (added by the Courts and Legal Services Act 1990 s 100).

3 These powers may be exercised by a judge in chambers or a master: RSC Ord 73 r 3 (1).

4 Arbitration Act 1950 s 12 (6) (a): see generally RSC Ord 23; and PRACTICE AND PROCEDURE. The power of the court to order security for costs cannot be ousted by an express contrary agreement between the parties: *Mavani v Ralli Bros Ltd* [1973] 1 All ER 555, [1973] 1 WLR 468.

   An arbitrator does not have the power to order security for costs unless the arbitration agreement confers on him such a power: see para 674 ante. For the factors which the court will take into consideration in deciding whether to exercise this power see *Mavani v Ralli Bros Ltd* supra; *K/S A/S Bani and K/S A/S Havbulki v Korea Shipbuilding and Engineering Corpn* [1987] 2 Lloyd's Rep 445, CA (where the court considered that an order for security for costs was appropriate where the proceedings were expensive and complex, and the claimant's financial position was precarious); *Bank Mellat v Helliniki Techniki SA* [1984] QB 291, [1983] 3 All ER 428, CA (where the court declined to make an order for security for costs where foreign parties had agreed to arbitrate in England under the rules of the International Chamber of Commerce); *Flender Werft AG v Aegean Maritime Ltd* [1990] 2 Lloyd's Rep 27. See also *Fal Bunkering of Sharjah v Grecale Inc of Panama* [1990] 1 Lloyd's Rep 369.

   An order for security for costs may be granted to a claimant advancing a counterclaim: see *Flender Werft AG v Aegean Maritime* supra; *Hitachi Shipbuilding and Engineering Co Ltd v Viafiel Compania Naviera SA* [1981] 2 Lloyd's Rep 498, CA; *Samuel J Cohl Co v Eastern Mediterranean Maritime Ltd, The Silver Fir* [1980] 1 Lloyd's Rep 371, CA.

   The court may order a permanent stay of the arbitration proceedings in the event of a failure by a party to comply with an order to provide security: *Dorval Tankers Pty Ltd v Two Arrows Maritime and Port Services Ltd (Pakistan Edible Oil Corpn Ltd, intervener)* [1984] 2 Lloyd's Rep 563, CA.

5 Arbitration Act 1950 s 12 (6) (c): see generally RSC Ord 38 r 2; and EVIDENCE.

6 Arbitration Act 1950 s 12 (6) (d): see generally RSC Ord 39; and EVIDENCE.

7 Arbitration Act 1950 s 12 (6) (e): see generally RSC Ord 29 rr 2, 4; and PRACTICE AND PROCEDURE.

8 Arbitration Act 1950 s 12 (6) (f): see generally RSC Ord 29 r 2 (3); and PRACTICE AND PROCEDURE. See also *Mantovani v Carapelli SpA* [1980] 1 Lloyd's Rep 375 at 382, CA, per Browne LJ. The court may order a permanent stay of the arbitration proceedings in the event of a failure by a party to comply with an order to pay the amount in dispute into court, thereby debarring the party in breach from pursuing or defending his claim: *Richco International Ltd v International Industrial Food Co SAL, The Fayrouz III* [1989] 1 All ER 613, [1989] 2 Lloyd's Rep 106.

9 Arbitration Act 1950 s 12 (6) (g): see generally RSC Ord 29 rr 2, 3; and PRACTICE AND PROCEDURE.

10 Arbitration Act 1950 s 12 (6) (h): see generally RSC Ord 29 r 1 and INJUNCTIONS, and RSC Ord 30 and RECEIVERS. See also *Cie du Sénégal et de la Côte Occidentale d'Afrique v Smith & Co and Woods & Co* (1883) 53 LJ Ch 166; *Pini v Roncoroni* [1892] 1 Ch 633; *Law v Garrett* (1878) 8 ChD 26, CA. The court may grant a Mareva injunction under either the Arbitration Act 1950 s 12 (6) (h) or the Supreme Court Act 1981 s 37: *The Rena K* [1979] QB 377 at 407–408, [1979] 1 All ER 397 at 418 per Brandon J. See also *Bank Mellat v Helliniki Techniki SA* [1984] QB 291 at 302, [1983] 3 All ER 428 at 432, CA, per Kerr LJ. As to Mareva injunctions see INJUNCTIONS.

11 Administration of Justice Act 1970 s 4 (4), Sch 3 para 5 (1).
12 Ibid Sch 3 para 5 (2).

678. Extending the power of arbitrator or umpire. If any party to a reference under an arbitration agreement fails within the time specified in the order or, if no time is so specified, within a reasonable time, to comply with an order made by the arbitrator or umpire in the course of the reference, then, on the application of the arbitrator or umpire or of any party to the reference, the High Court may make an order extending the powers of the arbitrator or umpire[1]. If such an order is made by the High Court, the arbitrator or umpire has power, to the extent and subject to any conditions specified in that order, to continue with the reference in default of appearance or of any other act by one of the parties in like manner as a judge of the High Court might continue with proceedings in that court where a party fails to comply with an order of that court or a requirement of rules of court[2].

In the case of a judge-arbitrator or judge-umpire this power is exercisable as in the case of any other reference to arbitration and also by the judge-arbitrator or judge-umpire himself[3], and anything done in the exercise of this power is done by him in his capacity as judge of the High Court and has effect as if done by that court[4].

1 Arbitration Act 1979 s 5 (1). The application must be made to a judge in chambers: RSC Ord 73 r 3 (2).
2 Arbitration Act 1979 s 5 (2). The provisions of s 5 have effect notwithstanding anything in the arbitration agreement but do not derogate from any powers conferred on an arbitrator or umpire whether by an arbitration agreement or otherwise: s 5 (5). 'Appearance', referred to in s 5, now means acknowledgment of service: see para 616 note 7 ante.
3 Ibid s 5 (3).
4 Ibid s 5 (4). The provisions of s 5 have effect notwithstanding anything in the arbitration agreement but do not derogate from any powers conferred on any arbitrator or umpire, whether by an arbitration agreement or otherwise: s 5 (5).

679. Determination of preliminary point of law. On an application[1] to the High Court made by any of the parties to a reference with the consent of an arbitrator or umpire who has entered on the reference, or with the consent of all the other parties, the High Court has jurisdiction[2] to determine any question of law[3] arising in the course of the reference[4]. However, the High Court must not entertain an application made with the consent of an arbitrator or umpire, but without the consent of all the other parties, unless it is satisfied that the determination of the application might produce substantial savings in costs to the parties, and the question of law is one in respect of which leave to appeal from the award would be likely to be given[5] by the court[6]. Unless the High Court gives leave, no appeal lies to the Court of Appeal from a decision of the High Court to entertain or not to entertain an application made with the consent of the arbitrator or umpire, but without the consent of all the other parties[7].

For the purposes of appeals to the Court of Appeal, such a decision of the High Court is deemed to be a judgment of the court within the meaning of the Supreme Court Act 1981[8], but no appeal will lie from such a decision unless the High Court or the Court of Appeal gives leave to appeal, and it is certified by the High Court that the question of law to which the decision relates either is one of general public importance or is one which for some other special reason should be considered by the Court of Appeal[9]. The criteria for granting leave to appeal to the Court of Appeal are at least as strict[10] as those[11] relating to appeals against determination of an appeal by the High Court[12].

1 The application must be made by originating motion to a single judge in court: RSC Ord 73 r 2 (1). The application must be made and notice thereof served within 14 days after the arbitrator or umpire has consented to the application being made, or the other parties have so consented: RSC Ord 73 r 5 (3).

2 See *Chapman v Charlwood Alliance Properties* (1981) 260 Estates Gazette 1041.

3 The provisions of the Arbitration Act 1979 s 2 are subject only to the provisions relating to exclusion agreements and have effect not withstanding anything in any agreement purporting to prohibit or restrict access to the High Court, or to restrict the jurisdiction of that court, or to prohibit or restrict the making of a reasoned award: s 3 (4).

4 Ibid s 2 (1). No application with the consent of an arbitrator or umpire may be made under this section if an exclusion agreement has been entered into by the parties: s 3 (1). There are certain classes of contract in respect of which the parties cannot enter into an exclusion agreement: see s 4. See also *Babanaft International Co SA v Avant Petroleum Inc, The Oltenia* [1982] 3 All ER 244, [1982] 1 WLR 871, [1982] 2 Lloyd's Rep 99, CA; *Gebr Broere BV v Saras Chimica SpA* [1982] 2 Lloyd's Rep 436; *Vasso (Owners) v Vasso (Cargo owners), The Vasso* [1983] 3 All ER 211, [1983] 1 WLR 828, [1983] 2 Lloyd's Rep 346. The Arbitration Act 1979 s 2 (1) applies in relation to the determination of a dispute by the arbitral tribunal arising from an agreement made in connection with the construction and operation of the Channel Tunnel system: Channel Tunnel Act 1987 s 15 (3), (4). As to the 'arbitral tribunal' see s 2 (10). No court in any part of the United Kingdom has jurisdiction to determine any matter over which the arbitral tribunal assumes jurisdiction: s 15 (5).

5 Ie under the Arbitration Act 1979 s 1 (3) (b); see para 710 post.

6 Ibid s 2 (2). The conditions in s 2 (2) do not apply where the application is brought with the consent of all the parties other than the applicant. See *Vasso (Owners) v Vasso (Cargo owners), The Vasso* [1983] 3 All ER 211, [1983] 1 WLR 838, [1983] 2 Lloyd's Rep 346.

7 Arbitration Act 1979 s 2 (2A) (added by the Supreme Court Act 1981 s 148 (3) (a)).

8 Ie the Supreme Court Act 1981 s 16.

9 Arbitration Act 1979 s 2 (3) (amended by the Supreme Court Act 1981 ss 148 (3) (b), 152 (1), Sch 5).

10 *Babanaft International Co SA v Avant Petroleum Inc, The Oltenia* [1982] 3 All ER 244, [1982] 1 WLR 871, [1982] 2 Lloyd's Rep 99, CA.

11 Defined in *Geogas SA v Trammo Gas Ltd, The Baleares* [1991] 2 All ER 110, [1991] 2 WLR 794, CA; affd [1991] 3 All ER 554, [1991] 1 WLR 776, HL.

12 Ie under the Arbitration Act 1979 s 1.

680. Issue of subpoena. Any party to a reference under an arbitration agreement may sue out a writ of subpoena ad testificandum or a writ of subpoena duces tecum[1], but no person may be compelled under any such writ to produce any document which he could not be compelled to produce on the trial of an action, and the High Court or a judge thereof may order that a writ of subpoena ad testificandum or of subpoena duces tecum shall issue to secure the attendance before an arbitrator or umpire of a witness wherever he may be within the United Kingdom[2]. The High Court or a judge thereof may also order that a writ of habeas corpus ad testificandum shall issue to bring up a prisoner for examination before an arbitrator or umpire[3]. In the case of a judge-arbitrator or judge-umpire these powers are exercisable as in the case of any other reference to arbitration, but are exercisable also by the judge-arbitrator or judge-umpire himself[4], and anything he does in the exercise of these powers is done by him in his capacity as a judge of the High Court and has effect as if done by that court; this is without prejudice to any power vested in the arbitrator or umpire in his capacity as such[5].

1 See generally RSC Ord 38 rr 14–19; and EVIDENCE. An application under the Arbitration Act 1950 s 12 (4) for an order that a writ of subpoena ad testificandum or duces tecum shall issue to compel the attendance before an arbitrator or umpire of a witness may, if the attendance of the witness is required within the district of any district registry, be made at that registry, instead of at the Admiralty and Commercial Registry, at the option of the applicant: RSC Ord 73 r 4. For forms see 6 Court Forms (2nd Edn) (1989 Issue) 130–132, Forms 55–58.

2 Arbitration Act 1950 s 12 (4).

3 Ibid s 12 (5). For forms see 6 Court Forms (1989 Issue) 132–133, Forms 59–61.

4 Administration of Justice Act 1970 s 4 (4), Sch 3 para 5 (1).
5 Ibid Sch 3 para 5 (2).

9. THE AWARD, REMISSION, APPEALS AND ENFORCEMENT

(1) THE AWARD

(i) The Award

681. Content of award. The award must be complete in that it must determine all disputes which the parties referred to arbitration[1]. An incomplete award is invalid and unenforceable[2] and will normally be remitted by the court to the arbitrator[3]. Conversely, the award must not determine matters which were not referred to arbitration. If it does, the award is invalid and unenforceable unless it is possible to sever the part of the award which determines matters within the reference from the part of the award which determines matters outside the reference, in which case the former part of the award is valid and the latter part of the award is invalid[4]. The court should approach an award with a desire to support it rather than destroy it[5], and presume, unless and until the contrary is shown, that the arbitrator has by his award determined those matters, and those matters alone, which were referred to him. The burden of proving that the arbitrator has failed to award on matters which were referred, or that he has awarded on matters not referred, lies on the party who seeks to impeach the award[6].

The award may be expressed in such language as the arbitrator thinks fit, provided that its meaning is certain[7]. If the meaning of the award is uncertain, the award is invalid and unenforceable[8].

The award must be final and, therefore, an award is invalid and unenforceable if it leaves some of the matters in dispute to be determined either by the arbitrator at a later date[9] or by a third party[10]. Similarly, a conditional award is invalid for want of finality unless the award provides an alternative in case the condition is not fulfilled[11].

Unless a contrary intention is expressed therein, every arbitration agreement is, where such a provision is applicable to the reference, deemed to contain a provision that the arbitrator or umpire may, if he thinks fit, make an interim award[12].

1 However, where all matters in dispute between the parties are referred to arbitration, the award is valid if it deals with all the disputes which were placed before the arbitrator, even though there may be other disputes which were not brought to his attention: *Rees v Walters* (1847) 16 M & W 263; *Hawksworth v Brammall* (1840) 5 My & Cr 281; *Abraham and Westminster Improvements Co* (1849) 14 LTOS 203.
2 *Bradford v Bryan* (1741) Willes 268; *Hewitt v Hewitt* (1841) 1 QB 110; *Re Marshall and Dresser* (1842) 3 QB 878; *Richardson v Worsley* (1850) 5 Exch 613; *Wilkinson v Page* (1842) 1 Hare 276.
3 *Panchaud Frères SA v R Pagnan & Flli* [1974] 1 Lloyd's Rep 394, CA; *Lambert and Krzyiak Ltd v British Commercial Overseas Co Ltd* (1923) 16 Ll L Rep 51.
4 *Duke of Buccleuch v Metropolitan Board of Works* (1870) LR 5 Exch 221 at 229 per Blackburn J; revsd on another point (1872) LR 5 HL 418; *Selby v Whitbread & Co* [1917] 1 KB 736; *Leadbetter v Marylebone Corpn* [1904] 2 KB 893, CA; *Williams Bros v E T Agius Ltd* [1914] AC 510, HL; see also *Re Wright and Cromford Canal Co* (1841) 1 QB 98.
5 *Selby v Whitbread & Co* [1917] 1 KB 736 at 748 per McCardie J; *Christopher Brown Ltd v Genossenschaft Oesterreichischer Waldbesitzer Holwirtschaftsbetriebe Registrierte GmbH* [1954] 1 QB 8 at 10, [1953] 2 All

ER 1039 at 1041, per Devlin J; *Aktiebolaget Legis v V Berg & Sons Ltd* [1964] 1 Lloyd's Rep 203 at 214 per Roskill J.

6 *Bland & Co Ltd v Russian Bank for Foreign Trade* (1906) 11 Com Cas 71; *Jewell v Christie* (1867) LR 2 CP 296; *Davies v Pratt* (1855) 17 CB 183 at 188 per Jervis CJ; *Harrison v Creswick* (1853) 13 CB 399; *Obaseki Bros v Reif & Son Ltd* [1952] 2 Lloyd's Rep 364.

7 *Giacomo Costa Fu Andrea v British Italian Trading Co Ltd* [1963] 1 QB 201 at 218, [1962] 2 All ER 53 at 63, CA, per Diplock LJ; *Lock v Vulliamy* (1833) 5 B & Ad 600 at 602 per Denman CJ.

8 *River Plate Products Netherlands BV v Etablissement Coargrain* [1982] 1 Lloyd's Rep 628; *Margulies Bros Ltd v Dafnis Thomaides & Co (UK) Ltd* [1958] 1 All ER 777, [1958] 1 WLR 398; *Re Tidswell* (1863) 33 Beav 213; *Waddle v Downman* (1844) 12 M & W 562; *Plummer v Lee* (1837) 2 M & W 495 at 499; *Mortin v Burge* (1836) 4 Ad & El 973; *Re Tribe and Upperton* (1835) 3 Ad & El 295; *Hopcraft v Hickman* (1824) 2 Sim & St 130; see also *Manchester Carriage and Tramways Co Ltd v Swinton and Pendlebury UDC* [1906] AC 277, HL.

9 Unless the arbitrator is making an interim award, in which case he should make clear the purpose of the award: see *Stockport Metropolitan Borough Council v O'Reilly* [1978] 1 Lloyd's Rep 595.

10 *Re Goddard and Mansfield* (1850) 1 LM & P 25; *Johnson v Latham* (1850) 1 LM & P 348; *Tomlin v Fordwich Corpn* (1836) 5 Ad & El 147

11 *Nickels v Hancock* (1855) 7 De GM & G 300; *Baillie v Edinburgh Oil Gas Light Co* (1835) 3 Cl & Fin 639.

12 Arbitration Act 1950 s 14. Any reference in Part I of the Act (ss 1–34) to an award includes an interim award: s 14.

682. Form of award. Unless the agreement of reference prescribes the form in which the award is to be made, it may be made in such form as the arbitrator or umpire thinks fit[1]. It is usual, although unnecessary, to insert recitals in an award[2], in which the arbitrator or umpire sets out the nature and circumstances of the dispute. Inaccurate recitals do not affect the validity of the award[3]. Collateral writings not attached or referred to in the award cannot form part of it[4]. However, in the absence of an express disclaimer, reasons not attached to the award, but issued together with it, form part of the award[5].

There is no duty on the arbitrator to give reasons for the award. However, where an award is made, and it appears to the court that the award does not or does not sufficiently set out the reasons for the award, the court has power to order the arbitrator or umpire to state the reasons[6] for his award in sufficient detail to enable the court to consider any question of law[7] arising out of the award, in order that an appeal may be brought[8]. Where the award is made without any reasons being given, the court must not make any such order unless it is satisfied either that before the award was made one of the parties to the reference gave notice to the arbitrator or umpire that a reasoned award would be required or that there is some special reason why such a notice was not given[9].

An award which is made by more than one arbitrator must be executed by all the arbitrators[10].

1 *Everard v Paterson* (1816) 6 Taunt 625; *Eardley v Steer* (1835) 4 Dowl 423.

2 *Spence v Eastern Counties Rly Co* (1839) 7 Dowl 697; *Baker v Hunter* (1847) 16 M & W 672.

3 *Thames Ironworks and Shipbuilding Co Ltd v R* (1869) 10 B & S 33; *Baker v Hunter* (1847) 16 M & W 672; *White v Sharp* (1844) 12 M & W 712; *Trew v Burton* (1833) 1 Cr & M 533.

4 *Leggo v Young* (1855) 16 CB 626; *Holgate v Killick* (1861) 7 H & N 418; *Kent v Elstob* (1802) 3 East 18. See also *Produce Brokers Co Ltd v Olympia Oil and Cake Co Ltd* [1916] 1 AC 314, HL.

As to the incorporation of documents or contracts into the award see generally *Aktiebolaget Legis v Berg & Sons Ltd* [1964] 1 Lloyd's Rep 203; *Giacomo Costa Fu Andrea v British Italian Trading Co Ltd* [1963] 1 QB 201, [1962] 2 All ER 53, CA; *Blaiber & Co Ltd v Leopold Newborne (London) Ltd* [1953] 2 Lloyd's Rep 427, CA.

5 *Pearl Marin Shipping A/B v Putro Cingolani SAS, The General Valdes* [1982] 1 Lloyd's Rep 17, CA. The reasons given may be taken into consideration by the court in deciding whether to set aside or remit the award.

6 For an award to constitute a reasoned award under the Arbitration Act 1979, the arbitrator or umpire should set out what, on his view of the evidence, did or did not happen and should explain why, in the light of what happened, he reached his decision and what that decision is: *Bremer Handelsgesellschaft mbH v Westzucker GmbH (No 2)* [1981] 2 Lloyd's Rep 130 at 132, CA, per Donaldson LJ.

7 There is no provision in the Arbitration Act 1979 for an appeal on a question of fact.

8 Ibid s 1 (5). See para 711 post . The application to the court will be made by any of the parties to the reference with the consent of all the other parties to the reference, or with the leave of the court (provided that there is no 'exclusion agreement'; see para 707 post): Arbitration Act 1979 s 1 (5) (a), (b).

9 Ibid s 1 (6).

10 It is no longer necessary for the arbitrators to sign the award at the same time and place: *European Grain and Shipping Ltd v Johnston* [1983] QB 520, [1982] 3 All ER 989, CA. (For the previous position see *Wade v Dowling* (1854) 4 E & B 44; *Anning v Hartley* (1858) 27 LJ Ex 145.)

683. Alteration of award. An arbitrator or umpire who has made his award is functus officio[1]. The effect of this, at common law, was that the arbitrator or umpire could not alter the award in any way whatsoever, even if the alteration was to correct a clerical mistake[2]. However, the current position[3] is that unless a contrary intention is expressed in the arbitration agreement, the arbitrator or umpire has power[4] to correct in an award any clerical mistake[5] or error arising from any accidental slip or omission[6]. This power cannot be invoked by an arbitrator or umpire to correct an award or judgment in which he assesses the evidence wrongly or misconstrues or misappreciates the law[7].

1 See para 684 post.

2 *Mordue v Palmer* (1870) 6 Ch App 22, where it was held that an arbitrator could not correct a mistake by a clerk in copying his draft order; see also *Henfree v Bromley* (1805) 6 East 309; *Irvine v Elnon* (1806) 8 East 54; *Ward v Dean* (1832) 3 B & Ad 234; *Trew v Burton* (1833) 1 Cr & M 533; *Brooke v Mitchell* (1840) 6 M & W 473 at 477; *Re Calvert and Wyler* (1899) 106 LT Jo 288; *Re Stringer and Riley Bros* [1901] 1 KB 105; and cf *Mountain v Parr* [1899] 1 QB 805, CA.

3 Arbitration Act 1950 s 17. The so-called 'slip rule' gives the arbitrator the same power to correct errors as is given to the High Court under RSC Ord 20 r 10, and the authorities on RSC Ord 20 r 10 are of assistance in considering the scope of the arbitrator's powers under the Arbitration Act 1950 s 17: see *Mutual Shipping Corpn of New York v Bayshore Shipping Co of Monrovia, The Montan* [1985] 1 All ER 520, [1985] 1 WLR 625, [1985] 1 Lloyd's Rep 189, CA. The power conferred by the Arbitration Act 1950 s 17 is rigidly limited to mere clerical mistakes or errors arising from an accidental slip or omission: see *Mutual Shipping Corpn of New York v Bayshore Shipping Co of Monrovia, The Montan* supra (where it was held that an award in which the arbitrator transposed the parties was an accidental slip giving rise to an error in the award); *Sutherland & Co v Hannevig Bros Ltd* [1921] 1 KB 336 (where it was held that the arbitrator had not made an error arising from any accidental slip or omission in awarding certain costs to one of the disputants and that he could not correct this award under the slip rule); *Re Great Western Rly Co and Postmaster-General* (1903) 19 TLR 636; *Pedler v Hardy* (1902) 18 TLR 591 at 592; and cf *Re Stringer and Riley Bros* [1901] 1 KB 105. See also *R v Cripps, ex p Muldoon* [1984] 1 QB 686, [1984] 2 All ER 705, CA; *Fuga AG v Bunge AG* [1975] 2 Lloyd's Rep 192. As to the power to add a direction as to costs see the Arbitration Act 1950 s 18 (4).

4 'Where he is minded to exercise this power, he should notify the parties and give them an opportunity to make representations and, if so minded, to challenge in the courts the applicability of the power to the facts of the particular situation': *Mutual Shipping Corpn of New York v Bayshore Shipping Co of Monrovia, The Montan* [1985] 1 All ER 520 at 527, [1985] 1 WLR 625 at 634, [1985] 1 Lloyd's Rep 189 at 194, CA, per Sir John Donaldson MR.

5 See *Sutherland & Co v Hannevig Bros Ltd* [1921] 1 KB 336 at 340–341 per Rowlatt J ('. . . a clerical mistake . . . is something almost mechanical — a slip of the pen or something of that kind').

6 Eg an oversight by an arbitrator in failing to award interest on a principal sum awarded: *Pancommerce SA v Veecheema BV* [1983] 2 Lloyd's Rep 304, CA. See *Food Corpn of India v Marastro Compania Naviera SA of Panama, The Trade Fortitude* [1986] 3 All ER 500, [1987] 1 WLR 134, [1986] 2 Lloyd's Rep 209, CA, where the respondent failed to establish an accidental slip or omission.

7 *Mutual Shipping Corpn of New York v Bayshore Shipping Co of Monrovia, The Montan* [1985] 1 All ER 520 at 526, [1985] 1 WLR 625 at 633, [1985] 1 Lloyd's Rep 189 at 193, CA, per Sir John Donaldson MR.

684. Effect of award. The effect of the award is such as the agreement of reference expressly or impliedly prescribes. Where no contrary intention is expressed and where such a provision is applicable, every arbitration agreement is deemed to contain a provision that the award is to be final and binding on the parties and any persons claiming under them respectively[1]. The making of an award, therefore, extinguishes the right on which the claim was founded[2] and gives rise to a new cause of action based on a term implied into every arbitration agreement that the parties will perform the award of the arbitrator[3].

Consequently, the making of an award determines the authority of the arbitrator and renders him functus officio[4]. However, this general rule is subject to the following qualifications: the arbitrator has the power to correct clerical mistakes or errors arising from any accidental slip or omission[5]; if the award is an interim award, the arbitrator's authority is determined only in respect of the matters dealt with in the interim award[6]; if the court remits the award to the arbitrator he has authority to make a fresh award on the matters remitted[7]. As a general rule, the effect of an award as between the parties to an arbitration agreement is to preclude either party from bringing fresh proceedings in respect of the cause of action which has been determined by the award[8] or in respect of an issue which was necessarily determined by the award[9]. Furthermore, once the award has been made, a party will not be allowed to raise in fresh proceedings an issue which should with reasonable diligence have been raised in the original proceedings[10]. The award gives rise to an estoppel analogous to that created by the judgment in an action in personam[11]. Therefore, where the arbitrator has awarded damages for breach of contract the successful party cannot commence further proceedings in personam[12] in respect of the same breach[13]. This is the case even though the damages payable under the award have not been paid[14]. However, where the arbitrator has awarded the payment of a debt, as opposed to the payment of damages, the award does not bar a further action for the original debt[15]. Similarly, where the award is merely declaratory of a party's right to be paid or the amount to be paid, that party is able to bring fresh proceedings to enforce that right[16].

An award of damages for breach of contract will bar further proceedings to recover further damages arising from the same cause of action[17] because of the rule that damages resulting from one cause of action, including anticipated future damages, must be assessed and recovered once and for all in the same proceedings[17]. However, this rule may not apply where there is a contrary arbitral practice in a particular trade[18].

1 Arbitration Act 1950 s 16.
2 *Gascoyne v Edwards* (1826) 1 Y & J 19; *Allen v Milner* (1831) 2 Cr & J 47; *Commings (Cummings) v Heard* (1869) LR 4 QB 669. See also *Norske Atlas Insurance Co Ltd v London General Insurance Co Ltd* (1927) 43 TLR 541.
3 *Purslow v Baily* (1705) 2 Ld Raym 1039; *Bremer Oeltransport GmbH v Drewry* [1933] 1 KB 753, CA; *F J Bloemen Pty Ltd v Gold Coast City Council* [1973] AC 115, [1972] 3 All ER 357, PC. But see *Norske Atlas Insurance Co Ltd v London General Insurance Co Ltd* (1927) 43 TLR 541. See para 712 post.
4 See para 683 ante, for the effect of this on the arbitrator's power to alter the award.
5 See the Arbitration Act 1950 s 17; and para 683 ante.
6 *Fidelitas Shipping Co Ltd v V/O Exportchleb* [1966] 1 QB 630, [1965] 2 All ER 4, [1965] 1 Lloyd's Rep 223, CA.
7 See para 690 et seq post. See *Aktiebolaget Legis v Berg & Sons Ltd* [1964] 1 Lloyd's Rep 203 at 213–214 per Roskill J.
8 *Whitehead v Tattersall* (1839) 1 Ad & El 491; *Parkes v Smith* (1850) 15 QB 297; *Commings (Cummings) v Heard* (1869) LR 4 QB 669; *Ayscough v Sheed, Thomson & Co Ltd* (1924) 40 TLR 707, HL; *Aktiebolaget Legis v Berg & Sons Ltd* [1964] 1 Lloyd's Rep 203.

9 *Fidelitas Shipping Co Ltd v V/O Exportchleb* [1966] 1 QB 630, [1965] 2 All ER 4, [1965] 1 Lloyd's Rep 223, CA, as discussed in *Carl Zeiss Stiftung v Rayner & Keeler Ltd (No 2)* [1967] 1 AC 853, [1966] 2 All ER 536, HL; *Middlemiss & Gould (a firm) v Hartlepool Corpn* [1973] 1 All ER 172 at 176, [1972] 1 WLR 1643 at 1647–1648, CA, per Lord Denning MR and Edmund-Davies LJ.

10 *Fidelitas Shipping v V/O Exportchleb* [1966] 1 QB 630, [1965] 2 All ER 4, [1965] 1 Lloyd's Rep 223, CA; *Yat Tung Investment Co Ltd v Dao Heng Bank Ltd* [1975] AC 581, [1975] 2 WLR 690, PC; *Dallal v Bank Mellat* [1986] QB 441, [1986] 1 All ER 239; *Arnold v National Westminster Bank plc* [1991] 3 All ER 41, [1991] 2 WLR 1177, HL. See also *Smith v Johnson* (1812) 15 East 213; *Trimingham v Trimingham* (1835) 4 Nev & MKB 786; *Dunn v Murray* (1829) 9 B & C 780; *Hawksworth v Brammall* (1840) 5 My & Cr 281; *Henderson v Henderson* (1843) 3 Hare 100; *Rees v Waters* (1847) 16 M & W 263; *Smalley v Blackburn Rly Co* (1857) 2 H & N 158. The court may either exercise its inherent jurisdiction to strike out such a claim as an abuse of process or restrain the claimant from referring the matter to arbitration. But where a cause of action falls outside the terms of an arbitration agreement, a party may not be precluded from raising it in subsequent proceedings: *Gueret v Auduoy* (1893) 62 LJQB 633; *Crane v Hegemann-Harris Co Inc* [1939] 4 All ER 68, CA; *Cie Graniere SA v Fritz Kopp AG* [1980] 1 Lloyd's Rep 463, CA; *Telfair Shipping Corpn v Inersea Carriers SA, The Caroline P* [1985] 1 All ER 243, [1985] 1 WLR 553, [1983] 2 Lloyd's Rep 351; *Excomm Ltd v Guan Guan Shipping (Pte) Ltd, The Golden Bear* [1987] 1 Lloyd's Rep 330. See also *Purser & Co (Hillingdon) Ltd v Jackson* [1977] QB 166, [1976] 3 All ER 641. Similarly, where a cause of action existed without actually being a matter in difference at the time of the reference, a party may not be precluded from raising it in subsequent proceedings: *Ravee v Farmer* (1791) 4 Term Rep 146. This will be most obviously the case where a claim has been fraudulently concealed from the claimant: *Charter v Trevelyan* (1844) 11 Cl & Fin 714.

11 See ESTOPPEL vol 16 paras 1525 et seq, 1543 et seq.

12 *F J Bloemen Pty Ltd v Gold Coast City Council* [1973] AC 115, [1972] 3 All ER 357, PC. This is not so in the case of an action in rem: see *The Rena K* [1979] QB 377, [1979] 1 All ER 397, [1978] 1 Lloyd's Rep 545.

13 The successful party's remedy is to enforce the award, as to which see paras 712–716 post.

14 *Gascoyne v Edwards* (1826) 1 Y & J 19.

15 *Allen v Milner* (1831) 2 Cr & J 47, as explained in *Commings (Cummings) v Heard* (1869) LR 4 QB 669; *Adler (trading as Argo Rederei) v Soutos (Hellas) Maritime Corpn, The Argo Hellas* [1984] 1 Lloyd's Rep 296.

16 *F J Bloemen Pty Ltd v Gold Coast City Council* [1973] AC 115 at 126, [1972] 3 All ER 357 at 363, PC, per Lord Pearson.

17 *Conquer v Boot* [1928] 2 KB 336; *Naamlooze Vennootschap Handels-en-Transport Maatschappij 'Vulcan' v A/S J Ludwig Mowinckels Rederi* [1938] 2 All ER 152 at 156, 60 Ll L Rep 217 at 223, HL; *Cie Graniere SA v Fritz Kopp AG* [1978] 1 Lloyd's Rep 511 at 521; *Telfair Shipping Corpn v Inersea Carriers SA, The Caroline P* [1983] 2 Lloyd's Rep 351 at 353. See also *H E Daniels Ltd v Carmel Exporters and Importers Ltd* [1953] 2 QB 242, [1953] 2 All ER 401, [1953] 2 Lloyd's Rep 103; *Speak v Taylor* (1894) 10 TLR 224; *Brunsden v Humphrey* (1884) 14 QBD 141; *Dunn v Murray* (1829) 9 B & C 780.

18 *E E and B Smith (1928) Ltd v Wheatsheaf Mills Ltd* [1939] 2 KB 302, [1939] 2 All ER 251. But see also *H E Daniels Ltd v Carmel Exporters and Importers Ltd* [1953] 2 QB 242, [1953] 2 All ER 401, [1953] 2 Lloyd's Rep 103.

(ii) Remedies

685. Payment of money; declaratory relief; indemnity. The most usual form of relief provided for in an award is the payment of money by one party to the other, whether as a debt or as damages. An arbitrator is empowered to order that such payment be made in a foreign currency[1].

An award may also contain a declaration as to the respective rights of the parties or a declaration that one party is entitled to be indemnified by the other in respect of a liability or expenditure incurred by him.

1 *Jugoslavenska Oceanska Plovidba v Castle Investment Co Inc* [1974] QB 292, [1973] 3 All ER 498, [1973] 2 Lloyd's Rep 1, CA; *Services Europe Atlantique Sud (SEAS) v Stockholms Rederiaktiebolag SVEA, The Folias* [1979] AC 685, [1979] 1 All ER 421, [1979] 1 Lloyd's Rep 1, HL.

686. Specific performance. Unless a contrary intention is expressed therein, every arbitration agreement is, where such a provision is applicable to the reference, deemed to contain a provision that the arbitrator or umpire shall have the same power as the High Court to order specific performance of any contract other than a contract relating to land or any interest in land[1].

1 Arbitration Act 1950 s 15; and see generally SPECIFIC PERFORMANCE.

687. Interest. Unless a contrary agreement is expressed therein, every arbitration agreement is, where such a provision is applicable to the reference, deemed to contain a provision that the arbitrator or umpire may, if he thinks fit, award simple interest at such rate as he thinks fit on any sum which is the subject of the reference but which is paid before the award, for such period ending not later than the date of payment as he thinks fit; and on any sum which he awards, for such period ending not later than the date of the award as he thinks fit[1].

These powers are without prejudice to any other powers of the arbitrator or umpire to award interest[2]. Although they are discretionary powers, an award will normally be remitted to the arbitrator if a principal sum is awarded without interest[3].

Once an award has been made and unless it otherwise directs, interest accrues on the sum awarded from the date of the award and at the same rate[4] as a judgment debt[5].

1 Arbitration Act 1950 s 19A (1) (added by the Administration of Justice Act 1982 s 15 (6), Sch 1 Pt IV). The Arbitration Act 1950 s 19A (1) (as added) has retrospective effect: *Food Corpn of India v Marastro Compania Naviera SA of Panama, The Trade Fortitude* [1986] 3 All ER 500, [1987] 1 WLR 134, [1986] 2 Lloyd's Rep 209, CA.
2 Arbitration Act 1950 s 19A (2) (added by the Administration of Justice Act 1982 s 15 (6), Sch 1 Pt IV).
3 *Panchaud Frères SA v R Pagnan & Flli* [1974] 1 Lloyd's Rep 394, CA; *P J Van Der Zijden Wildhandel NV v Tucker and Cross Ltd* [1976] 1 Lloyd's Rep 341 (a failure to award interest or deal with interest is a technical misconduct); *Thos P Gonzales Corpn v F R Waring (International) (Pty) Ltd* [1978] 1 Lloyd's Rep 494 at 505; affd [1980] 2 Lloyd's Rep 160, CA; *Warinco AG v Andre & Cie SA* [1979] 2 Lloyd's Rep 298. If the failure to award interest was an accidental omission, this might be remedied by the arbitrator under the Arbitration Act 1950 s 17 (the 'slip rule'): see *Pancommerce SA v Veecheema BV* [1983] 2 Lloyd's Rep 304; and para 683 ante.
4 The rate (which is determined by Orders in Council made under the Administration of Justice Act 1970 s 44) is 15 per cent per annum: Judgment Debts (Rate of Interest) Order 1985, SI 1985/437.
5 Arbitration Act 1950 s 20. This provision is effectively a term of the award implied by statute: *Continental Grain Co v Bremer Handelsgesellschaft mbH (No 2)* [1984] 2 Lloyd's Rep 121. The applicable rate in respect of an award is the rate under the Orders in Council at the time that judgment or the award is entered up: *Roco Guiseppe & Figli v Tradax Export SA* [1983] 3 All ER 598, [1984] 1 WLR 742. Although an award may provide that the sum awarded shall not carry interest, it cannot provide that it bears interest at a rate other than at the same rate as a judgment debt: *Timber Shipping Co SA v London and Overseas Freighters Ltd* [1972] AC 1, [1971] 2 All ER 599, [1971] 1 Lloyd's Rep 523, HL.

(iii) Costs of the Arbitration

688. Agreement between the parties. As a general rule, the parties may make such agreement with regard to the costs of the arbitration as they think fit[1]. However, any provision in the arbitration agreement to the effect that the parties or any party to the agreement shall in any event pay their or his own costs of the reference or award, or any part thereof, is void and the agreement is to be read as if the provision were not contained in it[2].

1 See *Fitzsimmons v Lord Mostyn* [1904] AC 46, HL; *Mansfield v Robinson* [1928] 2 KB 353 at 358. The power to deal with the costs of the reference includes the power to deal with the costs of the award: *Re Walker and Brown* (1882) 9 QBD 434.
2 Arbitration Act 1950 s 18 (3). However, such a provision is not void where the agreement is to refer a dispute which has already arisen: s 18 (3).

689. Powers of arbitrator. Unless a contrary intention is expressed therein[1], every arbitration agreement is deemed to include a provision that the costs of the reference and award are to be in the discretion[2] of the arbitrator or umpire, who may direct to and by whom and in what manner these costs or any part thereof are to be paid, and may tax or settle the amount of costs to be so paid or any part thereof, and may award costs to be paid as between solicitor and client[3]. Any costs directed by an award to be paid are, unless the award otherwise directs, taxable in the High Court[4]. If no provision is made by an award with respect to the costs of the reference, any party to the reference may, within 14 days of the publication of the award or such further time as the High Court or a judge thereof may direct, apply to the arbitrator for an order directing by and to whom those costs shall be paid, and thereupon the arbitrator must, after hearing any party who may desire to be heard, amend his award by adding to it such directions as he may think proper with respect to the payment of the costs of the reference[5]. In the case of a reference to a judge-arbitrator the application may be made at any time[6]. The High Court has power to make declarations and orders to charge property recovered or preserved in an arbitration with the payment of solicitors' costs[7]. This power applies in the case of a reference to a judge-arbitrator or judge-umpire, but in such cases the declaration or order may also be made by the arbitral tribunal itself[8].

1 See para 688 ante.
2 The arbitrator must exercise the discretion conferred on him: *Re Arbitration between Becker, Shillan & Co and Barry Bros* [1921] 1 KB 391. He must exercise the discretion in each case and must not apply an invariable rule of practice: *James Allen (Liverpool) Ltd v London Export Corpn Ltd* [1981] 2 Lloyd's Rep 632. As to what amounts to an exercise of the discretion see *Bradshaw v Air Council* [1926] Ch 329.
    In exercising his discretion as to costs, the arbitrator must apply the same principles as are applied by the High Court: see *Lloyd del Pacifico v Board of Trade* (1930) 46 TLR 476; *Stotesbury v Turner* [1943] KB 370; *Matheson & Co Ltd v A Tabah & Sons* [1963] 2 Lloyd's Rep 270.
    In particular, the arbitrator must exercise his discretion judicially and in accordance with the principles laid down by the House of Lords in *Donald Campbell and Co v Pollak* [1927] AC 732, HL. If the arbitrator exercises his discretion unjudicially, that part of the award may be remitted to him for reconsideration (*L E Cattan v A Michaelides and Co* [1958] 2 All ER 125, [1958] 1 WLR 717; *Warinco AG v Andre and Cie SA* [1979] 2 Lloyd's Rep 298; *Patroclus Shipping Co v Société Secopa* [1980] 1 Lloyd's Rep 405; *Archital Luxfer Ltd v Henry Boot Construction Ltd* [1981] 1 Lloyd's Rep 642) or the court may set it aside and, by consent of the parties, make its own determination (*Smeaton Hanscomb & Co Ltd v Sassoon I Setty, Son & Co (No 2)* [1953] 2 All ER 1588, [1953] 1 WLR 1481; *Lewis v Haverfordwest RDC* [1953] 2 All ER 1599, [1953] 1 WLR 1486). A reasoned award as to costs may be challenged by appeal to the High Court, leave having first been obtained pursuant to the Arbitration Act 1979 s 1: *Blexen Ltd v G Percy Trentham Ltd* [1990] 42 EG 133, CA. The remedy of remission may also be available in an appropriate case: *King v Thomas McKenna Ltd* [1991] 1 All ER 653, [1991] 2 WLR 1234, CA. As to remission see para 692 post.
    If the arbitrator exercises his discretion judicially, the costs order will not be set aside even if founded on a mistake of law: *Heaven and Kesterton Ltd v Sven Widaeus A/B* [1958] 1 All ER 420, [1958] 1 WLR 248. Unless it is clear that the arbitrator has acted unjudicially the court will seek to give effect to the award: *P Rosen & Co v Dowley and Selby* [1943] 2 All ER 172.
    In exercising his discretion judicially an arbitrator should, as a general rule, award the successful party his costs, as in the High Court where 'costs follow the event'. The arbitrator should not depart from this general rule in the absence of special circumstances: *Lewis v Haverfordwest RDC* supra. The following do not constitute special circumstances justifying a departure from the general rule: where neither party had made any serious effort to settle the dispute (*Lewis v Haverford West RDC* supra);

where the successful party took a technical point; where there is a defence that the respondent was always willing to put right the matters complained of (*Dineen v Walpole* [1969] 1 Lloyd's Rep 261, CA); where the successful party does not win the entirety of his claim (*Demolition and Construction Co Ltd v Kent River Board* [1963] 2 Lloyd's Rep 7 at 15); where there was a preliminary friendly discussion which took place without prejudice and the refusal of an offer made without prejudice (*Stotesbury v Turner* supra). See also *Smeaton Hanscomb & Co Ltd v Sassoon I Setty, Son & Co (No 2)* supra; *Heaven and Kesterton v Sven Widaeus A/B* [1958] 1 All ER 420, [1958] 1 WLR 248; *Heaven and Kesterton v Etablissements François Albiac & Cie* [1956] 2 Lloyd's Rep 316 at 322. An arbitrator does not exercise his discretion judicially when he takes into account matters which are unconnected with the proceedings, for example, the fact that, in his view, the conduct of the successful party before the reference commenced was immoral (*Lloyd del Pacifico v Board of Trade* supra at 332, 334).

The courts have considered it appropriate for an arbitrator to depart from the general rule in the following circumstances: where the successful claimant has delayed in making his claim and the award is small (*Evmar Shipping Corpn v Japan Line Ltd, The Evmar* [1984] 2 Lloyd's Rep 581); where the successful party fails on an issue which took up a great deal of time (*Heaven and Kesterton v Sven Widaeus A/B* supra; *Lewis Emanuel & Son Ltd v Sammut* [1959] 2 Lloyd's Rep 629 at 635; *Ismail v Polish Ocean Lines, The Chiechocinek (No 2)* [1980] 1 Lloyd's Rep 97); where the successful party recovered only a trivial sum in comparison with that claimed and failed on a number of important issues (*Perry v Stopher* [1959] 1 All ER 713, [1959] 1 WLR 415, CA). Where the respondent made an offer which was rejected by the successful claimant, the respondent may be awarded the costs incurred by him after the date of the offer (*Tramountana Armadora SA v Atlantic Shipping Co SA* [1978] 2 All ER 870, [1978] 1 Lloyd's Rep 391). See also *Matheson & Co Ltd v Tabah & Sons* supra; *Centrala Morska Importowo Eksportowa v Companhia Nacional De Navegacao SARL* [1975] 2 Lloyd's Rep 69; *Blue Horizon Shipping Co SA v E D and F Man Ltd, The Aghios Nicolaos* [1980] 1 Lloyd's Rep 17.

Where there is an unusual order as to costs, an arbitrator is not under a duty to state the reasons for the order (*Perry v Stopher* supra; *Heaven and Kesterton v Sven Widaeus A/B* supra; *Matheson & Co v Tabah & Sons* supra; *Dineen v Walpole* supra; *L Figueiredo Navegecas SA v Reederei Richard Schroeder KG, The Eric Schroeder* [1974] 1 Lloyd's Rep 192 at 193; *Centrala Morska Importowo Eksportowa (known as Centromor) v Companhia Nacional de Navegacao SARL* [1975] 2 Lloyd's Rep 69), although it is desirable that reasons be given in such circumstances (*Smeaton Hanscomb & Co Ltd v Sassoon I Setty, Son & Co (No 2)* supra per Devlin J; *The Erich Shroeder* supra at 193). Where, however, the arbitrator choses to state his reasons for the order as to costs, the court can look at those reasons to see whether the discretion has been exercised judicially (*Heaven and Kesterton Ltd v Sven Widaeus A/B* supra; *Stotesbury v Turner* supra; *Lloyd del Pacifico v Board of Trade* supra). If the reasons given are worded in such a way that a meaning cannot be ascribed to the relevant sentence without a substantial reconstruction of it, the reasons as given cannot of themselves justify a departure from the general rule and the proper course is for the court to remit the award to the arbitrator for further consideration: *Leif Hoegh & Co A/S v Maritime Mineral Carriers Ltd, The Marques de Bolarque* [1982] 1 Lloyd's Rep 68.

The arbitrator or umpire does not have a discretion in respect of costs of argument on an appeal to the High Court as these are a matter for the court: *Higham v Havant and Waterloo UDC* [1951] 2 TLR 87 at 90, CA; *Arnhold Karberg & Co v Blythe, Green, Jourdain & Co* [1915] 2 KB 379 at 393 per Scrutton J. Although these decisions relate to costs of arguing a special case, the principle should apply equally to appeals under the Arbitration Act 1979.

3 Arbitration Act 1950 s 18 (1). As to costs see generally PRACTICE AND PROCEDURE; SOLICITORS; RSC Ord 62 r 28.
4 Arbitration Act 1950 s 18 (2). See also RSC Ord 62 r 2 (2).
5 Arbitration Act 1950 s 18 (4).
6 Administration of Justice Act 1970 s 4 (4), Sch 3 para 7 (1).
7 Arbitration Act 1950 s 18 (5).
8 Administration of Justice Act 1970 Sch 3 para 7 (2), (3).

(2) REMISSION OR SETTING ASIDE OF AWARD

(i) Jurisdiction and Procedure

690. Jurisdiction. In all cases of reference to arbitration, the High Court or a judge thereof or, in the case of a judge-arbitrator or judge-umpire, the Court of

Appeal, may remit the matters referred, or any of them, to the reconsideration of the arbitrator or umpire[1]. Where an arbitrator or umpire has misconducted himself or the proceedings, or an arbitration or award has been improperly procured, the High Court or, in the case of a judge-arbitrator or judge-umpire, the Court of Appeal, may set the award aside[2]. The court's jurisdiction derives from statute, and there is no inherent general supervisory jurisdiction[3]. An application to remit or set aside must be heard by a Commercial judge unless such judge otherwise directs[4].

The court has no power to make orders of certiorari or prohibition addressed to an arbitrator unless he is acting under statutory powers[5].

1   Arbitration Act 1950 s 22 (1); Administration of Justice Act 1970 s 4 (4), Sch 3 para 9 (1); *Fuga AG v Bunge AG* [1975] 2 Lloyd's Rep 192. The power to remit or set aside an award applies to all cases of reference to arbitration. Many other provisions of the relevant statutes, eg the Arbitration Act 1950 s 26 (enforcement) and the Arbitration Act 1979 s 1 (appeals), apply only to written arbitration agreements (1950 Act s 32). As to the application of this power to arbitrations under special statutes see para 601 note 2 ante.

2   Arbitration Act 1950 s 23 (2); Administration of Justice Act 1970 Sch 3 para 9 (1).

3   *Exormisis Shipping SA v Oonsoo, the Democratic Peoples Republic of Korea and the Korean Foreign Transportation Corpn* [1975] 1 Lloyd's Rep 402.

4   RSC Ord 73 r 6 (1). See the Guide to Commercial Court Practice: RSC Ord 72/A1.

5   *R v National Joint Council for Craft of Dental Technicians (Disputes Committee), ex p Neate* [1953] 1 QB 704, [1953] 1 All ER 327.

691. Procedure. An application to remit or set aside an award[1] must be made by originating motion[2] within 21 days after the award has been made and published to the parties[3]. The notice of motion[4] must state in general terms the grounds of the application[5], and, where the motion is founded on affidavit evidence, a copy of every affidavit[6] intended to be used must be served with the notice of motion[7]. If the grounds of the application are that the arbitrator or umpire has misconducted himself or the proceedings, the notice of motion and affidavit must be served on him[8].

Affidavits by the arbitrator or umpire may be used[9], or, in cases of exceptional difficulty in ascertaining the facts, his evidence may be taken orally[10], since the evidence of an arbitrator or umpire is admissible upon every point which may be considered to be a matter of fact with reference to the making of the award. He may state what course the proceedings took before him, what claims were made by either party, and what claims were admitted; but his evidence is not admissible to explain, aid or contradict his award[11].

An order to remit or set aside an award may be made on such terms as to costs or otherwise as the court thinks just[12]. On an application to set aside an award the court may order that any money made payable by the award must be paid into court or otherwise secured pending the determination of the application[13].

From the decision of the court on any such application an appeal lies to the Court of Appeal with the leave of the court or of the Court of Appeal[14].

1   For the jurisdiction see para 690 ante.

2   RSC Ord 73 r 2 (1) (a), (c).

3   RSC Ord 73 r 5 (1). The motion is to a Commercial judge (RSC Ord 73 r 6 (1)). The court may extend the time limit either before or after it has expired: RSC Ord 3 r 5 (1), (2). See *Universal Cargo Carriers Corpn v Citati* [1957] 3 All ER 234, [1957] 1 WLR 979, CA; *Ismail v Polish Ocean Lines (No 2)* [1977] 2 Lloyd's Rep 134; *Industria de Oleos Pacaembu SA v NV Bunge* [1982] 1 Lloyd's Rep 490. Taking up the award and payment of the arbitrator's fees is not waiver of the right to apply for remission: *Sokratis Rokopoulos v Esperia SpA, The Aros* [1978] 1 Lloyd's Rep 456; cf *European Grain and Shipping Ltd v Johnston* [1983] QB 520, [1982] 3 All ER 989, [1982] 2 Lloyd's Rep 550, CA, where

a party who had taken advantage of the award could not thereafter apply to set it aside.

As to what is meant by an award being 'made and published' see *Brooke v Mitchell* (1840) 6 M & W 473; *Bulk Transport Corpn v Sissy SS Co Ltd, The Archipelagos and The Delfi* [1979] 2 Lloyd's Rep 289; *Musselbrook v Dunkin* (1833) 9 Bing 605; *Macarthur v Campbell* (1833) 5 B & Ad 518.

4 See 6 Court Forms (2nd Edn) (1989 Issue) 140–141, 142–143, Forms 71, 74.

5 RSC Ord 73 r 5 (5). See *Mercier v Pepperell* (1881) 19 ChD 58. For the grounds see para 692 post.

6 See 6 Court Forms (2nd Edn) (1989 Issue) 141, 143, Forms 72, 75.

7 RSC Ord 73 r 5 (5). Failure to comply with this requirement does not render the proceedings a nullity; rather the court has a discretion whether to set them aside wholly or in part: RSC Ord 2 r 1 (2).

8 He then has a choice whether (1) to take a full part in the proceedings as an active party or (2) to file an affidavit setting out any facts which he considers may be of assistance to the court or (3) to take no action, in which case it will be assumed only that he has no wish to do more than accept the decision of the court: *Port Sudan Cotton Co v Gavindaswamy Chettiar & Sons* [1977] 1 Lloyd's Rep 166. See also *Modern Engineering (Bristol) Ltd v C Miskin & Sons Ltd* [1981] 1 Lloyd's Rep 135, CA; *Bank Mellat v GAA Development and Construction Co* [1988] 2 Lloyd's Rep 44 at 47. The arbitrator or umpire may recover his costs if the application fails.

9 *Mills v Bowyers' Society* (1856) 3 K & J 66.

10 *Leiserach v Schalit* [1934] 2 KB 353.

11 *Duke of Buccleuch v Metropolitan Board of Works* (1872) LR 5 HL 418 at 462; *A-G for Manitoba v Kelly* [1922] 1 AC 268 at 279, PC; and see *Recher & Co v North British and Mercantile Insurance Co* [1915] 3 KB 277; *Kiril Mischeff Ltd v Constant Smith & Co* [1950] 2 KB 616, [1950] 1 All ER 890. See also *Ward v Shell-Mex and BP Ltd* [1952] 1 KB 280, [1951] 2 All ER 904; *Top Shop Estates Ltd v Danino* (1984) 273 Estates Gazette 197.

12 Arbitration Act 1950 s 28 (amended by the Arbitration Act 1975 s 8 (2)).

13 Arbitration Act 1950 s 23 (3).

14 RSC Ord 59 r 1A (7) (b) (iii).

(ii) When Court will Set Aside or Remit Award

692. Grounds for remission or setting aside. There are five broad grounds on which awards have been remitted to the reconsideration of the arbitrator or umpire[1] or have been set aside. They are the following:

(1) that the arbitrator or umpire has misconducted himself or the proceedings[2];

(2) that there is some defect or error patent on the face of the award[3], as, for example, where the award is uncertain[4] or incomplete[5];

(3) that the arbitrator or umpire has admittedly made a mistake, and desires the award to be remitted in order that he may correct it, as, for example, where by mistake the arbitrator omitted to give credit for a payment which had been duly proved[6], or by an oversight directed payment of the sums awarded to the wrong person[7];

(4) that material evidence, which could not with reasonable diligence have been discovered before the award was made, has since been obtained[8]; an award will not be remitted to discover evidence to develop a new presentation of a case[9];

(5) that, without misconduct, a mishap or misunderstanding has caused an aspect of the dispute which has been the subject of the reference not to be considered and adjudicated upon as fully as, or in a manner which, the parties were entitled to expect, and it would be inequitable to allow the award to take effect without further consideration by the arbitrator[10].

The jurisdiction may not, however, be invoked on the basis that the arbitrator has made an erroneous finding of fact or has based his award on a wrong principle or mistaken reasoning[11]. In such cases the appeal procedure[12] must be used. But where an error of law causes the arbitrator to refuse to allow a prospective party to take part in the reference, the proper course is an application to remit, not an appeal[13].

1 See *Re Montgomery, Jones & Co and Liebenthal & Co's Arbitration* (1898) 78 LT 406 at 409, CA, per Chitty LJ. For the court's power to remit on other grounds see infra.
2 Arbitration Act 1950 s 23 (2). As to what constitutes misconduct see para 694 post.
3 Other than error of fact or law on the face of the award, which is no longer a ground: see the Arbitration Act 1979 s 1 (1).
4 *Ellis v Desilva* (1881) 6 QBD 521, CA; *Re Fearon and Flinn* (1869) LR 5 CP 34; *Montrose Canned Foods v Eric Wells (Merchants) Ltd* [1965] 1 Lloyd's Rep 597 (failure to quantify damages). See also *Olefinio Zucchi SpA v Northern Sales Ltd* [1965] 2 Lloyd's Rep 496 at 522.
5 *Re Arbitration between Becker, Shillan & Co and Barry Bros* [1921] 1 KB 391 (costs); *Lambert and Kuzyiak Ltd v British Commercial Overseas Co Ltd* (1923) 16 Ll L Rep 51; *P J Van der Zijden Wildhandel NV v Tucker and Cross Ltd* [1976] 1 Lloyd's Rep 341. Remission for this purpose is largely superseded by the Arbitration Act 1979 s 1 (5): *Bulk Oil (Zug) AG v Sun International Ltd (No 2)* [1984] 1 Lloyd's Rep 531. See also para 706 et seq post, which deal with the power of High Court to remit an award on a question of law which is the subject of an appeal.
6 *Flynn v Robertson* (1869) LR 4 CP 324.
7 *The Mello* (1948) 81 Ll L Rep 230.
8 *Re Keighley, Maxsted & Co and Durant & Co* [1893] 1 QB 405, CA; *Sprague v Allen & Sons* (1899) 15 TLR 150; Before the court will remit an award for the admission of fresh evidence, the party seeking leave must show that: (1) he did not have the evidence at the time of the arbitration; (2) he could not have got it by the exercise of due diligence; (3) it would have been likely to have had a substantial effect on the result; and (4) he had no opportunity to ask the arbitrators to delay issuing the award while the evidence was procured: *Whitehall Shipping Co Ltd v Kompass Schiffahrtskontor GmbH, The Stainless Patriot* [1979] 1 Lloyd's Rep 589; *Nicoban Shipping Co v Alam Maritime Ltd, The Evdokia* [1980] 2 Lloyd's Rep 107; *Aiden Shipping Ltd v Interbulk Ltd, The Vimeira (No 2)* [1985] 2 Lloyd's Rep 377 at 400.
9 *Sinason-Teicher Inter-American Grain Corpn v Oilcakes and Oilseeds Trading Co Ltd* [1954] 2 All ER 497, [1954] 1 WLR 935; affd [1954] 3 All ER 468, [1954] 1 WLR 1394, CA; *Tsakiroglou & Co Ltd v Transgrains SA* [1958] 1 Lloyd's Rep 562.
10 *King v Thomas McKenna Ltd* [1991] 1 All ER 653, [1991] 2 WLR 1234, CA. Where the mishap has been caused by the fault of the party seeking remission, relief will not necessarily be refused, but strict terms may be imposed: *King v Thomas McKenna Ltd* supra. See also *GKN Centrax Gears Ltd v Matbro Ltd* [1976] 2 Lloyd's Rep 555 at 581, CA, per Bridge LJ; *Sokratis Rokopoulos v Esperia SpA, The Aros* [1978] 1 Lloyd's Rep 456; *Bulk Oil Zug AG v Sun International Ltd (No 2)* [1984] 1 Lloyd's Rep 531; *Cie Nationale Algerienne de Navigation v Hecate Shipping Co* [1985] 2 Lloyd's Rep 588 at 591; *Overseas Fortune Shipping Pte Ltd v Great Eastern Shipping Co Ltd, The Singapore Fortune* [1987] 1 Lloyd's Rep 270 at 277.
11 *Gillespie Bros v Thompson Bros & Co* (1922) 13 Ll L Rep 519 at 524, CA; *Oleficio Zucci SpA v Northern Sales Ltd* [1965] 2 Lloyd's Rep 496, approved in *GKN Centrax Gears Ltd v Matbro Ltd* [1976] 2 Lloyd's Rep 555 at 580, CA; *Bulk Oil (Zug) AG v Sun International Ltd (No 2)* [1984] 1 Lloyd's Rep 531. See also *Nello Simoni v A/S M/S Straum* (1949) 83 Ll L Rep 157; *Tersons Ltd v Stevenage Development Corpn* [1963] 2 Lloyd's Rep 333 at 359–360.
12 *Mutual Shipping Corpn of New York v Bayshore Shipping Co of Monrovia, The Montan* [1985] 1 All ER 520 at 525, [1985] 1 WLR 625 at 631, [1985] 1 Lloyd's Rep 189 at 192, CA. Neither s 22 nor s 23 of the Arbitration Act 1950 is available as a back door method of circumventing the restrictions created by the 1979 Act: *Moran v Lloyd's* [1983] 1 Lloyd's Rep 472 at 475. See para 706 et seq post.
13 *Montedipe SpA v JTP-RO Jugotanker, The Jordan Nicolov* [1990] 2 Lloyd's Rep 11.

693. Reasons for setting aside as opposed to remission. The question whether an award should be remitted or set aside altogether is one for the court's discretion, which will be exercised with regard to all the circumstances of the case[1]. However, an award will normally be set aside, rather than remitted, where there has been a serious miscarriage of justice. Thus in the case of misconduct, the appropriate remedy depends on the nature of the misconduct[2] and upon the surrounding circumstances. Where the arbitrator has so conducted himself that a reasonable person would think that there was a real likelihood that the arbitrator could not or would not fairly determine the issues on the basis of the evidence and argument to be adduced before him, the award should be set aside, not remitted[3]. It is also likely to be set aside where it has been improperly procured, for example by fraud.

On the other hand, in the case of the arbitrator's admitted mistake, remission is the normal remedy[4]. In most cases it will be appropriate to remit where further findings are required[5], or where the error is inadvertent[6].

1 *Odlum v Vancouver City and Canadian Northern Pacific Rly Co* (1915) 85 LJPC 95; and see *Kiril Mischeff Ltd v Constant Smith & Co* [1950] 2 KB 616 at 621, [1950] 1 All ER 890 at 893.
2 Normally the award will be set aside rather than remitted when that course is in accordance with ordinary notions of justice: see eg *Re Fuerst Bros & Co Ltd and Stephenson* [1951] 1 Lloyd's Rep 429; *E Rotheray & Sons Ltd v Carlo Bedarida & Co* [1961] 1 Lloyd's Rep 220.
3 *Ardhalian v Unifert International SA, The Elissan* [1984] 2 Lloyd's Rep 84, CA; see also *Modern Engineering (Bristol) Ltd v C Miskin & Son Ltd* [1981] 1 Lloyd's Rep 135, CA.
4 See para 692 ante and the cases cited in notes 5 and 6 thereto.
5 See the cases cited in para 692 notes 3, 4 ante.
6 *Royal Commission on Sugar Supply v Kwik-Hoo-Tong Trading Society* (1922) 11 Ll L Rep 163.

694. What constitutes misconduct. Misconduct has been described as 'such a mishandling of the arbitration as is likely to amount to some substantial miscarriage of justice'[1]. Most cases depend as much upon the terms of the reference and on the surrounding circumstances as upon the conduct of the arbitrator or umpire, and it is therefore difficult to provide an exhaustive definition of the term.

Where an arbitrator fails to comply with the terms, express or implied[2], of the arbitration agreement[3], that will amount to misconduct. But, whether or not he complies with those terms, he will misconduct himself if he acts in a way that is contrary to public policy[4]. In particular, it would be misconduct to act in a way which is, or appears to be, unfair[5]. Misconduct committed in good faith is sometimes referred to as 'technical misconduct', though all allegations of misconduct assert a breach of duty[6]. It is not misconduct to make an erroneous finding of law or fact[7].

Misconduct has been found to have occurred in the following instances[8], some of which would also give the court jurisdiction to intervene on other grounds: (1) where the arbitrator or umpire fails to decide all the matters which were referred to him[9]; (2) where by his award the arbitrator or umpire purports to decide matters which have not in fact been included in the agreement of reference[10]; (3) where the award is uncertain[11]; (4) where there has been irregularity in the proceedings[12], but where the complaining party continues with the reference after knowing of the irregularity, he may impliedly agree to that manner of proceeding, or may waive his right to object[13]; (5) where the arbitrator or umpire has acted unfairly and in breach of the rules of natural justice[14]; (6) where the arbitrator or umpire delegates any part of his authority[15], whether to a stranger[16] or to one of the parties[17], or even to a co-arbitrator[18]; (7) where the arbitrator or umpire accepts the hospitality of one of the parties, being hospitality offered with the intention of influencing his decision or actually influencing it[19]; (8) where the arbitrator or umpire appears to be biased[20] or has an interest in the subject matter of the reference[21]; (9) where the arbitrator or umpire takes a bribe from either party[22].

1 *Williams v Wallis and Cox* [1914] 2 KB 478 at 485. It is a question of fact and degree: *Mabanaft GmbH v Consentino Shipping Co SA, The Achillet* [1984] 2 Lloyd's Rep 191.
2 See paras 671, 674 ante.

3 *London Export Corpn Ltd v Jubilee Coffee Roasting Co Ltd* [1958] 1 All ER 494 at 497, [1958] 1 WLR 271 at 277 per Diplock J; affd [1958] 2 All ER 411, [1958] 1 WLR 661, CA; *Margulies Bros Ltd v Dafnis Thomaides & Co (UK) Ltd* [1958] 1 All ER 777 at 781, [1958] 1 WLR 398 at 402 per Diplock J.

4 There may be a variety of grounds of public policy on which an award may be set aside (*London Export Corpn Ltd v Jubilee Coffee Roasting Co Ltd* [1958] 1 All ER 494 at 497, [1958] 1 WLR 271 at 277 per Diplock J; affd [1958] 2 All ER 411, [1958] 1 WLR 661, CA), eg that its effect is to enforce an illegal contract (see *David Taylor & Son Ltd v Barnett Trading Co* [1953] 1 All ER 843, [1953] 1 WLR 562).

5 'I apprehend that an award obtained in violation of the rules of natural justice even where there was no breach of the agreed procedure would be set aside on grounds of public policy; as, for instance, where an arbitrator manifested obvious bias too late for an application for his removal to be effective before he made his award. Contrast *Catalina SS (Owners) v Norma (Owners)* (1938) 61 Ll L Rep 360': *London Export Corpn Ltd v Jubilee Coffee Roasting Co Ltd* [1958] 1 All ER 494 at 498, [1958] 1 WLR 271 at 278 per Diplock J; see also *Oswald v Earl Grey* (1855) 24 LJQB 69; *Faure Fairclough Ltd v Premier Oil and Cake Mills Ltd* [1968] 1 Lloyd's Rep 237.

6 *Thomas Borthwick (Glasgow) Ltd v Faure Fairclough Ltd* [1968] 1 Lloyd's Rep 16.

7 *Moran v Lloyd's* [1983] 1 Lloyd's Rep 472, CA; *Bulk Oil (Zug) AG v Sun International Ltd(No 2)* [1984] 1 Lloyd's Rep 531.

8 Though the Arbitration Act 1979 does not deal with misconduct, the policy underlying the Act may affect the discretion of the court in remitting or setting aside an award: *Italmare SpA v Stellar Chartering and Brokerage Inc, The Marina di Cassano* [1984] 2 Lloyd's Rep 577; see also *Bulk Oil (Zug) AG v Sun International Ltd (No 2)* [1984] 1 Lloyd's Rep 531.

9 See the cases cited in para 692 note 4 ante; also *Re O'Conor and Whitlaw's Arbitration* (1919) 88 LJKB 1242, CA. See also *Turner v Turner* (1827) 3 Russ 494. The award will not be set aside for excluding one of the matters referred, if that matter was not in dispute between the parties at the date of the agreement (*Cockburn v Newton* (1841) 2 Man & G 899); nor if the matter excluded was not specifically brought before the arbitrator (*Rees v Waters* (1847) 16 M & W 263; and see *Hawksworth v Brammall* (1840) 5 My & Cr 281). Unless required by the agreement, the award will not be set aside because the arbitrator has not found separately on each matter referred (*Whitworth v Hulse* (1866) LR 1 Exch 251). A point not expressly dealt with may be dealt with by implication: *Middlemiss and Gould (a firm) v Hartlepool Corpn* [1973] 1 All ER 172, [1972] 1 WLR 1643, CA.

10 *Re Roywood Investments Ltd and London Life Insurance Co* [1971] 3 OR 385 (construction of lease instead of determination of rent and value); *Price v Popkin* (1839) 10 Ad & El 139; *Re Green & Co and Balfour, Williamson & Co* (1890) 63 LT 97; affd 63 LT 325, CA; and see *Faviell v Eastern Counties Rly Co* (1848) 2 Exch 344 at 349; and *Bowes v Fernie* (1838) 4 My & Cr 150 (award containing unauthorised directions); *Turner v Swainson* (1836) 1 M & W 572 (directions affecting third parties); *Walford, Baker & Co v Macfie & Sons* (1915) 84 LJKB 2221; and see *May v Mills* (1914) 30 TLR 287 (wrong contract construed). However excess of jurisdiction over costs alone is not sufficient to invalidate the award: see *Cockburn v Newton* (1841) 2 Man & G 899. The arbitrator cannot reserve to himself the right to deal with future differences arising on the award: *Manser v Heaver* (1832) 3 B & Ad 295; *Re Tandy and Tandy* (1841) 9 Dowl 1044.

11 The award will be remitted if it is uncertain or not in a form capable of being enforced as a judgment: *Margulies Bros Ltd v Dafnis Thomaides & Co (UK) Ltd* [1958] 1 All ER 777, [1958] 1 WLR 398.

12 *London Export Corpn Ltd v Jubilee Coffee Roasting Co Ltd* [1958] 1 All ER 494, [1958] 1 WLR 271; affd [1958] 2 All ER 411, [1958] 1 WLR 661, CA. See also *Oswald v Earl Grey* (1855) 24 LJQB 69 (failure to give parties notice of the time and place of meeting; however, the award will not be set aside on this ground if nothing is done at the meeting: *Re Morphett* (1845) 2 Dow & L 967); *Banks v Banks* (1835) 1 Gale 46 (agreement requiring evidence to be taken orally but arbitrator admitting affidavits); *Phipps v Ingram* (1835) 3 Dowl 669; *Williams v Wallis and Cox* [1914] 2 KB 478 (arbitrator refusing to admit evidence. In such a case the supporting affidavit should state the arbitrator's reasons for refusal: *Bradley v Ibbetson* (1851) 2 LM & P 583; and see *Re Maunder* (1883) 49 LT 535); *Faure Fairclough Ltd v Premier Oil and Cake Mills Ltd* [1968] 1 Lloyd's Rep 237 (examination of witnesses was taken out of the parties' hands); *E Rotheray & Sons Ltd v Carlo Bedarida & Co* [1961] 1 Lloyd's Rep 220 (failure to order translation of foreign documents); *Re Fuerst Bros & Co Ltd and Stephenson* [1951] 1 Lloyd's Rep 429 (umpire hearing one arbitrator without the other); *European Grain and Shipping Ltd v Johnston* [1983] QB 520, [1982] 3 All ER 989, [1982] 2 Lloyd's Rep 550, CA (arbitrator signed the award in blank, and took no part in the discussion); *Montedipe SpA v JTP-RO Jugotanker, The Jordan Nicolov* [1990] 2 Lloyd's Rep 11 (refusal to allow assignee to participate in the reference); *Indian Oil Corpn v Coastal (Bermuda) Ltd* [1990] 2 Lloyd's Rep 407 (failure clearly to advise party to amend pleadings).

13 See para 695 post.

14 *London Export Corpn Ltd v Jubilee Coffee Roasting Co Ltd* [1958] 1 All ER 494, [1958] 1 WLR 271; affd [1958] 2 All ER 411, [1958] 1 WLR 661, CA; *Oswald v Earl Grey* (1855) 24 LJQB 69 (hearing one party but refusing to hear the other); *The Myron, Myron (Owners) v Tradax Export SA Panama City RP* [1970] 1 QB 527, [1969] 2 All ER 1263, [1969] 1 Lloyd's Rep 411 (deciding in default of defence without clear warning); *Re Gregson and Armstrong* (1894) 70 LT 106; *Re Hick* (1819) 8 Taunt 694; *Harvey v Shelton* (1844) 7 Beav 455; *Hickman & Co v Roberts* [1913] AC 229, HL (taking instructions from or talking with one party in the absence of the other); *Walker v Frobisher* (1801) 6 Ves 70; *Dobson and Sutton v Groves* (1844) 6 QB 637; *Re Plews and Middleton* (1845) 6 QB 845; *Re Tidswell* (1863) 33 Beav 213; *Re Brook, Delcomyn and Badart* (1864) 16 CBNS 403; *Re O'Conor and Whitlaw's Arbitration* (1919) 88 LJKB 1242, CA; *W Ramsden & Co Ltd v Jacobs* [1922] 1 KB 640; and see *Bache v Billingham* [1894] 1 QB 107 at 112, CA; *Re Brien and Brien* [1910] 2 IR 84; *Government of Ceylon v Chandris* [1963] 1 Lloyd's Rep 214 at 225–226 per Megaw J; approved *The Myron, Myron (Owners) v Tradax Export SA Panama City RP* [1970] 1 QB 527 at 534, [1969] 2 All ER 1263 at 1266, [1969] 1 Lloyd's Rep 411 at 416 (taking evidence in the absence of a party unless, perhaps, it is affirmatively shown that it could not have affected the award: *Eastcheap Dried Fruit Co v NV Gebroeders Catz Handelsvereeniging* [1962] 1 Lloyd's Rep 283; *Sociedad Iberica de Molturacion SA v Nidera Handelscompagnie BV* [1990] 2 Lloyd's Rep 240; see also *Grand Trunk Rly Co of Canada v R* [1923] AC 150 at 166, PC; but cf *Royal Commission on Sugar Supply v Trading Society Kwik-Hoo-Tong* (1922) 38 TLR 684, DC, per Greer J); *Owen v Nicholl* [1948] 1 All ER 707, CA (arbitrator using knowledge he has acquired in a different capacity); *Pitt v Dawkra* (undated) cited in 2 Vern 251 (making award without hearing witnesses whom he has promised to hear). *Société Franco-Tunisienne d'Armement-Tunis v Government of Ceylon, The Massalia* [1959] 3 All ER 25, [1959] 1 WLR 787, CA (deciding the case on a point not put to the parties); *Modern Engineering (Bristol) Ltd v C Miskin & Son Ltd* [1981] 1 Lloyd's Rep 135, CA (producing award before hearing full argument); *Fox v P G Wellfair Ltd* [1981] 2 Lloyd's Rep 514, CA (acting on private opinion without disclosing it, though an arbitrator may act on his general knowledge of the relevant trade: *Jordeson & Co v Stora, Kopparbergs Bergslags AB* (1931) 41 Ll L Rep 201; *Wilson v Glover* [1969] NZLR 365; *FR Waring (UK) Ltd v Administracao Geral do Acucar e do Alcool EP* [1983] 1 Lloyd's Rep 45). As to when an arbitrator may proceed ex parte see *Gladwin v Chilcote* (1841) 9 Dowl 550; *Scott v Van Sandau* (1844) 6 QB 237; *Tryer v Shaw* (1858) 27 LJ Ex 320; *Re Hewitt and Portsmouth Waterworks Co* (1862) 10 WR 780.

15 The arbitrator may delegate, to the proper officer of the court, the ascertainment of the amount of costs: *Holdsworth v Wilson* (1863) 4 B & S 1 at 8; *Simpson v IRC* [1914] 2 KB 842; *Matthews v IRC* [1914] 3 KB 192, CA; see also *Knott v Long* (1735) 2 Stra 1025 and *Cargey v Aitcheson* (1823) 2 B & C 170.

16 *Johnson v Latham* (1850) 1 LM & P 348; *Tomlin v Fordwich Corpn* (1836) 5 Ad & El 147.

17 *Pedley v Goddard* (1796) 7 Term Rep 73 at 77.

18 *Little v Newton* (1841) 2 Man & G 351; *Re Tandy and Tandy* (1841) 9 Dowl 1044.

19 *Re Hopper* (1867) LR 2 QB 367; *Moseley v Simpson* (1873) LR 16 Eq 226. To induce the court to interfere on such a ground there must be something more than mere suspicion: *Crossley v Clay* (1848) 5 CB 581. See also *Re Maunder* (1883) 49 LT 535.

20 *Catalina (Owners) v Norma (Owners)* (1938) 61 Ll L Rep 360, 82 Sol Jo 698, DC; *Veritas Shipping Corpn v Anglo-Canadian Cement Ltd* [1966] 1 Lloyd's Rep 76; see also *Schofield v Allen* (1904) 48 Sol Jo 176, CA. The test is whether there exist grounds from which a reasonable person would think that there was a real likelihood of bias (*Tracomin SA v Gibbs Nathaniel (Canada) Ltd and George Jacob Bridge* [1985] 1 Lloyd's Rep 586. See also *Metropolitan Properties Co (FGC) Ltd v Lannon* [1969] 1 QB 577, [1968] 3 All ER 304, CA; *Hannam v Bradford Corpn* [1970] 2 All ER 690, [1970] 1 WLR 937, CA; *R v Liverpool City Justices, ex p Topping* [1983] 1 All ER 490, [1983] 1 WLR 937, DC, *Ardahalian v Unifert International SA, The Elissar* [1984] 2 Lloyd's Rep 84, CA).

21 *Blanchard v Sun Fire Office* (1890) 6 TLR 365; see also *Parker v Burroughs* (1702) Colles 257 (where Titus Oates was the arbitrator); *Kemp v Rose* (1858) 1 Giff 258 (the interest need not be pecuniary); *Kimberley v Dick* (1871) LR 13 Eq 1; and *Sellar v Highland Rly Co* 1919 SC (HL) 19. Where the interest of the arbitrator was known to the parties when he was appointed, his award will only be set aside if actual prejudice or bias is shown: *Ranger v Great Western Rly Co* (1854) 5 HL Cas 72; and see *Eckersley v Mersey Docks and Harbour Board* [1894] 2 QB 667, CA; *Ives and Barker v Willans* [1894] 2 Ch 478, CA; *Bright v River Plate Construction Co Ltd* [1900] 2 Ch 835. Where, on the other hand, his interest was unknown, it is not necessary to show actual bias: *Dimes v Proprietors of Grand Junction Canal* (1852) 3 HL Cas 759; *Ghiradosi v Minister of Highways for British Columbia* [1966] SCR 367, 56 DLR (2d) 469 (Can SC).

22 Hearsay evidence of an admission of bribery by the arbitrator is not admissible on normal principles, however the arbitrator may be called to give evidence: *Re Whiteley and Roberts* [1891] 1 Ch 558.

695. Waiver of objection. The parties may waive objection to any kind of irregularity in the conduct of a reference[1]. Continuing to take part in the reference knowing of the irregularity may amount either to waiver of the irregularity, or to an implied agreement to the irregular procedure[2]. But the waiver or agreement must be made with full knowledge of the irregularity[3]. The parties cannot, however, agree in advance to oust the supervisory jurisdiction of the court[4].

1 *Ritchie v W Jacks & Co* (1922) 10 Ll L Rep 519, CA; *Bignall v Gale* (1841) 2 Man & G 830; *Re Backhouse and Taylor* (1851) 20 LJQB 233; *Thomas v Morris* (1867) 16 LT 398; *Moseley v Simpson* (1873) LR 16 Eq 226; *Drew v Drew and Leburn* (1855) 2 Macq 1 at 8–9; *Mills v Bowyers' Society* (1856) 3 K & J 66; *Re Clout and Metropolitan and District Railway Cos* (1882) 46 LT 141, DC; *Biglin v Clarke* (1905) 49 Sol Jo 204 DC; *Fletcher v Robertson* (1919) 56 SLR 305; *Wessanen's Koninklijke Fabrieken NV v Isaac Modiano Brother & Sons Ltd* [1960] 3 All ER 617, [1960] 1 WLR 1243, [1960] 2 Lloyd's Rep 257; *Government of Ceylon v Chandris* [1963] 1 Lloyd's Rep 214; *Faure Fairclough Ltd v Premier Oil and Cake Mills Ltd* [1968] 1 Lloyd's Rep 237. See also *Re Salkeld and Slater and Harrison* (1840) 12 Ad & El 767.
2 *Star International Hong Kong (UK) Ltd v Bergbau-Handel GmbH* [1966] 2 Lloyd's Rep 16.
3 *Earl Darnley v London, Chatham and Dover Rly Co* (1867) LR 2 HL 43.
4 *Czarnikow v Roth, Schmidt & Co* [1922] 2 KB 478 at 488, CA; *Re Davstone Estates Ltd's Leases, Manprop Ltd v O'Dell* [1969] 2 Ch 378 at 386, [1969] 2 All ER 849 at 854 per Ungoed-Thomas J.

(iii) Effect of Order for Remission or Setting Aside Award

696. Effect of remission of award. The effect of remission is to revive the jurisdiction of the arbitrator with regard to the matters remitted[1]. The whole or only a part of an award may be remitted. The court may also, expressly or impliedly, restrict the revival of the arbitrator's jurisdiction to reconsideration of a particular aspect of a matter referred[2]. Where the whole of an award is remitted, it becomes wholly ineffective, and the arbitrator resumes his authority in the reference. Even where only some of the matters referred are remitted, it may be that there is nevertheless no enforceable award even as to the matters not remitted[3]. The court may make it a condition of remission that the applicant should pay such part of the award as would not be affected[4]. The arbitrator may not make fresh findings in relation to matters not remitted[5].

1 *Aiden Shipping Ltd v Interbulk Ltd, The Vimeira (No 1)* [1985] 2 Lloyd's Rep 410n, CA.
2 *Aiden Shipping Ltd v Interbulk Ltd, The Vimeira (No 1)* [1985] 2 Lloyd's Rep 410n, CA.
3 *Johnson v Latham* (1851) as reported in 20 LJQB 236 at 238 per Erle J.
4 *Congimex SARL (Lisbon) v Continental Grain Export Corpn (New York)* [1979] 2 Lloyd's Rep 346 at 356, CA, per Donaldson J. The Court of Appeal did not deal with this point in allowing an appeal: [1979] 2 Lloyd's Rep 346 at 357.
5 *Aiden Shipping Ltd v Interbulk Ltd, The Vimeira (No 1)* [1985] 2 Lloyd's Rep 410n, CA.

697. Evidence on reconsideration by arbitrator. Where an award is remitted to the reconsideration of the arbitrator or umpire, his original powers are thereby revived in relation to the matters remitted[1]. It is his duty to hear such further evidence as the parties may wish to present[2], unless the remission is merely for the purpose of correcting some formal defect or making some alteration in the award which would not involve the hearing of further evidence[3].

1 *Aiden Shipping Ltd v Interbulk Ltd, The Vimeira (No 1)* [1985] 2 Lloyd's Rep 410n, CA.
2 *Nickalls v Warren* (1844) 6 QB 615; and see *Baker v Hunter* (1847) 16 M & W 672; *Bjorn-Jensen & Co v Lysaght (Australia) Ltd, The Gamma* [1979] 1 Lloyd's Rep 494.
3 *Howett v Clements* (1845) 1 CB 128; *Bird v Penrice* (1840) 6 M & W 754; *Re Morris and Morris* (1856) 6 E & B 383.

698. Time for second award. Where an award is remitted, the arbitrator or umpire, as the case may be, must, unless the order remitting the award otherwise directs, make his second award within three months after the date of the order[1].

1 Arbitration Act 1950 s 22 (2).

699. Effect of setting aside award. On being set aside, the award is deprived of all legal effect, and the position is left as though it had never been made. Since the object of setting an award aside, rather than remission, is normally that the reference should go before a differently constituted tribunal, it has been assumed that the effect is to prevent the original arbitrator resuming his jurisdiction[1]. However, removal of the arbitrator would seem to require an order under section 23 (1) of the Arbitration Act 1950 as well as one under section 23 (2).

Where an award is set aside because the court takes the view that the original tribunal should cease to deal with the reference, a party could, if any question were raised as to the powers of the original arbitrator or umpire, apply either for an order for his removal[2] or for an order revoking the arbitration agreement[3].

1 *Stockport Metropolitan Borough Council v O'Reilly* [1983] 2 Lloyd's Rep 70 at 79.
2 Arbitration Act 1950 s 23 (1).
3 Ibid s 25 (2) (b).

700. Limitation of actions. Where the High Court orders that an award be set aside or orders, after the commencement of an arbitration[1], that the arbitration agreement[2] shall cease to have effect with respect to the dispute referred[3], the court may further order that the period between the commencement of the arbitration and the date of the order be excluded in computing the time prescribed by the Limitation Act 1980 or any other limitation enactment for the commencement of proceedings, including arbitration, with respect to the dispute referred[4].

1 See para 650 ante.
2 See the Limitation Act 1980 s 34 (7).
3 See para 636 note 7 and para 660 ante.
4 Limitation Act 1980 s 34 (5).

(iv) Challenging Validity of Award

701. Void and voidable awards. If there exist grounds upon which an award ought to be remitted or set aside[1], the award may be either void or voidable. Where an arbitrator exceeds his jurisdiction[2], or fails to make anything that could properly be called a decision[3], his award is void. Where the arbitrator only partially exceeds his jurisdiction, the award is void as to that part[4].

In all other cases the award is valid until it is in fact set aside or remitted[5]. Unless a defect in an award is of such a character as to render the award void, or unenforceable[6], no party may rely upon that defect in any legal proceedings without first successfully applying to have the award set aside or remitted[7].

1 See paras 690–695 ante.
2 See the cases cited in para 694 note 10 ante; and *Davies v Price* (1862) 6 LT 713; *Mordue v Palmer* (1870) 6 Ch App 22; *Pedler v Hardy* (1902) 18 TLR 591; *Jungheim Hopkins & Co v Foukelmann* [1909] 2 KB

948. In *Re Marshall and Dresser* (1843) 3 QB 878, the award was held not to be binding because it was uncertain; however, in such circumstances it is more likely that an award would be remitted or set aside: *River Plate Products Netherlands BV v Etablissement Coargrain* [1982] 1 Lloyd's Rep 628.
3 *Bache v Billingham* [1894] 1 QB 107, CA.
4 *Manser v Heaver* (1832) 3 B & Ad 295.
5 *Bache v Billingham* [1894] 1 QB 107 CA. But cf *Cook International Inc v Handelmaatschappij Jean Delvaux and Braat, Scott and Meadows* [1985] 2 Lloyd's Rep 225, and the comment on that case in Mustill and Boyd *Commercial Arbitration* (2nd Edn, 1989) p 576 note 7.
6 See paras 702, 712 post.
7 *Bache v Billingham* [1894] 1 QB 107 CA; *Re Lord and Lord* (1855) 5 E & B 404; *Thorburn v Barnes* (1867) LR 2 CP 384; *White, Tomkins and Courage v Cie Lyonnaise de Madagascar* (1921) 7 Ll L Rep 134; *L Oppenheim v Mahomed Haneef* [1922] 1 AC 482, PC; *Scrimaglio v Thornett and Fehr* (1924) 131 LT 174, CA; *Birtley District Co-operative Society Ltd v Windy Nook and District Industrial Co-operative Society Ltd* [1959] 1 All ER 43, [1959] 1 WLR 142; *Termarea SRL v Rederiaktieboleget Sally, The Dalny* [1979] 2 Lloyd's Rep 439 at 442. See also *H E Daniels Ltd v Carmel Exporters and Importers Ltd* [1953] 2 QB 242, [1953] 2 All ER 401 (failure to ask for a special case).

702. Void awards. Where an award is void, as opposed to merely voidable[1], a party may apply to the court for a declaration that he is not bound by the award[2] and, if necessary and appropriate, for an injunction restraining enforcement of the award until the issue of validity of the award has been decided. Alternatively he may rely upon the defect in the award as a defence to proceedings to enforce it[3].

An application for such a declaration may be combined with proceedings to set aside or remit the award[4]. However, proceedings to set aside or remit cannot stand as a counterclaim in an application to enforce the award[5].

1 See para 701 ante.
2 See *Kaukomarkkinat O/Y v 'Elbe' Transport-Union GmbH, The Kelo* [1985] 2 Lloyd's Rep 85.
3 *Davies v Price* (1862) 6 LT 713; *Oil Products Trading Co Ltd v Société Anonyme Société de Gestion d'Entreprises Coloniales* (1934) 150 LT 475. Where a party challenges an award and fails, he cannot thereafter rely upon a different defect in the award as a defence: *Hall and Wodehouse Ltd v Panorama Hotel Properties Ltd* [1974] 2 Lloyd's Rep 413 at 419, CA, per Megaw LJ.
4 See RSC Ord 73 r 2 (3); *Luanda Exportadora v Tamari & Sons* [1967] 2 Lloyd's Rep 353.
5 *Birtley District Co-operative Society Ltd v Windy Nook and District Industrial Co-operative Society Ltd* [1959] 1 All ER 43, [1959] 1 WLR 142; *Termarea SRL v Rederiaktieboleget Sally, The Dalny* [1979] 2 Lloyd's Rep 439 at 442; see also *Pedler v Hardy* (1902) 18 TLR 591. For the procedure for setting aside or remitting see para 691 ante.

703. Waiver of objection to jurisdiction. Where a party wishes to challenge any award on the grounds that the arbitrator had no jurisdiction in the reference at all, but also wishes to defend the arbitration proceedings on the merits, he must protest the jurisdiction of the arbitrator and make it clear that his participation is without prejudice to his challenge to the jurisdiction[1]. Otherwise he may be taken to have waived his objection to jurisdiction[2], or alternatively to have made an ad hoc arbitration agreement[3].

1 *Davies v Price* (1862) 6 LT 713; *Ringland v Lowndes* (1864) 33 LJCP 337; *Ronaasen & Son v Metsanomistajain Metsakeskus O/Y* (1931) 40 Ll L Rep 267; *Dalmia Dairy Industries Ltd v National Bank of Pakistan* [1978] 2 Lloyd's Rep 223 at 233 (Kerr J), 280 (CA); *Westminster Chemicals and Produce Ltd v Eicholz and Loeser* [1954] 1 Lloyd's Rep 99 at 105; *Allied Vision Ltd v VPS Film Entertainment GmbH* [1991] 1 Lloyd's Rep 392. See also *Hamlyn v Betteley* (1880) 6 QBD 63 at 65; *Henry v Geoprosco International Ltd* [1976] QB 726, [1975] 2 All ER 702, CA.
2 *Compania Maritima Zorroza SA v Sesostris SA, The Marques de Bolarque* [1984] 1 Lloyd's Rep 652.
3 *Furness Withy (Australia) Pty Ltd v Metal Distributors (UK) Ltd, The Amazonia* [1990] 1 Lloyd's Rep 236, CA; see also *Almare Societa di Navigazione SpA v Derby and Co Ltd, The Almare Prima* [1989] 2 Lloyd's Rep 376.

704. Appeal from High Court. An appeal lies to the Court of Appeal from every order made by the High Court on an application in the matter of an arbitration[1], but the notice of appeal must be served within four weeks from the date on which the order was sealed or otherwise perfected[2], unless the period is extended by the High Court on application made before the expiration of that period[3] or by the Court of Appeal[4].

In all appeals, other than those arising out of applications made under the Arbitration Act 1979[5], an appeal to the Court of Appeal lies without leave.

1 Supreme Court Act 1981 s 16. As to appeals direct to the House of Lords see the Administration of Justice Act 1969 s 12 (amended by the Supreme Court Act 1981 s 152 (4), Sch 7); and COURTS.
2 RSC Ord 59 r 4 (1).
3 RSC Ord 59 r 15.
4 RSC Ord 3 r 5 (1), (2).
5 Ie the Arbitration Act 1979 ss 1, 2 (as to which see para 706 et seq post).

705. Appeal from Court of Appeal. Appeal lies from any order made by the Court of Appeal to the House of Lords, by leave of the Court of Appeal or of the House of Lords[1].

1 Appellate Jurisdiction Act 1876 s 3 (1); Administration of Justice (Appeals) Act 1934 s 1 (1): see COURTS.

(3) APPEALS

706. Appeals under the Arbitration Act 1979. The old procedure for statement of a case for a decision of the High Court[1] has ceased to have effect and the High Court no longer has jurisdiction to set aside or remit an award on the ground of error of fact or law on the face of the award[2]. Instead, the Arbitration Act 1979 has created a procedure by way of appeal to the High Court[3] on any question of law arising out of an award made on an arbitration agreement. However, an appeal may only be brought with the consent of all the other parties to the reference, or with the leave of the court[4]. The award must sufficiently set out the reasons for the award to enable the court to consider any question of law arising out of it[5]. On the determination of such an appeal, the court may by order confirm, vary or set aside the award, or remit the award to the reconsideration of the arbitrator or umpire together with the court's opinion on the question of law which was the subject of the appeal[6]. There is a limited power to grant leave to appeal to the Court of Appeal on the determination of an appeal by the High Court, on the grant or refusal by the High Court of leave to appeal, or on the making of or refusal to make an order for remission for further reasons[7].

1 Ie under the Arbitration Act 1950 s 21 (repealed).
2 Arbitration Act 1979 ss 1 (1), 8 (3).
3 Ibid s 1. The provisions of this section are subject only to the provisions relating to exclusion agreements and have effect notwithstanding anything in any agreement purporting to prohibit or restrict access to the High Court, or to restrict the jurisdiction of that court, or to prohibit or restrict the making of a reasoned award: s 3 (4).
4 Ibid s 1 (3). See also para 710 post. Leave cannot be given where there is an exclusion agreement: see para 707 post.
5 If it does not, the court has a limited power to remit the award for reasons, or further reasons: see para 708 post.

6 Arbitration Act 1979 s 1 (2), (8). Where the award is so remitted, the arbitrator or umpire must, unless the order otherwise directs, make his award within three months after the date of the order: s 1 (2).

7 See para 711 post.

707. Exclusion agreements. If the parties to a reference have entered into an agreement in writing excluding the right of appeal in relation to an award, the High Court must not grant leave to appeal with respect to a question of law arising out of that award[1], and must not grant leave to make an application for an order that the arbitrator or umpire concerned state reasons in relation to that award[2]. Furthermore, no application may be made[3] in relation to such award for determination of a preliminary point of law by the court[4].

Exclusion agreements are of no effect in relation to certain arbitration awards or questions of law arising in the course of certain references. These are awards made on, or questions of law arising in the course of a reference under, a statutory arbitration[5], an award made on, or a question of law arising in the course of a reference under, a domestic arbitration agreement[6], unless the exclusion agreement is entered into after the commencement of the arbitration in which the award is made or, as the case may be, in which the question of law arises[7]; and an award or a question of law arising in the course of a reference relating, in whole or in part, to a question or claim falling within the Admiralty jurisdiction of the High Court, or a dispute arising out of a contract of insurance, or a dispute arising out of a commodity contract[8], unless the exclusion agreement is entered into after the commencement of the arbitration in which the award is made or, as the case may be, in which the question of law arises, or the award or question relates to a contract which is expressed to be governed by a law other than the law of England and Wales[9]. The Secretary of State may by order[10] provide that the provision relating to maritime, insurance and commodity arbitrations is to cease to have effect or, subject to specified conditions, is not to apply to any exclusion agreement made in relation to an arbitration award of a specified description[11].

1 Ie under Arbitration Act 1979 s 1 (3) (b); and see para 706 ante.
2 Ie under ibid s 1 (5) (b); and see para 708 post.
3 Ie with the consent of the arbitrator or umpire under ibid 2 (1) (a); and see para 679 ante.
4 Ibid s 3 (1). An exclusion agreement may be expressed so as to relate to a particular award to awards under a particular reference or to any other description of awards, whether arising out of the same reference or not. An agreement may be an exclusion agreement whether it is entered into before or after the passing of the Act and whether or not it forms part of an arbitration agreement: s 3 (2).
   Where an arbitration agreement, other than a domestic arbitration agreement (see note 6 infra), provides for disputes between the parties to be referred to arbitration and a dispute to which the agreement relates involves the question whether a party has been guilty of fraud, and the parties have entered into an exclusion agreement which is applicable to any award made on the reference of that dispute, then, except in so far as the exclusion agreement otherwise provides, the High Court must not exercise its powers under the Arbitration Act 1950 s 24 (2) to take steps necessary to enable the question to be determined by the High Court in relation to that dispute (see para 636 note 7 ante): Arbitration Act 1979 s 3 (3).
5 Ie such an arbitration as is referred to in the Arbitration Act 1950 s 31 (1) (see para 601 ante): Arbitration Act 1979 s 3 (5).
6 A 'domestic arbitration agreement' means an arbitration agreement which does not provide, expressly or by implication, for arbitration in a state other than the United Kingdom and to which neither an individual who is a national of, or habitually resident in, any state other than the United Kingdom, nor a body corporate which is incorporated in, or whose central management and control in exercised in, any state other than the United Kingdom, is a party at the time when the arbitration agreement is entered into: ibid s 3 (7).
7 Ibid s 3 (6).

8 A 'commodity contract' means a contract for the sale of goods regularly dealt with on a commodity market or exchange in England or Wales which is specified for the purposes of this section by an order made by the Secretary of State, and of a description so specified: ibid s 4 (2). As to the making of orders see note 10 infra. See the Arbitration (Commodity Contracts) Order 1979, SI 1979/754.
9 Arbitration Act 1979 s 4 (1).
10 Ie by statutory instrument subject to annulment in pursuance of a resolution of either House of Parliament: ibid s 4 (4).
11 Ibid s 4 (3).

708. The reasoned award. An arbitrator will normally give an explanation of the reasons for his award, and those reasons may or may not be incorporated as part of the award[1]. Only if they are so incorporated may they be relied upon in relation to an appeal[2]. An award is a reasoned award only if it incorporates reasons stated in sufficient detail for the court to consider any question of law arising out of it[3]. If a party wishes the arbitrator to make a reasoned award he must, before the award is made, give notice to the arbitrator or umpire concerned that a reasoned award is required[4]. Otherwise, in any case where an award is made without any reason being given, in the absence of some special reason why such a notice was not given the court cannot order the arbitrator or umpire concerned to state the reasons for his award[5].

If it appears to the High Court that the award does not or does not sufficiently set out the reasons for the award, the court may, with the consent of the parties or the leave of the court, order the arbitrator or umpire concerned to state the reasons for his award in sufficient detail to enable the court, should an appeal be brought[6], to consider any question of law arising out of the award[7]. Application is by originating summons to a Commercial judge in chambers[8]. The court will not, however, make such an order where there is an exclusion agreement[9], where a reasoned award was neither requested nor given, where the question of law for which leave is sought is whether there was any evidence to support a particular finding of fact and the arbitrator was not asked specifically to set out the evidential basis of his finding[10], or where there is no real prospect of leave being granted in any event[11]. If the point was not taken before the arbitrator, and as a result the necessary facts were not found, an order for further reasons will only be granted in very special circumstances, if at all[12].

An applicant for an order that the arbitrator or umpire concerned state his reasons may not adduce evidence extrinsic to the award, except that he may refer to the fact that he made specific submissions to the arbitrator and requested a reasoned award in relation to them[13].

1 The arbitrator may ensure the non-incorporation of his reasons by using a formula such as 'reasons not forming part of the award': *Intermare Transport GmbH v International Copra Export Corpn, The Ross Isle and Ariel* [1982] 2 Lloyd's Rep 589; *Mutual Shipping Corpn v Bayshore Shipping Co Ltd, The Montan* [1985] 1 All ER 520, [1985] 1 WLR 625, [1985] 1 Lloyd's Rep 189, CA.
2 Though they may be relied on for other purposes: *Mutual Shipping Corpn v Bayshore Shipping Co Ltd, The Montan* [1985] 1 All ER 520, [1985] 1 WLR 625, [1985] 1 Lloyd's Rep 189, CA.
3 *Trave Schiffahrtsgesellschaft mbH & Co KG v Ninemia Maritime Corpn, The Niedersachsen (No 2)* [1986] QB 802, [1986] 2 All ER 244, [1986] 1 Lloyd's Rep 393, CA.
4 The request may be in conditional form, eg that reasons should be given only if the result is adverse to the party making the request. It should be accompanied by a formulation of the question of law on which the party may wish to appeal, though this is not essential.
5 Arbitration Act 1979 ss 1 (5), (6).
6 Under ibid s 1 (3).
7 Ibid s 1 (5).
8 RSC Ord 73 r 3.

9 See para 707 ante.
10 *Athens Cape Naviera SA v Deutsche Dampfschiffahrts-gesellschaft 'Hansa' Aktiengesellschaft, The Baren-bels* [1985] 1 Lloyd's Rep 528, CA; *Mondial Trading Co GmbH v Gill and Duffus Zuckerhandels-gesellschaft mbH* [1980] 2 Lloyd's Rep 376; *Universal Petroleum Co Ltd v Handels und Transport-gesellschaft mbH* [1987] 2 All ER 737, [1987] 1 WLR 1178, [1987] 1 Lloyd's Rep 517, CA.
11 *Universal Petroleum Co Ltd v Handels und Transportgesellschaft mbH* [1987] 2 All ER 737, [1987] 1 WLR 1178, [1987] 1 Lloyd's Rep 517, CA; *Kansa General Insurance Co Ltd v Bishopsgate Insurance plc* [1988] 1 Lloyd's Rep 503.
12 *Petraco (Bermuda) Ltd v Petromed International SA* [1988] 3 All ER 454, [1988] 1 WLR 896, [1988] 2 Lloyd's Rep 357, CA; *Bremer Handelsgesellschaft mbH v Westzucker GmbH (No 2)* [1981] 2 Lloyd's Rep 130, CA.
13 *Universal Petroleum Co Ltd v Handels und Transportgesellschaft mbH* [1987] 2 All ER 737, [1987] 1 WLR 1178, [1987] 1 Lloyd's Rep 517, CA; *Kansa General Insurance Co Ltd v Bishopsgate Insurance plc* [1988] 1 Lloyd's Rep 503.

709. Procedure on application for leave to appeal. The application for leave to appeal is made by originating summons for hearing by a Commercial judge in chambers[1], unless any such judge otherwise directs[2]. The appeal itself is by notice of originating motion. The summons for leave to appeal, where leave is required, and the notice of originating motion must be served and the appeal entered, within 21 days after the award and reasons have been made and published to the parties[3]. The notice of originating motion and the originating summons must state the grounds of the appeal and application for leave and, where the application is founded on evidence by affidavit, or is made with the consent of the other parties, a copy of every affidavit intended to be used, or, as the case may be, of every consent given in writing, must be served with that notice[4]. The statement of the grounds of the appeal must specify the relevant parts of the award and reasons, and a copy of the award and reasons, or the relevant parts thereof, must be lodged with the court and served with the notice of originating motion[5]. The statement of the grounds of the appeal should also contain specific reference to any authority relied on[6]. Any affidavit by the respondent to a prospective appeal dealing with the one-off nature of the question in the appeal must be lodged with the court and served on the applicant not less than two clear days before the hearing of the application for leave[7]. If the respondent wishes to contend that the award should be upheld on grounds not expressed or not fully expressed in the award and reasons he must, not less than two clear days before the hearing of the application, lodge with the court and serve on the applicant a notice specifying the grounds of his contention[8].

1 RSC Ord 73 r 3 (2), (3).
2 RSC Ord 73 r 6. The Commercial Court will retain applications relating to disputes that would qualify as commercial actions if they were brought before the court: see RSC Ord 72 r 1 (2). Rent review arbitrations are normally transferred to the Chancery Division and construction arbitrations to an official referee: *Tate and Lyle Industries Ltd v Davy McKee (London) Ltd* [1990] 1 QB 1068, [1990] 1 All ER 157, [1990] 1 Lloyd's Rep 116, CA; see also *Ipswich Borough Council v Fisons plc* [1989] 2 All ER 737; affd on different grounds [1990] Ch 709, [1990] 1 All ER 730, CA.
3 RSC Ord 73 r 5 (2). See also para 691 text and note 3 ante.
4 RSC Ord 73 r 5 (5), (7).
5 RSC Ord 73 r 5 (6).
6 *Practice Direction* [1985] 2 Lloyd's Rep 300. A copy should be provided of any authority not contained in the Law Reports, Weekly Law Reports, All England Law Reports, English Reports or Lloyd's Law Reports.
7 RSC Ord 73 r 5 (8).
8 RSC Ord 73 r 5 (9).

710. Principles on which leave to appeal is granted. The court has no jurisdiction to entertain an appeal unless, having regard to all the circumstances, the determination of the question of law could substantially affect the rights of one or more parties to the arbitration agreement[1]. Only if that requirement is satisfied does the court go on to consider whether leave to appeal should be granted.

Where the question of law in relation to which leave is sought is a one-off question because, for example, it depends upon construction of a non-standard contractual term or upon application of a legal principle to an unusual set of facts[2], leave will not normally be given unless it is apparent to the judge upon a mere perusal of the reasoned award itself[3] that the arbitrator was obviously wrong. Otherwise the parties should be left to accept, for better or for worse, the decision of the tribunal that they had chosen to decide the matter in the first instance[4]. Where, on the other hand, the question of law is not a one-off question, for example because it concerns the interpretation of a clause in general use in a particular trade, or because it concerns the application of a legal principle to facts which are likely to recur, it will normally be enough to demonstrate that there is a strong prima facie case that the arbitrator was wrong[5]. In an exceptional case, where the question of law is of great general importance, it may be enough to show that the point is capable of serious argument[6]. Leave will also normally be given where there is a conflict of judicial authority, as opposed to a mere conflict of dicta[7].

In an application for leave to appeal, as in the appeal itself, the court may look only at material incorporated into the reasoned award[8]. However, where a party wishes to contend that the question of law does or does not concern a term of a contract or an event which is not a one-off term or event, evidence to that effect should be given by affidavit[9].

1 Arbitration Act 1979 s 1 (4).
2 *Pioneer Shipping Ltd v BTP Tioxide Ltd, The Nema* [1982] AC 724, [1981] 2 All ER 1030, [1981] 2 Lloyd's Rep 239, HL; *Antaios Compania Naviera SA v Salen Rederierna AB* [1985] AC 191, [1984] 3 All ER 229, [1984] 2 Lloyd's Rep 235, HL. See also *BVS SA v Kerman Shipping Co SA* [1982] 1 All ER 616, [1982] 1 WLR 166, [1982] 1 Lloyd's Rep 62; *Marrealeza Compania Naviera SA v Tradax Export SA, The Nichos A* [1982] 1 Lloyd's Rep 52; *Retla Steamship Co v Gryphon Shipping Co SA, The Evimeria* [1982] 1 Lloyd's Rep 55; *National Rumour Co SA v Lloyd-Libra Navegacao SA* [1982] 1 Lloyd's Rep 472. The same considerations apply in construction of rent review clauses: *Ipswich Borough Council v Fisons plc* [1990] Ch 709, [1990] 1 All ER 730, CA.
3 *Pioneer Shipping Ltd v BTP Tioxide Ltd, The Nema* [1982] AC 724 at 742, [1981] 2 All ER 1030 at 1040, [1981] 2 Lloyd's Rep 239 at 247, HL, per Lord Diplock.
4 *Pioneer Shipping Ltd v BTP Tioxide Ltd, The Nema* [1982] AC 724 at 743, [1981] 2 All ER 1030 at 1040, [1981] 2 Lloyd's Rep 239 at 247, HL, per Lord Diplock.
5 *Pioneer Shipping Ltd v BTP Tioxide Ltd, The Nema* [1982] AC 724, [1981] 2 All ER 1030, [1981] 2 Lloyd's Rep 239, HL; *Antaios Compania Naviera SA v Salen Rederierna AB* [1985] AC 191, [1984] 3 All ER 229, [1984] 2 Lloyd's Rep 235, HL. See also *Italmare Shipping Co v Ocean Tanker Co Inc, The Rio Sun* [1982] 1 All ER 517, [1982] 1 WLR 158, [1981] 2 Lloyd's Rep 489, CA; *Astro Valiente Compania Naviera SA v Pakistan Ministry of Food and Agriculture, The Emmanuel Colocotronis* [1982] 1 All ER 578, [1982] 1 Lloyd's Rep 297; *Tor Line AB v Alltrans Group of Canada Ltd, The TFL Prosperity* [1982] 1 Lloyd's Rep 617, CA; *Phoenix Shipping Co v Apex Shipping Corpn, The Apex* [1982] 1 Lloyd's Rep 476; *Seaworld Ocean Line Co SA v Catseye Marine Co Ltd, The Kalaniya* [1989] 1 Lloyd's Rep 30, CA (appeal from an award by judge-arbitrator).
6 *Bulk Oil (Zug) AG v Sun International Ltd* [1984] 1 All ER 386, [1984] 1 WLR 147, [1983] 2 Lloyd's Rep 587, CA.
7 *Antaios Compania Naviera SA v Salen Rederierna AB* [1985] AC 191 at 203–204, [1984] 3 All ER 229 at 235, [1984] 2 Lloyd's Rep 235 at 240, HL, per Lord Diplock.
8 See para 708 ante; *Universal Petroleum Co Ltd v Handels und Transport GmbH* [1987] 2 All ER 737, [1987] 1 WLR 1178, [1987] 1 Lloyd's Rep 517, CA; *Athens Cape Naviera SA v Deutsche Dampf-*

schiffahrtsgesellschaft 'Hansa' Aktiengesellschaft, The Barenbels [1985] 1 Lloyd's Rep 528, CA. See also
Warde v Feedex International Inc [1984] 1 Lloyd's Rep 310.
9 RSC Ord 73 r 5 (7), (8).

711. Appeal to the Court of Appeal. The Court of Appeal has jurisdiction to
hear appeals from decisions of the High Court granting or refusing leave to appeal
an award[1], granting or refusing leave to apply for an order for the arbitrator to state
his reasons[2], ordering or refusing to order the arbitrator to state his reasons[3] or
deciding whether or not to entertain an application for determination of a preliminary point of law[4]. If the High Court refuses, despite the consent of the parties[5], to
determine a preliminary point, an appeal against that refusal lies with the leave of
the High Court or the Court of Appeal. In all the other cases mentioned above, an
appeal only lies with the leave of the High Court[6], and the Court of Appeal has no
jurisdiction to give leave to appeal. Nor does the Court of Appeal have jurisdiction
to hear an appeal against refusal by the High Court of leave to appeal to the Court of
Appeal[7]. In the case of grant or refusal of leave to appeal to the High Court, leave to
appeal to the Court of Appeal will only be given if the judge considers that the
guidelines laid down by the appellate courts need amplification, elucidation or
adaptation to changing practices, and in any other case he will not only refuse leave
to appeal to the Court of Appeal but will give no reasons for his decision to grant or
refuse leave to appeal to the High Court[8].

Provided that the High Court or the Court of Appeal give leave and that it is
certified by the High Court that the question of law to which its decision relates
either is one of general public importance or is one which for some other special
reason ought to be considered by the Court of Appeal[9], an appeal lies to the Court
of Appeal on the determination of an appeal to the High Court or on the determination by the High Court of a preliminary point of law. The guidelines laid down
for the granting of leave to appeal to the High Court[10] do not apply to the granting
of leave to appeal to the Court of Appeal[11]. The House of Lords has no jurisdiction
to hear an appeal from the Court of Appeal's grant or refusal of leave to appeal from
the High Court[12].

1 Ie under the Arbitration Act 1979 s 1 (3) (b); see para 706 ante.
2 Ie under ibid s 1 (5) (b); see para 708 ante.
3 Ie under ibid s 1 (5).
4 Ie under ibid s 2; see para 679 ante.
5 Ie under ibid s 2 (1) (b).
6 Ibid ss 1 (6A), 2 (2A) (added by the Supreme Court Act 1981 s 148 (2)–(4)).
7 *Aden Refinery Co Ltd v Ugland Management Co Ltd, The Ugland Obo One* [1987] QB 650, [1986] 3 All
   ER 737, [1986] 2 Lloyd's Rep 336, CA.
8 Arbitration Act 1979 s 1 (6A) (as added: see note 6 supra); *Antaios Compania Naviera SA v Salen
   Rederierna AB* [1985] AC 191, [1984] 3 All ER 229, [1984] 2 Lloyd's Rep 235, HL. See also *BVS SA v
   Kerman Shipping Co SA, The Kerman* [1982] 1 All ER 616, [1982] 1 WLR 166, [1982] 1 Lloyd's Rep
   62; *Petraco (Bermuda) Ltd v Petromed International SA* [1988] 3 All ER 454, [1988] 1 WLR 896, [1988] 2
   Lloyd's Rep 357, CA.
9 Arbitration Act 1979 s 1 (7), 2 (3). There is no appeal to the Court of Appeal against refusal of a
   certificate by the High Court: *National Westminster Bank plc v Arthur Young McClelland Moores & Co
   (a firm)* (Practice Note) [1985] 2 All ER 817, [1985] 1 WLR 1123n, CA. Nor may a second application
   be made in the light of subsequent Court of Appeal decisions: *National Westminster Bank plc v Arthur
   Young McClelland Moores & Co (a firm) (No 2)* [1991] 3 All ER 21.
10 *Pioneer Shipping Ltd v BTP Tioxide Ltd, The Nema* [1982] AC 724, [1981] 2 All ER 1030, [1981] 2
   Lloyd's Rep 239, HL.
11 *Geogas SA v Trammo Gas Ltd, The Baleares* [1991] 2 All ER 110, [1991] 2 WLR 794, CA. The
   majority of the Court of Appeal decided that neither *Babanaft International v Avant Petroleum* [1982]

3 All ER 244, [1982] 1 WLR 871, [1982] 2 Lloyd's Rep 99, CA, nor *Venezolana (CA) de Navegacion v Bank Line Ltd, The Roachbank* [1988] 2 Lloyd's Rep 337, CA, was a binding decision to the effect that the guidelines applied.

12 *Geogas SA v Trammo Gas Ltd, The Baleares* [1991] 3 All ER 554, [1991] 1 WLR 776, HL.

(4) ENFORCEMENT OF AWARD

(i) Action on the Award

712. Enforcement by action. There is an implied promise in every arbitration agreement that the parties will perform the award[1]. If a party to an arbitration agreement acts in breach of this implied promise by failing to comply with the award, the successful party may bring an action to enforce the award in any court of competent jurisdiction[2]. This remedy is available to a successful party whether the award arises out of a written or an oral arbitration agreement. The plaintiff in an action on the award may claim the following relief: judgment for the amount of the award[3]; a declaration that the award is binding[4]; in appropriate cases, specific performance of the award[5]; damages for failure to perform the award[6]; an injunction restraining the unsuccessful party from failing to comply with the award[7]. Judgment may be granted on an award in a foreign currency[8].

In an action on the award[9], the plaintiff must prove the following[10]: (1) the making of the contract which contains the submission; (2) that the dispute arose within the terms of the submission; (3) that the arbitrators were duly appointed in accordance with the clause containing the submission; (4) the making of the award; and (5) that the amount awarded has not been paid or that the award has not otherwise been performed. The burden of proof is on the plaintiff; if he fails to establish any one of these matters the action on the award will fail. In an action on the award, an arbitrator may be called to give evidence as to what occurred at the arbitration proceedings[11].

An action on the award may be defended on any of the following grounds: that the arbitration agreement was never entered into by the parties; that a valid award was never made; that the award as alleged was never made; that the award is void because the arbitrator exceeded his jurisdiction or acted without jurisdiction[12]; that the authority of the arbitrator was validly revoked before the award was made[13]. It is no defence to an action on the award that there has been misconduct or a mistake on the part of the arbitrator and, in these circumstances, the proper course it to have the award set aside[14].

The limitation period[15] in respect of an action on the award begins to run from the date of the failure to honour the award[16]

1 *Purslow v Baily* (1704) 2 Ld Raym 1039 at 1040 per Holt CJ; *Bremer Oeltransport GmbH v Drewry* [1933] 1 KB 753, CA; *F J Bloemen Pty Ltd v Gold Coast City Council* [1973] AC 115, [1972] 3 All ER 357, PC. See also para 684 text and note 3 ante.

2 See *King v Bowen* (1841) 8 M & W 625; *China Steam Navigation Co v Van Laun* (1905) 22 TLR 26. An action in rem may be brought to enforce an award made where a dispute under a charterparty has been referred to arbitration: *The St Anna* [1983] 2 All ER 691, [1983] 1 WLR 895, [1983] 1 Lloyd's Rep 637.

3 Or judgment for unpaid interest under the Arbitration Act 1950 s 20, even though the amount of the award has been paid: *Coastal States Trading (UK) Ltd v Mebro Mineraloel-Handelsgesellschaft mbH* [1986] 1 Lloyd's Rep 465

4 See *Birtley District Co-operative Society v Windy Nook and District Industrial Co-operative Society (No 2)* [1960] 2 QB 1, [1959] 1 All ER 623; *Selby v Whitbread & Co* [1917] 1 KB 736; *Merrifield, Ziegler & Co v Liverpool Cotton Association Ltd* (1911) 105 LT 97.

5 *Wood v Griffith* (1818) 1 Swan 43 at 54; *Nickels v Hancock* (1855) 7 De GM & G 300; *Blackett v Bates* (1865) 1 Ch App 117; *Selby v Whitbread & Co* [1917] 1 KB 736 at 753 per McCardie J. See also *Hall v Hardy* (1733) 3 P Wms 187 at 190.

6 *Birtley District Co-operative Society v Windy Nook and District Industrial Co-operative Society (No 2)* [1960] 2 QB 1, [1959] 1 All ER 623; *Dalmia Dairy Industries Ltd v National Bank of Pakistan* [1978] 2 Lloyd's Rep 223 at 273–274 per Kerr J; on appeal [1978] 2 Lloyd's Rep 223, CA.

7 *Birtley District Co-operative Society v Windy Nook and District Industrial Co-operative Society (No 2)* [1960] 2 QB 1, [1959] 1 All ER 623.

8 *Jugoslavenska Oceanska Plovidba v Castle Investment Co Inc* [1974] QB 292, [1973] 3 All ER 498, [1973] 2 Lloyd's Rep 1, CA, approved in *Miliangos v George Frank Textiles Ltd* [1976] AC 443, [1975] 3 All ER 801, [1976] 1 Lloyd's Rep 201, HL. The date for the conversion of the amount into sterling was said in *Jugoslavenska Oceanska Plovidba v Castle Investment Co Inc* supra, to be the date of the award and in *Miliangos v George Frank Textiles Ltd* supra, to be the date when leave to enforce is given by the court.

9 For Forms see 6 Court Forms (2nd Edn) (1989 Issue) 156–163, Forms 94–106.

10 These requirements were set out by Devlin J in *Christopher Brown Ltd v Genossenschaft Oesterreichisch-er Waldbesitzer Holzwirtschaftsbetriebe Registrierte GmbH* [1954] 1 QB 8 at 9, [1953] 2 All ER 1039 at 1040. See also *Kianta Osakeyhito v Britain and Overseas Trading Co* [1953] 2 Lloyd's Rep 569; affd [1954] 1 Lloyd's Rep 247 at 250–251, CA.

11 *Duke of Buccleuch v Metropolitan Board of Works* (1872) LR 5 HL 418; followed in *O'Rourke v Railways Comr* (1890) 15 App Cas 371; *Recher & Co v North British and Mercantile Insurance Co* [1915] 3 KB 277. See also *Ellis v Saltau* (1808) 4 C & P 327n; *Johnson v Durant* (1830) 4 C & P 327.

12 *Christopher Brown Ltd v Genossenschaft Oesterreichischer Waldbesitzer Holzwirtschaftsbetriebe Registrierte GmbH* [1954] 1 QB 8 at 10, [1953] 2 All ER 1039 at 1041 per Devlin J. See also *Wyndham v Jackson* [1938] 2 All ER 109, CA; *Crane v Hegeman-Harris Co Inc* [1939] 4 All ER 68; *Kruse v Questier & Co Ltd* [1953] 1 QB 669, [1953] 1 All ER 954.

13 See the Arbitration Act 1950 s 1. See also para 661 et seq ante.

14 *Thorburn v Barnes* (1867) L R 2 CP 384, approved in *L Oppenheim & Co v Mahomed Haneef* [1922] 1 AC 482, PC; *Bache v Billingham* [1894] 1 QB 107 at 111.

15 See the Limitation Act 1980 s 7.

16 *Agromet v Motoimport Ltd v Maulden Engineering Co (Beds) Ltd* [1985] 2 All ER 436, [1985] 1 WLR 762.

(ii) Summary Enforcement

713. Enforcement as a judgment. An award on an arbitration agreement may, by leave of the High Court or a judge thereof, be enforced in the same manner as a judgment or order to the same effect, and where leave is so given, judgment may be entered in terms of the award[1]. This remedy is only available to a successful party where the award arises out of a written arbitration agreement[2].

The court will grant leave to enforce the award as a judgment unless there is either a real ground for doubting the validity of the award[3] or the award is not in a form in which it can be enforced as a judgment[4]. Where the court refuses to grant leave to enforce, a party is left to enforce the award by action[5]. The court may grant leave to enforce an award made in a foreign currency[6].

An application to the High Court for leave to enforce the award may be made by originating summons[7] or ex parte on affidavit[8]. The application is made before a master[9] or a Commercial judge in chambers[10]. In the case of a judge-arbitrator or judge-umpire leave to enforce the award may be given by the judge-arbitrator or judge-umpire himself[11].

The application for leave must be supported by an affidavit[12]: (1) exhibiting the arbitration agreement and the original award or, in either case, a copy thereof; (2) stating the name and the usual or last known place of abode or business of the applicant ('the creditor') and the person against whom it is sought to enforce the award ('the debtor'); (3) stating either that the award has not been complied with or the extent to which it has not been complied with at the date of the application.

An order giving leave to enforce an award must be drawn up by or on behalf of the creditor and must be served on the debtor by delivering a copy to him personally at his usual or last known place of abode or business or in such other manner as the court may direct[13]. Service of the order out of the jurisdiction is permissible without leave[14]. Within 14 days after service of the order or, if the order is to be served outside the jurisdiction, within such other period as the court may fix, the debtor may apply to set aside the order and the award must not be enforced until after the expiration of that period or, if the debtor applies within that period to set aside the order, until after the application is finally disposed of[15].

1 Arbitration Act 1950 s 26 (1) (added by the Administration of Justice Act 1977 s 17 (2)). For the history of the law relating to the enforcement of awards see *Duff Development Co Ltd v Kelantan Government* [1924] AC 797 at 817–818, HL. As to the enforcement of High Court judgments or orders see EXECUTION.

If the amount sought to be recovered does not exceed the county court limit and a county court so orders, it is recoverable (by execution issued from the county court or otherwise) as if payable under an order of that court and is not enforceable under the Arbitration Act 1950 s 26 (1): s 26 (2) (added by the Administration of Justice Act 1977 s 17 (2) and amended by the County Courts Act 1984 s 148 (1), Sch 2 para 22 (a)).

An application to the High Court under this section precludes an application to a county court, and an application to a county court under this section precludes an application to the High Court: Arbitration Act 1950 s 26 (3) (as added: see supra).

Where an award for the payment of money has been partially satisfied, the court may grant leave to enforce the balance: *Continental Grain Co v Bremer Handelsgesellschaft mbH (No 2)* [1984] 2 Lloyd's Rep 121. Where a successful party seeks to enforce an award but accepts a reduction in the amount of the money awarded, the court may grant leave to enforce the balance: *E D and F Man Ltd v Société Anonyme Tripolitaine des Usines Raffinage de Sucre* [1970] 2 Lloyd's Rep 416.

2 See Arbitration Act 1950 ss 26, 32.

3 *Middlemiss and Gould (a firm) v Hartlepool Corpn* [1973] 1 All ER 172 at 175,[1972] 1 WLR 1643 at 1647, CA, not following *Re Boks & Co and Peters, Rushton & Co Ltd* [1919] 1 KB 491, CA. See also *May v Mills* (1914) 30 TLR 287; *Grech v Board of Trade* (1932) 92 LJKB 956, CA; *Frank Fehr & Co v Kassam Jivraj & Co Ltd* (1949) 82 Ll L Rep 673; *Union Nationale des Co-operatives Agricoles de Cereales v Robert Catterall & Co Ltd* [1959] 2 QB 44, [1959] 1 All ER 721, CA; *Hall and Wodehouse Ltd v Panorama Hotel Properties Ltd* [1974] 2 Lloyd's Rep 413, CA.

4 *Margulies Bros Ltd v Dafnis Thomaides & Co (UK) Ltd* [1958] 1 All ER 777 at 780, [1958] 1 WLR 398 at 401–402 per Diplock J. The court has jurisdiction to remit an award for the payment of money to enable the arbitrator to amend the award and put it in a form capable of being enforced as a judgment: *Margulies Bros Ltd v Dafnis Thomaides & Co (UK) Ltd* supra.

5 See para 712 ante.

6 *Jugoslavenska Oceanska Plovidba v Castle Investment Co Inc* [1974] QB 292, [1973] 3 All ER 498, [1973] 2 Lloyd's Rep 1, CA; *Miliangos v George Frank Textiles Ltd* [1976] AC 443, [1975] 3 All ER 801, [1976] 1 Lloyd's Rep 201, HL. As to the date of conversion see para 712 text and note 8 ante.

The court will not grant leave to enforce an award which requires payment in a foreign currency: *Dalmia Cement Ltd v National Bank of Pakistan* [1975] QB 9, [1974] 3 All ER 189, [1974] 2 Lloyd's Rep 98.

7 RSC Ord 5 r 3. Service out of the jurisdiction of an originating summons for leave to enforce an award is permissible with the leave of the court whether or not the arbitration is governed by English law: RSC Ord 73 r 7 (1A); RSC Ord 11 r 9. For the procedure see RSC Ord 73 r 7 (2), (3).

8 RSC Ord 73 r 10 (1). The court hearing the application may, however, direct that an originating summons be issued: RSC Ord 73 r 10 (1). If the court directs a summons to be issued, it must be in Form No 10 in Appendix A (expedited form): RSC Ord 73 r 10 (2).

9 RSC Ord 73 r 3 (1).

10 See RSC Ord 73 rr 3 (1), 6.

11 Administration of Justice Act 1970 s 4 (4), Sch 3 para 12.

12 RSC Ord 73 r 10 (3).

13 RSC Ord 73 r 10 (4).

14 RSC Ord 73 r 10 (5).

15 RSC Ord 73 r 10 (6). See also RSC Ord 73 r 10 (7).

(iii) Foreign Awards

714. General. The award of a foreign arbitrator may, depending upon the circumstances in which it was made, be enforced either by an action on the award[1] or by way of summary procedure. The successful party may apply for the summary enforcement of the award as follows: under the Arbitration Act 1950[2]; as a 'foreign' award, under Part II of the Arbitration Act 1950[3]; as a 'convention' award, under the Arbitration Act 1975[4].

1 See para 712 ante.
2 Ie the Arbitration Act 1950 s 26; see para 713 ante. It is clear from the wording of s 26 that it is not limited to English awards. Consequently, the award of a foreign arbitrator may be enforced under s 26 whether or not it is also a 'convention' or a 'foreign' award: see *Dalmia Cement Ltd v National Bank of Pakistan* [1975] QB 9, [1974] 3 All ER 189, [1974] 2 Lloyd's Rep 98 (dealing with a 'foreign' award). See also the Arbitration Act 1950 s 40.
3 See para 716 post.
4 See para 715 post. Where a 'convention' award is also a 'foreign' award under Part II of the Arbitration Act 1950 (ss 35–42), Part II does not apply to it: Arbitration Act 1975 s 2. Therefore, an award within the provisions of the Arbitration Act 1975 must be enforced as a 'convention' award and not as a 'foreign' award under Part II of the Arbitration Act 1950.

715. 'Convention awards'. The Arbitration Act 1975 gives effect to the New York Convention on the Recognition and Enforcement of Foreign Arbitral Awards. It provides that a 'convention award'[1] is enforceable either by action or in the same manner as the award of an arbitrator is enforceable by virtue of the Arbitration Act 1950[1]. A 'convention award' is an award made in pursuance of an arbitration agreement in the territory of a state, other than the United Kingdom, which is party to the New York Convention[2].

Enforcement of a convention award will not be refused except in the circumstances set out in the Arbitration Act 1975[3]. These are as follows[4]: (1) that a party to the arbitration agreement was (under the law applicable to him) under some incapacity; or (2) that the arbitration agreement was not valid under the law to which the parties subjected it or, failing any indication thereon, under the law of the country where the award was made; or (3) that the party against whom the award is invoked was not given proper notice of the appointment of the arbitrator or of the arbitration proceedings or was otherwise unable to present his case; or (4) that the award deals with a difference not contemplated by or not falling within the terms of the submission to arbitration or contains decisions on matters beyond the scope of the submission to arbitration[5]; or (5) that the composition of the arbitral authority or the arbitral procedure was not in accordance with the agreement of the parties or, failing such agreement, with the law of the country where the arbitration took place; or (6) that the award has not yet become binding[6] on the parties, or has been set aside or suspended by a competent authority of the country in which, or under the law of which, it was made[7]. The burden of proving the existence of any of these circumstances lies on the party opposing enforcement of the award[8].

The party seeking to enforce a convention award must produce the following documents[9]: (a) the duly authenticated original award or a duly certified copy of it; (b) the original arbitration agreement or a duly certified copy of it; and (c) where the award or agreement is in a foreign language, a translation of it certified by an official or sworn translator or by a diplomatic or a consular agent.

1 Arbitration Act 1975 s 3 (1). See also the Arbitration Act 1950 s 26; and para 713 ante.

2 A 'convention award' is defined as an award made in pursuance of an arbitration agreement in the territory of a state, other than the United Kingdom, which is a party to the New York Convention: Arbitration Act 1975 s 7 (1). An award is 'made' in the place where it is signed, in the absence of a provision in the arbitration agreement or the rules governing the conduct of the arbitration requiring some further formality before the award becomes effective: *Hiscox v Outhwaite (No 1)* [1991] 3 All ER 641, [1991] 3 WLR 297, HL. An 'arbitration agreement' is defined as an agreement in writing (including an agreement contained in an exchange of letters or telegrams) to submit to arbitration present or future differences capable of settlement by arbitration: s 7 (1).

The Arbitration (Foreign Awards) Order 1984, SI 1984/1168, Sch 2, and the Arbitration (Foreign Awards) Order 1989, SI 1989/1348, Schedule, set out the states which are parties to the New York Convention: Algeria, Antigua, Argentina, Australia (including all the external territories for the international relations of which Australia is responsible), Austria, Bahrain, Barbados, Belgium, Belize, Benin, Botswana, Bulgaria, Burkina Faso, Byelorussian Soviet Socialist Republic, Cambodia, Cameroon, Canada, Central African Republic, Chile, China, Columbia, Costa Rica, Cuba, Cyprus, Czechoslovakia, Denmark (including Greenland and the Faroe Islands), Djibouti, Dominica, Ecuador, Egypt, Finland, France (including all the territories of the French Republic), Germany, Ghana, Greece, Guatemala, Haiti, Holy See, Hungary, India, Indonesia, Republic of Ireland, Israel, Italy, Japan, Jordan, Kenya, Korea, Kuwait, Luxembourg, Madagascar, Malaysia, Mexico, Monaco, Morocco, Netherlands (including the Netherlands Antilles), New Zealand, Niger, Nigeria, Norway, Panama, Peru, Philippines, Poland, Romania, San Marino, Singapore, South Africa, Spain, Sri Lanka, Sweden, Switzerland, Syria, Tanzania, Thailand, Trinidad and Tobago, Tunisia, Ukranian Socialist Soviet Republic, Union of Soviet Socialist Republics, the United States of America (including all the territories for the international relations of which the United States of America is responsible), Uruguay, Yugoslavia.

An award made in the territory of a foreign state which is a party to the convention is enforceable in the United Kingdom irrespective of whether the state in question was a party to the convention at the date either of the award or of the arbitration agreement: *Minister of Public Works of the Kuwait State Government v Sir Frederick Snow & Partners (a firm)* [1984] AC 426, [1984] 1 All ER 733, [1984] 1 Lloyd's Rep 458, HL.

2 Arbitration Act 1975 s 3 (1). The summary procedure referred to is that under the Arbitration Act 1950 s 26.

3 Arbitration Act 1975 s 5 (1). The presence of assets in the United Kingdom is not a prerequisite to enforcement: *Rosseel NV v Oriental Commercial and Shipping (UK) Ltd* [1990] 3 All ER 545, [1990] 1 WLR 1387, CA.

4 Arbitration Act 1975 s 5 (2) (a)–(f).

5 This provision is subject to ibid s 5 (4), which provides that a convention award which contains decisions on matters not submitted to arbitration may be enforced to the extent that it contains decisions on matters submitted to arbitration which can be separated from those on matters not so submitted.

6 An agreement between the parties entered into before the award was made, to the effect that any proceedings to confirm or vacate the award once made would be brought in the United States of America, does not detract from the binding nature of the award when it is made and is, therefore, ineffective to prevent its enforcement as a convention award: *Rosseel NV v Oriental Commercial and Shipping (UK) Ltd* [1990] 3 All ER 545, [1990] 1 WLR 1387, CA.

7 See *Hiscox v Outhwaite (No 1)* [1991] 3 All ER 641, [1991] 3 WLR 297, HL.

8 See *Deutsche Schachtbau und Tiefbohrgessellschaft mbH v Ras al Khaimah National Oil Co* [1987] 2 All ER 769, [1987] 2 Lloyd's Rep 246, CA; revsd on other grounds [1990] 1 AC 295, [1988] 2 All ER 833, [1988] 2 Lloyd's Rep 293, HL.

9 Arbitration Act 1975 s 4.

716. 'Foreign awards'. Part II of the Arbitration Act 1950[1] provides that an award to which it applies, referred to as a 'foreign award'[2], is enforceable either by action or in the same manner as the award of an arbitrator is enforceable by virtue of section 26 of the 1950 Act[3]. Part II applies to awards[4] in the following circumstances[5]: (1) where the award is made in pursuance of an arbitration agreement to which the Protocol on Arbitration Clauses (1923) applies[6]; and (2) where the arbitration agreement is made between persons one of whom is subject to the jurisdiction of a state party to the Geneva Convention on the Execution of Foreign

Arbitral Awards (1927)[7], the other of whom is a person subject to the jurisdiction of some other such state[8]; and (3) where the arbitration agreement was made in a territory to which the Geneva Convention on the Execution of Foreign Arbitral Awards (1927) applies.

For a foreign award to be enforceable under Part II of the Arbitration Act 1950 the following conditions must be satisfied[9]: (a) the award must have been made in pursuance of an agreement for arbitration which was valid under the law by which it was governed; (b) the award must have been made by the tribunal provided for in the agreement or constituted in manner agreed upon by the parties; (c) the award must have been made in conformity with the law governing the arbitration procedure; (d) the award must have become final in the country in which it was made[10]; (e) the award must have been in respect of a matter which may lawfully be referred to arbitration under the law of England. Furthermore, the enforcement of the award must not be contrary to the public policy or the law of England[11].

A foreign award is not enforceable under Part II of the Arbitration Act 1950 if the court dealing with the case is satisfied as follows[12]: (i) that the award has been annulled in the country in which it has been made; or (ii) that the party against whom it is sought to enforce the award was not given notice of the arbitration proceedings in sufficient time to enable him to present his case, or was under some legal incapacity and was not properly represented; or (iii) that the award does not deal with all the questions referred or contains decisions on matters beyond the scope of the arbitration agreement[13].

If a party seeking to resist the enforcement proves that there is any ground entitling him to contest the validity of the award[14], the court may, if it thinks fit, either refuse to enforce the award or adjourn the hearing until after the expiration of such period as appears to the court to be reasonably sufficient to enable that party to take the necessary steps to have the award annulled by the competent tribunal[15].

The party seeking to enforce a foreign award must produce the following documents[16]: (A) the original award or a copy thereof duly authenticated in manner required by the law of the country in which it was made; (B) evidence proving that the award has become final; (C) such evidence as may be necessary to prove that the award is a foreign award; (D) such evidence as may be necessary to prove that the award was made in pursuance of an arbitration agreement which was valid under the law by which it was governed; (E) such evidence as may be necessary to prove that the award has been made by the tribunal provided for in the agreement or constituted in manner agreed upon by the parties; and (F) such evidence as may be necessary to prove that the award has been made in conformity with the law governing the arbitration procedure.

If any document required to be produced is in a foreign language, it is the duty of the party seeking to enforce the award to produce a translation certified as correct by a diplomatic or consular agent of the country to which that party belongs, or certified as correct in such other manner as may be sufficient according to the law of England[17].

1 The effect of the Arbitration Act 1950 Pt II (ss 35–42) is to put a foreign award in the same position as an English award in relation to enforcement, subject to fulfilling the conditions set out in s 37: see *Union Nationale des Co-operatives Agricoles de Cereales v Robert Catterall & Co Ltd* [1959] 2 QB 44 at 50, [1959] 1 All ER 721 at 723, CA, per Lord Evershed MR. Part II of the 1950 Act does not apply to awards made on an arbitration agreement governed by English law: s 40 (b).

2 Ibid s 35 (1).

3 Ibid s 36 (1). See also para 713 ante.

4 Other than 'convention awards', which are enforceable under the Arbitration Act 1975. Convention awards are not, therefore, enforceable under Part II of the Arbitration Act 1950 as 'foreign awards': Arbitration Act 1975 s 2.

5 Arbitration Act 1950 s 35 (1).

6 This is set out in the Arbitration Act 1950 Sch 1. The contracting states for the purposes of the
protocol are as follows: Albania (TS 56 (1925); Cmd 2577); Austria (TS 29 (1928); Cmd 3266);
Bahamas (TS 43 (1931); Cmd 4015); Belgium (TS 56 (1925); Cmd 2577); Brazil (TS 38 (1932); Cmd
4249); British Guiana (TS 32 (1926); Cmd 2804); British Honduras (TS 32 (1926); Cmd 2804);
Burma (excluding Karenni States) (TS 75 (1938); Cmd 5930); Ceylon (TS 75 (1926); Cmd 2804);
Czechoslovakia (TS 43 (1931); Cmd 4015); Danzig (TS 75 (1938); Cmd 5930); Denmark (TS 56
(1925); Cmd 2577); Estonia (TS 33 (1929); Cmd 3491); Falkland Islands and Dependencies (TS 32
(1926); Cmd 2804; and TS 39 (1934); Cmd 4809); Finland (TS 56 (1925); Cmd 2577); France (TS 29
(1928); Cmd 3266); Gambia (Colony and Protectorate) (TS 32 (1926); Cmd 2804; and TS 39 (1934);
Cmd 4809); Germany (TS 56 (1925); Cmd 2577); Gibraltar (TS 32 (1926); Cmd 2804); Gold Coast
(including Ashanti, Northern Territories and Togoland under British Mandate) (TS 32 (1926); Cmd
280; and TS 43 (1931); Cmd 4015); Greece (TS 32 (1926); Cmd 2804); India (TS 56 (1937); Cmd
5654); Iraq (TS 32 (1926); Cmd 2804); Italy (TS 56 (1925); Cmd 2577); Jamaica (including Turks and
Caicos Islands and the Cayman Islands) (TS 32 (1926); Cmd 280; and TS 43 (1931); Cmd 4015); Japan
(including Chosen, Taiwan, Karafuto, leased territory of Kwangtung and Japanese Mandated
Territories) (TS 28 (1928); Cmd 326; and TS 33 (1929); Cmd 3491); Kenya (Colony and Protectorate) (TS 32 (1926); Cmd 2804; and TS 39 (1934); Cmd 4809); Leeward Islands (TS 32 (1926); Cmd
2804); Luxembourg (TS 52 (1930); Cmd 3816); Malta (TS 32 (1926); Cmd 2804); Monaco (TS 29
(1927); Cmd 3022); Netherlands (including Netherlands Indies, Surinam and Curaçao) (TS 56
(1925); Cmd 2577; TS 75 (1938); Cmd 5930; and TS 31 (1940); Cmd 6253); Newfoundland (TS 56
(1925); Cmd 2577); New Zealand (TS 32 (1926); Cmd 2804); Northern Rhodesia (TS 32 (1926);
Cmd 2804); Norway (TS 29 (1927); Cmd 3022); Palestine (excluding Trans-Jordan) (TS 32 (1926);
Cmd 2804; and TS 39 (1934); Cmd 4809); Poland (TS 43 (1931); Cmd 4015); Portugal (TS 52 (1930);
Cmd 3816); Roumania (TS 56 (1925); Cmd 2577); St Helena (TS 32 (1926); Cmd 2804); Siam (TS 52
(1930); Cmd 3816); Southern Rhodesia (TS 56 (1925); Cmd 2577); Spain (TS 32 (1926); Cmd 2804);
Sweden (TS 33 (1926); Cmd 3491); Switzerland (TS 29 (1928); Cmd 3266); Tanganyika Territory
(TS 32 (1926); Cmd 2804); Trans-Jordan (TS 39 (1934); Cmd 4809); Uganda (TS 33 (1929); Cmd
3491); United Kingdom of Great Britain and Northern Ireland (TS 4 (1925); Cmd 2312); Windward
Islands (Grenada, St Lucia, St Vincent) (TS 32 (1926); Cmd 2804); Zanzibar (TS 32 (1926); Cmd
2804).

　　The names of these states are those by which they were known at the date on which they became
contracting states; many have subsequently changed.

7 This is set out in the Arbitration Act 1950 Sch 2. The Arbitration (Foreign Awards) Order 1984, SI
1984/1168, Sch 1, lists the states which are parties to the Geneva Convention and the territories to
which the convention applies. The states listed are as follows: the United Kingdom of Great Britain
and Northern Ireland, Anguilla, British Virgin Islands, Cayman Islands, Falkland Islands, Falkland
Islands Dependencies, Gibraltar, Hong Kong, Montserrat, Turks and Caicos Islands, Antigua and
Barbuda, Austria, Bahamas, Bangladesh, Belgium, Belize, Czechoslovakia, Denmark, Dominica,
Finland, France, Germany, Greece, Grenada, Guyana, India, Republic of Ireland, Israel, Italy,
Japan, Kenya, Luxembourg, Malta, Mauritius, Netherlands (including Curaçao), New Zealand,
Pakistan, Portugal, Romania, St Christopher and Nevis, St Lucia, Spain, Sweden, Switzerland,
Tanzania, Thailand, Western Samoa, Yugoslavia, Zambia.

　　Orders in Council made under the Arbitration (Foreign Awards) Act 1930 (repealed) have
continued to have effect under the Arbitration Act s 35 (3); although none has been revoked they are
largely superseded by the Arbitration (Foreign Awards) Order 1984, SI 1984/1168. For a list of these
states see 2 Halsbury's Statutes (4th Edn) 569–570, notes to the Arbitration Act 1950 s 35.

8 Arbitration Act 1950 s 35 (1) (b). See also *Dalmia Cement Ltd v National Bank of Pakistan* [1975] QB 9,
[1974] 3 All ER 189, [1974] 2 Lloyd's Rep 98.

9 These conditions are set out in the Arbitration Act 1975 s 37 (1).

10 For the purposes of the Arbitration Act 1950 Pt II, an award is not deemed to be final if any
proceedings for the purpose of contesting the validity of the award are pending in the country in
which it was made: s 39.

11 Ibid s 37 (1).

12 These conditions are set out in the Arbitration Act 1950 s 37 (2).

13 Provided that, if the award does not deal with all the questions referred, the court may, if it thinks fit,
either postpone the enforcement of the award or order its enforcement subject to the giving of such
security by the person seeking to enforce it as the court thinks fit: ibid s 37 (2).

14 Other than the non-existence of the conditions specified in s 37 (1) (a)–(c) or the existence of the
   conditions specified in s 37 (2) (b), (c): ibid s 37 (3).
15 Ibid s 37 (3).
16 Ibid s 38 (1).
17 Ibid s 38 (2).

10. CONFLICT OF LAWS

717. Proper law of the arbitration agreement. The proper law of the arbitration agreement governs its validity, interpretation and effect[1]. That proper law
is determined in accordance with the general principles of the conflict of laws,
namely the law chosen by the parties or, in the absence of such choice, the law of
the country with which the agreement is most closely connected[2]. An agreement to
submit future disputes to arbitration usually forms part of a substantive contract,
for example a contract of sale, but is to be treated as a separate contract[3] and though
normally its proper law will be the same as the proper law of the substantive
contract of which it forms part, that may exceptionally not be the case[4]. Once a
particular dispute has arisen, its reference by the parties to arbitration gives rise to a
further contract separate from the agreement to submit future disputes to arbitration and with its own proper law[5].

1 *Whitworth Street Estates (Manchester) Ltd v James Miller & Partners Ltd* [1970] AC 583, [1970] 1 All ER
  796, HL.
2 See CONFLICT OF LAWS. It should be noted that art 1 (2) (d) of the Rome Convention (the Convention
  on the law applicable to contractual obligations, opened for signature by European Community
  member states in Rome on 19 June 1980), incorporated into English law by the Contracts (Applicable Law) Act 1990, excludes from its scope arbitration agreements, so their proper law continues
  to be determined by common law principles.
3 *Bremer Vulkan Schiffbau und Maschinenfabrik v South India Shipping Corpn* [1981] AC 909, [1981] 1 All
  ER 289, [1981] 1 Lloyd's Rep 253, HL.
4 *Black-Clawson International Ltd v Papierwerke Waldhof-Aschaffenburg AG* [1981] 2 Lloyd's Rep 446.
5 *Black-Clawson International Ltd v Papierwerke Waldhof-Aschaffenburg AG* [1981] 2 Lloyd's Rep 446,
  where the proper law of the contract regulating the individual reference to arbitration had to be
  ascertained for the purpose of determining whether it had been terminated by frustration or
  repudiation.

718. Curial law of the arbitration. The curial (or procedural) law governs the
arbitration proceedings, namely the conduct of the arbitration and supervisory
powers of the court[1]. In the absence of any choice of law, the curial law will be the
law of the seat of the arbitration, that is the country in which the arbitration is
held[2].

1 *Whitworth Street Estates (Manchester) Ltd v James Miller & Partners Ltd* [1970] AC 583, [1970] 1 All ER
  796, [1970] 1 Lloyd's Rep 269, HL.
2 *Whitworth Street Estates (Manchester) Ltd v James Miller & Partners Ltd* [1970] AC 583, [1970] 1 All ER
  796, [1970] 1 Lloyd's Rep 269, HL; *Bank Mellat v Helliniki Techniki SA* [1984] QB 291 at 301, [1983] 3
  All ER 428 at 431, CA. The seat of the arbitration will normally be stipulated in the arbitration
  agreement or some subsequent document, but does not imply that all meetings or hearings of the
  tribunal need be held in that country: *Naviera Amazonica Peruana SA v Compania Internacional de
  Seguros del Peru* [1988] 1 Lloyd's Rep 116 at 120–121, CA.

11. FOREIGN INVESTMENT DISPUTES

(1) INTRODUCTION

719. International investment disputes. Facilities have been provided by the Arbitration (International Investment Disputes) Act 1966 pursuant to a convention[1] for submission to conciliation[2] or arbitration[3] of disputes relating to international investment. These facilities are open only to contracting states and their nationals[4]. The Act applies the convention to England[5] and, with certain exceptions, adaptations and modifications, to Scotland[6], Northern Ireland[7] and the following territories[8]: (1) Antigua, Bahamas, Bermuda, British Honduras[9], British Solomon Islands Protectorate[10], Cayman Islands, Dominica, Falkland Islands, Fiji, Gibraltar, Gilbert and Ellice Islands Colony[11], Grenada, Hong Kong, Mauritius, Montserrat, St Christopher, Nevis and Anguilla, St Helena, St Lucia, St Vincent, Seychelles, Swaziland, Turks and Caicos Islands, and the Virgin Islands[12]; (2) Guernsey[13]; (3) Tonga[14]; (4) Jersey[15].

1 Ie the Convention on the Settlement of Investment Disputes between States and Nationals of Other States, signed at Washington on 18 March 1965. The convention is set out in the Arbitration (International Investment Disputes) Act 1966, Schedule. The convention is hereinafter referred to as the Convention on the Settlement of Investment Disputes or, simply, the convention. The purpose of the convention is to promote an atmosphere of mutual confidence between states and foreign investors, thus stimulating a larger flow of private international capital into countries which ratify it, and to safeguard the interests of private investors, including companies, who, unlike states, have no recourse to the International Court of Justice.
2 Arbitration (International Investment Disputes) Act 1966 s 1, Schedule (Convention on the Settlement of Investment Disputes) Ch III (arts 28–35).
3 Ibid Schedule Ch IV (arts 36–55).
4 See ibid Schedule art 25 (1).
5 Ibid s 1 (amended by the Administration of Justice Act 1977 ss 4, 32, Sch 5, and the Supreme Court Act 1987 s 152, Sch 5).
6 Arbitration (International Investment Disputes) Act 1966 s 7.
7 Ibid s 8.
8 See ibid s 6.
9 Now Belize: see COMMONWEALTH vol 6 (Reissue) para 889.
10 Now Solomon Islands: see COMMONWEALTH vol 6 (Reissue) para 966.
11 Now Kiribati and Tuvalu: see COMMONWEALTH vol 6 (Reissue) paras 936, 937, 972.
12 Arbitration (International Investment Disputes) Act 1966 (Application to Colonies, etc) Order 1967, SI 1967/159 (amended by SI 1967/249).
13 Arbitration (International Investment Disputes) Act 1966 (Guernsey) Order 1968, SI 1968/1199.
14 Arbitration (International Investment Disputes) Act 1966 (Application to Tonga) Order 1967, SI 1967/585.
15 Arbitration (International Investment Disputes) (Jersey) Order 1979, SI 1979/572.

720. Jurisdiction. Disputes falling within the scope of the convention[1] include any legal dispute arising out of an investment, between a contracting state (or any designated constituent sub-division or agency thereof) of the one part and a private person of the other part[2]. The private person may be a natural or juridical person, and must not be a national of the state concerned[3]. However, a juridical person may be agreed to be treated as a non-national by reason of non-national control[4]. The submission to the procedures of the convention must be by mutual agreement[5], but once agreement is given, it may not be withdrawn unilaterally[6]. Consent of the parties to arbitration under the convention is, unless otherwise stated, deemed to be consent to such arbitration to the exclusion of any other remedy[7]. A contracting state must not give diplomatic protection or bring an international claim in a case where one of its nationals and another contracting state have submitted or consented to arbitration unless that other state has failed to abide by the award[8].

1 Ie the Convention on the Settlement of Investment Disputes, as to which see para 719 ante.
2 Arbitration (International Investment Disputes) Act 1966 s 1, Schedule art 25 (1).
3 See ibid Schedule art 25 (2).
4 See ibid Schedule art 25 (2) (b).
5 See ibid Schedule arts 25 (1), (3), 28 (2), 36 (2).
6 Ibid Schedule art 25 (1).
7 Ibid Schedule art 26.
8 Ibid Schedule art 27.

721. International organisation. The convention facilities are provided by the International Centre for Settlement of Investment Disputes[1] with a seat at the principal office of the International Bank for Reconstruction and Development[2], an Administrative Council[3] and a secretariat[4]. The secretariat includes a Secretary-General (and deputy or deputies),[5] who performs the function of registrar and who has power to authenticate arbitral awards rendered pursuant to the convention, and to certify copies thereof[6]. The centre maintains a Panel of Conciliators and a Panel of Arbitrators[7]. The members of the panels are designated by the contracting states and by the president of the bank[8] who is ex officio chairman of the Administrative Council[9]. The expenditure of the centre should be met from the charges for the use of its facilities and other receipts. If this is not possible the excess should be borne by the contracting states either in proportion to their contributions to the capital stock of the bank or, in the case of states which are not members of the bank, in accordance with rules adopted by the council[10].

Persons designated to serve on the panels must be persons of high moral character and recognised competence in the fields of law, commerce, industry or finance, who may be relied on to exercise independent judgment; competence in the field of law is of particular importance in the case of persons on the Panel of Arbitrators[11]. A person may serve on both panels[12]. The chairman, in designating persons to serve on the panels, must pay due regard to the importance of assuring representation on the panels of the principal legal systems of the world and of the main forms of economic activity[13].

1 Arbitration (International Investment Disputes) Act 1966 s 1, Schedule art 1 (1). As to the Convention on the Settlement of Investment Disputes see para 719 ante.
2 Arbitration (International Investment Disputes) Act 1966 Schedule art 2. The centre is in Washington. Arbitration and conciliation proceedings are held at the seat of the centre, but the parties may agree to hold the proceedings at the seat of the Permanent Court of Arbitration at The Hague, or some other approved place: Schedule arts 62, 63.
3 See ibid Schedule art 3. The Administrative Council consists of one representative (with an alternate representative) of each contracting state; that representative (and alternate) is, in the absence of contrary designation, the governor appointed by the state to the bank: Schedule art 4. The council adopts the financial and administrative regulations of the centre, and the rules for the institution and conduct of arbitrations and conciliations under the convention: Schedule art 6. Members of the council receive no remuneration from the centre: Schedule art 8. As to meetings, voting and the number needed for a quorum see Schedule art 7.
4 See ibid Schedule art 3, 9–11.
5 See ibid Schedule art 9. As to the appointment and qualification of the Secretary-General and deputy, and the carrying out by deputies of the Secretary-General's functions during his absence or incapacity, see Schedule art 10.

6 Ibid Schedule art 11.
7 Ibid Schedule arts 3, 12.
8 Ibid Schedule art 13. The term of office of a member of a panel is a renewable period of six years: Schedule art 15. As to designations see Schedule art 16 (2).
10 Ibid Schedule art 17; and see note 3 supra as to the adoption of rules. The Treasury discharges the United Kingdom government's obligations under this provision; money for the purpose is provided by Parliament: s 5.
11 Ibid Schedule art 14 (1).
12 Ibid Schedule art 16 (1).
13 Ibid Schedule art 14 (2).

722. Status, immunities and privileges. The centre has full international legal personality including capacity to contract, buy and sell property and institute legal proceedings[1]. The centre, its property and assets is immune from all legal process save where immunity is waived by a statement certified by the Secretary-General[2]. Its archives are inviolable[3]. It is exempt from taxation and customs duties, with certain exceptions as to customs duties on goods for resale, and duties or taxes which form part of the price of goods or are no more than charges for services rendered[4].

The chairman and other members of the Administrative Council, persons acting as conciliators or arbitrators or members of a committee appointed to consider whether or not an award should be annulled, persons appearing in proceedings under the convention as parties, agents, counsel, advocates, witnesses or experts and the officers and employees of the secretariat enjoy immunity from legal process with respect to acts performed by them in the exercise of their functions, except where the centre waives this immunity in a statement certified by the Secretary-General[5].

Except in the case of local nationals, no tax may be levied on or in respect of expense allowances paid by the centre to the chairman or members of the Administrative Council, or on or in respect of salaries, expense allowances or other emoluments paid by the centre to officials or employees of the secretariat[6]. No tax can be levied on or in respect of fees or expense allowances received by persons acting as conciliators, or arbitrators, or members of a committee appointed to consider whether or not an award should be annulled, in proceedings under the convention, if the sole jurisdictional basis for the tax is the location of the centre or the place where the proceedings are conducted or the fees or allowances are paid[7].

1 Arbitration (International Investment Disputes) Act 1966 ss 1, 4 (1), Schedule art 18. See generally FOREIGN RELATIONS. As to the convention see para 719 ante; as to the centre see para 721 ante.
2 Ibid s 4 (1), (3), Schedule art 20.
3 Ibid s 4 (1), Schedule art 23 (1).
4 Ibid s 4 (1), (2), Schedule art 24 (1).
5 Ibid s 4 (1), (3), Schedule arts 21, 22, 52 (3).
6 Ibid s 4 (1), Schedule art 24 (2).
7 Ibid s 4 (1), Schedule arts 24 (3), 52 (3).

723. Conciliation. Conciliation is initiated by one of the parties giving a written request to the Secretary-General[1], who sends a copy to the other party[2]. The request must contain information concerning the issues in dispute, the identity of the parties and their consent to conciliation[3]. The Secretary-General then registers the request and sends notice of registration to the parties; if, however, the dispute is manifestly outside the jurisdiction of the centre, he refuses to register and the parties are notified of the refusal to register[4].

As soon as possible thereafter a Conciliation Commission is constituted[5] consisting of a sole conciliator or any uneven number of conciliators appointed as the parties agree[6] or, in default of agreement, three conciliators, one appointed by each party and the third (who acts as president of the commission) appointed by agreement of the parties[7]. If, however, the commission has not been constituted within 90 days after notice of registration of the request has been despatched to the parties, or such other period as the parties may agree, the chairman, at the request of either party and after consulting both parties as far as possible, appoints any conciliator not yet appointed[8]. The parties, though not the chairman, may appoint persons not on the Panel of Conciliators, provided they have the qualities required of panel members[9]. Provision is made for the replacement of conciliators who cannot act[10].

The Conciliation Commission is the judge of its own competence[11] and jurisdiction[12] and acts in accordance with the convention, the conciliation rules in effect on the date when the parties consented to conciliation, rules agreed by the parties, and, if the point is otherwise uncovered, its own rules[13].

The commission clarifies the issues in dispute between the parties and endeavours to bring about an agreement between them. The parties must co-operate in good faith and give their most serious consideration to the commission's recommendations[14]. If agreement is reached the commission draws up a report noting the issues in dispute and recording that agreement has been reached. If at any stage of the proceedings it appears that there is no likelihood of agreement between the parties, or if one party fails to appear or participate in the proceedings, the proceedings are closed and the commission reports accordingly[15].

The parties bear their own expenses, but share the expenses of the centre (as determined by the Secretary-General) and the commission (as determined by the commission or as agreed in advance with the commission)[16].

Except by agreement the views expressed or statements or admissions or offers of settlement made by the other party or the report or any recommendations made by the commission cannot be invoked or relied on by a party in subsequent proceedings, whether before arbitrators or in a court of law or otherwise[17].

1 As to the Secretary-General see para 721 ante.
2 Arbitration (International Investment Disputes) Act 1966 s 1, Schedule art 28 (1). As to the convention see para 719 ante.
3 Ibid Schedule art 28 (2).
4 Ibid Schedule art 28 (3).
5 Ibid Schedule art 29 (1).
6 Ibid Schedule art 29 (2) (a).
7 Ibid Schedule art 29 (2) (b).
8 Ibid Schedule art 30.
9 Ibid Schedule art 31. As to the panel and its members see para 721 ante.
10 See ibid Schedule arts 56–58.
11 Ibid Schedule art 32 (1).
12 See ibid Schedule art 32(2).
13 See ibid Schedule art 33.
14 Ibid Schedule art 34 (1).
15 Ibid Schedule art 34 (2).
16 See ibid Schedule arts 59–61.
17 See ibid Schedule art 35.

(2) THE TRIBUNAL AND THE ARBITRATION

724. Request for arbitration. When a dispute has been submitted to arbitration under the convention[1], legal proceedings may be stayed[2].

Arbitration under the convention is initiated by one of the parties giving to the Secretary-General[3] a written request[4] containing information concerning the issues in dispute, the identity of the parties and their consent to arbitration[5]. The Secretary-General sends a copy of the request to the other party[6], and registers the request, sending notice of the registration to the parties[7]. If, however, the dispute is manifestly outside the centre's jurisdiction[8], he refuses to register and notifies the parties accordingly[9].

1 Ie the Convention on the Settlement of Investment Disputes, as to which see para 719 ante.
2 Arbitration Act 1950 s 4 (1) (see para 616 ante); Arbitration (International Investment Disputes) Act 1966 s 3 (2).
3 As to the Secretary-General see para 721 ante.
4 Arbitration (International Investment Disputes) Act 1966 s 1, Schedule art 36 (1).
5 Ibid Schedule art 36 (2).
6 Ibid Schedule art 36 (1).
7 Ibid Schedule art 36 (3).
8 As to the centre see para 721 ante.
9 Arbitration (International Investment Disputes) Act 1966 Schedule art 36 (3).

725. Arbitral Tribunal. As soon as possible after registration of a request an Arbitral Tribunal is constituted[1] by a sole arbitrator or any uneven number of arbitrators as the parties agree[2] or, in default of agreement, three arbitrators, one appointed by each party and the third, who functions as president of the tribunal, appointed by agreement of the parties[3]. If, however, the tribunal has not been constituted within 90 days after the dispatch of notice of registration of the request, or such other period as the parties may agree, the chairman[4], at the request of either party and after consulting both parties as far as possible, appoints any arbitrator not yet appointed[5]. The parties, though not the chairman, may appoint persons not on the Panel of Arbitrators, provided they have the qualifications needed by panel members[6]. Provision is made for the replacement of arbitrators who cannot act[7].

The Arbitral Tribunal is the judge of its own competence[8] and jurisdiction[9], and decides disputes in accordance with such rules of law or equity as the parties agree[10]. In the absence of agreement the tribunal applies the law of the contracting state party, including its rules on the conflict of laws, and such rules of international law as may be applicable[11]. It may not bring in a finding of *non liquet*[12] on the ground of silence or obscurity of the law[13].

1 Arbitration (International Investment Disputes) Act 1966 s 1, Schedule art 37 (1). As to the convention see para 719 ante.
2 Ibid Schedule art 37 (2) (a).
3 Ibid Schedule art 37 (2) (b).
4 Ie the chairman of the Administrative Council: see para 721 ante.
5 Arbitration (International Investment Disputes) Act 1966 Schedule art 38. Arbitrators appointed by the chairman must not be co-nationals of either party (Schedule art 38), and, except in the case of agreed appointments, the majority of the arbitrators must not be co-nationals of the parties (Schedule art 39).
6 Ibid Schedule art 40. As to the panel and its members see para 721 ante.
7 See ibid Schedule arts 56–58.

8 Ibid Schedule art 41 (1).
9 See ibid Schedule art 41 (2).
10 See ibid Schedule art 42 (1), (3).
11 Ibid Schedule art 42 (1).
12 'It is not clear'.
13 Arbitration (International Investment Disputes) Act 1966 Schedule art 42 (2).

726. The arbitration. The arbitration is conducted in accordance with the convention[1], the arbitration rules in effect on the date when the parties consented to arbitration, rules agreed by the parties, and, if the point is otherwise uncovered, in accordance with the tribunal's own rules[2]. The Arbitration Act 1950 does not apply to the proceedings[3], but the Lord Chancellor may by order direct that its provisions relating to the attendance of witnesses and the production of documents[4] shall apply[5].

Except as the parties otherwise agree, the tribunal may at any stage of the proceedings call for the production of documents or other evidence[6], visit the scene connected with the dispute and conduct inquiries there[7], and recommend any provisional measures which should be taken to preserve the rights of either party[8].

Failure of a party to appear or present his case is not deemed an admission of the other party's assertions[9], but the other party may, on such failure, request the tribunal to deal with the questions submitted and render an award. Before rendering such an award the tribunal must notify, and grant a period of grace to, the party in default unless satisfied that the default will continue[10].

Unless the parties otherwise agree the tribunal must on the request of a party determine any incidental or additional claims or counterclaims arising out of the subject matter of the dispute provided that they are within the scope of the consent of the parties and are otherwise within the centre's jurisdiction[11].

1 Ie the Convention on the Settlement of Investment Disputes, as to which see para 719 ante.
2 Arbitration (International Investment Disputes) Act 1966 s 1, Schedule art 44.
3 Ibid s 3 (2).
4 Ie the provisions of the Arbitration Act 1950 s 12: see para 671 ante.
5 Arbitration (International Investment Disputes) Act 1966 s 3 (1) (a). At the date at which this volume states the law no such order had been made.
6 Ibid Schedule art 43 (a).
7 Ibid art 43 (b).
8 Ibid Schedule art 47.
9 Ibid Schedule art 45 (1).
10 Ibid Schedule art 45 (2).
11 Ibid Schedule art 46.

(3) THE AWARD; REGISTRATION AND ENFORCEMENT

(i) The Award

727. The award. The Arbitral Tribunal's award, which must deal with every question submitted and state the reasons on which it is based[1], is decided by a majority vote[2]. It must be in writing, signed by the members of the tribunal who voted for it[3]. Any tribunal member may attach to the award his individual opinion, whether he dissents from the majority or not, or a statement of his dissent[4].

Unless the parties otherwise agree the tribunal assesses the expenses of the parties and decides as part of the award how and by whom those expenses and those of the centre (as determined by the Secretary-General) and the tribunal (as determined by the tribunal or as agreed in advance with the tribunal) shall be borne[5].

For purposes of enforcement in the United Kingdom 'award' includes any decision interpreting, revising or annulling an award and any decision as to costs which is to form part of the award[6].

The centre must not publish the award unless the parties consent[7].

The Secretary-General must promptly dispatch certified copies of the award to the parties, and the award is deemed to have been rendered on the date when the certified copies were dispatched[8]. A decision on rectification of the award[9] becomes part of the award and must be notified to the parties in the same manner as the award[10]. Certain time limits with regard to the revision and annulment of the award by the centre run from the date on which the award was rendered[11]. However, in cases where there has been a decision on rectification these time limits run from the date on which that decision was rendered[12] and this date is, it seems, the date on which notification of that decision was dispatched to the parties. Hereinafter the expression 'date of the award' is used to refer to whichever of these dates is applicable.

1 Arbitration (International Investment Disputes) Act 1966 s 1, Schedule art 48 (3). As to the convention see para 719 ante.
2 Ibid Schedule art 48 (1).
3 Ibid Schedule art 48 (2).
4 Ibid Schedule art 48 (4).
5 See ibid Schedule arts 59–61. As to the centre and the Secretary-General see para 721 ante.
6 Ibid s 1 (7) (a).
7 Ibid Schedule art 48 (5).
8 Ibid s 1 (7) (b) and Schedule art 49 (1).
9 See para 728 post.
10 Arbitration (International Investment Disputes) Act 1966 s 1, Schedule art 49 (2).
11 See ibid arts 49 (2), 51 (2), 52 (2), and paras 728, 729 post.
12 Ibid Schedule art 49 (2).

728. Rectification, interpretation, revision and annulment of award. On the request of a party made within 45 days after the date of the award[1] the Arbitral Tribunal may, after notice to the other party, decide any question it had omitted to decide in the award, and must rectify any clerical, arithmetical or similar error in the award[2]. Its decision becomes part of the award[3].

If any dispute arises between the parties as to the meaning or scope of an award, either party may request interpretation of the award by an application in writing addressed to the Secretary-General[4]. The request is, if possible, submitted to the tribunal which rendered the award; if that is not possible a new tribunal is constituted in the normal way[5]. The tribunal may, if it considers that the circumstances so require, stay enforcement of the award pending its decision[6].

Either party may apply in writing to the Secretary-General to have the award reviewed on the ground of fresh, decisive evidence unknown to the tribunal and unknown to the applicant (otherwise than by negligence) at the date the award was rendered[7]. The application must be made within 90 days after discovery of the evidence and in any event within three years after the date of the award[8]. The application is if possible submitted to the tribunal which rendered the award; if that is not possible a new tribunal is constituted in the normal way[9]. The tribunal may, if it considers that the circumstances so require, stay enforcement of the award pending its decision; if the applicant requests a stay in his application, enforcement is stayed provisionally until the tribunal rules on the request[10].

Either party may by written application to the Secretary-General made within 120 days after the date of the award[11], and in any event within three years after the date of the award, request annulment of the award on one or more of the following grounds: (1) that the tribunal was not properly constituted[12]; (2) that the tribunal manifestly exceeded its powers[13]; (3) that there was corruption on the part of a member of the tribunal[14]; (4) that there was a serious departure from a fundamental rule of procedure[15]; or (5) that the award failed to state the reasons on which it was based[16].

Such requests are dealt with by an ad hoc committee of three persons chosen by the chairman from the Panel of Arbitrators, not being members of the original tribunal, co-nationals of the parties or members of the original tribunal, persons designated to the panel by the states of the parties, or persons who have acted as conciliators in the same dispute[17]. The procedure is mutatis mutandis the same as in the original arbitration[18].

The committee may, if it considers that circumstances so require, stay enforcement of the award pending its decision; if the applicant requests a stay of enforcement of the award in his application, enforcement is stayed provisionally until the committee rules on the request[19].

If the award is annulled, the dispute must, at the request of either party, be submitted to a new tribunal constituted in the normal way[20].

1　As to the date of the award see para 727 ante.
2　Arbitration (International Investment Disputes) Act 1966 s 1, Schedule art 49 (2). As to the convention see para 719 ante.
3　Ibid Schedule art 49 (2).
4　Ibid Schedule art 50 (1). As to the Secretary-General see para 721 ante.
5　Ibid Schedule art 50 (2). As to the constitution of the tribunal see para 725 ante.
6　Ibid Schedule art 50 (2).
7　Ibid Schedule art 51 (1). As to the date the award was rendered see para 727 ante.
8　Ibid Schedule art 51 (2).
9　Ibid Schedule art 51 (3). As to the constitution of the tribunal see para 725 ante.
10　Ibid Schedule art 51 (4).
11　Ibid Schedule art 52 (2). See also note 14 infra. As to the date of the award see para 727 ante.
12　Ibid Schedule art 52 (1) (a). As to the constitution of the tribunal see para 725 ante.
13　Ibid Schedule art 52 (1) (b).
14　Ibid Schedule art 52 (1) (c). In this case the application must be made within 120 days after the discovery of the corruption, and in any event within three years after the date of the award: art 52 (2).
15　Ibid Schedule art 52 (1) (d).
16　Ibid Schedule art 52 (1) (e). The award is required by art 48 (3) to state the reasons on which it is based.
17　Ibid Schedule art 52 (3). As to the chairman of the Administrative Council, and the panel see para 721 ante; as to conciliation see para 623 ante.
18　Ibid Schedule art 52 (4), applying arts 41–45, 48, 49, 53, 54: see paras 725–727 ante, and para 729 post.
19　Ibid Schedule art 52 (5).
20　Ibid Schedule art 52 (6). As to the constitution of the tribunal see para 725 ante.

729. Recognition and enforcement of award under convention. The award is binding on the parties and is not subject to any appeal or to any other remedy except as provided for in the convention[1]. Each contracting state recognises an award as binding and enforces the pecuniary obligations imposed by that award within its territories as if it were a final judgment of a court of that state[2]. A party seeking recognition or enforcement in the territories of a contracting state must furnish to a competent court or other authority which such state shall have designated for this purpose a copy of the award certified by the Secretary-General[3].

1 Arbitration (International Investment Disputes) Act 1966 s 1, Schedule art 53. Cf, however, para 733 post. As to the convention see para 719 ante.
2 Ibid Schedule art 54 (1).
3 Ibid Schedule art 54 (2). As to the Secretary-General see para 721 ante.

730. Recognition and enforcement of award under United Kingdom law. An award is enforceable against the Crown in any manner in which a judgment would be enforceable against the Crown[1].

1 Arbitration (International Investment Disputes) Act 1966 s 1 (8).

(ii) Registration and its Effect

731. Registration of award generally. The award is registered in respect of the pecuniary obligations imposed by the award and for the reasonable costs of and incidental to registration[1]. However, if at the date of the application for registration[2] the pecuniary obligations have been partly satisfied, the award can be registered only in respect of the balance, and if those obligations have been wholly satisfied, the award cannot be registered[3].

1 Arbitration (International Investment Disputes) Act 1966 s 1 (4).
2 As to the application for registration see para 733 post.
3 Arbitration (International Investment Disputes) Act 1966 s 1 (5).

732. Effect of registration of award. As respects the pecuniary obligations which it imposes the award is of the same force and effect for the purposes of execution as a judgment of the High Court given at the date of the award under the convention[1] and entered on the date of registration under the Act, and so far as relates to such pecuniary obligations: (1) proceedings may be taken on the award[2], (2) the sum for which the award is registered carries interest[3], and (3) the High Court has the normal control over the execution of the award[4].

1 Ie the Convention for the Settlement of Investment Disputes, as to which see para 719 ante.
2 Arbitration (International Investment Disputes) Act 1966 s 2 (1) (a).
3 Ibid s 2 (1) (b).
4 Ibid s 2 (1) (c).

733-900. Procedure for registration of award. A person seeking recognition or enforcement of an award under the convention[1] (hereinafter called the 'judgment creditor', the other party being called the 'judgment debtor'[2]) is entitled to apply to the High Court[3] to have the award registered[4]. The application is made by originating summons to which no appearance need be entered[5], supported by an affidavit[6], exhibiting a copy of the award certified by the Secretary-General[7] and, where the award is not in the English language, a translation of it in that language certified by a notary public or authenticated by affidavit[8], stating the name, trade or business and the usual or last known place of abode or business of the judgment creditor and the judgment debtor respectively so far as known to the deponent[9]; and stating to the best of the deponent's information or belief:

(1) that the judgment creditor is entitled to enforce the award[10];
(2) as the case may require, either that at the date of the application the award has not been satisfied, or the amount in respect of which it remains unsatisfied[11];
(3) that the award does not fall within any of the following cases, in which case no award may be ordered to be registered, namely:
   (a) the original tribunal acted without jurisdiction;
   (b) the judgment debtor was not within the tribunal's jurisdiction or did not voluntarily appear or otherwise submit or agree to submit to the jurisdiction of that tribunal;
   (c) the judgment debtor, being the respondent in the arbitration, was not duly served with the process of the original tribunal and did not appear, not-withstanding that he was ordinarily within the jurisdiction of the tribunal or agreed to submit to its jurisdiction;
   (d) the award was obtained by fraud;
   (e) the judgment debtor can satisfy the registering court either that an appeal is pending or that he is entitled and intends to appeal against the award;
   (f) the award was in respect of a cause of action which for reasons of public policy or some other similar reason could not have been entertained by the registering court[12].

The affidavit must state whether at the date of the application the enforcement of the award has been stayed[13], provisionally or otherwise, pursuant to the convention and whether any, and if so what, application has been made pursuant to the convention which, if granted, might result in a stay of the enforcement of the award[14].

Where it appears to the court[15] on granting leave to register an award, or on an application made by the judgment debtor by summons supported by affidavit[16] after an award has been registered: (i) that the enforcement of the award has been stayed, whether provisionally or otherwise, pursuant to the convention[17], or (ii) that an application has been made pursuant to the convention which, if granted, might result in a stay of the enforcement of the award[18], the court must, or in case (ii) may, stay execution of the award for such time as it considers appropriate in the circumstances[19].

A register of the awards ordered to be registered is kept in the Central Office of the Supreme Court under the direction of the Senior Master, and particulars are entered in the register of any execution issued on such an award[20].

Notice of registration of an award must be served on the judgment debtor[21], stating: (A) full particulars of the award registered and the order for registration[22], and (B) the name and address of the judgment creditor or of his solicitor or agent on whom and at which any summons issued by the judgment debtor may be served[23].

Any party wishing to issue execution on a registered award must produce to the proper officer an affidavit of service of the notice of registration of the award and any order made by the court in relation to the award[24].

1 Ie the Convention on the Settlement of Investment Disputes, as to which see para 719 ante.
2 RSC Ord 73 r 9 (1). RSC Ord 73 r 9, which prescribes the procedure for registration of an award, was made under the Arbitration (International Investment Disputes) Act 1966 s 1 (6) (amended by the Supreme Court Act 1981 s 152 (1), Sch 5).
3 This includes a judge in chambers and a master of the Queen's Bench Division: RSC Ord 71 r 1, applied by RSC Ord 73 r 9 (2).

4 Arbitration (International Investment Disputes) Act 1966 s 1 (2).
5 RSC Ord 73 r 9 (3). No time limit for applying has been prescribed.
6 RSC Ord 71 r 3 (1), applied by RSC Ord 73 r 9 (2).
7 RSC Ord 73 r 9 (4) (a). See para 729 ante.
8 RSC Ord 71 r 3 (1) (a), applied by RSC Ord 73 r 9 (2).
9 RSC Ord 71 r 3 (1) (b), applied by RSC Ord 73 r 9 (2).
10 RSC Ord 71 r 3 (1) (c) (i), applied by RSC Ord 73 r 9 (2).
11 RSC Ord 71 r 3 (1) (c) (ii), applied by RSC Ord 73 r 9 (2).
12 This appears to follow him from the combined effect of the Administration of Justice Act 1920 s 9 (2) and RSC Ord 71 r 3 (1) (c) (iii), applied by RSC Ord 73 r 9 (2). It is not entirely clear whether it should be inferred from the prescribed contents of the affidavit that the judgment debtor can resist registration and/or enforcement of the award, if he can show that some matter deposed to in the affidavit is untrue, by replying on local English law. On the one hand the Convention on the Settlement of Investment Disputes provides (see arts 53, 54 (1); and para 729 ante) that the award shall be as binding as a final judgment of the court of a contracting state; on the other hand it is not normal to require an affidavit to establish some fact, unless that fact is material.
13 As to stay under the convention see para 724 ante.
14 RSC Ord 73 r 9 (4) (b).
15 See note 3 supra.
16 RSC Ord 73 r 9 (7).
17 RSC Ord 73 r 9 (6) (a).
18 RSC Ord 73 r 9 (6) (b).
19 RSC Ord 73 r 9 (6); Arbitration (International Investment Disputes) Act 1966 s 2 (2) (amended by the Supreme Court Act 1981 s 152 (1), Sch 5).
20 RSC Ord 73 r 9 (5).
21 RSC Ord 71 r 7 (1), applied by RSC Ord 73 r 9 (2). The notice must be served personally or by, sending it to the judgment debtors usual or last known place of abode or business, unless the court otherwise orders: RSC Ord 71 r 7 (1). Service out of the jurisdiction is permissible without leave, and RSC Ord 11, rr 5, 6, 8, apply as if the notice were notice of a writ: RSC Ord 71 r 7 (2).
22 RSC Ord 71 r 7 (3) (a), applied by RSC Ord 73 r 9 (2).
23 RSC Ord 71 r 7 (3) (b), applied by RSC Ord 73 r 9 (2).
24 RSC Ord 71 r 10 (3), applied by RSC Ord 73 r 9 (2).

ARCHITECTS

See BUILDING CONTRACTS, ARCHITECTS AND ENGINEERS

ARMED CONFLICT

See WAR AND ARMED CONFLICT

ARMY

See ROYAL FORCES

ATTACHMENT OF DEBT

See COUNTY COURTS; EXECUTION

ATTACHMENT OF EARNINGS

See BANKRUPTCY AND INSOLVENCY; COUNTY COURTS; DIVORCE

ATOMIC ENERGY

See ELECTRICITY AND NUCLEAR POWER

AUCTION

1. THE AUCTIONEER

(1) DEFINITION; QUALIFICATIONS; APPOINTMENT

901. 'Auction' and 'auctioneer'. An auction[1] is a manner of selling or letting property by bids, usually to the highest bidder by public competition. The prices which the public are asked to pay are the highest which those who bid can be tempted to offer by the skill and tact of the auctioneer under the excitement of open competition[2]. Although the word 'auction' is derived from the Latin *auctio*, an increase, a 'Dutch auction' is one where property is offered at a certain price and then successively at lower prices until one is accepted[3].

An auctioneer[4] is an agent[5] who sells goods or other property by auction.

1 There is no comprehensive statutory definition of an auction. The Mock Auctions Act 1961 (see para 943 post) refers to the necessity for competitive bidding.

2 See *Frewen v Hays* (1912) 106 LT 516 at 518, PC, per Lord Macnaghten and *Bexwell v Christie* (1776) 1 Cowp 395 at 397 per Lord Mansfield. However, there exist auctions where the lot goes to the highest bidder but the element of open competition is lacking in that bidders are unaware of rival bids. Postal auctions provide an example. These are conducted in a manner similar to that of selling by tenders.
3 See *Demerara Turf Club Ltd v Wight* [1918] AC 605, PC.
4 The use of the term 'auctioneer' in an apprenticeship deed or other instrument formerly imported that the person so described was duly licensed: see *Creaser v Hurley* (1915) 32 TLR 149. As to the abolition of the requirement of an auctioneer's licence see para 904 post.
5 *Wheatley v Smithers* [1906] 2 KB 321, DC; revsd on appeal on the facts [1907] 2 KB 684, CA. He is not, however, an agent when he sells his own goods or property: see para 906 post.

902. Auctioneers in partnership. A partnership for the purpose of carrying on the business of auctioneering is not subject to any restriction as to the number of persons who may constitute the partnership provided that not less than three-quarters of the partners are members of either the Royal Institution of Chartered Surveyors, the Chartered Land Agents' Society, the Chartered Auctioneers' and Estate Agents' Institute or the Incorporated Society of Valuers and Auctioneers[1]. Nor is a limited partnership for the purpose of carrying on such a business subject to any such restriction, provided that the partnership consists of persons not less than three-quarters of the total number of whom are members of the Incorporated Society of Valuers and Auctioneers or the Royal Institution of Chartered Surveyors and provided also that not more than one quarter are limited partners[2].

It has been held that a firm of auctioneers is not a trading partnership, and therefore a member of the firm has no implied authority to bind his partners by giving a bill of exchange in the firm name[3].

1 See the Companies Act 1985 s 716 (3); Partnerships (Unrestricted Size) No 1 Regulations 1968, SI 1968/1222; and PARTNERSHIP.
2 See the Limited Partnership Act 1907 s 4 (2) (amended by the Banking Act 1979 ss 46 (b), 51 (2), Sch 7 (repealed)); the Companies Act 1985 s 717 (2); the Limited Partnerships (Unrestricted Size) No 1 Regulations 1971, SI 1971/782; and PARTNERSHIP.
3 *Wheatley v Smithers* [1906] 2 KB 321, DC; revsd on appeal on the facts [1907] 2 KB 684, CA, but the Court of Appeal declined to express any view as to whether an auctioneer was a trader. See further BILLS OF EXCHANGE; PARTNERSHIP.

903. Qualifications for practice. No special qualification is required by one who carries on the business of an auctioneer. Any person is at liberty to do so, provided that he complies with the Companies legislation[1], where it applies. An auctioneer is under no obligation to become a member of a professional association, but if he does so, he is bound by the rules of conduct laid down by the association of which he is a member[2].

1 See COMPANIES.
2 *Faraday v Auctioneers' and Estate Agents' Institute of United Kingdom* [1936] 1 All ER 496, CA.

904. Licensing requirements. An auctioneer does not require any general auctioneers' licence for the purposes of carrying on his business[1], and a person hawking goods from place to place for sale by auction no longer requires a hawker's licence[2]. However, several London boroughs have introduced codes of practice and licence conditions relating to auctions conducted within their localities[3]. These regulate such matters as display of name, conduct of bidding, post-sale advertising and declarations as to ownership of goods.

An auctioneer requires an excise licence for the sale of excisable commodities[4].

An auctioneer may sell by auction, expose for sale by auction or have in his possession for sale by auction a firearm or ammunition[5] without being registered as a firearms dealer, provided that he has obtained a permit for the purpose from the chief officer of police for the area in which the auction is held, and complies with the terms of the permit[6]; and he or his servant may be in possession of firearms or ammunition in the ordinary course of his business as an auctioneer without holding a firearms certificate[7]. Any person who makes a statement which he knows to be false for the purpose of procuring, whether for himself or for another, the grant of a permit commits an offence[8].

The offence of carrying, without lawful authority or reasonable excuse, a loaded shotgun, loaded air weapon, or any other firearm together with suitable ammunition, in a public place may be committed if, at the material time, the public have or are permitted to have access, whether on payment or otherwise, to the premises or place[9].

An auctioneer who advances money on bills of sale with a view to obtaining business, and not with the primary object of lending money, does not require to take out a licence as a moneylender[10].

The exportation of certain classes of goods may be subject to licensing under powers derived from the Import, Export and Customs Powers (Defence) Act 1939[11]. Most antiques and collectable items produced more than 50 years before exportation are subject to an open general export licence but those which are not require a specific licence[12]. Regular exporters may obtain bulk licences. Sales at auction in contravention of this licensing regime will render the auctioneer, as agent of the vendor liable to criminal penalties[13].

1 The excise duty on auctioneers' licences was abolished, and the provisions of the Auctioneers Act 1845 requiring auctioneers' licences were repealed, by the Finance Act 1949 s 14, Sch 11 Pt I (repealed).

2 Local Government Act 1966 ss 35, 43, Sch 3 Pt I, Sch 6 Pt I (repealed), repealing the Hawkers Act 1888.

3 The conditions are made pursuant to the Greater London Council (General Powers) Act 1984 s 28(3).

4 See the Customs and Excise Management Act 1979 s 101. As to the commodities that are excisable, and for licensing requirements, see CUSTOMS AND EXCISE.

5 For the definitions of 'firearm' and 'ammunition' see respectively the Firearms Act 1968 s 57 (1), (2); and see the Firearms (Amendment) Act 1988.

6 Firearms Act 1968 s 9 (2). If he has no such permit, or if he does not comply with the terms of his permit, he commits an offence under s 3 (1). See further CRIMINAL LAW; POLICE.

7 Ibid s 9 (1). For offences in relation to s 9 (1) see the Firearms (Amendment) Act 1988 s 14; and CRIMINAL LAW vol 11 (1) (Reissue) para 211.

8 Firearms Act 1968 s 9 (3).

9 Ibid ss 19, 57 (4).

10 *Furber v Fieldings Ltd* (1907) 23 TLR 362. As to moneylenders' licences see the Consumer Credit Act 1974 Pt III (ss 21–42); and HIRE PURCHASE.

11 Import, Export and Customs Powers (Defence) Act 1939 s 1; see TRADE AND LABOUR vol 47 para 328 et seq.

12 See the Export of Goods (Control) Order 1987, SI 1987/2070, art 2, Sch 1 Pt I Group B.

13 For penalties see TRADE AND LABOUR vol 47 para 324.

905. Form of contract between vendor and auctioneer. There are no special rules affecting the form of contract between the vendor and the auctioneer, and, subject to the ordinary exceptions common to all forms of agency, the contract may be either verbal or in writing[1].

---

1 See AGENCY vol 1 (2) (Reissue) para 19 et seq; *Coles v Trecothick* (1804) 9 Ves 234. For forms of auctioneer's appointment see 3 Forms & Precedents (5th Edn) 399–401, Forms 6, 8.

(2) AUCTIONEER'S AUTHORITY

906. Agency of auctioneer. An auctioneer is primarily the agent of the vendor. He can, however, sell his own property and a purchaser can take no objection to the sale on that ground[1]. Hitherto, the auctioneer was also treated as the purchaser's agent[2] for the limited purpose of signing on his behalf such notes or memoranda of sale as were formerly required[3], but this is no longer the case.

It is clear that the auctioneer is the agent of the vendor. Whereas an estate agent has (usually) only a revocable mandate to bring about a stipulated result[4] the auctioneer is a 'skilled agent to whom complete control of operations is given by the owner of the goods'[5]. He is employed, therefore, as an independent contractor rather than as an employee[6].

1 *Flint v Woodin* (1852) 22 LJ Ch 92.
2 See *Chaney v Maclow* [1929] 1 Ch 461, CA; *Sims v Landray* [1894] 2 Ch 318; *Bell v Balls* [1897] 1 Ch 663, 66 LJ Ch 397; *Van Praagh v Everidge* [1902] 2 Ch 266, 71 LJ Ch 598; revsd on the ground that there was no sufficient memorandum [1903] 1 Ch 434, 72 LJ Ch 260, CA; *Phillips v Butler* [1945] Ch 358, [1945] 2 All ER 258.
3 The requirement for written formalities was contained in the Law of Property Act 1925 s 40, which has now been replaced by the Law of Property (Miscellaneous Provisions) Act 1989 s 2 requiring written contracts but not in relation to public auctions of land. As to the present position see para 914 post; and see SALE OF LAND vol 42 para 27.
4 *Luxor (Eastbourne) Ltd v Cooper* [1941] AC 108, [1941] 1 All ER 33, HL.
5 *Walker v Crabb* (1917) 61 Sol Jo 219 at 220 per Atkin J.
6 *Walker v Crabb* (1917) 61 Sol Jo 219.

907. Extent of authority. Apart from express instructions enlarging or limiting it, the implied authority of the auctioneer is a general authority to sell by auction[1] and deal in the way usual and customary amongst auctioneers[2]. The authority does not extend so as to make the vendor liable for injury caused by the auctioneer's negligence to a person attending the sale unless the vendor has instructed the auctioneer to do any unlawful act or thing whereby the injury was caused[3].

An auctioneer has no implied authority to conclude a sale by private contract[4], even if the sale proves abortive and he is offered more than the reserve price[5]. If however, the vendor accepts a purchaser introduced by the auctioneer, and himself concludes a sale to that purchaser by private treaty, the auctioneer has a right to claim remuneration[6].

In some cases, where property has not reached its reserve and has been bought in, and immediately afterwards the auctioneer has sold the property at the reserve price to a person present at the bidding, the sale has been held good as, in effect, a sale by auction[7]. The true ratio decidendi of these cases, however, would seem to be that the instructions to sell were primarily to raise a minimum price pursuant to a court order or terms of compromise of a dispute, with sale by auction merely being stipulated as a convenient method of sale. Moreover, both of these cases involved claims by principals to enforce contracts against reluctant purchasers. Such claims could have succeeded simply on the basis of ratification. It would therefore be unsafe to regard these cases as authority for the proposition that a power to sell otherwise than by auction would be implied. In the one case[8] where a vendor was held bound by a private treaty sale effected by the auctioneer after the reserve was not reached at auction the overriding object of the sale was held to be to achieve a minimum price howsoever obtained, the auction being merely the preferred method.

1 *Howard v Braithwaite* (1812) 1 Ves & B 202 at 210; *Hawkins v Rogers* [1951] IR 48 at 59 per Dixon J. See also *Toulmin v Millar* (1887) 3 TLR 836, HL, per Lord Watson.
2 *Collen v Gardner* (1856) 21 Beav 540.
3 *Walker v Crabb* (1916) 33 TLR 119; here the auctioneer was liable in respect of injuries caused by an unruly mare. The vendor was not liable, notwithstanding that the sale was carried out on his premises, because both the sale and the chattel were entirely within the control of the auctioneer.
4 *Marsh v Jelf* (1862) 3 F & F 234.
5 *Daniel v Adams* (1764) Amb 495; *Re Loft* (1844) 2 LTOS 397.
6 *Green v Bartlett* (1863) 14 CBNS 681. See also para 923 post. The authority to sell otherwise than by auction was here express.
7 *Else v Barnard, ex p Courtauld* (1860) 28 Beav 228; *Bousfield v Hodges* (1863) 33 Beav 90.
8 *Garnier v Bruntlett* (1974) 236 Estates Gazette 867 (sale to realise security).

908. Sale below reserve price. If a reserve is fixed[1] by the vendor and the sale or lot is expressed to be subject to a reserve, the auctioneer has no authority to sell below it[2]. If he purports to do so no contract is concluded between the vendor and purchaser since all bids amount only to conditional offers and any acceptance is similarly conditional on the reserve being reached or exceeded[3]. Moreover the auctioneer cannot be liable to the disappointed buyer for breach of any warranty of authority to sell to the highest bidder below reserve in the face of an express 'subject to reserve sale'[4].

Where the sale is notified to be subject to the vendor's right to fix a reserve the auctioneer is similarly unable to sell below any reserve actually set and the purchaser is put on notice as to whether one has been fixed[5].

It may be that an auctioneer announces a sale to be without reserve where, in fact, the vendor has fixed one. In such a case a valid contract may be brought about enforceable by a purchaser who has bid below the reserve[6].

Conversely if no reserve is fixed and the auctioneer rightly advertises the sale as 'without reserve', liability may attach to the auctioneer if, subsequently, the vendor withdraws the lot, buys it in or fixes a reserve so that it is not sold to the highest bidder. Although no sale will in these circumstances be achieved the auctioneer may be liable on a collateral contract that the sale be without reserve[7]. It is suggested that in such a case the auctioneer would be able to look to the vendor-principal for indemnification[8].

1 It should be expressly set. The courts may not imply the setting of reserves: *Nelson v Hicks* (1899) QR 15 SC 465 (no implication that sales were subject to reserves by reason only of the fact that the goods were sent to the auctioneer accompanied by invoices).
2 *McManus v Fortescue* [1907] 2 KB 1, CA.
3 *McManus v Fortescue* [1907] 2 KB 1, CA.
4 *McManus v Fortescue* [1907] 2 KB 1, CA.
5 *Fay v Miller, Wilkins & Co* [1941] Ch 360, [1941] 2 All ER 18, CA. The auctioneers were liable, however, for breach of warranty of authority having, in this case, gone on to effect a memorandum as then required by the Law of Property Act 1925 s 40 (now repealed: see para 906 ante) thus, it was held, rendering the contract no longer conditional.
6 *Rainbow v Howkins* [1904] 2 KB 322, DC. The case was decided on the basis that the auctioneer had apparent authority to sell without reserve in the absence of any express notice to the contrary. This was expressly doubted in *McManus v Fortescue* [1907] 2 KB 1, CA, where, however, the existence of a reserve was expressly notified. The finding of apparent authority defeated the claim for breach of warranty of authority. The buyers also failed to enforce the contract of sale, notwithstanding that

the auctioneer was held to be authorised to effect it, since no memorandum as then required by the Sale of Goods Act 1893 s 4 (repealed) was signed.

7 *Warlow v Harrison* (1859) 1 E & E 309. The contract is made by the auctioneer making a unilateral offer to this effect which is accepted by the highest bona fide bidder by virtue of his bid: see at 316–317 per Martin B (obiter). This analysis was employed in *Tully v Irish Land Commission* (1961) 97 ILT 174. Contrast *Fenwick v Macdonald, Fraser & Co Ltd* (1904) 6 F 850.

8 *Warlow v Harrison* (1859) 1 E & E 309. See further para 947 post.

909. Authority to receive payment. An auctioneer has implied authority to receive the deposit on sales both of land and of goods[1], but no implied authority, by virtue of his agency alone, to receive the purchase money[2]. Thus a purchaser who pays the purchase money to an auctioneer who lacks express authority to receive it is not discharged from liability to the vendor. Where in a sale of goods, as is generally the case, the conditions contemplate that the auctioneer is to complete the sale, the position is different and he is then usually authorised to receive the purchase money[3]. This does not mean necessarily that he is under a duty to collect the price[4].

The auctioneer has authority to receive payment of the deposit by cash. He may accept a cheque[5], provided he exercises reasonable caution, but cannot be compelled to do so[6]. This authority is confined to cheques presently payable, and does not extend to receiving payment of the deposit by bill of exchange or post-dated cheque[7]. He cannot give credit[8], or allow a set-off due from the vendor to the purchaser[9]. Otherwise the auctioneer has no right, in the absence of express instructions, to take payment of the purchase money otherwise than in cash[10].

Where the auctioneer has received payment by cheque or bill of exchange without or in excess of any express or implied authority, the vendor is not bound by the payment: the purchaser still remains liable[11], and the auctioneer may be sued by the vendor for any damages sustained by him[12]. Where the auctioneer does receive the deposit he should do so as agent for the vendor rather than as stakeholder in order to protect his lien[13]. Normally, however, he will hold it as stakeholder[14].

1 *Mynn v Joliffe* (1834) 1 Mood & R 326; *Williams v Millington* (1788) 1 Hy Bl 81; *Capel v Thornton* (1828) 3 C & P 352; *Butwick v Grant* [1924] 2 KB 483, DC.
2 *Drakeford v Piercy* (1866) 7 B & S 515; *Butwick v Grant* [1924] 2 KB 483, DC.
3 *Sykes v Giles* (1839) 5 M & W 645.
4 See *Fordham v Christie Manson & Woods Ltd* (1977) 121 Sol Jo 529, 244 Estates Gazette 213; and para 922 post.
5 *Farrer v Lacy, Hartland & Co* (1885) 31 ChD 42, CA.
6 *Johnston v Boyes* [1899] 2 Ch 73.
7 *Williams v Evans* (1866) LR 1 QB 352; *Pape v Westacott* [1894] 1 QB 272, CA.
8 See note 7 supra.
9 *Brown v Staton* (1816) 2 Chit 353.
10 *Earl Ferrers v Robins* (1835) 2 Cr M & R 152; *Sykes v Giles* (1839) 5 M & W 645.
11 *Sykes v Giles* (1839) 5 M & W 645; and see *Hodgens v Keon* [1894] 2 IR 657, and *Boothman v Byrne* (1923) 57 ILT 36.
12 *Earl Ferrers v Robins* (1835) 2 Cr M & R 152.
13 See para 924 post.
14 See para 948 post.

910. Authority to warrant. It used to be the case that an auctioneer had no authority, except by express instructions, to give a warranty at the auction; and that an unauthorised warranty would not bind the vendor[1]. However, it has now been held that an agent may have usual or apparent authority to make warranties binding on his principal[2]. This proposition was considered in the context of auctions with regard to a representation relating to the property made by the auctioneer before sale. It was held that the vendor was not liable for misrepresentation since he had expressly drawn the attention of the public to the limits placed upon the auctioneer's authority to make binding representations[3].

Where the auctioneer does make unauthorised representations, he could be personally liable to the purchaser for breach of warranty of authority[4]. He will also have to indemnify his vendor if he makes representations rendering the latter liable to the purchaser; for example in misrepresentation.

If a vendor makes it clear that his descriptions are to be applied to the lots the auctioneer will be liable to him for any loss caused by his failure to do so[5].

1 *Payne v Lord Leconfield* (1882) 51 LJQB 642. See also ANIMALS para 222 ante.
2 See *Mendelssohn v Normand Ltd* [1970] 1 QB 177 at 183–184, [1969] 2 All ER 1215 at 1218, CA, per Lord Denning MR (an oral promise or a representation of fact made by one party, which induces the other to contract, can be relied on provided apparent authority to make such a statement exists).
3 See *Overbrooke Estates v Glencombe Properties Ltd* [1974] 3 All ER 511, [1974] 1 WLR 1335. This suggests that in the absence of such a notification the representation could have been binding on the vendor. Clearly, where the vendor does authorise the representation, he will be bound by it: *Museprime Properties Ltd v Adhill Properties Ltd* (1990) 61 P & CR 111.
4 See para 952 post.
5 *Brown v Draper* (1975) 233 Estates Gazette 929.

911. Delegation of authority. An agent has no power, without the authority of his principal, to delegate his agency to another. It follows that an auctioneer employed to sell must, in general, effect the sale himself[1]. Thus, he cannot delegate to his clerk[2], unless the principal has clearly assented. Different considerations would arise where the principal instructs a firm of auctioneers rather than an individual, but it would seem that even then only a person practising as an auctioneer would be impliedly authorised[3].

The context in which the question of delegation has most commonly arisen is that of signature by a clerk of the memoranda formerly required in sales both of land and of goods. Such signature might be made on behalf of either vendor or purchaser. Whilst the authorities themselves are not particularly strong, there exist categorical dicta that the auctioneer has no usual or implied authority to delegate the signing of a memorandum to his clerk so as to bind the vendor[4].

It appears to be free from doubt that there is no implied power to delegate signature to the clerk so as to bind the purchaser[5]. All matters incidental to the sale which it might be useful to delegate should be expressly agreed between the parties[6]. It is within the clerk's authority to receive the deposit[7].

1 *Coles v Trecothick* (1804) 9 Ves 234; *Henderson v Barnewall* (1827) 1 Y & J 387.
2 *Coles v Trecothick* (1804) 9 Ves 234; *Henderson v Barnewall* (1827) 1 Y & J 387; *Bird v Boulter* (1833) 4 B & Ad 443.
3 *Wilson & Sons v Pike* [1949] 1 KB 176, [1948] 2 All ER 267, CA. See also para 914 post.
4 *Gosbell v Archer* (1835) 2 Ad & El 500 (although here the clerk clearly signed only as a witness); *Peirce v Corf* (1874) LR 9 QB 210 (clerk signing sales ledger not shown to bidders); however, contrast *Dyas v Stafford* (1881) 7 LR Ir 590.
5 *Bell v Balls* [1897] 1 Ch 663. See also paras 906 ante, 914 post.

6 For a vendor's letter including authorisation for the auctioneer to delegate to a suitably qualified and experienced practitioner, see 3 Forms & Precedents (5th Edn) 401, Form 8.
7 *Gosbell v Archer* (1835) 2 Ad & El 500.

912. Termination of authority. The agency of the auctioneer is normally an agency for sale by auction only[1], and therefore, when the property has been knocked down, the auctioneer's authority is at an end except for the purpose of carrying out the contract made at the auction. He cannot introduce into it any stipulations as to title[2]. Normally the auctioneer cannot accept rescission of the contract[3].

1 *Seton v Slade* (1802) 7 Ves 265 at 276 per Lord Eldon LC; and see *Blackburn v Scholes* (1810) 2 Camp 341.
2 *Seton v Slade* (1802) 7 Ves 265.
3 *Nelson v Aldridge* (1818) 2 Stark 435; and contrast *Stevens v Legh* (1853) 22 LTOS 84, where the vendor failed in his action for breach of contract against the auctioneer who had returned the purchase price after fraud had been discovered. It is fairly common for auctioneers' conditions to provide expressly for a right to accept rescission, eg where a forgery is discovered.

913. Revocation of authority. Up to the time of the conclusion of the sale, and until the property is finally knocked down, the auctioneer's authority is revocable either expressly or in any of the events which ordinarily determine agencies[1], unless the contract is such as to give the auctioneer an authority coupled with an interest[2].

The authority can be withdrawn even though the auctioneer has incurred expenses[3] and advertised the property for sale[4], since the advertisement is the act of the auctioneer, and he has no ostensible authority to make representations as to the existence or extent of his own authority. The auctioneer will be liable in trespass if, after the determination of his authority, he insists on entering the vendor's premises for the purpose of effecting a sale[5].

If the authority has in fact been revoked, the auctioneer can give the highest bidder no right to the property, even though the bidder is unaware of the revocation[6]. It remains to be decided whether, unlike an estate agent, an auctioneer can recover damages, on the revocation of his authority, for preventing him from earning his commission[7]. It may be said that an auctioneer contracts to put the property to auction, and is therefore obliged, in contradistinction to an estate agent, to endeavour to sell the property in that fashion.

1 *Warlow v Harrison* (1859) 1 E & E 309; but if the property is sold 'without reserve', revocation after bidding had commenced would render the auctioneer, and thus his principal liable on the collateral contract to sell to the highest bona fide bidder. See para 908 ante; and AGENCY vol 1 (2) (Reissue) para 182 et seq.
2 Eg if an auctioneer is entrusted with goods for sale to repay previous advances, the authority is irrevocable: see *Charlesworth v Mills* [1892] AC 231 at 243, HL. See also AGENCY vol 1 (2) (Reissue) paras 183–188. The authority is not, however, irrevocable if the auctioneer pays money on the understanding that he is to sell the goods and recoup himself from the proceeds of sale: *Chinnock v Sainsbury* (1860) 30 LJ Ch 409.
3 *Taplin v Florence* (1851) 10 CB 744. The auctioneer does not, however, lose his right to be indemnified against the expenses he has incurred: see para 925 post.
4 *Warlow v Harrison* (1859) 1 E & E 309; *Taplin v Florence* (1851) 10 CB 744.
5 *Taplin v Florence* (1851) 10 CB 744.
6 *Manser v Back* (1848) 6 Hare 443.

7 See para 906 ante; and *Luxor (Eastbourne) Ltd v Cooper* [1941] AC 108, [1941] 1 All ER 33, HL. See
  also *Warlow v Harrison* (1859) 1 E & E 309 at 317. It is common for auctioneers' conditions of trading
  specifically to provide for payment in the event of withdrawal of lots.

914. Nature and exercise of authority to sign contract. As has been stated[1] it
is no longer the case that a contract for the sale or other disposition of an interest in
land made at public auction must be evidenced in writing and the requirement of
writing in the case of sales of land[2] does not apply. Thus the well established
implied authority to sign a memorandum evidencing the sale on behalf of the
vendor and purchaser no longer is of relevance. In order to achieve evidential
certainty of the terms of the contract of sale, which can now be made orally, it can
be made a term of that contract that the parties sign a contract containing the terms.

Alternatively, the terms under which the bidding is conducted may prevent a
contract arising at the fall of the hammer and provide that one only comes into
existence when such signed documentation is effected. If, in this latter situation, it
is sought to permit the auctioneer to act as agent in signing, that authority must be
expressly given.

1 See para 906 note 3 ante.
2 Laid down in the Law of Property (Miscellaneous Provisions) Act 1989 s 2.

(3) AUCTIONEER'S DUTIES TO VENDOR

(i) General Duties

915. Exercise of skill and knowledge. Being a person who professes to carry
on a business requiring skill and knowledge, an auctioneer must display such skill
and knowledge in acting for his vendor as is reasonably to be expected from
competent auctioneers, and must follow the course of business ordinarily recognised by custom[1] or prescribed by statute[2]. In the exercise of skill and knowledge
by an auctioneer the standard of care will vary depending upon whether he is
regarded as a specialist or a general practitioner[3]. If the former, he will not be liable
if, albeit that there is a body of professional opinion which considers that the
actions were wrong, there also exists an equally competent body of professional
opinion which supports the manner in which the auctioneer carried out his duty[4].
An auctioneer who is a 'general practitioner' will be regarded as negligent only if it
is found that no auctioneer of ordinary skill and care would have acted as he did[5].

An auctioneer will be liable in damages for a breach of any duty, nominal where
no material injury results[6], or substantial and of an amount to compensate the
vendor for any actual loss sustained through the negligence of the auctioneer[7], or of
persons employed by him[8]. It is not negligence for an auctioneer, in the exercise of
his judgment, not to insist upon a payment of a deposit by a purchaser[9]. It has been
held to be negligent to allow the purchaser to take away the goods before he has
paid the price[10].

1 *Russell v Hankey* (1794) 6 Term Rep 12; *Denew v Daverell* (1813) 3 Camp 451; *Jones v Nanney* (1824)
  13 Price 76.
2 Supply of Goods and Services Act 1982 s 13 (implied term of care and skill); *Coppen v Moore (No 2)*
  [1898] 2 QB 306; *Christie, Manson and Woods v Cooper* [1900] 2 QB 522.
3 *Luxmoore-May v Messenger May Baverstock (a firm)* [1990] 1 All ER 1067, [1990] 1 WLR 1009, CA,
  applying *Maynard v West Midlands Regional Health Authority* [1985] 1 All ER 635, [1984] 1 WLR 634,
  HL.

4 See *Alchemy (International) Ltd v Tattersalls (Ltd)* (1985) 276 Estates Gazette 675.
5 *Luxmoore-May v Messenger May Baverstock (a firm)* [1990] 1 All ER 1067, [1990] 1 WLR 1009, CA.
6 *Hibbert v Bayley* (1860) 2 F & F 48.
7 *Parker v Farebrother* (1853) 21 LTOS 128.
8 *Lord North's Case* (1557) 2 Dyer 161a.
9 *Cyril Andrade Ltd v Sotheby & Co* (1931) 47 TLR 244. Cf *Hibbert v Bayley* (1860) 2 F & F 48, where there was a condition that the highest bidder should immediately pay a deposit, and it was held to be negligent to allow him to leave without doing so. In the former case the deposit was only payable by the purchaser 'if required to do so'.
10 *Brown v Staton* (1816) 2 Chit 353.

916. Duty to describe the property accurately. The auctioneer will generally be under an obligation in tort, and may be specifically in contract, to describe the vendor's property with such care as is necessary in order to ensure that a proper price is obtained[1]. This may involve a duty to research and value[2] a lot.

Unless the contract between the auctioneer and the vendor permits the auctioneer to apply his own descriptions to the property he must apply any descriptions expressly or impliedly instructed[3] and if he fails to do so will be liable in damages for the difference between the price achieved and that which the property would have realised if it had been described as instructed[4].

If the auctioneer describes the property without authority or in breach of his duty to the vendor so that the latter becomes liable to the purchaser (for example, under the Misrepresentation Act 1967), the auctioneer will be liable to indemnify the vendor for causing that loss; it is otherwise if the misdescriptions are authorised[5].

1 *Cuckmere Brick Co Ltd v Mutual Finance Ltd* [1971] Ch 949, [1971] 2 All ER 633, CA.
2 *Luxmoore-May v Messenger May Baverstock (a firm)* [1990] 1 All ER 1067, [1990] 1 WLR 1009, CA.
3 *Brown v Draper & Co* (1975) 119 Sol Jo 300, 233 Estates Gazette 929, CA.
4 *Brown v Draper & Co* (1975) 119 Sol Jo 300, 233 Estates Gazette 929, CA.
5 *Museprime Properties Ltd v Adhill Properties Ltd* (1990) 61 P & CR 111.

917. Duties in respect of goods. Since the auctioneer is a bailee for reward, he must exercise ordinary care and diligence in keeping the goods entrusted to him[1]. He has a possession coupled with an interest in goods which he is employed to sell, and not a bare custody[2], and is liable for any loss or damage which may occur through his default or negligence[3]. If he has contracted to store goods as a bailee he is in breach of contract if he arranges for someone else to take possession of them, since the contract is one of which his personal care is of the essence[4]. If he has undertaken to insure goods which he is employed to sell he must give notice to his principal if, for any reason, he is unable to effect the insurance[5].

In the absence of authority from the vendor, it is the duty of the auctioneer not to part with possession of the goods until the purchaser has paid the price. If the auctioneer does so and the purchaser fails to pay, the auctioneer will be liable to the vendor for the amount[6].

Except where his right of lien exists[7], an auctioneer must redeliver goods to the vendor on demand, either before sale if the authority to sell is revoked, or after sale if the goods are unsold. Like other bailees, he is estopped from setting up the title of a third person against the bailor, unless the bailment is determined by what is equivalent to an eviction by title paramount, and the auctioneer defends upon the right and title and by the authority of such third person[8]. Even with such authority he cannot set up the jus tertii if he was aware of the adverse claim at the time when he accepted his employment[9].

1 *Maltby v Christie* (1795) 1 Esp 340. The auctioneer may contract out of his liability as bailee and otherwise: *Spriggs v Sotheby Parke Bernet & Co Ltd* [1986] 1 Lloyd's Rep 487, CA (a pre-Unfair Contract Terms Act 1977 case where the exclusion clause was upheld). See BAILMENT para 1569 post.
2 *Williams v Millington* (1788) 1 Hy Bl 81 at 85; *Woolfe v Horne* (1877) 2 QBD 355.
3 *Lilley v Doubleday* (1881) 7 QBD 510; *McMahon v Field* (1881) 7 QBD 591, CA.
4 *Edwards v Newland* [1950] 2 KB 534, [1950] 1 All ER 1072, CA, applying *British Waggon Co and Parkgate Waggon Co v Lea & Co* (1880) 5 QBD 149, DC.
5 *Callander v Oelrichs* (1838) 5 Bing NC 58.
6 *Brown v Staton* (1816) 2 Chit 353; see para 915 ante.
7 See para 924 post.
8 *Biddle v Bond* (1865) 6 B & S 225; *Thorne v Tilbury* (1858) 3 H & N 534 at 537. See also BAILMENT. Whereas the limitations on the right to plead the jus tertii are abolished by the Torts (Interference with Goods) Act 1977 s 8, it is questionable whether the auctioneer is thereby enabled to resist claims by vendors to return the property or their proceeds of sale. Section 1 refers to an action for wrongful interference as one to which the provisions of the Act apply. A vendor seeking the return of his property or their proceeds could invariably claim under the terms of the contract of agency, and that appears to be outside the Act.
9 *Re Sadler, ex p Davies* (1881) 19 ChD 86.

(ii) Fiduciary Duties

918. Fiduciary duties owed to the vendor. There are duties owed to the vendor which arise out of the fiduciary relationship inherent in the agency: duties which are imposed so that there cannot be a position such that the auctioneer's duty to the vendor and his own interests conflict. These are (1) bidding on behalf of the purchaser[1]; (2) purchasing the vendor's property[2]; (3) obtaining a secret profit[3]; and (4) the duty to account[4].

1 See para 919 post.
2 See para 920 post.
3 See para 921 post.
4 See para 922 post.

919. Bidding on behalf of the purchaser. Accepting commission bids on behalf of the purchaser creates an obvious potential conflict of interest[1] since the auctioneer is then acting for two parties whose interests are antithetical. Most auctioneers do accept commissions to bid for potential purchasers and this will be unobjectionable only if the consent of the vendor is obtained[2]. This is usually done by making it clear in the conditions of trading that the auctioneer is willing to accept commissions.

1 *Fullword v Hurley* [1928] 1 KB 498, CA: 'If and so long as the agent is the agent of one party he cannot engage to become the agent of another . . .'; cf *Bexwell v Christie* (1776) 1 Cowp 395, where obiter the contrary was suggested. See also *Fordham v Christie Manson & Woods* (1977) 121 Sol Jo 529, 244 Estates Gazette 213 at 215 per May J.
2 *Fullword v Hurley* [1928] 1 KB 498, CA.

920. Purchase by auctioneer. A purchase by the auctioneer himself without the vendor's consent is voidable, and will be set aside at the instance of the vendor, even after a long lapse of time, unless there is evidence that the vendor consented to the purchase after disclosure of all material facts known to the auctioneer[1]. It is not enough to put the vendor on inquiry; the auctioneer must make a full disclosure of all material facts[2]. If he purchases without such disclosure he becomes a trustee of the property for his principal and is strictly accountable as such[3]. The burden of proof that there was full disclosure and that the vendor acquiesced in the sale lies on the auctioneer[4].

Even after such full disclosure the auctioneer will not, however, be entitled to commission on the sale unless the principal has expressly agreed to pay commission in the changed circumstances[5]. The presumption is that the auctioneer has then ceased to be an agent and has become a contracting principal. The same principles apply if he has only a part interest in the purchase; for example, if he is one of a syndicate or if he is a shareholder in a purchasing company[6]. The embargo on the auctioneer buying his principal's property ceases once the auctioneer's agency is terminated[7].

1 *Oliver v Court* (1820) 8 Price 127; *Salomons v Pender* (1865) 3 H & C 639; and see *Ex p Lacey* (1802) 6 Ves 625; *Sanderson v Walker* (1807) 13 Ves 601; *Downes v Grazebrook* (1817) 3 Mer 200.
2 *Dunne v English* (1874) LR 18 Eq 524; *Boston Deep Sea Fishing and Ice Co v Ansell* (1888) 39 ChD 339, CA; *Oliver v Court* (1820) 8 Price 127; *Baskett v Cafe* (1851) 4 De G & Sm 388; *Lees v Nuttall* (1835) 2 My & K 819; *Whitcomb v Minchin* (1820) 5 Madd 91.
3 *Lees v Nuttall* (1835) 2 My & K 819.
4 *Wentworth v Lloyd* (1863) 32 Beav 467.
5 *Hocker v Waller* (1924) 29 Com Cas 296; *Great Luxembourg Rly Co v Magnay (No 2)* (1858) 25 Beav 586; *McPherson v Watt* (1877) 3 App Cas 254, HL; *Salomons v Pender* (1865) 3 H & C 639; *Lees v Nuttall* (1835) 2 My & K 819.
6 *Wentworth v Lloyd* (1863) 32 Beav 467; *Salomons v Pender* (1865) 3 H & C 639.
7 *Young v Hill, Ford & Newton* (1883) 2 NZLR 62; contrast *Oliver v Court* (1820) 8 Price 127 (agency continued after auctioneer left the rostrum).

921. Obtaining a secret profit. It is an inexorable rule drawn from the law of trusts that an auctioneer must not use his position to gain a profit from the transaction from a third party[1]. Any such profit, such as discounts on printing costs, must be passed to the vendor unless he consents to the profit being made[2].

1 *Hippisley v Knee Bros* [1905] 1 KB 1.
2 *Hippisley v Knee Bros* [1905] 1 KB 1. It is thought that this will only apply if, as is nowadays unusual, the auctioneer invoices the vendor separately for such items. See AGENCY vol 1(2) (Reissue) para 105.

922. Duty to account. Whilst there is no duty to obtain the purchase money[1] an auctioneer must account for any money received by him on the vendor's behalf[2], and be ready to pay it over to him. He is in a fiduciary position in respect of such money[3], and an order to pay can be made against him as trustee, which, if disobeyed, renders him liable to committal for contempt[4].

In general, payment should be made to the vendor, and not to his solicitors except by his express directions[5]. The relevance of the fact that the duty arises out of the fiduciary relationship between the auctioneer and his vendor client is that the vendor can trace the property in the hands of his agent in priority to the latter's ordinary trade and other creditors[6].

1 *Fordham v Christie Manson and Woods* (1977) 121 Sol Jo 529, 244 Estates Gazette 213; see para 909 ante.
2 For a statement of claim for an account see 6 Court Forms (2nd Edn) (1989 Issue) 194–195, Form 25.
3 *Re Cotton, ex p Cooke* (1913) 108 LT 310, CA.
4 *Crowther v Elgood* (1887) 34 ChD 691, CA; see CONTEMPT OF COURT. See, however, *Henry v Hammond* [1913] 2 KB 515, where *Crowther v Elgood* supra does not appear to have been cited.
5 *Brown v Farebrother* (1888) 58 LJ Ch 3. See, as to payment in sales under court direction, SALE OF LAND; and 35 Court Forms (2nd Edn) (1991 Issue) 16–17. As to deposits see para 948 post.

6 *Re Cotton, ex p Cooke* (1913) 108 LT 310, CA. Contrast where the auctioneer sells as principal: *Murphy v Jonathon Howlett (a firm)* (1960) 176 Estates Gazette 311.

(4) AUCTIONEER'S RIGHTS AGAINST VENDOR

923. Remuneration. The remuneration payable to an auctioneer by a private vendor may be fixed by express agreement as to both its amount and the events on which it is to be paid[1].

In order to found a legal claim for commission or other remuneration there must be a contractual relationship[2]. The contract on which the relationship is based may be implied from the circumstances or may arise from custom or usage. Where a valid claim to remuneration arises but the amount has not been agreed the auctioneer will be entitled to a fair and reasonable amount[3].

Where a letter is written to the principal setting out the terms on which remuneration is payable[4] and the principal does not dissent from them he may be taken to have assented to them[5]. A failure to dissent, however, will not by itself create a contract in contradistinction to incorporating terms into an existing mandate[6].

In most instances, where the services of the auctioneer have been fully performed, a customary rate of payment will be treated as the measure of a reasonable amount[7].

The scale of payments to auctioneers is fixed by law in the case of a sale under a distress[8], sales under the Insolvency Act 1986[9], and sales by the sheriff under a writ of fieri facias[10], and it is also fixed on a sale of land under the directions of the High Court[11]. Before commission will be payable the auctioneer will have to show that the events upon the happening of which he has acquired a vested right to commission have happened[12]. What these events are will vary from case to case[13].

The auctioneer may be entitled to commission on a sale to a purchaser introduced by the auctioneer even where no sale by auction has been actually effected, if the terms of the contract so stipulate[14], and he may be entitled to commission on a sale before the date of the auction when the purchaser is found by his client, the vendor, but not if the sale is effected by some third party with the right to sell[15].

An auctioneer who is also a trustee cannot make a profit out of the execution of the trust, unless authorised by the terms of the trust to do so, and therefore, in the absence of such authorisation, cannot in general claim remuneration for the sale of trust property of which either he or his partner is trustee[16].

The right to claim commission may be lost by the auctioneer's negligence[17] or misconduct[18].

There is no room for any implied term that the vendor will not revoke his auctioneer's authority to sell and thus prevent the commission being earned[19], but if the vendor has unjustifiably prevented its being earned by breaking his contract with the purchaser the court will imply such a term[20]. If the justifiable revocation prevents the auctioneer from bringing about the event upon which commission is payable none is recoverable, but a reasonable sum may be. It has been held that a quantum meruit claim can be maintained[21], but this contradicts earlier authority[22] equating the position of estate agents and auctioneers, which is to be preferred. There seems nothing, however, to prevent the auctioneer from making express contractual provision for situations where he is prevented from earning his commission.

The rationale against the auctioneer being paid commission or a reasonable sum, in the absence of express provision, where he has not brought about the event on which it is to be payable does not apply to expenses paid out and these are recoverable[23].

If two auctioneers claim commission in respect of the sale of the same property, the vendor cannot interplead unless the claims are adverse, that is, unless they are claims to the same money[24].

1 *Re Page (No 3)* (1863) 32 Beav 487; *Beningfield v Kynaston* (1887) 3 TLR 279, CA; *Peacock v Freeman* (1888) 4 TLR 541, CA. For general rules and construction of contracts as to the payment of commission see AGENCY vol 1(2) (Reissue) para 115 et seq.
2 *Toulmin v Millar* as reported in (1887) 58 LT 96, HL, per Lord Watson.
3 *Manson v Baillie* (1855) 2 Macq 80; *Miller v Beal* (1879) 27 WR 403.
4 See 3 Forms & Precedents (5th Edn) 389–392, Form 1.
5 *John E Trinder & Partners v Haggis* [1951] WN 416, CA, Denning LJ dissenting.
6 *Way and Waller Ltd v Ryde* [1944] 1 All ER 9, CA.
7 Auctioneers today tend to charge a flat percentage of the sale price.
8 See the Law of Distress Amendment Act 1888 s 8 (2), and the Distress for Rent Rules 1988, SI 1988/2050, rr 10, 11, App I.
9 Provisions relating to bankruptcy and companies winding up are now contained in the Insolvency Act 1986 and the Insolvency Rules 1986, SI 1986/1925; see BANKRUPTCY; COMPANIES.
10 See the Sheriffs Act 1887 s 20 (2), and the Writs of Fieri Facias, Sheriffs' or Sheriffs' Officers' Fees Order 1920, SR & O 1920/1250 (amended by SI 1956/502, SI 1956/2081, SI 1962/2417, SI 1971/808 and SI 1982/89).
11 See *Practice Direction* [1983] 1 All ER 160, [1983] 1 WLR 86, made under RSC Ord 31 r 2 (2) (g); and see the Supreme Court Practice 1991 para 31/2/2. The charges will normally be regarded as reasonable if they do not exceed the normal rate of commission charged on a sole agency basis up to a maximum of 2.5% of the sale price exclusive of VAT. The charges are to include all commission, valuations, expenses and disbursements except for surveys, which will be at the court's discretion. An application must be made to the court to approve fees if the agent's charges fall outside these limits or if there is a sale of investment or business property or farm property, or where property is sold in lots or by valuation. The limits do not apply in sales of property for patients of the Court of Protection where an agreement has been concluded prior to invocation of the court's jurisdiction, and there is discretion vested in the taxing officer in matrimonial cases where either the party condemned in costs has not agreed to the higher rates or where the costs fall to be paid out of the legal aid fund.
12 *Luxor (Eastbourne) Ltd v Cooper* [1941] AC 108, [1941] 1 All ER 33, HL (an estate agency case). Contra if he has a sole agency: *Gross Fine and Krieger Chalfen v Gaynor* (1974) 233 Estates Gazette 1015.
13 Cf *Peacock v Freeman* (1888) 4 TLR 541, CA (no commission payable where land knocked down to a purchaser but rescinded by the vendor in accordance with the conditions of sale, commission being payable if the property was 'sold') and *Skinner v Andrews and Hall* (1910) 26 TLR 340, CA (commission payable in similar circumstances, the contract providing for commission to be payable on a 'sale .. under the hammer').
14 *Green v Bartlett* (1863) 14 CBNS 681. See also *Bayley v Chadwick* (1878) 39 LT 429, HL; and *Clark v Smythies* (1860) 2 F & F 83. The question whether the sale is the result of the auctioneer's intervention is in each case a question of fact: see *Lumley v Nicholson* (1886) 34 WR 716.
15 *John Meacock & Co v Abrahams (Loescher, third party)* [1956] 3 All ER 660, [1956] 1 WLR 1463, CA (mortgagors, the vendor client being the mortgagee).
16 *Matthison v Clarke* (1854) 3 Drew 3, where the auctioneer was merely a mortgagee with a power of sale. See also *Salomons v Pender* (1865) 3 H & C 639; *Broad v Selfe* (1863) 2 New Rep 541; *Kirkman v Booth* (1848) 11 Beav 273. As to the inability of trustees to charge for services see TRUSTS.
17 *Denew v Daverell* (1813) 3 Camp 451; *Duncan v Blundell* (1820) 3 Stark 6; *Jones v Nanney* (1824) 13 Price 76.
18 *White v Chapman* (1815) 1 Stark 113; see further AGENCY vol 1 (2) (Reissue) para 122.
19 *Luxor (Eastbourne) Ltd v Cooper* [1941] AC 108, [1941] 1 All ER 33, HL.
20 *Alpha Trading Ltd v Dunnshaw-Patten Ltd* [1981] QB 290, [1981] 1 All ER 482,CA.
21 *Frank Swain (a firm) v Whitfield Corpn Ltd* (1962) 183 Estates Gazette 479, CA.
22 *John Meacock & Co v Abrahams (Loescher, third party)* [1956] 3 All ER 660, [1956] 1 WLR 1463, CA.

23 *Chinnock v Sainsbury* (1860) 30 LJ Ch 409 per Romilly MR but only as reported in (1860) 3 LT at 259.
See also similar dicta in *John Meacock & Co v Abrahams (Loescher, third party)* [1956] 3 All ER 660 at
663, [1956] 1 WLR 1463 at 1467, CA, per Lord Denning LJ.
24 *Greatorex v Shackle* [1895] 2 QB 249 at 252 per Wright J; and see INTERPLEADER.

924. Lien. By the custom of their business, auctioneers have a lien on goods
entrusted to them for sale and on the deposit and purchase money, for their charges
and remuneration[1]. They also have a lien on documents of title to land. The lien not
only entitles the auctioneer to retain the goods against claims thereto by the
principal-vendor but also allows him to resist claims to the goods made by the
purchaser in support of his rights against the vendor and he will not in that situation
be susceptible to a claim in tort for wrongful interference with goods[2].

This lien attaches to goods whether they are sold at the auctioneer's premises or
at those of the vendor[3]. It is a charge on the proceeds of sale in priority to any
assignment by the vendor, and the auctioneer cannot be compelled to marshal the
proceeds of several sales in order to give effect to the rights of an assignee of the
purchase money of certain of the sales[4]. The lien will be lost if the auctioneer waives
it[5] and he may be estopped from establishing it by having earlier denied the
vendor's title[6].

1 *Williams v Millington* (1788) 1 Hy Bl 81. As to agents' liens see generally AGENCY vol 1 (2) (Reissue)
paras 126–130. But see also *Skinner v Trustee of the Property of Reed* [1967] Ch 1194, [1967] 2 All ER
1286 (no lien on deposit received by auctioneer as stakeholder where outstanding incumbrances
exceed the amount of the purchase price or the balance of it because the property never became that
of the vendor; see further para 948 post).
2 *Lane v Tewson* (1841) 12 Ad & El 116n.
3 *Williams v Millington* (1788) 1 Hy Bl 81; *Robinson v Rutter* (1855) 4 E & B 954.
4 *Webb v Smith* (1885) 30 ChD 192, CA.
5 *Scarfe v Morgan* (1838) 4 M & W 270.
6 *Dirks v Richards* (1842) 4 Man & G 574. It is thought that merely accepting alternative security will
not amount to abandonment of the lien.

925. Indemnity. The vendor is bound to indemnify the auctioneer[1] for any
damages sustained by the auctioneer in the ordinary course of his employment as
the natural consequence of the contract of agency and, in the absence of any
agreement to the contrary, for any expenses incurred[2]. Where an auctioneer is sued
and claims an indemnity he may serve a third party notice on his principal[3].

The vendor's duty to indemnify the auctioneer extends to a case where property
for sale has been received by an auctioneer in good faith from a principal who was
not the true owner, and the auctioneer has been held liable for conversion[4]. But the
indemnity does not extend to cases where the auctioneer has been sued and
damages have been recovered from him for some act which is not a wrongful act
done in pursuance of his employment, unless the auctioneer defends with the
principal's express or implied authority[5]. The judgment against the auctioneer
creates no estoppel against the principal unless he had such authority[6]. The auctioneer will not be entitled to an indemnity where he incurs a liability by virtue of a
mistake of the law[7] or where he has been negligent[8].

1 *Williams v Lister & Co (Llewellyn Bros, third parties)* (1913) 109 LT 699, CA; *Adamson v Jarvis* (1827) 4
Bing 66. As to an agent's right of indemnity generally see AGENCY vol 1 (2) (Reissue) paras 123–125;
and for a form of express indemnity see 3 Forms & Precedents (5th Edn) 405, Form 14.

2 Among the expenses properly incurred is money paid to protect the goods from distress as long as they remain the vendor's property, but money paid after the sale and when the property in them has passed to the purchaser is not chargeable against the vendor: *Sweeting v Turner* (1871) LR 7 QB 310; *Chinnock v Sainsbury* (1860) 30 LJ Ch 409; *Brittain v Lloyd* (1845) 14 M & W 762.

3 Ie under RSC Ord 16; see PRACTICE AND PROCEDURE vol 37 para 254 et seq.

4 *Spurrier v Elderton* (1803) 5 Esp 1; *Adamson v Jarvis* (1827) 4 Bing 66. On a sale on behalf of the sheriff an auctioneer is not entitled to indemnity against the sheriff: *Farebrother v Ansley* (1808) 1 Camp 343.

5 *Halbronn v International Horse Agency and Exchange Ltd* [1903] 1 KB 270; *Frixione v Tagliaferro & Sons* (1856) 10 Moo PCC 175 at 200 (doubted in *Williams v Lister & Co (Llewellyn Bros, third parties)* (1913) 109 LT 699, CA); and see also *Tomlinson v Scottish Amalgamated Silks Ltd (Liquidators)* 1935 SC 1, HL.

6 *Halbronn v International Horse Agency and Exchange Ltd* [1903] 1 KB 270; *Frixione v Tagliaferro & Sons* (1856) 10 Moo PCC 175.

7 *Capp v Topham* (1805) 6 East 392 (failure to avoid auction duty being payable on abortive sale).

8 *Jones v Nanney* (1824) 13 Price 76.

(5) AUCTIONEER IN RELATION TO THIRD PERSONS

(i) Liabilities

926. Liability for conversion. An action for conversion lies against an auctioneer who, with or without knowledge of the true ownership of goods, has dealt with the property in and possession of those goods without the true owner's consent or authority[1], unless the case is governed by the Factors Act 1889[2]. The auctioneer's liability is strict; he is liable to the true owner even if he is completely ignorant of the want of title or the right to sell of the vendor-principal[3].

A mere advertisement for sale without an actual sale does not constitute a conversion. Greater difficulty, however, surrounds situations where the auctioneer does not effect the sale itself but plays some role in bringing the vendor and purchaser together. If the auctioneer is in possession of the goods but the vendor and purchaser effect a private treaty sale, it has been suggested that no act of conversion has been committed by the auctioneer[4]. However, it has been held that where auctioneers had an elaborate provisional bid procedure, designed to bring about a private treaty sale where the lot had not been sold at auction, they were liable in conversion and could not be said to be mere conduits[5].

Where an auctioneer deals or purports to deal both with possession and with property in the goods he will be liable in conversion[6].

Normally the sale of goods not owned by the vendor-principal effected by the auctioneer will not vest title in the purchaser[7]. Even where it does, by virtue of the recognised exceptions to the general principle[8] this does not assist the auctioneer since the sale was not only intended to, but also had the effect of, depriving the owner of property.

It has been suggested that when goods are delivered to an auctioneer by a mercantile agent acting in the course of his ordinary business who is in possession of the goods with the true owner's consent, the auctioneer is not liable for dealing with the goods, provided the dealing is in good faith and without notice of the true owner's claim[9]. However, that requires the delivery to the auctioneer to be treated as a 'disposition' and that this is so has been denied[10].

If the auctioneer has notice of the adverse claim of the true owner, he is thereafter liable for the value, not only of goods sold by him, but also of those unsold by him and returned to his principal[11].

When the auctioneer's liability is established, the measure of damages is the true value of the goods, normally at the time when the judgment is given[12], and not merely the sum realised at the auction[13].

The auctioneer may also be liable for failing to deliver the goods up to the true owner who claims them, but he is entitled to make reasonable enquiries[14]. In appropriate cases he may interplead[15].

There can, however, be no liability if the principal had title at the time of sale. This may involve a question of foreign law[16].

1   *Barker v Furlong* [1891] 2 Ch 172;*Consolidated Co v Curtis & Son* [1892] 1 QB 495;*Brown v Hickin-botham* (1881) 50 LJQB 426, CA; *Featherstonhaugh v Johnson* (1818) 8 Taunt 237; *Adamson v Jarvis* (1827) 4 Bing 66; *Cochrane v Rymill* (1879) 40 LT 744, CA; *Hardacre v Stewart* (1804) 5 Esp 103. See further TORT. For a statement of claim see 6 Court Forms (2nd Edn) (1989 Issue) 203, Form 41.
2   See *Shenstone & Co v Hilton* [1894] 2 QB 452; *Waddington & Sons v Neale & Sons* (1907) 96 LT 786. As to dispositions under the Factors Act 1889 see AGENCY vol 1(2) (Reissue) para 160.
3   *Union Transport Finance Ltd v British Car Auctions Ltd* [1978] 2 All ER 385, CA.
4   *Cochrane v Rymill* (1879) 40 LT 744, CA (obiter, the auctioneer in fact being liable because there had been a clear dealing with the property here by the auctioneer, he having given the vendor an advance on the proceeds of sale and having a lien on the goods). See also other cases where the auctioneer has been held not liable in conversion because he has acted as a mere conduit: *National Mercantile Bank v Rymill* (1881) 44 LT 767, CA (sale by private treaty before auction, auctioneer taking his commission and giving delivery order to purchaser); *Turner v Hockey* (1887) 56 LJQB 301 (mere communication of offer: see explanation given in *Consolidated Co v Curtis & Son* [1892] 1 QB 495 at 502–503); *Barker v Furlong* [1891] 2 Ch 172 (mere setting of price (obiter)).
5   *R H Willis & Son (a firm) v British Car Auctions Ltd* [1978] 2 All ER 392, [1978] 1 WLR 438, CA, casting doubt on *National Mercantile Bank v Rymill* (1881) 44 LT 767, CA, and *Turner v Hockey* (1887) 56 LJQB 301.
6   *Barker v Furlong* [1891] 2 Ch 172.
7   'Nemo dat quod non habet': see the Sale of Goods Act 1979 s 21 (1); and see SALE OF GOODS vol 41 para 744 et seq.
8   Ibid ss 21–25. See SALE OF GOODS vol 41 para 744 et seq and MARKETS AND FAIRS vol 29 para 624 et seq (market overt).
9   See *Shenstone & Co v Hilton* [1894] 2 QB 452. See also AGENCY vol 1(2) (Reissue) para 160.
10 *Waddington & Sons v Neale & Sons* (1907) 96 LT 786.
11 *Davis v Artingstall* (1880) 49 LJ Ch 609.
12 *Sachs v Miklos* [1948] 2 KB 23, [1948] 1 All ER 67, CA.
13 *Davis v Artingstall* (1880) 49 LJ Ch 609 at 610. See also DAMAGES.
14 *Lee v Bayes and Robinson* (1856) 18 CB 599; *Turner v Ford* (1846) 15 M &W 212.
15 See para 932 post.
16 *Winkworth v Christie, Manson & Woods Ltd* [1980] Ch 496, [1980] 1 All ER 1121.

927. Other duties to third parties. An auctioneer owes a general duty of care to third parties who attend auctions and especially duties to ensure their safety whilst at the auction premises over which the auctioneer has control. This could include the vendor's premises[1]. He also may in appropriate circumstances be liable in nuisance[2].

1   *Walker v Crabb* (1916) 33 TLR 119.
2   *Benjamin v Storr* (1874) LR 9 CP 400.

928. Executorship de son tort. If an auctioneer intermeddles with the estate of a deceased person without the authority of a properly constituted executor, he may render himself liable as an executor de son tort[1].

1   See EXECUTORS vol 17 paras 753–762; *Nulty v Fagan* (1888) 22 LR Ir 604.

929. Racial discrimination. It is unlawful for a person to discriminate on the grounds of colour, race or ethnic or racial origins in the provision of professional services or in the disposal of housing accommodation or business or other premises[1].

1 See the Race Relations Act 1976; and BRITISH NATIONALITY.

(ii) Rights

930. Right to possession of goods. By virtue of his lien and special property an auctioneer can maintain an action for trespass or conversion against persons wrongfully interfering with or converting goods[1]. He has, however, no such property in, or right of action in respect of, unsevered fixtures because these are land and an auctioneer employed to sell such fixtures has only a right to detach and remove them and not, before such severance, possession of them[2].

1 *Williams v Millington* (1788) 1 Hy Bl 81 at 85 per Heath J; *Robinson v Rutter* (1855) 4 E & B 954 at 956. See also para 917 ante.
2 *Davis v Danks* (1849) 3 Exch 435.

931. Privilege from distress. Goods delivered to an auctioneer for sale are privileged from distress whilst on the auctioneer's premises, as being chattels delivered to a person exercising a public trade to be dealt with in the way of his trade or employ[1]. The privilege attaches to the goods either at the auctioneer's ordinary place of business or on premises temporarily hired for the auction, and even though the auctioneer's occupation of the premises is not lawful[2]. It also extends to goods in the yard of a house[3]. It does not, however, cover goods which are on the owner's premises; such goods remain liable to distraint although they are the subject matter of a sale by auction[4]. The law is now largely governed by statute[5].

1 See DISTRESS; *Adams v Grane and Osborne* (1833) 1 Cr & M 380; the privilege is granted for the benefit of trade.
2 *Brown v Arundell* (1850) 10 CB 54 .
3 *Williams v Holmes* (1853) 8 Exch 861.
4 *Lyons v Elliott* (1876) 1 QBD 210.
5 Law of Distress Amendment Act 1908, which gives the goods owner, suffering distress, not being interested in the premises where distraint is carried out, the right to serve notice of his interest in the goods. See DISTRESS vol 13 para 251 et seq.

932. Interpleader by auctioneer. Where adverse claims are made to goods or money in the hands of an auctioneer, the auctioneer may interplead[1] subject to the ordinary rules governing interpleader[2]. In order to interplead the auctioneer must be subject to an action or expect to be sued in respect of the goods[3]. If that is not the case but a third party disputes the vendor's right to sell the auctioneer will be advised not to put the lot up for sale without securing an express indemnity from the vendor.

1 See RSC Ord 17 r 1 (1) (a), and CCR Ord 33 rr 6, 7. For interpleader summonses see 22 Court Forms (2nd Edn) (1980 Issue) 424–425, 441, Forms 27, 50.
2 See INTERPLEADER. For the application to auctioneers of the ordinary rules as to the identity of the

property claimed see *Wright v Freeman* (1879) 48 LJQB 276; *Hoggart v Cutts* (1841) 1 Cr & Ph 197. As to collusion, see *Thompson v Wright* (1884) 13 QBD 632; *Ingham v Walker* (1887) 3 TLR 448, CA.
3 RSC Ord 17 r 1 (1) (a).

2. THE AUCTION SALE AND THE DEPOSIT

(1) CONDUCT OF THE AUCTION

933. Time and place of sale. There are no special restrictions affecting the time and place when and where a sale by auction may be held[1], and an auctioneer has the same right of admission to a public market to exercise his calling as have traders entering to sell their own goods[2].

It may be illegal to auction goods in a shop[3] by retail sale on a Sunday[4]. It is questionable whether a sale of land by auction is properly regarded as a sale by retail or whether a place used for such sales is, from that fact alone, a shop.

There is no restriction on sales by auction on Sundays otherwise than by retail in a shop or elsewhere, that is, where the sales are to persons buying with a view to resale and not for their own consumption[5].

A sale by auction should not be held at any place in contravention of any person's legal rights, for example, in a house in respect of which restrictive covenants against sales by auction exist[6], or under such circumstances as to constitute an infringement of market rights[7]. An injunction will not be granted to restrain the sale by auction on leasehold premises of furniture belonging to the house[8].

Any place at which a public auction is held, even though a private house, is for the time being a 'place of public resort' for the purposes of the criminal law[9].

In livestock sales there are special statutory controls relating to the premises[10].

1 *Keith v Reid* (1870) LR 2 Sc & Div 39, HL. The restriction on sales on Sundays imposed by the Sunday Observance Act 1677 s 1, was repealed as obsolete by the Statute Law (Repeals) Act 1969 s 1, Schedule Pt IV.
2 *London Corpn v Lyons Son & Co (Fruit Brokers) Ltd* [1936] Ch 78, CA; and see *Nicholls v Tavistock UDC* [1923] 2 Ch 18.
3 'Shop' includes any premises where any retail trade or business is carried on, and 'retail trade or business' includes, inter alia, retail sales by auction: Shops Act 1950 s 74 (1).
4 See ibid s 47; and TRADE AND LABOUR.
5 See TRADE AND LABOUR. See also *Phillips v Parnaby* [1934] 2 KB 299, DC; *Dolton, Bournes and Dolton Ltd v Osmond* [1955] 2 All ER 258, [1955] 1 WLR 621, CA.
6 *Toleman v Portbury* (1872) LR 7 QB 344.
7 *Elwes v Payne* (1879) 12 ChD 468. See also *Abergavenny Improvement Comrs v Straker* (1889) 42 ChD 83; and, further, *Hailsham Cattle Market Co v Tolman* [1915] 2 Ch 1, CA.
8 *Reeves v Cattell* (1876) 24 WR 485. Cf *Moses v Taylor* (1862) 11 WR 81.
9 *Sewell v Taylor* (1859) 7 CBNS 160, a case under the Vagrancy Act 1824. See further CRIMINAL LAW. See also para 904 text and note 9 ante.
10 See para 938 post.

934. Advertisement of auction. The advertisement of an auction is merely an intimation of an intention to sell, and therefore, in the absence of fraud, intending purchasers who attend an auction have no right of action if the property is not put up for sale[1]. Even when the property is put up, it may be withdrawn before the fall of the hammer[2].

When, however, the advertisement amounts to a representation of fact that the auctioneer is authorised to sell, and this representation is fraudulent, persons incurring expense on the faith of it can sue the auctioneer in tort[3].

1 *Harris v Nickerson* (1873) LR 8 QB 286.
2 *Fenwick v Macdonald, Fraser & Co* (1904) 6 F 850; but see para 947 note 2 post.
3 *Richardson v Silvester* (1873) LR 9 QB 34.

935. Particulars and conditions of sale. It is customary for an auctioneer to settle the particulars and conditions of sale[1] on sales of goods, but not on sales of real property[2].

When he undertakes to settle the conditions, he must do so with the skill and knowledge which may reasonably be expected of one who practises as an auctioneer[3]; and if he sells without imposing conditions which are usual and prudent for the vendor's protection, he may, even in the case of a sale of real property, be held liable for negligence at the suit of the vendor[4].

It is necessary in order that the conditions of sale may be incorporated into the contract of sale that they be communicated to bidders and this can be done by notice, for example by exhibition in the auction room[5] or by reproduction in the auction catalogue. Such communication must take place before the conclusion of the contract[6].

Most conditions affect the vendor, auctioneer and the purchaser, that is the highest bidder. Some however affect bidders generally[7]. If such conditions are to bind bidders generally they must do so by virtue of the court finding a collateral contract between the auctioneer and the bidders[8].

Conditions of an exclusionary nature or those modifying or limiting the liability of the auctioneer or vendor are subject to statutory control[9] whereby they may be rendered void[10] or subject to a test of reasonableness[11]. A sale by auction is not, in any circumstances, treated as a consumer sale for the purposes of the provisions relating to the exclusion of terms implied by the Sale of Goods Act 1979[12].

A number of conditions are implied by this statute[13]. In relation to auctions, those of widest application are the implied conditions of correspondence with description and merchantability. Auction sales are sales by description and are thus affected by the statutory provision[14]. Descriptions, especially statements about provenance in fine art sales, are invariably subject to some form of express caveat or exclusion of liability in auction conditions. To be valid, these must satisfy the test of reasonableness[15]. As regards merchantability, the implied term only applies to sellers who sell in the course of a business[16]. Where, as is frequently the case, the auctioneer sells on behalf of a principal who is not selling in the course of a business the implied condition will still apply unless either the auctioneer takes steps to bring to the notice of the buyer the fact that the vendor is a private seller or the buyer knows that fact[17].

1 See SALE OF GOODS; SALE OF LAND. For forms of conditions on a sale of goods by auction see 3 Forms & Precedents (5th Edn) 394–398, Forms 3, 4; for forms on sale of land see 3 Forms & Precedents (5th Edn) 398–399, Form 5 and 38 Forms & Precedents (5th Edn) 85–100, Forms 25–27. In *Couchman v Hill* [1947] KB 554 at 559, [1947] 1 All ER 103 at 105, CA, Scott LJ expressed the view that a printed condition that the vendor will take no responsibility for errors of description of things or animals specifically offered for sale on inspection is reasonable for visible defects, but not for qualities which are invisible, and he recommended the point for consideration by the auctioneers' associations. Cf *Druce & Co Ltd v Leveson* (1952) 102 L Jo 721, where the purchaser was held to have assented to a printed condition to which attention was drawn by the auctioneer.
2 *Pike v Wilson* (1854) 1 Jur NS 59.
3 See para 915 ante.

4 *Denew v Daverell* (1813) 3 Camp 451.
5 *Mesnard v Aldridge* (1801) 3 Esp 271; *Bywater v Richardson* (1834) 1 Ad & El 508; and cf *Torrance v Bolton* (1872) 8 Ch App 118 (property described in printed particulars: subsequent oral description not enough to show purchaser not misled). See, further, *Scriven Bros & Co v Hindley & Co* [1913] 3 KB 564. As to the construction of a particular condition see *Robinson, Fisher and Harding v Behar* [1927] 1 KB 513, where a condition that lots uncleared 'shall' be resold was held to be purely permissive.
6 *Dennant v Skinner and Collom* [1948] 2 KB 164, [1948] 2 All ER 29.
7 Eg conditions relating to the conduct of the auction: control of bidding, withdrawal of bids, etc.
8 As found in *Shandel v Jacobs* [1949] (1) SA 320.
9 See the Unfair Contract Terms Act 1977, which applies to contracts made after 1 February 1978: s 31 (2); and see SALE OF GOODS vol 41 paras 700–702 and CONTRACT vol 9 para 366A.
10 Unfair Contract Terms Act 1977 s 6 (1) (seller's implied undertakings as to title).
11 Ibid s 6 (3).
12 Ibid s 12 (2).
13 See the Sale of Goods Act 1979 ss 12–15.
14 Ibid s 13.
15 Unfair Contract Terms Act 1977 s 11, Sch 2. See note 11 supra.
16 Sale of Goods Act 1979 s 14 (2).
17 Ibid s 14 (5).

936. Sale in lots. Where goods are put up for sale by auction in lots, each lot is prima facie deemed to be the subject of a separate contract of sale[1]. For stamp purposes[2], the sale of each lot must be treated as a separate contract[3].

1 Sale of Goods Act 1979 s 57 (1).
2 See STAMP DUTIES.
3 *Roots v Lord Dormer* (1832) 4 B & Ad 77; *Watling v Horwood* (1847) 12 Jur 48; *A-G v Cohen* [1937] 1 KB 478, [1937] 1 All ER 27, CA.

937. Property subject to fixed agricultural charge. An auctioneer selling by auction property subject to a fixed agricultural charge[1] is not concerned to see that the statutory obligations governing the right to sell the property[2] have been complied with notwithstanding that he may be aware of the existence of the charge[3].

1 As to fixed agricultural charges see the Agricultural Credits Act 1928 s 5 (3); and AGRICULTURE vol 1 (2) (Reissue) paras 551, 552.
2 See ibid s 6 (1), (2); and AGRICULTURE vol 1 (2) (Reissue) para 552.
3 Ibid s 6 (3).

938. Sale of cattle in mart. Unless exempted by order of the Minister of Agriculture, Fisheries and Food[1], an auctioneer must not sell cattle[2] at any mart where cattle are habitually or periodically sold, unless such facilities for weighing cattle are provided at the mart as are required in the case of sale of cattle at a market or fair to which the Markets and Fairs (Weighing of Cattle) Acts 1887 and 1891 apply[3].

Default in complying with these requirements renders the auctioneer or his employer, if he is employed by any person, liable on summary conviction to a fine not exceeding level 2 on the standard scale, or, if the offence is continuing, £10 a day[4].

Further, an auctioneer must not offer for sale in any market, fair or mart in or near which a statutory weighing machine is provided[5] any cattle[6] fit for immediate slaughter unless they have been weighed on the machine and their weight as so ascertained is disclosed to intending purchasers at the time of the offer for sale[7]. The penalty for not complying with this provision is a fine not exceeding level 1 on the standard scale[8]. The minister[9] may by order declare that this provision shall not apply to any market, fair or mart[10].

1 The minister (formerly the Board of Agriculture: see the Ministry of Agriculture and Fisheries Act 1919 s 1 and the Transfer of Functions (Ministry of Food) Order 1955, SI 1955/554) may delegate his functions to the Meat and Livestock Commission: see the Agriculture Act 1967 s 4 (1); and AGRICULTURE vol 1 (2) (Reissue) para 804.

2 'Cattle' includes, for this purpose, rams, ewes, wethers, lambs and swine: Markets and Fairs (Weighing of Cattle) Act 1887 s 3. Cf note 6 infra. As to the sale of cattle generally see ANIMALS para 218 et seq ante. As to markets see generally MARKETS AND FAIRS.

3 Markets and Fairs (Weighing of Cattle) Act 1891 s 4 (1) ; Markets and Fairs (Weighing of Cattle) Act 1926 s 2 (amended by the Statute Law (Repeals) Act 1975 s 1, Schedule and, as regards local authorities which were market authorities, by the Food and Drugs Act 1938 ss 101, 103, Sch 4 Pt I and the London Government Act 1963 s 93 (1), Sch 18 Pt II).

4 Markets and Fairs (Weighing of Cattle) 1891 s 4 (3) (amended by virtue of the Criminal Justice Act 1982 ss 38, 46). In any enactment contained in an Act passed either before or after the Criminal Justice Act 1982 'the standard scale' has the meaning given by s 37: s 75 (a). A standard scale of fines for summary offences was introduced by the Criminal Justice Act 1982 s 37 (1). Where any enactment contained in an Act passed either before or after that Act provides (1) that a person convicted of a summary offence is liable on conviction to a fine or a maximum fine by reference to a specified level on the standard scale, or (2) confers power by subordinate instrument to make a person liable on conviction of a summary offence, whether or not created by the instrument, to a fine or a maximum fine by reference to a specified level on the standard scale, it is to be construed as referring to the standard scale for which s 37 provides as that scale has effect from time to time by virtue either of that section or of an order under the Magistrates' Courts Act 1980 s 143: Criminal Justice Act 1982 s 37 (3). In relation to Acts passed before the Criminal Justice Act 1982, this provision applies where references to the standard scale are substituted by s 46 as read with s 38 or s 40. At the date at which this volume states the law, the standard scale is as follows, in relation to offences committed after 1 May 1984: level 1, £50; level 2, £100; level 3, £400; level 4, £1,000; level 5, £2,000: s 37 (2) (amended by the Criminal Penalties etc (Increase) Order 1984, SI 1984/447, art 2 (4), Sch 4). As from a day to be appointed, the levels are increased to £200, £500, £1,000, £2,500 and £5,000 respectively: Criminal Justice Act 1991 s 17 (1).

5 Ie in order to comply with the Markets and Fairs (Weighing of Cattle) Acts 1887 and 1891. A weighing machine provided under those Acts includes one provided under the Food Act 1984 s 57: s 57 (2).

6 'Cattle' means, for this purpose, bulls, cows, oxen and heifers: Markets and Fairs (Weighing of Cattle) Act 1926 s 1 (3). Cf note 2 supra.

7 Ibid s 1 (1).

8 Ibid s 1 (2) (amended by virtue of the Criminal Justice Act 1982 ss 38, 46). As to the standard scale see note 4 supra. At the date at which this volume states the law, level 1 on that scale is at £50.

9 See note 1 supra.

10 Markets and Fairs (Weighing of Cattle) Act 1926 s 1 (4).

939. Display of auctioneer's name and address. Before beginning an auction[1] the auctioneer must place or cause to be placed a ticket or board bearing his true and full christian and surname and his residence painted, printed or written thereon in large letters publicly visible and legible, and a copy of the Auctions (Bidding Agreements) Act 1927 and of the Auctions (Bidding Agreements) Act 1969, in some conspicuous part of the auction room and must keep them there during the whole time the auction is being held[2].

The penalty for a contravention of this provision on conviction is a fine[3].

1 In addition to the statutory provisions regulating sales which are dealt with in this title, see the following other titles: SALE OF LAND, for sales under RSC Ord 31 by order of the High Court; BANKRUPTCY, for sales on behalf of a trustee in bankruptcy; DISTRESS, for sales under distress; COMPANIES, for sales in the winding up of companies; CONSTITUTIONAL LAW , for sales of Crown land; EXECUTION, for sales by a sheriff; EXECUTORS, for sales by personal representatives; INNS, for sales of goods deposited with innkeepers; MORTGAGE, for sales by mortgagees; TRUSTS, for sales of trust property.

2 Auctioneers Act 1845 s 7; Auctions (Bidding Agreements) Act 1927 s 3; Auctions (Bidding Agreements) Act 1969 s 4.
3 Auctioneers Act 1845 s 7. It is thought that the offence is triable on indictment only, with an unlimited fine on conviction; see the Criminal Law Act 1977 s 32 (1).

940. Notification of reserve and of vendor's right to bid. A sale by auction may be notified to be subject to a reserve price[1], and a right to bid at an auction may be reserved expressly by or on behalf of the seller[2]. When the sale of land or goods is subject to a reserve price, or when the vendor reserves a right to bid or to employ persons to bid on his behalf, the fact must be notified before the sale[3]. It is not necessary, in sales either of land or of goods to state whether the sale is subject to or without reserve, but in land sales it must be stated either that the sale is on such terms or that a right to bid is reserved. In both land and goods sales it must be stated before the sale if the vendor reserves the right to bid or to employ a puffer[4]. Any words may be used to render it clear, when such is the case, that the sale is without reserve[5].

Unless notification is made[6], it is illegal for the vendor or any one on his behalf[7] to make a bid, or for the auctioneer knowingly to take such a bid, and any sale contravening this rule may be treated as fraudulent by the purchaser[8].

Where the vendor reserves a right to bid, he or any one, but only one, person on his behalf may bid at the auction[9], and the conditions announced as governing his right must be strictly complied with[10].

1 Sale of Goods Act 1979 s 57 (3). It seems to have been formerly a rule in equity that, where a sale of land was not notified to be without reserve, one bidder might, even without express stipulation, be employed to prevent a sale at an undervalue: *Green v Baverstock* (1863) 14 CBNS 204 at 208 per Willes J; but see *Mortimer v Bell* (1865) 1 Ch App 10 per Lord Cranworth LC.
2 Sale of Goods Act 1979 s 57 (3).
3 Sale of Land by Auction Act 1867 s 5; Sale of Goods Act 1979 s 57 (3).
4 Sale of Land by Auction Act 1867 s 5; Sale of Goods Act 1979 s 57 (3). A 'puffer' is a person appointed to bid on the part of the owner: Sale of Land by Auction Act 1867 s 3.
5 *Hills and Grant Ltd v Hodson* [1934] Ch 53; *Gilliat v Gilliat* (1869) LR 9 Eq 60, and dictum of Lord Romilly MR which, it is suggested, is not reflective of the words used in the 1867 Act.
6 Notification of a reserve price is not in itself a reservation of the right to bid: *Gilliat v Gilliat* (1869) LR 9 Eq 60; see the Sale of Goods Act 1979 s 57 (3).
7 See *Parnell v Tyler* (1833) 2 LJ Ch 195, where it was held that even the employment by a third person of the vendor's solicitor's clerk invalidated the sale.
8 Sale of Goods Act 1979 s 57 (4), (5). This section enacts the common law rule. The buyer has alternative remedies to sue for the tort or to avoid the contract. See generally *Crowder v Austin* (1826) 3 Bing 368 (highest bidder to be purchaser; seller whose servant pushed up bidding cannot recover price); *R v Marsh* (1831) 1 Cr & J 406 (bona fide bid for himself by seller's agent); *Thornett v Haines* (1846) 15 M & W 367 (sale without reserve; puffer employed without notice by vendor; buyer may recover deposit from auctioneer); *Green v Baverstock* (1863) 14 CBNS 204 (highest bidder to be purchaser; action by auctioneer for non-clearance of goods). As to improper or fraudulent acts likely to prevent the goods put up from realising their fair value, such as damping the sale or 'knock out', see para 944 post.
9 Sale of Land by Auction Act 1867 s 6; Sale of Goods Act 1979 s 57 (6); *Thornett v Haines* (1846) 15 M & W 367; For form of acceptance of appointment to bid on vendor's behalf see 3 Forms & Precedents (5th Edn) 401–402, Form 9.
10 *Parfitt v Jepson* (1877) 46 LJQB 529, where the vendor reserved a right to bid once, and the sale was set aside because he bid three times.

941. Conditions of sale and oral modifications. Oral statements made by the auctioneer may or may not form part of the contract of sale[1]. Oral statements made to the purchaser by the auctioneer before the sale may amount to conditions or warranties[2] which override the written conditions of sale[3].

There used to be a distinction drawn between sales of goods and those of land as regards the effect of oral modifications of the conditions[4]. The difficulty in the case of land sales was that parol evidence could not be introduced to vary a written contract[5]. Now that there is no requirement of writing to render a contract for the sale of land by auction valid or enforceable[6], that distinction may no longer be maintained. Oral statements may be used, where the contract is reduced to writing, to show that the written version was not what was actually agreed or that the contract is void for mistake[7].

Oral corrections of misdescriptions in the particulars at the time of the sale may defeat the purchaser's right to enforce specific performance with compensation[8].

1 *Druce & Co Ltd v Leveson* (1952) 102 L Jo 721 (purchaser taken to have assented to conditions of sale forming part of contract where she heard auctioneer make oral reference to conditions of sale prior to the sale); as to what statements are and are not part of the contract see CONTRACT; SALE OF GOODS; SALE OF LAND. Statements by the auctioneer may, however, amount to an offence under the Trade Descriptions Act 1968; see para 956 post and TRADE MARKS.

2 The distinction between a condition, which gives a right to reject the thing sold and treat the contract as ended by the breach of the condition, and a warranty, which gives a right of action for damages for breach, is considered in CONTRACT. A party entitled to the benefit of a condition may, in effect, turn it into a warranty by electing to claim damages: see *Wallis, Son and Wells v Pratt and Haynes* [1911] AC 394, HL.

3 *Couchman v Hill* [1947] KB 554, [1947] 1 All ER 103, CA (confirmatory description (heifer unserved) made by auctioneer and vendor before sale overrode stultifying condition in printed terms); and see *Harling v Eddy* [1951] 2 KB 739, [1951] 2 All ER 212, CA (vendor's oral guarantee of soundness of heifer amounted to a condition of the contract). As to warranty on sale of animals see ANIMALS para 218 et seq ante .

4 With goods if there was no requirement of written evidence and no written contract, oral statements could modify the conditions of sale: *Eden v Blake* (1845) 13 M & W 614.

5 *Gunnis v Erhart* (1789) 1 Hy Bl 289; *Shelton v Livius* (1832) 2 Cr & J 411; *Ogilvie v Foljambe* (1817) 3 Mer 53; *Higginson v Clowes* (1805) 15 Ves 516; *Clowes v Higginson* (1813) 1 Ves & B 524; *Winch v Winchester* (1812) 1 Ves & B 375; *Anson v Towgood* (1820) 1 Jac & W 637.

6 See para 906 note 3 ante.

7 *Swaisland v Dearsley* (1861) 30 LJ Ch 652; *Winch v Winchester* (1812) 1 Ves & B 375; *Manser v Back* (1848) 6 Hare 443; *Re Hare and O'More's Contract* [1901] 1 Ch 93.

8 *Farebrother v Gibson* (1875) 1 DeG & J 602.

942. Bidding. The method of bidding and the amount of the bids are usually regulated by the conditions of sale[1].

Until the property is actually knocked down there is no complete contract of sale. A bid is a mere offer, and can be retracted by the bidder at any time before the auctioneer announces the completion of the sale by the fall of the hammer, or in other customary manner[2].

Fictitious bids made by a third person without the privity of the vendor or the auctioneer do not invalidate the sale, nor do they affect the vendor's right to specific performance[3].

If an auctioneer pretends to accept bids which have not been made, an action will lie against him for the deposit and interest upon it[4]. He might also be sued in fraud, and where fraud is alleged in an action brought by the purchaser against the auctioneer and the vendor for rescission of the contract, the auctioneer cannot claim to be dismissed from the action upon paying the deposit into court[5]. It remains to be decided whether the auctioneer 'taking bids out of the air' – a practice by no means unknown – is guilty of obtaining property by deception[6]. All the main constituents of the offence appear to be committed but there may be problems relating to causation, especially where genuine bids intervene.

If two or more persons take part in a mock auction, by means of sham bidders and bidding, to induce persons to buy at excessive prices, they are guilty of a criminal conspiracy[7].

1 Where the conditions provide that, in case any dispute arises respecting a bid, the auctioneer may determine the bid or the property may, at the vendor's option, either be put up again at the last undisputed bid or be withdrawn there is a sufficient dispute respecting an overlooked bid even though the property was knocked down to the only bid seen by the auctioneer: *Richards v Phillips* [1969] 1 Ch 39 at 53, [1968] 2 All ER 859, CA.
2 Sale of Goods Act 1979 s 57 (2); *Payne v Cave* (1789) 3 Term Rep 148. In an unconditional sale of specific goods the property in the goods passes on the fall of the hammer: Sale of Goods Act 1979 s 18 r 1; *Dennant v Skinner and Collom* [1948] 2 KB 164, [1948] 2 All ER 29.
3 *Union Bank of London v Munster* (1887) 37 ChD 51.
4 *Heatley v Newton* (1881) 19 ChD 326, CA.
5 See note 4 supra.
6 See the Theft Act 1968 s 15, and CRIMINAL LAW vol 11 (1) (Reissue) para 567.
7 *R v Lewis* (1869) 11 Cox CC 404; see CRIMINAL LAW vol 11 (1) (Reissue) para 60 et seq.

943. Mock auctions. It is an offence to promote or conduct, or to assist in the conduct of, a mock auction at which one or more lots consisting of or including one or more of the following articles are offered for sale[1]: any plate, plated articles, linen, china, glass, books, pictures, prints, furniture, jewellery, articles of household or personal use or ornament and any musical or scientific instrument or apparatus[2].

A sale of goods by way of competitive bidding[3] is taken to be a mock auction if, but only if, during the course of the sale[4]:

(1) any such lot is sold to a person bidding for it[5], and either it is sold to him at a price lower than the amount of his highest bid for that lot, or part of the price at which it is sold to him is repaid or credited to him or is stated[6] to be so repaid or credited[7]; or

(2) the right to bid for any such lot is restricted, or is stated[8] to be restricted, to persons who have bought or agreed to buy one or more articles[9]; or

(3) any articles are given away or offered as gifts[10].

The penalty on summary conviction is a fine not exceeding the prescribed sum, or imprisonment for a term not exceeding three months, or both, and the penalty on conviction on indictment is an unlimited fine or two years imprisonment, or both[11].

1 Mock Auctions Act 1961 s 1 (1).
2 Ibid s 3 (2).
3 Ie a sale of goods at which the persons present, or some of them, are invited to buy articles by way of competitive bidding, this expression including any mode of sale whereby prospective purchasers may be enabled to compete for the purchase of articles, whether by way of increasing bids or by the offer of articles to be bid for at successively decreasing prices or otherwise: ibid s 3 (1). See *Lomas v Rydeheard* (1975) 119 Sol Jo 233, DC (seller calling out successively decreasing prices but not asking for offers until he reached his final price); *Clements v Rydeheard* [1978] 3 All ER 658, DC (offering boxes at fixed price and selecting purchasers who put up hands; purchasers of later lots similarly selected from amongst those who had purchased boxes). The competition need not relate to the price: *Allen v Simmons* [1978] 3 All ER 662, [1978] 1 WLR 879, DC. The words 'or otherwise' are not to be construed ejusdem generis with the preceding words: *R v Pollard* (1983) 148 JP 679, CA.
4 Anything done in or about the place where a sale of goods by way of competitive bidding is held, if done in connection with the sale, must be taken to be done during the course of it, whether it is done at the time when any articles are being sold or offered for sale by way of competitive bidding or before or after any such time: Mock Auctions Act 1961 s 3 (5).

5 The reference to sale to a person bidding includes a reference to a purported sale to a person stated to have bid, whether that person exists or not: ibid: s 3 (4).

6 Ie stated by or on behalf of the person conducting the sale, by an announcement made to the persons present: ibid s 3 (3).

7 Ibid s 1 (3) (a). This does not apply if it is proved that the reduction, repayment or credit was on account of a defect discovered after the highest bid in question had been made, being a defect of which the person conducting the sale was unaware when that bid was made, or was on account of damage sustained after that bid was made: s 1 (4). Any bid stated to have been made is conclusively presumed to have been made, and to have been a bid of the amount stated: s 3 (4).

8 See note 6 supra.

9 Mock Auctions Act 1961 s 1 (3) (b).

10 Ibid s 1 (3) (c).

11 Ibid s 1 (2) (amended by virtue of the Magistrates' Courts Act 1980 s 32 (7) and the Criminal Law Act 1977 s 32 (1)). Where an offence committed by a body corporate is proved to have been committed with the consent or connivance or to be attributable to any neglect on the part of any director, manager, secretary or other similar officer or any person purporting to act in such capacity, he, as well as the body corporate, is deemed guilty and is liable to be proceeded against and punished accordingly: Mock Auctions Act 1961 s 2. The prescribed sum is that prescribed under the Magistrates' Courts Act 1980 s 32 and at the date at which this volume states the law is £2,000: s 32 (9) (amended by the Criminal Penalties etc (Increase) Order 1984, SI 1984/447, art 2, Sch 1); see MAGISTRATES vol 29 para 397. As from a day to be appointed, the prescribed sum is increased to £5,000: Criminal Justice Act 1991 s 17 (2).

944. Damping the sale and bidding agreements. Improper or fraudulent acts, which are likely to prevent the property put up from realising its fair value and to 'damp' the sale, will invalidate any purchase by persons guilty of or privy to such acts, so that the purchaser will be disentitled to specific performance and the auctioneer will be justified in withdrawing the property[1]. Furthermore if a person maliciously makes false statements with the consequence that no sale results the unsuccessful vendor can sue for malicious falsehood[2].

At common law an agreement between two or more persons not to bid against each other at an auction, even if amounting to what is popularly known as a 'knock-out', is not illegal, nor does it invalidate the sale[3].

Where two or more persons agree not to bid against each other at an auction on the understanding that the successful purchaser shall convey part of the property purchased to the other or others, equity will give relief if the purchaser fails to implement his promise[4].

By statute a dealer[5] who offers or agrees to give or gives any gift or consideration to any other person as an inducement or reward for abstaining or for having abstained from bidding at a sale by auction, either generally or for any particular lot, and any person who attempts to obtain or agrees to accept or accepts any such gift or consideration from a dealer as such inducement or reward is guilty of an offence and liable, on summary conviction, to a fine not exceeding the prescribed sum[6] or imprisonment for a term not exceeding six months, or both, or, on conviction on indictment to a fine or imprisonment for a term not exceeding two years or both[7]. A prosecution may not be instituted without the consent of the Attorney General or Solicitor General[8].

A written agreement made before an auction whereby a dealer agrees with one or more persons to purchase goods at that auction bona fide on a joint account is not a contravention of the statute provided a copy of the agreement is deposited with the auctioneer before any purchase is made in pursuance of it[9]. A copy of the Auctions (Bidding Agreements) Act 1927 is one of the particulars required to be conspicuously displayed in the auction room[10].

1 *Twining v Morrice* (1788) 2 Bro C C 326; *Mason v Armitage* (1806) 13 Ves 25; *Fuller v Abrahams* (1821) 6 Moore CP 316.
2 *Mayer v Pluck* (1971) 223 Estates Gazette 33, 219.
3 *Rawlings v General Trading Co* [1921] 1 KB 635, CA; *Cohen v Roche* [1927] 1 KB 169, followed in *Harrop v Thompson* [1975] 2 All ER 94, [1975] 1 WLR 545.
4 *Pallant v Morgan* [1953] Ch 43, [1952] 2 All ER 951; *Chattock v Muller* (1878) 8 ChD 177: the successful purchaser buys for himself and the person who refrains from bidding jointly.
5 'Dealer' means a person who in the normal course of his business attends sales by auction for the purpose of purchasing goods with a view to reselling them: Auctions (Bidding Agreements) Act 1927 s 1 (2). It is submitted that the Act does not apply to sales of land by auction.
6 As to the prescribed sum see para 943 note 11 ante.
7 Auctions (Bidding Agreements) Act 1927 s 1 (1); Criminal Justice Act 1967 s 92 (1), (9), Sch 3 Pt I; Auctions (Bidding Agreements) Act 1969 s 1 (1). It was held before the passing of the Act of 1969 (which introduced trial on indictment) that the offence, being the creation of statute and not an offence at common law, was triable only as provided by the Act of 1927 and not on indictment, and that a count in an indictment which alleged a conspiracy to contravene the Act and, on the facts, amounted substantially to the statutory offence, was bad: *R v Barnett* [1951] 2 KB 425, [1951] 1 All ER 917, CCA. Since the offence is now triable on indictment it would seem that a charge of conspiracy to contravene the Act will now lie.
8 Auctions (Bidding Agreements) Act 1927 s 1 (3).
9 Ibid s 1 (1) proviso.
10 Ibid s 3, requiring the Auctioneers Act 1845 (para 939 ante) to have such effect.

945. Convicted persons not to attend auctions. On a conviction under the Auctions (Bidding Agreements) Act 1927[1] the court may order that the person convicted, or that person and any representative of him, must not, on a summary conviction, for a period of not more than a year or, in the case of a conviction on indictment, not more than three years, enter upon any premises where goods intended for sale by auction are on display, or attend or participate in any way in any sale by auction, without leave of the court[2].

In any proceedings against a person in respect of a contravention of such an order by entering upon premises, it is a defence to prove that he did not know, and had no reason to suspect, that goods intended for auction were on display there[3]. Where the proceedings are in respect of a contravention of such an order consisting in a person having done something as the representative of another, it is a defence for him to prove that he did not know, and had no reason to suspect, that the other was the subject of such an order[4]. A person is not guilty of an offence of contravening such an order by reason only of his selling property by auction or causing it to be so sold[5]. A copy of the Auctions (Bidding Agreements) Act 1969 is one of the particulars to be conspicuously displayed in the auction room[6].

1 Ie a conviction under the Auctions (Bidding Agreements) Act 1927 s 1 (1); see para 944 ante.
2 Auctions (Bidding Agreements) Act 1969 s 2 (1). Contravention of an order is punishable on summary conviction by a fine of not more than the prescribed sum, and on conviction on indictment by imprisonment up to two years or by a fine or both: s 2 (2) (amended by virtue of the Magistrates' Courts Act 1970 s 32 (7)). As to the prescribed sum (presently £2,000) see para 943 note 11 ante.
3 Auctions (Bidding Agreements) Act 1969 s 2 (3).
4 Ibid s 2 (3).
5 Ibid s 2 (4).
6 Ibid s 4, which provides that the reference to the Act in the Auctions (Bidding Agreements) Act 1927 includes a reference to the 1969 Act. See para 944 ante.

946. Seller's right to avoid contract. Where goods are purchased at an auction by a person who has entered into an agreement[1] with another or others that the other or the others, or some of them, shall abstain from bidding for the goods, and he or the other party, or one of the other parties, to the agreement is a dealer[2], the seller may avoid the contract under which the goods are purchased[3].

Where a contract is avoided by virtue of this provision, then, if the purchaser has obtained possession of the goods and restitution thereof is not made, the persons who were parties to the agreement[4] are jointly and severally liable to make good to the vendor any loss he sustained by reason of the operation of the agreement[5].

1 This does not include an agreement to purchase the goods bona fide on a joint account.
2 For the meaning of 'dealer' see para 944 note 5 ante.
3 Auctions (Bidding Agreements) Act 1969 s 3 (1), (5).
4 Ie the agreement that one or some of them should abstain from bidding for the goods the subject of the contract.
5 Auctions (Bidding Agreements) Act 1969 s 3 (2).

947. Withdrawal of property. Before the completion of the sale the vendor may withdraw the property from the auction, provided that the sale is subject to a reserve which has not been reached[1].

Where the sale is not subject to a reserve price and the property has been withdrawn during the auction, it has been suggested that the vendor or the auctioneer, if the latter has not disclosed his principal, is liable to an action for damages by the highest bidder on an implied undertaking that the sale shall be without reserve, but the point is not free from doubt[2].

1 *McManus v Fortescue* [1907] 2 KB 1, CA.
2 See para 908 ante. The view that an action will lie for breach of such implied undertaking is supported by the judgment of the majority of the Exchequer Chamber in *Warlow v Harrison* (1859) 1 E & E 309. See also, for dicta somewhat in favour of this view, *Harris v Nickerson* (1873) LR 8 QB 286 at 288 and *Johnston v Boyes* [1899] 2 Ch 73 at 77. The ratio decidendi in *Fenwick v Macdonald, Fraser & Co Ltd* (1904) 6 F 850, namely that, since the bidder has a right to retract his bid until the completion of the sale, there can be no complete contract, and therefore neither the vendor nor the purchaser is bound until that time, is countered by the analysis that there is a separate collateral contract. That contract comprises an offer by the auctioneer to sell to the person who makes himself the highest bona fide bidder and an acceptance by that performance. This latter view is founded on the assumption that the case is indistinguishable from such cases as *Denton v Great Northern Rly Co* (1856) 5 E & B 860; see judgment in *Warlow v Harrison* supra; *Williams v Carwardine* (1833) 4 B & Ad 621 (see *Re Agra and Masterman's Bank, ex p Asiatic Banking Corpn* (1867) 2 Ch App 391); and *Carlill v Carbolic Smoke Ball Co* [1893] 1 QB 256, CA (see *Johnston v Boyes* supra), where an offer addressed to a number of persons was held to give contractual rights to any one of those persons complying with the conditions of the offer.

(2) THE DEPOSIT

948. Auctioneer as stakeholder. In the absence of special agreement[1], the auctioneer receives the deposit as stakeholder for the vendor and the purchaser[2], and it is his duty to hold it until the completion or rescission of the contract, and to pay it to the party ultimately entitled[3].

If the auctioneer pays the money prematurely to either vendor[4] or purchaser, and it turns out that the person paid was not entitled to it, the auctioneer is liable to make good the money to the party to the contract eventually held to be entitled[5].

Where the purchaser is entitled to the return of the deposit, the auctioneer can set up the purchaser's right to the money in answer to any claim to it made by the vendor[6].

An auctioneer may exercise his lien for his charges and disbursements against the deposit where the sale goes off by reason of the purchaser's default, or against the vendor, where the sale is completed and the deposit becomes part of the purchase price[7]. If, however, the incumbrances are greater than the purchase price or, where the vendor has become bankrupt, the balance of it, the auctioneer can be in no better position than the vendor, and cannot enforce his lien against the deposit[8]. Where the vendor charges the proceeds of sale to the purchaser subsequently to the sale the lien will take priority[9].

The auctioneer should be ready to account for the deposit[10], but he is not liable to invest the deposit so as to be accountable for interest on it for the period during which he rightfully holds it as stakeholder, nor until demand for repayment has been made by some person entitled to receive it[11]. If the auctioneer as stakeholder does invest the deposit there are dicta suggesting that he is entitled to keep the interest[12].

1 In land sales the contract normally will have an express provision that the auctioneer is to hold the deposit as stakeholder: see the National Conditions of Sale and the Law Society's Conditions of Sale.
2 *Harington v Hoggart* (1830) 1 B & Ad 577. See *Edwards v Hodding* (1814) 5 Taunt 815, where it was held that a solicitor who was also the auctioneer received the purchase money as auctioneer and not as solicitor and agent for the vendor. As to the receipt of a cheque by the auctioneer in payment of the deposit, see paras 909 ante, 949 post.
3 *Gray v Gutteridge* (1828) 1 Man & Ry KB 614; *Yates v Farebrother* (1819) 4 Madd 239; *Edwards v Hodding* (1814) 5 Taunt 815; *Burrough v Skinner* (1770) 5 Burr 2639; *Furtado v Lumley* (1890) 54 JP 407; *Spurrier v Elderton* (1803) 5 Esp 1; *Spittle v Lavender* (1821) 2 Brod & Bing 452; *Berry v Young* (1788) 2 Esp 640n; *Stevens v Legh* (1853) 22 LTOS 84. It has been decided that the auctioneer may pay over to the vendor even when the latter is in insolvent circumstances (*White v Bartlett* (1832) 9 Bing 378); see the Insolvency Act 1986 for provisions relating to insolvency.
4 For a form of indemnity in such a case see 3 Forms & Precedents (5th Edn) 405, Form 14.
5 *Burrough v Skinner* (1770) 5 Burr 2639; *Furtado v Lumley* (1890) 54 JP 407; *Edwards v Hodding* (1814) 5 Taunt 815.
6 *Stevens v Legh* (1853) 22 LTOS 84; *Murray v Mann* (1848) 2 Exch 538. See also para 912 ante.
7 *Skinner v Trustee of the Property of Reed (a Bankrupt)* [1967] Ch 1194 at 1200, [1967] 2 All ER 1286 at 1289 per Cross J.
8 See note 7 supra.
9 *Webb v Smith* (1885) 30 ChD 192, CA.
10 *Brown v Staton* (1816) 2 Chit 353; *Crosskey v Mills* (1834) 1 Cr M & R 298.
11 *Lee v Munn* (1817) 8 Taunt 45; *Harington v Hoggart* (1830) 1 B & Ad 577; *Gaby v Driver* (1828) 2 Y & J 549.
12 *Potters (a firm) v Loppert* [1973] Ch 399 at 414–415, [1973] 1 All ER 658 at 669 per Pennycuick V-C; contrast *Burt v Claude Cousins & Co Ltd* [1971] 2 QB 426 [1971] 2 All ER 611, CA. The view in the former case is preferred since it maintains the distinction between the position of one who takes as stakeholder and one who is an agent.

949. Loss of deposit. Where the deposit is lost either by infraction of the auctioneer or otherwise (for example, his insolvency) it would seem that the loss falls on the vendor rather than the purchaser[1]. Whilst, in principle this seems to treat the auctioneer as though he were the vendor's agent, the rationale seems to be that it is the vendor who selects the auctioneer to be the stakeholder and must take the risk of loss occasioned by his lack of honesty or financial stability.

1 The authorities are mainly fairly ancient and are not entirely compelling: *Fenton v Browne* (1807) 14 Ves 144 (but there the auctioneer clearly held the deposit as agent of the vendor, and where, as will be the case absent specific provision, he holds it as stakeholder the position should be that risk should fall on whichever party ultimately becomes entitled to it; see para 948 ante); *Smith v Jackson and Lloyd* (1816) 1 Madd 618 (vendor treated as having the benefit of the stake because it was part payment and he could require investment of it: the first rationale is not convincing, where, as here, completion did not take place and the second justification is, it is submitted, wrong; see para 948 ante); *Rowe v May* (1854) 18 Beav 613 (but there the auctioneer seems to have been treated as agent of the vendor rather than the stakeholder: see per Lord Romilly MR at 616–617).

(3) AUCTIONEER'S LIABILITIES TO PURCHASER

950. Liability on contract. Where an auctioneer sells for an undisclosed principal, he is personally liable on the contract[1]. Where an auctioneer discloses the fact that he is selling as an agent, but does not name his principal, he is personally liable on the contract unless a contrary intention appears, the presumption being that the purchaser is only willing to contract with the unknown man if the auctioneer makes himself personally liable. This presumption does not, however, arise in the case of the sale of a specific chattel which the purchaser knows is not the auctioneer's property[2].

The extent of his liability and the nature of his obligations, for example, as to warranty of title or delivery of the property sold, must in each case depend on the contract of sale and the circumstances of the case[3]. He does not, however, make himself a party to the contract of sale as does an agent acting for an undisclosed principal when he acts merely for an unidentified one[4] and it seems that the extent of the liability is one for non-delivery[5]. The duty to deliver is the other side of the coin that gives the auctioneer the right to sue for the price[6].

Contracts for the sale or other disposition of an interest in land made at public auction are now both valid and enforceable on the fall of the hammer without writing or evidence in writing[7]. It is possible to provide that that contract be only one to enter into a written agreement of sale (that is, to restrict it to an agreement to sell and not of sale). In such circumstances the auctioneer might be empowered to sign the second, written contract of sale on behalf of the vendor[8] and it is possible for the auctioneer to sign in such a way that he attracts personal liability on the contract[9].

1 *Hanson v Roberdeau* (1792) Peake 120; *Franklyn v Lamond* (1847) 4 CB 637; *Evans v Evans* (1835) 3 Ad & El 132; see also *Page v Sully* (1918) 63 Sol Jo 55. Whilst this may be regarded as axiomatic since the purchaser is unaware of the fact of the agency, there have been dicta to the contrary on the basis that an auctioneer can only sell another's property: see eg *Mainprice v Westley* (1865) 6 B & S 420 at 429 per Blackburn J. That view is clearly erroneous, for an auctioneer can sell his own property: *Flint v Woodin* (1852) 9 Hare 618.
2 *Benton v Campbell, Parker & Co* [1925] 2 KB 410 at 414–415 per Salter J. There are dicta in *Mainprice v Westley* (1865) 6 B & S 420 suggesting that the auctioneer may escape liability by contracting merely as agent without disclosing his principal's name.
3 *Wood v Baxter* (1883) 49 LT 45; *Payne v Elsden* (1900) 17 TLR 161; *Salter v Woollams* (1841) 2 Man & G 650.
4 *Wood v Baxter* (1883) 49 LT 45.
5 *Wood v Baxter* (1883) 49 LT 45; and see also *Hanson v Roberdeau* (1792) Peake 120 and *Franklyn v Lamond* (1847) 4 CB 637 where failure to deliver was, in each case, the complaint. *Benton v Campbell, Parker & Co* [1925] 2 KB 410 establishes that the auctioneer does not give any warranty as to title, save that he knows of no defect in that of the vendor; and see *Rainbow v Howkins* [1904] 2 KB 322 at 325, DC, preferring *Woolfe v Horne* (1877) 2 QBD 355 to *Mainprice v Westley* (1865) 6 B & S 420 ('We are of opinion, on the authority of *Woolfe v Horne*, which is a more recent decision than *Mainprice v Westley*, . . that an action for wrongful refusal to deliver a chattel sold at public auction may in some circumstances successfully be brought against the auctioneer, although the principal's name is disclosed to the buyer at the time of the sale'). The court did not define the circumstances, and it is only possible to state the proposition in the form in the text.
6 *Benton v Campbell, Parker & Co* [1925] 2 KB 410. See para 955 post.
7 See para 906 note 3 ante.
8 As now permitted by the Law of Property (Miscellaneous Provisions) Act 1989 s 2 (3). The power previously was only to sign the evidentiary memorandum under the Law of Property Act 1925 s 40 (repealed).
9 See *Fisher v Marsh* (1865) 6 B & S 411. This statutory power enabling contracts for the sale of land to be signed by agents is novel and it remains to be seen what the ambit of such a liability might be.

951. Auctioneer joined as defendant. If the auctioneer is made a defendant to an action by the purchaser for specific performance or rescission, he will in general be dismissed from the action on paying the balance of the deposit into court after deducting his charges; but he will not be so dismissed if relief is claimed against him personally on some ground, such as his misconduct at the auction[1].

1 *Heatley v Newton* (1881) 19 ChD 326, CA, where the allegations involved fraud so that payment into court of the deposit did not discharge the auctioneer. See also *Annesley v Muggridge* (1816) 1 Madd 593; *Yates v Farebrother* (1819) 4 Madd 239, both cases involving suits by vendors for the deposit but the principles apply equally to claims by the purchaser. In *Earl of Egmont v Smith* (1877) 6 ChD 469 it was suggested that if the deposit was small, the defendant should be joined only if he does not pay the sum into court.

952. Breach of warranty of authority and fraud. Where an auctioneer sells property without or in excess of his authority, he is, like other agents, liable to the purchaser for breach of warranty of authority[1]. Where the auctioneer sells goods of which his principal is not the true owner a liability in conversion will arise and if the purchaser finds himself sued by the true owner he may in turn seek to recover from the auctioneer. The auctioneer will only be liable for breach of warranty as to his vendor's title if he has expressly warranted it[2].

The purchaser is entitled to sue the auctioneer personally for any fraud to which the auctioneer is privy[3].

1 *Anderson v John Croall & Sons Ltd* (1904) 6 F 153. See also *Fay v Miller, Wilkins & Co* [1941] Ch 360, [1941] 2 All ER 18, CA. In this case (see para 908 ante) the auctioneers were liable to the purchaser for breach of warranty of authority in knocking the property down below the reserve because they took the further step of signing the then required memorandum in writing on his behalf. This was said to waive the conditional nature of the bid and its acceptance. Now that the memorandum is no longer required and both land and chattel sales are effected at the fall of the hammer the position would seem to be the same in both types of sale; namely that purporting to sell under a reserve when the purchaser is on notice either of the existence of one or of the right of the vendor to fix one, will not give rise to liability on the part of the auctioneer for breach of warranty of authority. As to warranty of an agent's authority see AGENCY vol 1 (2) (Reissue) paras 172, 173.
2 See generally para 926 ante.
3 *Heatley v Newton* (1881) 19 ChD 326, CA.

953. Liability as bailee. Normally specific goods are sold at auction. In such sales property in the goods will, unless a contrary intention appears, pass to the buyer on the fall of the hammer[1]. Thereafter, the goods will belong to the purchaser. If, as is sometimes provided by the auction conditions, the purchaser is entitled to a certain time to collect the goods, in the interim the auctioneer will hold them as bailee for him. He will then be under a duty to take reasonable care of them[2]. If the property and risk in the goods does not pass to the purchaser until, say, he has paid for and collected them there will be no such liability on the part of the auctioneer to the purchaser but he will remain bailee for the vendor, whose goods they still are.

1 Sale of Goods Act 1979 s 18 r 1. See *Dennant v Skinner and Collom* [1948] 2 KB 164, [1948] 2 All ER 29.
2 The auctioneer's duty is not that of a bailee for reward, as to which see BAILMENT para 1838 post.

954. Liability for misrepresentations. Whilst the auctioneer will not incur personal civil liability to the purchaser for misrepresentations under the Misrepresentation Act 1967[1] there seems no reason in principle why he should not, in appropriate circumstances, be liable in tort to the purchaser for deceit[2], negligent misstatement[3] or contractually on a collateral warranty where he induces the formation of the contract of sale by making a false representation[4].

1 *Resolute Maritime Inc v Nippon Kaiji Kyokai, The Skopas* [1983] 2 All ER 1, [1983] 1 WLR 857; see MISREPRESENTATION.
2 *Derry v Peek* (1889) 14 App Cas 337, 58 LJ Ch 864, HL; see MISREPRESENTATION.
3 Under *Hedley Byrne & Co Ltd v Heller & Partners Ltd* [1964] AC 465, [1963] 2 All ER 575, HL; see MISREPRESENTATION; NEGLIGENCE.
4 See *Andrews v Hopkinson* [1957] 1 QB 229, [1956] 3 All ER 422; and CONTRACT.

(4) AUCTIONEER'S RIGHTS AGAINST PURCHASER

955. When auctioneer may sue in own name. An auctioneer may, by reason of his lien on or special property in goods, maintain an action[1] in his own name for the price of goods sold and delivered by him[2]. This is so even where he sells and delivers as agent for a disclosed principal[3], but this right does not extend, in the absence of special contract, to suing for the purchase money of land if he sells as agent for a disclosed principal[4], or for the use and occupation of land let by him by auction[5].

There are dicta which suggest that the right to sue, apart from those cases where the auctioneer sues on a quite separate contract, is dependant on the continued existence of the lien[6]. However, it is suggested that the better view is that it arises out of the lien but does not depend on continued possession; where, as is often the case, the auctioneer wishes to sue just because he has parted with the possession, which is the basis of the lien, he sues on an implied contract arising out of the delivery without payment[7].

Where the auctioneer is suing on his own account and not merely for the principal, as where he has already accounted for the sale price to him, he will be unaffected by any set-off which the purchaser may have against the vendor[8]. If the auctioneer can be taken to have assented to such a settlement or had notice not to account to the vendor he may be disentitled to recover from the purchaser[9]. He will also be unable to recover if it has been agreed that the price should be satisfied otherwise than by payment[10].

Once, however, the auctioneer has been paid his fees and charges he cannot recover in circumstances where there is a set-off, since he is then merely suing for his principal[11]. Where the goods sold are not the property of the vendor, and are claimed by the true owner before payment by the purchaser, the auctioneer cannot maintain an action for the price even though the purchaser has taken away the goods under an express promise to pay[12].

1 For forms in actions by auctioneers see 6 Court Forms (2nd Edn) (1989 Issue) 179–190, 209–211, Forms 16, 49–52.
2 *Williams v Millington* (1788) 1 Hy Bl 81. See also *Benton v Campbell, Parker & Co Ltd* [1925] 2 KB 410 at 416 per Salter J: 'The auctioneer sues for the price by virtue of his special property and his lien, and also, in most cases, by virtue of his contract with the buyer, that the price shall be paid into his hands, and not by virtue of the contract of sale'. And see *Wilson & Sons v Pike* [1949] 1 KB 176 at 182, [1948] 2 All ER 267 at 269, CA, per Tucker LJ. For a statement of claim, see 6 Court Forms (2nd Edn) (1985 Issue) 185, Form 9. This right to sue in his own name does not impose a duty to get in the purchase money: *Fordham v Christie Manson & Woods Ltd* (1977) 121 Sol Jo 529, 244 Estates Gazette 213. Note that the auctioneer's right extends to the whole price, not merely that necessary to cover his own charges: *Chelmsford Auctions Ltd v Poole* [1973] QB 542, [1973] 1 All ER 810, CA.

3 *Williams v Millington* (1788) 1 Hy Bl 81. See *Freeman v Farrow* (1886) 2 TLR 547, where an auctioneer was held entitled to sue even where the sale was effected by the owner himself on the auctioneer's premises, the contract having specifically provided therefor. But in sales outside the ring in cattle auctions the analysis is different: see *Murphy v Howlett* (1960) 176 Estates Gazette 311; and see *Mackenzie v Cormack* 1950 SC 183, where it was held that an auctioneer, although acting on behalf of a disclosed principal, could sue the purchaser for the payment of the price of the goods sold to him irrespective of whether the sale was conducted in the auction room or on the vendor's premises. See also *Cleave v Moore* (1857) 28 LTOS 255; *Hodgens v Keon* [1894] 2 IR 657, where an auctioneer who had taken an IOU in respect of a deposit on the sale of land was allowed to sue the purchaser; but the ratio decidendi was that by so doing the auctioneer had in fact advanced the money to the purchaser. See also *Robinson, Fisher and Harding v Behar* [1927] 1 KB 513. In this situation the auctioneer's rights to sue are unaffected by factors vitiating the contract of sale: *Hindle v Brown* (1907) 98 LT 44; affd (1908) 98 LT 791, CA. Where a purchaser fails to pay the deposit as required by the conditions of sale, the auctioneer may put up the property for sale again and the purchaser will be denied specific performance: *Morrow v Carty* [1957] NI 174.
4 *Cherry v Anderson* (1876) IR 10 CL 204.
5 *Evans v Evans* (1835) 3 Ad & El 132; *Fisher v Marsh* (1865) 6 B & S 411.
6 *Coppin v Walker* (1816) 7 Taunt 237.
7 *Coppin v Craig* (1816) 7 Taunt 243. *Coppin v Walker* (1816) 7 Taunt 237 can be explained on the basis that the auctioneer's actions negatived any such implication of a contract.
8 *Robinson v Rutter* (1855) 4 E & B 954; *Manley & Sons Ltd v Berkett* [1912] 2 KB 329.
9 *Grice v Kenrick* (1870) LR 5 QB 340.
10 *Bartlett v Purnell* (1836) 4 Ad & El 792.
11 *Holmes v Tutton* (1855) 5 E & B 65; *Manley & Sons Ltd v Berkett* [1912] 2 KB 329.
12 *Dickenson v Naul* (1833) 4 B & Ad 638.

(5) SALES OF GOODS GIVING RISE TO CRIMINAL SANCTIONS

956. Misdescribed goods. An auctioneer, no less than anyone else who in the course of a trade or business applies a false trade description to any goods or supplies or offers to supply any goods to which such a description is applied, commits a criminal offence[1].

It is possible to attempt to disclaim the description (as is often done with regard to odometer readings in auctions of second-hand motor cars) but to avoid liability under the Trade Descriptions Act it is necessary that such a disclaimer be as bold, precise and compelling as the description itself and brought to the notice of any person to whom the goods may be supplied[2]. Disclaimers which take the form of an assurance that all care is taken to describe a lot accurately, commonplace in art sales where questions of attribution may be crucial, may be effective but the assurance may itself give rise to criminal sanctions if such care has not, in fact, been taken; it will then potentially be a false description as to services[3].

An auctioneer will be able to rely on the defences of mistake or accident if he can show, on the balance of probabilities, that his commission of the offence was due to a mistake, or reliance on information supplied to him, or the act of a third party, or accident or some other cause beyond his control and that he took all reasonable precautions and exercised all due diligence to avoid the commission of the offence[4].

1 Under the Trade Descriptions Act 1968 s 1 (1) (a), (b). See *Derbyshire County Council v Vincent* (1990) Times, 19 June. See also TRADE MARKS vol 48 para 290 et seq. As to prohibited sales generally see SALE OF GOODS vol 41 paras 654–671.
2 *Norman v Bennett* [1974] 3 All ER 351, [1974] 1 WLR 1229, DC.
3 See the Trade Descriptions Act 1968 s 14.

4 Ibid s 24. See TRADE MARKS vol 48 para 315.

957. Unhallmarked gold, silver or platinum. An auctioneer is guilty of an offence, which is one of strict liability[1], if in the course of his trade or business he applies to an unhallmarked item a description indicating that it is wholly or partly made of gold, silver or platinum, or if he supplies or offers to supply such an item to which such a description is applied[2].

Goods are unhallmarked if they do not bear the approved hallmarks and the sponsor's mark, or if they have been the subject of improper alteration[3]. Problems may be encountered particularly with imported items, especially those manufactured in countries where there exists self-regulatory hallmarking, the items being marked by the manufacturer rather than some official assay office.

1 *Chilvers v Rayner* [1984] 1 All ER 843, [1984] 1 WLR 328, DC.
2 Hallmarking Act 1973 s 1(1). See generally TRADE MARKS vol 48 para 328 et seq.
3 Ibid s 2 (4).

958. Unsafe and dangerous goods. There are numerous regulations made under statutes[1] whereby it is an offence to sell or have in one's possession for the purpose of sale a wide range of goods which are unsafe or do not conform to certain standards. Whereas the Consumer Protection Act 1961 (repealed) contained a specific exception for those, such as auctioneers, selling as agents, the later Acts do not. It is also specifically an offence to sell pharmaceuticals[2].

Auctioneers undertaking 'household clearances' need to be particularly on guard.

1 See the Consumer Protection Act 1987 ss 11, 50 (5). By virtue of the Consumer Protection Act 1987 (Commencement No 1) Order 1987, SI 1987/1680, arts 5–9, and the Interpretation Act 1978 s 17 (2) (b) all the regulations made under the Consumer Protection Act 1961 (repealed) and the Consumer Safety Act 1978 (repealed) are to have effect as if made under Consumer Protection Act 1987. See also SALE OF GOODS vol 41 para 659 et seq.
2 See the Medicines Act 1968; and MEDICINE vol 30 para 621 et seq.

959. Unroadworthy vehicles. It is a criminal offence for an auctioneer to sell or supply, or to offer to sell or supply, or to expose for sale unroadworthy vehicles[1]. The offence is not committed if the auctioneer proves that it was sold, etc for export or that he had reasonable cause to believe that it would not be used on a road in Great Britain or in that unlawful condition[2]. If such a vehicle is sold, the contract made at auction is not invalidated by any infringement of the statutory provisions[3].

The offence is punishable on summary conviction by a fine not exceeding level 5 on the standard scale[4].

1 Road Traffic Act 1988 s 75. See further SALE OF GOODS vol 41 para 670 and ROAD TRAFFIC vol 40 para 146.
2 Road Traffic Act 1988 s 75 (6).
3 Ibid s 75 (7).
4 See the Road Traffic Offenders Act 1988 s 9, Sch 2 Pt I. As to standard scale see para 938 note 4 ante. At the date at which this volume states the law, level 5 on that scale is at £2,000.

960. Wild birds, wild animals and endangered species. Except in relation to wild birds specified in the Wildlife and Countryside Act 1981[1], the sale or offering or exposing for sale of any live wild bird, or an egg or any part of such, or any dead wild bird or any part of, or anything derived from it, is an offence unless authorised under a licence by the appropriate authority[2].

The position is the same with regard to certain live or dead wild animals[3]. Endangered species are dealt with, as to restrictions upon importation and exportation, by the Endangered Species (Import and Export) Act 1976[4], which subjects their sale to a licensing system.

1 See the Wildlife and Countryside Act 1981 s 6, Sch 3 (birds which may be sold).
2 Wildlife and Countryside Act 1981 ss 6 (1), (2), 16 (4). The 'appropriate authority' for these purposes is the Secretary of State: s 16 (9) (b). A person guilty of an offence under s 6 (1), (2) is liable on summary conviction to fine not exceeding level 3 on the standard scale: s 21 (1) (b) (amended by virtue of the Criminal Justice Act 1982 s 46). As to offences committed concerning more than one bird see the Wildlife and Countryside Act 1981 s 21 (5). As to the standard scale see para 938 note 4 ante. At the date at which this volume states the law, level 3 on that scale is at £400. Commission of an offence under s 6 in relation to a bird specified in Sch 1 is punishable by a special penalty, being level 5 on the standard scale: ss 6 (4), 21 (1) (a) (as amended: see supra). At the date at which this volume states the law, level 5 on that scale is £2,000.
3 Ibid s 9 (5), Sch 5 (Sch 5 amended by virtue of the Wildlife and Countryside Act 1981 (Variation of Schedules) Orders 1988, SI 1988/288, 1989, SI 1989/906 and 1991, SI 1991/367). A person guilty of an offence under the Wildlife and Countryside Act 1981 s 9 (5) (a) is liable, subject to s 21 (5), on summary conviction to a fine not exceeding level 5 on the standard scale: s 21 (2) (amended by virtue of the Criminal Justice Act 1982 s 46). As to the standard scale see para 938 note 4 ante. At the date at which this volume states the law, level 5 on that scale is at £2,000.
4 See the Endangered Species (Import and Export) Act 1976 (amended by the Wildlife and Countryside Act 1981 s 15 (1), Sch 10 and the Endangered Species (Import and Export) Act 1976 (Modification) Orders 1982, SI 1982/1230, 1983, SI 1983/1609 and 1985, SI 1985/1502); and ANIMALS paras 241–246 ante.

961–1000. Firearms and other offensive weapons. It is an offence if by way of trade or business an auctioneer sells, exposes for sale or transfer, or has in his possession for sale, any firearm[1] or ammunition to which the Firearms Act 1968 applies[2] without being registered as a firearms dealer[3] or obtaining a permit from the chief officer of police for the area in which the auction is held and complying with the terms of the permit[4]. It is similarly an offence to sell or transfer to any person in the United Kingdom, other than a registered firearms dealer, any firearm or ammunition to which the 1968 Act applies, unless that person produces the relevant certificate authorising him to purchase or acquire it or shows that he is entitled to do so without such[5].

The criminal offences are not committed in the sale of antique firearms sold, transferred, purchased, acquired or possessed as a curiosity or ornament[6]. Firearms are regarded as antique if they are 100 years old but they may be so regarded even if they are of less age[7]. However, they will not be regarded as antique if manufactured this century and, it has been suggested, if they could still be used as a weapon of war[8].

Other offensive weapons[9] are treated separately[10]. It is an offence to sell or expose for sale such weapons, punishable on summary conviction by a term of imprisonment not exceeding six months or a fine not exceeding level 5 on the standard scale, or both[11]. There is a general exclusion for antiques, which are simply defined as weapons over 100 years old[12].

1 As to firearms generally see CRIMINAL LAW vol 11 (1) (Reissue) para 197 et seq; POLICE vol 36 para 332 et seq; TRADE AND LABOUR vol 47 para 374 et seq.
2 See the Firearms Act 1968 ss 1, 3. See also the Firearms (Amendment) Act 1988, which redefines many types of firearms. The 1988 Act creates new offences which subject auctioneers to liability for

failing to take proper care of firearms or ammunition and failing to report loss of such: s 14; see CRIMINAL LAW vol 11 (1) (Reissue) para 211.

3 Firearms Act 1968 s 3 (1).
4 Ibid s 9 (2); see para 904 ante.
5 Ibid s 3 (2), subject to s 8 (2).
6 Ibid s 58 (2). It is not a defence that one has an honest belief that the firearm is an antique if in fact or law it is not: *R v Howells* [1977] QB 614, [1977] 3 All ER 417, CA; *R v Hussain* [1981] 2 All ER 287, [1981] 1 WLR 416, CA.
7 *Richards v Curwen* [1977] 3 All ER 426, [1977] 1 WLR 747; *Bennett v Brown* (1980) 71 Cr App Rep 109, DC.
8 *Bennett v Brown* (1980) 71 Cr App Rep 109, DC.
9 See the Criminal Justice Act 1988 (Offensive Weapons) Order 1988, SI 1988/2019, art 2, Schedule; the order was made under the Criminal Justice Act 1988 s 141 (2). The list includes swordsticks and knives and a number of exotic oriental weapons. It also includes more prosaic items such as knuckledusters.
10 See the Criminal Justice Act 1988 s 141 (offensive weapons).
11 Ibid s 141 (2). As to the standard scale see para 938 note 4 ante. At the date at which this volume states the law, level 5 on that scale is at £2,000.
12 Criminal Justice Act 1988 (Offensive Weapons) Order 1988 Schedule para 2.

AVIATION

11. LIABILITIES

For aircraft of Her Majesty's forces	.	.	.	*see*	ROYAL FORCES
carriers generally .	.	.	.	.	CARRIERS
collisions at sea	.	.	.	.	SHIPPING
Crown, actions by or against	.	.	.	.	CROWN PROCEEDINGS
customs	.	.	.	.	CUSTOMS AND EXCISE
damages	.	.	.	.	CARRIERS; DAMAGES; NEGLIGENCE
fatal accidents	.	.	.	.	NEGLIGENCE
immigration	.	.	.	.	BRITISH NATIONALITY
insurance .	.	.	.	.	INSURANCE
liquor licensing	.	.	.	.	INTOXICATING LIQUOR
mails	.	.	.	.	POST OFFICE
ministers of the Crown .	.	.	.	.	CONSTITUTIONAL LAW
negligence .	.	.	.	.	NEGLIGENCE
nuisance .	.	.	.	.	NUISANCE
prize law .	.	.	.	.	PRIZE
radio	.	.	.	.	TELECOMMUNICATIONS
rating	.	.	.	.	RATING
safety regulations .	.	.	.	.	HEALTH AND SAFETY AT WORK
salvage	.	.	.	.	SHIPPING
sanitary regulations	.	.	.	.	PUBLIC HEALTH
seizure on patent claims .	.	.	.	.	PATENTS
treaties and conventions generally	.	.	.	.	FOREIGN RELATIONS LAW
wreck	.	.	.	.	SHIPPING

1. INTRODUCTION: AIR CONVENTIONS AND AIR LAW

(1) INTERNATIONAL AIR CONVENTIONS

1001. Nature of conventions. A large part of the English law relating to civil aviation is directly or indirectly derived from the provisions of conventions on international aerial navigation and cognate matters. These conventions are the outcome of agreements between numbers of sovereign states providing for the mutual and uniform regulation of air traffic and matters incidental thereto. They are, however, in the nature of multilateral treaties between states, and form part of English municipal law[1] only so far as they are incorporated therein by domestic legislation[2].

1 Cf *Republic of Italy v Hambros Bank Ltd and Gregory* [1950] Ch 314, [1950] 1 All ER 430. See further CONSTITUTIONAL LAW.

2 For the direct incorporation of the Warsaw Convention as amended at The Hague (see para 1009 post) see the Carriage by Air Act 1961; and para 1528 et seq post. For indirect incorporation see eg the Civil Aviation Act 1982 and the orders and regulations made thereunder (see paras 1025, 1026 post) giving effect to the Chicago Convention (see para 1002 post). As to international conventions see generally FOREIGN RELATIONS LAW.

1002. The Chicago Convention. At a conference held at Chicago a convention on International Civil Aviation[1] was signed on 7 December 1944 by 38 states[2]; this is known as the Chicago Convention. The convention came into force on 4 April 1947[3], and superseded the Paris Convention 1919[4] and the Havana (Pan-American) Convention 1928[5]. Its professed object is to lay down principles and make arrangements in order that international civil aviation may be developed in a safe and orderly manner and that international air transport services may be established on the basis of equality of opportunity, and may be operated soundly and economically[6].

The convention provides, however, that in case of war or national emergency its provisions do not affect the freedom of action of contracting states involved, whether as belligerents or as neutrals[7].

1 For the text of the convention see Cmd 8742; TS 8 (1953). The convention has been amended by a number of protocols and is supplemented by 18 annexes. For United Kingdom legislation giving effect to the convention see the Civil Aviation Act 1982 and the orders and regulations made thereunder (see paras 1025, 1026 post).

2 More than 160 states have ratified the Chicago Convention. As to the status of the convention and of the various protocols of amendment see Shawcross & Beaumont: Air Law (4th Edn) vol 2.

3 Ie 30 days after the deposit of the twenty-sixth instrument of ratification: see the Chicago Convention art 91 (b). The Air Navigation Act 1947 was enacted to enable the provisions of the convention to be incorporated into United Kingdom law, but was repealed and replaced by the Civil Aviation Act 1949, certain provisions of which were, in turn, replaced by provisions of the Civil Aviation Act 1968 and the Civil Aviation Act 1971; the Civil Aviation Act 1982 repealed and replaced the Civil Aviation Acts 1949 to 1971. For each state ratifying or adhering after 4 April 1947 the convention came into force on the thirtieth day after the deposit of its instrument of ratification or the receipt of its notification of adherence: Chicago Convention arts 91 (b), 92 (b).

4 Ie the Convention relating to the Regulation of Aerial Navigation, signed at Paris on 13 October 1919 (Cmd 1609): see further note 5 infra.

5 Ie the Convention on Commercial Aviation, signed at Havana on 20 February 1928 (League of Nations Treaty Series No 2963). The parties to the Chicago Convention undertook (see art 80) to denounce the Paris or Havana Conventions if they were parties to either. Contracting states also accepted the convention as abrogating all obligations and understandings between them which were inconsistent therewith, and undertook not to enter into any such obligations or understandings (art 82). Arrangements not inconsistent with the convention may be made, but these, as well as existing aeronautical agreements, must be registered with the Council of ICAO (arts 81 and 83). As to ICAO see paras 1020–1022 post.

6 See the preamble to the Chicago Convention.

7 Ibid art 89.

1003. Scope of Chicago Convention. The Chicago Convention recognises that every state has complete and exclusive sovereignty over the airspace above its territory[1]. It applies only to civil aircraft and not to state aircraft[2].

The convention lays down the conditions upon which civil aircraft are to have the right to fly over and land in the territory of other contracting states[3]; it provides for the nationality[4] and registration[5] of aircraft, and for the adoption of measures to facilitate air navigation[6]; and it lays down conditions to be fulfilled with respect to aircraft[7].

1 Chicago Convention (Cmd 8742) art 1. The territory of a state is deemed to be the land areas and territorial waters adjacent thereto under the sovereignty, suzerainty, protection or mandate of the state: art 2.

2 Ibid art 3 (a). Aircraft used in military, customs and police services are deemed to be state aircraft: art 3 (b). State aircraft may not fly over or land in the territory of another contracting state without special authorisation: art 3 (c). Although 'state aircraft' was defined in the Air Navigation Order 1949, SI 1949/349, art 71 (1) (revoked), it does not figure in the definitions of the Air Navigation Order 1989, SI 1989/2004, art 106 (1).

3 Chicago Convention arts 5–16. See further para 1004 post.

4 The Chicago Convention art 17 provides that aircraft have the nationality of the state in which they are registered; see further para 1267 post.

5 Chicago Convention arts 18–21.

6 Ibid art 23 (customs and immigration procedures); art 24 (customs duty); art 25 (aircraft in distress); art 26 (investigation of accidents); art 27 (exemption from seizure on patent claims); art 28 (air navigation facilities and standard systems).

7 Ibid arts 29–36. Provisions concern documents to be carried in aircraft (art 29); certificates of airworthiness (art 31); and licensing of personnel (art 32).

1004. Flight over territory of contracting states. Each contracting state agrees, by the terms of the Chicago Convention, that all aircraft of other contracting states, being aircraft not engaged in scheduled international air services[1], have the right, subject to the observance of the terms of the convention, to make flights into or in transit non-stop across its territory and to make stops for non-traffic purposes[2] without obtaining prior permission[3].

No scheduled international air service may be operated over or into the territory of a contracting state except with the special permission or other authorisation of that state, and in accordance with the terms of such permission or authorisation[4]. Each contracting state has the right to refuse permission to the aircraft of other contracting states to take on in its territory passengers, mail and cargo carried for remuneration or hire and destined for another point within its territory[5].

1 The convention does not define 'scheduled international air services', but the Council of ICAO (see para 1022 post) has adopted the following definition: a scheduled international air service is a series of flights that possesses all the following characteristics: (a) it passes through the airspace over the territory of more than one state: (b) it is performed by aircraft for the transport of passengers, mail or cargo for remuneration, in such a manner that each flight is open to use by members of the public; (c) it is operated, so as to serve traffic between the same two or more points, either (i) according to a published timetable or (ii) with flights so regular or frequent that they constitute a recognisable systematic series: see ICAO document 7278–C/841, part 1 (1952). As to the operation of such services see text and note 4 infra and para 1006 post.

2 'Stop for non-traffic purposes' means a landing for any purpose other than taking on or discharging passengers, cargo or mail: Chicago Convention art 96 (d); but it is clear from the context that aircraft have the right to take on or discharge passengers or goods not carried for remuneration, for art 5 provides that aircraft, if engaged in the carriage of passengers, cargo or mail for remuneration or hire on other than scheduled international air services, also have the privilege (subject to the provisions of art 7 (see the text and note 5 infra), which relates to cabotage) of taking on or discharging passengers, cargo or mail subject to the right of any state where such embarkation or discharge takes place to impose such regulations, conditions or limitations as it may consider desirable. See generally the 'Analysis of the Rights Conferred by Article 5 of the Chicago Convention', issued by ICAO (ICAO Document 7278–C/841, Pt II). As to the English law on this subject see para 1528 et seq post.

3 Chicago Convention art 5. The state overflown has, however, the right to require the aircraft to land; and each contracting state reserves the right, for reasons of safety of flight, to require aircraft desiring to proceed over regions which are inaccessible or without adequate air navigation facilities to follow prescribed routes or to obtain special permission for such flights: art 5. For the meaning of 'territory of a state' see para 1003 note 1 ante. As to the exclusion of liability for trespass see para 1684 post.

4 Chicago Convention art 6. As to possible conflicts within Europe between the rights conferred on individual states by the Chicago Convention and the liberal policies of the EEC see EUROPEAN COMMUNITIES vol 52 paras 18.239–18.244.

5 Ibid art 7. The class of traffic thus prohibited is termed 'cabotage'. For the corresponding prohibition in English law see para 1651 post. See also note 4 supra.

1005. Restriction of access to foreign aircraft. Where it appears to the Secretary of State[1] that a foreign state is contravening an international agreement relating to civil aviation to which that state and the United Kingdom are parties, by prohibiting any one or more aircraft registered in the United Kingdom from either flying over its territory or landing in it, the Secretary of State may take measures against aircraft registered in, or owned by, that state or operated under the direction of nationals of that state[2] when they have landed in the United Kingdom, save where the aircraft landed in accordance with a permission granted by the Secretary of State[3].

Thus the Secretary of State may direct the manager of an aerodrome, or the occupier of land, on which such a foreign aircraft has landed to take such measures as to prevent any person, save a constable, from gaining access to the aircraft[4]. Notwithstanding the general restriction, a person may gain access to the aircraft either for the purpose of preparing the aircraft for a flight out of the United Kingdom, or where he has the permission of a constable to do so, or he is acting in the exercise of his powers or he is a person so specified by the direction[5].

Where the Secretary of State has given such a direction, a constable or any specified person may enter any part of the aerodrome or land on which the aircraft is present and go into or onto the aircraft, if need be by force, to ensure that the direction is being complied with or to get the aircraft to be moved, if the direction so requires[6]. The aircraft may be moved to a part of the aerodrome where its presence does not interfere with the operation of the aerodrome or, if it has landed outside an aerodrome, to an aerodrome where it can be prepared for its flight out of the country[7]. A constable or a specified person may require the commander of the aircraft, or other person reasonably believed to be in possession of documents relating to the aircraft, to produce such documents, and may remove and detain the documents; these documents must be returned to the commander of the aircraft when the relevant constable or specified person is satisfied that the aircraft is being prepared for a flight out of the United Kingdom[8].

Such a direction given by the Secretary of State has effect notwithstanding any contract, enactment or rule of law; thus, no proceedings, whether civil or criminal, lie against any person in any United Kingdom court by reason of what he may or may not have done, or others on his behalf, in compliance with such a direction[9]. However, the direction does not affect any liability to pay airport charges incurred in respect of the aircraft or the right to detain and sell the aircraft for unpaid airport charges[10].

Where a person fails, without reasonable excuse, to comply with such a direction, intentionally obstructs a constable or a specified person acting in the exercise of his powers or gains access to an aircraft without lawful authority or reasonable excuse when he knew of the existence of the direction relating to the aircraft in question and did not gain access in accordance with such a direction, that person is guilty of an offence[11].

1 As to the Secretary of State see para 1032 post.
2 Aviation and Maritime Security Act 1990 s 48 (1); s 48 does not apply where the prohibition only affects Crown aircraft: s 48 (2). Steps taken by a foreign state to prevent certain aircraft from flying over, or landing in its territory are taken to prohibit them from doing so: s 48 (3).
3 Ibid s 48 (4); s 48 applies to an aircraft which has landed in the United Kingdom and is situated either at an aerodrome, or on land outside an aerodrome where it has landed or has been moved with the consent of the occupier: s 48 (4) (a)–(c).
4 Ibid s 48 (5). A person gains access to an aircraft if, and only if, he goes into or onto the aircraft, carries out any work on the aircraft or delivers anything to the aircraft or to persons on board the aircraft: s 48 (13).
5 Ibid s 48 (5) (a)–(c). The person to whom the direction is given may himself be prohibited from gaining access to the aircraft save in specified circumstances: s 48 (6).
6 Ibid s 48 (7) (a). As to offences see text and note 11 infra.
7 Ibid s 48 (7) (b).
8 Ibid s 48 (7) (c)–(d), (10).

9 Ibid s 48 (8).
10 Ibid s 48 (9). As to airport charges and the power to detain and sell an aircraft for unpaid airport charges see paras 1376–1381 post.
11 Ibid s 48 (11). The penalty for such offences is on summary conviction a fine not exceeding the statutory maximum and on conviction on indictment a fine or imprisonment for a term not exceeding two years or both: s 48 (12). The statutory maximum is the prescribed sum within the meaning of the Magistrates' Courts Act 1980 s 32, which may be amended by order under s 143 of that Act. At the date at which this volume states the law, that sum is at £2,000: s 32 (9) (amended by the Criminal Penalties etc (Increase) Order 1984, SI 1984/447). As from a day to be appointed, the prescribed sum is increased to £5,000: Criminal Justice Act 1991 s 17 (2).

1006. Scheduled international air services. The special permission or other authorisation which is required for the operation of scheduled international air services[1] may be granted by means of a bilateral treaty between the states concerned or by virtue of the adherence of the states concerned to an international agreement regarding such matters. Two such agreements already exist: the International Air Services Transit Agreement 1944 (commonly known as the 'Two Freedoms' Agreement), and the International Air Transport Agreement 1944 (commonly known as the 'Five Freedoms' Agreement), both of which were signed, the former by 32 states and the latter by 20 states, at the Chicago Conference in 1944[2].

Each of the parties to the 'Two Freedoms' Agreement, which include the United Kingdom, grants to all other parties to the agreement two freedoms of the air in respect of scheduled international air services: the privilege to fly across its territory without landing and the privilege to land for non-traffic purposes[3].

Each of the parties to the 'Five Freedoms' Agreement, to which the United Kingdom is not a party, grants to all other parties the two freedoms set out above and three further freedoms of the air in respect of scheduled services: the privilege to put down passengers, mail and cargo taken on in the territory of the state whose nationality the aircraft possesses; the privilege to take on passengers, mail and cargo destined for the territory of that same state; and the privilege to take on passengers, mail and cargo destined for the territory of any other party to the Agreement and the privilege to put down passengers, mail or cargo coming from any such territory[4].

1 As to this requirement see para 1004 ante; and for the meaning of 'scheduled international air services' see para 1004 note 1 ante.
2 The text of both agreements is set out in Cmd 6614 and that of the former also in Cmd 8742. As to the status of both agreements see Shawcross & Beaumont: Air Law (4th Edn) vol 2.
3 International Air Services Transit Agreement 1944 (Cmd 6614) art 1, s 1. Article 5 provides that 'territory' has the same meaning as in the Chicago Convention art 2: see para 1003 note 1 ante. Presumably 'stop for non-traffic purposes' has the same meaning as in the convention: see para 1004 note 2 ante. As to English law see paras 1025–1027 post.
4 International Air Transport Agreement 1944 (Cmd 6614) art 1, s 1. Article 7 provides that 'territory' has the same meaning as in the Chicago Convention art 2: see para 1003 note 1 ante.

1007. Annexes to the Chicago Convention. Each contracting state undertakes to collaborate in securing the highest practicable degree of uniformity in regulations, standards, procedures and organisation in relation to aircraft, personnel, airways and auxiliary services in all matters in which such uniformity will facilitate and improve air navigation[1]. To secure this end the International Civil Aviation Organisation (ICAO)[2], which is a body brought into being by the convention, is to adopt and amend from time to time international standards and recommended practices and procedures dealing with a variety of subjects[3], which are to be designated annexes to the convention[4].

1 Chicago Convention (Cmd 8742) art 37. See arts 12 (uniformity of regulations relating to flight and manoeuvre of aircraft), 23 (uniformity of customs and immigration procedures), and 28 (air navigation facilities and standard systems).
2 This organisation is considered in paras 1021, 1022 post.
3 Chicago Convention art 37.
4 Ibid art 54 (l). Annexes are adopted by the Council of ICAO (as to which see para 1022 post). Provisions for the adoption, amendment and coming into force of annexes are contained in the Chicago Convention art 90. Annexes do not strictly bind the contracting states: art 38 provides, in the case of any state which finds it impracticable to comply with any such international standard or deems it necessary to adopt regulations or practices differing therefrom, for notification to ICAO of the state's departure from the set rules. There are the following annexes to the convention: Annexes 1 (personnel licensing), 2 (Rules of the air), 3 (Meteorology service for international air navigation), 4 (Aeronautical charts), 5 (Units of measurement to be used in air-ground communications), 6 (Operation of aircraft), 7 (Aircraft nationality and registration marks), 8 (Airworthiness of aircraft), 9 (Facilitation), 10 (Aeronautical telecommunications), 11 (Air traffic services), 12 (Search and rescue), 13 (Aircraft accident investigation), 14 (Aerodromes), 15 (Aeronautical information services), 16 (Aircraft Noise), 17 (Security) and 18 (Safe transport of dangerous goods by air). These annexes are obtainable from HM Stationery Office, the CAA or direct from ICAO; amendments are available from ICAO on specific request by holders of annexes who order them when they are announced in the ICAO Journal. There is also a number of other important publications for air navigation services. In all cases care must be taken to ensure that the most up-to-date edition is obtained.

1008. Disputes. Disputes between contracting states as to the interpretation or application of the Chicago Convention are decided by the Council of ICAO[1], with an appeal to an ad hoc arbitral tribunal agreed by the parties or to the International Court of Justice[2].

1 As to the Council of ICAO see para 1022 post.
2 See the Chicago Convention art 84. Procedure is provided by art 85 for appointing an arbitral court where the parties to the dispute cannot agree a tribunal, and one or more of them have not accepted the Statute of the International Court of Justice.

1009. The Warsaw Convention. The Warsaw Convention[1], which was signed on 12 October 1929, is expressed to be a convention for the unification of certain rules relating to international carriage[2] by air. The convention was amended by the Hague Protocol[3], signed on 28 September 1955, by the Guatemala Protocol[4], signed on 8 March 1971 and by the Montreal Protocols, signed on 25 September 1975[5]. The Warsaw Convention, as amended[6], establishes uniform rules governing the rights, duties and liabilities of carriers and their passengers, and of consignors, carriers and consignees of cargo by air, in the case of carriage to which the convention applies[7].

The amended convention applies to such carriage even where it is performed by the state or by legally constituted public bodies[8], but by an Additional Protocol[9] to the amended convention each high contracting party[10] reserves to itself the right to declare at the time of ratification or accession that it should not apply to carriage so performed[11]. Any high contracting party may declare that the acceptance which it gives to the amended convention does not apply to all or any of its colonies or other territories subject to its sovereignty, but may subsequently accede separately in the name of such territory[12].

1 The convention was drawn up in a French text only (see Cmd 4284). The Carriage by Air Act 1932 gave effect to the provisions of the convention which was set out in Sch 1 to the Act. That Act was repealed and replaced by the Carriage by Air Act 1961, and Sch 1 to the 1961 Act contains the provisions of the Warsaw Convention, as amended by the Hague Protocol, in English and in French. The authentic trilingual (English, French and Spanish) text of the convention was published as Cmnd 4198 and the authentic quadrilingual text (English, French, Russian and Spanish) as Cmnd 7192. For a detailed consideration of the convention see paras 1528 et seq post: for a list of parties see the Carriage by Air (Parties to Convention) Order 1988, SI 1988/243, or the ICAO list (see Shawcross & Beaumont (4th Edn) vol 2); see also para 1534 note 2 post. Although the Carriage by Air Act 1961 s 2 provides that Orders in Council made from time to time may conclusively certify who are the high contracting parties to the convention, these Orders in Council are usually out of date by reference to a current list maintained by ICAO: unfortunately the ICAO list is not in any way authoritative, but it is generally regarded as accurate, in the absence of current information from the Polish government. In place of the present system, there is a case for the acceptance as conclusive evidence of a certificate of the government of the Republic of Poland as to who are, on a particular day, high contracting parties. The present system may be in breach of the United Kingdom's obligations under the convention in view of its inaccuracy. There is no apparent reason why Orders in Council should not be made more frequently, for example, every time a change is notified by the Polish government: see the Warsaw Convention art 39. In practice, problems arise rarely, but they can arise and have arisen.

2 For the meaning of 'international carriage' see para 1533 post.

3 The Hague Protocol (Cmd 9824) was drawn up in English and in French; in the case of inconsistency the French text prevails, as the Warsaw Convention was drawn up only in French.

4 The Guatemala Protocol (Cmnd 4691) was drawn up in English, French and Spanish; in case of inconsistency the French text prevails. Only ten states have ratified the Guatemala Protocol which thus has not come into force; as to Montreal Protocol No 3, which is designed to take over from the Guatemala Protocol, see paras 1605–1628 post.

5 The Montreal Protocols (Cmnd 6480–6483) were drawn up in English, French, Russian and Spanish; in case of inconsistency, the French text prevails.

6 The Carriage by Air Act 1961 gives effect to the provisions of the Warsaw Convention as amended by the Hague Protocol: see note 1 supra. For a detailed consideration of the amended convention see para 1540 et seq post.

7 See the Warsaw Convention as amended by the Hague Protocol art 1, reproduced in the Carriage by Air Act 1961 Sch 1 Pt I art 1.

8 Ibid Sch 1 Pt I art 2 (1).

9 This is appended to the text of the amended Warsaw Convention: see the Carriage by Air Act 1961 Sch 1.

10 For the meaning of 'high contracting party' see para 1534 post.

11 Canada, Chile, Congo, Cuba, Ethiopia, the Philippines and the United States of America have availed themselves of this provision: see the Carriage by Air (Parties to Convention) Order 1988, SI 1988/243, art 4, Sch 2; and para 1537 post.

12 See the Warsaw Convention art 40. This article was not amended by subsequent protocols, and although it figured in the Carriage by Air Act 1932 (repealed) it is not reproduced in the Carriage by Air Act 1961. The United Kingdom acceded to the convention for its overseas territories: at the attainment of independence the former colonies either regarded themselves as bound by the accession of the United Kingdom on their behalf or decided that their own accession would take effect either from the date of their independence or from some later date. As to the effect of the convention in overseas territories see the Carriage by Air (Parties to Convention) Order 1988, SI 1988/243, art 2 and Sch 1; and para 1529 post.

1010. The Guadalajara Convention. A convention supplementary to the Warsaw Convention was signed at Guadalajara on 18 September 1961[1]. It is a convention for the unification of certain rules relating to international carriage by air performed by a person other than the contracting carrier[2]. The object is to give the actual carrier[3] the same protection as that to which the contracting carrier is entitled under either the Warsaw Convention, or the Warsaw Convention as amended at The Hague in 1955[4]. The United Kingdom is a party to this convention[5].

1 The convention was drawn up in English, French and Spanish (see Cmnd 1568); in case of inconsistency the French text prevails. The Carriage by Air (Supplementary Provisions) Act 1962 gives effect to the provisions of the convention, which is set out in the Schedule to the Act.
2 For the meaning of 'contracting carrier' see para 1539 note 5 post.
3 For the meaning of 'actual carrier' see para 1539 note 4 post.
4 The scope of the convention is limited either to the Warsaw Convention or to the Warsaw Convention as amended at The Hague in 1955; it does not apply to carriage by air which is not governed by either the unamended or the amended Warsaw Convention. See further paras 1539, 1543 post.
5 For a list of the parties to the Guadalajara Convention see Shawcross & Beaumont (4th Edn) vol 2.

1011. International Health Regulations. The International Health Regulations[1] adopted by the XXIInd World Health Assembly at Boston on 25 July 1969 contain detailed provisions designed to prevent the spread of disease through international air navigation[2].

1 Cmnd 4650 (originally published as Cmnd 4528). The regulations were amended by the XXVIth World Health Assembly in 1973.
2 For English legislation see the Public Health Act 1936 s 143 (amended by the London Government Act 1963 s 93 (1), Sch 19 Pt II and the Public Health (Control of Disease) Act 1984 s 78, Sch 3); the Civil Aviation Act 1982 s 36 (amended by the Public Health (Control of Disease) Act 1984 s 78, Sch 3); and the Public Health (Control of Disease) Act 1984 ss 13–15, 76; as well as the Public Health (Aircraft) Regulations 1979, SI 1979/1434, and the Public Health (Aircraft) (Isle of Man) Regulations 1982, SI 1982/1784. See further paras 1107, 1230, 1231 post.

1012. The Convention of Rome. As with the Convention of Rome 1933[1], the United Kingdom signed, but has not ratified, the Convention of Rome 1952[2]. The object of the 1933 convention was the unification of rules relating to damage caused by aircraft to third parties on the surface. The convention regulated the incidence of liability and the circumstances in which liability attaches, and contained provisions for the limitation of liability and for compulsory insurance. Detailed regulations as to insurance requirements were contained in the Insurance Protocol to the Convention of Rome (1933) 1938[3]. The 1952 convention is intended to replace the 1933 instrument with more workable propositions[4].

1 The convention (Cmd 5056), which was signed on 23 May 1933, has been ratified by only five signatories.
2 The 1952 convention (Cmd 8886), which was signed on 7 October 1952, has been ratified by 36 states.
3 This was signed in September 1938, but was ratified by only Brazil and Guatemala.
4 A protocol to amend the 1952 convention was signed on 23 September 1978 in Montreal; it has only been ratified by two states. For the lists of parties to the 1933, 1938, 1952 and 1978 instruments see Shawcross & Beaumont (4th Edn) vol 2.

1013. The Geneva Convention on international recognition of rights in aircraft. The United Kingdom has signed, but has not ratified[1], the Convention on the International Recognition of Rights in Aircraft, signed at Geneva on 19 June 1948[2]. Her Majesty may by Order in Council make such provision as appears to be necessary or expedient for giving effect to the convention[3].

1 Ie at the date at which this volume states the law.
2 Cmd 7510. The convention is drawn up in English, French and Spanish, each text being of equal authenticity. The convention has been in force since 3 October 1953. For a list of parties see Shawcross & Beaumont (4th Edn) vol 2.

3 Civil Aviation Act 1982 s 90. No such order has been made at the date at which this volume states the law.

1014. The Tokyo Convention. The Tokyo Convention was signed on 14 September 1963 and deals with offences and certain other acts committed on board aircraft[1]. The acts concerned are those which might or do jeopardise the safety of the aircraft or of persons or property therein or which jeopardise the good order and discipline on board the aircraft; offences against penal law are within the scope of the convention[2]. The convention regulates the powers of the aircraft commander and of states which are parties to the convention in connection with such acts and offences[3].

1 For the text of the convention, which came into force on 4 December 1969, see Cmnd 2261 and Cmnd 4230 (republication). Much of the convention was enacted in the law of the United Kingdom by the Tokyo Convention Act 1967 most provisions of which were repealed by, and re-enacted in, the Civil Aviation Act 1982; see further para 1662 post.
2 Tokyo Convention art 1: see further para 1664 post.
3 Tokyo Convention arts 5–10, 12–15: see further paras 1664–1667 post. For a list of countries which have ratified the convention see the Tokyo Convention (Certification of Countries) Order 1977, SI 1977/1258 (supplemented by SI 1978/1534). See also para 1677 note 3 post.

1015. The Hague Convention on hijacking. The Hague Convention on hijacking was signed on 16 December 1970 and is expressed to be a convention for the suppression of unlawful seizure of aircraft[1]. It defines the offence as the act committed by a person who, on board an aircraft in flight, by force or threat or any other form of intimidation, seizes or exercises control of that aircraft or attempts to perform any such act, or who is an accomplice of a person who performs or attempts to perform any such act[2]. The convention regulates the powers and duties, in connection with such an offence, of the state in which the offender is present[3].

1 The convention, which came into force on 14 October 1971, was drawn up in English, French, Russian and Spanish, each text being of equal authenticity. For the text of the convention see Cmnd 4577, and the Extradition (Hijacking) Order 1971, SI 1971/2102, Sch 1; for a list of the states which are parties to it see Schs 2, 3 (amended by SI 1982/146, SI 1985/1989, SI 1986/2012, SI 1987/2041 and SI 1988/2243 and by the Aviation Security (Anguilla) Order 1987, SI 1987/451). The Hijacking Act 1971 gave effect to the convention; the statute was repealed by, and re-enacted in, the Aviation Security Act 1982.
2 Hijacking Convention art 1. For a detailed consideration of the convention see para 1666 et seq post.
3 Hijacking Convention arts 4–12: see the Aviation Security Act 1982 and paras 1666–1672 post.

1016. Montreal Convention and Protocol. A convention for the suppression of unlawful acts against the safety of civil aviation was signed in Montreal on 23 September 1971 to deal with those offences not covered by the Tokyo and Hague Conventions[1]. The convention is concerned with acts of violence against the person which may destroy, damage or endanger the safety of, aircraft (in flight or in service) or air navigation facilities[2]. The convention was supplemented by a protocol signed in Montreal on 24 February 1988 to include in its scope such acts committed at an airport serving international civil aviation[3].

1 The convention was drawn up in the English, French, Russian and Spanish languages, each text being of equal authenticity. For the text of the convention, which came into force on 25 October

1973, see Cmnd 4822 and the Extradition (Aviation Security) Order 1991, SI 1991/1699, Sch 1; for a list of countries which have ratified the convention see Schs 2, 3. The convention was given effect in English law by the Protection of Aircraft Act 1973 which has subsequently been repealed and re-enacted in the Aviation Security Act 1982; see further paras 1665–1672 post. As to the Tokyo and Hague Conventions see respectively paras 1014 and 1015 ante.

2 Montreal Convention art 1; see further para 1664 post.

3 For the text of the protocol, which came into force on 6 August 1989, see Cm 378. The dispositions of the protocol were enacted in the law of the United Kingdom by the Aviation and Maritime Security Act 1990 which amends the Aviation Security Act 1982; see further para 1664 post.

1017. Regional conventions and agreements. A number of conventions and agreements has been signed to set up regional organisations. Some of these conventions were made under the auspices of ICAO[1], such as those establishing the various regional Civil Aviation Conferences[2]; others are the result of concerted efforts to solve specific problems at a local level, such as those relating to commercial rights[3], tariffs[4], airworthiness[5], air traffic control[6], capacity[7] or those relating to a specific region[8].

1 As to ICAO see paras 1020–1022 post.

2 Ie the European Civil Aviation Conference (ECAC), the Latin American Civil Aviation Commission (LACAC), the African Civil Aviation Commission (AFCAC) established respectively in 1954, 1973 and 1969. Among a number of functions bestowed on these organisations is to be found the drafting of conventions and agreements; see eg the role of ECAC in the Paris Agreements of 1967 and 1987; see further notes 4 and 7 infra.

3 Eg the Multilateral Agreement on commercial rights of non-scheduled air services in Europe, signed in Paris on 30 April 1956, to which the United Kingdom is a party (for text see Cmnd 1099. As to non-scheduled air services see para 1004 ante.

4 Eg the International Agreement on the procedure for the establishment of tariffs for scheduled air services, signed in Paris on 10 July 1967, to which the United Kingdom is a party (for text see Cmnd 3746) and the International Agreement on the procedure for the establishment of tariffs for intra-European scheduled air services, signed in Paris on 16 June 1987, to which the United Kingdom is not a party. As to scheduled air services see para 1006 ante.

5 Eg the Multilateral Agreement relating to certificates of airworthiness for imported aircraft, signed in Paris on 22 April 1960, to which the United Kingdom is a party (for text see Cmnd 1687). As to certificates of airworthiness see paras 1284–1294 post.

6 Eg the International Convention relating to co-operation for the safety of air navigation (Eurocontrol), signed in Brussels on 13 December 1960, to which the United Kingdom is a party; for text see Cmnd 2114. The Eurocontrol convention has been added to and amended by a number of protocols and agreements signed in Brussels in 1970, 1978 and 1981 (see Cmnds 5140, 7477 and 8662). As to Eurocontrol see para 1023 post; as to air traffic control see paras 1384–1408 post.

7 Eg the International Agreement on the sharing of capacity on intra-European scheduled air services, signed in Paris on 16 June 1987, to which the United Kingdom is not a party. As to capacity see para 1198 post.

8 Eg the Civil Aviation Council of Arab States (CACAS) created in 1965.

1018. Treaty on outer space. A treaty on the principles governing the activities of states in the exploration and use of outer space, including the moon and other celestial bodies, drawn up on the initiative of the United Nations[1], was signed at Washington, London and Moscow on 27 January 1967[2].

1 See Resolutions of the United Nations General Assembly (II) of 3 November 1947, 1884 (XVIII) of 17 October 1963, and 1962 (XVIII) of 13 December 1963.

2 For the text of the Treaty on Outer Space see Cmnd 3198. The treaty was drawn up in English, Russian, French, Spanish and Chinese, each text being of equal authenticity. The United States, United Kingdom and Union of Soviet Socialist Republics were designated as depositary governments with whom instruments of ratification and of accession are to be deposited. The treaty has

come into force upon the deposit of instruments of ratification by five governments, including the three depositary governments.

1019. Bilateral treaties. Besides the principal international aeronautical conventions already mentioned, there exist numerous bilateral treaties[1] made between independent states for regulating such matters as the mutual right of flight into and over each other's territory, and the operation of scheduled international air services between such territories[2].

 1 All aeronautical agreements existing at the date of the Chicago Convention and all arrangements subsequently made between the parties to the convention must be registered with ICAO (as to which see para 1020 post): see the Chicago Convention (Cmd 8742) arts 81 and 83. The texts of all agreements so registered are published by ICAO.
 2 See the Chicago Convention art 6; and para 1006 ante. As to possible conflicts within Europe between the provisions of individual bilateral agreements and EEC law see EUROPEAN COMMUNITIES vol 52 paras 18.239–18.244. Agreements for scheduled services entered into by the United Kingdom are usually published by HM Stationery Office as Command Papers. For a full list of bilateral agreements to which the United Kingdom is a party see Shawcross & Beaumont: Air Law (4th Edn) vol 2.

(2) INTERNATIONAL BODIES

1020. International Civil Aviation Organisation. The International Civil Aviation Organisation (ICAO) was brought into being by Part II of the Chicago Convention 1944[1]. It consists of an assembly, a council and certain subordinate bodies[2]. The aims and objects of ICAO are to develop the principles and techniques of international air navigation and to foster the planning and development of international air transport for a number of specified ends[3].

Pursuant to the Chicago Convention[4], the United Kingdom has granted to ICAO corporate capacity and immunities identical to those of foreign sovereigns[5]; similarly, diplomatic immunity is given in varying measures to the representatives of member governments and their staff, to certain high officials of the organisation and their families, and to other officials[6].

 1 Cmd 8742. The permanent seat of ICAO is Montreal: Chicago Convention art 45. An authoritative list of the countries who are at any particular time members of ICAO may be obtained from the Secretary General of ICAO at Montreal; see also Shawcross & Beaumont: Air Law (4th Edn) vol 2.
 2 Chicago Convention art 43. As to the assembly see para 1021 post; as to the council see para 1022 post; and as to subordinate bodies see para 1024 post.
 3 Chicago Convention art 44.
 4 ICAO enjoys in the territory of each contracting state such legal capacity as may be necessary for the performance of its functions, and full juridical personality is to be granted wherever compatible with the constitution and law of the state concerned: ibid art 47. Article 60 contains provisions regarding immunities and privileges.
 5 See the Diplomatic Privileges (International Civil Aviation Organisation) Order 1949, SI 1949/134, arts 1–7. That order has effect under the International Organisations Act 1968: see s 12 (5). See further FOREIGN RELATIONS LAW.
 6 Diplomatic Privileges (International Civil Aviation Organisation) Order 1949 arts 8–11 (amended by SI 1954/1465).

1021. Assembly of ICAO. The Assembly of ICAO[1] meets annually[2]. All contracting states have the right to be represented and to vote at meetings[3]; decisions are normally taken by a majority of votes[4]. The assembly's main duties are to elect the contracting states to be represented on the council[5], to examine and decide on matters referred to it by the council, and generally to deal with matters not specifically assigned to the council[6].

The Assembly has created a Legal Committee[7], a Committee on Joint Support of Air Navigation[8], a Committee on Aviation Environmental Protection[9] and a Finance Committee[10].

1 As to ICAO see para 1020 ante.
2 Chicago Convention (Cmd 8742), art 48 (a).
3 Ibid art 48 (b).
4 Ibid art 48 (c). Exceptions are made under art 93 (admission to the convention of states not members of the United Nations to be by a four-fifths vote); and by art 94 (amendments to the convention to be by a two-thirds vote).
5 As to the council see para 1022 post.
6 See the Chicago Convention art 49.
7 See ICAO Doc 7669 LC/139. The Legal Committee advises the Council (see further para 1022 post) as to the interpretation and amendment of the Chicago Convention as well as other matters of public international air law; it prepares draft conventions on civil aviation to be adopted in conferences by the greatest possible number of states.
8 See ICAO Doc 7325–C/852 (A1–7). The committee is responsible for the provision, maintenance and improvement of airports and air navigation facilities.
9 See ICAO Doc 9499. This committee is the result of the amalgamation of the Committee on Aircraft Noise and the Committee on Aircraft Engine Emissions in 1983.
10 See ICAO Doc 7325 (A1–58).

1022. Council of ICAO. The Council of ICAO[1] is a permanent body, composed of thirty-three contracting states elected by the Assembly[2]; elections take place every three years[3]. The Council elects a president who holds office for three years[4]. Voting in Council is by a majority of the members[5].

The Council has certain mandatory[6] and certain discretionary functions[7]. Among its mandatory functions are the appointment of an Air Transport Committee[8], the establishment of an Air Navigation Commission[9], the appointment of a Secretary General and other officers[10], the notification of infractions to the convention[11] and the adoption of annexes to the convention[12].

In addition the Council has power to give financial assistance to a contracting state for the purpose of improving air navigation facilities in that state and, with the consent of the state, itself to provide and maintain such facilities therein[13].

1 As to ICAO see para 1020 ante.
2 As to the Assembly see para 1021 ante.
3 Chicago Convention (Cmd 8742) art 50 (a), as amended. The membership of the Council was increased on three occasions; see the Assembly Resolutions amending art 50 (a) in 1961, 1971 and 1976: ICAO Docs 8167 (A13–P/2), 8931 (A17–A–P/7) and 9118 (A21–P/6). In electing members the Assembly must give adequate representation to certain classes of state: Chicago Convention art 50 (b).
4 Ibid art 51.
5 Ibid art 52. The adoption of annexes to the convention requires a two-thirds vote: art 90. As to annexes see para 1007 ante.
6 Chicago Convention art 54.
7 Ibid art 55.
8 Ibid art 54 (d).
9 Ibid art 54 (e). The Commission is composed of twelve persons appointed from among persons nominated by contracting states (art 56); its duties, set out in art 57, include considering, and recommending to the council for adoption, modification of annexes to the convention (as to which see para 1007 ante).
10 Chicago Convention art 54 (h).

11 Ibid art 54 (j), (k). For provisions as to disputes and default see arts 84–88.
12 Ibid art 54 (l). As to annexes see para 1007 ante.
13 See the Chicago Convention arts 68–76.

1023. Eurocontrol. A convention relating to co-operation for the safety of air navigation was signed at Brussels on 13 December 1960[1]. It establishes a European organisation for the safety of air navigation, called 'Eurocontrol'[2]. The convention was to remain in force for 20 years; it was prolonged for a further 20 years by a Protocol signed in Brussels on 12 February 1981[3].

The particular aim of Eurocontrol was to provide for the common organisation of air traffic control services in the upper air space[4]. Two organs were created for that purpose: a permanent commission for the safety of air navigation, and an air traffic services agency[5]. The commission is composed of representatives of the contracting parties[6]. Its role was to promote the adoption of measures and the installation of facilities for air navigation safety as well as an orderly and rapid flow of air traffic[7]; these tasks have remained but are only part of a general policy[8]. For the first 20 years of its existence, the agency provided air traffic services, applied the regulations in force in the territories of the contracting states and established the tariffs which Eurocontrol was entitled to collect from users[9]. Since the coming into force of the 1981 protocol prolonging the life of the 1960 convention, the agency is responsible for the performance of the tasks prescribed by the convention or entrusted to it by the commission[10].

1 The Brussels Convention (Cmnd 2114; see also the Additional Protocol of 6 July 1970 (Cmnd 5140) as amended by the Protocol of 21 November 1978 (Cmnd 7477)) was drawn up in English, French, German and Dutch; in case of inconsistency the French text prevails. The convention came into force on 1 March 1963. Belgium, Germany, France, Luxembourg, the Netherlands and the United Kingdom were the original signatories; Ireland, then Portugal and Spain, Greece and Turkey have since adhered to the convention. The Civil Aviation Act 1982 and the Civil Aviation (Eurocontrol) Act 1983 make provision in connection with the convention: see paras 1370–1375 post.
   Following the establishment of Eurocontrol, a Multilateral Agreement relating to the collection of route charges was signed in Brussels in 1970 (for text see Cmnd 4916) with the main purpose of ensuring uniformity of charges for the use of air traffic services; the agreement was signed by the original signatories to the Brussels Convention and Ireland, and acceded to by Austria, Portugal, Spain and Switzerland. See further note 3 infra.
2 Brussels Convention art 1.2.
3 For the text of the protocol see Cmnd 8662. The protocol amends as well as prolongs the life of the convention. The 1970 Multilateral Agreement relating to route charges was replaced at the same time by the 1981 Multilateral Agreement; for text see Cmnd 8662. Eurocontrol has a broader role with the co-ordination of air traffic services throughout the relevant airspace while at the same time is not directly responsible for the provision of such services unless specifically agreed with a contracting state; this revised role of Eurocontrol entails a lesser financial burden on the organisation: see the Brussels Convention arts 1.1 and 2 (amended by the 1981 Protocol).
4 See the Brussels Convention art 1 (1). This organisation is entitled to the exemptions and reliefs accorded to international organisations: see the Civil Aviation (Eurocontrol) Act 1983, s 2. It has the legal capacity of a body corporate under the municipal laws of the contracting parties: see the Civil Aviation Act 1982 Sch 4 para 1.
5 Brussels Convention art 1.2 (amended by the 1981 Protocol).
6 See the Brussels Convention art 5 (amended by the 1981 Protocol). To allow both civil and military interests to be represented, each contracting state may appoint several delegates although it will only have one vote: art 5.1 (as so amended); when negotiating the establishment and collection of charges (see art 2.1 (l) (as so amended)), the commission is enlarged to include representatives of non-member states which are parties to the Multilateral Agreement relating to route charges: art 5.2 (for the Multilateral Agreement see note 1 supra).
7 See the original art 6 of the Brussels Convention which has been amended to become the new art 2 (see note 8 infra). The commission makes recommendations and decisions and gives directives to the agency: art 6 (amended by the 1981 Protocol).

8 Brussels Convention art 2 (amended by the 1981 Protocol).
9 See the original arts 14, 17–20 and 38 of the Brussels Convention; arts 14, 20 and 38 have been
   revoked by the 1981 Protocol and the relevant provisions are now arts 15–17 (as amended by the
   1981 Protocol). As to charges payable for navigation services provided in the United Kingdom see
   para 1377 post. As to penalties and jurisdiction see para 1380, 1381 post.
10 Brussels Convention art 1.2 (amended by the 1981 Protocol).

1024. Non-governmental bodies. There is also in existence a number of private or semi-private organisations which are active in the field of international aviation of which perhaps the most important is the International Air Transport Association (IATA), an association of air transport service operators which has done much work for securing uniformity in the traffic documents and conditions of carriage applicable to transport by air[1], although it is often criticised as being monopolistic because of its fare-fixing activities. This has led to competition from charter airlines, whose own organisation is the International Air Charter Association (IACA). The Fédération Aéronautique Internationale (FAI) has done much to facilitate private international air travel and sporting flying.

1 As to IATA conditions of contract and general conditions of carriage see para 1531 post.

(3) UNITED KINGDOM LAW

1025. The legislation. To a great extent English municipal air law is regulated by statute and by statutory instruments made under statutory powers. The principal statutes include the Civil Aviation Act 1982, which confers comprehensive enabling powers for the regulation of civil aviation, and the Airports Act 1986, which deals with the regulation and use of airport facilities.

Much of the legislation gives effect in English law to international agreements: the Civil Aviation Act 1982 contains provisions for carrying out the requirements of the Chicago Convention[1]; the Carriage by Air Act 1961 enacts in the law of the United Kingdom the provisions of the Warsaw Convention as amended at The Hague in 1955[2] and the Carriage by Air and Road Act 1979 the provisions of that Convention as further amended at Montreal in 1975[3]; the Carriage by Air (Supplementary Provisions) Act 1962 gives effect to the Guadalajara Convention[4]; and the Aviation Security Act 1982 enables the rules of international agreements for the protection of civil aviation to be applied in the United Kingdom[5].

1 See the Civil Aviation Act 1982 s 60. As to the Chicago Convention see para 1002 ante.
2 As to the amended Warsaw Convention see para 1009 ante; as to international and non-international
   carriage see paras 1528–1656 post.
3 See paras 1009 ante, 1592–1628 post.
4 As to the Guadalajara Convention see paras 1010 ante, 1539 post.
5 See paras 1014–1016 ante, 1663 post.

1026. The subordinate legislation. The legislation contains provisions for subordinate legislation covering a wide range of subjects, and taking the form of Orders in Council, orders, regulations and rules. Orders in Council under these provisions are made by Her Majesty in Council, in practice upon the advice of the responsible minister, who is usually the Secretary of State for Transport[1], on whom is conferred the power to make orders, regulations and rules. In certain cases Orders in Council may confer power to make regulations[2].

Among the great and growing mass of subordinate legislation regulating civil aviation the most notable instruments are the Air Navigation Order 1989[3], the Air Navigation (General) Regulations 1981[4], the Rules of the Air Regulations 1990[5], the Civil Aviation Authority Regulations 1991[6], the Carriage by Air Acts (Application of Provisions) Order 1967[7], which, by virtue of powers contained in the Carriage by Air Act 1961 and the Carriage by Air (Supplementary Provisions) Act 1962 applies with modifications the amended Warsaw Convention and the Guadalajara Convention to various types of international and non-international carriage by air, the Civil Aviation (Investigation of Air Accidents) Regulations 1989[8], and the Air Navigation (Noise Certification) Order 1990[9].

1 As to the Secretary of State see para 1032 post.
2 See Civil Aviation Act 1982 s 102, Sch 13 Pt II, Pt III para 3 (1).
3 SI 1989/2004 (amended by SI 1990/2154 and SI 1991/1726).
4 SI 1981/57 (amended by SI 1985/528, SI 1987/2078 and SI 1989/669).
5 SI 1990/2241.
6 SI 1991/1672.
7 SI 1967/480 (amended by SI 1969/1083, SI 1979/931 and SI 1981/440).
8 SI 1989/2062.
9 SI 1990/1514.

1027. Application of common law. The legislation already referred to deals specifically with aeronautical matters. In addition it will be found that many questions arising in connection with civil aviation are wholly or partially governed by the rules of the common law or by statutes of general application. Thus, in the field of tort, the law of negligence is relevant in relation to certain classes of accident arising out of the operation of aircraft[1]; and the law of trespass and nuisance may in some cases govern the liability of aircraft owners and operators for damage caused to persons or property on the surface of the ground or water[2]. The law of contract, and in particular the general law relating to carriers, requires consideration in connection with matters arising out of the carriage of passengers or goods by air[3]. In addition, in spite of the fact that such international conventions as the Warsaw Convention[4] and the Rome Convention[5] have as their principal object the avoidance of problems involving the conflict of laws, it is nevertheless thought that such problems will arise in practice[6].

1 As to negligence generally see NEGLIGENCE.
2 See para 1689 post. As to trespass and nuisance generally see TRESPASS; NUISANCE.
3 As to the law relating to the carriage of passengers and cargo by air see paras 1528–1650 post. See also CONTRACT; CARRIERS.
4 See para 1009 ante.
5 See para 1012 ante.
6 See CONFLICT OF LAWS.

(4) TERRITORIAL SCOPE OF ENACTMENTS

1028. Extra-territorial effect of certain instruments. The question whether a particular enactment extends, as part of the law of the United Kingdom, to acts done outside the United Kingdom[1] depends in each case upon the true construction of the provision itself and of the statute or subordinate instrument as a whole[2]. The Civil Aviation Act 1982 confers express power to make subordinate instruments having extra-territorial operation, in so far as they apply to aircraft registered in the

United Kingdom, wherever the aircraft may be, or prohibit, require or regulate the doing of anything by its occupants or personnel, wherever they may be, or the doing of anything in relation to such aircraft by Commonwealth citizens or citizens of the Republic of Ireland, wherever they may be[3], or to any aircraft on or in the neighbourhood of offshore installations[4].

1 Ie outside England, Wales, Scotland and Northern Ireland.
2 The presumption is that British statutes apply only to the United Kingdom unless a contrary intention clearly appears; see *Treacy v DPP* [1971] AC 537, [1971] 1 All ER 110, HL; and STATUTES. In many sections of the Civil Aviation Act 1982, any reference to a country or territory includes, unless the context otherwise requires, reference to its territorial waters: s 106.
3 Ibid s 102, Sch 13 Pt II, Pt III para 6 (1). 'Personnel' includes for this purpose the commander or other person in charge of the aircraft and all other crew members: Sch 13 Pt III para 6 (3).
4 Ibid Sch 13 Pt III para 6 (5). For the meaning of 'offshore installation' see the Mineral Workings (Offshore Installations) Act 1971; and PETROLEUM PRODUCTION vol 35 para 1244.

(5) CROWN AND MILITARY AIRCRAFT

1029. Application of enactments to Crown aircraft. The Civil Aviation Act 1982 does not apply to aircraft belonging to or exclusively employed in the service of the Crown[1]; but certain provisions of that Act[2] and any Orders in Council, orders or regulations made thereunder may, by Order in Council, be applied with or without modification to such aircraft[3]. The Air Navigation Order 1989[4] is in fact made to apply, except where otherwise expressly stated, to all aircraft belonging to or in the service of the Crown other than military aircraft[5]. Where, however, a military aircraft is flown by a civilian pilot and is not commanded by a person acting in the course of his duty as a member of any of Her Majesty's forces, or as a member of a visiting force or international headquarters, certain provisions of the Air Navigation Order 1989 must be complied with[6].

Any regulations made for the investigation of accidents to aircraft may be made to apply to Crown aircraft[7].

1 This is the effect of the Civil Aviation Act 1982 s 101 (1) (a), which refers to the fact that ss 60–62, 73–77, 81, 87, 89, 91, 96 and 97 and Sch 13 Pt III do not, in the absence of an exercise of the power conferred by s 101, apply to these aircraft.
2 Ie those referred to in note 1 supra and those to which ibid Sch 13 Pt III para 5 applies.
3 Ibid s 101 (1) (a), (2), Sch 13 Pt III para 5. Section 76 applies to Crown aircraft by virtue of the Civil Aviation (Crown Aircraft) Order 1970, SI 1970/289 (referring to the predecessor s 40 of the Civil Aviation Act 1949).
4 SI 1989/2004.
5 See the Air Navigation Order 1989 art 103 (1)–(3). 'Military aircraft' means the naval, military or air force aircraft of any country, any aircraft being constructed for those forces under a contract entered into by the Secretary of State, and any aircraft in respect of which he has certified that the aircraft is to be treated for the purposes of the Order as a military aircraft: art 106 (1) (amended by SI 1991/1726).
6 Air Navigation Order 1989 art 103 (4). For the meaning of 'visiting force' and 'international headquarters' see para 1264 notes 11, 12 post. For the provisions which must be complied with see para 1268 note 6 post.
7 See the Civil Aviation Act (Application to Crown Aircraft) Order 1959, SI 1959/1309, art 2, which applied the provisions of the Civil Aviation Act 1949 s 10 (now re-enacted as the Civil Aviation Act 1982 s 75 (investigation of accidents)) to all Crown aircraft, both civil and military. The Civil Aviation (Investigation of Air Accidents) Regulations 1989, SI 1989/2062, appear to apply to all Crown civil aircraft (see the Civil Aviation Act (Application to Crown Aircraft) Order 1959 art 4, which refers to the predecessor regulations). See also para 1500 et seq post.

1030. Claims by and against the Crown. The law relating to civil salvage service rendered to or by aircraft[1] applies, with some exceptions[2], to salvage services rendered to or by any of Her Majesty's aircraft[3] as if rendered to or by an aircraft belonging to a private person[4].

In the case of imminent national danger or great emergency or for the purposes of warlike operations or other operations carried out in connection with the warlike activity of any person, the Secretary of State may revive certain provisions of the Crown Proceedings Act 1947 which do not otherwise apply in respect of any act or omission committed after 15 May 1987[5]. These provide that no action in tort lies against the Crown or any officer of the Crown for death or personal injury suffered by a member of the armed forces of the Crown if it was suffered in consequence of the nature or condition of any aircraft being used for the time being for the purpose of the armed forces of the Crown, provided that it is certified that the death or injury otherwise qualifies for entitlement to an award[6].

1 See para 1501 post.
2 See the Crown Proceedings Act 1947 s 8 (1), excluding the Merchant Shipping Act 1894 ss 552–554 which are applied by the Aircraft (Wreck and Salvage) Order 1938, SR & O 1938/136 (provisions as to valuation, detention and sale of salvage property by receiver and agreements as to salvage do not apply to Crown property salvaged). As to the application of wreck and salvage rules to aircraft, see para 1501 post.
3 'Her Majesty's aircraft' does not include aircraft belonging to Her Majesty otherwise than in right of her United Kingdom government: Crown Proceedings Act 1947 s 38 (2).
4 Ibid s 8.
5 Crown Proceedings (Armed Forces) Act 1987 ss 1, 2. As to the Secretary of State see para 1032 post.
6 Crown Proceedings Act 1947 s 10 (2). See further CROWN PROCEEDINGS.

2. ADMINISTRATION AND FINANCE

(1) THE CENTRAL AUTHORITY

1031. The Department of Transport. Since the advent of aircraft, a long succession of governmental or quasi-governmental bodies has been responsible for civil aviation, from the Home Office[1], the Air Ministry and the Air Council[2], the Ministry of Civil Aviation[3], the Ministry of Transport and Civil Aviation[4], the Ministry of Supply and Ministry of Aviation[5], the Board of Trade and the Ministry of Technology[6], the Department of Trade and Industry and the Ministry of Aviation Supply[7], and the Department of Trade[8] to the Department of Transport[9].

In 1971, following the recommendations of the 'Edwards Report'[10], an entirely new administrative system was set up which provided for the creation of a Civil Aviation Authority. This body corporate was made responsible for the economic, technological and operational regulation of the civil air transport industry[11].

1 See the Aerial Navigation Act 1911.
2 See the Air Navigation Acts 1919 and 1920: the Air Council was responsible for all aerial navigation, including civil aviation, until the passing of the Air Navigation Act 1936, which transferred all civil aviation functions of the Air Council to the Secretary of State for Air (see the Air Navigation Act 1936 s 23).

3 See the Ministry of Civil Aviation Act 1945 and the Civil Aviation Acts 1946 and 1949.
4 See the Transfer of Functions (Ministry of Civil Aviation) Order 1953, SI 1953/1204, which amalgamated the Ministry of Civil Aviation with the Ministry of Transport.
5 See the Minister of Aviation Order 1959, SI 1959/1768; the aviation functions of the Minister of Transport and Civil Aviation were transferred to the Minister of Supply, whose title became Minister of Aviation.
6 See the Transfer of Functions (Civil Aviation) Order 1966, SI 1966/741, and the Transfer of Functions (Civil Aviation) (No 2) Order 1966, SI 1966/1015, as well as the Ministry of Aviation (Dissolution) Order 1967, SI 1967/155.
7 See the Secretary of State for Trade and Industry Order 1970, SI 1970/1537; the Ministry of Technology became the Ministry of Aviation Supply in 1970 and was dissolved in 1971, its last functions being transferred to the Secretary of State for Defence: see the Ministry of Aviation Supply (Dissolution) Order 1971, SI 1971/719.
8 See the Secretary of State (New Departments) Order 1974, SI 1974/692, and the Ministers of the Crown Act 1975.
9 See the Transfer of Functions (Trade and Industry) Order 1983, SI 1983/1127.
10 'British Air Transport in the Seventies': Report of the Committee of Inquiry into Civil Air Transport (Cmnd 4018).
11 The Civil Aviation Authority was created by the Civil Aviation Act 1971 (now replaced by the Civil Aviation Act 1982); see further paras 1044–1062 post.

1032. Secretary of State's aviation functions. The Secretary of State for Transport[1] is charged with the general duty of organising, carrying out and encouraging measures for the development of civil aviation, for the designing, development and production of civil aircraft, for the promotion of safety and efficiency in their use, and for research into questions relating to air navigation[2].

The Secretary of State is not authorised to produce civil aircraft[3], and the acquisition and disposal by him of aircraft, aero-engines and aviation equipment is subject to Treasury approval[4].

1 As to the appointment of the Secretary of State, his parliamentary secretaries and other officers, and for ancillary provisions as to the Secretary of State see CONSTITUTIONAL LAW. As to the transfer of functions to the Secretary of State see para 1031 ante.
2 Civil Aviation Act 1982 s 1 (1).
3 Ibid s 1 (2). The Industrial Expansion Act 1968 s 12, the Rolls Royce (Purchase) Act 1971 s 1 (2) and the Concorde Aircraft Act 1973 s 1 amending the Industrial Expansion Act 1968 s 8, have, however, allowed the Secretary of State to take part in the production of civil aircraft in special circumstances.
4 Civil Aviation Act 1982 s 1 (3).

1033. Power to provide aerodromes and acquire and manage land. The Secretary of State[1] has power to establish and maintain aerodromes[2] for the purposes of civil aviation[3] and to provide and maintain roads, apparatus and buildings in connection with such aerodromes[4].

He may, for the purposes of his functions connected with civil aviation, acquire land by agreement or be authorised to acquire land compulsorily[5], and he may authorise the Civil Aviation Authority to acquire land compulsorily for any purpose in connection with the performance of its functions[6].

He has power to manage, sell, let or exchange any land vested in him[7], and to manage and, subject to the terms of the lease, to sublet land taken on lease by him, or to assign the lease[8].

He may, with Treasury approval, make grants or loans in respect of any expenses incurred or to be incurred by any person in investigating the need for, or for the expansion of, an aerodrome in any part of Great Britain, in establishing or expanding any such aerodrome, in maintaining any such aerodrome or in providing or maintaining roads, approaches, apparatus, equipment, buildings or other accommodation, and for making good any losses incurred by any person in the operation of, or in the provision of any services at, any such aerodrome[9].

1 As to the Secretary of State see para 1032 ante.
2 For the meaning of 'aerodrome' see para 1102 post.
3 The last definition of 'purposes of civil aviation' was given by the Civil Aviation Act 1949 (now repealed), which provided that 'purposes of civil aviation' included all purposes connected with air navigation except purposes of defence of the realm by air, and 'defence of the realm by air' included the air force and the administration of all matters relating to it: see s 63 (1).
4 Civil Aviation Act 1982 s 25 (1). Four aerodromes were transferred to the British Airports Authority (now BAA plc) under the Airports Authority Act 1965 s 1 (repealed) (see further para 1108 et seq post), and nine aerodromes were transferred to the Civil Aviation Authority under the Civil Aviation Act 1971 s 14 (1), Sch 2 (see further para 1114 post). As to the Secretary of State's duties in relation to aerodromes see para 1113 et seq post, and as to financial assistance by means of loans see the text to note 9 infra.
5 Civil Aviation Act 1982 s 41 (1); the Acquisition of Land Act 1981 (without Pt VI) has effect in the case of compulsory purchase of land in England and Wales: Civil Aviation Act 1982 s 41 (2); see further para 1113 post.
6 Ibid s 42 (1); see further para 1114 post.
7 Ibid s 41 (3); power to pay or receive money for equality of exchange is included. The Secretary of State's power of sale must be exercised subject, in the case of land acquired under the Defence of the Realm (Acquisition of Land) Act 1916, to the right of pre-emption given by s 5 of the 1916 Act to the original owner of the land: Civil Aviation Act 1982 s 41 (3). See further COMPULSORY ACQUISITION.
8 Ibid s 41 (4).
9 Ibid s 34 (1). Any such loan must be repaid to the Secretary of State at such times and by such methods, and, except where he made it free of interest, is subject to the payment of such interest, as he may with Treasury approval direct: s 34 (3).

1034. Other powers in relation to land. The Secretary of State[1] has power, by order, to provide for the creation of easements and other rights over land in his favour, including rights to carry out and maintain works, structures and apparatus upon any specific land[2] in order to secure that the relevant land is used safely and efficiently for the purposes of civil aviation, that appropriate services are provided in relation to that land or that civil aircraft are navigated safely and efficiently[3]; to prohibit or restrict the use of any area of land or water as a civil aerodrome so as to secure that aerodromes, either vested in him or under his control or owned or managed by the Civil Aviation Authority, are safe for the arrival and departure of aircraft[4]; and to declare any area of land to be subject to control, so that directions may be given to require, inter alia, the demolition of buildings or the cutting down of trees on the land or to extinguish private rights[5]. He may also exercise these powers where the land or relevant apparatus, structures or work are vested in Eurocontrol, the Civil Aviation Authority or the licensee of an aerodrome[6].

The Secretary of State has power to authorise the proprietors of licensed aerodromes to erect warning lights and other apparatus on buildings in the vicinity of those aerodromes[7]. In certain cases he has a supplementary power to authorise persons to enter upon land not belonging to him for the purpose of carrying out surveys[8]. He also has power by order to authorise the stopping up or diversion of highways for civil aviation purposes[9].

1 As to the Secretary of State see para 1032 ante.
2 Civil Aviation Act 1982 s 44 (2); see paras 1119–1126 post.
3 Ibid s 44 (1) (a)–(c).
4 Ibid s 45 (1); see paras 1138–1141 post.
5 Ibid s 46 (1),(2); see paras 1127–1133 post.

6 See ibid ss 44 (2), (12), 45 (1), 46 (10); and paras 1119 et seq post, 1127 et seq post, 1138 et seq post. As to Eurocontrol see para 1023 ante; as to the Civil Aviation Authority see paras 1044–1059 post; and as to the licensee of an aerodrome see para 1154 et seq post.
7 Ibid s 47 (1); see para 1203 post.
8 Ibid s 50 (1), (2); see para 1142 post.
9 Ibid s 48; see para 1134 post.

1035. Power to make byelaws. The Secretary of State[1] may make byelaws in respect of any aerodrome owned or managed by him for regulating the use and operation of the aerodrome and the conduct of all persons while within the aerodrome[2].

1 As to the Secretary of State see para 1032 ante.
2 See the Airports Act 1986 s 63 (1); and para 1237 post.

1036. Powers and duties under Orders in Council. The Secretary of State[1] is invested by the Air Navigation Order 1989 with various powers in connection with the administration and control of civil aviation. These include powers in relation to the regulation and control of all aircraft in or over the United Kingdom and territorial waters adjacent thereto[2]. He prescribes the form and manner of keeping records of flight times and duty periods[3]. He also has powers in relation to aerodromes[4] and the control of noise and vibration there[5], the detention of aircraft[6], and the cancellation, suspension and variation of permission granted to aircraft which are not registered in the United Kingdom either in respect of carriage for valuable consideration[7] or in respect of aerial photography and survey[8]. He may make regulations with regard to any matters dealt with in that order[9].

1 As to the Secretary of State see para 1032 ante.
2 See para 1264 post.
3 See para 1367 post.
4 See paras 1182, 1189 post.
5 See paras 1185–1188 post.
6 See para 1459 post.
7 See para 1651 post.
8 See para 1471 post.
9 See the Air Navigation Order 1989, SI 1989/2004, arts 47 (carriage of dangerous goods), 69 (air traffic control): see paras 1654, 1394 et seq post.

1037. Expenses defrayed by Parliament. The Secretary of State's[1] salary and expenses, including any salaries or remuneration paid to his parliamentary secretaries and to the other secretaries, officers and servants appointed by him, are defrayed out of money provided by Parliament[2].

Any contribution payable by Her Majesty's government to the expenses of the International Civil Aviation Organisation (ICAO)[3] under the Chicago Convention[4], and such expenses of any delegate or representative appointed in connection with that convention as may be approved by the Treasury, are payable out of money provided by Parliament[5]. So also are any expenses incurred by Her Majesty's government for the purpose of that part of the convention[6] which relates to the provision of airports and other air navigation facilities[7]. All sums received by Her Majesty's government in repayment of expenses relating to the provision of airports and air navigation facilities under the Chicago Convention[8] and all fees paid under an Air Navigation Order are paid into the Consolidated Fund[9].

1 As to the Secretary of State see para 1032 ante.
2 As to the salaries etc payable to the Secretary of State, his parliamentary secretaries and his officers and servants see further CONSTITUTIONAL LAW.
3 As to ICAO see para 1020 ante.
4 As to the Chicago Convention (Cmd 8742), art 61 of which provides for finance, see para 1002 ante.
5 Civil Aviation Act 1982 s 61 (7) (a), (b).
6 Ie the Chicago Convention ch XV (arts 68–76).
7 Civil Aviation Act 1982 s 61 (7) (c).
8 Ibid s 61 (8) (a); as to such repayment see the Chicago Convention art 76.
9 Civil Aviation Act 1982 s 61 (8) (b).

1038. Expenses in connection with Civil Aviation Authority. The Secretary of State[1] may make grants to the Civil Aviation Authority (CAA)[2] out of money provided by Parliament[3], and may lend to the authority sums issued by the Treasury out of the National Loans Fund[4].

1 As to the Secretary of State see para 1032 ante.
2 As to the CAA see para 1044 post.
3 Civil Aviation Act 1982 s 12 (1) (a).
4 Ibid s 12 (2)–(4). Sums received by the Secretary of State in repayment of loans must be paid into the National Loans Fund: s 12 (4). As to the fund see CONSTITUTIONAL LAW.

1039. Directions and functions in respect of international relations. After consultation with the Civil Aviation Authority (CAA)[1], the Secretary of State[2] may give the CAA directions to do a particular thing which it has power to do, or to refrain from doing a particular thing, if the Secretary of State considers it appropriate to give such directions which concern national security, any obligation, aim or wish of the United Kingdom with respect to an international organisation or an international agreement, or in connection with any matter which may affect the international relations of the United Kingdom, or in relation to the environmental issues that are noise, vibration, pollution and other disturbance attributable to aircraft[3].

In this context it should be noted that the CAA takes an active part in the framing of United Kingdom aviation policy to be pursued by British airlines at traffic conferences of IATA[4]. In such matters the CAA acts as the aeronautical authority for the United Kingdom and approves or disapproves IATA tariff resolutions, and ensures the implementation of those approved. None the less, the Secretary of State remains responsible for international relations and, where formal negotiations with foreign governments are required, provides the United Kingdom government with all necessary advice and assistance, it being recognised that the necessary expert knowledge lies with the CAA.

1 As to the CAA see para 1044 post.
2 As to the Secretary of State see para 1032 ante.
3 Civil Aviation Act 1982 s 6.
4 As to IATA see para 1024 ante.

1040. Secretary of State for Defence. Until 1982, the Secretary of State for Defence had wide powers to control civil aircraft in time of war or great national emergency[1]; these powers belong now to the Secretary of State for Transport[2]. However, some of the powers of the Secretary of State for Transport must be exercised by him in collaboration with the Secretary of State for Defence. Thus, they must act jointly in directing whether to apply the regulations relating to the investigation of an accident involving civil and military aircraft or installations[3]. Similarly, the Secretary of State for Defence acts jointly with the Secretary of State for Transport when appointing the Air Traffic Control Board[4] and with the Civil Aviation Authority in the provision of air navigation services within the National Air Traffic Services[5].

1 See the Civil Aviation Act 1949 s 9 (repealed by the Civil Aviation Act 1982 s 109 (3), Sch 16). The functions of the Minister of Aviation Supply had been transferred to the Secretary of State for Defence and the Ministry of Aviation Supply dissolved by the Ministry of Aviation Supply (Dissolution) Order 1971, SI 1971/719. For the history of the Ministry of Aviation Supply see the Minister of Aircraft Production (Transfer of Functions) Order 1940, SR & O 1940/762, and the Ministry of Aircraft Production (Dissolution) Order 1946, SR & O 1946/374; and see also the Ministry of Supply Act 1939, the Minister of Aviation Order 1959, SI 1959/1768, the Ministers of the Crown Act 1964, the Transfer of Functions (Civil Aviation) Order 1966, SI 1966/741, the Transfer of Functions (Civil Aviation) (No 2) Order 1966, SI 1966/1015, the Ministry of Aviation (Dissolution) Order 1967, SI 1967/155, the Secretary of State for Trade and Industry Order 1970, SI 1970/1537, and the Ministry of Aviation Supply (Dissolution) Order 1971, SI 1971/719. See also the Industrial Expansion Act 1968 s 12.
2 See the Civil Aviation Act 1982 ss 62, 63.
3 See the Air Navigation (Investigation of Air Accidents involving Civil and Military Aircraft or Installations) Regulations 1986, SI 1986/1953, reg 3 (1); see further para 1507 post.
4 See the Civil Aviation Authority (Air Navigation Services) Directions 1976 para 7; these directions are published as an Annex B to the White Paper 'Future Civil Aviation Policy' (Cmnd 6400) and were made under the Civil Aviation Act 1971 s 28 (2) (now the Civil Aviation Act 1982 s 72 (2)).
5 See the Civil Aviation Authority (Air Navigation Services) Directions 1976 para 3; and note 4 supra.

(2) LOCAL AUTHORITIES

1041. Provision of aerodromes. A local authority[1] may, with the consent of the Secretary of State[2] and subject to any conditions which he may impose, establish and maintain aerodromes[3], and may provide and maintain roads, equipment, buildings and other accommodation in connection therewith[4], and may provide facilities at aerodromes established or maintained by some other person under special arrangements made with that person[5]. The local authority may also, with the authorisation of the Secretary of State, carry on, in connection with the aerodrome which it maintains, any particular ancillary business which it would otherwise have no power to carry on[6].

A local authority may acquire land by agreement[7], or may be authorised by the Secretary of State to purchase land compulsorily[8]. Land, including rights in or over land adjacent to the site of an aerodrome established, or to be established, by a local authority, may be acquired for the purpose of securing that the land is not used so as to interfere with, or cause danger to, aircraft using the aerodrome[9]. These powers may be exercised by a local authority outside as well as within its area[10]. A local authority may make byelaws in respect of any aerodrome owned or managed by it[11].

1 'Local authority' means, in England and Wales, a county council, the council of a district or London borough or the Common Council of the City of London: Civil Aviation Act 1982 s 105 (1) (amended by the Local Government Act 1985 s 102 (2), Sch 17); see also the Airports Act 1986 s 12 (1), which refers to the definition given by the Local Government Act 1972 of a local authority as a county, district or London borough council, the Greater London Council (now extinct) or the Common Council of the City of London: s 179, Sch 30.

2 As to the Secretary of State see para 1032 ante.

3 For the meaning of 'aerodrome' see para 1102 post. Capital controls over local authorities' airport undertakings are provided for by the Airports Act 1986 in addition to the Local Government, Planning and Land Act 1980 ss 72, 75: see LOCAL GOVERNMENT. As to the circumstances when a local authority, known as the 'principal council', is directed by the Secretary of State to transfer its airport undertaking to a public airport company under its control, see paras 1042, 1110 post

4 Civil Aviation Act 1982 s 30 (1), (2).

5 Ibid s 30 (1) (b).

6 See ibid s 31. The power may be granted subject to such conditions as the Secretary of State may think fit: s 31 (1).

7 See ibid s 30 (4). The provisions of the Compulsory Purchase Act 1965 Pt I (ss 1–32), except ss 4–8, 10, 31, and, if the land is in Scotland, the Lands Clauses Consolidation Acts, except the provisions relating to the purchase and taking of land otherwise than by agreement, apply to such acquisition: Civil Aviation Act 1982 s 30 (8); and see the Compulsory Purchase Act 1965 s 38, Sch 6. As to the 1965 Act see COMPULSORY ACQUISITION.

8 Civil Aviation Act 1982 s 30 (4). The Acquisition of Land (Authorisation Procedure) Act 1981 applies: see the Civil Aviation Act 1982 s 30 (5). See generally COMPULSORY ACQUISITION.

9 Civil Aviation Act 1982 s 30 (6).

10 Ibid s 30 (7). As to local authorities' rights over land generally see LOCAL GOVERNMENT.

11 See the Airports Act 1986 s 63; see para 1035 ante.

1042. Public airport companies. The Secretary of State[1] may direct a local authority, known as the principal council[2], to form a company to operate as a commercial undertaking the airport which it controls[3] where the annual turnover of that airport has exceeded £1 million for at least two of the last three financial years prior to the time of the direction[4]. In pursuance of the direction, the principal council must prepare a scheme transferring all property, rights and liabilities from the controlling authority to the airport company and submit it to the Secretary of State for approval[5]. A local authority may invest in any public airport company not under its control provided the Secretary of State has consented to the operation[6].

1 As to the Secretary of State see para 1032 ante.

2 A 'principal council', in relation to England and Wales, means the council of a non-metropolitan county, of a district, or of a London borough: Airports Act 1986 s 12 (1); as to the meaning of 'local authority' see para 1041 note 1 ante.

3 Airports Act 1986 s 13; and see paras 1110–1112 post.

4 Ibid s 14; and see para 1110 post. 'Annual turnover', in relation to the business carried on at an airport by the airport operator, means the aggregate, as stated or otherwise shown in the accounts of the business, of all sums received in the course of the business during a financial year, including grants from a public or local authority but excluding capital receipts and loans made by any person: s 14 (2). 'Airport operator' means the person for the time being having the management of an airport, or in relation to a particular airport the management of that airport: s 82 (1).

5 Ibid s 15; and see para 1110 post. Sections 21 and 22 provide capital controls in relation to investments in public airport companies in addition to the Local Government, Planning and Land Act 1980 ss 72, 75; further, capital finance transactions of bodies, such as public airport companies, under local authority control are within its capital finance control: see the Local Government and Housing Act 1989 Pt IV (ss 39–66) and the Public Airport Companies (Capital Finance) Order 1990, SI 1990/719 (amended by SI 1991/423), made under s 39 of the 1989 Act (description of effects of capital financing transactions of a public airport company and its subsidiaries for the local authority in control): see generally LOCAL GOVERNMENT.

6 Airports Act 1986 s 20 (3); the consent of the Secretary of State for a local authority to invest in a public airport company does not replace the consent needed by a local authority to establish and maintain an aerodrome under the Civil Aviation Act 1982 s 30 (1) (a) (see para 1041 ante): Airports Act 1986 s 20 (4). As to investments in public airport companies see para 1112 post. As to the power for a local authority to make loans to a public airport company where the company is a subsidiary of

two or more councils (a composite authority) and the local authority is one of those councils, albeit not the majority shareholder, see *R v Bolton Borough Council, ex p Manchester City Council* (1991) Times, 19 April; and see paras 1110–1112 post.

1043. Other functions of local authorities. The duty of enforcing and executing regulations made by the Secretary of State for Health in relation to sanitary control at aerodromes falls in most cases upon local authorities[1].

The Secretary of State for Transport[2] and any other person having the management of an aerodrome are required to provide facilities for consultation with local authorities affected by that aerodrome[3]; the Secretary of State is also required to consult with the local authorities affected before making any order declaring land to be subject to control in the interests of civil aviation[4].

Local land charges and certain orders made by the Secretary of State in relation to land must be registered in the register of local land charges maintained by the local authority in whose area the land lies[5].

Local authorities are involved, as planning authorities, where any person wishes to establish, maintain or develop an aerodrome[6].

1 See the Public Health (Aircraft) Regulations 1979, SI 1979/1434, reg 4, made under the Public Health Act 1936 s 143. See also the Civil Aviation Act 1982 s 36; and para 1230 post.
2 As to the Secretary of State see para 1032 ante.
3 Civil Aviation Act 1982 ss 26 (Secretary of State) and 35 (amended by the Airports Act 1986 s 83 (5), Sch 6 Pt II) (airport manager); and see the Aerodromes (Designation) (Facilities for Consultation) Orders 1986, SI 1986/1348, and 1989, SI 1989/1489, made under the Civil Aviation Act 1982 s 35; see para 1179 post.
4 Civil Aviation Act 1982 s 46 (5); see para 1130 post.
5 See ibid s 55 (1); and para 1151 post.
6 See the Town and Country Planning Act 1990; see generally LOCAL GOVERNMENT; TOWN AND COUNTRY PLANNING.

(3) THE CIVIL AVIATION AUTHORITY

(i) Constitution and Functions

1044. Constitution. The Civil Aviation Authority (CAA) consists of six to sixteen members including the chairman and one or two deputy chairmen, all of whom are appointed by the Secretary of State[1]. Appointment and tenure of office, remuneration[2], meetings and proceedings are regulated by statute[3].

The CAA is a body corporate[4]. It is not regarded as the servant or agent of the Crown or as enjoying any status, privilege or immunity of the Crown, and it is not exempt from any tax, duty, rate, levy or any other charge; its property is not regarded as property of, or held on behalf of, the Crown[5]. The CAA is a tribunal under the supervision of the Council on Tribunals[6].

1 Civil Aviation Act 1982 s 2 (2) (amended by the Airports Act 1986 s 72). As to the Secretary of State see para 1032 ante.
2 Remuneration is determined by the Secretary of State with the consent of the Treasury: Civil Aviation Act 1982 s 2 (3), Sch 1 para 6.
3 Ibid Sch 1 paras 9–11.
4 Ibid s 2 (1).
5 Ibid s 2 (4). But the authority must act on behalf of the Crown when performing functions under an Air Navigation Order which falls to be performed by the Crown in pursuance of the Chicago

Convention or under an Order in Council when such functions appear to Her Majesty to relate to the exercise of powers or the discharge of obligations of the United Kingdom under an international agreement: s 20 (2).

6 The Tribunals and Inquiries Act 1971 has effect as if for the purposes of certain of its functions the CAA were a tribunal specified in Sch 1 Pt I of the Act but s 8 (under which certain consents are required for the removal of members) does not apply: Civil Aviation Act 1982 s 7 (3); see ADMINISTRATIVE LAW. The functions concerned are those prescribed for the purposes of the Civil Aviation Act 1982 s 7 (2), which include functions under Air Navigation Orders and functions concerning air transport licensing and air travel organisers' licences: see the Civil Aviation Authority Regulations 1991, SI 1991/1672, and the Civil Aviation (Air Travel Organisers' Licensing) Regulations 1972, SI 1972/223, made under the Civil Aviation Act 1971 s 26 (now replaced by the Civil Aviation Act 1982 s 71). Regulations made under s 7 (2) of the 1982 Act may make provision for withholding information furnished to the CAA and for imposing, on summary conviction for any contravention of the regulations, a fine not exceeding level 3 on the standard scale: Civil Aviation Act 1982 s 7 (2) (a), (b) (amended by virtue of the Criminal Justice Act 1982 ss 40, 46).

In any enactment contained in an Act passed either before or after the Criminal Justice Act 1982 'the standard scale' has the meaning given by s 37: s 75 (a). A standard scale of fines for summary offences was introduced by the Criminal Justice Act 1982 s 37 (1). Where any enactment contained in an Act passed either before or after that Act provides (1) that a person convicted of a summary offence is liable on conviction to a fine or a maximum fine by reference to a specified level on the standard scale, or (2) confers power by subordinate instrument to make a person liable on conviction of a summary offence, whether or not created by the instrument, to a fine or a maximum fine by reference to a specified level on the standard scale, it is to be construed as referring to the standard scale for which s 37 provides as that scale has effect from time to time by virtue either of that section or of an order under the Magistrates' Courts Act 1980 s 143: Criminal Justice Act 1982 s 37 (3). In relation to Acts passed before the Criminal Justice Act 1982, this provision applies where references to the standard scale are substituted by s 46 as read with s 38 or s 40. At the date at which this volume states the law, the standard scale is as follows, in relation to offences committed after 1 May 1984: level 1, £50; level 2, £100; level 3, £400; level 4, £1,000; level 5, £2,000: s 37 (2) (amended by the Criminal Penalties etc (Increase) Order 1984, SI 1984/447, art 2 (4), Sch 4). As from a day to be appointed, the fines are increased as follows: level 1, £200; level 2, £500; level 3, £1,000; level 4, £2,500; level 5, £5,000: Criminal Justice Act 1991 s 17 (1).

1045. General powers and functions. The CAA has power to provide for the licensing of air transport and the licensing of the provision of accommodation in aircraft, for air navigation services, for the operation of aerodromes and for assistance and information generally[1]. The CAA has the duty to regulate the use of airports and to ensure their economic viability[2]. The CAA's functions also concern the registration of aircraft, the safety of air navigation and aircraft (including airworthiness), the control of air traffic, the certification of operators of aircraft, and the licensing of aircrews and aerodromes[3]. The CAA appoints the members and designates the chairman of the Airworthiness Requirements Board[4].

Other general functions are conferred on the CAA by the Civil Aviation Act 1982 and may be conferred on it by other enactments[5]. It may do anything which is calculated to facilitate or is conducive or incidental to the performance of its functions, and for the same purpose may do elsewhere than in the United Kingdom such things as it considers appropriate[6].

Although the CAA may delegate a great number of its functions[7], certain prescribed functions may not be performed on its behalf by any other person[8].

1 Civil Aviation Act 1982 s 3 (b). These functions are conferred on the CAA by or under Pt II (ss 25–59). As to licensing see paras 1066–1101 post; as to air navigation services see paras 1370–1381 post; as to aerodromes see paras 1102 et seq post.
2 Airports Act 1986 Pts III, IV (ss 29 –56); see paras 1156 et seq post.
3 Civil Aviation Act 1982 s 3 (c). These functions are conferred on the CAA by or under Air Navigation Orders. As to aircraft registration see paras 1276–1283 post; as to certification and safety

see paras 1284–1331 post; as to air traffic control see paras 1394–1408 post; as to aircraft operators and crew see paras 1340–1369 post; as to the licensing of aerodromes see paras 1154, 1155 post.

4 Ibid s 85 (3); see para 1060 post.

5 Ibid s 3 (a), (d).

6 See ibid s 20 (1). However, these wide powers are limited in matters, concerned with the formation or acquisition of a body corporate or the loan of money to or entry into a guarantee for the benefit of a body corporate, for which the consent of the Secretary of State is required: s 20 (1) (b).

7 See ibid s 7 (2) and the Civil Aviation Authority Regulations 1991, SI 1991/1672, reg 6 which regulates the conduct of the CAA when performing any function defined by an Air Navigation Order (eg registration and certification of aircraft, licensing of personnel and aerodromes, validation and approval of documents); see paras 1066–1071 post.

8 See the Civil Aviation Act 1982 s 7 (1) and the Civil Aviation Authority Regulations 1991 reg 15 which provides for a special quorum and for regulating the authority's conduct in connection with air transport licensing; see paras 1072–1091 post. As to the provision of accommodation in aircraft see the Civil Aviation (Air Travel Organisers' Licensing) Regulations 1972, SI 1972/223, reg 5; and see paras 1092–1101 post.

1046. General objectives. The CAA must perform its functions in the best possible manner to secure that British airlines[1] provide air transport services[2] which satisfy all substantial categories of public demand, at the lowest charges consistent with a high standard of safety and an economic return to efficient operators on the sums invested in providing those services[3]. The CAA must also encourage the sound development of the United Kingdom civil air transport industry[4] and further the reasonable interests of users of air transport services[5].

1 'British airline' means an undertaking having power to provide air transport services and appearing to the authority to have its principal place of business in the United Kingdom, the Channel Islands or the Isle of Man, and to be controlled by persons who are either United Kingdom nationals or are for the time being approved by the Secretary of State for the purposes of the Civil Aviation Act 1982 s 4 (2): s 4 (2). A 'United Kingdom national' is an individual who is (1) a British citizen, a British Dependent Territories citizen, a British National (Overseas) or a British Overseas citizen, (2) a British subject under the British Nationality Act 1981 or (3) a British protected person within the meaning of that Act: Civil Aviation Act 1982 s 105 (1) (amended by the Hong Kong (British Nationality) Order 1986, SI 1986/948, art 8, Schedule). As to the Secretary of State see para 1032 ante.

2 'Air transport service' means a service for the carriage by air of passengers or cargo, and 'cargo' includes mail: Civil Aviation Act 1982 s 105 (1).

3 Ibid s 4 (1) (a). The public demand must be reasonable in so far as the services that British airlines may provide are concerned.

4 See ibid s 4 (1) (a).

5 Ibid s 4 (1) (b).

1047. Directions by Secretary of State. After consultation with the CAA the Secretary of State[1] may give the authority directions of a general character as to the performance of its functions in the interests of national security[2]. The Secretary of State may also give the CAA directions as to its financial functions[3], in time of war or national emergency[4], to meet obligations of the United Kingdom[5] and in matters concerning the regulation of civil aviation[6] or the protection of the environment[7].

The CAA has a duty to comply with any direction given by the Secretary of State[8].

1 As to the Secretary of State see para 1032 ante.

2 See the Civil Aviation Act 1982 s 6 (1), (2) (a).

3 See ibid ss 8 (4), 12 (1) (b), 13, 15 (1) (b); and paras 1048–1056 post.

4 See ibid s 63 (3); and para 1064 post.
5 See ibid s 6 (2) (b)–(e).
6 See ibid ss 36 (1) (health control), 66 (3) and 67 (3) and (5) (air transport licensing) and 72 (2) (air navigation services).
7 Ibid s 6 (2) (f) (noise, vibration, pollution or other disturbance caused by civil aircraft); see paras 1305–1311 post.
8 Ibid s 20 (3). Directions given in pursuance of s 6, 63 (3) or 72 (2) (see notes 2, 4–7 supra) must be set out in the CAA's annual report to the Secretary of State: s 21 (2) (a).

(ii) Financial Provisions

1048. General duties. The CAA must conduct its affairs so as to secure that its revenue is sufficient to meet charges properly chargeable to revenue account[1]. It must also act on lines settled with the approval of the Secretary of State[2] and secure that any of its subsidiaries acts on those lines when framing and carrying out proposals involving it in substantial outlay on capital account[3].

1 Civil Aviation Act 1982 s 8 (1).
2 As to the Secretary of State see para 1032 ante.
3 Civil Aviation Act 1982 s 8 (2), which also applies to any decision to hire equipment the purchase of which at the time of the hire would have involved such an outlay unless the CAA hires the equipment from a subsidiary or the subsidiary hires such equipment from the CAA: s 8 (2) (b), (3).

1049. The initial debt. The CAA assumed on 16 November 1973[1] a debt to the Secretary of State[2] in respect of property and rights transferred to it[3]. The scheme of payment is determined from time to time by the Secretary of State with Treasury approval[4].

1 See the Civil Aviation Act 1982 s 9 (1) as well as the Civil Aviation Act 1971 s 7 (repealed) and the Civil Aviation Authority (Vesting Date) (No 1) Order 1972, SI 1972/140.
2 As to the Secretary of State see para 1032 ante.
3 Civil Aviation Act 1982 s 9, Sch 3 paras 1–5. This debt, referred to as the initial debt, concerned aerodromes and other undertakings listed in the Civil Aviation Act 1971 Sch 2 (repealed).
4 Civil Aviation Act 1982 s 9 (2). Any sums received by the Secretary of State by way of interest on, or repayment of, the initial debt must be paid into the National Loan Fund: s 9 (3).

1050. Borrowing powers. The CAA may borrow such sums as it may require for performing its functions[1] from the Secretary of State[2] in all circumstances[3], from the Commission of the European Communities or the European Investment Bank with the consent of the Secretary of State when borrowing in sterling otherwise than by way of a temporary loan for capital purposes or for fulfilling a guarantee entered into by the CAA[4], and from any other person with the consent of or in accordance with a general authorisation given by the Secretary of State whether in sterling or in another currency[5].

No such consent or authorisation may be given by the Secretary of State without the approval of the Treasury[6].

The aggregate outstanding in respect of the principal of any money borrowed by the CAA and the initial debt must not exceed £750 million[7].

1 Civil Aviation Act 1982 s 10 (1).
2 As to the Secretary of State see para 1032 ante.
3 See the Civil Aviation Act 1982 s 10 (2), (3).

4 Ibid s 10 (2).
5 Ibid s 10 (3); the reference to a currency other than sterling includes a reference to units of account defined by reference to more than one currency: s 10 (7) (added by the Civil Aviation Authority (Borrowing Powers) Act 1990 s 1 (3)).
6 Civil Aviation Act 1982 s 10 (4).
7 Ibid s 10 (6) (amended by the Civil Aviation Authority (Borrowing Powers) Act 1990 s 1 (2)). As to the initial debt see para 1049 ante.

1051. Government grants and loans. The Secretary of State[1] may make to the CAA out of money provided by Parliament grants of such amounts as he thinks fit[2].

The Secretary of State may also lend to the CAA, for capital purposes or for fulfilling a guarantee entered into by the CAA[3], any sums[4] which the Treasury may issue to the Secretary of State out of the National Loans Fund[5]. Determinations as to the scheme of repayment are given by the Secretary of State[6], and the sums received by the Secretary of State are paid into the National Loans Fund[7].

All such loans and determinations can only be made by the Secretary of State with Treasury approval[8].

1 As to the Secretary of State see para 1032 ante.
2 Civil Aviation Act 1982 s 12 (1) (a). The Secretary of State may direct that the whole or part of the grant is not to be used otherwise than for the purposes of such of the CAA's functions as are specified in the direction: s 12 (1) (b). See also para 1038 ante.
3 See ibid s 10; and para 1050 ante.
4 Ibid s 12 (2).
5 Ibid s 12 (4).
6 Ibid s 12 (3).
7 Ibid s 12 (4).
8 Ibid s 12 (2), (3).

1052. Treasury guarantees. The Treasury may guarantee the repayment of the principal of, the payment of interest on, and the discharge of any other financial obligation relating to, any sums which the CAA borrows from a person other than the Secretary of State[1]. Sums required by the Treasury for fulfilling these guarantees are charged on and issued out of the Consolidated Fund[2]. Where sums are issued in fulfilment of such a guarantee, the CAA must make such payments as the Treasury directs towards repayment of those sums and payment of interest[3].

A statement of any guarantee thus given must be laid before each House of Parliament by the Treasury immediately after it has been given: and where any sum has thus been issued for fulfilling a guarantee, the Treasury must, as soon as possible after the end of each financial year, lay before each House of Parliament a statement relating to that sum[4].

1 Civil Aviation Act 1982 s 14 (1) (amended by the Miscellaneous Financial Provisions Act 1983 s 4 (1), Sch 2). The manner and the conditions of the guarantee are determined by the Treasury: Civil Aviation Act 1982 s 14 (1). As to the Secretary of State see para 1032 post.
2 Civil Aviation Act 1982 s 14 (3).
3 Ibid s 14 (4).
4 Ibid s 14 (2). The obligation begins with the year in which the sum is issued and ends with that in which all liability in respect of the principal of the sum and in respect of interest thereon is finally discharged: s 14 (2). For the meaning of 'financial year' see para 1056 note 8 post.

1053. Charges payable to Civil Aviation Authority. After consultation with the Secretary of State[1] the CAA may determine a scheme of charges to be paid to it in respect of the performance of its functions as specified in the scheme[2]. The scheme may specify the amount of the charge and the manner in which it must be paid, or may provide for different charges[3].

Regulations may also determine charges which are to be paid to the CAA or may secure that no charge is payable to it in respect of such of its functions as may be prescribed[4]. Such regulations may prescribe the amount of a charge or the manner in which it must be paid[5].

In so far as a scheme and regulations made different provisions with respect to the same matter the provisions made by the scheme must be disregarded[6].

Where provision for a charge has been made it is the duty of the CAA to charge accordingly as respects the performance of the function; however, the CAA may waive the whole or part of the charge if it thinks fit to do so in a particular case[7]. It may also enter into an agreement for the payment of charges as determined in the agreement in respect of the performance by the CAA of any of its functions, other than a function in respect of which provision is made for the making of a charge or of no charge[8].

No charges may be determined in respect of the provision of air navigation services, and provision may not be made by or under an Air Navigation Order for the payment of fees to the CAA[9].

1 As to the Secretary of State see para 1032 ante.
2 Civil Aviation Act 1982 s 11 (1).
3 Ibid s 11 (1). The scheme may specify a scale of charges by reference to which the amount is to be ascertained, and it may provide that the charges will be of such amount, not exceeding that specified in the scheme, as may be decided by the CAA having regard to the expense incurred by it in performing the function in question and to such other factors as may be so specified; the time at which and the person by whom any charge is to be paid may also be specified: s 11 (1) (a)–(c). The scheme comes into force on a specified date at least 60 days after its publication: s 11 (2).
4 Ibid s 11 (3). Regulations had been made under the Civil Aviation Act 1971 s 9 (now replaced by s 11 of the 1982 Act), but were revoked and not replaced: see the Civil Aviation Authority (Charges) (Revocation) Regulations 1978, SI 1978/1633, revoking the Civil Aviation Authority (Charges) Regulations 1976, SI 1976/1396.
5 Civil Aviation Act 1982 s 11 (3) (a), (b); the time at which and the person by whom the charge must be paid, as well as a maximum or minimum charge or a scale of charges, may also be prescribed in the scheme: s 11 (3).
6 Ibid s 11 (4).
7 Ibid s 11 (5).
8 Ibid s 11 (6).
9 Ibid s 11 (7). As to air navigation services see paras 1370–1381 post.

1054. Reserves. The Secretary of State[1] may, with Treasury approval, give directions to the CAA in regard to the establishment or management of reserves, or the application of any reserves for the purposes of the authority[2].

The Secretary of State may also, with Treasury approval and after consultation with the CAA, direct the CAA to pay to him the whole or part of the sums standing to the credit of any of its reserves[3].

1 As to the Secretary of State see para 1032 ante.
2 Civil Aviation Act 1982 s 8 (4).
3 Ibid s 13 (2).

1055. Application of revenue. If, in any accounting year[1], the Civil Aviation Authority's revenue exceeds the total sum properly chargeable by the authority to revenue account for that year, the excess must be applied in such manner as the Secretary of State[2], with Treasury approval and after consultation with the authority, may direct[3]. The Secretary of State may direct that the whole or part of the excess be paid to him[4].

1 'Accounting year' means the period of 12 months ending with 31 March: Civil Aviation Act 1982 s 105 (1).
2 As to the Secretary of State see para 1032 ante.
3 Civil Aviation Act 1982 s 13 (1).
4 Ibid s 13 (1).

1056. Accounts and audit. Proper accounts and proper records must be kept by the CAA[1], which must prepare, in respect of each accounting year[2], a statement of accounts, showing the state of affairs and the profit or loss of the authority, in such form as the Secretary of State[3] with Treasury approval directs[4]. As soon as the accounts of the CAA and the statement have been audited[5], the CAA must send a copy of the statement together with any auditors' report to the Secretary of State[6], who is then required to lay before each House of Parliament a copy of every document so received[7].

As respects each financial year[8], the Secretary of State must prepare an account of sums issued to him[9] or received by him[10] and of the sums required to be paid into the National Loans Fund[11], and of the disposal by him of such sums[12]; the Secretary of State must send a copy of the account to the Comptroller and Auditor General not later than the end of November next following that year[13].

The Comptroller and Auditor General examines, certifies and reports on each statement and account so sent to him and lays copies of them and of his report before each House of Parliament[14].

1 Civil Aviation Act 1982 s 15 (1) (a).
2 For the meaning of 'accounting year' see para 1055 note 1 ante.
3 As to the Secretary of State see para 1032 ante.
4 Civil Aviation Act 1982 s 15 (1) (b).
5 The accounts and the statement are audited by auditors appointed annually by the Secretary of State after consultation with the CAA: see the Civil Aviation Act 1982 s 15 (2) (a) (substituted by the Civil Aviation Authority (Auditing of Accounts) Order 1984, SI 1984/65, and amended by the Companies Consolidation (Consequential Provisions) Act 1985 s 30, Sch 2).
6 Civil Aviation Act 1982 s 15 (1) (c) (substituted by the Civil Aviation Authority (Auditing of Accounts) Order 1984).
7 Civil Aviation Act 1982 s 15 (2) (b) (as substituted: see note 6 supra).
8 'Financial year' means the 12 months ending with 31 March: Interpretation Act 1978 s 5, Sch 1.
9 In pursuance of the Civil Aviation Act 1982 s 12 (4) (loans); see para 1051 ante.
10 In pursuance of ibid s 13 (excess of revenue); see para 1055 ante.
11 In pursuance of ibid ss 12 (4) (loans) or 9 (initial debt); see respectively paras 1051, 1049 ante.
12 Ibid s 15 (4) (a).
13 Ibid s 15 (4) (b).
14 Ibid s 15 (4).

(iii) Miscellaneous Provisions

1057. Annual report. As soon as possible after the end of each accounting year[1], the CAA must make to the Secretary of State[2] a report on the performance of its functions during that year[3], setting out any direction[4] given by the Secretary of State during that year unless he has notified the CAA that in his opinion it would be against the national interest to do so[5]. The report must also include any statement of policy which the CAA may have published during that time[6], particulars of any case in which the CAA has decided not to proceed with advice given by the Airworthiness Requirements Board[7], and such information as may be specified by the Secretary of State with respect to the CAA's plans, activities and financial position[8]. The Secretary of State must lay a copy of the report before each House of Parliament[9].

1 For the meaning of 'accounting year' see para 1055 note 1 ante.
2 As to the Secretary of State see para 1032 ante.
3 Civil Aviation Act 1982 s 21 (1).
4 Ie any direction under ibid s 6 (national interest: see para 1047 ante), s 63 (3) (control in time of war or emergency: see para 1064 post) or s 72 (2) (air navigation services: see para 1372 post).
5 Ibid s 21 (2) (a).
6 Ibid s 21 (2) (b); as to statements of policy by the CAA see s 69 and para 1073 post.
7 Ibid s 21 (2) (c); as to the board see s 85 (2) and para 1060 post.
8 Ibid s 21 (2) (d).
9 Ibid s 21 (3).

1058. General duty to provide assistance. The CAA is under the duty to provide the Secretary of State[1] or any other person specified by him with such assistance and advice as he may require in connection with any of his functions relating to civil aviation[2]. Thus the CAA may advise the Secretary of State before the latter directs any aircraft operator to modify or alter his aircraft in order to protect them against acts of violence[3]; the CAA may make recommendations to the Secretary of State concerning aerodromes generally[4] and airport capacity in particular[5]; and may provide technical assistance and advice[6]. The CAA is entitled to recover from the Secretary of State a sum equal to any expense reasonably incurred in providing assistance or advice[7].

1 As to the Secretary of State see para 1032 ante.
2 Civil Aviation Act 1982 s 16 (1). The CAA may refuse to provide assistance or advice for a person other than the Secretary of State if the Secretary of State does not undertake to pay for it, unless that person pays such charge as is provided for or, if no charge is provided for, such reasonable charge as the CAA determines: s 16 (3).
3 Aviation Security Act 1982 ss 12 (3), 15 (3); see para 1243 post.
4 Civil Aviation Act 1982 s 16 (2); see further para 1102 et seq post.
5 Airports Act 1986 s 69; see para 1198 post.
6 Civil Aviation Act 1982 s 16 (5).
7 Ibid s 16 (4).

1059. Duty to provide information. The CAA is under a duty to furnish to the Secretary of State[1] such information as it has or can reasonably be expected to obtain relating to the CAA or to civil aviation[2]. The Secretary of State may specify the information that he requires, but the CAA must give him notice of any proposal to merge or any merger of a body holding an air transport licence with another body[3]. Notice of matters affecting international relations or involving noise, vibration, pollution or other disturbance attributable to aircraft must also be given to him[4].

The CAA is entitled to recover from the Secretary of State a sum equal to any expense reasonably incurred in furnishing such information[5].

The CAA may require licence holders, recipients of approval given by the CAA, persons who have held themselves out as ones who may enter into contracts to make available accommodation for persons or goods on aircraft, and persons carrying on business as manufacturers of aircraft or aircraft engines or equipment or as insurers of aircraft, to furnish certain information to it[6].

Provision may be made by regulations for requiring those persons to furnish such information to the Secretary of State as may be prescribed[7].

Failure to supply information required is punishable on summary conviction with a fine not exceeding level 3 on the standard scale[8] and knowingly or recklessly furnishing information which is false in a material particular is punishable on summary conviction with a fine not exceeding the statutory maximum or, on conviction on indictment, with a fine or imprisonment for a term not exceeding two years or both[9]; and the CAA may revoke any relevant licence, certificate or approval[10].

No information relating to a particular person which has been furnished to the CAA may be disclosed save with that person's written consent[11] or where the CAA determines that the information may be disclosed after the person concerned was given the opportunity of making representations[12] or where the person concerned is dead or is a body corporate which has ceased to exist[13]. The CAA may also determine that the information is of the same kind as information for which it had determined disclosure and thus can be disclosed[14].

1 As to the Secretary of State see para 1032 ante.
2 Civil Aviation Act 1982 s 17 (1) (a). For the purpose of such information, the Secretary of State has access to all relevant documents under the CAA's control: s 17 (1) (b).
3 Ibid s 17 (1) (c).
4 Ibid s 17 (1) (d). As to noise, vibration and pollution see paras 1185–1188 post.
5 Ibid s 17 (3).
6 See ibid s 84 (1), (2).
7 Ibid s 84 (3). No such regulations had been made at the date at which this volume states the law.
8 See ibid s 84 (4) (a) (amended by virtue of the Criminal Justice Act 1982 ss 38, 46). As to the standard scale see para 1044 note 6 ante. At the date at which this volume states the law, level 3 on that scale is at £400. The failure to provide the information is an offence notwithstanding the fact that at the relevant time the person concerned may not have been in the United Kingdom and is neither a United Kingdom national or a United Kingdom incorporated body corporate: Civil Aviation Act 1982 s 84 (4). For the meaning of 'United Kingdom national' see para 1046 note 1 ante.
9 See ibid s 84 (4) (b). As to the statutory maximum see the Civil Aviation Act 1982 s 105 (1); and para 1005 note 11 ante.
10 Ibid s 84 (4) (c).
11 Ibid s 23 (1) (a); as to exceptions see s 23 (4). Unauthorised disclosure by the CAA, a member or employee of the CAA or an officer of the Secretary of State is an offence punishable on summary conviction with a fine not exceeding the statutory maximum or, on conviction on indictment, with a fine or (save in the case of the CAA) imprisonment for a term not exceeding two years or both: see s 23 (5). As to the statutory maximum see note 9 supra.
12 Ibid s 23 (1) (b); as to exceptions and penalties see note 11 supra.
13 Ibid s 23 (1) (c); as to exceptions and penalties see note 11 supra.
14 Ibid s 23 (1) (d); as to cases where the CAA determines that information can be disclosed see s 23 (1) (b), (c); as to exceptions and penalties see note 11 supra.

(iv) The Airworthiness Requirements Board

1060. Constitution. The Civil Aviation Authority (CAA) has the duty to consult a body known as the Airworthiness Requirements Board[1] on matters concerning the standards of design, construction and maintenance of aircraft and cognate matters[2]. The board may consult experts for the purpose of giving such advice[3].

The board consists of 12 to 20 persons appointed by the CAA and representative of interests concerned with civil aviation: one person each is nominated by manufacturers, operators, insurers and pilots; members of the CAA may be appointed as members of the board[4].

1 See the Civil Aviation Act 1982 s 85 (2). The Air Registration Board established under the Civil Aviation Act 1949 s 7 was dissolved by the Civil Aviation Act 1971 s 27 (1) (repealed).
2 See the Civil Aviation Act 1982 s 85 (1).
3 Ibid s 85 (2) (b).
4 See ibid s 85 (3). As to the tenure of office of members, staff and procedure see s 85 (4) and Sch 11. The CAA designates as chairman of the board a member of the board whom the board has nominated: see s 85 (3).

1061. Functions. Standards of design, construction and maintenance by reference to which certificates of airworthiness[1] for aircraft are to be granted or renewed and whether an aircraft of a new type satisfies the standards of design and construction for the issue of such a certificate are matters on which the Civil Aviation Authority (CAA) must consult the Airworthiness Requirements Board[2]. When the board considers it appropriate it may give advice to the CAA on any other matters which appear to it to relate to such standards[3].

1 As to certificates of airworthiness see paras 1284–1294 post. In securing a high standard of aviation safety the CAA must give effect to safety requirements deriving from international agreements, in particular the Chicago Convention and its annex 8 (airworthiness of aircraft) (as to the Chicago Convention and its annexes see paras 1002, 1007 ante).
2 Civil Aviation Act 1982 s 85 (1), (2) (a) (i). See further para 1289 post. The Civil Aviation (Air Registration Board) Order 1967, SI 1967/1060, art 4, required the Air Registration Board (the predecessor of the CAA and the Airworthiness Requirements Board) to have regard to the standards and recommended practices adopted by ICAO (as to which see para 1020 ante); this provision does not appear in the current legislation. The Civil Aviation Act 1982 s 20 (2) (a), however, stipulates that the CAA shall act on behalf of the Crown in performing any function which in pursuance of the Chicago Convention (as amended, and including the annexes) falls to be performed on behalf of the Crown.
3 Civil Aviation Act 1982 s 85 (2) (a) (ii).

1062. Decision by Civil Aviation Authority. The Civil Aviation Authority (CAA) must consider all advice given by the Airworthiness Requirements Board[1] and decide any question as to whether or not a matter is one on which consultations are required[2]. If the CAA decides not to proceed in accordance with any advice given by the board, the CAA must inform the board in writing of its reasons and, if the advice was given in consequence of consultations which the CAA was required to make, must publish particulars of the case[3].

1 Civil Aviation Act 1982 s 85 (1) (b).
2 Ibid s 85 (1) (a). As to consultations see para 1060 ante.
3 Ibid s 85 (1) (c). As to consultations see para 1060 ante.

(4) NATIONAL EMERGENCIES

1063. Control of aviation in time of emergency. In time of war, whether actual or imminent, or of great national emergency, the Secretary of State has power, by order made by statutory instrument[1], to regulate or prohibit, either absolutely or subject to any conditions contained in the order, the navigation of all or any descriptions of aircraft over the whole or any part of the United Kingdom or any specified area of sea[2]. He may also by order provide for taking possession of and using for the purposes of Her Majesty's naval, military or air forces any aerodrome, or any aircraft, plant, machinery, material or other things found thereon, and for regulating or prohibiting the use, erection, building, maintenance or establishment of any aerodrome or flying school[3]. Such an order may provide for the imposition of penalties, for the detention of aircraft[4] or for the taking of any steps, including firing on aircraft, which may be specified in the order to secure its compliance[5]. Any person suffering direct injury or loss owing to the operation of such an order is entitled to compensation[6].

1 Civil Aviation Act 1982 s 102 (1); see para 1026 ante.
2 Ibid s 62 (1) (a). See also WAR.
3 Ibid s 62 (1) (b).
4 See ibid s 62 (2) and Sch 13 Pt III para 4 (1); any such provision may be made as appears necessary or expedient for securing such detention. For other powers of detention see para 1339 post.
5 Ibid s 62 (2), applying s 60 (3) (l).
6 Ibid s 62 (3). Compensation is to be fixed, in default of agreement, by the Lands Tribunal, and the principles of the Land Compensation Act 1961 (see COMPULSORY ACQUISITION) apply with the necessary modifications where possession is taken of any land: Civil Aviation Act 1982 s 62 (4).

1064. Control of Civil Aviation Authority in time of emergency. In time of war, whether actual or imminent, or of great national emergency, the Secretary of State[1] may by order require that all or any property or rights of or under the control of the Civil Aviation Authority (CAA)[2] be placed at his disposal, and while such an order is in force he may give the CAA such directions as he thinks fit, and where those directions conflict with the requirements of any enactment or instrument relating to the CAA those requirements must be disregarded[3].

1 As to the Secretary of State see para 1032 ante.
2 As to the CAA see para 1044 ante.
3 See the Civil Aviation Act 1982 s 63 (1), (3).

1065. Control of British air transport undertakings in time of emergency. In time of war, whether actual or imminent, or of great national emergency, the Secretary of State[1] may by order require that the whole or any part of the relevant undertaking of any British air transport business[2] or any property or rights of any such business be placed at his disposal[3]. While such an order is in force the managers of the business must comply with any direction which the Secretary of State may have given them[4].

To secure compliance therewith, an order so made may provide for the imposition of penalties[5] and for the detention of aircraft[6]. Any person who suffers direct injury or loss owing to the operation of such an order is entitled to receive compensation from the Secretary of State[7].

1 As to the Secretary of State see para 1032 ante.
2 References to a British air transport business are references to any person or body appearing to the Secretary of State to have his or its principal place of business in the United Kingdom whose business includes the provision of commercial air transport services; in relation to such business, the 'relevant undertaking' means that part of its undertaking which consists of the provision of commercial air transport services; 'commercial air transport services' means services for the carriage by air of passengers and cargo for hire or reward (or valuable consideration): see the Civil Aviation Act 1982 s 63 (2).

3 Ibid s 63 (1) (a), (b). See also WAR.
4 Ibid s 63 (4).
5 **Ibid s 63 (5)**: the order may provide for the imposition of a fine not exceeding the statutory maximum on summary conviction and on conviction on indictment a fine or imprisonment for a term not exceeding two years or both. As to the statutory maximum see para 1005 note 11 ante. At the date at which this volume states the law, the statutory maximum is £2,000.
6 See ibid Sch 13 Pt III para 4 (1). For other powers of detention see para 1339 post.
7 Ibid s 63 (6); the amount of the compensation is fixed by the Lands Tribunal where no agreement can be reached; the principles of the Land Compensation Act 1961 apply with the necessary modifications where possession is taken of any land. See also COMPULSORY ACQUISITION.

3. LICENSING

(1) FUNCTIONS UNDER AIR NAVIGATION ORDER

1066. Licensing regulations. The Civil Aviation Authority Regulations 1991[1] prescribe, in relation to the Air Navigation Order 1989[2], the procedure to be followed by the Civil Aviation Authority (CAA)[3] in connection with the performance by it of its functions under the Air Navigation Order to register aircraft, to issue certificates, licences, approvals and ratings and to receive reports of reportable occurrences[4]. The regulations also prescribe the procedure to be followed in relation to air transport licensing[5] by the CAA under the Civil Aviation Act 1982[6].

1 SI 1991/1672.
2 SI 1989/2004 (amended by SI 1990/2154 and SI 1991/1726).
3 As to the CAA see para 1044 ante.
4 See the Civil Aviation Authority Regulations 1991 reg 6. As to the regulation of aircraft safety see also the Civil Aviation Act 1982 s 85; and see paras 1060–1062 ante. As to reportable occurrences see para 1496 post.
5 For the meaning of 'air transport licensing' see para 1072 post.
6 See the Civil Aviation Authority Regulations 1991 regs 15–31. See also the Civil Aviation Act 1982 ss 64–68; and paras 1072–1091 post.

1067. Scope of functions. The functions conferred on the Civil Aviation Authority (CAA)[1] by or under the Air Navigation Order concern the registration of aircraft[2], the certification of operators of aircraft[3], the certification of airworthiness of aircraft[4], noise certification[5], the certification of compliance with the requirements for the emission by aircraft engines of unburned hydrocarbons[6], personnel licensing[7], the licensing of aerodromes[8], the validation of any certificate or licence[9], the approval of equipment and the approval or authorisation of persons[10], the approval of schemes for the regulation of the flight times of aircraft crew[11] and the receipt of reports of reportable occurrences[12]. The Civil Aviation Authority Regulations provide for the regulation of the conduct of the CAA and other persons in connection with the performance by the CAA of these functions[13].

1 As to the CAA see para 1044 ante.
2 Civil Aviation Authority Regulations 1991, SI 1991/1672, reg 6 (1) (a): see the Air Navigation Order 1989, SI 1989/2004, arts 3–5; and paras 1276–1283 post.
3 Civil Aviation Authority Regulations 1991 reg 6 (1) (b): see the Air Navigation Order 1989 art 6; and paras 1340–1342 post.
4 Civil Aviation Authority Regulations 1991 reg 6 (1) (c): see the Air Navigation Order 1989 arts 7–18; and paras 1284–1294 post. As to the Airworthiness Requirements Board see the Civil Aviation Act 1982 s 85; and para 1060 ante.

5 Civil Aviation Authority Regulations 1991 reg 6 (1) (d): see the Air Navigation (Noise Certification) Order 1990, SI 1990/1514; and paras 1305–1311 post. As to noise and vibration generally see the Civil Aviation Act 1982 ss 78–80; and paras 1185–1188 post.

6 Civil Aviation Authority Regulations 1991 reg 6 (1) (e): see the Air Navigation (Aeroplane and Aeroplane Engine Emission of Unburned Hydrocarbons) Order 1988, SI 1988/1994; and paras 1295–1300 post.

7 Civil Aviation Authority Regulations 1991 reg 6 (1) (f): see the Air Navigation Order 1989 arts 19–25; and paras 1343–1358 post.

8 Civil Aviation Authority Regulations 1991 reg 6 (1) (g): see the Air Navigation Order 1989 art 78; and para 1154 post.

9 Civil Aviation Authority Regulations 1991 reg 6 (1) (h): see the Air Navigation Order 1989 art 22; and para 1356 post.

10 Civil Aviation Authority Regulations 1991 reg 6 (1) (i): see the Air Navigation Order 1989 arts 20 and 13 respectively; and paras 1344 and 1306 respectively post.

11 Civil Aviation Authority Regulations 1991 reg 6 (1) (j): see the Air Navigation Order 1989 art 58; and para 1367 post.

12 Civil Aviation Authority Regulations 1991 reg 6 (1) (k): see the Air Navigation Order 1989 art 94; and paras 1494–1496 post.

13 Civil Aviation Act 1982 s 7 (2).

1068. Decision on application. A decision in relation to the registration of an aircraft, or to the grant of a certificate, licence, approval, authorisation or rating[1], may be made on behalf of the Civil Aviation Authority (CAA)[2] only by a member or employee of the CAA[3].

In the event of a refusal to register an aircraft because it would be inexpedient in the public interest for the aircraft to be registered in the United Kingdom or where the CAA refuses to grant, validate or vary a certificate, licence, approval, authorisation or rating, or grants an application in terms different from those applied for, the CAA must serve[4] on the applicant a notice stating the reasons for the decision; within 14 days from the service of the notice the applicant may request a review by the CAA[5].

Notice of a proposal to cancel the registration of an aircraft, or to revoke, suspend or vary a certificate, licence, approval, authorisation, validation or rating, must be served, together with the reasons for such a proposal, on the person concerned[6], who may, within 14 days from the service of the notice, serve on the CAA a request that the case be decided by the CAA and not by any other person on its behalf[7].

1 'Rating' means a rating on a personnel licence and 'personnel licence' means a licence authorising a person to act as a member of a flight crew (see para 1360 post), an aircraft maintenance engineer (see para 1304 post), an air traffic controller (see para 1385 post), a student air traffic controller (see para 1386 post) or an aerodrome flight information service officer (see para 1387 post): Civil Aviation Authority Regulations 1991, SI 1991/1672, reg 3 (1).

2 As to the CAA see para 1044 ante.

3 Civil Aviation Authority Regulations 1991 reg 6 (2). As to exceptions see para 1071 post.

4 A document may be served on a person by delivering it to him, by leaving it at his proper address, by post or by telex or similar means, and where the person is a body corporate it may be served on its secretary: ibid reg 4 (1). A person's proper address is his last known address or, in the case of a body corporate, its registered or principal office: reg 4 (2).

5 Ibid reg 6 (3); as to exceptions see para 1071 post.

6 'The person concerned' means, in relation to aircraft registration, the applicant for registration or the person in whose name the aircraft is registered, and, in relation to a certificate, licence, approval, authorisation, validation or rating, the holder or former holder of, or applicant for, the certificate, licence, approval, authorisation, validation or rating: ibid reg 3 (1).

7 Ibid reg 6 (4); as to exceptions see para 1071 post.

1069. Failure of test or examination. A person notified of his failure of a test or examination for a personnel licence[1] may within 14 days from service of the notification[2] request the Civil Aviation Authority (CAA)[3] to determine whether the test or examination was properly conducted[4]. Appeal lies to the county court[5] from the CAA's decision that a person is not a fit person to hold a personnel licence[6], but no appeal lies from a decision that a person is not qualified to hold the licence by reason of any deficiency in his knowledge, experience, competence, skill or physical or mental fitness[7].

1 For the meaning of 'personnel licence' see para 1068 note 1 ante.
2 See para 1068 ante.
3 As to the CAA see para 1044 ante.
4 Civil Aviation Authority Regulations 1991, SI 1991/1672, reg 6 (5).
5 Ie the county court for the district in which the decision was made: CCR Ord 4 r 9. The appeal is brought by filing in the court office, within 21 days after the date of the decision, a copy of the decision and a request for entry of the appeal: see CCR Ord 3 r 6; and COUNTY COURTS.
6 See the Air Navigation Order 1989, SI 1989/2004, art 105 (1); the CAA must be a respondent to any appeal: art 105 (3); the CAA's decision is deemed to have been taken on the day on which it furnished a statement of its reasons for the decision to the applicant, the holder or former holder, as the case may be: art 105 (4).
7 Ibid art 105 (1) proviso.

1070. Review of decision by Civil Aviation Authority. The function of deciding a case where a request for review has been duly served on the Civil Aviation Authority (CAA)[1] is a function which may not be performed on behalf of the CAA by any other person; for the purpose of making a decision in such a case, the quorum of the CAA is one member[2]. The CAA may appoint technical assessors to sit with it[3]. Before reaching its decision the CAA must consider any representations which may have been served[4] upon it by the persons concerned[5] within 21 days of the service of notification of the original decision[6]. When the CAA makes a decision in such a case, it must furnish to the person concerned a statement of its reasons for the decision[7].

1 Ie under the Civil Aviation Authority Regulations 1991, SI 1991/1672, reg 6 (3)–(5): see para 1068 et seq ante. As to the CAA see para 1044 ante.
2 Ibid reg 6 (6) (a).
3 Ibid reg 6 (6) (b). No person who participated in the decision or proposal or in giving or assessing the test or examination which is to be the subject of the CAA's decision may be appointed as an assessor: reg 6 (6) (b).
4 As to service of documents see para 1068 note 4 ante.
5 For the meaning of 'person concerned' see para 1068 note 6 ante.
6 Civil Aviation Authority Regulations 1991 reg 6 (7).
7 Ibid reg 7.

1071. Exceptions. Nothing in the regulation of the conduct of the Civil Aviation Authority (CAA)[1] prevents it from provisionally cancelling the registration of an aircraft, or from provisionally suspending or varying any certificate, licence, approval, authorisation, validation or rating[2] pending inquiry into or consideration of the case[3]. Nor do those provisions apply to the variation of any document incorporated by reference in a certificate of airworthiness[4] or where, following a direction given by the Secretary of State, the CAA refuses to register or cancels or amends a registration of aircraft or again refuses to grant, grants in different terms, revokes, suspends or varies a certificate, licence, approval, authorisation or rating[5]; or where the CAA refuses to grant an aerodrome licence or grants it on different terms or proposes to revoke, suspend or vary an aerodrome licence otherwise than on the application of the holder, or where, in the cases of substitution of ordinary aerodrome licence and public use aerodrome licence, the CAA refuses the application made by the holder of the aerodrome licence or proposes to make a substitution otherwise than on the holder's application[6].

Further, there is no right of review in respect of a medical certificate or certificate of test or experience relating to a personnel licence[7], although there is a right to request a determination that the relevant test was properly conducted[8].

1 See the Civil Aviation Authority Regulations 1991, SI 1991/1672, reg 6; and paras 1068–1070 ante. As to the CAA see para 1044 ante.
2 For the meaning of 'rating' see para 1068 note 1 ante.
3 Civil Aviation Authority Regulations 1991 reg 6 (8) (a).
4 Ibid reg 6 (8) (b). As to such certificates see para 1284 post.
5 Ibid reg 6 (8) (c).
6 Ibid reg 6 (9) (b), (10); as to aerodrome licences see paras 1154, 1155 post.
7 Ibid reg 6 (9) (a). For the meaning of 'personnel licence' see para 1068 note 1 ante.
8 Ibid reg 6 (5); see para 1069 ante.

(2) FUNCTIONS IN RELATION TO AIR TRANSPORT LICENSING

(i) Introduction

1072. Meaning of 'air transport licensing'. An air transport licence is a licence granted by the Civil Aviation Authority (CAA)[1] authorising the use of an aircraft for the carriage for reward of passengers or cargo, including mail[2].

In order to comprehend the system of air transport licensing created by the Civil Aviation Act 1971, now replaced by the Civil Aviation Act 1982, it is necessary to refer to the Civil Aviation Authority Regulations[3] and the CAA's Official Record – Air Transport Licensing[4].

The function of making a decision on air transport licensing is one which may not be performed on the CAA's behalf by any other person[5].

1 As to the CAA see para 1044 ante.
2 See the Civil Aviation Act 1982 ss 64 (1) (a), 105 (1).
3 SI 1991/1672; see para 1066 ante.
4 Any notice or other matter (other than a schedule of terms under the Civil Aviation Authority Regulations 1991 reg 18) required by those regulations or by the Civil Aviation Act 1982 ss 11 (2), 64 (3), 65 (1) or (6) or 85 (1), to be published must be published by the CAA in its official record: Civil Aviation Authority Regulations 1991 reg 5. Series 1 of the Official Record is amended from time to time. The contents are as follows:
　　General guidance; classes of licences; specification of flights which do not require an air transport licence; application for grant of licence; revocation, suspension or variation of licences; continuation of expired licences; application for variation of schedules; objections and representations; preliminary meetings; hearings and decisions of the CAA; appeals to the Secretary of State against decisions of the CAA; publication of licensing particulars, applications, decisions, etc; scheme of charges.
　　In addition there are 11 schedules: Definitions of expressions used in the Official Record and in air transport licences; Standard conditions of air transport licences; United Kingdom domestic air tariff and cabotage air passenger tariff (as to cabotage see para 1004 text and note 5 ante); Standard

provisions with respect to tariffs; Standard conditions for advance booking charters between the United Kingdom and specified countries or territories; Standard conditions for advance booking charters between the United Kingdom and Canada; Standard conditions for advance booking charters between the United Kingdom and the United States of America; Standard conditions for advance booking charters between the United Kingdom and Ghana; Inclusive tour charter terms for journeys between the United Kingdom and the United States of America; Schedule of advance booking charter terms for journeys between the United Kingdom and Switzerland; and Schedule of inclusive tour and travel only charter terms for journeys between the United Kingdom and Europe.

5 Civil Aviation Act 1982 s 7 (1); Civil Aviation Authority Regulations 1991 reg 15.

1073. Statement of policies. The Civil Aviation Authority (CAA)[1] must from time to time publish a statement of the policies which it intends to apply in the performance of its functions in relation to air transport licensing[2]. It may also be required by notice of the Secretary of State to publish a statement of policy in respect of a particular point[3]. In either case, the CAA must consult representatives of the civil air transport industry and of users of air transport services before publishing its statement[4].

1 As to the CAA see para 1044 ante.
2 Civil Aviation Act 1982 s 69 (1). See the statements published on 8 January 1985, Official Record Series 2, CAP 501, and on 27 January 1988, Official Record Series 2, Misc No 808.
3 Civil Aviation Act 1982 s 69 (2); the statement must be published within six months of the notice.
4 Ibid s 69 (3).

(ii) Preliminaries to the Hearing

1074. Applications for air transport licence. The Civil Aviation Authority (CAA)[1] may refuse to consider an application for the grant, revocation, suspension or variation of an air transport licence unless it is made in the prescribed manner[2]. The CAA must publish particulars of the application[3]; it may, however, dispense with publication if this is unlikely to prejudice any interested persons having a right to be heard[4].

1 As to the CAA see para 1044 ante.
2 Civil Aviation Authority Regulations 1991, SI 1991/1672, reg 16 (1). An application for the grant of a licence must be made in writing (Civil Aviation Act 1982 s 65 (1)); it must be served on the CAA not less than six months before the beginning of the period for which it is proposed to be in effect; it must contain particulars specified under s 65 (1) in the official record (as to which see para 1072 note 4 ante), any other application must be so served not less than six months before the revocation, suspension or variation is to take effect, and a signed copy of any such application made other than by the holder must be served on the holder: Civil Aviation Authority Regulations 1991 reg 16 (1) (a), (b), (2). The application must be accompanied by the appropriate fee: reg 16 (1) (c); and see the Civil Aviation Act 1982 s 11 and the Official Record Series 1 s 12 (amended 30 January 1990), No 121 as to any scheme of charges which the CAA may make. An application for the revocation, suspension or variation of a licence may be made by any person mentioned in the Civil Aviation Authority Regulations 1991 reg 25 (1) (b)–(d) (see para 1081 note 2 post): reg 16 (6).
3 Ibid reg 16 (3).
4 See ibid reg 16 (3) proviso. As to who has a right to be heard see reg 25 (1); and para 1081 note 2 post.

1075. Revocation, suspension or variation of licences without application. If the Civil Aviation Authority (CAA)[1] proposes to revoke, suspend or vary an air transport licence, otherwise than in pursuance of an application made to it, on the ground that it is not satisfied as to the holder's experience or resources and financial arrangements[2], it must publish particulars of the proposal in its official record[3] after serving[4] on the holder of the licence not less than 21 days' notice of its intention to publish such particulars together with its reasons for its proposal[5], and after considering any representations made by him before the expiration of the notice[6].

The CAA may revoke, suspend or vary an air transport licence where it is not satisfied that the holder is a United Kingdom national after serving a 21 day notice of its intention to consider the matter and having considered any representation which the holder may have made[7].

The CAA may dispense with publication of the particulars where such dispensation either has the consent of the licence holder, in the case of a proposal to revoke or suspend[8], or is unlikely to prejudice any interests, in the case of varying a licence[9]. The CAA will not publish the particulars of its proposal where the Secretary of State has directed it to revoke, suspend or vary a licence[10], or to re-hear a case[11], where the CAA is under a duty to revoke, suspend or vary a licence under the Airports Act 1986[12] or where it is satisfied that no interest will be prejudiced and the licence holder consents to the non-publication[13].

1 As to the CAA see para 1044 ante.
2 The CAA may suspend a licence after serving on the licence holder 6 days' notice of its proposal to suspend the licence together with its reasons where it is not satisfied as to the holder's experience or resources and financial arrangements: Civil Aviation Authority Regulations 1991, SI 1991/1672, reg 17 (3). As to experience in the field of aviation or resources and financial arrangements needed to satisfy the CAA see the Civil Aviation Act 1982 s 66 (3) (a), (b); and see para 1080 post.
3 Civil Aviation Authority Regulations 1991 regs 5, 17 (1) (c). As to the official record see para 1072 note 4 ante.
4 As to service see para 1068 note 4 ante.
5 Civil Aviation Authority Regulations 1991 reg 17 (1) (a).
6 Ibid reg 17 (1) (b).
7 Ibid reg 17 (4); the same applies to a body incorporated under the law of any part of the United Kingdom or of a relevant overseas territory or associated state and controlled by United Kingdom nationals: reg 17 (4). As to nationality requirements see para 1080 post.
8 Ibid reg 17 (1) proviso.
9 See note 2 supra.
10 Civil Aviation Authority Regulations 1991 reg 17 (2) (a).
11 Ibid reg 17 (2) (a). As to appeals and re-hearings see regs 27, 29; and paras 1086, 1087 post.
12 Ibid reg 17 (2) (b). See also the Airports Act 1986 s 31 requiring that air transport licensing functions are performed in compliance with any traffic distribution rules in force under the 1986 Act; see further para 1196 post.
13 Civil Aviation Authority Regulations 1991 reg 17 (2) (c).

1076. Provisional variation of licence for damaging behaviour. Where the holder of an air transport licence applies to the Civil Aviation Authority (CAA)[1] for the variation of an air transport licence held by another person in order to restrain him from engaging in behaviour damaging to the applicant's business, he may require in view of the urgency of the matter a preliminary hearing of the application so that his competitor's licence is provisionally varied pending the hearing[2].

Within 20 days of the date of service of the application[3], the CAA must hold a preliminary hearing if it is satisfied that there is enough evidence as to the respondent's behaviour[4] and that its statutory duties, its statement of policies and the urgency of the matter warrant the hearing[5]. The CAA will hear both applicant and respondent as well as any other person whom it wishes to hear[6], including those persons whom it must consult before a hearing[7]. The CAA must give a decision within five days of the end of the preliminary meeting: the decision can only be a decision provisionally to vary or to refuse provisionally to vary the respondent's licence[8]. A provisional variation has effect until the time the decision taken by the CAA in a full hearing takes effect[9].

1 As to the CAA see para 1044 ante.
2 See the Civil Aviation Authority Regulations 1991, SI 1991/1672, reg 24 (1). The applicant's statement must give particulars of the behaviour complained of and the extent to which his business is being or is likely to be damaged by that behaviour (reg 24 (1) (b)); a copy of the application must be served by the applicant on the respondent on the same day as the application is being served on the CAA (reg 24 (1) (d)). The respondent has five days to make representations and serve them on the CAA and the applicant: reg 24 (2). As to service see para 1068 note 4 ante.
3 Notice of the time and place of the preliminary hearing must be given at least ten days before the date: see reg 24 (3), (4); similarly, if the CAA decides not to hold a preliminary hearing, it must so notify the parties within ten days of the service of the application: reg 24 (3), (4).
4 See ibid reg 24 (5) (a).
5 See ibid reg 24 (5) (b). As to the statutory duties and statements of policies of the CAA see respectively paras 1045, 1073 ante.
6 See ibid reg 24 (6)–(8); regs 21 (consultations), 22 (furnishing of information), 26 (1), (4), (6), (7) (procedure) apply to the preliminary hearing as they apply to a full hearing: see paras 1079, 1081 post.
7 See ibid reg 24 (9). As to consultations see para 1079 post.
8 See ibid reg 24 (10), (11); the decision notice must contain the terms of the variation (if so decided) and the date, time and place of the hearing (see reg 24 (10) (a)–(c)) and the CAA must give the reasons for its decision within ten days of the end of the preliminary hearing: reg 24 (10).
9 See ibid reg 24 (11). As to a full hearing see para 1081 post.

1077. Objections and representations. Within 21 days of the publication of an application, or of the publication of a proposal by the Civil Aviation Authority (CAA)[1] for the grant, revocation, suspension or variation of an air transport licence, or within three days of notification by the CAA that the application or proposal has been made and will not be published, any person may enter an objection to, or make a representation about, the application or proposal[2], and a copy of the objection or representation must be served within the specified time limits[3] on the applicant, if any, on any other person who holds a licence to which the application or proposal relates, and on any person or body which the CAA is obliged to consult[4].

1 As to the CAA see para 1044 ante.
2 Civil Aviation Authority Regulations 1991, SI 1991/1672, reg 20 (1); save for a provisional variation: reg 20 (1).
3 Ie within 24 hours after service on the CAA by the person making the objection or representation where he is the holder of an air transport licence, or by the CAA within seven days of the day of service on the CAA in any other case: ibid reg 20 (3); as to service see para 1068 note 4 ante.
4 Ibid reg 20 (3). Upon being so served the applicant must, if so required, serve the person making the objection or representation with a copy of the application: reg 20 (4). As to bodies which the CAA must consult see reg 21; and para 1079 post.

1078. Environmental cases. The Civil Aviation Authority (CAA)[1] may receive an environmental application or make an environmental proposal for the grant or variation of an air transport licence[2] authorising the holder to operate either a helicopter under 3,000 feet or any aircraft the operation of which will or may cause an exceptional amount of noise, vibration, pollution or other disturbance[3]. The CAA must designate the application or proposal as an environmental case and publish a notice of this designation[4]. Objections or representations[5] on grounds of noise, vibration, pollution or other disturbance must be served within 42 days of the date of publication of the designation notice[6].

1   As to the CAA see para 1044 ante.
2   As to the application for an air transport licence see para 1074 ante.
3   Civil Aviation Authority Regulations 1991, SI 1991/1672, reg 19 (1) (a), (b); the provision does not include applications or proposals which do not relate to a licence to operate a regular and frequent service or to a proposal by the CAA to vary a licence on the ground that it is no longer satisfied as to the experience or resources and financial arrangements of the licence holder (see further para 1080 post): reg 19 (1) (i), (ii). As to environmental disturbances see paras 1185–1188 post.
4   Ibid reg 19 (2); as to publication see reg 5.
5   As to objections and representations see para 1077 ante.
6   Civil Aviation Authority Regulations 1991 reg 20 (2); as to service see para 1068 note 4 ante.

1079. Preliminaries to hearings. Before the date fixed for the hearing of a case, the Civil Aviation Authority (CAA)[1] must furnish to any person or body who is entitled to be heard[2] or which it is required to consult[3] all information which the CAA has obtained in connection with the case[4].

The CAA may hold a preliminary meeting to discuss the conduct of the case with all parties[5], persons whom the CAA wishes to hear in relation to the case and those persons consulted by the CAA who responded in writing[6].

The CAA must also consult such persons in the Channel Islands as have been notified by the Bailiff of Jersey, the Bailiff of Guernsey or the President of the States of Alderney to the Secretary of State for the Home Department in any case concerning the Channel Islands, the Isle of Man Department of Highways, Ports and Properties in any case concerning the Isle of Man, and the Secretary of State[7] in any case concerning Gibraltar[8].

1   As to the CAA see para 1044 ante.
2   As to who has a right to be heard see para 1081 note 2 post.
3   See the text to notes 7, 8 infra.
4   Civil Aviation Authority Regulations 1991, SI 1991/1672, reg 22. However, the CAA may not disclose any information provided by the Secretary of State where the latter has certified that a disclosure would not be in the public interest (reg 22 proviso (i)) and, where it may disclose information, it must first consult the person or body who furnished such information although it may not disclose information relating to the commercial or financial affairs of the person or body who provided it if it cannot be disclosed without disadvantage to that person or body which, by comparison with the advantage to the public and the prospective recipient, is unwarranted (reg 22 proviso (ii)).
5   'Party' means a person who has a right to be heard: ibid regs 3 (1), 25 (1). As to these persons see para 1081 note 2 post.
6   Ibid reg 23. As to consultations by the CAA see text and note 8 infra. Any such person may attend in person or be represented by an authorised representative: reg 23 (2).
7   As to the Secretary of State see para 1032 ante.
8   Civil Aviation Authority Regulations 1991 reg 21. Such consultation is not necessary where the application or licence is for not more than four flights in any one direction between the same two places, or where the CAA is acting in pursuance of its duty under the Civil Aviation Act 1982 ss 65 (2) or (3) or 66 (3), or where the CAA is compelled to refuse, revoke, suspend or vary a licence under the Airports Act 1986 s 31 (see para 1075 note 12 ante): Civil Aviation Authority Regulations 1991 reg 21 proviso (i)–(iii).

(iii) The Hearing

1080. Considerations for decision. It is the duty of the Civil Aviation Authority (CAA)[1] to perform its functions so as to secure that the services provided by

British airlines[2] satisfy public demand at the lowest cost consistent with the highest standard of safety and an economic return to efficient operators as well as securing the sound development of the civil air transport industry[3]; the CAA must also endeavour to further the reasonable interests of users of air transport services[4].

While the CAA has a number of duties to fulfil in the performance of its air transport licensing functions, it must see that these duties impose the minimum restrictions on the civil air transport industry and the services which it provides[5].

The CAA must ensure that British airlines compete effectively with other airlines on international routes having regard to any advice from the Secretary of State[6] and the most effective use of airports in the United Kingdom[7]. Regard must also be given to the effect that any new service, which the applicant proposes to offer under the new licence, may have on services already provided by British airlines, particularly, where the existing services and the new service are similar in terms of route or where several applicants propose to provide similar services, the CAA must consider whether any benefit can arise from allowing several airlines to offer similar services[8].

A further consideration that has to be taken into account is the need to reduce as much as possible any adverse effects on the environment and any disturbance to the public from noise, vibration, atmospheric pollution or any other cause attributable to the use of aircraft[9].

The CAA must refuse to grant a licence if it is not satisfied that the applicant is a fit person to operate aircraft under the authority of a licence having regard to his and his employees' experience and past activities[10], that his resources and financial arrangements are adequate[11] and that he is either a United Kingdom national[12] or a body incorporated under the law of any part of the United Kingdom or of a relevant overseas territory[13] or an associated state and is controlled by United Kingdom nationals[14].

The same criteria[15] apply to the making of a decision to revoke, suspend or vary an air transport licence either on the application of a person other than the licence holder[16] or on the proposal of the CAA.[17]

1 As to the CAA see para 1044 ante.
2 'British airline' means an undertaking having power to provide air transport services and appearing to the CAA to have its principal place of business in the United Kingdom, the Channel Islands or the Isle of Man and to be controlled by persons who are either United Kingdom nationals or are for the time being approved by the Secretary of State: Civil Aviation Act 1982 s 4 (2). As to United Kingdom nationals see note 12 infra.
3 See the Civil Aviation Act 1998 s 4 (1); and para 1047 ante.
4 Ibid s 4 (2).
5 See ibid s 68 (4).
6 Ibid s 68 (1) (a); negotiations for traffic rights between states are conducted at governmental level; see further para 1004 ante. As to the Secretary of State see para 1032 ante.
7 Ibid s 68 (1) (b); as to the use of airports see paras 1196–1197 post (traffic distribution rules and orders limiting aircraft movements at airports under the Airports Act 1986 ss 31, 32).
8 Civil Aviation Act 1982 s 68 (2).
9 Ibid s 68 (3); as to environmental disturbances see paras 1185–1188 post.
10 Ibid s 65 (2) (a).
11 Ibid s 65 (2) (b).
12 Ibid s 65 (3) (a). 'United Kingdom national' means an individual who is either a British citizen, a British Dependent Territories citizen, a British National (Overseas) or a British Overseas citizen, or a person who under the British Nationality Act 1981 is a British subject, or a British protected person within the meaning of the 1981 Act: Civil Aviation Act 1982 s 105 (1) (amended by the Hong Kong (British Nationality) Order 1986, SI 1986/948, art 8, Schedule); see further BRITISH NATIONAL-ITY.

13 'Relevant overseas territory' means any of the Channel Islands, the Isle of Man, any colony and any country or place outside Her Majesty's dominions in which for the time being Her Majesty has jurisdiction: Civil Aviation Act 1982 s 105 (1); see COMMONWEALTH.
14 Civil Aviation Act 1982 s 105 (3) (b). 'Associated state' is not defined. Before deciding that a licence holder is neither a United Kingdom national nor such a body the CAA must serve on him 21 days' notice of its intention to consider the matter, and consider any representations he makes before the expiration of that period: Civil Aviation Authority Regulations 1991, SI 1991/1672, reg 17 (4).
15 This includes the provisions of the Civil Aviation Act 1982 s 4: see text and note 3 supra.
16 See the Civil Aviation Act 1982 s 66 (1).
17 See ibid s 66 (2). As to the application of the criteria see s 66 (3); and text and notes 10–14 supra.

1081. Hearings. No decision to grant, refuse to grant, revoke, suspend or vary an air transport licence may be made by the Civil Aviation Authority (CAA)[1] until all persons having a right to be heard[2] have had the opportunity of being heard[3] by the CAA, sitting with such of its employees as it thinks fit[4]. Any person who has a right to be heard is a party to the case[5].

Fourteen days' written notice of the date, time and place of the hearing must be served[6] by the CAA on persons intended to be heard[7], but in cases considered by the CAA to be of compelling urgency a hearing may be held without such previous notice, provided sufficient notice is given[8].

Hearings must be held in public, unless the CAA decides otherwise[9]. If the CAA thinks fit, any person heard by it may appear in person or be represented, may produce oral and written evidence and may examine witnesses[10]. The proceedings are recorded and a transcript may be made available on terms[11]. Failure to give any notice or any other procedural irregularity does not invalidate the action taken by the CAA[12].

1 As to the CAA see para 1044 ante.
2 The following persons have a right to be heard: the applicant, the holder of any air transport licence or air operator's certificate or aerodrome licence and persons representative of those who have served objections or representations whether they expressed the views of passengers or shippers of cargo or whether they were made on the ground of environmental disturbance: Civil Aviation Authority Regulations 1991, SI 1991/1672, reg 25 (1). However, no person other than the applicant and the holder of the licence to which the application relates has a right to be heard unless he has made an objection or representation and has then stated that he wishes to be heard (reg 25 (1) proviso (i)), and no person may be heard before the CAA makes a decision in a case where the Secretary of State has directed that the licence be granted, refused, revoked, suspended or varied or where it is the duty of the CAA to refuse, revoke, suspend or vary the licence under the Airports Act 1986 s 31: Civil Aviation Authority Regulations 1991 reg 25 (1) proviso (ii). Save in a case where the Secretary of State has given such a direction, the CAA may, if it thinks fit, hear a person who has no right to be heard, provided he has made an objection or representation and has then stated that he wishes to be heard: reg 25 (2).
3 See ibid reg 25 (1).
4 Ibid reg 26 (1). For the purpose of conducting a hearing and making a decision the quorum of the CAA is two members: see reg 15 (2).
5 Ibid reg 3 (1); this provision does not apply to persons who are to be heard by the CAA although they have no right to be heard: see reg 3 (1); and note 2 supra.
6 As to service see para 1068 note 4 ante.
7 Civil Aviation Authority Regulations 1991 reg 25 (3). The same notice must be served on any person consulted by the CAA who has responded in writing: reg 25 (3); as to consultations see para 1079 ante. A similar notice must be published in the official record not less than seven days before the date of the hearing, and must be exhibited in a public place: reg 25 (3). As to the official record see para 1072 note 4 ante.
8 See ibid reg 25 (3) proviso.
9 Ibid reg 26 (4).
10 Ibid reg 26 (2). The CAA may allow a person who has no right to be heard to exercise the same rights as a party to the case: reg 26 (2); and see text and notes 2, 5 supra. A person consulted by the CAA

who has responded in writing may attend the hearing and be given the opportunity by the CAA to make observations to which all parties and other persons heard may respond: reg 26 (5); as to consultations see para 1079 post; as to parties to the case see note 5 supra.

11 See ibid reg 26 (7), (8).

12 See ibid reg 26 (6).

1082. Decisions. The Civil Aviation Authority (CAA)[1] may either grant an air transport licence to the applicant in the terms[2] requested by him or in those terms with such modification as it thinks fit, or may refuse to grant a licence[3].

The CAA may publish particulars of and reasons for any decision with respect to a licence or an application for a licence[4].

1 As to the CAA see para 1044 ante.

2 As to the terms of a licence see para 1083 post.

3 Civil Aviation Act 1982 s 65 (1). The CAA may refuse a licence for any reason; it is not confined to the reasons specified in s 65 (2) and (3) (failure to be satisfied as to the experience or resources and financial arrangements of the applicant; see para 1080 ante): s 65 (4).

4 Ibid s 67 (4).

1083. Terms of licences. An air transport licence may contain such terms as the Civil Aviation Authority (CAA)[1] thinks fit[2]. The terms may be, or include, terms settled by a person other than the CAA[3] and may include terms as to the charges which are to be made and the goods, services and other benefits which are and are not to be furnished in connection with a charter contract to which the licence relates[4].

If the CAA establishes a schedule of terms and includes in a licence a term that the holder must comply with terms set out in the schedule, then any proposal by the CAA to vary the schedule or any part of it must be treated as a proposal to vary every licence containing that term[5]. The holder of an air transport licence which includes a term requiring compliance with a schedule of terms may apply for the variation of the schedule; his application is to be treated as an application for the variation of every air transport licence containing the same term[6].

1 As to the CAA see para 1044 ante.

2 Civil Aviation Act 1982 s 65 (5).

3 Ibid s 65 (5) (a).

4 Ibid s 65 (5) (b).

5 See the Civil Aviation Authority Regulations 1991, SI 1991/1672, reg 18 (1). When a licence contains such a term relating to a schedule the CAA must publish the schedule and any variations to it in its official record or otherwise: reg 18 (2). As to the official record see para 1072 note 4 ante.

6 See ibid reg 18 (3).

1084. Statement of reasons. Where the Civil Aviation Authority (CAA)[1] takes a decision in relation to an air transport licence, it must give a statement of its reasons to all parties[2] to the case, save that no statement need be given if the licence was granted in the terms of the application without there having been an objection or a specific request for reasons by any party[3].

If, however, the CAA believes that it would not be in the interests of national security or relations with other states for reasons to be given, the Secretary of State[4] may, on notice given by the CAA, direct it to refrain from giving reasons[5]. Further, if the giving to a relevant person[6] of reasons containing details of the commercial or financial affairs of any other person would cause disadvantage to that person which, by comparison with the advantage to the public and the relevant person of its disclosure to him, is unwarranted, then the CAA may refrain from giving, or may exclude that material from, the statement of reasons[7].

1 As to the CAA see para 1044 ante.
2 Ie to the applicant or, as the case may be, the holder or former holder of the licence, and to any other person who has made an objection or has requested a statement of reasons.
3 Civil Aviation Act 1982 s 67 (2).
4 As to the Secretary of State see para 1032 ante.
5 See the Civil Aviation Act 1982 s 67 (3).
6 Ie one of the persons mentioned in note 2 supra.
7 See the Civil Aviation Act 1982 s 67 (3).

1085. Renewal of licences. If the holder of a current air transport licence applies for the grant of another licence in continuation of or substitution for a current licence, the current licence does not cease to be in force by reason only of its expiration unless either the Civil Aviation Authority (CAA)[1] has decided the application, or the time for appealing has expired or any appeal in respect of the application is determined or abandoned or, if an appeal is successful, the licence granted in consequence of the appeal comes into force[2].

1 As to the CAA see para 1044 ante.
2 Civil Aviation Act 1982 s 65 (6).

(iv) Appeals

1086. Appeals to Secretary of State. Every party[1] to a case before the Civil Aviation Authority (CAA)[2] has a right of appeal to the Secretary of State[3]. An appeal is made by written notice of appeal signed by or on behalf of the appellant, stating the grounds of appeal and the arguments relied on[4], and served[5] on the Secretary of State, the CAA, all other parties, any persons heard by the CAA[6] and any person or body consulted by it[7] within 21 days from the notification by the CAA of its decision[8].

Any party to the appeal[9] or any person or body consulted by the CAA may, within 14 days of service of the notice of the appeal, serve on the Secretary of State, the appellant and the CAA a written submission giving reasons why the CAA's decision should or should not be upheld[10], but neither the appellant nor any other party to the appeal may submit to the Secretary of State evidence which was not before the CAA when it reached its decision[11].

Within 28 days of receiving notice of an appeal, the CAA may make a written submission to the Secretary of State in connection with the appeal, including an amplification and explanation of the reasons for its decision[12]. Within 14 days of the expiry of this 28 day period the appellant may serve upon the Secretary of State a reply to any submission made by any party to the appeal or by the CAA[13].

Before deciding an appeal, the Secretary of State may ask the appellant, any other person who has made a submission or the CAA to give any amplification or explanation of any submission which he may require[14]. He may also obtain from the CAA any information, relating to the commercial or financial affairs of the informant, which it withheld from any person having the right to be heard as in its opinion its disclosure was unwarranted; the CAA and the person who gave the information can make written submissions to the Secretary of State in connection with that information[15].

1 Any party who has the right to be heard (see para 1081 note 2 ante) is deemed to be a party: see the Civil Aviation Authority Regulations 1991, SI 1991/1672, regs 3 (1), 25 (1). In the case of an appeal from a decision rendered at a preliminary hearing for the provisional variation of an air transport licence on the grounds of damaging behaviour, reference to every party is a reference to the applicant and the respondent: reg 28 (2) (a); as to the provisional variation of a licence for damaging behaviour see para 1076 ante.
2 As to the CAA see para 1044 ante.
3 Civil Aviation Authority Regulations 1991 reg 27 (1). As to the Secretary of State see para 1032 ante.
4 Ibid reg 27 (2).
5 As to service see para 1068 note 4 ante.
6 Ie under the Civil Aviation Authority Regulations 1991 reg 25 (2); see para 1081 note 2 ante. In the case of an appeal from a decision as to the provisional variation of a licence on the grounds of damaging behaviour, the notice of appeal must be served on those persons whom the CAA may have heard at the preliminary hearing under reg 24 (6): reg 28 (2) (b); and see note 1 supra.
7 Ie under ibid reg 21; see para 1079 ante.
8 Ibid reg 27 (3), (4). The period is extended if a transcript has been ordered (see reg 27 (4)) but reduced to five days in the case of allocation of scarce bilateral capacity (see reg 27 (9)) or of appeal in respect of a provisional variation of a licence on the grounds of damaging behaviour (see reg 28 (2) (c); and para 1076 ante) and, in the latter case, any reference to a transcript is to be ignored (see reg 28 (2) (c)).
9 Ie all those persons served with notice of the appeal pursuant to ibid reg 27 (3) (c)–(e); see note 6 supra.
10 Ibid reg 27 (6). The period of 14 days is reduced to five days in the case of allocation of scarce bilateral capacity (see reg 27 (9)) or of appeal in respect of a provisional variation of a licence on the grounds of damaging behaviour (see reg 28 (2) (d); and para 1076 ante).
11 Ibid reg 27 (11).
12 Ibid reg 27 (7). It must serve a copy on the appellant and on all those persons served with the notice of appeal: reg 27 (7). The period of service of the CAA's submission is reduced to eight days in the case of allocation of scarce bilateral capacity (see reg 27 (9)) or of appeal in respect of a provisional variation of a licence on the grounds of damaging behaviour (see reg 28 (2) (e); and para 1076 ante).
13 Ibid reg 27 (8). The period of 14 days is reduced to four days in the case of allocation of scarce bilateral capacity (reg 27 (9)) or of appeal in respect of a provisional variation of a licence on the grounds of damaging behaviour (see reg 28 (2) (f); and para 1076 ante).
14 See ibid reg 27 (10) (a). He must give the appellant the opportunity of replying to any such amplification or explanation: reg 27 (10) (a).
15 See ibid reg 27 (10) (b). As to the furnishing of information by the authority see reg 22; and para 1079 ante.

1087. Decisions on appeal. The Secretary of State[1] may uphold the decision of the Civil Aviation Authority (CAA)[2] or direct it to rehear the case, or to reverse or to vary its decision[3]. The Secretary of State must notify the CAA, appellant and persons and bodies served with the notice of appeal of his decision and the reasons for it, and the CAA must publish the notification[4].

The decision of the Secretary of State is neither invalidated by any procedural irregularity, which he may ask to be righted, save for the service of the appellant's notice of appeal on the Secretary of State[5] nor can it be attacked on the ground that he consulted foreign authorities in matters relating to national security or foreign relations even though they could have affected the appeal[6].

1 As to the Secretary of State see para 1032 ante.
2 As to the CAA see para 1044 ante.
3 Civil Aviation Authority Regulations 1991, SI 1991/1672, reg 29 (1). The Secretary of State may order the appellant to pay to any other party to the appeal either a specified sum for costs or the taxed amount of the costs whether or not in the county court, any such costs being recoverable if the

county court so orders by execution in that court or otherwise as if payable under a county court
order: see reg 29 (4).
4 Ibid reg 29 (2). While directing the CAA to rehear a case, the Secretary of State must notify all the
relevant persons whether or not the CAA's first decision is to have effect pending its further
decision: reg 29 (3).
5 Ibid reg 29 (7).
6 Ibid reg 29 (6). As to national interest and relations with other countries or territories see the Civil
Aviation Act 1982 s 6; and para 1047 ante.

(v) Supplementary Provisions

1088. Transfer of licences. The Civil Aviation Authority (CAA)[1] may allow
the transfer of an air transport licence either if the sole holder has died[2] or in
connection with the reconstruction of a body corporate or the amalgamation of any
bodies corporate[3]. The procedure is the same as that of an application for the
variation of a licence[4]. No transfer is allowed if the CAA would be bound[5] to refuse
to grant a licence to the proposed transferee[6].

1 As to the CAA see para 1044 ante.
2 See the Civil Aviation Act 1982 s 67 (1) and the Civil Aviation Authority Regulations 1991, SI
1991/1672, reg 30 (1) (a). The person treated as the holder of the licence may apply to the CAA for
the transfer of the licence to a person entitled to an interest in the deceased person's estate: see reg 30
(2) (a).
3 See ibid reg 30 (1) (b). The person treated as the holder of the licence may apply to the CAA for the
substitution of his own name in the licence: see reg 30 (2) (b).
4 Ibid reg 30 (4). The application must state the grounds on which it is based and be served on the CAA
within 21 days from the day on which the applicant became entitled to make it; if no application is
made during that period, the licence ceases at the end of the 21 day period to be treated as if granted to
a person other than the grantee: reg 30 (3). Regulations 27 and 29 (appeals) apply: reg 30 (4). As to
applications for variation see paras 1080–1084 ante; as to appeals see paras 1086, 1087 ante.
5 Ie under the Civil Aviation Act 1982 s 65 (2) or (3): see para 1080 ante.
6 Civil Aviation Authority Regulations 1991 reg 30 (5).

1089. Surrender of licences. The Civil Aviation Authority (CAA)[1] may require
any person who has possession or control of an air transport licence which it has
revoked or varied to surrender it for cancellation or variation; failure to comply
with such a requirement is an offence[2].

1 As to the CAA see para 1044 ante.
2 Civil Aviation Authority Regulations 1991, SI 1991/1672, reg 31. The penalty on summary
conviction is a fine not exceeding level 2 on the standard scale: reg 31. As to the standard scale see
para 1044 note 6 ante. At the date at which this volume states the law, level 2 on that scale is at £100.

1090. Charges. Charges payable to the Civil Aviation Authority (CAA)[1] in
connection with matters arising under the Civil Aviation Act 1982[2] in respect of air
transport licensing are to be found in the scheme published in the CAA's official
record[3].

1 As to the CAA see para 1044 ante.
2 See the Civil Aviation Act 1982 s 11 (1), (2); and para 1053 ante.
3 Official Record Series 1.

1091. Offences. Any operator[1] who knows, or ought to have known, that an
aircraft is flown for the carriage for reward of passengers and cargo without, or in
breach of the terms of, an air transport licence is guilty of an offence[2].

Any other person than an operator who makes available accommodation for the carriage of passengers or cargo on an aircraft on a flight[3] and who knows, or ought to know, before the flight that the aircraft is to be flown without, or in breach of the terms of, an existing air transport licence is guilty of an offence[4].

It is immaterial whether the contravention occurred outside the United Kingdom if the operator committing the offence was a United Kingdom national[5] or a body incorporated under the law of any part of the United Kingdom or of a relevant overseas territory[6], or a person (other than a United Kingdom national or such a body) maintaining a place of business in the United Kingdom[7].

If the Civil Aviation Authority (CAA)[8] suspects that a contravention is about to take place, it may direct the commander of the aircraft not to take off, or it may detain the aircraft; failure to comply with any such direction is an offence[9].

Any person who knowingly or recklessly furnishes to the CAA or the Secretary of State[10] information which is false in a material particular for the purpose of obtaining for himself or any other person the grant, variation or cancellation of a suspension of an air transport licence is guilty of an offence[11].

1 For the meaning of 'operator' see para 1340 post.
2 Civil Aviation Act 1982 s 64 (5) (a). The penalty on summary conviction is a fine not exceeding the statutory maximum, or on conviction on indictment a fine or imprisonment for a term not exceeding two years or both: s 64 (8). As to the statutory maximum see para 1005 note 11 ante. At the date at which this volume states the law, the statutory maximum is £2,000. For the meaning of 'reward' see para 1092 note 6 post.
3 'Flight' means a journey by air beginning when the aircraft in question takes off and ending when it lands: ibid s 105 (1).
4 Ibid s 64 (5) (b). For the penalty see s 64 (8); and note 2 supra.
5 For the meaning of 'United Kingdom national' see para 1080 note 12 ante.
6 For the meaning of 'relevant overseas territory' see para 1080 note 13 ante.
7 Civil Aviation Act 1982 s 64 (6).
8 As to the CAA see para 1044 ante.
9 Civil Aviation Act 1982 s 64 (7). For the penalty see s 64 (8); and note 2 supra. For rights of detention in other circumstances see para 1339 post.
10 As to Secretary of State see para 1032 ante.
11 Civil Aviation Act 1982 s 67 (6). The penalty prescribed is the same as that specified in note 2 supra: s 67 (6).

(3) PROVISION OF ACCOMMODATION IN AIRCRAFT

1092. Air travel organiser's licence. No person in the United Kingdom may make available, either as a principal or as an agent, accommodation for the carriage of persons or cargo[1] on flights[2] in any part of the world, nor may any such person hold himself out as a person who, either as a principal or as an agent or without disclosing his capacity, may make such accommodation available, unless he is the operator[3] of the relevant aircraft or holds and complies with the terms of an air travel organiser's licence or is exempted from the need to hold such a licence[4]. A person who contravenes this provision commits an offence[5].

However, no licence is required either by an operator of aircraft for the carriage of persons for reward[6] who makes available or holds himself out as a person who may make available such accommodation where he has reason to believe that at the time of the flight he will be the operator of the relevant aircraft[7]; or by a person who makes available, or holds himself out as a person who may make available, such accommodation where he is the agent acting on behalf and with the authority of the licence holder, the operator or a person otherwise exempted by the Civil Aviation Authority (CAA)[8] from the need to hold a licence[9].

The CAA may by instrument exempt from the need to hold a licence any person or class or description of persons specified in it, and may revoke or vary the instrument by subsequent instrument[10].

1 'Cargo' includes mail: Civil Aviation Act 1982 s 105 (1).
2 For the meaning of 'flight' see para 1091 note 3 ante.
3 For the meaning of 'operator' see para 1340 post.
4 See the Civil Aviation Act 1982 s 71 (1) and the Civil Aviation (Air Travel Organisers' Licensing) Regulations 1972, SI 1972/223, reg 2 (1). No person may give the wrong indication, whether directly or not, that he holds an air travel organiser's licence: reg 2 (1B) (added by SI 1975/1049).
5 See the Civil Aviation (Air Travel Organisers' Licensing) Regulations 1972 reg 2 (1A), (5) (amended by SI 1975/1049): the offence is punishable on summary conviction by a fine not exceeding £400 or, on conviction on indictment, by a fine or imprisonment for a term not exceeding two years or both.
6 'Reward' includes any kind of consideration received or to be received wholly or partly in connection with the flight irrespective of the person by whom or to whom the consideration has been or is to be given: Civil Aviation Act 1982, 105 (1).
7 Civil Aviation (Air Travel Organisers' Licensing) Regulations 1972 reg 2 (2) (a).
8 As to the CAA see para 1044 ante.
9 Civil Aviation (Air Travel Organisers' Licensing) Regulations 1972 reg (2) (b) (amended by SI 1981/314).
10 See the Civil Aviation Act 1982 s 71 (1) and the Civil Aviation (Air Travel Organisers' Licensing) Regulations 1972 reg 2 (3). The instrument does not come into force until published in the official record: regs 1 (2), 2 (4). As to the official record see para 1072 note 4 ante.

1093. Applications. An application for the grant of an air travel organiser's licence must be made to the Civil Aviation Authority (CAA)[1] in writing[2]. An application may be made by the holder of a licence for it to be revoked, suspended or varied at any time, but a licence holder may not apply for the variation of a schedule of terms included in the licence[3]. The CAA may refuse to consider an application unless it is accompanied by the appropriate fee and is served on the CAA not less than six months before the date on which the licence or its revocation, suspension or variation is to take effect[4].

1 As to the CAA see para 1044 ante.
2 Civil Aviation (Air Travel Organisers' Licensing) Regulations 1972, SI 1972/223, reg 3 (1).
3 Ibid reg 4 (1). As to schedules of terms see para 1096 post.
4 Ibid regs 3 (1) proviso, 4 (2). As to the fee payable under the Civil Aviation Act 1982 s 11 see the scheme of charges published by the CAA in its Official Record Series 1; as to the computation of time see the Civil Aviation (Air Travel Organisers' Licensing) Regulations 1972 reg 1 (5), (6) (periods are exclusive of the first day but inclusive of the last day, and Saturdays, Sundays, Christmas Day, Good Friday and bank holidays are disregarded). As to the service of documents see reg 1 (3), (4), which corresponds to the Civil Aviation Authority Regulations 1991, SI 1991/1672, reg 4: see para 1068 note 4 ante.

1094. Criteria for decision. Before granting an air travel organiser's licence the Civil Aviation Authority (CAA)[1] must be satisfied that the applicant is a fit person to make available accommodation for the carriage of persons on flights[2], and that the resources of the applicant and the financial arrangements made by him are adequate for discharging his obligations as a licence holder[3].

While in determining whether the applicant is a fit person it must have regard to his and his employees' past activities generally, the CAA is not obliged to refuse a licence on the grounds that it considers that he has insufficient experience in making available accommodation for the carriage of persons on flights[4].

1 As to the CAA see para 1044 ante.
2 Civil Aviation (Air Travel Organisers' Licensing) Regulations 1972, SI 1972/223, reg 3 (2) (a). As to appeals see para 1098 post.
3 Ibid reg 3 (2) (b).
4 See ibid reg 3 (2) (a).

1095. Decisions. The Civil Aviation Authority (CAA)[1] may either grant an air travel organiser's licence to the applicant in the terms of the application or in those terms with such modifications as the CAA thinks fit, or it may refuse to grant a licence[2].

The CAA may also revoke, suspend or vary a licence on the holder's application[3], and if no longer satisfied that the holder is a fit person or that his resources and financial arrangements are adequate for discharging his obligations, the CAA must revoke or suspend[4] or vary the licence[5].

Where the CAA proposes to grant a licence in terms other than those requested by the applicant, or to refuse to grant a licence, or to revoke, suspend or vary a licence otherwise than on the holder's application, it must serve on the applicant or the holder 21 days' notice of the proposal and the reasons for it[6] and consider any representation the applicant or the holder may serve on the authority before the expiration of the notice[7]. Where the CAA makes a decision[8] after such a proposal, it must furnish a statement of its reasons for the decision to the applicant or the holder[9].

1 As to the CAA see para 1044 ante.
2 See the Civil Aviation Act 1982 s 71 (2) (a) and the Civil Aviation (Air Travel Organisers' Licensing) Regulations 1972, SI 1972/223, reg 3 (1).
3 See the Civil Aviation Act 1982 s 71 (2) (c) and the Civil Aviation (Air Travel Organisers' Licensing) Regulations 1972 reg 4 (1).
4 The CAA may provide, by written notice on the holder, that the licence shall not be effective during a period specified in the notice; a further notice may render the licence effective on and after a date specified in such notice which, however, does not prejudice the CAA's powers to suspend the licence again or to revoke or vary it: ibid reg 4 (4). The CAA may also suspend a licence after a short notice of 72 hours where it is no longer satisfied as to the holder's fitness or resources and financial arrangements in respect of the activities in which he is engaged: see reg 6 (2).
5 Ibid reg 4 (3).
6 Ibid reg 6 (1) (a). As to service of notice and computation of time see reg 1 (3)–(6); and para 1093 note 4 ante.
7 Ibid reg 6 (1) (b).
8 For a decision to revoke, suspend or vary a licence on the CAA's proposal, to grant or vary a licence in terms other than those requested by the applicant, or to refuse to grant a licence, the quorum of the CAA is one member; any other decision to grant, revoke suspend or vary a licence may be made on behalf of the CAA only by a member or employee of the CAA: ibid reg 5 (2), (3).
9 Ibid reg 6 (3). The CAA may publish in its official record particulars of, and reasons for, any of its decisions: reg 6 (4). As to the official record see para 1072 note 4 ante.

1096. Terms of licences. The Civil Aviation Authority (CAA)[1] may prescribe such terms for an air travel organiser's licence as it thinks fit, and in particular may include terms as to the minimum charges to be made and the goods, services and other benefits which are or are not to be furnished[2].

If the CAA establishes any schedule of terms and includes in a licence a term that the licence holder must comply with that schedule as varied from time to time, the

CAA may at any time propose to vary that schedule, any such proposal then being treated as a proposal to vary the licence[3].

1 As to the CAA see para 1044 ante.
2 See the Civil Aviation Act 1982 s 71 (2) (b) and the Civil Aviation (Air Travel Organisers' Licensing) Regulations 1972, SI 1972/223, reg 3 (3).
3 Ibid reg 7 (1). The CAA must publish the schedule and any variation of it in its official record: reg 7 (2). As to the variation of a licence see para 1095 ante; as to the official record see para 1072 note 4 ante.

1097. Renewal of licences. If the holder of a current air travel organiser's licence applies for the grant of another licence in continuation of, or in substitution for, his current licence, the current licence does not cease to be in force by reason only of the expiration of its term but remains in force until the Civil Aviation Authority (CAA)[1] gives its decision on the application[2].

1 As to the CAA see para 1044 ante.
2 Civil Aviation (Air Travel Organisers' Licensing) Regulations 1972, SI 1972/223, reg 3 (4) (amended by SI 1979/5). The application must contain the particulars relating to fitness, resources and financial arrangements which the CAA may have specified in a notice four months before the expiration of the licence (or at the time of the grant if the licence had a term of less than six months) (Civil Aviation (Air Travel Organisers' Licensing) Regulations 1972 reg 3 (4) (a) (as so amended)); it must be accompanied by the right fee and made not later than three months (or, in the case of a licence for a term of three months or less, half the term) before the expiration of the terms of the licence (reg 3 (4) (b)–(c)). This provision does not apply in the case of an application being withdrawn and is without prejudice to the CAA's power to revoke, suspend or vary the licence: reg 3 (4) (as so amended). As to fees see the Official Record Series 1.

1098. Appeals. An appeal lies to a county court[1] from any decision of the Civil Aviation Authority (CAA)[2] that a person is not a fit person to hold an air travel organiser's licence[3]. The CAA is a respondent to any such appeal[4].

If the court is satisfied on the evidence submitted to the CAA that it was wrong in deciding as it did, the court may reverse the CAA's decision and the CAA must give effect to the court's determination[5].

1 Ie the county court for the district in which the decision was made: CCR Ord 4 r 9. The appeal is brought by filing in the court office, within 21 days of the date of the decision, a copy of the decision and a request for entry of the appeal: see CCR Ord 3 r 6; and COUNTY COURTS.
2 As to the CAA see para 1044 ante.
3 See the Civil Aviation Act 1982 s 71 (2) (d) and the Civil Aviation (Air Travel Organisers' Licensing) Regulations 1972, SI 1972/223, reg 8 (1). The CAA's decision is deemed to have been taken on the date on which it furnished a statement of its reasons for the decision: reg 8 (4).
4 Ibid reg 8 (3)
5 Ibid reg 8 (1).

1099. Transfer of licences. The Civil Aviation Authority (CAA)[1] may grant an application[2] for the transfer of an air travel organiser's licence or for the substitution of the name in the licence if the sole holder has died or if such transfer or substitution is applied for in connection with the reconstruction of a body corporate or the amalgamation of any bodies corporate[3]. However, the CAA may not grant an application for such a transfer if it would be bound to refuse the application if it were an application for the grant of a licence to that person[4]. In such circumstances, the provisions relating to appeals apply[5].

1 As to the CAA see para 1044 ante.
2 The application, which must state the grounds on which it is based, must be served on the CAA within 20 days from the date on which the applicant became entitled to make it; if no application is made during that period the licence ceases at the end of the period to be treated as if granted to a person other than the grantee: Civil Aviation (Air Travel Organisers' Licensing) Regulations 1972, SI 1972/223, reg 9 (3).
3 Ibid reg 9 (2). From the time of the transfer or sale of the business, the licence is to be treated as if it had been granted to the deceased's legal personal representative, ie a person constituted executor, administrator or other representative of a deceased person by probate, administration or other instrument (reg 9 (5)) or to the new body corporate (see reg 9 (1)).
4 Ibid reg 9 (4). For grounds for refusal see para 1094 ante.
5 Ibid reg 9 (4). As to appeals see reg 8; and para 1098 ante.

1100. Surrender of licences. The Civil Aviation Authority (CAA)[1] may require any person who has possession or control of an air travel organiser's licence which has been revoked or varied to surrender it for cancellation or variation; failure to comply with such a requirement is an offence[2].

1 As to the CAA see para 1044 ante.
2 See the Civil Aviation Act 1982 s 71 (2) (e) and the Civil Aviation (Air Travel Organisers' Licensing) Regulations 1972, SI 1972/223, reg 10. The penalty on summary conviction is a fine not exceeding £100: reg 10.

1101. Offences. Any person who for the purpose of obtaining for himself or another person an air organiser's licence, the variation or the cancellation of a suspension of a licence, knowingly or recklessly furnishes to the Civil Aviation Authority (CAA)[1] any information which is false in a material particular, is guilty of an offence[2].

Any person is guilty of an offence when he makes available accommodation for the carriage of passengers or cargo on an aircraft on a flight and knows or ought to have known before the flight either that the accommodation would be provided on a flight in contravention of section 64 of the Civil Aviation Act 1982 or in breach of the terms of an air transport licence[3]. It is immaterial whether the contravention occurs outside the United Kingdom if any part of the negotiations resulting in the making available of the accommodation takes place in the United Kingdom, whether by post or other means[4].

1 As to the CAA see para 1044 ante.
2 See the Civil Aviation Act 1982 s 71 (2) (e) and the Civil Aviation (Air Travel Organisers' Licensing) Regulations 1972, SI 1972/223, reg 11. The penalty on summary conviction is a fine not exceeding £400 and on conviction on indictment a fine or imprisonment for a term not exceeding two years or both: reg 11.
3 Civil Aviation Act 1982 s 64 (5) (b). Although s 71 (2) (f) provides that the Secretary of State may make regulations for the purpose of repealing s 64 (5) (b) and part of s 64 (6), no such provision appears in the Civil Aviation (Air Travel Organisers' Licensing) Regulations 1972 or in any other regulations made at the date at which this volume states the law. As to the penalty see the Civil Aviation Act 1982 s 64 (8); and para 1091 note 2 ante.
4 Ibid s 64 (6).

4. AERODROMES AND LAND

(1) TYPES AND PROVISION OF AERODROMES

1102. Meaning of 'aerodrome'. 'Aerodrome' means any area of land or water designed, equipped, set apart or commonly used for affording facilities for the landing and departure of aircraft, and includes any area or space, whether on the ground, on the roof of a building or elsewhere, which is designed, equipped or set apart for affording facilities for the landing and departure of aircraft capable of descending or climbing vertically[1], but does not include any area the use of which for affording facilities for the landing and departure of aircraft has been abandoned and has not been resumed[2].

1 Civil Aviation Act 1982 s 105 (1).
2 See the Air Navigation Order 1989, SI 1989/2004, art 106 (1). For the meaning of 'aerodrome' in the Customs and Excise Management Act 1979 see para 1227 note 14 post.

1103. Provision of aerodromes. Specific powers to establish aerodromes[1] are conferred upon the Secretary of State for Transport[2], on the Secretary of State for Defence[3], on naval, military and air force authorities[4] for the discharge of their various functions, and, with the consent of the Secretary of State for Transport, on local authorities[5]. Any person, firm or company may establish an aerodrome[6] and public bodies may transfer their ownership of aerodromes to private companies[7]. The Civil Aviation Authority (CAA) may not establish or acquire any new aerodrome since 1982[8], but it may continue to operate those aerodromes which had been transferred to it by the Civil Aviation Act 1971 or which it had acquired under that Act[9] and, with the consent of the Secretary of State[10], it may manage any aerodrome which it does not own[11].

Restrictions upon the establishment of aerodromes by any person or company arise from statutory provisions relating to town and country planning[12], environmental disturbances[13] and the harmonious flow of air traffic[14].

1 For the meaning of 'aerodrome' see para 1102 ante.
2 See the Civil Aviation Act 1982 s 25; and para 1033 ante. As to the Secretary of State see 1109para 1032 ante. As to his position under the town and country planning legislation see para 1104 post. As to his duties in relation to aerodromes vested in him see para 1177 post.
3 For the Secretary of State's civil aviation powers and functions see para 1040 ante.
4 For the powers of naval, military and air force authorities to acquire and use land for the discharge of their functions see ROYAL FORCES.
5 See the Civil Aviation Act 1982 s 30; and para 1041 ante.
6 But see ibid s 45 (4) under which no compensation is payable in respect of restrictions or prohibitions imposed on an aerodrome established without the consent of the Secretary of State for Transport after 1 August 1946.
7 See the Airports Act 1986 Pts I (ss 1–11) (Transfer of undertakings of British Airports Authority) and II (ss 12–28) (Transfer of airport undertakings of local authorities); see further, respectively, paras 1109, 1110 post.
8 See the Civil Aviation Act 1982 s 28 (1). As to the CAA see para 1044 ante.
9 Ie under the Civil Aviation Act 1971 s 14, Sch 2 (repealed).
10 As to the Secretary of State see para 1032 ante.
11 Civil Aviation Act 1982 s 28 (1). Similarly, the CAA may not discontinue the use of any aerodrome which it owns or manages without the consent of the Secretary of State: s 28 (2).
12 See para 1104 post.
13 See paras 1185–1188 post.
14 See paras 1195–1200 post.

1104. Town and country planning. Any development or change of use of land which is undertaken or made by the Crown, or by a government department on the Crown's behalf, is exempt from regulation by the legislation relating to town and country planning[1]. No planning permission is therefore required for the establishment of an aerodrome by the Secretary of State for Transport[2], the Secretary of State for Defence or naval, military or air force authorities, or for the construction or use of buildings in connection with such an aerodrome. Such permission would, however, be required before any other person or undertaking could establish an aerodrome or could construct or use buildings in connection with it[3].

1 This is because the Town and Country Planning Act 1990 has only a limited application to the Crown: see Pt XIII (ss 293–302); and TOWN AND COUNTRY PLANNING.
2 As to the Secretary of State see para 1032 ante.
3 See the Town and Country Planning Act 1990 ss 55–69; and see the Town and Country Planning General Development Order 1988, SI 1988/1813, art 3, Sch 2 Pt 18, which specifies permitted development at aerodromes. See further TOWN AND COUNTRY PLANNING.

1105. Government, Civil Aviation Authority and other aerodromes. 'Government aerodrome' in the Air Navigation Order means any aerodrome[1] in the United Kingdom which is in the occupation of any government department or visiting force[2]. Government aerodromes may be notified[3] by the Civil Aviation Authority (CAA)[4], with the concurrence of the Secretary of State[5], as available for take-off and landing by aircraft engaged on flights for the purpose of the public transport[6] of passengers or for instruction in flying[7] or by any classes of such aircraft[8].

The CAA may also cause to be notified[9] any aerodrome owned or managed by it as available for take-off and landing as above described[10].

An aircraft engaged on flights for the above purposes may not take off or land at any place in the United Kingdom other than a government or CAA aerodrome which has been so notified, or in respect of which the person in charge has given specific permission, or an aerodrome licensed under the Air Navigation Order for the take-off and landing of aircraft engaged in such flights[11]. There is nevertheless no general requirement that all aerodromes should be licensed.

1 For the meaning of 'aerodrome' see para 1102 ante.
2 Air Navigation Order 1989, SI 1989/2004, art 106 (1).
3 'Notified' means set forth in a document published by the CAA and entitled 'United Kingdom Notam' or 'United Kingdom Air Pilot', and for the time being in force: ibid art 106 (1).
4 As to the CAA see para 1044 ante.
5 As to the Secretary of State see para 1032 ante.
6 For the meaning of 'public transport' see para 1272 post.
7 As to instruction in flying see para 1358 post.
8 Air Navigation Order 1989 art 77 (b).
9 See note 3 supra.
10 Air Navigation Order 1989 art 77 (a). See also paras 1114, 1178 post.
11 See ibid art 76 (1). As to the licensing of aerodromes see art 78; and para 1154 post.

1106. Customs and excise airports. Customs and excise airports are aerodromes[1] which the Secretary of State[2] has by order[3] designated, with the concurrence of the Commissioners of Customs and Excise, and subject to such conditions as they may think fit to be places for the landing or departure of aircraft for the purpose of the enactments relating to customs[4]. The Secretary of State has power, with the concurrence of the Commissioners of Customs and Excise, to revoke by order any designation so made[5].

All aircraft arriving in the United Kingdom from abroad, or leaving for abroad, must land at or depart from a customs airport[6].

1 For the meaning of 'aerodrome' see para 1102 ante.
2 As to the Secretary of State see para 1032 ante.
3 By the Civil Aviation (Customs and Excise Airports) Order 1985, made under the Air Navigation Order 1985, SI 1985/1643 (revoked), the following aerodromes have been designated as customs and excise airports: Aberdeen (Dyce), Belfast (Aldergrove), Biggin Hill, Birmingham, Blackpool, Bournemouth (Hurn), Bristol (Lulsgate), Cambridge, Cardiff, Coventry, East Midlands, Edinburgh, Exeter, Gatwick, Glasgow, Heathrow, Humberside, Leeds and Bradford, Liverpool, Luton, Lydd, Manchester, Manston, Newcastle (Woolsington), Norwich, Plymouth (Roborough), Prestwick, Shoreham, Southampton, Southend, Stansted, Sumburgh and Tees-side. The designation of Staverton was revoked by the Civil Aviation (Customs and Excise Airports) (De-designation of Staverton) Order 1986.
4 Air Navigation Order 1989, SI 1989/2004, art 86 (1). The order may be subject to such conditions as the Secretary of State and the commissioners think fit: art 86 (1). As to customs enactments see paras 1220–1228 post; and CUSTOMS.
5 Air Navigation Order 1989 art 86 (2).
6 See paras 1220–1228 post.

1107. Sanitary airports. A sanitary airport is a customs and excise airport[1] which has been designated in accordance with the International Health Regulations 1969[2], as adopted by the World Health Organisation, which require the governmental authority responsible for health administration in each country to designate as sanitary airports a number of airports in its territory, the number depending upon the volume of the country's international traffic[3]. Every sanitary airport is required to have at its disposal an organised medical service with staff, equipment and premises and other facilities necessary for implementing the International Health Regulations[4].

If the medical officer at an airport other than a sanitary airport considers that there should be applied to an aircraft alighting there, or to any person carried on such an aircraft, sanitary measures which can only be applied at a sanitary airport, he may direct the commander of the aircraft to ensure that the aircraft, or that person, proceeds to a sanitary airport[5].

1 As to customs and excise airports see para 1106 ante.
2 As to the International Health Regulations 1969 (Cmnd 4650) see para 1011 ante.
3 International Health Regulations 1969 art 19; see the Public Health (Aircraft) Regulations 1979, SI 1979/1434, regs 2 (1), 4; and para 1230 post.
4 See the Public Health (Aircraft) Regulations 1979 reg 5.
5 Ibid reg 22.

(2) ESTABLISHMENT OF AERODROMES

(i) Introduction

1108. Introduction. As seen previously[1], aerodromes are, or have been, established by the government[2], the Civil Aviation Authority (CAA)[3], local authorities[4] or private entities and individuals[5]. The Airports Act 1986 provides for public bodies, whether nationalised companies or local authorities, to transfer their property, rights and liabilities in aerodromes to private companies[6].

1 See para 1102 ante.
2 Ie the Secretary of State for Transport or the Secretary of State for Defence; see further paras 1032, 1103 ante.
3 As to the CAA see paras 1044, 1103 ante.
4 As to local authorities see paras 1041–1043, 1103 ante.
5 See para 1103 ante.
6 See the Airports Act 1986 Pts I, II (ss 1–11, 12–28); and paras 1109–1112 post.

(ii) Transfer to a Public Company

1109. British Airports Authority. Before the passing of the Airports Act 1986, the establishment and management of a number of aerodromes was regulated by the Airports Authority Acts 1965 to 1975[1]. These statutes had provided for the creation of the British Airports Authority and the management of the aerodromes which had been vested in it[2]. In 1986, all property, rights and liabilities of the British Airports Authority were vested in BAA plc, a company nominated by the Secretary of State and registered under the Companies Act 1985 with seven subsidiary airport companies[3] before shares in BAA plc were offered to the public and admitted to the Official List of the Stock Exchange[4].

1 The Airports Authority Act 1965 and the Airports Authority Act 1968 were repealed by the Airports Authority Act 1975 which, in turn, was repealed by the Airports Act 1986.
2 The aerodromes were the London airports of Gatwick, Heathrow and Stansted and the Scottish airports of Aberdeen, Edinburgh, Glasgow and Prestwick.
3 See the Airports Act 1986 s 2 together with the Airports Act 1986 (Commencement No 1 and Appointed Day) Order 1986, SI 1986/1228, and the Airports Act 1986 (Nominated Company) Order 1986, SI 1986/1229. As to the financial structure of BAA plc, its power to issue securities, government investment and application of the Trustee Investments Act 1961 in relation to investment in the successor company see the Airports Act 1986 ss 3–11. As to the transfer scheme and corporation tax liability see ss 75 and 77. See generally COMPANIES.
4 As to the privatisation of the British Airports Authority see the Government's White Paper on Airports Policy (Cmnd 9542).

1110. Airport undertakings of local authority. The Secretary of State[1] may direct a local authority, known as the principal council[2], to form a company to operate as a commercial undertaking the airport which it controls[3] where the annual turnover of that airport exceeds £1 million for at least two of the last three financial years prior to the direction[4]. In pursuance of the direction, the principal council must prepare a scheme transferring all properties, rights and liabilities from the controlling authority to the airport company, to be known as a public airport company[5], and submit it to the Secretary of State for approval[6].

1 As to the Secretary of State see para 1032 ante.
2 A 'principal council', in relation to England and Wales, means the council of a non-metropolitan county, of a district or of a London borough: Airports Act 1986 s 12 (1). Where an airport is jointly controlled by several principal councils, the Secretary of State addresses his direction to one of the councils which must consult the other councils before forming the company: s 13 (3); reference to a composite authority is a reference to a controlling authority consisting of two or more principal councils, the councils concerned being referred to as the constituent councils of that authority: s 16 (2) (a). For a discussion of s 16 (1), (2) see *R v Bolton Borough Council, ex p Manchester City Council* (1991) Times, 19 April; and see further para 1112 post as to the controlling authority of a public airport company. As to the meaning of 'local authority' see para 1041 note 1 ante.
3 See ibid s 13; and para 1111 post.
4 Ibid s 14; and see para 1112 post. 'Annual turnover', in relation to the business carried on at an airport by the airport operator, means the aggregate, as stated or otherwise shown in the accounts of the

business, of all sums received in the course of the business during a financial year, including grants from a public or local authority but excluding capital receipts and loans made by any person: s 14 (2).
5 See ibid s 16; and para 1111 post.
6 Ibid s 15; and see para 1111 post.

1111. Public airport companies. A public airport company is a company which carries on the business of operating an airport as a commercial undertaking and is for the time being a subsidiary of either a single principal council or several such councils[1], collectively known as a composite authority[2]. For the purposes of Part II of the Airports Act 1986[3], a public airport company is an associated company of a principal council where the latter is its controlling authority or one of the constituent councils of a composite authority where the latter is its controlling authority[4].

A public airport company is a company limited by shares and registered under the Companies Act 1985[5]. The board of directors must have at least three of its members (or one quarter, whichever is less) fully employed by the company and qualified so to act by reason of their experience in airport management[6]. No director who is a paid officer or an employee of the company or of one of its subsidiaries may be elected to or remain a member of any of the councils controlling the company[7]. A director who is not remunerated by the company and is a member of any of the controlling councils may remain such a member although he will be disqualified to participate in some of the council's activities[8] or may be excluded from a council meeting by standing orders[9]. No person who is a full-time officer or employee of a principal council may hold any office or employment with a public airport company associated with that controlling authority[10].

1 Airports Act 1986 s 16 (1). As to the constitution of a public airport company see para 1110 ante; for the meaning of 'principal council' see para 1110 note 2 ante.
2 See ibid s 16 (2) (b); and para 1110 note 2 ante.
3 Ie ibid ss 12–28; see further paras 1110 ante.
4 Ibid s 16 (3); as to the controlling authority see para 1112 post.
5 See ibid s 13 (2); and para 1110 ante. See also generally COMPANIES.
6 See ibid s 17 (1). The Secretary of State may direct, with such qualifications as he thinks fit, that s 17(1) does not apply to a company which has made satisfactory arrangements for the management of the airport by persons other than its officers or employees: see s 17 (2), (3).
7 See ibid s 18 (1); as to the controlling authority see para 1112 post. As to prosecution for an offence under s 18 see note 8 infra. The same provision applies to a director of a subsidiary of a public airport company as it applies to a director of such a company: 18 (7).
8 See ibid s 18 (2). The ban applies equally to committee and sub-committee meetings as it applies to full council meetings: s 18 (6). The director concerned may not participate in any meeting relating to a contract between the company or one of its subsidiaries and the council or vote on any question relating to such a contract (including a contract with one of the constituent councils in the case of a composite authority) or to any other matter relating to the activities of the company or such a subsidiary: s 18 (2) (a), (b). Prosecution for an offence under s 18 can only be instituted by the Director of Public Prosecutions: s 18 (4). Contravention of s 18 (2) renders the offender liable on summary conviction to a fine not exceeding level 4 on the standard scale unless he can prove that he had no knowledge of the involvement of the company or its subsidiary concerned: s 18 (3); as to offences and penalties see para 1141 post. As to the standard scale see para 1044 note 6 ante. At the date at which this volume states the law, level 4 on that scale is at £1,000. The same provisions apply to a director of a subsidiary of a public airport company as they apply to a director of such a company: s 18 (7).
9 Ibid s 18 (5). Consideration of a contract between the company or one of its subsidiaries and the council or of any other matter relating to the company or such a subsidiary are the circumstances justifying the exclusion: see s 18 (5) (a), (b). The exclusion applies equally to committee and sub-committee meetings as it applies to full council meetings: s 18 (6).
10 Airports Act 1986 s 19.

1112. Controlling authority. The controlling authority of a public airport company is the principal council or principal councils of which it is a subsidiary[1]. It is the duty of the controlling authority to ensure that the right number of directors of the company are full-time employees of the company and suitably qualified unless otherwise directed by the Secretary of State[2]. It must also satisfy itself that the company does not engage, or let one of its subsidiaries engage, in activities in which the controlling authority has no power to engage[3]. These duties are joint duties of all the constituent councils where the controlling authority is a composite authority[4].

The controlling authority may give help to the public airport company by contracting with it for the supply of administrative, professional or technical services[5] or by providing financial backing for the establishment and operation of the company by means of loans, guarantees or grants or even by meeting creditors' demands in case of the winding up of the company[6]. The controlling authority may also invest in the company either by subscribing for shares on the formation of the company[7] or by acquiring shares or securities in consideration for any property, rights or liabilities which it may have transferred to the company[8] or, at any time, by subscribing, taking up or acquiring any security of the company[9]. Where a local authority is not a controlling authority of a public airport company, it may none the less acquire securities in that company, provided it has the consent of the Secretary of State[10]. In the same way that it can invest in a company, a controlling authority may dispose of the securities which it has acquired[11]; it may do so by providing for an employees' share scheme[12].

1 As to the formation of a public airport company and the meaning of 'principal council' see paras 1110, 1111 ante.
2 Airports Act 1986 s 17 (1); as to the directors of a public airport company see para 1111 ante. As to the direction of the Secretary of State dispensing the company from the provisions of s 17 (1) see s 17 (2), (3); and para 1111 note 6 ante. As to the Secretary of State see para 1032 ante.
3 Ibid s 17 (4); as to a composite authority see note 4 infra.
4 Ibid s 17 (5); in the case of a composite authority s 17 (4) refers to activities in which none of the constituent councils has power to engage: s 17 (5). For the meaning of 'composite authority' and 'constituent councils' see para 1110 note 2 ante.
5 See ibid s 24. The services rendered must be charged at proper commercial rates: s 24 (2) and the accounts of the principal council must include a separate account for each contract with the company: s 24 (2). As to rights of inspection the Local Government Finance Act 1982 s 24 applies to any such separate account as it does to any statement of accounts prepared by the council: Airports Act 1986 s 24 (3) (a); see generally LOCAL GOVERNMENT.
6 See ibid s 25. The terms of any loan made in respect of the working capital or the assets of the company may not be any more favourable than they would be for the council had the council itself had to borrow at that particular time: see s 25 (4). As to guarantees, the council guarantees the repayment of the principal of, the payment of interest on, and the discharge of any other financial obligation in connection with, loans made in respect of working capital (s 25 (2)); the council may also give guarantees when it disposes of some of its securities under s 20 (2) (s 25 (5) (a); see text and note 11 infra), when the company is either disposing of its assets or some of them or incurring losses affecting the viability of its business (s 25 (5) (b), (6)) or for the benefit of persons dealing or proposing to deal with the company while it is being wound up (s 25 (7)). It was held in *R v Bolton Borough Council, ex p Manchester City Council* (1991) Times, 19 April that where a number of local authorities had shares in a public airport company, the company was a subsidiary of all the councils and, accordingly, all the councils had power to make loans to the company under the Airports Act 1986, regardless of the amount of shares which they held.
7 See ibid s 13; and para 1111 ante.
8 See ibid s 15; and para 1111 ante.
9 Ibid s 20 (1). As to the provision of facilities at aerodromes by a local authority see para 1041 ante. As to investment by a local authority which is not the controlling authority see s 20 (3); and text to note 10 infra.

10 Ibid s 20 (3).
11 Ibid s 20 (2). The statute formally provides for the avoidance of restrictions on the disposal by the holder of any security in a public airport company which he may retain: see s 26.
12 See ibid s 20 (5) in which 'employees' share scheme' means a scheme for encouraging or facilitating the holding of shares or debentures in a public airport company by or for the benefit of employees or former employees of the company or of one of its subsidiaries or of relatives of such employees: s 20 (6).

(3) ACQUISITION AND CONTROL OF LAND

(i) Acquisition of Land

1113. Secretary of State's power to acquire land. The Secretary of State[1] has power for the purposes of civil aviation[2] and any purpose connected with the discharge of his functions[3] to acquire land or any rights in or over land by agreement or compulsorily[4]. The Secretary of State may authorise an airport operator to acquire land compulsorily for any purpose connected with the performance of the operator's functions[5].

When a person grants or agrees to grant to the Secretary of State any right[6], for whatever period and whether capable of subsisting as a legal estate or not, in relation to land in which the grantor has an interest, the grant or agreement is binding upon any person deriving title or otherwise claiming under the grantor to the same extent as it binds the grantor[7]. Where a right in or in relation to land has been so granted or has been agreed to be so granted, it is a local land charge[8].

1 As to the Secretary of State see para 1032 ante.
2 For the meaning of 'purposes of civil aviation' see para 1033 note 3 ante.
3 For the Secretary of State's power to establish and maintain aerodromes, and his other functions see para 1033 ante.
4 Civil Aviation Act 1982 s 41 (1). The Acquisition of Land Act 1981, save for Pt VI (ss 32, 33), has effect with respect of such compulsory purchase: Civil Aviation Act 1982 s 41 (2) (a). For the Secretary of State's powers in relation to land acquired see para 1033 ante. The Secretary of State has power to manage, sell, let or exchange land vested in him (see s 41 (3)), although this provision does not affect the pre-emption right conferred on a person from whom land was acquired under the Defence of the Realm (Acquisition of Land) Act 1916 in the case of the subsequent sale of the land (Civil Aviation Act 1982 s 41 (3)). The Secretary of State may also manage and sublet any land which he has taken on lease, within the terms of the lease, or assign the lease: see s 41 (4).
5 See the Airports Act 1986 s 59 (1); see further para 1117 post. The Acquisition of Land Act 1981 (apart from Pt VI) applies to the compulsory purchase of land by an airport operator authorised by the Secretary of State as it applies in the case of compulsory purchase of land by the Secretary of State: see s 59 (1) (a); and note 4 supra.
6 Among these rights are included rights to enter on the land, to carry out and maintain works on the land, or to install or maintain structures or apparatus on, under, over or across the land, and rights restrictive of the user of the land: Civil Aviation Act 1982 s 43 (2). Any reference to the carrying out of works on land are to be construed as including a reference to the making of excavations on the land or to the carrying out of levelling operations on the land: s 104 (2)
7 Ibid s 43 (1). This applies notwithstanding that it would not have been thus binding under the ordinary rules of law: s 43 (1). As to the binding effect of agreements in relation to land, and as to rights capable of subsisting as legal estates, see REAL PROPERTY.
8 See ibid s 55 (1) (a) and the Local Land Charges Rules 1977, SI 1977/985 (amended by SI 1978/1638 and SI 1989/951); the provision applies to any grant or agreement to grant dated after 25 October 1968. Failure to register does not affect the enforceability of the charge but a purchaser may be entitled to compensation: Local Land Charges Act 1975 s 10; see LAND CHARGES.

1114. Civil Aviation Authority's power to acquire land. At the time of the creation of the Civil Aviation Authority (CAA)[1], property in a certain number of aerodromes and other undertakings[2] was vested in the CAA, together with the rights and liabilities that this vesting implied[3]. The CAA may, with the authorisation of the Secretary of State[4] and for any purposes connected with the performance of its functions, acquire land[5] compulsorily[6] or by agreement[7].

Any land vested in the CAA by virtue of the Civil Aviation Acts 1971[8] and 1982[9] is deemed for all purposes to have been acquired by the CAA for the purposes of its undertakings[10].

1 As to the CAA see para 1044 ante.
2 Ie the aerodromes at Aberdeen, Benbecula, Inverness, Islay (Port Ellen), Kirkwall, Stornoway, Sumburgh, Tiree and Wick (see the Civil Aviation Act 1971 Sch 2 para 1 (1) (a) (repealed)), and the National Air Traffic Services, the Civil Aviation Flying Unit, the Fire Service Training School at Stansted, the Secretary of State's medical unit at Heathrow, and the unit of the Directorate of Operational Research and Analysis at Heathrow (Sch 2 para 1 (1) (b) (repealed)). The eight Scottish aerodromes were transferred to a wholly owned subsidiary of the CAA, Highlands and Islands Airports Limited, on 1 April 1986, following the recommendations set out in the government's White Paper on Airports Policy (Cmnd 9542).
3 See the Civil Aviation Act 1971 s 14 (1), Sch 2; following the repeal of the 1971 Act by the Civil Aviation Act 1982, matters arising out of the transfer to the CAA of aerodromes and other undertakings are dealt with by Schedule 3 to the 1982 Act: s 22. The vesting date for the purposes of Sch 2 to the 1971 Act was 1 April 1972: Civil Aviation Authority (Vesting Date) (No 1) Order 1972, SI 1972/140.
4 As to the Secretary of State see para 1032 ante.
5 For the purposes of acquiring land, any person authorised by the Secretary of State may enter upon any of the land in order to make a survey after eight days' notice of the intended entry has been served on the occupier (see the Civil Aviation Act 1982 s 50 (1) (a), (2), (4) (a)); and where displacement of persons is necessary, the CAA must secure that suitable accommodation is provided (see s 52 (1) (c), (2), (3)). Provisions as to consecrated land and burial grounds (Town and Country Planning Act 1990 ss 238–240) have effect in relation to any land acquired by the CAA: Civil Aviation Act 1982 s 54 (amended by the Planning (Consequential Provisions) Act 1990 s 4, Sch 2 para 55 (4)). See generally CREMATION AND BURIAL; COMPULSORY ACQUISITION.
6 Civil Aviation Act 1982 s 42 (1). Provisions of the Acquisition of Land Act 1981 (other than Pt VI (ss 32, 33)) apply as if the CAA were a local authority: Civil Aviation Act 1982 s 42 (1). See COMPULSORY ACQUISITION.
7 Provisions of the Compulsory Purchase Act 1965 Pt I (ss 1–32) (so far as applicable), other than ss 4–8, 27 and 31, apply: see the Civil Aviation Act 1982 s 42 (4). See COMPULSORY ACQUISITION.
8 See note 3 supra.
9 See the Civil Aviation Act 1982 s 42.
10 Ibid s 42 (5).

1115. Grant of land to Civil Aviation Authority. Any person having an interest in land may grant or agree to grant to the Civil Aviation Authority (CAA)[1] any right in or in relation to the land[2]. This grant or agreement is binding upon any person deriving title or otherwise claiming under the grantor to the same extent as it is binding upon the grantor[3]. Where a right in, or in relation to, land is granted or is agreed to be granted, this right is a local land charge[4].

1 As to the CAA see para 1044 ante.
2 Civil Aviation Act 1982 s 43 (1). The right granted or agreed to be granted may be in perpetuity or for any other period and whether capable of subsisting as a legal estate or not; it may be a right to enter upon the land, a right to carry out and maintain works on the land, a right to install or maintain structures or apparatus on, under, over or across the land, or a right restrictive of the user of the land: see s 43 (2); and see para 1116 note 3 post. See generally REAL PROPERTY.
3 Civil Aviation Act 1982 s 43 (1). The grant or agreement is binding upon that person notwithstanding that it would not have been binding upon that person apart from these provisions: s 43 (1).
4 Ibid s 55 (1) (a). Failure to register does not affect the enforceability of a charge but a purchaser may be entitled to compensation: Local Land Charges Act 1975 s 10; see LAND CHARGES.

1116. Planning decisions and the Civil Aviation Authority. A local planning authority[1] is entitled to recover from the Civil Aviation Authority (CAA)[2] a sum equal to the compensation[3] payable where the planning authority is liable to pay compensation and where the liability is attributable to a planning decision[4], if such planning decision was necessary in order to secure either the safety of aerodromes, or the safety of persons or buildings in respect of aircraft using aerodromes owned by the CAA, or the safe and efficient operation of apparatus owned by the CAA and provided for the purpose of assisting air traffic control or as an aid to air navigation[5].

Where a purchase notice is served[6] in respect of such a planning decision, any local authority deemed[7] to have served a notice to treat in respect of the interest to which the purchase notice relates may by notice[8] require the CAA to purchase the interest from the local authority[9].

Any dispute relating to such a planning decision is referred to and determined by the Secretary of State[10].

1 References to a local planning authority include, in relation to England and Wales, references to any authority to which the functions of a local planning authority are delegated: Civil Aviation Act 1982 s 53 (6). See generally TOWN AND COUNTRY PLANNING.
2 As to the CAA see para 1044 ante.
3 See the Town and Country Planning Act 1990 ss 107, 108, 114, 144 (2), 279 (1), which relate to compensation for certain planning restrictions, for purchase notices which do not take effect and in respect of undertakers' operational land.
4 See the Civil Aviation Act 1982 s 53 (1) (amended by the Planning (Consequential Provisions) Act 1990 s 4, Sch 2 para 55 (3) (a)). 'Planning decision' means a decision made on an application under the Town and Country Planning Act 1990 Pt III (ss 55–106): Civil Aviation Act 1982 s 53 (6) (amended by the Planning (Consequential Provisions) Act 1990 Sch 2 para 55 (3) (e)).
5 See the Civil Aviation Act 1982 s 53 (1) (b) (as amended: see note 4 supra). Where the CAA pays such a sum the planning authority must pay to it any amount received by the planning authority in respect of compensation under the Town and Country Planning Act 1990 ss 111, 112 (recovery of compensation on subsequent development): Civil Aviation Act 1982 s 53 (2) (amended by the Planning (Consequential Provisions) Act 1990 Sch 2 para 55 (3) (b)).
6 See the Town and Country Planning Act 1990 s 137.
7 See ibid ss 139 (3), 143 (1); and TOWN AND COUNTRY PLANNING.
8 Notice in writing must be given to the CAA not later than one month from the time when the amount of compensation payable by the local authority for the interest is agreed or determined: Civil Aviation Act 1982 s 53 (3).
9 Ibid s 53 (3) (amended by the Planning (Consequential Provisions) Act 1990 Sch 2 para 55 (3) (c)). The purchase price is a sum equal to the amount of compensation so agreed or determined: Civil Aviation Act 1982 s 53 (3). The CAA is deemed to have contracted with the local authority to purchase the interest at that price where such a notice is given to the CAA and subject to any agreement between the local authority and the CAA: s 53 (4).
10 Ibid s 53 (5) (amended by the Planning (Consequential Provisions) Act 1990 Sch 2 para 55 (3) (d)).

1117. Airport operator's power to acquire land. With the authorisation of the Secretary of State[1] an airport operator[2] may acquire land compulsorily for any purpose connected with the performance of his functions[3]. He may also acquire land by agreement[4].

The airport operator may not dispose of any land acquired compulsorily and forming part of an airport or being attached to an airport and being administered with the airport as a single unit[5] within 25 years of the date of acquisition[6]. The exceptions to this provision are a disposal in order to provide services or facilities associated with the operation of an airport[7], a disposal of a leasehold interest in the land for a period of less than seven years[8] or a disposal which has the consent of the Secretary of State[9].

1 As to the Secretary of State see para 1032 ante.
2 As to airport operators see para 1042 note 4 ante.
3 See the Airports Act 1986 s 59 (1). Provisions of the Acquisition of Land Act 1981, other than Pt V (ss 32, 33), apply: Airports Act 1986 s 59 (1). See COMPULSORY ACQUISITION.
4 For the purpose of acquisition by agreement the provisions of the Compulsory Purchase Act 1965 Pt I (ss 1–32) (so far as applicable), other than ss 4–8, 27 and 31, apply: Airports Act 1986 s 59 (2) (a). See COMPULSORY ACQUISITION.
5 Or the land had been part of an airport or attached and administered with an airport at some time since the date of the acquisition.
6 See the Airports Act 1986 s 60 (1), (2); the same applies to any interest or right in or over such land: s 60 (1), (2).
7 Ibid s 60 (2) (a).
8 Ibid s 60 (2) (b).
9 Ibid s 60 (2) (c); the Secretary of State may attach any conditions which he thinks necessary: s 60 (3).

1118. Planning decisions and airport operators. A local planning authority[1] is entitled to recover from an airport operator[2] a sum equal to the compensation[3] payable where the planning authority is liable to pay compensation and where the liability is attributable to a planning decision[4] relating to the safety of aerodromes, the prevention of damage to persons or buildings from aircraft using the airport owned by the operator or the safe and efficient operation of apparatus owned by the operator and provided for air traffic control or air navigation purposes[5].

Where a purchase notice is served[6] in respect of such a planning decision, any local authority deemed[7] to have served a notice to treat in respect of the interest to which the purchase notice relates may by notice[8] require the operator to purchase the interest from the local authority[9].

Any dispute relating to such a planning decision is referred to and determined by the Secretary of State[10].

1 References to a local planning authority include, in relation to England and Wales, references to any authority to which the functions of a local planning authority are delegated: Airports Act 1986 s 61 (6). See generally TOWN AND COUNTRY PLANNING.
2 As to airport operators see para 1042 note 4 ante.
3 See the authorities referred to in para 1116 notes 3–5 ante.
4 'Planning decision' means a decision made on an application under the Town and Country Planning Act 1990 Pt III (ss 55–106): Airports Act 1986 s 61 (6) (amended by the Planning (Consequential Provisions) Act 1990 s 4, Sch 2 para 73 (2) (e)).
5 Airports Act 1986 s 61 (1) (amended by the Planning (Consequential Provisions) Act 1990 Sch 2 para 73 (2) (a)). Where the operator pays such a sum, the planning authority must repay him any amount which it received in respect of compensation under the Town and Country Planning Act 1990 ss 111, 112 (recovery of compensation on subsequent development): Airports Act 1986 s 61 (2) (amended by the Planning (Consequential Provisions) Act 1990 Sch 2 para 73 (2) (b)).
6 See the Town and Country Planning Act 1990 s 137.
7 See ibid ss 139 (3), 143 (1); and TOWN AND COUNTRY PLANNING.
8 Notice in writing must be given to the operator not later than one month from the time when the amount of compensation payable by the local authority for the interest is agreed or determined: see the Airports Act 1986 s 61 (3).
9 Ibid s 61 (3) (amended by the Planning (Consequential Provisions) Act 1990 Sch 2 para 73 (2) (c)). The purchase price is a sum equal to the amount of compensation so agreed or determined: see the Airports Act 1986 s 61 (3). The operator is deemed to have contracted with the local authority to purchase the interest at that price where such a notice is given to the operator and subject to any agreement between the local authority and the operator: s 61 (4).
10 Ibid s 61 (5) (amended by the Planning (Consequential Provisions) Act 1990 Sch 2 para 73 (2) (d)).

(ii) Acquisition of Rights over Land

1119. Power to obtain rights over land. The Secretary of State[1] may make an order creating easements or servitudes over land or other rights[2] in respect of land where he is satisfied that it is necessary to do so[3]. The aim of the order is to secure either the safe and efficient use for civil aviation purposes[4] of any land which is vested in him, in Eurocontrol[5] or in the Civil Aviation Authority (CAA)[6] or was acquired by an airport operator[7], or which any of the above proposes to acquire[8], or the provision of any services required in relation to such land[9], or the safe and efficient navigation of civil aircraft[10] in which case the rights are created in favour of the Secretary of State[11], in all other cases the rights being created for the benefit of the relevant authority or person[12].

1 As to the Secretary of State see para 1032 ante.
2 Such rights include rights to carry out and maintain works on any land and to install and maintain structures and apparatus on, under, over or across any land; see further para 1113 note 6 ante.
3 See the Civil Aviation Act 1982 s 44 (1) and the Airports Act 1986 s 59 (4) (in respect of airport operators). For the procedure in connection with such orders see para 1122 post.
4 For the meaning of 'civil aviation purposes' see para 1033 note 3 ante.
5 As to Eurocontrol see para 1023 ante.
6 As to the CAA see para 1044 ante.
7 As to airport operators see para 1042 note 4 ante.
8 Civil Aviation Act 1982 s 44 (1) (a); and see note 3 supra.
9 Ibid s 44 (1) (b); and see note 3 supra.
10 Ibid s 44 (1) (c); and see note 3 supra.
11 Ibid s 44 (2) (b).
12 Ibid s 44 (2) (a).

1120. Entry on land. Any order[1] creating rights in relation to land may contain such consequential, incidental and supplemental provisions as appear to the Secretary of State[2] to be necessary for the aim of the order, including provisions for authorising persons to enter on land for the purpose of carrying out, installing, maintaining or removing any works, structures or apparatus[3].

Entry may not be made in pursuance of such a provision unless notice is served on the occupier not less than seven days before the entry is made, stating that on a named day entry will be made in pursuance of these powers, and specifying the purpose for which the entry will be made[4]. Entry may however be made without notice in case of emergency or for the purpose of performing any functions required from time to time in connection with the maintenance or use of any works, structures or apparatus[5].

If any land is damaged in the exercise of such a power of entry, the Secretary of State[6] or the Civil Aviation Authority (CAA) or the airport operator, as the case may be, must pay such compensation to the persons interested in the land as may be just[7].

1 See para 1119 ante.
2 As to the Secretary of State see para 1032 ante.
3 Civil Aviation Act 1982 s 44 (3); and see para 1119 note 3 ante, as to airport operators. Obstruction is an offence: see para 1121 post. As to works see para 1119 note 2 ante.
4 See ibid s 44 (4). As to service of notice see para 1152 post.
5 Ibid s 44 (5).
6 The Secretary of State is the person involved when the order was made either in his favour or in favour of Eurocontrol: see ibid s 44 (6) (a); and paras 1032, 1119 ante.

7 See ibid s 44 (6). Any dispute as to whether compensation is payable, or as to its amount or the person to whom it is payable, must be referred to and determined by the Lands Tribunal: s 44 (6). As to such determination see COMPULSORY ACQUISITION. As to the CAA see para 1044 ante.

1121. Ownership of and interference with structures, etc; offences. The ownership of anything which is placed on or under, or affixed to, any land in pursuance of an order[1] creating rights in relation to land does not pass to the owner of the land by reason only that the thing is so placed or affixed[2].

Moreover, while any such order is in force it is an offence for anyone, except with the consent of the relevant person or authority in whose favour the order was made[3], wilfully to interfere with any works[4] carried out on, or with anything installed on, over, under or across, any land in pursuance of the order[5]. It is also an offence wilfully to obstruct any person in the exercise of a power of entry conferred by such an order[6]. In neither case, however, may proceedings be instituted except by or with the consent of the Secretary of State or the Director of Public Prosecutions, or by the Civil Aviation Authority (CAA) where the order was made in its favour[7].

If any such offence is committed by a body corporate, any person who was at the time of the commission of the offence a director (by whatever name he is called), general manager, secretary or other similar officer of that body or any person purporting to act in such capacity is deemed to be guilty of the offence, together with the body corporate, if it is proved that it was committed with his consent or connivance or that it is attributable to any neglect on his part[8].

1 See para 1119 ante.
2 Civil Aviation Act 1982 s 44 (7). The rule might be otherwise at common law; as to the ownership of things affixed to land see REAL PROPERTY. See also para 1207 post.
3 Ie the Secretary of State, acting on his own behalf or that of Eurocontrol, the Civil Aviation Authority or the airport operator; see para 1119 ante.
4 References to interference with works must be construed in accordance with the meaning of 'works' set out in para 1113 note 6 ante.
5 Civil Aviation Act 1982 s 44 (7). An offence of wilful interference is punishable on summary conviction by imprisonment for a term not exceeding three months or a fine not exceeding level 5 on the standard scale or both: s 44 (10) (amended by virtue of the Criminal Justice Act 1982 ss 38, 46). As to the standard scale see para 1044 note 6 ante. At the date at which this volume states the law, level 5 on that scale is at £2,000.
6 Civil Aviation Act 1982 s 44 (10). An offence of obstruction is punishable on summary conviction by a fine not exceeding level 3 on the standard scale: s 44 (10) (as amended: see note 5 supra). As to the standard scale see para 1044 note 6 ante. At the date at which this volume states the law, level 3 on that scale is at £400.
7 Civil Aviation Act 1982 s 44 (11). As to the CAA see para 1044 ante.
8 See ibid s 99 (1); this provision applies also, where a body corporate is managed by its members, to the acts and defaults of a member in connection with his functions of management as if he were a director of the body corporate: s 99 (2).

1122. Procedure for making orders. The procedure for making orders of this nature is strictly regulated[1]. Orders in respect of land vested in the Civil Aviation Authority (CAA)[2] or an airport operator[3], or which one of the above proposes to acquire, are made on the application of the CAA or the operator as the case may be[4].

Before the making of the order notices stating its effect and specifying the time[5] within which and the manner in which objections to the making of the order may be made must be published by the Secretary of State[6] or, as the case may be, by the

CAA or the operator in one or more newspapers circulating in the district in which the land is situated, and must be served upon every owner, lessee and occupier of any of the land, and upon every local authority[7] within whose area any of the land is situated[8]. If no objection is duly made by any such person or local authority, or if all objections are withdrawn, the Secretary of State may make the order[9]. If any objection duly made is not withdrawn the Secretary of State must, before making the order, either cause a public local inquiry to be held or afford any person who has made such an objection an opportunity of being heard by a person whom he has appointed for the purpose[10]. After considering the objection and the report of the person who held the inquiry or before whom the hearing was held, the Secretary of State may, if he thinks fit, make the order[11].

Immediately after an order has been made, the Secretary of State, the CAA or the operator, as the case may be, must publish in one or more newspapers circulating in the district in which the land is situated a notice stating that the order has been made, and naming a place where a copy of it may be seen at all reasonable hours. A similar notice must be served on every person who, having duly objected to the order, has not withdrawn his objection[12]. Subject to the provisions as to appeal[13], the order becomes operative six weeks after the date on which the notice is first published[14].

1   See the Civil Aviation Act 1982 s 44 (8), Sch 7. As to the order see para 1119 ante.
2   As to the CAA see para 1044 ante.
3   As to airport operators see para 1042 note 4 ante; as to the application of the Civil Aviation Act 1982 s 44 in relation to an airport operator as it applies to the CAA see the Airports Act 1986 s 59 (3), (4); and para 1119 ante.
4   See the Civil Aviation Act 1982 Sch 7 para 1; and note 3 supra.
5   From the day the notice was served, the time may not be less than 28 days (or 42 days in the case of an application by the CAA or an operator): ibid Sch 7 para 1 (1), (2).
6   As to the Secretary of State see para 1032 ante.
7   For the meaning of 'local authority' see para 1041 note 1 ante.
8   See the Civil Aviation Act 1982 Sch 7 para 1. As to service see para 1152 post.
9   Ibid Sch 7 para 2.
10   Ibid Sch 7 para 3.
11   Ibid Sch 7 para 3. Notwithstanding these provisions, the Secretary of State may require a person to state the grounds of his objection in writing and, if satisfied that it relates solely to matters which can be dealt with by the tribunal assessing compensation, may disregard it in considering whether to make the order: Sch 7 para 4.
12   See ibid Sch 7 para 5 (1), (2). As to the registration of orders as local land charges see para 1151 post.
13   See ibid Sch 7 para 7; and para 1123 post.
14   See ibid Sch 7 para 8. As to service see para 1152 post.

1123. Questioning validity of orders. No order[1] may be questioned, whether before or after it has been made, in any legal proceedings[2] except on the ground that the order or any provision in it is not within the powers of the Secretary of State[3], or that some statutory requirement[4] in relation to the making of the order has not been complied with[5]. In either of these cases a person aggrieved by the order may, within six weeks of the first publication of notice that the order has been made[6], apply to the High Court[7]. The court may make an interim order suspending the operation of the order, or of any provision therein, until the final determination of the proceedings[8]. If the court is satisfied that the order or any provision in it is not within the Secretary of State's powers, or that the applicant's interests have been substantially prejudiced by non-compliance with any statutory requirement, it may quash the order or any provision in it whether generally or in so far as it affects the applicant[9].

1 As to the orders concerned see para 1119 ante.
2 See the Civil Aviation Act 1982 Sch 7 para 7.
3 As to the Secretary of State see para 1032 ante.
4 Ie the Civil Aviation Act 1982 s 44 (8), Sch 7.
5 See ibid Sch 7 para 8.
6 See para 1122 ante.
7 Civil Aviation Act 1982 Sch 7 para 7. The application is made by originating motion to a single
   Queen's Bench judge, and the notice of motion must state the grounds: RSC Ord 94 r 1. See further
   PRACTICE AND PROCEDURE.
8 Civil Aviation Act 1982 Sch 7 para 7 (a). Unless the order is quashed or suspension is granted on one
   or other of the grounds set out in the text, the order becomes operative six weeks after notice of the
   making of it is first published: Sch 7 para 8.
9 Ibid Sch 7 para 7 (b).

1124. Compensation. Any person having an interest in land the value of which
is diminished in consequence of the coming into operation of an order creating
rights in relation to land[1] is entitled to recover compensation for it from the
appropriate person[2].

If an interest in land is subject to a mortgage[3], compensation is assessed as if the
interest were not so subject[4], but a mortgagee is entitled to claim compensation and
the compensation payable for the interest in land is paid to such of the claimants as
the Secretary of State thinks proper, and is applied by that claimant in such manner
as the parties interested agree, or, if they do not agree, as is determined by
arbitration[5].

1 As to such orders see para 1119 ante.
2 Civil Aviation Act 1982 s 44 (8), Sch 7 para 10 (1); the 'appropriate person' means the Civil Aviation
   Authority (CAA) or an airport operator in the case of an order under s 44 made in favour of the CAA
   or the operator and the Secretary of State in any other case: see Sch 7 para 10 (2), applying Pt I para 5
   (2); and, as to the position of the operator, the Airports Act 1986 s 59 (3), (4). As to the CAA see para
   1044 ante; as to operators see para 1340 post; as to the Secretary of State see para 1032 ante. The Land
   Compensation Act 1961 (see COMPULSORY ACQUISITION) applies to the recovery of the compensation:
   Civil Aviation Act 1982 Sch 7 para 10 (1).
3 'Mortgage' includes an equitable charge or other incumbrance: ibid Sch 7 para 11 (2).
4 Ibid Sch 7 para 11 (1) (a). A compensation claim may be made by any mortgagee of the interest, but
   without prejudice to the making of a claim by the person entitled to the interest: Sch 7 para 11 (1) (b).
   A mortgagee is not entitled to claim compensation in respect of his interest as such: Sch 7 para 11 (1)
   (c).
5 Ibid Sch 7 para 11 (1) (d).

1125. Land held by statutory undertakers. Where an order[1] made by the
Secretary of State[2] provides for the creation of an easement over, or of any other
right in or in relation to, land held by a statutory undertaker[3] for the purposes of the
carrying on of his undertaking, and where the Secretary of State, upon a representation made to him within the time during which an objection to the making of the
order may be entered[4], is satisfied that the easement or right could not be enjoyed
without serious detriment to the carrying on of the undertaking, and certifies to
that effect, the order becomes subject to special parliamentary procedure[5].

Special provisions apply to the recovery of compensation by statutory undertakers from the appropriate person where any such order has been made[6].

1 See para 1119 ante.
2 As to the Secretary of State see para 1032 ante.
3 For the meaning of 'statutory undertaker' see para 1144 post.

4 See para 1122 ante.
5 Civil Aviation Act 1982 s 44 (9). The provisions of the Statutory Orders (Special Procedure) Act
 1945, thus become applicable: see s 1 (1) and see the Civil Aviation Act 1982 s 44 (8), Sch 7 para 9; as
 to these provisions see PARLIAMENT. The provisions of the 1982 Act Sch 7 paras 7, 8 (see para 1123
 ante), giving a right to apply to the High Court in certain circumstances, remain applicable (save that
 for the reference in Sch 7 para 7 to the time notice of the order is first published there must be
 substituted a reference to the time it becomes operative under the 1945 Act) in the case of orders to
 which the 1945 Act is thus made applicable, except where the order is confirmed by Act of
 Parliament under s 6 of that Act: Civil Aviation Act 1982 Sch 7 para 9.
6 Ibid Sch 7 para 12. As to these special provisions see para 1145 et seq post. For the meaning of
 'appropriate person' see para 1124 note 2 ante.

1126. Rights over Eurocontrol land. Provisions which enable the Secretary of
State[1] by order to obtain rights over land[2] apply in relation to land, structures,
works and apparatus vested in or occupied by Eurocontrol[3] or proposed to be
acquired, occupied or installed by Eurocontrol, as they apply in relation to land,
structures, works or apparatus vested in or proposed to be acquired by the
Secretary of State[4].

Any easements, servitudes or rights created by order under those provisions
may be created in favour of Eurocontrol[5].

1 As to the Secretary of State see para 1032 ante.
2 See para 1119 ante.
3 As to Eurocontrol see para 1023 ante.
4 See the Civil Aviation Act 1982 s 44 (12).
5 Ibid s 44 (2) (a).

(iii) Power to exercise Control over Land

1127. Control over land. If the Secretary of State[1] is satisfied that it is necessary
to do so in order to secure the safe and efficient use for civil aviation purposes[2],
including the testing of aircraft designed for civil aviation, of any land, structures,
works or apparatus vested in a relevant authority[3] or which such authority proposes to acquire or install, he may declare by order[4] that any land specified in the
order shall be subject to control by directions[5]. The existence of this power does
not prejudice the Secretary of State's powers to acquire land so as to secure the
observance of any requirement, even though such observance could have been
secured by means of this power[6].

1 As to the Secretary of State see para 1032 ante.
2 For the meaning of 'civil aviation purposes' see para 1033 note 3 ante.
3 The relevant authorities for the purposes of the Civil Aviation Act 1982 s 46 are the Secretary of State
 (as to whom see para 1032 ante), Eurocontrol (as to which see para 1023 ante), the Civil Aviation
 Authority (CAA) (as to which see para 1044 ante) and the licensee of any aerodrome licensed under
 an Air Navigation Order (as to which see para 1154 post): s 46 (10); and see the Airports Act 1986 s 59
 (3), (4), which assimilates any relevant airport operator to the CAA in so far as the application of s 46
 of the 1982 Act is concerned.
4 For provisions as to the making of such orders see para 1130 post.
5 Civil Aviation Act 1982 s 46 (1).
6 Ibid s 46 (8). For the Secretary of State's powers to acquire land see para 1113 ante.

1128. Power to give directions. Where an order of this nature[1] is in force the
Secretary of State[2] may, in pursuance of any general or special authority given by

the order, give directions for requiring the total or partial demolition of any building or structure within the area to which the order relates[3]; for restricting the height of trees upon any land within the area, or requiring such trees to be cut down or reduced in height[4]; for extinguishing any private right of way over land within the area[5]; for restricting the installation of cables, mains, pipes, sewers, wires or other apparatus upon, across, under or over any land within the area[6]; for extinguishing, at the expiration of such period as may be determined in the directions, any subsisting right of installing or maintaining such apparatus[7]; or for requiring that, before the expiration of such period as may be determined by the directions, any such apparatus shall be removed from the land[8].

1 See para 1127 ante.
2 As to the Secretary of State see para 1032 ante.
3 Civil Aviation Act 1982 s 46 (2) (a).
4 Ibid s 46 (2) (b); see the Forestry (Exceptions from Restriction of Felling) Regulations 1951, SI 1951/1725, reg 4 (a) (amended by SI 1959/96), exempting from the provisions of the Forestry Act 1967 s 9 (1) (which prohibits the felling of growing trees without a licence), the felling of trees where the Secretary of State for Defence or the Secretary of State for Trade and Industry (now the Secretary of State for Transport; see para 1031 et seq ante) has certified that the tree obstructs the approach of aircraft to, or their departure from, any aerodrome, or hinders the safe and efficient use of air navigation or aircraft landing installations; the regulations are saved by Sch 6 para 1 (1). See further FORESTRY.
5 Civil Aviation Act 1982 s 46 (2) (c).
6 Ibid s 46 (2) (d) (amended by the Water Act 1989 s 190 (1), Sch 25 para 67 (1)).
7 Civil Aviation Act 1982 s 46 (2) (e).
8 Ibid s 46 (2) (f).

1129. Incidental provisions in orders. An order made under the foregoing powers[1] may contain any consequential, incidental or supplemental provision which appears to the Secretary of State[2] to be necessary or expedient for the purposes of the order; in particular provisions may be included for empowering persons authorised by him to remove, pull or cut down or alter so as to bring into conformity with the requirements of any directions given under the order, any building, structure, tree or apparatus which contravenes those requirements[3].

1 See para 1127 ante.
2 As to the Secretary of State see para 1032 ante.
3 Civil Aviation Act 1982 s 46 (3).

1130. Procedure for making orders. Any order made under these powers[1] is subject to special parliamentary procedure[2]. Before making an order, the Secretary of State[3] must consult every local authority[4] within whose area the whole or any part of the land to which the proposed order will relate is situated[5], in addition to complying with the other preliminary requirements as to notices, objections and local inquiries which the application of special parliamentary procedure involves[6].

1 See para 1127 ante.
2 Civil Aviation Act 1982 s 46 (4).
3 As to the Secretary of State see para 1032 ante.
4 For the meaning of 'local authority' see para 1041 note 1 ante.
5 Civil Aviation Act 1982 s 46 (5).
6 See ibid s 46 (5), (6). For these preliminary requirements see the Statutory Orders (Special Procedure) Act 1945 Sch 1; and PARLIAMENT. As to the registration of such orders as local land charges see para 1151 post. The notices in respect of land, structures, works and apparatus as vested must be

given by the relevant authority, as to which see para 1127 note 3 ante. For provisions as to notices see para 1152 post.

1131. Directions. Immediately after the Secretary of State[1] has given a direction[2] by virtue of an order exercising control over land[3] the appropriate person[4] must publish in one or more newspapers circulating in the district a notice stating that the direction has been given[5]. It must in all cases serve notice of the direction upon every owner, lessee or occupier of the land to which the direction relates[6], or, in the case of a direction for extinguishing a right of way[7], of any land to which the right of way is appurtenant[8], and upon every local authority in whose area any of the land is situated[9]. In the case of a direction restricting the installation of apparatus, or extinguishing rights to install or maintain apparatus, notice must also be served upon every person whose rights to install or maintain apparatus are affected by the direction[10]. Finally, the relevant authority must serve notice, in the case of a direction requiring the removal of apparatus, upon the person entitled to maintain that apparatus[11].

The same provisions apply to applications to the High Court in respect of the giving of any direction as apply to such applications in respect of orders by which the Secretary of State obtains rights over land in his favour[12].

1 As to the Secretary of State see para 1032 ante.
2 As to the power to give directions see para 1128 ante. As to the registration of such directions as local land charges see para 1151 post.
3 As to such orders see para 1127 ante.
4 For the purposes of the Civil Aviation Act 1982 Sch 9, 'appropriate person' means any relevant authority for whom the order was made, save if the order is for the benefit of Eurocontrol where it means the Secretary of State: Civil Aviation Act 1982 s 46 (7), Sch 9 para 11. For the meaning of 'relevant authority' see para 1127 note 3 ante; as to Eurocontrol see para 1023 ante.
5 See ibid Sch 9 para 1.
6 See ibid Sch 9 para 1 (2) (b). For provisions as to service see para 1152 post.
7 Ie under ibid s 46 (2) (c); see para 1128 ante.
8 Ibid Sch 9 para 1 (2) (a).
9 Ibid Sch 9 para 1 (2) (b).
10 Ibid Sch 9 para 1 (2) (c).
11 Ibid Sch 9 para 1 (2) (d).
12 Ibid Sch 9 para 2, applying Sch 7 Pt II (paras 7–9), as to which see para 1123 ante.

1132. Compensation. Any person having an interest in land[1] the value of which is diminished in consequence of the coming into operation of a direction[2] is entitled to compensation from the appropriate person[3]. Compensation must also be paid to anyone who sustains damage by being disturbed in the enjoyment of any right in or over land, even though the damage does not consist in the diminution in value of an interest in land[4]. In addition the appropriate person must pay compensation in respect of any expenditure reasonably incurred by any person for the purpose of carrying out work required by the direction[5].

Any compensation will be reduced by the value of any timber, apparatus or other materials removed in compliance with the order[6].

Any dispute as to whether compensation is payable, as to its amount, or as to the persons to whom it is payable must be referred to and determined by the Lands Tribunal[7].

Special provisions apply to the recovery of compensation by statutory undertakers[8] in the case of directions affecting buildings, structures or apparatus held or

Vol 2: Aviation

used, or rights of way enjoyed, by the undertaker for the purposes of his undertaking, or affecting rights to install or maintain apparatus for those purposes[9].

1 For special provisions where land is mortgaged see the Civil Aviation Act 1982 Sch 7 para 11, applied by s 46 (7), Sch 9 para 4: see further para 1124 ante.
2 See para 1131 ante.
3 For the meaning of 'appropriate person' see para 1131 note 4 ante. The Land Compensation Act 1961 s 5 (see COMPULSORY ACQUISITION) has effect for the purpose of assessing such compensation so far as it is applicable and subject to any necessary modifications: Civil Aviation Act 1982 Sch 9 para 8.
4 Ibid Sch 9 para 5.
5 Ibid Sch 9 para 6.
6 Ibid Sch 9 para 7.
7 Ibid Sch 9 para 9. As to such determination see COMPULSORY ACQUISITION.
8 For the meaning of 'statutory undertakers' see para 1144 post.
9 Civil Aviation Act 1982 Sch 9 para 10. As to these special provisions see para 1145 post.

1133. Control over Eurocontrol land. Provisions which enable the Secretary of State[1] to exercise control over land in order to secure the safe and efficient use for civil aviation purposes of land, structures, works or apparatus vested in him or which he proposes to acquire or install[2], apply in relation to land, structures, works and apparatus vested in or occupied by Eurocontrol[3] or proposed to be acquired, occupied or installed by Eurocontrol as they apply in relation to land, structures, works or apparatus vested in or proposed to be acquired or installed by the Secretary of State[4].

1 As to the Secretary of State see para 1032 ante.
2 See para 1127 ante.
3 As to Eurocontrol see para 1023 ante.
4 See the Civil Aviation Act 1982 s 46 (10).

(iv) Highways

1134. Power to stop up and divert highways. The Secretary of State[1] may authorise by order the stopping-up or diversion of any highway, including a highway stopped up or diverted under any enactment other than the Civil Aviation Act 1982[2], if he is satisfied that it is necessary to do so in order to secure the safe and efficient use for civil aviation purposes[3], including the testing of aircraft designed for civil aviation, of any land vested in or proposed to be acquired by him, the Civil Aviation Authority (CAA)[4] or a relevant airport operator[5].

1 As to the Secretary of State see para 1032 ante.
2 See the Civil Aviation Act 1982 s 48 (8).
3 For the meaning of 'civil aviation purposes' see para 1033 note 3 ante.
4 As to the CAA see para 1044 ante.
5 Civil Aviation Act 1982 s 48 (1); as to the airport operator and his assimilation to the CAA for the purposes of s 48 (save subsection (9): see infra) see the Airports Act 1986 s 59 (3), (4); and see paras 1119, 1127 ante, 1138, 1151 post. The conferment of this power does not prejudice any power conferred on the Secretary of State by any other enactment to stop up or divert highways: Civil Aviation Act 1982 s 48 (8); see further HIGHWAYS. Where an order relating to telegraphic lines affected by the stopping-up, diversion or improvement of a highway is made under the Town and Country Planning Act 1990 s 247, references in s 256 (1)–(4) to that order include references to an order made under the Civil Aviation Act 1982 s 48 in relation to land vested in the CAA or which the CAA proposes to acquire: see s 48 (9) (amended by the Planning (Consequential Provisions) Act 1990 s 4, Sch 2 para 55 (1)). As to provisions relating to telecommunication apparatus installed on

land owned by an airport operator and over which the highway to be stopped up, diverted or improved passes see the Airports Act 1986 s 62 (1) (b), (2), the Telecommunications Act 1984 s 10, Sch 2 para 23 and the Public Utilities Street Works Act 1950; see further HIGHWAYS; TELECOMMUNICATIONS.

1135. Supplementary provisions. Any order for the stopping-up or diversion of a highway[1] may provide for securing the provision or improvement of any highway where necessary in consequence of the stopping-up or diversion[2]; for directing that any highway so provided or improved shall be maintainable at public expense, and for specifying which authority is to be the highway authority for it[3]; for directing that a highway provided or improved in consequence of the stopping-up or diversion of a trunk road shall itself be a trunk road[4]; for the retention or removal of cables, mains, sewers, pipes, wires or similar apparatus placed along, across, over or under a stopped up or diverted highway, and for the extinguishment, modification or preservation of any rights as to the use or maintenance of that apparatus[5]; for authorising or requiring the provision of such apparatus, in relation to any highway to be improved or provided, in lieu of apparatus removed from a highway under the order, and for conferring rights as to the use or maintenance of apparatus so provided[6]; and for requiring the Secretary of State[7] or any other specified authority or person to pay or contribute to the cost of doing any work provided for by the order[8], or to repay or make contributions in respect of any compensation paid by the highway authority in respect of restrictions formerly placed, under the Restriction of Ribbon Development Act 1935[9], upon the highway now stopped up or diverted[10]. The order may contain any consequential, incidental and supplemental provisions which appear to the Secretary of State to be necessary or expedient for the purposes of the order[11].

1 See para 1134 ante.
2 Civil Aviation Act 1982 s 48 (3) (a).
3 Ibid s 48 (3) (b), (c). As to highway authorities and the repair of highways see HIGHWAYS.
4 Ibid s 48 (3) (d). As to trunk roads see HIGHWAYS.
5 Ibid s 48 (3) (e) (amended by the Water Act 1989 s 190 (1), Sch 25 para 67 (2)).
6 Civil Aviation Act 1982 s 48 (3) (f).
7 As to the Secretary of State see para 1032 ante.
8 Civil Aviation Act 1982 s 48 (3) (g) (i).
9 See the Restriction of Ribbon Development Act 1935 ss 1, 2; and see TOWN AND COUNTRY PLANNING.
10 Civil Aviation Act 1982 s 48 (3) (g) (ii).
11 Ibid s 48 (4).

1136. Procedure for making orders. Any order for the stopping-up or diversion of highways[1] made by the Secretary of State[2] is subject to special parliamentary procedure[3].

The provisions of the Statutory Orders (Special Procedure) Act 1945[4] relating to the notices to be given and the other requirements to be complied with before an order is made apply to the making of such an order[5]. Notice[6] of the proposed order must be displayed at the ends of that part of the highway which is to be stopped up or diverted[7], must be sent to every local authority[8] in whose area any highway to be stopped up or diverted, or to be provided or improved, under the order, is situated[9], and must be served on any water, gas or electricity undertakers having any cables, mains, sewers, pipes or wires along, across, under or over any highway to be stopped up or diverted under the order[10].

1 See para 1134 ante.
2 As to the Secretary of State see para 1032 ante.
3 See the Civil Aviation Act 1982 s 48 (5).
4 See the Statutory Orders (Special Procedure) Act 1945 s 2, Sch 1; and PARLIAMENT.
5 Civil Aviation Act 1982 s 48 (5).
6 For provisions as to notices see para 1152 post.
7 Civil Aviation Act 1982 s 48 (6) (a).
8 'Local authority' here includes in England a parish council and the parish meeting of a rural parish not having a separate parish council and in Wales a council of a community and the community in the case of a community without a council: ibid s 48 (7) (a). See also para 1041 note 1 ante.
9 Ibid s 48 (6) (b).
10 Ibid s 48 (6) (c) (amended by the Water Act 1989 s 190 (1), Sch 25 para 67 (2)). 'Electricity undertaker' here includes the Post Office and the operator of a telecommunications code system; and 'water undertaker' means the National Rivers Authority, a water undertaker or a sewerage undertaker: Civil Aviation Act 1982 s 48 (7) (b), (c) (amended and added respectively by the Telecommunications Act 1984 s 109 (1), Sch 4 para 84 and the Water Act 1989 Sch 25 para 67 (2)).

1137. Compulsory purchase of land. The Secretary of State[1] may be authorised to purchase land compulsorily for the purpose of providing or improving any highway in pursuance of an order authorising the stopping-up or diversion of any highway[2], or for any other purpose for which land is required in connection with such an order[3].

For the same purposes, the Civil Aviation Authority (CAA) may exercise its right under the Civil Aviation Act 1982[4] to acquire land compulsorily[5].

1 As to the Secretary of State see para 1032 ante.
2 See para 1134 ante.
3 Civil Aviation Act 1982 s 49 (1). The provisions of the Acquisition of Land Act 1981 apply to such a compulsory purchase: Civil Aviation Act 1982 s 49 (2). For special provisions as to compensation for land held by statutory undertakers see paras 1144–1148 post. See generally COMPULSORY ACQUISITION.
4 Ie under the Civil Aviation Act 1982 s 42; see para 1114 ante. As to the CAA see para 1044 ante.
5 See ibid s 49 (3).

(v) Power to restrict Use of Aerodromes

1138. Use of aerodromes restricted for the purposes of safety. The Secretary of State[1] may by order impose such prohibitions or restrictions on the use of any area of land or water as a place for the arrival and departure of civil aircraft as he thinks expedient in order to secure the safe arrival and departure of aircraft at any aerodrome[2] or part of an aerodrome which is either vested in him or is under his control or which is either owned or managed by the Civil Aviation Authority (CAA)[3] or a relevant airport operator[4]. However, no imposition of any such prohibition or restriction is allowed in relation to tidal waters beyond those of the territorial waters adjacent to the United Kingdom[5].

1 As to the Secretary of State see para 1032 ante.
2 For the meaning of 'aerodrome' para 1102 ante.
3 As to the CAA see para 1044 ante.
4 Civil Aviation Act 1982 s 45 (1); and see the Airports Act 1986 s 59 (3), (4) as to the assimilation of the airport operator to the CAA; see further paras 1119, 1127, 1134 ante, 1151 post. As to the Secretary of State's power to establish and maintain aerodromes see para 1033 ante. As to the restriction on a local authority's powers to appropriate an aerodrome to other purposes see para 1041 ante. For planning restrictions see para 1104 ante. As to the power of the Secretary of State to restrict the use of

aerodromes and land adjacent for the purposes of security see the Aviation Security Act 1982 and the Aviation and Maritime Security Act 1990; and generally para 1243 et seq post.
5 Civil Aviation Act 1982 s 45 (2). For the meaning of 'territorial waters' see FOREIGN RELATIONS.

1139. Procedure for making orders. The same procedural provisions apply to the making of orders prohibiting or restricting the use of land for the arrival and departure of civil aircraft[1] as apply in the case of orders[2] creating rights over land[3].

In the case of orders imposing prohibitions or restrictions on the use of water[4], the Secretary of State[5] must, before making the order, publish notice of his intention to make it in such manner as he thinks best calculated to bring it to the attention of persons who will be affected by it[6]. Immediately after the order has been made, he must publish in one or more newspapers circulating in the district to which the order relates a notice stating that the order has been made and naming a place where a copy of the order may be seen at all reasonable hours; he must also serve a similar notice on any person who in his opinion will be affected by the order[7].

The same provisions apply in respect of applications to the High Court concerning the making of any order of this nature, whether or not relating to water, as they apply in the case of orders creating rights over land[8].

1 See para 1138 ante.
2 See para 1119 ante.
3 See the Civil Aviation Act 1982 s 45 (3), applying Sch 7 Pt I (paras 1–6); as to which see para 1122 ante. Orders in respect of aerodromes owned or managed by the Civil Aviation Authority (CAA) or the relevant airport operator are made on the application of the appropriate person: see Sch 7 paras 1 (2), 5 (2); and see para 1138 note 4 ante as to the assimilation of the airport operator to the CAA. As to the CAA see para 1044 ante; as to the airport operator see para 1042 note 4 ante.
4 See para 1138 ante.
5 As to the Secretary of State see para 1032 ante.
6 Civil Aviation Act 1982 s 45 (3) (a).
7 Ibid s 45 (3) (b). There is no provision for the holding of an inquiry. As to service see para 1152 post.
8 See ibid s 45 (3), applying Sch 7 Pt II (paras 7–9; as to which see para 1123 ante) and Sch 8.

1140. Compensation. Any person having an interest in land[1] to which an order prohibiting or restricting its use[2] relates is entitled to recover compensation from the Secretary of State[3] or, in the case of an aerodrome owned or managed by the Civil Aviation Authority (CAA)[4] or the relevant airport operator[5], from the appropriate person, if the value of his interest is diminished by the coming into operation of the order[6]. Compensation may similarly be recovered by any person who sustains damage, consisting not in the diminution in value of an interest in land, but in the disturbance in the use of land or water by reason of the coming into operation of the order[7]. Any dispute as to whether compensation is payable or as to its amount or the persons to whom it is payable must be referred to and determined by the Lands Tribunal[8].

No compensation is payable, however, in respect of the imposition of prohibitions or restrictions upon the use of an aerodrome which was first established as such after 31 July 1946[9] unless it was so established with the Secretary of State's consent[10].

1 For special provisions where land is mortgaged see the Civil Aviation Act 1982 Sch 7 para 11, applied by s 45 (4), Sch 8 para 3: see para 1124 ante.
2 See para 1138 ante.

3 As to the Secretary of State see para 1032 ante.
4 As to the CAA see para 1044 ante.
5 As to the relevant airport operator see paras 1138 note 4 ante (assimilation to the CAA) and 1042 note 4 ante generally.
6 See the Civil Aviation Act 1982 Sch 8 para 1. The Land Compensation Act 1961 s 5, so far as applicable and subject to any necessary modifications, has effect for the purpose of assessing such compensation: Civil Aviation Act 1982 Sch 8 para 4. See generally COMPULSORY ACQUISITION.
7 Ibid Sch 8 para 3.
8 Ibid Sch 8 para 5. As to such determination see COMPULSORY ACQUISITION.
9 Ie the date of the passing of the Civil Aviation Act 1946 (now repealed).
10 Civil Aviation Act 1982 s 45 (4).

1141. Offences. Any person[1] who contravenes the provisions of an order imposing prohibitions or restrictions on the use of land or water[2] is liable to penalties in respect of each offence[3]. Where an offence against such an order is committed on tidal waters outside the ordinary jurisdiction of a court of summary jurisdiction, the offence may be tried by the court of summary jurisdiction having jurisdiction over that part of the United Kingdom which is nearest to the place where the offence was committed[4].

1 The Civil Aviation Act 1982 s 99 provides that directors, general managers, secretaries or other officers of corporate bodies are liable in certain circumstances for offences committed by those bodies and applies to any offence committed under s 45 (restricted use of aerodromes): see s 99 (4); see also para 1121 ante.
2 See para 1138 ante.
3 The maximum penalty on summary conviction is a fine not exceeding the statutory maximum or three months' imprisonment or both; or on conviction on indictment, a fine or two years' imprisonment or both: ibid s 45 (5). As to the statutory maximum see para 1005 note 11 ante. At the date at which this volume states the law, the statutory maximum is £2,000. Proceedings may not be instituted except by or with the consent of the Secretary of State or the Director of Public Prosecutions (s 45 (7) (a)), although this consent is not required where the offence is against an order made on the application of the Civil Aviation Authority (CAA) or the airport operator: s 45 (7). As to the Secretary of State see para 1032 ante; as to the CAA see para 1044 ante; as to the airport operator see para 1138 note 4 ante (assimilation to the CAA) and para 1154 post generally.
4 See ibid s 45 (6). For the local limits of jurisdiction of courts of summary jurisdiction see MAGISTRATES.

(vi) Power of Entry for Survey

1142. Power of entry for purposes of survey. Any person authorised by the Secretary of State[1] in writing may at all reasonable times, on producing his authority from the Secretary of State if so required, enter upon any relevant land in order to make a survey[2]. Such a survey may be needed where, in pursuance of the provisions of the Civil Aviation Act 1982 providing for aerodromes and other land[3], the Secretary of State has made or confirmed[4] or is considering making or confirming an order authorising the compulsory purchase of land[5], or has made or is considering making an order providing for the creation of easements over, or other rights in, or in relation to, land[6], or declaring any area of land to be subject to control by directions[7], which either the Secretary of State, the Civil Aviation Authority (CAA)[8] or the relevant airport operator[9] requires to be made[10].

Admission to land which is occupied may only be demanded as of right if 24 hours' or, in the case of an order relating to the CAA or an airport operator, eight days' notice of the intended entry has been served on the occupier[11]. It is an offence to obstruct a person so authorised in the exercise of any power conferred by the foregoing provisions[12].

1 As to the Secretary of State see para 1032 ante.
2 Civil Aviation Act 1982 s 50 (2). A survey is any survey required to be made for the purpose of any steps to be taken in consequence of the order or for the purpose of determining whether the order should be made or, as the case may be, confirmed or for the purpose of ascertaining whether the land would be suitable for the purposes for which it is proposed to acquire it: see s 50 (3).
3 Ie the Civil Aviation Act 1982 Pt II (ss 25–59).
4 Ie where the order is made on the application of the CAA or an airport operator: see ibid s 50 (1), which refers to the CAA and the licensee of an aerodrome licensed under an Air Navigation Order (see further para 1044 ante as to the CAA and para 1154 post as to the licensee of an aerodrome); see also the Airports Act 1986 s 59, which assimilates a relevant airport operator to the CAA in so far as the application of the Civil Aviation Act 1982 s 50 is concerned; and see para 1143 post.
5 For the Secretary of State's powers to make such orders see paras 1041 (in relation to local authorities), 1113 (general powers), and 1134 (highways) ante.
6 See para 1119 ante.
7 See para 1127 ante.
8 As to the CAA see note 4 supra.
9 As to the relevant airport operator see note 4 supra.
10 See the Civil Aviation Act 1982 s 50 (1).
11 See ibid s 50 (4). For provisions as to notices see para 1152 post.
12 See ibid s 50 (5). The penalty on summary conviction is a fine not exceeding level 2 on the standard scale: s 50 (5) (amended by virtue of the Criminal Justice Act 1982 s 46). As to the standard scale see para 1044 note 6 ante. At the date at which this volume states the law, level 2 on that scale is at £100. Proceedings may not be instituted except by or with the consent of the Secretary of State or the Director of Public Prosecutions save where the CAA or the relevant airport operator concerned with the specific order wishes to institute proceedings: Civil Aviation Act 1982 s 50 (6). As to provisions making directors, general managers, secretaries or other officers of corporate bodies liable in certain circumstances for offences committed by those bodies see s 99 (1); and see para 1121 ante.

1143. Compensation. If any land is damaged in the exercise of a power of entry or in the making of any survey[1], the Secretary of State[2], the Civil Aviation Authority (CAA)[3] or the relevant airport operator[4], as the case may be, must pay such compensation to the persons interested in the land as is just[5]. Any dispute as to whether compensation is payable, as to its amount or as to the persons to whom it is payable, must be referred to and determined by the Lands Tribunal[6].

1 See para 1142 ante.
2 As to the Secretary of State see para 1032 ante.
3 As to the CAA see para 1044 ante.
4 As to the relevant airport operator and his assimilation to the CAA see paras 1119, 1127, 1134, 1138 and 1142 note 4 ante. As to the licensee of an aerodrome licensed under an Air Navigation Order see para 1142 note 4 ante and para 1154 post.
5 Civil Aviation Act 1982 s 50 (7).
6 Ibid s 50 (7). As to such determination see COMPULSORY ACQUISITION.

(vii) Statutory Undertakers

1144. Meaning of 'statutory undertaker'. A 'statutory undertaker' in this context is any person, including the Civil Aviation Authority (CAA)[1], the Post Office, airports permitted to levy airport charges[2], airports owned or managed by the CAA[3] or a local authority[4], who is authorised by any Act, whether public general or local, or by any order or scheme made under or confirmed by any Act, to construct, work or carry on any railway, light railway, tramway, road transport, water transport, canal, inland navigation, dock, harbour, pier or lighthouse undertaking or any undertaking for the supply of hydraulic power[5]. 'Statutory undertaking' has a corresponding meaning[6]. The National Rivers Authority, every water undertaker and every sewerage undertaker are deemed to be statutory undertakers and their undertakings statutory undertakings for these purposes[7], and the holder of a licence under the Electricity Act 1989 is deemed to be a statutory undertaker and his undertaking a statutory undertaking for certain purposes[8].

1 See the Civil Aviation Act 1982 s 19 (1), Sch 2. For the purposes of the law relating to rating, the CAA's undertaking is treated as not being a public utility undertaking: s 19 (3). As to the CAA see para 1044 ante.
2 See the Airports Act 1986 s 57 (1); see further para 1157 post. Airports owned by the BAA (now BAA plc; as to which see para 1109 ante) and airports either owned by a principal council (or by a metropolitan county passenger transport authority) or jointly owned by several councils (or by such an authority and one or more such councils) (as to such airports see para 1041 ante) are excluded from the meaning of 'statutory undertaker': s 57 (2).
3 See para 1105 ante.
4 For the meaning of 'local authority' see para 1041 note 1 ante.
5 See the Civil Aviation Act 1982 s 105 (1) (amended by the Telecommunications Act 1984 s 109, Sch 7 and the Gas Act 1986 s 67 (3), (4), Sch 8 Pt I para 17, Sch 9 Pt I).
6 Civil Aviation Act 1982 s 105 (1).
7 Water Act 1989 Sch 25 para 1 (1), (2) (xxviii).
8 Ie for the purposes of the Civil Aviation Act 1982 s 53 or, in the case of a licence holder entitled to exercise any power of compulsory acquisition under the Electricity Act 1989 Sch 3, for the purposes of the Civil Aviation Act 1982 ss 47–49, 51, Sch 9: Electricity Act 1989 s 112 (1), Sch 16 paras 1 (1) (xxxv), 2 (2) (h), (9).

1145. Application of special provisions. The instances in which the special provisions relating to statutory undertakers[1] apply are where land held by a statutory undertaker for the purpose of the carrying on of his undertaking is compulsorily purchased[2], where any order is made for the creation of an easement over, or of any other right in, or in relation to, such land[3], or where a direction is given[4] which affects any building, structure or apparatus held or used by an undertaker for the purposes of his undertaking, or affects any of his rights to install or maintain apparatus for these purposes, or affects any right of way enjoyed by him for these purposes[5]. Even in these cases the special provisions do not apply unless the Secretary of State[6], upon representation being made to him before the expiration of the time within which objections may be made to the making of the order[7] or, in the case of a direction affecting buildings or structures, of the time within which an application may be made to the court with respect to the direction[8], has certified that the land, building or structure, as the case may be, is, by reason of its nature or situation, comparable less with the generality of land, buildings or structures than with land, buildings or structures held for the purpose of carrying on statutory undertakings[9].

1 For the meaning of 'statutory undertaker' see para 1144 ante.
2 Ie under the Civil Aviation Act 1982 s 41, 42 or 48 (see paras 1113, 1114, 1134 ante): s 51 (1) (a). The special provisions do not apply where land held by a statutory undertaker is compulsorily purchased by a local authority under s 30: s 51 (1) (a); see para 1041 ante. As to the assessment of compensation by the Lands Tribunal see para 1146 note 1 post.
3 Ie under ibid s 41 or 44 (see paras 1113 and 1119 ante): s 51 (1) (b). The special provisions do not apply where an order provides for the creation under s 30 in favour of a local authority of an easement over, or other right in, or in relation to, land held by a statutory undertaker: s 51 (1) (b); see para 1041 ante.
4 Ie under ibid s 46 (see paras 1127–1132 ante).
5 Ibid s 51 (1) (c).

6 As to the Secretary of State see para 1032 ante.
7 As to the time within which objections may be made in relation to compulsory acquisition of land
   under the Civil Aviation Act 1982 ss 41, 42, 48 see the Acquisition of Land Act 1981; and see
   COMPULSORY ACQUISITION; and in relation to orders creating easements and other rights under the
   Civil Aviation Act 1982 s 44 see para 1122 note 5 ante.
8 As to the time within which application may be made to the court see para 1123 text to note 6 ante.
9 See the Civil Aviation Act 1982 s 51 (6).

1146. Assessment of compensation. In default of agreement, the compensation
to be paid to a statutory undertaker in any of these cases must be assessed by the
Lands Tribunal[1], and the amount of the compensation must be calculated in
accordance with the rules laid down by the Town and Country Planning Act 1990[2]
in relation to such compensation with certain minor modifications[3].

Those rules, as modified, provide that the compensation payable shall include
the amount of any expenditure reasonably incurred for the purpose of any adjustment of the carrying on of the undertaking necessitated by the acquisition; the
estimated amount of any decrease in net receipts by the undertaking in consequence
of the adjustment or, where no adjustment is made, of any decrease attributable to
the acquisition; and in the case of the imposition of a requirement to remove
apparatus or to demolish buildings or structures, any reasonable expense incurred
in complying with the requirement, reduced by the value of the apparatus removed
or materials salvaged[4].

In the case, however, of compensation for compulsory purchase, the person
carrying on the undertaking may elect, by written notice given to the Secretary of
State before the expiration of two months from the date on which notice to treat
was served, that the compensation for all or any of the land acquired shall be
assessed in accordance with the enactments which would apply apart from these
special provisions[5].

1 See the Civil Aviation Act 1982 s 51 (1); this provision does not apply to compulsory acquisition of
   land by the Civil Aviation Authority (CAA) under s 42 (as to which see para 1114 ante): s 51 (1). See
   also the Lands Tribunal (Statutory Undertakers Compensation Jurisdiction) Order 1952, SI 1952/
   161, art 3. As to the CAA see para 1044 ante. See further COMPULSORY ACQUISITION.
2 See the Town and Country Planning Act 1990 s 280 (2)–(5), (7), (8).
3 See the Civil Aviation Act 1982 s 51 (2) (a), (5) (amended by the Planning (Consequential Provisions)
   Act 1990 s 4, Sch 2 para 55 (2) (a), (b)).
4 See the Town and Country Planning Act 1990 s 280 (2). See further COMPULSORY ACQUISITION.
5 Civil Aviation Act 1982 s 51 (4). The Land Compensation Act 1961 s 5 (5) (which relates to
   compensation on the basis of equivalent reinstatement), does not apply to the assessment of
   compensation when such an election has been made: Civil Aviation Act 1982 s 51 (4). For the
   enactments and rules by which compensation is assessed apart from the special provisions see the
   Acquisition of Land Act 1981; and COMPULSORY ACQUISITION.

1147. Adjustment of undertakers' functions. Where it appears to the Secretary of State[1], upon a representation[2] made by a statutory undertaker, that, in
order to facilitate any adjustment of the carrying on of the undertaking, necessitated by an order made or proposed to be made, or by a direction given or proposed
to be given, under certain provisions of the Civil Aviation Act 1982[3], it is expedient
to extend or modify the undertaker's powers or duties in relation to the carrying on
of the undertaking, the Secretary of State may make an order providing for such
extension or modification[4]. An order so made may empower the undertaker to
acquire any land either compulsorily or by agreement, and to erect or construct any

buildings or works, specified in the order[5]; it may apply to such acquisition or construction enactments[6] relating to the acquisition of land and the construction of works[7] and contain such incidental and supplemental matters as appear expedient to the Secretary of State[8]. Any such order is subject to special parliamentary procedure[9].

1 As to the Secretary of State see para 1032 ante.
2 As soon as may be after making the representation the undertaker must publish, in such form and manner as the Secretary of State directs, a notice giving such particulars of the subject of the representation as may be directed, and specifying how and when objections to the making of the order on the representation may be made; he must also, if so directed, serve a similar notice on specified persons: Civil Aviation Act 1982 s 51 (7), Sch 10 para 3. As to notices see para 1152 post.
3 Ie the provisions of the Civil Aviation Act 1982 Pt II (ss 25–59, except s 30, which relates to the acquisition of land by local authorities (see para 1041 ante)): s 51 (7) (amended by the Planning (Consequential Provisions) Act 1990 s 4, Sch 2 para 55 (2) (c)). See paras 1113, 1119, 1127, 1134, 1138 ante and 1203 post.
4 Civil Aviation Act 1982 Sch 10 para 1. See generally the Town and Country Planning Act 1990 ss 275–277; and TOWN AND COUNTRY PLANNING.
5 Civil Aviation Act 1982 Sch 10 para 2 (a).
6 These include the Land Compensation Act 1961: see COMPULSORY ACQUISITION.
7 Civil Aviation Act 1982 Sch 10 para 2 (b).
8 Ibid Sch 10 para 2. See also Sch 10 para 4 (amended by the Planning (Consequential Provisions) Act 1990 Sch 2 para 55 (5) (a)), which applies the Town and Country Planning Act 1990 s 278 as if references therein to s 275 or 276 included a reference to the Civil Aviation Act 1982 Sch 10 Pt I (paras 1–5).
9 Ibid Sch 10 para 5; see PARLIAMENT.

1148. Relief from undertakers' obligations. If, on a representation[1] made by a statutory undertaker, the Secretary of State[2] is satisfied that the making of any order or the giving of any direction under certain provisions of the Civil Aviation Act 1982[3] has rendered impracticable the fulfilment of any obligation incurred by the undertaker in connection with the carrying on of the undertaking, he may by order direct that the undertaker shall be relieved of that obligation, either absolutely, or to such extent as is specified in the order[4].

If any objection is made to the making of such an order and is not withdrawn before the order is made, the making of the order is subject to special parliamentary procedure[5].

1 As soon as may be after making the representation the undertaker must, as directed, either publish in such manner as may be directed a notice giving such particulars of the subject of the representation as directed and specifying how and when objections to the making of the order may be made, or serve such a notice on specified persons, or both: Civil Aviation Act 1982 s 51 (7), Sch 10 para 7. As to notices see para 1152 post.
2 As to the Secretary of State see para 1032 ante.
3 Ie under the Civil Aviation Act 1982 Pt II (ss 25–59); see para 1147 note 3 ante.
4 Ibid Sch 10 para 6; see also Sch 10 para 8 (amended by the Planning (Consequential Provisions) Act 1990 s 4, Sch 2 para 55 (5) (b)), which applies the Town and Country Planning Act 1990 s 278 as if references therein to s 277 included a reference to the Civil Aviation Act 1982 Sch 10 Pt II (paras 6–9).
5 Ibid Sch 10 para 9; see PARLIAMENT.

(viii) Displacement from Land

1149. Duty to secure alternative accommodation. Where the Secretary of State[1] has acquired land for purposes connected with the discharge of his functions² or with aerodromes³, or gives a direction⁴ in relation to any land, and where the use of the land or the execution of the direction implies the displacement of persons residing in premises on that land⁵, he has a duty to secure that any such person displaced by reason of the order or direction is provided with reasonable residential accommodation⁶. The residential accommodation, to suit reasonable requirements, on reasonable terms, is provided for those persons who require it in consequence of the displacement, in so far as such accommodation is not otherwise available to them⁷. The provision of such accommodation need not be made in advance of a displacement if the Secretary of State is satisfied that for reasons of exceptional public importance it is essential that the displacement should be effected before such accommodation can be found⁸.

The same duty falls upon the Civil Aviation Authority (CAA)⁹ or the relevant airport operator¹⁰ where land was acquired for purposes connected with the discharge of functions and the use of the land therefor involves the displacement of persons there resident¹¹.

1 As to the Secretary of State see para 1032 ante.
2 As to the Secretary of State's functions see para 1032 et seq ante.
3 See the Civil Aviation Act 1982 ss 41, 43–45, 48–49; and paras 1113–1141 ante.
4 Ie under ibid s 46: see para 1127 ante and see notes 6, 11 infra.
5 See ibid s 52 (1).
6 See ibid s 52 (2). Where an order has been made under s 46 in favour of Eurocontrol (see para 1127 ante), the duty to re-house falls on the Secretary of State: see s 52 (1) (d), (2) (b).
7 See ibid s 52 (2). As to the rehousing of persons displaced from land see also the Land Compensation Act 1973 ss 39–43; and COMPULSORY ACQUISITION.
8 See the Civil Aviation Act 1982 s 52 (3).
9 As to the CAA see para 1044 ante.
10 As to the assimilation of an airport operator to the CAA for the purposes of the Civil Aviation Act 1982 s 52 see the Airports Act 1986 s 59 (3), (4); see also paras 1119, 1127, 1134, 1138 ante, 1151 post.
11 See the Civil Aviation Act 1982 s 52 (1) (c), (2) (a), (3) (a) and the Airports Act 1986 s 59 (4). The same duty befalls the licensee of an aerodrome where the Secretary of State has made an order under s 46 (see para 1127 ante): see s 52 (1) (d), (2) (c), (3) (a). As to the licensing of aerodromes see para 1154 et seq post.

(ix) Miscellaneous Provisions as to Land

1150. Consecrated land and burial grounds. Certain provisions of the Town and Country Planning Act 1990¹ are applied in relation to land acquired by the Secretary of State², the Civil Aviation Authority (CAA)³ or the relevant airport operator⁴, so as to allow them or anyone acting on their behalf to use the land for any purpose for which they acquired it and in any manner, whether or not involving the erection of buildings or the carrying out of work, even though the land or part of it consists of consecrated land or a burial ground, and notwithstanding any obligation or restriction imposed under ecclesiastical law or otherwise as respects such land⁵.

1 Ie the Town and Country Planning Act 1990 ss 238–240; see CREMATION AND BURIAL.
2 As to the Secretary of State see para 1032 ante.
3 As to the CAA see para 1044 ante.
4 As to the relevant airport operator and his assimilation to the CAA for the purposes of the Town and Country Planning Act 1990 ss 238–240 see the Airports Act 1986 s 59 (6) (amended by the Planning (Consequential Provisions) Act 1990 s 4, Sch 2 para 73 (1)); and see paras 1119, 1127, 1134, 1138 ante, 1151 post.

5 Civil Aviation Act 1982 s 54 (amended by the Planning (Consequential Provisions) Act 1990 Sch 2 para 55 (4)).

1151. Registration of certain orders. All orders providing for the creation in favour of the Secretary of State[1], Eurocontrol[2], the Civil Aviation Authority (CAA)[3] or the relevant airport operator[4] of easements over land or of other rights in or in relation to land[5], prohibiting or restricting the use of any land as an aerodrome[6], or declaring areas of land to be subject to control by directions, and any direction given under such an order[7], must be registered in the register of local land charges kept by any local authority[8] in whose area the land affected or any part of it is situated[9].

1 As to the Secretary of State see para 1032 ante.
2 As to Eurocontrol see para 1023 ante.
3 As to the CAA see para 1044 ante.
4 As to the relevant airport operator and his assimilation to the CAA for purposes connected with the acquisition of rights over land see the Airports Act 1986 s 59 (3), (4); and see paras 1119, 1127, 1138 ante.
5 Ie orders made under the Civil Aviation Act 1982 s 44; see para 1119 ante.
6 Ie orders made under ibid s 45; see para 1138 ante. Orders imposing prohibitions or restrictions on the use of water are not registrable: s 55 (1) (b) (ii).
7 Ie orders made under ibid s 46; see para 1127 ante.
8 As to local authorities see para 1041 note 1 ante.
9 See the Civil Aviation Act 1982 s 55 (1). As to the registration of local land charges see LAND CHARGES.

1152. Service of notices. Any notice required to be served upon a person for the purposes of the provisions of the Civil Aviation Act 1982 relating to land and aerodromes[1] may be served upon that person either by delivering it to him, or by leaving it at his proper address[2], or by sending it by registered post or by the recorded delivery service[3]. Any notice required to be served upon an incorporated company[4] or body will be duly served if served upon its secretary or clerk[5].

If it is not practicable after reasonable inquiry to ascertain the name or address of any owner, lessee or occupier of land on whom a notice is to be served, it may be served by addressing it to him by the description 'owner', 'lessee' or 'occupier' of the land (describing it) to which the notice relates, and by delivering it to some person on the premises, or, if there is no such person, by affixing it, or a copy of it, to some conspicuous part of the premises[6].

1 Ie the Civil Aviation Act 1982 ss 25–59.
2 A person's proper address is, in the case of the secretary or clerk of any incorporated company or body, that of the registered or principal address of the company or body, and in any other case, the person's last known address: ibid s 56 (3). Where, however, the person has furnished an address for service, that address is his proper address: s 56 (3).
3 Ibid s 56 (1).
4 As to service on a company see the Companies Act 1985 s 725; and COMPANIES.
5 Civil Aviation Act 1982 s 56 (2).
6 Ibid s 56 (4).

1153. Exemption from stamp duty. Stamp duty[1] is not payable on any conveyance of land or on any instrument creating or disposing of any right in or in relation to land, if the Secretary of State[2] is a party to the conveyance or instrument and certifies that the duty would fall to be defrayed as part of his expenses[3], provided that such expenses are connected to the performance of his civil aviation functions or, in the case of a conveyance of land, the conveyance is made for purposes relating to the establishment of aerodromes[4]. This exemption does not apply to the Civil Aviation Authority or to any airport operator.

1 See STAMP DUTIES.
2 As to the Secretary of State see para 1032 ante.
3 Civil Aviation Act 1982 s 59 (2).
4 Ibid s 59 (2) (a), (b).

(4) LICENSING OF AERODROMES

1154. Licensed aerodromes. The Civil Aviation Authority (CAA)[1] may license any aerodrome in the United Kingdom which is neither a government aerodrome nor a CAA aerodrome[2], subject to such conditions as it thinks fit, for the take-off and landing of aircraft[3] flying for the purpose either of the public transport of passengers[4], or of instruction in flying[5], or of flying tests for the grant of a pilot's licence or the inclusion of a rating in a licence[6]. Aircraft engaged on such flights may also take off and land at government aerodromes or CAA aerodromes notified as available to such aircraft or for which a particular permission was given[7].

The CAA may grant an aerodrome licence to any applicant where it is satisfied that his competence can secure that the aerodrome and its relevant airspace are safe for use by aircraft and that the aerodrome itself is safe for such use[8]. The licence is granted with such conditions as the CAA thinks fit and remains in force as therein specified, subject to the CAA's powers of revocation, suspension or variation[9].

The licensee of the aerodrome must give any information as to the terms of the licence to any person requesting it[10]. He may not cause or permit any condition of the licence to be contravened in relation to an aircraft engaged on such flights as described above[11], although the licence does not cease to be valid by reason only of the contravention[12].

1 As to the CAA see para 1044 ante.
2 For the meaning of 'aerodrome', 'government aerodrome' and 'CAA aerodrome' see paras 1102–1107 ante.
3 The Air Navigation Order 1989, SI 1989/2004, art 76 defines those aircraft which must take off and land from a licensed aerodrome when they are flying for specific purposes: aeroplanes of a maximum total weight authorised, whether they exceed 2,730 kg or not, helicopters, gyroplanes and gliders; see art 76 (2) (a)–(d).
4 For the meaning of 'public transport' see para 1272 post.
5 As to instruction in flying see para 1358 post.
6 See the Air Navigation Order 1989 arts 76 (1), (2), 78 (1). 'Licensed aerodrome' means an aerodrome licensed under the Air Navigation Order: art 106 (1). As to licensing see paras 1066–1071 ante; as to pilots' licences and ratings see Sch 8.
7 See ibid art 76 (1) (b).
8 Ibid art 78 (1). In reaching its decision, the CAA examines the applicant's previous conduct and experience, his equipment, organisation, staffing, maintenance and other arrangements and, as regards the aerodrome, it pays particular attention to the physical characteristics of the aerodrome and of its surroundings.
9 Ibid art 78 (2); as to a public use condition see para 1155 post; as to the CAA's powers to revoke, suspend or vary see art 66; and para 1422 post.
10 Ibid art 78 (4) (a).
11 The penalty for an offence is, on summary conviction, a fine not exceeding £1,000: ibid art 99 (5), Sch 12 Pt A.

12 Ibid art 78 (5).

1155. Public use aerodrome licence. When applying for an aerodrome licence, an applicant may request, or the Civil Aviation Authority (CAA)[1] may decide to grant, a 'licence for public use': such a licence is similar to an ordinary aerodrome licence save that it is subject to the special condition that the aerodrome shall, at all times when it is available for the take-off or landing of aircraft, be so available to all persons on equal terms and conditions[2].

During the period of validity of the licence, an ordinary aerodrome licence may be substituted for a public use aerodrome licence and a public use aerodrome licence for an ordinary aerodrome licence[3]. The substitution is made by the CAA either, in both cases, on the application of the licensee or, in the case of a public use aerodrome licence to be replaced by an ordinary aerodrome licence, on the application of another aerodrome licensee or of an air operator's certificate holder[4] or of an air transport licence holder[5] or exceptionally of an aircraft operator[6]. The CAA may also propose the substitution of a public use aerodrome licence for an ordinary aerodrome licence[7].

1 As to the CAA see para 1044 ante.
2 Air Navigation Order 1989, SI 1989/2004, art 78 (3). This provision is expressed to be without prejudice to the generality of art 78 (2), as to which see para 1154 ante. As to licensing see paras 1066–1071 ante. Any contravention is punishable on summary conviction by a fine not exceeding £400: art 99 (4).
3 See the Civil Aviation Authority Regulations 1991, SI 1991/1672, regs 10–14. These provisions relate to the publication of the application, objections and representations, furnishing of information and hearing.
4 As to an aircraft operator's certificate see paras 1340–1342 post.
5 As to air transport licensing see paras 1072–1091 ante.
6 See the Civil Aviation Authority Regulations 1991 reg 10 (1), (2).
7 Ibid regs 6 (10) (b), 10 (4).

(5) ECONOMIC REGULATION OF AERODROMES

(i) Permission to levy Airport Charges

1156. Aerodromes subject to economic regulation. Airports whose annual turnover[1] of business in at least two of the last three financial years exceeded £1 million[2] are subject to economic regulation by the Civil Aviation Authority (CAA)[3]. Government and CAA aerodromes[4] are not subject to economic regulation[5], nor are aerodromes which have been exempted by determination of the Secretary of State[6] when their annual turnover had fallen below the relevant sum in two of the last three financial years[7].

Where an aerodrome is subject to economic regulation, no airport charges[8] may be levied there unless they are levied by the airport operator to whom a permission to levy airport charges has been granted by the CAA and while the permission is in force in respect of that airport[9].

1 'Annual turnover' in relation to business carried on at an airport by the airport operator means the aggregate, as stated or otherwise shown in the accounts of the business, of all sums received in the course of the business during a financial year, including grants from any public or local authority but excluding capital receipts and loans made by any person: Airports Act 1986 s 14 (2), referred to by s 37 (9).

2 The sum of £1 million is the 'relevant sum' fixed by ibid s 14 (1); it may be increased by the Secretary of State: see ss 14 (3) and 37 (9), which refers to s 14.

3 Ibid s 37 (2). As to the CAA see para 1044 ante. The Airports Act 1986 imposes a restriction on the disclosure of information (as provided for by s 73) with respect to any particular business which has been obtained under the Act (s 74 (1)); disclosure of information in contravention of that restriction is an offence, punishable on summary conviction by a fine not exceeding the statutory maximum, and on conviction on indictment by imprisonment for a maximum term of two years or a fine or both (s 74 (5)). As to the statutory maximum see para 1005 note 11 ante. At the date at which this volume states the law, the statutory maximum is £2,000. As to exceptions to the restriction see s 74 (2)–(4).

4 As to government and CAA aerodromes see para 1105 ante.

5 Airports Act 1986 s 37 (4) (a), (b).

6 As to the Secretary of State see para 1032 ante.

7 Airports Act 1986 s 37 (4) (c). Such determination is made by the Secretary of State either of his own motion or on the application of the airport operator (s 37 (6)); it does not preclude the airport from being subjected to economic regulation once more at a later date (s 37 (7) (a)), nor does it affect any rights or liabilities accrued before the determination is made (s 37 (7) (b)).

8 'Airport charges', in relation to an airport, means (a) charges levied on operators of aircraft in connection with the landing, parking or taking-off of aircraft at an airport, including charges that are to any extent determined by reference to the number of passengers on board the aircraft, but excluding charges payable by virtue of regulations under the Civil Aviation Act 1982 s 73 (air navigation services: see paras 1376–1381 post) and (b) charges levied on aircraft passengers in connection with their arrival at, or departure from, the airport by air: Airports Act 1986 s 36 (1).

9 Ibid s 37 (1). As to the grant by the CAA of a permission to levy airport charges see the Civil Aviation Authority (Economic Regulation of Airports) Regulations 1986, SI 1986/1544; and para 1157 post. If a person levies airport charges in contravention of the Airports Act 1986 s 37 (1), he is not guilty of any offence by reason only of that contravention but he may not claim the airport charges so levied and any airport charges paid to him are recoverable from him: s 37 (8).

1157. Grant of permission to levy airport charges. When an airport is due to become subject to economic regulation[1], the airport operator must, within the nine months[2] preceding that time, apply to the Civil Aviation Authority (CAA)[3] for the grant in respect of the airport of a permission to levy airport charges[4].

The permission is deemed to be in force from the date of the application to the CAA for its grant or from the day when the airport becomes subject to economic regulation, whichever comes later[5]; the permission enters into force from the day it is granted[6] and remains so until it is revoked[7] or the airport ceases to be subject to economic regulation by determination of the Secretary of State[8].

The permission is granted when all the formalities are fulfilled, including the production of documents and the furnishing of accounts, estimates or other information further required by the CAA and relevant to the imposition of any condition on the permission[9].

1 As to aerodromes subject to economic regulation see para 1156 ante.

2 For airports which on 1 October 1986 had an annual turnover exceeding £1 million during two of the last three years preceding that date, the period was only six months: see the Airports Act 1986 s 37 (2).

3 The application had to be made to the Secretary of State when, before 1 April 1987, he notified the CAA that he was taking over its functions in respect of the airports mentioned in the notification and which were to be subjected to economic regulation by that same date (six months after the entry into force of the relevant statutory provisions): ibid s 53 (1); and see note 2 supra. Permission to levy airport charges was granted by the Secretary of State for the seven airports which succeeded to the British Airports Authority on its dissolution: see Official Record Series 6 No 2 Pt 3. As to the Secretary of State see para 1032 ante; as to the CAA see para 1044 ante.

4 Airports Act 1986 s 38 (1). The application must be in writing, contain all particulars as set by notice by the CAA and be accompanied by the specified fee: s 38 (2). The CAA must publicise the application and as much of its contents as it thinks fit: see the Civil Aviation Authority (Economic

Regulation of Airports) Regulations 1986, SI 1986/1544, reg 7 (1); and the CAA's Official Record Series 6 Pt 1.

5 See the Airports Act 1986 s 38 (3).

6 Ibid s 38 (7) (a). Where the date when the airport becomes subject to economic regulation is later than the date when the permission is granted, the permission enters into force on the later day: s 38 (7) (b).

7 Ibid s 38 (7). Revocation is for contravention of a compliance order: see s 49 (9); and para 1419 post.

8 Ibid s 38 (7). As to an airport ceasing to be subject to economic regulation see s 37 (5); and para 1156 ante.

9 See ibid s 38 (4). Where the applicant fails to comply with any requirement made by the CAA, the latter may give him further time to fulfil his obligation but has to refuse the application if the applicant cannot comply within the extra time: s 38 (5). The grant or refusal of the application must be notified to the applicant by the CAA; s 38 (6). As to service of documents see the Civil Aviation Authority (Economic Regulation of Airports) Regulations 1986 reg 5.

(ii) Conditions

1158. Imposition of conditions. Where an airport is subject to economic regulation[1] and has been granted a permission to levy airport charges[2], the granting authority[3] must impose conditions known as mandatory conditions[4] relating to the accounts of the airport operator and to the levying of airport charges where the airport has been designated for the purpose by order of the Secretary of State[5]. Conditions can also be imposed on other airports at the discretion of the Civil Aviation Authority (CAA)[6].

In imposing conditions the objectives of the CAA are, taking into account such international obligations of the United Kingdom which the Secretary of State may have notified to the CAA[7], to further the reasonable interests of users of airports within the United Kingdom, to promote the efficient, economic and profitable operation of such airports, to encourage investments in new facilities at airports in time to satisfy anticipated demands by the users of such airports and to impose the minimum restrictions that are consistent with the performance by the CAA of its functions[8].

The airport operator must comply with either mandatory or discretionary conditions imposed with the permission to levy airport charges[9].

1 As to aerodromes subject to economic regulation see para 1156 ante.

2 As to permission to levy airport charges see para 1157 ante; for the meaning of 'airport charges' see para 1156 note 8 ante.

3 Ie the Civil Aviation Authority (CAA) (as to which see para 1044 ante); but see the role of the Secretary of State, in the first six months after the royal assent was given to the Airport Act 1986, in respect of the seven airports issued from the dissolution of the British Airports Authority; para 1157 note 3 ante.

4 See further para 1159 post.

5 Airports Act 1986 s 40 (1) and see para 1159 post. Nothing requires or authorises the CAA to impose or modify conditions otherwise than on granting a permission to levy airport charges or while such a permission is in force: s 39 (5).

6 Ibid s 41 (1) and see para 1162 post.

7 Ibid s 39 (3); as to the international obligations of the United Kingdom see para 1001 et seq ante.

8 Ibid s 39 (2).

9 Ibid s 39 (1); as to the enforcement of the duty to comply with the conditions see ss 48–50 and paras 1170–1175 post.

1159. Mandatory conditions. Where an airport is designated for the purpose[1], the Civil Aviation Authority (CAA)[2] must impose conditions on the airport operator either when it grants the permission to levy airport charges[3] or within the period of nine months following the designation if this occurred after the grant of the permission[4]. The conditions concern the transparency of accounts[5] and the levying of airport charges[6].

1 As to the designation of airports for the purpose of economic regulation see the Airports Act 1986 s 40 (1); see also the Economic Regulation of Airports (Designation) Order 1986, SI 1986/1502, made under the 1986 Act s 40 and designating Gatwick Airport (London), Heathrow Airport (London), Manchester International Airport and Stansted Airport (London). The Secretary of State, in this instance, designated particular airports for the purposes of s 40; he may also designate classes of airports by reference to their annual turnover (as to which see para 1156 note 1 ante) or to any other matter: s 40 (10).
2 As to the CAA see para 1044 ante. As to the role of the Secretary of State see para 1157 note 3 ante.
3 Airports Act 1986 s 40 (1) (a); and see note 4 infra. As to permission to levy airport charges see para 1157 ante; as to the meaning of 'airport charges' see para 1156 note 8 ante. As to reference to the Monopolies and Mergers Commission (MMC) see paras 1164–1166 post.
4 Ibid s 40 (1) (b). The CAA must serve on the airport operator a notice containing the conditions which it intends to impose and make its decision within two months after considering any representation which the airport operator may have made: Civil Aviation Authority (Economic Regulation of Airports) Regulations 1986, SI 1986/1544, reg 8. The same rules apply where the CAA wishes to modify the conditions: reg 8.
5 See para 1160 post.
6 See para 1161 post.

1160. Mandatory conditions: accounts. The mandatory conditions as to accounts require that the accounts[1] disclose all subsidies relating to operational activities[2] carried on at the airport and furnished either by a third party[3] or by the operator himself out of funds attributable to other activities[4]. These accounts must also show under different headings the aggregate income and expenditure attributable to the levying of the airport charges[5], to the operational activities taken into account in fixing the airport charges[6] and to any business carried on by the airport operator at other airports which he also manages[7].

Where accounts are not required to be delivered to the registrar of companies[8], the Civil Aviation Authority (CAA)[9] may impose such conditions as it thinks appropriate as regards the publication of those accounts[10].

1 Reference to the accounts of the airport operator is a reference to accounts delivered to the registrar of companies in accordance with the Companies Act 1985: Airports Act 1986 s 40 (2); see, however, text and note 8 infra .
2 'Operational activities' in relation to an airport, means any activities which are carried on wholly or mainly for the benefit of users of the airport or the revenues from which are wholly or mainly attributable to payments by such users: ibid ss 30 (4), 36 (1). Compare the meaning of 'operational activities' with that of 'relevant activities' which is not so restrictive: see s 36 (1) and para 1162 note 8 post.
3 Ibid s 40 (2) (a) (i). The identity of the third party must be indicated; the subsidy may take the form of a loan on non-commercial terms or otherwise: s 40 (2) (a) (i).
4 Ibid s 40 (2) (a) (ii).
5 Ibid s 40 (2) (a) (iii). As to the levying of airport charges see para 1157 ante.
6 Ibid s 40 (2) (a) (iv). The operational activities may be carried out either by the operator or by a third party: s 40 (2) (a) (iv).
7 Ibid s 40 (2) (a) (v).
8 As to the non-delivery of accounts to the registrar of companies see COMPANIES.
9 As to the CAA see para 1044 ante.
10 Airports Act 1986 s 40 (2) (b).

1161. Mandatory conditions: airport charges. The mandatory conditions as to airport charges regulate the maximum amounts that the airport operator may levy by way of airport charges over a period of five years[1]. The maximum limit may be fixed by reference to the aggregate of accounts so levied at the airport and any other airport which together serve the same area and are either managed by the same airport operator or owned by the same person or group of companies and operated as a group of airports[2]. These conditions may not be imposed by the Civil Aviation Authority (CAA)[3] without prior reference to the Monopolies and Mergers Commission (MMC)[4], save as otherwise directed by the Secretary of State[5] and only once it has received the MMC's report[6].

The conditions may provide for an overall limit or for different limits to apply to different categories of airport charges or for a combination of such limits[7] or again for different limits to apply in relation to different periods of time falling within the five year period[8]. They may also impose restrictions in increases, or require reductions, in such airport charges[9].

The conditions are reviewed and prolonged, with or without modification, at the end of the five year period[10].

1 Airports Act 1986 s 40 (3). The period begins on a date specified by the Civil Aviation Authority (CAA), being a date not more than 12 months after the date on which the conditions were imposed: s 40 (3). The CAA may determine the extension of the five year period by no more than one year, after consultation with the operator: see s 40 (7). For the meaning of airport charges see para 1156 note 8 ante. As to the levying of airport charges see para 1157 ante.

2 Ibid s 52 (1) (2). The reference to airports serving the same area in the United Kingdom is construed in accordance with s 31 (6) (s 52 (2)), ie a reference to airports in the case of which a substantial number of the passengers departing from, or arriving at, the airports by air (other than those interrupting their flights there or transferring from one flight to another) have as their original points of departure, or (as the case may be) as their ultimate destinations, places situated within the same area in the United Kingdom (s 31 (6)). As to groups of companies see s 52; and generally COMPANIES.

3 As to the CAA see para 1044 ante.

4 As to references to the MMC see para 1164–1166 post.

5 Airports Act 1986 s 40 (9). As to the Secretary of State see para 1032 ante.

6 See ibid s 46 (1).

7 Ibid s 40 (5) (a) (i)–(iii).

8 Ibid s 40 (5) (c); where the CAA determines to extend the period in such a case, the limit applying to the last of those periods applies to the additional period for which the conditions are to remain in force, unless otherwise agreed by the CAA and the operator: s 40 (8).

9 Ibid s 40 (5) (b).

10 Ibid s 40 (4). Conditions may not be modified otherwise than in pursuance of s 40 (4) save with the agreement of the airport operator: s 40 (6). Reference to the MMC is needed before the CAA may modify the conditions: s 40 (9); the provisions described in the text and notes 4–9 supra apply to such modifications as they apply to the imposition of conditions: see s 40 (5), (8), (9).

1162. Discretionary conditions. The Civil Aviation Authority (CAA)[1] may impose on a non-designated airport[2] subject to economic regulation[3] the same conditions regarding accounts as are mandatory for designated airports[4], either at the time of granting a permission to levy airport charges[5] or later while the permission is in force[6].

The CAA may also impose such conditions as it considers appropriate, either at the time of granting a permission to levy airport charges or later, on an airport, whether or not it has been designated, if the airport operator is pursuing a course of conduct the adverse effects of which the CAA wishes to remedy or prevent[7]. The course of conduct of the airport operator to which the CAA may object can be: (1) the adoption, in relation to his relevant activities, of trade practices or pricing policies which unreasonably discriminate against any class of users, or particular users of the airport or which unfairly exploit his bargaining position relative to airport users generally[8]; or (2) the adoption of practices which unreasonably discriminate against persons applying for, or granted, rights to carry out relevant activities at the airport[9] or which unfairly exploit his bargaining position relative to grantees of such rights[10] or unreasonably limit the number of such rights that are granted[11]; or (3) the fixing of airport charges at levels insufficient to cover the costs to which they relate, or at artificially low levels[12] and which thus materially harm, or are intended so to harm, the business of an operator at any other airport in the United Kingdom[13].

1 As to the CAA see para 1044 ante. As to the role of the CAA in imposing discretionary conditions see para 1163 post.
2 As to the designation of airports see para 1159 ante.
3 As to aerodromes subject to economic regulation see para 1156 ante.
4 As to mandatory accounts conditions see para 1160 ante; as to mandatory conditions generally see paras 1158–1161 ante.
5 As to permission to levy airport charges see para 1157 ante; as to the meaning of airport charges see para 1156 note 8 ante.
6 Airports Act 1986 s 41 (1).
7 Ibid s 41 (2). As to the operator's course of conduct see text and notes 8–13 infra.
8 Ibid s 41 (3) (a). 'Relevant activity' in relation to an airport means the provision at the airport of any services or facilities for the purposes of the landing, taking-off or parking of aircraft, the servicing of aircraft (including the supply of fuel), or the handling of passengers or their baggage or of cargo at all stages, while on airport premises (including transfer of passengers, baggage or cargo): s 36 (1). Cf the meaning of 'operational activities' which is less restrictive: see s 36 (1); and para 1160 note 2 ante.
9 See ibid s 41 (3) (b) (i), (ii).
10 Ibid s 41 (3) (b) (i).
11 Ibid s 41 (3) (b) (ii).
12 Ibid s 41 (3) (c) (i). The reference to artificially low levels is a reference to such levels being significantly lower than they would otherwise have been either (i) by reason of a subsidy (furnished either by a third party, to the operator, in connection with his business relating to airport operational activities (see para 1160 note 2 ante), or by the operator out of funds attributable to other activities), or (ii) where the airport operator is a company, by reason of any conduct of the company resulting in failure to achieve a reasonable return, or to distribute a reasonable proportion of profits or to reach a level of borrowing appropriate to its equity share capital: s 41 (4); and see s 41 (5) as to how the CAA determines what is reasonable or appropriate conduct in the case of a company.
13 Ibid s 41 (3) (c) (ii).

1163. Discretionary conditions: role of the Civil Aviation Authority. Where the Civil Aviation Authority (CAA)[1] proposes to impose (or modify) discretionary accounts conditions[2], it must notify the airport operator of its intentions and consider any representations which the latter may have served on, or made to, the CAA within two months of service of the notice by the CAA, before making the decision whether to impose such conditions[3].

Where the CAA proposes to make discretionary conditions in respect of the airport operator's course of conduct[4], it must first investigate the conduct of the operator before deciding whether to impose (or modify) conditions in order to remedy or prevent what the CAA considers may be adverse effects of the course of conduct[5]. Before carrying out the investigation, the CAA must notify the operator of its intention and of its reasons therefor[6] and after completion of the investigation publish a report stating whether the operator is pursuing an objectionable course of conduct and, if so, what condition it intends to impose (or modify)[7]. Before imposing any such condition, the CAA must notify the operator[8] of the course of conduct which it has investigated and of its proposals[9]. If within the prescribed period[10], the operator objects to the proposals, the CAA must not proceed with the implementation of its proposals but may refer the matter to the Monopolies and Mergers Commission[11].

1 As to the CAA see para 1044 ante.
2 As to discretionary accounts conditions see para 1162 ante.
3 Civil Aviation Authority (Economic Regulation of Airports) Regulations 1986, SI 1986/1544, reg 10.
4 As to the meaning of 'course of conduct' see para 1162 ante.
5 Ibid reg 11 (1); Airports Act 1986 s 41 (3); see para 1162 ante.
6 Civil Aviation Authority (Economic Regulation of Airports) Regulations 1986 reg 11 (2) (a). The notice, together with an indication of the matters to be investigated, must be published to attract the attention of any person who may have an interest in the investigation: reg 11 (2) (b).
7 Ibid reg 11 (3). A decision as to the form and content of the report may be taken by a member of the CAA only after consideration of representations made to the CAA in the course of its investigation: reg 11 (4).
8 A copy of the notice must also be served on any person who may have adopted the same course of conduct as the operator as a consequence of the latter's practices or policies: reg 11 (6).
9 Airports Act 1986 s 41 (6).
10 Ie one month: Civil Aviation Authority (Economic Regulation of Airports) Regulations 1986 reg 4 (c).
11 See the Airports Act 1986 ss 41 (6) (a), (b), 43 (3). The decision to refer to the Monopolies and Mergers Commission (MMC) may be taken only after consideration of objections made within one month of service of notice by the CAA: see the Civil Aviation Authority (Economic Regulation of Airports) Regulations 1986 regs 4 (c), 11 (5). As to references to the MMC see para 1164 et seq post.

(iii) References to the Monopolies and Mergers Commission

1164. Ground for reference: mandatory conditions. Before imposing (or modifying) any mandatory conditions in respect of airport charges[1], the Civil Aviation Authority (CAA)[2] must make a reference to the Monopolies and Mergers Commission (MMC) unless otherwise directed by the Secretary of State[3].

The MMC is thus requested to investigate and report on a number of questions relating to the maximum amounts to be levied by the airport operator by way of airport charges at the airport over the relevant five year period[4], to the course of conduct of the airport operator[5], and to the possibility of remedying or preventing any adverse effect that that course of conduct might have had or might be expected to have[6]. The CAA must give the MMC all the information and assistance possible in order to help it with its investigation, and the MMC must take account of such information for the purpose of carrying out its investigation [7].

1 As to the mandatory conditions in respect of airport charges see para 1161 ante. No reference to the Monopolies and Mergers Commission (MMC) (see note 3 infra) is required for accounts conditions, as to which see para 1160 ante.
2 As to the CAA see para 1044 ante.
3 Airports Act 1986 ss 40 (9), 43 (1). As to the MMC see generally TRADE AND LABOUR. Particulars of the reference, and any variation thereof, must be published by the CAA in order to bring it to the attention of persons likely to be affected by it: s 44 (4) (a); copies of the reference (or variation) must be sent to the Secretary of State and to the airport operator: s 44 (4) (b). As to the provisions of the Fair Trading Act 1973 applying in relation to such references see the Airports Act 1986 s 44 (3), and see generally TRADE AND LABOUR. As to the MMC report see para 1166 post.
4 Ibid s 43 (1) (a). The CAA may specify in the reference any view that it may have formed as to the appropriate amount and any conditions (or modifications) which implement its view on the maximum amounts: s 44 (1) (a) (i), (iv).
5 Ibid s 43 (1) (b), (2) (a); the course of conduct referred to is the one adopted by the airport operator in relation to any airport charges levied by him at the airport, any operational activities carried on by

him and relating to the airport or any granting of rights to third parties to carry on operational activities at the airport: s 43 (2) (a) (i)–(iii). The CAA may specify in the reference any course of conduct of the airport operator which he may have pursued and has operated, or might operate, against the public interest and any conditions (or modifications) which could remedy or prevent those adverse effects: s 44 (1) (a) (ii), (iv). As to such courses of conduct see para 1162 ante.

6 Ibid s 43 (1) (b) and (2) (b). The CAA may specify in the reference any effect adverse to the public interest caused, or likely to be caused by an objectionable course of conduct of the airport operator and any conditions (or modifications) which would remedy or prevent those adverse effects: s 44 (1) (a) (iii), (iv).

7 Ibid s 44 (2).

1165. Ground for reference: discretionary conditions. Where the Civil Aviation Authority (CAA)[1] notifies an airport operator that it proposes to impose (or modify) conditions in relation to airport charges[2] to remedy or prevent the adverse effects caused or likely to be caused by his course of conduct[3] and where the operator objects to the proposals, the CAA must refer the case to the Monopolies and Mergers Commission (MMC) before implementing its proposals[4].

The MMC is thus requested to investigate and report on the questions whether the airport operator has, during the last 12 months[5] pursued the course of conduct which the CAA proposes to change[6] and if so, whether such conduct operated, or might operate, against the public interest[7] and if so, whether the adverse effects to the public interest which it had or might have could be remedied or prevented by the imposition (or modification) of conditions in relation to the airport[8]. The CAA may vary the reference by adding or excluding any specified matter[9].

The CAA must give the MMC all information and assistance possible in order to help it with its investigation, and the MMC must take account of such information for the purpose of carrying out of its investigation [10].

1 As to the CAA see para 1044 ante.
2 For the meaning of 'airport charges' see para 1156 note 8 ante.
3 As to the course of conduct of an airport operator see para 1162 ante.
4 Airports Act 1986 s 41 (6); and see paras 1162, 1163 ante. As to the MMC report see para 1166 post. Particulars of the reference, and any variation thereof, must be published by the CAA in order to bring it to the attention of persons likely to be affected by it: s 44 (4) (a); copies of the reference (or variation) must be sent to the Secretary of State and to the airport operator: s 44 (4) (b).
5 See ibid s 43 (6) (b).
6 Ibid s 43 (3) (a); and see notes 7, 8 infra.
7 Ibid s 43 (3) (b). The CAA may specify in the reference (or variation) any effects adverse to the public interest which, in its opinion, the relevant course of conduct has had or might have: s 44 (1) (b) (i). As to variation of reference see text and note 9 infra.
8 Ibid s 43 (3) (c). The CAA may specify in the reference (or variation) any conditions (or modifications) by which, in its opinion, the adverse effects of the relevant course of conduct could be remedied or prevented: s 44 (1) (b) (ii); as to variation of references see text and note 9 infra.
9 Ibid s 43 (4).
10 See ibid s 44 (2).

1166. Monopolies and Mergers Commission Report. When making its report, the Monopolies and Mergers Commission (MMC) must include definite conclusions on the questions comprised in the reference[1] and specify the effects, if any, adverse to the public interest which the course of conduct of the airport operator might have occasioned, or might be expected to occasion[2] as well as conditions or (modifications) which should be imposed to remedy or prevent those adverse effects[3]. The MMC's conclusions relating to the maximum amounts of airport charges to be levied are made in the form of recommendations[4].

In determining whether any particular point has operated, or might operate, against the public interest, the MMC must have regard to the objectives of the CAA under the relevant part of the Airports Act 1986[5]. In the case of a matter relating to the grant of rights to a third party[6], the MMC must consider the furtherance of the reasonable interests of the person granted such rights[7]. If the MMC concludes, on a reference, that an airport operator is party to an agreement to which the Restrictive Trade Practices Act 1976 applies, it must not indicate whether the provisions of that agreement have operated, or might be expected to operate against the public interest[8].

The report is sent to the CAA[9] which forwards copies to the Secretary of State and to the airport operator concerned before publishing it, subject to any direction given by the Secretary of State as to the exclusion of matter from the report[10].

1 Airports Act 1986 s 45 (1) (a). The report must also include such account of the MMC's reasons as is expedient for facilitating the proper understanding of the questions and conclusions: s 45 (1) (a). As to the grounds for reference to the MMC see paras 1164, 1165 ante.
2 Ibid s 45 (1) (b). As to objectionable courses of conduct pursued by an airport operator see para 1162 ante.
3 Ibid s 45 (1) (c).
4 Ibid s 45 (2); as to the limits or restrictions which the MMC may recommend see s 40 (5) and para 1161 ante; as to the imposition (or modification) of conditions see para 1167 post.
5 Ibid s 43 (5) (a); as to the objectives of the CAA under s 39 (2) see para 1158 ante.
6 See para 1160 ante.
7 Airports Act 1986 s 43 (5) (b).
8 Ibid s 45 (3). As to the Restrictive Trade Practices Act 1976 see TRADE AND LABOUR.
9 Airports Act 1986 s 45 (5). The expenses of the MMC in preparing reports in relation to references made by the CAA are covered by annual charges payable by airport operators: s 47; and see the Economic Regulation of Airports (Expenses of the Monopolies and Mergers Commission) Regulations 1986, SI 1986/1543. As to the CAA see para 1044 ante.
10 Airports Act 1986 s 45 (6). A direction to exclude any matter from a report may be made if it appears to the Secretary of State that the publication of that matter would be against the public interest or against the commercial interests of any person; the direction must be given within 21 days after he receives the copy of the report: s 45 (7); and see para 1163 note 11 ante.

1167. Imposition of mandatory conditions following report. The conclusions of the Monopolies and Mergers Commission (MMC) relating to the maximum amounts that should be capable of being levied by the airport operator by way of airport charges take the form of recommendations as to what those maximum amounts should be[1]. Where the Civil Aviation Authority (CAA) [2] is required to impose conditions as to the regulation of such maximum amounts, and a reference to the MMC has been made in pursuance of that requirement [3], the CAA must impose the conditions when it has received the report of the MMC containing the recommendations [4]. Before imposing the conditions, however, the CAA must have regard to the recommendations made by the MMC [5].

Where the MMC concludes in its report that the airport operator has pursued, or might pursue, a course of conduct detrimental to the public interest the adverse effects of which could be remedied or prevented by the imposition (or modification) of specified conditions[6] the CAA must impose (or modify) such conditions in respect of the airport as it thinks appropriate[7]. However, notwithstanding those conclusions, the Secretary of State may direct that the CAA is not to impose (or modify) any such condition[8].

The CAA must publish a notice of the conditions or modifications which it intends to impose, together with, if the proposed conditions or modifications do not accord with the MMC's report, a statement of the reasons for not implementing that report [9]. The notice must be published in such manner as to bring the matter to the attention of persons likely to be affected by the condition [10]. A decision as to the form of the conditions or modifications to be imposed may be taken by a member of the CAA only after consideration of written representations served on the CAA within 30 days after the date of the notice [11].

Finally the CAA must publish in like manner particulars of the conditions or modifications which it has imposed, and where they do not accord with the MMC's report as to the maximum airport charges or as to the remedying or prevention of the adverse effects of particular courses of conduct [12], a statement of its reasons for not implementing the report[13].

1 Airports Act 1986 s 45 (2). Such recommendations may contain provisions doing any of the things referred to in s 40 (5) (a)–(c): s 45 (2) (see para 1161 ante). As to the regulation of maximum amounts of airport charges, and the requirement for a reference to the MMC as to what those amounts should be, see ss 40 (3), (9), 43 (1); paras 1161, 1164 ante.
2 As to the CAA see para 1044 ante.
3 See ibid s 40 (9).
4 Ibid s 46 (1).
5 Ibid s 46 (4).
6 See ibid s 46 (2) (a)–(d).
7 See ibid s 46 (2).
8 Ibid s 46 (3); as to the Secretary of State see para 1032 ante.
9 Civil Aviation Authority (Economic Regulation of Airports) Regulations 1986, SI 1986/1544, reg 12 (1).
10 Ibid reg 12 (2).
11 Ibid reg 12 (3).
12 See text and notes 6–8 supra; and para 1168 post.
13 Airports Act 1986 s 46 (5).

1168. Imposition of discretionary conditions following report. Where the Monopolies and Mergers Commission (MMC) concludes in its report that an airport operator's course of conduct[1] detrimental to the public interest has operated, or might operate, with specified adverse effect which could be remedied or prevented by the imposition (or modification) of conditions, and where those conditions are specified, the Civil Aviation Authority (CAA)[2] must impose such conditions (or modifications) in relation to the relevant airport as it considers appropriate to remedy or prevent those adverse effects[3]. Before making its conditions (or modifications) the CAA must have regard to the conditions (or modifications) suggested in the report of the MMC[4].

The CAA must publish particulars of the conditions (or modifications) and, if they do not accord with those suggested in the report, a statement of its reasons for not implementing the report, so as to bring the matter to the attention of persons likely to be affected by the conditions[5].

1 As to the course of conduct of an airport operator see para 1162 ante.
2 As to the CAA see para 1044 ante.
3 Airports Act 1986 s 46 (2).
4 Ibid s 46 (4).
5 Ibid s 46 (5); as to the manner for the conditions to be published see the Civil Aviation Authority (Economic Regulation of Airports) Regulations 1986, SI 1986/1544, reg, 12; see para 1167 text and notes 9–11 ante.

1169. Duration and modification of conditions. All conditions imposed by the Civil Aviation Authority (CAA)[1] remain in force for such period or indefinitely as is determined by the CAA at the time of the imposition[2], save for mandatory airport charges conditions which, by statute, remain in force for five years[3].

Where a condition is imposed for a limited period, it may be extended[4]; where a condition is imposed for an unlimited period, the CAA must specify that it is a condition for an unlimited duration[5].

Mandatory account conditions may at any time be modified or revoked by the CAA provided in the latter case that they are replaced with further conditions[6].

Mandatory airport charges conditions may only be modified by the CAA at the end of the statutory five year period, save with the agreement of the airport operator concerned[7], and at the end of each succeeding period of five years[8].

Discretionary account conditions imposed on non-designated airports[9] may at any time be modified or revoked by the CAA (without obligation of replacement in the latter case)[10].

Discretionary airport charges conditions which have not been imposed in pursuance of a reference to the Monopolies and Mergers Commission (MMC)[11] may at any time be modified or revoked by the CAA[12]. However, where the CAA wishes to modify such conditions in order more effectively to secure the purpose for which they had been made it may not take this course of action where either reference to the MMC is required by reason of the airport operator objecting to the modification[13] or a previous reference had resulted in a modification of a condition[14].

All conditions made by the CAA after reference to the MMC in respect of the course of conduct of the airport operator may be modified or revoked by the CAA as long as such modification or revocation does not permit the occurrence or recurrence of the adverse effects intended to be remedied or prevented[15].

1 As to the CAA see para 1044 ante.
2 See the Airports Act 1986 s 51 (1). As to the notification of the imposition see the Civil Aviation Authority (Economic Regulation of Airports) Regulations 1986, SI 1986/1544, reg 5.
3 Airports Act 1986 s 40 (3).
4 Ibid s 51 (2). Notice of the proposed extension and the reasons therefor must be served on the operator, who has two months to make representations which must be considered by the CAA before it decides upon the extension: Civil Aviation Authority (Economic Regulation of Airports) Regulations 1986 reg 16. As to notification of the extension see note 2 supra.
5 Airports Act 1986 s 51 (1) (b).
6 Ibid s 51 (3); as to notification of the modification or revocation see note 2 supra. As to the mandatory account conditions see para 1160 ante.
7 See ibid s 40 (6).
8 Ibid s 40 (4), (6). Before making such a modification, the CAA must refer to the Monopolies and Mergers Commission (MMC) unless otherwise directed by the Secretary of State: s 40 (9) and see para 1161 ante as to the mandatory airport charges conditions. As to references to the MMC see para 1164 et seq ante. As to notification of the modification or revocation see note 2 supra.
9 As to the designated and non-designated airports see para 1159 note 1 ante.
10 Ibid s 51 (3). As to discretionary account conditions see para 1162 ante. As to notification of modification or revocation see note 2 supra.
11 As to the reference to the MMC in respect of discretionary airports charges conditions see para 1165 ante.
12 Ibid s 51 (4). As to notification of modification or revocation see note 2 supra.
13 See ibid s 51 (4) (a), (5); as to discretionary airport charges conditions see para 1162 ante.
14 See ibid s 51 (4) (b); as to reference to the MMC see para 1165 ante.
15 Ibid s 51 (6). As to notification of modification or revocation see note 2 supra.

(iv) Enforcement of Conditions

1170. Breach of airport conditions; complaints. Either a person on whom any airport charges have been levied by the relevant airport operator[1], or another airport operator[2] may complain to the Civil Aviation Authority (CAA)[3] that the airport operator is failing to comply with airport charges conditions imposed in relation to the airport which he operates[4]. The CAA must investigate the complaint unless it considers it frivolous[5]. It may also investigate the complaint of any other person if it thinks fit[6].

1 As to airport charges permitted to be levied by an airport operator see para 1157 ante; as to conditions relating to airport charges see paras 1161, 1162 ante.
2 The claim must be that the business carried on by the claimant at another airport in the United Kingdom has been or is being materially harmed by the alleged failure of the relevant airport operator to comply with the conditions which had been imposed: Airports Act 1986 s 48 (1) (b) (ii).
3 As to the CAA see para 1044 ante.
4 Ibid s 48 (1) (a). As to the imposition of airport charges conditions see para 1161 ante.
5 Ibid s 48 (1).
6 Ibid s 48 (2).

1171. Breach of airport charges conditions: investigation and hearing. After investigation of a complaint, the Civil Aviation Authority (CAA)[1] notifies the complainant and the relevant airport operator of its findings and of the action which it proposes to take, or that it intends to take no action [2].

Either party to the complaint may ask, within the prescribed time[3], to be heard by the CAA who, after hearing the parties, decides whether there has been, or is, failure on the part of the airport operator to comply with any condition[4].

The CAA may decide to take no action[5] or to make a compliance order[6] or to modify any relevant condition[7].

1 As to the CAA see para 1044 ante.
2 Civil Aviation Authority (Economic Regulation of Airports) Regulations 1986, SI 1986/1544, reg 13 (1).
3 Ie 21 days: ibid reg 13 (3).
4 The parties are served 21 days' notice of the date, time and place of the hearing and a copy or summary of the information gathered by the CAA in the investigation, provided it does not harm the public interest or the provider of information: ibid reg 13 (3), (4). The hearing is conducted by one or two members of the CAA, in private, each party appearing in person or being represented producing evidence and witnesses as the case may be, all proceedings being recorded: reg 13 (5)–(8). The decision as to compliance and action to be taken is made by those members of the CAA who heard the case; the decision and its reasons are served on the parties although the statement of reasons may be withheld by the CAA if disclosure of particular commercial or financial information to a relevant person might be to the unwarranted disadvantage of another person by comparison with the advantage which the disclosure might give to the relevant person and the public: reg 13 (9).
5 See ibid reg 13 (1), (2).
6 See para 1173 et seq post.
7 See para 1172 post.

1172. Breach of airport charges conditions: modification of conditions. Once the Civil Aviation Authority (CAA)[1] is satisfied that an airport operator has, as complained of, failed to comply with an airport charges condition[2], it may modify such a condition, unless it is a mandatory airport charges condition in which case the agreement of the airport operator is needed[3]. The modification of the condition must not permit any occurrence or recurrence of any effect adverse to the public interest which the Monopolies and Mergers Commission (MMC) had specified in a report following a reference in respect of the relevant airport[4].

1 As to the CAA see para 1044 ante.
2 As to the complaints and their investigation see paras 1170, 1171 ante.
3 See the Airports Act 1986 ss 48 (3) (b), 40 (6).
4 Ibid s 48 (4). As to references to the MMC see para 1164 et seq ante.

1173. Breach of airport charges conditions: compliance order. Once the Civil Aviation Authority (CAA)[1] is satisfied that an airport operator has failed to comply with an airport charges condition[2], it may make an order to secure his compliance with the condition and to remedy any loss, damage or injustice which the failure to comply caused to any person[3].

A compliance order requires the relevant airport operator to do, or not to do, specified things[4] and takes effect as soon as a copy is served on the airport operator unless otherwise specified[5]; it may be revoked by the CAA at any time[6].

The validity of a compliance order may not be questioned[7] save by application to the court on the ground that the order is not within the powers of the CAA[8] or that the requirements of the Civil Aviation Authority Regulations[9], in respect of the procedure to be followed by the CAA in the performance of its functions, have not been complied with[10].

The court may decide to reject the application or quash the order, in its entirety or in part[11].

1 As to the CAA see para 1044 ante.
2 See para 1171 ante.
3 Airports Act 1986 s 48 (3) (a). If the failure to comply has ended and is unlikely to occur again, the order need not contain any compliance provisions and may deal only with remedial matters: s 48 (5).
4 Ibid s 48 (6) (a).
5 Ibid s 48 (6) (b), (7). As to service of documents see the Civil Aviation Authority (Economic Regulation of Airports) Regulations 1986, SI 1986/1544, reg 5.
6 Airports Act 1986 s 48 (6) (c).
7 Ibid s 49 (3).
8 Ibid s 49 (1) (a). The application must be made within 42 days from the date of service of a copy of the order: s 49 (1).
9 Ie the Civil Aviation Authority Regulations 1991, SI 1991/1672, made under the Civil Aviation Act 1982 s 7 (2) as extended by the Airports Act 1986 s 36 (3) to functions granted to the CAA by Part IV (ss 36–56) of the 1986 Act.
10 Airports Act 1986 s 49 (1) (b). The court in question is the High Court: s 49 (11). As to the time within which to make the application see note 8 supra.
11 See ibid s 49 (2). Procedural irregularities do not invalidate the action taken by the CAA, which may take such necessary steps to remedy any prejudice which it may have caused before curing the irregularity: Civil Aviation Authority (Economic Regulation of Airports) Regulations 1986 reg 18.

1174. Breach of airport charges conditions: effect of compliance order. The obligation to comply with a compliance order[1] is a duty owed by the relevant airport operator to any person who may be affected by the contravention of the order[2]. No criminal proceedings may be brought against any person solely on the ground that he contravened the order[3]. Civil proceedings may, however, be brought by the aggrieved party against a person who either caused a breach of duty entailing loss or damage[4], or acted in such a manner that it induced a breach of duty or interfered with the performance of the duty and caused loss or damage[5]. Civil proceedings may also be brought by the Civil Aviation Authority (CAA)[6] for an injunction or interdict to enforce the compliance order[7].

Where the aircraft operator contravenes a compliance order and it appears that he is unlikely to comply with it in the immediate future, the CAA may revoke the permission to levy airport charges which it had granted him in respect of the airport to which the contravention relates[8].

1 As to compliance orders see para 1173 ante.
2 Airports Act 1986 s 49 (5).
3 See ibid s 49 (4): 'contravention', in relation to a compliance order, includes any failure to comply with it: s 49 (11). This provision also applies to aiding, abetting, counselling, procuring, conspiracy, attempt and incitement: s 49 (4).
4 Ibid s 49 (6) (a). It is a defence for the person against whom the proceedings are brought to show that he took all reasonable steps and exercised all due diligence to avoid contravening the order: s 49 (7).
5 Ibid s 49 (6) (b); 'act', in relation to any person includes any failure to do an act which he is under a duty to do, and 'done' is construed accordingly: s 49 (11).
6 As to the CAA see para 1044 ante.
7 Airports Act 1986 s 49 (8).
8 Ibid s 49 (9); for the meaning of 'contravention' see note 3 supra. As to the notice of the CAA's proposal to revoke the permission, the statement of respects in which the operator contravened the compliance order, and the grounds for revoking the permission see the Civil Aviation Authority (Economic Regulation of Airports) Regulations 1986, SI 1986/1544, reg 14 (1); as to the decision to revoke see reg 14 (2).
    Where the permission is revoked because of the airport operator's contravention, a permission may not be granted in respect of the airport in question so long as the operator remains the airport operator unless it appears to the CAA that he would comply with a condition corresponding to the one whose breach gave rise to the compliance order: Airports Act 1986 s 49 (10). As to the decision by the CAA to reinstate a permission see the Civil Aviation Authority (Economic Regulation of Airports) Regulations 1986 reg 14 (3). As to permission to levy airport charges see para 1157 ante.

1175. Breach of accounts conditions. Failure to comply with either mandatory or discretionary accounts conditions[1] renders the airport operator guilty of an offence and liable to a fine[2]. Whether or not criminal proceedings are brought against the operator, the Civil Aviation Authority (CAA)[3] may impose, in the case of the breach of a mandatory condition, new conditions requiring the publication of any matter which the operator should have disclosed[4]. If the operator fails to comply with the new conditions before the end of the period given for compliance he is again guilty of an offence[5].

In any such proceedings, it is a defence for the operator to show that he took all reasonable steps to secure compliance with the condition and, as the case may be, within the time allowed[6].

1 As to accounts conditions see paras 1160, 1162 ante.
2 Airports Act 1986 s 50 (1); the penalty is, on summary conviction, a fine not exceeding the statutory maximum, and on conviction on indictment, a fine: s 50 (1) (a), (b). As to the statutory maximum see para 1005 note 11 ante. At the date at which this volume states the law, the statutory maximum stands at £2,000. Where an airport operator is not required to deliver his accounts to the registrar of companies in accordance with the Companies Act 1985, but the CAA has imposed some appropriate conditions with respect to the publication of accounts and where the operator fails to comply with those conditions before the end of the period allowed for compliance, he is guilty of an offence and liable on summary conviction to a fine not exceeding level 5 on the standard scale and on a second or subsequent conviction to a fine of one-tenth of the amount corresponding to that level for each day on which the contravention is continued: s 50 (2) (a), (b); and see para 1160 ante as to account conditions made under s 40 (2) (b). As to the standard scale see para 1044 note 6 ante. At the date at which this volume states the law, level 5 on that scale is at £2,000.
3 As to the CAA see para 1044 ante
4 Airports Act 1986 s 50 (3).

5 Ibid s 50 (3). As to the penalty see s 50 (2) (a); note 2 supra.
6 Ibid s 50 (4).

(6) MANAGEMENT OF AERODROMES

(i) Duties in relation to Aerodromes

1176. Duty not to discriminate. It is the duty of the Civil Aviation Authority (CAA)[1] to secure that at all times when an aerodrome in the United Kingdom which it owns or manages is available for the landing or departure of aircraft it is so available to all persons on equal terms[2].

Where an airport is licensed for public use[3], the principal condition of the licence is that the airport is available to all persons on equal terms and conditions at all times when it is available for the take-off or landing of aircraft[4]. It is the duty of the aerodrome licence holder to notify the times during which the aerodrome is so available to aircraft engaged on flights for the purpose of the public transport of passengers or instruction in flying[5]. The licence holder may not contravene or cause or permit to be contravened any condition of the licence, including the non-discrimination condition[6].

1 As to the CAA see para 1044 ante.
2 Civil Aviation Act 1982 s 28 (4). As to restrictions relating to noise and vibration see s 78; and paras 1185–1188 post.
3 As to licences for public use see para 1155 ante.
4 Air Navigation Order 1989, SI 1989/2004, art 78 (3). The right of access may be curtailed by an interlocutory injunction where the aircraft operator has not paid the increased airport charges to which he objects: see *Air Canada v Secretary of State for Trade* [1981] 3 All ER 336. As to the binding effect of reasonable conditions see *British Airports Authority v British Airways Board* (1981) 1 S&B AvR VII/17.
5 Ibid art 78 (4) (b). As to flying for public transport purposes see para 1272 post; as to instruction in flying see para 1358 post.
6 See ibid art 78 (5). The offender is liable on summary conviction to a fine not exceeding £1,000: art 99 (5), Sch 12 Pt A.

1177. Secretary of State's duty in relation to aerodromes. The Secretary of State[1] must appoint, for each aerodrome[2] vested in him, an officer to be responsible to him for all the services provided there on his behalf, including signalling services, flying control services and services connected with the execution of works[3].

In the management and administration of any aerodrome vested in him, the Secretary of State must make such provisions as he thinks necessary to ensure that adequate facilities for consultation are provided for local authorities[4] in whose area the aerodrome or any part of it is situated, for local authorities whose areas are in that neighbourhood, and for other organisations representing the interests of persons concerned with that locality[5].

1 As to the Secretary of State see para 1032 ante.
2 For the meaning of 'aerodrome' see para 1102 ante.
3 Civil Aviation Act 1982 s 25 (2). As to the prevention of the spread of diseases at aerodromes see para 1230 post.
4 For the meaning of 'local authority' see para 1041 note 1 ante.
5 Civil Aviation Act 1982 s 26.

1178. Civil Aviation Authority's duty in relation to aerodromes. The Civil Aviation Authority (CAA)[1] is under a duty to provide at the aerodromes[2] in the United Kingdom which it owns or manages such services and facilities as it considers necessary or desirable for their operation[3]. It may, with the Secretary of State's[4] consent, appoint another person to manage on its behalf any aerodrome which it owns or manages[5].

1 As to the CAA see para 1044 ante.
2 For the meaning of 'aerodrome' see para 1102 ante. See also paras 1105, 1114 ante.
3 Civil Aviation Act 1982 s 28 (3). In carrying out this duty it must have regard to the development of air transport and to efficiency, economy and safety of operation: s 28 (3).
4 As to the Secretary of State see para 1032 ante.
5 Civil Aviation Act 1982 s 28 (5). As to the duty to provide consultation facilities see para 1179 post.

1179. Duty in relation to other aerodromes. The person having the management of any aerodrome[1] designated for the purpose by order[2] made by the Secretary of State[3], must provide, for users of the aerodrome, for any local authority[4] (or, if a local authority manages the aerodrome, for any other local authority) in whose area the aerodrome or any part of it is situated or whose area is in that neighbourhood, and for any other organisation representing the interests of persons concerned with that locality, adequate facilities for consultation with respect to any matter concerning the management or administration of the aerodrome which affects their interests[5].

1 For the meaning of 'aerodrome' see para 1102 ante.
2 The order must be made by statutory instrument, and may be varied or revoked by another such order which is subject to annulment in pursuance of a resolution of either House of Parliament: Civil Aviation Act 1982 s 102 (1). See the Aerodromes (Designation) (Facilities for Consultation) Order 1986, SI 1986/1348, and the Aerodromes (Designation) (Facilities for Consultation) Order 1989, SI 1989/1489: Civil Aviation Act 1982 s 35 (1) (amended by the Airports Act 1986 s 83 (5), Sch 6 Pt II).
3 Civil Aviation Act 1982 s 35 (2). As to the Secretary of State see para 1032 ante.
4 For the meaning of 'local authority' see para 1041 note 1 ante.
5 Civil Aviation Act 1982 s 35 (2).

1180. Records at aerodromes. Where an aerodrome is provided with an aeronautical radio station[1] which is used for the provision of an air traffic control service by an air traffic control unit[2], the person in charge of the aeronautical radio station must provide apparatus capable of recording the terms or content of any radio message or signal transmitted to any aircraft, either alone or in common with other aircraft, or received from any aircraft, by the air traffic control unit at the aerodrome[3].

The apparatus must be of a type approved by the Civil Aviation Authority (CAA)[4] in relation to the particular aeronautical radio station, must be installed, modified and maintained in a manner so approved[5], and must be in use at all times when the aeronautical radio station is operating to provide an air traffic control service[6].

The person in charge must ensure[7] that each record includes the identification of the aeronautical radio station, the date or dates on which it was made, a means of determining the time when the message or signal was transmitted, the aircraft to or from which and the frequency on which it was transmitted or received, and the time at which the record started and finished[8].

The person in charge must preserve[9] each record for 30 days, or such longer period as the CAA directs, from the date on which the message or signal was recorded, and must cause it to be produced to any authorised person[10] within a reasonable time of his requesting it[11].

The person in charge must also keep written records of functional tests, flight checks and particulars of any overhaul, repair, replacement or modification of the particular aeronautical radio station[12]. Such record must be preserved for one year or such longer period as the CAA directs and must be produced to any authorised person within a reasonable time of the request[13].

1 An 'aeronautical radio station' means a radio station on the surface, which transmits or receives signals for the purpose of assisting aircraft: Air Navigation Order 1989, SI 1989/2004, art 106 (1). See further para 1435 post.
2 For the meaning of 'air traffic control unit' see para 1394 note 1 post.
3 Air Navigation Order 1989 art 80 (2). The penalty for contravention of this and other requirements set out in this paragraph is on summary conviction a fine not exceeding £1,000: art 99 (5), Sch 12 Pt A. The provisions of art 80 do not apply in respect of aeronautical radio stations in the charge of the Secretary of State or the Civil Aviation Authority: art 80 (8).
4 As to the CAA see para 1044 ante.
5 If the apparatus ceases to be capable of recording, the person in charge must ensure that the matters to be recorded are recorded in writing: Air Navigation Order 1989 art 80 (5). As to contravention see note 3 supra.
6 Ibid art 80 (3).
7 As to contravention see note 3 supra.
8 Ibid art 80 (4).
9 Where a person ceases to be in charge he, or, if he dies, his personal representatives, must continue to preserve the record as if he had not ceased to be in charge; if another person becomes the person in charge the original person in charge or his personal representative must deliver the record to him on demand, and the new person in charge then has the duty of dealing with the record as if he were the original person in charge: ibid art 80 (7). As to contravention see note 3 supra.
10 For the meaning of 'authorised person' see para 1193 note 2 post.
11 Air Navigation Order 1989 art 80 (6).
12 Ibid art 80 (1) (a); and see note 3 supra in respect of aeronautical radio stations in the charge of the Secretary of State or the CAA.
13 Ibid art 80 (1) (b).

(ii) Charges

1181. Financing of aerodromes. Aerodromes may be financed by loans or grants made by the Secretary of State[1] or local authorities[2], by investments made by local authorities[3] or any other person and by charges established and levied by airport operators on users of aerodromes[4].

In order to ensure fair trading practices, the Airports Act 1986[5] distinguishes between those airports whose annual turnover[6] exceeds £1 million and the others, closely regulating the conduct of the former, particularly in the levying of airport charges[7].

1 See the Civil Aviation Act 1982 s 34; and para 1033 ante. As to the Secretary of State see para 1032 ante.
2 See the Airports Act 1986 s 25; and para 1112 ante. As to the local authorities see para 1041 ante.
3 See ibid s 20 (1), (3); and para 1042 ante.
4 See the Air Navigation Order 1989, SI 1989/2004, art 81 and para 1182 post; and the Airports Act 1986 s 37 and para 1183 post.
5 See the Airports Act 1986 ss 36–56.
6 For the meaning of 'annual turnover' see para 1156 note 1 ante.

7 See further paras 1156, 1157 ante.

1182. Charges at aerodromes. The licensee of an aerodrome licensed for public use[1] may establish charges for the use of the aerodrome or of any facilities provided at the aerodrome for the safety, efficiency or regularity of air navigation[2]. In order to encourage the use of quieter aircraft and to diminish the inconvenience from aircraft noise, the aerodrome authority[3] may fix, or be directed[4] by the Secretary of State[5] to fix the charges by reference, inter alia, to the amount of noise caused by the relevant aircraft or to the extent or nature of any inconvenience due to such noise[6]. The aerodrome licensee must furnish to the Secretary of State when required by him, such particulars of those charges as he may require[7].

1 As to licences for public use see para 1155 ante.
2 Air Navigation Order 1989, SI 1989/2004, art 81. As to the non-payment of charges see paras 1183, 1184 post. The penalty for contravention is on summary conviction a fine not exceeding £1,000: art 99 (4).
3 An 'aerodrome authority' means a person owning or managing an aerodrome licensed under an Air Navigation Order: Civil Aviation Act 1982 s 38 (3).
4 Ibid s 38 (2) (amended by the Airports Act 1986 s 83 (5), Sch 6 Pt II). The order may contain directions as to the manner in which those charges are to be fixed: Civil Aviation Act 1982 s 38 (2).
5 As to the Secretary of State see para 1032 ante.
6 Civil Aviation Act 1982 s 38 (1). As to noise generally see paras 1185–1188 post.
7 Air Navigation Order 1989 art 81.

1183. Detention of aircraft for unpaid airport charges. Where default is made in the payment of airport charges[1] incurred in respect of any aircraft at an aerodrome owned or managed by any government department or a local authority[2], or at any other aerodrome designated for this purpose by an order made by the Secretary of State[3], the aerodrome authority[4] may: (1) detain, pending payment, either the aircraft[5] in respect of which the charges were incurred, whether or not they were incurred by the person who is its operator[6] at the time the detention begins, or any other aircraft of which the person in default is the operator at the time detention begins[7]; and (2) sell the aircraft in order to satisfy the charges[8].

The power of detention and sale extends to any equipment of the aircraft carried in it, and to any stores carried in it for use in connection with its operation, whether or not the equipment and stores are the operator's property[9]; and the power of detention extends to any aircraft documents[10] carried in the aircraft[11].

The power of detention may be exercised on the occasion on which the charges were incurred or on any subsequent occasion when the aircraft is on the relevant aerodrome or on any other aerodrome owned or managed by the aerodrome authority concerned[12].

The aerodrome authority may not so detain or continue to detain an aircraft if the operator or any other person claiming an interest in it disputes that the charges are due[13] and gives the authority, pending the determination of the dispute, sufficient security for the payment of the charges alleged to be due[14].

1 'Airport charges' means charges payable to an aerodrome authority for the use of, or for services provided at, an aerodrome, but does not include charges payable by virtue of regulations made under the Civil Aviation Act 1982 s 73 (charges for air navigation services; see paras 1376–1381 post); 'aerodrome authority', in relation to any aerodrome, means the person owning or managing it (see paras 1176–1179 ante): see s 88 (10). For the meaning of 'aerodrome' see para 1102 ante. Airport charges must relate to specific aircraft: see *Havelet Leasing Ltd v Cardiff-Wales Airport Ltd* (1988) 1 S&B AvR IV/111.

2 For the meaning of 'local authority' see para 1041 note 1 ante.
3 Civil Aviation Act 1982 s 88 (10) (amended by the Airports Act 1986 s 83 (5), Sch 6 Pt I), under which were made the Aerodromes (Designation) (Detention and Sale of Aircraft) Order 1986, SI 1986/312, the Aerodromes (Designation) (Detention and Sale of Aircraft) (No 2) Order 1986, SI 1986/1347, the Aerodromes (Designation) (Detention and Sale of Aircraft) Order 1987, SI 1987/1377, the Aerodromes (Designation) (Detention and Sale of Aircraft) (No 2) Order 1987, SI 1987/2229, and the Aerodromes (Designation) (Detention and Sale of Aircraft) Order 1990, SI 1990/1527. As to the Secretary of State see para 1032 ante.
4 For the meaning of 'aerodrome authority' see note 1 supra.
5 As to equipment, stores and documents see the text to notes 10–12 infra.
6 As to aircraft operators see para 1340 post.
7 Civil Aviation Act 1982 s 88 (1) (a). For an application see *R v Civil Aviation Authority, ex p Emery Air Freight Corpn* (1988) 1 S&B AvR IV/105, CA. The detention must be begun by an overt act: see *Havelet Leasing Ltd v Cardiff-Wales Airport Ltd* (1988) 1 S&B AvR IV/111. As to whether leave of the court or consent of the administrator of a company is required where an administration order has been made under the Insolvency Act 1986 before the aircraft authority can exercise its right to detain aircraft see *Bristol Airport plc v Powdrill* [1990] Ch 744, [1990] 2 All ER 493, 1 S&B AvR IV/121, CA. As to other powers of detention see para 1339 post. As to forbidding access to an airport as long as disputed increased charges are not paid see *Air Canada v Secretary of State for Transport* [1981] 3 All ER 336; and para 1176 note 4 ante.
8 Ibid s 88 (1) (b). As to sale see para 1184 post.
9 Ibid s 88 (7).
10 'Aircraft documents' means any certificate of registration, maintenance or airworthiness, log books and any similar document: ibid s 88 (10).
11 Ibid s 88 (8).
12 Ibid s 88 (9).
13 Ibid s 88 (2) (a). Alternatively, if such person disputes that the aircraft detained is the one in respect of which the charges were incurred the aerodrome authority may not continue to detain the aircraft, provided the provisions of s 88 (2) (b) are complied with: s 88 (2) (a).
14 Ibid s 88 (2) (b).

1184. Sale of aircraft for unpaid airport charges. An aerodrome authority[1] may not sell an aircraft detained for unpaid airport charges[2] without the leave of the High Court[3]. The aerodrome authority must, in the prescribed manner[4], bring the proposed application to the attention of those persons who may be affected by the determination of the court[5] so that they may become parties to the proceedings on the application if need be[6].

The application to the court should be made by originating summons, which the defendant must acknowledge[7]. On the hearing of the application the court may not give leave except on proof that a sum is due to the authority for airport charges, that default has been made in its payment and that the aircraft is liable to sale by reason of the default[8]. If leave is given the authority must secure that the aircraft is sold for the best price that can reasonably be obtained[9]. The proceeds of any sale must be applied in the following order: (1) payment of customs or excise duty or value added tax due in consequence of the aircraft having been brought into the United Kingdom; (2) payment of expenses incurred by the aerodrome authority in detaining, keeping and selling the aircraft and in applying for leave to sell it; (3) payment of airport charges found due; and (4) payment of charges[10] for air navigation services[11]. Any surplus must be paid to or among the persons whose interests in the aircraft have been divested by reason of the sale[12].

Nothing in these provisions prejudices an authority's right to recover any charges, or any part of them, by action[13].

1 For the meaning of 'aerodrome authority' see para 1183 note 1 ante.
2 See para 1183 ante. For the meaning of 'airport charges' see para 1183 note 1 ante. As to the extension of the power of sale to equipment and stores see para 1183 text to note 9 ante.

3 Civil Aviation Act 1982 s 88 (3), (10).
4 See the Civil Aviation (Airport Charges) (Sale of Detained Aircraft) Regulations 1971, SI 1971/1134, made under the Civil Aviation Act 1968 s 14 (4) (repealed) and saved by the Civil Aviation Act 1982 s 109 (1), Sch 14 para 3.
5 Ibid s 88 (4) (a).
6 Ibid s 88 (4) (b). While failure to comply with these requirements is actionable as against the authority at the suit of any person suffering loss in consequence, it is not a ground for impugning the validity of a sale: s 88 (5).
7 RSC Ord 12 r 9; see PRACTICE AND PROCEDURE.
8 Civil Aviation Act 1982 s 88 (3).
9 Ibid s 88 (4). As to the sale of aircraft see para 1332 post. As to failure to comply with this provision see note 5 supra. If aircraft documents (as to which see para 1183 note 10 ante) were detained with an aircraft which is sold, the aerodrome authority must transfer them to the purchaser: s 88 (8).
10 As to these charges see paras 1376–1381 post.
11 Civil Aviation Act 1982 s 88 (6).
12 Ibid s 88 (6).
13 Ibid s 88 (12).

(iii) Noise and Vibration

1185. Noise and vibration on aerodromes. No action lies in respect of nuisance by reason only of the noise and vibration caused by aircraft on an aerodrome[1] to which the appropriate provisions of the Civil Aviation Act 1982[2] apply by virtue of an Air Navigation Order[3] as long as the provisions of that order are duly complied with[4].

The Secretary of State[5] may prescribe the conditions under which noise and vibration may be caused by aircraft, including military aircraft[6], on government aerodromes or aerodromes owned or managed by the Civil Aviation Authority (CAA)[7], licensed aerodromes[8], or on aerodromes at which the manufacture, maintenance or repair of aircraft is carried out by persons carrying on business as aircraft manufacturers or repairers[9]. Noise and vibration may be caused on any such aerodrome provided it is caused by aircraft taking off or landing or moving on the ground or on water, or by aircraft engines being operated for the purpose of ensuring their satisfactory performance or of bringing them up to a proper temperature for, or at the end of, a flight, or of insuring that the instruments, accessories or other components of the aircraft are in a satisfactory condition[10].

1 For the meaning of 'aerodrome' see para 1102 ante.
2 Ie the Civil Aviation Act 1982 s 77 (2).
3 The Air Navigation Order 1989, SI 1989/2004, art 83, made under the Civil Aviation Act 1982 ss 60 (see para 1026 ante), 77 (1), applies s 77 (2) to any aerodrome to which the Secretary of State has applied conditions: see infra.
4 Ibid s 77 (2). Compensation may, in certain circumstances, be recovered where the value of land is depreciated by noise, vibration or other physical factors caused by the use of an aerodrome: see the Land Compensation Act 1973 ss 1–19; and COMPULSORY ACQUISITION. But such compensation is recoverable only if the aerodrome concerned is one to which the Civil Aviation Act 1982 s 77 (2) applies.
5 As to the Secretary of State see para 1032 ante.
6 For the meaning of 'military aircraft' see para 1029 note 5 ante.
7 As to the CAA see para 1044 ante.
8 For the meaning of 'licensed aerodrome' see para 1154 note 5 ante.
9 Air Navigation Order 1989 art 83. As to manufacture and repairs see paras 1275, 1324–1331 post.
10 Air Navigation (General) Regulations 1981, SI 1981/57, reg 12. As to noise certificates for aircraft see paras 1305–1311 post. As to nuisance caused by noise and vibration see para 1687 post; and generally NUISANCE.

1186. Aircraft operators' duties as to noise and vibration. The Secretary of State[1] may provide by notice that it is the duty of the operator[2] of an aircraft to secure that, after the aircraft takes off or before it lands at a designated aerodrome[3], the requirements specified in the notice are complied with, for the purpose of limiting or of mitigating the effect of noise and vibration connected with the taking-off or landing of aircraft at that aerodrome[4].

If it appears to him that any such requirement has not been complied with the Secretary of State may, after considering any representation that the operator may make to him, give to the person managing the aerodrome a direction requiring him to secure that facilities for using the aerodrome are withheld to the extent specified in the direction from the operator's aircraft and servants[5].

The Secretary of State may limit by notice the number of occasions on which aircraft of specified descriptions may be permitted to take off or land at the aerodrome during specified periods, other than in an emergency of a specified description[6]; specify the maximum number of occasions when particular aircraft are permitted to take off or land at the aerodrome during specified periods[7] and determine, after consulting any body representative of operators using the aerodrome[8], the operators who will be entitled to arrange for their aircraft to take off or land and the number of occasions on which their aircraft may take off or land during those periods[9]. If it appears to the Secretary of State that an aircraft is about to take off in contravention of the limitations thus imposed, any person authorised by him in that behalf may detain the aircraft for such period as that person considers appropriate for preventing the contravention, and may for this purpose enter on any land[10]. The same provision applies when it appears to a person authorised by the airport manager that an aircraft is about to take off in contravention of the imposed restriction or prohibition: that person, or a person whom he has authorised, may detain the aircraft in order to prevent the contravention and, for that purpose, enter on any land[11].

1 As to the Secretary of State see para 1032 ante.
2 For the meaning of 'operator' see para 1340 post.
3 As to designated aerodromes see the Civil Aviation (Designation of Aerodromes) Order 1981, SI 1981/651, made under the Civil Aviation Act 1971 s 29B (repealed) and saved by the Civil Aviation Act 1982 s 109 (1), Sch 14 para 3.
4 Ibid s 78 (1).
5 Ibid s 78 (2). It is the duty of the person managing the aerodrome to comply with the direction: s 78 (2). See para 1187 post.
6 Ibid s 78 (3) (a). It is the duty of the person managing the aerodrome to secure that the limitations are complied with: s 78 (3). The Secretary of State may, by notice, determine that a particular occasion be disregarded (see s 78 (5) (f)), or a particular occasion may be disregarded if the circumstances for disregard are specified by notice and the airport operator determines that the occasion is to be disregarded while notifying the Secretary of State appropriately (see s 78 (4)).
7 Ibid s 78 (3) (b).
8 See ibid s 78 (5) (a).
9 Ibid s 78 (3) (c). It is the duty of the person managing the aerodrome to secure that the limitations are complied with: s 78 (3). Nothing, however, requires him to prevent an aircraft from landing at the aerodrome: s 78 (5) (e).
10 Ibid s 78 (5) (c). As to other powers of detention see para 1339 post.
11 Ibid s 78 (5) (d).

1187. Aerodrome managers' duties as to noise and vibration. The person managing a designated aerodrome[1] must comply with directions given to him by the Secretary of State[2] for the purpose of limiting, or of mitigating the effect of, noise and vibration connected with the taking-off or landing of aircraft at the aerodrome[3].

After consulting that person, the Secretary of State may by order require him, at his own expense, to provide, maintain and operate specified equipment for measuring noise in the vicinity of the aerodrome, to make reports to the Secretary of State with respect to the noise so measured, and to permit any person authorised by the Secretary of State to inspect that equipment on demand at any time[4].

If the person managing the aerodrome fails to provide, maintain and operate the equipment, or fails to make reports or allow inspection[5], the Secretary of State may, after considering any representations made by that person, take such steps as he considers appropriate for remedying that failure, and recover from that person, in any court of competent jurisdiction, any expense attributable to the taking of those steps[6].

1 As to designated aerodromes see para 1186 note 3 ante.
2 As to the Secretary of State see para 1032 ante. As to such directions see para 1186 ante.
3 Civil Aviation Act 1982 s 78 (6).
4 Ibid s 78 (8). For other duties of the person managing the aerodrome see para 1186 notes 6, 9 ante.
5 Failure to make reports and permit inspection is an offence carrying a penalty, on summary conviction, of a fine not exceeding level 3 on the standard scale; if the failure continues after a conviction a further offence, carrying a like penalty, is committed on every day the failure continues: ibid s 78 (9) (i), (ii) (amended by virtue of the Criminal Justice Act 1982 ss 38, 46). For the purpose of conferring jurisdiction, the offence is deemed to have been committed in any place where the offender may for the time being be: Civil Aviation Act 1982 s 99 (3), (5). As to the standard scale see para 1044 note 6 ante. At the date at which this volume states the law, level 3 on that scale is at £400.
6 Ibid s 78 (9) (a), (b), which is without prejudice to the power of the Secretary of State apart from that paragraph to recover the expenses mentioned therein: s 78 (10).

1188. Grants towards cost of sound-proofing dwellings. If it appears to the Secretary of State[1] that dwellings near a designated aerodrome[2] require further protection from noise and vibration attributable to the use of the aerodrome than can be given by the Civil Aviation Act 1982[3], he may make a scheme, by statutory instrument, requiring the person for the time being managing the aerodrome to make grants towards the cost of insulating those dwellings against noise[4].

The scheme, made after consultation with the relevant manager[5], must specify the areas and expenditure in respect of which, the persons in respect of whom, the rate at which, and the conditions on which, grants may be paid[6]; it may require the relevant manager to give an applicant a written statement of reasons where a grant is refused[7]; it may authorise or require local authorities to deal with applications and payments as the relevant manager's agents[8]; and it may make different provisions with respect to different areas or different circumstances[9].

1 As to the Secretary of State see para 1032 ante.
2 As to designated aerodromes see para 1186 note 3 ante.
3 See the Civil Aviation Act 1982 s 78; and paras 1186, 1187 ante.
4 Ibid s 79 (1). Any such statutory instrument is subject to annulment in pursuance of a resolution of either House of Parliament: s 79 (8). Such instruments, being local, are not listed in this work. For an example, however, see the Heathrow Airport–London Noise Insulation Grants Scheme 1989, SI 1989/247.
5 Civil Aviation Act 1982 s 79 (6).
6 Ibid s 79 (2).
7 Ibid s 79 (3).
8 Ibid s 79 (4); for the purpose of s 79, 'local authority' does not include the council of a county: s 79 (7). See further para 1041 ante.
9 Ibid s 79 (5).

(7) ACCESS; LIGHTS; OBSTRUCTIONS; TRAFFIC MARKINGS

(i) Access

1189. Access to government and Civil Aviation Authority aerodromes. The Civil Aviation Authority (CAA)[1] may cause to be notified[2], subject to such conditions as it thinks fit, any aerodrome[3] owned or managed by it[4] and, with the concurrence of the Secretary of State[5], any government aerodrome[6], as an aerodrome available for the take-off and landing by aircraft engaged on flights for the purpose of public transport[7] of passengers or for instruction in flying[8] or by any classes of such aircraft[9].

1 As to the CAA see para 1044 ante.
2 For the meaning of 'notified' see para 1105 note 3 ante.
3 For the meaning of 'aerodrome' see para 1102 ante.
4 See para 1105 ante.
5 As to the Secretary of State see para 1032 ante.
6 For the meaning of 'government aerodrome' see para 1105 ante.
7 For the meaning of 'public transport' see para 1272 post.
8 As to instruction in flying see para 1358 post.
9 Air Navigation Order 1989, SI 1989/2004, art 77.

1190. Prohibition on discrimination. The person in charge of any aerodrome[1] in the United Kingdom which is open for public use[2] by aircraft registered in the United Kingdom, whether or not the aerodrome is a licensed aerodrome[3], must cause the aerodrome and all air navigation facilities provided there to be available for use by aircraft registered in other contracting states[4] or in any part of the Commonwealth[5] on the same terms and conditions as for use by aircraft registered in the United Kingdom[6].

1 For the meaning of 'aerodrome' see para 1102 ante.
2 As to licences for public use see para 1155 ante.
3 For the meaning of 'licensed aerodrome' see para 1154 note 6 ante.
4 'Contracting state' means any state, including the United Kingdom, which is a party to the Chicago Convention (as to which see para 1002 ante): Air Navigation Order 1989, SI 1989/2004, art 106 (1).
5 'The Commonwealth' means the United Kingdom, the Channel Islands, the Isle of Man, the countries mentioned in the British Nationality Act 1981 Sch 3 and all other territories forming part of Her Majesty's dominions or in which Her Majesty has jurisdiction: Air Navigation Order 1989 art 106 (1). See further BRITISH NATIONALITY.
6 Ibid art 82. The penalty for contravention is on summary conviction a fine not exceeding £400: art 99 (4).

1191. Aerodromes other than government or Civil Aviation Authority aerodromes. An aircraft engaged on a flight for the purpose of the public transport[1] of passengers, or of instruction in flying[2], or of carrying out flying tests[3] may not take off or land[4] at any place in the United Kingdom other than: (1) a government aerodrome[5] or a Civil Aviation Authority (CAA) aerodrome[6] notified[7] as available[8] or in respect of which the person in charge has given his permission for the particular aircraft to take off or land, as the case may be[9]; or (2) an aerodrome licensed[10] for the take-off and landing of such aircraft[11].

The taking-off or landing must be in accordance with any condition subject to which the aerodrome may have been licensed or notified or subject to which such permission may have been given[12].

The foregoing provisions apply to all aircraft so engaged with very few exceptions which concern mainly aircraft engaged on a non-scheduled flight[13] and gliders being flown under arrangements made by a flying club and carrying no person other than a club member[14].

1 For the meaning of 'public transport' see para 1272 post.
2 As to instruction in flying see para 1358 post.
3 As to flying tests for pilots' licences and ratings see the Air Navigation Order 1989, SI 1989/2004, Sch 8 (amended by SI 1991/1726).
4 The penalty for an offence is, on summary conviction, a fine not exceeding £1,000: Air Navigation Order 1989 art 99 (5), Sch 12 Pt A.
5 For the meaning of 'government aerodrome' see para 1105 ante.
6 See para 1105 ante.
7 For the meaning of 'notified' see para 1105 note 3 ante.
8 As to availability see para 1189 ante.
9 Air Navigation Order 1989 art 76 (1) (b).
10 See para 1154 ante.
11 Air Navigation Order 1989 art 76 (1) (a).
12 Ibid art 76 (1).
13 See ibid art 76 (2) (b) (i), (c) concerning aeroplanes of a maximum total weight authorised not exceeding 2,730 kg, helicopters and gyroplanes. The obligation to use licensed aerodromes, or government or CAA aerodromes applies to aeroplanes of a maximum total weight authorised not exceeding 2,730 kg engaged on a flight intended to begin and end at the same aerodrome, or on a flight for the purpose of the public transport of passengers at night (art 76 (2) (b) (ii), (iv)) and to all above mentioned aircraft when engaged on a flight for the purpose of instruction in flying (art 76 (2) (b) (iii), (c)). For the meaning of 'maximum total weight authorised' see para 1314 note 5 post.
14 See ibid art 76 (2) (d).

1192. Use of aerodrome at night. It is the duty of the person in charge of an area which is neither a licensed aerodrome[1] nor a government[2] or Civil Aviation Authority (CAA) aerodrome[3] and which is intended to be used for take-off or landing by night[4] by a helicopter engaged on a flight for the public transport[5] of passengers to ensure that there is adequate lighting in operation in the area for the pilot to make a safe take-off or to land safely after he has recognised the area and the landing direction[6]. Further, a helicopter flying for the purpose of the public transport of passengers at night may not use such a place to take off or land where the lighting is inadequate[7].

There are no statutory provisions as to the use of aerodromes at night by aircraft other than helicopters.

1 As to licensed aerodromes see para 1154 ante.
2 As to government aerodromes see para 1105 ante.
3 As to the CAA see para 1044 ante; as to CAA aerodromes see para 1105 ante.
4 'Night' means the time from half an hour after sunset until half an hour before sunrise (both times inclusive), sunset and sunrise being determined at surface level: Air Navigation Order 1989, SI 1989/2004, art 106 (1) (amended by SI 1991/1726).
5 For the meaning of 'public transport' see para 1272 post.
6 Air Navigation Order 1989 art 76 (3) (a).
7 Ibid art 76 (3) (b). The penalty for contravention is on summary conviction a fine not exceeding £1,000: art 99 (5), Sch 12 Pt A.

1193. Right of access to aerodromes and other places. The Civil Aviation Authority (CAA)[1] and any authorised person[2] have the right of access at all reasonable times to any aerodrome[3] for the purpose of inspecting either the aerodrome[4], any aircraft on it, or any document which the CAA or authorised person has power to demand under the Air Navigation Order[5], or for the purpose of detaining any aircraft under that order[6].

The CAA and any authorised person also have the right of access at all reasonable times to any place where an aircraft has landed, for the purpose of inspecting the aircraft or any document which the CAA or authorised person has power to demand under that order, or for the purpose of detaining the aircraft under that order[7].

Impeding a person acting in the exercise of his powers under the order is an offence[8].

1 As to the CAA see para 1044 ante.
2 'Authorised person' means any constable and any person authorised by the CAA (whether by name, or by class or description) either generally or in relation to a particular case or class of cases: see the Air Navigation Order 1989, SI 1989/2004, art 106 (1).
3 Access to a government aerodrome or to an aerodrome owned or managed by the CAA may only be obtained with the permission of the person in charge of it: ibid art 96. As to such aerodromes see para 1105 ante.
4 Ibid art 96 (a). As to the right to inspect aircraft see paras 1258, 1313 post.
5 Ibid art 96 (b). As to the right to demand documents see paras 1418–1421 post.
6 Ibid art 96 (b). As to the right to detain aircraft see para 1339 post. As to the right to search aerodromes, air navigation installations, aircraft and persons under the Aviation Security Act 1982 and the Aviation and Maritime Security Act 1990 see para 1247 et seq post.
7 Air Navigation Order 1989 art 96 (c); see also notes 4–6 supra.
8 Ibid art 97. The penalty is on summary conviction a fine not exceeding £1,000: art 99 (5), Sch 12 Pt A.

1194. Trespass on aerodromes. Any person who trespasses on any land which forms part of a licensed aerodrome[1] is liable on summary conviction to a fine[2], but no one is liable to this penalty unless it is proved that, at the material time, notices warning trespassers of their liability under this provision were posted, so as to be readily seen and read by members of the public, in such positions on or near the boundary of the aerodrome as appear to the court to be proper[3].

1 As to licensed aerodromes see para 1154 ante.
2 Civil Aviation Act 1982 s 39 (1); the fine may not exceed level 1 on the standard scale: s 39 (1) (amended by virtue of the Criminal Justice Act 1982 s 46). As to the standard scale see para 1044 note 6 ante. At the date at which this volume states the law, level 1 on that scale is at £50. As to the prevention of theft see para 1240 post. As to unauthorised entry into restricted zones of aerodromes or air navigation installations designated by order under the Aviation Security Act 1982 amended by the Aviation and Maritime Security Act 1990 see para 1263 post.
3 Civil Aviation Act 1982 s 39 (2).

1195. Regulation of access. Access to aerodromes may be restricted by the Secretary of State[1] in the interests either of national security or of foreign relations or in respect of international obligations of the United Kingdom[2]. The Secretary of State exercises such control over airport operators through general or specific directions given after consultation with the airport operators most likely to be affected by the direction and any organisation representative of their interests[3]. Where the interests of foreign relations or the private commercial interests of a person may be affected by the disclosure of the direction, the latter will not be disclosed[4]; it is an offence for a person notified that the direction is not to be disclosed to reveal the contents of such a direction[5]. Such direction overrules any requirement made by any other enactment or instrument which would otherwise apply to the relevant airport operator[6].

1 As to the Secretary of State see para 1032 ante.
2 See the Airports Act 1986 s 30 (1).
3 Ibid s 30 (1), (9); in the case of a specific direction, the consultation involves only the particular person to whom the direction is given: see s 30 (9).
4 See ibid s 30 (7). Unless disclosure is overruled, the Secretary of State must lay a copy of the direction before each House of Parliament (s 30 (6)) and where the Secretary of State decides that the direction is not to be disclosed, he must notify the relevant persons accordingly (s 30 (7)).
5 Ibid s 30 (8); the penalty is, on summary conviction, a fine not exceeding the statutory maximum and on conviction on indictment, imprisonment for a term not exceeding two years or a fine, or both: s 30 (8). As to the statutory maximum see para 1005 note 11 ante. At the date at which this volume states the law, the statutory maximum is £2,000.
6 Ibid s 30 (5). As to directions given to the Civil Aviation Authority in the national interest see para 1064 ante.

1196. Traffic distribution rules. The Secretary of State[1] may make rules to distribute air traffic between two or more airports serving the same area in the United Kingdom[2]. Before making traffic distribution rules, the Secretary of State must consult the Civil Aviation Authority (CAA)[3], which must in turn consult any airport and aircraft operators[4] likely to be affected by the rules and any relevant organisation representing such operators before it can give its advice to the Secretary of State[5].

The traffic distribution rules may specify classes or descriptions of air traffic which are either permitted to use any of the relevant airports, or restricted, or prohibited, from using such airports[6]; they may also provide for their coming into operation at such time or in such circumstances as they specify[7]. Nothing else may be included in those rules[8].

The CAA has a duty to take into account any traffic distribution rules in force when it is performing its air transport licensing functions so as to prevent any conflict[9].

1 As to the Secretary of State see para 1032 ante.
2 See the Airports Act 1986 s 31 (1), under which were made the Traffic Distribution Rules 1991 for Airports serving the London Area. The reference to airports serving the same area in the United Kingdom is a reference to airports in the case of which a substantial number of the passengers departing from, or arriving at, the airports by air (other than those interrupting their flight there or transferring from one flight to another) have as their original points of departure, or (as the case may be) as their ultimate destinations, places situated within the same area in the United Kingdom: Airports Act 1986 s 31 (6).
3 As to the CAA see para 1044 ante.
4 As to airport operators see para 1042 note 4 ante; as to aircraft operators see para 1340 post.
5 Airports Act 1986 s 31 (4). As to the matters to be taken into account by the Civil Aviation Authority when giving advice see s 34 and para 1199 post. Requirements for consultation are satisfied provided the subject matter of the rules is contained in the CAA's advice and the rules are made within five years of the giving of the advice: s 31 (5). The advice given to the Secretary of State is published by the CAA; see eg 'The need for traffic distribution rules: advice to the Secretary of State for Transport', CAP 578, published on 22 January 1991.
6 Airports Act 1986 s 31 (3) (a), (b).
7 Ibid s 31 (3) (c).
8 See ibid s 31 (3).
9 Ibid s 31 (2); as to the air transport licensing functions of the CAA see paras 1072–1091 ante.

1197. Power to limit aircraft movements. Where it appears that the existing runway capacity of a particular airport is not fully utilised for a substantial proportion of the time during which it is available for take-off and landing[1], the Secretary of State[2] may make an order imposing either an overall limit on the number of aircraft movements[3] during a specified period[4], or such other limits to apply to aircraft movements in circumstances or cases specified in the order as the Secretary of State thinks appropriate[5].

Before making the order, the Secretary of State must consult the Civil Aviation Authority (CAA)[6], the airport operator to be affected by the order, other aircraft operators who may also be so affected and their representative organisations as well as local authorities which may be concerned by operations at the airport[7].

The order may provide that some aircraft movements are not to be taken into account in certain circumstances and therefor provide for the manner in which the number of those movements is calculated[8]. The order may neither establish a level of movements lower than the highest level of any corresponding movements at the airport during any equivalent period within the last three years prior to the order[9], nor limit the number of movements to a number inferior to the preceding such order[10].

The CAA has a duty to take into account the existence of any aircraft movement limitation at any particular airport when it is exercising its air transport licensing functions[11]. And it is the duty of the airport operator to ensure compliance with any aircraft movement limit imposed at his airport[12].

1 See the Airports Act 1986 s 32 (2).
2 As to the Secretary of State see para 1032 ante.
3 'Movement' in relation to an airport, means a take-off or landing by an aircraft at the airport: ibid s 29 (1).
4 Ibid s 32 (1) (a).
5 Ibid s 32 (1) (b).
6 As to the CAA see para 1044 ante.
7 Airports Act 1986 s 32 (6). As to the matters to be taken into account by the CAA see para 1199 post. As to air operators generally see para 1340 post. 'Local authority' means a local authority within the meaning of the Local Government Act 1972 or the Common Council of the City of London: see the Airports Act 1986 ss 32 (7), 12 (1); see also para 1041 ante.
8 See ibid s 32 (4).
9 Ibid s 32 (5) (a).
10 Ibid s 32 (5) (b).
11 Ibid s 32 (3). As to the air transport licensing functions of the CAA see paras 1072–1091 ante.
12 Ibid s 32 (3).

1198. Schemes for allocating capacity at airports. Where an order limiting aircraft movements at an airport is in force[1], or where it appears to the Secretary of State[2] that the demand for the use of the airport is getting greater than its operational capacity can manage, the Secretary of State may require, by direction, the Civil Aviation Authority (CAA)[3] to prepare a scheme allocating capacity at the airport[4].

Before giving any such direction the Secretary of State must consult the CAA[5], and before the CAA submits the scheme to the Secretary of State for approval it must consult the relevant airport operator, any aircraft operator likely to be affected by the scheme and any appropriate organisation representing airport or aircraft operators[6].

The scheme may provide for an aircraft operator either to acquire the right to use the airport or to pay a special charge in respect of such use[7]. Where the scheme provides for the acquisition of rights, it will specify the manner and period of their allocation, their transferability and any other necessary conditions[8]. Where the scheme provides for the payment of special charges to the airport operator it may specify different charges for different aircraft operators in different circumstances[9].

The scheme may provide that all aircraft operators have to acquire the right to use the airport as well as pay special charges to the airport operator[10] and it may make as many exceptions as it considers relevant[11].

The scheme enters into force when it has been approved by the Secretary of State[12]. It may be varied or revoked by the CAA, replaced or not by a subsequent scheme[13]; it ceases to have effect if the order limiting aircraft movements at the airport[14] and in pursuance of which the scheme had been made[15] is revoked by the Secretary of State[16].

It is the duty of the airport operator to give effect to the scheme while it is in force[17].

1 See para 1197 ante.
2 As to the Secretary of State see para 1032 ante.
3 As to the CAA see para 1044 ante.
4 Airports Act 1986 s 33 (1).
5 Ibid s 33 (2).
6 Ibid s 33 (6); as to the matters to be taken into account by the CAA see s 34; and para 1199 post. As to the airport operators see para 1042 note 4 ante; as to the aircraft operators see para 1340 post.
7 See ibid s 33 (3) (a), (b).
8 See ibid 33 (4) (a) (i)–(iv).
9 See ibid s 33 (4) (b).
10 See ibid s 33 (3).
11 Ibid s 33 (4) (c).
12 Ibid s 33 (5); the Secretary of State may make any modification to the scheme as he thinks fit after consultation with the CAA and specify the date of coming into force of the scheme.
13 See ibid s 33 (8) (a), (b). The revocation or termination of the scheme does not prejudice the recovery of sums owed to the aircraft operator under the scheme: s 33 (9).
14 See para 1197 ante.
15 See the Airports Act 1986 s 33 (1) (a).
16 Ibid s 33 (8).
17 Ibid s 33 (7).

1199. Matters to be taken into account by the Civil Aviation Authority. Where the Civil Aviation Authority (CAA)[1] is to give advice to the Secretary of State[2] under the Airports Act 1986 in so far as the regulation of the use of airports is concerned[3] or where it has been directed to prepare a scheme for allocating capacity at airports[4] it must take into account a number of points which are not included in its general objectives as set by the Civil Aviation Act 1982[5].

Thus the CAA must have regard to the general framework provided by any of the international obligations of the United Kingdom which the Secretary of State may have notified to it as well as to any advice which the latter may have given with respect to the relations of the United Kingdom with a country or territory outside the United Kingdom[6]. The matters which the CAA must take into account are the need to secure the sound development of civil aviation within the United Kingdom, the reasonable interests of users of air transport services and any policy considerations notified by the Secretary of State[7].

1 As to the CAA see para 1044 ante.
2 As to the Secretary of State see para 1032 ante.
3 Ie the Airports Act 1986 ss 31–33; see paras 1194–1198 ante.
4 See para 1198 ante.
5 Airports Act 1986 s 34 (1). As to the general objectives for the CAA set by the Civil Aviation Act 1982 s 4 see para 1046 ante.
6 See the Airports Act 1986 s 34 (2) (a), (b).
7 Ibid s 34 (3). As to policy considerations see para 1073 ante.

1200. Restrictions under the Air Navigation Order. The Air Navigation Order made under the Civil Aviation Act 1982[1] may restrict the availability of airports to aircraft through the conditions which the Civil Aviation Authority (CAA)[2] may attach to an aerodrome licence[3]; thus such a licence may limit the use of the airport to specified aircraft or to specified circumstances without the need for an order by the Secretary of State[4].

1 See the Air Navigation Order 1989, SI 1989/2004, made under the Civil Aviation Act 1982 s 60 (3).
2 As to the CAA see para 1044 ante.
3 As to licensed aerodromes see para 1154 ante; as to access to aerodromes see paras 1189–1200 ante.
4 See the Airports Act 1986 s 35 and the Air Navigation Order 1989 art 78 (2); see para 1189 ante. As to the power to limit aircraft movements at airports see para 1197 ante; as to the Secretary of State see para 1032 ante

(ii) Lights

1201. Aeronautical lights. No aeronautical beacon or ground light[1] may be established, maintained or altered in the United Kingdom except with the permission of the Civil Aviation Authority (CAA)[2] and in accordance with any conditions which may be prescribed or subject to which the permission may be granted[3]. In the case of an aeronautical beacon, which is or may be visible from any waters within the area of a general lighthouse authority[4], the CAA must not give its permission except with the consent of that authority[5].

A person must not intentionally or negligently damage or interfere with any aeronautical ground light established by or with the permission of the CAA[6].

1 'Aeronautical beacon' means an aeronautical ground light which is visible either continuously or intermittently to designate a particular point on the surface of the earth; 'aeronautical ground light' means any light specifically provided as an aid to air navigation, other than a light displayed on an aircraft: Air Navigation Order 1989, SI 1989/2004, art 106 (1).
2 As to the CAA see para 1044 ante.
3 Air Navigation Order 1989 art 84 (1). The penalty for contravention is on summary conviction a fine not exceeding £1,000: art 99 (5), Sch 12 Pt A. See also the Civil Aviation Act 1982 s 109, Sch 14 para 7, which provides that nothing contained in ss 39, 41, 43, 47, 60, 62, 73–77, 81, 87, 89, 96, 97, 107 (2) or in any instrument made thereunder (which includes the Air Navigation Order 1989) shall prejudice or affect the rights, powers or privileges of any general or local lighthouse authority (as to which see SHIPPING).
4 'General lighthouse authority' has the same meaning as in the Merchant Shipping Act 1894 s 634 (ie in respect of England and Wales and the Channel Islands and adjacent seas and islands, Trinity House): Air Navigation Order 1989 art 106 (1).
5 Ibid art 84 (1) (a) proviso
6 Ibid art 84 (2). As to the penalty for contravention see note 3 supra.

1202. Dangerous lights. A person may not exhibit in the United Kingdom any light which is liable by reason of its glare to endanger aircraft taking off from or landing at an aerodrome[1] or which, by reason of its liability to be mistaken for an aeronautical ground light[2], is liable to endanger aircraft[3].

If any light which appears to the Civil Aviation Authority (CAA)[4] to be such a light is exhibited, the CAA may cause a notice to be served[5] on the person who is the occupier of the place where the light is exhibited or having charge of the light, directing him, within a reasonable specified time, to take specified steps for extinguishing or screening the light and for preventing for the future the exhibition of any other light which may similarly endanger aircraft[6]. Where such a light is or may be visible from any waters within the area of a general lighthouse authority[7] the CAA's powers may not be exercised except with that authority's consent[8].

1 For the meaning of 'aerodrome' see para 1102 ante.
2 For the meaning of 'aeronautical ground light' see para 1201 note 1 ante.
3 Air Navigation Order 1989, SI 1989/2004, art 85 (1). The penalty for contravention is on summary conviction a fine not exceeding £1,000: art 99 (5), Sch 12 Pt A
4 As to the CAA see para 1044 ante.
5 The notice may be served either personally or by post, or by affixing it in some conspicuous place near to the light: Air Navigation Order 1989 art 85 (3).
6 Ibid art 85 (2). The penalty for contravention is on summary conviction a fine not exceeding £1,000: art 99 (5), Sch 12 Pt A.
7 For the meaning of 'general lighthouse authority' see para 1201 note 4 ante.
8 Air Navigation Order 1989 art 85 (4).

(iii) Obstructions

1203. Obstructions near licensed aerodromes. If the Secretary of State[1] is satisfied that, in order to avoid danger to aircraft flying in darkness or conditions of bad visibility in the vicinity of any aerodrome licensed for public use[2], provision ought to be made for giving warning to such aircraft, whether by lighting or otherwise, of the presence of any building, structure or erection in that vicinity, he may by order[3] authorise the proprietor of the aerodrome[4], and any person acting under the proprietor's instructions, to execute, install, maintain, operate and, as occasion requires, to repair or alter, any works and apparatus which may be necessary for enabling such warning to be given in the manner specified in the order, and, so far as may be necessary for exercising any of the powers conferred by the order, to enter upon and pass over any land specified in the order, with or without vehicles[5].

No order may be made, however, if it appears to the Secretary of State that satisfactory arrangements have been made and are being carried out for giving warning to aircraft of the presence of a particular building, structure or erection[6].

1 As to the Secretary of State see para 1032 ante.
2 See the Civil Aviation Act 1982 s 47 (1). As to the licensing of aerodromes see paras 1154, 1155 ante.
3 As to the making of such orders, and their contents, see paras 1204, 1205 post.
4 'Proprietor of the aerodrome' means the person carrying on or entitled to carry on the business of an aerodrome on the premises in question: Civil Aviation Act 1982 s 47 (10).
5 Ibid s 47 (1).
6 Ibid s 47 (2).

1204. Procedure for making orders. Before making an order relating to obstruction warnings[1] the Secretary of State[2] must cause to be published, in such manner as he thinks best for informing persons concerned, notice of the proposal to make the order and of the place where copies of the draft order may be obtained free of charge[3]; and he must take into consideration any representation made to him with respect to the order by any person appearing to him to have an interest in any land which would be affected by it. Representations must be made within a specified period, being not less than two months after publication of the notice[4]. At the end of that period the Secretary of State may make the order with any modifications he thinks proper[5].

1 See para 1203 ante.

2 As to the Secretary of State see para 1032 ante.
3 Civil Aviation Act 1982 s 47 (3) (a).
4 Ibid s 47 (3) (b).
5 Ibid s 47 (3).

1205. Contents of order. Every order relating to obstruction warnings[1] must contain a provision that except in a case of emergency, no works shall be executed on any land in pursuance of the order unless, at least 14 days previously, the proprietor of the aerodrome[2] concerned has served in the manner prescribed by the order on the occupier of the land, and on every other person known by the proprietor to have an interest in it, a written notice containing such particulars of the proposed works, and of the manner in which and the time at which it is proposed to execute them, as may be prescribed by or in accordance with the order[3]. The order must also contain a provision that if within 14 days after service of a notice on any such person the proprietor receives a written intimation of objection on that person's part, specifying the grounds of objection, no steps may be taken in pursuance of the notice without the specific sanction of the Secretary of State[4], unless and except in so far as the objection is withdrawn[5].

1 See para 1203 ante.
2 For the meaning of 'proprietor of the aerodrome' see para 1203 note 4 ante.
3 Civil Aviation Act 1982 s 47 (4).
4 As to the Secretary of State see para 1032 ante.
5 Civil Aviation Act 1982 s 47 (4).

1206. Compensation. Every order relating to obstruction warnings[1] must provide for requiring the proprietor of the aerodrome[2] to which the order relates to pay to any person having an interest in any land affected by the order compensation[3] for loss or damage suffered in consequence of the order; and any expense reasonably incurred in connection with the lawful removal of any apparatus installed in pursuance of such an order, and so much of any expense incurred in connection with the repair, alteration, demolition or removal of any building, structure or erection to which the order relates as is attributable to the operation of the order, is deemed to be loss or damage suffered in consequence of the order[4].

1 See para 1203 ante.
2 For the meaning of 'proprietor of the aerodrome' see para 1203 note 4 ante.
3 The compensation must be determined, in default of agreement, by a single arbitrator appointed by the Lord Chief Justice: Civil Aviation Act 1982 s 47 (4). As to compensation in respect of planning decisions relating to aerodrome safety, etc see para 1116 ante.
4 Ibid s 47 (5).

1207. Ownership of materials; offences. The ownership of anything placed in or affixed to land in pursuance of an order relating to obstruction warnings[1] does not pass to the owner of the land by reason only that the thing is so placed or affixed[2], and so long as the order is in force in respect of the aerodrome it is an offence punishable on summary conviction, wilfully to interfere, without the consent of the proprietor of the aerodrome[3], with any works or things which to the knowledge of the person interfering, were executed or placed in, on or over the land in pursuance of the order[4].

It is also an offence, punishable on summary conviction, wilfully to obstruct a person in the exercise of any of the powers conferred by such an order[5].

1 See para 1203 ante.
2 See para 1121 ante.
3 For the meaning of 'proprietor of the aerodrome' see para 1203 note 4 ante.
4 Civil Aviation Act 1982 s 47 (6). The penalty is imprisonment for a term not exceeding six months, or a fine not exceeding level 4 on the standard scale, or both: s 47 (7) (amended by virtue of the Criminal Justice Act 1982 ss 38, 46). As to the standard scale see para 1044 note 6 ante. At the date at which this volume states the law, level 4 on that scale is at £1,000.
5 Civil Aviation Act 1982 s 47 (7). The penalty is a fine not exceeding level 3 on the standard scale: s 47 (7) (as amended: see note 4 supra). As to the standard scale see para 1044 note 6 ante. At the date at which this volume states the law, level 3 on that scale is at £400.

1208. Savings as to work done by owners of buildings. No order relating to obstruction warnings[1] may operate so as to restrict the doing of any work for the purpose of repairing, altering, demolishing or removing a building, structure or erection, provided that notice of the doing of the work is given as soon as may be to the proprietor of the aerodrome[2], and that the giving of warning of the presence of the building, structure or erection in the manner provided by the order is not interrupted[3].

1 See para 1203 ante.
2 For the meaning of 'proprietor of the aerodrome' see para 1203 note 4 ante.
3 Civil Aviation Act 1982 s 47 (8).

1209. Statutory undertakers. Any order relating to obstruction warnings[1] which affects any property held by a statutory undertaker[2] for the purpose of his undertaking must be so framed as to avoid interference with the proper carrying on of the undertaking[3]. Except in an emergency, no person may enter in pursuance of such an order upon any land so held, unless he has given the statutory undertaker at least three clear days' notice of his intention so to do[4] and, when entry is made, the person entering must comply with any reasonable directions given to him by or on behalf of the undertaker to prevent interference with the proper carrying on of the undertaking[5].

If statutory undertakers show that by reason of the operation of such an order they have been obliged to take special measures to secure the safety of persons thus entering their land or otherwise acting under the order in relation to any of the undertakers' property, the proprietor of the aerodrome[6] concerned must pay to the undertakers the amount of any expenses reasonably incurred by them[7].

1 See para 1203 ante.
2 For the meaning of 'statutory undertaker' see para 1144 ante.
3 Civil Aviation Act 1982 s 47 (9) (a).
4 In addition the provisions of ibid s 47 (4), (5) (as to which see paras 1205, 1206 ante) must be complied with: s 47 (9).
5 Ibid s 47 (9) (b).
6 For the meaning of 'proprietor of the aerodrome' see para 1203 note 4 ante.
7 Civil Aviation Act 1982 s 47 (9). Any dispute as to whether any sum is so payable, or as to the amount of any sum payable, must, unless the parties otherwise agree, be referred for determination to a single arbitrator appointed by the Lord Chief Justice: s 47 (9) (c).

1210. Control of advertisements and hoardings. When exercising the powers conferred on them by the town and country planning legislation in relation to the grant or refusal of consent to the display of advertisements, local planning authorities must have regard, inter alia, to the safety of persons who may use any airfield affected or who are likely to be affected by any display of advertisements, and must in particular consider whether any such display is likely to obscure or hinder the ready interpretation of any signal for the control or safety of navigation by air[1].

1 Town and Country Planning (Control of Advertisements) Regulations 1989, SI 1989/670, reg 4 (1) (b), having effect as if made under the Town and Country Planning Act 1990 ss 220, 221: see the Planning (Consequential Provisions) Act 1990 s 2. See further TOWN AND COUNTRY PLANNING.

(iv) Ground Markings and Traffic Signals

1211. Rules of the air: aerodromes. Detailed rules are laid down in relation to ground marks and signals by day and night[1], which must be complied with at all licensed aerodromes[2] and at any government aerodrome[3] or aerodrome managed by the Civil Aviation Authority (CAA)[4] which has been notified[5] as available[6] for use by civil aircraft[7].

A signal or marking to which a meaning is given by the Rules of the Air Regulations 1990[8], or which is required by those rules to be used in circumstances or for a purpose specified therein, may not be used except with that meaning or for that purpose[9], and no signal must be made by a person in an aircraft, or on an aerodrome or at any place at which an aircraft is landing or taking off, which may be confused with any signal specified in the rules, nor should any signal known to be a signal in use for signalling to or from any of Her Majesty's naval, military or air force aircraft be made without lawful authority[10].

1 'Day' means the time from half an hour before sunrise until half an hour after sunset (both times exclusive), sunset and sunrise being determined at surface level: Air Navigation Order 1989, SI 1989/2004, art 106 (1) (amended by SI 1991/1726), applied by the Rules of the Air Regulations 1990, SI 1990/2241, reg 2, Schedule r 1 (2). For the meaning of 'night' see para 1192 note 4 ante.
2 For the meaning of 'licensed aerodrome' see para 1154 note 6 ante.
3 For the meaning of 'government aerodrome' see para 1105 ante.
4 As to such aerodromes see para 1105 ante; as to the CAA see para 1044 ante.
5 For the meaning of 'notified' see para 1105 note 3 ante.
6 As to such availability see para 1105 ante.
7 See the Rules of the Air Regulations 1990, made under the Air Navigation Order 1989 art 69 (1).
8 SI 1990/2241.
9 Rules of the Air Regulations 1990 Schedule r 3 (1).
10 Ibid Schedule r 3 (2).

1212. Rules for aerodrome signals and markings by day. The Rules of the Air Regulations 1990[1] contain provisions in respect of signals in the signals area[2], markings for paved runways and taxiways and on unpaved manoeuvring areas[3], signals visible from the ground[4], lights and pyrotechnic signals for the control of aerodrome traffic[5], marshalling signals, whether from a marshaller to an aircraft or from an aircraft pilot to a marshaller[6], distress, urgency and safety signals[7] and warning signals to aircraft in flight[8].

1 SI 1990/2241.
2 See the Rules of the Air Regulations 1990 reg 2, Schedule r 42.
3 See ibid Schedule rr 43, 44.
4 See ibid Schedule r 45.
5 See ibid Schedule r 46.
6 See ibid Schedule rr 47, 48.

591 Aerodromes and Land Para 1215

591 Aerodromes and Land Para 1215

7 See ibid Schedule r 49; and para 1486 post.
8 See ibid Schedule r 50; and para 1486 post.

(8) MOVEMENT OF AIRCRAFT ON LAND AND SEA

(i) Aerodrome Traffic Rules

1213. Visual signals. The commander[1] of a flying machine[2] on, or in the pattern of traffic at , an aerodrome[3] must observe such visual signals as may be displayed at or directed to him from the aerodrome by the authority of the person in charge of it, and must obey any instructions which may be given to him by means of such signals[4]. He may, however, decide not to obey the marshalling signals[5] if in his opinion it is inadvisable to do so in the interests of safety[6].

1 'Commander' in relation to an aircraft means the member of the flight crew designated as commander by the operator (ie the person having the management of the aircraft) or, failing such a person, the person who is for the time being the pilot in command: Air Navigation Order 1989, SI 1989/2004, art 106 (1), applied by the Rules of the Air Regulations 1990, SI 1990/2241, reg 2, Schedule r 1 (2). For the meaning of 'pilot in command' see para 1343 note 2 post.
2 For the meaning of 'flying machine' see para 1269 post, applied by the Rules of the Air Regulations 1990 Schedule r 1 (2). Rules 30–37, in so far as they are expressed to apply to flying machines, must also be observed, so far as practicable, in relation to all other aircraft: r 29.
3 For the meaning of 'aerodrome' see para 1102 ante.
4 Rules of the Air Regulations 1990 Schedule r 30.
5 Ie under ibid Schedule r 47: these are signals given by a marshaller to an aircraft either, by day, by hand or by circular bats or, by night, by torches or illuminated wands.
6 Ibid Schedule r 30 proviso.

1214. Movement of aircraft on aerodromes. An aircraft may not taxi on the manoeuvring area[1] or the apron[2] of an aerodrome without the permission of the person in charge of the aerodrome[3] or the permission of the air traffic control unit[4] if the aerodrome has such a unit being notified as being on watch[5].

1 'Manoeuvring area' means the part of an aerodrome provided for the take-off and landing of aircraft and for the movement of aircraft on the surface, excluding the apron and any part of the aerodrome provided for the maintenance of aircraft: Rules of the Air Regulations 1990, SI 1990/2241, reg 2, Schedule r 1 (1).
2 'Apron' means the part of an aerodrome provided for the stationing of aircraft for the embarkation and disembarkation of passengers, the loading and unloading of cargo and for parking: ibid Schedule r 1 (1).
3 As to airport operators see para 1042 note 4 ante.
4 As to air traffic control units see para 1394 note 1 post.
5 Rules of the Air Regulations 1990 Schedule r 31.

1215. Manoeuvring areas. A person or vehicle may not go on to any part of an aerodrome under the control of the person in charge of the aerodrome without that person's permission and except in accordance with any conditions subject to which that permission was granted[1]. Similarly, a vehicle or person may not go or move on the manoeuvring area[2] of an aerodrome having an air traffic control unit[3] without such permission and except in accordance with any such conditions[4]. Any such permission may be either general or in respect of a particular person or vehicle or class of persons or vehicles[5].

1　Rules of the Air Regulations 1990, SI 1990/2241, reg 2, Schedule r 32 (1).
2　For the meaning of 'manoeuvring area' see para 1214 note 1 ante.
3　For the meaning of 'air traffic control unit' see para 1394 note 1 post.
4　Rules of the Air Regulations 1990 Schedule r 32 (2). As to right of way on the ground see para 1216 post.
5　Ibid Schedule r 32 (3).

1216. Right of way on the ground. Flying machines[1] and vehicles on any part of a land aerodrome provided for the use of aircraft and under the control of the person in charge of the aerodrome must give way to aircraft which are taking off or landing; vehicles and flying machines which are not taking off or landing must give way to vehicles towing aircraft; and vehicles which are not towing aircraft must give way to aircraft[2].

A vehicle must overtake another vehicle so that the other vehicle is on the left of the overtaking vehicle, and must keep to the left when passing another vehicle which is approaching head-on or approximately so[3].

Where there is a risk of collision between two flying machines, each must alter its course to the right if they are approaching head-on[4] or, if they are on converging courses, the one which has the other on its right must give way to the other and avoid going ahead of it unless well clear[5]. A flying machine being overtaken has the right-of-way while the overtaking flying machine must keep out of its way by altering its course to the left until it has passed the other flying machine well clear[6].

Notwithstanding any air traffic control clearance[7] it remains the duty of the commander[8] of an aircraft to take all possible measures to ensure that his aircraft does not collide with any other aircraft or with any vehicle[9].

1　For the meaning of 'flying machine' see para 1269 post. As to the application of these rules to other aircraft see para 1213 note 2 ante.
2　Rules of the Air Regulations 1990, SI 1990/2241, reg 2, Schedule r 33 (1), (3).
3　Ibid Schedule r 33 (5).
4　Ibid Schedule r 33 (4) (a).
5　Ibid Schedule r 33 (4) (b).
6　Ibid Schedule r 33 (4) (c).
7　'Air traffic control clearance' means authorisation by an air traffic control unit for an aircraft to proceed under conditions specified by that unit: ibid Schedule r 1 (1). For the meaning of 'air traffic control unit' see para 1394 note 1 post.
8　For the meaning of 'commander' see para 1213 note 1 ante.
9　Rules of the Air Regulations 1990 Schedule r 33 (2). As to the rules for avoiding collision between two flying machines in the air see para 1480 post.

(ii) Application of Sea Collision Rules

1217. Aircraft on or near the water. The International Regulations for Preventing Collisions at Sea 1972 as amended[1] are known as the Collision Regulations and apply to seaplanes[2] on the surface of the water anywhere in the world if they are registered in the United Kingdom or within the United Kingdom and its territorial waters if they are foreign registered[3].

The Collision Regulations must be followed by all seaplanes on the high seas and in all waters connected therewith navigable by seagoing vessels[4].

An aircraft must not fly closer than 500 feet to any vessel[5] save for the purpose of saving life[6], unless it is in the service of the police authority for any area of the United Kingdom[7].

1 For these regulations, see the Merchant Shipping (Distress Signals and Prevention of Collisions) Regulations 1989, SI 1989/1798, Schedule, made under the Merchant Shipping Act 1979 ss 21, 49. See para 1218 post and, generally, SHIPPING.
2 'Seaplane' includes any aircraft designed to manoeuvre on the water: Merchant Shipping (Distress Signals and Prevention of Collisions) Regulations 1989 Schedule r 3 (e), which does not refer to flying boats although the Civil Aviation Act 1982 s 97 does, as did all previous legislation and statutory instruments.
3 Collision Regulations (Seaplanes) Order 1989, SI 1989/2005, art 2.
4 See the Merchant Shipping (Distress Signals and Prevention of Collisions) Regulations 1989 Schedule r 1 (a).
5 Rules of the Air Regulations 1990, SI 1990/2241, reg 2, Schedule r 5 (1) (e).
6 Ibid Schedule r 5 (3).
7 Ibid Schedule r 5 (2) (b).

1218. Provisions as to observance of sea collision rules. Those provisions of the Merchant Shipping Acts 1894 and 1979[1] which provide for the observance of the International Regulations for Preventing Collisions at Sea[2], and for offences and penalties in connection with contraventions[3], which preserve the operation of local rules of navigation in harbours, rivers and other inland waters[4] and which enable the regulations to be applied to ships of foreign countries when beyond the limits of British jurisdiction[5], apply, with certain modifications, in relation to seaplanes[6] on the surface of the water as they apply in relation to ships and vessels[7].

1 For the application to seaplanes of the power conferred by the Merchant Shipping Acts 1894 and 1979 to make regulations for preventing collisions at sea see para 1217 ante.
2 See para 1217 note 1 ante.
3 See the Merchant Shipping Act 1894 s 419; and SHIPPING.
4 See ibid s 421; and SHIPPING.
5 See ibid s 424; and SHIPPING. The regulations must be observed by all foreign ships (see s 418 (2)), and (by virtue of the Civil Aviation Act 1982 s 97) by all foreign seaplanes when within British jurisdiction. See SHIPPING.
6 'Seaplane' includes a flying boat and any other aircraft designed to manoeuvre on the water: Civil Aviation Act 1982 s 97 (7) (erroneously numbered s 97 (6)).
7 Ibid s 97 (1).

1219. Application of other enactments to seaplanes. Rules may be made under the Dockyard Ports Regulations Act 1865[1] concerning the lights or signals to be carried or used and the steps to be taken to avoid collisions between vessels in dockyard ports[2]. For the purpose of that Act and the rules seaplanes are deemed to be vessels when on the surface of the water[3]. Any power or duty conferred or imposed on a conservancy or harbour authority by any enactment to make byelaws for the regulation of ships or vessels must be construed as including a power or duty to make byelaws for the regulation of seaplanes on the surface of the water and for authorising the harbour master or other authority to exercise over them the like functions as he can over ships[4], but the byelaws cannot authorise the alteration of a seaplane's structure or equipment[5]. References to 'vessel' in the Harbours, Docks and Piers Clauses Act 1847[6] include any aircraft on the surface of the water, being an aircraft which is designed to float or manoeuvre on water[7].

1 See further SHIPPING.
2 See the Dockyard Ports Regulations Act 1865 s 7: rules relating to seaplanes are made on the joint recommendation of the Secretary of State for Defence and the Secretary of State for Transport: see the preamble to the Collision Regulations (Seaplanes) Order 1989, SI 1989/2005.
3 Civil Aviation Act 1982 s 97.

4 Ibid s 97 (4), (6); see further SHIPPING. This provision applies also to hovercraft: see para 1270 note 3 post.
5 Ibid s 97 (5).
6 Ie in the Harbours, Docks and Piers Clauses Act 1847 s 28, relating to the exemption of certain vessels from harbour rates.
7 Civil Aviation Act 1982 s 97 (3).

(9) CUSTOMS RULES

1220. Application of customs rules. The provisions of the Customs and Excise Management Act 1979 relating to aircraft[1] apply in relation to all aircraft, including aircraft belonging to or employed in the service of the Crown other than military aircraft[2].

1 The Customs and Excise Management Act 1979, which consolidates previous customs enactments, is dealt with largely in CUSTOMS AND EXCISE. In the following paragraphs, however, those provisions which closely concern the operation of aircraft are noted. In addition, reference should be made to the following sections of that Act: ss 68 (5) (aircraft liable to forfeiture if goods which may only be exported if consigned to a particular place or person are delivered to some other person), 75 (explosives: see also paras 1653, 1654 post), 84 (penalty for signalling to smugglers), 141 (forfeiture of aircraft used in connection with goods liable to forfeiture). Goods such as liquor and tobacco, carried in an aircraft, as merchandise for sale by retail to persons carried therein are treated as stores for the purposes of the Customs and Excise Acts: s 1 (4), and see s 61 as to stores; see also the Alcoholic Liquor Duties Act 1979 and the Tobacco Products Duty Act 1979; and LICENSING and CUSTOMS AND EXCISE generally. See also the sections referred to in paras 1224 note 10, 1227 notes 4–11 post.
2 Customs and Excise Management Act 1979 s 4 (1). 'Military aircraft' includes naval and air force aircraft and any aircraft commanded by a person in naval, military or air force service detailed for the purpose of such command: s 4 (2).

1221. Customs and excise airports. The Commissioners of Customs and Excise may, in any customs and excise airport[1], approve a part of, or a place at, that airport, called an 'examination station', for the loading and unloading of goods and the embarkation and disembarkation of passengers[2]. The commissioners may also approve, in any customs airport, places, called 'transit sheds', for the deposit of goods[3] imported at the airport and not yet cleared out of charge[4].

1 For the meaning of 'customs and excise airport' see para 1106 ante.
2 Customs and Excise Management Act 1979 s 22.
3 'Goods' includes stores and baggage, and 'stores' means goods for use in an aircraft, and includes fuel and spare parts and other articles of equipment, whether or not for immediate fitting: ibid s 1 (1); as to liquor and tobacco carried on aircraft for retail to passengers and treated as stores see para 1220 note 1 ante. See also ss 39, 61, 68 (provisions as to aircraft stores).
4 Ibid s 25 (1). As to the clearance of goods and passengers see CUSTOMS AND EXCISE.

1222. Duty to land at and take off from a customs and excise airport. Save as permitted by the Commissioners of Customs and Excise, the commander[1] of an aircraft entering the United Kingdom from a place outside the United Kingdom must not cause or permit the aircraft to make its first landing after arrival in the country at any place other than a customs and excise airport[2] and, so long as the aircraft is carrying passengers or goods[3] brought in the aircraft from a place outside the United Kingdom and not yet cleared, must not cause or permit it to make any subsequent landing at any place other than a customs and excise airport; and any person importing or concerned in importing any goods in any aircraft must not bring the goods into the United Kingdom at any place other than a customs and excise airport[4].

Save as permitted by the commissioners, every person departing on a flight to a place or area outside the United Kingdom must do so from a customs and excise airport; and the commander of an aircraft engaged in a flight from a customs and excise airport to a place or area outside the United Kingdom must not cause or permit it to land at any place in the United Kingdom other than a customs and excise airport specified in the application for clearance for that flight[5].

1 'Commander' includes any person having or taking the charge or command of the aircraft: Customs and Excise Management Act 1979 s 1 (1).
2 For the meaning of 'customs and excise airport' see para 1106 ante.
3 For the meaning of 'goods' see para 1221 note 3 ante.
4 Customs and Excise Management Act 1979 s 21 (1); references in s 21 to a place or area outside the United Kingdom do not include references to a place or area in the Isle of Man: s 21 (8) (added by the Isle of Man Act 1979 s 13, Sch 1 para 4). Contravention renders an offender liable on summary conviction to a penalty of level 4 on the standard scale or to imprisonment for a term not exceeding three months or both: Customs and Excise Management Act 1979 s 21 (6) (amended by virtue of the Criminal Justice Act 1982 ss 38, 46). As to the standard scale see para 1044 note 6 ante. At the date at which this volume states the law, level 4 on that scale is at £1,000. As to proceedings, offences and penalties see the Customs and Excise Management Act 1979 ss 145–155, 171; and CUSTOMS AND EXCISE. As to landings in case of necessity see para 1223 post.
5 Ibid s 21 (3). Contravention renders the offender liable as set out in note 4 supra. As to applications for clearance see para 1225 post.

1223. Landings in cases of necessity. The provisions referred to in the preceding paragraph do not apply where the aircraft in question is required under or by virtue of any enactment relating to air navigation, or is compelled by accident, stress of weather or other unavoidable cause, to land at a place other than a customs and excise airport[1]. In any such case, however, the commander[2] of the aircraft must immediately report the landing to an officer of customs and excise[3] or a constable; he must not without the consent of such an officer permit any goods[4] carried in the aircraft to be unloaded from, or any of the crew or passengers to depart from the vicinity of, the aircraft, and must comply with any directions given by such an officer with respect to any such goods; in addition no passenger or member of the crew may, without the consent of such an officer or a constable, leave the immediate vicinity of the aircraft[5]. Nothing in these provisions, however, prohibits the departure of crew or passengers from the vicinity of, or the removal of goods from, an aircraft when that is necessary for reasons of health, safety or the preservation of life or property[6].

1 Customs and Excise Management Act 1979 s 21 (4). For enactments under which aircraft may be required to land see para 1488 post (prohibited areas).
2 For the meaning of 'commander' see para 1222 note 1 ante.
3 The term used in the Customs and Excise Management Act 1979 is 'officer', which is defined by s 1 (1) as a person commissioned by the Commissioners of Customs and Excise; but see also s 8 (2), (3); and see further CUSTOMS AND EXCISE.
4 'Goods' includes stores and baggage: ibid s 1 (1).
5 Ibid s 21 (4) (a), (b). A person failing to comply with any of these provisions is liable as set out in para 1222 note 4 ante.
6 Ibid s 21 (5).

1224. Arrival at customs and excise airport. Provision is made by regulations[1] as to the procedure to be adopted by the commander[2] of an aircraft upon arrival in the United Kingdom at a customs and excise airport[3]. Thus he must, unless prevented by circumstances over which he has no control[4], take the aircraft to the examination station[5], he must deliver to the proper officer[6] a general declaration, particulars of the goods[7] on board and a list in duplicate of the stores[8], produce to him such other documents relating to the flight as the latter may require and all goods in the aircraft save those permitted to remain on board as they are to be carried to another customs and excise airport or to a foreign destination, he must unload all goods except those which are to be carried on to another customs and excise airport or to a foreign destination and are permitted to remain in the aircraft and deposit these goods in a transit shed[9] at the airport[10].

1 See the Aircraft (Customs and Excise) Regulations 1981, SI 1981/1259, made under the Customs and Excise Management Act 1979 ss 2, 56 (2), 66, which apply to arrival at any customs and excise airport. Reference to a destination in the United Kingdom includes the Isle of Man: see s 35 (9) (added by the Isle of Man Act 1979 s 13, Sch 1 para 6).
2 Any act required to be performed by the commander, other than that of taking the aircraft to the examination station, may be carried out on his behalf by a responsible person authorised for that purpose by the owner of the aircraft: Aircraft (Customs and Excise) Regulations 1981 reg 4 (3). For the meaning of 'commander' see para 1222 note 1 ante.
3 For the meaning of 'customs and excise airport' see para 1106 ante.
4 Aircraft (Customs and Excise) Regulations 1981 reg 4 (2); and see para 1223 ante.
5 For the meaning of 'examination station' see para 1221 ante.
6 'Proper officer' means the person appointed or authorised in that behalf by the Commissioners of Customs and Excise: Customs and Excise Management Act 1979 s 1(1). Charges and hours of attendance are prescribed by notice issued by the commissioners.
7 For the meaning of 'goods' see para 1221 note 3, ante.
8 For the meaning of 'stores' see para 1221 note 3, ante.
9 For the meaning of 'transit shed' see para 1221 ante.
10 Aircraft (Customs and Excise) Regulations 1981 reg 4 (1). See also the Customs and Excise Management Act 1979 s 35 (5) (failure to report: penalty of level 3 on the standard scale and unreported goods may be detained); s 35 (6) (failure to answer questions: penalty of level 3 on the standard scale); s 35 (7) (breaking bulk, altering stowage etc after aircraft arrives within 12 nautical miles of United Kingdom coast: penalty of level 3 on the standard scale); s 42 and the Aircraft (Customs and Excise) Regulations 1981 regs 5, 6 (restrictions on unloading of goods and removal from examination station and transit shed; penalty of level 3 on the standard scale); Customs and Excise Management Act 1979 s 49 (forfeiture of goods improperly imported); s 50 (improper importation: liable to arrest; and penalty on summary conviction of the prescribed sum or three times the value of the goods, whichever is the greater, or imprisonment for a term not exceeding six months; on conviction on indictment, a penalty of any amount or imprisonment for a term not exceeding two years, or both; more severe punishment for offences involving drugs or forged or counterfeit goods); s 67 (unauthorised unloading in United Kingdom of goods retained on board for export: forfeiture of goods; penalty of three times the value of the goods or level 3 on the standard scale, whichever is the greater); s 141 (forfeiture of aircraft used in connection with goods liable to forfeiture; as to the scope of the forfeiture provisions of s 141 see *Customs and Excise Comrs v Air Canada* (1990) 1 S&B AvR IV/151, Times, 15 June, CA): see CUSTOMS. The references to sums on the standard scale are substituted by virtue of the Criminal Justice Act 1982 ss 38, 46; and to arrest by the Police and Criminal Evidence Act 1984 s 114 (1). As to the standard scale see para 1044 note 6 ante; at the date at which this volume states the law, level 3 on that scale is at £400. As to the prescribed sum (presently £2,000) see para 1005 note 11 ante. As to proceedings, offences and penalties, see the Customs and Excise Management Act 1979 ss 145–155, 171; and CUSTOMS.

1225. Clearance outward of aircraft: loading and embarkation. Except as permitted by the Commissioners of Customs and Excise, no aircraft may depart from any customs and excise airport[1] from which it commences, or at which it touches down during, a flight to an eventual destination outside the United Kingdom, until clearance of the aircraft for that departure has been obtained from the proper officer[2] at the airport[3].

The proper officer may at any time refuse clearance of an aircraft or, where clearance has been granted and the aircraft is at any customs and excise airport, may demand that the clearance be returned to him for the purpose of detaining the aircraft in pursuance of any power or duty conferred or imposed by or under any enactment[4] or for the purpose of securing compliance with any provision relating to the importation or exportation of goods[5].

No goods may be loaded[6] on an aircraft about to depart from a customs and excise airport on a flight to an eventual destination outside the United Kingdom except at the examination station[7] and with the authority of the proper officer; and no passenger may embark, nor may the commander[8] or any other person permit any passenger to embark, on such an aircraft except at the examination station[9].

1 For the meaning of 'customs and excise airport' see para 1106 ante.
2 For the meaning of 'proper officer' see para 1224 note 6 ante.
3 Customs and Excise Management Act 1979 s 64 (1); s 64 applies to the Isle of Man: Isle of Man Act 1979 s 13, Sch 1 para 13. The commissioners may give directions as to the procedure for obtaining clearance, and as to the documents to be produced and information to be supplied by an applicant for clearance: Customs and Excise Management Act 1979 s 64 (2). The commander of an aircraft which departs from a customs airport without a necessary clearance is liable to a fine not exceeding level 3 on the standard scale: s 64 (6) (amended by virtue of the Criminal Justice Act 1982 ss 38, 46). As to the standard scale see para 1044 note 6 ante; at the date at which this volume states the law, level 3 on that scale is at £400.
  Any person concerned with loading goods into an aircraft requiring clearance before application has been made for clearance may be arrested and is liable on summary conviction to a penalty of the prescribed sum or three times the value of the goods or imprisonment for a term not exceeding six months, or both, and on conviction on indictment, to a penalty of any amount or imprisonment for a term not exceeding two years, or both; and the goods may be forfeited: Customs and Excise Management Act 1979 s 64 (7), (8) (amended by the Police and Criminal Evidence Act 1984 s 114 (1)). As to the prescribed sum see para 1005 note 11 ante. At the date at which this volume states the law, that sum is £2,000. As to proceedings, offences and penalties see the Customs and Excise Management Act 1979 ss 145–155, 171; and CUSTOMS.
4 As to detention powers under the Civil Aviation Act 1981 and the Air Navigation Order 1989, SI 1989/2004, see para 1326 post.
5 Customs and Excise Management Act 1979 s 65 (1). As to the making of the demand, see s 65 (2). On the making of a demand the clearance forthwith becomes void, and if the demand is not complied with the commander is liable to a fine not exceeding level 3 on the standard scale: s 65 (3) (amended by virtue of the Criminal Justice Act 1982 ss 38, 46). As to the standard scale see note 3 supra. For the meaning of 'goods' see para 1221 note 3, ante.
6 As to unauthorised unloading see the Customs and Excise Management Act 1979 s 67; and para 1224 note 10 ante.
7 For the meaning of 'examination station' see para 1221 ante.
8 For the meaning of 'commander' see para 1222 note 1 ante.
9 See the Aircraft (Customs and Excise) Regulations 1981, SI 1981/1259, reg 8. A person contravening the regulations is liable to a fine not exceeding level 4 on the standard scale and the goods may be forfeited: Customs and Excise Management Act 1979 s 66 (2) (amended by the Finance Act 1981 s 10 (2), Sch 7 Pt II para 5 and by virtue of the Criminal Justice Act 1982 ss 38, 46). As to the standard scale see note 3 supra. At the date at which this volume states the law, level 4 on that scale is at £1,000.

1226. Power to prevent flight. Any customs and excise officer[1] or constable may, if it appears to him that an aircraft is intended or is likely to depart for a destination outside the United Kingdom and the Isle of Man from any place other than a customs and excise airport[2] or from a customs and excise airport before clearance outwards is given, give such instructions and take such steps by way of detention of the aircraft or otherwise as appear to him to be necessary in order to prevent the flight[3]. A person who contravenes any such instructions is liable to a fine of level 4 on the standard scale or to imprisonment for a term not exceeding three months, or both[4]; and if an aircraft flies in contravention of any such instruction or flies notwithstanding any steps taken to prevent the flight, the owner, as well as the commander[5], is similarly liable unless he proves that the flight took place without his consent or connivance[6].

1 For the meaning of 'officer' see para 1223 note 3 ante.
2 For the meaning of 'customs and excise airport' see para 1106 ante.
3 Customs and Excise Management Act 1979 s 34 (1) (amended by the Isle of Man Act 1979 s 13, Sch 1). For the power to detain an aircraft while certain expenses of watching, guarding or removing goods or protecting the revenue remain unpaid see the Customs and Excise Act 1979 s 29. As to customs clearance see para 1225 ante. For other powers to prevent flight see para 1459 post.
4 Ibid s 34 (2) (amended by virtue of the Criminal Justice Act 1982 ss 38, 46). As to the standard scale see para 1044 note 6 ante. At the date at which this volume states the law, level 4 on that scale is at £1,000. As to proceedings, offences and penalties, see the Customs and Excise Management Act 1979 ss 144–155, 171; and CUSTOMS.
5 For the meaning of 'commander' see para 1222 note 1 ante.
6 Customs and Excise Management Act 1979 s 34 (3) (amended by virtue of the Criminal Justice Act 1982 ss 38, 46). As to the standard scale see note 4 supra.

1227. Power to inspect aircraft, aerodromes, records, etc. The commander[1] of an aircraft must permit a customs and excise officer[2] at any time to board the aircraft and inspect it and any goods[3] loaded in it and all documents relating to the aircraft or to goods or persons carried in it, and an officer has the right of access at any time to any place to which access is required for the purpose of any such inspection[4].

At any time while an aircraft is at a customs and excise airport[5] any officer and any other person duly engaged in preventing smuggling may board the aircraft, remain there and rummage in any part of it[6]. The proper officer[7] has free access to every part of any aircraft at a customs and excise airport, and may cause any goods to be marked before they are unloaded, may lock up, seal, mark or otherwise secure any goods carried on the aircraft or any place or container in which they are carried, and may break open any locked place or container of which the keys are withheld[8]. There is also a general power to examine and take account of any goods loaded into any aircraft[9], and any goods found concealed on board are liable to forfeiture[10], and there is power to search any person on board or who has landed from any aircraft and any person at a customs and excise airport[11].

An authorised officer[12] of a council has power to enter an aircraft to examine any imported food intended for sale for human consumption[13].

The person in control of any aerodrome[14] must permit an officer at any time to enter upon and inspect the aerodrome and all buildings and goods on it[15]; and the person in control of a licensed aerodrome[16] or, if the Commissioners of Customs and Excise so require, of any other aerodrome, must keep a record of all aircraft arriving at or departing from it, must keep that record available and produce it on demand to any officer together with all other documents kept on the aerodrome which relate to the movement of aircraft, and must permit an officer to make copies of and take extracts from any such record or document[17].

1 For the meaning of 'commander' see para 1222 note 1 ante.
2 For the meaning of 'officer' see para 1223 note 3 ante.
3 For the meaning of 'goods' see para 1221 note 3 ante.
4 Customs and Excise Management Act 1979 s 33 (1). A person contravening or failing to comply with this provision is liable to a fine not exceeding level 4 on the standard scale or imprisonment for a term not exceeding three months or both: s 33 (4) (amended by virtue of the Criminal Justice Act

1982 ss 38, 46). As to the standard scale see para 1044 note 6 ante. At the date at which this volume states the law, level 4 on that scale is at £1,000. As to proceedings, offences and penalties see the Customs and Excise Management Act 1979 ss 145–155, 171; and CUSTOMS.
5   For the meaning of 'customs and excise airport' see para 1106 ante.
6   Customs and Excise Management Act 1979 s 27 (1).
7   For the meaning of 'proper officer' see para 1224 note 6 ante.
8   Customs and Excise Management Act 1979 s 28 (1). If the lock, mark or seal is wilfully opened, altered or broken or the goods concerned are secretly conveyed away the commander is liable to a fine not exceeding level 4 on the standard scale: s 83 (amended by virtue of the Criminal Justice Act 1982 s 46). As to the standard scale see note 4 supra.
9   See the Customs and Excise Management Act 1979 s 159 (amended by the Isle of Man Act 1979 s 13, Sch 1, the Police and Criminal Evidence Act 1984 s 114 (1), the Finance Act 1984 s 8, Sch 4 Pt II para 5 and the Finance Act 1988 s 12 (1) (a)).
10 Customs and Excise Management Act 1979 s 28 (2); as to forfeiture see also ss 139–144; and CUSTOMS. If the commander cannot account for missing cargo, or if an aircraft is used to carry anything liable to forfeiture, the aircraft is liable to forfeiture: Customs and Excise Management Act 1979 ss 90, 141. As to the scope of the forfeiture provisions of s 141 see *Customs and Excise Comrs v Air Canada* (1990) 1 S&B AvR IV/151, Times, 15 June, CA.
11 Customs and Excise Management Act 1979 s 164.
12 For the meaning of 'authorised officer' see the Food Act 1984 s 76, the Imported Food Regulations 1984, SI 1984/1918, reg 2 (1); and FOOD.
13 Food Act 1984 s 88: see FOOD.
14 'Aerodrome' means any area of land or water designed, equipped, set apart or commonly used for affording facilities for the landing and departure of aircraft: Customs and Excise Management Act 1979 s 1 (1).
15 Ibid s 33 (2). For the penalties see note 4 supra.
16 As to the licensing of aerodromes see para 1154 ante.
17 Customs and Excise Management Act 1979 s 33 (3). For the penalties see note 4 supra.

1228. Carrying away officers. If any aircraft departs from any place carrying on board without his consent any customs and excise officer[1] or other government officer, the commander[2] of the aircraft is liable to a fine of level 3 on the standard scale[3]. In addition, the amount of any expenses incurred by the Commissioners of Customs and Excise or by any government department by reason of the carrying away of any officer may be recovered summarily as a civil debt from the commander or from the owner of the aircraft concerned[4].

1   For the meaning of 'officer' see para 1223 note 3 ante.
2   For the meaning of 'commander' see para 1222 note 1 ante.
3   Customs and Excise Management Act 1979 s 32 (1) (amended by virtue of the Criminal Justice Act 1982 ss 38, 46). As to the standard scale see para 1044 note 6 ante. At the date at which this volume states the law, level 3 on that scale is at £400. As to proceedings, offences and penalties see the Customs and Excise Management Act 1979 ss 145–155, 171; and CUSTOMS.
4   Ibid s 32 (2). As to the summary recovery of civil debts see the Magistrates' Courts Act 1980 ss 58, 97; and MAGISTRATES.

(10) OTHER PROVISIONS AFFECTING AERODROMES

1229. Entry into United Kingdom of persons from overseas. Subject to certain exceptions[1] a person who is not a British citizen[2] may not enter the United Kingdom unless given leave to do so[3] by an immigration officer[5], who may examine persons who arrive in the United Kingdom by aircraft, including transit passengers, members of the crew and others not seeking entry[5]. The commander of the aircraft is required to furnish immigration officers with a passenger list and particulars of the crew[6]. The commander must take all reasonable steps to ensure that persons on board the aircraft do not disembark save in conformity with immigration requirements[7].

The owner or agent of an aircraft employed to carry passengers for reward must not, without the Secretary of State's[8] approval, arrange for the aircraft to call at an airport in the United Kingdom other than a port of entry[9] for the purpose of disembarking passengers[10].

Where a person requiring leave to enter arrives by aircraft in the United Kingdom without valid documents[11], the owner or agent of the aircraft is liable to a fine[12]. Where a person is refused leave to enter and the airline is directed to remove him[13], the owner of the aircraft must pay him any expenses due to custody, accommodation and maintenance of that person between his arrival and removal[14].

1 See the Immigration Act 1971 ss 1 (3) (arrival from Channel Islands, Isle of Man or Republic of Ireland), 8 (crew members, diplomats and military personnel). As to crew members see also Sch 2 para 12. As to free movement of persons within the European Community see the EEC Treaty arts 48, 49; EC Council Regulation 1612/68 (amended by EC Council Regulation 312/76) and EC Commission Regulation 1251/70; and EUROPEAN COMMUNITIES. As to immigration see further BRITISH NATIONALITY.

2 As to British citizenship see the British Nationality Act 1981 ss 1–14, 36, Sch 2 paras 2–6; and BRITISH NATIONALITY.

3 Immigration Act 1971 s 3 (1) (amended by the British Nationality Act 1981 s 39 (6), Sch 4 para 2). The Prevention of Terrorism (Temporary Provisions) Acts 1984 and 1989 further limit the right of entry; see further CRIMINAL LAW.

4 Immigration Act 1971 s 4 (1).

5 Ibid Sch 2 para 2 (amended by the British Nationality Act 1981 Sch 4 para 2). The owner or agent of an aircraft must supply landing or embarkation cards in such form as the Secretary of State may direct for persons who are not British citizens disembarking or embarking in the United Kingdom, and such persons must produce such cards to immigration officers: see the Immigration Act 1971 Sch 2 para 5 and the Immigration (Landing and Embarkation Cards) Order 1975, SI 1975/65.

6 Immigration Act 1971 Sch 2 para 27 (2); Immigration (Particulars of Passengers and Crew) Order 1972, SI 1972/1967 (amended by SI 1975/380).

7 Immigration Act 1971 Sch 2 para 27.

8 As to the Secretary of State see the Interpretation Act 1978 s 5, Sch 1, Sch 2 para 4 (1). The Secretary of State here concerned is the Secretary of State for the Home Department.

9 For this purpose the Secretary of State may designate ports of entry: Immigration Act 1971 s 33 (3): see the Immigration (Ports of Entry) Order 1987, SI 1987/177, Schedule, which designates the following airports: Aberdeen, Belfast, Birmingham, Bournemouth (Hurn), Bristol, Cardiff (Wales), East Midlands, Edinburgh, Gatwick, Glasgow, Heathrow, Leeds/Bradford, Liverpool, Luton, Manchester, Newcastle, Norwich, Prestwick, Southampton, Southend, Stansted and Teesside.

10 Immigration Act 1971 Sch 2 para 26 (1).

11 Ie passport with photograph (or equivalent document), visa.

12 Immigration (Carriers Liability) Act 1987 s 1 (4); the fine is a sum of £1,000 payable to the Secretary of State on demand. No liability is incurred where the owner of the aircraft can show that the documents were produced at the time of embarkation: s 1 (2).

13 See the Immigration Act 1971 Sch 2 para 8· the direction must be given within two months of the refusal to give leave to enter; as to the difficulties in calculating the period see *R v Immigration Officer, ex p Shah* [1982] 2 All ER 264, [1982] 1 WLR 545.

14 Immigration Act 1971 Sch 2 para 19 (1), the Secretary of State having defrayed the expenses under Sch 2 para 10 (3).

1230. Prevention of spread of diseases. The Secretary of State for Health and the Secretary of State for Wales, in pursuance of statutory powers and duties conferred upon them[1], have made regulations[2] for preventing danger to public health from aircraft arriving at any place in England and Wales, including aerodromes vested in or under the control of the Secretary of State for Transport and the Civil Aviation Authority (CAA), and for preventing the spread of infection by means of aircraft leaving any such place or aerodrome.

At aerodromes vested in or under the control of the Secretary of State for Transport, or owned or managed by the CAA, the authority by whom the regulations are to be enforced is the Secretary of State for Health, but provision is made for allowing or requiring local authorities to undertake this duty[3]. At other aerodromes and places the local authority concerned is the enforcing authority[4].

The regulations[5] deal separately with incoming and outgoing aircraft. In the case of incoming aircraft arriving at a customs and excise airport[6], provision is made for the inspection of the aircraft by the medical officer at the airport[7], for taking measures such as the examination, detention and disinfection of persons on board or leaving the aircraft[8], for requiring the commander of the aircraft to answer questions, supply information, and notify deaths or cases of infectious disease on board the aircraft[9], for authorising the detention of the aircraft for medical examination[10], for requiring the aircraft to proceed to a sanitary airport[11] and for taking other precautionary measures[12]. The regulations also provide for the procedure to be followed in the case of incoming aircraft alighting elsewhere than at a customs and excise airport[13]. The regulations are relaxed to a considerable extent in the case of any aircraft which has commenced its voyage within an 'excepted area' comprising the United Kingdom, the Channel Islands, the Isle of Man, the Republic of Ireland, Belgium, France, Greece, Italy, Luxembourg, the Netherlands and Spain, and has not during the voyage alighted outside that area[14].

In the case of outgoing aircraft, provision is made for the examination of persons proposing to embark, for prohibiting their embarkation[15] and for the taking of additional precautions in the case of infected places[16].

1 The Secretary of State for Health is empowered to make regulations for, inter alia, the purposes set out in the text, by the Public Health (Control of Disease) Act 1984 s 13. The Secretary of State for Transport (as to whom see para 1032 ante) and the Civil Aviation Authority (see para 1044 et seq ante) have a duty to make arrangements for the same purposes in relation to aerodromes vested in or under the control of that Secretary of State or owned or managed by the CAA: Civil Aviation Act 1982 s 36 (1). The provisions of the Public Health (Control of Disease) Act 1984 s 13 have effect subject to certain minor modifications in relation to government aerodromes and CAA aerodromes (as to which see para 1105 ante): see ss 13, 14, 76. See further PUBLIC HEALTH.
2 See the Public Health (Aircraft) Regulations 1979, SI 1979/1434, which are designed to carry out the provisions of the International Health Regulations (Cmnd 4650) adopted by the World Health Assembly in 1969 and amended in 1973: see para 1011 ante. Power to do so was given by the Public Health Act 1936 s 143 (1), the Civil Aviation Act 1949 s 18 (1), the Airports Authority Act 1965 s 13 (1), and the Civil Aviation Act 1971 s 32 (1), now replaced by the Public Health (Control of Disease) Act 1984 s 13 and the Civil Aviation Act 1982 s 36: see further PUBLIC HEALTH.
3 Public Health (Aircraft) Regulations 1979 reg 4 (1). A local authority is the enforcing authority if it has undertaken duties at the aerodrome under the Civil Aviation Act 1982 s 36 (2).
4 See the Public Health (Aircraft) Regulations 1979 reg 4 (1) (b)–(d). See further PUBLIC HEALTH.
5 The Public Health (Aircraft) Regulations 1979 are treated further in PUBLIC HEALTH, to which reference should be made for the provisions of regs 32, 33 (where measures are required to be taken by the commander of an aircraft, the responsible authority may, at his request, itself carry out the measures, but may, if it thinks fit, recover the expenses from him); and of reg 36 (commander not willing to comply with any provision of the regulations must notify the medical officer, who may require the aircraft to leave the aerodrome immediately; in those circumstances the aircraft may not alight at any other place in England or Wales). See also reg 29 (compliance with directions given, etc, under the regulations), and the Public Health (Control of Disease) Act 1984 s 13 (penalties for breach of regulations etc).
6 For the meaning of 'customs and excise airport' see para 1106 ante.
7 Public Health (Aircraft) Regulations 1979 reg 7.
8 Ibid regs 8–10.
9 Ibid regs 11–12.

10 Ibid regs 14–19.
11 Ibid reg 22. For the meaning of 'sanitary airport' see para 1107 ante.
12 See further PUBLIC HEALTH.
13 Public Health (Aircraft) Regulations 1979 reg 25.
14 Ibid regs 2 (1), 26.
15 Ibid reg 27.
16 Ibid reg 28.

1231. Pests; infestation and fumigation. The provisions of the Prevention of Damage by Pests Act 1949[1] may be applied by Order in Council in relation to aircraft as they apply to land, with such exceptions and modifications as may be specified in the order[2]. The Act deals with measures to keep down rats and mice[3] and to prevent the infestation of food[4], and requires, among other things, a person whose business consists of or includes the transport of food to give notice to the Minister of Agriculture, Fisheries and Food if it comes to his notice that any infestation is present in any premises or vehicle which is or is likely to be used in the course of that business[5]. The use of particular premises or vehicles for the storage or transport of food may be prohibited[6].

Regulations may be made as to the fumigation of premises and articles, including any aircraft, with a view to securing the health, safety and welfare of people at work[7].

1 See PUBLIC HEALTH.
2 Prevention of Damage by Pests Act 1949 s 23. No such order was in force on the date at which this volume states the law.
3 See the Prevention of Damage by Pests Act 1949 Pt I (ss 1–12). As to deratting and disinfection of aircraft see the Public Health (Aircraft) Regulations 1979, SI 1979/1434, reg 13; and see para 1230 ante.
4 See the Prevention of Damage by Pests Act 1949 Pt II (ss 13–18).
5 Ibid ss 13, 28 (1) (amended by the Transfer of Functions (Ministry of Food) Order 1955, SI 1955/554, art 3).
6 Prevention of Damage by Pests Act 1949 s 14.
7 See the Health and Safety at Work etc Act 1974 ss 1, 15, Sch 3. This power had not been exercised in relation to aircraft at the date at which this volume states the law. Accidents occasioning loss of human life or personal injury due to fumigation must be notified to the Health and Safety Executive. See further PUBLIC HEALTH.

1232. Aviation fuel installations. When an aviation fuel installation[1] is located on an aerodrome[2], the person in charge of the installation may not allow aviation fuel[3] to be delivered to the installation until he is satisfied that the storing and dispensing equipment will not make the fuel unfit for aviation use[4], that the installation is properly marked[5] and the fuel has been sampled at delivery, is of the correct grade and is fit for use in aircraft[6]. The aviation fuel may not be dispensed from the installation to an aircraft before the person in charge is satisfied that it has been sampled[7].

The person in charge of the installation must keep records of grades, quantities and dates of aviation fuel deliveries, of samples taken and of particulars concerning the maintenance and cleaning of the installation[8].

The person in charge may not allow any aviation fuel to be dispensed for use in an aircraft when he knows or has reason to believe that the fuel is unfit for such use[9]. Where the Civil Aviation Authority (CAA)[10] believes that aviation fuel may be delivered in contravention of the Air Navigation Order 1989[11] it may direct the person in charge of the installation not to permit the fuel to be dispensed from that installation until the direction is revoked[12].

1 'Aviation fuel installation' means any apparatus or container, including a vehicle, designed, manufactured or adapted for the storage of avaition fuel or for the delivery of such fuel to an aircraft: Air Navigation Order 1989, S1 1989/2004, art 87 (4).
2 For the meaning of 'aerodrome' see para 1102 ante.
3 'Aviation fuel' means fuel intended for use in aircraft: Air Navigation Order 1989 art 87 (4).
4 Ibid art 87 (1) (a) (i); and see note 7 infra.
5 Ibid art 87 (1) (a) (ii); and see note 7 infra.
6 Ibid art 87 (1) (a) (iii); and see note 7 infra.
7 Ibid art 87 (1) (b). Sub-paragraph (1) does not apply to aviation fuel removed from one aircraft and intended for use in another aircraft operated by the same operator as the first aircraft: art 87 (1) proviso. Contravention renders the offender liable on summary conviction to a fine not exceeding £1,000: art 99 (5), Sch 12 Pt A.
8 Ibid art 87 (2). The records must be kept for 12 months: art 87 (2). As to contravention see note 7 supra.
9 Ibid art 87 (3) (a). Contravention renders the offender liable on summary conviction to a fine not exceeding £2,000 and on conviction on indictment to a fine or imprisonment for a term not exceeding two years or both: art 99 (6), Sch 12 Pt B.
10 As to the CAA see para 1044 ante.
11 Ie the Air Navigation Order 1989 art 87.
12 Ibid art 87 (3) (b); as to penalties see note 9 supra.

1233. Obstruction of authorised person. A person must not wilfully obstruct or impede any person acting in the exercise of his powers or the performance of his duties under the Air Navigation Order 1989[1].

1 Air Navigation Order 1989, SI 1989/2004, art 97. The penalty for contravention is on summary conviction a fine not exceeding £1,000: art 99 (5), Sch 12 Pt A. As to powers and duties conferred by the order see eg para 1193 ante (right of access to aerodromes etc), paras 1405–1408 post (production of documents), para 1313 post (inspection of aircraft) and para 1459 post (preventing flight in contravention of regulations).

1234. Miscellaneous powers and duties. Commanders of aircraft on landing or departing are under an obligation to produce specified documents to authorised persons[1], and aircraft arriving from or departing for a place out of the United Kingdom must comply with customs requirements[2]. Other duties before, during and after flight are considered elsewhere in this title[3].

Authorised persons have rights of access to aerodromes[4], and trespassers are liable to penalties[5].

1 See paras 1405–1408 post.
2 See paras 1220–1228 ante.
3 See paras 1426–1499 post.
4 See para 1193 ante.
5 See para 1194 ante.

1235. Exemptions as to shops. Shops in which the only trade or business carried on is that of the sale of aircraft supplies or accessories to travellers are exempted from the statutory provisions requiring the closing of shops on early closing days[1]. The statutory provisions relating to general closing hours[2], and the provisions of closing orders made by local authorities[3], do not prevent the sale of aircraft supplies or accessories for immediate use, so long as the shop is kept open only for such time as is necessary for serving the customer[4]; and the provisions relating to Sunday closing[5] do not prevent a shop being open on Sundays for the sale of aircraft supplies or accessories[6].

Special provision is made as to the hours of employment of persons between the ages of 16 and 18 in shops carrying on the business of serving customers with supplies or accessories for aircraft sold for immediate use[7].

The statutory provisions as to Sunday trading[8] do not prevent the sale, dispatch or delivery of victuals, stores or other necessaries, including butchers' meat[9], required by any person for an aircraft on its arrival at, or immediately before its departure from, an aerodrome[10].

The statutory provisions relating to early closing days and hours of closing in shops[11] and to Sunday trading[12] do not apply to shops, or sales otherwise than at a shop of goods by or on behalf of a person carrying on a retail trade or business at a shop, at a designated airport[13].

1 Shops Act 1950 s 1 (6), Sch 1 (amended by the Shops (Early Closing Days) Act 1965 ss 1 (1), 2, 3). As to the provisions referred to see the Shops Act 1950 s 1 (as so amended); and TRADE AND LABOUR.
2 See ibid s 2 (amended by the Statute Law (Repeals) Act 1974); and TRADE AND LABOUR.
3 See the Shops Act 1950 s 8 (amended by the Statute Law (Repeals) Act 1974 and the Local Government, Planning and Land Act 1980 ss 1 (4), 194, Sch 4 para 1 (1), Sch 34 Pt IV); and TRADE AND LABOUR.
4 Shops Act 1950 ss 2 (3) (b), 8 (5) (b), Sch 2 para 1 (h).
5 See ibid s 47; and TRADE AND LABOUR.
6 Ibid s 47 proviso, Sch 5 para 1 (h).
7 See ibid s 26; and TRADE AND LABOUR.
8 See ibid Pt IV (ss 47–59); and TRADE AND LABOUR.
9 See ibid ss 61, 65.
10 Ibid s 56 (1) (a); see also *NAS Airport Services Ltd v Hotel and Catering Industry Training Board (No 2)* [1970] 3 All ER 928, [1970] 1 WLR 1576, CA; and TRADE AND LABOUR.
11 See the Shops Act 1950 Pt I (ss 1–16); and TRADE AND LABOUR.
12 See the Shops Act 1950 Pt IV.
13 Shops (Airports) Act 1962 s 1 (1) (amended by the Airports Act 1986 s 70). The aerodromes designated by order made by the Secretary of State for Transport under the Shops (Airports) Act 1962 are to be found in the Airports (Shops) Order 1977, SI 1977/1397; the East Midlands Airport Shops Order 1977, SI 1977/1919; the Cardiff-Wales Airport Shops Order 1980, SI 1980/774; the Airports Shops Orders 1985, SI 1985/654 and 1985/1739; the Exeter Airport Shops Order 1986, SI 1986/981; the Sumburgh Airport Shops Order 1987, SI 1987/837; the London City Airport Shops Order 1987, SI 1987/1983; and the Manston Airport Shops Order 1990, SI 1990/1044. See TRADE AND LABOUR.

1236. Exemption from licensing hours. In the case of any international airport specified in an order of the Secretary of State[1], licensed premises within the airport's examination station[2] are exempt from the prohibition[3] on the sale, supply or consumption of intoxicating liquor outside permitted hours[4].

1 As to these airports see the Airports Licensing (Liquor) Order 1983, SI 1983/1217, specifying Birmingham, Bristol, Cardiff-Wales, East Midlands, London-Gatwick, London-Heathrow, London-Stansted, Luton, Manchester International and Newcastle airports; the Airports Licensing (Liquor) Order 1985, SI 1985/653, specifying Leeds/Bradford and Southampton airports; the Airports Licensing (Liquor) (No 2) Order 1985, SI 1985/1730, specifying Bournemouth (Hurn), Humberside, Liverpool, Norwich and Tees-side airports; the Southend Airport Licensing (Liquor) Order 1986, SI 1986/525; and the London City Airport Licensing (Liquor) Order 1987, SI 1987/1982. As to the Secretary of State see para 1032 ante.
2 For the meaning of 'examination station' see para 1221 ante.

3 See the Licensing Act 1964 s 59; and INTOXICATING LIQUOR.
4 Licensing Act 1964 s 87: see para 1652 post. This provision applies also to hovercraft (see para 1270 note 3 post) and has been brought into operation at Pegwell Bay Hoverport by the Pegwell Bay Hoverport Licensing (Liquor) Order 1972, SI 1972/1335, and at Dover Hoverport by the Dover Hoverport Licensing (Liquor) Order 1978, SI 1978/225.

(11) POLICING AND PROTECTION OF AERODROMES

(i) Control of Aerodromes

1237. Byelaws. Where an airport is either designated for the purpose or is managed by the Secretary of State[1], the airport operator[2], whether he is the Secretary of State or some other person, may make byelaws in respect of any aerodrome owned or managed by him, for regulating the use and operation of the aerodrome and the conduct of all persons while within the aerodrome[3].

Before making byelaws, the Secretary of State must give public notice of the proposed byelaws to allow representations to be made and to be considered prior to the publication of the statutory instrument embodying them[4]. And in the case of any other airport operator, the latter must ensure that his airport has been designated for the purpose[5] and he must have the proposed byelaws confirmed by the Secretary of State for them to have any effect[6].

The Secretary of State may revoke a byelaw made by another airport operator in respect of noise, vibration and pollution caused by aircraft on or above the aerodrome[7] where he has designated the airport for the purposes of noise regulation under the Civil Aviation Act 1982[8] or where he is of the opinion that the byelaw is inconsistent with general safety or with any international obligation of the United Kingdom[9].

Any person contravening these byelaws is liable on summary conviction to a fine specified in the byelaws, being a fine not exceeding level 4 on the standard scale[10].

1 As to the Secretary of State see para 1032 ante. The Secretary of State's power is exercisable by statutory instrument: Airports Act 1986 s 63 (7). Such instruments, being local, are not listed in this work.
2 As to airport operators see para 1042 note 4 ante. As to the powers of the Civil Aviation Authority (CAA) in respect of aerodromes see para 1178 ante. As to airports managed by local authorities see para 1110 ante. The Local Government Act 1972 ss 236 (9) (notice of byelaws) and 237 (penalties) do not apply to byelaws made by a local authority under the Airports Act 1986 s 63: see s 63 (8).
3 Ibid s 63 (1). Where the airport has been designated for the purposes of the Aviation Security Act 1982 (as to which see para 1239 post), the manager may make byelaws to extend to the whole of the aerodrome and to require persons to leave the aerodrome or state their name and address and the purpose of their presence on the aerodrome if so requested by a relevant constable: Aviation Security Act 1982 s 28 (1). As to the powers of the regular police on a designated airport see para 1239 post.
4 Airports Act 1986 s 63 (6), (7).
5 See ibid s 63 (1) (a). As to airports designated under s 63 (1) see the Airports Byelaws (Designation) Order 1987, SI 1987/380, and the Airports Byelaws (Designation) (No 2) Order 1987, SI 1987/2246.
6 See the Airports Act 1986 s 63 (5), Sch 3.
7 See ibid s 63 (2) (b).
8 As to airports designated under the Civil Aviation Act 1982 s 78 see para 1186 ante.
9 See the Airports Act 1986 s 64 (3).
10 Ibid s 64 (1), (2). As to the operation of byelaws prohibiting the unauthorised offer of services see *Robertson v Bannister* [1973] RTR 109, DC; or the entry into the airport otherwise than as a bona fide airline passenger see *Cinnamond v British Airports Authority* [1980] 2 All ER 368, [1980] 1 WLR 582,

CA; or public demonstrations interfering with the use of airport see *British Airports Authority v Ashton* [1983] 3 All ER 6, [1983] 1 WLR 1079, DC.

1238. Special constables. Persons nominated by the Secretary of State[1] may be appointed by any two justices of the peace to be special constables on any premises vested in the Secretary of State or under his control[2]. Any person so appointed must be sworn in by the justices duly to execute the office of constable on those premises, and, when sworn, has on those premises the powers and privileges and is liable to the duties and responsibilities of a constable[3]. All special constables thus appointed are under the exclusive control of the Secretary of State, who has power to suspend or terminate their appointment[4].

Where an aerodrome is neither a government aerodrome nor an airport designated for the purposes of the Aviation Security Act 1982, the aerodrome manager may maintain an aerodrome constabulary[5].

1 As to the Secretary of State see para 1032 ante.
2 Civil Aviation Act 1982 s 57 (1). As to special constables generally see POLICE.
3 Ibid s 57 (2). As to the powers, privileges, duties and responsibilities of constables see POLICE.
4 Ibid s 57 (3). As to the control of ordinary constables see POLICE.
5 See para 1239 post.

1239. Policing of airports. The Aviation Security Act 1982[1] enables the regular police[2] to take over the policing of designated civil airports from the aerodrome constabulary[3]. The Secretary of State[4], after consulting the aerodrome manager, police authorities and the chief officer of police for the area concerned[5], may designate by order[6] an aerodrome to be policed by the regular police in the interests of the preservation of the peace and the prevention of crime[7]. So long as the aerodrome has been so designated, any relevant constable[8] is entitled to enter any part of the aerodrome irrespective of the manager[9] and may act to the exclusion of any existing aerodrome constabulary[10].

The Secretary of State may make supplementary orders where an aerodrome becomes, or ceases to be, a designated airport, such as provisions relating to aerodrome byelaws[11], transfer of personnel and preservation of pension rights[12]. As regards the policing of the airport the manager of such a designated airport is responsible for making all necessary payments and for providing suitable accommodation and facilities[13].

1 See the Aviation Security Act 1982 Pt III (ss 25–31).
2 As to the regular police see POLICE.
3 'Aerodrome constabulary' means, in relation to any aerodrome, any body of constables which the manager of the aerodrome has power to maintain at the aerodrome: Aviation Security Act 1982 s 31 (1). As to the designation of airports see text and note 6 infra.
4 As to the Secretary of State see para 1032 ante.
5 See the Aviation Security Act 1982 s 25 (2). The relevant police area in relation to any aerodrome is that area in which the aerodrome is wholly or mainly situated: see s 31 (1).
6 Ibid s 25 (1), (2): the order must be made by statutory instrument and, where it contains a statement that it is made with the consent of the airport manager and the police authority, it may be annulled in pursuance of a resolution of either House of Parliament; if it does not contain such a statement it must be laid before Parliament in draft, which must be approved by resolution of each House of Parliament before the order can be made: s 25 (3).
7 Ibid s 25 (1). This provision re-enacts the Policing of Airports Act 1974 s 1 (1) (repealed), under which were made all existing orders designating airports for the purpose of their policing; the designated airports are Heathrow (see the Policing of Airports (Heathrow) Order 1974, SI 1974/

1671), Stansted (see SI 1975/168), Gatwick (see SI 1975/375), Glasgow (see SI 1975/443), Prestwick (see SI 1975/445), Edinburgh (see SI 1975/447), Birmingham (see SI 1976/590) and Manchester (SI 1976/1045).

8   A 'relevant constable' in relation to an aerodrome means any constable under the direction and control of the chief officer of police for the relevant police area: Aviation Security Act 1982 s 31 (1); and see note 5 supra. As to the rights of a relevant constable in a designated airport see s 28 (2), (3) (forceful removal of persons, services, animals or things and arrest without warrant).

9   Ibid s 26 (1) (a); this provision is without prejudice to any right of entry existing apart from it: s 26 (2).

10   Ibid s 26 (1) (b); for the meaning of 'aerodrome constabulary' see note 3 supra.

11   The Secretary of State may amend aerodrome byelaws in order to transfer to relevant constables (see note 8 supra) any functions conferred by the byelaws until then on members of an aerodrome constabulary (see note 3 supra); to extend the byelaws to the whole of the aerodrome if not done so by the airport manager under ibid s 28 (1) or the Airports Act 1986 s 63 (see para 1237 ante); or to include in any such byelaws any requirement for people to leave the aerodrome or make specified statements if required by a relevant constable (see s 28 (1) (b) of the 1982 Act; and para 1237 note 3 ante): see the Aviation Security Act 1982 s 30 (2) (b).

12   Ibid s 30. As to such supplementary orders see the orders made under the Policing of Airports Act 1974 s 6 (repealed), which preceded the Aviation Security Act 1982 s 30, and concerning Heathrow (SI 1974/1672 and SI 1980/93), Stansted (SI 1975/169 and SI 1980/94), Gatwick (SI 1975/376 and SI 1980/92), Glasgow (SI 1975/444), Prestwick (SI 1975/446), Birmingham (SI 1976/591) and Manchester (SI 1976/1046).

13   See the Aviation Security Act 1982 s 26 (3), (4); if no agreement is reached between the manager and the police authority, the Secretary of State may determine the amount of payments or the provision of facilities: s 26 (3).

1240. Prevention of theft. Any relevant constable[1] may, in any designated airport[2], stop any airport employee[3] whom he suspects to have stolen, or unlawfully obtained, something on such an aerodrome[4]; he may stop and search any vehicle or aircraft carrying an airport employee when he suspects that anything stolen, or unlawfully obtained, could be found in or on the vehicle or aircraft[5]. He may also stop any person who is leaving a cargo area[6] in a designated aerodrome, and may inspect any goods carried by that person[7]. He may also stop and search any vehicle or aircraft which is leaving the area and inspect it and any goods carried in or on it[8], and he may detain in the area any such goods for which there is not produced a document[9] signed by a person authorised by the airport manager in that behalf authorising their removal from the area, and may detain any vehicle or aircraft which was carrying goods so liable to detention[10].

The constable has no power to search any person[11] unless the person is an airport employee and the constable has reasonable grounds to suspect him of having in his possession or conveying in any manner anything stolen or unlawfully obtained on any such aerodrome[12]. He has power to stop, search and detain any vehicle or aircraft if he has reasonable grounds to suspect that anything stolen or unlawfully obtained on any such aerodrome may be found in or on the vehicle or aircraft[13].

1   For the meaning of 'relevant constable' see para 1239 note 8 ante.

2   As to designated airports see para 1239 ante.

3   'Airport employee' means, in relation to any aerodrome and in the context of prevention of theft, any person in the employment of the manager of the aerodrome and any person employed otherwise than by the manager to work on the aerodrome: Aviation Security Act 1982 s 27 (5).

4   See ibid s 27 (1) (a).

5   See ibid s 27 (1) (b); the constable must have reasonable grounds for his suspicions before he may without warrant search and detain the vehicle or aircraft concerned. These powers extend to any vehicle whether or not it carries an airport employee and include the power to stop and detain an aircraft when the occurrence takes place in a cargo area of a designated airport: s 27 (4). As to 'cargo area' see note 6 infra.

6 In the context of the prevention of theft, 'cargo area' means any area which appears to the Secretary of State to be used wholly or mainly for the storage or handling of cargo in an aerodrome and is designated by order made by the Secretary of State for the purpose of the prevention of theft: ibid s 27 (6). The order is made by statutory instrument: s 27 (8). See eg the Heathrow Airport–London (Cargo Area Designation) Order 1970, SI 1970/958. As to the Secretary of State see para 1032 ante.
7 Aviation Security Act 1982 s 27 (2) (a).
8 Ibid s 27 (2) (b).
9 As to documents in respect of cargo see paras 1432, 1433 post.
10 Aviation Security Act 1982 s 27 (2) (c).
11 Ibid s 27 (3).
12 Ibid s 27 (1) (a).
13 Ibid s 27 (1) (b).

1241. Control of road traffic. Road traffic enactments[1] apply to all roads within a designated airport[2] whether or not the public has access to them[3]. After consultation with the airport operator[4] the Secretary of State[5] may by order[6] direct that those enactments be modified as necessary to confer on the airport operator functions usually exercised by a highway authority or a local authority[7] or on the chief officer of the airport constabulary[8] functions usually exercised by a chief officer of police[9], save that the chief officer of police keeps and exercises his functions where the airport has been designated under the Aviation Security Act 1982[10].

Where an aerodrome has been designated under the Aviation Security Act 1982[11], traffic wardens appointed by the police authority for the relevant police area[12] may exercise their functions on the aerodrome and enter it as against the manager of the aerodrome[13].

1 'Road traffic enactments' means the enactments, whether passed before or after the Airports Act 1986, relating to road traffic, including the lighting and parking of vehicles, and any order or other instrument having effect by virtue of such enactments: Airports Act 1986 ss 65 (6), 63 (3).
2 'Designated airport' means an airport designated for the purposes of the control of road traffic by order made by the Secretary of State: ibid s 65 (6).
3 Ibid s 65 (1); as to exemptions see note 6 infra.
4 Ibid s 65 (4). This provision does not apply to government aerodromes: s 65 (4); see further para 1105 ante.
5 As to the Secretary of State see para 1032 ante.
6 The order may exempt particular roads or lengths of roads to which the public does not have access, requiring the airport operator to indicate the exempted roads or lengths of roads in a specified manner: ibid s 65 (3).
7 Ibid s 65 (2) (a). As to local authorities see para 1041 ante.
8 'Airport constabulary' means, in relation to an airport owned or managed by the Secretary of State, the special constables appointed under the Civil Aviation Act 1982 s 57 and, in relation to any airport owned or managed by a local authority, any body of constables which that authority has power to maintain at that airport: Airports Act 1986 s 65 (6); see further para 1238 ante.
9 Ibid s 65 (2) (b).
10 See the Aviation Security Act 1982 s 29 (1) (amended by the Airports Act 1986 s 83 (1), Sch 4 para 9). For the meaning of 'designated airport' see para 1239 ante.
11 Ie under the Aviation Security Act 1982 s 25; see para 1239 ante.
12 For the meaning of 'relevant police area' see para 1239 note 5 ante.
13 Aviation Security Act 1982 s 29 (2) (a).

1242. Custody and disposal of lost property and abandoned vehicles. The Secretary of State[1] has made under the Civil Aviation Act 1949 provision by regulations[2], for securing the safe custody and redelivery of any property which, while not in proper custody, is found on any premises belonging to him or under his control[3]. Since the passing of the Airports Act 1986, lost property is no more the concern of the Secretary of State. It is for the airport operator to include in the airport byelaws[4] the means to secure the safe custody and redelivery of lost property[5]; the byelaws may provide for requiring charges to be paid in respect of any such property before it is redelivered[6], and for authorising the disposal of any such property if it is not redelivered before the expiration of any period specified in the regulations[7].

After consulting the airport operator the Secretary of State may make orders in respect of abandoned vehicles, adapting certain provisions of the Refuse Disposal (Amenity) Act 1978[8] in their application to land and parking areas within a building in any designated airport[9], and he may adapt the road traffic enactments in respect of abandoned vehicles[10] not only as respects their application to roads within such aerodromes but also as respects their application to other land and parking areas within a building within those aerodromes[11].

The aerodrome must have been designated for the purpose[12].

1 As to the Secretary of State see para 1032 ante.
2 See the British Airports Authority (Lost Property) Regulations 1972, SI 1972/1027, made under the Civil Aviation Act 1949 s 56 (repealed) and saved by the Civil Aviation Act 1982 and the Airports Act 1986 s 83 (4), Sch 5 para 11 (2). A person finding lost property must hand it in to an employee or constable, who must deliver it to the lost property office unless a claimant first gives evidence of ownership and his name and address, which must be reported (regs 4, 5). The lost property office must retain property in safe custody, although it must return official documents (eg licences and passports) to the issuing authority and, where the name and address of the owner of property are ascertainable (for which purpose property may be opened and examined: reg 9), he must be notified (reg 6). Property is handed to claimants without fee or reward on giving evidence of ownership and their names and addresses (reg 7). Property unclaimed for three months may be sold for the best obtainable price, although perishable or objectionable property may be sold or disposed of sooner (reg 8 (1)–(3)). The owner is entitled to the proceeds of sale after costs are deducted (reg 8 (4)). Records of property found and claimants' names and addresses must be kept (reg 6).
3 See the Civil Aviation Act 1949 s 56, replaced by the Civil Aviation Act 1982 s 58, which was repealed by the Airports Act 1986. Lost property is now included in byelaws made by the airport manager: see infra.
4 As to byelaws see para 1237 ante.
5 See the Airports Act 1986 s 63 (2) (j).
6 Ibid s 63 (2) (j) (i).
7 Ibid s 63 (2) (j) (ii).
8 Ie the Refuse Disposal (Amenity) Act 1978 ss 3–5 and s 8 so far as it relates to s 3, and any regulations made thereunder; see PUBLIC HEALTH.
9 Airports Act 1986 s 66 (1), (3). 'Designated airport' means an airport designated for the purposes of s 66 by order made by the Secretary of State: s 66 (5); and see note 12 infra.
10 Ie the Road Traffic Regulations Act 1984 ss 99–102 and any regulations made thereunder: see ROAD TRAFFIC.
11 Airports Act 1986 s 66 (2), (3).
12 See ibid s 66 (1), (5) and the Airports (Designation) (Removal and Disposal of Vehicles) Order 1990, SI 1990/54.

(ii) Powers of the Secretary of State

1243. Protection against acts of violence. As well as providing for the protection of aircraft and of persons or property on board aircraft[1], the Aviation Security Act 1982 as amended by the Aviation and Maritime Security Act 1990 provides for the protection against acts of violence[2] of aerodromes, of persons present at any time in any part of an aerodrome, of property present, permanently or not, at any time in any part of an aerodrome, and of air navigation installations which do not form part of an aerodrome[3].

1 As to the protection of aircraft and of persons or property on board thereof against acts of violence see para 1665 et seq post.

2 'Act of violence', for the purposes of the Aviation Security Act 1982 Pt II (ss 10–24A), means any act (whether actual or potential, and whether done or to be done in the United Kingdom or elsewhere) which either, being an act done in Great Britain, constitutes, or if done in Great Britain would constitute, the offence of murder, attempted murder, manslaughter, culpable homicide or assault, or an offence under the Offences against the Person Act 1861 ss 18, 20–24, 28 or 29, under the Explosive Substances Act 1883 s 2 or under the Criminal Damage Act 1971 s 1: Aviation Security Act 1982 s 10 (2).

3 Ibid s 10 (1). 'Air navigation installation' means any building, works, apparatus or equipment used wholly or mainly for the purpose of assisting air traffic control or as an aid to air navigation, together with any land contiguous or adjacent to any such building, works, apparatus or equipment and used wholly or mainly for purposes connected therewith: s 38 (1).

1244. Power to require information. The Secretary of State[1] may by notice require United Kingdom aircraft operators[2], aerodrome managers[3], the occupier of land forming part of an aerodrome and any person having access to an aerodrome restricted zone[4] for the purpose of his business[5], as well as authorities responsible for United Kingdom air navigation installations[6], to provide him with information concerning the measures which they are taking to protect aerodromes, aircraft, persons and property therein and air navigation installations against acts of violence[7].

The notice may also require the person on whom it is served to give further information if at any time the information first given becomes inaccurate by any change of circumstances[8].

Any person who without reasonable excuse fails to comply with any requirement imposed by such a notice, or in furnishing any information required knowingly or recklessly makes a statement which is false in a material particular is guilty of an offence[9].

1 As to the Secretary of State see para 1032 ante.

2 For the meaning of 'aircraft operator' see para 1340 post.

3 'Manager', in relation to an aerodrome, means the person (whether the Civil Aviation Authority (CAA) (as to which see para 1044 ante), a local authority or any other person) by whom the aerodrome is managed. Aviation Security Act 1982 s 38 (1) (amended by the Airports Act 1986 s 83 (5), Sch 6 Pt I).

4 As to restricted zones see para 1245 post.

5 For the purposes of the Aviation Security Act 1982 Pt II (ss 10–24A), a person is permitted to have access to a restricted zone of an aerodrome or air navigation installation if he is permitted to enter that zone or if arrangements exist for permitting any of his employees or agents to enter that zone: s 24A (2) (added by the Aviation and Maritime Security Act 1990 s 8, Sch 1 para 16). See further para 1245 post.

6 For the purposes of the Aviation Security Act 1982 the authority responsible for an air navigation installation is either the CAA where it has provided it or uses it wholly or mainly, or, in any other case, the manager of an aerodrome by whom the air navigation installation is provided or is wholly or mainly used: s 38 (2). For the meaning of 'air navigation installation' see para 1243 note 3 ante.

7 Aviation Security Act 1982 s 11 (1) (substituted by the Aviation and Maritime Security Act 1990 Sch 1 para 2). The notice must specify a date, not earlier than seven days from the date on which the notice is served, before which the information required must be furnished: Aviation Security Act 1982 s 11 (2) (amended by the Aviation and Maritime Security Act 1990 Sch 1 para 2). The notice may at any time be revoked or varied by a further notice: Aviation Security Act 1982 s 11 (6) (as so amended).

8 Ibid s 11 (3) (as amended: see note 7 supra). The information must be furnished by a date specified in the notice, not being earlier than seven days from the date on which the change of circumstances occurs: s 11 (4) (as so amended).
9 Ibid s 11 (5) (as amended: see note 7 supra). The penalty on summary conviction is a fine not exceeding the statutory maximum and on conviction on indictment a fine or imprisonment for not more than two years, or both: s 11 (5). As to the statutory maximum see para 1005 note 11 ante. At the date at which this volume states the law, the statutory maximum is £2,000.

1245. Designation of restricted zones. The manager of an aerodrome[1], either of his own accord or when requested by the Secretary of State[2], may, or must in the latter case[3], apply to the Secretary of State for the designation of the whole or part of the aerodrome as a restricted zone[4] for the purposes of aviation security[5]. The aerodrome manager must consult the person responsible for any air navigation installation[6] to be found on the aerodrome before making the application[7]. The Secretary of State may approve the application, with or without modification[8], and designate the restricted zone accordingly[9]. The designation is either permanent or for specified days or times of day, for the whole of the aerodrome or parts thereof[10].

In relation to an air navigation installation in the United Kingdom which does not form part of an aerodrome, the above provisions apply as if reference to an aerodrome was reference to an air navigation installation[11].

Unauthorised presence in a restricted zone, whether of an aerodrome or of an air navigation installation outside an aerodrome, renders the person present in the restricted zone without lawful authority or reasonable excuse guilty of an offence[12]. Notices stating that the area concerned is a restricted zone must be posted so as to be readily seen and read by persons entering the restricted zone[13].

1 For the meaning of 'aerodrome manager' see para 1244 note 3 ante.
2 As to the Secretary of State see para 1032 ante.
3 The Secretary of State may make the designation without an application by the aerodrome manager where the latter fails to apply within the specified period when required to do so: Aviation Security Act 1982 s 11A (6) (added by the Aviation and Maritime Security Act 1990 s 8, Sch 1 para 3).
4 'Restricted zone', in relation to an aerodrome or air navigation installation, means any part of the aerodrome or installation designated under the Aviation Security Act 1982 s 11A or, where the whole of the aerodrome or installation is so designated, that aerodrome or installation: s 24A (1) (added by the Aviation and Maritime Security Act 1990 Sch 1 para 16).
5 Aviation Security Act 1982 s 11A (1) (as added: see note 3 supra). The application is made in the form and manner required by the Secretary of State: s 11A (3) (as so added).
6 For the meaning of 'air navigation installation' see para 1243 note 3 ante.
7 Aviation Security Act 1982 s 11A (2) (a) (as added: see note 3 supra). The manager must send a copy of the application to the authority responsible for the installation: s 11A (2) (b) (as so added).
8 If the Secretary of State wishes to modify the application, he must consult the aerodrome manager and the authority responsible for the air navigation installation part of the aerodrome before making the designation: ibid s 11A (5) (as added: see note 3 supra).
9 Ibid s 11A (4) (as added: see note 3 supra). The designation may be revoked or varied at any time, the provisions of s 11A (1)–(9) (as so added) applying to such revocation or variation: s 11A (10) (as so added).
10 Ibid s 11A (7) (as added: see note 3 supra).
11 Ibid s 11A (9) (as added: see note 3 supra).
12 Ibid s 21C (1) (added by the Aviation and Maritime Security Act 1990 s 5). The penalty for the offence is, on summary conviction, a fine not exceeding level 5 on the standard scale: Aviation Security Act 1982 s 21C (3) (as so added). As to the standard scale see para 1044 note 6 ante. At the date at which this volume states the law, level 5 on that scale is at £2,000.
13 Ibid s 21C (2) (as added: see note 12 supra). The unauthorised entry into a restricted zone may not be penalised if it cannot be proved that, at the material time, the notices were posted as prescribed: s 21C (2) (as so added).

1246. Power to impose restrictions in relation to aircraft. The Secretary of State[1] may direct the operator[2] of one or more aircraft registered or operating in the United Kingdom, or the manager[3] of an aerodrome in the United Kingdom not to permit persons or property on board the relevant aircraft or to come into proximity to the aircraft unless searches of those persons or that property have been carried out by constables[4] or other specified persons[5]. He may also direct the aircraft operator or the aerodrome manager not to allow the aircraft to fly unless it has been so searched[6].

The Secretary of State may further direct such an operator or manager not to let the aircraft fly unless specified modifications or alterations of the aircraft or apparatus or equipment installed in the aircraft have been carried out or specified additional apparatus or equipment is installed[7].

Any direction given to a person not to cause or permit anything to be done must be construed as requiring him to take all practicable and necessary steps in the circumstances to prevent that thing from being done[8].

Any person who without reasonable excuse fails to comply with such a direction is guilty of an offence[9] and is guilty of a further offence if, when he has been convicted of such an offence, without reasonable excuse the failure continues after the conviction[10].

1 As to the Secretary of State see para 1032 ante.
2 For the meaning of 'aircraft operator' see para 1340 post. The direction given to the aircraft operator must specify whether it relates either to all aircraft of which he is the operator or will become the operator, or to a class of such aircraft or to one or more such aircraft, whether it relates to all persons or only to one or more persons or to persons of one or more descriptions, and whether it relates to property of every description or to particular property or property of one or more descriptions: Aviation Security Act 1982 s 12 (5). A direction may be given to a person appearing to be about to become such an operator, although it may not take effect until he actually becomes such an operator: see s 12 (8).
3 For the meaning of 'aerodrome manager' see para 1244 note 3 ante. The direction given to the aerodrome manager must specify whether it relates to all aircraft in any part of the aerodrome at the time when the direction is given or at any subsequent time or to a class of such aircraft, whether it relates to all persons or only to one or more persons or persons of one or more descriptions and whether it relates to property of every description or to particular property, or property of one or more descriptions: Aviation Security Act 1982 s 12 (6). A direction may be given to a person appearing to be about to become such a manager although it may not take effect until he actually becomes such a manager: see s 12 (8).
4 'Constable' includes any person having the powers and privileges of a constable: ibid s 38 (1).
5 Ibid s 12 (1) (a).
6 Ibid s 12 (1) (b).
7 Ibid s 12 (2). Before giving such a direction, the Secretary of State must inform the Civil Aviation Authority (CAA) (as to which see para 1044 ante) of the proposed requirements and take account of any advice which the CAA may give him in respect of those proposals: s 12 (3). The modifications, alterations or installation of additional apparatus or equipment must be carried out within the period specified in the direction which does not take effect before the end of that period: s 12 (4). As to limitations on the scope of the direction see para 1251 post.
8 Ibid s 12 (7).
9 Ibid s 12 (9) (amended by the Aviation and Maritime Security Act 1990 s 8, Sch 1 para 4). The penalty is, on summary conviction, a fine not exceeding the statutory maximum, and on conviction on indictment, a fine or imprisonment for a term not exceeding two years or both: Aviation Security Act 1982 s 12 (9). As to the statutory maximum see para 1005 note 11 ante. At the date at which this volume states the law, the statutory maximum is £2,000.
10 Ibid s 12 (10) (added by the Aviation and Maritime Security Act 1990 Sch 1 para 4); the penalty is on summary conviction a fine not exceeding one-tenth of level 5 on the standard scale for each day on which the failure continues: Aviation Security Act 1982 s 12 (10) (as so added). As to the standard scale see para 1044 note 6 ante. At the date at which this volume states the law, level 5 on that scale is at £2,000.

1247. Power to require aerodrome managers to promote searches. The Secretary of State[1] may direct the manager of an aerodrome to use his best endeavours to secure that searches of the aerodrome and aircraft, persons or property in any part of the aerodrome are searched by constables or other specified persons[2]. Where such a direction is in force, any constable or specified person who has reasonable cause to suspect that certain dangerous articles statutorily banned[3] are or may be brought into any part of the aerodrome may, without a warrant, search any part of the aerodrome or any aircraft, vehicle, goods, property or person for the time being in any part of the aerodrome[4]. For that purpose, he may enter any building or works and enter upon any land in the aerodrome even by force and he may stop any such aircraft, vehicle, goods, property or person and detain it or him as need be[5].

Any person who without reasonable excuse fails to comply with such a direction or who intentionally obstructs a person acting in the exercise of a power so conferred on him is guilty of an offence[6]. Where a person is convicted of the offence of failure to comply, he is guilty of a further offence if without reasonable excuse the failure continues after the conviction[7].

1 As to the Secretary of State see para 1032 ante.
2 Aviation Security Act 1982 s 13 (1), (2). For the meaning of 'aerodrome manager' and 'constable' see respectively paras 1244 note 3 and 1246 note 4 ante.
3 As to offences in relation to certain dangerous articles such as firearms, explosives etc see the Aviation Security Act 1982 s 4; and para 1670 post. 'Firearm' includes an air gun or air pistol: s 38 (1).
4 Ibid s 13 (3).
5 Ibid s 13 (3) (a), (b).
6 Ibid s 13 (4) (a), (b) (amended by the Aviation and Maritime Security Act 1990 s 8, Sch 1 para 5). The penalty is on summary conviction a fine not exceeding the statutory maximum and on conviction on indictment a fine or imprisonment for a term not exceeding two years or both: Aviation Security Act 1982 s 13 (4) (i), (ii). As to the statutory maximum see para 1005 note 11 ante. At the date at which this volume states the law, the statutory maximum is £2,000.
7 Ibid s 13 (4A) (added by the Aviation and Maritime Security Act 1990 Sch 1 para 5). The penalty on summary conviction is a fine not exceeding one-tenth of level 5 on the standard scale for each day on which the failure continues: Aviation Security Act 1982 s 13 (4A) (as so added). As to the standard scale see para 1044 note 6 ante. At the date at which this volume states the law, level 5 on that scale is at £2,000.

1248. Power to require other persons to promote searches. A person who occupies any land forming part of an aerodrome in the United Kingdom or is permitted to have access to a restricted zone[1] of such an aerodrome for the purposes of his business activities may be directed by the Secretary of State[2] to use his best endeavours to secure that such searches as are specified in the direction are carried out by constables or other specified persons[3].

A direction given to the occupier of the land must specify that the searches concern the land which he occupies and persons or property which may at any time be on that land[4]. In so far as a person permitted access to a restricted zone is concerned, the direction must specify that the searches concern any land which he occupies outside the aerodrome for the purposes of his business and persons or property which may at any time be on that land[5].

Any person who without reasonable excuse fails to comply with such a direction is guilty of an offence[6] and is guilty of a further offence if, when he has been convicted of such an offence, without reasonable excuse the failure continues after the conviction[7].

1 As to restricted zones see para 1245 ante.

2 As to the Secretary of State see para 1032 ante.

3 Aviation Security Act 1982 s 13A (1) (added by the Aviation and Maritime Security Act 1990 s 2). For the meaning of 'constable' see para 1246 note 4 ante.

4 Aviation Security Act 1982 s 13A (2) (a) (as added: see note 3 supra).

5 Ibid s 13A (2) (b) (as added: see note 3 supra).

6 Ibid s 13A (3) (as added: see note 3 supra). The penalty is on summary conviction a fine not exceeding the statutory maximum and on conviction on indictment a fine or imprisonment for a term not exceeding two years or both: s 13A (3) (as so added). As to the statutory maximum see para 1005 note 11 ante. At the date at which this volume states the law, the statutory maximum is £2,000.

7 Ibid s 13A (4) (as added: see note 3 supra). The penalty on summary conviction is a fine not exceeding one-tenth of level 5 on the standard scale for each day on which the failure continues: s 13A (4) (as so added). As to the standard scale see para 1044 note 6 ante. At the date at which this volume states the law, level 5 on that scale is at £2,000.

1249. Other directions given by the Secretary of State. The Secretary of State[1] may direct an aircraft operator[2], an aerodrome manager[3], the occupier of any land forming part of an aerodrome or a person authorised to have access to a restricted zone[4] for the purpose of his business activities to take specified measures, in respect of aircraft, aerodromes, specified land or specified activities carried on by the relevant person in the restricted zone, as the case may be[5]. Such measures may include the provision of personnel charged with the duty of guarding against acts of violence[6] aircraft, the aerodrome, persons or property in any part of the aerodrome or that part under the control of the person so directed; and in respect of a person having access to a restricted zone, to guard any land outside the aerodrome which he occupies for business purposes, vehicles, equipment and goods connected with those purposes and any aircraft under his control[7].

Such a direction is of either a general or a specific character[8], may not require any search or modification or alteration of aircraft or installation of equipment or apparatus on such aircraft[9] and may be given to a person appearing to become one of those to whom such a direction may be given[10]. Such a direction may not be construed as requiring any person directed to construct, execute, alter, demolish or remove any building or works on land outside the aerodrome to do anything which would be actionable at the suit of persons having rights on that land[11].

Any person who, without reasonable excuse, fails to comply with such a direction or, intentionally, interferes with any building constructed or works executed on any land or with anything installed on, under, over or across any land, in compliance with such a direction, is guilty of an offence[12]. Where a person is convicted of an offence of failure to comply with such a direction, he is guilty of a further offence if, without reasonable excuse, the failure continues after the conviction[13].

1 As to the Secretary of State see para 1032 ante.

2 For the meaning of 'aircraft operator' see para 1340 post. The direction may concern all aircraft registered or operating in the United Kingdom of which he is the operator at the time when the direction is given or any subsequent time, or such aircraft or class of aircraft as specified by the direction: Aviation Security Act 1982 s 14 (1A) (a) (added by the Aviation and Maritime Security Act 1990 s 3).

3 For the meaning of 'manager' see para 1244 note 3 ante.

4 As to restricted zones see para 1245 ante.

5 See the Aviation Security Act 1982 s 14 (1), (1A) (substituted and added respectively by the Aviation and Maritime Security Act 1990 s 3). As to limitation on the scope of such a direction see para 1251 post.

6 For the meaning of 'acts of violence' see para 1243 note 2 ante.

7 See the Aviation Security Act 1982 s 14 (2) (as substituted: see note 5 supra).

8 Ibid s 14 (3).
9 Ibid s 14 (5). As to searches see paras 1247, 1248 ante; as to modifications or alterations to aircraft, installation of equipment or apparatus on aircraft see para 1246 ante.
10 Aviation Security Act 1982 s 14 (6) (as amended: see note 5 supra); the direction takes effect only when the person concerned becomes such a person to whom s 14 applies: s 14 (6) (as so amended).
11 Ibid s 16 (6) (substituted by the Aviation and Maritime Security Act 1990 s 8, Sch 1 para 8). The ownership of any property is not affected by reason only that it is placed on or under, or affixed to, any land in compliance with such a direction: Aviation Security Act 1982 s 14 (8).
12 Ibid s 14 (7) (amended by the Aviation and Security Act 1990 Sch 1 para 6). The penalty is on summary conviction a fine not exceeding the statutory maximum and on conviction on indictment a fine or imprisonment for a term not exceeding two years or both: Aviation Security Act 1982 s 14 (7). As to the statutory maximum see para 1005 note 11 ante. At the date at which this volume states the law, the statutory maximum is £2,000.
13 Ibid s 14 (7A) (added by the Aviation and Maritime Security Act 1990 Sch 1 para 6). The penalty is on summary conviction a fine not exceeding one-tenth of level 5 on the standard scale for each day on which the failure continues: Aviation Security Act 1982 s 14 (7A) (as so added). As to the standard scale see para 1044 note 6 ante. At the date at which this volume states the law, level 5 on that scale is at £2,000.

(iii) Directions

1250. Matters included in directions. Apart from the provision of personnel to guard aircraft, aerodromes, persons or property[1] against acts of violence[2], the Aviation Security Act 1982 provides for a number of matters which may be included in certain directions[3].

Thus a direction imposing restrictions in relation to aircraft[4] or requiring the promotion of searches[5] may specify the minimum number of persons who may carry out searches, their qualifications, the manner in which any such search is to be carried out and any apparatus, equipment or other aids to be used for such purpose[6]. The direction may also require the person concerned to inform the chief officer of police for the police area in which the searches are to be carried out that the Secretary of State[7] considers it appropriate that constables should be authorised to carry, and should carry, firearms when carrying out the searches[8].

Where a direction requires modifications or alterations to aircraft or the installation of additional apparatus or equipment on an aircraft[9], it must include the requirement that such actions are undertaken by persons approved by the Civil Aviation Authority (CAA)[10].

Any other direction[11] may specify the minimum number of persons to be employed for the purposes of any measures to be taken by the person to whom the direction is given and the qualifications which the persons so employed must have as well as any apparatus, equipment or other aids to be used for those purposes[12].

1 See para 1247 ante.
2 For the meaning of 'acts of violence' see para 1243 note 2 ante.
3 See the Aviation Security Act 1982 s 15 (amended by the Aviation and Maritime Security Act 1990 s 8, Sch 1 para 7).
4 See para 1246 ante.
5 See paras 1247, 1248 ante.
6 Aviation Security Act 1982 s 15 (1) (as amended: see note 3 supra).
7 As to the Secretary of State see para 1032 ante.
8 Aviation Security Act 1982 s 15 (5) (substituted by the Aviation and Maritime Security Act 1990 Sch 1 para 7). For the meaning of 'constables' see para 1246 note 4 ante.
9 See para 1246 ante.
10 Aviation Security Act 1982 s 15 (2) (as substituted: see note 8 supra). As to the CAA see para 1044 ante.

11 Ie a direction made under the Aviation Security Act 1982 s 14: see para 1249 ante.
12 Ibid s 15 (4) (as amended: see note 3 supra).

1251. Limitations on scope of directions. A direction by the Secretary of State[1] may not require or authorise any person to carry a firearm[2].

Such a direction may not apply to any military, customs or police aircraft[3].

Such a direction may not apply to an aircraft operated by a foreign government unless it is being used for the carriage of passengers or cargo for reward[4].

Such a direction may not be construed as authorising an act of violence[5] although constables[6] or other specified persons[7] may use reasonable force when exercising powers conferred on them by the Aviation Security Act 1982[8].

Such a direction has no effect outside the United Kingdom, save in relation to aircraft registered in the United Kingdom, and may not require anything to be done (or not done) in contravention of any provision of the local law, save for any such provision relating to breach of contract[9].

No derogation from any exemption or immunity of the Crown in relation to Part II of the Aviation Security Act 1982 is permissible[10].

1 'Direction' in this context means a direction under the Aviation Security Act 1982 s 12, 13, 13A or 14: s 16 (8) (amended by the Aviation and Maritime Security Act 1990 s 8, Sch 1 para 8). See paras 1246–1249 ante; as to the Secretary of State see para 1032 ante.
2 Aviation Security Act 1982 s 16 (1). As to exceptions concerning constables see para 1250 ante.
3 Ibid s 16 (2).
4 Ibid s 16 (3). As to the carriage of passengers and cargo for reward see para 1272 ante.
5 For the meaning of 'act of violence' see para 1243 note 2 ante.
6 For the meaning of 'constables' see para 1246 note 4 ante.
7 Ie persons specified in the direction exercising powers conferred by the Aviation Security Act 1982 s 7 (1) or 13 (3): see para 1247 ante.
8 Ibid s 16 (4) (as amended: see note 1 supra).
9 Ibid s 16 (5).
10 Ibid s 16 (7). Part II of the Act comprises ss 10–24A.

1252. General or urgent directions. A direction[1] need not be addressed to a particular person, but may be framed in general terms applicable to all persons to whom such a direction may be given or to any class of such persons to which that particular person belongs[2].

Where it appears to the Secretary of State[3] that an exception from a given direction is urgently needed, he may notify, otherwise than in writing, the person subject to the direction and authorise him to disregard, within the specified terms, such a direction[4]. The notification ceases to have effect either when a direction, in writing, is given to that same person varying or revoking the original direction or at the end of a period of 30 days from the date on which the notification was given if no new direction in writing is given[5].

1 Ie any direction made under the Aviation Security Act 1982 s 12, 13, 13A or 14; see paras 1246–1249 ante.
2 Ibid s 17 (1) (amended by the Aviation and Maritime Security Act 1990 s 8, Sch 1 para 9).
3 As to the Secretary of State see para 1032 ante.
4 See the Aviation Security Act 1982 s 17 (2), (4) (s 17 (2) amended by the Aviation and Maritime Security Act 1990 Sch 1 para 9).
5 Aviation Security Act 1982 s 17 (3).

1253. Effects of directions. Where a direction[1] requires anything to be done or not done in the United Kingdom, the direction has effect notwithstanding anything contained either in any contract[2] or in any statute or rule of law; thus no proceedings in any United Kingdom court[3], whether civil or criminal, lie against a person carrying out such a direction[4].

Where a direction requires anything to be done or not done outside the United Kingdom, the direction has effect notwithstanding anything contained in any contract; thus where there is inconsistency between the direction and a contract and without prejudice to any proceedings in a court other than a United Kingdom court, the direction must be construed as requiring compliance with it even though such compliance would be in breach of contract[5]. No proceedings for breach of contract in a United Kingdom court lie against a person complying with the direction outside the United Kingdom provided the contract is a United Kingdom contract[6].

1 As to such directions see paras 1246–1249 ante. Reference to a direction in the Aviation Security Act 1982 s 19 includes a reference to an enforcement notice: s 19 (4A) (added by the Aviation and Maritime Security Act 1990 s 8, Sch 1 para 10); as to enforcement notices see para 1255–1257 post.
2 The contract may be a United Kingdom contract or not; a 'United Kingdom contract' means a contract which is either expressed to have effect in accordance with the law of the United Kingdom or of part of the United Kingdom or, not being so expressed, is a contract the law applicable to which is the law of the United Kingdom or of part of the United Kingdom: Aviation Security Act 1982 s 19 (5) (amended by the Contracts (Applicable Law) Act 1990 s 5, Sch 4 para 5).
3 'United Kingdom court' means a court exercising jurisdiction in any part of the United Kingdom under the law of the United Kingdom or of part of the United Kingdom: ibid s 19 (5).
4 Ibid s 19 (2).
5 Ibid s 19 (3).
6 Ibid s 19 (4).

1254. Objections to directions. Any person required by a direction under the Aviation Security Act 1982 to construct, execute, alter, demolish or remove a building or other works[1] may by notice served on the Secretary of State[2] object to the direction on the grounds that the measures to be taken are unnecessary, or excessively onerous or inconvenient and must be modified[3].

The Secretary of State, after considering the grounds of the objection[4], may either confirm the direction as originally given or with modifications or may withdraw the direction. The direction takes effect when it is confirmed, with or without modifications, by a notice served on the objector[5].

1 See para 1249 ante.
2 As to the Secretary of State see para 1032 ante.
3 Aviation Security Act 1982 s 18 (1), (2). There may not be any objection where the direction states that the measures are urgently required and that it is to take effect immediately: s 18 (1) (b). The notice of objection must be served within 30 days of the date on which the direction was given: s 18 (2). The objection suspends the effects of the direction: see s 18 (3).
4 The objector may require to be heard: see ibid s 18 (3).
5 Ibid s 18 (3).

(iv) Enforcement Notices

1255. Enforcement notices. Where an authorised person[1] believes that a person has failed to comply with any general requirement[2] of a direction given to him under the Aviation Security Act 1982[3], he may serve on that person an enforcement notice specifying those requirements which have not been complied with and the measures that ought to be taken to remedy the situation[4].

The enforcement notice may specify in greater detail the measures which were only described in general terms in the direction[5]. It may also be so framed as to give a choice between different ways of complying with the specified general requirements[6].

Where a direction imposes restrictions in relation to aircraft[7], the enforcement notice must require the person to whom the direction was given not to effect searches until the specified measures have been taken[8] within a reasonable specified period[9]. Similarly, where a direction requires aerodrome managers or other persons to promote searches[10] or to take other measures[11], the enforcement notice must either require that the specified measures are taken within a specified period[12] or that specified things are not done until the specified measures are taken[13].

Any person who, without reasonable excuse, fails to comply with an enforcement notice is guilty of an offence[14] and is guilty of a further offence if, after such conviction, the failure to comply is continued without reasonable excuse[15]. Any person who intentionally interferes with any building constructed or works executed or anything installed in compliance with an enforcement notice is guilty of an offence[16].

1 'Authorised person' means a person authorised in writing by the Secretary of State for the purposes of the Aviation Security Act 1982 Pt II (ss 10–24A): s 24A (1) (added by the Aviation and Maritime Security Act 1990 s 8, Sch 1 para 16). As to the Secretary of State see para 1032 ante.

2 For the purposes of the Aviation Security Act 1982 s 18A (added by the Aviation and Maritime Security Act 1990 s 4), a requirement of a direction given by the Secretary of State under s 12, 13, 13A or 14 (see paras 1246–1249 ante) is a 'general requirement' if the provision imposing the requirement has been included in two or more directions given to different persons and is framed in general terms applicable to all the persons to whom those directions are given: s 18A (2) (as so added).

3 Ie under ibid s 12, 13, 13A or 14; see note 2 supra.

4 Ibid s 18A (1) (as added: see note 2 supra). Before he may serve the notice, the authorised person must inform the Civil Aviation Authority (CAA) of the proposed measures and take account of any advice the CAA may give him: s 18A (3) (as so added). As to the CAA see para 1044 ante.

5 Ibid s 18B (1) (added by the Aviation and Maritime Security Act 1990 s 4). The enforcement notice may not impose a requirement which could not have been imposed by the Secretary of State: Aviation Security Act 1982 s 18B (1) (as so added).

6 Ibid s 18B (2) (as added: see note 5 supra).

7 See para 1246 ante.

8 Aviation Security Act 1982 s 18B (3) (as added: see note 5 supra).

9 Ibid s 18B(4) (as added: see note 5 supra).

10 See paras 1247, 1248 ante.

11 See para 1249 ante.

12 Aviation Security Act 1982 s 18B (5) (a) (as added: see note 5 supra). Where the measures consist in construction, execution, alteration, demolition or removal of buildings or other works, the period must be at least 30 days from the date of service of the notice, and seven days in any other case: s 18B (5) (a) (i), (ii) (as so added).

13 Ibid s 18B (5) (b) (as added: see note 5 supra).

14 Ibid s 18C (1) (added by the Aviation and Maritime Security Act 1990 s 4). The penalty is on summary conviction a fine not exceeding the statutory maximum and on conviction on indictment a fine: Aviation Security Act 1982 s 18C (1) (a), (b) (as so added). The 'statutory maximum' is the prescribed sum within the meaning of the Magistrates' Courts Act 1980 s 32: Aviation Security Act 1982 s 38. As to that sum see para 1005 note 11 ante. At the date at which this volume states the law, the prescribed sum is £2,000 .

15 Ibid s 18C (2) (as added: see note 14 supra). The penalty is on summary conviction a fine not exceeding one-tenth of level 5 on the standard scale for each day on which the failure continues: s 18C (2) (as so added). As to the standard scale see para 1044 note 6 ante. At the date at which this volume states the law, level 5 on that scale is at £2,000 .

16 Ibid s 18C (3) (as added: see note 14 supra). The penalty is on summary conviction a fine not exceeding the statutory maximum and on conviction on indictment a fine: s 18C (3) (as so added). See also note 14 supra.

1256. Effects of enforcement notices. The ownership of any property is not affected by being placed on, or under, or affixed to, any land in compliance with an enforcement notice[1].

Where a person is served with an enforcement notice, that person is not considered, for the purposes of prosecution, to have failed to comply with the direction[2] by reason of the matters specified in the notice[3]. The fact that the notice specifies certain general requirements[4] of the direction as not having been complied with may not be, in any proceedings, evidence that any other requirement of the direction has been complied with[5].

1 Aviation Security Act 1982 s 18E (3) (added by the Aviation and Maritime Security Act 1990 s 4).
2 'Direction' in the Aviation Security Act 1982 s 18E (as added: see note 1 supra) means a direction under s 12, 13, 13A or 14 of the Act: s 18E (7) (as so added); see further paras 1246–1249 ante.
3 Ibid s 18E (4) (as added: see note 1 supra); this provision does not apply to any proceedings started before the service of the notice: s 18E (5) (as so added).
4 For the meaning of 'general requirement' see para 1255 note 2 ante.
5 Aviation Security Act 1982 s 18E (6) (as added: see note 1 supra)

1257. Objections to enforcement notices. The person on whom an enforcement notice[1] is served may serve on the Secretary of State[2] a notice in writing of his objection to the enforcement notice[3]. The grounds of the objection must be specified in the notice and may be either that the general requirements[4] of the direction had been complied with, or that a requirement imposed by the enforcement notice could not have been imposed by the relevant direction or that such a requirement is either unnecessary or is excessively onerous or inconvenient and should be modified[5].

The Secretary of State must consider the grounds of the objection[6] and serve on the objector a notice in writing which either confirms the enforcement notice as originally served or with modifications or cancels the enforcement notice[7].

When an objection to an enforcement notice has been served, the latter does not take effect until confirmed, with or without modifications, by the Secretary of State[8], save where the enforcement notice required the recipient not to cause or permit things to be done[9] in respect of aircraft[10] or searches[11].

1 As to enforcement notices see para 1255 ante.
2 As to the Secretary of State see para 1032 ante.
3 Aviation Security Act 1982 s 18D (1) (added by the Aviation and Maritime Security Act 1990 s 4). The notice must be served within seven days of the date on which the enforcement notice was served, save where the enforcement notice specifies measures involving buildings and other works, in which case the period for service is 30 days: s 18D (2).
4 For the meaning of 'general requirements' see para 1255 note 2 ante.
5 Aviation Security Act 1982 s 18D (3) (as added: see note 3 supra).
6 The objector is entitled to be heard by a person appointed by the Secretary of State: ibid s 18D (4) (as added: see note 3 supra).
7 Ibid s 18D (4) (as added: see note 3 supra).
8 Ibid s 18D (5) (b) (as added: see note 3 supra).
9 As to the construction of an enforcement notice requiring a person not to cause or permit anything to be done see para 1255 text and notes 7–9 ante.
10 See para 1246 ante.
11 Aviation Security Act 1982 s 18D (5) (a) (as added: see note 3 supra). As to searches see paras 1247, 1248 ante.

(v) Miscellaneous

1258. Inspection of aircraft and aerodromes. In order to enable the Secretary of State[1] to determine whether to give a direction under Part II of the Aviation Security Act 1982[2] or whether such a direction or enforcement notice[3] is being or has been complied with, an authorised person[4] has power to inspect aircraft registered or operating in the United Kingdom, aerodromes in the United Kingdom or land outside such an aerodrome and occupied for business purposes by a person who for business purposes either also occupies land within an aerodrome or has access to a restricted zone of an aerodrome[5].

Inspectors may test property found in aircraft[6], subject aerodromes and property found thereon or on relevant land outside the aerodrome to such tests as they think necessary[7], ascertain and test any security practice or procedure established by the person in charge[8] and require information from aircraft operators, aerodrome managers or land occupiers[9]. For inspection purposes, an authorised person may, without using force, enter an aircraft and detain it, enter any building or works and enter upon any land in an aerodrome as well as on land outside an aerodrome[10].

Any person who without reasonable excuse fails to furnish information as required by an authorised person or knowingly or recklessly makes a statement which is false in a material particular is guilty of an offence[11].

1 As to the Secretary of State see para 1032 ante.
2 See the Aviation Security Act 1982 ss 10–24A.
3 As to enforcement notices see para 1255 ante.
4 For the meaning of 'authorised person' see para 1255 note 1 ante.
5 Aviation Security Act 1982 s 20 (1) (amended by the Aviation and Maritime Security Act 1990 s 8, Sch 1 para 11). As to restricted zones see para 1245 ante.
6 Aircraft themselves may not be tested, nor may any apparatus or equipment installed in them; see note 7 infra.
7 Aviation Security Act 1982 s 20 (2) (a) (as amended: see note 5 supra).
8 Aviation Security Act 1982 s 20 (2) (aa) (added by the Aviation and Maritime Security Act 1990 Sch 1 para 11).
9 Aviation Security Act 1982 s 20 (2) (b) (as amended: see note 5 supra).
10 Ibid s 20 (3), (4) (s 20 (3) as amended: see note 5 supra).
11 Ibid s 20 (5) (as amended: see note 5 supra). The penalty is, on summary conviction, a fine not exceeding the statutory maximum and on conviction on indictment a fine or imprisonment for a term not exceeding two years or both: s 20 (5). The statutory maximum is the prescribed sum within the meaning of the Magistrates' Courts Act 1980 s 32: Aviation Security Act 1982 s 38. As to that sum see para 1005 note 11 ante. At the date at which this volume states the law, the prescribed sum is £2,000 .

1259. Air navigation installations. Certain provisions of the Aviation Security Act 1982[1] have effect in relation to air navigation installations[2] in the United Kingdom[3].

Where an air navigation installation does not form part of an aerodrome, those provisions have effect as if any reference in them to an aerodrome were a reference to such an air navigation installation and any reference to the manager of an aerodrome were a reference to the authority responsible for such an air navigation installation[4].

Where an air navigation installation is part of an aerodrome in the United Kingdom, those provisions have effect as if reference in them to an aerodrome were a reference either to an aerodrome or to an air navigation installation which forms part of an aerodrome or to so much of an aerodrome as does not consist of an air navigation installation[5].

The Secretary of State[6] may give certain directions to the authority responsible for one or more air navigation installations so as to relate to all installations for which it is responsible or to specified installations or classes of installations[7].

1 Ie the Aviation Security Act 1982 ss 11, 13, 13A, 14–16, 20.
2 For the meaning of 'air navigation installation' see para 1243 note 3 ante.
3 Aviation Security Act 1982 s 21 (1) (amended by the Aviation and Maritime Security Act 1990 s 8, Sch 1 para 12). Modification of those provisions relating to the service of notices and the giving of directions is provided by the Aviation Security Act 1982 s 21 (4).
4 Ibid s 21 (2). As to the authority responsible for an air navigation installation see para 1244 note 6 ante. This provision does not apply in relation to a direction under s 13 (3) (see para 1247 ante), except in certain circumstances: see s 21 (5).
5 Ibid s 21 (3) (a)–(c); and accordingly a notice under s 11 (see para 1244 ante) or a direction under s 13 or 14 (see paras 1247, 1249 ante) may be served or given in respect of the whole of the aerodrome, in respect of the air navigation installation separately or in respect of so much of the aerodrome as does not consist of an air navigation installation: s 21 (3). This provision does not apply in relation to a direction under s 13 (3) (see para 1247 ante), except in certain circumstances: see s 21 (5).
6 As to the Secretary of State see para 1032 ante.
7 Aviation Security Act 1982 s 21 (6).

1260. Duty to report occurrences. For the purpose of protecting aircraft, aerodromes and air navigation installations[1] against acts of violence[2], the Secretary of State[3] may make regulations[4] requiring specified persons to report to him any occurrence of a specified description, including occurrences taking place outside the United Kingdom which concern aircraft registered in the United Kingdom[5]. The regulations may also provide for offences, such as false statements knowingly or recklessly made, and penalties[6].

1 For the meaning of 'air navigation installation' see para 1243 note 3 ante.
2 For the meaning of 'acts of violence' see para 1243 note 2 ante.
3 As to the Secretary of State see para 1032 ante.
4 At the date at which this volume states the law, no such regulations had been made.
5 Aviation Security Act 1982 s 21G (1), (4) (added by the Aviation and Maritime Security Act 1990 s 7). Before making the regulations, the Secretary of State must consult any organisation representing persons who may be affected by such regulations: s 21G (2) (as so added). The regulations must specify the manner in which, and the period within which, a report must be made: s 21G (1) (as so added) .
6 Ibid s 21G (3) (as added: see note 5 supra). The maximum penalties which can be prescribed by regulations are: (1) in the case of knowingly or recklessly making a false statement, on summary conviction a fine not exceeding the statutory maximum, and on conviction on indictment a fine or imprisonment for up to two years or both; and (2) in any other case, on summary conviction a fine not exceeding level 5 on the standard scale: s 21G (3) (a), (b) (as so added). As to the statutory maximum see para 1005 note 11 ante; at the date at which this volume states the law, it is set at £2,000. As to the standard scale see para 1044 note 6 ante; at the date at which this volume states the law, level 5 on the scale is at £2,000.

1261. Air cargo agents. For the purpose of protecting aircraft, aerodromes and air navigation installations[1] against acts of violence[2], the Secretary of State[3] may make regulations[4] in relation to persons, known as air cargo agents, who carry on a business of handling cargo[5] to be delivered to an aircraft operator[6] for carriage from any United Kingdom aerodrome by a civil aircraft[7].

The regulations may provide for the maintenance of a list of approved air cargo agents[8], for the authorisation for such approved air cargo agents to enter a restricted zone of an aerodrome for business purposes[9] and for different rules to apply to different classes of air cargo agents, or to different cases[10].

1 For the meaning of 'air navigation installation' see para 1243 note 3 ante.
2 For the meaning of 'acts of violence' see para 1243 note 2 ante.
3 As to the Secretary of State see para 1032 ante.
4 At the date at which this volume states the law, no such regulations had been made.
5 'Cargo' includes stores and mail and 'stores' means any goods intended for sale or use on an aircraft including spare parts and other articles of equipment, whether or not for immediate fitting: Aviation Security Act 1982 s 21F (6) (added by the Aviation and Maritime Security Act 1990 s 6).
6 As to aircraft operators see para 1340 post.
7 Aviation Security Act 1982 s 21F (1) (as added: see note 5 supra). Before making the regulations, the Secretary of State must consult organisations representing persons who may be affected by the regulations: s 21F (3).
8 Ibid s 21F (2) (a) (as added: see note 5 supra). The regulations would specify how a name would be included or removed from the list in accordance with criteria defined in the regulations: s 21F (2) (a) (as so added).
9 Ibid s 21F (2)(b) (as added: see note 5 supra). As to restricted zones see para 1245 ante.
10 Ibid s 21F (2) (d)–(f) (as added: see note 5 supra).

1262. Compensation and reimbursement of expenses. If the value of any land to which a person is entitled is depreciated in consequence of the taking of measures[1] in compliance with a particular direction[2] or enforcement notice[3], or the person having such an interest suffers loss in consequence of such measures by being disturbed in his enjoyment of any of that land, that person is entitled to compensation equal to the amount of the depreciation or loss[4]. If any land other than the land on which the measures are taken is injuriously affected by the taking of those measures, any person having an interest in that other land is entitled to compensation equal to the amount of any loss he suffers in consequence[5].

Any such compensation to which a person is entitled is payable to him by the person who took the measures[6].

1 Ie measures taken by the person to whom the direction was given or on whom the enforcement notice was served (see paras 1249, 1255 ante): Aviation Security Act 1982 s 22 (1) (amended by the Aviation and Maritime Security Act 1990 s 8, Sch 1 para 13).
2 See para 1249 ante.
3 See para 1255 ante.
4 Aviation Security Act 1982 s 22 (2). For further provision regarding the details and calculation of compensation, including the power to make regulations in that behalf, see s 22 (5), Sch 1. At the date at which this volume states the law, no such regulations were in force.
5 Ibid s 22 (3).
6 Ibid s 22 (4) (as amended: see note 1 supra).

1263. Offences relating to security at aerodromes. The Aviation Security Act 1982 (as amended by the Aviation and Maritime Security Act 1990) provides for a number of offences in order to ensure a better protection of aircraft, aerodromes and air navigation installations.

It is thus an offence:
(1) to fail to comply without reasonable excuse with a direction or an enforcement notice given or served under Part II of the 1982 Act[1];
(2) to obstruct intentionally a person acting in the exercise of his functions or an authorised person in the exercise of his powers[2];
(3) to interfere intentionally with buildings constructed or works executed in compliance with such a direction or enforcement order[3];

(4) to fail to give the required information to the Secretary of State or an authorised person[4]; and

(5) to furnish information false in a material particular, knowingly or recklessly[5].

The penalty for these offences is, on summary conviction, a fine not exceeding the statutory maximum and, on conviction on indictment, a fine or imprisonment for a term not exceeding two years or both[6].

It is a further offence to continue to fail to comply with such a direction or enforcement order after having been convicted for such a failure. The penalty is, on summary conviction, a fine not exceeding one-tenth of level 5 on the standard scale for each day on which the failure continues[7].

It is also an offence:

(a) to make, knowingly or recklessly, false statements relating to baggage, cargo or stores[8] or in connection with identity documents[9];

(b) to go, or to remain without authorisation, on any part of a restricted zone of an aerodrome or of an air navigation installation outside an aerodrome[10];

(c) to get into or onto an aircraft without authorisation or to remain on an aircraft after being requested to leave[11]; and

(d) to pretend to be an authorised person[12].

The penalty for these last offences is, on summary conviction, a fine not exceeding level 5 on the standard scale[13].

1 See the Aviation Security Act 1982 ss 12 (9), 13 (4) (a), 13A (3) and 14 (7) (ss 12 (9), 13 (4) (a), 14 (7) amended by the Aviation and Maritime Security Act 1990 s 8, Sch 1 paras 4 (2), 5 (2), 6 (2) respectively; the 1982 Act s 13A (3) added by the 1990 Act s 3); and see paras 1245–1249 ante. The 1982 Act Pt II comprises ss 10–24A.

2 See the Aviation Security Act 1982 ss 13 (4) (b) (amended by the Aviation and Maritime Security Act 1990 s 8, Sch 1 para 5 (2)), 21E (1) (a) (added by the 1990 Act s 5); and see paras 1247–1258 ante.

3 See the Aviation Security Act 1982 s 14 (7) (b) (amended by the Aviation and Maritime Security Act 1990 Sch 1 para 6 (2)); and see para 1249 ante.

4 See the Aviation Security Act 1982 ss 11 (5) (a), 20 (5) (b) (amended by the Aviation and Maritime Security Act 1990 Sch 1 paras 2 (6), 11 (5) respectively); and see paras 1244, 1258 ante.

5 See the Aviation Security Act 1982 ss 11 (5) (b), 20 (5) (c); and see paras 1244, 1258 ante.

6 See the Aviation Security Act 1982 ss 11 (5), 12 (9), 13 (4), 13A (3), 14 (7), 20 (5) and 21E (2) (all as added or amended: see notes 1–4 supra); and see paras 1244, 1246–1249, 1258 ante. As to the statutory maximum see para 1005 note 11 ante; at the date at which this volume states the law, it is set at £2,000.

7 See the Aviation Security Act 1982 ss 12 (10), 13 (4A), 13A (4) and 14 (7A) (ss 12 (10), 13 (4A), 14 (7A) added by the Aviation and Maritime Security Act 1990 Sch 1 paras 4 (3), 5 (3), 6 (3) respectively; the 1982 Act s 13A (4) as added: see note 1 supra) ; and see paras 1246–1249 ante.

8 See the Aviation Security Act 1982 s 21A (1) (added by the Aviation and Maritime Security Act 1990 s 5).

9 See the Aviation Security Act 1982 s 21B (1) (as added: see note 8 supra).

10 See ibid s 21C (1) (as added: see note 8 supra) and see para 1245 ante.

11 See ibid s 21D (1) (as added: see note 8 supra).

12 See ibid s 21E (1) (b) (as added: see note 8 supra).

13 See ibid ss 21A (4), 21B (5), 21C (3), 21D (2) and 21E (3) (all as added: see note 8 supra). As to the standard scale see para 1044 note 6 ante. At the date at which this volume states the law, level 5 on that scale is at £2,000.

5. AIRCRAFT

(1) INTRODUCTORY

1264. Introduction: Air Navigation Order. The Air Navigation Order 1989[1], which has been amplified in many respects by regulations made under it[2], applies, unless the context otherwise requires, to or in relation to all aircraft registered in the United Kingdom wherever they may be[3], and, in so far as they apply to other aircraft, to all other aircraft when within the United Kingdom or on, or in the neighbourhood of, an offshore installation[4]. The Civil Aviation Authority (CAA)[5] may direct that specified provisions of the order and of regulations made under it are to apply to British-controlled aircraft not registered in the United Kingdom[6].

Many of the provisions of the Air Navigation Order 1989 are, however, confined to aircraft registered in the United Kingdom; but where an aircraft flies within the United Kingdom unregistered when it should be registered[7], and flies in such a manner or in such circumstances that an offence against the order or any regulations made thereunder would have been committed if it had been registered in the United Kingdom, the same offence is deemed to have been committed in respect of the aircraft[8].

Except where otherwise expressly stated, the order applies to all aircraft belonging to or employed in the service of the Crown[9], but not to military aircraft[10] and aircraft of visiting forces[11] or belonging to international headquarters[12]. In general the order does not apply to small aircraft[13], and the CAA may exempt from most of its provisions or from those of regulations made under it any aircraft or persons or classes of aircraft or persons, either absolutely or conditionally[14].

1 SI 1989/2004 (amended by SI 1990/2154).
2 See the Air Navigation (General) Regulations 1981, SI 1981/57 (amended by SI 1985/528, SI 1987/2078 and SI 1989/669), made under the Air Navigation Order 1980, SI 1980/1965, art 66 (revoked); the Air Navigation (Dangerous Goods) Regulations 1985, SI 1985/1939 (amended by SI 1986/2129), made under the Air Navigation Order 1985, SI 1985/1643, art 44 (1) (revoked) ; the Air Navigation (Restriction of Flying) (Nuclear Installations) Regulations 1988, SI 1988/1138, made under the Air Navigation Order 1985 art 69 (revoked); the Air Navigation (Restriction of Flying) (Security Establishments in Northern Ireland) Regulations 1989, SI 1989/2117, made under the Air Navigation Order 1985 art 69 (revoked); the Air Navigation (Restriction of Flying) (High Security Prisons) Regulations 1989, SI 1989/2118 (amended by SI 1991/1679), made under the Air Navigation Order 1985 art 69 (revoked), and the Rules of the Air Regulations 1990, SI 1990/2241.
3 Air Navigation Order 1989, SI 1989/2004, art 100 (1) (a). As to the registration and nationality of aircraft see paras 1276–1283 post.
4 Ibid art 100 (1) (b).
5 As to the CAA see para 1044 ante.
6 Air Navigation Order 1989 art 102: this applies to any aircraft specified in the direction, being an aircraft under the management of a person who is qualified to hold a legal or beneficial interest by way of ownership in an aircraft registered in the United Kingdom: art 102. As to these persons see para 1277 post.
7 See para 1276 post.
8 Air Navigation Order 1989 art 3 (2). As to offences see para 1662 et seq post.
9 Ibid art 103 (1).
10 See ibid art 103 (3); as to exemptions see para 1268 post. For the meaning of 'military aircraft' see para 1029 note 5 ante.
11 'Visiting force' means any such body, contingent or detachment of the forces of any country as is a visiting force for the purposes of the provisions of the Visiting Forces Act 1952 which apply to that country by virtue of s 1 (1) (a), or which from time to time apply to that country by virtue of s 1 (1) (b), and of any Order in Council made under s 1 designating that country for the purpose of all the

provisions of that Act following s 1 (2): Air Navigation Order 1989 art 106 (1). See further ROYAL FORCES.

12 Ibid art 103 (2). 'International headquarters' means an international headquarters designated by Order in Council under the International Headquarters and Defence Organisations Act 1964 s 1: Air Navigation Order 1989 art 106 (1). See further FOREIGN RELATIONS LAW.

13 Ibid art 109. For provisions which do apply see arts 51 (endangering safety; see para 1456 post), 75 (balloons, kites and airships; see para 1408 post) and 106 (1), (4) (interpretation). By 'small aircraft' is meant any balloon which at any stage of its flight is not more than 2 metres in any linear dimension including any basket or other equipment attached to the balloon; any kite weighing not more than 2 kg; any other aircraft weighing not more than 7 kg without its fuel, or any parachute including a parascending parachute: art 109 (a)–(d). For the meaning of 'parascending parachute' see para 1408 note 1 post.

14 Ibid art 104. There can be no exemption from arts 67, 88, 92 (restrictions on foreign aircraft engaged in carriage for hire or reward or aerial photography and survey; see paras 1471, 1531 post), 89 (filing and approval of tariffs), 93 (flights over any foreign country: see para 1472 post) and 105 (right of appeal to county court in licensing matters: see paras 1304, 1349, 1384 post).

1265. Application to Channel Islands and Isle of Man. Legislation exists to extend the Air Navigation Order 1989[1] to the Channel Islands and the Isle of Man as part of the law of those places, with certain modifications and adaptations[2]. The Air Navigation (General) Regulations 1972[3] have been modified and adapted so as to apply in the Channel Islands[4]. In the Isle of Man, the Air Navigation Order 1976[5] and the Air Navigation (General) Regulations 1976[6] have been extended under the Civil Aviation Act 1982[7]. In 1987, the Tynwald enacted the Airports and Civil Aviation Act 1987 (Isle of Man) which gives power to the Isle of Man Department of Highways, Ports and Properties to apply specified United Kingdom legislation to the Isle of Man, and thus replace the present Order in Council with Manx orders[8].

1 SI 1989/2004 (amended by SI 1990/2154) .
2 See the Civil Aviation Act 1982 s 108 (1) (amended by the Airports Act 1986 s 83 (1), Sch 4 para 8 (2)) . The Air Navigation Order 1989 has not yet been extended to the Channel Islands but previous orders had been: see the Air Navigation (Jersey) Order 1972, SI 1972/452, and the Air Navigation (Guernsey) Order 1981, SI 1981/1805.
3 Ie SI 1972/322
4 See the Air Navigation (General) (Guernsey) Regulations 1972, SI 1972/486, and the Air Navigation (General) (Jersey) Regulations 1972, SI 1972/487.
5 Ie SI 1976/1783.
6 Ie SI 1976/1982.
7 See the Air Navigation (Isle of Man) Order 1979, SI 1979/929 (made under the Civil Aviation Act 1949 (repealed)) and the Air Navigation (General) (Isle of Man) Regulations 1979, SI 1979/1184.
8 The legislation listed is the Carriage by Air Act 1961, the Carriage by Air (Supplementary Provisions) Act 1962, the Tokyo Convention Act 1967, the Civil Aviation Act 1982, the Aviation Security Act 1982 and the Airports Act 1986.

1266. Application to dependent territories. Flying in dependent territories is regulated by the Air Navigation (Overseas Territories) Order 1989[1], the provisions of which substantially correspond, with necessary modifications, to the provisions of the Air Navigation Order 1989[2].

Thus, in relation to each particular territory, the Air Navigation (Overseas Territories) Order 1989 applies, unless the contrary intention appears, to or in relation to all aircraft registered there wherever they may be and to all other aircraft when they are there[3]. Further, the power to make regulations for the purpose of the order is exercisable by the Governor[4].

1 Ie SI 1989/2395 (amended by SI 1991/189 and SI 1991/1697). For the territories to which the order applies see Sch 16 to the 1989 Order.
2 Ie SI 1989/2004 (amended by SI 1990/2154).
3 Air Navigation (Overseas Territories) Order 1989 art 92.
4 Ibid art 98.

1267. British and foreign aircraft. Under the Chicago Convention[1] aircraft have the nationality of the state in which they are registered, and, while the registration may be changed from one state to another, no aircraft can validly be registered in more than one state[2]. Further, every aircraft engaged in international air navigation must bear its appropriate nationality and registration marks[3].

1 Cmd 8742: see para 1002 ante.
2 Chicago Convention arts 17, 18. No aircraft may be registered in the United Kingdom if it is already registered elsewhere: Air Navigation Order 1989, SI 1989/2004, art 4 (2) (a); see para 1277 post.
3 Chicago Convention art 20. As to nationality and registration marks on United Kingdom aircraft see para 1283 post.

1268. Military aircraft. With certain exceptions[1] the Air Navigation Order 1989[2] does not apply to military aircraft[3].

Where a military aircraft is flown by a civilian pilot and is not commanded by a person acting in the course of his duty as a member of any of Her Majesty's forces or as a member of a visiting force[4] or international headquarters[5], certain provisions of the order[6] apply on the occasion of that flight[7].

1 Ie the Air Navigation Order 1989, SI 1989/2004, arts 56 (4), (8) (exhibition of flying), 69 (1) (a) (power to make rules of the air requiring aircraft to give way to military aircraft), 83 (noise and vibration: see para 1185 ante). See also text and notes 4–6 infra.
2 Ie SI 1989/2004.
3 Air Navigation Order 1989 art 103 (3). For the meaning of 'military aircraft' see para 1029 note 5 ante.
4 For the meaning of 'visiting force' see para 1264 note 11 ante.
5 For the meaning of 'international headquarters' see para 1264 note 12 ante.
6 Ie the Air Navigation Order 1989 arts 50–52 (endangering safety of aircraft, person or property; drunkenness: see paras 1456, 1457 post), 74 (prohibiting or restricting flying: see paras 1487, 1501 post) and, so far as applicable, art 69 (amended by SI 1990/2154) (rules of the air: see paras 1382, 1383 post).
7 Air Navigation Order 1989 art 103 (4).

1269. Classification of aircraft. The term 'aircraft' is not defined in the Civil Aviation Act 1982 or in the Air Navigation Order 1989, but the order contains a table setting out a general classification of aircraft[1], and the expressions appearing in this classification have the meanings there assigned to them[2].

In this classification aircraft are either lighter than air aircraft or heavier than air aircraft[3].

Lighter than air aircraft include non-power driven aircraft (free and captive balloons) and power driven aircraft (airship).

Heavier than air aircraft include non-power driven aircraft (glider and kite) and power driven aircraft, that is, flying machines (aeroplane (landplane), aeroplane (seaplane[4]), aeroplane (amphibian), aeroplane (self-launching motor glider), and rotorcraft (gyroplane and helicopter))[5].

1 Air Navigation Order 1989, SI 1989/2004, Sch 1 Pt A. Reference is made in arts 4 (6) and 24 (2) to column 4 of this table: the descriptions set out in column 4 are those in the parentheses or, as the case may be, the outer parentheses, in text to notes 3–5 infra.

2 Ibid art 106 (4) .
3 Ibid Sch 1 Pt A.
4 'Seaplane' includes a flying boat and any other aircraft designed to manoeuvre on water: ibid art 106 (1), applying the Civil Aviation Act 1982 s 97 (6) .
5 Air Navigation Order 1989 Sch 1 Pt A.

1270. Hovercraft. A hovercraft is a vehicle which is designed to be supported when in motion wholly or partly by air expelled from the vehicle to form a cushion of which the boundaries include the ground, water or other surface beneath the vehicle[1].

A hovercraft is not to be treated as an aircraft[2] except as otherwise provided by and under the Hovercraft Act 1968[3].

1 Hovercraft Act 1968 s 4 (1); see also the Hovercraft (General) Order 1972, SI 1972/674 (amended by SI 1989/1351). See generally SHIPPING.
2 Hovercraft Act 1968 s 4 (3).
3 See ibid s 1 (1) (h) and the Hovercraft (Application of Enactments) Order 1972, SI 1972/971 (amended by SI 1978/1913, SI 1979/1309, SI 1982/715, SI 1983/796, SI 1989/1351 and SI 1990/2594); and see the Civil Aviation Act 1982 s 100 which allows the inclusion of the 1982 Act and any instrument made thereunder.

1271. Categories of aircraft. For the purpose of certificates of airworthiness[1] aircraft are divided into six categories: transport category (passenger) aircraft, which may fly for any purpose; transport category (cargo) aircraft, which may fly for any purpose except for the public transport of passengers[2]; aerial work[3] category aircraft, which may fly for any purpose other than public transport; private category aircraft[4], which may fly for any purpose other than public transport or aerial work; and special category aircraft, which may fly for any purpose, other than public transport, specified in the certificate of airworthiness but not including the carriage of passengers unless expressly permitted[5].

1 As to certificates of airworthiness see paras 1284–1294 post.
2 As to public transport aircraft see para 1272 post.
3 As to aerial work see para 1273 post.
4 As to private aircraft see para 1274 post.
5 Air Navigation Order 1989, SI 1989/2004, Sch 3.

1272. Public transport aircraft. 'Public transport aircraft' means an aircraft flying or intended by the operator of the aircraft to fly for the purpose of public transport[1]. An aircraft in flight[2] is deemed to fly for the purpose of public transport if valuable consideration[3] is given or promised for the carriage of passengers or cargo[4] on that flight[5]; or if passengers or cargo are carried gratuitously on that flight by an air transport undertaking[6]; or if, for the purposes of the provisions relating to airworthiness and equipment[7], valuable consideration is given or promised for the right to fly the aircraft on that flight otherwise than under a hire-purchase or conditional sale agreement[8].

An aircraft registered outside the United Kingdom[9] may not take on board or discharge passengers or cargo in the United Kingdom if these passengers or cargo are carried or to be carried for a valuable consideration unless the Secretary of State[10] has granted permission for such carriage to the operator[11] or charterer of the aircraft, or to the government of the country in which the aircraft is registered, and in accordance with any condition to which the permission may be subject[12].

An aircraft operated by an association of persons flies for the purpose of public transport because, notwithstanding the relationship between the association and its members or members carried in or having the right to fly the aircraft, valuable consideration is deemed by the Air Navigation Order 1989 to be given[13].

1 Air Navigation Order 1989, SI 1989/2004, art 106 (1).
2 For the meaning of 'in flight' see para 1460 post.
3 'Valuable consideration' means any right, interest, profit or benefit, forbearance, detriment, loss or responsibility accruing, given, suffered or undertaken pursuant to an agreement, which is of more than a nominal nature: Air Navigation Order 1989 art 106 (1).
4 'Cargo' includes mail and animals: ibid art 106 (1).
5 Ibid art 107 (2) (a).
6 Ibid art 107 (2) (b); this provision does not apply to the employees of the undertaking or, if a body corporate, to the directors of that body (including the Civil Aviation Authority) or inspectors on duty for the purposes of the order, nor does the provision apply to cargo intended to be used by such passengers or by such an undertaking. 'Air transport undertaking' means an undertaking whose business includes the carriage by air of passengers or cargo for valuable consideration: art 106 (1).
7 See ibid Pt III (arts 7–18); and para 1284 et seq post.
8 Ibid art 107 (2) (c); this provision does not apply to a single-seater aircraft of which the maximum total authorised weight does not exceed 910 kg; for the meaning of 'maximum total weight authorised' see para 1314 note 5 post. Notwithstanding that an aircraft may be flying for the purpose of public transport by reason of this provision, it is not deemed to be flying for the purpose of the public transport of passengers unless valuable consideration is given for the carriage of those passengers: art 107 (2) proviso; nor does the provision apply in the case of a glider owned or operated by a flying club where the valuable consideration is given or promised, and the glider is flown, by a member of the flying club: art 107 (2) proviso. 'Hire-purchase agreement' has the same meaning as in the Consumer Credit Act 1974 s 189: Air Navigation Order 1989 art 106 (1): see HIRE PURCHASE. As to charter flights see paras 1336–1338 post.
9 The aircraft may be registered in a state which is a party to the Chicago Convention (see para 1002 ante) or in any other foreign state: ibid art 88 (1).
10 As to the Secretary of State see para 1032 ante.
11 For the meaning of 'operator' see para 1340 post.
12 Air Navigation Order 1989 art 88 (1); any breach of a condition subject to which the permission was granted is a contravention: art 88 (2). The penalty for contravention is on summary conviction a fine not exceeding £2,000 and on conviction on indictment a fine or imprisonment for a term not exceeding two years, or both: art 99 (6), Sch 12 Pt B. For the Secretary of State's power to prevent flight in contravention of the provision see para 1459 post.
13 Ibid art 107 (3).

1273. Aerial work aircraft. An aerial work aircraft is an aircraft, other than a public transport aircraft[1], flying or intended by the operator to fly for any purpose, other than public transport, for which a valuable consideration[2] is given or promised in respect of the flight or the purpose of the flight[3]. But if the only valuable consideration is a remuneration for the services of the pilot, the flight is deemed a private flight[4].

Examples of aerial work flights are flights for the purpose of dropping persons by parachute in accordance with any written permission of the Civil Aviation Authority (CAA)[5], flights to get an aircraft to and from the position where a parachute drop is to take place[6], flights to give instruction in flying[7] or to conduct flying tests[8] or flights for aerial application[9].

1 As to public transport aircraft see para 1272 ante.
2 For the meaning of 'valuable consideration' see para 1272 note 3 ante.
3 See the Air Navigation Order 1989, SI 1989/2004, arts 106 (1), 107 (1).
4 Ibid art 107 (1) proviso.
5 See ibid art 107 (9) (a). As to the CAA see para 1044 ante.
6 Ibid art 107 (9) (b), (c).

7 See ibid art 24; and para 1358 post.
8 See ibid art 21, Sch 8 Pt C para 3; and para 1349 post.
9 See ibid arts 43 and 45; and paras 1467–1469 post.

1274. Private flight. An aircraft[1] is on a private flight when the flight is undertaken neither for the purpose of public transport nor for the purpose of aerial work[2]. The Air Navigation Order sets out five types of private flights together with the conditions which they must fulfil[3].

Where an aircraft flies in a race, contest or exhibition of flying, the flight is a private flight, for the purposes of crew licensing, provided that any payment made covers only the direct costs[4] of the flight and a proportion of the annual costs[5], that any prize awarded to the pilot does not exceed £500 save with the permission of the Civil Aviation Authority (CAA)[6] and that no valuable consideration was given or promised for the main purpose of giving a particular pilot the right to fly the aircraft[7].

Where an aircraft carries passengers whose contributions are given or promised to a registered charity which is not the operator of the aircraft[8], the flight is a private flight provided that the CAA gave permission for the flight and that no valuable consideration was given or promised for the main purpose of giving a particular pilot the right to fly the aircraft[9].

Where an aircraft carries no more than four persons including the pilot, each bearing a proportion of the direct costs of the flight[10], the flight is a private flight provided that the pilot is not employed or hired by the aircraft operator carried on the flight, that no valuable consideration was given or promised for the main purpose of giving a particular pilot the right to fly the aircraft, and that the flight had not been advertised[11].

Where an aircraft is flown by a pilot in employment and where the pilot asks of his employer or of a body corporate of which the pilot is a director a contribution to cover only the direct costs (or part thereof) of the flight which the pilot would otherwise have to pay[12], the flight is a private flight provided that neither the pilot nor any passenger in the aircraft was legally obliged to be carried, and that no valuable consideration was given or promised for the main purpose of giving a particular pilot the right to fly the aircraft[13].

Where an aircraft jointly owned by a number of persons, each of whom is a natural person, and registered in their names[14], or owned by a company[15], is in flight, the flight is a private flight provided that the only payment made is for the direct costs of the flight or in respect of the annual costs, by one or more of the joint owners or registered shareholders[16].

1 As to aircraft in joint ownership see text and notes 14–16 infra.
2 Air Navigation Order 1989, SI 1989/2004, art 106 (1). As to public transport aircraft see para 1272 ante; as to aerial work aircraft see para 1273 ante.
3 See ibid art 107 (4)–(8); and text and notes 4–16 infra.
4 'Direct costs' means, in respect of a flight, the costs actually and necessarily incurred in connection with that flight without a view to profit but excluding any remuneration payable to the pilot for his services as such: ibid art 106 (1).
5 'Annual costs' in relation to the operation of an aircraft means the best estimate reasonably practicable at the time of a particular flight in respect of the year commencing on the first day of January preceding the date of the flight, of the costs of keeping and maintaining and the indirect costs of operating the aircraft, such costs in either case excluding direct costs and being those actually and necessarily incurred without a view to profit: ibid art 106 (1); as to direct costs see note 4 supra.

6 As to the CAA see para 1044 ante.
7 Air Navigation Order 1989 art 107 (4). As to aircraft in joint ownership see text and notes 14–16 infra; as to crew licensing see para 1343 et seq post; as to valuable consideration see para 1272 note 3 ante.
8 See ibid art 107 (5). As to registered charities see CHARITIES.
9 Ibid art 107 (5). For the meaning of 'valuable consideration' see para 1272 note 3 ante.
10 See ibid art 107 (6) proviso (i), (ii); for the meaning of 'direct costs' see note 4 supra.
11 Ibid art 107 (6). Advertising of the flight is permitted within the premises of the flying club provided all persons carried on the flight aged 18 or over are members of the flying club: art 107 (6) proviso (iii). For the meaning of 'valuable consideration' see para 1272 note 3 ante.
12 Ibid art 107 (7) (amended by SI 1990/2154). 'Director' has the same meaning as in the Companies Act 1989 s 53 (1): Air Navigation Order 1989 art 106 (1) (as so amended); see COMPANIES. For the meaning of 'direct costs' see note 4 supra.
13 Ibid art 107 (7) proviso; for the meaning of 'valuable consideration' see para 1272 note 3 ante.
14 See ibid art 107 (8) (a) (i) (amended by SI 1991/1726); each person must hold at least a five per cent beneficial share in the aircraft which is registered in either the names of all the joint owners or in the name of one or more of the joint owners as trustee or trustees for all the joint owners: Air Navigation Order 1989 art 107 (8) (a) (i) (aa), (bb).
15 See ibid art 107 (8) (a) (ii); each shareholder must be a natural person and hold at least five per cent of the shares in the company, and the aircraft must be registered in the name of the company: art 107 (8) (a) (ii) (as amended: see note 14 supra).
16 Ibid art 107 (8) (b). For the meaning of 'direct costs' and of 'annual costs' see respectively notes 4, 5 supra.

(2) MANUFACTURE, REGISTRATION AND MARKING OF AIRCRAFT

1275. Liabilities of aircraft manufacturers. A manufacturer of aircraft may be liable to a purchaser in respect of the faulty design or construction of an aircraft, by reference to the terms of the contract between them and the ordinary law relating, for example, to the sale of goods [1].

In addition, the manufacturer is strictly liable if death or personal injury or, subject to certain qualifications, loss of or damage to any property (including land) is caused wholly or partly by a defect in the product (including a component part of another product) [2].

An employer is liable in negligence where an employee suffers personal injury, death or disease in the course of his employment in consequence of a defect in an aircraft provided by his employer for the purposes of the employer's business, but without prejudice to the law relating to contributory negligence [3].

1 See generally CONTRACT; DAMAGES; NEGLIGENCE; SALE OF GOODS.
2 Consumer Protection Act 1987 Pt I (ss 1–9); see generally CONTRACT; SALE OF GOODS.
3 Employer's Liability (Defective Equipment) Act 1969 s 1 (1) (a); see *Coltman v Bibby Tankers Ltd, The Derbyshire* [1988] AC 276, [1987] 3 All ER 1068, 1 S&B AvR I/165, HL; and EMPLOYMENT.

1276. Necessity for registration. No aircraft may fly over the United Kingdom unless it is registered in some part of the Commonwealth[1], or in a contracting state[2], or in some other country in relation to which there is in force an agreement between Her Majesty's United Kingdom government and the government of that country making provision for the flight over the United Kingdom of aircraft registered in that country[3].

However, a glider may fly unregistered[4] and any aircraft may fly unregistered on a flight beginning and ending in the United Kingdom without passing over any other country and which is in accordance with certain special conditions[5]. Kites and captive balloons do not need to be registered[6].

1 Air Navigation Order 1989, SI 1989/2004, art 3 (1) (a). For the meaning of 'Commonwealth' see para 1190 note 5 ante.
2 Ibid art 3 (1) (b). For the meaning of 'contracting state' see para 1190 note 4 ante.
3 Air Navigation Order 1989 art 3 (1) (c). Contravention is an offence: see art 3 (2); and para 1264 ante. The penalty for contravention is on summary conviction a fine not exceeding £1,000: art 99 (5), Sch 12 Pt A. As to the persons liable see para 1577 post. As to offences and penalties see further paras 1576–1580 post. For the power to direct that an unregistered aircraft shall not be flown, see art 95 (1); and para 1459 post.
4 See ibid art 3 (1) proviso (i). A glider is deemed to be registered in the United Kingdom for the purposes of arts 13 (equipment: see para 1312 post), 14 (radio equipment: see para 1318 post), 20 (flight crew licences: see para 1344 post) and 35 (pre-flight action: see para 1426 post), on any flight wholly within the United Kingdom which is not for the purpose of public transport (see para 1272 ante) or aerial work (defined in para 1273 ante).
5 Ibid art 3 (1) proviso (ii). The conditions referred to are the 'B' conditions set out in Sch 2, as to which see para 1287 post.
6 Ibid art 3 (1) proviso (iii).

1277. Eligibility of aircraft for registration. No aircraft may be registered or continue to be registered in the United Kingdom if it appears to the Civil Aviation Authority (CAA)[1] that it is already registered outside the United Kingdom[2], or that it could more suitably be registered in some other part of the Commonwealth[3], or that it would be inexpedient in the public interest for it to be or continue to be registered in the United Kingdom[4].

Further, no aircraft may be so registered if it appears to the CAA that an unqualified person holds any legal or beneficial interest by way of ownership in the aircraft or any share in it[5]; if, however, the holder of the interest resides or has a place of business in the United Kingdom the CAA may register the aircraft if satisfied that the aircraft may otherwise be properly registered[6]. The persons qualified to hold such an interest are the Crown, Commonwealth citizens and citizens of the Republic of Ireland, British protected persons, bodies incorporated in and having their principal place of business in some part of the Commonwealth, and firms carrying on business in Scotland[7]. If an aircraft is chartered by demise to a qualified person[8], the CAA may register the aircraft in the charterer's name if satisfied that the aircraft may otherwise be properly so registered[9].

1 The CAA is the authority for the registration of aircraft in the United Kingdom, and keeps the register on its premises: Air Navigation Order 1989, SI 1989/2004, art 4 (1). As to the CAA see para 1044 ante.
2 Ibid art 4 (2) (a).
3 Ibid art 4 (2) (c). For the meaning of 'Commonwealth' see para 1190 note 5 ante.
4 Ibid art 4 (2) (d).
5 Ibid art 4 (2) (b). Reference to an interest in an aircraft does not include reference to an interest in an aircraft to which a person is entitled only by virtue of his membership of a flying club: art 4 (15). 'Beneficial interest' has the same meaning as in the Merchant Shipping Act 1894 s 57 (as to which see SHIPPING): Air Navigation Order 1989 art 106 (1).
6 Ibid art 4 (4): the holder of the interest must not cause or permit the aircraft, while it is registered in pursuance of this provision, to be used for the purpose of public transport (as to which see para 1272 ante) or aerial work (as to which see para 1273 ante).
7 Ibid art 4 (3).
8 This applies whether or not an unqualified person is entitled as owner to a legal or beneficial interest in the aircraft: ibid art 4 (5).
9 Ibid art 4 (5). Subject to the provisions of art 4 the aircraft may remain so registered during the continuation of the charter: art 4 (5).

1278. Application for registration of aircraft. Application for the registration of an aircraft must be made to the Civil Aviation Authority (CAA)[1] in writing, and must include or be accompanied by such particulars and evidence relating to the aircraft[2] and its ownership and chartering as the CAA requires to enable it to determine whether the aircraft may properly be registered in the United Kingdom[3] and to issue the registration certificate[4].

1 As to the CAA see para 1044 ante.
2 The application must include the proper description of the aircraft according to column 4 of the general classification of aircraft, as to which see para 1269 ante.
3 As to eligibility for registration see para 1277 ante.
4 Air Navigation Order 1989, SI 1989/2004, art 4 (6). As to the registration certificate see para 1279 post.

1279. The registration certificate. When satisfied upon an application for registration that an aircraft may properly be registered[1] the Civil Aviation Authority (CAA)[2] must register it, wherever it may be, and must include in the register the number of the registration certificate, the nationality mark[3] of the aircraft, the registration mark[4] assigned to it, the name of the constructor of the aircraft and its designation, the aircraft's serial number, the name and address of each person entitled as owner to a legal interest or share in the aircraft or of the charterer by demise[5] and, if it be the case, an indication that the aircraft is registered in special circumstances[6].

The CAA must furnish to the person in whose name the aircraft is registered a registration certificate including the particulars entered in the register and the date of issue[7].

1 As to eligibility for registration see para 1277 ante.
2 As to the CAA see para 1044 ante.
3 See para 1283 post.
4 See para 1283 post.
5 See para 1277 ante.
6 Air Navigation Order 1989 art 4 (7). As to these special circumstances see art 4 (4), (5); and para 1277 ante.
7 Ibid art 4 (8). For an exception see para 1280 post.

1280. Aircraft dealer's certificate. The Civil Aviation Authority (CAA)[1] may grant to any qualified person[2] an aircraft dealer's certificate if it is satisfied that he has a place of business in the United Kingdom for buying and selling aircraft[3].

The CAA is not required to furnish a registration certificate[4] to the holder of an aircraft dealer's certificate who has made to the CAA a statement that a particular aircraft is to fly only in accordance with special conditions[5].

1 As to the CAA see para 1044 ante.
2 As to qualified persons see the Air Navigation Order 1989, SI 1989/2004, art 4 (3); and para 1277 ante.
3 Ibid art 4 (9).
4 As to registration certificates see para 1279 ante.
5 Air Navigation Order 1989 art 4 (8) proviso. The conditions referred to are the 'C' conditions set out in Sch 2, under which an operator holding an aircraft dealer's certificate may fly an aircraft in the United Kingdom only for the purpose of testing, demonstration with a view to sale, and delivery, etc.

1281. Notice of change of circumstances. The registered owner[1] of an aircraft registered in the United Kingdom must forthwith inform the Civil Aviation

Authority (CAA)² in writing of any change in the particulars furnished on the application for registration³, of the destruction of the aircraft or its permanent withdrawal from use and, if it was registered in the name of a charterer by demise, of the termination of the charter⁴.

Any person who becomes the owner of an aircraft registered in the United Kingdom must inform the CAA in writing to that effect within 28 days⁵.

1 'Registered owner' means the person in whose name the aircraft is registered: Air Navigation Order 1989, SI 1989/2004, art 4 (8). Reference to the registered owner includes, in the case of a deceased person, his legal personal representative and, in the case of a body corporate which has been dissolved, its successor: art 4 (15). As to the transfer of air transport licences see para 1088 ante.
2 As to the CAA see para 1044 ante.
3 As to the application see para 1278 ante.
4 Air Navigation Order 1989 art 4 (11). As to demise charters see para 1277 ante.
5 Ibid art 4 (12).

1282. Amendment, cancellation and nullity of registration. The Civil Aviation Authority (CAA)¹ may amend the register² at any time when it appears necessary or appropriate to do so for giving effect to the provisions relating to the registration and marking of aircraft³ or for bringing up to date or correcting the particulars on the register⁴. It may also, if it thinks fit, cancel the registration of an aircraft, and must do so if satisfied that there has been a change in ownership⁵; nothing, however, requires it to cancel a registration if in its opinion it would be inexpedient in the public interest to do so⁶.

Where, after an aircraft has been registered in the United Kingdom, an unqualified person⁷ becomes entitled to a legal or beneficial interest by way of ownership or a share in the aircraft, the registration becomes void and the registered owner⁸ must forthwith return the registration certificate to the CAA⁹.

1 As to the CAA see para 1044 ante.
2 As to the register see para 1279 ante.
3 Ie the Air Navigation Order 1989, SI 1989/2004, Pt I (arts 3–5).
4 Ibid art 4 (13).
5 Ibid art 4 (13). The registration of an aircraft which is the subject of an undischarged registered mortgage cannot be cancelled unless all persons shown in the register as mortgagees consent to the cancellation: art 4 (17). As to the mortgage of aircraft see para 1334 post.
6 Ibid art 4 (16).
7 As to unqualified persons see para 1277 ante.
8 For the meaning of 'registered owner' see para 1281 note 1 ante.
9 Air Navigation Order 1989 art 4 (10): this provision is subject to art 4 (4), (5), as to which see para 1277 ante. The registration of an aircraft which is the subject of an undischarged registered mortgage does not become void by virtue of this provision: Air Navigation Order 1989 art 4 (17). As to the mortgage of aircraft see para 1334 post.

1283. Nationality and registration marks. An aircraft, other than one permitted to fly without being registered¹, must not fly unless it bears painted on it or affixed to it, in the manner required by the law of the country in which it is registered, the nationality and registration marks required by that law². Further, an aircraft must not bear any marks purporting to indicate that it is registered in a country in which it is not registered³; or that it is a state aircraft of a particular country if it is not such an aircraft, unless the appropriate authority of that country has sanctioned the bearing of such marks⁴.

1 See para 1276 ante.

2 Air Navigation Order 1989, SI 1989/2004, art 5 (1). The penalty for contravention of this and other provisions set out in this paragraph is on summary conviction a fine not exceeding £1,000: art 99 (5), Sch 12 Pt A. An aircraft registered in the United Kingdom must bear marks complying, before 1 November 1992, with the Air Navigation Order 1989 Sch 1 Pt B1 or Pt B2 and, on and after that date, with Sch 1 Pt B2 (renumbered and added respectively by SI 1991/1726): Air Navigation Order 1989 art 5 (2) (substituted by SI 1991/1726). The nationality mark, a capital 'G', is followed by a hyphen and a group of four capital letters comprising the registration mark: Air Navigation Order 1989 Sch 1 Pt B1 para 1, Pt B2 para 1. As to the position, size, width, spacing, clarity and visibility of the marks, see Sch 1 Pt B1 paras 2, 4, Pt B2 paras 2, 3, 5. They must also be inscribed, with the registered owner's name and address, on a fireproof metal plate: Sch 1 Pt B1 para 3, Pt B2 para 4. For the power to direct that an aircraft not properly marked shall not fly see art 95 (1); and para 1459 post.
3 Ibid art 5 (3) (a) (substituted by SI 1990/2154). Marks approved by the CAA for the purposes of flight in accordance with the 'B' conditions are deemed not to purport to indicate that the aircraft is so registered: Air Navigation Order 1989 art 5 (3) (a) proviso (as so substituted and as amended by SI 1991/1726). As to the 'B' conditions see the Air Navigation Order 1989 Sch 2; and para 1287 post. As to contravention see note 2 supra.
4 Ibid art 5 (3) (b). As to contravention see note 2 supra. 'State aircraft', which was defined in earlier Air Navigation Orders, is not defined in the current order.

(3) CERTIFICATES

(i) Certificates of Airworthiness

1284. Necessity for certificate of airworthiness. Subject to certain exceptions[1], an aircraft may not fly unless there is in force in respect of it a certificate of airworthiness[2] duly issued or rendered valid under the law of the country in which the aircraft is registered, and any conditions subject to which the certificate was issued or rendered valid are complied with[3].

1 See paras 1285–1287 post.
2 'Certificate of airworthiness' includes any validation of it, and any flight manual, performance schedule or other document, whatever its title, incorporated by reference in that certificate relating to the certificate of airworthiness: Air Navigation Order 1989, SI 1989/2004, art 106 (1).
3 Ibid art 7 (1). The penalty for contravention is on summary conviction a fine not exceeding £2,000 and on conviction on indictment a fine or imprisonment for a term not exceeding two years or both: art 99 (6), Sch 12 Pt B. For the power to direct that an aircraft shall not fly if this provision is not complied with see art 95 (1); and para 1459 post.

1285. Flights permitted without certificate of airworthiness. An aircraft may fly without a certificate of airworthiness where the flight begins and ends in the United Kingdom, provided the aircraft is a glider not being used for the public transport[1] of passengers or a balloon flying on a private flight[2]; or a glider not being used for aerial work[3]; or a kite[4]; or an aircraft flying in accordance either with special conditions[5] or with the conditions of a permit to fly issued by the Civil Aviation Authority (CAA)[6] in respect of that aircraft[7].

1 For the meaning of 'public transport' see para 1272 ante.
2 Air Navigation Order 1989, SI 1989/2004, art 7 (1) proviso (a), (b) (amended by SI 1991/1726). For the meaning of 'private flight' see para 1274 ante.
3 Air Navigation Order 1989 art 7 (1) proviso (a). For the meaning of 'aerial work' see para 1273 ante.
4 Ibid art 7 (1) proviso (c).
5 Ibid art 7 (1) proviso (d). The conditions referred to are the 'A' and 'B' conditions set out in Sch 2, as to which see paras 1286, 1287 post.

6 As to the CAA see para 1044 ante.
7 Air Navigation Order 1989 art 7 (1) proviso (e).

1286. 'A' conditions. The 'A' conditions apply where, prior to flight, an application has been made for the issue or renewal of a certificate of airworthiness in respect of the aircraft, or of a validation of such a certificate[1], or for the approval of modifications[2] to the aircraft[3]. The aircraft may then fly without a certificate being in force, provided that the flight is carried out solely for the purpose of qualifying for such issue, renewal or approval[4], or may proceed to or from a place at which any inspection, test or weighing of, or the installation of equipment in, the aircraft is to take place for one of those purposes[5]. The aircraft must, however, be either an aircraft in respect of which a certificate of airworthiness or a validation has previously been in force under the Air Navigation Order or an aircraft identical in design with an aircraft in respect of which such a certificate is or has been in force[6]. It must carry the minimum flight crew[7], but may carry no passengers or cargo except passengers performing duties in connection with the flight[8], and it must not fly over any congested area[9] of a city, town or settlement except in order to take off from or land at an aerodrome[10] in accordance with normal aviation practice[11]. The aircraft and its engines must be certified as fit for flight by an aircraft maintenance engineer[12].

1 As to the issue, validation and renewal of certificates see paras 1288–1293 post.
2 As to the approval of modifications see para 1329 post.
3 Air Navigation Order 1989, SI 1989/2004, Sch 2 A (2) (a).
4 Ibid Sch 2 A (2) (a).
5 Ibid Sch 2 A (2) (b).
6 Ibid Sch 2 A (1).
7 Ibid Sch 2 A (4): this is the minimum specified in a previous certificate for the aircraft or for an aircraft of identical design. Nevertheless the aircraft must carry such crew as to ensure its safety: Sch 2 A (7). See further paras 1359–1365 post.
8 Ibid Sch 2 A (5).
9 'Congested area' means any area which is substantially used for residential, industrial, commercial or recreational purposes: ibid art 106 (1); see further para 1490 note 2 post.
10 Ie a government aerodrome owned or managed by the Civil Aviation Authority (as to which see para 1044 ante), or a licensed aerodrome (defined in para 1154 ante): ibid Sch 2 A (6).
11 Ibid Sch 2 A (6).
12 Ibid Sch 2 A (3). As to certificates of maintenance see paras 1301–1304 post.

1287. 'B' conditions. The 'B' conditions apply where the flight is made under the supervision of a person approved by the Civil Aviation Authority (CAA)[1] for the purpose; it is subject to any additional conditions specified in the approval[2]. The aircraft may fly only for the purpose of experimenting with or testing the aircraft or its engines and its equipment, or enabling the aircraft to qualify for the issue or validation of a certificate of airworthiness[3] or the approval of modifications[4], or proceeding to or from a place at which any experiment, test, inspection or weighing of, or the installation of equipment in, the aircraft for those purposes is to take place[5]. The aircraft must, if registered, be marked in accordance with the Air Navigation Order[6] and, if unregistered, must be marked in a manner approved for this purpose[7]. It must carry such flight crew as is necessary to ensure its safety[8], but may carry no passengers or cargo except persons, whether employed by the operator or by manufacturers of component parts of the aircraft, carrying out, during the flight, duties in connection with the purposes of the flight, persons approved by the CAA to report on the aircraft, and other persons carrying out a technical evaluation of the aircraft or its operation[9]. It may not be flown over any congested area[10] of a city, town or settlement except in accordance with procedures approved by the CAA in relation to that flight[11].

1 As to the CAA see para 1044 ante.
2 Air Navigation Order 1989, SI 1989/2004, Sch 2 B (1).
3 As to the issue, validation and renewal of certificates see paras 1288–1293 post.
4 As to the approval of modifications see para 1329 post.
5 Air Navigation Order 1989 Sch 2 B (3).
6 See para 1283 ante.
7 Air Navigation Order 1989 Sch 2 B (2): the provisions of arts 14, 16, 20, 35, 38, 61 and 63 relating to radio equipment, log books, crew licences, pre-flight action, operation of radio, documents and records, must, so far as applicable, be complied with as if the aircraft were registered.
8 Ibid Sch 2 B (4).
9 Ibid Sch 2 B (5). As to reports see art 8 (8) (added by SI 1990/2154).
10 For the meaning of 'congested area' see 1286 note 9 ante.
11 Air Navigation Order 1989 Sch 2 B (6).

1288. Issue of certificates of airworthiness. The Civil Aviation Authority (CAA)[1] may issue a certificate of airworthiness in respect of an aircraft if satisfied that it is fit to fly, having regard to the design, construction, workmanship and materials of the aircraft including, in particular, any engines fitted to it, and of any equipment carried in the aircraft which it considers necessary for its airworthiness; and also having regard to the results of flying trials and other tests[2]. If the CAA refuses to grant a certificate, there is a right of review of the decision to refuse[3]. Where the CAA has issued a certificate in respect of a prototype or modification of a prototype it may dispense with flying trials in the case of any other aircraft if satisfied that it conforms to the prototype or modification[4].

1 As to the CAA see para 1044 ante.
2 Air Navigation Order 1989, SI 1989/2004, art 8 (1). As to aircraft engine emissions certificates see para 1295 post.
3 Civil Aviation Authority Regulations 1991, SI 1991/1672, reg 6 (3): see para 1070 ante.
4 Air Navigation Order 1989 art 8 (1) proviso.

1289. Consultation with Airworthiness Requirements Board. The Civil Aviation Authority (CAA)[1] must consult the Airworthiness Requirements Board[2] on all matters appearing to the CAA to be of significance as respects the standards of design, construction and maintenance by reference to which certificates of airworthiness for aircraft are to be granted or renewed[3], and must also consult the board as to whether an aircraft of a new type satisfies the standards of design and construction required for the issue of such a certificate[4].

1 As to the CAA see para 1044 ante.
2 As to the board and its functions see paras 1060, 1061 ante.
3 See the Air Navigation Order 1989, SI 1989/2004, arts 7–9.
4 Civil Aviation Act 1982 s 85 (1). As to the CAA's powers in relation to the board see para 1062 ante.

1290. Particulars and conditions in certificates of airworthiness. Every certificate of airworthiness must specify such categories of aircraft as are, in the opinion of the Civil Aviation Authority (CAA)[1], appropriate to the aircraft concerned[2], and may also designate the performance group to which the aircraft belongs[3].

The certificate of airworthiness is issued subject to the condition that the aircraft shall be flown only for the purposes indicated in relation to the appropriate category[4], and may be issued subject to such other conditions relating to the airworthiness of the aircraft as the CAA thinks fit[5].

A flight manual, performance schedule or other document incorporated by reference in the certificate of airworthiness[6] may be varied by the CAA on sufficient ground being shown to its satisfaction, whether or not after due inquiry[7].

1 As to the CAA see para 1044 ante.
2 Air Navigation Order 1989, SI 1989/2004, art 8 (2). As to the categories of aircraft see Sch 3; and para 1271 ante.
3 Ibid art 8 (4). This provision is for the purposes of art 30 (1), as to which see para 1430 post.
4 Ibid art 8 (2).
5 Ibid art 8 (3).
6 See the definition of 'certificate of airworthiness' in para 1284 note 2 ante.
7 Air Navigation Order 1989 art 66 (5).

1291. Validation of overseas certificates of airworthiness. Where a certificate of airworthiness has been issued in respect of an aircraft under the law of any country other than the United Kingdom, the Civil Aviation Authority (CAA)[1] may, subject to such conditions as it thinks fit, issue a certificate of validation rendering that certificate of airworthiness valid for the purposes of the Air Navigation Order 1989 [2].

1 As to the Civil Aviation Authority see para 1044 ante.
2 Air Navigation Order 1989, SI 1989/2004, art 8 (5).

1292. Validity of certificates. A certificate of airworthiness or validation remains in force only for the period specified in it[1], but it may be renewed[2]. In some circumstances where modifications are made to an aircraft it may be necessary to obtain a new certificate[3].

1 Air Navigation Order 1989, SI 1989/2004, art 8 (6). A certificate may, however, be revoked, varied or suspended by the Civil Aviation Authority: see art 66; and para 1422 post.
2 See para 1293 post.
3 See para 1294 post.

1293. Renewal of certificates. Subject to the foregoing provisions[1], the Civil Aviation Authority (CAA)[2] may from time to time renew a certificate of airworthiness or a validation for such further period as it thinks fit[3].

1 See paras 1288–1292 ante.
2 As to the CAA see para 1044 ante.
3 Air Navigation Order 1989, SI 1989/2004, art 8 (6). A certificate may, however, be revoked, varied or suspended by the CAA: see art 66; and para 1422 post.

1294. Discontinuance of certificates. A certificate of airworthiness or a certificate of validation ceases to be in force if the aircraft or such of its equipment as is necessary for its airworthiness is overhauled, repaired or modified[1], or if any part is removed or replaced, otherwise than in a manner and with material of a type approved by the Civil Aviation Authority (CAA)[2]; or until the completion of any inspection required for the purpose of ascertaining whether the aircraft remains airworthy[3]; or until completion to the CAA's satisfaction of any modification required for that purpose[4].

1 As to overhauls, repairs and modifications see para 1327 post.
2 Air Navigation Order 1989, SI 1989/2004, art 8 (7) (a). As to the CAA see para 1044 ante.
3 Ibid art 8 (7) (b).
4 Ibid art 8 (7) (c).

(ii) Certificates as to Aircraft Engine Emissions

1295. Certified engine types. An aircraft powered by gas turbine engines or by turbojet or turbofan engines may not land or take off in the United Kingdom unless the aircraft or the engines are of a type certified as complying with requirements relating to fuel venting[1], or smoke emissions[2] or unburned hydrocarbons emissions[3]. However, these prohibitions do not apply to aircraft flying in accordance with the 'A' conditions or the 'B' conditions in the Air Navigation Order 1989[4] or to aircraft landing or taking off at a prescribed place[3].

1 See the Air Navigation (Aircraft and Aircraft Emissions) Order 1986, SI 1986/599, art 4. The prohibition applies to every aircraft powered by gas turbine engines whose date of manufacture was, or in respect of which a certificate of airworthiness was first issued, on or after 1 May 1986. As to certification see para 1296 et seq post.
2 Ibid art 5. The prohibition applies to every turbojet or turbofan engine whose date of manufacture was on or after 1 May 1986. As to certification see para 1296 et seq post.
3 See the Air Navigation (Aeroplane and Aeroplane Engine Emission of Unburned Hydrocarbons) Order 1988, SI 1988/1994, art 4. The prohibition applies to every aeroplane powered by turbojet or turbofan engines and every turbojet or turbofan engine the date of manufacture of which was on or after 1 January 1989 whether they were intended for propulsion of aeroplanes at subsonic speeds (in which case only those engines with a rated output greater than 26.7 kN are affected) or at supersonic speeds: art 3. The orders apply to aircraft, together with the engines fitted thereto, belonging to or exclusively employed in the service of Her Majesty: see art 11 (1) and the Air Navigation (Aircraft and Aircraft Emissions) Order 1986 arts 12 (1). As to certification see para 1296 et seq post.
4 Ie in the Air Navigation Order 1989, SI 1989/2004, Sch 2; see paras 1286, 1287 ante.
5 Air Navigation (Aircraft and Aircraft Engine Emissions) Order 1986 art 6; Air Navigation (Aeroplane and Aeroplane Engine Emission of Unburned Hydrocarbons) Order 1988 art 4 (2). As to other exemptions see para 1300 post.

1296. Certification by the Civil Aviation Authority. The Civil Aviation Authority (CAA)[1] certifies a type of aircraft or a type of engine as complying with requirements relating to fuel venting[2], or a type of turbojet or turbofan engine as complying with requirements relating to smoke emission[3] or to the emission of unburned hydrocarbons[4] when it is satisfied as to the compliance with such requirements. The applicant must furnish all evidence and subject the aircraft or engines to such tests and trials as the CAA may require[5]. The CAA may accept for the purposes of such certification reports from such persons as it may have approved[6].

A declaration in the official record of the CAA is evidence that a type of aircraft or a type of engine is certified[7].

1 As to the CAA see para 1044 ante.

2 See the Air Navigation (Aircraft and Aircraft Engine Emissions) Order 1986, SI 1986/599, art 7 (1). The design and construction of the aircraft or the engine must prevent the intentional discharge into the atmosphere of liquid fuel from the fuel nozzle manifolds when the engine is shut down after a normal flight or following ground operations: art 7 (1).
3 See ibid art 7 (2), (4), (5), Sch 1 Pt I (subsonic aircraft), Pt II (supersonic aircraft) (see para 1295 note 2 ante). 'Smoke' means the carbonaceous materials in exhaust emissions which obscure the transmission of light: art 2 (1).
4 See the Air Navigation (Aeroplane and Aeroplane Engine Emission of Unburned Hydrocarbons) Order 1988, SI 1988/1994, art 5 (1), (3), (4), Sch 2 Pt I (subsonic aeroplanes), Pt II (supersonic aeroplanes) (see para 1295 note 3 ante).
5 Air Navigation (Aircraft and Aircraft Engine Emissions) Order 1986 art 7 (3); Air Navigation (Aeroplane and Aeroplane Engine Emission of Unburned Hydrocarbons) Order 1988 art 5 (2).
6 Air Navigation (Aircraft and Aircraft Engine Emissions) Order 1986 art 7 (7); Air Navigation (Aeroplane and Aeroplane Engine Emission of Unburned Hydrocarbons) Order 1988 art 5 (6).
7 Air Navigation (Aircraft and Aircraft Engine Emissions) Order 1986 art 7 (6) and Air Navigation (Aeroplane and Aeroplane Engine Emission of Unburned Hydrocarbons) Order 1988 art 5 (5). Article 6 of the 1988 Order specifically provides for the revocation, suspension and variation of any certification, approval, exemption (see para 1300 post) or document issued under the order (see art 6 (1)), such a decision to be published in the official record (art 6 (2)) and followed by the surrender by the holder of the document (art 6 (3)); any breach of a condition attached to the document invalidates it during the continuance of the breach (art 6 (4)). As to penalties see para 1299 post.

1297. Certification by foreign authority. Certificates relating to aircraft engine emissions[1] may be issued by the competent authority of a state party to the Chicago Convention[2] or of a country prescribed as one which applies standards which in the opinion of the Secretary of State[3] are substantially equivalent to those required for a certification by the Civil Aviation Authority[4].

1 As to the necessity for certificates relating to aircraft engine emissions see para 1295 ante.
2 As to the Chicago Convention see para 1002 ante.
3 As to the Secretary of State see para 1032 ante.
4 See the Air Navigation (Aircraft and Aircraft Engine Emissions) Order 1986, SI 1986/599, arts 4 (b), (c), 5 (b), (c) and the Air Navigation (Aeroplane and Aeroplane Engine Emission of Unburned Hydrocarbons) Order 1988, SI 1988/1994, art 4 (1) (b), (c). As to the Civil Aviation Authority see para 1044 ante.

1298. Power to prevent aircraft flying. Where the Civil Aviation Authority (CAA)[1] or an authorised person[2] believes that an aircraft is intended or likely to be flown in contravention of the provisions regulating the emissions of aircraft engines[3], the CAA or the authorised person may direct the operator or the commander of the aircraft that he is not to allow the aircraft to make any flight as specified in the direction until the direction has been revoked. If necessary, the aircraft may be detained[4].

The operator or the commander of the aircraft is guilty of an offence if he fails without reasonable excuse to comply with the direction[5].

1 As to the CAA see para 1044 ante.
2 An 'authorised person' means any constable and any person authorised by the CAA (whether by name or by class or description) either generally or in relation to a particular case or class of cases: Air Navigation (Aircraft and Aircraft Engine Emissions) Order 1986, SI 1986/599, art 2 (1); Air Navigation (Aeroplane and Aeroplane Engine Emission of Unburned Hydrocarbons) Order 1988, SI 1988/1994, art 2 (1).
3 See para 1295 ante.
4 Air Navigation (Aircraft and Aircraft Engine Emissions) Order 1986 art 8 (1); Air Navigation (Aeroplane and Aeroplane Engine Emission of Unburned Hydrocarbons) Order 1988 art 7 (1). For the purposes of these provisions the CAA or an authorised person may enter upon and inspect the

aircraft; see the 1986 Order art 8 (3) and the 1988 Order art 7 (3). They also have the right of access a all reasonable times to any aerodrome, or to any other place where an aircraft has landed, in order to inspect or to detain an aircraft: see the 1986 Order art 9 and the 1988 Order art 8.

1299. Offences. Where any provision relating to the certification of aircraf engine emissions[1] is contravened, the operator and the commander of the aircraf are deemed to have contravened the provision unless they prove that the contra-vention occurred without their consent or connivance and that they exercised al due diligence to prevent the offence[2]. Where it is proved that an act or omission wa: unavoidable in spite of the exercise of reasonable care by the person involved, thi: act or omission is deemed not to be a contravention by that person[3].

A person may not intentionally obstruct or impede any person acting in the exercise of his powers or the performance of his duties[4].

1 See para 1295 ante.
2 Air Navigation (Aircraft and Aircraft Engine Emissions) Order 1986, SI 1986/599, art 11 (1); Ai Navigation (Aeroplane and Aeroplane Engine Emission of Unburned Hydrocarbons) Order 1988 SI 1988/1994, art 10 (1). A contravention of any provision of those orders renders the offender liabl on summary conviction to a fine not exceeding £1,000: see the Air Navigation (Aircraft and Aircraf Engine Emissions) Order 1986 art 11 (3) and the Air Navigation (Aeroplane and Aeroplane Engin Emission of Unburned Hydrocarbons) Order 1988 art 10 (3).
3 Air Navigation (Aircraft and Aircraft Engine Emissions) Order 1986 art 11 (2); Air Navigatio (Aeroplane and Aeroplane Engine Emission of Unburned Hydrocarbons) Order 1988 art 10 (2).
4 Air Navigation (Aircraft and Aircraft Engine Emissions) Order 1986 art 10; Air Navigatio (Aeroplane and Aeroplane Engine Emission of Unburned Hydrocarbons) Order 1988 art 9.

1300. Exemptions. After consulting the Secretary of State[1], the Civil Aviatior Authority (CAA)[2] may exempt from any of the provisions of the Air Navigatior (Aircraft and Aircraft Engine Emissions) Order 1986[3] or of the Air Navigatior (Aeroplane and Aeroplane Engine Emission of Unburned Hydrocarbons) Orde 1988[4] or of any regulations made thereunder any aircraft, aircraft engine or persor (or classes of aircraft, aircraft engines or persons) either absolutely or as it think fit[5].

1 As to the Secretary of State see para 1032 ante.
2 As to the CAA see para 1044 ante.
3 Ie SI 1986/599.
4 Ie SI 1988/1994.
5 Air Navigation (Aircraft and Aircraft Engine Emissions) Order 1986 art 13; Air Navigatio (Aeroplane and Aeroplane Engine Emission of Unburned Hydrocarbons) Order 1988 art 12. As to aircraft flying under the 'A' conditions or the 'B' conditions or landing or taking off at a prescribe place see para 1295 notes 4, 5 ante.

(iii) Certificates of Maintenance Review

1301. Maintenance schedules and certificates of maintenance review. Ar aircraft registered in the United Kingdom must not fly for the purposes of public transport[1] or aerial work[2] unless the aircraft, including in particular its engines, together with its equipment and radio station, is maintained in accordance with ar approved[3] maintenance schedule and there is in force in respect of that aircraft a certificate of maintenance review certifying that maintenance has been carried ou in accordance with that schedule[4].

1 For the meaning of 'public transport' see para 1272 ante.
2 For the meaning of 'aerial work' see para 1273 ante.
3 The schedule is approved by the Civil Aviation Authority (CAA) in relation to the particular aircraft: Air Navigation Order 1989, SI 1989/2004, art 9 (1) (a). The schedule must specify the occasion on which a review must be carried out: art 9 (2). As to the CAA see para 1044 ante.
4 Ibid art 9 (1) (b). The penalty for contravention is on summary conviction a fine not exceeding £1,000: art 99 (5) , Sch 12 Pt A .

1302. Issue of certificates of maintenance review. A certificate of maintenance review may be issued only by a person authorised by the Civil Aviation Authority (CAA)[1] in a particular case[2] or by a person approved by the CAA as being competent to issue such certificates[3] or by the holder of an aircraft maintenance engineer's licence[4] granted either under the Air Navigation Order 1989 [5], or under the law of a country other than the United Kingdom and rendered valid under that order[6], or under the law of any such country as may be prescribed in accordance with the privileges endorsed on the licence and subject to any conditions which may be prescribed[7].

Upon approving a maintenance schedule the CAA may direct that certificates of maintenance review relating to that schedule may be issued only by the holder of such a licence as is so specified[8].

The person issuing the certificate of maintenance review must verify that maintenance has been carried out in accordance with the maintenance schedule, that, where required by the CAA, the aircraft has been inspected and modified and thereafter certified in the relevant certificate of release to service[9], that defects entered in the technical log[10] have been rectified or deferred as provided by the CAA and that certificates of release to service have been properly issued[11].

Certificates of maintenance review, which must be issued in duplicate[12], must be preserved by the operator for a period of two years after they have been issued[13].

1 As to the CAA see para 1044 ante.
2 Air Navigation Order 1989, SI 1989/2004, art 9 (3) (b).
3 Ibid art 9 (3) (c).
4 As to the licensing of maintenance engineers see para 1304 post; as to licensing under the Air Navigation Order 1989 generally see the Civil Aviation Authority Regulations 1991, SI 1991/1672, reg 6; and paras 1066–1071 ante.
5 Air Navigation Order 1989 art 9 (3) (a) (i).
6 Ibid art 9 (3) (a) (ii).
7 Ibid art 9 (3) (a) (iii). For the countries prescribed for this purpose see the Air Navigation (General) Regulations 1981, SI 1981/57, reg 13.
8 Air Navigation Order 1989 art 9 (3) proviso.
9 As to certificates of release to service see para 1325 note 2 post.
10 As to the technical log see para 1303 post.
11 Air Navigation Order 1989 art 9 (4). All necessary information must be made available by the operator of the aircraft: art 9 (4).
12 Ibid art 9 (5). One of the duplicates must be carried in the aircraft when so required by art 61 (see para 1415 post), and the other must be kept by the operator elsewhere than in the aircraft: art 9 (5).
13 Ibid art 9 (6).

1303. Entries in technical log. On the termination by an aircraft registered in the United Kingdom of every flight[1] for the purposes of public transport[2] or aerial work[3], the commander of the aircraft must enter into a technical log the times at which the aircraft took off and landed[4], particulars of any defect in any part of the aircraft or its equipment which is known to him, and which affects the airworthiness or safe operation of the aircraft, or, if no such defect is known to him, an entry to that effect[5] and any other airworthiness or operation particulars required by the Civil Aviation Authority (CAA)[6]. He must sign and date the entries[7].

Upon the rectification of any defect entered in a technical log a copy of the certificate of release to service[8] must be entered in the log in such a manner as to be readily identifiable with the entry of the defect to which it relates[9].

The technical log must be carried in the aircraft when so required[10], and copies of the entries must be kept on the ground[11]. It must be preserved by the operator for a period of two years after the aircraft has been destroyed or has been permanently withdrawn from use, or for such shorter period as permitted by the CAA[12].

1 Where a number of consecutive flights begin and end on the same day with the same commander and, save where each flight is for the purposes of dropping or projecting any material for agricultural, public health or similar purposes, where each such flight begins and ends at the same aerodrome, the commander may make the entries at the end of the last flight unless he is aware of defect during any earlier flight: Air Navigation Order 1989, SI 1989/2004, art 10 (2) proviso.
2 For the meaning of 'public transport' see para 1272 ante.
3 For the meaning of 'aerial work' see para 1273 ante.
4 Air Navigation Order 1989 art 10 (2) (a).
5 Ibid art 10 (2) (b).
6 Ibid art 10 (2) (c). As to the CAA see para 1044 ante.
7 See ibid art 10 (2).
8 See para 1331 post.
9 Air Navigation Order 1989 art 10 (3).
10 Ie by ibid art 61: see para 1416 post.
11 Air Navigation Order 1989 art 10 (4).
12 Ibid art 10 (5).

1304. Licensing of maintenance engineers. The Civil Aviation Authority (CAA)[1] may grant to any person a licence to act as an aircraft maintenance engineer where it is satisfied that the applicant is a fit person to hold the licence and is qualified by his knowledge and experience to do so[2]. The applicant must furnish such evidence and undergo such examinations and tests as the CAA may require to establish that he has sufficient knowledge, experience, competence and skill in aeronautical engineering[3].

The holder of an aircraft maintenance engineer's licence is entitled to issue certificates of maintenance review[4], certificates of release to service[5] or certificates of fitness for flight under the 'A' conditions[6].

An appeal lies to a county court from any decision of the CAA that a person is not a fit person to hold such a licence, and, if satisfied that on the evidence submitted to the CAA it was wrong in so deciding, the court may reverse the decision[7]. No appeal lies, however, from a decision that the applicant was not qualified by reason of deficiency in his knowledge, experience, competence, skill or physical or mental fitness[8].

The licence remains in force for a period specified in it, not exceeding five years but it may be renewed from time to time[9]. Upon receiving the licence the applicant must sign it in ink with his ordinary signature[10].

The CAA may issue a certificate rendering valid any licence as an aircraft maintenance engineer granted under the law of any country other than the United Kingdom[11].

1 As to the CAA see para 1044 ante.
2 Air Navigation Order 1989, SI 1989/2004, art 12 (1). As to the licensing procedure see the Civil Aviation Authority Regulations 1991, SI 1991/1672, reg 6; and paras 1066–1071 ante.

3 Air Navigation Order 1989 art 12 (1).
4 Ibid art 12 (2) (a); and see para 1301 ante.
5 Ibid art 12 (2) (b); and see para 1331 post.
6 Ibid art 12 (2) (c); and see para 1286 ante.
7 Ibid art 105 (1). The CAA must be a respondent to the appeal: art 105 (3). Its decision is deemed to
  have been taken on the date on which it furnished the applicant with a statement of its reasons for the
  decision: art 105 (4). As to the venue and procedure see para 1098 note 1 ante.
8 Ibid art 105 (1) proviso.
9 Ibid art 12 (3). This is subject to art 66: see para 1422 post.
10 Ibid art 12 (5).
11 Ibid art 12 (4).

(iv) Noise Certificates

1305. Necessity for noise certificates. An aircraft requiring a noise certificate[1]
may not take off or land in the United Kingdom unless there is in force in respect of
that aircraft a noise certificate and any conditions subject to which the certificate
was issued are complied with[2].

However, this provision does not apply to an aircraft flying in accordance with
the 'A' or 'B' conditions set out in the Air Navigation Order 1989 [3], or to an aircraft
landing or taking off at a prescribed place[4].

The Air Navigation (Noise Certification) Order 1990 does not apply to or in
relation to visiting forces[5], international headquarters[6] and any military aircraft[7],
and the Civil Aviation Authority (CAA)[8] may, after consultation with the Secretary of State[9], exempt any person or aircraft, as it thinks fit[10].

The provisions of the order apply to aircraft registered in the United Kingdom
wherever they may be and to other aircraft when they are within the United
Kingdom[11].

1 As to the aircraft which require noise certificates see para 1306 post. 'Noise certificate' means a
  certificate issued or validated or other document approved by the competent authority of a state to
  the effect that the aircraft to which the certificate or document relates complies with the applicable
  noise certification requirements in force in that state: Air Navigation (Noise Certification) Order
  1990, SI 1990/1514, art 3 (1).
2 Ibid art 5 (1) (a), (b). For the penalty for contravention see para 1311 note 1 post.
3 As to the 'A' and 'B' conditions see paras 1286, 1287 ante.
4 Air Navigation (Noise Certification) Order 1990 art 5 (3). 'Prescribed place' means a place prescribed by regulations made by the Secretary of State under that order: art 3 (1). Regulations may
  make different provisions for different classes of aircraft and for different circumstances and any
  incidental or supplementary provision as is necessary or expedient: art 3 (3).
5 For the meaning of 'visiting force' see para 1264 note 11 ante. Definitions in the Air Navigation
  Order 1989, SI 1989/2004, are applied by the Air Navigation (Noise Certification) Order 1990 art 3
  (2).
6 For the meaning of 'international headquarters' see para 1264 note 12 ante.
7 Air Navigation (Noise Certification) Order 1990 art 15 (2), (3). Subject to art 15 (2), (3), the order
  applies to Crown aircraft: see art 15 (1). For the meaning of 'military aircraft' see para 1029 note 5
  ante.
8 As to the CAA see para 1044 ante.
9 As to the Secretary of State see para 1032 ante.
10 Air Navigation (Noise Certification) Order 1990 art 16.
11 Ibid art 17 (1) (a), (b). The same extra-territorial effect applies to the commander of an aircraft
  registered in the United Kingdom wherever he may be (art 17 (1) (c)) and to Commonwealth
  citizens, British protected persons or citizens of the Republic of Ireland in relation to an aircraft
  registered in the United Kingdom, wherever they may be (art 17 (1) (d)).

1306. Aircraft to which noise certificate requirements apply. The requirement for an aircraft to have a noise certificate does not apply to every aircraft[1]. It does, however, apply to every propeller driven aeroplane having a maximum total weight authorised of 9,000 kg or less[2], to every aeroplane capable of sustaining level flight at a speed in excess of Flight Mach 1.0[3], to every microlight aeroplane[4], to every other subsonic aeroplane which requires, in accordance with its certificate of airworthiness[5], a runway of more than 610 metres for take-off at maximum total weight authorised[6], and to every helicopter[7].

1 As to exemptions see para 1305 ante.
2 Air Navigation (Noise Certification) Order 1990, SI 1970/1514, art 4 (a). As to the applicable standards see art 6 (5)–(8), Sch 1 Pts I, II, IV–VI. As to the determination of the applicable standards see para 1307 post.
3 Ibid art 4 (b). The standards applicable to supersonic aircraft are that the noise made by the aircraft must not be louder than that made by the prototype when the noise level of the prototype is measured in accordance with Sch 1 Pt I para 2: art 6 (9). The aircraft must conform to a prototype in respect of which a certificate of airworthiness was applied for before 1 January 1975 and not rejected and for which a certificate of airworthiness was first issued on or after 26 November 1981, and the same condition applies to an aircraft conforming to a delivered version of such a prototype: art 6 (9) (a), (b). As to the determination of applicable standards see para 1307 post.
4 Ibid art 4 (c). As to the applicable standards see art 6 (12), Sch 1 Pts VII, VIII. As to the determination of applicable standards see para 1307 post.
5 As to certificates of airworthiness see paras 1284–1294 ante.
6 Air Navigation (Noise Certification) Order 1990 art 4 (d). For the meaning of 'maximum total weight authorised' see para 1314 note 5 post. Subsonic aeroplanes registered in the United Kingdom after 1 November 1990 and powered by turbojet or turbofan engines which either have a maximum total weight authorised of more than 34,000 kg or can seat more than 19 passengers must not take off or land in the United Kingdom or in any other member state of the European Community unless the Civil Aviation Authority (as to which see para 1044 ante) has issued a noise certificate to the effect that the aircraft complies with the standards set in art 6 (3), Sch 1 Pt II: see art 5 (2). As to the applicable standards to other aeroplanes having turbojet or turbofan engines see art 6 (2), (4), Sch 1 Pts II, III. As to the determination of applicable standards see para 1307 post.
7 Ibid art 4 (e). As to the applicable standards see art 6 (10), Sch 1 Pt IX. As to the determination of applicable standards see para 1307 post.

1307. Issue of noise certificates. A noise certificate may be issued either by the competent authority of the country in which the aircraft is registered, being either a prescribed country[1] or a state, party to the Chicago Convention[2], or, where the application is made to the Civil Aviation Authority (CAA)[3], by that authority[4].

The CAA must be satisfied that the aircraft complies with the applicable standards[5] specified in the Air Navigation (Noise Certification) Order 1990[6] in relation to the noise made by the aircraft, and for this purpose the applicant must furnish such evidence and submit the aircraft to such trials and tests as the CAA may require[7]. The CAA may accept reports furnished by a person whom it may approve as qualified to furnish such reports[8].

The CAA may issue the certificate subject to such conditions as it thinks fit, and must, except in respect of microlight aeroplanes, make the certificate subject to a condition as to the maximum total weights at which the aircraft may take off and land[9].

No aircraft may land or take off in the United Kingdom, and no aircraft registered in the United Kingdom may fly over the United Kingdom or elsewhere, unless it carries the noise certificate which it is required to carry under the law of the country in which it is registered[10].

1 The country is prescribed as one which applies standards which in the opinion of the Secretary of State are substantially equivalent to those required for the issue of a noise certificate by the CAA (see note 3 infra): Air Navigation (Noise Certification) Order 1990, SI 1990/1514, art 5 (1) (a) (i) (bb). For microlight aeroplanes, the country does not need to be prescribed as long as in the opinion of the CAA it applies substantially equivalent standards to those required by the CAA for the issue of a noise certificate: art 5 (1) (a) (ii) (bb).
2 Ibid art 5 (1) (a) (i) (cc). As to the Chicago Convention see para 1002 ante.
3 As to the CAA see para 1044 ante.
4 Air Navigation (Noise Certification) Order 1990 art 5 (1) (a) (i) (aa), (ii) (aa).
5 For the purposes of determining the standard applicable to an aircraft where the interval between the application for a certificate of airworthiness for a prototype aircraft and the first issue of such a certificate for an aircraft of that type exceeds five years, the date on which the application was made is deemed to be five years before the date of the first issue of the certificate, unless otherwise directed by the CAA: ibid art 6 (11) (a). The same applies when a certificate of airworthiness is modified: see art 6 (11) (b).
6 See ibid Sch 1.
7 Ibid art 6 (1).
8 Ibid art 6 (16).
9 Ibid art 6 (13).
0 Ibid art 7 (1), (2). If, however, the flight by an aircraft registered in the United Kingdom is intended to begin and end at the same aerodrome, the certificate may be kept there: art 7 (2) proviso. The aircraft commander must produce the certificate within a reasonable time after being requested to do so by an authorised person: art 8. For the meaning of 'commander' see para 1213 note 1 ante.

1308. Validity of noise certificates. A noise certificate remains in force without limit of time[1]. However, it may cease to be sufficient if a modification to the aircraft affects the aircraft's ability to comply with the required noise standards[2]; and until completion of any inspection or test required by the Civil Aviation Authority (CAA)[3] for the purpose of ascertaining whether the aircraft continues to comply with the required noise standards[4].

1 Air Navigation (Noise Certification) Order 1990, SI 1990/1514, art 6 (14). As to the revocation, suspension or variation of certificates see para 1309 post.
2 Ibid art 6 (15) (a): this provision concerns any modification made otherwise than in a manner and with material of a type approved by the CAA (see note 3 infra) either generally or in relation to a class of aircraft or to the particular aircraft.
3 As to the CAA see para 1044 ante.
4 Air Navigation (Noise Certification) Order 1990 art 6 (15) (b).

1309. Revocation, suspension and variation of noise certificates. The Civil Aviation Authority (CAA)[1] may, if it thinks fit, provisionally suspend a noise certificate, approval, exemption or other document issued under the Air Navigation (Noise Certification) Order 1990 pending inquiry into or consideration of the case, and may, after due inquiry, revoke, suspend or vary any such certificate[2]. Where a noise certificate, approval, exemption or other document has been revoked, suspended or varied, the holder, or any person having possession or custody of it, must surrender it to the CAA[3].

The breach of any condition subject to which any noise certificate, approval, exemption or other document has been issued renders the certificate invalid during the continuance of the breach[4].

1 As to the CAA see para 1044 ante.
2 Air Navigation (Noise Certification) Order 1990, SI 1990/1514, art 9 (1).
3 Ibid art 9 (2).
4 Ibid art 9 (3).

1310. Power to prevent aircraft flying. Where the Civil Aviation Authorit (CAA)[1] or an authorised person[2] believes that an aircraft is intended or likely to b flown in contravention of the provisions requiring noise certification[3], the CAA c the authorised person may direct the operator or the commander of the aircraft tha he is not to permit the aircraft to make any flight as specified in the direction unt the latter is revoked[4]. If necessary, the aircraft may be detained[5]. For such pu poses, the CAA or the authorised person may enter upon and inspect any aircraft[6]

1 As to the CAA see para 1044 ante.
2 An 'authorised person' means any constable and any person authorised by the CAA (whether b name or by class or description) either generally or in relation to a particular case or class of cases: A Navigation (Noise Certification) Order 1990, SI 1990/1514, art 3 (1).
3 See ibid art 5; and para 1305 ante.
4 Ibid art 11 (1). As to offences and penalties see para 1311 post.
5 Ibid art 11 (1).
6 Ibid art 11 (3).

1311. Offences in relation to noise certificates. A person must not, wit intent to deceive, either use a revoked or suspended noise certificate or one t which he is not entitled; or lend to, or allow a noise certificate to be used by, an other person; or make any false representation in order to obtain the issue, renew or variation of a noise certificate[1]; and no person may purport to issue a nois certificate unless he has been authorised to do so[2].

If the operator or the commander of an aircraft fails without reasonable excuse t comply with a direction given to him by the Civil Aviation Authority (CAA)[3] c by an authorised person preventing the aircraft from flying , he is guilty of a offence[4]; and if any provision of the Air Navigation (Noise Certification) Ord 1990 is contravened in relation to an aircraft, the operator and the commander c that aircraft are deemed to have contravened that provision[5].

A person must not intentionally obstruct or impede any person acting in th exercise of his powers or the performance of his duties under the order[6].

Where a contravention is likely to be committed, the CAA has power to prever the aircraft from flying[7]. The CAA has a right of access to any aerodrome and an other place to inspect an aircraft for the purpose of ascertaining whether th provisions of the order are being complied with[8].

Where it is proved that an act or omission was unavoidable in spite of the exercis of reasonable care by the person involved, the act or omission is deemed not to hav contravened the order[9].

1 Air Navigation (Noise Certification) Order 1990, SI 1990/1514, art 10 (1). The penalty on summar conviction is a fine not exceeding level 4 on the standard scale: art 14 (4). As to the standard scale s para 1044 note 6 ante. At the date at which this volume states the law, level 4 on that scale is at £1,00
2 Ibid art 10 (2). For the penalty see note 1 supra.
3 As to the CAA see para 1044 ante.
4 Air Navigation (Noise Certification) Order 1990 art 11 (2); as to the power to prevent aircraft flyin see para 1310 ante.
5 Ibid art 14 (1). However, there is a defence that the contravention occurred without the consent c connivance of the accused and that he exercised all due diligence to prevent the contravention: art 1 (1). For the penalty see note 1 supra.
6 Ibid art 13. For the penalty see note 1 supra.
7 See para 1310 ante.
8 See the Air Navigation (Noise Certification) Order 1990 art 12.

9 Ibid art 14 (2).

(4) EQUIPMENT AND REPAIRS

(i) General Equipment

1312. Equipment of aircraft. An aircraft must not fly unless it is so equipped as to comply with the law of the country in which it is registered and to enable lights and markings to be displayed and signals to be made in accordance with the Air Navigation Order 1989 [1].

Where an aircraft is registered in the United Kingdom, the equipment required to be provided is that specified in the order[2]; it must be of a type approved by the Civil Aviation Authority (CAA)[3] and must be installed in a manner so approved[4]. The CAA may direct that such an aircraft must carry such additional or special equipment or supplies as it may specify in order to facilitate the aircraft's navigation, the carrying out of search and rescue operations or the survival of the persons carried in the aircraft[5].

The position of equipment for emergency use must be indicated by clear markings in or on the aircraft, and in particular in every public transport aircraft[6] registered in the United Kingdom there must be exhibited prominently in every passenger compartment or provided individually for each passenger a notice containing pictorial instructions and information as to the brace position to be adopted in the event of an emergency landing, the method of use of the safety belts or safety harnesses, the location of emergency exits and how they are to be used, and where lifejackets, escape slides, liferafts and oxygen masks are to be found and how they are to be used [7].

All equipment installed or carried in an aircraft must be so installed or stowed and kept stowed, maintained and adjusted as not to be a source of danger in itself or to impair the airworthiness of the aircraft or the proper functioning of any equipment or service necessary for the aircraft's safety[8].

1 Air Navigation Order 1989, SI 1989/2004, art 13 (1). The penalty for contravention of this and other requirements set out in this paragraph is on summary conviction a fine not exceeding £1,000: art 99 (5), Sch 12 Pt A . Article 13, does not apply to radio apparatus except that specified in Sch 4: art 13 (8). As to radio see paras 1318–1323 post.
2 See ibid Sch 4, which specifies the equipment to be carried by different types of aircraft in the case of flights of different types for different purposes, at different times and heights over different places and under different flight rules. With the permission of the CAA (see note 3 infra) an aircraft registered in the United Kingdom may in special circumstances take off without all the required equipment or with equipment not in a fit condition for use, save for radio communication apparatus: art 15.
3 As to the CAA see para 1044 ante.
4 Air Navigation Order 1989 art 13 (2). In particular, equipment capable of establishing the aircraft's position in relation to an earlier position, and equipment capable of establishing automatically the altitude must, when carried in an aircraft registered in the United Kingdom, be of a type approved by the CAA: art 13 (7).
5 Ibid art 13 (3). The equipment carried must be so installed, stowed, maintained and adjusted as to be readily accessible and capable of being used by the person for whose use it is intended: art 13 (4).
6 For the meaning of 'public transport aircraft' see para 1272 ante.
7 Air Navigation Order 1989 art 13 (5).
8 Ibid art 13 (6).

1313. Inspection for airworthiness purposes. The Civil Aviation Authority (CAA)[1] may cause such inspections, investigations, tests, experiments and flight trials to be made as it deems necessary[2], and any person authorised in writing by the CAA may therefore at any reasonable time inspect any part, or material intended to be incorporated or used in the manufacture of any part, of the equipment of an aircraft, and may for that purpose go upon any aerodrome or enter any aircraft factory[3].

1 As to the CAA see para 1044 ante.
2 Ie for the purposes of the Air Navigation Order 1989, SI 1989/2004, Pt III (arts 7–18: airworthiness and equipment of aircraft).
3 Ibid art 18. See also para 1288 ante.

1314. Exits in aircraft. In every public transport aircraft[1] registered in the United Kingdom which is carrying passengers, every exit from the aircraft and every internal door in it must be in working order , and during take-off and landing and during any emergency, be kept free from obstruction, and must not be fastened by locking or otherwise so as to prevent, hinder or delay its use by passengers[2]. Every exit intended to be used by passengers in normal circumstances must be marked 'EXIT', and every exit intended for use by passengers in an emergency only must be marked 'EMERGENCY EXIT'[3]. Every exit must be marked with instructions in English and with diagrams to indicate the correct method of opening it[4]. Where the maximum total weight authorised[5] of the aircraft exceeds 3,600 kg the aircraft must be marked on the exterior of the fuselage to show the break-in areas[6] and where the maximum total weight authorised exceeds 5,700 kg, every emergency exit must be marked on the exterior of the aircraft by a band outlining the exit[7].

1 For the meaning of 'public transport aircraft' see para 1272 ante.
2 Air Navigation Order 1989, SI 1989/2004, art 49 (1), (2). The penalty for contravention of this and other requirements set out in this paragraph is on summary conviction a fine not exceeding £1,000: art 99 (5), Sch 12 Pt A. For the circumstances in which an exit may be obstructed or an internal door may be locked see art 49 (2) proviso; and para 1427 post. Where one exit becomes inoperative at a place where it is not reasonably practicable for it to be repaired or replaced , the aircraft may carry passengers until it next lands at a place where the repair or replacement can be made, provided the number of passengers and position of seats are in accordance with arrangements approved by the CAA (as to which see para 1044 ante) and the exit is visibly condemned: art 49 (8).
3 Ibid art 49 (3).
4 Ibid art 49 (4) (a). The markings, which must be painted red and kept clean and unobscured (art 49 (7)), must be placed on or near the inside surface of the door and, if it is openable from the outside, on or near the exterior surface (art 49 (4) (b)).
5 'Maximum total weight authorised', in relation to an aircraft, means the maximum total weight of the aircraft and its contents at which the aircraft may take off anywhere in the world, in the most favourable circumstances in accordance with the certificate of airworthiness in force in respect of the aircraft: ibid art 106 (1)).
6 Ibid art 49 (5) (a): 'break-in areas' are areas which can, for the purpose of rescue in an emergency, be most readily and effectively broken into by persons outside the aircraft. These areas must be rectangular, marked by right-angle corner markings, with ' CUT HERE IN EMERGENCY' marked across the centre: art 49 (5) (b), (c). These provisions do not apply to helicopters: art 49 (5)

proviso (added by SI 1991/1726). The markings must be painted red, and kept clean and unobscured: Air Navigation Order 1989 art 49 (7).
7 Ibid art 49 (6); the band must be at least five centimetres wide.

1315. Aircraft log books. In addition to any other log books required by or under the Air Navigation Order 1989 [1], there must be kept in respect of every aircraft registered in the United Kingdom an aircraft log book, a separate log book for each engine and a separate log book for each variable pitch propeller[2].

Each entry must be made as soon as is practicable after the occurrence to which it relates[3]; it may refer to other documents, which will therefore be deemed to be part of the log book[4].

It is the duty of the operator[5] of the aircraft to keep the required log books in accordance with the foregoing provisions and to preserve them until a date two years after the destruction or permanent withdrawal of the aircraft or of that part of the aircraft to which they relate[6].

1 See paras 1303 ante, 1357, 1455 post.
2 Air Navigation Order 1989, SI 1989/2004, art 16 (1). As to the particulars to be included in each see Sch 6. 'Log book' in the case of an aircraft log book, engine log book or variable pitch propeller log book includes a record kept either in a book or by any other means approved by the Civil Aviation Authority (as to which see para 1044 ante) in the particular case: art 106 (1). The penalty for contravention of this and other requirements set out in this paragraph is on summary conviction a fine not exceeding £1,000: art 99 (5), Sch 12 Pt A.
3 Ibid art 16 (2); an entry may not be made more than seven days after the expiration of the certificate of maintenance review (if any) in force in respect of the aircraft at the time of the occurrence art 16 (2) (a).
4 Ibid art 16 (3).
5 For the meaning of 'operator' see para 1340 post.
6 Air Navigation Order 1989 art 16 (4), (5). This is subject to art 65: see para 1409 post.

1316. Aircraft weight schedules. Where a certificate of airworthiness[1] is in force in respect of a flying machine[2] or glider, the aircraft concerned must be weighed and the position of its centre of gravity determined at such times and in such manner as the Civil Aviation Authority (CAA)[3] may require in the case of that aircraft[4]. The operator[5] of the aircraft must then prepare a weight schedule showing either the basic weight of the aircraft[6], or such other weight as may be approved by the CAA, and either the position of the centre of gravity when the aircraft contains only the items included in the basic weight[7], or such other position of the centre of gravity as may be approved by the CAA.

The operator must preserve the weight schedule until the expiry of a period of six months following the next occasion on which the aircraft is weighed[8].

1 As to certificates of airworthiness see paras 1284–1294 ante.
2 As to the meaning of 'flying machine' see para 1269 ante.
3 As to the CAA see para 1044 ante.
4 Air Navigation Order 1989, SI 1989/2004, art 17 (1). The penalty for contravention of this and other requirements set out in this paragraph is on summary conviction a fine not exceeding £1,000: art 99 (5), Sch 12 Pt A.
5 For the meaning of 'operator' see para 1340 post.
6 The basic weight of the aircraft is the weight of the aircraft empty together with the weight of unusable fuel and unusable oil in the aircraft and of such items of equipment as are indicated in the weight schedule: Air Navigation Order 1989 art 17 (2).
7 Ibid art 17 (2).
8 Ibid art 17 (3): this is subject to art 65, as to which see para 1409 post.

1317. Minimum navigation performance and area navigation equipment. An aircraft registered in the United Kingdom may not fly in prescribed airspace[1] unless it is equipped with navigation systems which enable it to maintain the prescribed navigation performance capability[2]. The Civil Aviation Authority (CAA)[3] must approve, in writing and with such conditions as it thinks fit[4], such navigation systems as well as the manner in which they are installed and maintained and the relevant operating procedures[5]. The equipment must be operated in accordance with such approved procedures[6].

An aircraft may not fly in controlled airspace notified as an area navigation route or area[7] unless it is equipped with area navigation equipment[8] which (1) if the aircraft is registered in the United Kingdom, is approved by the CAA in relation to the purpose for which it is to be used and is installed and maintained in a manner approved by the CAA, or (2) if the aircraft is not registered in the United Kingdom, complies with the law of the country in which the aircraft is registered in so far as that law requires it to be so equipped when flying within any specified areas[9]. An aircraft when flying in notified controlled airspace[10] which is not an area navigation route or area must not be navigated by means of area navigation equipment unless (a) if the aircraft is registered in the United Kingdom, the equipment is approved by the CAA in relation to the purpose for which it is to be used and installed and maintained in a manner approved by the CAA, or (b) if the aircraft is not registered in the United Kingdom, the equipment complies with the law of the country in which the aircraft is registered[11]. In all the above cases, the equipment must be capable of being operated so as to enable the aircraft to maintain the navigation accuracy notified in respect of the airspace in which the aircraft is flying, and be so operated[12].

1 The airspace is prescribed for the purposes of the Air Navigation Order 1989, SI 1989/2004, art 39.
2 Ibid art 39 (1) (a).
3 As to the CAA see para 1044 ante.
4 Air Navigation Order 1989 art 39 (2).
5 Ibid art 39 (1) (b), (c).
6 Ibid art 39 (1) (d).
7 Ie controlled airspace notified for the purpose of ibid art 39A (1) (added by SI 1991/1726). For the meaning of 'controlled airspace' see para 1395 post.
8 'Area navigation equipment' means equipment carried on board an aircraft which enables the aircraft to navigate on any desired flight path within the coverage of appropriate ground based navigation aids or within the limits of that on-board equipment or a combination of the two: Air Navigation Order 1989 art 106 (1) (amended by SI 1991/1726).
9 Air Navigation Order 1989 arts 39A (1), 39B (1) (as added. see note 7 supra). The CAA's approval must be in writing and may be subject to conditions: see art 39A (3) (as so added).
10 Ie controlled airspace notified for the purpose of ibid art 39A (2) (as added: see note 7 supra).
11 Ibid arts 39A (2), 39B (2) (as added: see note 7 supra).
12 Ibid arts 39A (1), 39B (1) (as added: see note 7 supra).

(ii) Radio Equipment

1318. Necessity for radio equipment. An aircraft may not fly unless it is so equipped with radio and radio navigation equipment as to comply with the law of the country in which the aircraft is registered, and to enable communications to be made, and the aircraft to be navigated, in accordance with the provisions of the Air Navigation Order 1989 [1].

1 Air Navigation Order 1989, SI 1989/2004, art 14 (1). Without prejudice to this provision, aircraft must be equipped with radio and radio navigation equipment in accordance with Sch 5: art 14 (2).

The penalty for contravention is on summary conviction a fine not exceeding £1,000: art 99 (5), Sch 12 Pt A.

1319. Approval of radio equipment. All radio and radio navigation equipment installed in an aircraft registered in the United Kingdom or carried on such an aircraft for use therewith must be of a type approved by the Civil Aviation Authority (CAA)[1] in relation to the purpose for which it is to be used, and must be installed in a manner approved by the CAA[2].

Any modification to the equipment or to the manner in which it is installed must receive the CAA's approval[3].

1 As to the CAA see para 1044 ante.
2 Air Navigation Order 1989, SI 1989/2004, art 14 (5); in the case of a glider permitted by art 3 (1) to fly unregistered (see para 1276 ante), the manner in which its radio equipment is installed need not be approved by the CAA. The penalty for contravention is on summary conviction a fine not exceeding £1,000: art 99 (5), Sch 12 Pt A.
3 Ibid art 14 (5).

1320. Radio equipment to be carried in aircraft. All aircraft must be equipment with radio and radio navigation equipment in accordance with the requirements of the Air Navigation Order 1989[1]. The Civil Aviation Authority (CAA)[2] may in any particular case direct that an aircraft registered in the United Kingdom must carry specified additional or special radio or radio navigation equipment to facilitate the navigation of the aircraft, the carrying out of search and rescue operations or the survival of the persons carried in the aircraft[3]. The radio and radio navigation equipment must always be maintained in serviceable condition unless otherwise prescribed[4].

1 Air Navigation Order 1989, SI 1989/2004, art 14 (2); as to the equipment see Sch 5. Requirements relating to radio equipment which previously applied only to aircraft registered in the United Kingdom have been extended to aircraft registered elsewhere when flying within the United Kingdom. The provisions in the text to note 3, however, apply only to aircraft registered in the United Kingdom. The penalty for contravention of this and other requirements set out in this paragraph is on summary conviction a fine not exceeding £1,000: art 99 (5), Sch 12 Pt A.
2 As to the CAA see para 1044 ante.
3 Air Navigation Order 1989 art 14 (3).
4 Ibid art 14 (4). As to flights permitted when equipment is unserviceable see para 1312 note 2 ante.

1321. Particular radio equipment to be carried. All aircraft within the United Kingdom when flying under instrument flight rules[1] within controlled airspace notified for the purpose[2] or when flying within controlled airspace notified for the purpose[3], and all aircraft (other than gliders) within the United Kingdom when flying at or above flight level[4] 245 or within airspace notified for the purpose[5] must be equipped with radio equipment capable of maintaining direct two-way communication with the appropriate aeronautical radio stations[6], unless the appropriate air traffic control unit[7] otherwise permits, and all aircraft registered in the United Kingdom must carry such equipment wherever they may be[8].

Radio navigation equipment capable of enabling the aircraft to be navigated on the intended route must be carried by all single-engined aircraft registered in the United Kingdom, wherever they may be, when flying for the purpose of public transport[9] under visual flight rules[10] except over a route on which navigation is effected solely by visual reference to landmarks[11].

All aircraft registered in the United Kingdom, wherever they may be, flying for the purpose of public transport under instrument flight rules must carry radio equipment capable of receiving from the appropriate aeronautical radio stations meteorological broadcasts relevant to the intended flight on all occasions[12] and must, while making an approach to landing, carry radio navigation equipment capable of receiving signals from one or more aeronautical radio stations on the surface to enable the aircraft to be guided to a point from which a visual landing can be made at the aerodrome at which it is to land[13].

All aircraft within the United Kingdom making an approach to landing at an aerodrome notified[14] for the purpose must, unless the appropriate air traffic control unit otherwise permits, carry radio navigation equipment capable of enabling the aircraft to make an approach to landing using the instrument landing system[15].

All aircraft within the United Kingdom when flying under instrument flight rules within controlled airspace and all aircraft (other than gliders) within the United Kingdom when flying at or above flight level 100 or when flying within such airspace as may be notified for the purpose must, unless the appropriate air traffic control unit otherwise permits, carry radio equipment capable of replying to an interrogation from secondary surveillance radar units on the surface and of being operated in accordance with instructions from the appropriate air traffic control unit[16].

All aircraft within the United Kingdom when flying under instrument flight rules within controlled airspace and all aircraft (other than gliders) within the United Kingdom when flying at or above flight level 245 must, unless the appropriate air traffic control unit otherwise permits, carry specified radio navigation equipment capable of enabling the aircraft to be navigated along the intended route[17].

All aircraft registered in the United Kingdom, wherever they may be, when flying for the purpose of public transport under instrument flight rules or (in the case of multi-engined aircraft) visual flight rules must carry specified radio navigation equipment capable of enabling the aircraft to be navigated on the intended route[18].

Contravention of any of the above provisions is an offence[19].

1 As to instrument flight rules see paras 1399–1404 post.
2 Ie notified for the purposes of the Air Navigation Order 1989, SI 1989/2004, Sch 5 para 2 (1) (a). For the meaning of 'controlled airspace' see para 1395 post.
3 Ie notified for the purposes of ibid Sch 5 para 2 (1) (b).
4 For the meaning of 'flight level' see para 1401 note 2 post.
5 Ie notified for the purposes of the Air Navigation Order 1989 Sch 5 para 2 (2) (b).
6 For the meaning of 'appropriate aeronautical radio station' see para 1435 note 4 post.
7 For the meaning of 'appropriate air traffic control unit' see para 1394 note 1 post.
8 Air Navigation Order 1989 art 14 (2), Sch 5 paras 2 (1) (a), (b), (2) (a), (b), (4), 3 Scale A (amended by SI 1991/1726).
9 For the meaning of 'public transport' see para 1272 ante.
10 As to visual flight rules see para 1398 post.
11 Air Navigation Order 1989 Sch 5 paras 2 (4) (a), (c), 3 Scale B.
12 Ibid Sch 5 paras 2 (4) (a), 3 Scale C.
13 Ibid Sch 5 paras 2 (4) (a) (i), 3 Scale D.
14 For the meaning of 'notified' see para 1105 note 3 ante.
15 Air Navigation Order 1989 Sch 5 paras 2 (1) (c), 3 Scale G.
16 Ibid Sch 5 paras 2 (1) (a), (2), 3 Scale E.
17 Ibid Sch 5 paras 2 (1) (a), (2) (a), 3 Scale F.

18 Ibid Sch 5 paras 2 (4) (a), (b), 3 Scale H, which sets out exceptions as to the carriage of such radio navigation equipment.
19 The penalty for contravention is on summary conviction a fine not exceeding £1,000: ibid art 99 (5), Sch 12 Pt A.

1322. Flight radio operator. An aircraft registered in the United Kingdom must carry a flight radio operator as a member of the flight crew[1] when the aircraft is required to be equipped with radio communications apparatus[2]; if the flight radio operator is required to operate radiotelegraph apparatus, he must be carried in addition to any other person who is required to be carried to perform other duties[3]. He must be the holder of an appropriate licence[4].

1 As to the flight crew see paras 1359–1364 post.
2 As to radio communications apparatus see paras 1318–1321 ante.
3 Air Navigation Order 1989, SI 1989/2004, art 19 (5). The penalty for contravention is on summary conviction a fine not exceeding £1,000: art 99 (5), Sch 12 Pt A. As to the radio operator's duties while the aircraft is in flight, see paras 1452–1455 post.
4 See ibid art 20 (1), Sch 8 Pt A para 5. As to exceptions within the United Kingdom, the Channel Islands and the Isle of Man see art 20 (1) (a) (flight radiotelephony operator who does not hold a licence). As to licensing generally see paras 1066–1071 ante. Flight radio operators must be tested by or on behalf of the operator as to their competence to perform their duties: Sch 10 Pt B para 1 (4). As to the training of the flight crew see para 1436 post.

1323. Commander's duties. Before an aircraft takes off the commander[1] of the aircraft must satisfy himself that the radio equipment required to be carried in the circumstances of the intended flight is carried and is in a fit condition for use[2].

1 For the meaning of 'commander' see para 1213 note 1 ante.
2 Air Navigation Order 1989, SI 1989/2004, art 35 (b). The penalty for contravention is on summary conviction a fine not exceeding £1,000: art 99 (5), Sch 12 Pt A. As to commander's pre-flight duties generally see paras 1426–1429 post. As to the operation of radio in the aircraft see para 1454 post.

(iii) Overhauls, Repairs and Modifications

1324. Repairer's contractual obligations. In a contract for the repair of an aircraft or its equipment there are implied terms as to the skill with which, and the time within which, the work will be done. These terms are implied by virtue of the Supply of Goods and Services Act 1982, which applies to contracts for repair[1]. It is rare in practice for the contract for the repair, maintenance or overhaul of an aircraft to be made otherwise than on the basis of detailed express terms.

1 See generally SALE OF GOODS.

1325. Repairer's liability to third parties. If repairs to an aircraft are negligently carried out, the repairer may be directly liable in damages to third parties who are injured by reason of such negligence[1].
If any part of an aircraft or its equipment has been overhauled, repaired, replaced or modified a certificate of release to service issued by a duly qualified engineer must be in force before the aircraft is flown[2], but this does not necessarily enable the negligent repairer to escape the consequences of his negligence. An engineer who

negligently certifies repairs may be liable for damages for breach of contract if damage results. A third party with whom the engineer is in no contractual relationship may have a right of action against the engineer in respect of the negligent certification[3]. These issues have not yet been tested in the English courts.

1 See CONTRACT and NEGLIGENCE.
2 See the Air Navigation Order 1989, SI 1989/2004, art 11 (1); and para 1330 post. It is submitted that there is no obligation on an aircraft owner or operator to examine overhaul, repair, replacement or modification work if the appropriate certificate of release to service has been granted. It must be noted that 'certificate of release to service' means a certificate that the part of the aircraft or of its equipment to which the certificate relates has been overhauled, repaired, replaced or modified, as the case may be in a manner and with material of a type approved by the Civil Aviation Authority (CAA) either generally or in relation to a class of aircraft or the particular aircraft and which identifies the overhaul, repair, replacement or modification to which it relates and includes particulars of the work done; in relation to an inspection required by the CAA it certifies that the inspection has been made in accordance with the CAA's requirements and that any consequential repair or replacement has been carried out as aforesaid: art 11 (5). As to the CAA see para 1044 ante.
3 See *Hawke v Waterloo-Wellington Flying Club Ltd* (1972) 22 DLR (3d) 266; and generally NEGLIGENCE.

1326. Lien for repairs. The repairer of an aircraft delivered to him for repair has a lien upon it for the price of the repairs actually executed[1] but, where no improvement to the machine has been effected, no lien exists for the cost of maintenance not amounting to repair[2].

1 See generally BAILMENT; LIEN. Cf *Hatton v Car Maintenance Co Ltd* [1915] 1 Ch 621; *Albemarle Supply Co Ltd v Hind & Co* [1928] 1 KB 307, CA. See also *Wilson v Lombank Ltd* [1963] 1 All ER 740, [1963] 1 WLR 1294; *Tappenden (trading as English and American Autos) v Artus* [1964] 2 QB 185, [1963] 3 All ER 213, CA. It is submitted that the law relating to bailments of and liens over aircraft is no different from that relating to bailments of and liens over, for example, motor vehicles.
2 *Hatton v Car Maintenance Co Ltd* [1915] 1 Ch 621. It is thought that in many cases 'maintenance' will amount to repair so as to give rise to a lien: see *Albermarle Supply Co Ltd v Hind & Co* [1928] 1 KB 307 at 313, CA, per Lord Hanworth MR, and at 318 per Scrutton LJ. As to the effect of a mortgage upon a lien see para 1335 post.

1327. Requirements as to overhauls, repairs, replacements and modifications. Detailed regulations as to overhaul, repair, replacement of parts and modification exist and must be complied with in respect of aircraft registered in the United Kingdom[1].

1 See the Air Navigation Order 1989, SI 1972/2004, art 11; and paras 1329–1331 post.

1328. Consultations on maintenance standards. The Civil Aviation Authority (CAA) [1] must consult the Airworthiness Requirements Board[2] on all matters which appear to the CAA to be of significance as respects the standards of design, construction and maintenance of aircraft by reference to which certificates of airworthiness[3] are to be granted or renewed, and as to whether any aircraft of a new type satisfies such standards[4]. The CAA must consider all advice given to it by that board, and if it decides to proceed otherwise than in accordance with such advice, must inform the board of its reasons and in certain circumstances must publish details of the case[5]. The board must advise the CAA on all such matters on which it is consulted and on any other matters appearing to the board to relate to such matters[6], and may consult such persons as it considers appropriate for the purpose of giving such advice[7].

1 As to the CAA see para 1044 ante.
2 As to the board see para 1060 ante.
3 As to certificates of airworthiness see paras 1284–1294 ante.
4 Civil Aviation Act 1982 s 85 (1). Any question whether a matter is one in which consultations are required is to be decided by the CAA: s 85 (1) (a).
5 Ibid s 85 (1) (b), (c).
6 Ibid s 85 (2) (a).
7 Ibid s 85 (2) (b).

1329. Installation of equipment after overhaul, repair or modification. No equipment required to be provided for an aircraft, except certain navigational, first-aid and other emergency equipment[1], and no radio equipment (whether for use in the aircraft or in any survival craft carried in it), may be installed or placed on board for use in an aircraft registered in the United Kingdom after being overhauled, repaired, modified or inspected unless a certificate of release to service[2] in respect of it is in force at the time of the installation and relating to the overhaul, repair, modification or inspection[3].

1 Ie no equipment provided in compliance with the Air Navigation Order 1989, SI 1989/2004, art 13 (2), Sch 4, except Sch 4 para 3.
2 For the meaning of 'certificate of release to service' see para 1325 note 2 ante.
3 Air Navigation Order 1989 art 11 (4). The penalty for contravention of this provision is, on summary conviction, a fine not exceeding £1,000: art 99 (5), Sch 12 Pt A.

1330. Flight prohibited until requirements complied with. An aircraft registered in the United Kingdom in respect of which a certificate of airworthiness[1] has been issued or rendered valid may not fly if any part of the aircraft or such of its equipment as is necessary for its airworthiness has been overhauled, repaired, replaced, modified or inspected unless there is in force a certificate of release to service[2] in respect thereof[3].

This provision does not, however, apply to light aircraft[4]; and does not apply to an aircraft on which a repair has been carried out at such a place that it is not reasonably practicable for the repair to be carried out in such a manner that a certificate of release to service can be issued, or for such a certificate to be issued while the aircraft is there; the aircraft may be flown to the nearest place where such a certificate can be issued, taking into account the safety of the aircraft and any hazard to the liberty or health of any person on board[5].

1 As to certificates of airworthiness see paras 1284–1294 ante.
2 For the meaning of 'certificate of release to service' see para 1325 note 2 ante.
3 Air Navigation Order 1989, SI 1989/2004, art 11 (1). The penalty for contravention of this provision is, on summary conviction, a fine not exceeding £1,000: art 99 (5), Sch 12 Pt A.
4 Ie an aircraft the maximum total weight authorised of which (defined in para 1154 note 3 ante) does not exceed 2,730 kg and in respect of which a certificate of airworthiness of the special category (as to which see para 1271 ante) is in force: ibid art 11 (2). There is no prohibition on flying such an aircraft where repairs and replacements of a description prescribed in the Air Navigation (General) Regulations 1981, SI 1981/57, have been carried out personally by the owner or operator of the aircraft, being the holder of a pilot's licence (as to which see para 1348 post), who must use equipment and parts of a type approved by the Civil Aviation Authority (CAA) (as to which see para 1044 ante) and must record the relevant entries in a log book: Air Navigation Order 1989 art 11 (3).

5 Ibid art 11 (1) proviso; the commander (defined in para 1213 note 1 ante) must cause written particulars of the flight, and the reasons for making it, to be given to the CAA within ten days thereafter.

1331. Issue and preservation of certificates of release to service. A certificate of release to service[1] may be issued only by either the holder of a licence as an aircraft maintenance engineer granted under the Air Navigation Order 1989[2] or under the law of a country other than the United Kingdom[3], or by a person approved generally or authorised in a particular case by the Civil Aviation Authority (CAA)[4], or, in relation to the adjustment and compensation of direct reading magnetic compasses, by the holder of an airline transport pilot's licence (aeroplanes), a senior commercial pilot's licence (aeroplanes) or a flight navigator's licence[5]. Contravention of this provision is an offence[6].

Although there is no specific provision in the Air Navigation Order for the preservation of certificates of release to service, such certificates must be available for delivery by the operator of an aircraft to any other person who becomes the operator[7].

1 For the meaning of 'certificate of release to service' see para 1325 note 2 ante.
2 Air Navigation Order 1989, SI 1989/2004, art 11 (6) (a) (i); see para 1304 ante.
3 Ie either (1) granted under the law of a country other than the United Kingdom and validated under the Air Navigation Order 1989; or (2) granted under the law of any country prescribed by the Air Navigation (General) Regulations 1981, SI 1981/57; or (3) granted or issued by or under the law of any state, being a party to the Chicago Convention (see para 1002 ante) in which the repair, replacement or modification of an aircraft of which the maximum total weight authorised (defined in para 1314 note 5 ante) does not exceed 2,730 kg has been carried out: Air Navigation Order 1989 art 11 (6) (a) (ii), (iii), (b).
4 Ibid art 11 (6) (c), (d). As to the CAA see para 1044 ante.
5 Ibid art 11 (6) (e). As to pilots' licences see para 1348 post.
6 The penalty for contravention is, on summary conviction, a fine not exceeding £1,000: ibid art 99 (5), Sch 12 Pt A.
7 See ibid art 65 proviso (a); and para 1411 post.

(5) DEALINGS WITH AIRCRAFT

(i) Sale, Bailment and Mortgage

1332. Sale of aircraft. The sale of aircraft is governed by the ordinary law relating to the sale of goods[1], so that the extent to which the seller of an aircraft, whether he is a manufacturer or not, is liable to a purchaser if the aircraft does not comply with the contract or is defective depends upon the terms and circumstances of the particular sale[2]. When a seller, in breach of contract or as a result of his negligence, sells an aircraft which is defective, the purchaser may in some circumstances be able to recover from the seller the amount of any sums paid by way of damages to third parties. In these respects, it is submitted, an aircraft is no different from a motor car.

A contract for the sale of an aircraft which, to the knowledge of the seller, is intended to be flown in contravention of statutory provisions is void as being a contract for an illegal purpose[3].

It is submitted that the law relating to the hire purchase and credit sale of aircraft is the same law as that which applies to other classes of goods. It is essential, in considering the law relating to the hire purchase and credit sale of aircraft, to consult current statutory instruments relating to minimum deposits and maximum periods of repayment, if any[4].

1 See generally SALE OF GOODS. As to the effect on registration of change of ownership of an aircraft see para 1281 ante. The definition of 'goods' in the Restrictive Trade Practices Act 1976 s 43 (1) includes aircraft; accordingly, agreements relating to the sale, resale or export of an aircraft may be subject to that Act. See further TRADE AND LABOUR.
2 See CONTRACT; DAMAGES; NEGLIGENCE; SALE OF GOODS; TRADE AND LABOUR.
3 *Commercial Air Hire Ltd v Wrightways Ltd* [1938] 1 All ER 89 (aircraft to be flown without approval of modifications (cf para 1330 ante); *Vinall v Howard* [1953] 2 All ER 515 (cheque in payment also unenforceable); and see *Northland Airlines Ltd v Dennis Ferranti Meters Ltd* (1970) 114 Sol Jo 845, CA. As to illegal contracts see generally CONTRACT.
4 See HIRE PURCHASE.

1333. Bailment of aircraft. The ordinary law of bailment applies where an aircraft is delivered to a bailee for safe custody or for any other purpose such as repair; the standard of care to be taken by the bailee will vary as the bailment is gratuitous or for valuable consideration, and may be modified by special contract[1]. In general the bailee will be excused if he can show that the loss or destruction of chattels, while lawfully in his care, took place without negligence or default attributable to him or his agents acting within the scope of their authority[2]. The measure of damages for negligence or default may include not only the actual loss or damage, but also allowance by way of a hiring charge if the aircraft was profit-earning equipment[3].

1 See BAILMENT paras 1829–1833 (gratuitous loan for use), 1858–1862 (hire) post; and see *Vendair (London) Ltd v Giro Aviation Co Ltd* [1961] 1 Lloyd's Rep 283.
2 See BAILMENT para 1859 post; and *F Hills & Sons Ltd v British Airways Ltd* (1936) 56 Ll L Rep 20.
3 See generally BAILMENT.

1334. Mortgage of aircraft. Statutory provisions[1] exist as to the mortgaging of aircraft registered in the United Kingdom[2]. Such an aircraft, or such an aircraft together with any store of spare parts for it, may be made security for a loan or other valuable consideration[3].

The mortgagee or prospective mortgagee may apply[4] to enter any mortgage of an aircraft[5] or notice of intention to apply to enter a contemplated mortgage (a 'priority notice'), as the case may be, in the register of aircraft mortgages kept by the Civil Aviation Authority (CAA)[6], whereupon the CAA must enter the mortgage or priority notice in the register, noting the time and date of entry[7], and notify the applicant, the mortgagor and the owner[8] accordingly[9].

The removal of an aircraft from the register of aircraft does not affect any entry in the register of aircraft mortgages[10]. The provisions of the Bills of Sale Acts 1878 and 1882[11], in so far as they relate to bills of sale and other documents given by way of security for the payment of money, do not apply to any registered mortgage of an aircraft[12].

Where a registered mortgage is discharged, the mortgagor must send the CAA a notification[13], countersigned by the mortgagee, and a copy of the document of discharge or receipt for the mortgage money, or other document which shows, to the satisfaction of the CAA, that the mortgage has been discharged , whereupon the CAA will enter the notification in the register, mark the relevant entries 'Discharged' and notify the mortgagee, the mortgagor and the owner that it has done so[14].

On paying the appropriate charge, any person may inspect the register or apply to the CAA for the supply of a certified copy of any entry in it or a notification whether there are any entries relating to a particular aircraft[15]. All persons are taken to have express notice of all facts appearing in the register[16].

An aircraft owned by a limited company may be charged by way of debenture, which must be registered with the registrar of companies[17]. Like any other chattel, an aircraft may be pledged by delivery of possession to a pledgee[18].

1 See the Civil Aviation Act 1982 s 86; Mortgaging of Aircraft Order 1972, SI 1972/1268 (amended by SI 1981/611 and SI 1986/2001).

2 Ie registered in the register of aircraft maintained by the Civil Aviation Authority: Mortgaging of Aircraft Order 1972 art 2 (2). As to the registration of aircraft see paras 1276–1283 ante.

3 Ibid art 3. The order gives no guidance as to the form of an aircraft mortgage for use in England and Wales: Sch 2 contains a form to be used in the case of Scotland only. It is submitted that any form of words which makes plain that the particular aircraft is being made security for the particular loan is sufficient to create an aircraft mortgage in the case of England and Wales; it is suggested that all that is needed are the words 'hereby mortgage', particularly as this phrase corresponds with the form prescribed in Sch 2 for aircraft mortgages in Scotland and with the form used for ships under the Merchant Shipping Act 1894 Sch 1 Pt I Form B.

4 Application to enter a mortgage or priority notice in the register must be made to the CAA in the forms prescribed in the Mortgaging of Aircraft Order 1972 Sch 1 Pts I, II, accompanied by the appropriate charge and, in the case of a mortgage, by a certified copy of it and, if it is in a language other than English, a certified translation: arts 4 (2), 5 (2), 6 (2). Where two or more aircraft are the subject of more than one mortgage, separate applications must be made: art 6 (1). For the charges see the CAA's Official Record, Series 4.

5 'Mortgage of an aircraft' includes a mortgage which extends to any store of spare parts for that aircraft, but does not otherwise include a mortgage created as a floating charge: Mortgaging of Aircraft Order 1972 art 2 (2).

6 Ibid arts 4 (1), 5 (1). As to the CAA see para 1044 ante.

7 Ibid art 7 (1). Applications are entered in the register in the order they were received: art 7 (2). The CAA must specify in its official record the days and times on which its office is open for such registrations; any application delivered when the office is closed is treated as received when the office is next opened: art 7 (3). As to the amendment of entries on change of circumstances see art 8, Sch 1 Pt III. Application may be made by originating summons to the Chancery Division of the High Court for the amendment of the register so as to rectify errors in it: art 10; RSC Ord 93 r 18 (1). Every person, other than the plaintiff, who is registered as mortgagor or mortgagee must be made a defendant, and a copy of the originating summons must be sent to the CAA, which is entitled to be heard: RSC Ord 93 r 18 (2), (3). On being served with the order the CAA must amend the register accordingly: Mortgaging of Aircraft Order 1972 art 10.

8 'Owner' means the person shown as the owner of the mortgaged aircraft on the application for registration of the aircraft in the United Kingdom nationality register maintained by the CAA: ibid art 2 (2).

9 Ibid art 7 (4). For the effect of the registration of the mortgage on the registration of the aircraft see para 1282 ante.

10 Ibid art 12. For the position on the insolvency of the mortgagor see the Insolvency Act 1986 s 285 (4); and *Bristol Airport plc v Powdrill* [1990] Ch 744, [1990] 2 All ER 493, 1 S&B AvR IV/121, CA.

11 See BILLS OF SALE.

12 Mortgaging of Aircraft Order 1972 art 16 (1).

13 For the form of notification see ibid Sch 1 Pt IV (substituted by SI 1981/611).

14 Mortgaging of Aircraft Order 1972 art 9 (substituted by SI 1981/611).

15 Mortgaging of Aircraft Order 1972 art 11 (1)–(3). A certified copy of an entry is admissible evidence of the entry: art 11 (4). No such application affects the priority of any mortgage: art 11 (5). As to priorities see para 1335 post.

16 Mortgaging of Aircraft Order 1972 art 13. The registration of a mortgage is not, however, evidence of its validity: art 13.

17 Companies Act 1985 s 395 (1) (amended by the Insolvency Act 1985 s 109 (1), Sch 6 para 10; substituted as from a day to be appointed by the Companies Act 1989 s 93); Mortgaging of Aircraft Order 1972 art 16 (2). See COMPANIES.

18 See generally PLEDGES AND PAWNS.

1335. Priority of mortgages. A mortgage of an aircraft entered in the register of aircraft mortgages[1] has priority over any other mortgage of or charge on that aircraft, other then another mortgage entered in that register[2], although where two or more mortgages are registered they have priority, as between themselves, according to the times at which they were registered[3]. Where a priority notice is registered and the contemplated mortgage referred to in it is made and registered within 14 days thereafter, the mortgage is deemed to have priority from the time when the priority notice was registered[4].

These priorities have effect notwithstanding any express, implied or constructive notice affecting the mortgagee[5].

The foregoing does not give a registered mortgage priority over any possessory lien in respect of work done, at any time, on the aircraft on the express or implied authority of any person entitled to possession of the aircraft, or over any statutory right to detain the aircraft[6].

1 See para 1334 ante.
2 Mortgaging of Aircraft Order 1972, SI 1972/1268, art 14 (1).
3 Ibid art 14 (2). Nevertheless, mortgages made before 1 October 1972 and registered before 31 December 1972 have priority over mortgages made on or after 1 October 1972, and as between themselves have the same priority as they would have had apart from the order: art 14 (2) proviso (i).
4 Ibid art 14 (2) proviso (ii): this is without prejudice to art 14 (2) proviso (i), as to which see note 3 supra. In reckoning the 14 days no account is taken of days on which the Civil Aviation Authority's office is not open for registering mortgages: art 14 (3). As to the CAA see para 1044 ante.
5 Ibid art 14 (4).
6 Ibid art 14 (5). As to liens see para 1326 ante; as to powers of detention see para 1339 post.

(ii) Charter of Aircraft

1336. Classes of charter contract. The owner of an aircraft may by a contract of charter put his aircraft at the disposal of a charterer for a specified flight or flights or for a specified period of time. Such contracts fall into two essentially different categories, depending upon the extent to which the control of the aircraft is transferred to the charterer or remains with the owner[1].

In the one case the charter operates as a demise of the aircraft itself to the charterer, to which there may or may not be added the services of a crew. Such a contract is often referred to as a 'bare-hull charter', a 'dry charter' or a 'dry lease'; under it the charterer becomes for most purposes the owner of the aircraft, the crew, whether supplied by the owner or the charterer, being the servants of the charterer and under his control in all respects[2]. In such a case the charterer is the operator[3].

In the other case, usually known as a 'time and voyage charter', 'wet charter' or 'wet lease', the contract merely confers upon the charterer the right to use the carrying space of the aircraft for the purpose of conveying passengers or goods upon a specified flight or flights or during a specified period, and to have the services of the crew of the aircraft for that purpose; the crew in such circumstances remain the owner's servants, although the charterer may acquire limited rights to direct them as to the flights to be undertaken, but not as to the manner in which they are to be performed[4]. In such a case the owner is the operator[5].

1 Cf the distinction, in relation to the charter of ships, between charterparties which operate by way of demise of the ship, and those which do not so operate. See further SHIPPING.
2 As to such charters see para 1337 post.

3 As to the operator see para 1340 post.
4 As to such charters see para 1338 post.
5 As to the operator see para 1340 post.

1337. Bare-hull charters. Where the charter is a 'bare-hull charter'[1], the rights and liabilities inter se of the owner and the charterer depend primarily upon the individual contract[2]. In the absence of express terms it seems that the owner impliedly undertakes that the aircraft chartered is as fit for the purpose for which it is chartered as reasonable care and skill can render it[3], and that any crew supplied are reasonably competent and skilful.

As regards liabilities to third parties, the statutory liability for damage caused to persons or property on the surface[4] falls upon the charterer if the aircraft has been chartered for a period exceeding 14 days and no operative member of the crew is in the employment of the owner; otherwise the owner remains liable[5]. Passengers on aircraft subject to a bare-hull charter normally enter into contracts of carriage with the operator, so that it is unlikely that any question of the contracting carrier being different from the actual carrier can arise unless the passengers are transferred for carriage to an aircraft operated by another operator without a fresh contract of carriage being made[6].

Similarly, any common law liabilities which may arise from the operation of the aircraft fall upon the charterer[7].

The charterer, for his part, is under an implied obligation, where no express provision is made, to exercise all reasonable care in using the aircraft, and is liable for any damage caused to it during the period of the charter, unless he can prove that it was not due to his negligence nor to that of his servants[8].

1 Such charters are also known as 'dry charters' or 'dry leases': see para 1336 ante.
2 It would be unusual for a public transport aircraft (defined in para 1272 ante) to be chartered on a bare-hull basis without a written agreement: see *Autair International Airways Ltd v Claydon Aviation Ltd* [1965] 1 Lloyd's Rep 74.
3 Cf *Reed v Dean* [1949] 1 KB 188 (hire of launch), and *Hyman v Nye* (1881) 6 QBD 685 (hire of carriage); see also *Aslan v Imperial Airways Ltd* (1933) 149 LT 276 (no absolute warranty of airworthiness).
4 Ie the liability imposed by the Civil Aviation Act 1982 s 76 (2): see para 1685 post.
5 See para 1685 post.
6 For the distinction between 'actual carriers' and 'contracting carriers' and its effect see para 1539 notes 4, 5 post.
7 Cf *Baumwoll Manufactur von Carl Scheibler v Furness* [1893] AC 8, HL. Common law liabilities fall generally on the person who, by himself or his servants, is in control. As to common law liabilities which may arise see para 1678 et seq post.
8 See BAILMENT.

1338. Time and voyage charters. The rights and liabilities[1] of the owner and charterer inter se depend, in a time and voyage charter[2], upon the terms of the particular contract, but it is thought that, in the absence of express terms, where the contract does not operate by way of demise, the owner impliedly undertakes that the aircraft is and will be as fit for the purpose for which it is chartered as reasonable care and skill can make it[3], that the crew are properly qualified, and that reasonable care and skill will be exercised in the carriage of the passengers or goods, as the case may be[4]. It would be rare for a commercial time and voyage charter not to be based upon a written agreement.

As between the owner of an aircraft and a time and voyage charterer, it is unusual for the charterer to be a contracting carrier[5], since the standard form of charter agreement usually provides that the time and voyage charterer contracts as agent only for the passengers, who contract as principals with the owner of the aircraft for their carriage. There are usually express contractual terms confirming this relationship in the contracts between most tour operators and the passengers to be carried pursuant to charter arrangements made by them[6].

Similarly any common law liability which arises in respect of damage caused to persons or property on the surface falls upon the owner of the aircraft[7].

1 As to the common law liabilities which may arise see para 1678 et seq post; and see *Romulus Films Ltd v William Dempster Ltd* [1952] 2 Lloyd's Rep 535, a case as to the damages recoverable for delay in performing a charter contract.
2 These charters are also known as 'wet charters' or 'wet leases': see para 1336 ante.
3 See *Aslan v Imperial Airways Ltd* (1933) 149 LT 276; and cf *Hyman v Nye* (1881) 6 QBD 685; *Readhead v Midland Rly Co* (1867) LR 2 QB 412; on appeal (1869) LR 4 QB 379; and cf also *Reed v Dean* [1949] 1 KB 188.
4 See *Fosbroke-Hobbes v Airwork Ltd and British-American Air Services Ltd* [1937] 1 ALL ER 108.
5 For the meaning of 'contracting carrier' see para 1539 note 5 post.
6 Ie in most time and voyage charters the charterer will not be a carrier for the purposes of the carriage by air legislation (as to which see generally para 1528 et seq post)
7 Cf para 1337 ante. As to common law liabilities see para 1688 post.

(iii) Powers of Detention

1339. Powers of detention of aircraft. The Civil Aviation Authority (CAA)[1] and other authorised persons have wide powers to give instructions and take steps by way of detention or otherwise in order to prevent the flight of an aircraft where the contravention of particular provisions of the Air Navigation Order 1989 is apprehended or where other specified conditions are satisfied[2].

There is also power to detain in the United Kingdom foreign aircraft which are alleged to infringe patents or designs entitled to protection in the United Kingdom[3]. Aircraft and their spare parts may, however, be exempt from seizure on patent claims where a declaration has been made by Order in Council that the benefits of the provisions of the Chicago Convention which confer exemption from seizure on such claims apply to the country or territory in which the aircraft is registered[4].

Aircraft in respect of which default is made in the payment of airport charges at specified aerodromes, whether they be the particular aircraft in respect of which the default was made or aircraft of which the person in default is the operator, may be detained and sold[5].

Other powers of detention arise in time of emergency[6], and where it is suspected that a breach of an air transport licence[7] or of provisions as to fuel venting or smoke emissions of aircraft engines[8] is about to take place, and to enforce customs and excise requirements[9] or the payment of charges for air navigation services[10].

The registration of an aircraft mortgage does not give the registered mortgage any priority over any statutory right of detention[11].

1 As to the CAA see para 1044 ante.
2 See the Air Navigation Order 1989, SI 1989/2004, art 95; and para 1459 post.
3 Civil Aviation Act 1982 s 89 (5), Sch 12; and see PATENTS.
4 See ibid s 89 (1)–(4); the Chicago Convention (Cmd 8742) art 27; and PATENTS. The Aircraft (Exemption from Seizure on Patents Claims) Order 1977, SI 1977/829, declares that the provisions apply to the countries listed in the Schedule to the order.
5 See the Civil Aviation Act 1982 s 88; *R v Civil Aviation Authority, ex p Emery Air Freight Corpn* (1988) 1 S&B AvR IV/105, Times, 13 January, CA; *Havelet Leasing Ltd v Cardiff-Wales Airport Ltd* (1988) 1

S&B AvR IV/111 (charges must relate to a specific aircraft); *Bristol Airport plc v Powdrill* [1990] Ch
744, [1990] 2 All ER 493, 1 S&B AvR IV/121, CA; and paras 1183, 1184 ante.
6   See the Civil Aviation Act 1982 s 63 (1) (b), (4); and paras 1063, 1065 ante.
7   See ibid s 64 (7); and para 1091 ante.
8   See the Air Navigation (Aircraft and Aircraft Engine Emissions) Order 1986, SI 1986/599, arts 4, 5;
and para 1295 et seq ante.
9   See the Customs and Excise Management Act 1979 ss 29, 34. See paras 1220–1228 ante and generally
CUSTOMS AND EXCISE.
10 See the Civil Aviation Act 1982 s 74 (4); and para 1380 post.
11 See the Mortgaging of Aircraft Order 1972, SI 1972/1268, art 14 (5); and para 1335 ante.

6. OPERATORS AND CREW

(1) AIR OPERATORS

1340. Air operators. The operator, in relation to an aircraft, is the person who
for the time being has the management of the aircraft[1].

However, in so far as the provisions of the Air Navigation Order 1989 relating to
airworthiness and equipment[2] are concerned, when by virtue of any charter or
other agreement for the hire or loan of an aircraft a person other than an air
transport undertaking[3] or an aerial work undertaking[4] has the management of that
aircraft for a period not exceeding 14 days, the agreement is deemed, for the
purpose of determining who is the operator, not to have been entered into[5].

1   Civil Aviation Act 1982 s 105 (1); Air Navigation Order 1989, SI 1989/2004, art 106 (3).
2   Ie ibid Pt III (arts 7–18): see paras 1284–1304, 1312–1331 ante.
3   For the meaning of 'air transport undertaking' see para 1272 note 6 ante.
4   For the meaning of 'aerial work' see para 1273 ante.
5   Air Navigation Order 1989 art 106 (3) proviso.

1341. Air operators' certificates. An aircraft registered in the United Kingdom, may not fly on any flight for the purpose of public transport[1] otherwise than
under and in accordance with the terms of an air operator's certificate granted to the
operator[2] of the aircraft by the Civil Aviation Authority[3].

1   For the meaning of 'public transport' see para 1272 ante.
2   For the meaning of 'operator' see para 1340 ante.
3   Air Navigation Order 1989, SI 1989/2004, art 6 (1). The penalty for contravention is on summary
conviction a fine not exceeding £2,000 and on conviction on indictment a fine or imprisonment for a
term not exceeding two years, or both: art 99 (6), Sch 12 Pt B. As to the Civil Aviation Authority see
para 1044 ante. For the power to direct that an aircraft shall not fly if this provision is not complied
with see art 95 (1); and para 1459 post.

1342. Criteria for decision. Before granting an air operator's certificate the
Civil Aviation Authority (CAA)[1] must be satisfied that the applicant is competent,
having regard in particular to his previous conduct and experience, his equipment,
organisation, staffing, maintenance and other arrangements, to secure the safe
operation of aircraft[2].

The certificate may be granted subject to such conditions as the CAA thinks fit[3],
it remains in force for the period specified in it, it certifies that the holder is a

competent person to operate aircraft safely, and it specifies the types of aircraft to be used and the description and purposes of flights for which they may be used[4].

1 As to the CAA see para 1044 ante.
2 Air Navigation Order 1989, SI 1989/2004, art 6 (2). As to the licensing procedure see the Civil Aviation Authority Regulations 1991, SI 1991/1672, reg 6; and paras 1066–1071 ante.
3 This is subject to the Air Navigation Order 1989 art 66, as to which see para 1422 post.
4 Ibid art 6 (1), (2).

(2) AIRCRAFT CREW

(i) Personnel Licensing

1343. Control of aircraft by young persons. No person under the age of 17 years may have the sole control of any aircraft in motion[1], although a person aged 16 or over may act as pilot in command[2] of a glider[3].

1 This is the minimum age at which a person may hold the necessary pilot's licence: see the Air Navigation Order 1989, SI 1989/2004, arts 20 (1), 21 (1), Sch 8 Pt A paras 1–4. See further paras 1344–1358 post.
2 'Pilot in command' means a person who for the time being is in charge of the piloting of the aircraft without being under the direction of any other pilot in the aircraft: ibid art 106 (1).
3 Ibid art 25. The penalty for contravention is on summary conviction a fine not exceeding £400: art 99 (4).

1344. Necessity for licences for members of flight crews. No person may act as a member of the flight crew[1] of an aircraft registered in the United Kingdom unless he holds an appropriate licence[2] granted or rendered valid under the Air Navigation Order 1989[3]. However, within the United Kingdom, the Channel Islands, and the Isle of Man , and subject to a series of conditions, a person may without holding such a licence act as a flight radiotelephony operator[4], or as pilot in command of an aircraft for the purpose of becoming qualified for the grant or renewal of a pilot's licence or the inclusion or variation of any rating in such a licence[5], or as pilot in command of a balloon[6]. No person may act as a member of the flight crew of an aircraft registered outside the United Kingdom unless, in the case of an aircraft flying for the purpose of public transport[7] or aerial work[8], he holds an appropriate licence granted or rendered valid under the law of the country in which the aircraft is registered[9] or, in the case of any other aircraft, he holds an appropriate licence granted or rendered valid under the law of the country in which the aircraft is registered or under the Air Navigation Order 1989 and the Civil Aviation Authority (CAA)[10] does not in a particular case give a direction to the contrary[11]. A licence granted by a contracting state[12] or a relevant overseas territory[13] is deemed to be a licence rendered valid under the Air Navigation Order unless the CAA in the particular case otherwise directs[14], but it does not entitle the holder to act as a member of the flight crew of any aircraft flying for the purpose of public transport or aerial work or on any flight in respect of which his services are remunerated[15] or to act as pilot of an aircraft flying in controlled airspace notified for this purpose in compliance with instrument flight rules or to give instruction in flying[16].

No licence need be held by a person, other than a flight radio operator, acting as a member of the flight crew of a glider which is not flying for the purpose of public transport or aerial work[17].

1 'Flight crew' means those members of the crew of the aircraft who respectively undertake to act as pilot, flight navigator, flight engineer and flight radio operator of the aircraft: Air Navigation Order 1989, SI 1989/2004, art 106 (1). A cabin attendant carried under art 19 (7) does not act as a member of the flight crew: art 19 (7) (b); see para 1365 post. As to the flight crew see paras 1359–1364 post.
2 'Appropriate licence', for the purpose of ibid art 20, means a licence which entitles the holder to perform the functions which he undertakes in relation to the aircraft concerned and the flight on which it is engaged: art 20 (7).
3 Ibid art 20 (1). As to the grant and validation of such licences see paras 1347–1356 post. The penalty for contravention of this and other requirements set out in this paragraph is on summary conviction a fine not exceeding £1,000 : art 99 (5), Sch 12 Pt A. For the power to direct that an aircraft shall not fly if these provisions are not complied with see art 95 (1); and para 1459 post.
4 Ibid art 20 (1) proviso (a).
5 Ibid art 20 (1) proviso (b)–(d). As to ratings see paras 1350–1352 post.
6 Ibid art 20 (1) proviso (e).
7 For the meaning of 'public transport' see para 1272 ante.
8 For the meaning of 'aerial work' see para 1273 ante.
9 Air Navigation Order 1989 art 20 (2) (a).
10 As to the CAA see para 1044 ante.
11 Air Navigation Order 1989 art 20 (2) (b).
12 For the meaning of 'contracting state' see para 1190 note 4 ante.
13 'Relevant overseas territory' means any colony and any country or place outside Her Majesty's dominions in which for the time being Her Majesty has jurisdiction: Air Navigation Order 1989 art 106 (1).
14 Ibid art 20 (3).
15 Ibid art 20 (3) (a).
16 Ibid art 20 (3) (b) (amended by SI 1991/1726).
17 Air Navigation Order 1989 art 20 (8). If the aerial work consists of the giving of instruction in flying in a glider owned or operated by a flying club of which the person giving and the person receiving instruction are both members, the licence is not required: art 20 (8) (b).

1345. Practice flights to qualify for pilot's licences. Unless the certificate of airworthiness[1] in force in respect of the aircraft otherwise requires, a person who does not hold an appropriate licence granted or rendered valid under the Air Navigation Order 1989 may act as pilot of an aircraft registered in the United Kingdom for the purpose of undergoing training or tests for the grant or renewal of a pilot's licence or for the inclusion, renewal or extension of a rating[2] thereon[3].

However, no other person may be carried on the aircraft except a person carried as a member of the flight crew, a person authorised by the Civil Aviation Authority (CAA)[4] to witness or conduct such training or tests, or, if the pilot in command of the aircraft holds an appropriate licence, a person carried for the purpose of being trained or tested as a member of the flight crew[5]. Further, the person acting as the pilot without holding the appropriate licence must either have been serving as a qualified pilot in Her Majesty's forces within the preceding six months and not be aware of any deterioration in his physical fitness rendering him unfit for the licence for which he intends to qualify[6], or hold a pilot's, flight engineer's or flight navigator's licence and be undergoing the training or test to qualify for a pilot's licence or additional rating and be acting under the supervision of a person who holds an appropriate licence[7].

1 As to certificates of airworthiness see paras 1284–1294 ante.
2 As to ratings see paras 1350–1352 post.
3 Air Navigation Order 1989, SI 1989/2004, art 20 (1), (4).
4 As to the CAA see para 1044 ante.
5 Air Navigation Order 1989 art 20 (4) (a).
6 Ibid art 20 (4) (b) (i).
7 Ibid art 20 (4) (b) (ii).

1346. Members of forces in flight crews. A person may act as a member of the flight crew[1] of an aircraft registered in the United Kingdom without being the holder of an appropriate licence if he is acting in the course of his duty as a member of any of Her Majesty's naval, military or air forces[2].

1 For the meaning of 'flight crew' see para 1344 note 1 ante.
2 Air Navigation Order 1989, SI 1989/2004, art 20 (6).

1347. Indorsement as to international standards. Where a licence is indorsed to the effect that the holder does not satisfy in full the relevant international standard, the holder may not act as a member of the flight crew[1] (1) of an aircraft registered in the United Kingdom in or over the territory of a contracting state[2], except in accordance with a permission granted by the competent authorities[3] of that state, where the licence has been granted or rendered valid under the Air Navigation Order 1989[4], or (2) of any aircraft in or over the United Kingdom except in accordance with a permission granted by the Civil Aviation Authority (CAA)[5] when the licence has been granted or rendered valid under the law of a contracting state other than the United Kingdom, whether or not the licence is or is deemed to be rendered valid under the Air Navigation Order[6].

1 For the meaning of 'flight crew' see para 1344 note 1 ante.
2 For the meaning of 'contracting state' see para 1190 note 4 ante.
3 'Competent authority' means, in relation to the United Kingdom, the CAA, and in relation to any other country the authority responsible under the law of that country for promoting the safety of civil aviation: Air Navigation Order 1989, SI 1989/2004, art 106 (1).
4 Ibid art 20 (9) (a). The penalty for contravention of this and any other provision set out in this paragraph is on summary conviction a fine not exceeding £1,000 : art 99 (5), Sch 12 Pt A.
5 As to the CAA see para 1044 ante.
6 Air Navigation Order 1989 art 20 (9) (b). As to the penalty see note 4 supra.

1348. Classes of licence. The Civil Aviation Authority (CAA)[1] may grant licences, subject to such conditions as it thinks fit, in a variety of classes for pilots, flight navigators, flight engineers, flight radiotelephony operators and flight radio-telegraphy operators[2].
A pilot's licence may be for aeroplanes and be either a private, basic commercial, commercial, senior commercial or airline transport pilot's licence[3]; it may be for helicopters and gyroplanes and be either a private, commercial or airline transport pilot's licence[4]; it may be a private pilot's licence for balloons and airships or a commercial pilot's licence for airships or for balloons[5]; or it may be a commercial pilot's licence for gliders[6].
There is only one flight navigator's licence and one flight engineer's licence; a flight radiotelephony operator's licence may be either general or restricted; and a flight radiotelegraphy operator's licence may be a temporary licence where the holder may only operate under the supervision of a person who holds a full radiotelegraphy licence[7].

1 As to the CAA see para 1044 ante.
2 See the Air Navigation Order 1989, SI 1989/2004, art 21 (1), and, as to the minimum age for and period of validity and privileges of each licence see Sch 8 Pt A.
3 See ibid Sch 8 Pt A para 1 (amended by SI 1991/1726). No Senior Commercial Pilot's Licence (Aeroplanes) has been granted since 4 December 1989 to any person who was not on 3 December 1989 the holder of such a licence and any such licence remains in force until either the end of the

period indicated in the licence or 3 December 1994, whichever is earlier: Air Navigation Order 1989 art 21 (2).
4 See ibid Sch 8 Pt A para 2 (amended by SI 1991/1726).
5 See the Air Navigation Order 1989 Sch 8 Pt A para 3.
6 See ibid Sch 8 Pt A para 4.
7 See ibid Sch 8 Pt A para 5.

1349. Criteria for grant of licences. Before granting a licence to act as a member of a flight crew[1] the Civil Aviation Authority (CAA)[2] must be satisfied that the applicant is a fit person to hold the licence and is qualified by reason of his knowledge, experience, competence, skill, physical and mental fitness to act in the capacity to which the licence relates; for this purpose the applicant must furnish such evidence and undergo such examinations and tests, including in particular medical examinations[3], as the CAA may require[4].

Appeal lies to the county court from any decision of the CAA that a person is not a fit person to hold a licence, except where it bases its decision on any deficiency of the applicant in his knowledge, experience, competence, skill, physical or mental fitness[5]. The CAA must be a respondent to the appeal[6]. If the court reverses its decision the CAA must give effect to the court's determination[7].

1 For the meaning of 'flight crew' see para 1344 note 1 ante; as to the classes of licences see para 1348 ante.
2 As to the CAA see para 1044 ante.
3 See further para 1354 post.
4 Air Navigation Order 1989, SI 1989/2004, art 21 (1). As to licensing procedure see paras 1066–1071 ante. As to training see para 1436 post. The CAA may approve any course of training or instruction and a person to provide such a course, and may authorise a person to conduct examinations or tests, subject to such conditions as it thinks fit: art 21 (12).
5 Ibid art 105 (1).
6 Ibid art 105 (3). The CAA's decision is deemed to have been taken on the date on which it furnished the applicant with a statement of reasons for its decision: art 105 (4). As to the venue and procedure see para 1098 note 1 ante.
7 Ibid art 105 (1).

1350. Privileges and ratings of licences. Subject to any conditions attached to a licence to act as a member of a flight crew[1], a licence of any class entitles the holder to perform the functions specified in the Air Navigation Order 1989 [2].

The Civil Aviation Authority (CAA)[3] may include in a licence a rating[4] and must include a valid medical certificate[5], a valid certificate of test or experience appropriate to the functions to be performed[6], or to the functions to which the rating relates[7].

1 For the meaning of 'flight crew' see para 1344 note 1 ante; as to the classes of licence see para 1348 ante.
2 Air Navigation Order 1989, SI 1989/2004, art 21 (4), Sch 8 Pt A (amended by SI 1991/1726).
3 As to the CAA see para 1044 ante.
4 Air Navigation Order 1989 art 21 (3). For the various ratings and their privileges see Sch 8 Pt B (amended by SI 1991/1726). As to ratings see para 1351 post. As to exceptions see para 1352 post.
5 Air Navigation Order 1989 art 21 (8) (a): this does not apply in the cases of a flight radiotelephony operator's licence. As to medical examinations see para 1354 post. Where the holder of a licence has reason to believe that his physical or mental condition renders him temporarily or permanently unfit to perform any of his functions, he is not entitled to perform such functions: art 21 (9) (a); as to injury, illness or pregnancy see para 1355 post.
6 Ibid art 21 (5). Where the holder of a licence fails the test he is not entitled to fly in the capacity for which that test would have qualified him had he passed it: art 21 (7). As to certificates of test or

experience see Sch 8 Pt C. The test may be conducted in a flight simulator, which must be approved by the CAA subject to such conditions as it thinks fit: art 21 (11). As to the approval of courses and instruction see para 1349 note 4 ante.

7 Ibid art 21 (6); as to failure see note 6 supra.

1351. Ratings. Where the Civil Aviation Authority (CAA)[1] is satisfied that the applicant for a licence to act as a member of a flight crew[2] is qualified to act in the capacity to which a rating[3] relates, the CAA may include that rating in the licence subject to such conditions as it thinks fit; the rating is then deemed to form part of the licence and entitles the holder to perform the functions attaching to that rating[4].

1 As to the CAA see para 1044 ante.
2 For the meaning of 'flight crew' see para 1344 note 1 ante; as to the classes of licence see para 1348 ante.
3 For the ratings and the privileges attaching to them see the Air Navigation Order 1989, SI 1989/2004, Sch 8 Pt B (amended by SI 1991/1726). As to tests being conducted in a flight simulator approved by the CAA see para 1350 note 6 ante.
4 Air Navigation Order 1989 art 21 (3), (4).

1352. Exceptions to ratings. Nothing in the Air Navigation Order 1989 prevents the holder of a pilot's licence from acting as pilot of an aircraft certificated for a single pilot operation when, with the permission of the Civil Aviation Authority (CAA)[1], he is testing a person for the purpose of that person's being examined for the grant of a flight crew licence[2], obtaining a certificate of test or experience[3] or a rating[4], notwithstanding that the type of aircraft used for the test is not specified in the aircraft rating in the pilot's licence or that the licence or personal flying log book does not include a valid certificate of test or experience in respect of the type of aircraft[5].

1 As to the CAA see para 1044 ante.
2 See the Air Navigation Order 1989, SI 1989/2004, art 21 (1); and para 1349 ante.
3 See ibid art 21 (5); and para 1350 ante.
4 See ibid art 21 (3), (6); and para 1351 ante.
5 Ibid art 21 (10).

1353. Validity and renewal of licences. When receiving a licence to act as a member of a flight crew[1], the holder must forthwith sign his name on it in ink with his ordinary signature[2].

The licence remains in force for the periods indicated in the licence, not exceeding those specified in the Air Navigation Order 1989 [3]. It may be renewed by the Civil Aviation Authority (CAA)[4] from time to time upon its being satisfied that the applicant is a fit person and is duly qualified[5]. If no period is indicated, it remains in force for the lifetime of the holder[6].

1 For the meaning of 'flight crew' see para 1344 note 1 ante; as to the classes of licences see para 1348 ante.
2 Air Navigation Order 1989, SI 1989/2004, art 21 (1) (c).
3 Ibid art 21 (1) (d): this is subject to art 66, as to which see para 1422 post. For the periods of validity see Sch 8 Pt A.
4 As to the CAA see para 1044 ante.
5 Air Navigation Order 1989 art 21 (1) (d).
6 Ibid art 21 (1) (d).

1354. Medical examinations. Every applicant for and holder of a licence to act as a member of a flight crew[1], other than as a flight radio telephony operator [2] granted by the Civil Aviation Authority (CAA)[3] must on such occasions as the CAA requires submit himself to medical examination by a person approved by the CAA, who will report to the CAA[4]. On the basis of this examination the CAA or any person approved by it as competent to do so may issue a medical certificate to the effect that the applicant for or the holder of the licence is assessed as being fit to perform the functions to which the licence relates[5].

The certificate contains such conditions as the CAA thinks fit, is valid for such period as is specified in it, and is deemed to form part of the licence[6].

1 For the meaning of 'flight crew' see para 1344 note 1 ante; as to the classes of licence see para 1348 ante.
2 See the Air Navigation Order 1989, SI 1989/2004, art 21 (8) (a).
3 As to the CAA see para 1044 ante.
4 Air Navigation Order 1989 art 21 (8) (b).
5 Ibid art 21 (8) (c)
6 Ibid art 21 (8) (c).

1355. Injury, illness or pregnancy. The holder of a licence to act as a member of a flight crew which includes a medical certificate[1] who suffers any personal injury or illness of 20 days or more involving incapacity to undertake the functions to which his licence relates, or, in the case of a woman, has reason to believe that she is pregnant, must inform the Civil Aviation Authority (CAA)[2] in writing of the injury or pregnancy as soon as possible or of the illness as soon as 20 days have elapsed[3]. The medical certificate is deemed to be suspended upon the occurrence of such an injury or the elapse of 20 days of such illness or the confirmation of the pregnancy[4]. In the case of injury or illness the suspension ceases upon the holder being medically examined and pronounced fit to resume his functions, or upon the CAA exempting the holder from the requirement of a medical examination, subject to such condition as the CAA thinks fit[5]. Where a pregnancy is confirmed, the suspension may be lifted for such period and subject to such conditions as the CAA thinks fit and it ceases when the holder has been medically examined after the pregnancy has ended and she has been pronounced fit to resume her functions[6].

1 This paragraph applies only in relation to holders of licences which include medical certificates and therefore does not apply to a flight radiotelephony operator's licence: see the Air Navigation Order 1989, SI 1989/2004, art 21 (8) (a), (9) (b). For the meaning of 'flight crew' see para 1344 note 1 ante; as to the classes of licence see para 1348 ante.
2 As to the CAA see para 1044 ante.
3 Air Navigation Order 1989 art 21 (9) (b).
4 Ibid art 21 (9) (b).
5 Ibid art 21 (9) (b) (aa): the CAA makes the arrangements under which the medical examination takes place.
6 Ibid art 21 (9) (b) (bb): the CAA makes the arrangements under which the medical examination takes place.

1356. Validation of licences. The Civil Aviation Authority (CAA)[1] may issue a certificate of validation rendering valid for the purposes of the Air Navigation Order 1989 any licence to act as a member of a flight crew[2] granted under the law of any country other than the United Kingdom[3].

1 As to the CAA see para 1044 ante.
2 For the meaning of 'flight crew' see para 1344 note 1 ante; as to the classes of licences see para 1348 ante.

3 Air Navigation Order 1989, SI 1989/2004, art 22: the certificate may be issued subject to such
conditions and for such period as the CAA thinks fit.

1357. Personal flying log books. A personal flying log book must be kept by
every member of the flight crew[1] of an aircraft registered in the United Kingdom,
and by any person who flies for the purpose of qualifying for the grant or renewal
of a licence to be such a member[2].

The personal flying log book must contain particulars of the holder's name and
address, of any licence he holds, and of the name and address of his employer (if
any)[3]. Particulars of all flights he has made as a member of the flight crew of the
aircraft or for the purpose of qualifying for the grant or renewal of a licence under
the Air Navigation Order 1989 must be recorded at the end of each flight or as soon
as is reasonably practicable , including the date, duration and places of arrival and
departure of each flight, the type and registration marks of the aircraft, the capacity
in which he acted, any special condition including night flying and instrument
flying, and particulars of any test or examination undertaken while in flight[4].

1 For the meaning of 'flight crew' see para 1344 note 1 ante.
2 Air Navigation Order 1989, SI 1989/2004, art 23 (1). As to the preservation of the log book see para
  1410 post.
3 Ibid art 23 (1) (a)–(c).
4 Ibid art 23 (2). Particulars of any test or examination taken in a flight simulator must also be recorded
  in the log book: art 23 (4).

1358. Flying instructors. No person may give instruction in flying to any
person flying or about to fly a flying machine or glider [1] for the purpose of
becoming qualified for: (1) the grant of a pilot's licence[2]; or (2) the inclusion or
variation of any rating, other than an aircraft rating, in a pilot's licence[3]; unless
certain requirements are complied with[4]. These are (i) that the instructor must hold
a duly granted or validated licence entitling him to act for the purpose and in the
circumstances as pilot in command[5]; (ii) that the instructor's licence includes a
flying instructor's rating or an assistant flying instructor's rating entitling him to
give the instruction[6]. These provisions do not apply to any instruction in flying to a
person for the purpose of becoming qualified for the inclusion in his licence of an
aircraft rating entitling him to act as pilot of a multi-engined or certain other
aircraft[7], where the pupil has previously been entitled under the Air Navigation
Order 1989 or qualified in any of Her Majesty's forces to act as pilot of such an
aircraft[8].

1 As to the classification of aircraft see para 1269 ante.
2 Air Navigation Order 1989, SI 1989/2004, art 24 (2) (a).
3 Ibid art 24 (2) (b).
4 See ibid art 24 (1). The penalty for contravention is on summary conviction a fine not exceeding
  £1,000: art 99 (5), Sch 12 Pt A.
5 Ibid art 24 (1) (a). As to the grant and validation of licences see paras 1348–1356 ante. For the meaning
  of 'pilot in command' see para 1343 note 2 ante.
6 Ibid art 24 (1) (b).
7 Ie an aircraft of any class appearing in ibid Sch 1 Pt A column 4; see para 1269 ante.
8 Ibid art 24 (2) proviso.

(ii) Aircraft Crew

1359. Necessity for flight crew. No aircraft may fly unless it carries a flight crew[1] of the number and description required by the law of the country in which it is registered[2].

1 For the meaning of 'flight crew' see para 1344 note 1 ante.
2 Air Navigation Order 1989, SI 1989/2004, art 19 (1). The penalty for contravention is on summary conviction a fine not exceeding £1,000: art 99 (5), Sch 12 Pt A. As to the power to direct that an aircraft shall not fly if the provisions as to the flight crew are not complied with see art 95 (1) (a); and para 1459 post. As to licensing of the crew see para 1344 et seq ante.

1360. Flight crew for United Kingdom aircraft. An aircraft registered in the United Kingdom must carry a flight crew[1] adequate in number and description to ensure the safety of the aircraft and of at least the number and description specified in the certificate of airworthiness[2] or, if no such certificate is required to be in force, the certificate of airworthiness if any, last in force in respect of that aircraft[3].

1 For the meaning of 'flight crew' see para 1344 note 1 ante.
2 As to certificates of airworthiness see paras 1284–1294 ante.
3 Air Navigation Order 1989, SI 1989/2004, art 19 (2). The penalty for contravention is on summary conviction a fine not exceeding £1,000: art 99 (5), Sch 12 Pt A. As to licensing of the flight crew see para 1344 et seq ante.

1361. Carriage of two pilots. A flying machine[1] registered in the United Kingdom and flying for the purpose of public transport[2], and having a maximum total weight authorised[3] of 5,700 kg or more[4], must carry not less than two pilots as members of the flight crew[5]. Both pilots must remain at the controls of the aircraft during take-off and landing[6].

1 As to the classification of aircraft see para 1269 ante.
2 For the meaning of 'public transport' see para 1272 ante.
3 For the meaning of 'maximum total weight authorised' see para 1314 note 5 ante.
4 Since 1 January 1990, an aircraft registered in the United Kingdom, flying for the purpose of public transport in circumstances where the aircraft commander must comply with instrument flight rules (as to which see para 1399 post), having a maximum total weight authorised of 5,700 kg or less and powered by turbine jets, or turbine propeller engines or piston engines must carry at least two pilots as members of the flight crew, unless, in the case of piston engine or turbine propeller engine powered aircraft (carrying less than ten passengers in the latter case), it is equipped with an approved and serviceable autopilot: Air Navigation Order 1989, SI 1989/2004, art 19 (3) (b).
5 Ibid art 19 (3) (a). The penalty for contravention is on summary conviction a fine not exceeding £1,000: art 99 (5), Sch 12 Pt A.
6 See ibid art 33 (1); and para 1446 post.

1362. Carriage of flight navigators. An aircraft registered in the United Kingdom and flying for the purpose of public transport[1] must carry either navigational equipment approved by the Civil Aviation Authority (CAA)[2] or a flight navigator as a member of the flight crew[3], in addition to any other person who is required to be carried to perform other duties, if on its planned route or planned diversion the aircraft is intended to be more than 500 nautical miles[4] from the point of take-off and to pass over a specified area[5]. He must be the holder of an appropriate licence[6].

1 For the meaning of 'public transport' see para 1272 ante.

2 As to the CAA see para 1044 ante.
3 For the meaning of 'flight crew' see para 1344 note 1 ante.
4 'Nautical mile' means the international nautical mile, ie 1,852 metres: Air Navigation Order 1989, SI 1989/2004, art 106 (1).
5 Ibid art 19 (4). For details of the specified areas (ie the Arctic, Antarctic, Sahara, South America, Pacific Ocean, Australia, Indian Ocean, North Atlantic Ocean, South Atlantic Ocean, Northern Canada, Northern Asia and Southern Asia) see Sch 7 (substituted by SI 1990/2154). The penalty for contravention is on summary conviction a fine not exceeding £1,000: Air Navigation Order 1989 art 99 (5), Sch 12 Pt A.
6 See ibid art 21 (1), Sch 8 Pt A para 5. As to licensing generally see paras 1066–1071 ante. Flight navigators must be tested by or on behalf of the operator as to their competence to perform their duties: Sch 10 Pt B para 1 (4). As to the training of the flight crew see para 1436 post.

1363. Carriage of flight radio operators. An aircraft registered in the United Kingdom and required to be equipped with radio communication equipment[1] must carry a flight radio operator as a member of the flight crew[2], who, if he is required to operate radiotelegraphy apparatus, must be carried in addition to any other person carried to perform other duties on board the aircraft[3].

1 See the Air Navigation Order 1989, SI 1989/2004, art 14; and para 1318 ante.
2 For the meaning of 'flight crew' see para 1344 note 1 ante.
3 Air Navigation Order 1989 art 19 (5). The penalty for contravention is on summary conviction a fine not exceeding £1,000: art 99 (5), Sch 12 Pt A.

1364. Carriage of additional flight crew. If a appears to the Civil Aviation Authority (CAA)[1] expedient to do so in the interests of safety, it may direct the operator[2] of an aircraft registered in the United Kingdom that his aircraft may not fly in such circumstances as it specifies unless they carry such additional persons as members of the flight crew[3] as it specifies[4].

1 As to the CAA see para 1044 ante.
2 For the meaning of 'operator' see para 1340 ante.
3 For the meaning of 'flight crew' see para 1344 note 1 ante.
4 Air Navigation Order 1989, SI 1989/2004, art 19 (6). The penalty for contravention is on summary conviction a fine not exceeding £1,000: see art 99 (5), Sch 12 Pt A.

1365. Other persons to be carried. Where an aircraft registered in the United Kingdom carries 20 passengers or more, or can carry more than 35 passengers according to its certificate of airworthiness[1] on a flight for the purpose of public transport[2], the crew[3] of the aircraft must include cabin attendants[4] carried for the purpose of performing, in the interests of the safety of passengers, duties assigned by the operator[5] or the commander of the aircraft[6]; the aircraft should carry one cabin attendant for every 50 seats installed in the aircraft unless otherwise agreed with the Civil Aviation Authority (CAA)[7]. These persons do not act as members of the flight crew[8].

If it appears to the CAA expedient to do so in the interests of safety, the CAA may direct the operator that the aircraft may not fly in such circumstances as it specifies unless they carry such additional persons as cabin attendants as it specifies[9].

1 As to certificates of airworthiness see paras 1284–1294 ante.
2 For the meaning of 'public transport' see para 1272 ante.

3 Although the Air Navigation Order 1989, SI 1989/2004, art 19 (7) includes cabin attendants in the crew of an aircraft, and art 106 (1) defines 'crew' as meaning a member of the flight crew or a cabin attendant, cabin attendants are specifically excluded from the flight crew in the definition of 'cabin attendant': see note 4 infra. For the meaning of 'flight crew' see para 1344 note 1 ante.

4 'Cabin attendant' in relation to an aircraft means a person on a flight for the purpose of public transport carried for the purpose of performing in the interests of safety of passengers duties to be assigned by the operator or the commander of the aircraft but who shall not act as a member of the flight crew: ibid art 106 (1).

5 For the meaning of 'operator' see para 1340 ante.

6 Air Navigation Order 1989 art 19 (7) (a), (b). The penalty for contravention of this and any other provision in this paragraph is on summary conviction a fine not exceeding £1,000: art 99 (5), Sch 12 Pt A.

7 Ibid art 19 (7) (c) and proviso. As to the CAA see para 1044 ante.

8 See ibid arts 19 (7) (b), 106 (1); and note 3 supra.

9 Ibid art 19 (8).

(iii) Fatigue of Crew

1366. Application of provisions as to fatigue of crew. Most of the provisions relating to the fatigue of aircraft crew[1] apply only to an aircraft registered in the United Kingdom which is either engaged on a flight for the purpose of public transport[2] or is operated by an air transport undertaking[3].

In particular , they do not apply in relation to a flight made only for the purpose of instruction in flying by or on behalf of a flying club or flying school, or a person who is not an air transport undertaking[4].

1 Ie, the Air Navigation Order 1989, SI 1989/2004, Pt VI (arts 57–60): see paras 1367–1369 post.

2 For the meaning of 'public transport' see para 1272 ante .

3 Air Navigation Order 1989 art 57 (1). For the meaning of 'air transport undertaking' see para 1272 note 6 ante.

4 Ibid art 57 (1) proviso.

1367. Operator's duties as to fatigue of crew. An aircraft[1] may not fly before the operator has established a scheme regulating the flight times for every member of the crew [2] of that aircraft[3]. The scheme must be approved by the Civil Aviation Authority (CAA)[4] and incorporated into the operations manual[5] or a similar document[6].

The operator must ensure that the provisions are observed by all members of the crew[7], and that any particular member of the crew does not fly in the aircraft where he knows, or has reason to believe, that such a person is suffering from, or is likely to suffer from such fatigue that he may endanger the safety of the aircraft or of its occupants[8].

The operator may not allow a person to fly as a member of the aircraft's flight crew unless he has an accurate and up-to-date record of all the flight times[9] and particulars of the functions performed in the course of such flight times of that person during the last 28 days[10] before the flight[11].

1 As to the aircraft to which this provision applies see para 1366 ante.

2 'Crew' means a member of the flight crew, a person carried on the flight deck who is appointed by the operator of the aircraft to give or to supervise the training, experience, practice and periodical tests required in respect of the flight crew, or a cabin attendant: Air Navigation Order 1989, SI 1989/2004, art 106 (1). For the meaning of 'flight crew' see para 1344 ante

3 Ibid art 58 (1) (a). The penalty for contravention is on summary conviction a fine not exceeding £2,000 and on conviction on indictment a fine or imprisonment for a term not exceeding two years, or both: art 99 (6), Sch 12 Pt B. As to operators see para 1340 ante.

4 As to the CAA see para 1044 ante.
5 As to the operations manual see para 1438 post.
6 Air Navigation Order 1989 art 58 (1) (b), (c). As to the penalty for contravention see note 2 supra.
7 Ibid art 58 (1) (d). As to the penalty for contravention see note 2 supra.
8 Ibid art 58 (2). As to the penalty for contravention see note 2 supra.
9 'Flight time', in relation to any person, means all time spent by that person in an aircraft whether or not registered in the United Kingdom (other than an aircraft of which the maximum weight authorised does not exceed 1,600 kg and which is not flying for the purpose of public transport or aerial work) while it is in flight and he is carried therein as a member of the crew thereof: ibid art 57 (2) (a). For the meaning of 'in flight' see para 1460 post. However, for the purposes of the 1989 Order Pt VI, a helicopter is deemed to be in flight from the moment it first moves under its own power in order to take off until the rotors are next stopped: art 57 (3). For the meaning of 'maximum total weight authorised' see para 1314 note 5 ante, of 'aerial work' see para 1273 ante, and of 'flight crew' see para 1344 note 1 ante.
10 'Day' means a continuous period of 24 hours beginning at Midnight Co-ordinated Universal Time: ibid art 57 (2) (b).
11 Ibid art 58 (3). The record must be preserved until a date 12 months after the relevant flight: art 58 (4). The penalty for contravention is on summary conviction a fine not exceeding £1,000: art 99 (5), Sch 12 Pt A.

1368. Crew's responsibilities. A person may not act as a member of the crew of an aircraft[1] where he knows, or suspects, that he is suffering from, or is likely to suffer from, such fatigue that it may endanger the safety of the aircraft or of its occupants[2]. A person may not act as a member of the flight crew of an aircraft [3] unless he ensures that the aircraft operator[4] knows of his flight times[5] during the 28 days[6] preceding the flight[7].

1 As to the aircraft to which this provision applies see para 1366 ante. For the meaning of 'crew' see para 1367 note 2 ante.
2 Air Navigation Order 1989, SI 1989/2004, art 59 (1). See also the aircraft operator's duties in respect of fatigue of crew: para 1354 ante. The penalty for contravention is on summary conviction a fine not exceeding £2,000 and on conviction on indictment a fine or imprisonment for a term not exceeding two years, or both: art 99 (6), Sch 12 Pt B.
3 See note 1 supra. For the meaning of 'flight crew' see para 1344 note 1 ante.
4 As to aircraft operators see para 1340 ante.
5 For the meaning of 'flight time' see para 1367 note 9 ante.
6 For the meaning of 'day' see para 1367 note 10 ante.
7 Air Navigation Order 1989 art 59 (2). The penalty for contravention is on summary conviction a fine not exceeding £1,000: art 99 (5), Sch 12 Pt A.

1369. Flight crew's responsibilities as to flight times. A person may not act as a member of the flight crew[1] of an aircraft registered in the United Kingdom where the aggregate of all his flight times[2] either exceeds 100 hours during the period of 28 consecutive days[3] expiring at the end of the day on which the flight begins[4] or exceeds 900 hours during the period of 12 months expiring at the end of the month preceding the day on which the flight begins[5].

These provisions do not apply to a flight made in an aircraft not flying for the purpose of public transport[6] or aerial work[7] and of which the maximum total weight authorised[8] does not exceed 1,600 kg[9]; nor do they apply to a flight made in an aircraft neither flying for the purpose of public transport nor being operated by an air transport undertaking[10] where, when the flight begins, the aggregate amount of the flight times of the person concerned does not exceed 25 hours since he was last medically examined and found fit[11].

1 For the meaning of 'flight crew' see para 1344 note 1 ante.

2 For the meaning of 'flight times' see para 1367 note 9 ante.
3 For the meaning of 'day' see para 1367 note 10 ante.
4 Air Navigation Order 1989, SI 1989/2004, art 60 (a). The penalty for contravention is on summary conviction a fine not exceeding £1,000: art 99 (5), Sch 12 Pt A.
5 Ibid art 60 (b). As to the penalty for contravention see note 4 supra.
6 For the meaning of 'public transport' see para 1272 ante.
7 For the meaning of 'aerial work' see para 1273 ante.
8 For the meaning of 'maximum total weight authorised' see para 1314 note 5 ante.
9 Air Navigation Order 1989 art 60 proviso (i).
10 For the meaning of 'air transport undertaking' see para 1272 note 6 ante.
11 Air Navigation Order 1989 art 60 proviso (ii).

7. AIR NAVIGATION SERVICES

(1) AIR NAVIGATION SERVICES

(i) General Provisions

1370. Eurocontrol. The European Organisation for the Safety of Air Navigation (Eurocontrol) was established by a convention signed in 1960, when it was agreed that international control of air traffic within Europe was necessary[1]. The Civil Aviation (Eurocontrol) Act 1962 was passed to make provision in connection with the convention, to provide for the recovery of charges for services provided for aircraft, and for purposes connected with these matters. Further, provisions as to charges payable to other international organisations or governments outside the United Kingdom were set out in the Civil Aviation Act 1968[2]; these provisions together with those of the Civil Aviation (Eurocontrol) Act 1962 were consolidated and incorporated in the Civil Aviation Act 1982[3]. The Civil Aviation (Eurocontrol) Act 1983 was passed to make further provision with respect to Eurocontrol[4].

The Secretary of State[5] may make regulations for requiring the payment of charges in respect of air navigation services to international organisations (other than Eurocontrol) , any government outside the United Kingdom , the Secretary of State, the Civil Aviation Authority or Eurocontrol [6].

1 As to Eurocontrol see generally para 1023 ante.
2 Civil Aviation Act 1968 s 15 (repealed) .
3 See the Civil Aviation Act 1982 ss 73, 74; and paras 1376–1381 post.
4 In addition, the Civil Aviation (Eurocontrol) Act 1983 amended the Civil Aviation Act 1982 ss 24, 73 (4), Sch 4 paras 1, 3 and added s 74A.
5 As to the Secretary of State see para 1032 ante.
6 Civil Aviation Act 1982 s 73 (1) (b). As to the Civil Aviation Authority see para 1044 ante; as to the regulations see para 1377 post.

1371. Civil Aviation Authority's functions. The Civil Aviation Authority (CAA)[1] must perform such functions in respect of air navigation services[2] and the control of air navigation as are provided for by statute or regulations[3].

1 As to the CAA see para 1044 ante.
2 'Air navigation services' includes information, directions and other facilities furnished, issued or provided in connection with the navigation or movement of aircraft and includes the control of

movement of vehicles in any part of an aerodrome used for the movement of aircraft: Civil Aviation Act 1982 s 105 (1). For the meaning of 'aerodrome' see para 1102 ante.

3 See ibid s 3 (b).

1372. Civil Aviation Authority's duties. It is the duty of the Civil Aviation Authority (CAA)[1] to provide air navigation services[2] in the United Kingdom and for any area outside the United Kingdom for which the United Kingdom has undertaken to provide those services in pursuance of international arrangements[3]; and to join with the Secretary of State[4], in such manner as he may direct, in providing specified air navigation services in respect of specified areas, in defraying the costs of providing such services[5], and in discharging any liability to a third party which is incurred by the CAA and the Secretary of State, together or separately, in providing the services[6].

Without prejudice to any right of action in respect of an act or omission which takes place in the course of providing air navigation services, no action lies in respect of a failure by the CAA to perform these duties[7].

1 As to the CAA see para 1044 ante.
2 For the meaning of 'air navigation services' see para 1371 note 2 ante.
3 Civil Aviation Act 1982 s 72 (1). As to Eurocontrol see para 1370 ante.
4 As to the Secretary of State see para 1032 ante.
5 Civil Aviation Act 1982 s 72 (2) (a), (b). The CAA must join with the Secretary of State for Defence in the performance of such duties: Civil Aviation Authority (Air Navigation Services) Directions 1976 set as Annex B to the Future Civil Aviation Policy, Cmnd 6400 (the Policy has been revoked, but the directions remain); and para 1373 post.
6 Civil Aviation Act 1982 s 72 (2) (c).
7 Ibid s 72 (3).

1373. National Air Traffic Services. The Civil Aviation Authority (CAA)[1] must collaborate with the Secretary of State for Defence in exercising its functions in providing air navigation services[2] through the joint organisation known as the National Air Traffic Services (NATS)[3]. Such services must be available to all classes of civil and military aircraft both within United Kingdom national airspace and within any airspace for which the United Kingdom has undertaken to provide services[4].

NATS must secure safe separation of aircraft while facilitating the most expeditious flow, the greatest possible freedom and the optimum utilisation of aircraft; its services must be operated in such a way as to reconcile the differing civil and military air traffic operational needs; a common standard of service to all aircraft within a given airspace is to be provided; and the requirements of all air user interests, including general aviation, must be taken into account[5].

1 As to the CAA see para 1044 ante.
2 For the meaning of 'air navigation services' see para 1371 note 2 ante.
3 Civil Aviation Authority (Air Navigation Services) Directions 1976 (as to which see para 1372 note 5 ante) para 3. Disagreements between the CAA and the Secretary of State for Defence must be referred by the CAA to the Secretary of State for Transport for consideration in consultation with the Secretary of State for Defence where no agreement can be reached: Civil Aviation Authority (Air Navigation Services) Directions 1976 para 10.
4 Ibid para 4; see para 1372 ante.
5 Ibid para 5.

1374. Functions of NATS. The functions exercised jointly through NATS[1] include the provision of services within any airspace, other than United Kingdom national airspace, for which the United Kingdom has undertaken to make such provision[2]; ensuring that international agreements binding the United Kingdom are observed; the provision of services to aircraft in the upper airspace[3]; the provision and operation of approach and aerodrome control services[4]; advising on air traffic control[5] matters concerning airspace, other than United Kingdom national airspace, for which the United Kingdom has undertaken to make provision; and the establishment of aerodromes[6].

1 See para 1373 ante.
2 See para 1372 ante.
3 Ie to enable the Secretary of State (as to whom see para 1032 ante) to discharge his functions under a contract between the Secretary of State and Eurocontrol. As to Eurocontrol see para 1370 ante.
4 Ie at such civil aerodromes as may be determined by the Civil Aviation Authority or at such Ministry of Defence airfields as may be agreed with the Secretary of State for Defence.
5 As to air traffic control see paras 1382–1407 post.
6 Civil Aviation Authority (Air Navigation Services) Directions 1976 (as to which see para 1372 note 5 ante) para 6.

1375. Air Traffic Control Board. The Civil Aviation Authority[1] assists the Air Traffic Control Board appointed by the Secretary of State for Defence and the Secretary of State for Transport in any review of the navigation services which the board may from time to time carry out, and may refer to the board for advice any questions of special difficulty arising between NATS[2] and operators of aircraft which cannot be resolved in discussion[3].

1 As to the CAA see para 1044 ante.
2 As to NATS see para 1373 ante.
3 Civil Aviation Authority (Air Navigation Services) Directions 1976 (as to which see para 1372 note 5 ante) para 7. The board's composition is not stated in the directions.

(ii) Charges

1376. Costs of services. Arrangements are made between the Civil Aviation Authority (CAA)[1] and the Secretary of State for Defence to share the costs of providing facilities and services. Where a facility or service is to be provided on a cost-sharing basis through NATS[2] the cost, if not included in the existing arrangements, is to be borne proportionately by the CAA and the Secretary of State for Defence having regard to the extent to which the facility or service is expected to be used by civil and military aircraft respectively[3].

1 As to the CAA see para 1044 ante.
2 As to NATS see para 1373 ante.
3 Civil Aviation (Air Navigation Services) Directions 1976 (as to which see para 1372 note 5 ante) para 9.

1377. Regulations as to charges. The Secretary of State[1] may make regulations[2] requiring the payment of charges for air navigation services[3] provided for aircraft by Eurocontrol, or any international organisation or any government outside the United Kingdom in pursuance of an agreement to which the United Kingdom is a party, or the Secretary of State, or the Civil Aviation Authority (CAA)[4], or any other persons[5]. Payments under the regulations are to be made either to Eurocon-

rol, or to such an organisation or government, or to the Secretary of State, or to
he CAA[6].

The rates of the charges are determined by the Secretary of State either in
pursuance of tariffs approved under an international agreement to which the
United Kingdom is, or is to become, a party[7] or, when the payment is to be made
o the Secretary of State or the CAA, with the consent of the Treasury[8]. The
charges may be prescribed in units of account defined by reference to more than
one currency and may be paid and recovered either in such units or in their
equivalent in such currencies as may be prescribed[9].

The regulations may prescribe different charges in relation to different classes or
descriptions of aircraft or to aircraft used in different circumstances, may provide
for the payment of interest on unpaid charges, and may dispense with the charges
in specified cases[10]. Failure without reasonable cause to comply with any requirement of the regulations is an offence punishable on summary conviction by a fine
not exceeding level 3 on the standard scale[11].

The Secretary of State may make regulations providing for the payment of an
annual charge in respect of aircraft for which there is in force a certificate of
airworthiness at the time the charge is payable and requiring the CAA to refund so
much of the payment as is equal to the amount which the operator or owner owes
to Eurocontrol for flights made by the aircraft over the United Kingdom during
the relevant period of 12 months[12].

1 As to the Secretary of State see para 1032 ante.
2 See the Civil Aviation (Navigation Service Charges) Regulations 1991, SI 1991/470; and the Civil
  Aviation (Route Charges for Navigation Services) Regulations 1989, SI 1989/303 (amended by SI
  1989/2257 and SI 1990/2482) .
3 For the meaning of 'air navigation services' see para 1371 note 2 ante.
4 As to the CAA see para 1044 ante.
5 Civil Aviation Act 1982 s 73 (1).
6 See ibid s 73 (1). As to the charges see the regulations cited in note 2 supra.
7 See the Civil Aviation Act 1982 s 73 (6) (b), (c). In compliance with s 73 (6) (b) (ii), (c) (ii), the
  Secretary of State may determine the rates which in his opinion are likely to be approved before or
  within one month after the date on which the regulations come into force, under any international
  agreement to which the United Kingdom is likely to be a party before or within one month after that
  date. See the Civil Aviation (Route Charges for Navigation Services) Regulations 1989 (as amended:
  see note 2 supra).
8 Civil Aviation Act 1982 s 73 (6) (a).
9 Ibid s 73 (1A) (added by the Civil Aviation (Air Navigation Charges) Act 1989 s 1).
0 Civil Aviation Act 1982 s 73 (6). Charges for air navigation services are specifically excluded from
  the charges for which either the CAA may make a scheme or the Secretary of State may make
  regulations under s 11: s 11 (7); see para 1053 ante.
1 Ibid s 74 (1) (amended by virtue of the Criminal Justice Act 1982 ss 38, 46) . As to the standard scale
  see para 1044 note 6 ante. At the date at which this volume states the law, level 3 on that scale is at
  £400
2 Civil Aviation Act 1982 s 73 (2). As to certificates of airworthiness see paras 1284–1294 ante.

378. Payments and liabilities. The liability for any charges payable for air
navigation services[1] is imposed upon the operators of aircraft for which the
navigation services are available[2], upon the managers of aerodromes used by such
aircraft, or upon the owners of the aircraft; and it may be imposed partly upon the
operators of aircraft, partly upon the owners of aircraft and partly upon the
managers of aerodromes[3].

Payments may be made elsewhere than in the United Kingdom, and are recover able in the United Kingdom wherever they are payable, without prejudice to thei recovery elsewhere[4].

Any sum received by the Secretary of State[5] must be paid into the Consolidate Fund, and regulations may provide for regulating the disposal by the Civil Avi ation Authority (CAA)[6] of sums received by it[7].

1 As to charges see para 1377 ante. For the meaning of 'air navigation services' see para 1371 note ante.
2 Civil Aviation Act 1982 s 73 (3). Where charges are payable to an international organisation othe than Eurocontrol or to a government outside the United Kingdom (see para 1377 ante), liability ma be imposed upon the operator or owner of any aircraft whether or not it is registered in the Unite Kingdom, whether or not it was flying over the United Kingdom and whether or not the service were provided from a place in the United Kingdom: s 73 (4) (amended by the Civil Aviatio (Eurocontrol) Act 1983 s 3 (2)).
3 Civil Aviation Act 1982 s 73 (3).
4 See ibid s 73 (1), (3). As to payments in units of account defined by reference to more than on currency see para 1377 ante.
5 As to the Secretary of State see para 1032 ante.
6 As to the CAA see para 1044 ante.
7 Civil Aviation Act 1982 s 73 (9).

1379. Records. To facilitate the assessment and collection of charges for ai navigation services[1], regulations may impose on aircraft operators and aerodrom managers the duty to make and preserve[2] records of aircraft movements, t produce to international organisations, including Eurocontrol, to government outside the United Kingdom, to the Secretary of State[2] or to the Civil Aviatior Authority (CAA)[3] for inspection, any such record and all other records required t be preserved[4]; and to furnish to those persons such particulars of any such record as may be prescribed[5].

Certain records may be used as evidence in any legal proceedings[6].

1 For the meaning of 'air navigation services' see para 1371 note 2 ante.
2 As to the Secretary of State see para 1032 ante.
3 As to the CAA see para 1044 ante.
4 As to the preservation of certain documents and records see paras 1409–1414 post.
5 Civil Aviation Act 1982 ss 73 (7), 74 (1) (amended by virtue of the Criminal Justice Act 1982 ss 38 46) . For offences relating to the unlawful disclosure of information or false information see the Civi Aviation Act 1982 s 74 (2), (3) (amended by virtue of the Criminal Justice Act 1982 ss 38, 46) . Thes requirements may be imposed upon the operator of any aircraft whether or not it is registered in th United Kingdom, whether or not it is in or over the United Kingdom at the time when the service are provided and whether or not those services are provided from a place in the United Kingdom s 73 (8).
6 Ibid s 96 (2), (3). As to evidence see generally para 1659 post; and the Civil Aviation (Documentar Evidence) Regulations 1972, SI 1972/187, which designate the persons who may certify document and records.

1380. Detention of aircraft. Regulations may authorise the detention of ai aircraft[1] in the case of default in the payment of any charge for air navigatior services[2] payable by the operator; the aircraft detained may be either the aircraft ir respect of which the charge was incurred or any other aircraft operated by th operator in default[3]. The same provision applies in the case of default in complying with any requirements in respect of records[4].

1 As to the detention of aircraft in other circumstances see para 1339 ante.

2 For the meaning of 'air navigation services' see para 1371 note 2 ante.
3 Civil Aviation Act 1982 s 74 (4) (a): see the Civil Aviation (Navigation Services Charges) Regulations 1991, SI 1991/470, regs 11–18, Sch 2 and the Civil Aviation (Route Charges for Navigation
Services) Regulations 1989, SI 1989/303, regs 10–18. As to the right of the Civil Aviation Authority
to detain an aircraft operated at the time of detention by a successor to the person in default see *R v
Civil Aviation Authority, ex p Emery Air Freight Corpn* (1988) 1 S&B AvR IV/105, Times, 13 January,
CA.
4 Civil Aviation Act 1982 s 74 (4) (b).

1381. Jurisdiction of courts. A court in any part of the United Kingdom has
jurisdiction to hear and determine claims for charges or interest payable to Eurocontrol[1], the Secretary of State[2] or the Civil Aviation Authority (CAA)[3], notwithstanding that the person against whom the claim is made is not resident within the
court's jurisdiction[4]. It has also jurisdiction to hear and determine claims for
damages against Eurocontrol notwithstanding that the wrongful act, neglect or
default did not take place within the court's jurisdiction or that Eurocontrol is not
present within that jurisdiction[5], but the court has no jurisdiction in respect of
damage or injury wholly sustained within or over a country to which the provisions of the Civil Aviation Act 1982 relating to Eurocontrol do not extend[6].

Where the relevant authority[7] of a state, party to the Multilateral Agreement
relating to Route Charges[8] has determined whether or not a sum is due to
Eurocontrol in respect of air navigation services[9] provided by Eurocontrol or some
other person, that determination is enforceable, or recognised, as the case may be,
in the United Kingdom[10].

1 As to Eurocontrol see para 1370 ante.
2 As to the Secretary of State see para 1032 ante.
3 As to the CAA see para 1044 ante.
4 Civil Aviation Act 1982 s 74 (6).
5 Ibid Sch 4 para 3 (1) (amended by the Civil Aviation (Eurocontrol) Act 1983 s 2).
6 Civil Aviation Act 1982 Sch 4 para 3 (2).
7 For the meaning of 'relevant authority' see ibid s 74A (8) (added by the Civil Aviation (Eurocontrol)
Act 1983 s 1).
8 See para 1023 ante.
9 For the meaning of 'air navigation services' see para 1371 note 2 ante.
10 Civil Aviation Act 1982 s 74 A (1) (added by the Civil Aviation (Eurocontrol) Act 1983 s 1). As to the
procedure to be followed for such enforcement see the Civil Aviation Act 1982 s 74A (2)–(7) (as so
added).

(2) RULES OF THE AIR

(i) General Provisions

1382. Rules of the Air. The Secretary of State[1] may make regulations[2] prescribing the manner in which aircraft may move or fly[3], the lights and other signals to be
shown or made by aircraft or persons[4], the lighting and marking of aerodromes[5],
and any other provisions for securing the safety of aircraft in flight and in movement and the safety of persons and property on the surface[6].

1 As to the Secretary of State see para 1032 ante.
2 See the Rules of the Air Regulations 1990, SI 1990/2241.
3 See paras 1456–1483 post.
4 See paras 1484–1486 post.

5 See paras 1211, 1212 ante.
6 Air Navigation Order 1989, SI 1989/2004, art 69 (1) (amended by SI 1990/2154).

1383. Non-compliance with and departure from rules. It is an offence to contravene, to permit the contravention of, or to fail to comply with, the Rules of the Air[1].

The rules may, however, be departed from to the extent necessary for avoiding immediate danger[2], in which case the commander[3] of the aircraft must cause written particulars of the departure and of the circumstances giving rise to it to be given within 10 days to the competent authority[4] of the country in whose territory the departure was made or, if the departure was made over the high seas, to the Civil Aviation Authority (CAA)[5]. Departure from the rules is also lawful to the extent necessary for complying with the law of any country other than the United Kingdom within which the aircraft then is[6], or for complying with Military Flying Regulations[7] or Flying Orders to Contractors[8] issued by the Secretary of State[9] where the commander of the aircraft is acting as such in the course of his duty as a member of any of Her Majesty's naval, military or air forces[10].

Nothing in the rules exonerates any person from the consequences of any neglect in the use of lights or signals[11] or of the neglect of any precautions required by ordinary aviation practice or by special circumstances[12].

1 Air Navigation Order 1989, SI 1989/2004, art 69 (2) (amended by SI 1990/2154) . The penalty for contravention is on summary conviction a fine not exceeding £1,000: Air Navigation Order 1989 art 99 (5), Sch 12 Pt A (as so amended).
2 Ibid art 69 (3) (a). See also para 1403 text to notes 11, 12 post.
3 For the meaning of 'commander' see para 1213 note 1 ante.
4 For the meaning of 'competent authority' see para 1347 note 3 ante.
5 Air Navigation Order 1989 art 69 (4) (as amended: see note 1 supra). The penalty for contravention is on summary conviction a fine not exceeding £400: art 99 (4). As to the Civil Aviation Authority see para 1044 ante.
6 Ibid art 69 (3) (b).
7 Joint Service Publication 318.
8 Aviation Publication 67.
9 As to the Secretary of State see para 1032 ante.
10 Air Navigation Order 1989 art 69 (3) (c).
11 See paras 1484–1486 post.
12 Air Navigation Order 1989 art 69 (5) (as amended: see note 1 supra) .

(ii) Air Traffic Controllers

1384. Licensing of air traffic controllers. Subject to such conditions as it thinks fit the Civil Aviation Authority (CAA)[1] may grant a licence to any person to act as an air traffic controller or student air traffic controller or aerodrome flight information service officer[2], upon its being satisfied that the applicant is a fit person to hold the licence and is qualified by reason of his knowledge, experience, competence, skill, physical and mental fitness so to act, for which purpose the applicant must furnish evidence and undergo such examinations and tests as the CAA may require[3].

An appeal lies to a county court from any decision of the CAA that a person is not a fit person to hold such a licence, and if the court is satisfied that on the evidence submitted to the CAA it was wrong in so deciding, it may reverse the decision[4].

No appeal lies, however, from a decision that the applicant was not qualified by reason of deficiency in his knowledge, experience, competence, skill, physical or mental fitness[5].

1 As to the CAA see para 1044 ante.
2 A licence may not be granted to a person under 18 to act as a student air traffic controller or as an aerodrome flight information service officer, nor may it be granted to a person under 20 years if it includes an aerodrome control rating, an approach control rating or an area control rating and nor may it be granted to a person under 21 years if it includes any other rating: Air Navigation Order 1989, SI 1989/2004, art 70 (1) proviso (a)–(c). For the meaning of 'aerodrome flight information service' see para 1387 note 2 post.
3 Ibid art 70 (1). Applicants for and holders of licences must submit to such examinations and tests, and furnish such evidence as to their knowledge, experience, competence and skill on such occasions as the CAA may require and, in the case of air traffic controller's or student air traffic controller's licences, must undergo a medical examination by an approved person when required by the CAA: art 70 (7), (8). As to licences generally see paras 1066–1071 ante.
4 Ibid art 105 (1). The CAA must be a respondent to an appeal: art 105 (3). Its decision is deemed to have been taken on the date on which it furnished the applicant with a statement of its reasons for the decision: art 105 (4). As to the venue and procedure see para 1098 note 1 ante.
5 Ibid art 105 (1) proviso.

1385. Air traffic controller's licence. A licence to act as an air traffic controller[1] must include the ratings[2] specifying the type of air traffic control service[3] which the holder is competent to provide, and a list of the places at which and the type of radar equipment, if any, with the aid of which he may provide the service[4]. If for a period of 90 days the holder has not provided at a particular place the type of air traffic control service specified in the rating, the rating ceases to be valid for that place at the end of that period, and the holder must forthwith inform the Civil Aviation Authority (CAA)[5] that the rating has ceased to be valid and forward the licence to the CAA to enable it to endorse the licence accordingly[6].

1 As to applications for such a licence see para 1384 ante.
2 As to ratings see para 1389 post.
3 For the meaning of 'air traffic control service' see para 1394 note 1 post.
4 Air Navigation Order 1989, SI 1989/2004, art 70 (2).
5 As to the CAA see para 1044 ante.
6 Air Navigation Order 1989 art 70 (2).

1386. Student air traffic controller's licence. A licence to act as a student air traffic controller[1] is valid only for the purpose of authorising the holder to provide air traffic control service[2] under the supervision of another person present at the time who is the holder of an air traffic controller's licence which includes a rating[3] specifying the type of air traffic control service which is being provided by the student air traffic controller, and valid at the place in question[4].

1 As to applicants for such a licence see para 1384 ante.
2 For the meaning of 'air traffic control service' see para 1394 note 1 post.
3 As to ratings see para 1389 post.
4 Air Navigation Order 1989, SI 1989/2004, art 70 (3).

1387. Aerodrome flight information service officer's licence. A licence to act as an aerodrome flight information service officer[1] is valid only for the purpose of authorising the holder to provide an aerodrome flight information service[2] at a specified aerodrome[3]. If for a period of 180 days the holder has not at any time provided such service at the aerodrome, his licence ceases to be valid for that aerodrome at the end of that period[4].

1　As to applications for such a licence see para 1384 ante.
2　'Aerodrome flight information service' is to be construed in accordance with the meaning of 'aerodrome flight information unit', which means a person appointed by the Civil Aviation Authority (as to which see para 1044 ante) or by any other person maintaining an aerodrome to give information by means of radio signals to aircraft flying or intending to fly within the aerodrome traffic zone (as to which see para 1395 post) of that aerodrome: Air Navigation Order 1989, SI 1989/2004, art 106 (1).
3　Ibid art 70 (4).
4　Ibid art 70 (4).

1388. Validity of licences. A licence to act as an air traffic controller, as a student air traffic controller, or as an aerodrome flight information service officer is not valid unless signed in ink by the holder[1].

Such licence remains in force for the period indicated in the licence and may be renewed from time to time by the Civil Aviation Authority (CAA)[2] upon its being satisfied that the applicant is a fit person and is qualified to act[3]. The CAA has the right to suspend, revoke or vary the licence[4].

The holder of an air traffic controller's or student air traffic controller's licence must not provide any type of air traffic control service unless his licence includes a valid medical certificate [5].

1　Air Navigation Order 1989, SI 1989/2004, art 70 (5).
2　As to the CAA see para 1044 ante.
3　Air Navigation Order 1989 art 70 (6). If no period is indicated in the licence it remains in force for the lifetime of the holder: art 70 (6). As to the qualifications see para 1384 ante.
4　See ibid art 66 .
5　Ibid art 70 (10). This certificate is deemed to form part of the licence: art 70 (9). As to the issue of medical certificates see art 70 (9).

1389. Ratings. A licence holder may not perform any of the functions in respect of a rating at any of the places listed in the licence[1] unless his licence includes that rating and the rating is valid for the place at which and the type of radar equipment, if any, with the aid of which the functions are performed, or unless he is supervised by a person who is present at the time and who is the holder of an air traffic controller's licence authorising him to provide at that aerodrome or other place the type of air traffic control service which is being provided[2].

Seven classes of ratings are set out in the Air Navigation Order 1989 : (1) aerodrome control rating, (2) approach control rating, (3) approach radar control rating, (4) precision approach radar control rating, (5) area control rating, (6) area radar control rating and (7) area radar control (aerodrome) rating[3]. The holder of a licence which includes ratings of two or more of these classes may not at any one time perform the functions specified in respect of more than one of them[4].

1　See para 1391 post.
2　See the Air Navigation Order 1989, SI 1989/2004, arts 70 (2) (a)–(c), 71 (2) (a), (b). The penalty for contravention of art 70 is on summary conviction a fine not exceeding £400, and of art 71 (except art 71 (4)) a fine on summary conviction not exceeding £1,000: art 99 (4), (5), Sch 12 Pt A.
3　Ibid art 71 (2), Sch 9 para 2 (amended by SI 1990/2154) . The air traffic control services which the holder is entitled to perform are specified there in respect of each rating.

4 Air Navigation Order 1989 Sch 9 para 1. The functions of any one or more of the following groups of ratings may, however, be exercised at the same time: ratings (1) and (2); ratings (2) and (3) (with exceptions); ratings (5) and (6): Sch 9 para 1 proviso.

1390. Flight information service manual. A person may not provide an aerodrome flight information service[1] at any aerodrome unless it is provided in accordance with the standards and procedures laid down in an aerodrome information service manual concerning that aerodrome[2]. From time to time the Civil Aviation Authority (CAA)[3] may request that it is shown the manual and that additions or amendments are made to it[4].

1 For the meaning of 'aerodrome flight information service' see para 1387 note 2 ante.
2 Air Navigation Order 1989, SI 1989/2004, art 72 (a).
3 As to the CAA see para 1044 ante.
4 Air Navigation Order 1989 art 72 (b), (c).

1391. Prohibition of unlicensed air traffic controllers and aerodrome flight service officers. A person may not provide at any place any type of air traffic control service[1] or an aerodrome flight information service[2] or hold himself out, whether by use of a radio call sign or in any other way, as a person who may provide any type of air traffic control service or an aerodrome flight information service unless he is the holder of, and complies with the terms of, (1) in the case of an air traffic control service (a) a valid student air traffic controller's licence and under the supervision of the holder of a valid air traffic controller's licence present at the time[3]; or (b) a valid air traffic controller's licence authorising him to provide that type of service at that place[4]; or (c) a valid air traffic controller's licence which does not authorise him to provide that type of service there, provided he is supervised at the time by the holder of a valid air traffic controller's licence which authorises that holder to provide at that place the type of air traffic control service which is being provided[5]; or (2) in the case of an aerodrome flight information service, an aerodrome flight information service officer's licence granted under the Air Navigation Order 1989[6] authorising him to provide such a service at that place[7].

A licence to provide air traffic control service is not required by any person acting in the course of his duty as a member of any of Her Majesty's naval, military or air forces or a visiting force[8].

1 For the meaning of 'air traffic control service' see para 1394 note 1 post.
2 See para 1387 note 2 ante.
3 Air Navigation Order 1989, SI 1989/2004, arts 70 (3), 71 (1) (a) (i): see para 1386 ante.
4 Ibid art 71 (1) (a) (ii).
5 Ibid art 71 (1) (a) (iii).
6 See para 1387 ante.
7 Air Navigation Order 1989 art 71 (1) (b). The penalty for contravention of any of these provisions is on summary conviction a fine not exceeding £1,000: art 99 (5), Sch 12 Pt A.
8 Ibid art 71 (1) proviso.

1392. Other prohibitions. A person may not provide any type of air traffic control service[1] or aerodrome flight information service[2] unless he has identified himself in such a manner as may be notified[3].

Nothing in an air traffic controller's licence permits any person providing an air traffic control service or making signals to an aircraft to operate manually any direction-finding equipment for the purpose of providing air traffic control service to that aircraft or to another aircraft[4].

However, the holder of a valid air traffic controller's licence may provide, at any place for which the licence includes a valid rating[5], information to aircraft in flight in the interests of safety[6].

1 For the meaning of 'air traffic control service' see para 1394 note 1 post.
2 For the meaning of 'aerodrome flight information service' see para 1387 note 2 ante.
3 Air Navigation Order 1989, SI 1989/2004, art 71 (3).
4 Ibid art 71 (4). The penalty for contravention is on summary conviction a fine not exceeding £400 : art 99 (4).
5 As to ratings see para 1389 ante.
6 Air Navigation Order 1989 art 71 (5).

1393. Incapacity, pregnancy or drunkenness of air traffic controllers. The holder of a valid air traffic controller's licence must inform the Civil Aviation Authority (CAA)[1] in writing as soon as possible of any personal injury or illness involving incapacity to undertake his functions throughout a period of 20 consecutive days[2]. The licence is deemed to be suspended upon the elapse of that period, but the suspension ceases when the holder, being medically examined, is pronounced fit to resume his functions under the licence[3], or upon the CAA exempting him from such medical examination subject to such conditions as it may think fit[4].

A woman licence holder who has reason to believe that she is pregnant must inform the CAA in writing as soon as possible[5].

When exercising the privileges of an air traffic controller's licence, a person must not be under the influence of drink or a drug to such an extent as to impair his capacity to exercise such privileges[6].

1 As to the CAA see para 1044 ante.
2 Air Navigation Order 1989, SI 1989/2004, art 73 (1) (a).
3 Ibid art 73 (2) (a). The CAA makes the arrangements for the examination: art 73 (2) (a).
4 Ibid art 73 (2) (b).
5 Ibid art 73 (1) (b).
6 Ibid art 73A (added by SI 1991/1726). Contravention is an offence punishable on summary conviction by a fine not exceeding £2,000 and on conviction on indictment by a fine or imprisonment for a term not exceeding two years or by both: Air Navigation Order 1989 art 99 (6), Sch 12 Pt B (amended by SI 1991/1726).

(iii) Control of Air Traffic

1394. Provision of air traffic services. A person may only provide an air traffic control service[1] under and in accordance with the terms of the approval which the Civil Aviation Authority (CAA)[2] has granted him. When applying for such an approval, he must satisfy the CAA that he is competent to provide a service which is safe for use by aircraft, having regard to his organisation, staffing, equipment, maintenance and other arrangements[3].

The person in charge of an aerodrome[4] which has equipment for providing holding aid, let-down aid or approach aid by radio or radar must inform the CAA in advance of the periods during, and times at, which any of that equipment is to be in operation for the purpose of providing such aid and must cause an air traffic control service to be provided, during any period and at such times as are notified, for any aircraft flying in the aerodrome traffic zone[5] (or in its vicinity) whether or not it is flying by visual reference to the surface[6].

Where the CAA directs that an air traffic control service, or an aerodrome flight information service[7] or means of two-way radio communication[8] must be provided at a particular aerodrome, specifying if need be, the periods during, and times at, which such service or means must be provided, the person in charge of that aerodrome must ensure that such service or means are provided as directed[9].

The obligations to cause an air traffic control service to be provided arising either from the initiative of the person in charge of the aerodrome[10] or from a direction made by the CAA[11] are without prejudice to each other[12].

1 'Air traffic control service' is to be construed in accordance with the meaning of 'air traffic control unit', which means a person appointed by the CAA or by any other person maintaining an aerodrome or place to give instructions or advice or both instructions and advice by means of radio signals to aircraft in the interests of safety but does not include a person so appointed solely to give information to aircraft; and 'appropriate air traffic control unit' means, in relation to an aircraft, either the air traffic control unit serving the area in which the aircraft is for the time being or the air traffic control unit serving the area which the aircraft intends to enter and with which unit the aircraft is required to communicate prior to entering that area: Air Navigation Order 1989, SI 1989/2004, art 106 (1) (amended by SI 1991/1726).
2 As to the CAA see para 1044 ante.
3 Air Navigation Order 1989 art 69A (1) (added by SI 1990/2154).
4 Government aerodromes are excluded. As to aerodromes see para 1102 ante.
5 For the meaning of 'aerodrome traffic zone' see para 1395 post.
6 Air Navigation Order 1989 art 69A (2) (as added: see note 3 supra) .
7 As to 'aerodrome flight information service' see para 1387 note 2 ante.
8 The person in charge of an aerodrome provided with means of two-way radio communication may not cause or permit any call sign to be used for a purpose other than a purpose for which that call sign has been notified: Air Navigation Order 1989 art 69B (added by SI 1990/2154). As to radio equipment see paras 1318–1323 ante.
9 Air Navigation Order 1989 art 69A (3) (as added: see note 3 supra).
10 See the Air Navigation Order 1989 art 69A (2) (as added: see note 3 supra).
11 See ibid art 69A (3) (as added: see note 3 supra) .
12 Ibid art 69A (4) (as added: see note 3 supra).

1395. Meaning of 'aerodrome traffic zone', 'control area', 'control zone' and 'controlled airspace'. 'Aerodrome traffic zone' means the airspace in the vicinity of an aerodrome which is notified[1] for the purposes of flying within such an airspace[2]. It is that airspace extending from the surface to a height of 2,000 feet above the level of the aerodrome within the area bounded by a circle centred on the notified mid-point of the longest runway of the aerodrome and having a radius of two nautical miles[3], where that runway is notified as being 1,850 metres long or less, or two and a half nautical miles where the longest runway is notified as being over 1,850 metres long[4]. In the case of an aerodrome on an offshore installation, the aerodrome traffic zone is that airspace extending from mean sea level to 2,000 feet above mean sea level and within one and a half nautical miles of the offshore installation[5]. However, any part of any of that airspace which is within the aerodrome traffic zone of another aerodrome notified as a controlling aerodrome may not be included in the aerodrome traffic zone of the non-controlling aerodrome[6].

A 'control area' is controlled airspace which has been further notified as a control area and which extends upwards from a notified altitude or flight level; a 'control zone' is controlled airspace which has been further notified as a control zone and which extends upwards from the surface; and 'controlled airspace' means airspace which has been notified as Class A, Class B, Class C, Class D or Class E airspace[7].

1 For the meaning of 'notified' see para 1105 note 3 ante.
2 See the Air Navigation Order 1989, SI 1989/2004, art 106 (1). The entry for 'aerodrome traffic zone' was amended by SI 1990/2154 to take account of the Rules of the Air Regulations 1990, SI 1990/2241. As to flights in an aerodrome traffic zone see para 1476 post.
3 For the meaning of 'nautical mile' see para 1362 note 4 ante.
4 Air Navigation Order 1989 art 106 (1).
5 Ibid art 106 (1).
6 Ibid art 106 (1).
7 Ibid art 106 (1) (amended by SI 1991/1726). Class A, B, C, D or E airspace means airspace respectively notified as such: Air Navigation Order 1989 art 106 (1) (as so amended).

1396. Weather reports and forecasts. Immediately before an aircraft flies, its commander[1] must examine the current reports and forecasts of the weather conditions on the proposed flight paths in order to determine whether instrument meteorological conditions[2] prevail or are likely to prevail during any part of the flight[3].

An aircraft which is unable to communicate by radio with an air traffic control unit[4] at the aerodrome of destination may not begin a flight to an aerodrome within a control zone[5] if the information which it is reasonably practical for the commander to obtain indicates that the aircraft will arrive at that aerodrome when ground visibility[6] is less than five nautical miles[7] or the cloud ceiling[8] is less than 1500 feet, unless he has obtained permission to enter the aerodrome traffic zone[9] from an air traffic control unit at that aerodrome[10].

1 For the meaning of 'commander' see para 1213 note 1 ante.
2 'Instrument meteorological conditions' means weather preventing flight in compliance with the visual flight rules: Air Navigation Order 1989, SI 1989/2004, art 106 (1). As to these rules see para 1398 post.
3 Rules of the Air Regulations 1990, SI 1990/2241, Schedule r 16 (1). As to weather conditions see generally paras 1440–1445 post; as to the commander's pre-flight action see para 1426 post.
4 For the meaning of 'air traffic control unit' see para 1394 note 1 ante.
5 For the meaning of 'control zone' see para 1395 ante.
6 'Ground visibility' means the horizontal visibility at ground level: Rules of the Air Regulations 1990 Schedule r 1 (1).
7 For the meaning of 'nautical mile' see para 1362 note 4 ante.
8 For the meaning of 'cloud ceiling' see para 1441 note 5 post.
9 For the meaning of 'aerodrome traffic zone' see para 1395 ante. For the meaning of 'notified' see para 1105 note 3 ante.
10 Rules of the Air Regulations 1990 Schedule r 16 (2).

1397. Visual and instrument flight rules. An aircraft must always be flown in accordance with the visual flight rules (VFR)[1] or the instrument flight rules (IFR)[2], in addition to complying with the general flight rules[3]. In the United Kingdom an aircraft must be flown in accordance with the instrument flight rules when it is flying at night[4] whether in a control zone[5] or not[6]. However, in a control zone, in the case of a special VFR flight[7], the aircraft must be flown as directed by the appropriate air traffic control unit[8].

1 As to the visual flight rules see para 1398 post.
2 As to the instrument flight rules see paras 1399–1404 post.
3 Rules of the Air Regulations 1990, SI 1990/2241, Schedule r 22.

4 For the meaning of 'night' see para 1192 note 4 ante.
5 Rules of the Air Regulations 1990 Schedule r 22 proviso (b). For the meaning of 'control zone' see para 1395 ante.
6 Ibid Schedule r 22 proviso (a).
7 For the meaning of 'special VFR flight' see para 1398 note 8 post.
8 Rules of the Air Regulations 1990 Schedule r 22 proviso (b).

1398. Visual flight rules (VFR). In order to comply with the visual flight rules, an aircraft flying outside (and above 3,000 feet above mean sea level) or within controlled airspace[1] must remain at least one nautical mile[2] horizontally and 1,000 feet vertically away from cloud and in a flight visibility[3] of at least five nautical miles[4]. The same applies where the aircraft is flying outside notified airspace[5].

When the aircraft is flying outside controlled or notified airspace it may be flown at or below 3,000 feet above mean sea level if it remains at least one nautical mile horizontally and 1,000 feet vertically away from cloud and in a flight visibility of at least three nautical miles[6].

In a control zone[7], in the case of a special VFR flight[8], the aircraft must be flown in accordance with any instructions given by the appropriate air traffic control unit[9].

When an aircraft is flying within airspace notified as being subject to special rules[10], it must be flown in accordance with the provisions relating to flight outside such airspace or controlled airspace by aircraft flying above 3,000 feet above mean sea level[11] and, in the case of a flight for which the appropriate air traffic control unit has given a special VFR clearance, such aircraft must fly clear of cloud, within sight of the surface and, in accordance with any special instructions given by the air traffic control unit[12].

1 For the meaning of 'controlled airspace' see para 1395 ante.
2 For the meaning of 'nautical mile' see para 1362 note 4 ante.
3 'Flight visibility' means the visibility forward from the flight deck of an aircraft in flight: Air Navigation Order 1989, SI 1989/2004, art 106 (1).
4 See the Rules of the Air Regulations 1990, SI 1990/2241, Schedule r 23 (a) (i), (b).
5 See ibid Schedule r 23 (a); as to such notified airspace see r 36; and text and notes 10–12 infra.
6 Ibid Schedule r 23 (a) (ii). The same applies to helicopters although it may also suffice for them to remain clear of cloud and in sight of the surface: r 23 (a) (iii). This last provision can also apply to aircraft flying at a speed of 140 knots or less and which remains clear of cloud, in sight of the surface and in a flight visibility of at least one nautical mile: r 23 (a) (ii) proviso.
7 For the meaning of 'control zone' see para 1395 ante.
8 'Special VFR flight' means a flight made in instrument meteorological conditions or at night in a control zone or in a control zone notified for the purpose of the Rules of the Air Regulations 1990 Schedule r 21, in respect of which the appropriate air traffic control unit has given permission for the flight to be made in accordance with special instructions from that unit instead of in accordance with the instrument flight rules: Schedule r 23 (b). As to r 21 see para 1405 post. For the meaning of 'instrument meteorological conditions' see para 1396 note 2 ante; for the meaning of 'night' see para 1192 note 4 ante; and as to the instrument flight rules see paras 1399–1404 post.
9 Ibid Schedule r 23 (b) proviso. See para 1397 ante. For the meaning of 'air traffic control unit' see para 1394 note 1 ante.
10 As to such notified airspace see ibid Schedule r 36; and para 1406 post. This is not to be confused with r 21, as to which see para 1405 post.
11 Ibid Schedule r 23 (c) (ii).
12 Ibid Schedule r 23 (c) (i).

1399. Instrument Flight Rules (IFR): application. Where an aircraft is flying outside controlled airspace[1], the applicable instrument flight rules are the minimum height rules[2] and the quadrantal and semi–circular rules[3].

Where an aircraft is flying within controlled airspace, the applicable instrument flight rules are those concerning minimum height[4], flight plan and air traffic clearance[5] and position reports[6].

1 For the meaning of 'controlled airspace' see para 1395 ante.
2 As to minimum height rules see the Rules of the Air Regulations 1990, SI 1990/2241, Schedule r 25; and para 1400 post.
3 Ibid Schedule r 24 (a). As to quadrantal and semi-circular rules see r 26; and para 1401 post.
4 See note 2 supra.
5 As to flight plan and air traffic control clearance rules see the Rules of the Air Regulations 1990 Schedule r 27; and para 1402 et seq post.
6 Ibid Schedule r 24 (b). As to position reports rules see r 28; and para 1404 post.

1400. IFR: minimum height. In order to comply with the instrument flight rules[1], and without prejudice to the provisions in respect of low flying[2], an aircraft, whether flying outside or within controlled airspace[3], may not fly at a height of less than 1,000 feet above the highest obstacle within a distance of five nautical miles[4] unless it is necessary to do so in order to take off or land, or it is flying on a route notified[5] for the purpose, or it has otherwise been authorised by the competent authority[6] or it is flying at an altitude not exceeding 3,000 feet above mean sea level and remains clear of cloud and in sight of the surface[7].

1 See paras 1399 ante, 1401–1404 post.
2 See paras 1489–1493 post.
3 For the meaning of 'controlled airspace' see para 1395 ante.
4 For the meaning of 'nautical mile' see para 1362 note 4 ante.
5 For the meaning of 'notified' see para 1105 note 3 ante.
6 For the meaning of 'competent authority' see para 1347 note 3 ante.
7 Rules of the Air Regulations 1990, SI 1990/2241, Schedule r 25 (a)–(d).

1401. Quadrantal and semi-circular rules. In order to comply with the instrument flight rules, an aircraft, when in level flight above 3,000 feet above mean sea level or above the appropriate transition altitude[1], whichever is the higher, must be flown at a level appropriate to its magnetic track[2]. The level of flight must be measured by an altimeter set, in the case of a flight over the United Kingdom, to a pressure setting of 1,013·2 millibars[3] or, in the case of any other flight according to the system published by the competent authority[4], in relation to the area over which the aircraft is flying[5].

An aircraft may, however, fly at a level other than the required level if it is flying in conformity with instructions given by an air traffic control unit[6] or in accordance with either notified[7] en-route holding patterns or with holding procedures notified in relation to the aerodrome[8].

1 'Transition altitude' means the altitude so notified in relation to flight over such area or areas as may be notified: Rules of the Air Regulations 1990, SI 1990/2241, Schedule r 26.
2 Ibid Schedule r 26. 'Flight level' means one of a series of levels of equal atmospheric pressure, separated by notified intervals and each expressed as the number of hundreds of feet which would be indicated at that level on a pressure altimeter calibrated in accordance with the international standard atmosphere and set to 1,013·2 millibars: Air Navigation Order 1989, SI 1989/2004, art 106 (1). Levels of flight are set out in the Rules of the Air Regulations 1990 Schedule r 26, Tables I, II.
3 Ibid Schedule r 26 (a).
4 For the meaning of 'competent authority' see para 1347 note 3 ante.
5 Rules of the Air Regulations 1990 Schedule r 26 (b).
6 For the meaning of 'air traffic control unit' see para 1394 note 1 ante.

7 For the meaning of 'notified' see para 1105 note 3 ante.
8 Rules of the Air Regulations 1990 Schedule r 26 proviso.

1402. IFR: flight plans. In order to comply with the instrument flight rules, the commander[1] of an aircraft must cause a flight plan to be communicated to the appropriate air traffic control unit[2] before the aircraft either takes off from a point within controlled airspace[3] or flies within any controlled airspace[4]. The flight plan must contain such particulars of the intended flight as may be necessary to enable the unit to issue an air traffic control clearance[5] or for search and rescue purposes[6].

After the aircraft has flown in controlled airspace the commander must forthwith inform the air traffic control unit when the aircraft lands within or leaves the controlled airspace, unless he has requested the unit to cancel his flight plan[7].

1 For the meaning of 'commander' see para 1213 note 1 ante.
2 For the meaning of 'air traffic control unit' see para 1394 note 1 ante.
3 For the meaning of 'controlled airspace' see para 1395 ante.
4 Rules of the Air Regulations 1990, SI 1990/2241, Schedule r 27 (1).
5 As to air traffic control clearance see para 1403 post.
6 Rules of the Air Regulations 1990 Schedule r 27 (2).
7 Ibid r 27 (5).

1403. IFR: air traffic control clearance. Before an aircraft either takes off from a point within controlled airspace[1] or otherwise flies within any controlled airspace, the commander[2] must, in order to comply with the instrument flight rules, obtain from the appropriate air traffic control unit[3] an air traffic control clearance[4] based on his flight plan[5].

The commander of the aircraft must fly in conformity with the clearance issued for the flight, as amended by any further instructions given by an air traffic control unit and with the holding and instrument approach procedures notified[6] in relation to the aerodrome of destination unless otherwise authorised by the air traffic control unit there[7]. He is not, however, required to comply with these provisions if he is able to fly in uninterrupted visual meteorological conditions[8] for so long as he remains in controlled airspace, and he has informed the appropriate air traffic control unit of his intention to continue the flight in accordance with visual flight rules[9] and has requested that unit to cancel his flight plan[10].

In the case of any departure from these provisions for the purpose of avoiding immediate danger[11], the commander must as soon as possible inform the appropriate air traffic control unit of the deviation as well as making a written report to the competent authority[12].

1 For the meaning of 'controlled airspace' see para 1395 ante.
2 For the meaning of 'commander' see para 1213 note 1 ante.
3 For the meaning of 'air traffic control unit' see para 1394 note 1 ante.
4 'Air traffic control clearance' means authorisation by an air traffic control unit for an aircraft to proceed under conditions specified by that unit: Rules of the Air Regulations 1990, SI 1990/2241, Schedule r 1 (1).
5 Ibid Schedule r 27 (1). As to flight plans see para 1402 ante.
6 For the meaning of 'notified' see para 1105 note 3 ante.
7 Rules of the Air Regulations 1990 Schedule r 27 (3) (a)–(b).
8 'Visual meteorological conditions' means weather permitting flight in accordance with visual flight rules: Air Navigation Order 1989, SI 1989/2004, art 106 (1).
9 As to visual flight rules see paras 1397, 1398 ante.
10 Rules of the Air Regulations 1990 Schedule r 27 (3) proviso.

11 See the Air Navigation Order 1989 art 69 (3) (amended by SI 1990/2154) ; and para 1383 ante.
12 Rules of the Air Regulations 1990 Schedule r 27 (4). As to such written reports see the Air
    Navigation Order 1989 art 69 (4) (amended by SI 1990/2154); and para 1383 ante.

1404. IFR: position reports. In order to comply with the instrument flight rules
the commander[1] of an aircraft in IFR flight[2] who flies in or is intending to enter
controlled airspace[3] must report to the appropriate air traffic control unit[4] the time,
and the aircraft's position and altitude at such reporting points or at such intervals
of time as may be notified[5] for that purpose or as may be directed by that unit[6].

1 For the meaning of 'commander' see para 1213 note 1 ante.
2 'IFR flight' means a flight conducted in accordance with the instrument flight rules: Rules of the Air
   Regulations 1990, SI 1990/2241, Schedule r 1 (1).
3 For the meaning of 'controlled airspace' see para 1395 ante.
4 For the meaning of 'air traffic control unit' see para 1394 note 1 ante.
5 For the meaning of 'notified' see para 1105 note 3 ante.
6 Rules of the Air Regulations 1990 Schedule r 28.

1405. Flight in notified airspace. In relation to flights in visual meteorological
conditions[1] in notified[2] controlled airspace[3], the commander[4] of an aircraft must
comply with the rules as to flight plans[5], air traffic control clearances[6] and position
reports[7] as if the flights were IFR flights[8].

1 For the meaning of 'visual meteorological conditions' see para 1403 note 8 ante.
2 For the meaning of 'notified' see para 1105 note 3 ante.
3 For the meaning of 'controlled airspace' see para 1395 ante.
4 For the meaning of 'commander' see para 1213 note 1 ante.
5 See para 1402 ante.
6 See para 1403 ante. The commander may not elect to continue the flight in accordance with visual
   flight rules as he could were he flying in controlled airspace: see Rules of the Air Regulations 1990, SI
   1990/2241, Schedule rr 21 proviso, 27 (3) proviso.
7 See para 1404 ante.
8 Rules of the Air Regulations 1990 Schedule r 21. This rule does not apply to the commander of a
   glider if the glider is flown in accordance with any notified conditions in respect of that airspace:
   r 21A. As to notified airspace for the purposes of r 36 see para 1406 post. For the meaning of 'IFR
   flight' see para 1404 note 2 ante.

1406. Notified airspace: special rules for certain aerodromes. The special
rules concerning the airspace above certain aerodromes[1] apply to all aircraft unless
otherwise authorised by the air traffic control unit[2] at the aerodrome, save gliders
and mechanically driven aircraft[3] without radio equipment in certain circumstances[4]. The rules apply to the notified[5] airspace during the notified hours of
watch of the air traffic control unit at the aerodrome[6].

An aircraft may not fly within the notified airspace without the permission of the
appropriate air traffic control unit, which the commander[7] of the aircraft must
obtain before so flying; the commander must also inform the unit of the aircraft's
position, level and track[8]. While the aircraft is flying within such an airspace, the
commander must ensure that a continuous radio watch is maintained and he must
comply with any instruction given by the air traffic control unit[9]. The aircraft must
remain at least one nautical mile[10] horizontally and 1,000 feet vertically away from
cloud and in a flight visibility of at least five nautical miles unless the commander
holds a licence with a valid instrument rating[11] or the aircraft is given a special VFR
clearance to take off or land within such a notified airspace[12].

1 For a list of the aerodromes concerned see the Rules of the Air Regulations 1990, SI 1990/2241, Schedule r 36 (1). As for special rules for the Upper Heyford Mandatory Radio Area, Cross-Channel air traffic, the Upper Flight Information Regions and the Scottish Terminal Control Area, see rr 36A–40.
2 For the meaning of 'air traffic control unit' see para 1394 note 1 ante.
3 As to mechanically driven aircraft see para 1269 ante.
4 See the Rules of the Air Regulations 1990 Schedule r 36 (3) (c), (4).
5 For the meaning of 'notified' see para 1105 note 3 ante.
6 See the Rules of the Air Regulations 1990 Schedule r 36 (3), (4).
7 For the meaning of 'commander' see para 1213 note 1 ante.
8 Rules of the Air Regulations 1990 Schedule r 36 (3) (a).
9 Ibid Schedule r 36 (3) (b).
10 For the meaning of 'nautical mile' see para 1362 note 4 ante.
11 Rules of the Air Regulations 1990 Schedule r 36 (4); as to pilots' licences and ratings see paras 1348–1351 ante.
12 Ibid Schedule r 36 (4) (a)–(c). For the purposes of r 36, 'special VFR clearance' means a clearance given by the appropriate air traffic control unit to an aircraft for flight within airspace notified for the purposes of any paragraph of r 36 if the aircraft remains clear of cloud, within sight of the surface and is flown in accordance with any special instructions given by that unit: r 36 (2).

1407. Notification of arrival and departure. The commander[1] of an aircraft who has caused notice of its intended arrival at an aerodrome to be given to the air traffic control unit[2] or other authority there must ensure that that unit or authority is informed as quickly as possible of any change of intended destination and any estimated delay in arrival of 45 minutes or more[3].

When landing, or prior to departure, the commander of an aircraft must ensure that the event is notified to the person in charge of the aerodrome or to the air traffic control unit[4] or aerodrome flight information unit[5] at the aerodrome[6]. Whether or not the flight will take place in controlled airspace[7], the commander of an aircraft of which the maximum total weight authorised exceeds 5,700 kg must cause a flight plan[8] containing particulars of the intended flight for search and rescue purposes to be given to the relevant air traffic control unit where the aerodrome of destination is more than 40 kilometres from the point of take-off in the United Kingdom[9].

1 For the meaning of 'commander' see para 1213 note 1 ante.
2 For the meaning of 'air traffic control unit' see para 1394 note 1 ante.
3 Rules of the Air Regulations 1990, SI 1990/2241, Schedule r 20 (1).
4 For the meaning of 'air traffic control unit' see para 1394 note 1 ante.
5 For the meaning of 'aerodrome flight information service' see para 1387 note 2 ante.
6 Rules of the Air Regulations 1990 Schedule r 20 (2).
7 As to flights in controlled airspace see para 1399 ante.
8 As to flight plans see para 1402 ante.
9 Rules of the Air Regulations 1990 Schedule r 20 (3). As to flights across any boundary of airspace notified as either the London or Scottish Flight Information Region, save for their common boundary, see r 20 (4).

1408. Balloons, kites, airships, gliders and parascending parachutes. Within the United Kingdom certain flights by balloons, kites, airships, gliders and parascending parachutes[1] are not allowed without the written permission of the Civil Aviation Authority (CAA)[2] and, where permitted, must be made in accordance with any conditions subject to which that permission may be granted[3].

Thus, subject to the foregoing provisions, a captive balloon or kite may not be flown at a height of more than 60 metres above ground level or within 60 metres of any vessel, vehicle or structure[4]; a captive balloon may not be flown within five kilometres of an aerodrome[5]; a balloon exceeding two metres in any linear dimension at any stage of its flight, including any basket or other equipment attached to it, may not be flown in controlled airspace notified for this purpose[6]; a kite may not be flown within five kilometres of an aerodrome[7]; an airship may not be moored[8] and a glider or parascending parachute may not be launched by winch and cable or by ground tow to a height of more than 60 metres above ground level[9].

1 'Parascending parachute' means a parachute which is towed by a cable in such a manner as to cause it to ascend: Air Navigation Order 1989, SI 1989/2004, art 106 (1).
2 As to the CAA see para 1044 ante.
3 Air Navigation Order 1989 art 75 (1). As to the lights and markings to be displayed see the Rules of the Air Regulations 1990, SI 1990/2241, Schedule rr 14, 15.
4 Air Navigation Order 1989 art 75 (1) (a).
5 Ibid art 75 (1) (b). A captive balloon when in flight must be securely moored and must not be left unattended unless fitted with a device which ensures its automatic deflation if it breaks free: art 75 (2).
6 Ibid art 75 (1) (c) (amended by SI 1991/1726). For the meaning of 'controlled airspace' see para 1395 ante; for the meaning of 'notified' see para 1105 note 3 ante.
7 Air Navigation Order 1989 art 75 (1) (d).
8 Ibid art 75 (1) (e).
9 Ibid art 75 (1) (f).

8. OPERATION OF AIRCRAFT

(1) DOCUMENTS AND RECORDS

(i) Preservation of Documents

1409. Preservation and delivery of documents and records. The operator[1] of an aircraft is required to preserve specified documents and records; if he ceases to be the operator of a particular aircraft he must continue to preserve the documents and records relating to it as if he had not ceased to be the operator, and in the event of his death the duty falls upon his personal representative[2].

However, the original operator or his personal representative must deliver to the new operator of an aircraft which remains registered in the United Kingdom the certificates of maintenance review and release to service[3], log books[4], weight schedule[5] and any record made by a flight data recorder[6] which are in force or have been preserved[7]. Similarly the operator or his personal representative must deliver to the relevant operator such log books relating to an engine or variable pitch propeller removed from an aircraft and installed in another aircraft[8], and such records of flight times concerning a person who becomes a member of the flight crew of a public transport aircraft[9] registered in the United Kingdom and operated by another person[10]. The person to whom these documents are delivered must deal with them as if he were the first mentioned operator[11].

1 For the meaning of 'operator' see para 1340 ante.
2 Air Navigation Order 1989, SI 1989/2004, art 65.
3 As to certificates of maintenance review and release to service see paras 1301 and 1331 ante, respectively; as to their preservation see para 1411 post.
4 As to log books see paras 1303, 1315, 1357 ante, 1455 post; as to their preservation see para 1410 post.
5 As to weight schedules see para 1316 ante; as to their preservation see para 1411 post.
6 As to flight data recorders and their preservation see para 1414 post.

7 Air Navigation Order 1989 art 65 proviso (a).
8 Ibid art 65 proviso (b); see para 1315 ante.
9 For the meaning of 'public transport aircraft' see para 1272 ante.
10 Air Navigation Order 1989 art 65 proviso (c); see para 1367 ante.
11 Ibid art 65 proviso .

1410. Preservation of log books. Log books must be preserved for a specified period: thus, a technical log[1] must be preserved by the operator[2] until a date two years after the date on which the aircraft has been destroyed or permanently withdrawn from use or for such shorter period as the Civil Aviation Authority (CAA)[3] may permit[4]; aircraft, engine and variable pitch propeller log books[5] must be preserved by the operator until a date two years after the date of destruction or permanent withdrawal from use of the aircraft, engine or propeller, as the case may be[6]; telecommunications log books[7] must be preserved by the operator of the aircraft until a date six months after the date of the last entry[8]; and any personal flying log book[9] required to be kept by every member of the flight crew of an aircraft registered in the United Kingdom, every member flying for the purpose of qualifying for the grant or renewal of a licence and every person flying for the purpose of undergoing tests or receiving flying instruction for the purpose of admission into Her Majesty' s forces, must be preserved so that it can be produced to an authorised person[10], within a period of two years after the date of the last entry[11].

1 See para 1303 ante.
2 For the meaning of 'operator' see para 1340 ante.
3 As to the CAA see para 1044 ante.
4 Air Navigation Order 1989, SI 1989/2004, art 10 (5); this is subject to art 65: see para 1409 ante. The penalty for contravention of this provision or of the provisions described in notes 6, 8 infra is, on summary conviction, a fine not exceeding £1,000: art 99 (5), Sch 12 Pt A.
5 See para 1315 ante.
6 Air Navigation Order 1989 art 16 (5). This is subject to art 65: see para 1409 ante. For the penalty for contravention see note 4 supra .
7 As to telecommunications log books see para 1455 post.
8 Air Navigation Order 1989 art 38 (7). As to the penalty for contravention see note 4 supra.
9 See ibid art 23; and para 1357 ante.
10 For the meaning of 'authorised person' see para 1193 note 2 ante.
11 Air Navigation Order 1989 art 63 (4). The penalty for contravention of this provision is, on summary conviction, a fine not exceeding £400: art 99 (4).

1411. Preservation of certificates and weight schedules. Subject to the general provisions as to the preservation of records[1], the operator[2] of an aircraft must preserve all certificates of maintenance review[3] for a period of two years after the date of issue [4]; all certificates of release to service[5] must be inserted in the technical log[6] and thus kept for the period for which the operator is required to preserve the log books[7] relating to the same part of the aircraft or to the same equipment or apparatus[8]; and the weight schedule[9] must be kept until the expiration of a period of six months following the next occasion on which the aircraft is weighed[10].

1 See the Air Navigation Order 1989, SI 1989/2004, art 65; and para 1409 ante.
2 For the meaning of 'operator' see para 1340 ante.
3 See paras 1301–1304 ante.
4 Air Navigation Order 1989 art 9 (6). The penalty for contravention of this provision is, on summary conviction, a fine not exceeding £400: art 99 (4).
5 As to certificates of release to service see para 1331 ante.

6 Air Navigation Order 1989 art 10 (3); as to the technical log see para 1303 ante.
7 See para 1410 ante.
8 Air Navigation Order 1989 art 10 (3), (5). The penalty for contravention of this provision, or of that described in note 10 infra, is, on summary conviction, a fine not exceeding £1,000: art 99 (5), Sch 12 Pt A.
9 As to weight schedules see para 1316 ante.
10 Air Navigation Order 1989 art 17 (3). For the penalty for contravention see note 8 supra.

1412. Preservation of load sheets. A copy of the load sheet and of the instructions given by the operator[1] must be preserved by him until the expiration of a period of six months after the completion of the flights to which they relate[2].

1 See paras 1432, 1433 post. For the meaning of 'operator' see para 1340 ante.
2 Air Navigation Order 1989, SI 1989/2004, art 29 (5). The penalty for contravention of this provision is, on summary conviction, a fine not exceeding £1,000: art 99 (5), Sch 12 Pt A.

1413. Preservation of records of flight times and duty and rest periods. The operator[1] of an aircraft must preserve all records of flight times[2] of each member of the aircraft's crew for a period of 12 months after the end of the flight to which they relate[3].

1 For the meaning of 'operator' see para 1340 ante.
2 See paras 1366–1369 ante.
3 Air Navigation Order 1989, SI 1989/2004, art 58 (4). This is subject to art 65, as to which see para 1409 ante. The penalty for contravention of this provision is, on summary conviction, a fine not exceeding £400: art 99 (4).

1414. Flight data recorders and cockpit voice recorders. Where a flight data recorder, or a cockpit voice recorder, or a combined voice recorder/flight data recorder is required to be carried in an aircraft[1], it must be in use from the beginning of the take-off run until the end of the landing run[2].

The operator[3] must preserve the record made by the flight data recorder[4], together with the means of identifying the record with the flight to which it relates, for such period as the Civil Aviation Authority[5] may in a particular case direct[6].

1 See the Air Navigation Order 1989, SI 1989/2004, art 40 (1), Sch 4 para 4 (4)–(7). The penalty for not using the flight data recorder, or for contravention of the provisions described in notes 2, 4, 6 infra, is a fine not exceeding £1,000: art 99 (5), Sch 12 Pt A. For the power to direct that an aircraft shall not fly if these provisions cannot be complied with see art 95 (1); and para 1459 post.
2 Ibid art 40 (1). As to the penalty for contravention see note 1 supra.
3 For the meaning of 'operator' see para 1340 ante.
4 The operator must preserve the last 25 hours of recording by a recorder required in an aeroplane, and at least one representative flight, ie a flight including take-off, climb, cruise, descent, approach to landing and landing: Air Navigation Order 1989 art 40 (2) (a), (b). As to the penalty for contravention see note 1 supra. There are additional requirements as to the preservation of records made by flight data recorders or cockpit voice recorders carried on helicopters: see art 40 (3)–(5) (amended by SI 1991/1726).
5 As to the Civil Aviation Authority see para 1044 ante.
6 Air Navigation Order 1989 art 40 (2). This is subject to art 65: see para 1409 ante. For the penalty for contravention see note 1 supra.

(ii) Carriage of Documents

1415. Prohibition of flight without appropriate documents. An aircraft may not fly unless it carries the documents which it is required to carry under the law of the country in which it is registered[1].

1 Air Navigation Order 1989, SI 1989/2004, art 61 (1). The penalty for contravention of this provision is, on summary conviction, a fine not exceeding £400: art 99 (4). For the documents which must be carried by an aircraft registered in the United Kingdom see para 1416 post.

1416. Documents to be carried by aircraft registered in the United Kingdom. An aircraft registered in the United Kingdom must, when in flight[1], whether within the United Kingdom or elsewhere, carry a noise certificate[2] which is required to be in force in respect of that aircraft[3] and no aircraft may land or take off in the United Kingdom unless it carries a noise certificate as required under the law of the country of registration[4].

The Air Navigation Order[5] makes no provision in respect of documents to be carried by an aircraft registered in the United Kingdom when it is either on a flight which is not international air navigation[6] or when it is flying for a purpose other than public transport[7] or aerial work[8]; however, where the flight is intended to begin and end at the same aerodrome and does not include passage over the territory of any country other than the United Kingdom, all documents, including the noise certificate, may be kept at that aerodrome[9].

In all other cases an aircraft registered in the United Kingdom must, when in flight, carry the following documents[10]:

(1) in every case, the aircraft radio station licence and the current telecommunications log[11], the certificate of airworthiness[12] and the licences of the members of the flight crew[13];

(2) whenever the flight is international air navigation, the certificate of registration[14] and a copy of the procedures to be observed if an aircraft is intercepted [15];

(3) when the flight is for the purpose of public transport, one copy of each certificate of maintenance review[16], the technical log[17], one copy of the load sheet[18] and the operations manual[19]; and

(4) when the flight is for the purpose of aerial work, one copy of each certificate of maintenance review and the technical log[20].

When an aircraft is flying in accordance with the terms of a permission granted to the operator allowing such aircraft to fly in special circumstances with minimum equipment[21], it must carry the permission unless otherwise authorised[22].

1 For the meaning of 'in flight' see para 1460 post.
2 As to noise certificates see para 1305 ante.
3 Air Navigation (Noise Certification) Order 1990, SI 1990/1514, art 7 (2). See, however, the text to note 9 infra. The penalty for contravention of this provision, or of that described in note 4 infra, is, on summary conviction, a fine not exceeding level 3 on the standard scale: art 14 (3). As to the standard scale see para 1044 note 6 ante. At the date at which this volume states the law, level 3 on that scale is at £400.
4 Ibid art 7 (1). As to the penalty for contravention see note 3 supra.
5 Ie the Air Navigation Order 1989, SI 1989/2004.
6 'International air navigation' means any flight which includes passage over the territory of any country other than the United Kingdom, except any of the Channel Islands, the Isle of Man, any country to which there is power to extend the Civil Aviation Act 1982 under s 108 (1) (see para 1028 ante), or any British Protected State: Air Navigation Order 1989 art 61, Sch 11.
7 For the meaning of 'public transport' see para 1272 ante.
8 For the meaning of 'aerial work' see para 1273 ante.
9 Air Navigation (Noise Certification) Order 1990 art 7 (2) proviso; Air Navigation Order 1989 art 61 (2) proviso.
10 Ibid art 61 (2), Sch 11. The penalty for contravention of this provision is, on summary conviction, a fine not exceeding £400: art 99 (4).
11 Ibid Sch 11 Document A. As to telecommunications log books see para 1455 post.

12 Ibid Sch 11 Document B. As to certificates of airworthiness see para 1288 ante.
13 Ibid Sch 11 Document C. As to flight crew licensing see paras 1343–1358 ante.
14 Ibid Sch 11 Document G. As to registration see paras 1276–1283 ante.
15 Ibid Sch 11 Document I.
16 Ibid Sch 11 Document E. As to certificates of maintenance review see paras 1301–1304 ante.
17 Ibid Sch 11 Document F. As to technical logs see para 1303 ante.
18 Ibid Sch 11 Document D. As to load sheets see para 1433 post.
19 Ibid Sch 11 Document H. As to operations manuals see para 1438 post.
20 Ibid Sch 11. As to certificates of maintenance review and technical logs see notes 16, 17 supra.
21 As to minimum equipment requirements see para 1312 ante.
22 Air Navigation Order 1990 Sch 11 Document J, proviso

1417. Records to be kept. The operator of a public transport aircraft registered in the United Kingdom must keep a record in a manner prescribed [1] of every flight by that aircraft during which it flew at an altitude of more than 49,000 feet together with the total dose of cosmic radiation to which the aircraft was exposed during the flight and the names of the members of the crew of the aircraft during the flight[2].

1 At the date at which this volume states the law, no regulations prescribing the manner of keeping such a record were in force.
2 Air Navigation Order 1989, SI 1989/2004, art 62. The penalty for contravention of this provision is, on summary conviction, a fine not exceeding £400: art 99 (4).

(iii) Production of Documents and Records

1418. Production of documents by commander. The commander[1] of an aircraft must, within a reasonable time after being requested to do so by an authorised person[2], produce to that person the following documents: the certificates of registration[3] and airworthiness[4] of the aircraft for the time being in force, the licences of the flight crew[5], and such other documents as the aircraft is required to carry[6] when in flight[7].

1 For the meaning of 'commander' see para 1213 note 1 ante.
2 For the meaning of 'authorised person' see para 1193 note 2 ante.
3 As to certificates of registration see para 1279 ante.
4 As to certificates of airworthiness see para 1288 ante.
5 As to the licences of the flight crew see paras 1343–1358 ante.
6 Ie by the Air Navigation Order 1990, SI 1990/2004, art 61; see para 1416 ante.
7 Air Navigation Order 1990, art 63 (1). The penalty for contravention of this provision is, on summary conviction, a fine not exceeding £400: art 99 (4).

1419. Production of documents by operator. The operator[1] of an aircraft registered in the United Kingdom must, within a reasonable time after being requested to do so by an authorised person[2], cause to be produced to that person such of the following documents or records, being documents or records required to be in force, carried, produced or made available, as that person may have requested: the aircraft radio station licence and current telecommunications log book[3]; the certificates of registration[4] and airworthiness[5]; the aircraft, engine and variable pitch propeller log books[6]; the weight schedule[7]; any records of flight times, duty periods and rest periods[8]; the parts of the operations manual relevant to the duties of each member of the crew of the aircraft[9]; the record made by any flight data recorder[10]; the record made from any cosmic radiation detection equipment

together with the record of the names of crew members on flights over 49,000
feet[11]; and, in the case of public transport aircraft[12] or aerial work aircraft[13], the
following additional documents: a copy of the load sheet[14]; the operations manual[15]; a copy of each certificate of maintenance review[16]; and the technical log[17].

1 For the meaning of 'operator' see para 1340 ante.
2 For the meaning of 'authorised person' see para 1193 note 2 ante.
3 As to radio communications see paras 1452–1455 post.
4 As to certificates of registration see para 1279 ante.
5 As to certificates of airworthiness see para 1288 ante.
6 As to log books see para 1315 ante.
7 As to the weight schedule see para 1316 ante.
8 As to records see para 1367 ante.
9 As to this operations manual see para 1438 post. For the meaning of 'operating staff' see para 1438
   note 4 post.
10 As to the flight data recorder see para 1414 ante.
11 As to records of cosmic radiation see para 1417 ante.
12 For the meaning of 'public transport aircraft' see para 1272 ante.
13 For the meaning of 'aerial work aircraft' see para 1273 ante.
14 As to the load sheet see para 1433 post.
15 As to the operations manual see para 1438 post.
16 As to certificates of maintenance review see paras 1301–1304 ante.
17 Air Navigation Order 1989, SI 1989/2004, art 63 (2). The penalty for contravention of this provision
   is, on summary conviction, a fine not exceeding £400: art 99 (4). As to the technical log see para 1303
   ante.

1420. Production of licences. The holder of a licence granted or rendered valid
under the Air Navigation Order[1] must within a reasonable time after being
requested to do so by an authorised person[2] cause the licence, including any
certificate of validation[3], to be produced to that person[4]. It is a sufficient compliance with this provision, in the case of a licence not required[5] to be carried in an
aircraft or kept at an aerodrome, if the licence is produced within five days after the
request has been made, at a police station in the United Kingdom specified at the
time of the request, by the person to whom the request is made[6].

The same applies to a medical certificate issued to a person to the effect that he is
fit to act as pilot in command of an aircraft for the purpose of becoming qualified
for the grant or renewal of a pilot's licence or variation of a rating therein[7].

1 Ie the Air Navigation Order 1989, SI 1989/2004.
2 For the meaning of 'authorised person' see para 1193 note 2 ante.
3 As to certificates of validation see para 1291 ante.
4 Air Navigation Order 1989 art 63 (3). The penalty for contravention of this provision is, on
   summary conviction, a fine not exceeding £400: art 99 (4).
5 Ie by ibid art 61: see para 1416 ante.
6 Ibid art 63 (3).
7 See ibid arts 63 (3) (b), 20 (1) (b) (ii); and para 1344 ante.

1421. Production of log books. Every person required to keep a personal flying
log book[1] must cause it to be produced within a reasonable time to an authorised
person[2] after being requested to do so by him within two years after the date of the
last entry in it[3].

1 Ie under the Air Navigation Order 1989, SI 1989/2004, art 23; see para 1357 ante.
2 For the meaning of 'authorised person' see para 1193 note 2 ante.
3 Air Navigation Order 1989 art 63 (4). The penalty for contravention of this provision is, on
   summary conviction, a fine not exceeding £400: art 99 (4).

(iv) General Provisions as to Documents

1422. Civil Aviation Authority's powers as to revocation, suspension or variation of certificates, etc. The Civil Aviation Authority (CAA) [1] may provisionally suspend or vary any certificate, licence, approval, permission, exemption, authorisation or other document issued, granted or having effect under the Air Navigation Order and, where satisfied after due inquiry that there are sufficient grounds, may revoke, suspend or vary any such document [2]. There is a limited right of appeal [3].

Where any such document has been revoked, suspended or varied the holder or any person having possession or custody of it must surrender it to the CAA within a reasonable time after being requested to do so [4].

1 As to the CAA see para 1044 ante. In relation to a permission granted under the Air Navigation Order 1989, SI 1989/2004, arts 88, 92, the power is exercised by the Secretary of State, from whom there is no appeal: arts 66 (4), 67 (7); see art 67 and paras 1272 text and note 10–12 ante, 1423, 1471 post. As to the Secretary of State see para 1032 ante.

2 Ibid art 66 (1). A flight manual, performance schedule or other document incorporated by reference in a certificate of airworthiness (see para 1288 ante) may be varied whether or not after due inquiry: art 66 (5).

3 See, as to review by the CAA, the Civil Aviation Authority Regulations 1991, SI 1991/1672, reg 6, and in particular, reg 6 (6), which must be read in the context of the Civil Aviation Act 1982 s 7 (1): see paras 1045, 1070 ante. As to appeals to the Secretary of State see para 1086 ante.

4 Air Navigation Order 1989 art 66 (2). The penalty for contravention of this provision is, on summary conviction, a fine not exceeding £400: art 99 (4).

1423. Secretary of State's powers as to revocation, suspension or variation of permissions, etc. Where the Secretary of State [1] has granted a permission to an operator, charterer or foreign government to allow an aircraft registered outside the United Kingdom to take on board or discharge any passengers or cargo in the United Kingdom for valuable consideration [2], he may revoke, suspend or vary that permission after having notified the permit-holder of his intention and after due consideration of the case [3]. The same applies to a permission given to the operator or charterer of an aircraft registered outside the United Kingdom to allow the aircraft to fly over the United Kingdom for the purpose of aerial photography, aerial survey or other aerial work [4].

However, the urgency of the case may compel the Secretary of State to suspend or vary provisionally the permit without complying with the statutory requirements [5]. As soon as reasonably practicable and after due consideration of the case, the Secretary of State may either revoke the provisional suspension or variation or make a definitive revocation, suspension or variation [6].

The power to revoke, suspend or vary such a permission may be exercised by the Secretary of State whenever he believes that the holder should no longer, or not to the same extent, be entitled to exercise the rights attached to the permission [7]. The reasons for such a belief may be an act or omission by the permit-holder [8], or his breach of a condition attached to the permission [9], or the termination of a bilateral agreement with the relevant state [10], or the inconsistent or prejudicial actions of the holder or of the government or of the aeronautical authorities of the state [11], or new circumstances concerning the holder affecting his qualification to keep the permit [12].

1 As to the Secretary of State see para 1032 ante.

2 See para 1272 ante; for the meaning of 'valuable consideration' see para 1272 note 3 ante.
3 Air Navigation Order 1989, SI 1989/2004, arts 67 (1), (2), 88 (see para 1272 ante) . The absence of 'due inquiry' on the part of the Secretary of State vitiates his decision: see *R v Secretary of State for Transport, ex p Philippine Airlines Inc* (1984) 1 S&B AvR IV/31, Times, 17 October, CA, where it was held that the Secretary of State must construe the bilateral agreement before revoking the permit.
4 Air Navigation Order 1989 arts 67 (1), (2), 92. See para 1471 post.
5 Ibid art 67 (3). As to whether the Secretary of State is entitled to suspend a permit provisionally pending inquiry see *R v Secretary of State for Transport, ex p Pegasus Holidays (London) Ltd* [1989] 2 All ER 481, [1988] 1 WLR 990, 1 S&B AvR II/1.
6 Air Navigation Order 1989 art 67 (3) (a), (b). The permit-holder or any other person in whose possession or custody it is must surrender it within a reasonable time: art 67 (5). The penalty for contravention of this requirement is, on summary conviction, a fine not exceeding £400: art 99 (4).
7 Ibid art 67 (4).
8 Ibid art 67 (4).
9 Ibid art 67 (4) (a). The breach of any condition renders the permit invalid while the breach continues: art 67 (6). There is no limitation to the power of the Secretary of State to attach conditions to the permit; see eg *Pan American World Airways Inc v Department of Trade* [1976] 1 Lloyd's Rep 257, CA, and *Seaboard World Airlines Inc v Department of Trade* [1976] 1 Lloyd's Rep 42, QB.
   Where conditions require that the chartered aircraft be operated by crews of the country of registration and that the charterer ensures that the foreign licence requirements be complied with, the Secretary of State may suspend provisionally the permit where the pilot's ability gives serious grounds for concern: see *R v Secretary of State for Transport, ex p Pegasus Holidays (London) Ltd* [1989] 2 All ER 481, [1988] 1 WLR 990, 1 S&B AvR II/1.
10 Air Navigation Order 1989 art 67 (4) (b).
11 Ibid art 67 (4) (c).
12 Ibid art 67 (4) (d).

1424. Breach of condition of certificate, etc. The breach of any condition subject to which any certificate, licence, approval, permission, exemption or other document has been granted or issued, or which has effect under the Air Navigation Order 1989 , renders the document invalid during the continuance of the breach in the absence of provision to the contrary in the document[1].

1 Air Navigation Order 1989, SI 1989/2004, art 66 (3). This provision does not apply to a licence issued in respect of an aerodrome (art 66 (3)) ; as to which see paras 1154, 1155 ante.

1425. Offences relating to documents and records. A person must not, with intent to deceive, use any document[1] issued or required by or under the Air Navigation Order 1989 which has been forged, altered, revoked or suspended, or to which he is not entitled; he must not lend any document issued or having effect or required by or under the order to, or allow it to be used by, any other person; and he must not make any false representation for the purpose of procuring for himself or any other person the grant, issue, renewal or variation of any such document[2].

A person must not intentionally damage, alter or render illegible any log book or other record required by or under the order to be maintained or any entry made in it; he must not knowingly make, or procure or assist in the making of, any false entry in it or material omission from it; and he must not destroy it during the period for which it is required under the order to be preserved[3].

A person must not knowingly make any entry incorrect in a material particular in, or any material omission from, a load sheet[4].

A person must not purport to issue a certificate unless he is authorised to do so, and must not issue a certificate unless he has satisfied himself that all statements in it are correct[5].

1 The term 'document' in this paragraph includes any certificate, licence, approval, permission or other document, and reference to such a document includes a copy or purported copy thereof: see the Air Navigation Order 1989, SI 1989/2004, art 68 (1).

2 Ibid art 68 (1). The penalty for contravention of this and, save where otherwise stated, the other provisions set out in this paragraph, is, on summary conviction, a fine not exceeding £2,000, and on conviction on indictment, a fine or imprisonment for up to two years or both: art 99 (6), Sch 12 Pt B.

3 Ibid art 68 (2). As to contravention see note 2 supra. All entries in such log books and records must be made in ink or indelible pencil: Air Navigation Order 1989 art 68 (3). The penalty for contravention of art 68 (3) is, on summary conviction, a fine not exceeding £400: art 99 (4).

4 Ibid art 68 (4). As to contravention see note 2 supra.

5 Ibid art 68 (5), (6). As to contravention see note 2 supra.

(2) DUTIES BEFORE FLIGHT

(i) General Duties

1426. Action by commander. Before any aircraft registered in the United Kingdom takes off[1], the commander[2] of the aircraft must satisfy himself[3]: (1) that the flight can safely be made, taking into account the latest information as to the route and aerodromes[4] to be used, the weather reports and forecasts[5], and any alternative course of action which can be adopted if the flight cannot be completed as planned[6]; (2) that the equipment, including radio apparatus, required to be carried is carried and is in a fit condition for use[7]; (3) that the aircraft is in every way fit for the proposed flight and that any required certificates of maintenance review[8] are and will remain in force during the flight[9]; (4) that the load carried by the aircraft is of such a weight and is so distributed and secured that it may safely be carried on the flight[10]; (5) in the case of a flying machine[11] or airship, that sufficient fuel, oil and engine coolant, if required, is carried for the flight, including a safe margin for contingencies[12]; (6) in the case of an airship or balloon, that sufficient ballast is carried for the flight[13]; (7) in the case of a flying machine, that, having regard to the performance of the machine in the conditions to be expected on the flight, and to any obstructions at the places of departure and intended destination and on the intended route, it is capable of safely taking off, reaching and maintaining a safe height thereafter and making a safe landing at the place of intended destination[14]; and (8) that any pre-flight check system established by the operator[15] and set forth in the operations manual[16] or elsewhere has been complied with by each member of the crew[17].

1 As to customs formalities before taking-off see paras 1220–1228 ante; as to the production of documents before flight see para 1225 ante.

2 For the meaning of 'commander' see para 1213 note 1 ante. As to the commander's duties in respect of passengers see para 1447 et seq post.

3 The penalty for contravention of any of the provisions of this paragraph is, on summary conviction, a fine not exceeding £1,000: Air Navigation Order 1989, SI 1989/2004, art 99 (5), Sch 12 Pt A.

4 For the meaning of 'aerodrome' see para 1102 ante.

5 As to weather reports and forecasts see para 1396 ante.

6 Air Navigation Order 1989 art 35 (a).

7 Ibid art 35 (b) (i); the flight may alternatively commence under and in accordance with the terms of a permission granted under art 15 (minimum equipment): see art 35 (b) (ii); and para 1312 note 2 ante. For the requirements as to the carriage of equipment and radio equipment see paras 1312–1323 ante.

8 As to certificates of maintenance review see paras 1301–1304 ante.

9 Air Navigation Order 1989 art 35 (c).

10 Ibid art 35 (d). As to the loading of public transport aircraft see para 1432 post.

11 As to what constitutes a 'flying machine' see para 1269 ante.

12 Air Navigation Order 1989 art 35 (e). In the case of a flight for the purpose of public transport, the commander must satisfy himself that instructions in the operations manual relating to fuel, oil and engine coolant have been complied with: art 35 (e). For the meaning of 'public transport' see para 1272 ante.

13 Air Navigation Order 1989 art 35 (f).

14 Ibid art 35 (g). For weight and performance requirements in the case of public transport aircraft see paras 1430, 1431 post.

15 For the meaning of 'operator' see para 1340 ante.

16 As to the operations manual see para 1438 post.

17 Air Navigation Order 1989 art 35 (h).

1427. Obstruction of exits and doors. Where a public transport aircraft[1] registered in the United Kingdom is carrying passengers, every exit[2] and internal door in the aircraft must be in working order and , during take-off and landing and during any emergency, must be kept free of obstruction and must not be fastened by locking or otherwise so as to prevent, hinder or delay its use by passengers[3].

However, if an exit is not required for use by passengers, cargo may obstruct it[4]; further, the commander[5] of the aircraft may have a door between the flight crew compartment and any adjacent compartment to which the passengers have access locked or bolted for the purpose of preventing access by passenger to the flight crew compartment[6].

1 For the meaning of 'public transport aircraft' see para 1272 ante.

2 As to exits see para 1314 ante.

3 Air Navigation Order 1989, SI 1989/2004, art 49 (1), (2). The penalty for contravention of this provision is, on summary conviction, a fine not exceeding £1,000: art 99 (5), Sch 12 Pt A. Nothing applies to any internal door which is so placed that it cannot interfere with the exit of passengers in an emergency if it is not in working order: art 49 (2) proviso (c).

4 The Civil Aviation Authority (CAA) must approve the arrangements under which the exit is not so required, either generally or in relation to a class of aircraft or a particular aircraft: ibid art 49 (2) proviso (a). As to the CAA see para 1044 ante.

5 For the meaning of 'commander' see para 1213 note 1 ante.

6 Air Navigation Order 1989 art 49 (2) proviso (b). This action by the commander has become the practice in view of hijacking offences, as to which see para 1666 post.

1428. Action by commander of aircraft towing glider. The commander[1] of an aircraft which is about to tow a glider must satisfy himself, before the towing aircraft takes off[2]: (1) that the tow rope is in good condition and is of adequate strength for the purpose, and that the combination of towing aircraft and glider, with regard to its performance in the expected conditions and to any obstructions at the place of departure or on the route, is capable of safely taking off, reaching and maintaining a safe height at which to separate, and that thereafter the towing aircraft can make a safe landing at the place of intended destination[3]; (2) that signals have been agreed and communication established with persons suitably stationed so as to enable the glider to take off safely[4]; and (3) that emergency signals have been agreed between the commanders of the towing aircraft and of the glider[5].

The glider must be attached to the towing aircraft by means of the tow rope before the aircraft takes off[6].

1 For the meaning of 'commander' see para 1213 note 1 ante.

2 The penalty for contravention of any of the provisions of this paragraph is, on summary conviction, a fine not exceeding £1,000: Air Navigation Order 1989, SI 1989/2004, art 99 (5), Sch 12 Pt A.

3 Ibid art 41 (3) (a).

4 Ibid art 41 (3) (b).

5 Ibid art 41 (3) (c). These signals are to be used, respectively, by the commander of the towing aircraft to indicate that the tow must be released immediately by the glider, and by the commander of the glider to indicate that the tow cannot be released: art 41 (3) (c).

6 Ibid art 41 (4). As to the penalty for contravention see note 2 supra.

1429. Exhibitions of flying. A person[1] may hold an exhibition of flying which he believes more than 500 persons are likely to attend provided he has obtained the permission in writing of the Civil Aviation Authority (CAA)[2] for that exhibition of flying and complies with any specified conditions[3]. The CAA grants such a permission when it is satisfied that the applicant is a fit and competent person to organise the proposed event safely[4]. The permission may be subject to such conditions as the CAA thinks fit and remains in force for the period specified therein[5].

A person may act as pilot of an aircraft participating in an exhibition of flying for which a permission is required provided he holds an appropriate display authorisation for the intended flight, granted by the CAA, and he complies with any of its conditions[6]. The CAA grants such an authorisation when it is satisfied that the applicant is a fit person and is particularly qualified to participate in an exhibition of flying[7]. The authorisation remains in force for the period specified therein, which may not exceed two years[8].

The commander of an aircraft may participate in an exhibition of flying for which a permission is required provided he is satisfied before he participates that the exhibition organiser has been granted his permission, the flight can comply with any condition specified in the permission and the pilot has been granted the appropriate display authorisation[9]. He must further comply with any condition subject to which the permission may have been given[10].

The exhibition organiser may not allow any person to act as pilot of an aircraft participating in an exhibition of flying for which a permission is required unless that person holds the appropriate display authorisation[11]. He may not permit any military aircraft to participate in such an exhibition unless he complies with any conditions relating to military aircraft subject to which the permission was granted[12].

An exhibition of flying permission is not required by an exhibition organiser for an organised event which is taking place at a Ministry of Defence or visiting forces acrodrome, or other Ministry of Defence premises[13], or for which the exhibition organiser could not reasonably foresee seven days before the event that it would be attended by more than 500 persons[14]. Nor are exhibitions of flying permissions and display authorisations required in the case of an aircraft race or contest whether or not such a race or contest is held in association with an exhibition of flying[15].

1 For the purposes of art 56 of the Air Navigation Order 1989, SI 1989/2004, the person acting as the organiser of an exhibition of flying is referred to as 'the exhibition organiser': art 56 (1).

2 As to the CAA see para 1044 ante.

3 Air Navigation Order 1989 art 56 (1). The penalty for contravention of this provision, or of any of the other provisions described in this paragraph is, on summary conviction, a fine not exceeding £1,000: art 99 (5), Sch 12 Pt A. As to exemptions see text and notes 13–15 infra.

4 Ibid art 56 (4); the CAA must have regard to the applicant's previous conduct and experience, his organisation, staffing and other arrangements: art 56 (4). As to the granting of permissions generally see para 1045 ante.

5 Air Navigation Order 1989 art 56 (4); the permission may be revoked, suspended or varied as the CAA thinks fit: see art 66; and para 1422 ante.

6 Air Navigation Order 1989 art 56 (2) (c). As to contravention see note 3 supra.
7 Ibid art 56 (5). The CAA must be satisfied as to the applicant's knowledge, experience, competence, skill, physical and mental fitness to fly in accordance with the authorisation, and for that purpose the applicant must furnish such evidence and undergo such examinations and tests as the CAA may require of him: art 56 (5) (a); such examinations and tests are conducted by a person authorised by the CAA: art 56 (5) (b).
8 Ibid art 56 (6). As to revocation, suspension or variation of the authorisation see note 5 supra.
9 Ibid art 56 (2) (a) (i)–(iii). As to contravention see note 3 supra.
0 Ibid art 56 (2) (b). As to contravention see note 3 supra.
1 Ibid art 56 (3). As to contravention see note 3 supra.
2 Ibid art 56 (8). As to contravention see note 3 supra.
3 Ibid art 56 (7).
4 Ibid art 56 (1) proviso.
5 Ibid art 56 (9).

(ii) Public Transport Aircraft

A. WEIGHT AND PERFORMANCE

430. Weight and performance requirements in general. The requirements s to weight and performance which must be complied with before an aircraft egistered in the United Kingdom is permitted to fly for the purpose of public transport[1] are prescribed in great detail[2]. They do not, however, apply in the case f a public transport aircraft[3] used solely for the purpose of training persons to erform duties in aircraft[4].

The ability of an aircraft to comply with these provisions must be based on the nformation as to its performance contained in its certificate of airworthiness or, if hat is insufficient, on the best information available to the commander[5].

1 For the meaning of 'public transport' see para 1272 ante.
2 See the Air Navigation Order 1989, SI 1989/2004, art 30 (1), and the Air Navigation (General) Regulations 1981, SI 1981/57, regs 5–11. The penalty for contravention is, on summary conviction, a fine not exceeding £1,000: Air Navigation Order 1989 art 99 (5), Sch 12 Pt A.
3 For the meaning of 'public transport aircraft ' see para 1272 ante.
4 Air Navigation Order 1989 art 30 (1).
5 Ibid art 30 (2). As to the certificate of airworthiness see paras 1284–1294 ante; for the meaning of 'commander' see para 1213 note 1 ante.

431. Purpose of weight and performance requirements. The purpose of the veight and performance requirements is to ensure that the performance of the ircraft is adequate for safety at all stages of the intended flight, taking into account he factors, such as temperature, altitude and weather conditions, which affect the erformance of the aircraft. The requirements vary in detail according to whether he aircraft has no performance group classification in its certificate of airworthiess, has a Group A classification, or has a Group C, D, E or X classification[1].

1 See generally the Air Navigation (General) Regulations 1981, SI 1981/57, regs 6–11 (amended by SI 1985/528, SI 1987/2078 and SI 1989/669). As to certificates of airworthiness see paras 1284–1294 ante.

B. LOAD SHEETS

432. Operator's instructions. The operator[1] of an aircraft registered in the Jnited Kingdom must not cause or permit it to be loaded for a flight for the purpose of public transport[2], or any load to be suspended from it[3], except under th supervision of a person whom he has furnished with written instructions as to th distribution and securing of the load[4].

These instructions must indicate the weight of the aircraft prepared for service and must show the position of the centre of gravity of the aircraft at that weight This requirement does not, however, apply in relation to a flight if the aircraft maximum total weight authorised does not exceed 1,150 kilogrammes[7]; or, i relation to a flight solely for the purpose of training any person to perform duties i an aircraft, or in relation to a flight intended to begin and end at the sam aerodrome, where in either case the aircraft's maximum total weight authorise does not exceed 2,730 kilogrammes and the flight is not intended to last more tha 60 minutes[8]; or where, the aircraft being a helicopter, its maximum total weigl authorised does not exceed 3,000 kilogrammes and its total seating capacity is fiv or less[9].

The operator must not cause or permit the aircraft to be loaded in contraventio of these instructions[10].

1 For the meaning of 'operator' see para 1340 ante.
2 For the meaning of 'public transport' see para 1272 ante.
3 As to the carriage of cargo see paras 1568–1582, 1600–1604, 1619–1627, 1645–1650 post.
4 Air Navigation Order 1989, SI 1989/2004, art 29 (1). It must be ensured that the load may safely 1 carried on the flight and that the conditions relating to loading and included in the certificate airworthiness are complied with: art 29 (1). The penalty for contravention of this provision, and the other provisions described in this paragraph is, on summary conviction, a fine not exceedir £1,000: art 99 (5), Sch 12 Pt A. For the power to direct that an aircraft shall not fly if these provisior are not complied with see art 95 (1); and para 1459 post.
5 Ie the aggregate of the basic weight shown in the weight schedule (as to which see ibid art 17; ar para 1316 ante) and the weight of such additional items in or on the aircraft as the operator thinks 1 to include: art 29 (2). The instructions must also indicate these additional items: art 29 (2) .
6 Ibid art 29 (2).
7 Ibid art 29 (2) proviso (a).
8 Ibid art 29 (2) proviso (b). For the meaning of 'maximum total weight authorised' see para 1314 no 5 ante.
9 Ibid art 29 (2) proviso (c).
10 Ibid art 29 (3). As to contravention see note 4 supra.

1433. Load sheets. The person supervising the loading of the aircraft mus before the commencement of a flight for the purpose of public transport[1], prepar and sign a load sheet in duplicate containing particulars of the aircraft's nationalit and registration marks, the flight, the total weight of the aircraft as loaded, th weights of the several items from which this has been calculated[2], the manner i which the load is distributed, and the resulting position of the centre of gravity, an must include a certificate signed by the person responsible for the loading that th aircraft has been loaded in accordance with the loading instructions[3]. He mu: then, unless he is the commander[4] of the aircraft, submit the load sheet fc examination to the commander, who must sign it[5].

These provisions do not apply where no instructions are required from th operator[6], or where the load upon the next intended flight is to be undisturbe from the previous flight and the commander makes and signs an endorsement t that effect on the load sheet for the previous flight[7].

A copy of the load sheet must be carried in the aircraft when so required[8] until th completion of the flights to which it relates, and a copy of the load sheet and of th operator's instructions must be preserved by the operator for six months and mu:

‎t be carried in the aircraft⁹ unless it is not reasonably practicable to keep it on the
ound, in which case it may be carried in an approved container provided the
‎‑craft is an aeroplane of which the maximum total weight authorised does not
ceed 2,370 kilogrammes or is a helicopter¹⁰.

For the meaning of 'public transport' see para 1272 ante.
These include in particular the weight of the aircraft prepared for service (for the meaning of which
see para 1432 note 5 ante) and the respective total weights of the passengers, crew, baggage and
cargo, calculated in accordance with the Air Navigation (General) Regulations 1981, SI 1981/57, reg
4 (2)–(4): reg 4 (1).
Air Navigation Order 1989, SI 1989/2004, art 29 (4); Air Navigation (General) Regulations 1981 reg
4 (1). The penalty for contravention of this provision is, on summary conviction, a fine not
exceeding £1,000: Air Navigation Order 1989 art 99 (5), Sch 12 Pt A. As to the loading instructions
see para 1432 ante. As to the carriage of cargo see paras 1568–1582, 1600–1604, 1619–1627,
1645–1650 post.
For the meaning of 'commander' see para 1213 note 1 ante.
Air Navigation Order 1989 art 29 (4). As to contravention see note 3 supra.
See ibid art 29 (2) proviso (a)–(c) and (4) proviso (b); and para 1432 ante.
Ibid art 29 (4) proviso (a).
See ibid art 61, Sch 11; and para 1416 ante.
Ibid art 29 (5). For the penalty for contravention see note 3 supra .
Ibid art 29 (5) proviso.

34. Passenger compartment baggage. The operator of an aircraft registered
 the United Kingdom and flying for the purpose of the public transport of
ssengers¹ must not cause or permit baggage to be carried in the passenger
mpartment of the aircraft unless it can be properly secured². Where the aircraft
 n seat more than 30 passengers, such baggage must not exceed the capacity of the
aces provided for stowing baggage as approved by the Civil Aviation Authority
‑AA) ³. However, baggage which exceeds that capacity may be carried in the
mpartment if it is so carried in accordance with the terms of a written permission
anted by the CAA with such conditions as it thinks fit⁴.

As to the public transport of passengers see para 1272 ante.
Air Navigation Order 1989, SI 1989/2004, art 29 (6). The penalty for contravention of this provision
is, on summary conviction, a fine not exceeding £1,000: art 99 (5), Sch 12 Pt A.
Ibid art 29 (6). As to the CAA see para 1044 ante.
See ibid arts 29 (6), 37 (2) (d) (ii).

C. OPERATOR'S DUTIES

35. Operator's responsibilities. The operator¹ of an aircraft registered in the
nited Kingdom must not permit the aircraft to fly for the purpose of public
nsport² without first designating a pilot to be the commander³ for the flight and
:isfying himself that the aeronautical radio stations⁴ and navigational aids serving
 intended route are adequate for the safe navigation of the aircraft and that all
rodromes⁵ which might be used are suitable for the purpose and, in particular,
 adequately manned and equipped to ensure the safety of the aircraft and its
ssengers⁶.

For the meaning of 'operator' see para 1340 ante.
For the meaning of 'public transport' see para 1272 ante.
For the meaning of 'commander' see para 1213 note 1 ante.
'Aeronautical radio station' means a radio station on the surface which transmits or receives signals
for the purpose of assisting aircraft, and 'appropriate aeronautical radio station' in relation to an

aircraft means such a station serving the area in which the aircraft is for the time being: ⸱
Navigation Order 1989, SI 1989/2004, art 106 (1).
5 For the meaning of 'aerodrome' see para 1102 ante.
6 Air Navigation Order 1989 art 28 (1). The penalty for contravention of this provision is,
summary conviction, a fine not exceeding £1,000: art 99 (5), Sch 12 Pt A. The operator need ⸱
satisfy himself of the adequacy of fire-fighting, search, rescue or other services required only at
the occurrence of an accident: art 28 (1) proviso.

1436. Duty to ensure training and practice of crew. The operator[1] of
aircraft registered in the United Kingdom must not permit any person to be
member of its crew during a flight[2] for the purpose of public transport[3] unless th
person has had specified training, experience, practice and periodical tests[4], a⸱
unless the operator has satisfied himself that that person is competent to perfor
his duties and, in particular, to use the equipment provided in the aircraft[5].

1 For the meaning of 'operator' see para 1340 ante.
2 This does not apply to a flight for the sole purpose of training persons to perform duties in aircr⸱
Air Navigation Order 1989, SI 1989/2004, art 28 (2).
3 For the meaning of 'public transport' see para 1272 ante.
4 The training and tests specified in relation to members of the crew are contained in the ⸱
Navigation Order 1989 Sch 10 Pt B.
5 Ibid art 28 (2). The operator must preserve, produce and furnish information respecting reco⸱
relating to these matters in accordance with Sch 10 Pt B: art 28 (2). The penalty for contravention
this provision is, on summary conviction, a fine not exceeding £1,000: art 99 (5), Sch 12 Pt A. As
licensing see para 1349 ante.

**1437. Duty to avoid practice of emergency manoeuvres on passeng
flights.** The operator[1] of an aircraft registered in the United Kingdom must n⸱
permit any member of the flight crew[2], during any flight for the purpose of t⸱
public transport[3] of passengers, to simulate emergency manoeuvres and pr⸱
cedures which the operator has reason to believe would adversely affect the flig
characteristics of the aircraft[4].

1 For the meaning of 'operator' see para 1340 ante.
2 For the meaning of 'flight crew' see para 1344 note 1 ante.
3 For the meaning of 'public transport' see para 1272 ante.
4 Air Navigation Order 1989, SI 1989/2004, art 28 (3). The penalty for contravention of this provisi
is, on summary conviction, a fine not exceeding £1,000: art 99 (5), Sch 12 Pt A.

1438. Operations manual. The operator[1] of a public transport aircraft[2] regi⸱
tered in the United Kingdom[3] must make available to each member of his opera
ing staff[4] an operations manual[5]; he must ensure that each copy of the manual
kept up to date[6] and that on each flight every member of the crew has access to
copy of it[7]; and he must, if the Civil Aviation Authority (CAA) [8] so require
furnish the CAA with a copy of the manual not less than 30 days prior to the flig
of the aircraft to which the manual relates, failing which the aircraft may not fly
he must furnish to the CAA any amendments or additions before or immediate
after they come into effect[10]; and he must make such amendments or additions
the manual as the CAA requires to ensure the safety of the aircraft or of persons ⸱
property carried in it or the safety, efficiency or regularity of air navigation[11].

1 For the meaning of 'operator' see para 1340 ante.

2 For the meaning of 'public transport aircraft' see para 1272 ante.

3 This provision does not apply to an aircraft for the time being used solely for flights not intended to exceed 60 minutes which are either solely for the purpose of training persons to perform duties in an aircraft or intended to begin and end at the same aerodrome: Air Navigation Order 1989, SI 1989/2004, art 26 (1) (a), (b).

4 For the purpose of ibid art 26 and Sch 10, 'operating staff' means the servants and agents employed by the operator, whether or not as members of the crew , to ensure that flights are conducted in a safe manner, and includes an operator who himself performs those functions: art 26 (4).

5 Ibid art 26 (2) (a) (i). As to the contents of the manual see para 1439 post. The penalty for contravention of this and the other requirements set out in this paragraph is, on summary conviction, a fine not exceeding £1,000: art 99 (5), Sch 12 Pt A.

6 Ibid art 26 (2) (a) (ii). As to contravention see note 5 supra.

7 Ibid art 26 (2) (a) (iii). As to contravention see note 5 supra.

8 As to the CAA see para 1044 ante.

9 Air Navigation Order 1989 art 26 (3) (a).

0 Ibid art 26 (3) (b). If the amendment or addition concerns the operation of an aircraft to which the operations manual did not previously relate, that aircraft may not fly for the purpose of public transport as long as the amendment or addition has not been furnished to the CAA: art 26 (3) (b) proviso.

1 Ibid art 26 (3) (c).

1439. Contents of operations manual. The operations manual[1] must contain all such information and instructions as may be necessary to enable the operating staff[2] to perform their duties[3], but it need not contain any information or instructions available in a flight manual accessible to the persons by whom the information or instructions may be required[4].

In particular, it must contain information and instructions relating to the crew to be carried in the aircraft[5], the capacities in which they are to act and the order and circumstances in which crew members are to assume command[6]; the respective duties of crew members and other members of the operating staff[7]; the limits on flight times, duty periods and rest periods[8]; necessary technical particulars as to the aircraft, its engines, equipment and performance[9]; the computing of the aircraft's fuel and oil needs[10] and of any oxygen and oxygen equipment required to be carried[11], including the circumstances in which the crew and passengers are to use oxygen[12]; the check system to be followed on take-off, landing and in an emergency[13]; the maintenance of a radio watch[14]; the reporting of meteorological observations[15]; minimum altitudes for safe flight[16]; aerodrome operating minima [17]; emergency flight procedures, including the giving of assistance to another aircraft or a vessel in distress[18]; procedures for the use of cosmic radiation detection equipment if the aircraft is to fly over 49,000 feet[19]; labelling, marking and loading of dangerous goods as well as crew responsibilities and emergency procedures in this respect[20]; and particulars of permission to carry minimum equipment[21].

In addition there must be contained in a route guide, which may be in the form of separate volume, information and instructions relating to communication, navigational aids, aerodromes, local regulation, in-flight procedures, approach and landing procedures, and such other information as the operator may deem necessary for the proper conduct of flight operations[22]. In relation to any flight which is not one of a series of flights between the same two places it is sufficient if, to the extent that it is not practicable to comply with this requirement, and the requirement as to the reporting of meteorological observations, the manual contains such information and instructions as will enable the equivalent data to be ascertained before take-off[23].

1 As to the operations manual see para 1438 ante.

2 For the meaning of 'operating staff' see para 1438 note 4 ante.

3 Air Navigation Order 1989, SI 1989/2004, art 26 (2) (b). The penalty for contravention of th provision is, on summary conviction, a fine not exceeding £1,000: art 99 (5), Sch 12 Pt A.

4 Ibid art 26 (2) (b) proviso.

5 As to the crew see paras 1359–1365 ante.

6 Air Navigation Order 1989 art 26 (2) (b), Sch 10 Pt A para (i).

7 Ibid Sch 10 Pt A para (ii).

8 Ibid Sch 10 Pt A para (iii); see art 58 (1) (c) (i); and para 1367 ante.

9 Ibid Sch 10 Pt A para (iv).

10 Ibid Sch 10 Pt A para (v); the instructions must take account of all circumstances likely to b encountered, including the possibility of failure of one or more of the aircraft's engines.

11 Ibid Sch 10 Pt A para (vi). For the requirement to carry oxygen see art 13 (2), Sch 4 para 5 Scale L1 c L2.

12 Ibid Sch 10 Pt A para (ix).

13 Ibid Sch 10 Pt A para (vii).

14 Ibid Sch 10 Pt A para (viii).

15 Ibid Sch 10 Pt A para (xi).

16 Ibid Sch 10 Pt A para (xii); the minimum altitudes must not be lower than any which may b applicable under the law of the United Kingdom or of the countries being flown over. As t minimum altitudes see paras 1489–1493 post.

17 Ibid Sch 10 Pt A para (xiii): see art 31; and para 1441 post.

18 Ibid Sch 10 Pt A para (xiv).

19 Ibid Sch 10 Pt A para (xv).

20 Ibid Sch 10 Pt A para (xvi).

21 Ibid Sch 10 Pt A para (xvii); and see art 15 .

22 Ibid Sch 10 Pt A para (x).

23 Ibid Sch 10 Pt A proviso.

D. MINIMUM WEATHER CONDITIONS

1440. United Kingdom aircraft. There are detailed provisions for regulatin₁ flights by public transport aircraft[1] registered in the United Kingdom by referenc to the weather conditions existing at the time of take-off or landing[2].

The provisions apply to every such aircraft except an aircraft which is for th time being used solely for flights not intended to exceed 60 minutes in duration which are either flights solely for training persons to perform duties in an aircraft or flights intended to begin and end at the same aerodrome[3].

1 For the meaning of 'public transport aircraft' see para 1272 ante.

2 See paras 1441–1443 post. As to the general duties imposed by the Rules of the Air Regulations upo persons in command of aircraft in relation to weather conditions see also para 1396 ante. See also par 1026 ante.

3 Air Navigation Order 1989, SI 1989/2004, art 26 (1).

1441. Aerodrome operating minima. The operator[1] of a public transpor aircraft[2] registered in the United Kingdom must establish and include in th operations manual[3] relating to the aircraft particulars of aerodrome operatin₁ minima appropriate to every aerodrome of intended departure or landing an₁ every alternate aerodrome[4]. 'Aerodrome operating minima' means, in relation t₁ the operation of an aircraft at an aerodrome, the cloud ceiling[5] and runway visua range[6] for take-off, and the decision height[7] or minimum descent height[8] an₁ runway visual range and visual reference for landing, which are the minimum fo the operation of that aircraft at that aerodrome[9].

In no case may the aerodrome operating minima so specified be less favourable
an any declared for the aerodrome in question by the competent authority[10],
lless that authority otherwise permits in writing[11].

In establishing the aerodrome operating minima the operator must take into
count various matters relating to the physical characteristics of the aircraft, the
mposition of its crew, the characteristics of the aerodrome and its surroundings,
e dimensions of the runways, and any approach, landing or take-off aids there,
d must establish for each runway which may be selected aerodrome operating
inima appropriate to each likely set of circumstances[12].

For the meaning of 'operator' see para 1340 ante.
For the meaning of 'public transport aircraft' see para 1272 ante.
As to the operations manual see para 1438 ante.
Air Navigation Order 1989, SI 1989/2004, art 26 (2) (b), Sch 10 Pt A para (xiii), and art 31 (1) (a). If
inclusion of aerodrome operating minima in the operations manual is not practical, such information must be given in writing to the commander of the aircraft before the commencement of the
flight and a copy thereof kept outside the aircraft for a period of three months: art 31 (1) (a) proviso.
The operations manual should contain sufficient data and information to allow the commander to
calculate the appropriate aerodrome operating minima for aerodromes the use of which could not
reasonably have been foreseen prior to the flight: art 31 (1) (b). For the meaning of 'commander' see
para 1213 note 1 ante.
'Cloud ceiling' means the vertical distance from the elevation of the aerodrome to the lowest part of
any cloud visible from the aerodrome which is sufficient to obscure more than half the sky so visible:
ibid art 106 (1).
'Runway visual range' in relation to a runway means the distance in the direction of take-off or
landing over which the runway lights or surface markings may be seen from the touchdown zone as
calculated by either human observation or instruments in the vicinity of the touchdown zone or
where this is not reasonably practicable in the vicinity of the mid-point of the runway; and the
distance, if any, communicated to the commander of an aircraft by or on behalf of the person in
charge of the aerodrome as being the runway visual range is to be taken to be the runway visual range
for the time being: ibid art 106 (1).
'Decision height' in relation to the operation of an aircraft at an aerodrome means the height in a
precision approach at which a missed approach must be initiated if the required visual reference to
continue that approach has not been established: ibid art 106 (1). 'Precision approach' means an
instrument approach using Instrument Landing System, Microwave Landing System or Precision
Approach Radar for guidance in both azimuth and elevation: art 106 (1).
'Minimum descent height' in relation to the operation of an aircraft at an aerodrome means the
height in a non-precision approach below which descent may not be made without the required
visual reference: ibid art 106 (1). A 'non-precision approach' is an instrument approach using
non-visual aids for guidance in azimuth or elevation which is not a precision approach: art 106 (1).
For the meaning of 'precision approach' see note 7 supra.
Ibid art 106 (1).
For the meaning of 'competent authority' see para 1347 note 3 ante.
Air Navigation Order 1989 art 31 (2).
Ibid art 31 (3).

42. Regulation of flights according to aerodrome operating mini-
a. No aircraft to which the provisions as to aerodrome operating minima apply[1]
ay (1) commence a flight at a time when either the cloud ceiling[2] or the runway
sual range[3] at the aerodrome of departure is less than the minimum specified for
ke-off from that aerodrome[4]; or (2) commence a flight if, according to the
formation available to its commander[5], it would not be able, without contra-
ntion of the minimum height provisions[6], to land at the aerodrome of intended
stination at the estimated time of arrival there and at any alternate aerodrome[7] at
y time at which according to a reasonable estimate the aircraft would arrive
ere[8]; or (3) descend from a height of 1,000 feet or more above the aerodrome to a

height less than 1,000 feet above the aerodrome if the runway visual range[9] there
less than the specified minimum for landing[10]; or (4) continue its approach
landing[11] at any aerodrome by flying below the relevant specified decision height
or descend below the minimum descent height [13] unless, in either case, from such
height the specified visual reference for landing is established and maintained[1]
Contravention of these requirements is an offence[15].

1 See para 1441 text and notes 2, 3 ante.
2 For the meaning of 'cloud ceiling' see para 1441 note 5 ante.
3 For the meaning of 'runway visual range' see para 1441 note 6 ante.
4 Air Navigation Order 1989, SI 1989/2004, art 31 (4) (a).
5 For the meaning of 'commander' see para 1213 note 1 ante.
6 Ie the Air Navigation Order 1989, art 31 (5) or (6); see text and notes 9–11 infra.
7 As to alternate aerodromes see para 1443 post.
8 Air Navigation Order 1989 art 31 (4) (b).
9 For the meaning of 'runway visual range' see para 1441 note 6 ante.
10 Air Navigation Order 1989 art 31 (5) (amended by SI 1991/1726).
11 'Approach to landing' means that portion of the flight of the aircraft, when approaching to land,
    which it is descending below a height of 1,000 feet above the relevant specified decision height
    minimum descent height: Air Navigation Order 1989 art 106 (1). For the meanings of 'decisi
    height' and 'minimum descent height' see para 1441 notes 7, 8 respectively ante.
12 For the meaning of 'decision height' see para 1441 note 7 ante.
13 For the meaning of 'minimum descent height' see para 1441 note 8 ante.
14 Air Navigation Order 1989 art 31 (6).
15 Such an offence is punishable on summary conviction by a fine not exceeding £1,000: ibid art 99 (;
    Sch 12, Part A.

1443. Selection of alternate aerodromes. If according to the available info
mation a public transport aircraft[1] registered in the United Kingdom would, a
regards any particular flight, be required[2] to be flown in accordance with instr
ment flight rules[3] at the aerodrome of intended landing, the commander[4] of th
aircraft must, prior to taking off, select an alternate aerodrome unless no aer
drome suitable for that purpose is available[5].

1 For the meaning of 'public transport aircraft' see para 1272 ante. As to excepted aircraft see para 14
   ante.
2 Ie required by the Rules of the Air (as to which see paras 1026, 1382, 1383 ante).
3 As to instrument flight rules see paras 1399–1404 ante.
4 For the meaning of 'commander' see para 1213 note 1 ante.
5 Air Navigation Order 1989, SI 1989/2004, art 31 (7) (amended by SI 1990/2154) .

1444. Foreign aircraft. A public transport aircraft[1] registered in a country oth
than the United Kingdom must not fly unless the operator[2] has furnished to th
Civil Aviation Authority (CAA) [3] such particulars as it requires relating to aer
drome operating minima specified by the operator for aerodromes in the Unite
Kingdom for the purpose of limiting their use by the aircraft for take-off c
landing, including any instructions given by the operator in relation to suc
aerodrome operating minima[4]. The aircraft may not fly in or over the Unite
Kingdom unless the operator has made such amendments or additions to th
aerodrome operating minima so specified and instructions so given as the CA
may require to ensure the aircraft's safety or the safety, efficiency or regularity c
air navigation[5].

Where the operator has thus laid down aerodrome operating minima in relatio
to a United Kingdom aerodrome, the aircraft must not take off or land there i

contravention of such aerodrome operating minima or instructions[6]; in particular, the aircraft must not, when making a descent to an aerodrome, descend from a height of 1,000 feet or more above the aerodrome to a height less than 1,000 feet above the aerodrome if the runway visual range[7] there is less than the relevant specified minimum for landing[8].

A public transport aircraft registered in a country other than the United Kingdom may not continue an approach to landing[9] at any aerodrome by flying below the relevant specified decision height or descend below the relevant minimum descent height unless, in either case, from such a height the specified visual reference for landing is established and maintained[10].

Contravention by any person of any of the provisions described above is an offence punishable on summary conviction by a fine not exceeding £1,000 [11].

1 For the meaning of 'public transport aircraft' see para 1272 ante.
2 For the meaning of 'operator' see para 1340 ante.
3 As to the CAA see para 1044 ante.
4 Air Navigation Order 1989, SI 1989/2004, art 32 (1). For the penalty for contravention of this and the other requirements set out in this paragraph see text and note 11 infra .
5 Ibid art 32 (1).
6 Ibid art 32 (2), (5) .
7 For the meaning of 'runway visual range' see para 1441 note 6 ante.
8 Air Navigation Order 1989 art 32 (3) (amended by SI 1991/1726).
9 For the meaning of 'approach to landing' see para 1442 note 11 ante.
10 Air Navigation Order 1989 art 32 (4). For the meanings of 'decision height' and 'minimum descent height' see para 1441 notes 7, 8 respectively ante.
11 Ibid art 99 (5), Sch 12 Pt A.

1445. Non-public transport aircraft. When descending to an aerodrome for which there is a notified runway instrument approach, an aircraft which is not a public transport aircraft[1] may not descend from a height of 1,000 feet or more above the aerodrome to a height less than 1,000 feet above the aerodrome if the runway visual range[2] there is less than the specified minimum for landing[3].

Such an aircraft may not continue an approach to landing[4] on such a runway by flying below the relevant specified decision height[5] or descend below the specified minimum descent height[6] unless, in either case, from such height the specified visual reference for landing is established and is maintained[7].

1 For the meaning of 'public transport aircraft' see para 1272 ante.
2 For the meaning of 'runway visual range' see para 1441 note 6 ante.
3 Air Navigation Order 1989, SI 1989/2004, art 32A (1), (2) (added by SI 1990/2154 and amended by SI 1991/1726).
4 For the meaning of 'approach to landing' see para 1442 note 11 ante.
5 For the meaning of 'decision height' see para 1441 note 7 ante.
6 For the meaning of 'minimum descent height' see para 1441 note 8 ante.
7 Air Navigation Order 1989 art 32A (3) (as added: see note 3 supra).

(3) FLYING

(i) Commanders' Duties

1446. Pilots remaining at controls. The commander[1] of an aircraft registered in the United Kingdom must cause one pilot to remain at the controls at all times while the aircraft is in flight[2].

Where the aircraft is required to carry two pilots[3] the commander must cause both pilots to remain at the controls during take-off and landing; and, if it carries two or more pilots, whether or not it is required to do so, and is engaged on a flight for the purpose of public transport[4] of passengers, the commander must himself remain at the controls during take-off and landing[5].

Contravention of any of the provisions described above is an offence punishable on summary conviction by a fine not exceeding £1,000[6].

1 For the meaning of 'commander' see para 1213 note 1 ante.
2 Air Navigation Order 1989, SI 1989/2004, art 33 (1). Each pilot at the controls must be secured in his seat by either a safety belt or a safety harness; a safety harness must be used at take-off and landing if it is required by art 13 to be provided: art 22 (2). As to art 13 see para 1312 ante.
3 For the requirement to carry two pilots see para 1361 ante.
4 For the meaning of 'public transport' see para 1272 ante.
5 Air Navigation Order 1989 art 33 (1).
6 Ibid art 99 (5), Sch 12 Pt A.

1447. Wearing of survival suits. Each member of the crew of an aircraft registered in the United Kingdom must wear a survival suit where it is required to be worn[1]. Failure to do so is an offence punishable on summary conviction by a fine not exceeding £400[2].

1 Air Navigation Order 1989, SI 1989/2004, art 34. As to the requirement to wear a survival suit see art 13 and Sch 4 para 4 (13) (b) (v) (ee) and para 5 Scale I; and para 1312 ante.
2 Ibid art 99 (4).

1448. Passenger briefing by commander. The commander[1] of an aircraft registered in the United Kingdom, must, before take-off, take all reasonable steps to ensure that the passengers are made familiar with the position and method of use of the emergency exits and the safety and emergency devices[2] intended for their individual use in the case of an emergency[3].

In any emergency, the commander must take all reasonable steps to ensure that all passengers are instructed in the emergency action which they should take[4].

Contravention of either of the requirements described above is an offence punishable on summary conviction by a fine not exceeding £1,000[6].

1 For the meaning of 'commander' see para 1213 note 1 ante.
2 These devices are safety belts, safety harnesses, oxygen breathing equipment, lifejackets, floor path lighting system and all other devices required by or under the Air Navigation Order 1989, SI 1989/2004: art 36 (a).
3 Ibid art 36 (a).
4 Ibid art 36 (b).
5 Ibid art 99 (5), Sch 12 Pt A.

1449. Public transport of passengers. The commander[1] of an aircraft registered in the United Kingdom, when on a flight for the purpose of the public transport[2] of passengers, must ensure that passengers are given a demonstration of the method of using lifejackets where the flight is intended to reach a point more than 30 minutes flying time from the nearest land, or to proceed beyond gliding distance from land, or where the aircraft could be forced to land onto water in an emergency[3].

The commander must also take all reasonable steps to ensure that, before the aircraft takes off and before it lands, the crew and any other persons carried to assist

passengers are properly secured in their seats[4]; that passengers are properly secured
in their seats by safety belts or safety harnesses from the moment when, after the
embarkation of its passengers for the purpose of taking off, the aircraft first moves
until after it has taken off, and before it lands until it comes to rest for the purpose of
the disembarkation of its passengers, and whenever by reason of turbulent air or
any emergency occurring during the flight he considers the precaution necessary[5];
and that at such times baggage in the passenger compartment is properly secured
whether in approved storage spaces if the aircraft seats more than 30 passengers or
in accordance with the written permission of the Civil Aviation Authority
(CAA)[6].

Except where a pressure greater than 700 millibars is maintained in the aircraft
throughout the flight, the commander must take all reasonable steps to ensure that
the method of using oxygen equipment is demonstrated to all passengers[7], that
passengers and cabin attendants are recommended to use oxygen when reaching a
specified flight level[8] and that during any period when the aircraft is flying above
flight level 100 oxygen is used by all the flight crew[9].

Contravention of any of the above provisions is an offence punishable on
summary conviction by a fine not exceeding £1,000[10].

1 For the meaning of 'commander' see para 1213 note 1 ante.
2 For the meaning of 'public transport' see para 1272 ante.
3 See the Air Navigation Order 1989, SI 1989/2004, art 37 (2) (a). In the case of the possibility of a
  forced landing onto water, the demonstration need not be given until after the decision has been
  taken to divert to such a destination: art 37 (2) (a) (ii) proviso. In the case of a seaplane, the
  demonstration must be given before take-off: art 37 (2) (b).
4 Ibid art 37 (2) (c).
5 Ibid art 37 (2) (d) (i) (amended by SI 1991/1726). Children under the age of two years must be secured
  by means of a child restraint device: Air Navigation Order 1989 art 37 (2) (d) (i).
6 Ibid art 37 (2) (d) (ii) (amended by SI 1991/1726). As to passenger compartment baggage see para
  1434 ante. As to the CAA see para 1044 ante.
7 See the Air Navigation Order 1989 art 37 (2) (e) (i) (which concerns aircraft whose certificate of
  airworthiness was issued on or after 1 January 1989) and (f) (i) (which concerns aircraft whose
  certificate of airworthiness was issued prior to 1 January 1989): the demonstration must take place
  before the aircraft reaches flight level 100 for the former or flight level 130 for the latter. For the
  meaning of 'flight level' see para 1401 note 2 ante.
8 Ibid art 37 (2) (e) (ii) (flight level 120), (f) (ii) (flight level 130).
9 Ibid art 37 (2) (e) (iii), (f) (iii).
10 Ibid art 99 (5), Sch 12 Pt A.

1450. Weather reports and forecasts. The commander[1] of an aircraft must
examine, immediately before the aircraft flies, the current reports and forecasts of
the weather conditions on the proposed flight path in order to determine whether
instrument meteorological conditions[2] prevail or are likely to prevail during any
part of the flight[3].

The aircraft may not begin a flight to an aerodrome within a control zone[4] when
it is unable to communicate by radio with an air traffic control unit[5] at that
aerodrome, and if the information available to the commander of the aircraft
indicates that it will arrive at that aerodrome in poor visibility[6]; he may, however,
obtain permission from the relevant air traffic control unit to enter the aerodrome
traffic zone[7].

Breach of the above provisions is an offence punishable on summary conviction
by a fine not exceeding £1,000 [8].

1 For the meaning of 'commander' see para 1213 note 1 ante.

2 For the meaning of 'instrument meteorological conditions' see para 1396 note 2 ante.
3 Rules of the Air Regulations 1990, SI 1990/2241, Schedule r 16 (1).
4 For the meaning of 'control zone' see para 1395 ante.
5 For the meaning of 'air traffic control unit' see para 1394 note 1 ante.
6 Ie when the ground visibility is less than five nautical miles or the cloud ceiling is less than 1,500 feet: Rules of the Air Regulations 1990 Schedule r 16 (2). For the meaning of 'nautical mile' see para 1362 note 4 ante.
7 Ibid Schedule r 16 (2). For the meaning of 'aerodrome traffic zone' see para 1395 ante. As to air traffic control generally see paras 1382–1408 ante.
8 Air Navigation Order 1989, SI 1989/2004, arts 69 (2), 99 (5), Sch 12 Pt A (art 69 (2) and Sch 12 Pt A amended by SI 1990/2154). The 1989 Order art 69 (as so amended) provides that it is an offence to contravene, permit the contravention of, or fail to comply with, the Rules of the Air.

1451. Commander's authority. Every person in an aircraft registered in the United Kingdom must obey all lawful commands which the commander[1] of that aircraft may give for the purpose of securing the safety of the aircraft and of persons or property carried in it, or for the safety, efficiency or regularity of air navigation[2]. Failure to do so is an offence punishable on summary conviction by a fine not exceeding £1,000 [3].

1 For the meaning of 'commander' see para 1213 note 1 ante.
2 Air Navigation Order 1989, SI 1989/2004, art 54.
3 Ibid art 99 (5), Sch 12 Pt A. As to crimes committed on board aircraft see para 1662 et seq post.

(ii) Aircraft Radio Stations

1452. Compliance with aircraft radio station licence. The radio station in an aircraft must be operated, whether or not the aircraft is in flight, in accordance with the conditions of the licence issued in respect of that station under the law of the country in which the aircraft is registered, and by a person duly licensed or otherwise permitted to operate the radio station under that law[1].

1 Air Navigation Order 1989, SI 1989/2004, art 38 (1) . Contravention is punishable on summary conviction by a fine not exceeding £1,000: art 99 (5), Sch 12 Pt A. In the United Kingdom the licence is governed by the Wireless Telegraphy Act 1949, as to which see TELECOMMUNICATIONS.

1453. Radio watch. Where an aircraft is required to be equipped with radio communication apparatus[1], a member of the flight crew[2] must maintain a continuous radio watch, while the aircraft is in flight, by listening to the signals transmitted upon the frequency notified[3] or designated by a message received from an appropriate aeronautical radio station[4] for use by that aircraft[5].

However, the radio watch may be discontinued or continued on another frequency when such a message so permits[6]; and the watch may be kept by a device installed in the aircraft if the appropriate aeronautical radio station has been informed, has raised no objection and if that station is notified or, in the case of a station in a country other than the United Kingdom, otherwise designated as transmitting a signal suitable for that purpose[7].

1 As to the radio equipment to be carried see para 1320 ante.
2 For the meaning of 'flight crew' see para 1344 note 1 ante.
3 For the meaning of 'notified' see para 1105 note 3 ante.
4 For the meaning of 'appropriate aeronautical radio station' see para 1435 note 4 ante.

5 Air Navigation Order 1989, SI 1989/2004, art 38 (2) . The penalty for contravention is, on summary conviction, a fine not exceeding £1,000: art 99 (5), Sch 12 Pt A.
6 Ibid art 38 (2) proviso (a).
7 Ibid art 38 (2) proviso (b).

1454. Operation of radio in aircraft. Where an aircraft is required to be equipped with radio or radio navigation equipment a member of the flight crew must operate that equipment as instructed by the relevant air traffic control unit[1] or as notified in relation to any notified airspace in which the aircraft is flying[2].

The radio station in an aircraft must not be operated so as to cause interference which impairs the efficiency of aeronautical telecommunications or navigational services[3].

In accordance with general international aeronautical practice, emissions are restricted to emissions of the class and frequency for the time being in use in the airspace in which the aircraft is flying; to distress, urgency and safety messages and signals; to messages and signals relating to the flights of the aircraft; and to such public correspondence messages as may be permitted by or under the aircraft radio station licence[4].

Where a flying machine[5] registered in the United Kingdom is engaged on a flight for the purpose of public transport[6] the pilot and the flight engineer (if any) may not use a hand-held microphone while the aircraft is flying in controlled airspace[7] below flight level[8] 150 or is taking off or landing[9].

Contravention of the above provisions is an offence punishable on summary conviction by a fine not exceeding £1,000 [10] .

1 For the meaning of 'air traffic control unit' see para 1394 note 1 ante.
2 Air Navigation Order 1989, SI 1989/2004, art 38 (3).
3 Ibid art 38 (4).
4 Ibid art 38 (4) (a)–(d). As to the licence see para 1452 ante.
5 For the meaning of 'flying machine' see para 1269 ante.
6 For the meaning of 'public transport' see para 1272 ante.
7 For the meaning of 'controlled airspace' see para 1395 text to note 7 ante.
8 For the meaning of 'flight level' see para 1401 note 2 ante.
9 Air Navigation Order 1989 art 38 (8).
10 Ibid art 99 (5), Sch 12 Pt A.

1455. Telecommunication log book. A telecommunication log book must be kept in every aircraft registered in the United Kingdom and equipped with radio communication apparatus[1].

The following entries must be made in it: identification of the aircraft radio station; date and time of the beginning and end of every radio watch[2] maintained and of its frequency; date, time and particulars of all signals and messages sent or received including distress signals or distress messages; particulars of any action taken upon the receipt of a distress signal or distress message; and particulars of any failure or interruption of radio communications and the cause thereof[3].

The flight radio operator maintaining radio watch must sign the entries indicating the times at which he began and ended the watch[4], and the operator[5] of the aircraft must preserve the log book until a date six months after the date of the last entry in it[6].

Contravention of the above provisions is an offence punishable on summary conviction by a fine not exceeding £1,000 [6].

1 Air Navigation Order 1989, SI 1989/2004, art 38 (5). A telecommunication log book is not required in respect of communication by radiotelephony with a radio station on land or on a ship which provides a radio service for aircraft: art 38 (5) proviso. As to preservation of the log book see para 1410 ante.
2 As to the radio watch see para 1453 ante.
3 Air Navigation Order 1989 art 38 (5) (a)–(e).
4 Ibid art 38 (6).
5 For the meaning of 'operator' see para 1340 ante.
6 Air Navigation Order 1989 art 38 (7).
7 Ibid art 99 (5), Sch 12 Pt A.

(iii) General Safety Provisions

1456. Dangerous flying and similar acts. Where an aircraft is flown in such a manner as to be the cause of unnecessary danger to any person or property on land or water, the pilot or the person in charge of the aircraft, and also the owner[1] unless he proves to the satisfaction of the court that the aircraft was so flown without his actual fault or privity, is liable on summary conviction to a fine not exceeding level 4 on the standard scale or to imprisonment for a term not exceeding six months or to both[2].

Further, a person may not recklessly or negligently either act in a manner likely to endanger an aircraft or any person in it[3] or cause or permit an aircraft to endanger any person or property[4].

There is power under the Air Navigation Order to direct that an aircraft shall not fly if it appears that it is intended or likely to be flown so as to be a cause of danger to any person or property, whether or not in the aircraft[5].

1 'Owner' includes any person by whom the aircraft is hired at the time of the offence: Civil Aviation Act 1982 s 81 (2).
2 Ibid s 81 (1) (amended by virtue of the Criminal Justice Act 1982 ss 38, 46). This provision is in addition to and not in derogation of the powers conferred by the Civil Aviation Act 1982 s 60 of making Orders in Council for the regulation of flying and the imposition of penalties: s 81 (3). As to these regulations see the Air Navigation Order 1989, SI 1989/2004: the relevant provisions are considered in this section of the title. As to the standard scale see para 1044 note 6 ante. At the date at which this volume states the law, level 4 on that scale is at £1,000.
3 Air Navigation Order 1989 art 50. The penalty for the contravention of this provision or of that described in the text to note 4 infra is, on summary conviction, a fine not exceeding £2,000, or, on conviction on indictment, a fine or imprisonment for up to two years or both: art 99 (6), Sch 12 Pt B. As to crimes committed on board aircraft see para 1662 et seq post.
4 Air Navigation Order 1989 art 51. As to the penalty for contravention see note 3 supra. As to dropping things from aircraft see paras 1467, 1468 post.
5 See the Air Navigation Order 1989 art 95 (1) (b); and para 1459 post.

1457. Smoking or drunkenness in aircraft. Notices indicating when smoking is prohibited must be exhibited in every aircraft registered in the United Kingdom so as to be visible from each passenger seat[1]. A person may not smoke in any compartment of such an aircraft at a time when smoking is prohibited in that compartment by a notice exhibited by or on behalf of the commander[2].

No one may enter or be in any aircraft when drunk[3], nor may any person, while acting as a member of the crew[4] or being carried in an aircraft for the purpose of so acting, be under the influence of drink or a drug to such an extent as to impair his capacity so to act[5].

1 Air Navigation Order 1989, SI 1989/2004, art 53 (1). Contravention of this provision or of that described in the text to note 2 infra is an offence punishable on summary conviction by a fine not exceeding £1,000: art 99 (5), Sch 12 Pt A.
2 Ibid art 53 (2). As to the penalty see note 1 supra; for the meaning of 'commander' see para 1213 note 1 ante.
3 Ibid art 52 (1). The penalty for the contravention of this provision or of that described in the text to notes 4, 5 infra is, on summary conviction, a fine not exceeding £2,000, or, on conviction on indictment, a fine or imprisonment for up to two years or both: art 99 (6), Sch 12 Pt B.
4 For the meaning of 'crew' see para 1365 note 3 ante.
5 Air Navigation Order 1989 art 52 (2). As to the penalty for contravention see note 3 supra.

1458. Access to parts of aircraft during flight. A person may not be in or on any part of an aircraft in flight[1] which is not a part designed for the accommodation of persons, and, in particular, a person may not be on the wings or undercarriage of the aircraft[2]. However, a person may have temporary access to any part of the aircraft for the purpose of doing anything necessary for the safety of the aircraft or of any person, animal or goods in it; or to any part of the aircraft in which cargo or stores are carried and to which proper means of access during flight is provided[3].

Further, a person may not be in or on any object, other than a glider or flying machine, towed by or attached to an aircraft in flight[4].

1 For the meaning of 'in flight' see para 1460 post.
2 Air Navigation Order 1989, SI 1989/2004, art 48. Contravention of this provision or of that described in the text to note 4 infra is an offence punishable on summary conviction by a fine not exceeding £1,000: art 99 (5), Sch 12 Pt A.
3 Ibid art 48 proviso (a), (b).
4 Ibid art 48.

1459. Power to prevent flight. If it appears to the Civil Aviation Authority (CAA) [1] or to any authorised person[2] that an aircraft is intended or likely to be flown in such circumstances that the flight would be in contravention of specified provisions of the Air Navigation Order[3], the CAA or authorised person may direct the operator[4] or the commander[5] of the aircraft that he is not to permit the aircraft to make the particular flight or any other flight of a description specified in the direction until the CAA or authorised person has revoked the direction[6]. The CAA or authorised person may enter upon and inspect any aircraft for the purpose of these provisions[7], and may take such steps as are necessary to detain the aircraft[8]. Similarly, the CAA or authorised person may take the same action where it appears that an aircraft may be flown in contravention of the requirements for a noise certificate[9].

The same direction may be given or steps taken where it appears to the CAA or to any authorised person that an aircraft is intended or likely to be flown in such circumstances that the flight would be in contravention of any other provision of the Air Navigation Order or any regulations made under it and be a cause of danger to any person or property whether or not in the aircraft[10]; or while in a condition unfit for the flight, whether or not the flight would otherwise be in contravention of any provision of the order or of any regulations made under it[11].

Finally, if it appears to the Secretary of State[12] or any authorised person[13] that an aircraft is intended or likely to be flown in contravention of the provisions of the order which restrict the use of aircraft registered in the United Kingdom over any foreign country[14] or of aircraft registered outside the United Kingdom for carriage for valuable consideration[15] in respect of aerial photography and survey[16], the Secretary of State or that person may direct the operator or commander of the aircraft that he is not to permit the aircraft to make the particular flight or any other flight of a description specified in the direction until the direction has been revoked by him[17]. The Secretary of State or any authorised person may take such steps as are necessary to detain the aircraft and, for the purpose of these provisions, he or any authorised person may enter upon any aerodrome or aircraft in order to detain the aircraft[18].

1   As to the CAA see para 1044 ante.
2   For the meaning of 'authorised person' in this context see para 1193 note 2 ante.
3   Air Navigation Order 1989, SI 1989/2004, art 95 (1) (a). The provisions specified are arts 3 (requirement for aircraft to be registered: see para 1276 ante), 5 (nationality and registration mark: see para 1283 ante), 6 (issue of air operators' certificates: see para 1341 ante), 7 (requirement for certificates of airworthiness to be in force: see para 1284 ante), 19 (composition of crew: see para 1359 et seq ante), 20 (licences of members of flight crew: see para 1344 ante), 29 (operator's responsibilities in respect of loading public transport aircraft: see para 1432 ante), 40 (use of flight recording systems and preservation of records: see para 1414 ante), 46 (carriage of munitions of war: see para 1653 post) and 47 (carriage of dangerous goods: see para 1654 post).
4   For the meaning of 'operator' see para 1340 ante.
5   For the meaning of 'commander' see para 1213 note 1 ante.
6   Air Navigation Order 1989 art 95 (1) (a) . The penalty for flying in contravention of such a direction is, on summary conviction, a fine not exceeding £2,000, or, on conviction on indictment, a fine or imprisonment for up to two years or both: art 99 (6), Sch 12 Pt B.
7   Ibid art 95 (2).
8   Ibid art 95 (1). For other powers of detention see para 1339 ante.
9   Air Navigation (Noise Certification) Order 1990, SI 1990/1514, art 11; and see para 1311 ante.
10   Air Navigation Order 1989 art 95 (1) (b). As to the penalty for contravention of such a direction see note 6 supra.
11   Ibid art 95 (1) (c). As to the penalty for contravention of such a direction see note 6 supra. For other powers to prevent flight see paras 1311, 1330 ante.
12   As to the Secretary of State see para 1032 ante.
13   For the purposes of the Air Navigation Order 1989 art 95 (3), (4) (but not for the purposes of art 95 (1), (2): see note 2 supra), 'authorised person' means any constable and any person authorised by the Secretary of State, whether by name or by class or description either generally or in relation to a particular case or class of cases: art 106 (1).
14   See ibid art 93; and para 1472 post .
15   See ibid art 88; and para 1272 ante.
16   See ibid art 92; and para 1471 post.
17   Ibid art 95 (3). As to the penalty for contravention of such a direction see note 6 supra.
18   Ibid art 95 (3), (4).

(iv) General Flight Rules

1460. Meaning of 'flight'. For the purposes of the Air Navigation Order an aircraft is deemed to be in flight either, in the case of a piloted flying machine[1], from the moment when, after the crew embarks for the purpose of taking off, it first moves under its own power until the moment when it next comes to rest after landing[2]; or, in the case of a pilotless flying machine or a glider, from the moment when it first moves for the purpose of taking off until the moment when it next comes to rest after landing[3]; or, in the case of an airship, from the moment when it first becomes detached from the surface until the moment when it next becomes attached thereto or comes to rest thereon[4]; or, in the case of a free balloon, from the moment when the balloon, including the canopy and basket, becomes separated from the surface until the moment it next comes to rest[5]; or, in the case of a captive balloon from the moment when the balloon, including the canopy and basket, becomes separated from the surface apart from a restraining device attaching it to the surface, until the moment when it next comes to rest[6]. The expressions 'a flight' and 'to fly' must be construed accordingly[7].

1 For the classification of aircraft see para 1269 ante.
2 Air Navigation Order 1989, SI 1989/2004, art 106 (2) (a).
3 Ibid art 106 (2) (b).
4 Ibid art 106 (2) (c).
5 Ibid art 106 (2) (d).
6 Ibid art 106 (2) (e).
7 Ibid art 106 (2). For the meaning of 'flight' in the Aviation Security Act 1982 s 38 (3) see para 1666 note 1 post.

1461. Commander's responsibility. If any provision of the Air Navigation Order or of the Rules of the Air Regulations or other regulations made under the order is contravened in relation to an aircraft, the commander[1] as well as the operator[2] is, without prejudice to any other person's liability, deemed to have contravened the provision unless he proves that the contravention occurred without his consent or connivance and that he exercised all due diligence to prevent it[3]. Every person on board must obey the commander's lawful commands[4].

It is an offence to contravene or permit the contravention of or to fail to comply with the Rules of the Air[5] save in circumstances in which departure from those rules is lawful[6].

1 For the meaning of 'commander' see para 1213 note 1 ante.
2 For the meaning of 'operator' see para 1340 ante.
3 Air Navigation Order 1989, SI 1989/2004, art 99 (1).
4 See ibid art 54; and para 1451 ante.
5 Air Navigation Order 1989 art 69 (2) (amended by SI 1990/2154); see para 1383 ante. The penalty for summary conviction of this offence is a fine not exceeding £1,000: Air Navigation Order 1989 art 99 (5), Sch 12 Pt A (as so amended).
6 Ibid art 69 (3) (as amended: see note 5 supra); see para 1383 ante.

1462. Reporting hazardous conditions. On meeting with hazardous conditions in the course of a flight, or as soon as possible thereafter, the commander[1] of an aircraft must send to the appropriate air traffic control unit[2] by the quickest means available particulars of such conditions as may be pertinent to the safety of other aircraft[3].

1 For the meaning of 'commander' see para 1213 note 1 ante.
2 For the meaning of 'appropriate air traffic control unit' see para 1394 note 1 ante.
3 Rules of the Air Regulations 1990, SI 1990/2241, Schedule r 4. As to contraventions of the Rules of the Air see para 1461 ante.

1463. Flight over water. A flying machine[1] registered in the United Kingdom when flying over water for the purpose of public transport[2] must fly at such an altitude as would enable the aircraft to reach a place at which it may safely land either, if it has only one engine, in the event of the failure of that engine or, if it has more than one engine, in the event of the failure of one of those engines and with the remaining engine or engines operating within the maximum continuous power conditions specified in the aircraft's certificate of airworthiness[3].

Where a certificate of airworthiness designates an aircraft as being of performance group[4] X and the aircraft has not more than two power units, the aircraft may not fly over water for the purpose of public transport so as to be more than 60 minutes flying time[5] from the nearest shore[6]. Where a certificate of airworthiness designates a helicopter as being of performance group B or A2 it may not fly over water for the purpose of public transport unless it is equipped with flotation apparatus approved by the Civil Aviation Authority (CAA)[7].

Contravention of the above provisions is an offence punishable on summary conviction by a fine not exceeding £1,000[8].

1 For the meaning of 'flying machine' see para 1269 ante.
2 For the meaning of 'public transport' see para 1272 ante.
3 Air Navigation Order 1989, SI 1989/2004, art 30 (3). As to certificates of airworthiness see paras 1284–1294 ante.
4 As to performance groups see para 1431 ante.
5 For this purpose flying time must be calculated at normal cruising speed with one power unit inoperative: Air Navigation Order 1989 art 30 (4).
6 Ibid art 30 (4).
7 See ibid art 30 (5), (6); as to performance groups see para 1431 ante; as to the CAA see para 1044 ante.
8 Ibid art 99 (5), Sch 12 Pt A.

1464. Towing of gliders. An aircraft in flight may not tow a glider unless the certificate of airworthiness[1] of the towing aircraft issued or rendered valid under the law of the country in which the aircraft is registered includes an express provision that it may be used for that purpose[2]. The length of the combination of towing aircraft, tow rope and glider in flight must not exceed 150 metres[3].

1 As to certificates of airworthiness see paras 1284–1294 ante.
2 Air Navigation Order 1989, SI 1989/2004, art 41 (1). The penalty for contravention of this provision and of that described in the text to note 3 infra is, on summary conviction, a fine not exceeding £1,000: art 99 (5), Sch 12 Pt A. As to the precautions to be taken by the commander of the towing aircraft before take-off see para 1428 ante.
3 Ibid art 41 (2). As to the penalty see note 2 supra.

1465. Towing of other articles. An aircraft in flight may not, by means external to the aircraft, tow any article other than a glider[1] unless the certificate of airworthiness[2] of that aircraft issued or rendered valid under the law of the country in which it is registered includes an express provision that it may be used for that purpose[3].

An aircraft in flight may not tow any article, other than a glider, at night or when flight visibility[4] is less than one nautical mile[5]. The length of the combination of towing aircraft, tow rope and article in tow must not exceed 150 metres[6].

Contravention of the above provisions is an offence punishable on summary conviction by a fine not exceeding £1,000[7].

An aircraft in flight may, however, tow in a reasonable manner any radio aerial, any instrument being used for experimental purposes, or any signal, apparatus or article required or permitted by or under the Air Navigation Order to be towed or displayed by an aircraft in flight[8].

1 As to the towing of gliders see para 1464 ante.
2 As to certificates of airworthiness see paras 1284–1294 ante.
3 Air Navigation Order 1989, SI 1989/2004, art 42. The provisions of art 42 do not apply to aircraft flying in accordance with the 'B' conditions (see para 1287 ante) and do not permit the towing of gliders otherwise than in accordance with art 41 (see para 1464 ante): art 42 (7) (c), (d).

4 For the meaning of 'flight visibility' see para 1398 note 3 ante.
5 Air Navigation Order 1989 art 42 (3). For the meaning of 'nautical mile' see para 1362 note 4 ante.
6 Ibid art 42 (4).
7 Ibid art 99 (5), Sch 12 Pt A.
8 Ibid art 42 (7) (a).

1466. Picking up persons and articles. An aircraft in flight must not pick up or raise any person, animal or article unless the certificate of airworthiness[1] issued or rendered valid in respect of that aircraft under the law of the country in which it is registered includes an express provision that the aircraft may be used for that purpose[2]; nor may it launch or pick up tow ropes, banners or similar articles otherwise than at an aerodrome[3]. A helicopter must not fly at any height over a congested area[4] of a city, town or settlement at any time when an article, person or animal is suspended from the helicopter[5].

Contravention of the above provisions is an offence punishable on summary conviction by a fine not exceeding £1,000[6].

These provisions do not, however, prohibit the picking up or raising of any person, animal or article in an emergency or for the purpose of saving life[7], and do not apply to any aircraft flying in accordance with the 'B' conditions[8].

1 As to certificates of airworthiness see paras 1284–1294 ante.
2 Air Navigation Order 1989, SI 1989/2004, art 42 (1).
3 Ibid art 42 (2). As to the launching and picking up of tow ropes, etc at aerodromes see the Rules of the Air Regulations 1990, SI 1990/2241, Schedule r 34.
4 For the meaning of 'congested area' see para 1286 note 9 ante.
5 Air Navigation Order 1989 art 42 (5). Unless he has duties to perform in connection with the person, article or animal to be picked up by, or lowered from, the helicopter, no passenger may be carried in the helicopter when such a person, article or animal is suspended therefrom: art 42 (6). Further as to the use of helicopters see para 1467 post.
6 Ibid art 99 (5), Sch 12 Pt A.
7 Ibid art 42 (7) (b).
8 Ibid art 36 (5) (c). As to the 'B' conditions see para 1287 ante.

1467. Dropping of articles and animals. Articles and animals, whether or not attached to a parachute, must not be dropped[1] or permitted to drop from an aircraft so as to endanger persons or property[2]; and articles and animals, whether or not attached to a parachute, must not be dropped or permitted to drop to the surface from an aircraft flying over the United Kingdom except under and in accordance with the terms of an aerial application certificate[3].

Contravention of the above provisions is an offence punishable on summary conviction by a fine not exceeding £1,000[6].

These prohibitions do not, however, apply to the dropping of articles by or with the authority of the commander[5] of the aircraft in certain circumstances, namely the dropping of articles for the purpose of saving life, the jettisoning of fuel or other articles in case of emergency, the dropping of ballast in the form of fine sand or water, the dropping of articles solely for the purpose of navigating the aircraft, the dropping at an aerodrome of ropes, banners or articles towed by the aircraft, the dropping of articles for the purpose of public health or as a measure against weather conditions, surface icing or oil pollution (or training therefor) with the permission of the Civil Aviation Authority (CAA) and the dropping of wind drift indicators for the purpose of enabling parachute descents with the permission of the CAA[6].

Further, the foregoing prohibitions do not apply to the lowering of any animal or article from a helicopter to the surface, if the certificate of airworthiness[7] of that helicopter issued or rendered valid under the law of the country in which it is registered includes an express provision that it may be used for that purpose[8].

1 For the purpose of the Air Navigation Order 1989, SI 1989/2004, art 43, 'dropping' includes projecting and lowering: art 43 (3).
2 Ibid art 43 (1).
3 Ibid art 43 (2). As to aerial application certificates see para 1469 post.
4 Ibid art 99 (5), Sch 12 Pt A.
5 For the meaning of 'commander' see para 1213 note 1 ante.
6 Air Navigation Order 1989 art 43 (2) proviso (a)–(g). As to the dropping of tow ropes, banners, etc see the Rules of the Air Regulations 1990, SI 1990/2241, Schedule r 34. As to the CAA see para 1044 ante.
7 As to certificates of airworthiness see paras 1284–1294 ante.
8 Air Navigation Order 1989 art 43 (4). See also para 1466 text to note 4 ante.

1468. Dropping of persons. A person may not drop[1], be dropped or be permitted to be dropped to the surface or jump from an aircraft in flight over the United Kingdom without a written permission granted by the Civil Aviation Authority (CAA) [2]; and notwithstanding the grant of such a permission a person may not drop, be dropped or be permitted to be dropped from an aircraft in flight so as to endanger persons or property[3].

Dropping of persons may not occur unless the aircraft has a valid certificate of airworthiness[4] including an express provision that it may be used for that purpose; further, the aircraft must be operated in accordance with the above written permission granted by the CAA[5].

When requested, every applicant for, and every holder of, such a permission must produce a parachuting manual to the CAA and make any amendment or modification to it as so requested. The parachuting manual must contain all information and instructions necessary and be available to every employee of the holder of the permission, or person engaged in parachuting activities conducted by him, so that such employees, or persons, may perform their duties[6].

Contravention of the above provisions is an offence punishable on summary conviction by a fine not exceeding £1,000[7].

The prohibitions as to the dropping of persons do not apply to the descent of persons by parachute from an aircraft in an emergency[8], nor to the lowering of any person in an emergency or for the purpose of saving life[9]. They do not apply either to the lowering of any person from a helicopter to the surface, if the certificate of airworthiness of that helicopter issued or rendered valid under the law of the country in which it is registered includes an express provision that it may be used for that purpose[10].

1 For the purpose of the Air Navigation Order 1989, SI 1989/2004, art 44, 'dropping' includes projecting and lowering: art 44 (2).
2 Ibid art 44 (1). As to the CAA see para 1044 ante.
3 Ibid art 44 (3).
4 As to certificates of airworthiness see paras 1284–1294 ante.
5 Air Navigation Order 1989 art 44 (4).
6 Ibid art 44 (5).
7 Ibid art 99 (5), Sch 12 Pt A.
8 Ibid art 44 (6).
9 Ibid art 44 (7).
10 Ibid art 44 (8).

1469. Aerial application certificates. An aircraft may not be used for the dropping of articles[1] for the purpose of agriculture, horticulture or forestry[2], or for training therefor, otherwise than under and in accordance with the terms of an aerial application certificate granted to the operator by the Civil Aviation Authority (CAA) [3].

An aerial application certificate is granted to an applicant where the CAA is satisfied that that person is fit to hold such a certificate and is competent to secure the safe operation of the aircraft on flights to drop articles for agriculture, horticulture or forestry purposes, having regard to his previous conduct and experience, his equipment, organisation, staffing and other arrangements[4].

The certificate may include any condition which the CAA thinks fit including conditions to ensure that neither the aircraft nor any article dropped therefrom endangers persons or property in the aircraft or elsewhere[5].

An aerial application manual must be made available by every applicant for or any holder of, an aerial application certificate, to the CAA and to every member of his operating staff[6]; it must contain all information and instructions necessary for the operating staff to perform their duties; and it must be amended, or added to, when required by the CAA[7].

1   As to the dropping of articles generally see para 1467 ante.
2   Until 1985, control over crop-spraying operations was exercised on an ad hoc basis by the grant of conditional exemptions under the Air Navigation Order (as to such exemptions see para 1264 ante).
3   Air Navigation Order 1989, SI 1989/2004, art 45 (1). As to the CAA see para 1044 ante. Contravention of this provision, and of that described in the text to notes 6, 7 infra, is punishable on summary conviction by a fine not exceeding £1,000: art 99 (5), Sch 12 Pt A.
4   Ibid art 45 (2).
5   Ibid art 45 (2). The certificate remains in force for the period specified in the certificate unless revoked, suspended or varied under art 66: see para 1422 ante.
6   'Operating staff' has the same meaning as in ibid art 26 (4): art 45 (4); see para 1438 note 4 ante.
7   Ibid art 45 (3). As to the penalty for contravention see note 3 supra.

1470. Aerial advertising and propaganda. No aircraft while in the air over any part of the United Kingdom or its territorial waters may be used, whether wholly or in part, for emitting or displaying any advertisement or other communication in such a way that the advertisement or communication is audible or visible from the ground[1].

This prohibition does not, however, apply to the emission or display of any communication solely for one or more of the following purposes, namely: (1) compliance with any law relating to the aircraft, the safety of the aircraft or any person or property in it, air rescue operations where there is danger to persons or property, or civil defence, military or police purposes[2]; (2) to the use by any aircraft of identifying marks or inscriptions[3]; (3) to the use of an aircraft for the display of any mark or inscription on a banner towed behind the aircraft[4]; (4) to the use of any airship for such display on the body of the airship and for communicating information by means of an illuminated sign[5]; (5) to the use of any balloon which is not more than one metre in any linear dimension for the display of any mark or inscription on its body[6]; (6) to the use of free balloons displaying identifying marks or inscriptions on their body or on the basket or other equipment attached thereto[7]; or (7) the use of a captive balloon for the display of any mark or inscription provided a number of conditions is fulfilled[8].

1   Civil Aviation Act 1982 s 82 (1). Any person who uses an aircraft, or knowingly causes or permits it to be used, in contravention of this provision is liable on summary conviction to a fine not exceeding

level 4 on the standard scale or imprisonment for a term not exceeding three months or both: s 82 (2) (amended by virtue of the Criminal Justice Act 1982 ss 38, 46). As to the standard scale see para 1044 note 6 ante. At the date at which this volume states the law, level 4 on that scale is at £1,000. If an offence committed by a body corporate is proved to have been committed with the consent or connivance of, or to be attributed to the neglect of, any director, manager, secretary or other officer, he too is guilty of the offence: Civil Aviation Act 1982 s 99 (1). For the purpose of conferring jurisdiction any offence is deemed to have been committed in any place where the offender may for the time being be: s 99 (3).

2 Civil Aviation (Aerial Advertising) Regulations 1983, SI 1983/1885, reg 4 (1).

3 Ibid reg 4 (2); this provision does not apply to kites or balloons (save as provided in reg 4 (6): see note 7 infra). The identifying marks or inscriptions concern the owner or charterer of the aircraft, the manufacturers of the aircraft and of the aircraft engines and the types of the aircraft and of the aircraft engines: reg 4 (2) (i)–(vii).

4 Ibid reg 4 (3); as to the towing of articles see para 1465 ante.

5 Ibid reg 4 (4).

6 Ibid reg 4 (5).

7 Ibid reg 4 (6).

8 Civil Aviation (Aerial Advertising) (Captive Balloons) Regulations 1984, SI 1984/474, reg 3. The captive balloon must not be flown at more than 60 metres above ground level, must be more than one metre, but not more than seven metres in any linear dimension, must not have a total capacity of more than 700 cubic feet and must not have attached to it, or to its mooring cable, any banner, pennant or other thing on which it is possible to display any communication: reg 3 (i)–(iv).

1471. Aerial photography and survey. An aircraft registered in a contracting state[1] other than the United Kingdom, or in a foreign country, may not fly over the United Kingdom for the purpose of aerial photography or aerial survey or any other form of aerial work, whether or not valuable consideration is given or promised, except with the permission of the Secretary of State[2], who grants such permission to the operator[3] or charterer of the aircraft subject to such conditions as he thinks fit[4].

The Secretary of State may provisionally suspend or vary the permission for inquiry, and, on sufficient grounds shown to his satisfaction, may revoke, suspend or vary the permission[5], in which case the holder of the permission must surrender the permission to the Secretary of State within a reasonable time after being required to do so[6].

1 For the meaning of 'contracting state' see para 1190 note 4 ante.

2 As to the Secretary of State see para 1032 ante.

3 For the meaning of 'operator' see para 1340 ante.

4 Air Navigation Order 1989, SI 1989/2004, art 92 (1). As to aerial work see para 1273 ante. For the meaning of 'valuable consideration' see para 1651 note 4 post As to the effect on the validity of the permit of breach of the conditions see para 1424 ante. Contravention of this provision or breach of a condition is an offence punishable on summary conviction by a fine not exceeding £2,000, and on conviction on indictment by a fine or imprisonment for up to two years or both: arts 92 (2), 99 (6), Sch 12 Pt B.

5 Ibid art 67 (1), (4), (7). See also paras 1422, 1423 ante.

6 Ibid art 67 (5), (7). See further para 1423 ante.

1472. Flights over foreign countries. The operator[1] or commander[2] of an aircraft registered in the United Kingdom[3] which is being flown over any foreign country must not allow that aircraft to be used so as to prejudice the security, public order, public health or safe air navigation of that country[4].

Where there are grounds for the aeronautical authorities[5] of that country to believe that an aircraft is being used for such prejudicial purposes[6], or where the particular flight has not been duly authorised[7], the operator or commander of the aircraft must comply with any directions given by such authorities unless the lives of persons on board the aircraft or the safety of the aircraft would be thereby endangered[8].

1 For the meaning of 'operator' see para 1340 ante.
2 For the meaning of 'commander' see para 1213 note 1 ante.
3 Aircraft not registered in the United Kingdom but whose operator's principal place of business or permanent residence is in the United Kingdom are assimilated to aircraft registered in the United Kingdom for the purposes of the Air Navigation Order 1989, SI 1989/2004, art 93; see art 93 (1), (3).
4 Ibid art 93 (1). A person does not contravene art 93 (1) if he neither knew nor suspected that the aircraft was being used for prejudicial purposes: art 93 (2). As to the penalty for contravention see note 8 infra.
5 The 'appropriate aeronautical authorities' include any person, whether a member of a country's military or civil authorities, authorised under the law of the foreign country to issue directions to aircraft flying over that country: ibid art 93 (6).
6 Ibid art 93 (3) (b).
7 Ibid art 93 (3) (a).
8 Ibid art 93 (3); such a requirement is without prejudice to any other requirement to comply with directions of an aeronautical authority: art 93 (5). A person does not contravene art 93 (3) if he neither knew nor suspected that directions were being given by the appropriate aeronautical authorities: art 93 (4). The penalty for contravention of any provision of art 93 is, on summary conviction, a fine not exceeding £2,000, or, on conviction on indictment, a fine or imprisonment for up to two years or both: art 99 (6), Sch 12 Pt B.

1473. Aerobatic manoeuvres. An aircraft may not carry out any aerobatic manoeuvre[1] over the congested area[2] of any city, town or settlement; or within controlled airspace[3] except with the consent of the appropriate air traffic control unit[4].

1 'Aerobatic manoeuvres' includes loops, spins, rolls, bunts, stall turns, inverted flying or any other similar manoeuvre: Air Navigation Order 1989, SI 1989/2004, art 106 (1).
2 For the meaning of 'congested area' see para 1286 note 9 ante.
3 For the meaning of 'controlled airspace' see para 1395 ante.
4 Rules of the Air Regulations 1990, SI 1990/2241, Schedule r 18. Contravention of the Rules of the Air is an offence: Air Navigation Order 1989 art 69 (2) (amended by SI 1990/2154) ; see para 1461 ante. For the meaning of 'appropriate air traffic control unit' see para 1394 note 1 ante.

1474. Practice flights. An aircraft may not be flown in simulated instrument flight[1] conditions unless it is equipped with dual controls, and an additional pilot, called a safety pilot, is carried in the second control seat to render any necessary assistance to the pilot flying the aircraft and who is to have a competent observer to assist him if his field of vision is not adequate on all sides of the aircraft[2]. Aircraft may not carry out instrument approach practice in the United Kingdom when flying in visual meteorological conditions[3] unless the flight has been notified to the appropriate air traffic control unit[4] and, if the flight is not under simulated instrument flight conditions, a competent observer is carried who has an adequate field of vision and can readily communicate with the pilot flying the aircraft[5].

1 'Simulated instrument flight' means a flight during which mechanical or optical devices are used in order to reduce the field of vision or the range of visibility from the cockpit: Rules of the Air Regulations 1990, SI 1990/2241, Schedule r 6.
2 Ibid Schedule r 6. Contravention of the Rules of the Air is an offence: Air Navigation Order 1989, SI 1989/2004, art 69 (2) (amended by SI 1990/2154); see para 1461 ante.
3 For the meaning of 'visual meteorological conditions' see para 1403 note 8 ante.
4 For the meaning of 'appropriate air traffic control unit' see para 1394 note 1 ante; for the meaning of 'notified' see para 1105 note 3 ante.

5 Rules of the Air Regulations 1990 Schedule r 7. As to contravention see note 2 supra.

(v) Aerodrome Flight Rules

1475. Operation on or near aerodromes. The commander[1] of a flying machine on any part of an aerodrome provided for the use of the aircraft[2] must, notwithstanding any air traffic control clearance[3], take all possible measures to ensure that his aircraft does not collide with any other aircraft or with any vehicle[4].

Where an aircraft is flying in the aerodrome traffic zone[5] of an aerodrome where no air traffic control unit[6] is for the time being notified[7] as being on watch, or is moving on such an aerodrome, the commander must conform to, or avoid, the pattern of traffic formed by other aircraft in operation, make all turns to the left unless ground signals otherwise indicate, and take off and land in the direction indicated by such signals or, if no such signals are displayed, into the wind unless good aviation practice otherwise demands[8].

A flying machine or glider may not land at such an aerodrome unless the runway is clear of other aircraft[9], and after landing a flying machine must move clear of the landing area in use as soon as possible[10].

1 For the meaning of 'commander' see para 1213 note 1 ante.
2 See the Rules of the Air Regulations 1990, SI 1990/2241, Schedule r 33 (1).
3 For the meaning of 'air traffic control clearance' see para 1216 note 7 ante.
4 Rules of the Air Regulations 1990 Schedule rr 17 (1) (a), 33 (2). Contravention of the Rules of the Air is an offence: Air Navigation Order 1989, SI 1989/2004, art 69 (2) (amended by SI 1990/2154); see para 1461 ante . As to the rules for avoiding collisions see the Rules of the Air Regulations 1990 Schedule rr 17, 33 (3)–(5); and paras 1480–1482 post.
5 For the meaning of 'aerodrome traffic zone' see para 1395 ante.
6 For the meaning of 'air traffic control unit' see para 1394 note 1 ante.
7 For the meaning of 'notified' see para 1105 note 3 ante.
8 Rules of the Air Regulations 1990 Schedule rr 17 (5), (7) (a), 35 (2). As to contravention see note 4 supra.
9 Ibid Schedule r 17 (7) (b). For special provisions where take-off and landing is not confined to runways see r 17 (7) (c). As to contravention see note 4 supra.
10 Ibid Schedule r 17 (7) (d). As to contravention see note 4 supra.

1476. Aerodrome traffic zones. An aircraft may not fly within a zone which the commander[1] of the aircraft knows or ought reasonably to know to be the aerodrome traffic zone[2] of an aerodrome, unless he has the permission of the appropriate air traffic control unit[3] or he has obtained information to enable the flight to be conducted with safety within the zone either from the aerodrome flight information unit[4], if there is no air traffic control unit, or from the aerodrome air/ground radio station at that aerodrome if there is neither air traffic control unit nor aerodrome flight information unit[5].

The commander of the aircraft must cause a continuous watch to be maintained on the appropriate radio frequency for air traffic control communications, or if that is not possible, cause a watch to be kept for such instructions as may be issued by visual means[6]; where the aircraft is fitted with means of communication with the ground, its position and height must be given to the appropriate air traffic control unit, aerodrome flight information unit or air/ground radio station on entering the zone and just before leaving it[7].

1 For the meaning of 'commander' see para 1213 note 1 ante.

2 For the meaning of 'aerodrome traffic zone' see para 1395 ante.
3 For the meaning of 'air traffic control unit' see para 1394 note 1 ante.
4 For the meaning of 'aerodrome flight information unit' see para 1387 note 2 ante.
5 Rules of the Air Regulations 1990, SI 1990/2241, Schedule r 35 (2). This provision applies to
  government aerodromes (as to which see para 1105 ante) at such times as are notified, to aerodromes
  having an air traffic control unit or an aerodrome flight information unit during the notified hours of
  watch of such a unit and to licensed aerodromes having a means of two-way radio communication
  with aircraft during the notified hours of watch of the air/ground radio station: r 35 (1). As to the
  flight rules relating to notified airspace see para 1406 ante. Contravention of the Rules of the Air is an
  offence: Air Navigation Order 1989, SI 1989/2004, art 69 (2) (amended by SI 1990/2154); see para
  1461 ante.
6 Rules of the Air Regulations 1990 Schedule r 35 (3) (a). As to contravention see note 5 supra.
7 Ibid Schedule r 35 (3) (b). As to contravention see note 5 supra.

1477. Radio navigation aids. The commander[1] of an aircraft may not make use
of any radio navigation aid without complying with the notified and appropriate
restrictions and procedures unless authorised by an air traffic control unit[2], save
where he is required to comply with the provisions relating to flight plans[3] and air
traffic control clearance[4].

1 For the meaning of 'commander' see para 1213 note 1 ante.
2 Rules of the Air Regulations 1990, SI 1990/2241, Schedule r 37. For the meaning of 'air traffic control
  unit' see para 1394 note 1 ante. Contravention of the Rules of the Air is an offence: Air Navigation
  Order 1989, SI 1989/2004, art 69 (2) (amended by SI 1990/2154); see para 1461 ante.
3 As to flight plans see para 1402 ante.
4 Rules of the Air Regulations 1990 Schedule r 37 proviso. As to provisions relating to flight plans and
  air traffic control clearance see r 27; and paras 1402, 1403 ante.

1478. United Kingdom aerodrome flight rules. Additional rules must be
complied with by all aircraft operating in the vicinity of aerodromes in the United
Kingdom. In addition, special rules apply within a specified airspace above and
around particular aerodromes[1].

1 See the Rules of the Air Regulations 1990, SI 1990/2241, Schedule r 36; see further paras 1406 ante,
  1479–1482 post.

1479. Scope of United Kingdom aerodrome flight rules. The rules include
general provisions requiring arrivals and intended departures to be notified to the
air traffic control unit[1], if one exists[2].
  In addition there are rules regulating the flight of aircraft within a specified
airspace above and around aerodromes[3], regulating the direction in which aircraft
must land and the procedure for and manner of landing and regulating the manner
and direction of take-off and its control by signals, rules as to landing signals,
specifying the signals for prohibiting landing either temporarily or altogether, the
signal for instructing an aircraft to return and land, and the signals and communications for requesting permission to land and the replies thereto[4]; rules regulating
the movement of aircraft and vehicles on aerodromes[5]; and rules as to marshalling
signals, for giving various instructions to aircraft[6].

1 For the meaning of 'air traffic control unit' see para 1394 note 1 ante.
2 See the Rules of the Air Regulations 1990, SI 1990/2241, Schedule r 20; and para 1407 ante.
3 See ibid Schedule rr 36, 36A, 38–40; and para 1406 ante.
4 See ibid Schedule rr 30, 41–50.

5 See ibid Schedule rr 31–33.
6 See ibid Schedule rr 47, 48.

1480. Rules for avoiding aerial collisions. No aircraft[1] may be flown in such proximity to other aircraft as to create a collision danger[2], and aircraft must not fly in formation unless their commanders have agreed to do so[3].

An aircraft which is required by the rules to give way to another aircraft must avoid passing over or under it, or crossing ahead of it, unless passing well clear[4]. An aircraft which has the right of way must maintain its course and speed[5]. Notwithstanding that the flight is being made with air traffic control clearance[6], it remains the commander's duty to take all possible means to ensure that his aircraft does not collide with any other aircraft[7].

1 For the purpose of the Rules of the Air Regulations 1990, SI 1990/2241, Schedule r 17, a glider and the towing flying machine are considered to be a single aircraft under the command of the commander of the towing flying machine: r 17 (1) (f). For the meaning of 'commander' see para 1213 note 1 ante. As to the application of the general flight rules, in which the general rules for avoiding collisions are included, see paras 1460–1474 ante.
2 Ibid Schedule r 17 (1) (b). Contravention of the Rules of the Air is an offence: Air Navigation Order 1989, SI 1989/2004, art 69 (2) (amended by SI 1990/2154); see para 1461 ante.
3 Rules of the Air Regulations 1990 Schedule r 17 (1) (c). As to contravention see note 2 supra.
4 Ibid Schedule r 17 (1) (d). As to contravention see note 2 supra.
5 Ibid Schedule r 17 (1) (e). As to contravention see note 2 supra.
6 For the meaning of 'air traffic control clearance' see para 1216 note 7 ante.
7 Rules of the Air Regulations 1990 Schedule r 17 (1) (a). As to contravention see note 2 supra.

1481. Right-of-way rules in flight. Subject to the rules as to aircraft approaching head-on and overtaking[1], aircraft of different classes when converging in the air must give way as follows: flying machines must give way to airships, gliders and balloons; airships to gliders and balloons; and gliders to balloons[2]. Where two aircraft of the same class are at approximately the same altitude, the aircraft which has the other on its right must give way, but nevertheless mechanically driven aircraft must give way to aircraft which are towing other aircraft or objects[3].

Where two aircraft are approaching head-on or approximately so in the air and there is danger of collision, each must alter course to the right[4].

An aircraft being overtaken in the air has the right of way and the overtaking aircraft, whether climbing, descending or in horizontal flight, must keep out of the way of the other aircraft by altering course to the right and must not cease to keep out of the way of the other until the other has been passed and is clear, notwithstanding any change in the relative positions of the two[5], although a glider overtaking another glider in the United Kingdom may alter its course to the right or to the left[6].

1 See text and notes 4–6 infra.
2 Rules of the Air Regulations 1990, SI 1990/2241, Schedule r 17 (2) (a). There is power to make rules requiring aircraft to give way to military aircraft: see the Air Navigation Order 1989, SI 1989/2004, art 69 (1) (a); and para 1268 note 1 ante. Contravention of the Rules of the Air is an offence: Air Navigation Order 1989, SI 1989/2004, art 69 (2) (amended by SI 1990/2154); see para 1461 ante.
3 Rules of the Air Regulations 1990 Schedule r 17 (2) (b). As to contravention see note 2 supra.

4 Ibid Schedule r 17 (3). As to contravention see note 2 supra.
5 Ibid Schedule r 17 (4). As to contravention see note 2 supra.
6 Ibid Schedule r 17 (4) proviso.

1482. Right-of-way rules on landing and take-off. An aircraft landing or on final approach to land has the right of way over other aircraft in flight or on the ground or water[1]; and where two or more flying machines, gliders or airships are approaching any place for the purpose of landing, the aircraft at the lower altitude has the right of way, but must not take advantage of this rule to cut in front of another aircraft which is on final approach to land or overtake that aircraft[2]. Notwithstanding the foregoing, an aircraft whose commander[3] is aware that another aircraft is making an emergency landing must always give way to that aircraft, and at night, notwithstanding that it has permission to do so, must not attempt to land until it receives further permission to do so[4]. When an air traffic control unit[5] has communicated to any aircraft an order of priority for landing, the aircraft must approach to land in that order[6].

An aircraft about to take off must not attempt to do so until the commander is satisfied that there is no risk of collision with another aircraft[7].

1 Rules of the Air Regulations 1990, SI 1990/2241, Schedule r 17 (6) (a). Contravention of the Rules of the Air is an offence: Air Navigation Order 1989, SI 1989/2004, art 69 (2) (amended by SI 1990/2154); see para 1461 ante.
2 Rules of the Air Regulations 1990 Schedule r 17 (6) (b). As to contravention see note 1 supra.
3 For the meaning of 'commander' see para 1213 note 1 ante.
4 Rules of the Air Regulations 1990 Schedule r 17 (6) (b) proviso (ii). As to contravention see note 1 supra.
5 For the meaning of 'air traffic control unit' see para 1394 note 1 ante.
6 Rules of the Air Regulations 1990 Schedule r 17 (6) (b) proviso (i). As to contravention see note 1 supra.
7 See ibid Schedule r 17 (1) (a); and para 1480 ante.

1483. Right-hand side traffic. An aircraft which is flying within the United Kingdom in sight of the ground and following a road, railway, canal or coastline, or any other line of landmarks, must keep that line of landmarks on its left[1].

1 Rules of the Air Regulations 1990, SI 1990/2241, Schedule r 19. This rule does not apply to aircraft flying within controlled airspace (see r 21 and para 1405 ante) or within notified airspace (see r 36 and para 1406 ante) in accordance with instructions given by the appropriate air traffic control unit (as to which see para 1394 note 1 ante): r 19 proviso. Contravention of the Rules of the Air is an offence: Air Navigation Order 1989, SI 1989/2004, art 69 (2) (amended by SI 1990/2154); see para 1461 ante.

(vi) Lights and Signals

1484. Rules for night flying. By night[1] all aircraft must display the appropriate lights specified in the Rules of the Air Regulations[2], and may not display any other lights which might obscure or otherwise impair the visibility of or be mistaken for such lights; by day an aircraft fitted with an anti-collision light must display that light [3].

A flying machine[4] on a land aerodrome in the United Kingdom must display by night the lights which it would be required to display if it were flying[5] or certain specified lights[6], unless the aircraft is stationary on the apron[7] or a part of the aerodrome provided for the maintenance of aircraft[8]; if the aircraft is fitted with a red anti-collision light, this light must be displayed by day or night when the aircraft is stationary on the apron with its engines running[9].

While an aircraft is flying in the United Kingdom and any light which is required to be displayed by it in flight fails and cannot be immediately repaired or replaced, the aircraft must land as soon as, in the commander's[10] opinion, it can safely do so, unless authorised by the appropriate air traffic control unit[11] to continue its flight[12].

The commander may switch off, or reduce the intensity of, any flashing light where it adversely affects the performance of the duties of any member of the flight crew or subjects an outside observer to unreasonable dazzle[13].

1 For the meaning of 'night' see para 1192 note 4 ante.
2 See the Rules of the Air Regulations 1990, SI 1990/2241, Schedule rr 11–15; and para 1485 post.
3 Ibid Schedule r 9 (1). 'Anti-collision light' means in relation to rotorcraft a flashing red light and in relation to any other aircraft a flashing red or flashing white light and in either case showing in all directions for the purpose of enabling the aircraft to be more readily detected by pilots of distant aircraft: r 1 (1). Contravention of the Rules of the Air is an offence: Air Navigation Order 1989, SI 1989/2004, art 69 (2) (amended by SI 1990/2154); see para 1461 ante.
4 For the meaning of 'flying machine' see para 1269 ante.
5 As to these lights see para 1485 note 2 post.
6 See the Rules of the Air Regulations 1990 Schedule r 11 (2) (c), which specifies the lights listed in r 11 (2) (a), but all being flashing lights flashing together; see para 1485 note 2 post .
7 For the meaning of 'apron' see para 1214 note 2 ante.
8 Rules of the Air Regulations 1990 Schedule r 9 (2) (a). As to contravention see note 3 supra.
9 Ibid Schedule r 9 (2) (b). As to contravention see note 3 supra. A helicopter to which the Air Navigation Order 1989 art 26 applies (requirement of operations manual: see para 1438 ante), when stationary on an offshore installation, may switch off the anti-collision light as a signal to ground personnel that it is safe to approach the helicopter for embarkation or disembarkation, loading or unloading, in accordance with a procedure contained in the operations manual: Rules of the Air Regulations 1990 Schedule r 9 (2) proviso.
10 For the meaning of 'commander' see para 1213 note 1 ante.
11 For the meaning of 'appropriate air traffic control unit' see para 1394 note 1 ante.
12 Rules of the Air Regulations 1990 Schedule r 10 (1). If an anti-collision light fails when flying by day, the aircraft may continue to fly by day provided the light is repaired as soon as possible: r 10 (2).
13 Ibid Schedule r 9 (3).

1485. Lights and signals. The Rules of the Air contain detailed provisions as to the lights and other objects to be displayed by aircraft.

Separate provision is made as to the lights and other objects to be displayed by flying machines[1] in the air[2] or on a land aerodrome[3], by gliders[4], by free balloons[5], by captive balloons and kites[6], and by airships[7]. There are separate rules for seaplanes on the water[8].

1 For the meaning of 'flying machine' see para 1269 ante.
2 The lights specified for use are: (1) a green starboard light of at least five candela showing through an angle of 110 degrees from dead ahead in the horizontal plane; a similar red port light; a white light of at least three candela showing through angles of 70 degrees from dead astern to each side in the horizontal plane (Rules of the Air Regulations 1990, SI 1990/2241, Schedule r 11 (2) (a)) ; (2) the lights specified in (1) plus an anti-collision light (r 11 (2) (b)); (3) the lights specified in (1), but all being flashing lights, together with either or both of the following: (a) a flashing white light of at least 20 candela showing in all directions; and (b) a flashing red light of at least 20 candela showing through angles of 70 degrees from dead astern to each side in the horizontal plane (r 11 (2) (d)) . The lights are used in different combinations depending on the size of the aircraft (over or under a maximum total weight authorised of 5,700 kg: see para 1361 note 4 ante) and the date the type certificate was first issued (before or after 1 April 1988) and whether the aircraft is registered in the United Kingdom: r 11 (1). For the meaning of 'anti-collision light' see para 1484 note 3 ante.

3 See ibid Schedule r 9 (2); and para 1484 ante.
4 See ibid Schedule r 12.
5 See ibid Schedule r 13.
6 See ibid Schedule r 14.
7 See ibid Schedule r 15.
8 See the Merchant Shipping (Distress Signals and Prevention of Collisions) Regulations 1989, SI
   1989/1798 (and as applied to Guernsey: see SI 1989/2410), and the Collision Regulations (Seaplanes)
   Order 1989, SI 1989/2005 (amended by SI 1990/251 and as applied to Guernsey: see SI 1990/252);
   and SHIPPING.

1486. Distress, urgency, safety and warning signals. Distress, urgency and
safety signals to be made by aircraft in various circumstances are prescribed. A
number of radiotelephony[1], visual[2] and sound[3] distress signals are prescribed for
use or display, either separately or together, signifying that an aircraft is threatened
by grave and imminent danger and requests immediate assistance[4].

Prescribed visual urgency signals[5], given either together or separately, before
the sending of a message, signify that the commander[6] wishes to give notice of
difficulties which compel the aircraft to land but that immediate assistance is not
required[7]; and prescribed radiotelephony[8], visual[9] and sound[10] signals, given
either separately or together, indicate that the commander has an urgent message to
transmit concerning the safety of the aircraft itself, of another aircraft, of any
person on board the aircraft or within sight of it, or of any ship or vehicle[11].

Further, warning signals are prescribed to be made to an aircraft in flight when it
is in the vicinity of a Danger Area or an area where flying is either restricted or
prohibited by reason of national defence or public interest[12] and is therefore
required to leave the area or change its course to avoid the area[13].

1 Ie the spoken word 'Mayday'.
2 Ie the signal S O S (. . . — — — . . .); a succession of pyrotechnic lights fired at short intervals each
   showing a single red light; a parachute flare showing a red light.
3 Ie the sound signal S O S (. . . — — — . . .); a continuous sounding with any sound apparatus.
4 Rules of the Air Regulations 1990, SI 1990/2241, Schedule r 49 (1). For distress signals for use by
   seaplanes see the Merchant Shipping (Distress Signals and Prevention of Collisions) Regulations
   1989, SI 1989/1798, Annex IV (as to Guernsey see para 1485 note 8 ante); and SHIPPING.
5 Ie a succession of white pyrotechnic lights; the repeated switching on and off of the aircraft landing
   lights; the repeated switching on and off of its navigation lights in such a manner as to be clearly
   distinguished from ordinary flashing navigation lights.
6 For the meaning of 'commander' see para 1213 note 1 ante.
7 Rules of the Air Regulations 1990 Schedule r 49 (2).
8 Ie the spoken word 'Pan Pan'.
9 Ie the signal XXX (— . . — — . . — — . . —).
10 Ie the signal XXX (— . . — — . . — — . . —).
11 Ibid Schedule r 49 (3).
12 See the Air Navigation Order 1989, SI 1989/2004, art 74 (1) (a) (iii); and para 1487 post. A 'Danger
   Area' is airspace which has been notified as such within which activities dangerous to the flight of
   aircraft may take place or exist at such times as may be notified: art 106 (1).
13 Rules of the Air Regulations 1990 Schedule r 50 which prescribes, by day or night, a series of
   projectiles discharged at ten second intervals showing red and green lights or stars.

(vii) Airspace Restrictions

1487. Restriction of flying. The Secretary of State[1] may deem it necessary in
the public interest to restrict or prohibit flying by any aircraft in any airspace over
the United Kingdom or in the neighbourhood of an offshore installation, or by any

British-registered aircraft in certain other airspace², by reason of the intended gathering or movement of a large number of persons³, the intended holding of an aircraft race or contest or of an exhibition of flying⁴, or national defence or any other reason affecting the public interest⁵. He may, for any of these reasons, make regulations⁶ prohibiting, restricting or imposing conditions on flight either generally or in relation to any class of aircraft⁷. An aircraft must not fly in contravention of such regulations; if the aircraft commander becomes aware of the contravention, he must cause the aircraft to leave the area by the shortest route without descending while still over the area, unless otherwise instructed⁸.

1 As to the Secretary of State see para 1032 ante.
2 Ie any other airspace, being airspace in respect of which the United Kingdom government has undertaken to provide navigation services in pursuance of international arrangements: Air Navigation Order 1989, SI 1989/2004, art 74 (1) (a) (bb).
3 Ibid art 74 (1) (a) (i).
4 Ibid art 74 (1) (a) (ii). As to exhibitions of flying see para 1429 ante.
5 Ibid art 74 (1) (a) (iii).
6 For an example see the Air Navigation (Restriction of Flying) (Nuclear Installations) Regulations 1988, SI 1988/1138, which prohibit flight at any time below a specified height above any of 12 atomic energy establishments. Generally, being local or temporary, such orders are outside the scope of this work.
6 Air Navigation Order 1989 art 74 (1) (b).
7 Ibid art 74 (2). Contravention of the provisions of flying regulations or of the provisions described above is an offence punishable on summary conviction by a fine not exceeding £1,000: art 99 (5), Sch 12 Pt A. As to warnings to an aircraft in the vicinity of a prohibited area see para 1486 ante. See also para 1488 post.

1488. Flying in prohibited areas. Where restrictions have been imposed by regulations upon flying over any area of the United Kingdom by reason of national defence or any other reason affecting the public interest¹, or within airspace notified as a Danger Area², and the commander³ of an aircraft becomes aware that the aircraft is flying in contravention of such regulations, the aircraft must forthwith comply with instructions given by radio or by visual signal⁴ by the appropriate air traffic control unit⁵ or by the person responsible for safety within the relevant airspace⁶.

Certain visual signals are prescribed for warning an aircraft that it is in the vicinity of such an area and that it should change course⁷.

1 See the Air Navigation Order 1989, SI 1989/2004, art 74 (1) (a) (iii); and para 1487 ante.
2 For the meaning of 'Danger Area' see para 1486 note 12 ante.
3 For the meaning of 'commander' see para 1213 note 1 ante.
4 As to distress signals see para 1486 ante.
5 For the meaning of 'appropriate air traffic control unit' see para 1394 note 1 ante.
6 Air Navigation Order 1989 art 74 (3). Contravention of these provisions is an offence punishable on summary conviction by a fine not exceeding £1,000: art 99 (5), Sch 12 Pt A.
7 See the Rules of the Air Regulations 1990, SI 1990/2241, Schedule r 50; and para 1486 ante.

1489. Low flying generally. Provisions relating to dangerous flying are set out in the Civil Aviation Act 1982 and the Air Navigation Order¹, and provisions relating to minimum altitudes of flight are to be found in special regulations restricting flying² and in the Rules of the Air Regulations³.

In general, an aircraft⁴ may not fly closer than 500 feet to any person, vessel, vehicle or structure⁵. This rule does not, however, apply to any United Kingdom police aircraft[6], to aircraft taking part in any organised flying event[7], to aircraft landing or taking off in accordance with normal aviation practice[8], to gliders while hill-soaring[9], to aircraft allowed to drop articles or animals in specified circumstances[10], to aircraft flying under and in accordance with an aerial application certificate[11] or to aircraft flying for the purpose of picking up or dropping tow ropes, banners or other articles[12].

Exemption may be sought[13] and nothing in the provisions described above prohibits an aircraft from flying in such a manner as is necessary for the purpose of saving life[14].

1 See the Civil Aviation Act 1982 s 81, the Air Navigation Order 1989, SI 1989/2004, art 51; and para 1456 ante.
2 See para 1487 text and note 5 ante.
3 See the Rules of the Air Regulations 1990, SI 1990/2241, Schedule r 5 (text and notes 5–14 infra); and paras 1490–1493 post.
4 'Aircraft' includes helicopters: see para 1269 ante.
5 Rules of the Air Regulations 1990 Schedule r 5 (1) (e). For general exemptions see para 1493 post. Contravention of the Rules of the Air is an offence: see para 1461 ante. As to whether frequent low flights over school grounds form a basis for an action for trespass or nuisance see *Roedean School Ltd v Cornwall Aviation Co Ltd* (1926) Times, 3 July. See also *Lord Bernstein of Leigh v Skyviews and General Ltd* [1978] QB 479, [1977] 2 All ER 902, where it was held that there could be no successful action for trespass or nuisance provided the flights were at a reasonable height and complied with the statutory requirements; see further paras 1490–1493 post.
6 Rules of the Air Regulations 1990 Schedule r 5 (2) (b).
7 Ie an aircraft flying over or within 3,000 feet of an assembly of persons gathered for the purpose of witnessing or participating in an event consisting wholly or partly of an aircraft race or contest or an exhibition of flying (whether or not with a permission or display authorisation granted under the Air Navigation Order 1989 art 56: see para 1429 ante), if the aircraft is taking part in that race, contest or exhibition or is engaged on a flight arranged by, or made with the written consent of, the organisers of the event: Rules of the Air Regulations 1990 Schedule r 5 (2) (c).
8 Ibid Schedule r 5 (2) (d) (i).
9 Ibid Schedule r 5 (2) (d) (ii).
10 Ibid Schedule r 5 (2) (d) (iii); and see para 1467 ante.
11 Ibid Schedule r 5 (2) (d) (iv); and see para 1469 ante.
12 Ibid Schedule r 5 (2) (d) (v); and see paras 1466, 1467 ante.
13 See the Air Navigation Order 1989 art 104.
14 Rules of the Air Regulations 1990 Schedule r 5 (3). As to further exceptions see para 1493 post.

1490. Minimum flying height over congested areas. An aircraft other than a helicopter[1] must not fly over any congested area[2] of a city, town or settlement either below such height as would enable the aircraft to alight clear of the area and without danger to persons or property on the surface in the event of the failure of a power unit[3] or below a height of 1,500 feet above the highest fixed object within 2,000 feet of the aircraft, whichever of those heights is the higher[4].

The provision relating to the minimum height of 1,500 feet does not apply to an aircraft flying over a route notified[5] for the purposes of this rule, or on a special VFR flight[6] or on a flight for which a special VFR clearance was given[7], both in accordance with instructions given by the appropriate air traffic control unit[8].

1 As to helicopters see para 1491 post.
2 'Congested area', in relation to a city, town or settlement, means any area which is substantially used for residential, industrial, commercial or recreational purposes: Air Navigation Order 1989, SI 1989/2004, art 106 (1). See *Cameron v Smith* 1982 SLT 398n, 1 S&B AvR IV/1, HC of Justiciary, in which the importance of 'substantially' was underlined, as parts of a 'congested area' may not be used for the purposes specified in the order: it is a question of circumstances and degree whether such parts are still parts of the greater 'congested area'.

3 If the aircraft is towing a banner the height is calculated on the basis that the banner is not dropped within the congested area: see note 4 infra.
4 Rules of the Air Regulations 1990, SI 1990/2241, Schedule r 5 (1) (a). Contravention of the Rules of the Air is an offence: see para 1461 ante.
5 For the meaning of 'notified' see para 1105 note 3 ante.
6 For the meaning of 'special VFR flight' see para 1398 note 8 ante.
7 For the meaning of 'special VFR clearance' see the Rules of the Air Regulations 1990 Schedule r 36 (2); and para 1406 note 12 ante.
8 Rules of the Air Regulations 1990 Schedule r 5 (2) (a). For the meaning of 'appropriate air traffic control unit' see para 1394 note 1 ante.

1491. Minimum flying height of helicopters. A helicopter may not fly below such height as would enable it to alight without danger to persons or property on the surface in the event of failure of a power unit[1].

Except with the written permission of the Civil Aviation Authority (CAA)[2], a helicopter may not fly over a congested area[3] of a city, town or settlement, below a height of 1,500 feet above the highest fixed object within 2,000 feet of the helicopter[4]. Over a specified area of central London[5], a helicopter must not fly below such height as would enable it to alight clear of the area in the event of the failure of a power unit[6].

1 Rules of the Air Regulations 1990, SI 1990/2241, Schedule r 5 (1) (b). Helicopters are not required to clear the area in case of engine failure, as are other aircraft: see para 1490 ante. Contravention of the Rules of the Air is an offence: see para 1461 ante.
2 As to the CAA see para 1044 ante.
3 For the meaning of 'congested area' see para 1490 note 2 ante.
4 Rules of the Air Regulations 1990 Schedule r 5 (1) (c) (i). This provision does not apply to a helicopter flying on a route notified for the purposes of r 5, or on a special VFR flight or on a flight for which a special VFR clearance was given, both in accordance with instructions given by the appropriate air traffic control unit: r 5 (2) (a). For the meaning of 'notified' see para 1105 note 3 ante; for the meaning of 'special VFR flight' see para 1398 note 8 ante; for the meaning of 'special VFR clearance' see para 1406 note 12 ante; and for the meaning of 'appropriate air traffic control unit' see para 1394 note 1 ante. See also *Dickson v Miln* 1969 SLT 269 (helicopter taking off and landing in congested area).
5 Ie an area bounded by straight lines joining Kew Bridge, Brent reservoir, Gospel Oak station, Springfield Park, Bromley station, Hither Green, Herne Hill station, Wimbledon station, Castelnau reservoir and Kew Bridge, excluding so much of the bed of the river Thames as lies within that area between the ordinary high water marks on each of its banks: Rules of the Air Regulations 1990 Schedule r 5 (1) (c) (ii).
6 Ibid Schedule r 5 (1) (c) (ii).

1492. Minimum flying height over assemblies. An aircraft must not fly over or within 3,000 feet of any assembly[1] in the open air of more than 1,000 persons assembled for the purpose of witnessing or participating in any organised event, except with the written permission of the Civil Aviation Authority (CAA)[2] and the written consent of the organisers of the event[3]. Further, the aircraft may not fly below such height as would enable it to alight clear of the assembly in the event of failure of a power unit[4]. It is a good defence to a charge of contravening either of these provisions[5] to prove that the flight was made at a reasonable height and for a reason unconnected with the event[6].

United Kingdom police aircraft and aircraft taking part in an organised flying event[7] are generally excepted from these provisions[8].

1 For this purpose a procession may be an assembly: *DPP v Roffey* (1959) 123 JP 241, DC (aircraft flying within 3,000 feet of H-Bomb protest march).

As to the CAA see para 1044 ante.
Rules of the Air Regulations 1990, SI 1990/2241, Schedule r 5 (1) (d) (i). See also note 5 infra as to contravention of these provisions.
Ibid Schedule r 5 (1) (d) (ii).
Contravention of the Rules of the Air is an offence: see para 1461 ante.
Rules of the Air Regulations 1990 Schedule r 5 (1) (d) proviso.
Ie such an event as is described in para 1489 note 7 ante.
Rules of the Air Regulations 1990 Schedule r 5 (2) (b), (c); see para 1489 ante.

1493. General exceptions to low flying rules. Nothing in the rules relating to low flying[1] prohibits an aircraft from flying in such a manner as is necessary for the purpose of saving life[2], or prohibits any aircraft from flying in accordance with normal aviation practice for the purpose of taking off from, landing at, practising approaches to landing at[3], or checking navigational aids or procedures at, a government aerodrome[4], an aerodrome owned or managed by the Civil Aviation Authority (CAA)[5] or a licensed aerodrome[6] in the United Kingdom[7] or at any aerodrome in any other country[8]. Nor do the rules relating to low flying apply to captive balloons and kites[9].

1 Ie the Rules of the Air Regulations 1990, SI 1990/2241, Schedule r 5: see paras 1489–1492 ante.
2 Ibid Schedule r 5 (3).
3 The practising of approaches to landing must be confined to the airspace customarily used at the aerodrome concerned by aircraft when landing or taking off in accordance with normal aviation practice: ibid Schedule r 5 (4) proviso.
4 For the meaning of 'government aerodrome' see para 1105 ante.
5 As to the CAA see para 1044 ante.
6 For the meaning of 'licensed aerodrome' see para 1154 note 6 ante.
7 As to the classification of aerodromes see para 1105 ante.
8 Rules of the Air Regulations 1990 Schedule r 5 (4). There is no saving in respect of such uses of aerodromes outside these classes, such as private aerodromes in respect of which no licence is in force. Thus, in respect of the use of such aerodromes, care must be taken to avoid a contravention of r 5 (1) (a) or (e) (as to which see, respectively, paras 1490, 1489 ante).
9 Ibid Schedule r 5 (5).

1494. Entries in technical log. On the termination of every flight by an aircraft registered in the United Kingdom for the purpose of public transport[1] or aerial work[2] the commander[3] of the aircraft must enter in the technical log[4] the times at which the flight began and ended, particulars of any defect known to him which affects the airworthiness or safe operation of the aircraft, or a statement that no defects were observed, and any other particulars as to airworthiness or operation as the Civil Aviation Authority (CAA)[5] may require, and must sign and date the entries[6].

1 For the meaning of 'public transport' see para 1272 ante.
2 For the meaning of 'aerial work' see para 1273 ante.
3 For the meaning of 'commander' see para 1213 note 1 ante.
4 As to the technical log see further para 1303 ante.
5 As to the CAA see para 1044 ante.
6 Air Navigation Order 1989, SI 1989/2004, art 10 (2). As to the case where one entry may be made after a series of flights see para 1303 ante.

1495. Mandatory reporting of occurrences. Any known reportable occurrence[1] which is of a prescribed description[2] must be reported to the Civil Aviation

Authority (CAA)[3] by such person as specified in the Air Navigation Order[4]. Suc a report must be made within such time, by such means and must contain suc information as may be prescribed[5]. The person who reported the occurrence, c some other specified person[6], must make a further report, in the prescribe manner, containing information in his possession or control and relating to th specific reported occurrence[7].

Nothing requires a person to report an occurrence which he has reason to believ has been or will be reported by another person to the CAA[8]. A person may n make any report where he knows, or has reason to believe, that the report is false i any particular[9].

1 For the meaning of 'reportable occurrence' see para 1496 post.
2 The reportable occurrences are defined in the Air Navigation (General) Regulations 1981, 1981/57, reg 17 (1).
3 As to the CAA see para 1044 ante.
4 See the Air Navigation Order 1989, SI 1989/2004, art 94 (1) (i). As to persons responsible f reporting occurrences see para 1497 post. As to contravention see note 5 infra.
5 Ibid art 94 (1). For the time and manner of reporting and the information to be reported see the A Navigation (General) Regulations 1981 reg 17 (3) (the report must be made in writing ar dispatched within 96 hours of the occurrence to the CAA by the quickest available means) and ((relevant information). Contravention of this provision, and of that described in text and notes 6, infra, is an offence punishable on summary conviction by a fine not exceeding £1,000: Air Nav gation Order 1989 art 99 (5), Sch 12, Pt A.
6 Ie one of the persons responsible for reporting the occurrence; see para 1497 post.
7 Air Navigation Order 1989 art 94 (1) (ii); and see the Air Navigation (General) Regulations 1981 re 17 (3) (time and manner) and (4) (information). As to contravention see note 5 supra.
8 Air Navigation Order 1989 art 94 (3). This is subject to art 94 (1) (ii) (see text and note 7 supra): art (3). As to contravention see note 5 supra.
9 Ibid art 94 (4). Contravention of this provision is an offence punishable on summary conviction by fine not exceeding £2,000, and, on conviction on indictment by a fine or imprisonment for up to tw years or both: art 99 (6), Sch 12 Pt B.

1496. Reportable occurrence. A reportable occurrence is any incident relatin to an aircraft[1] or any defect in or malfunctioning of such an aircraft or any part c equipment thereof, being an incident, malfunctioning or defect endangering, c which if not corrected would endanger, the aircraft, its occupants or any oth person[2]. A reportable occurrence is also any defect or malfunctioning of an facility on the ground used or intended to be used for purposes of, or in connectio with, the operation of such an aircraft, being a defect or malfunctioning endange ing, or which if not corrected would endanger, such an aircraft or its occupants

However, an accident notified to the Secretary of State[4] in accordance with th relevant regulations[5] does not constitute a reportable occurrence for the purpos of the Air Navigation Order[6].

1 Ie an aircraft as described in para 1497 post.
2 Air Navigation Order 1989, SI 1989/2004, art 94 (2) (a).
3 Ibid art 94 (2) (b). As to persons responsible for reporting occurrences see para 1497 post.
4 As to the Secretary of State see para 1032 ante.
5 See the Civil Aviation (Investigation of Air Accidents) Regulations 1989, SI 1989/2062, and the A Navigation (Investigation of Air Accidents involving Civil and Military Aircraft or Installation Regulations 1986, SI 1986/1953, both made under the Civil Aviation Act 1982 s 75; see further par 1500–1527 post.
6 Air Navigation Order 1989 art 94 (2) proviso.

1497. Responsibility for reporting occurrences. Where a reportable incider has occurred[1], any of the following persons must report the occurrence to the Civ viation Authority (CAA)[2]: the operator[3] of a public transport aircraft[4] registered the United Kingdom and with a maximum total weight authorised of more than 300 kilogrammes[5]; the commander[6] of such an aircraft; any person whose business is to manufacture, repair or overhaul such an aircraft or any of its equipment or parts[7]; any person who signs a certificate of maintenance review, or release to service, in respect of such aircraft, equipment or part[8]; an air traffic controller[9]; the licensee or manager of a licensed aerodrome[10].

Where an aircraft operator has reason to believe that a report has been, or will be, made, he must preserve any relevant data from a flight data recorder or combined cockpit voice recorder/flight data recorder[11] for 14 days from the date on which the report is made to the CAA or for longer if so directed by the CAA[12].

For the meaning of 'reportable occurrence' see para 1496 ante.
As to the CAA see para 1044 ante.
For the meaning of 'operator' see para 1340 ante.
For the meaning of 'public transport aircraft' see para 1272 ante.
As to maximum total weight authorised see paras 1314 note 5 and 1430, 1431 ante.
For the meaning of 'commander' see para 1213 note 1 ante.
As to manufacturers' and repairers' liabilities see paras 1324–1326 ante.
As to maintenance review and release to service see, respectively, paras 1301–1304, 1327–1331 ante.
As to air traffic controllers see paras 1384–1393 ante.
Air Navigation Order 1989, SI 1989/2004, art 94 (1) (a)–(e). As to licensed aerodromes see paras 1154, 1155 ante. For the penalty for contravention of art 94 (1) see para 1495 note 5 ante.
As to flight data recorders and combined cockpit voice recorders/flight data recorders see para 1414 ante.
Air Navigation Order 1989 art 94 (5). The record may be erased if the aircraft is outside the United Kingdom and it is not reasonably practicable to preserve it until the aircraft reaches the United Kingdom: art 94 (5) proviso. As to the preservation of records see paras 1409–1414 ante. For the penalty for contravention of art 94 (5) see para 1495 note 5 ante.

1498. Notification of births and deaths in aircraft. If a birth or death occurs in any part of the world in an aircraft registered in the United Kingdom or if the death occurs outside the United Kingdom of a traveller[1] in such an aircraft who is killed in the journey[2] in consequence of an accident, the owner of the aircraft must, as soon as practicable but not later than six months after the occurrence, transmit to the Civil Aviation Authority (CAA)[3] a return of such birth or death in the prescribed form[4]. For this purpose the person in command[5] of an aircraft in which the birth or death occurs must forthwith record the particulars of it in the journey log book[6] or other appropriate document relating to the aircraft and must make the record available to the owner as soon as practicable[7]. The nationality of a child born in an aircraft is discussed elsewhere[8].

Where an aircraft has been bona fide demised, let or hired out for a period exceeding 14 days to any other person by the owner, and no pilot, commander, navigator or operative member of the crew is in the employment of the owner, the foregoing obligations must be performed by the person to whom the aircraft has been demised, let or hired out and not by the owner[9].

'Traveller' includes a member of the aircraft's crew: Civil Aviation (Births, Deaths and Missing Persons) Regulations 1948, SI 1948/1411, reg 2 (6).
A journey is deemed to commence when a traveller enters the aircraft for the purpose of the journey, and to continue until he alights from it on the completion of the journey, notwithstanding any intermediate stop or break in the journey: ibid reg 2 (2) (amended by SI 1972/323).
As to the CAA see para 1044 ante.
Civil Aviation (Births, Deaths and Missing Persons) Regulations 1948 reg 4 (1) (as amended: see note 2 supra). If the owner does not know any of the necessary particulars, he must transmit as many

of them as he can reasonably ascertain: reg 4 (1) proviso. For the prescribed forms see Appendices B as amended. As to particulars in the case of an illegitimate child see reg 8. The regulations we made under the Civil Aviation Act 1946 s 43 (repealed), but have effect as if made under the Ci Aviation Act 1982 s 83, by virtue of s 105 (3). Failure to comply with any of the requirements set o in this paragraph is punishable on summary conviction with a fine not exceeding level 2 on t standard scale: s 83 (2) (amended by virtue of the Criminal Justice Act 1982 s 46). As to the standa scale see para 1044 note 6 ante. At the date at which this volume states the law, level 2 on that scale at £100.

5 'Person in command' means, where a person other than the pilot is in command, that person, and any other case the pilot: Civil Aviation (Births, Deaths and Missing Persons) Regulations 1948 reg (5).

6 The journey log book is no longer required to be kept. For the necessity to keep log books, se however, paras 1303, 1315, 1357, 1455 ante, and for the meaning of 'log book' see para 1315 note ante.

7 Civil Aviation (Births, Deaths and Missing Persons) Regulations 1948 reg 4 (2) (as amended: s note 2 supra). If the person in command does not know and cannot readily ascertain all t particulars, he must record and make available such particulars as are readily ascertainable: reg 4 (proviso.

8 See BRITISH NATIONALITY.

9 Civil Aviation (Births, Deaths and Missing Persons) Regulations 1948 reg 4 (3).

1499. Records of births, deaths and missing persons. The Civil Aviatic Authority (CAA)[1] keeps separate records of births and deaths in aircraft registere in the United Kingdom, and also a record of persons reported to it as missir persons[2], that is, persons with respect to whom there are reasonable grounds fc believing that they have died in consequence of an accident to an aircraft registere in the United Kingdom[3], and it must send a certified copy of any entry in thes records to the registrar general for England, Scotland or Northern Ireland as ma be appropriate within seven days of the completion of the entry[4]. The CAA ma rectify an error or omission in its records[5].

1 As to the CAA see para 1044 ante.

2 Civil Aviation (Births, Deaths and Missing Persons) Regulations 1948, SI 1948/1411, reg 5 (amen ed by SI 1972/323). For the form of the records see the 1948 Regulations, Appendices C–E; as to t particulars in the case of illegitimate children see reg 8.

3 Ibid reg 2 (4) (as amended: see note 2 supra).

4 Ibid reg 6 (as amended: see note 2 supra). Rules for ascertaining the appropriate registrar are set out reg 7 (as so amended). The appropriate registrar must have the certified copies filed and preserved an Air Register Book of Births and Deaths: Civil Aviation Act 1982 s 83 (5). As to registratic authorities see REGISTRATION. Certificates of death and presumed death issued by the registr general from the register are accepted as evidence of death on application for a grant of represen tation: *Practice Note* (1953) 103 L Jo 299.

5 Civil Aviation (Births, Deaths and Missing Persons) Regulations 1948 reg 9 (1) (as amended: s note 2 supra). Within seven days after correcting an entry the CAA must send a copy of the correcte entry to the appropriate registrar general (reg 9 (2) (as so amended)), who must substitute th corrected entry for the corresponding entry which had been made in the Air Register Book of Birt and Deaths: Civil Aviation Act 1982 s 83 (7).

9. ACCIDENTS

(1) INTRODUCTORY

1500. Necessity under international law to provide for accident investi gation. The Chicago Convention provides that a state in which an accident to a aircraft occurs in the circumstances described in the relevant article must institute an inquiry into the circumstances of the accident in accordance, in so far as its laws permit, with the procedure recommended by the International Civil Aviation Organisation (ICAO)[1]. The state in which the aircraft is registered must be given the opportunity of appointing observers to be present at the inquiry, and the state holding the inquiry must communicate the report to that state[2]. The Council of ICAO adopted Annex 13 on Aircraft Accidents Inquiry on 11 April 1951[3].

1 See the Chicago Convention (Cmd 8742; TS 8) art 26. As to the convention see generally para 1002 ante. As to ICAO see para 1020 ante.
2 Chicago Convention art 26.
3 Following the eighth amendment to Annex 13, the seventh edition was published in May 1988. For a list of annexes to the convention see para 1007 ante.

1501. Application of wreck and salvage law. Any services rendered in assisting, or in saving life from or in saving the cargo or apparel of an aircraft in, on or over the sea or any tidal water, or on or over the shores of the sea or any tidal water, are deemed to be salvage services in all cases in which they would have been salvage services if they had been rendered in relation to a vessel[1]; and where salvage services are rendered by an aircraft to any property or person, the owner of the aircraft is entitled to the same reward for those services as he would have been had the aircraft been a vessel[2]. The position is the same notwithstanding that the aircraft concerned is a foreign aircraft and notwithstanding that the services in question are rendered elsewhere than within the limits of the territorial waters adjacent to any part of Her Majesty's dominions[3].

Those provisions of the Merchant Shipping Act 1894[4] and of any other Acts[5] which relate to wreck and salvage have, with necessary exceptions, adaptations and modifications, been applied in relation to aircraft as they apply in relation to vessels[6], and jurisdiction over salvage claims in relation to aircraft is conferred on all courts having Admiralty jurisdiction[7].

The master of a British ship registered in the United Kingdom on receiving at sea signals of distress or information from any source that an aircraft is in distress must, unless released from this obligation[8], proceed with all speed to the assistance of the persons in distress[9].

1 Civil Aviation Act 1982 s 87 (1): see ADMIRALTY vol 1 (1) (Reissue) para 323. As to the extent of tidal waters see WATER. For salvage law see SHIPPING vol 43 para 1027 et seq.
2 Civil Aviation Act 1982 s 87 (2).
3 Ibid s 87 (3).
4 See the Merchant Shipping Act 1894 Pt IX (ss 510–571); and SHIPPING vol 43 para 1007 et seq.
5 Including any local or special Act and any provisions of the Harbours, Docks and Piers Clauses Act 1847: Civil Aviation Act 1982 s 87 (5) (b).
6 See ibid s 87 (4) and the Aircraft (Wreck and Salvage) Order 1938, SR & O 1938/136, having effect under the Civil Aviation Act 1982 s 87 (1) by virtue of s 105 (3).
7 Ibid s 91. As to jurisdiction see para 1657 et seq post.
8 See the Merchant Shipping (Safety Convention) Act 1949 s 22 (1), (3), (4), (6); and SHIPPING vol 43 para 330.
9 Merchant Shipping (Safety Convention) Act 1949 s 22 (1).

1502. Power under municipal law to make regulations for accident investigation. Power was given by the Civil Aviation Act 1982 to make regulations providing for the investigation of any accident[1] arising out of or in the course of air navigation, and either occurring in or over the United Kingdom or occurring elsewhere to aircraft registered in the United Kingdom[2], and for carrying out any Annex to the Chicago Convention[3].

If any person contravenes or fails to comply with any regulations made under this power he is liable, on summary conviction, to a fine not exceeding level 5 on the standard scale or to imprisonment for a term not exceeding three months[4].

1 The Civil Aviation Act 1982 provides that the regulations may define 'accident' so as to correspond to the meaning adopted for the time being in Annex 13 to the Chicago Convention (Civil Aviation Act 1982 s 75 (2) (a)) and adds, without prejudice, that it is to be construed in s 75 as including any fortuitous or unexpected event by which the safety of an aircraft or any person is threatened (s 75 (4)); see further para 1504 post.
2 Ibid s 75 (1) (a), (2), (3). As to the regulations made see paras 1506, 1507, 1526 post.
3 Ibid s 75 (1) (b). As to Annex 13 see para 1500 ante; as to the Chicago Convention see para 1002 ante.
4 Civil Aviation Act 1982 s 75 (5) (amended by virtue of the Criminal Justice Act 1982 s 46). As to the standard scale see para 1044 note 6 ante. At the date at which this volume states the law, level 5 on that scale is at £2,000. See also para 1503 post.
5 Civil Aviation Act 1982 s 75 (6); and see the Merchant Shipping Act 1894 ss 530–537.

1503. Proceedings relating to aircraft accidents. Summary proceedings for an offence under any Order in Council[1] or any regulations made by virtue of such an Order may be instituted at any time within 12 months from the commission of the offence if it was committed in connection with the flight[2] of an aircraft in the course of which an accident[3] occurred and not more than six months after the commission of the offence if either public notice has been given that an investigation is being carried out or a public inquiry has been directed to be held[4].

1 Ie an Order in Council under the Civil Aviation Act 1982 s 60.
2 For the purposes of accident investigation, the flight of an aircraft is deemed to include any period from the moment when power is applied for the purpose of take-off until the moment when the landing run (if any) at the termination of that flight ends: ibid s 61 (4).
3 For the meaning of 'accident' see paras 1502 note 1 ante, 1504 post.
4 Civil Aviation Act 1982 s 61 (3). See also the Civil Aviation (Investigation of Air Accidents) Regulations 1989, SI 1989/2062, regs 10, 18, and the Air Navigation (Investigation of Air Accidents Involving Civil and Military Aircraft or Installations) Regulations 1986/1953, regs 12, 17. The fact that a direction has been given on any date may be proved by producing a certificate to that effect purporting to be signed by an officer of the Secretary of State: Civil Aviation Act 1982 s 61 (5).

1504. Meaning of 'accident'. 'Accident' includes an incident and a reportable accident[1].

'Incident' means any fortuitous or unexpected event, not being a reportable accident, by which the safety of an aircraft or any person is threatened[2].

'Reportable accident' means an occurrence associated with the operation of an aircraft which takes place between the time when any person boards the aircraft with the intention of flight[3] and such time as all persons have disembarked therefrom, in which (1) any person suffers death or serious injury[4] while in or upon the aircraft or by direct contact with any part of the aircraft (including any part which has become detached from the aircraft) or by direct exposure to jet blast, except when the death or serious injury is from natural causes, is self inflicted or is inflicted by other persons[5] or when the death or serious injury is suffered by a stowaway[6] hiding outside the areas normally available in flight to the passengers and members of the crew of the aircraft, or (2) the aircraft incurs damage or structural failure (other than engine failure or damage limited to the engine, its

owling or accessories, or to propellers, wing tips, antennae, tyres, brakes, fair-
gs, small dents or punctured holes in the aircraft skin) which adversely affects its
ructural strength, performance[7] or flight characteristics and which would nor-
ally require major repair or replacement of the affected component, or (3) the
rcraft is missing or is completely inaccessible[8].

See the Civil Aviation (Investigation of Accidents) Regulations 1989, SI 1989/2062, reg 2 (1) and the
Air Navigation (Investigation of Air Accidents involving Civil and Military Aircraft or Instal-
lations) Regulations 1986, SI 1986/1953, reg 2 (1). As to the definition given in the Civil Aviation
Act 1982 see s 75; and para 1502 ante.
See the Civil Aviation (Investigation of Accidents) Regulations 1989 reg 2 (1) and the Air Navigation
(Investigation of Air Accidents involving Civil and Military Aircraft or Installations) Regulations
1986 reg 2 (1). As to incidents which come under the definition of 'reportable occurrences' and must
be reported to the Civil Aviation Authority (as to which see para 1044 ante) see para 1496 ante.
For the meaning of 'flight' for the purposes of accident investigation see para 1503 note 2 ante.
'Serious injury' means an injury which is sustained by a person in a reportable accident and which
requires his stay in hospital for more than 48 hours commencing within seven days from the date on
which the injury was received; or results in a fracture of any bone (save simple fractures of fingers,
toes or nose); or involves lacerations which cause nerve, muscle or tendon damage or severe
haemorrhage; or involves injury to any internal organ; or involves second or third degree burns or
any burns affecting more than 5 per cent of the body surface; or involves exposure to infectious
substances or injurious radiation: Civil Aviation (Investigation of Accidents) Regulations 1989 reg 2
(1); Air Navigation (Investigation of Air Accidents involving Civil and Military Aircraft or
Installations) Regulations 1986 reg 2 (1).
As to crimes committed on board aircraft see para 1662 et seq post.
As to stowaways see para 1458 ante.
As to aircraft performance requirements see para 1430 et seq ante.
See the Civil Aviation (Investigation of Accidents) Regulations 1989 reg 2 (1) and the Air Navigation
(Investigation of Air Accidents involving Civil and Military Aircraft or Installations) Regulations
1986 reg 2 (1).

505. Purpose of accident investigation. The fundamental purpose of investi-
ating accidents[1] is to determine the circumstances and causes of an accident with a
ew to the preservation of life and the avoidance of accidents in the future; it is not
e purpose to apportion blame or liability[2].

For the meaning of 'accident' see para 1504 ante.
Civil Aviation (Investigation of Air Accidents) Regulations 1989, SI 1989/2062, reg 4; Air Navi-
gation (Investigation of Air Accidents involving Civil and Military Aircraft or Installations)
Regulations 1986, SI 1986/1953, reg 4.

(2) ACCIDENT INVESTIGATION

506. Regulations as to civil aviation accidents. The Civil Aviation (Investi-
ation of Air Accidents) Regulations[1] relate only to civil aviation and apply to
ccidents arising out of or in the course of air navigation which occur to civil
rcraft in or over the United Kingdom, or elsewhere to civil aircraft registered in
e United Kingdom[2] or elsewhere to aircraft registered outside the United King-
om for the purpose of obtaining information[3]. They do not apply to accidents to
hich the Air Navigation (Investigation of Air Accidents involving Civil and
ilitary Aircraft or Installations) Regulations[4] apply[5].
However, the two sets of regulations create very similar systems, and in the
suing paragraphs are treated so far as possible together.

The Civil Aviation (Investigation of Air Accidents) Regulations 1989, SI 1989/2062 and the Air
Navigation (Investigation of Air Accidents involving Civil and Military Aircraft or Installations)

Regulations 1986, SI 1986/1953, were made under the Civil Aviation Act 1982 s 75 and are t
successors of regulations themselves the result of the Report of the Committee on Civil Aircr.
Accidents Investigation and Licence Control, CAP 169 (1961). The committee was known as t
Cairns Committee after its chairman, Mr David Cairns QC.
2 Civil Aviation (Investigation of Air Accidents) Regulations 1989 reg 3 (a), (b).
3 Ibid reg 3 (c); and see reg 21 (3) and para 1508 post.
4 For the accidents to which the Air Navigation (Investigation of Air Accidents involving Civil a
   Military Aircraft or Installations) Regulations 1986 apply see para 1507 post.
5 Civil Aviation (Investigation of Air Accidents) Regulations 1989 reg 3.

1507. Regulations as to combined military and civil air accidents. The A
Navigation (Investigation of Air Accidents involving Civil and Military Aircra
or Installations) Regulations[1] apply where military and civil aircraft are involve
together in an accident or where an accident occurs to either a military or a civ
aircraft in circumstances touching both the military and the civil authorities.

Where a military aircraft[2] is involved in an accident arising out of or in the cour
of air navigation occurring in or over the United Kingdom or, if the aircra
belongs to Her Majesty, occurring anywhere, and both the Secretary of State f
Transport and the Secretary of State for Defence[3] are of the opinion that tl
accident was due to a collision with a civil aircraft, or that the accident took place c
a civil aerodrome, or that the accident took place in circumstances in which tl
Secretary of State for Transport was or might be concerned or interested, tl
Secretaries of State may direct that the accident be investigated under these reg
lations[4].

Similarly, where a civil aircraft is involved in an accident arising out of or in tl
course of air navigation and occurring in or over the United Kingdom or, if tl
aircraft is registered in the United Kingdom or belongs to Her Majesty, occurrir
anywhere, and the Secretaries of State are of the opinion that the accident was di
to a collision with a military aircraft, or that the accident took place on a milita
aerodrome or that the accident took place in circumstances in which the Secreta
of State for Defence or the military authorities were or might be concerned
interested and that the accident ought to be investigated under these regulation
the Secretary of State for Transport may direct, either alone or jointly with tl
Secretary of State for Defence, that the accident be investigated under the
regulations[5].

1 SI 1986/1953: see para 1506 note 1 ante.
2 An aircraft is treated for the purpose of the Air Navigation (Investigation of Air Accidents involvi
   Civil and Military Aircraft or Installations) Regulations 1986 as being a military aircraft if, but on
   if, it was at the relevant time an aircraft belonging to any of Her Majesty's forces or any of the forc
   of any country or if the Secretary of State for Defence certifies that by reason of circumstanc
   affecting the aircraft it ought to be so treated: reg 2 (5).
3 As to the Secretaries of State see paras 1032, 1040 ante.
4 Air Navigation (Investigation of Air Accidents involving Civil and Military Aircraft or Inst.
   lations) Regulations 1986 reg 3 (1).
5 Ibid reg 3 (2).

1508. Foreign aircraft. Where an accident has occurred in or over the Unit
Kingdom to a foreign-registered aircraft, the Secretary of State[1] may authorise
investigator duly appointed in that foreign country to carry out an investigation
the United Kingdom and must, so far as possible, facilitate his inquiry[2].

In any inspector's investigation[3] or public inquiry[4], an accredited representati
of the country in which an aircraft is registered or in which it was manufactured

which has furnished information in connection with the accident may take part in the investigation or inquiry: he is permitted to visit the scene of the accident, examine the wreckage, question witnesses, receive copies of all pertinent documents (saving all just exceptions), have access to all relevant evidence, make submissions and be accompanied by technical and other advisers[5].

1 As to the Secretary of State see para 1032 ante.
2 Civil Aviation (Investigation of Air Accidents) Regulations 1989, SI 1989/2062, reg 21 (1); Air Navigation (Investigation of Air Accidents involving Civil and Military Aircraft or Installations) Regulations 1986, SI 1986/1953, reg 20 (1).
3 See para 1513 post.
4 See para 1521 et seq ante.
5 Civil Aviation (Investigation of Air Accidents) Regulations 1989 reg 21 (2); Air Navigation (Investigation of Air Accidents involving Civil and Military Aircraft or Installations) Regulations 1986 reg 20 (2).

1509. Foreign aircraft: accident outside United Kingdom. Where an accident has occurred outside the United Kingdom to a foreign civil aircraft the chief inspector[1] may be asked by the duly competent authority to obtain information relevant to the investigation[2] of the accident; he may thus take the same measures as if the accident had taken place in the United Kingdom[3].

1 As to the chief inspector see para 1510 note 5 post.
2 As to the investigation see para 1512 et seq post.
3 Civil Aviation (Investigation of Air Accidents) Regulations 1989, SI 1989/2062, reg 21 (3).

1510. Notification and furnishing of information. Where a reportable accident[1] occurs, the commander[2] or, if he be killed or incapacitated, then the operator[3] and the aerodrome authority[4] where the accident occurred on or close to an aerodrome, must forthwith give notice, by the quickest means of communication available, to the chief inspector[5] and, where the accident occurs in or over the United Kingdom, must also notify the local police[6]. The owner, operator, commander or hirer of the aircraft involved may be required to provide further information[7].

The chief inspector may at any time publish, or have published, information relating to an accident, whether or not it is the subject of an investigation, of a review board or of a public inquiry[8].

1 For the meaning of 'accident' see para 1504 ante.
2 'Commander' in relation to an aircraft means a member of the crew designated as commander of that aircraft by the operator thereof, or failing such a person, the person who is for the time being the pilot in command of the aircraft: Civil Aviation (Investigation of Air Accidents) Regulations 1989, SI 1989/2062, reg 2 (1); Air Navigation (Investigation of Air Accidents involving Civil and Military Aircraft or Installations) Regulations 1986, SI 1986/1953, reg 2 (1) (in relation to a military aircraft, 'commander' means also the person who is for the time being in command of that aircraft).
3 'Operator' means the person for the time being having the management of the aircraft: Civil Aviation (Investigation of Air Accidents) Regulations 1989 reg 2 (1); Air Navigation (Investigation of Air Accidents involving Civil and Military Aircraft or Installations) Regulations 1986 reg 2 (1).
4 'Aerodrome authority' means in relation to any civil aerodrome the person for the time being having the management of the aerodrome: Civil Aviation (Investigation of Air Accidents) Regulations 1989 reg 2 (1); Air Navigation (Investigation of Air Accidents involving Civil and Military Aircraft or Installations) Regulations 1986 reg 2 (1).
5 'Chief inspector' means the Chief Inspector of Air Accidents appointed under the Civil Aviation (Investigation of Air Accidents) Regulations 1989 reg 8 (1) and includes any deputy chief inspector:

reg 2 (1); Air Navigation (Investigation of Air Accidents involving Civil and Military Aircraft or Installations) Regulations 1986 reg 2 (1).

6 Civil Aviation (Investigation of Air Accidents) Regulations 1989 reg 5 (1); Air Navigation (Investigation of Air Accidents involving Civil and Military Aircraft or Installations) Regulations 1986 reg 5 (1). The notice to the chief inspector must state the identifying abbreviation ACCID; the aircraft's type, model, nationality and registration marks; its last point of departure, position, latitude and longitude, and its next point of intended landing; the names of its owner, operator, hirer (if any) and commander; the date and Coordinated Universal Time of the accident; the numbers of crew members and passengers on board, persons killed, persons seriously injured, and persons killed or seriously injured elsewhere than in the aircraft; the nature of the accident; and brief particulars of the damage to the aircraft: Civil Aviation (Investigation of Air Accidents) Regulations 1989 reg 5 (2); Air Navigation (Investigation of Air Accidents involving Civil and Military Aircraft or Installations) Regulations 1986 reg 5 (2). For the penalty for contravention see para 1502 ante.

7 Civil Aviation (Investigation of Air Accidents) Regulations 1989 reg 5 (3); Air Navigation (Investigation of Air Accidents involving Civil and Military Aircraft or Installations) Regulations 1986 reg 5 (3).

8 Civil Aviation (Investigation of Air Accidents) Regulations 1989 reg 6; Air Navigation (Investigation of Air Accidents involving Civil and Military Aircraft or Installations) Regulations 1986 reg 6. As to investigations see para 1512 et seq post; as to the review board see para 1516 et seq post; as to public inquiries see para 1521 et seq post.

1511. Removal of damaged aircraft. Where a reportable accident[1] occurs in or over the United Kingdom, no person other than an authorised person[2] may have access to the aircraft, which must not be removed or otherwise interfered with except under the authority of the Secretary of State for Transport or the Secretary of State for Defence, as the case may be, unless this is necessary for extricating persons or animals, removing mails, valuables or dangerous goods or preventing destruction, danger or obstruction; other property may be removed from the aircraft if supervised by an inspector of accidents or a constable[3]. Where the aircraft is wrecked on the water, the aircraft or its contents may be moved to a place of safety[4]. A military aircraft may be moved or interfered with in order to save life or to remove any immediate hazard to human life[5].

1 As to the notification of accidents see para 1510 ante. For the meaning of 'accident' see para 1504 ante.

2 'Authorised person' means any person authorised by the Secretary of State for Transport or, in the case of combined military and civil air accidents by the Secretary of State for Defence, either generally or specially to have access to any aircraft involved in an accident, and includes any constable or customs and excise officer: Civil Aviation (Investigation of Air Accidents) Regulations 1989, SI 1989/2062, reg 7 (2); Air Navigation (Investigation of Air Accidents involving Civil and Military Aircraft or Installations) Regulations 1986, SI 1986/1953, reg 7 (2).

3 Civil Aviation (Investigation of Air Accidents) Regulations 1989 reg 7 (1) proviso (i); Air Navigation (Investigation of Air Accidents involving Civil and Military Aircraft or Installations) Regulations 1986 reg 7 (1) proviso (i). For the penalty for contravention see para 1502 ante.

4 Civil Aviation (Investigation of Air Accidents) Regulations 1989 reg 7 (1) proviso (ii); Air Navigation (Investigation of Air Accidents involving Civil and Military Aircraft or Installations) Regulations 1986 reg 7 (1) proviso (iii).

5 Ibid reg 7 (1) proviso (ii).

(3) INSPECTORS' INVESTIGATIONS

(i) Investigation

1512. Inspectors of accidents. For the purpose of investigating the circumstances and causes of accidents, the Secretary of State[1] must appoint persons as inspectors of air accidents, one of whom must be appointed as Chief Inspector of Air Accidents[2]. The chief inspector must determine whether or not an investigation is to be carried out[3]. The chief inspector, if he thinks fit, may himself carry out, or cause an inspector to carry out, an investigation of any accident to which the relevant regulations apply[4]. The inspector may seek such advice or assistance as he deems necessary and further assistance may be given by persons appointed for that purpose by the Secretary of State at the request of the chief inspector[5].

An inspector has power by summons to examine and require answers or information from persons, who may have to produce books and articles which he may retain, to take statements under oath, to have access to and examine any aircraft involved in the accident, requiring that it be preserved unaltered, and the place where it occurred, to remove and test the aircraft or any parts of it or any other aircraft if need be, to enter and inspect any place or building which he may consider necessary for the purposes of the investigation, and to take measures for the preservation of evidence[6].

An investigation into any accident is either a formal investigation or a field investigation[7].

1 As to the Secretary of State see para 1032 ante.
2 Civil Aviation (Investigation of Air Accidents) Regulations 1989, SI 1989/2062, reg 8 (1). See also the Air Navigation (Investigation of Air Accidents involving Civil and Military Aircraft or Installations) Regulations 1986, SI 1986/1953, reg 2 (1) (meaning of 'inspector' and 'chief inspector').
3 Civil Aviation (Investigation of Air Accidents) Regulations 1989 reg 8 (2); Air Navigation (Investigation of Air Accidents involving Civil and Military Aircraft or Installations) Regulations 1986 reg 8 (1).
4 Civil Aviation (Investigation of Air Accidents) Regulations 1989 reg 8 (2); Air Navigation (Investigation of Air Accidents involving Civil and Military Aircraft or Installations) Regulations 1986 reg 8 (1).
5 Civil Aviation (Investigation of Air Accidents) Regulations 1989 reg 8 (3); Air Navigation (Investigation of Air Accidents involving Civil and Military Aircraft or Installations) Regulations 1986 reg 8 (2).
6 Civil Aviation (Investigation of Air Accidents) Regulations 1989 reg 9; Air Navigation (Investigation of Air Accidents involving Civil and Military Aircraft or Installations) Regulations 1986 reg 9.
7 Civil Aviation (Investigation of Air Accidents) Regulations 1989 reg 10 (1). As to the distinction between formal investigation and field investigation see para 1513 et seq post.

1513. Formal investigation. The chief inspector[1] must give public notice, in such manner as he thinks fit, that formal[2] investigation is taking place, inviting persons who desire to make representations concerning the circumstances or cause of the accident to do so in writing within a specified time[3]. The investigation is held in private[4]. In the course of the investigation, the inspector may permit a person (whose expenses may be paid[5]) to appear before him[6] and he can determine that any investigation shall be discontinued[7], in which case no report[8] is made to the Secretary of State but information may be submitted to the Civil Aviation Authority (CAA)[9] in the interest of the avoidance of accidents in the future[10].

1 As to the chief inspector see paras 1510 note 5, 1512 ante.
2 A 'formal investigation' means an investigation which is intended to be the subject of a report by an inspector to the Secretary of State: Civil Aviation (Investigation of Air Accidents) Regulations 1989, SI 1989/2062, reg 2 (1). As to the Secretary of State see para 1032 ante. As to reports see para 1515 post.

3 Ibid reg 10 (2); Air Navigation (Investigation of Air Accidents involving Civil and Military Aircraft or Installations) Regulations 1986, SI 1986/1953, reg 10 (1).
4 Civil Aviation (Investigation of Air Accidents) Regulations 1989 reg 10 (3); Air Navigation (Investigation of Air Accidents involving Civil and Military Aircraft or Installations) Regulations 1986 reg 10 (2).
5 Persons summoned as witnesses are allowed such expenses as determined by the Secretary of State with the approval of the Treasury: Civil Aviation (Investigation of Air Accidents) Regulations 1989 reg 10 (5); Air Navigation (Investigation of Air Accidents involving Civil and Military Aircraft or Installations) Regulations 1986 reg 10 (4).
6 Civil Aviation (Investigation of Air Accidents) Regulations 1989 reg 10 (4); Air Navigation (Investigation of Air Accidents involving Civil and Military Aircraft or Installations) Regulations 1986 reg 10 (3).
7 Civil Aviation (Investigation of Air Accidents) Regulations 1989 reg 10 (6); Air Navigation (Investigation of Air Accidents involving Civil and Military Aircraft or Installations) Regulations 1986 reg 10 (5).
8 As to reports, whether made to the Secretary of State for Transport alone or jointly with the Secretary of State for Defence see para 1515 post.
9 As to the CAA see para 1044 ante.
10 Civil Aviation (Investigation of Air Accidents) Regulations 1989 reg 10 (7).

1514. Field investigation. A field investigation means an investigation which is not intended to be the subject of a report by the inspector to the Secretary of State[1].

Most provisions relating to a formal investigation[2] apply to a field investigation save that no public notice need be given that an investigation is to take place[3].

Where the investigation is discontinued, no public notice need be given[4], but the inspector must submit to the Civil Aviation Authority (CAA)[5] such information as he considers desirable in the interest of the avoidance of accidents in the future[6].

No provision for field investigation was made in the Air Navigation (Investigation of Air Accidents involving Civil and Military Aircraft or Installations) Regulations 1986[7].

1 Civil Aviation (Investigation of Air Accidents) Regulations 1989, SI 1989/2062, reg 2 (1). As to the Secretary of State see para 1032 ante. As to reports to the Secretary of State see para 1515 post.
2 See para 1513 ante.
3 See the Civil Aviation (Investigation of Air Accidents) Regulations 1989 reg 10 (2).
4 See ibid reg 10 (6); and para 1513 ante.
5 As to the CAA see para 1044 ante.
6 See the Civil Aviation (Investigation of Air Accidents) Regulations 1989 reg 11 (2).
7 SI 1986/1953.

1515. Reports. When the inspector has completed his investigation and before the chief inspector[1] submits the inspector's report to the Secretary of State[2], the inspector must notify the operator[3], commander[4] and any other person whose reputation is, in the inspector's opinion, likely to be adversely affected by the report[5] and must consider any representations which may be made to him by or on behalf of such notified persons[6]. Any such person must be served with a copy of the report[7].

The report to the Secretary of State must state the circumstances of the accident and conclusions as to the cause, together with any observations and recommendations made with a view to the preservation of life and avoidance of similar accidents in the future[8].

No person may disclose or permit to be disclosed any information contained in a notice or in a report which has been served upon him without the prior consent in writing of the chief inspector[9].

In the case of an investigation into a combined military and civil air accident a report must be made to the Secretaries of State[10] and, if in the inspector's opinion or that of the chief inspector, the investigation has been completed but for the investigation of matters affecting the discipline or internal administration of Her Majesty's forces or those of any foreign country, which are more appropriate for investigation by some other person or body, the investigation may be regarded as completed but for such matters being specifically mentioned in the report[11].

1 As to the chief inspector see paras 1510 note 5, 1512 ante.
2 As to the Secretary of State see para 1032 ante.
3 For the meaning of 'operator' see para 1510 note 3 ante.
4 For the meaning of 'commander' see para 1510 note 2 ante.
5 Civil Aviation (Investigation of Air Accidents) Regulations 1989, SI 1989/2062, reg 12 (1) (a); Air Navigation (Investigation of Air Accidents involving Civil and Military Aircraft or Installations) Regulations 1986, SI 1986/1953, reg 11 (1) (a) (the notice must be served on the Secretary of State for Defence in the case of a combined civil and military air accident). If the operator or commander or any person whose reputation may be adversely affected by the report is deceased, the inspector serves the notice on such person as appears to him to represent best the interest of the deceased in the matter: Civil Aviation (Investigation of Air Accidents) Regulations 1989 reg 12 (1) (a); Air Navigation (Investigation of Air Accidents involving Civil and Military Aircraft or Installations) Regulations 1986 reg 11 (1) (a). The notice must include particulars of any of the proposed analysis of facts and conclusions as to the causes of the accident which may affect the relevant person: Civil Aviation (Investigation of Air Accidents) Regulations 1989 reg 12 (2); Air Navigation (Investigation of Air Accidents involving Civil and Military Aircraft or Installations) Regulations 1986 reg 11 (2).
6 Civil Aviation (Investigation of Air Accidents) Regulations 1989 reg 12 (1) (b); Air Navigation (Investigation of Air Accidents involving Civil and Military Aircraft or Installations) Regulations 1986 reg 11 (1) (b). The representations must be in writing and must be served on the inspector within 28 days of the service of the notice: Civil Aviation (Investigation of Air Accidents) Regulations 1989 reg 12 (3); Air Navigation (Investigation of Air Accidents involving Civil and Military Aircraft or Installations) Regulations 1986 reg 11 (3). As to the extension of time see the Civil Aviation (Investigation of Air Accidents) Regulations 1989 reg 22 and the Air Navigation (Investigation of Air Accidents involving Civil and Military Aircraft or Installations) Regulations 1986 reg 21.
7 Civil Aviation (Investigation of Air Accidents) Regulations 1989 reg 12 (4); Air Navigation (Investigation of Air Accidents involving Civil and Military Aircraft or Installations) Regulations 1986 reg 11 (4).
8 Civil Aviation (Investigation of Air Accidents) Regulations 1989 reg 11 (1), (3); Air Navigation (Investigation of Air Accidents involving Civil and Military Aircraft or Installations) Regulations 1986 reg 10 (6), (7).
9 Civil Aviation (Investigation of Air Accidents) Regulations 1989 reg 12 (5).
10 As to the Secretaries of State see paras 1032, 1040 ante.
11 Air Navigation (Investigation of Air Accidents involving Civil and Military Aircraft or Installations) Regulations 1986 reg 10 (8).

(ii) Review

1516. Notice of review. A person notified[1] that his reputation is likely to be adversely affected by the report on an air accident[2] may, before the expiration of 21 days from the day on which he has been served with a copy of the inspector's report, serve on the Secretary of State for Transport[3] a notice of review[4] indicating that he wishes the findings and conclusions which appear to adversely affect his reputation to be reviewed by a review board[5] consisting of a person appointed by the Lord Chancellor, sitting with such technical advisers, if any, as may be so appointed[6]. In the case of a deceased person, notice may be given by his personal representative[7].

1 As to such notification, which includes the Secretary of State for Defence, see para 1515 ante.

2 As to the report see para 1515 ante.
3 As to the Secretary of State see para 1032 ante.
4 The notice must specify the findings and conclusions to be reviewed, state concisely the grounds on which they are challenged and the reasons why they may affect the reputation of the person requesting the review. Copies of it and of any representations made must be served on each of the persons on whom the inspector served notice of his proposed findings (see para 1513 ante) and on the Treasury Solicitor, who must be informed whether the person requesting the review proposes to be represented, with the name of his solicitor or other representative: Civil Aviation (Investigation of Air Accidents) Regulations 1989, SI 1989/2062, reg 13 (2)–(4); Air Navigation (Investigation of Air Accidents involving Civil and Military Aircraft or Installations) Regulations 1986, SI 1986/1953, reg 12 (2)–(4).
5 Civil Aviation (Investigation of Air Accidents) Regulations 1989 reg 13 (1); Air Navigation (Investigation of Air Accidents involving Civil and Military Aircraft or Installations) Regulations 1986 reg 12 (1).
6 Civil Aviation (Investigation of Air Accidents) Regulations 1989 reg 14 (1); Air Navigation (Investigation of Air Accidents involving Civil and Military Aircraft or Installations) Regulations 1986 reg 13 (1).
7 See the Civil Aviation (Investigation of Air Accidents) Regulations 1989 regs 12 (1), 13 (1); and the Air Navigation (Investigation of Air Accidents involving Civil and Military Aircraft or Installations) Regulations 1986 regs 11 (1), 12 (1).

1517. Preliminary meeting of review board. The Treasury Solicitor must give 21 days' notice of the date, time and place of the preliminary meeting to the person requesting the review and all persons on whom a copy of the notice of review[1] had been served[2]. Any person wishing to make any application to the board at the meeting must notify the Treasury Solicitor[3]. The meeting is held in public unless otherwise determined by the board in the interests of justice or in the public interest[4]. Applications for leave to appear, to give evidence, produce witnesses and examine witnesses by persons who may be affected by the review may be made at the preliminary meeting[5]. The board must listen to any representation as to whether the review should be proceeded with[6]: it may decide at any time thereafter that the findings and conclusions of the inspector's report do not adversely affect the reputation of the person requesting the review and thus not to proceed with the review in respect of those findings and conclusions[7].

Where the board decides to proceed with the review, the Treasury Solicitor must serve on all relevant persons 21 days' notice of the date, time and place of the hearing of the review[8].

1 As to the notice of review see para 1516 ante.
2 Civil Aviation (Investigation of Air Accidents) Regulations 1989, SI 1989/2062, reg 14 (2); Air Navigation (Investigation of Air Accidents involving Civil and Military Aircraft or Installations) Regulations 1986, SI 1986/1953, reg 13 (2). As to the Treasury Solicitor see CONSTITUTIONAL LAW.
3 See note 2 supra.
4 Civil Aviation (Investigation of Air Accidents) Regulations 1989 reg 14 (3).
5 Ibid reg 15 (2); Air Navigation (Investigation of Air Accidents involving Civil and Military Aircraft or Installations) Regulations 1986 reg 14 (2).
6 Civil Aviation (Investigation of Air Accidents) Regulations 1989 reg 14 (5).
7 Ibid reg 14 (4).
8 Ibid reg 14 (6); Air Navigation (Investigation of Air Accidents involving Civil and Military Aircraft or Installations) Regulations 1986 reg 13 (3). As to the hearing see para 1518 post.

1518. Proceedings of review board. The review board has all the powers of an inspector[1]. The hearing is held in public unless otherwise determined by the board in the interests of justice or in the public interest[2]. The Treasury Solicitor assists the review board, presents any evidence before it and may examine witnesses; the chief inspector[3] gives the board such assistance as is in his power[4]. The review board hears representations from the person requesting the review, who has the right to appear in person or by representative, to produce witnesses and to examine any other witnesses giving evidence at the review[5]. The inspector who made the report is entitled to be heard[6] as well as any person who may be affected by the review and who was granted leave to appear[7].

The proceedings start with the hearing of the person who requested the hearing and the production and examination of witnesses on his behalf, followed by the hearing of the other persons appearing before it[8]. Where new and important evidence is given, the chief inspector may apply to the board to discontinue the review and must then cause the investigation to be re-opened[9]. Where the board is satisfied at any time that any of the findings and conclusions of the inspector's report do not adversely affect the reputation of the person who required the review, it may discontinue such a review in respect of those findings and conclusions[10].

On completion of the review, the board reports to the Secretary of State, giving a summary of the proceedings at the hearing and either confirming or rejecting in whole or in part those findings and conclusions of the inspector which were the subject of the review, together with its reasons therefor, and the Secretary of State serves a copy of the report on all persons who appeared or were represented before the board[11].

1 Civil Aviation (Investigation of Air Accidents) Regulations 1989, SI 1989/2062, reg 15 (5); Air Navigation (Investigation of Air Accidents involving Civil and Military Aircraft or Installations) Regulations 1986, SI 1986/1953, reg 14 (4). The board has also the power to administer an oath or require a solemn affirmation from a witness: Civil Aviation (Investigation of Air Accidents) Regulations 1989 reg 15 (5); Air Navigation (Investigation of Air Accidents involving Civil and Military Aircraft or Installations) Regulations 1986 reg 14 (4). As to the powers of an inspector see para 1512 ante.
2 Civil Aviation (Investigation of Air Accidents) Regulations 1989 reg 14 (7); Air Navigation (Investigation of Air Accidents involving Civil and Military Aircraft or Installations) Regulations 1986 reg 13 (4).
3 As to the chief inspector see paras 1510 note 5, 1512 ante.
4 Civil Aviation (Investigation of Air Accidents) Regulations 1989 reg 14 (8); Air Navigation (Investigation of Air Accidents involving Civil and Military Aircraft or Installations) Regulations 1986 reg 13 (5).
5 Civil Aviation (Investigation of Air Accidents) Regulations 1989 reg 15 (1), (3); Air Navigation (Investigation of Air Accidents involving Civil and Military Aircraft or Installations) Regulations 1986 reg 14 (1), (3).
6 Civil Aviation (Investigation of Air Accidents) Regulations 1989 reg 15 (1); Air Navigation (Investigation of Air Accidents involving Civil and Military Aircraft or Installations) Regulations 1986 reg 14 (1).
7 Civil Aviation (Investigation of Air Accidents) Regulations 1989 reg 15 (2); Air Navigation (Investigation of Air Accidents involving Civil and Military Aircraft or Installations) Regulations 1986 reg 14 (2). As to leave to appear, to give evidence and to examine witnesses see para 1517 ante.
8 Civil Aviation (Investigation of Air Accidents) Regulations 1989 reg 15 (4). As to witnesses' expenses, they are determined by the Secretary of State for Transport, with the approval of the Treasury where the witness was summoned by the review board: reg 15 (7); Air Navigation (Investigation of Air Accidents involving Civil and Military Aircraft or Installations) Regulations 1986 reg 14 (6). As to the costs of the review board, they are specified by order of the board and payable by any person appearing or represented at the hearing: see the Civil Aviation (Investigation of Air Accidents) Regulations 1989 reg 15 (8) and the Air Navigation (Investigation of Air Accidents involving Civil and Military Aircraft or Installations) Regulations 1986 reg 14 (7).
9 Civil Aviation (Investigation of Air Accidents) Regulations 1989 reg 15 (6) (a); Air Navigation (Investigation of Air Accidents involving Civil and Military Aircraft or Installations) Regulations 1986 reg 14 (5) (a). As to investigations see para 1512 et seq ante.

10 Civil Aviation (Investigation of Air Accidents) Regulations 1989 reg 15 (6) (b); Air Navigation
   (Investigation of Air Accidents involving Civil and Military Aircraft or Installations) Regulations
   1986 reg 14 (5) (b). As to the case were a review is totally discontinued see note 11 infra.
11 Civil Aviation (Investigation of Air Accidents) Regulations 1989 reg 15 (9); Air Navigation
   (Investigation of Air Accidents involving Civil and Military Aircraft or Installations) Regulations
   1986 reg 14 (8). Where a review is totally discontinued, no report is made: Civil Aviation (Investigation of Air Accidents) Regulations 1989 reg 15 (6) (c); Air Navigation (Investigation of Air
   Accidents involving Civil and Military Aircraft or Installations) Regulations 1986 reg 14 (5) (c).

1519. Publication of reports. Unless there are good reasons to the contrary, the
Secretary of State[1] alone, or jointly with the Secretary of State for Defence as the
case may be[2], causes the inspector's report[3], and, where a review board has been
held, the review board's report[4], to be made public wholly or in part, although the
inspector's report will not be published before the expiry of the time for serving a
notice of review[5] or, if a review board is held, until the completion of the review[6].

1 As to the Secretary of State see para 1032 ante.
2 See para 1507 ante.
3 As to the inspector's report see para 1515 ante.
4 As to the review board's report see para 1518 ante.
5 As to notice of review see para 1516 ante.
6 Civil Aviation (Investigation of Air Accidents) Regulations 1989, SI 1989/2062, reg 16; Air Navigation (Investigation of Air Accidents involving Civil and Military Aircraft or Installations)
  Regulations 1986, SI 1986/1953, reg 15.

1520. Reopening of investigations or reviews. The chief inspector[1] may cause
an inspector's formal investigation[2] which has not been the subject of a review to be
reopened, and the Secretary of State, alone or jointly with the Secretary of State for
Defence as the case may be[3], may direct a review to be reheard or a review for
which a decision not to proceed had been taken to be heard; and the chief inspector
or Secretary of State, as the case may be, must do so if new and important evidence
has been discovered after the completion of the investigation or the completion of
curtailment of the investigation or if for any other reason there is ground for
suspecting that a miscarriage of justice has occurred[4]. Any investigation reopened
or review reheard is subject to the provisions of the regulations relating to an
investigation or review, as the case may be[5].

1 As to the chief inspector see paras 1510 note 5, 1512 ante.
2 For the meaning of a 'formal investigation' see para 1513 ante.
3 See para 1507 ante.
4 Civil Aviation (Investigation of Air Accidents) Regulations 1989, SI 1989/2062, reg 17 (1); Air
  Navigation (Investigation of Air Accidents involving Civil and Military Aircraft or Installations)
  Regulations 1986, SI 1986/1953, reg 16 (1). The Lord Chancellor may direct any rehearing to be
  before the original review board or some other review board appointed by him for the rehearing:
  Civil Aviation (Investigation of Air Accidents) Regulations 1989 reg 17 (2); Air Navigation
  (Investigation of Air Accidents involving Civil and Military Aircraft or Installations) Regulations
  1986 reg 16 (2).
5 Civil Aviation (Investigation of Air Accidents) Regulations 1989 reg 17 (3); Air Navigation
  (Investigation of Air Accidents involving Civil and Military Aircraft or Installations) Regulations
  1986 reg 16 (3).

(iii) Public Inquiry

1521. Preliminaries to holding of public inquiry. Where it appears to the
Secretary of State[1], alone or jointly with the Secretary of State for Defence as the

case may be[2], that it is expedient in the public interest to hold a public inquiry into the circumstances and causes of an accident or into any matter furthering the avoidance of such accidents in the future, he may direct a public inquiry to be held in accordance with the procedure set out in the regulations; any inspector's investigation is discontinued forthwith save for rendering assistance to the court and the Attorney General[3]. The regulations provide for the appointment by the Lord Chancellor of a judge or a barrister of not less than ten years' standing to act as commissioner, called 'the court', assisted by not fewer than two assessors, appointed by the Lord Chancellor, possessing aeronautical, engineering or other special skills or knowledge[4]. The case is remitted by the Secretary of State to the Attorney General, and is prepared and presented by the Treasury Solicitor under the Attorney General's direction with the assistance of the Chief Inspector of Accidents[5].

The Attorney General causes a notice of the date, time and place and the nature of the public inquiry to be served on all interested persons[6]. Any other person may by leave of the court appear and thus become a party to the proceedings[7].

At any time before the public inquiry, the court may hold a preliminary meeting at which directions may be given and preliminary or interlocutory orders as to the procedure made[8], as well as applications for leave to appear at the hearing[9].

1 As to the Secretary of State see para 1032 ante.
2 See para 1507 ante.
3 Civil Aviation (Investigation of Air Accidents) Regulations 1989, SI 1989/2062, reg 18 (1); Air Navigation (Investigation of Air Accidents involving Civil and Military Aircraft or Installations) Regulations 1986, SI 1986/1953, reg 17 (1).
4 Civil Aviation (Investigation of Air Accidents) Regulations 1989 reg 18 (2); Air Navigation (Investigation of Air Accidents involving Civil and Military Aircraft or Installations) Regulations 1986 reg 17 (2).
5 Civil Aviation (Investigation of Air Accidents) Regulations 1989 reg 18 (3); Air Navigation (Investigation of Air Accidents involving Civil and Military Aircraft or Installations) Regulations 1986 reg 17 (3). As to the chief inspector see paras 1510 note 5, 1512 ante.
6 Civil Aviation (Investigation of Air Accidents) Regulations 1989 reg 18 (4); Air Navigation (Investigation of Air Accidents involving Civil and Military Aircraft or Installations) Regulations 1986 reg 17 (4). These persons are the owner, operator, hirer and commander of the aircraft and any other person who in the Attorney General's opinion ought to be served, and those persons, and the Attorney General, are deemed to be parties to the proceedings: Civil Aviation (Investigation of Air Accidents) Regulations 1989 reg 18 (4), (5); Air Navigation (Investigation of Air Accidents involving Civil and Military Aircraft or Installations) Regulations 1986 reg 17 (4), (5). For the meanings of 'commander' and 'operator' see para 1510 notes 2, 3 ante.
7 Civil Aviation (Investigation of Air Accidents) Regulations 1989 reg 18 (6); Air Navigation (Investigation of Air Accidents involving Civil and Military Aircraft or Installations) Regulations 1986 reg 17 (6).
8 Civil Aviation (Investigation of Air Accidents) Regulations 1989 reg 18 (7); Air Navigation (Investigation of Air Accidents involving Civil and Military Aircraft or Installations) Regulations 1986 reg 17 (7). Notice of the date, time and place of the preliminary meeting is given by the Treasury Solicitor to all parties and to those persons who have notified the Treasury Solicitor of their wish to apply for leave to appear.
9 Civil Aviation (Investigation of Air Accidents) Regulations 1989 reg 18 (6); Air Navigation (Investigation of Air Accidents involving Civil and Military Aircraft or Installations) Regulations 1986 reg 17 (6).

1522. Holding of public inquiry. For the purposes of the inquiry, the court has all the powers of a magistrate's court[1]. It may enter and inspect any place, building or aircraft as appears requisite to the court, summon witnesses to give evidence and produce books, papers and other documents and administer oaths[2].

At the time and place appointed, the court may proceed with the inquiry whether or not the parties are present[3]. The inquiry is held in public court save where the interests of justice or the public interest otherwise warrant[4].

1 Civil Aviation (Investigation of Air Accidents) Regulations 1989, SI 1989/2062, reg 18 (8); Air Navigation (Investigation of Air Accidents involving Civil and Military Aircraft or Installations) Regulations 1986, SI 1986/1953, reg 17 (8). As to the court see para 1521 ante.
2 Civil Aviation (Investigation of Air Accidents) Regulations 1989 reg 18 (8) (a)–(c); Air Navigation (Investigation of Air Accidents involving Civil and Military Aircraft or Installations) Regulations 1986 reg 17 (8) (a)–(c). The assessors have the same powers of entry and inspection as the court: Civil Aviation (Investigation of Air Accidents) Regulations 1989 reg 18 (8); Air Navigation (Investigation of Air Accidents involving Civil and Military Aircraft or Installations) Regulations 1986 reg 17 (8). Affidavits and statutory declarations may be permitted by the court to be used as evidence at the hearing: Civil Aviation (Investigation of Air Accidents) Regulations 1989 reg 18 (9); Air Navigation (Investigation of Air Accidents involving Civil and Military Aircraft or Installations) Regulations 1986 reg 17 (9).
3 Civil Aviation (Investigation of Air Accidents) Regulations 1989 reg 18 (10); Air Navigation (Investigation of Air Accidents involving Civil and Military Aircraft or Installations) Regulations 1986 reg 17 (10). As to the parties to the hearing see para 1521 ante.
4 Civil Aviation (Investigation of Air Accidents) Regulations 1989 reg 18 (11); Air Navigation (Investigation of Air Accidents involving Civil and Military Aircraft or Installations) Regulations 1986 reg 17 (11). The inspector in charge of an investigation into an accident to which the inquiry relates and a member of the Council on Tribunals are entitled to be present at any proceedings held in private: Civil Aviation (Investigation of Air Accidents) Regulations 1989 reg 18 (12); Air Navigation (Investigation of Air Accidents involving Civil and Military Aircraft or Installations) Regulations 1986 reg 17 (12). As to the Council on Tribunals see ADMINISTRATIVE LAW vol 1 (1) (Reissue) paras 48–50.

1523. Proceeding of public inquiry. The hearing of a public inquiry opens with a speech by the Attorney General, followed by brief speeches by the other parties at the discretion of the Court. The proceedings continue with the production and examination of witnesses on behalf of the Attorney General, their cross-examination by the parties and re-examination by the Attorney General[1]; and then with the addresses by the parties to the court and the production of more witnesses or recall of witnesses already examined, their cross-examination and re-examination as well as the production and examination of further witnesses on behalf of the Attorney General, equally to be cross-examined and re-examined[2].

Subsequently, when the whole of the evidence in relation to the questions for the court's opinion has been concluded in accordance with the prescribed inquisitional procedure, any of the parties may address the court upon the evidence, and the court may be addressed in reply upon the whole case on behalf of the Attorney General[3].

In due course, the court reports to the Secretary of State for Transport, alone or jointly with the Secretary of State for Defence as the case may be[4], stating fully the circumstances of the case and the court's opinion touching the causes of the accident or on any particular matter referred to it, adding any recommendations it thinks fit to make with a view to the preservation of life and the avoidance of similar future accidents[5]. Each assessor either signs the report with or without reservations or states in writing his dissent from it; unless there are good reasons to the contrary, the report, reservations or dissent and reasons must be made public[6].

1 Civil Aviation (Investigation of Air Accidents) Regulations 1989, SI 1989/2062, reg 19 (1); Air Navigation (Investigation of Air Accidents involving Civil and Military Aircraft or Installations) Regulations 1986, SI 1986/1953, reg 18 (1). As to the parties to the hearing and to the court see para 1521 ante.

2 Civil Aviation (Investigation of Air Accidents) Regulations 1989 reg 19 (2); Air Navigation
   (Investigation of Air Accidents involving Civil and Military Aircraft or Installations) Regulations
   1986 reg 18 (2). Witnesses are allowed the same expenses as if they were attending before the High
   Court; disputes as to expenses are referred to a taxing master of the Supreme Court Taxing Office;
   the court may however in its discretion direct the expenses to be disallowed: Civil Aviation
   (Investigation of Air Accidents) Regulations 1989 reg 19 (7); Air Navigation (Investigation of Air
   Accidents involving Civil and Military Aircraft or Installations) Regulations 1986 reg 18 (7).
3 Civil Aviation (Investigation of Air Accidents) Regulations 1989 reg 19 (3); Air Navigation
   (Investigation of Air Accidents involving Civil and Military Aircraft or Installations) Regulations
   1986 reg 18 (3). The court may adjourn the inquiry from time to time or place to place either on its
   own volition or on request by any party, in which latter case the court may impose costs: Civil
   Aviation (Investigation of Air Accidents) Regulations 1989 reg 19 (4); Air Navigation (Investigation
   of Air Accidents involving Civil and Military Aircraft or Installations) Regulations 1986 reg 18 (4).
4 As to the Secretaries of State see para 1507 ante.
5 Civil Aviation (Investigation of Air Accidents) Regulations 1989 reg 19 (5); Air Navigation
   (Investigation of Air Accidents involving Civil and Military Aircraft or Installations) Regulations
   1986 reg 18 (5).
6 Civil Aviation (Investigation of Air Accidents) Regulations 1989 reg 19 (6); Air Navigation
   (Investigation of Air Accidents involving Civil and Military Aircraft or Installations) Regulations
   1986 reg 18 (6).

1524. Rehearing of public inquiry. Just as in the case of the reopening of an
investigation or review, so also a public inquiry which has been held may be
reheard wholly or in part and must be reheard if new and important evidence has
been discovered or if there is, in the opinion of the Secretary of State[1], ground for
suspecting a miscarriage of justice[2].

Where the Secretary of State for Transport, alone or jointly with the Secretary of
State for Defence as the case may be, directs an inquiry to be reheard, the rehearing
is held by the same court who held the hearing or by some other person as the Lord
Chancellor directs[3].

1 As to the Secretary of State for Transport acting jointly with the Secretary of State for Defence see
   para 1507 ante.
2 Civil Aviation (Investigation of Air Accidents) Regulations 1989, SI 1989/2062, reg 20 (1); Air
   Navigation (Investigation of Air Accidents involving Civil and Military Aircraft or Installations)
   Regulations 1986, SI 1986/1953, reg 19 (1). As to public inquiries see paras 1521–1523 ante; as to
   investigations see paras 1512–1515 ante; as to review see paras 1516–1520 ante.
3 Civil Aviation (Investigation of Air Accidents) Regulations 1989 reg 20 (2); Air Navigation
   (Investigation of Air Accidents involving Civil and Military Aircraft or Installations) Regulations
   1986 reg 19 (2). Any rehearing is subject to and conducted in accordance with the regulatory
   provisions relating to the holding of public inquiries: Civil Aviation (Investigation of Air Accidents)
   Regulations 1989 reg 20 (3); Air Navigation (Investigation of Air Accidents involving Civil and
   Military Aircraft or Installations) Regulations 1986 reg 19 (3). As to the holding of public inquiries
   see paras 1521–1523 ante.

(iv) Miscellaneous

1525. Obstruction. A person must not obstruct or impede the court[1], a review
board[2], an inspector[3], an assessor[4] or any person acting under the authority of the
Secretary of State[5] or the Secretaries of State[6] in the exercise of any powers or duties
relating to the investigation of accidents; nor may a person without reasonable
excuse, proof whereof lies on him, fail, after having had any expenses to which he
is entitled[7] tendered to him, to comply with any summons or requisition of the
court, a review board or an inspector holding an investigation[8].

1   As to the court see para 1521 ante.
2   As to review boards see para 1516 ante.
3   As to inspectors see para 1512 ante.
4   As to assessors see para 1521 ante.
5   As to the Secretary of State see para 1032 ante.
6   As to the Secretaries of State see para 1507 ante.
7   As to witnesses' expenses see the Civil Aviation (Investigation of Air Accidents) Regulations 1989
     SI 1989/2062, regs 10 (5), 15 (7), 19 (7), and the Air Navigation (Investigation of Air Accident:
     involving Civil and Military Aircraft or Installations) Regulations 1986, SI 1986/1953, regs 10 (4), 1₄
     (6), 18 (7); paras 1513 note 5, 1518 note 8, 1523 note 2 ante.
8   Civil Aviation (Investigation of Air Accidents) Regulations 1989 reg 23; Air Navigation (Investi-
     gation of Air Accidents involving Civil and Military Aircraft or Installations) Regulations 1986 reg
     22. For the penalty for contravention see para 1502 ante.

1526. Civil air accidents in Scotland, Northern Ireland, the Isle of Man anc the Channel Islands. The regulations relating to the investigation of accidents tc civil aircraft apply to Scotland and Northern Ireland with consequential amend-ments to take account of the different constitutional position and legal framework but their effect is in all respects identical there to their effect in England and Wales[1] They do not apply in the Isle of Man or the Channel Islands. Separate provision: provide for the investigation of accidents to civil aircraft in or over those islands[2]

  1   See the Civil Aviation (Investigation of Air Accidents) Regulations 1989, SI 1989/2062, regs 24, 25
  2   See the Civil Aviation (Investigation of Accidents) (Guernsey) Order 1972, SI 1972/962; the Civi
      Aviation (Investigation of Accidents) (Isle of Man) Regulations 1974, SI 1974/1519; and the Civi
      Aviation (Investigation of Accidents) (Jersey) Regulations 1975, SI 1975/1516.

1527. Combined military and civil air accidents in Scotland, Northerr Ireland, the Isle of Man and the Channel Islands. The regulations relating tc combined military and civil air accidents apply to Scotland and Northern Irelanc with consequential amendments to take account of the different constitutiona position and legal framework, but their effect is in all respects identical there tc their effect in England and Wales[1]. They do not apply in the Isle of Man or th₍ Channel Islands, in respect of which places there are no regulations specificall₎ directed towards the investigation of combined military and civil air accidents.

  1   See the Air Navigation (Investigation of Air Accidents involving Civil and Military Aircraft o
      Installations) Regulations 1986, SI 1986/1953, regs 23, 24.

10. CARRIAGE BY AIR

(1) THE LEGISLATION AND ITS SCOPE

1528. Legislation governing carriage by air. The law governing the carriag₍ of passengers and goods by air is to be found in a number of different sets of rules almost all of which are derived from the provisions of the Warsaw Convention o 1929, which has as its object the adoption of certain uniform rules relating tc international carriage by air[1], and from subsequent revised versions of that conven-tion. The original Warsaw Convention was amended by the Hague Protocol o 1955, producing a version generally referred to as the Warsaw-Hague Convention

The Guatemala Protocol of 1971 and a series of Additional Protocols agreed at Montreal in 1975 together produce a third version, referred to as the Warsaw-Hague-Montreal Convention, which has not yet come into force.

Each set of rules contains a special definition of international carriage[2], and the rules, which regulate and limit the liability of air carriers, apply only to carriage falling within the relevant definition.

International carriage performed by a person other than the contracting carrier is governed by the provisions of the Guadalajara Convention of 1961[3] as given the force of law in the United Kingdom by the Carriage by Air (Supplementary Provisions) Act 1962 and by the Carriage by Air Acts (Application of Provisions) Order 1967[4].

If the carriage is international carriage within the meaning of the Warsaw Convention of 1929, as amended at The Hague in 1955, it is governed by the Carriage by Air Act 1961 and the Carriage by Air (Supplementary Provisions) Act 1962[5]. If it is international carriage within the meaning of the unamended Warsaw Convention of 1929, which remains in force between a number of states[6], it is governed by Schedule 2 to the Carriage by Air Acts (Application of Provisions) Order 1967[7]. If it is international carriage of passengers or baggage within the meaning of the Warsaw Convention of 1929, as amended at The Hague in 1955 and by Montreal Additional Protocol No 3 of 1975, or of goods within the meaning of the Warsaw Convention of 1929, as amended at The Hague in 1955 and by Montreal Additional Protocol No 4 of 1975, it is governed by the Carriage by Air Act 1961 and the Carriage by Air (Supplementary Provisions) Act 1962, both as amended by the Carriage by Air and Road Act 1979 (which, except for certain minor provisions, is not yet in force)[8].

A further set of rules which are similar to, but by no means identical with, the rules governing international carriage, is applied to many types of non-international carriage by Schedule 1 to the Carriage by Air Acts (Application of Provisions) Order 1967[9]. These rules also apply to the carriage of mail or postal packets.

Other carriage by air is governed by common law rules as to carriage[10].

There are in addition a number of miscellaneous statutory provisions relevant to carriage by air[11].

1 See para 1009 ante. The convention is expressed to be 'a Convention for the unification of Certain Rules Relating to International Carriage by Air'; but see *Grein v Imperial Airways Ltd* [1937] 1 KB 50 at 74, [1936] 2 All ER 1258 at 1277–1278, CA, per Greene LJ.
2 For these definitions see paras 1541, 1585 and 1605 post.
3 See para 1010 ante.
4 SI 1967/480 (amended by SI 1969/1083, SI 1979/931 and SI 1981/440).
5 See paras 1533–1583 post.
6 See para 1534 post.
7 See note 4 supra and paras 1584–1604 post.
8 See paras 1605–1628 post. As to the provisions in force see the Carriage by Air and Road Act 1979 s 7 and orders made thereunder.
9 See note 4 supra and paras 1629–1650 post.
10 See para 1530 post.
11 See paras 1651–1656 post.

1529. Application of legislation to Isle of Man, Channel Islands and overseas territories. By Orders in Council made under powers conferred by the Carriage by Air Act 1961 and the Carriage by Air (Supplementary Provisions) Act

1962[1], those Acts, giving effect to the provisions of the Warsaw Convention, as amended at The Hague in 1955, and of the Guadalajara Convention of 1961 have, with necessary modifications, been made part of the law of[2] the Isle of Man[3], the bailiwicks of Jersey[4] and Guernsey[5] and a number of overseas territories[6].

Similarly, the Carriage by Air Acts (Application of Provisions) Order 1967[7], giving effect to two different sets of rules governing certain types of international and non-international carriage[8], has also been made part of the law of the Isle of Man[9], the Channel Islands[10] and a number of overseas territories[11].

1 See the Carriage by Air Act 1961 s 9, and the Carriage by Air (Supplementary Provisions) Act 1962 s 5.
2 The effect of the instruments referred to in notes 3–6 infra is to be distinguished from that of the instruments which state for the purposes of United Kingdom law the territories in respect of which the United Kingdom and other countries are high contracting parties to the convention; see para 1535 post; and the Carriage by Air (Parties to Convention) Order 1988, SI 1988/243.
3 See the Carriage by Air (Isle of Man) Order 1967, SI 1967/805. In relation to the Isle of Man, 'Isle of Man' must be substituted for 'United Kingdom' wherever the latter words occur in the Carriage by Air Act 1961 or the Carriage by Air (Supplementary Provisions) Act 1962: Carriage by Air (Isle of Man) Order 1967 Schedule paras 1, 12.
4 See the Carriage by Air (Jersey) Order 1967, SI 1967/803, which provides that 'Jersey' must be substituted for 'United Kingdom': cf note 3 supra.
5 See the Carriage by Air (Guernsey) Order 1967, SI 1967/804. The word 'Guernsey' (the island of Alderney is included in the Bailiwick) must be substituted for 'United Kingdom': cf note 3 supra.
6 See the Carriage by Air (Overseas Territories) Order 1967, SI 1967/809, which extends to the following dependent territories of the United Kingdom: Bermuda, British Antarctic Territory, British Indian Ocean Territory, British Virgin Islands, Cayman Islands, Sovereign Base Areas of Akrotiri and Dhekelia in Cyprus, Falkland Islands and Dependencies, Gibraltar, Hong Kong, Montserrat, St Helena and Ascension, and Turks and Caicos Islands: Sch 3. The order also formerly extended to the Bahamas, Belize, Fiji, Kiribati, Mauritius, Seychelles, Solomon Islands, and Tuvalu, all of which are now independent. See generally COMMONWEALTH.
7 SI 1967/480. For the power to apply the order to the places referred to see the Carriage by Air Act 1961 s 10, and the Carriage by Air (Supplementary Provisions) Act 1962 s 5.
8 See para 1528 ante.
9 See the Carriage by Air Act 1961 (Application of Provisions) (Isle of Man) Order 1967, SI 1967/808.
10 See the Carriage by Air Acts (Application of Provisions) (Jersey) Order 1967, SI 1967/806, and the Carriage by Air Acts (Application of Provisions) (Guernsey) Order 1967, SI 1967/807.
11 See the Carriage by Air Acts (Application of Provisions) (Overseas Territories) Order 1967, SI 1967/810. The territories to which this order applies are those listed in note 6 supra.

1530. Application of common law rules. Almost all carriage by air is governed by the Carriage by Air Act 1961 or the Carriage by Air Acts (Application of Provisions) Order 1967[1]. There are, however, certain special categories of carriage, of which the most important is gratuitous carriage not performed by an air transport undertaking, to which neither of these applies[2]. In any such case the carriage is subject to the ordinary law with regard to carriers, which is dealt with elsewhere[3]. There are as yet few English or Commonwealth cases in which the application of the common law rules to aircraft operation has been discussed[4], but it seems likely that the courts will proceed by analogy from cases relating to the operation of the various forms of land and water transport[5]; they may also give attention to the large number of United States cases. Where the law differs as between land and sea transport, there are some indications that the analogy of land transport will be preferred[6].

1 SI 1967/480 (amended by SI 1969/1083, SI 1979/931 and SI 1981/440). See para 1528 ante.
2 See para 1532 post. The international rules do not apply in the case of carriage performed in extraordinary circumstances outside the normal scope of an air carrier's business; see paras 1543,

1587 post. As to the exclusion of non-international rules by exemption of the Secretary of State see para 1630 post.
3 See CARRIERS; NEGLIGENCE. As to the law applicable to a contract see CONFLICT OF LAWS. See also para 1531 post.
4 See however *Aslan v Imperial Airways Ltd* (1933) 149 LT 276; *Fosbroke-Hobbes v Airwork Ltd and British-American Air Services Ltd* [1937] 1 All ER 108; and *Ludditt v Ginger Coote Airways Ltd* [1947] AC 233, [1947] 1 All ER 328, PC. For a case on the duty of care owed by a learner-driver which could, by analogy, be applied to a student pilot see *Nettleship v Weston* [1971] 2 QB 691, [1971] 3 All ER 581, CA: the duty of care is the same as that owed by every driver to a passenger, and is not affected by the instructor's knowledge of the learner's lack of skill and experience; but cf *Cook v Cook* (1986) 68 ALR 353 at 357 (Aust HC): 'It would . . affront the standards of the reasonable man . . to define the duty of care which a mentally retarded and completely unqualified and inexperienced person owed to a professional pilot who had persuaded him or her to attempt to pilot an aircraft in which they were both travelling as being the skill and care that are reasonably to be expected of a qualified and experienced pilot' . In practical terms no difficulty seems to arise in the application of common law rules, eg in collision cases (see para 1679 post) or in cases of accidents on aerodromes (see para 1680 post).
5 See the cases cited in note 4 supra.
6 See *Aslan v Imperial Airways Ltd* (1933) 149 LT 276.

1531. Contract of carriage. In the great majority of cases carriage by air is performed upon the terms of a contract made between the carrier and the passenger or consignor of cargo[1]. The contract is normally made by the passenger or consignor accepting a ticket or air waybill, put forward by the carrier, which contains the conditions of contract upon which the carrier agrees to perform the carriage and often, in addition, incorporates by reference the carrier's general conditions of carriage[2].

It is only in the few cases which are governed neither by the international nor by the non-international carriage rules[3] that the carrier is able, by special contract, to limit or exclude his liability[4]; but in that limited number of cases, the carrier, even though he may be a common carrier[5], whether of passengers or cargo, may validly limit[6] or completely exclude his liability[7]. The usefulness of exclusion clauses is, however, greatly reduced by the Unfair Contract Terms Act 1977 and by common law principles as to the interpretation of such clauses and as to the effect of deviation or of fundamental breach of contract[8].

1 In the case of gratuitous carriage, there will usually be no contract, at any rate in cases where the carriage is not performed by an air transport undertaking: as to such cases see para 1532 post.
2 The circumstances in which a person accepting such a document is bound by the conditions contained or referred to in it are considered in CARRIERS; see also *Fosbroke-Hobbes v Airwork Ltd and British-American Air Services Ltd* [1937] 1 All ER 108. In nearly all cases of international carriage and in many cases of non-international carriage the passenger ticket or air waybill will contain the standard IATA conditions of contract, which incorporate by reference general conditions of carriage based upon those recommended by IATA. As to IATA see para 1024 ante.
3 As to instances where neither set of rules applies see paras 1543, 1587, 1630 post. The most important instances , for this purpose, are international carriage performed in extraordinary circumstances outside the normal scope of an air carrier's business (see paras 1543, 1587 post) and any non-international carriage which may be exempted from the non-international rules (see para 1630 post).
4 In the case of carriage governed by the international or non-international rules any provision tending to relieve the carrier of liability or fix a lower limit than that laid down in the rules is null and void (see paras 1552, 1588, 1640, 1646 post); but the carrier may, and normally does (see note 2 supra), impose conditions or regulations which do not conflict with the rules (see paras 1541, 1547 post; and see *Rotterdamsche Bank NV v British Overseas Airways Corpn* [1953] 1 All ER 675, [1953] 1 WLR 493).
5 As to common carriers see CARRIERS. See *Aslan v Imperial Airways Ltd* (1933) 149 LT 276 at 278 per Mackinnon J (possibility of air carriers being common carriers); see also *Ludditt v Ginger Coote Airways Ltd* [1947] AC 233, [1947] All ER 328, PC.

6 A limitation, as opposed to an exclusion, of liability will not normally affect the right of dependants to claim full damages under the Fatal Accidents Act 1976: see *Nunan v Southern Rly Co* [1923] 2 KB 703; affd [1924] 1 KB 233, CA; and *Heatley v Steel Co of Wales Ltd* [1953] 1 All ER 489, [1953] 1 WLR 405, CA; but see *Grein v Imperial Airways Ltd* [1937] 1 KB 50 at 87, [1936] 2 All ER 1286, CA, per Greene LJ (effect of contract which excludes all duties in negligence and substitutes 'a modified system of insurance'). See generally NEGLIGENCE.

7 *Ludditt v Ginger Coote Airways Ltd* [1947] AC 233, [1947] 1 All ER 328, PC; *Aslan v Imperial Airways Ltd* (1933) 149 LT 276.

8 See CONTRACT.

1532. Gratuitous carriage. The liabilities arising from the gratuitous carriage[1] of passengers or cargo not performed by an air transport undertaking or by the Crown, are governed by the ordinary law of negligence[2], which imposes upon the owner or operator[3] of the aircraft performing the carriage separate responsibilities in relation to the actual performance of the carriage and in relation to the condition of the aircraft. He is under a duty to use reasonable care and skill in performing the carriage[4] and, if the fault is his own or that of some person for whose actions he is vicariously responsible, he is liable for damage caused by any breach of this duty[5].

1 Gratuitous carriage is carriage not performed 'for reward'; see para 1540 et seq post.

2 See generally NEGLIGENCE. The doctrine of res ipsa loquitur (see NEGLIGENCE) may be relied on in appropriate cases; see *Fosbroke-Hobbes v Airwork Ltd and British-American Air Services Ltd* [1937] 1 All ER 108; *Grein v Imperial Airways Ltd* [1937] 1 KB 50, [1936] 2 All ER 1258, CA. See also the Canadian cases of *McInnerny v McDougall* [1938] 1 DLR 22, [1937] 3 WWR 625 (Man); *Nysted and Anson v Wings Ltd* [1942] 3 WWR 39, [1942] 3 DLR 336 (Man); and *Malone and Moss v Trans-Canada Airlines* [1942] 3 DLR 369, [1942] OR 453 (Ont CA); the doctrine has been applied in a large number of United States cases; see *Higginbotham v Mobil Oil Corpn* 545 F 2d 422 (5th Cir, 1977), revsd on other grounds 436 US 618 (1978).

3 Liability falls upon the person actually responsible for the damage, ie in normal cases the pilot, who may be the owner or operator (having perhaps chartered the aircraft), and also upon any person, such as the owner or operator, if not the pilot, who is vicariously responsible for the pilot's actions (as to vicarious responsibility see EMPLOYMENT; TORT); see *Fosbroke-Hobbes v Airwork Ltd and British-American Air Services Ltd* [1937] 1 All ER 108 at 112 per Goddard J. Cf also *Samson v Aitchison* [1912] AC 844, PC, and *Pratt v Patrick* [1924] 1 KB 488.

4 See *McInnerny v McDougall* [1938] 1 DLR 22, [1937] 3 WWR 625 (Man), and cf *Harris v Perry & Co* [1903] 2 KB 219, CA, and *Pratt v Patrick* [1924] 1 KB 488. The duty may include giving warning to passengers of dangers inherent in the journey of which the owner or operator is aware: cf *Lewys v Burnett and Dunbar* [1945] 2 All ER 555. In relation to the gratuitous carriage of goods the responsibilities of the owner or operator are those of a gratuitous bailee; see generally BAILMENT; CARRIERS; NEGLIGENCE.

5 As to vicarious liability see EMPLOYMENT; TORT; and as to the measure of damages recoverable see NEGLIGENCE.

(2) INTERNATIONAL CARRIAGE: WARSAW AND GUADALAJARA CONVENTIONS

1533. Carriage to which the Warsaw Convention applies. The various versions of the Warsaw Convention each apply, subject to a very few exceptions[1], to all international carriage of persons, baggage or cargo performed by aircraft for reward[2]. They apply equally to gratuitous carriage by air performed by an air transport undertaking[3]. Which version of the convention is applicable depends upon the definition of 'international carriage' in each version[4]; the effect of the definitions is largely governed by the states which are high contracting parties to the relevant version of the convention[5].

1 For special categories of international carriage to which the convention does not apply see paras 1543, 1587, 1606 post.
2 Carriage by Air Act 1961 s 1 (1), Sch 1 art 1 (1) (Sch 1 replaced as from a day to be appointed by the Carriage by Air and Road Act 1979 s 1 (1), Sch 1) ; Carriage by Air Acts (Application of Provisions) Order 1967, SI 1967/480, art 5, Sch 2 Pt B art 1 (1). See generally *Grein v Imperial Airways Ltd* [1937] 1 KB 50, [1936] 2 All ER 1258, CA, and *Philippson v Imperial Airways Ltd* [1939] AC 332, [1939] 1 All ER 761, HL. 'Reward' is not defined, but in the Civil Aviation Act 1982 s 105 (1) it includes any form of consideration received or to be received wholly or partly in connection with a flight irrespective of the person by whom or to whom the consideration has been or is to be given; and cf the term 'for remuneration' in the Chicago Convention arts 5 and 7, which includes any kind of remuneration, monetary or otherwise . As to the Chicago Convention see paras 1002–1008 ante.
3 Carriage by Air Act 1961 Sch 1 art 1 (1). 'Air transport undertaking' is not defined in the Act, although it is defined in the Air Navigation Order 1989, SI 1989/2004, art 106 (1); see para 1272 note 6 ante. It is noteworthy that this definition has never been specifically applied to the carriage by air legislation, but it is submitted that it is appropriate to do so in considering it in relation to gratuitous carriage.
4 See paras 1541, 1585, 1605 post.
5 See para 1534 post.

1534. High contracting parties. The expression 'high contracting party' was not formally defined in the original Warsaw Convention text; as used in the Warsaw Convention of 1929, as amended at The Hague in 1955, it means a state whose ratification of or adherence to the amended convention has become effective and whose denunciation of it has not become effective[1].

For the purposes, however, of the Carriage by Air Act 1961 it is from time to time certified by Order in Council[2] who are the high contracting parties to the Warsaw Convention or that convention as amended at The Hague in 1955, in respect of what territories they are respectively parties[3], and to what extent they have availed themselves of the provisions enabling them to exclude the application of either convention to carriage performed by the state[4]. Any such order, except in so far as it has been superseded by a subsequent order, is for the purpose of any question arising out of the Carriage by Air Act 1961[5], conclusive evidence of the matters so certified[6], and it is conclusive not only that the states named are parties to either convention but also that states not named are not parties[7].

1 See the Warsaw Convention as amended at The Hague 1955, art 40A (1). See also *Philippson v Imperial Airways Ltd* [1939] AC 332, [1939] 1 All ER 761, HL, where it was held by Lords Atkin, Thankerton and Wright (Lords Russell of Killowen and Macmillan dissenting) that Belgium was in 1935 a high contracting party within the terms of the convention and of a contract based on it, although she had not then ratified the convention. A number of articles of the Warsaw Convention (Cmd 4284) have not been reproduced in the Carriage by Air Act 1961 although they were incorporated in the Carriage by Air Act 1932 (repealed); these articles mainly concern the coming into force of the convention: arts 37 (ratification and coming into force), 38 (accession to convention), 39 (denunciation) and 40 (separate accession and denunciation in name of colonies). Article 40A (1), added by the Hague Protocol, has not been reproduced in the Act of 1961.
2 See the Carriage by Air (Parties to Convention) Order 1988, SI 1988/243, Sch 1, which names the following as high contracting parties to the Warsaw Convention and to that convention as amended at The Hague in 1955: Afghanistan, Argentina, Australia, Austria, Bahamas, Bangladesh, Belgium, Belize, Benin, Botswana, Brazil, Bulgaria, Cameroon, Canada, Chile, China, Colombia, Congo, Cuba, Cyprus, Czechoslovakia, Denmark, Dominican Republic, Ecuador, Egypt, Fiji, Finland, France, Gabon, Grenada, Greece, Hungary, Iceland, India, Iran, Iraq, Republic of Ireland, Israel, Italy, Ivory Coast, Japan, Jordan, Kiribati, Kuwait, Laos, Lebanon, Lesotho, Libya, Liechtenstein, Luxembourg, Madagascar, Malawi, Malaysia, Mali, Mauritius, Mexico, Morocco, Nauru, Nepal, Netherlands, New Zealand, Niger, Nigeria, Norway, Oman, Pakistan, Papua New Guinea, Paraguay, Philippines, Poland, Portugal, Qatar, Romania, Saudi Arabia, Senegal, Seychelles, Singapore, Solomon Islands, South Africa, Spain, Sudan, Surinam, Swaziland, Sweden, Switzerland, Syria, Togo, Tonga, Trinidad and Tobago, Tunisia, Turkey, Tuvalu, Union of Soviet

Socialist Republics, United Kingdom, Vanuatu, Venezuela, Vietnam, Western Samoa, Yemen Arab Republic, Yugoslavia, Zambia and Zimbabwe.

The following states are not certified by the Order to be high contracting parties in respect of the unamended Warsaw Convention but to be parties to the Warsaw Convention of 1929, as amended at The Hague in 1955: Algeria, El Salvador, Federal Republic of Germany, German Democratic Republic, Guatemala, Korea (South), and Monaco.

The following states are not certified by the Order to be high contracting parties in respect of the Warsaw Convention as amended at The Hague 1955, although they are certified parties to the unamended Warsaw Convention: Antigua and Barbuda, Barbados, Botswana, Brunei, Burma, Cambodia, Chad, Dominica, Ethiopia, Finland, Gambia, Germany, Ghana, Guinea, Guyana, Indonesia, Jamaica, Jordan, Kenya, Liberia, Malta, Mauritania, Mongolia, Rwanda, St Christopher and Nevis, St Lucia, St Vincent and the Grenadines, Sierra Leone, Sri Lanka, Tanzania, Uganda, United Arab Emirates, United Kingdom (in respect of Anguilla), United States of America, Uruguay, and Zaire.

3 As to the territories in respect of which states are parties to the Warsaw Convention or the Warsaw-Hague Convention see para 1535 post.

4 Carriage by Air Act 1961 s 2 (1). As to this exclusion see para 1537 post.

5 The orders have no effect except in relation to the Carriage by Air Act 1961: see *Philippson v Imperial Airways Ltd* [1939] AC 332, [1939] 1 All ER 761, HL.

6 Carriage by Air Act 1961 s 2 (3).

7 See *Philippson v Imperial Airways Ltd* [1939] AC 332 at 350–351, [1939] 1 All ER 761 at 767–768, HL, per Lord Atkin, at 353, 770 per Lord Russell of Killowen and at 370, 781 per Lord Wright.

1535. Territories in respect of which a state is a party. The Warsaw Convention in all its versions reserves to each high contracting party[1] the right to declare, at time of signature, ratification or accession, that the acceptance it gives to the convention does not apply to all or any of its colonies, protectorates, territories under mandate or any other territory subject to its sovereignty or authority or any territory under its suzerainty[2].

An amendment made at The Hague in 1955 provides that for the purposes of the convention 'territory' means not only the metropolitan territory of a state but also all other territories for the foreign relations of which that state is responsible[3]. This provision must not be read as extending references in the convention to the territory of a high contracting party to include any territory in respect of which that high contracting party is not a party[4].

The United Kingdom is a high contracting party in respect of Great Britain and Northern Ireland, the Channel Islands, the Isle of Man and its overseas dependent territories[5].

1 As to high contracting parties see para 1534 ante.

2 Warsaw Convention art 40 (1) (see para 1534 note 1 ante). A high contracting party may subsequently accede to the convention in the name of any territory originally excluded (art 40 (2)) and may denounce the convention separately in respect of all or any of its colonies, etc (art 40 (3)).

3 Carriage by Air Act 1961 s 1 (1), Sch 1 art 40A (2) (Sch 1 replaced as from a day to be appointed by the Carriage by Air and Road Act 1979 s 1 (1), Sch 1).

4 Carriage by Air Act 1961 s 2 (2). See also Sch 1 Additional Protocol; and para 1537 post. The question whether a particular territory is a part of the territory in respect of which a state is a party to the convention is important for the purpose of deciding whether carriage is international or not; see para 1533 ante.

5 The overseas dependent territories are Anguilla, Bermuda, British Antarctic Territory, British Indian Ocean Territory, British Virgin Islands, Cayman Islands, Falkland Islands, Gibraltar, Hong Kong, Montserrat, St Helena and Ascension, South Georgia and the South Sandwich Islands, the Sovereign Base Areas of Akrotiri and Dhekelia, Turks and Caicos Islands: Carriage by Air (Parties to Convention) Order 1988, SI 1988/243, Sch 1.

1536. Carriage performed partly by air, partly otherwise. In the case of combined carriage performed partly by air and partly by any other mode of carriage, the provisions of the Warsaw Convention of 1929, or of the convention as amended at The Hague in 1955, apply only to the carriage by air, and then only if the carriage by air falls within the terms of those provisions[1]. However, where carriage of goods is partly by road and partly by air, and the vehicle carrying the goods is carried by air, without the goods being unloaded from the vehicle[2], the whole of the carriage will be governed by the Carriage of Goods by Road Act 1965[3].

Nothing in the Warsaw or Warsaw-Hague Conventions prevents the parties, in the case of combined carriage, from inserting in the document of air carriage conditions relating to other modes of carriage, provided that the provisions of the relevant convention are observed as regards the carriage by air[4].

1 Carriage by Air Act 1961 s 1 (1), Sch 1 art 31 (1) (Sch 1 replaced as from a day to be appointed by the Carriage by Air and Road Act 1979 s 1 (1), Sch 1); Carriage by Air Acts (Application of Provisions) Order 1967, SI 1967/480, art 5, Sch 2 Pt B art 31 (1). For an example see *Arctic Electronics (UK) Ltd v McGregor Sea & Air Services Ltd* [1985] 2 Lloyd's Rep 510. The Carriage by Air (Supplementary Provisions) Act 1962 applies to that part of the carriage which is performed by air; see para 1539 post.
2 Except in emergency cases falling within the Carriage of Goods by Road Act 1965 s 1, Schedule art 14.
3 Ibid Schedule art 2 (1). See also CARRIERS.
4 Carriage by Air Act 1961 Sch 1 art 31 (2); Carriage by Air Acts (Application of Provisions) Order 1967 Sch 2 Pt B art 31 (2).

1537. Carriage by state or by public bodies. The Warsaw Convention of 1929, and that convention as amended at The Hague in 1955, apply to carriage performed by the state or by legally constituted public bodies, provided that the carriage is otherwise within the terms of the amended convention[1]. They also apply to carriage by the Crown, whether the carriage is gratuitous or for reward[2]. The high contracting parties[3], however, reserved the right to declare, at the time of their ratification or accession, that it should not apply to international carriage by air performed directly by the state, its colonies, protectorates or mandated territories or by any other territory under its sovereignty, suzerainty or authority[4], but this right has only been exercised in a small number of cases[5].

1 Carriage by Air Act 1961 s 1 (1), Sch 1 art 2 (1) (Sch 1 replaced as from a day to be appointed by the Carriage by Air and Road Act 1979 s 1 (1), Sch 1); Carriage by Air Acts (Application of Provisions) Order 1967, SI 1967/480, Sch 2 Pt B art 2 (1). As to actions against high contracting parties, and as to their submission to the jurisdiction, see para 1546 post. It is submitted that whether carriage performed by an agency associated with a particular state is carriage performed directly by that state depends on whether the agency is regarded as a department of state or an alter ego of the government of that state: see *Krajina v Tass Agency* [1949] 2 All ER 274, CA; *Baccus SRL v Servicio Nacional del Trigo* [1957] 1 QB 438, [1956] 3 All ER 715, CA; *Mellenger v New Brunswick Development Corpn* [1971] 2 All ER 593, [1971] 1 WLR 604, CA; *Swiss Israel Trade Bank v Government of Salta and Banco Provincial de Salta* [1972] 1 Lloyd's Rep 497; *Trendtex Trading Corpn v Central Bank of Nigeria* [1977] QB 529, [1977] 1 All ER 881, CA.
2 Carriage by Air Acts (Application of Provisions) Order 1967 art 7.
3 For the meaning of 'high contracting party' see para 1534 ante.
4 Carriage by Air Act 1961 Sch 1 Additional Protocol; Carriage by Air Acts (Application of Provisions) Order 1967, Sch 2 Pt B Additional Protocol. As to the certification by Order in Council of the extent to which high contracting parties have availed themselves of the Additional Protocol see note 5 infra.
5 See the Carriage by Air (Parties to Convention) Order 1988, SI 1988/243, art 4, Sch 2. Canada, Chile, Congo, Cuba, Ethiopia, the Philippines and the United States of America are certified in the order as having availed themselves of the Additional Protocol.

1538. Prohibition on contracting out. Where a contract is entered into for carriage to which the Warsaw Convention or the Warsaw-Hague Convention applies, any clause contained in the contract and all special agreements entered into before the damage occurred by which the parties purport to infringe the rules laid down by the conventions, whether by deciding the law to be applied or by altering the rules as to jurisdiction[1], are null and void[2]. Nevertheless, for the carriage of cargo, arbitration clauses are allowed, subject to the conventions, if the arbitration is to take place within one of the jurisdictions in which an action must be brought[3].

However, nothing in either convention prevents the carrier either from refusing to enter into any contract of carriage or from making regulations which do not conflict with the provisions of that convention[4].

1 For the rules as to jurisdiction see para 1545 post.
2 Carriage by Air Act 1961 s 1 (1), Sch 1 art 32 (Sch 1 replaced as from a day to be appointed by the Carriage by Air and Road Act 1979 s 1 (1), Sch 1); Carriage by Air Acts (Application of Provisions) Order 1967, SI 1967/480, Sch 2 Pt B art 32. For a similar provision in respect of the Guadalajara Convention (as to which see para 1539 post) see the Carriage by Air (Supplementary Provisions) Act 1962 s 1, Schedule Pt I art IX (3).
3 Carriage by Air Act 1961 Sch 1 art 32 (see note 2 supra); Carriage by Air Acts (Application of Provisions) Order 1967 Sch 2 Pt B art 32. For a similar provision in respect of the Guadalajara Convention (as to which see para 1539 post) see the Carriage by Air (Supplementary Provisions) Act 1962 Schedule Pt I art IX (3). For the rules as to jurisdiction see para 1545 post.
4 Carriage by Air Act 1961 Sch 1 Pt I art 33 (see note 2 supra); Carriage by Air Acts (Application of Provisions) Order 1967 Sch 2 Pt B art 33.

1539. Carriage to which the Guadalajara Convention applies. The Guadalajara Convention, supplementary to the Warsaw Convention, for the Unification of Certain Rules Relating to International Carriage by Air Performed by a Person other than the Contracting Carrier[1], applies to international carriage[2] governed by the unamended Warsaw Convention[3] or any of the amended versions of that convention and performed wholly or in part by a person, called the actual carrier[4], other than the contracting carrier[5]. In general terms, it gives to an actual carrier the same rights and liabilities as a contracting carrier under the Warsaw system.

The provisions of the convention, as given the force of law, so far as they relate to the rights and liabilities of carriers, their servants and agents, passengers, consignors, consignees and other persons, by the Carriage by Air (Supplementary Provisions) Act 1962[6], apply to carriage by the Crown[7].

In the following paragraphs the convention provisions are mentioned when they are part of United Kingdom law and when necessary.

1 (Cmnd 1568). See the Carriage by Air (Supplementary Provisions) Act 1962 s 1 (1), Schedule and, generally and for a list of high contracting parties, see Shawcross & Beaumont: Air Law (4th Edn) vol 2.
2 For the meaning of 'international carriage' see paras 1541, 1585, 1605 post.
3 The Guadalajara Convention is supplementary to the Warsaw Convention; art 1 (a) gives the meaning of 'Warsaw Convention': either the convention signed in 1929 at Warsaw or the Warsaw Convention as amended at The Hague 1955. Subsequent amending Protocols ensure that as between the parties to them the Guadalajara Convention is supplementary to the new amended version of the Warsaw Convention: Montreal Additional Protocol No 3, art XIII; Montreal Additional Protocol No 4, art XXIII. See the Carriage by Air (Supplementary Provisions) Act 1962 s 2 (1) and note the prospective amendment of Schedule 1 to the Carriage by Air Act 1961 to which that section refers, by the Carriage by Air and Road Act 1979 (not yet in force).
4 'Actual carrier' means a person, other than the contracting carrier (as to whom see note 5 infra), who by virtue of authority from the contracting carrier performs the whole or part of the contemplated carriage, but who is not with respect to such part a successive carrier (as to whom see para 1542 post);

such authority is deemed in the absence of proof to the contrary: Carriage by Air (Supplementary Provisions) Act 1962 Schedule Pt I art 1 (c).

5 Ibid s 1 (1). 'Contracting carrier' means a person who as a principal makes an agreement for carriage governed by the Warsaw Convention (see note 3 supra) with a passenger or consignor or with a person acting on his behalf: Carriage by Air (Supplementary Provisions) Act 1962 Schedule Pt I art 1 (b).

6 Ibid s 1 (1).

7 Ibid s 6 (1).

(3) INTERNATIONAL CARRIAGE UNDER THE WARSAW-HAGUE PROVISIONS

(i) Introductory

1540. Warsaw-Hague Convention as part of English law. The provisions of the Warsaw Convention as amended at The Hague in 1955 so far as they relate to the rights and liabilities of carriers, their servants and agents, passengers, consignors, consignees and other persons, have the force of law in the United Kingdom in relation to any carriage by air to which the convention applies, irrespective of the nationality of the aircraft performing that carriage[1], and despite any attempt by the parties to the contract of carriage to exclude their operation or to substitute some other law as the law applicable to the contract[2]. A deviation from the carriage contracted for does not remove the carriage from the ambit of the convention or disentitle the carrier from relying on its provisions[3].

1 Carriage by Air Act 1961 s 1 (1). The English text of the Warsaw-Hague Convention appears in Pt I of Schedule 1 to the Act, the French text in Pt II; in the case of any inconsistency, the French text prevails: Carriage by Air Act 1961 s 1 (2). As to the carriage to which the convention applies see para 1541 post. The Carriage by Air Act 1961 s 1 (1) is amended and a new Schedule 1 to that Act substituted by the Carriage by Air and Road Act 1979 s 1 (1), as from a day to be appointed by order under s 7 (2), so as to apply instead the provisions of the Warsaw Convention of 1929, as amended at The Hague in 1955 and by Montreal Additional Protocols Nos 3 and 4 of 1975; see paras 1605-1628 post. However, when the relevant provisions of the Carriage by Air and Road Act 1979 are brought into force, provision will be made by Order in Council under the Carriage by Air Act 1961 s 10 for the continued operation of the earlier provisions.

2 See paras 1538 ante, 1544, 1588 post. See also *Grein v Imperial Airways Ltd* [1937] 1 KB 50 at 74-75, [1936] 2 All ER 1258 at 1277-1278, CA, per Greene LJ.

3 See *Rotterdamsche Bank NV v British Overseas Airways Corpn* [1953] 1 All ER 675 at 682, [1953] 1 WLR 493 at 502-503 per Pilcher J. As to deviation in shipping law see SHIPPING; and cf *Stag Line Ltd v Foscolo Mango & Co Ltd* [1932] AC 328, HL.

1541. International carriage within the Warsaw-Hague Convention. International carriage, for the purpose of the convention, means any carriage in which, according to the agreement between the parties[1], the place of departure and the place of destination[2], whether or not there is a break[3] in the carriage or a transhipment, are situated either within the territories of two high contracting parties[4], or within the territory of a single high contracting party if there is an agreed stopping place[5] within the territory of another state, even though that state is not a high contracting party[6]. Carriage between two points within the territory of a single high contracting party without an agreed stopping place within the territory of another state is not international carriage for the purposes of the convention.

1 The contract (or under para 3 (ie the Carriage by Air Act 1961 s 1 (1), Sch 1 art 1 (3)) the series of contracts forming this agreement) is, so to speak, the unit to which attention is to be paid in

considering whether or not the carriage under it is international or not; the fact that there is a break in the carriage is immaterial: see *Grein v Imperial Airways Ltd* [1937] 1 KB 50 at 77–78, [1936] 2 All ER 1258 at 1280, CA, per Greene LJ; *Collins v British Airways Board* [1982] QB 734, [1982] 1 All ER 302, 1 S&B AvR VII/155, CA. The passenger or consignor does not have to be a party to the contract or agreement for the carriage to be international within the meaning of the Act of 1961; see *Block v Cie Nationale Air France* 386 F 2d 323 (5th Cir, 1967), cert denied 392 US 905 (1968) (case of a child or a servant). The Carriage by Air Act 1961 Sch 1 is replaced as from a day to be appointed by the Carriage by Air and Road Act 1979 s 1 (1), Sch 1; see para 1540 note 1 ante.

2 The use of the singular in this expression indicates that in the minds of the parties to the convention every contract of carriage has one place of departure and one place of destination; an intermediate place at which the carriage may be broken is not regarded as a place of destination, and in the case of a return ticket the only place of destination is that of departure: see *Grein v Imperial Airways Ltd* [1937] 1 KB 50 at 78–79, [1936] 2 All ER 1258 at 1280–1281, CA, per Greene LJ; *Qureshi v KLM Royal Dutch Airlines* (1979) 102 DLR (3d) 205 (NS SC); and cf para 1545 post.

3 See *Grein v Imperial Airways Ltd* [1937] 1 KB 50 at 83, [1936] 2 All ER 1258 at 1283–1284, CA, per Greene LJ; *Egan v Kollsman Instrument Corpn* 234 NE 2d 199 (NY, 1967).

4 For the meaning of 'high contracting party' see para 1534 ante; for the meaning of 'territory of a high contracting party' see para 1535 ante.

5 An agreed stopping place is a place where, according to the contract, the aircraft by which the contract is to be performed will stop in the course of performing the contractual carriage, whatever the purpose of the descent may be, and whatever rights the passenger may have to break his journey at that place: see *Grein v Imperial Airways Ltd* [1937] 1 KB 50 at 80, [1936] 2 All ER 1258 at 1281–1282, CA, per Greene LJ.

6 Carriage by Air Act 1961 Sch 1 art 1 (2) (see note 1 supra). See also para 1533 ante.

1542. Carriage by successive air carriers. Carriage to be performed by several successive air carriers is deemed for the purpose of the Warsaw Convention of 1929, as amended at The Hague in 1955, to be one undivided carriage, if it has been regarded by the parties as a single operation, whether it has been agreed upon under the form of a single contract or of a series of contracts, and it does not lose its international character merely because one contract or a series of contracts is to be performed entirely within the territory of the same state[1].

In any such case each carrier who accepts passengers, baggage or cargo is subjected to the rules of the Warsaw Convention of 1929, as amended at The Hague in 1955, and is deemed to be one of the contracting parties to the contract of carriage in so far as the contract deals with that part of the carriage which is performed under his supervision[2].

1 Carriage by Air Act 1961 s 1 (1), Sch 1 art 1 (3) (Sch 1 replaced as from a day to be appointed by the Carriage by Air and Road Act 1979 s 1 (1), Sch 1; see para 1540 note 1 ante). See *Rotterdamsche Bank NV v British Overseas Airways Corpn* [1953] 1 All ER 675, [1953] 1 WLR 493 and *Collins v British Airways Board* [1982] QB 734, [1982] 1 All ER 302, 1 S&B AvR VII/155, CA, for cases of successive carriage, and *Stratton v Trans Canada Air Lines* (1961) 27 DLR (2d) 670; affd (1962) 32 DLR (2d) 736 (BC CA). It is important that both parties should regard the carriage as a single operation: *Lemly v Trans World Airlines Inc* 807 F 2d 26 (2nd Cir, 1986). There would be no successive carriage where a carrier, without the passenger's agreement, engaged another carrier to perform the whole or part of the carriage.

2 Carriage by Air Act 1961 Sch 1 art 30 (1). The question which carrier a passenger, consignor or consignee is permitted to sue is considered in para 1548 post.

1543. International carriage to which the Warsaw–Hague Convention does not apply. Notwithstanding that it may fall within the definition of international carriage[1], the Warsaw Convention of 1929, as amended at The Hague in 1955, does not apply to the carriage of mail and postal packages[2], or to the carriage of persons, baggage or cargo for the military authorities of the United Kingdom or of any other state specified in an Order in Council if the whole capacity of the aircraft has been reserved by or on behalf of those authorities[3]. Furthermore, it does not apply to gratuitous international carriage by a person, firm or company who or which is not an air transport undertaking[4].

The provisions of the amended convention relating to documents of carriage[5] do not apply in the case of carriage performed in extraordinary circumstances outside the normal scope of an air carrier's business[6].

1 For the meaning of 'international carriage' see para 1541 ante.
2 Carriage by Air Act 1961 s 1 (1), Sch 1 art 2 (2) (Sch 1 replaced as from a day to be appointed by the Carriage by Air and Road Act 1979 s 1 (1), Sch 1; see para 1540 note 1 ante). See also para 1629 post.
3 Carriage by Air Act 1961 s 7, giving effect to art 26 of the Hague Protocol. No such Order in Council was in force at the date at which this volume states the law.
4 See the Carriage by Air Act 1961 Sch 1 art 1 (1). For the meaning of 'air transport undertaking' for this purpose see para 1533 note 3 ante.
5 See ibid Sch 1 arts 3–9; and note 2 supra.
6 Ibid Sch 1 art 34.

1544. Actions subject to amended Warsaw Convention. In the cases which are covered by the rules examined below providing for the liability of the carrier for death of or injury to passengers[1], for damage to or destruction or loss of cargo or registered baggage or objects of which the passenger takes charge himself[2] and for damage caused by delay[3], any action for damages, however founded, can only be brought subject to the conditions and limits set out in the amended Warsaw Convention[4].

The application of the rules cannot be excluded by any contract between the parties to the carriage[5]. Any provisions tending to relieve the carrier of liability or to fix a lower limit of liability than that laid down in the rules is null and void[6].

1 See para 1559 post.
2 See para 1564 post.
3 See para 1583 post.
4 Carriage by Air Act 1961 s 1 (1), Sch 1 art 24 (1), (2) (Sch 1 replaced as from a day to be appointed by the Carriage by Air and Road Act 1979 s 1 (1), Sch 1; see para 1540 note 1 ante). In the case of liability for death of or injury to passengers this provision is without prejudice to the question as to who are the persons who have the right to bring suit and what are their respective rights: Carriage by Air Act 1961 Sch 1 art 24 (2). For actions against the carrier's servants or agents see para 1551 post.
5 Ibid Sch 1 art 32.
6 Ibid Sch 1 art 23: see further para 1623 post.

1545. Jurisdictions in which actions must be brought. An action for damages must be brought, at the plaintiff's option, in the territory of one of the high contracting parties[1], either before the court[2] having jurisdiction where the carrier is ordinarily resident[3] or has his principal place of business[4], or has an establishment by which the contract has been made[5], or before the court having jurisdiction at the place of destination[6].

In relation to carriage performed by an actual carrier[7], any action for damages must be brought, at the plaintiff's option, either as above provided[8] or before the court having jurisdiction at the place where the actual carrier is ordinarily resident or has his principal place of business[9].

Questions of procedure are governed by the law of the court seised of the case[10].

1 As to the high contracting parties see para 1534 ante.

2 For the purposes of the Carriage by Air Act 1961 'court' includes an arbitrator (in any arbitration allowed by the Warsaw Convention): s 14 (2).

3 Where the carrier is a company, 'ordinarily resident' probably refers to the place where the company has its central management and control; that is, in all save exceptional cases, where its board of directors meets to conduct its business; but cf *Rothmans of Pall Mall (Overseas) Ltd v Saudi Arabian Airlines Corpn* [1981] QB 368, [1980] 3 All ER 359, 1 S&B AvR VII/1, CA, where a number of possible interpretations are examined.

4 'Principal place of business' presumably means the place where the main part of the carrier's executive and managerial work is done; in the case of a company this is usually but not necessarily the same place as the place of its central management and control.

5 This will normally be where the ticket or air waybill is issued.

6 Carriage by Air Act 1961 s 1 (1), Sch 1 art 28 (1) (Sch 1 replaced as from a day to be appointed by the Carriage by Air and Road Act 1979 s 1 (1), Sch 1; see para 1540 note 1 ante). This provision is strictly applied: *Rotterdamsche Bank NV v British Overseas Airways Corpn* [1953] 1 All ER 675, [1953] 1 WLR 493. The 'place of destination' will be the place of destination mentioned in the contract of carriage and, in the case of successive carriage, the ultimate place of destination set out in that contract. In the case of a round trip, the place of destination is the same as that of departure: *Qureshi v KLM Royal Dutch Airlines* (1979) 102 DLR (3d) 205 (NS SC), following *Grein v Imperial Airways Ltd* [1937] 1 KB 50, [1936] 2 All ER 1258; *Petrire v Spantax SA* 756 F 2d 263 (2nd Cir, 1985), 1 S&B AvR VII/161. Service of a writ or of notice of a writ out of the jurisdiction is permissible with the leave of the court in cases under the Carriage by Air Act 1961: RSC Ord 11 r 1 (2) (b); see PRACTICE AND PROCEDURE. If an action is brought in an English court which has no jurisdiction by reason of the provisions in the text, the writ and subsequent proceedings may be set aside: see *Rotterdamsche Bank NV v British Overseas Airways Corpn* supra.

7 For the meaning of 'actual carrier' see para 1539 note 4 ante.

8 Ie before the court having jurisdiction as regards the contracting carrier.

9 Carriage by Air (Supplementary Provisions) Act 1962 s 1 (1), Schedule Pt I art VIII.

10 Carriage by Air Act 1961 Sch 1 art 28 (2).

1546. Claims against high contracting parties. Every high contracting party[1] to the amended Warsaw Convention who has not declared that the provisions of the amended convention shall not apply to international carriage by air performed by it[2] is deemed, for the purpose of any action brought in a court in the United Kingdom in accordance with the preceding provisions[3] to enforce a claim in respect of carriage undertaken by it, to have submitted to the jurisdiction of that court[4]. Rules of court provide for the procedure in such an action[5]. Nothing in this provision, however, authorises the issue of execution against the property of any high contracting party[6].

1 As to the high contracting parties see para 1534 ante.

2 Ie who has not availed itself of the additional protocol; see paras 1009, 1537 ante. See also the Carriage by Air Act 1961 s 2 (1).

3 Ie the provisions of ibid s 1 (1), Sch 1 para 28 (Sch 1 replaced as from a day to be appointed by the Carriage by Air and Road Act 1979 s 1 (1), Sch 1; see para 1540 note 1 ante); see para 1545 ante.

4 Carriage by Air Act 1961 s 8. The reference to Sch 1 art 28 includes a reference to the Carriage by Air (Supplementary Provisions) Act 1962 s 1 (1), Schedule Pt I art VIII: 1962 Act s 3 (3); see para 1545 ante. As to actions against sovereign powers, and their submission to the jurisdiction, see CONSTITUTIONAL LAW; FOREIGN RELATIONS LAW.

5 See RSC Ord 11 r 7, made under the Carriage by Air Act 1961 s 8.

6 Carriage by Air Act 1961 s 8. As to the immunity from process of overseas sovereign states see CONSTITUTIONAL LAW; FOREIGN RELATIONS LAW.

1547. Actions against actual carrier. In relation to the carriage performed by the actual carrier[1], an action for damages may be brought, at the plaintiff's option, against that carrier or against the contracting carrier[2], or against both together or separately; if the action is brought against only one of those carriers, that carrier has

1e right to require the other to be joined in the proceedings, the procedure and ffects being governed by the law of the court seised of the case[3].

1 For the meaning of 'actual carrier' see para 1539 note 4 ante.
2 For the meaning of 'contracting carrier' see para 1539 note 5 ante.
3 Carriage by Air (Supplementary Provisions) Act 1962 s 1 (1), Schedule Pt I art VII. The acts and omissions of the actual carrier and of his servants and agents acting within the scope of their employment are deemed, in relation to carriage performed by the actual carrier, to be also those of the contracting carrier: Schedule Pt I art III (1). The acts and omissions of the contracting carrier and of his servants and agents acting within the scope of their employment are deemed, in relation to carriage performed by the actual carrier, to be also those of the actual carrier: Schedule Pt I art III (2). In the latter case there is, however, a limitation on the liability; see para 1551 post. As to jurisdiction see paras 1545, 1546 ante.

548. Actions in cases of successive carriage. In cases where carriage is to be erformed by various successive air carriers[1] and the carriage is deemed for the urposes of the amended Warsaw Convention to be one undivided carriage, a assenger or his representative can take action, in case of injury, death or delay, nly against the carrier who performed the carriage during which the accident or he delay occurred, save in the case where, by express agreement, the first carrier as assumed liability for the whole journey[2]. As regards baggage or cargo, the assenger or consignor has a right of action against the first carrier, and the assenger or consignee who is entitled to delivery has a right of action against the 1st carrier and further, each may take action against the carrier who performed the arriage during which the destruction, loss, damage or delay took place; these arriers are jointly and severally liable to the passenger or to the consignor or onsignee[3].

1 For the meaning of 'successive carriage' see para 1542 ante.
2 Carriage by Air Act 1961 s 1 (1), Sch 1 art 30 (2) (Sch 1 replaced as from a day to be appointed by the Carriage by Air and Road Act 1979 s 1 (1), Sch 1; see para 1540 note 1 ante).
3 Carriage by Air Act 1961 Sch 1 art 30 (3). As to when the consignee has the right to delivery see para 1577 post; as to joint and several liability in contract see CONTRACT.

549. Defence of all necessary measures. The carrier can escape from the abilities imposed upon him by the amended Warsaw Convention if he proves that e and his servants and agents have taken all necessary measures to avoid the amage or that it was impossible for him or them to take such measures[1].

1 Carriage by Air Act 1961 s 1 (1), Sch 1 art 20 (Sch 1 replaced as from a day to be appointed by the Carriage by Air and Road Act 1979 s 1 (1), Sch 1; see para 1540 note 1 ante). A number of carriers waive this defence, including all carriers who are parties to the Montreal Agreement of 1966, as to which see para 1558 post. As to the meaning of the provision in the text see *Grein v Imperial Airways Ltd* [1937] 1 KB 50 at 69–71, [1936] 2 All ER 1258 at 1274–1276, CA, per Greer LJ; *Chisholm v British European Airways* [1963] 1 Lloyd's Rep 626; *Goldman v Thai Airways International Ltd* (1981) 125 Sol Jo 413; revsd on other grounds [1983] 3 All ER 693, [1983] 1 WLR 1186, 1 S&B AvR VII/101, CA; *Swiss Bank Corpn v Brink's-MAT Ltd* (14 November 1985, unreported), Bingham J; further proceedings [1986] QB 853, [1986] 2 All ER 188, 1 S&B AvR VII/195.

550. Contributory negligence. If the carrier proves[1] that the damage was aused by or contributed to by the negligence of the injured person, the court may, n accordance with the provisions of its own law, exonerate the carrier wholly or artly from his liability[2].

1   The carrier has the burden of proof: *Rustenburg Platinum Mines Ltd v South African Airways* [1977] Lloyd's Rep 564 at 577–578; affd [1979] 1 Lloyd's Rep 19, CA.
2   Carriage by Air Act 1961 s 1 (1), Sch 1 art 21 (Sch 1 replaced as from a day to be appointed by th Carriage by Air and Road Act 1979 s 1 (1), Sch 1; see para 1540 note 1 ante). The Carriage by Air Ac 1961 s 6 provides expressly that for this purpose the Law Reform (Contributory Negligence) Ac 1945, including that Act as applied to Scotland, and the Law Reform (Miscellaneous Provisions) Ac (Northern Ireland) 1948 s 2, are provisions of the law of the United Kingdom under which a cour may exonerate the carrier wholly or in part from his liability. As to contributory negligence se NEGLIGENCE. See *Goldman v Thai Airways International Ltd* [1983] 3 All ER 693, [1983] 1 WLR 1186, S&B AvR VII/101, CA.

1551. Limitation of liability generally.

The liability of the carrier is limited t certain maximum sums specified in the Carriage by Air Act 1961[1]. This limitatio may be affected in the carriage of passengers by the carrier agreeing to an increase limit by a special contract[2], or in baggage and cargo cases by the making of a specia declaration as to the value of the goods carried[3], and is inapplicable in certain othe cases[4].

In relation to the carriage performed by the actual carrier, no act or omission o the contracting carrier[5] will subject the actual carrier to liability exceeding th limits laid down in the amended Warsaw Convention, and no waiver of rights b the contracting carrier will affect the actual carrier unless agreed by him[6].

If an action is brought against such a carrier's servant or agent, the servant o agent is entitled, if he proves that he was acting within the scope of his employ ment, to invoke the provisions of the amended convention limiting the carrier' liability applicable to the carrier whose servant he is[7].

The aggregate of the amounts recoverable from the carrier[8], his servants an agents, may not exceed the limits provided for by the amended convention[9].

1   See the Carriage by Air Act 1961 s 1 (1), Sch 1 art 22 (Sch 1 replaced as from a day to be appointed b the Carriage by Air and Road Act 1979 s 1 (1), Sch 1; see para 1540 note 1 ante). As to the sums se paras 1561, 1567, 1582 post.
2   See paras 1561, 1590 post.
3   See paras 1567, 1582, 1590 post.
4   See para 1553 post.
5   See para 1547 note 3 ante. For the meanings of 'actual carrier' and 'contracting carrier' see para 153 notes 4, 5 ante.
6   Carriage by Air (Supplementary Provisions) Act 1962 s 1 (1), Schedule Pt I art III (2).
7   Carriage by Air Act 1961 s 1 (1), Sch 1 art 25A (1) (see note 1 supra); Carriage by Air (Supplementary Provisions) Act 1962 Schedule Pt I art v. Limits of liability may not be invoked if it is proved that th servant or agent acted in a manner which, under the amended convention, excludes the limitation o liability by the carrier: Schedule Pt I art v; Carriage by Air Act 1961 Sch 1 art 25A (3); see para 155 post.
8   In the case of carriage not performed by the contracting carrier, reference to the carrier includes her reference to both the contracting carrier and the actual carrier when an action has been brough against both of them; see para 1547 ante.
9   Carriage by Air Act 1961 Sch 1 art 25A (2) (see note 1 supra); Carriage by Air (Supplementary Provisions) Act 1962 Schedule Pt I art vi. None of the persons mentioned may be liable for a sum i excess of the limit applicable to him: Schedule Pt I art vi.

1552. Provisions relieving carrier of liability.

Any provision tending t relieve the carrier of liability or to fix a lower limit than that which is laid down i the amended Warsaw Convention is null and void, but the nullity of any suc provision does not involve the nullity of the whole contract, which remains subjec to the provisions of the amended convention[1].

1 Carriage by Air Act 1961 s 1 (1), Sch 1 art 23 (1) (Sch 1 replaced as from a day to be appointed by the Carriage by Air and Road Act 1979 s 1 (1), Sch 1; see para 1540 note 1 ante). This rule does not, however, apply to provisions governing loss or damage resulting from the inherent defect, quality or vice of the cargo carried: Carriage by Air Act 1961 Sch 1 art 23 (2). These provisions apply whether the carriage is performed by the contracting carrier or an actual carrier: see the Carriage by Air (Supplementary Provisions) Act 1962 s 1 (1), Schedule Pt I art IX (1), (2).

1553. Loss of carrier's right to limit liability. The limits of liability[1] do not apply if it is proved that the damage resulted from an act or omission of the carrier[2], his servants or agents, done with intent to cause damage[3] or done recklessly and with knowledge[4] that damage would probably result[5]; in the case of a servant or agent, it must also be proved that the servant or agent was acting within the scope of his employment[6].

The right to exclude or limit liability is also lost if, with the carrier's consent, the passenger embarks without a passenger ticket having been delivered to him[7], or if the ticket does not include the notice required by the amended Warsaw convention[8].

In respect of registered baggage, the right to exclude or limit liability is lost if the carrier takes charge of the baggage without a baggage check having been delivered[9] or if the baggage check does not include the notice required by the amended convention[10]. In the case of cargo, if, with the carrier's consent, cargo is loaded on board the aircraft without an air waybill having been made out[11], or if the air waybill does not include the notice required by the amended convention[12], the carrier is not entitled to avail himself of the right to limit or exclude his liability[13].

1 See the Carriage by Air Act 1961 s 1 (1), Sch 1 art 22 (Sch 1 replaced as from a day to be appointed by the Carriage by Air and Road Act 1979 s 1 (1), Sch 1; see para 1540 note 1 ante); and para 1551 ante.
2 In relation to carriage by an actual carrier, the carrier may be the actual carrier or the contracting carrier (defined in para 1539 notes 4, 5 ante); but no act or omission of the contracting carrier, his servants or agents, may subject the actual carrier to liability exceeding the limits of the amended convention: Carriage by Air (Supplementary Provisions) Act 1962 s 1 (1), Schedule Pt I art III (2).
3 Not necessarily the precise damage which actually occurred: *Goldman v Thai Airways International Ltd* [1983] 3 All ER 693, [1983] 1 WLR 1186, 1 S&B AvR VII/101, CA.
4 This phrase carries a subjective meaning: *Goldman v Thai Airways International Ltd* [1983] 3 All ER 693, [1983] 1 WLR 1186, 1 S&B AvR VII/101, CA. A similar interpretation is given to the phrase in the courts of almost all other countries, France being an exception.
5 Carriage by Air Act 1961 Sch 1 art 25; and see the Carriage by Air (Supplementary Provisions) Act 1962 Schedule Pt I art V.
6 Carriage by Air Act 1961 Sch 1 art 25; and see the Carriage by Air (Supplementary Provisions) Act 1962 Schedule Pt I art V.
7 See the Carriage by Air Act 1961 Sch 1 art 3 (2); and para 1557 post.
8 See ibid Sch 1 art 3 (1) (c); and para 1556 post.
9 Ibid Sch 1 art 4 (2); see para 1563 post.
10 See ibid Sch 1 art 4 (1) (c); and para 1562 post. The carrier's right to exclude or limit his liability is not lost if the baggage check is combined with or incorporated in a passenger ticket which complies with the requirements of the amended convention: Sch 1 art 4 (2).
11 See ibid Sch 1 arts 5–8; and paras 1568–1571 post.
12 See ibid Sch 1 art 8 (c); and para 1570 post.
13 Ibid Sch 1 art 9.

1554. Limitation of actions. The right to damages is extinguished[1] if an action[2] is not brought within two years, reckoned from the date of arrival at the destination, or from the date on which the aircraft ought to have arrived or on which the carriage stopped[3]. The same limitation applies to any action[4] against a carrier's[5] servant or agent which arises out of damage to which the amended Warsaw Convention relates, if the servant or agent was acting within the scope of his employment[6].

The two years' limitation rule must not be read as applying to any proceeding for contribution between tortfeasors[7]; however, no action[8] may be brought by tortfeasor to obtain contribution from a carrier[9] in respect of a tort to which the above-mentioned rule[10] applies, after the expiration of two years from the time when judgment is obtained against the person seeking to obtain the contribution[11].

The method of calculating the limitation period is determined by the law of the court seised of the case[12].

1　See *Aries Tanker Corpn v Total Transport Ltd, The Aries* [1977] 1 All ER 398, [1977] 1 WLR 185, HL *Proctor v Jetway Aviation* [1982] 2 NSWLR 264, revsd on other grounds [1984] 1 NSWLR 166 (NSW CA).
2　The Carriage by Air Act 1961 s 5, and art 29 of the amended convention as enacted by s 1 (1) of an Sch 1 to that Act, have effect as if references to an action include references to an arbitration: Carriage by Air Act 1961 s 5 (3) (Sch 1 replaced as from a day to be appointed by the Carriage by Air and Road Act 1979 s 1 (1), Sch 1; see para 1540 note 1 ante).
3　Carriage by Air Act 1961 Sch 1 art 29 (1). Note that the provisions of the Limitation Act 1980 s 3 and of RSC Ord 15 r 6 are inapplicable. For the practice in respect of changes of party see *Liff Peasley* [1980] 1 All ER 623, [1980] 1 WLR 781, CA. The two-year period may not be suspended or extended for any reason, the provisions in the Limitation Act 1980 Pt II (ss 28–33) allowing for extensions being inapplicable; a similar view is taken in almost all other countries.
4　See note 2 supra.
5　The Carriage by Air Act 1961 s 5 must be read as if references to a carrier included references to an actual carrier as well as to a contracting carrier: Carriage by Air (Supplementary Provisions) Act 1962 s 3 (2).
6　Carriage by Air Act 1961 s 5 (1).
7　Ibid s 5 (2) (amended by the Limitation Act 1963 s 4 (4) and by the Civil Liability (Contribution) Act 1978 s 9 (1), Sch 1 para 5 (2)).
8　See note 2 supra.
9　See note 5 supra.
10　Ie the Carriage by Air Act 1961 Sch 1 art 29 (1).
11　Civil Liability (Contribution) Act 1978 s 1 (3).
12　Carriage by Air Act 1961 Sch 1 art 29 (2).

1555. Death of person liable. In the case of the death of the person liable[1], an action for damages lies in accordance with the terms of the amended Warsaw Convention against those legally representing his estate[2].

1　Ie under the provisions imposing liability for injury to or death of passengers (see para 1559 post), for loss of or damage to baggage or cargo (see paras 1564, 1579 post), and for delay (see para 1583 post).
2　Carriage by Air Act 1961 s 1 (1), Sch 1 art 27 (Sch 1 replaced as from a day to be appointed by the Carriage by Air and Road Act 1979 s 1 (1), Sch 1; see para 1540 note 1 ante). See also the Law Reform (Miscellaneous Provisions) Act 1934 s 1 (5) (amended by the Carriage by Air Act 1961 s 14 (3), Sch 2); and EXECUTORS.

(ii) Carriage of Passengers under the Warsaw-Hague Provisions

1556. Contents of passenger tickets. In respect of the carriage of passengers, a ticket must be delivered containing:

(1) an indication of the places of departure and destination[1];
(2) if those places are within the territory[2] of a single high contracting party[3], one or more agreed stopping places[4] being within the territory of another state, an indication of at least one such stopping place[5]; and

(3) a notice to the effect that if the passenger's journey involves an ultimate
destination or stop in a country other than the country of departure, the
Warsaw Convention may be applicable, and that this governs and in most
cases limits the liability of carriers[6] for death or personal injury and in respect
of loss of or damage to baggage[7].

The passenger ticket constitutes prima facie evidence of the conclusion and
conditions of the contract of carriage[8].

1 Carriage by Air Act 1961 s 1 (1), Sch 1 art 3 (1) (a) (Sch 1 replaced as from a day to be appointed by the
  Carriage by Air and Road Act 1979 s 1 (1), Sch 1; see para 1540 note 1 ante).
2 For the meaning of 'territory' see para 1535 ante.
3 For the meaning of 'high contracting party' see para 1534 ante.
4 For the meaning of 'agreed stopping place' see para 1541 note 5 ante. As to the incorporation of the
  stopping place by reference see para 1570 note 4 post.
5 Carriage by Air Act 1961 Sch 1 art 3 (1) (b) (see note 1 supra).
6 'Carrier' is not defined in the Carriage by Air Act 1961. 'Contracting carrier' and 'actual carrier' are
  defined in the Carriage by Air (Supplementary Provisions) Act 1962; see para 1539 notes 4, 5 ante.
  As to charter flights see para 1336 et seq ante.
7 Carriage by Air Act 1961 Sch 1 art 3 (1) (c) (see note 1 supra). For the standard IATA text see IATA
  Resolution 724, reproduced in Shawcross & Beaumont: Air Law (4th Edn) vol 2, Appendix AB.
8 Carriage by Air Act 1961 Sch 1 art 3 (2) (see note 1 supra). As to defective passenger tickets see para
  1557 post.

1557. Absence, irregularity or loss of passenger ticket. The absence, irregularity or loss of the passenger ticket does not affect the existence or the validity of
the contract of carriage, which is, none the less, subject to the rules of the
Warsaw-Hague Convention[1]. Nevertheless, if, with the carrier's consent, a passenger embarks without a passenger ticket having been delivered[2], or if the ticket
does not include the required notice[3], the carrier is not entitled to avail himself of
the provisions of Article 22 of the convention[4] on the limitation of liability[5].

1 Carriage by Air Act 1961 s 1 (1), Sch 1 art 3 (2) (Sch 1 replaced as from a day to be appointed by the
  Carriage by Air and Road Act 1979 s 1 (1), Sch 1; see para 1540 note 1 ante). See *Preston v Hunting Air
  Transport Ltd* [1956] 1 QB 454, [1956] 1 All ER 443, decided under the Carriage by Air Act 1932
  (repealed).
2 See *Mertens v Flying Tiger Line Inc* 341 F 2d 851 (2d Cir, 1965), cert denied 382 US 816 (1965):
  delivery of ticket to a passenger once on board the aircraft is insufficient compliance. To similar
  effect is the non-international case of *Fosbroke-Hobbes v Airwork Ltd and British-American Air Services
  Ltd* [1937] 1 All ER 108.
3 See para 1556 item (3) ante. As to the standard of legibility of the ticket see para 1558 post.
4 See para 1561 post.
5 Carriage by Air Act 1961 Sch 1 art 3 (2) (see note 1 supra). An actual carrier is not obliged to deliver a
  ticket if the contracting carrier has done so, as the acts and omissions of either the contracting carrier
  or of the actual carrier are deemed to be acts and omissions of the other: Carriage by Air (Supplementary Provisions) Act 1962 s 1 (1), Schedule Pt I art III.

1558. Legibility of passenger ticket. There are no reported English cases on
the standard of legibility of a passenger ticket, or the adequacy of notice of
conditions or the terms of the contract of carriage contained in an airline ticket, as
factors relevant to the carrier's right to limit his liability to pay damages in respect
of the death of or personal injury to a passenger caused during the performance of a
contract of international carriage governed by any version of the Warsaw Convention[1]. The issue has, however, been extensively tested in the courts of the United
States and Canada[2].

It is submitted that if the issue were to be tested in the English courts now, i
should be decided upon a strict interpretation of the relevant provisions[3], and b
reference to common law principles relating to the adequacy and legibility o
written notice of contractual conditions[4]. It is further submitted that passenge
tickets printed to the current IATA standard[5] ought to meet any reasonabl
standard of legibility. To measure the legibility of tickets printed to the IAT/
standard by reference to the different standard required for the formal 'Advice t
International Passengers on Limitation of Liability' given in compliance with th
Montreal Agreement to passengers travelling on a contract of international car
riage on a journey to, from or with an agreed stopping place in the United States[6]
is not an appropriate test[7].

1 See the Carriage by Air Act 1961 s 1 (1), Sch 1 arts 3, 17, 22 (Sch 1 replaced as from a day to b
appointed by the Carriage by Air and Road Act 1979 s 1 (1), Sch 1; see para 1540 note 1 ante).
2 In _Lisi v Alitalia-Linee Aeree Italiane SpA_ 370 F 2d 508 (2d Cir, 1966), [1967] 1 Lloyd's Rep 140, aff
by an equally divided court 390 US 455 (1968), it was held that as the diminutive size of the type use
by the defendants on their tickets did not adequately bring the notice to the passenger's attention, th
requirements of the convention had not been complied with. This decision, and the many decision
of courts in the United States influenced by it, lost much of their authority as a result of _Chan v
Korean Air Lines Ltd_ 109 S Ct 1676 (1989). Both were decided by reference to the text of th
unamended Warsaw Convention. As to Canada see _Montreal Trust Co v Canadian Pacific Airlines L_
(1976) 72 DLR (3d) 257, [1977] 2 Lloyd's Rep 80 (Can SC).
3 Ie not on the basis propounded by Salmon LJ in _Samuel Montagu & Co Ltd v Swiss Air Transport C
Ltd_ [1966] 2 QB 306 at 316, [1966] 1 All ER 814 at 818, CA.
4 See CONTRACT; and see _Koskas v Standard Marine Insurance Co Ltd_ (1927) 27 Ll L Rep 59 at 61–62, CA
and _Budd v Peninsular and Oriental Steam Navigation Co_ [1969] 2 Lloyd's Rep 262.
5 IATA Resolution 724. It provides, inter alia, that the Hague Protocol notice must be printed in bol
8 point letters, preferably in Helvetica or similar large character letters, and that the text of th
conditions of contract must be printed in 6 point type of the same character. For the requirement t
give a notice to the effect that the Warsaw Convention may be applicable to the passenger's journe
see para 1556 item (3) ante.
6 Agreement CAB 18900, approved by the Civil Aeronautics Board on 13 May 1966. This agreemen
provides, inter alia, that, for passengers on a journey to, from or with an agreed stopping place in th
United States, carriers who are parties to the agreement waive their defence under the Warsav
Convention art 20, and, further, that carrier's liability to pay damages for death or personal injury i
limited to US $75,000 inclusive of legal fees and costs, in place of the limits provided for by th
unamended and amended conventions. One of the terms of the Montreal Agreement is that eac
carrier must furnish to each passenger whose transport is governed by the Warsaw Convention o
the Warsaw Convention as amended at The Hague in 1955 a notice, usually printed on the ticket o
on a separate ticket envelope, explaining the special contract. The notice, the terms of which are se
out in the agreement, must be printed in type as large as 10 point modern type and in ink contrastin
with the stock. For the text see Shawcross & Beaumont: Air Law (4th Edn) vol 2, Appendix AB. It i
submitted that the words 'agreed stopping place' in the Montreal Agreement have the same meanin
as in the unamended and amended conventions; see para 1541 note 5 ante.
7 See _Chan v Korean Air Lines Ltd_ 109 S Ct 1676 (1989), 1 S&B AvR VII/383.

1559. Liability for death of or injury to passengers. The carrier[1] is liable[2] fo
damage sustained in the event of the death or wounding of a passenger or any othe
bodily injury[3] suffered by a passenger if the accident[4] which caused the damage s
sustained took place on board the aircraft or in the course of any of the operations o
embarking or disembarking[5].

1 As to who is the carrier see para 1539 ante. As to who should be sued in the case of carriage b
successive carriers see para 1548 ante.
2 For defences available to the carrier see paras 1549, 1550 ante; for limitations on the damages whic
may be payable see para 1561 post.

3 The English courts have not addressed the question whether nervous shock or mental anguish comes within the phrase 'other bodily injury'. See *Eastern Airlines Inc v Floyd* 111 S Ct 1489 (1991), where the United States Supreme Court after a full review of the authorities decided that such mental injury was not included.

4 The term 'accident' is not defined. The United States Supreme Court has held that it is an unexpected or unusual event or happening that is external to the passenger; it is not sufficient if the passenger suffers injury as a result of his own internal reaction to the usual, normal and expected operation of the aircraft: *Air France v Saks* 105 S Ct 1338 (1985), 1 S&B AvR VII/165. A technical failure (for example a tyre failure on take-off or landing) or a terrorist attack will constitute an 'accident'; a heart-attack or a loss of hearing as a result of normal take-off and landing procedures will not.

5 Carriage by Air Act 1961 s 1 (1), Sch 1 art 17 (Sch 1 replaced as from a day to be appointed by the Carriage by Air and Road Act 1979 s 1 (1), Sch 1; see para 1540 note 1 ante). As to 'the operations of embarking and disembarking' see *Day v Trans World Airlines Inc* 528 F 2d 31 (2nd Cir, 1975), cert denied 429 US 890 (1976) and *Evangelinos v Trans World Airlines Inc* 550 F 2d 152 (3rd Cir, 1976), where the courts adopted a tripartite test, looking at the location of the passenger, the nature of his activity at the relevant time, and the degree of control over his movements exercised by the carrier. A passenger on the airport apron is likely to be within the scope of the 1961 Act Sch 1 art 17; one moving freely within the terminal, or who on disembarking has reached the baggage reclaim area, is unlikely so to be.

560. Claim on passenger's death. An occurrence leading to a passenger's death and giving rise to a claim[1] is treated as a wrongful act, neglect or default within the meaning of the Fatal Accidents Act 1976[2], and is governed by the system of that Act[3]. An action may also be brought under the Law Reform (Miscellaneous Provisions) Act 1934. Damages in excess of the statutory limit[4] may not be recovered; that limitation encompasses all claims arising under the Fatal Accidents Act 1976 or under the Law Reform (Miscellaneous Provisions) Act 1934, or under both those Acts[5].

1 Ie under the Carriage by Air Act 1961 s 1 (1), Sch 1 art 17 (Sch 1 replaced as from a day to be appointed by the Carriage by Air and Road Act 1979 s 1 (1), Sch 1; see para 1540 note 1 ante); see para 1559 ante.

2 See the Fatal Accidents Act 1976 s 1 (substituted by the Administration of Justice Act 1982 s 3); and NEGLIGENCE.

3 Carriage by Air Act 1961 s 3; this provision refers to the Fatal Accidents Act 1846, but see the Fatal Accidents Act 1976 s 6, Sch 1 para 2.

4 See the Carriage by Air Act 1961 Sch 1 art 22; and paras 1553 ante, 1561 post.

5 Ibid s 4.

561. Limitation of liability for passengers. In the carriage of passengers, the carrier's liability for each passenger is limited under the amended Warsaw Convention to the sum of 250,000 francs[1]. Where, in accordance with the law of the court seised of the case, damages may be awarded in the form of periodical payments, the equivalent capital value of such payments must not exceed 250,000 francs[2].

The sums in francs mentioned in the Carriage by Air Act 1961 are deemed to refer to French 'Poincaré' francs consisting of 65½ milligrammes of gold of millesimal fineness 900; they may be converted into national currency according to the value of gold at the date of the judgment[3]. For this purpose, the Secretary of State may by order specify the amounts to be taken as the sterling equivalents of the sums expressed in francs in the Act[4].

These limitations on liability apply whatever the nature of the proceedings; in particular they apply to the carrier's aggregate liability in all proceedings brought against him whether within or outside the United Kingdom[5]. However, the carrier and the passenger may by special contract agree to a higher limit of liability[6].

1 Carriage by Air Act 1961 s 1 (1), Sch 1 art 22 (1) (Sch 1 replaced as from a day to be appointed by th Carriage by Air and Road Act 1979 s 1 (1), Sch 1; see para 1540 note 1 ante). The limit applie whether the claim is for death, injury or delay; for cases where the carrier loses the right to limit h liability see paras 1553, 1557 ante.

2 Carriage by Air Act 1961 Sch 1 art 22 (1).

3 Ibid Sch 1 art 22 (5).

4 Ibid s 4 (4) (repealed as from a day to be appointed by the Carriage by Air and Road Act 1979 Sch 2 The Carriage by Air (Sterling Equivalents) Order 1986, SI 1986/1778, made under this powe specifies the amounts to be taken for the purposes of the Carriage by Air Act 1961 Sch 1 art 22 and (that article as applied by the Carriage by Air Acts (Application of Provisions) Order 1967, S 1967/480, as equivalent to the sums therein expressed in convention francs. The figures are:

CONVENTION FRANCS	POUNDS STERLING EQUIVALENT
250	13.63
5,000	272.67
125,000	6,816.68
250,000	13,633.40

The basis of this table was that approximately 15 convention francs formerly equalled one SD (Special Drawing Right) of the IMF, the value of which against sterling is readily ascertainable. Th order is only amended when variations in this value render the established conversion figur significantly out of line.

As to the Secretary of State see para 1032 ante.

5 Carriage by Air Act 1961 s 4 (1) (amended by the Civil Liability (Contribution) Act 1978 s 9 (1), (2 Sch 1 para 5 (1), Sch 2); see also para 1551 ante. The court may make, at any stage of the proceeding and of any other proceedings, any order appearing to be just and equitable to enforce the carrier liability: Carriage by Air Act 1961 s 4 (2). When liability is, or may be, enforceable in any othe proceedings, the court may award an amount less than the amount which it would have awarded : the limitation applied solely to the proceedings before it, or it may make any part of its awar conditional on the result of any other proceedings: s 4 (3). These limits do not prevent the court fror awarding, in addition, the whole or part of the court costs and of the other expenses of litigatio incurred by the plaintiff (Sch 1 art 22 (4)), save in the case where the damages awarded do not excee the sum offered in writing by the carrier to the plaintiff within six months of the occurrence of th damage or before the commencement of the action (Sch 1 art 22 (4)).

6 Ibid Sch 1 art 22 (1). One example of a special contract is that entered into by all carriers party to th Montreal Agreement (see para 1558 note 6 ante) where either the place of departure or the place c destination or an agreed stopping place is within the United States; in such cases, the limit on th carrier's liability is raised to US $75,000.

(iii) Carriage of Baggage under the Warsaw–Hague Provisions

1562. Contents of baggage check. The Carriage by Air Act 1961 draws . distinction between registered baggage and objects of which the passenger take charge himself, commonly called cabin or hand baggage. For the carriage o registered baggage[1], a baggage check must be delivered which, unless combine(with or incorporated in a passenger ticket which complies with the provisions o the amended Warsaw Convention[2], must contain:

(1) an indication of the places of departure and destination[3];

(2) if those places are within the territory[4] of a single high contracting party[5] one or more agreed stopping places[6] being within the territory of anothe state, an indication of at least one such stopping place[7]; and

(3) a notice to the effect that, if the carriage involves an ultimate destination o stop in a country other than the country of departure, the amended conven- tion may be applicable and that it governs and in most cases limits th liability of carriers[8] in respect of loss of or damage to baggage[9].

The baggage check constitutes prima facie evidence of the registration of th baggage and of the conditions of the contract of carriage[10].

1 For a discussion of the meaning of the term see *Collins v British Airways Board* [1982] QB 734, [1982] 1 All ER 302, 1 S&B AvR VII/155, CA.
2 See para 1556 ante. In practice, the baggage check and passenger ticket are almost always combined. See *Collins v British Airways Board* [1982] QB 734, [1982] 1 All ER 302, 1 S&B AvR VII/155, CA.
3 Carriage by Air Act 1961 s 1 (1), Sch 1 art 4 (1) (a) (Sch 1 replaced as from a day to be appointed by the Carriage by Air and Road Act 1979 s 1 (1), Sch 1; see para 1540 note 1 ante).
4 For the meaning of 'territory' see para 1535 ante.
5 For the meaning of 'high contracting party' see para 1534 ante.
6 For the meaning of 'agreed stopping place' see para 1541 note 5 ante.
7 Carriage by Air Act 1961 Sch 1 art 4 (1) (b) (see note 3 supra).
8 As to the construction of references to carriers see para 1539 ante.
9 Carriage by Air Act 1961 Sch 1 art 4 (1) (c) (see note 3 supra).
10 Ibid Sch 1 art 4 (2) (see note 3 supra). As to defective baggage checks see para 1563 post.

1563. Absence, irregularity or loss of baggage check. The absence, irregularity or loss of the baggage check does not affect the existence or validity of the contract of carriage, which is, none the less, subject to the rules of the amended Warsaw Convention[1]. Nevertheless, if the carrier takes charge of the baggage without a baggage check having been delivered, or if the baggage check, unless combined with or incorporated in the passenger ticket which complies with the provisions of the amended convention[2], does not include the notice required by that convention[3], the carrier is not entitled to avail himself of the provisions of Article 22 (2) of that convention[4] which limit his liability[5].

1 Carriage by Air Act 1961 s 1 (1), Sch 1 art 4 (2) (Sch 1 replaced as from a day to be appointed by the Carriage by Air and Road Act 1979 s 1 (1), Sch 1; see para 1540 note 1 ante).
2 See para 1556 ante.
3 See para 1562 item (3) ante.
4 See para 1567 post.
5 Carriage by Air Act 1961 Sch 1 art 4 (2) (see note 1 supra). As to liability for loss of or damage to baggage, and for delay, see paras 1564, 1628 post.

1564. Loss of or damage to baggage. The carrier[1] is liable for damage sustained in the event of the destruction or loss of, or of damage to, any registered baggage[2], if the occurrence which caused the damage so sustained took place during the carriage by air[3].

The carriage by air for this purpose comprises the period during which the baggage is in charge of the carrier, whether in an aerodrome or on board an aircraft or, in the case of a landing outside an aerodrome, in any place whatsoever[4]. It does not extend to any carriage by land, by sea or by river performed outside an aerodrome, but if such a carriage takes place in the performance of a contract for carriage by air for the purpose of loading, delivery or transhipment, any damage is presumed, subject to proof to the contrary, to have been the result of an event which took place during the carriage by air[5].

1 As to who is the carrier see paras 1539, 1542 ante.
2 For the meaning of 'registered baggage' see *Collins v British Airways Board* [1982] QB 734, [1982] 1 All ER 302, 1 S&B AvR VII/155, CA.
3 Carriage by Air Act 1961 s 1 (1), Sch 1 art 18 (1) (Sch 1 replaced as from a day to be appointed by the Carriage by Air and Road Act 1979 s 1 (1), Sch 1; see para 1540 note 1 ante). For requirements as to notice of complaint see para 1566 post; for defences available to the carrier see paras 1549, 1550 ante; for limitations on the damages which may be payable see para 1567 post.
4 Carriage by Air Act 1961 Sch 1 art 18 (2). See para 1579 post.
5 Ibid Sch 1 art 18 (3).

1565. Receipt without complaint as evidence. Receipt by the person entitled to delivery of baggage without complaint is prima facie evidence that the same has been delivered in good condition and in accordance with the document of carriage[1].

1 Carriage by Air Act 1961 s 1 (1), Sch 1 art 26 (1) (Sch 1 replaced as from a day to be appointed by the Carriage by Air and Road Act 1979 s 1 (1), Sch 1; see para 1540 note 1 ante). Any complaint made under the provisions of the amended Warsaw Convention has the same effect whether addressed to the contracting carrier or to the actual carrier: Carriage by Air (Supplementary Provisions) Act 1962 Schedule Pt I art IV. For the meanings of 'contracting carrier' and 'actual carrier' see para 1539 notes 4, 5 ante. As to the time within which complaints must be made see para 1566 post.

1566. Complaints of damage or delay to baggage. In the case of damage[1] to baggage, the person entitled to delivery must complain to the carrier forthwith after the discovery of the damage and at the latest within seven days[2] from the date of receipt[3]. In the case of delay, the complaint must be made at the latest within 21 days from the date on which the baggage has been placed at his disposal[4].

Every complaint must be made in writing upon the document of carriage or by separate notice in writing dispatched within the times aforesaid[5].

Failing complaint within these times, no action lies against the carrier, save in the case of fraud on his part[6].

1 Including loss of part of the baggage in question: Carriage by Air Act 1961 s 4A (added by the Carriage by Air and Road Act 1979 s 2); *Fothergill v Monarch Airlines Ltd* [1981] AC 251, [1980] 2 All ER 696, 1 S&B AvR I/9, HL. Complaint is not needed in the case of total loss or destruction.
2 'Days' means current days, not working days: Carriage by Air Act 1961 s 1 (1), Sch 1 art 35 (Sch 1 replaced as from a day to be appointed by the Carriage by Air and Road Act 1979 s 1 (1), Sch 1; see para 1540 note 1 ante).
3 Carriage by Air Act 1961 Sch 1 art 26 (2).
4 Ibid Sch 1 art 26 (2).
5 Ibid Sch 1 art 26 (3).
6 Ibid Sch 1 art 26 (4). Fraud, it is thought, refers to fraudulent concealment of the damage or of the right of action: cf *Denby v Seaboard World Airlines Inc* 737 F 2d 172 (2nd Cir, 1984).

1567. Limitation of liability for baggage. In the carriage of registered baggage, the carrier's liability is limited to a sum of 250 francs[1] per kilogramme, unless the passenger has made, at the time when the package was handed over to the carrier, a special declaration of interest in delivery at destination and has paid a supplementary sum if the case so requires; in that case the carrier will be liable to pay a sum not exceeding the declared sum, unless he proves that that sum is greater than the passenger's actual interest in delivery at destination[2].

In the case of loss, damage or delay of part of registered baggage, or of any object contained in it, the weight to be taken into consideration in determining the limit on the carrier's liability is only the total weight of the package or packages concerned; nevertheless, when such a loss affects the value of other packages covered by the same baggage check, the total weight of such package or packages must also be taken into consideration[3].

As regards objects of which the passenger takes charge himself, the carrier's liability is limited to 5,000 francs per passenger[4].

1 The sterling equivalent of 250 francs is £13.63: see the Carriage by Air (Sterling Equivalents) Order 1986, SI 1986/1778: see further para 1561 ante.
2 Carriage by Air Act 1961 s 1 (1), Sch 1 art 22 (2) (a) (Sch 1 replaced as from a day to be appointed by the Carriage by Air and Road Act 1979 s 1 (1), Sch 1; see para 1540 note 1 ante). As to the meaning of

'special declaration' and 'supplementary' see *Westminster Bank Ltd v Imperial Airways Ltd* [1936] 2 All ER 890; and see *Corocraft Ltd v Pan American Airways Inc* [1969] 1 QB 616 at 641, [1969] 1 All ER 82, CA.
3 Carriage by Air Act 1961 Sch 1 art 22 (2) (b). As to the calculation of the weight where this is not clearly recorded see *Bland v British Airways Board* [1981] 1 Lloyd's Rep 289, CA, and *Collins v British Airways Board* [1982] QB 734, [1982] 1 All ER 302, 1 S&B AvR VII/155, CA.
4 Carriage by Air Act 1961 Sch 1 art 22 (3). The sterling equivalent of 5,000 francs is £272.67: see the Carriage by Air (Sterling Equivalents) Order 1986, SI 1986/1778; and para 1561 ante.

(iv) Carriage of Cargo under the Warsaw-Hague Provisions

1568. Air waybills. Every carrier of cargo has the right to require the consignor to make out and hand over to him a document called an air waybill, and every consignor has the right to require the carrier to accept this document[1]. The carrier has the right to require the consignor to make out separate waybills where there is more than one package[2].

1 Carriage by Air Act 1961 s 1 (1), Sch 1 art 5 (1) (Sch 1 replaced as from a day to be appointed by the Carriage by Air and Road Act 1979 s 1 (1), Sch 1; see para 1540 note 1 ante). But as to the carrier's right to refuse to carry see para 1538 ante. As to the contents of an air waybill see para 1570 post.
2 Carriage by Air Act 1961 Sch 1 art 7. As to the absence, irregularity or loss of an air waybill see para 1571 post.

1569. Making out of air waybill. The air waybill must be made out by the consignor in three original parts and must be handed over with the cargo[1]. The first part must be marked 'for the carrier' and must be signed by the consignor; the second part must be marked 'for the consignee' and must be signed by the consignor and by the carrier and must accompany the cargo; and the third part must be signed by the carrier and handed by him to the consignor after the cargo has been accepted[2]. The carrier must sign prior to the loading of the cargo on board the aircraft[3]. The carrier's signature may be stamped; the consignor's signature may be printed or stamped[4].

If, at the consignor's request, the carrier makes out the air waybill, he is deemed, subject to proof to the contrary, to have done so on behalf of the consignor[5].

1 Carriage by Air Act 1961 s 1 (1), Sch 1 art 6 (1) (Sch 1 replaced as from a day to be appointed by the Carriage by Air and Road Act 1979 s 1 (1), Sch 1; see para 1540 note 1 ante).
2 Carriage by Air Act 1961 Sch 1 art 6 (2).
3 Ibid Sch 1 art 6 (3).
4 Ibid Sch 1 art 6 (4).
5 Ibid Sch 1 art 6 (5). As to the responsibility for the correctness of particulars and statements see para 1572 post.

1570. Contents of air waybill. The air waybill must contain:
   (1) an indication of the places of departure and destination[1];
   (2) if these places are within the territory[2] of a single high contracting party[3], one or more agreed stopping places[4] being within the territory of another state, an indication of at least one such stopping place[5]; and
   (3) a notice to the consignor to the effect that, if the carriage involves an ultimate destination or stop in a country other than the country of departure, the amended Warsaw Convention may be applicable and that it governs and in

most cases limits the liability of carriers in respect of loss of or damage to cargo⁶.

1 Carriage by Air Act 1961 s 1 (1), Sch 1 art 8 (a) (Sch 1 replaced as from a day to be appointed by the Carriage by Air and Road Act 1979 s 1 (1), Sch 1; see para 1540 note 1 ante).
2 For the meaning of 'territory' see para 1535 ante.
3 For the meaning of 'high contracting party' see para 1534 ante.
4 For the meaning of 'agreed stopping place' see para 1541 note 5 ante. In *Kraus v Koninklijke Luchtvaart Maatschappij NV (Royal Dutch Airlines)* 92 NYS 2d 315 (1949); affd 105 NYS 2d 351 (1951), it was held that the requirement was satisfied by a reference in the air consignment note (the document under the unamended Warsaw Convention which corresponds to the air waybill) to the carrier's timetable for the stopping places.
5 Carriage by Air Act 1961 Sch 1 art 8 (b).
6 Ibid Sch 1 art 8 (c). See authorities on the corresponding provision in the unamended Warsaw Convention cited in para 1596 note 4 post.

1571. Absence, irregularity or loss of air waybill. The absence, irregularity or loss of the air waybill does not affect the existence or validity of the contract of carriage, which is, none the less, governed by the rules of the amended Warsaw Convention[1].

If, with the carrier's consent, cargo is loaded on board an aircraft without an air waybill having been made out, or if the air waybill does not include the required notice referring to the application of the amended convention[2], the carrier is not entitled to avail himself of the provisions of Article 22 (2) of that convention[3] which limit his liability[4].

1 Carriage by Air Act 1961 s 1 (1), Sch 1 art 5 (2) (Sch 1 replaced as from a day to be appointed by the Carriage by Air and Road Act 1979 s 1 (1), Sch 1; see para 1540 note 1 ante). As to information and documents which must accompany the air waybill see para 1575 post.
2 See para 1570 item (3) ante.
3 See para 1582 post.
4 Carriage by Air Act 1961 Sch 1 art 9.

1572. Correctness of air waybill. The consignor is responsible for the correctness of the particulars and statements relating to the cargo which he inserts in the air waybill[1]. He must indemnify the carrier against all damage suffered by him, or by any other person to whom the carrier is liable, by reason of the irregularity, incorrectness or incompleteness of the particulars and statements furnished by the consignor[2].

1 Carriage by Air Act 1961 s 1 (1), Sch 1 art 10 (1) (Sch 1 replaced as from a day to be appointed by the Carriage by Air and Road Act 1979 s 1 (1), Sch 1; see para 1540 note 1 ante). As to the making out, signature and contents of the air waybill see paras 1569, 1570 ante.
2 Carriage by Air Act 1961 Sch 1 art 10 (2).

1573. Air waybill as evidence of contract. The air waybill is prima facie evidence of the conclusion of the contract, of the receipt of the cargo and of the conditions of carriage[1]. Further, the statements in it relating to the weight, dimensions and packing of the cargo, as well as those relating to the number of packages, are prima facie evidence of the facts stated; those relating to the quantity, volume and condition of the cargo do not constitute evidence against the carrier except so far as they both have been, and are stated in the air waybill to have been, checked by him in the consignor's presence, or relate to the apparent condition of the cargo[2].

1 Carriage by Air Act 1961 s 1 (1), Sch 1 art 11 (1) (Sch 1 replaced as from a day to be appointed by the Carriage by Air and Road Act 1979 s 1 (1), Sch 1; see para 1540 note 1 ante). As to evidence of the receipt of goods without complaint see para 1580 post.
2 Carriage by Air Act 1961 Sch 1 art 11 (2).

1574. Negotiability of air waybill. Nothing in the Warsaw Convention as amended at The Hague in 1955 prevents the issue of a negotiable air waybill[1], although in practice, having regard to the speed of air transport, negotiability of air waybills is not so much required as in the case of shipping documents.

1 Carriage by Air Act 1961 s 1 (1), Sch 1 art 15 (3) (Sch 1 replaced as from a day to be appointed by the Carriage by Air and Road Act 1979 s 1 (1), Sch 1; see para 1540 note 1 ante). As to the negotiability of such documents see BILLS OF EXCHANGE; see also SHIPPING.

1575. Information and documents accompanying air waybill. The consignor must furnish such information and attach to the air waybill such documents as are necessary to meet the formalities of customs, octroi[1] or police before the cargo can be delivered to the consignee; the consignor is liable to the carrier for any damage occasioned by the absence, insufficiency or irregularity of any such information or documents, unless the damage is due to the fault of the carrier or his servants or agents[2]. The carrier is under no obligation to inquire into the correctness or sufficiency of such information or documents[3].

1 Octroi is a duty levied in some continental countries on goods entering a town: Oxford English Dictionary.
2 Carriage by Air Act 1961 s 1 (1), Sch 1 art 16 (1) (Sch 1 replaced as from a day to be appointed by the Carriage by Air and Road Act 1979 s 1 (1), Sch 1; see para 1540 note 1 ante).
3 Carriage by Air Act 1961 Sch 1 art 16 (2).

1576. Disposition and stoppage of cargo in transit. Subject to his liability to carry out all his obligations under the contract of carriage[1], the consignor has the right to dispose of the cargo by withdrawing it at the aerodrome of departure or destination, or by stopping it in the course of the journey on any landing, or by calling for it to be delivered at the place of destination or in the course of the journey to a person other than the consignee named in the air waybill, or by requiring the cargo to be returned to the aerodrome of departure[2]. The consignor must not exercise this right of disposition in such a way as to prejudice the carrier or other consignors, and he must repay any expenses occasioned by the exercise of the right[3]. If it is impossible to carry out the consignor's orders, the carrier must so inform him forthwith[4]. If the carrier obeys the consignor's orders for the disposition of the cargo without requiring the production of the part of the air waybill delivered to the consignor[5], he will be liable, without prejudice to his right of recovery from the consignor, for any damage which may be caused thereby to any person who is lawfully in possession of that part of the air waybill[6].

The right conferred on the consignor ceases at the moment when the rights of the consignee to delivery begin[7]; nevertheless, if the consignee declines to accept the waybill or the cargo, or if he cannot be communicated with, the consignor resumes his right of disposition[8].

1 The provisions of the Carriage by Air Act 1961 s 1 (1), Sch 1 art 12, stated in this paragraph, can only be varied by express provisions in the air waybill: Sch 1 art 15 (2) (Sch 1 replaced as from a day to be appointed by the Carriage by Air and Road Act 1979 s 1 (1), Sch 1; see para 1540 note 1 ante).

2 Carriage by Air Act 1961 Sch 1 art 12 (1). In relation to carriage performed by an actual carrier (as defined in para 1539 note 4 ante), such orders of the consignor are effective only if addressed to the contracting carrier (as defined in para 1539 note 5 ante): Carriage by Air (Supplementary Provisions) Act 1962 Schedule Pt I art IV. As to stoppage in transit see, further, CARRIERS; SALE OF GOODS: it will depend upon the ordinary law, eg as to the sale of goods, whether the consignor's exercise of his right of stoppage is justified as against the consignee or third parties.

3 Carriage by Air Act 1961 Sch 1 art 12 (1).

4 Ibid Sch 1 art 12 (2). The provisions of art 12 do not affect either the relations of the consignor and consignee with each other or the mutual relations of third parties whose rights are derived from either the consignor or the consignee (Sch 1 Pt I art 15 (1)); they have nothing to do with any right of action against the carrier for loss of or damage to the goods: *Gatewhite Ltd v Iberia Lineas Aereas de España SA* [1990] 1 QB 326, [1989] 1 All ER 944, 1 S&B AvR VII/305.

5 See the Carriage by Air Act 1961 Sch 1 art 6 (2).

6 Ibid Sch 1 art 12 (3). As to the various parts of the air waybill see para 1569 ante.

7 Carriage by Air Act 1961 Sch 1 art 12 (4). As to when the consignee's rights begin see Sch 1 art 13; and para 1577 post.

8 Carriage by Air Act 1961 Sch 1 art 12 (4).

1577. Consignee's rights. Except where any of the rights of disposal or stoppage in transit have been exercised in accordance with the foregoing provisions[1], the consignee is entitled, on arrival of the cargo at the place of destination, to require the carrier to hand over to him the air waybill[2] and to deliver the cargo to him, on payment of the charges due and on complying with the conditions of carriage set out in the air waybill[3]. Unless it is otherwise agreed, it is the carrier's duty to give notice to the consignee as soon as the cargo arrives[4].

If the carrier admits the loss of the cargo, or if it has not arrived at the expiration of seven days[5] after the date on which it ought to have arrived, the consignee is entitled to put into force against the carrier the rights which flow from the contract of carriage[6].

1 See the Carriage by Air Act 1961 s 1 (1), Sch 1 art 12 (Sch 1 replaced as from a day to be appointed by the Carriage by Air and Road Act 1979 s 1 (1), Sch 1; see para 1540 note 1 ante); and para 1576 ante.

2 This can only be the second part of the air waybill: see the Carriage by Air Act 1961 Sch 1 art 6 (2); and para 1569 ante. As to the documents which must accompany the air waybill see para 1575 ante.

3 Ibid Sch 1 art 13 (1). As to a carrier's lien for charges see CARRIERS. The provisions of Sch 1 art 13 do not affect either the relations of the consignor and consignee with each other or the mutual relations of third parties whose rights are derived either from the consignor or from the consignee (Sch 1 art 15 (1)); and they can only be varied by express provision in the air waybill (Sch 1 art 15 (2)).

4 Ibid Sch 1 art 13 (2).

5 'Days' means current days not working days: ibid Sch 1 art 35.

6 Ibid Sch 1 art 13 (3).

1578. Enforcement of rights by consignor and consignee. The consignor and the consignee can respectively enforce in their own names all the rights given them by the foregoing provisions relating to disposition, stoppage in transit and delivery[1], whether they are acting in their own interest or in the interest of another, provided that they carry out the obligations imposed by the contract[2].

1 See the Carriage by Air Act 1961 s 1 (1), Sch 1 arts 12, 13 (Sch 1 replaced as from a day to be appointed by the Carriage by Air and Road Act 1979 s 1 (1), Sch 1; see para 1540 note 1 ante); and paras 1576, 1577 ante.

2 Carriage by Air Act 1961 Sch 1 art 14. The provisions of that article do not affect either the relations of the consignor or the consignee with each other or the mutual relations of third parties whose rights are derived either from the consignor or from the consignee (Sch 1 art 15 (1)); and they can only be varied by express provision in the air waybill (Sch 1 art 15 (2)).

1579. Loss of or damage to cargo. The carrier[1] is liable for damage sustained in the event of the destruction or loss of, or of damage to, any cargo, if the occurrence which caused the damage so sustained took place during the carriage by air[2].

The carriage by air for this purpose comprises the period during which the cargo is in charge of the carrier[3], whether in an aerodrome or on board an aircraft or, in the case of a landing outside an aerodrome, in any place whatsoever[4]. It does not extend to any carriage by land, by sea or by river performed outside an aerodrome, but if such a carriage takes place in the performance of a contract for carriage by air for the purpose of loading, delivery or transhipment, any damage is presumed, subject to proof to the contrary, to have been the result of an event which took place during the carriage by air[5].

1 As to who is the carrier see para 1539 ante.
2 Carriage by Air Act 1961 s 1 (1), Sch 1 art 18 (1) (Sch 1 replaced as from a day to be appointed by the Carriage by Air and Road Act 1979 s 1 (1), Sch 1; see para 1540 note 1 ante). The owner of the cargo may sue even if he is not named as consignee or consignor on the air waybill: *Gatewhite Ltd v Iberia Lineas Aereas de España SA* [1990] 1 QB 326, [1989] 1 All ER 944, 1 S&B AvR VII/305; *Tasman Pulp and Paper Co Ltd v Brambles J B O'Loghlen Ltd* [1981] 2 NZLR 225, 1 S&B AvR VII/25 (NZ HC). For requirements as to notice of complaint see para 1581 post; for defences available to the carrier see paras 1549, 1550 ante; for limitations on the damages which may be payable see para 1582 post.
3 For the meaning of this phrase see *Swiss Bank Corpn v Brink's-MAT Ltd* (14 November 1985, unreported), Bingham J; further proceedings [1986] QB 853, [1986] 2 All ER 188, 1 S&B AvR VII/195. In general, cargo remains in charge of the carrier until released to the consignee; the submission of the cargo by the carrier to the customs authorities is not determinative.
4 Carriage by Air Act 1961 Sch 1 art 18 (2) (see note 2 supra).
5 Ibid Sch 1 art 18 (3).

1580. Receipt without complaint as evidence. Receipt by the person entitled to delivery of cargo without complaint is prima facie evidence that the same has been delivered in good condition and in accordance with the document of carriage[1].

1 Carriage by Air Act 1961 s 1 (1), Sch 1 art 26 (1) (Sch 1 replaced as from a day to be appointed by the Carriage by Air and Road Act 1979 s 1 (1), Sch 1; see para 1540 note 1 ante). Any complaint made under the provisions of the amended Warsaw Convention has the same effect whether addressed to the contracting carrier or to the actual carrier: Carriage by Air (Supplementary Provisions) Act 1962 Schedule Pt I art IV. For the meanings of 'contracting carrier' and 'actual carrier' see para 1539 notes 4, 5 ante. As to the time within which complaints must be made see para 1581 post.

1581. Complaints of damage or delay to cargo. In the case of damage[1] to cargo, the person entitled to delivery must complain to the carrier forthwith after the discovery of the damage and at the latest within 14 days[2] from the date of receipt; in the case of delay, the complaint must be made at the latest within 21 days from the date on which the cargo has been placed at his disposal[3].

Every complaint must be made in writing upon the document of carriage or by separate notice in writing dispatched within the times aforesaid[4].

Failing complaint within these times, no action lies against the carrier, save in the case of fraud on his part[5].

1 Including loss of part of the cargo in question: Carriage by Air Act 1961 s 4A (added by the Carriage by Air and Road Act 1979 s 2); *Fothergill v Monarch Airlines Ltd* [1981] AC 251, [1980] 2 All ER 696, 1 S&B AvR I/9, HL. Complaint is not needed in the case of total loss or destruction.
2 'Days' means current days, not working days: Carriage by Air Act 1961 Sch 1 art 35 (Sch 1 replaced as from a day to be appointed by the Carriage by Air and Road Act 1979 s 1 (1), Sch 1; see para 1540 note 1 ante).

3 Carriage by Air Act 1961 Sch 1 art 26 (2).

4 Ibid Sch 1 art 26 (3).

5 Ibid Sch 1 art 26 (4). Fraud, it is thought, refers to fraudulent concealment of the damage or of the right of action: cf *Denby v Seaboard World Airlines Inc* 737 F 2d 172 (2nd Cir, 1984).

1582. Limitation of liability for cargo. In the carriage of cargo, the carrier's liability is limited to a sum of 250 francs[1] per kilogramme, unless the consignor has made, at the time when the package was handed over to the carrier, a special declaration of interest in delivery at destination and has paid a supplementary sum if the case so requires; in that case the carrier will be liable to pay a sum not exceeding the declared sum, unless he proves that that sum is greater than the consignor's actual interest in delivery at destination[2].

In the case of loss, damage or delay of part of the cargo, or of any object contained in it, the weight to be taken into consideration in determining the limit on the carrier's liability is only the total weight of the package or packages concerned; nevertheless, when such a loss affects the value of other packages covered by the same air waybill, the total weight of such package or packages must also be taken into consideration[3].

1 The sterling equivalent of 250 francs is £13.63: see the Carriage by Air (Sterling Equivalents) Order 1986, SI 1986/1778: see further para 1561 ante.

2 Carriage by Air Act 1961 s 1 (1), Sch 1 art 22 (2) (a) (Sch 1 replaced as from a day to be appointed by the Carriage by Air and Road Act 1979 s 1 (1), Sch 1; see para 1540 note 1 ante). As to the meaning of 'special declaration' and 'supplementary' see *Westminster Bank Ltd v Imperial Airways Ltd* [1936] 2 All ER 890; and see *Corocraft Ltd v Pan American Airways Inc* [1969] 1 QB 616 at 641, [1969] 1 All ER 82, CA.

3 Carriage by Air Act 1961 Sch 1 art 22 (2) (b).

(v) Delay to Passengers, Baggage or Cargo under the Warsaw–Hague Provisions

1583. Delay. The carrier[1] is liable for damage occasioned by delay in the carriage by air[2] of passengers, baggage or cargo[3]. Except where the carrier has contracted to perform the carriage within an agreed time, his obligation is to perform it within a reasonable time: no liability for delay arises until the agreed time or a reasonable time, as the case may be, has passed[4].

1 As to who is the carrier see para 1539 ante; as to who may be sued in the case of carriage by successive carriers see para 1548 ante.

2 For the meaning of this phrase see *Bart v British West Indian Airways Ltd* [1967] 1 Lloyd's Rep 239 (Guyana CA). A passenger who is denied boarding through overbooking by the carrier appears not to suffer delay in the carriage by air; any remedy, subject to the terms of the contract, will be for non-performance.

3 Carriage by Air Act 1961 s 1 (1), Sch 1 art 19 (Sch 1 replaced as from a day to be appointed by the Carriage by Air and Road Act 1979 s 1 (1), Sch 1; see para 1540 note 1 ante). For defences see paras 1549, 1550 ante; for limitations on the carrier's liability see paras 1567, 1582 ante; and for requirements as to notice of complaint in baggage and cargo cases see paras 1566, 1581 ante.

4 *Panalpina International Transport Ltd v Densil Underwear Ltd* [1981] 1 Lloyd's Rep 187.

(4) INTERNATIONAL CARRIAGE UNDER THE UNAMENDED WARSAW CONVENTION

(i) Introductory

1584. The unamended Warsaw Convention as part of English law. The unamended provisions of the Warsaw Convention of 1929 have effect as part of the law of the United Kingdom in relation to any international carriage by air to which the convention applies[1], and despite any attempt by the parties to the contract of carriage to exclude their operation or to substitute some other law as the law applicable to the contract[2]. A deviation from the carriage contracted for does not remove the carriage from the ambit of the convention or disentitle the carrier from relying on its provisions[3].

1 Carriage by Air Acts (Application of Provisions) Order 1967, SI 1967/480, art 5 (1), Sch 2.
2 See paras 1538, 1540 note 2, 1544 ante, 1588 post.
3 See para 1540 note 3 ante.

1585. International carriage within the unamended Warsaw Convention. International carriage, for the purpose of the unamended convention, means any carriage in which, according to the agreement between the parties, the place of departure and the place of destination, whether or not there is a break in the carriage or a transhipment, are situated either within the territories of two high contracting parties, or within the territory of a single high contracting party if there is an agreed stopping place within the territory subject to the sovereignty, suzerainty, mandate or authority of another state, even though that state is not a high contracting party[1]. Carriage between two points within the territory of a single high contracting party without an agreed stopping place within the territory of another state is not international carriage for the purposes of the convention.

1 Carriage by Air Acts (Application of Provisions) Order 1967, SI 1967/480, art 5, Sch 2 Pt B art 1 (2). For the meaning of 'high contracting party' see para 1534 ante; for the meaning of 'territory of a high contracting party' see para 1535 ante. See also para 1541 ante.

1586. Carriage by successive air carriers. Carriage to be performed by several successive air carriers is deemed for the purposes of the unamended Warsaw Convention to be one undivided carriage, if it has been regarded by the parties as a single operation, whether it has been agreed upon under the form of a single contract or of a series of contracts, and it does not lose its international character merely because one contract or a series of contracts is to be performed entirely within a territory subject to the sovereignty, suzerainty, mandate or authority of the same high contracting party[1].

In any such case each carrier who accepts passengers, baggage or cargo is subjected to the rules of the convention, and is deemed to be one of the contracting parties to the contract of carriage in so far as the contract deals with that part of the carriage which is performed under his supervision[2].

1 Carriage by Air Acts (Application of Provisions) Order 1967, SI 1967/480, art 5, Sch 2 Pt B art 1 (3). See also para 1542 ante.

2 Ibid Sch 2 Pt B art 30 (1). As to the question which carrier a passenger, consignor or consignee is permitted to sue see para 1548 ante.

1587. International carriage to which the unamended Warsaw Convention does not apply. Notwithstanding that it may fall within the definition of international carriage[1], the unamended Warsaw Convention does not apply to carriage performed under the terms of any international postal convention[2]. It does not apply to gratuitous international carriage by a person, firm or company who or which is not an air transport undertaking[3], to carriage performed by way of experimental trial by air navigation undertakings with the view to the establishment of a regular line of air navigation, or to carriage performed in extraordinary circumstances outside the normal scope of an air carrier's business[4].

1 For the meaning of 'international carriage' see para 1585 ante.
2 Carriage by Air Acts (Application of Provisions) Order 1967, SI 1967/480, art 5, Sch 2 Pt B art 2 (2). See also para 1629 post.
3 See ibid Sch 2 Pt B art 1 (1). As to the meaning of 'air transport undertaking' for this purpose see para 1533 note 3 ante.
4 Ibid Sch 2 Pt B art 34.

1588. Actions subject to the unamended Warsaw Convention. In the cases which are covered by the rules examined below providing for the liability of the carrier for death of or injury to passengers[1], for damage, destruction or loss to cargo or registered baggage or objects of which the passenger takes charge himself[2] and for damage caused by delay[3], any action for damages, however founded, can only be brought subject to the conditions and limits set out in the unamended Warsaw Convention[4].

The application of the rules cannot be excluded by any contract between the parties to the carriage[5]. Any provisions tending to relieve the carrier of liability or to fix a lower limit of liability than that laid down in the rules is null and void[6].

Actions under the unamended convention are subject to the same rules as are applied to actions under the Warsaw-Hague provisions in respect of the jurisdictions in which actions may be brought[7], the bringing of actions against high contracting parties[8] or actual carriers[9], successive carriage[10], the defence of contributory negligence[11], the limitation of actions[12] and liability for delay[13].

1 See paras 1593–1595 post and notes 7–12 infra.
2 See paras 1596–1604 post and notes 7–12 infra.
3 See para 1583 ante; and text to note 13 infra.
4 Carriage by Air Acts (Application of Provisions) Order 1967, SI 1967/480, art 5, Sch 2 Pt B art 24 (1), (2). In the case of liability for death or injury to passengers this provision is without prejudice to the question as to who are the persons who have the right to bring suit and what are their respective rights: Sch 2 Pt B art 24 (2). For actions against the carrier's servants or agents see para 1590 post.
5 Ibid Sch 2 Pt B art 32.
6 Ibid Sch 2 Pt B art 23.
7 Ibid Sch 2 Pt B art 28; see para 1545 ante.
8 Carriage by Air Act 1961 s 8, as applied with modifications by the Carriage by Air Acts (Application of Provisions) Order 1967 art 5 (3); see para 1546 ante.
9 See para 1547 ante.
10 See para 1548 ante.

11 Carriage by Air Acts (Application of Provisions) Order 1967 Sch 2 Pt B art 21; Carriage by Air Act 1961 s 6 as applied by the Carriage by Air Acts (Application of Provisions) Order 1967 art 6. See para 1550 ante.
12 Carriage by Air Acts (Application of Provisions) Order 1967 Sch 2 Pt B art 29; Carriage by Air Act 1961 s 5, as applied by the Carriage by Air Acts (Application of Provisions) Order 1967 art 6. See para 1554 ante.
13 See para 1583 ante.

1589. Defence of all necessary measures. The carrier can escape from the liabilities imposed upon him by the unamended Warsaw Convention if he proves that he and his servants and agents have taken all necessary measures to avoid the damage or that it was impossible for him or them to take such measures[1], and in the carriage of cargo and baggage if he proves that the damage was occasioned by negligent pilotage or negligence in the handling of the aircraft or in navigation and that in all other respects he and his servants and agents have taken all necessary measures to avoid the damage[2].

1 Carriage by Air Acts (Application of Provisions) Order 1967, SI 1967/480, art 5, Sch 2 Pt B art 20 (1); see para 1549 ante.
2 Ibid Sch 2 Pt B art 20 (2).

1590. Limitation of liability generally. The liability of the carrier is limited to certain maximum sums specified in the Carriage by Air Acts (Application of Provisions) Order 1967[1]. This limitation may be affected in the carriage of passengers by the carrier agreeing to an increased limit by a special contract[2], or in baggage and cargo cases by the making of a special declaration as to the value of the goods carried[3], and is inapplicable in certain other cases[4].

In relation to the carriage performed by the actual carrier, no act or omission of the contracting carrier[5] will subject the actual carrier to liability exceeding the limits laid down in the amended Warsaw Convention, and no waiver of rights by the contracting carrier will affect the actual carrier unless agreed by him[6].

If an action is brought against such a carrier's servant or agent, the servant or agent is entitled, if he proves that he was acting within the scope of his employment, to invoke the provisions of the amended convention limiting the carrier's liability applicable to the carrier whose servant he is[7].

The aggregate of the amounts recoverable from the carrier[8], his servants and agents, may not exceed the limits provided for by the amended convention[9].

1 See the Carriage by Air Acts (Application of Provisions) Order 1967, SI 1967/480, art 5, Sch 2 Pt B art 22. As to liability for passengers see para 1595 post; for baggage see para 1599 post; for cargo see para 1604 post.
2 See ibid Sch 2 Pt B art 22 (1); and para 1595 post.
3 See ibid Sch 2 Pt B art 22 (2); and paras 1598, 1604 post.
4 See para 1592 post.
5 See para 1547 note 2 ante. For the meanings of 'actual carrier' and 'contracting carrier' see para 1539 notes 4, 5 ante.
6 Carriage by Air (Supplementary Provisions) Act 1962 s 1 (1), Schedule Pt I art III (2).
7 Carriage by Air Acts (Application of Provisions) Order 1967 Sch 2 Pt B art 25A (1); Carriage by Air (Supplementary Provisions) Act 1962 Schedule Pt I art v. Limits of liability may not be invoked if it is proved that the servant or agent acted in a manner which, under the unamended convention, excludes the limitation of liability by the carrier: Schedule Pt I art v; Carriage by Air Acts (Application of Provisions) Order 1967 Sch 2 Pt B art 25A (3); see para 1592 post.
8 In the case of carriage not performed by the contracting carrier, reference to the carrier includes here reference to both the contracting carrier and the actual carrier when an action has been brought against both of them; see para 1547 ante.

9 Carriage by Air Acts (Application of Provisions) Order 1967 Sch 2 Pt B art 25A (2); Carriage by Air (Supplementary Provisions) Act 1962 Schedule Pt I art vi. None of the persons mentioned may be liable for a sum in excess of the limit applicable to him: Schedule Pt I art vi.

1591. Provisions relieving carrier of liability. Any provision tending to relieve the carrier of liability or to fix a lower limit than the limit which is laid down in the unamended Warsaw Convention is null and void, but the nullity of any such provision does not involve the nullity of the whole contract, which remains subject to the provisions of the unamended convention[1].

1 Carriage by Air Acts (Application of Provisions) Order 1967, SI 1967/480, art 5, Sch 2 Pt B art 23. These provisions apply whether the carriage is performed by the contracting carrier or an actual carrier: see the Carriage by Air (Supplementary Provisions) Act 1962 s 1 (1), Schedule Pt I art ix (1), (2).

1592. Loss of carrier's right to limit liability. The provisions of the un-amended Warsaw Convention which exclude or limit the carrier's liability[1] do not apply if the damage is caused by the wilful misconduct, or such default as in accordance with the law of the court seised of the case is considered to be equivalent to wilful misconduct, of the carrier or any servant or agent acting within the scope of his employment[2].

The carrier loses the right to avail himself of those same provisions if he accepts a passenger without a passenger ticket having been delivered to him[3]; or, in respect of registered baggage, if he accepts baggage without a baggage check having been delivered or if the baggage check does not include particulars of the number of the passenger ticket, the number and weight of the packages, and a statement that the carriage is subject to the rules relating to liability established by the unamended convention[4]; or, in the case of cargo, if he accepts cargo without an air waybill having been made out or if the air waybill does not contain prescribed particulars[5], including a statement that the carriage is subject to the rules relating to liability established by the unamended convention[6].

1 These appear to include the Carriage by Air Acts (Application of Provisions) Order 1967, SI 1967/480, art 5, Sch 2 Pt B arts 20–22 and 26 (4).
2 Ibid Sch 2 Pt B art 25; Carriage by Air (Supplementary Provisions) Act 1962 s 1 (1), Schedule Pt I art v. 'Wilful misconduct' goes beyond negligence; it involves knowledge that injury or damage will probably result and an intentional or reckless act or omission: *Horabin v British Overseas Airways Corpn* [1952] 2 All ER 1016; *Rustenburg Platinum Mines Ltd v South African Airways* [1977] 1 Lloyd's Rep 564, affd [1979] 1 Lloyd's Rep 19, CA.
3 Carriage by Air Acts (Application of Provisions) Order 1967, Sch 2 Pt B art 3 (2); *Preston v Hunting Air Transport Ltd* [1956] 1 QB 454, [1956] 1 All ER 443. See also *Ludecke v Canadian Pacific Air Lines Ltd* (1979) 98 DLR (3d) 52, [1979] 2 Lloyd's Rep 260 (Can SC).
4 See the Carriage by Air Acts (Application of Provisions) Order 1967 Sch 2 Pt B art 4 (4).
5 Those prescribed by ibid Sch 2 Pt B art 8 (a)–(i).
6 Ibid Sch 2 Pt B arts 8 (q), 9; this provision was described as 'absurd' in *Corocraft v Pan American Airways Inc* [1969] 1 QB 616, [1969] 1 All ER 82, CA.

(ii) Carriage of Passengers under the Unamended Warsaw Convention

1593. Contents of passenger tickets. In respect of the carriage of passengers, the carrier must deliver a passenger ticket containing the following particulars:

(1) the place and date of issue;

(2) the place of departure and of destination;

(3) the agreed stopping places, provided that the carrier may reserve the right to alter the stopping places in case of necessity, and that if he exercises that right, the alteration shall not have the effect of depriving the carriage of its international character;

(4) the name and address of the carrier or carriers; and

(5) a statement to the effect that the carriage is subject to the rules relating to liability established by the Warsaw Convention[1].

1 Carriage by Air Acts (Application of Provisions) Order 1967, SI 1967/480, art 5, Sch 2 Pt B 1 art 3 (1). See para 1556 ante. As to defective passenger tickets see para 1594 post.

1594. Absence, irregularity or loss of passenger ticket. The absence, irregularity or loss of the passenger ticket does not affect the existence or the validity of the contract of carriage, which is, none the less, subject to the rules of the unamended convention[1].

1 Carriage by Air Acts (Application of Provisions) Order 1967, SI 1967/480, art 5, Sch 2 Pt B art 3 (2). As to the effect of the carrier accepting a passenger without a passenger ticket having been delivered see para 1592 ante.

1595. Limitation of liability for passengers. In the carriage of passengers, the carrier's liability[1] for each passenger is limited under the unamended Warsaw Convention to the sum of 125,000 francs[2]. Where, in accordance with the law of the court seised of the case, damages may be awarded in the form of periodical payments, the equivalent capital value of such payments must not exceed 125,000 francs[3]. However, the carrier and the passenger may by special contract agree to a higher limit of liability[4].

1 Carriage by Air Acts (Application of Provisions) Order 1967, SI 1967/480, art 5, Sch 2 Pt B art 17, corresponding to the provisions stated in para 1559 ante.
2 Carriage by Air Acts (Application of Provisions) Order 1967 Sch 2 Pt B art 22 (1). As to these francs and their sterling equivalents see para 1561 ante.
3 Ibid Sch 2 Pt B art 22 (1).
4 Ibid Sch 2 Pt B art 22 (1).

(iii) Carriage of Baggage under the Unamended Warsaw Convention

1596. Contents of baggage checks. In respect of the carriage of baggage, other than small personal objects of which the passenger takes charge himself, the carrier must deliver a baggage check[1], which must be made out in duplicate, one part for the passenger and the other part for the carrier[2]. The baggage check must contain the following particulars:

(1) the place and date of issue;

(2) the place of departure and of destination;

(3) the name and address of the carrier or carriers;

(4) the number of the passenger ticket;

(5) a statement that delivery of the baggage will be made to the bearer of the baggage check;

(6) the number and weight of the packages;

(7) the amount of the value of the baggage at delivery[3]; and

(8) a statement that the carriage is subject to the rules relating to liability established by the Warsaw Convention[4].

1 Carriage by Air Acts (Application of Provisions) Order 1967, SI 1967/480, art 5, Sch 2 Pt B art 4 (1).
2 Ibid Sch 2 Pt B art 4 (2).
3 Ie the value declared in accordance with ibid Sch 2 Pt B art 22 (2); see para 1599 post.
4 Ibid Sch 2 Pt B art 4 (3). As to this statement see *Westminster Bank Ltd v Imperial Airways Ltd* [1936] 2 All ER 890 (a broad statement is insufficient compliance); but see *Samuel Montagu & Co Ltd v Swiss Air Transport Co Ltd* [1966] 2 QB 306, [1966] 1 All ER 814, CA (the air waybill is not required to contain the words of the convention verbatim); see also *Philippson v Imperial Airways Ltd* [1939] AC 332, [1939] 1 All ER 761, HL; *Seth v British Overseas Airways Corpn* 329 F 2d 302 (1st Cir 1961), cert denied [1964] 1 Lloyd's Rep 268, 379 US 858 (1964). As to defective baggage checks see para 1597 post.

1597. Absence, irregularity or loss of baggage check. The absence, irregularity or loss of the baggage check does not affect the existence or the validity of the contract of carriage, which is, none the less, subject to the rules of the unamended Warsaw Convention[1].

1 Carriage by Air Acts (Application of Provisions) Order 1967, SI 1967/480, art 5, Sch 2 Pt B art 4 (4). For the effect of the carrier accepting baggage without a baggage check having been delivered or where the baggage check does not contain certain of the prescribed particulars see para 1592 ante.

1598. Complaints of damage or delay to baggage. In the case of damage[1] to baggage, the person entitled to delivery must complain to the carrier forthwith after the discovery of the damage and at the latest within three days[2] from the date of receipt; in the case of delay, the complaint must be made at the latest within 14 days from the date on which the baggage has been placed at his disposal[3].

Every complaint must be made in writing upon the document of carriage or by separate notice in writing dispatched within the times aforesaid[4].

Failing complaint within these times, no action lies against the carrier, save in the case of fraud on his part[5].

1 Including loss of part of the baggage in question: Carriage by Air Act 1961 s 4A (added by the Carriage by Air and Road Act 1979 s 2); *Fothergill v Monarch Airlines Ltd* [1981] AC 251, [1980] 2 All ER 696, HL. Complaint is not needed in the case of total loss or destruction.
2 'Days' means current days, not working days: Carriage by Air Acts (Application of Provisions) Order 1967, SI 1967/480, art 5, Sch 2 Pt B art 35.
3 Ibid Sch 2 Pt B art 26 (2).
4 Ibid Sch 2 Pt B art 26 (3).
5 Ibid Sch 2 Pt B art 26 (4). See para 1566 note 6 ante.

1599. Limitation of liability for baggage. In the carriage of registered baggage, the carrier's liability[1] is limited under the unamended Warsaw Convention to the sum of 250 francs per kilogramme[2] unless the consignor has made, at the time when the package was handed over to the carrier, a special declaration of value at delivery and has paid a supplementary sum if the case so requires; in that case the carrier will be liable to pay a sum not exceeding the declared sum, unless he proves that that sum is greater than the actual value to the consignor at delivery[3].

1 Carriage by Air Acts (Application of Provisions) Order 1967, SI 1967/480, art 5, Sch 2 Pt B art 18, corresponding to the provisions set out in para 1564 ante.

2 Ibid Sch 2 Pt B art 22 (2). As to these francs and their sterling equivalents see para 1561 ante. Only the
   weight of the lost or damaged package is to be taken into account: *Data Card Corpn v Air Express
   International Corpn* [1983] 2 All ER 639, [1984] 1 WLR 198, 1 S&B AvR VII/95.
3 Carriage by Air Acts (Application of Provisions) Order 1967 Sch 2 Pt B art 22 (2).

(iv) Carriage of Cargo under the Unamended Warsaw Convention

1600. Air waybills. Every carrier of cargo has the right to require the consignor
to make out and hand over to him a document called an air waybill, and every
consignor has the right to require the carrier to accept this document[1]. The carrier
has the right to require the consignor to make out separate air waybills where there
is more than one package[2].

The air waybill must be made out by the consignor in three original parts and
must be handed over with the cargo[3]. The first part must be marked 'for the carrier'
and must be signed by the consignor; the second part must be marked 'for the
consignee' and must be signed by the consignor and by the carrier and must
accompany the cargo; and the third part must be signed by the carrier and handed
by him to the consignor after the cargo has been accepted[4]. The carrier must sign
on acceptance of the cargo [5]. The carrier's signature may be stamped; the consignor's signature may be printed or stamped[6].

If, at the consignor's request, the carrier makes out the air waybill, he is deemed,
subject to proof to the contrary, to have done so on behalf of the consignor[7].

1 Carriage by Air Acts (Application of Provisions) Order 1967, SI 1967/480, art 5, Sch 2 Pt B art 5 (1).
2 Ibid Sch 2 Pt B art 7.
3 Ibid Sch 2 Pt B art 6 (1).
4 Ibid Sch 2 Pt B art 6 (2).
5 Ibid Sch 2 Pt B art 6 (3).
6 Ibid Sch 2 Pt B art 6 (4).
7 Ibid Sch 2 Pt B art 6 (5).

1601. Contents of air waybills. The air waybill must contain the following
particulars:

(1) the place and date of its execution;
(2) the place of departure and of destination;
(3) the agreed stopping places, provided that the carrier may reserve the right
     to alter the stopping places in case of necessity, and that if he exercises that
     right the alteration shall not have the effect of depriving the carriage of its
     international character;
(4) the name and address of the consignor;
(5) the name and address of the first carrier;
(6) the name and address of the consignee if the case so requires;
(7) the nature of the cargo;
(8) the number of the packages, the method of packing and the particular
     marks or numbers upon them;
(9) the weight, the quantity and the volume or dimensions of the cargo;
(10) the apparent condition of the cargo and of the packing;
(11) the freight, if it has been agreed upon, the date and place of payment, and
     the person who is to pay for it;
(12) if the cargo is sent for payment on delivery, the price of the cargo, and if the
     case so requires, the amount of the expenses incurred;

(13) the amount of the value of the baggage at delivery[1];
(14) the number of parts of the air waybill;
(15) the documents handed to the carrier to accompany the air waybill;
(16) the time fixed for the completion of the carriage and a brief note of the route to be followed, if these matters are agreed upon; and
(17) a statement that the carriage is subject to the rules relating to liability established by the Warsaw Convention[2].

1 Ie the value declared in accordance with the Carriage by Air Acts (Application of Provisions) Order 1967, SI 1967/480, art 5, Sch 2 Pt B art 22 (2); see para 1604 post.
2 Ibid Sch 2 Pt B art 8. As to this statement see para 1596 ante.

1602. Absence, irregularity or loss of air waybill. The absence, irregularity or loss of the air waybill does not affect the existence or the validity of the contract of carriage, which is, none the less, subject to the rules of the unamended convention[1].

1 Carriage by Air Acts (Application of Provisions) Order 1967, SI 1967/480, art 5, Sch 2 Pt B art 5 (2) As to the effect of the carrier accepting cargo without an air waybill having been made out or where the air waybill does not contain certain of the prescribed particulars see para 1592 ante.

1603. Complaints of damage or delay to cargo. In the case of damage[1] to cargo, the person entitled to delivery must complain to the carrier forthwith after the discovery of the damage and at the latest within seven days[2] from the date of receipt; in the case of delay, the complaint must be made at the latest within 14 days from the date on which the cargo has been placed at his disposal[3].

Every complaint must be made in writing upon the document of carriage or by separate notice in writing dispatched within the times aforesaid[4].

Failing complaint within these times, no action lies against the carrier, save in the case of fraud on his part[5].

1 Including loss of part of the cargo in question: Carriage by Air Act 1961 s 4A (added by the Carriage by Air and Road Act 1979 s 2); _Fothergill v Monarch Airlines Ltd_ [1981] AC 251, [1980] 2 All ER 696, 1 S&B AvR I/9, HL. Complaint is not needed in the case of total loss or destruction.
2 'Days' means current days, not working days: Carriage by Air Acts (Application of Provisions) Order 1967, SI 1967/480, art 5, Sch 2 Pt B art 35.
3 Ibid Sch 2 Pt B art 26 (2).
4 Ibid Sch 2 Pt B art 26 (3).
5 Ibid Sch 2 Pt B art 26 (4). See para 1566 ante.

1604. Limitation of liability for cargo. In the carriage of cargo, the carrier's liability[1] is limited under the unamended Warsaw Convention to the sum of 250 francs per kilogramme[2] unless the consignor has made, at the time when the package was handed over to the carrier, a special declaration of value at delivery and has paid a supplementary sum if the case so requires; in that case the carrier will be liable to pay a sum not exceeding the declared sum, unless he proves that that sum is greater than the actual value to the consignor at delivery[3].

1 Carriage by Air Acts (Application of Provisions) Order 1967, SI 1967/480, art 5, Sch 2 Pt B art 18, corresponding to the provisions stated in para 1579 ante.
2 Ibid Sch 2 Pt B art 22 (2). As to these francs and their sterling equivalents see para 1561 ante.
3 Ibid Sch 2 Pt B art 22 (2).

(5) INTERNATIONAL CARRIAGE UNDER THE WARSAW-HAGUE-MONTREAL CONVENTION

(i) Introductory

1605. Application of Warsaw-Hague-Montreal Convention. The provisions of the Warsaw Convention as amended at The Hague in 1955 and by Protocols Nos 3 and 4 signed at Montreal in 1975 so far as they relate to the rights and liabilities of carriers, their servants and agents, passengers, consignors, consignees and other persons, have the force of law in the United Kingdom in relation to any carriage by air to which the convention applies[1].

International carriage, for the purpose of the convention, is defined and provision as to successive carriage is made in terms corresponding to those in the Warsaw-Hague text[2]. However, the reference to high contracting parties is to such parties to the Warsaw-Hague-Montreal version of the convention.

1 Carriage by Air Act 1961 s 1 (1); Carriage by Air and Road Act 1979 s 1 (1). The 1979 Act substitutes a new text of Sch 1 to the 1961 Act. The Carriage by Air (Supplementary Provisions) Act 1962 applies in relation to the new provisions as to those of the Warsaw-Hague Convention: see the Carriage by Air and Road Act 1979 s 1 (2), Sch 2. None of the relevant provisions of the Carriage by Air and Road Act 1979 had been brought into force at the date at which this volume states the law.
2 See paras 1541, 1542 ante.

1606. International carriage to which the Warsaw-Hague-Montreal Convention does not apply. Notwithstanding that the carriage of postal items may fall within the definition of international carriage[1], the Warsaw-Hague-Montreal Convention does not apply to such carriage except in so far as the carrier is liable to the relevant postal administration in accordance with the rules applicable to the relationship between the carriers and the postal administrations[2], or to the carriage of persons, baggage or cargo for the military authorities of the United Kingdom or of any other state specified in an Order in Council if the whole capacity of the aircraft has been reserved by or on behalf of those authorities[3]. In cases otherwise falling within its scope, it applies to carriage performed by the state or by legally constituted public bodies[4]. It does not apply to gratuitous international carriage by a person, firm or company who or which is not an air transport undertaking[5].

The provisions relating to documents of carriage[6] do not apply in the case of carriage performed in extraordinary circumstances outside the normal scope of an air carrier's business[7].

1 For the meaning of 'international carriage' see para 1605 ante.
2 Carriage by Air and Road Act 1979 s 1 (1), Sch 1 Pt I art 2 (2), (3). None of the relevant provisions of the Carriage by Air and Road Act 1979 had been brought into force at the date at which this volume states the law.
3 Carriage by Air Act 1961 s 7, giving effect to art 26 of the Hague Protocol. No such Order in Council was in force at the date at which this volume states the law.
4 Carriage by Air and Road Act 1979 Sch 1 Pt I art 2 (1).
5 See ibid Sch 1 Pt I art 1 (1).
6 See ibid Sch 1 Pt I arts 3–8.
7 Ibid Sch 1 Pt I art 34.

1607. Jurisdiction and limitation of actions. An action for damages must be brought, at the plaintiff's option, in the territory of one of the high contracting parties, either before the court[1] having jurisdiction where the carrier is ordinarily resident or has his principal place of business or has an establishment by which the contract has been made, or before the court having jurisdiction at the place of destination[2].

In respect of damage resulting from the death, injury or delay of a passenger or the destruction, loss, damage or delay of baggage, an action may also be brought before the court within the jurisdiction of which the carrier has an establishment if the passenger has his ordinary or permanent residence in the territory of the same high contracting party[3].

Questions of procedure are governed by the law of the court seised of the case[4].

The rules as to limitation of actions are in terms corresponding to those in the Warsaw–Hague provisions[5].

1 For this purpose 'court' includes an arbitrator (in any arbitration allowed by the convention): Carriage by Air Act 1961 s 14 (2).
2 Carriage by Air and Road Act 1979 s 1 (1), Sch 1 Pt I art 28 (1). See para 1545 ante. None of the relevant provisions of the Carriage by Air and Road Act 1979 had been brought into force at the date at which this volume states the law.
3 Ibid Sch 1 Pt I art 28 (2).
4 Ibid Sch 1 Pt I art 28 (3).
5 Ibid Sch 1 Pt I art 29; see para 1554 ante.

1608. Limitation of liability generally. The liability of the carrier is limited to certain specified maximum sums[1]. Misconduct by the carrier or his servants or agents has no effect on the applicable maxima, and these sums so far as they apply to the carriage of passengers and baggage may not be increased by special contract or by the making of a special declaration as to the value of the baggage[2].

Any provision tending to relieve the carrier of liability or to fix a lower limit than which is laid down is null and void, but the nullity of any such provision does not involve the nullity of the whole contract, which remains subject to the Warsaw–Hague–Montreal provisions[3].

1 See the Carriage by Air and Road Act 1979 s 1 (1), Sch 1 Pt I art 22 (1); and paras 1611, 1617, 1626 post. For the award of costs and lawyers' fees see Sch 1 Pt I art 22 (2). None of the relevant provisions of the Carriage by Air and Road Act 1979 had been brought into force at the date at which this volume states the law.
2 Cf the position under the Warsaw–Hague provisions; see para 1551 ante.
3 Carriage by Air and Road Act 1979 Sch 1 Pt I art 23 (1). This rule does not, however, apply to provisions governing loss or damage resulting from the inherent defect, quality or vice of the cargo carried: Sch 1 Pt I art 23 (2).

(ii) Carriage of Passengers under the Warsaw–Hague–Montreal Provisions

1609. Documents of carriage. In respect of the carriage of passengers, an individual or collective document of carriage must be delivered containing:

(1) an indication of the places of departure and destination; and
(2) if those places are within the territory of a single high contracting party, one or more agreed stopping places being within the territory of another state, an indication of at least one such stopping place[1].

Any other means which would preserve a record of the information indicated above may be substituted for the delivery of the document of carriage[2].

Non-compliance with the above requirements does not affect the existence or the validity of the contract of carriage, which is, none the less, subject to the rules of the Warsaw-Hague-Montreal Convention[3].

1　Carriage by Air and Road Act 1979 s 1 (1), Sch 1 Pt I art 3 (1). None of the relevant provisions of the 1979 Act had been brought into force at the date at which this volume states the law.
2　Ibid Sch 1 Pt I art 3 (2).
3　Ibid Sch 1 Pt I art 3 (3).

1610. Liability for death of or injury to passengers. The carrier is liable for damage sustained in the event of the death or personal injury of a passenger upon condition only that the event which caused the death or injury took place on board the aircraft or in the course of any of the operations of embarking or disembarking[1]. However, the carrier is not liable if the death or injury resulted solely from the state of health of the passenger[2].

1　Carriage by Air and Road Act 1979 s 1 (1), Sch 1 Pt I art 17 (1). None of the relevant provisions of the 1979 Act had been brought into force at the date at which this volume states the law. As to 'the operations of embarking and disembarking' see para 1559 note 5 ante. For the applicability of the Fatal Accidents Act 1976 and the Law Reform (Miscellaneous Provisions) Act 1934 see para 1560 ante.
2　Carriage by Air and Road Act 1979 Sch 1 Pt I art 17 (1).

1611. Limitation of liability for passengers. In the carriage of persons, the carrier's liability for each passenger is limited to the sum of 100,000 special drawing rights[1] for the aggregate of the claims, however founded, in respect of damage suffered as a result of the death or personal injury of each passenger[2]. Where, in accordance with the law of the court seised of the case, damages may be awarded in the form of periodic payments, the equivalent capital value of such payments must not exceed 100,000 special drawing rights[3].

Nothing in the Warsaw-Hague-Montreal provisions prevents a state from establishing and operating within its territory a system to supplement the compensation payable to claimants under the convention in respect of death or personal injury of passengers[4]. Such a scheme must satisfy certain prescribed conditions[5].

1　Special drawing rights are as defined by the International Monetary Fund; conversion to national currencies in judicial proceedings is to be made according to the value of the national currency in terms of special drawing rights at the date of the judgment: Carriage by Air and Road Act 1979 s 1 (1), Sch 1 Pt I art 22 (3). See para 1561 note 4 ante. None of the relevant provisions of the 1979 Act had been brought into force at the date at which this volume states the law.
2　Ibid Sch 1 Pt I art 22 (1) (a).
3　Ibid Sch 1 Pt I art 22 (1) (a).
4　Ibid Sch 1 Pt I art 35A.
5　Ibid Sch 1 Pt I art 35A. The conditions are (1) that the system must not impose upon the carrier or his servants or agents any liability additional to that provided by the convention; (2) that it must not impose upon the carrier any financial or administrative burden other than collecting contributions from passengers if required; (3) that it must not give rise to discrimination between carriers with regard to the passengers concerned and the benefits available to those passengers under the system must be extended to them regardless of the carrier whose services they have used; and (4) if a passenger has contributed to the system, any person suffering damage as a consequence of the death or personal injury of that passenger must be entitled to the benefits of the system: Sch 1 Pt I art 35A (a)–(d).

1612. Contributory negligence. In the carriage of passengers, if the carrier proves that the damage was caused by or contributed to by the negligence or other wrongful act or omission of the person claiming compensation[1], the carrier is wholly or partly exonerated from his liability to such person to the extent that such negligence or wrongful act or omission caused or contributed to the damage[2].

1 Or of the passenger, in the case where another person is the claimant.
2 Carriage by Air and Road Act 1979 s 1 (1), Sch 1 Pt I art 21 (1). Cf para 1550 ante. None of the relevant provisions of the 1979 Act had been brought into force at the date at which this volume states the law.

(iii) Carriage of Baggage under the Warsaw-Hague-Montreal Provisions

1613. Baggage checks. In respect of the carriage of checked baggage, a baggage check must be delivered which, unless combined with or incorporated in a passenger document of carriage, must contain:

(1) an indication of the places of departure and destination; and
(2) if those places are within the territory of a single high contracting party, one or more agreed stopping places being within the territory of another state, an indication of at least one such stopping place[1].

Any other means which would preserve a record of the information indicated above may be substituted for the delivery of the baggage check[2].

Non-compliance with the above requirements does not affect the existence or the validity of the contract of carriage, which is, none the less, subject to the rules of the Warsaw-Hague-Montreal Convention[3].

1 Carriage by Air and Road Act 1979 s 1 (1), Sch 1 Pt I art 4 (1). None of the relevant provisions of the 1979 Act had been brought into force at the date at which this volume states the law. As to passenger documents of carriage see para 1609 ante.
2 Ibid Sch 1 Pt I art 4 (2).
3 Ibid Sch 1 Pt I art 4 (3).

1614. Loss of or damage to baggage. The carrier is liable for damage sustained in case of destruction or loss of, or of damage to, baggage[1] upon condition only that the event which caused the destruction, loss or damage took place on board the aircraft or in the course of any of the operations of embarking or disembarking[2] or during any period within which the baggage was in charge of the carrier. However, the carrier is not liable if the damage resulted solely from the inherent defect, quality or vice of the baggage[3].

1 Including both checked baggage and objects carried by the passenger: Carriage by Air and Road Act 1979 s 1 (1), Sch 1 Pt I art 17 (3). None of the relevant provisions of the 1979 Act had been brought into force at the date at which this volume states the law.
2 See para 1559 note 5 ante.
3 Carriage by Air and Road Act 1979 Sch 1 Pt I art 17 (2).

1615. Receipt without complaint as evidence. Receipt by the person entitled to delivery of baggage without complaint is prima facie evidence that the same has been delivered in good condition and in accordance with the document of carriage[1].

1 Carriage by Air and Road Act 1979 s 1 (1), Sch 1 Pt I art 26 (1). None of the relevant provisions of the 1979 Act had been brought into force at the date at which this volume states the law.

1616. Complaints of damage or delay to baggage. In the case of damage[1] to baggage, the person entitled to delivery must complain to the carrier forthwith after the discovery of the damage and at the latest within seven days[2] from the date of receipt; in the case of delay, the complaint must be made at the latest within 21 days from the date on which the baggage has been placed at his disposal[3].

Every complaint must be made in writing upon the document of carriage or by separate notice in writing dispatched within the times aforesaid[4].

Failing complaint within these times, no action lies against the carrier, save in the case of fraud on his part[5].

1 Including loss of part of the baggage in question: Carriage by Air Act 1961 s 4A (added by the Carriage by Air and Road Act 1979 s 2 (which provision is in force)); *Fothergill v Monarch Airlines Ltd* [1981] AC 251, [1980] 2 All ER 696, 1 S&B AvR I/9, HL. Complaint is not needed in the case of total loss or destruction.
2 'Days' means current days, not working days: Carriage by Air and Road Act 1979 s 1 (1), Sch 1 Pt I art 35. Neither this nor any of the provisions of the 1979 Act cited in the following notes had been brought into force at the date at which this volume states the law.
3 Ibid Sch 1 Pt I art 26 (2).
4 Ibid Sch 1 Pt I art 26 (3).
5 Ibid Sch 1 Pt I art 26 (4). See para 1566 note 6 ante.

1617. Limitation of liability for baggage. In the carriage of baggage, the carrier's liability in the case of destruction, loss, damage or delay is limited to 1,000 special drawing rights for each passenger[1].

1 Carriage by Air and Road Act 1979 s 1 (1), Sch 1 Pt I art 22 (1) (c). As to special drawing rights see para 1611 note 1 ante. None of the relevant provisions of the 1979 Act had been brought into force at the date at which this volume states the law.

1618. Contributory negligence. In the carriage of baggage, if the carrier proves that the damage was caused by or contributed to by the negligence or other wrongful act or omission of the person claiming compensation, the carrier is wholly or partly exonerated from his liability to such person to the extent that such negligence or wrongful act or omission caused or contributed to the damage[1].

1 Carriage by Air and Road Act 1979 s 1 (1), Sch 1 Pt I art 21 (1). Cf para 1550 ante. None of the relevant provisions of the 1979 Act had been brought into force at the date at which this volume states the law.

(iv) Carriage of Cargo under the Warsaw-Hague-Montreal Provisions

1619. Air waybills. In respect of the carriage of cargo an air waybill must be delivered[1]. Any other means which would preserve a record of the carriage to be performed may with the consent of the consignor be substituted for the delivery of an air waybill. If such other means are used, the carrier must, if so requested by the consignor, deliver to the consignor a receipt for the cargo permitting identification of the consignment and access to the information contained in the record preserved by such other means[2].

The impossibility of using, at points of transit and destination, the other means does not entitle the carrier to refuse to accept the cargo for carriage[3].

The air waybill must be made out by the consignor in three original parts[4]. The first part must be marked 'for the carrier' and must be signed by the consignor; the second part must be marked 'for the consignee' and must be signed by the consignor and by the carrier and must accompany the cargo; and the third part must be signed by the carrier and handed by him to the consignor after the cargo has been accepted[5]. The signatures of the carrier and the consignor may be printed or stamped[6]. If, at the consignor's request, the carrier makes out the air waybill, he is deemed, subject to proof to the contrary, to have done so on behalf of the consignor[7].

Where there is more than one package, the carrier of cargo has the right to require the consignor to make out separate air waybills, and the consignor has the right to require the carrier to deliver separate receipts when other means of recording are used[8].

The air waybill (or receipt for the cargo) must contain:

(1) an indication of the places of departure and destination;
(2) if those places are within the territory of a single high contracting party, one or more agreed stopping places being within the territory of another state, an indication of at least one such stopping place; and
(3) an indication of the weight of the consignment[9].

Non-compliance with the above requirements does not affect the existence or the validity of the contract of carriage, which is, none the less, subject to the rules of the Warsaw-Hague-Montreal Convention[10].

1　Carriage by Air and Road Act 1979 s 1 (1), Sch 1 Pt I art 5 (1). None of the relevant provisions of the 1979 Act had been brought into force at the date at which this volume states the law.
2　Ibid Sch 1 Pt I art 5 (2).
3　Ibid Sch 1 Pt I art 5 (3).
4　Ibid Sch 1 Pt I art 6 (1).
5　Ibid Sch 1 Pt I art 6 (2).
6　Ibid Sch 1 Pt I art 6 (3).
7　Ibid Sch 1 Pt I art 6 (4).
8　Ibid Sch 1 Pt I art 7.
9　Ibid Sch 1 Pt I art 8. As to information and documents accompanying air waybills see Sch 1 Pt I art 16; and para 1575 ante.
10　Ibid Sch 1 Pt I art 9.

1620. Correctness of air waybill. The consignor is responsible for the correctness of the particulars and statements relating to the cargo inserted by him or on his behalf in the air waybill or furnished by him or on his behalf to the carrier for insertion in the receipt for the cargo or for insertion in the record preserved by other means[1]. The consignor must indemnify the carrier against all damage suffered by him, or by any other person to whom the carrier is liable, by reason of the irregularity, incorrectness or incompleteness of the particulars and statements furnished by the consignor or on his behalf[2].

Subject to the above, the carrier must indemnify the consignor against all damage suffered by him, or by any other person to whom the consignor is liable, by reason of the irregularity, incorrectness or incompleteness of the particulars and statements inserted by the carrier or on his behalf in the receipt for the cargo or in the record preserved by other means[3].

1　Carriage by Air and Road Act 1979 s 1 (1), Sch 1 Pt I art 10 (1). None of the relevant provisions of the 1979 Act had been brought into force at the date at which this volume states the law. As to other means see para 1619 ante.
2　Ibid Sch 1 Pt I art 10 (2).
3　Ibid Sch 1 Pt I art 10 (3).

1621. Air waybill as evidence of contract. The air waybill is prima facie evidence of the conclusion of the contract, of the acceptance of the cargo and of the conditions of carriage mentioned therein[1]. Further, the statements in it relating to the weight, dimensions and packing of the cargo, as well as those relating to the number of packages, are prima facie evidence of the facts stated; those relating to the quantity, volume and condition of the cargo do not constitute evidence against the carrier except so far as they both have been, and are stated in the air waybill to have been, checked by him in the consignor's presence, or relate to the apparent condition of the cargo[2].

1 Carriage by Air and Road Act 1979 s 1 (1), Sch 1 Pt I art 11 (1). None of the relevant provisions of the 1979 Act had been brought into force at the date at which this volume states the law.
2 Ibid Sch 1 Pt I art 11 (2).

1622. Rights of consignor and consignee. The provisions of the Warsaw-Hague-Montreal Convention relating to the right of:
(1) the consignor, to dispose of the cargo by withdrawing it at the aerodrome of departure or destination, or by stopping it in the course of the journey on any landing, or by calling for it to be delivered at the place of destination or in the course of the journey to a person other than the consignee named in the air waybill, or by requiring the cargo to be returned to the aerodrome of departure; and
(2) the consignee, on arrival of the cargo at the place of destination, to require the carrier to hand over to him the air waybill and to deliver the cargo to him, or in certain cases of loss or non-arrival of the cargo to put into force against the carrier the rights which flow from the contract of carriage,
correspond to those in the Warsaw-Hague Convention[1].

1 See the Carriage by Air and Road Act 1979 s 1 (1), Sch 1 Pt I arts 12–15; and paras 1576–1578 ante. None of the relevant provisions of the 1979 Act had been brought into force at the date at which this volume states the law.

1623. Loss of or damage to cargo. The carrier is liable for damage sustained in the event of the destruction or loss of, or of damage to, cargo, upon condition only that the occurrence which caused the damage so sustained took place during the carriage by air[1]. However, the carrier is not liable if he proves that the destruction or loss of, or damage to, the cargo resulted solely from one or more of the following: (1) inherent defect, quality or vice of that cargo; (2) defective packing of that cargo performed by a person other than the carrier or his servants or agents; (3) an act of war or an armed conflict; or (4) an act of public authority carried out in connection with the entry, exit or transit of the cargo[2].

The carriage by air for this purpose comprises the period during which the baggage or cargo is in charge of the carrier, whether in an airport or on board an aircraft or, in the case of a landing outside an airport, in any place whatsoever[3]. It does not extend to any carriage by land, by sea or by river performed outside an airport, but if such a carriage takes place in the performance of a contract for carriage by air for the purpose of loading, delivery or transhipment, any damage is presumed, subject to proof to the contrary, to have been the result of an event which took place during the carriage by air[4].

1 Carriage by Air and Road Act 1979 s 1 (1), Sch 1 Pt I art 18 (1). None of the relevant provisions of the 1979 Act had been brought into force at the date at which this volume states the law.

2 Ibid Sch 1 Pt I art 18 (2).
3 Ibid Sch 1 Pt I art 18 (3).
4 Ibid Sch 1 Pt I art 18 (4).

1624. Receipt without complaint as evidence. Receipt by the person entitled to delivery of cargo without complaint is prima facie evidence that the same has been delivered in good condition and in accordance with the document of carriage[1].

1 Carriage by Air and Road Act 1979 s 1 (1), Sch 1 Pt I art 26 (1). None of the relevant provisions of the 1979 Act had been brought into force at the date at which this volume states the law.

1625. Complaints of damage or delay to cargo. In the case of damage[1] to cargo, the person entitled to delivery must complain to the carrier forthwith after the discovery of the damage and at the latest within 14 days[2] from the date of receipt; in the case of delay, the complaint must be made at the latest within 21 days from the date on which the cargo has been placed at his disposal[3].

Every complaint must be made in writing upon the document of carriage or by separate notice in writing dispatched within the times aforesaid[4].

Failing complaint within these times, no action lies against the carrier, save in the case of fraud on his part[5].

1 Including loss of part of the cargo in question: Carriage by Air Act 1961 s 4A (added by the Carriage by Air and Road Act 1979 s 2 (a provision which is in force)); *Fothergill v Monarch Airlines Ltd* [1981] AC 251, [1980] 2 All ER 696, 1 S&B AvR I/9, HL. Complaint is not needed in the case of total loss or destruction.
2 'Days' means current days, not working days: Carriage by Air and Road Act 1979 s 1 (1), Sch 1 Pt I art 35. Neither this nor any of the provisions of the 1979 Act cited in the following notes had been brought into force at the date at which this volume states the law.
3 Ibid Sch 1 Pt I art 26 (2).
4 Ibid Sch 1 Pt I art 26 (3).
5 Ibid Sch 1 Pt I art 26 (4). See para 1566 note 6 ante.

1626. Limitation of liability for cargo. In the carriage of cargo, the carrier's liability is limited to a sum of 17 special drawing rights per kilogramme, unless the consignor has made, at the time when the package was handed over to the carrier, a special declaration of interest in delivery at destination and has paid a supplementary sum if the case so requires; in that case the carrier will be liable to pay a sum not exceeding the declared sum, unless he proves that that sum is greater than the consignor's actual interest in delivery at destination[1].

In the case of loss, damage or delay of part of the cargo, or of any object contained in it, the weight to be taken into consideration in determining the limit on the carrier's liability is only the total weight of the package or packages concerned; nevertheless, when such a loss affects the value of other packages covered by the same air waybill, the total weight of such package or packages must also be taken into consideration[2].

1 Carriage by Air and Road Act 1979 s 1 (1), Sch 1 Pt I art 22A (1) (a). As to special drawing rights see para 1611 note 1 ante. None of the relevant provisions of the 1979 Act had been brought into force at the date at which this volume states the law.
2 Ibid Sch 1 Pt I art 22A (1) (b). As to costs and legal expenses see Sch 1 Pt I art 22A (2).

1627. Contributory negligence. In the carriage of cargo, if the carrier proves that the damage was caused by or contributed to by the negligence or other wrongful act or omission of the person claiming compensation, or the person from whom he derives his rights, the carrier is wholly or partly exonerated from his liability to such person to the extent that such negligence or wrongful act or omission caused or contributed to the damage[1].

1 Carriage by Air and Road Act 1979 s 1 (1), Sch 1 Pt I art 21 (2). Cf para 1550 ante. None of the relevant provisions of the 1979 Act had been brought into force at the date at which this volume states the law.

(v) Delay to Passengers, Baggage or Cargo under the Warsaw-Hague-Montreal Provisions

628. Delay. The carrier is liable for damage occasioned by delay in the carriage by air of passengers, baggage or cargo[1]. The carrier is not liable, however, if he proves that he and his servants and agents have taken all necessary measures to avoid the damage or that it was impossible for him or them to take such measures[2].

1 Carriage by Air and Road Act 1979 s 1 (1), Sch 1 Pt I art 19. None of the relevant provisions of the 1979 Act had been brought into force at the date at which this volume states the law.
2 Ibid Sch 1 Pt I art 20. See para 1583 ante.

(6) NON-INTERNATIONAL CARRIAGE

(i) Introductory

629. Rules governing non-international carriage. The provisions of the Warsaw Convention as amended at The Hague in 1955[1] and the provisions of the Guadalajara Convention[2] have been applied, with substantial exceptions and modifications, to carriage by air, not being international carriage[3] within the meaning of either the Warsaw-Hague provisions or of the unamended Warsaw Convention.

The non-international rules apply to all such carriage by air for reward, and to gratuitous carriage by aircraft performed by an air transport undertaking[4] or by the Crown[5] if the place of departure or of destination or an agreed stopping place is within the United Kingdom or other British territory[6], with the exception of certain special classes of carriage[7]. The rules also apply to the carriage of mail and postal packages[8].

The rules are set out in the Carriage by Air Acts (Application of Provisions) Order 1967[9]. Orders have been made[10] applying substantially similar provisions as part of the law of the Channel Islands[11], the Isle of Man[12] and certain overseas territories[13].

1 See paras 1009, 1528 ante.
2 See paras 1010, 1528 ante.
3 For the meanings of 'international carriage' see paras 1541, 1585 ante.
4 Carriage by Air Acts (Application of Provisions) Order 1967, SI 1967/480, art 4 (a), Sch 1 Pt III A art 1.
5 Ibid art 7.
6 *Holmes v Bangladesh Biman Corpn* [1989] AC 1112, [1989] 1 All ER 852, 1 S&B AvR VII/355, HL.
7 For the excepted classes see para 1543 ante.
8 Carriage by Air Acts (Application of Provisions) Order 1967 art 4 (b); see also POST OFFICE, where the carriage of postal packets is considered.

9 SI 1967/480 (amended by SI 1969/1083, SI 1979/931 and SI 1981/440). The order was made und
the Carriage by Air Act 1961 s 10, and the Carriage by Air (Supplementary Provisions) Act 1962 s
(2).
10 These orders were made under the Carriage by Air Act 1961 ss 9, 10, and the Carriage by A
(Supplementary Provisions) Act 1962 s 5 (1), (2).
11 See the Carriage by Air Acts (Application of Provisions) (Jersey) Order 1967, SI 1967/806, and th
Carriage by Air Acts (Application of Provisions) (Guernsey) Order 1967, SI 1967/807.
12 See the Carriage by Air Acts (Application of Provisions) (Isle of Man) Order 1967, SI 1967/808.
13 See the Carriage by Air Acts (Application of Provisions) (Overseas Territories) Order 1967, S
1967/810, art 4, Sch 2.

1630. Carriage excepted from non-international rules. The Secretary c
State may, subject to such conditions as he thinks fit, exempt any carriage or clas
of carriage, or any person or class of person, from any of the requirements impose
by the Carriage by Air Acts (Application of Provisions) Order 1967[1].

1 Carriage by Air Acts (Application of Provisions) Order 1967, SI 1967/480, art 8. As to the transfer c
functions to the Secretary of State see para 1032 ante.

1631. Meaning of 'carrier'. The Carriage by Air Acts (Application of Pro
visions) Order 1967[1] applies the provisions of the Guadalajara Convention[2]
subject to minor modifications, to all non-international carriage to which the orde
applies[3]. The position of 'actual carriers' and 'contracting carriers'[4] is substantiall
the same as under the Carriage by Air (Supplementary Provisions) Act 1962[5].
   The position of servants and agents of the actual carrier or of the contractin
carrier is the same under the order[6] as under the Carriage by Air Act 1961[7] and th
Carriage by Air (Supplementary Provisions) Act 1962[8].

1 Ie SI 1967/480 (amended by SI 1969/1083, SI 1979/931 and SI 1981/440).
2 The Guadalajara Convention is set out in the Carriage by Air (Supplementary Provisions) Act 196:
see paras 1010, 1528, 1539 ante.
3 Carriage by Air Acts (Application of Provisions) Order 1967 art 4 (a), Sch 1 Pt II.
4 For the meaning of 'actual carrier' and 'contracting carrier' see para 1539 notes 4, 5 ante.
5 See the Carriage by Air Acts (Application of Provisions) Order 1967 Sch 1 Pt III B.
6 See ibid Sch 1 Pt III A arts 25, 25A.
7 See the Carriage by Air Act 1961 s 1 (1), Sch 1 arts 25, 25A; and paras 1551, 1553 ante.
8 See the Carriage by Air (Supplementary Provisions) Act 1962 s 1 (1), Schedule Pt 1 art v; and par
1551 ante.

1632. Liability of successive carriers. Where carriage is to be performed b
various successive carriers, each carrier who accepts passengers, baggage or carg
is subjected to the rules of the Carriage by Air Acts (Application of Provisions
Order 1967[1], and is deemed to be one of the contracting parties to the contract o
carriage in so far as the contract deals with that part of the carriage which i
performed under his supervision[2].

1 Ie SI 1967/480 (amended by SI 1969/1083, SI 1979/931 and SI 1981/440).
2 Ibid art 4 (a), Sch 1. Pt III A art 30 (1).

1633. Combined carriage. In the case of combined carriage partly by air an
partly by any other mode of carriage, the carrier is liable only for that part of th
carriage which is performed by air, provided that the carriage falls within the term

f the Carriage by Air Acts (Application of Provisions) Order 1967[1]. Nothing owever, prevents the parties from inserting in the document of air carriage onditions relating to other modes of carriage provided that the provisions of the rder are observed as regards the carriage by air[2].

1 See the Carriage by Air Acts (Application of Provisions) Order 1967, SI 1967/480, art 4 (a), Sch 1 Pt III A art 31 (1).
2 Ibid Sch 1 Pt III A art 31 (2). See also, generally, CARRIERS.

634. Prohibition of contracting out. Where a contract is entered into for arriage to which the non-international rules apply[1], any clause contained in the ontract and all special agreements entered into before the damage occurred by vhich the parties purport to infringe the rules by deciding the law to be applied are ull and void[2]. Nevertheless, for the carriage of cargo, arbitration clauses are llowed subject to the rules[3].

However, nothing in the rules prevents the carrier either from refusing to enter nto any contract of carriage or from making regulations which do not conflict vith the rules[4].

1 As to the carriage to which the rules apply see para 1629 ante.
2 Carriage by Air Acts (Application of Provisions) Order 1967, SI 1967/480, art 4 (a), Sch 1 Pt III A art 32; and as to the actual carrier, Pt III B art IX (3). The provisions relieving the carrier of liability or fixing a lower limit than that laid down by the rules are null and void; see paras 1639, 1640, 1646 post.
3 Ibid Sch 1 Pt III A art 32; and, as to the actual carrier, Pt III B art IX (3).
4 Ibid Sch 1 Pt III A art 33.

635. Carriage of passengers, baggage or cargo. Many provisions of the Carriage by Air Acts (Application of Provisions) Order 1967[1] relating to the carriage of passengers, baggage or cargo are the same as those set out in the Carriage by Air Act 1961; thus the definition of the conduct of the carrier which may give rise to unlimited liability[2], the liability of the carrier for delay[3] and the position in the event of the death of the person liable[4] are the same as under the Act of 1961.

However, the provisions of the Act of 1961 relating to the existence and contents of documents of carriage[5] have been excluded from the order[6]; the carrier's right to avail himself of such of the provisions of the order which limit or exclude his liability is not dependent on the existence of documents of carriage[7].

1 SI 1967/480.
2 See the Carriage by Air Acts (Application of Provisions) Order 1967, SI 1967/480, art 4 (a), Sch 1 Pt III A art 25; and see para 1553 ante.
3 See ibid Sch 1 Pt III A art 19; and see paras 1583 ante, 1636, 1640, 1646 post.
4 See ibid Sch 1 Pt III A art 27; and see para 1555 ante.
5 Ie the Carriage by Air Act 1961 Sch 1 Chapter 2 (arts 3–16).
6 Carriage by Air Acts (Application of Provisions) Order 1967 Sch 1 Pt I para (5).
7 If the carrier wishes to take advantage of the provisions of the 1967 Order concerning the limitation of liability (see Sch 1 Pt III A art 22) in respect of baggage or cargo of which he takes charge, it is necessary for him to record the number and weight of the bags or packages concerned (Sch 1 Pt III A art 22 (2) (b)).

(ii) Carriage of Passengers under the Non-international Rules

1636. Death of or injury to passengers. The carrier is liable for damage sustained in the event of death or wounding of a passenger or any other bodily injury
suffered by a passenger, if the accident which caused the damage so sustained took
place on board the aircraft, or in the course of any of the operations of embarking or
disembarking[1].

In the event of the death of a passenger the carrier is liable as under the Carriage
by Air Act 1961 except for the limit of damages recoverable[2], and actions under the
Fatal Accidents Act 1976 and the Law Reform (Miscellaneous Provisions) Act 1934
may lie against him[3].

The carrier is also liable for damage occasioned by delays in the carriage by air o
passengers[4].

In relation to the carriage performed by the actual carrier, an action for damages
may be brought, at the plaintiff's option, against that carrier or the contracting
carrier, or against both together or separately[5].

1 Carriage by Air Acts (Application of Provisions) Order 1967, SI 1967/ 480, art 4 (a), Sch 1 Pt III A ar
  17. See also para 1559 note 5 ante.
2 See para 1639 post.
3 See the Carriage by Air Acts (Application of Provisions) Order 1967 art 6, which refers to the
  Carriage by Air Act 1961 s 3; see para 1560 ante. As to actions by dependants see para 1637 post.
4 Carriage by Air Acts (Application of Provisions) Order 1967 Sch 1 Pt III A art 19.
5 Ibid Sch 1 Pt III B art VII.

1637. Actions for damages against carriers of passengers. Any action for
damages, however founded, can only be brought subject to the conditions and
limits set out in the Carriage by Air Acts (Application of Provisions) Order 1967[1].
However, in cases of death or injury to passengers the above-mentioned rule will
apply without prejudice to the questions as to who are the persons entitled to bring
suit and what are their respective rights[2]; in such cases actions under the Fatal
Accidents Act 1976 and under the Law Reform (Miscellaneous Provisions) Act
1934 may lie against the carrier[3]. In the case of the death of the person liable, an
action for damages lies against those legally representing his estate[4].

In relation to carriage performed by the actual carrier, an action for damages may
be brought, at the plaintiff's option, against that carrier or against the contracting
carrier, or against both, together or separately[5]. In the case of successive carriage,
the passenger or his representative can take action only against the carrier who
performed the carriage during which the damage or the delay occurred, save in a
case where, by express agreement, the first carrier has assumed liability for the
whole journey[6].

1 Carriage by Air Acts (Application of Provisions) Order 1967, SI 1967/480, art 4 (a), Sch 1 Pt III A art
  24 (1). As to liability for delay in the carriage of passengers see para 1636 ante.
2 Ibid Sch 1 Pt III A art 24 (2).
3 See ibid art 6 which refers to the Carriage by Air Act 1961 s 3; see para 1560 ante.
4 Carriage by Air Acts (Application of Provisions) Order 1967 Sch 1 Pt III A art 27. As to contributory
  negligence see para 1638 post.
5 Ibid Sch 1 Pt III B art VII. For the meaning of 'actual carrier' and 'contracting carrier' see para 1539
  notes 4, 5 ante.
6 Ibid Sch 1 Pt III A art 30 (2).

1638. Defences. The carrier is not liable if he proves that he and his servants or agents took all necessary measures to avoid the damage, or that it was impossible for him or them to take such measures[1]. Further, if the carrier proves that the damage was caused or contributed to by the injured person's negligence, the court may, in accordance with the provisions of its own law, exonerate the carrier wholly or partly from his liability[2].

The right to damages is extinguished if an action is not brought within two years reckoned from the date of arrival at the destination, or from the date on which the aircraft ought to have arrived or on which the carriage stopped[3].

1 Carriage by Air Acts (Application of Provisions) Order 1967, SI 1967/480, art 4 (a), Sch 1 Pt III A art 20.
2 Ibid Sch 1 Pt III A art 21. See also art 6, which refers to the Carriage by Air Act 1961 s 6 (contributory negligence; see para 1560 ante).
3 Carriage by Air Acts (Application of Provisions) Order 1967 Sch 1 Pt III A art 29 (1). The method of calculating the limitation period is determined by the law of the court seised of the case: Sch 1 Pt III A art 29 (2).

1639. Limitation of liability. In the absence of a special contract between the carrier and the passenger fixing a higher limit of liability, the carrier's liability for each passenger is limited to the sum of 100,000 special drawing rights[1]. Where, in accordance with the law of the court seised of the case, damages may be awarded in the form of periodical payments, the capital value of the payments must not exceed 100,000 special drawing rights[2].

However, the carrier may not avail himself of the limitation of liability if it is proved that the damage resulted from an act or omission of the carrier, his servants or agents, done with intent to cause damage or recklessly and with knowledge that damage would probably result; in the case of such an omission of a servant or agent it must also be proved that he was acting within the scope of his employment[3].

Any provision tending to relieve the carrier of liability or to fix a lower limit than that laid down is null and void[4].

1 Carriage by Air Acts (Application of Provisions) Order 1967, SI 1967/480, art 4 (a), Sch 1 Pt III A art 22 (1) (substituted by SI 1981/440). For the value of a special drawing right see the Carriage by Air Acts (Application of Provisions) Order 1967 Sch 1 Pt III A art 22 (5) (substituted by SI 1979/931); and paras 1561 note 4, 1611 note 1 ante.
2 Carriage by Air Acts (Application of Provisions) Order 1967 Sch 1 Pt III A art 22 (1) (as substituted: see note 1 supra).
3 Ibid Sch 1 Pt III A art 25; see para 1553 ante.
4 Carriage by Air Acts (Application of Provisions) Order 1967, Sch 1 Pt III A art 23 (1). The nullity of the provision does not, however, involve the nullity of the whole contract, which remains subject to the provisions of the Schedule: Sch 1 Pt I II A art 23 (1).

(iii) Carriage of Baggage under the Non-international Rules

1640. Liability for baggage. The carrier is liable for damage sustained in the event of the destruction or loss of, or of damage to, any registered baggage, if the occurrence which caused the loss took place during the carriage by air[1]. The carrier is also liable for damage occasioned by delay in the carriage of baggage by air[2]. Receipt by the person entitled to delivery of the baggage without complaint is prima facie evidence that it has been delivered in good condition[3].

Any provision tending to relieve the carrier of liability or to fix a lower limit than that provided by the Carriage by Air Acts (Application of Provisions) Order 1967

is null and void; but the nullity of any such provision does not involve the nullity o
the whole contract[4].

1 Carriage by Air Acts (Application of Provisions) Order 1967, SI 1967/ 480, art 4 (a), Sch 1 Pt III A ar
18 (1). The carriage by air within the meaning of this provision comprises the period which
the baggage is in charge of the carrier, whether in an aerodrome or on board an aircraft, or, in th
case of a landing outside an aerodrome , in any place whatsoever: Sch 1 Pt III A art 18 (2); but it doe
not extend to carriage by other means performed outside an aerodrome; if however, such carriag
takes place in the performance of a contract for carriage by air, for the purpose of loading, delivery o
transhipment, any damage is presumed, subject to proof to the contrary, to have been the result of ar
event which took place during the carriage by air: Sch 1 Pt III A art 18 (3).
2 Ibid Sch 1 Pt III A art 19.
3 Ibid Sch 1 Pt III A art 26 (1). As to complaints see para 1641 post.
4 Ibid Sch 1 Pt III A art 23 (1); Sch 1 Pt III B art IX (1).

1641. Complaints. In the case of damage, the person entitled to delivery mus
complain to the carrier forthwith after the discovery of the damage and, at th
latest, within seven days from the date of receipt of the baggage; in the case o
delay, the complaint must be made at the latest within 21 days from the date or
which the baggage has been placed at the disposal of the person entitled to
delivery[1]. The complaint must be made in writing, and must be dispatched within
the appropriate time limit[2].

Failing complaint within these time limits, no action lies against the carrier save
in the case of fraud on his part[3].

1 Carriage by Air Acts (Application of Provisions) Order 1967, SI 1967/ 480, art 4 (a), Sch 1 Pt III A ar
26 (2).
2 Ibid Sch 1 Pt III A art 26 (3).
3 Ibid Sch 1 Pt III A art 26 (4). See para 1566 note 6 ante. As to actions see para 1642 post.

1642. Actions for damages against carriers of baggage. Any action for damages, however founded, in the case of damage, destruction or loss of baggage, or ir
the case of delay, can only be brought subject to the conditions set out in the
Carriage by Air Acts (Application of Provisions) Order 1967[1].

In relation to carriage performed by an actual carrier[2], an action for damages may
be brought, at the plaintiff's option, against that carrier or against the contracting
carrier[3], or against both together or separately[4].

In the case of successive carriers[5], the passenger has a right of action against the
first carrier, and the passenger who is entitled to delivery has a right of action
against the last carrier; further, each passenger may take action against the carrie
who performed the carriage during which the destruction, loss, damage or delay
occurred[6].

1 See the Carriage by Air Acts (Application of Provisions) Order 1967, SI 1967/480, art 4 (a), Sch 1 P
III A arts 18–30 (especially art 24 (1)) .
2 For the meaning of 'actual carrier' see para 1539 note 4 ante.
3 For the meaning of 'contracting carrier' see para 1539 note 5 ante.
4 Carriage by Air Acts (Application of Provisions) Order 1967 Sch 1 Pt III B art VII.
5 As to successive carriers see para 1632 ante.
6 Carriage by Air Acts (Application of Provisions) Order 1967 Sch 1 Pt III A art 30 (3). The carriers will
be jointly and severally liable to the passenger: Sch 1 Pt III A art 30 (3). As to the position of the
carriers' servants and agents see para 1551 ante.

1643. Defences. The carrier has the same defences in the case of destruction, loss,
damage or delay of baggage as he has in the case of death, injury or delay of

passengers[1]; namely, (1) that all necessary measures have been taken to avoid the damage[2], (2) the passenger's contributory negligence[3], and (3) the extinguishment of the right of action[4].

The carrier has the additional defences that the damage took place when the baggage was not in his charge[5], and that complaints were not made in the prescribed period[6].

1 See para 1638 ante.
2 Carriage by Air Acts (Application of Provisions) Order 1967, SI 1967/480, art 4 (a), Sch 1 Pt III A art 20.
3 Ibid Sch 1 Pt III A art 21.
4 Ibid Sch 1 Pt III A art 29.
5 See ibid Sch 1 Pt III A art 18 (1), (2).
6 See ibid Sch 1 Pt III A art 26 (2).

1644. Limitation of liability. In relation to registered baggage, the carrier's liability is limited to a sum of 17 special drawing rights per kilogramme, in the absence of an agreement for a higher sum[1]. In the case of loss, damage or delay of part of registered baggage or of any object contained in it, the weight to be taken into consideration in determining the amount to which the carrier's liability is limited is only the total weight of the package or packages concerned; but when the loss, damage or delay of a part of the registered baggage, or of an object contained in it, affects the value of other packages covered by the same baggage check, the total weight of such package or packages is also to be taken into consideration in determining the limit of liability[2].

As regards objects of which the passenger takes charge himself, the carrier's liability is limited to 332 special drawing rights[3].

These limits of liability do not apply to the carrier if it is proved that the damage resulted from an act or omission of the carrier, his servants or agents, done with intent to cause damage or recklessly and with knowledge that damage would probably result; in the case of such act or omission of a servant or agent it must also be proved that he was acting within the scope of his employment[4].

1 Carriage by Air Acts (Application of Provisions) Order 1967, SI 1967/480, art 4 (a), Sch 1 Pt III A art 22 (2) (a) (substituted by SI 1979/931). For the value of a special drawing right see the Carriage by Air Acts (Application of Provisions) Order 1967 Sch 1 Pt III A art 22 (5) (as so substituted); and paras 1561 note 4, 1611 note 1 ante. The passenger may, at the time when the package is handed over to the carrier, make a special declaration of interest in delivery at destination, and pay a supplementary sum if the case so requires; the carrier is then liable for a sum not exceeding the declared sum unless he proves that that sum is greater than the passenger's actual interest in delivery at destination: Sch 1 Pt III A art 22 (2) (a) (as so substituted).
2 Ibid Sch 1 Pt III A art 22 (2) (b). Though no baggage check is required by this order, the habit of issuing a baggage check has remained, thus providing for the weight and number of pieces of baggage to be recorded, which is necessary if the carrier wishes to limit his liability.
3 Ibid Sch 1 Pt III A art 22 (3) (substituted by SI 1979/931). For the value of a special drawing right see the Carriage by Air Acts (Application of Provisions) Order 1967 Sch 1 Pt III A art 22 (5) (as so substituted).
4 Ibid Sch 1 Pt III A art 25.

(iv) Carriage of Cargo and Mail and Postal Packages under the Non-international Rules

1645. Applicable rules. The provisions of the Warsaw Convention as amended at The Hague in 1955 relating to the existence and contents of the air waybill, to the disposition and stoppage of cargo in transit, and to the rights of the consignor and consignee[1], do not apply to carriage by air under the non-international rules which does not fall within the definition of international carriage[2].

1 As to these provisions see paras 1568–1582 ante.
2 See the Carriage by Air Acts (Application of Provisions) Order 1967, SI 1967/480, art 4, Sch 1 Pt para (5), Pt II para (5), which makes modifications for this purpose to the Warsaw-Hague Convention.

1646. Liability for cargo. The carrier is liable for damage sustained in the event of destruction or loss of, or of damage to, any cargo, if the occurrence which caused the damage so sustained took place during the carriage by air[1]. The carrier is also liable for damage occasioned by delay in the carriage of cargo by air[2]. Receipt by the person entitled to delivery of cargo without complaint is prima facie evidence that the cargo has been delivered in good condition[3].

Any provision tending to relieve the carrier of liability or to fix a lower limit than that provided by the Carriage by Air Acts (Application of Provisions) Order 1967 is null and void[4]; but this rule does not apply to provisions governing loss or damage resulting from the inherent defect, quality or vice of the cargo carried[5].

The order contains no provision requiring the delivery of an air waybill[6].

1 Carriage by Air Acts (Application of Provisions) Order 1967, SI 1967/480, art 4, Sch 1 Pt III A art 18 (1). For the meaning of 'carriage by air' in this paragraph see para 1640 note 1 ante.
2 Ibid Sch 1 Pt III A art 19.
3 Ibid Sch 1 Pt III A art 26 (1). As to complaints see para 1647 post.
4 Ibid Sch 1 Pt III A art 23 (1); Pt III B art IX (1): the nullity of any such provision does not involve the nullity of the whole contract.
5 Ibid Sch 1 Pt III A art 23 (2); Pt III B art IX (2).
6 The delivery of an air waybill is not necessary to allow the carrier to limit his liability: see further para 1650 post.

1647. Complaints. In the case of damage, the person entitled to delivery must complain to the carrier forthwith after the discovery of the damage and, at the latest, within 14 days from the date of receipt of the cargo; in the case of delay, the complaint must be made at the latest within 21 days from the date on which the cargo has been placed at the disposal of the consignee[1]. The complaint must be made in writing, and must be dispatched within the appropriate time limit[2].

Failing complaint within these time limits, no action lies against the carrier save in the case of fraud on his part[3].

1 Carriage by Air Acts (Application of Provisions) Order 1967, SI 1967/480, art 4, Sch 1 Pt III A art 26 (2).
2 Ibid Sch 1 Pt III A art 26 (3).
3 Ibid Sch 1 Pt III A art 26 (4). See para 1566 note 6 ante. As to actions see para 1648 post.

1648. Actions for damages against carriers of cargo. Any action for damages, however founded, in the case of damage, destruction or loss of cargo, or in the case of delay, can only be brought subject to the conditions set out in the Carriage by Air Acts (Application of Provisions) Order 1967[1].

In relation to carriage performed by an actual carrier[2], an action for damages may be brought, at the plaintiff's option, against that carrier or against the contracting carrier[3] or against both together or separately[4].

In the case of successive carriers[5], the consignor has a right of action against the first carrier, and the consignee who is entitled to delivery has a right of action against the last carrier; further, the consignor and the consignee may each take action against the carrier who performed the carriage during which the destruction, loss, damage or delay occurred[6].

1 See the Carriage by Air Acts (Application of Provisions) Order 1967, SI 1967/480, art 4, Sch 1 Pt III A arts 18–30 (especially art 24 (1)).
2 For the meaning of 'actual carrier' see para 1539 note 4 ante.
3 For the meaning of 'contracting carrier' see para 1539 note 5 ante.
4 Carriage by Air Acts (Application of Provisions) Order 1967 Sch 1 Pt III B art VII.
5 As to successive carriers see para 1632 ante.
6 Carriage by Air Acts (Application of Provisions) Order 1967 Sch 1 Pt III A art 30 (3). The carriers will be jointly and severally liable to the consignor or consignee: Sch 1 Pt III A art 30 (3). As to the position of the carriers' servants and agents see para 1551 ante.

1649. Defences. If the carrier proves that all necessary measures were taken to avoid the damage or that it was impossible for him to take such measures, he is exonerated from his liability[1]; similarly, he may be wholly or partly exonerated if there has been contributory negligence on the part of the consignor or consignee[2]. The right to damages is extinguished if no action has been brought within the prescribed time of two years[3].

The carrier has also the additional defences that the damage took place when the cargo was not in his charge[4], or that the complaint was not made within the prescribed times[5].

1 See the Carriage by Air Acts (Application of Provisions) Order 1967, SI 1967/480, art 4, Sch 1 Pt III A art 20.
2 See ibid Sch 1 Pt III A art 21.
3 See ibid Sch 1 Pt III A art 29; and para 1554 ante.
4 See ibid Sch 1 Pt III A art 18 (1), (2).
5 See ibid Pt III A art 26 (2); and para 1647 ante.

1650. Limitation of liability. In relation to cargo, the carrier's liability is limited to a sum of 17 special drawing rights per kilogramme, in the absence of an agreement for a higher sum[1]. In the case of loss, damage or delay of part of the cargo, or of any object contained in it, the weight to be taken into consideration in determining the amount to which the carrier's liability is limited is only the total weight of the package or packages concerned; but when the loss, damage or delay of a part of the cargo, or of an object contained in it, affects the value of other packages covered by the same air waybill, the total weight of such packages is also to be taken into consideration in determining the limits of liability[2].

These limits of liability do not apply to the carrier if it is proved that the damage resulted from an act or omission of the carrier, his servants or agents, done with intent to cause harm or recklessly and with knowledge that damage would probably result; in the case of such an act or omission of a servant or agent it must also be proved that he was acting within the scope of his employment[3].

1 Carriage by Air Acts (Application of Provisions) Order 1967, SI 1967/480, art 4, Sch 1 Pt III A art 22 (2) (a) (substituted by SI 1979/931). For the value of a special drawing right see the Carriage by Air Acts (Application of Provisions) Order 1967 Sch 1 Pt III A art 22 (5) (as so substituted); and paras 1561 note 4, 1611 note 1 ante. The consignor may, at the time when the package is handed over to the carrier, make a special declaration of interest in delivery at destination, and pay a supplementary sum

if the case so requires; the carrier is then liable for a sum not exceeding the declared sum unless he proves that that sum is greater than the passenger's actual interest in delivery at destination: ibid Sch 1 Pt III A art 22 (2) (a) (as so substituted).
2 Ibid Sch 1 Pt III A art 22 (2) (b). Although no air waybill is required by the order, the practice of issuing an air waybill has remained, thus providing for the weight and number of packages to be recorded, which is necessary if the carrier wishes to avail himself of the provisions of the order limiting his liability.
3 Ibid Sch 1 Pt III A art 25.

(7) MISCELLANEOUS PROVISIONS AS TO CARRIAGE BY AIR

1651. Restriction on carriage by foreign aircraft in the United Kingdom. Aircraft registered in a contracting state to the Chicago Convention of 1944[1] other than the United Kingdom, or in a foreign country[2], may not take on board or discharge any passengers or cargo[3] in the United Kingdom, being passengers or cargo carried for valuable consideration [4], except with the permission of the Secretary of State[5] granted to the operator[6] or charterer[7] of the aircraft or to the government of the country in which the aircraft is registered[8] and in accordance with any conditions to which that permission may be subject[9]. Any breach by a person to whom a permission has been granted of any condition to which the permission was subject constitutes a contravention[10].

1 See the Air Navigation Order 1989, SI 1989/2004, art 106 (1), definition of 'Contracting State'. For the Chicago Convention see para 1002 et seq ante.
2 'Foreign country' for this purpose includes Hong Kong: Air Navigation Order 1989 art 106 (1).
3 'Cargo' includes mail and animals: ibid art 106 (1).
4 'Valuable consideration' means any right, interest, profit or benefit, forbearance, detriment, loss or responsibility accruing, given, suffered or undertaken pursuant to an agreement, which is of more than a nominal nature: ibid art 106 (1). As to carriage for reward see para 1533 ante.
5 As to the Secretary of State see para 1032 ante.
6 For the meaning of 'operator' see the Air Navigation Order 1989 art 106 (3); and para 1340 ante.
7 As to charterers see para 1336 et seq ante.
8 As to the registration of aircraft see paras 1267, 1275 ante.
9 Air Navigation Order 1989 art 88 (1). See also the Chicago Convention (Cmd 8742) arts 5, 7, and the Civil Aviation Act 1982 s 60 (3) (f).
10 Air Navigation Order 1989 art 88 (2). The penalty for contravention of this provision is, on summary conviction, a fine not exceeding £2,000, and on conviction on indictment, a fine, or imprisonment for up to two years, or both: art 99 (6), Sch 12 Pt B.

1652. Ancillary provisions regulating carriage of passengers. Aircraft engaged in the public transport[1] of passengers may land or depart only from licensed or other specified aerodromes[2], and must comply with the customs procedure[3].

A passenger commits an offence if he recklessly or negligently endangers the safety of an aircraft or of any person in it[4] or recklessly or negligently causes it to endanger any person or property[5], is drunk in an aircraft[6], smokes in a part of an aircraft where smoking is not permitted[7], or travels in any part of an aircraft not designed for the accommodation of persons[8].

A person may not secrete himself for the purpose of being carried in an aircraft without the consent of either the operator[9] or the commander[10] or of any other person entitled to give consent to his being carried in the aircraft[11].

Restrictions apply to immigrants arriving or departing by air[12].

1 For the meaning of 'public transport' in this context see the Air Navigation Order 1989, SI 1989/2004, art 107; and para 1272 ante.
2 Ibid art 76. See para 1105 text and note 11 ante.
3 See paras 1220–1228 ante.
4 Air Navigation Order 1989 art 50. The penalty on summary conviction of this offence is a fine not exceeding £2,000, and on conviction on indictment, a fine or imprisonment for a term not exceeding two years or both: art 99 (6), Sch 12 Pt B.
5 Ibid art 51. The penalty for this offence is as described in note 4 supra.
6 Ibid art 52 (1). The penalty for this offence is as described in note 4 supra.
7 Ibid s 53 (2). The penalty on summary conviction of this offence is a fine not exceeding £1,000: art 99 (5), Sch 12 Pt A.
8 Ibid art 48. The penalty for this offence is as described in note 7 supra.
9 For the meaning of 'operator' see ibid art 106 (3); and para 1340 ante.
10 For the meaning of 'commander' see ibid art 106 (1); and para 1213 note 1 ante.
11 Ibid art 55. The penalty for this offence is as described in note 4 supra. See also para 1458 ante. It is submitted that in the event of the death of or injury to a stowaway during carriage by air the carrier is not liable since such carriage can hardly be described as gratuitous carriage which, to be so, requires the carrier's consent.
12 See the Immigration Act 1971; para 1229 ante; and BRITISH NATIONALITY.

1653. Carriage of weapons and munitions of war. An aircraft must not carry munitions of war except where the written permission of the Civil Aviation Authority (CAA) has been obtained and the carriage is in accordance with any conditions in that permission, and the commander has, before the commencement of the flight, been informed in writing by the operator of the type, weight or quantity, and location of the munitions and of the relevant conditions of the CAA's permission[1]. In no case may a weapon or munition of war be carried in any compartment or apparatus to which passengers have access[2].

It is unlawful for any person to carry or have in his possession or to take or cause to be taken on board an aircraft, or to suspend or cause to be suspended beneath an aircraft, or to deliver or cause to be delivered for carriage thereon, any weapon or munition of war, unless: (1) it is part of the baggage of a passenger or consigned as cargo, is carried in a part of the aircraft (or apparatus attached to it) inaccessible to the passengers and, in the case of a firearm, is unloaded; and (2) particulars of the weapon or munition have been furnished by the passenger or consignor to the operator before the flight commences; and (3) the operator consents to the carriage of the relevant articles[3].

These provisions do not apply to any weapon or munition of war taken or carried on board an aircraft registered outside the United Kingdom if the weapon or munition of war concerned may under the law of the state of registration be lawfully taken or carried on board for the purpose of ensuring the safety of the aircraft or of persons on board[4].

1 Air Navigation Order 1989, SI 1989/2004, art 46 (1). 'Munitions of war' means any weapon, ammunition or article containing an explosive or noxious liquid, gas or other thing which is designed or made for use in warfare or against persons, including parts (whether components or accessories) for such weapon, ammunition or article: art 46 (5). As to the CAA see para 1044 ante.
    The penalty on summary conviction of this offence is a fine not exceeding £2,000, and on indictment, a fine or imprisonment for a term not exceeding two years, or both: art 99 (6), Sch 12 Pt B.
2 Ibid art 46 (2). The penalty for this offence is as described in note 1 supra.
3 Ibid art 46 (3). The penalty for this offence is as described in note 1 supra. For powers to prevent flights in contravention of this provision see art 95 (1) (a); and para 1459 ante. As to the application of the Air Navigation Order 1989 to the Crown and visiting forces and military aircraft see art 103; and para 1264 notes 9–11 ante.

4 Ibid art 46 (4).

1654. Carriage of dangerous goods. An aircraft must not carry or have loaded therein or suspended thereunder any dangerous goods[1] except where the written permission of the Civil Aviation Authority (CAA) has been obtained and the carriage is in accordance with any conditions in that permission and with the Technical Instructions for the Safe Transport of Dangerous Goods by Air[2]. It is unlawful for any person to take or cause to be taken on board an aircraft, or to suspend or cause to be suspended beneath an aircraft, or to deliver or cause to be delivered for loading on or suspension beneath an aircraft any goods which he knows or ought to know or suspect to be dangerous goods unless the Air Navigation (Dangerous Goods) Regulations 1985 are complied with[3].

Dangerous goods permitted to be carried in an aircraft may not be loaded as cargo unless the consignor has furnished the operator with the dangerous goods transport document prescribed by the 1985 Regulations[4], which also impose obligations upon the shipper in respect of the marking, labelling and packing of the goods[5] and on the operator in respect of the inspection and loading of the goods[6]. It is an offence to contravene or permit the contravention of the 1985 Regulations[7].

1 'Dangerous goods' means any article or substance which is capable of posing significant risk to health, safety or property when carried by air and which is classified in Part 2 of the Technical Instructions for the Safe Transport of Dangerous Goods by Air (as to which see note 2 infra): Air Navigation (Dangerous Goods) Regulations 1985, SI 1985/1939, reg 3 (1) (amended by SI 1988/2133 and SI 1990/2531).
2 Air Navigation (Dangerous Goods) Regulations 1985 reg 4 (1). The regulations were made under the Air Navigation Order 1985, SI 1985/1643, art 44 (1) (revoked) and now have effect under the Air Navigation Order 1989, SI 1989/2004, art 47. The Technical Instructions are published by the Council of ICAO, and the reference is to the 1991–1992 English language version: Air Navigation (Dangerous Goods) Regulations 1985 reg 3 (1) (amended by SI 1990/2531). As to ICAO see para 1020 et seq ante; as to the CAA see para 1044 ante.
3 Air Navigation (Dangerous Goods) Regulations 1985 reg 4 (2) (substituted by SI 1986/2133).
4 Air Navigation (Dangerous Goods) Regulations 1985 reg 5 (1). This does not apply, however, where the goods are specified in the Technical Instructions (see note 2 supra) as being goods in respect of which a dangerous goods transport document is not required: reg 5 (1). As to the contents of such a document see reg 5 (2).
5 See ibid reg 6 (amended by SI 1988/2133 and SI 1990/2531).
6 See the Air Navigation (Dangerous Goods) Regulations 1985 regs 7, 8 (reg 7 amended by SI 1986/2129, SI 1988/2123 and SI 1990/2531).
7 Air Navigation Order 1989 art 47 (2). The penalty on summary conviction of such an offence is a fine not exceeding £2,000, and on conviction on indictment, a fine or imprisonment for a term not exceeding two years, or both: art 99 (6), Sch 12 Pt B. As to the application of the Air Navigation Order 1989 to the Crown and visiting forces and military aircraft see art 103; and para 1264 ante. The provisions are in addition to and not in derogation from the provisions as to weapons and munitions of law set out in para 1653 ante: art 47 (3).

1655. Carriage of animals. The carriage of animals by air is governed by the Carriage by Air Act 1961 and the Carriage by Air (Supplementary Provisions) Act 1962[1], as well as by common law rules. The carrier has the duty to feed and water the animals in transit; and he will be liable if fear or restiveness of the animals causes damage through his negligence[2].

The Animal Health Act 1981 enables orders to be made prohibiting the importation of named species of animals and of other animal products[3]; prohibiting or prescribing conditions for the export of horses[4] and other species[5]; and protecting animals from unnecessary suffering during inland transit, including transit by an aircraft on a flight beginning or ending in Great Britain[6].

1 See para 1528 et seq ante.
2 See generally CARRIERS.
3 Animal Health Act 1981 s 10. For application in or over territorial waters see the Animal Health and Welfare Act 1984 s 3.
4 Animal Health Act 1981 ss 40–49.
5 Ibid s 39.
6 Ibid s 37. See generally ANIMALS; CARRIERS.

1656. Customs control. All cargo carried in aircraft is subject to the requirements of the law regarding customs control[1].

1 See paras 1220–1228 ante.

II. LIABILITIES

(1) JURISDICTION AND EVIDENCE

1657. Jurisdiction in civil matters. The question whether the English courts have jurisdiction over a particular matter arising in relation to aircraft or air navigation will ordinarily[1] fall to be decided by the general rules of English law[2].

A court in any part of the United Kingdom has jurisdiction to hear and determine a claim for charges or interest payable to the Secretary of State or the Civil Aviation Authority (CAA) or Eurocontrol by virtue of regulations as to charges for air navigation services[3] notwithstanding that the person against whom the claim is made is not resident within the jurisdiction of the court[4].

Her Majesty may make provision by Order in Council as to the courts in which proceedings may be taken for enforcing any claim in respect of aircraft, and in particular may provide for conferring jurisdiction in any such proceedings on any court exercising Admiralty jurisdiction and for applying to such proceedings any rules of practice or procedure applicable to proceedings in Admiralty[5]. This power has only been exercised so as to confer jurisdiction upon Admiralty courts in cases relating to wreck and salvage of aircraft[6].

1 There are specific provisions as to jurisdiction over actions brought under the terms of the Warsaw Convention: see Carriage by Air Act 1961 s 1 (1), Sch 1 art 28; Carriage by Air Acts (Application of Provisions) Order 1967, SI 1967/480, Sch 2 Pt B art 28; Carriage by Air and Road Act 1979 s 1 (1), Sch 1 Pt I art 28 (1), (2); paras 1544, 1588, 1607 ante.
2 See generally CONFLICT OF LAWS.
3 Ie made under Civil Aviation Act 1982 s 73; see para 1377 ante.
4 Ibid s 74 (6). As to the Secretary of State see para 1032 ante; as to the CAA see para 1044 ante; as to Eurocontrol see para 1023 ante.
5 Ibid s 91.
6 Ibid s 87. See para 1492 ante; and ADMIRALTY vol 1 (1) (Reissue) para 323; SHIPPING vol 43 para 1027 et seq.

1658. Jurisdiction in criminal matters. A number of special provisions modify the limits which the general law imposes on the criminal jurisdiction of the English courts[1].

For the purpose of conferring jurisdiction, any offence under the law in force in, or in a part of, the United Kingdom committed on board an aircraft in flight is deemed to have been committed in any place in the United Kingdom (or, as the case may be, in that part thereof) where the offender may for the time being be[2].

Any court in the United Kingdom having jurisdiction in respect of piracy[3] committed on the high seas has jurisdiction in respect of piracy committed by or against an aircraft, wherever that piracy is committed[4].

1 See CRIMINAL LAW.
2 Civil Aviation Act 1982 s 92 (3). See also s 99 (2), (5).
3 See para 1665 post.
4 Aviation Security Act 1982 s 5 (1). The provisions as to 'aircraft' in the Civil Aviation Act 1982 s 92 (5) (see para 1660 note 1 post) and s 101 (application to Crown aircraft) apply in this context: Aviation Security Act 1982 s 5 (2).

1659. Documentary evidence. In any legal proceedings, a document purporting to be certified by a designated authority or person[1] as being, or being a true copy of, or of part of, a document issued or record kept, in pursuance of an Air Navigation Order or the Civil Aviation (Licensing) Act 1960[2], by, or by the minister in charge of, a government department, by an official specified in such an order, or by the Air Registration Board or the Air Transport Licensing Board[3], is evidence of the matters appearing from that document[4]. The same applies to any document printed by either Her Majesty's Stationery Office or the Civil Aviation Authority (CAA) and purporting to be the publication known as 'United Kingdom Air Pilot' or a publication of the series known as 'Notam-United Kingdom'[5].

Any record made by, or by a person acting under the control of, a designated person or authority and purporting to show the position of an aircraft at any material time or the terms or contents of any message transmitted to or received from the aircraft is, if produced from the custody of the designated person or authority, evidence in any legal proceedings of the matters appearing from the record[6].

1 See the Civil Aviation (Documentary Evidence) Regulations 1972, SI 1972/187. Under these regulations, any document certified by the CAA as being, or as being a true copy of, an instrument made by the authority is evidence of that instrument; and a copy, certified by the CAA of the relevant issue of the CAA's official record is evidence of the publication of any notice or other matter by the CAA: reg 4. As to the CAA see para 1044 ante.
2 Now repealed.
3 Now replaced by the CAA.
4 Civil Aviation Act 1982 s 96 (1) (a).
5 Ibid s 96 (1) (b).
6 Ibid s 96 (2).

1660. Evidence by deposition in criminal cases. Where in any proceedings before a court in the United Kingdom for an offence committed on board an aircraft[1] the testimony of any person is required and the court is satisfied that this person cannot be found in the United Kingdom, any deposition[2] previously made on oath[3] by that person outside the United Kingdom is admissible provided that it was made in the presence of the person charged with the offence [4] before a judge or magistrate of a Commonwealth country or one which was part of Her Majesty's dominions or in which Her Majesty had jurisdiction[5] or before a consular officer of Her Majesty's Government in the United Kingdom[6]. The judge, magistrate or officer must sign, and thus authenticate, the deposition and certify that the person charged with the offence was present at the taking of the deposition[7].

1 'Aircraft' means any aircraft, whether or not a British-controlled aircraft, other than (a) a military aircraft or (b) an aircraft which, not being a military aircraft, belongs to or is exclusively employed in the service of Her Majesty in right of the United Kingdom: Civil Aviation Act 1982 s 92 (5). Her Majesty may, by Order in Council, apply any provisions of the Act, with or without modifications, to such aircraft as are mentioned in (b) above: s 101 (1) (b).
2 'Deposition' includes any affidavit, affirmation or statement made upon oath: ibid s 95 (5).
3 'Oath' includes an affirmation or declaration in the case of persons allowed by law to affirm or declare instead of swearing: ibid s 95 (5).
4 Ibid s 95 (1) (a).
5 Ibid s 95 (1) (b).
6 Ibid s 95 (1) (b). If a complaint is made to such a consular officer that an offence has been committed on a British-controlled aircraft while in flight elsewhere than in or over the United Kingdom, that officer may inquire into the case upon oath: s 95 (4). For the meaning of 'British-controlled aircraft' see para 1663 note 1 post; for the meaning of 'in flight' see para 1661 note 2 post.
7 Ibid s 95 (2). The certificate is sufficient evidence of the presence of the person charged with the offence at the making of the deposition, unless the contrary is proved, and it is not necessary in the proceedings to prove the signature or official character of the person appearing to have authenticated the deposition or given the certificate: s 95 (3).

1661. Taking of criminal proceedings. No proceedings for any offence under the law in force in, or in part of, the United Kingdom committed on board an aircraft[1] while in flight[2] elsewhere than in or over the United Kingdom may be instituted except by or with the consent of the Director of Public Prosecutions[3].

1 For the meaning of 'aircraft' see para 1660 note 1 ante.
2 The period during which an aircraft is in flight is deemed to include any period from the moment when power is applied for the purpose of the aircraft taking off on a flight until the moment when the landing run (if any) at the termination of that flight ends: Civil Aviation Act 1982 s 92 (4). A reference to an aircraft in flight includes a reference to an aircraft during any period when it is on the surface of the sea or land but not within the territorial limits of any country: s 92 (4).
3 Ibid s 92 (2). This is subject to any provision to the contrary in any Act passed after 14 July 1967: s 92 (2).

(2) OFFENCES

1662. General provisions. A large part of air law is criminal law, as a large proportion of it consists of regulations governing the use of aircraft, the breach of which is an offence. These include many provisions of the Air Navigation Order 1989[1], which has a degree of extra-territorial application[2]. The Order contains a table of penalties applying in the case of contravention of particular provisions[3].

If any provision of the Air Navigation Order 1989 or of any regulation made thereunder is contravened in relation to an aircraft, the operator[4] and the commander[5] of that aircraft are, without prejudice to the liability of any other person under the Order for that contravention, deemed to have contravened that provision unless they prove that the contravention occurred without their consent or connivance and that they exercised all due diligence to prevent it[6].

If it is proved that an act or omission[7] of any person was due to any cause not avoidable by the exercise of reasonable care by that person, the act or omission is deemed not to be a contravention by that person[8].

Where a person is charged with a contravention by reason of his having been a member of the flight crew[9] of an aircraft on a flight for the purpose of public transport[10] or aerial work[11] the flight is to be treated (without prejudice to the liability of any other person) as not having been for that purpose if he proves that he neither knew nor suspected that the flight was for that purpose[12].

1 SI 1989/2004.
2 Air Navigation Order 1989 art 100.
3 See ibid art 99 (4)–(6), Sch 12.
4 For the meaning of 'operator' see para 1663 note 1 post; a similar definition is applied by the Air Navigation Order 1989 art 106 (3) (see para 1340 ante).
5 For the meaning of 'commander' see para 1673 note 2 post; a similar definition applies under the Air Navigation Order 1989 art 106 (1) (see para 1213 note 1 ante).
6 Ibid art 99 (1).
7 Ie an act or omission which would otherwise have been a contravention by that person of a provision of the Order or of a regulation made under it: ibid art 99 (2).
8 Ibid art 99 (2).
9 As to flight crews see para 1343 et seq ante.
10 For the meaning of 'public transport' see para 1272 ante.
11 For the meaning of 'aerial work' see para 1273 ante.
12 Air Navigation Order 1989 art 99 (3).

1663. Offences on board aircraft. Any act or omission taking place on board a British-controlled aircraft[1] while in flight[2] elsewhere than in or over the United Kingdom, which if taking place in, or in a part of, the United Kingdom, would constitute an offence under the law in force in, or in that part of, the United Kingdom, constitutes that offence[3]. This provision does not, however, apply to any act or omission which is expressly or impliedly authorised by or under that law when taking place outside the United Kingdom[4].

1 'British-controlled aircraft' means an aircraft which is either (1) registered in the United Kingdom; or (2) not registered in any country but in the case of which the operator of the aircraft, or each person entitled as owner to any legal or beneficial interest in it, satisfies the requirements (a) that he is a person qualified to be the owner of such an interest in an aircraft registered in the United Kingdom and (b) that he resides or has his principal place of business in the United Kingdom; or (3) if registered in another country, is chartered by demise to a person who satisfies, or to persons each of whom satisfies, the foregoing requirements: Civil Aviation Act 1982 s 92 (5). For the meaning of 'aircraft' see para 1660 note 1 ante. 'Military aircraft' means an aircraft of the naval, military or air forces of any country, and any other aircraft certified as such under an Order in Council under the Civil Aviation Act 1982: s 92 (5). A certificate of the Secretary of State that an aircraft is or is not a military aircraft for this purpose is conclusive evidence of the fact: s 92 (5). 'Operator' means the person who has the management of an aircraft: s 105 (1).
2 As to the period during which an aircraft is in flight see para 1661 note 2 ante.
3 Civil Aviation Act 1982 s 92 (1).
4 Ibid s 92 (1).

1664. Crimes against aviation: international conventions. The United Kingdom is a party to, and has given effect to, a number of international conventions dealing with crimes against the safety of aviation. These include the Convention on Offences and certain other Acts Committed on board Aircraft, Tokyo 1963[1], the Convention for the Suppression of Unlawful Seizure of Aircraft, The Hague 1970[2], and the Convention for the Suppression of Unlawful Acts against the Safety of Civil Aviation, Montreal 1971[3]. Provision has also been made in English law to give effect to a Protocol for the Suppression of Unlawful Acts of Violence at Airports Serving International Aviation, Montreal 1988, which supplements the 1971 Montreal Convention but which is not yet in force.

1 As to this convention, published in Cmnd 2261, see para 1014 ante. For a list of countries in which the Tokyo Convention is in force see the Tokyo Convention (Certification of Countries) Order 1977, SI 1977/1258 (amended by SI 1978/1534).
2 As to this convention, published in Cmnd 4577, see para 1015 ante. For a list of countries in which the convention is in force see the Extradition (Hijacking) Order 1971, SI 1971/2102 (amended by SI 1982/146, SI 1985/1989, SI 1986/2012, SI 1987/451, SI 1987/2041 and SI 1988/2243).

3 As to this convention see para 1016 ante. For a list of countries in which the convention is in force see
   the Extradition (Aviation Security) Order 1991, SI 1991/1699, Schs 2, 3.

1665. Piracy by or against aircraft. The offence of piracy as provided for in the
Convention on the High Seas, Geneva 1958[1], is treated for the purposes of any
proceedings before a court in the United Kingdom[2] as constituting part of the law
of nations[3].

1 Piracy consists of any of the following acts: (1) any illegal acts of violence, detention or any act of
   depredation committed for private ends by the crew or passengers of a private ship or aircraft
   directed (a) on the high seas, against another ship or aircraft or against persons or property on board,
   (b) against a ship, aircraft, persons or property in a place outside the jurisdiction of any state; (2) any
   act of voluntary participation in the operation of a ship or aircraft with knowledge of facts making it
   a pirate ship or aircraft; (3) any act of inciting or of intentionally facilitating an act described in (1) or
   (2) above: Convention on the High Seas signed at Geneva on 29 April 1958 (Cmnd 584) art 15, set
   out in the Tokyo Convention Act 1967 Schedule. See SHIPPING.
2 For the jurisdiction of the English courts see para 1658 ante.
3 Tokyo Convention Act 1967 s 4 (amended by the Aviation Security Act 1982 s 40, Sch 3); Aviation
   Security Act 1982 s 5.

1666. Hijacking. A person on board an aircraft in flight[1] who unlawfully, by the
use of force or by threats of any kind, seizes the aircraft or exercises control of it
commits the offence of hijacking, whatever his nationality, whatever the state in
which the aircraft is registered and whether the aircraft is in the United Kingdom[2]
or elsewhere[3].

However, no offence of hijacking is committed if the aircraft is used in military[4],
customs or police service[5]; or if both the place of take-off and the place of landing
are in the territory of the state in which the aircraft is registered[6]. These exceptions
do not apply where the person seizing or exercising control of the aircraft is a
United Kingdom national[7]; or where the act is committed in the United Kingdom[8]; or where the aircraft is registered in the United Kingdom or is used in the
military or customs service of the United Kingdom or in the service of any police
force in the United Kingdom[9].

1 For the purposes of the Aviation Security Act 1982, the period during which an aircraft is in flight is
   deemed to include any period from the moment when all its external doors are closed following
   embarkation until the moment when any such door is opened for disembarkation and, in the case of
   a forced landing, any period until the competent authorities take over responsibility for the aircraft
   and for persons and property on board: Aviation Security Act 1982 s 38 (3) (a).
2 For the purposes of ibid s 1, the territorial waters of any state are treated as part of its territory: s 1 (5).
3 Ibid s 1 (1). The maximum penalty is life imprisonment: s 1 (3).
4 'Military service' includes naval and air force service: ibid s 38 (1).
5 Ibid s 1 (2) (a).
6 Ibid s 1 (2) (b). As to acts in the United Kingdom inducing or assisting a hijacking elsewhere see s 6
   (2). As to the state of registration in the case of aircraft operated by joint or international organisations see s 1 (4). No relevant instrument had been made at the date at which this volume states the
   law.
7 Ibid s 1 (2) (i). A United Kingdom national is a British citizen, a British Dependent Territories
   citizen, a British National (Overseas) or a British Overseas citizen, a person who is a British subject
   under the British Nationality Act 1981 or a British protected person within the meaning of that Act:
   Aviation Security Act 1982 s 38 (1) (amended by the Hong Kong (British Nationality) Order 1986,
   SI 1986/948, art 8, Schedule).

8 Aviation Security Act 1982 s 1 (2) (ii).
9 Ibid s 1 (2) (iii).

1667. Related violence against passengers or crew. Where a person of whatever nationality does on board any aircraft, wherever registered, and while outside
the United Kingdom, any act which if done in, or in a part of, the United Kingdom
would constitute a specified offence[1], his act constitutes that offence if it is done in
connection with the offence of hijacking[2] committed or attempted by him on
board that aircraft[3].

1 Ie murder, attempted murder, manslaughter, culpable homicide or assault, or an offence under the
   Offences Against the Person Act 1861 ss 18, 20–23, 28 or 29, or under the Explosive Substances Act
   1883 s 2; see CRIMINAL LAW.
2 See para 1666 ante.
3 Aviation Security Act 1982 s 6 (1).

1668. Destroying, damaging or endangering the safety of aircraft. It is an
offence for any person unlawfully[1] and intentionally to destroy an aircraft in
service[2] or so to damage such an aircraft as to render it incapable of flight or as to be
likely to endanger its safety in flight[3]; or to commit on board an aircraft in flight
any act of violence[4] which is likely to endanger the safety of the aircraft[5].

It is also an offence for any person unlawfully and intentionally to place, or cause
to be placed, on an aircraft in service any device or substance which is likely to
destroy the aircraft or so to damage it as to render it incapable of flight or as to be
likely to endanger its safety in flight[6].

Both offences may be committed in the United Kingdom or elsewhere, whatever the nationality of the offender or the state of registration of the aircraft[7].
However, no offence is committed if the aircraft is used in military[8], customs or
police service unless the act is committed in the United Kingdom or by a United
Kingdom national[9].

1 In relation to an act done outside the United Kingdom this means so that it would have been an
   offence under English law if committed in England: Aviation Security Act 1982 s 2 (6).
2 For the purposes of the Aviation Security Act 1982, an aircraft is taken to be in service during the
   whole of the period which begins with the pre-flight preparation of the aircraft for a flight and ends
   24 hours after the aircraft lands having completed that flight, and also at any other time while the
   aircraft is in flight (as to which see para 1666 note 1 ante): s 38 (3) (b).
3 Ibid s 2 (1) (a).
4 Ie an act done in the United Kingdom which constitutes the offence of murder, attempted murder,
   manslaughter, culpable homicide or assault, or an offence under the Offences Against the Person
   Act 1861 ss 18, 20–23, 28 or 29, or under the Explosive Substances Act 1883 s 2, or an act done
   elsewhere which would constitute such offence had it been done in the United Kingdom: Aviation
   Security Act 1982 s 1 (7). See CRIMINAL LAW.
5 Ibid s 2 (1) (b). The maximum penalty, on conviction on indictment, is life imprisonment: s 2 (5).
6 Ibid s 2 (2), which is not to be construed as limiting the scope of the offence under s 2 (1) or of any
   preliminary offence related thereto. The maximum penalty, on conviction on indictment, is life
   imprisonment: s 2 (5).
7 Ibid s 2 (3).
8 See para 1666 note 4 ante.
9 Aviation Security Act 1982 s 2 (4). As to acts done in the United Kingdom which induce or assist the
   commission of an offence elsewhere see ibid s 6 (2). For the meaning of 'United Kingdom national'
   see para 1666 note 7 ante.

1669. Other acts endangering the safety of aircraft. It is an offence for any
person unlawfully[1] and intentionally to destroy or damage any property used for

the provision of air navigation facilities[2], or to interfere with the operation of any such property, where the destruction, damage or interference is likely to endanger the safety of aircraft in flight[3].

It is also an offence for any person intentionally to communicate any information which is false, misleading or deceptive in a material particular, where the communication of the information endangers or is likely to endanger the safety of aircraft in flight[4]. It is a defence for the person charged to prove that he believed, and had reasonable grounds for believing, that the information was true, or that, when he communicated the information, he was lawfully employed to perform duties which consisted of or included the communication of information and that he communicated the information in the performance of those duties[5].

The provisions stated in this paragraph do not apply unless the relevant act is committed in the United Kingdom, or, where it is committed elsewhere, the person committing it is a United Kingdom national[6], or the commission of the act endangers or is likely to endanger the safety in flight of a civil aircraft[7] registered in the United Kingdom or chartered by demise to a lessee whose principal place of business[8] is in the United Kingdom, or is committed on board such an aircraft, or on board a civil aircraft which lands in the United Kingdom with the person who committed the act still on board[9].

1 See para 1668 note 1 ante.
2 This includes any land, building or ship so used, and any apparatus or equipment so used whether it is on board an aircraft or elsewhere: Aviation Security Act 1982 s 3 (2). If the act is committed outside the United Kingdom and the property is so situated and is not used for the provision of air navigation facilities in connection with international air navigation, the offence can only be committed by a United Kingdom national: s 3 (6). For the meaning of 'United Kingdom national' see para 1666 note 7 ante.
3 Ibid s 3 (1). The maximum penalty, on conviction on indictment, is imprisonment for life: s 3 (7). As to the period during which an aircraft is deemed to be in flight see para 1666 note 1 ante.
4 Ibid s 3 (3). The maximum penalty, on conviction on indictment, is imprisonment for life: ibid s 3 (7).
5 Ibid s 3 (4).
6 See note 2 supra.
7 Ie any aircraft other than an aircraft used in military, customs or police service: Aviation Security Act 1982 s 3 (8). For the meaning of 'military service' see para 1666 note 4 ante.
8 If he has no place of business, his permanent residence.
9 Aviation Security Act 1982 s 3 (5). As to acts done in the United Kingdom which induce or assist the commission of an offence elsewhere see s 6 (2).

1670. Dangerous articles. It is an offence for any person without lawful authority or reasonable excuse (proof of which lies on him) to have with him certain dangerous articles in (1) any aircraft registered in the United Kingdom wherever it may be, (2) any other aircraft at a time when it is in, or in flight over, the United Kingdom, (3) any part of an aerodrome in the United Kingdom, or (4) any air navigation installation in the United Kingdom which does not form part of an aerodrome[1]. The articles concerned are any firearm, any article having the appearance of being a firearm (whether capable of being discharged or not), any explosive, any article manufactured or adapted (whether in the form of a bomb, grenade or otherwise) to have the appearance of being an explosive (whether capable of producing a practical effect by explosion or not), any article marked or labelled so as to indicate that it is or contains an explosive, and any other article

made or adapted for use for causing injury to or incapacitating a person or
destroying or damaging property, or intended by the person having it with him for
such use (whether by him or by any other person)[2].

1 Aviation Security Act 1982 s 4 (1).
2 Ibid s 4 (2). For the circumstances in which a person may be deemed to have an article with him see
   s 4 (3), (5). The maximum penalty is, on summary conviction, a fine not exceeding the statutory
   maximum or imprisonment for three months or both, or, on conviction on indictment, a fine or
   imprisonment for five years or both: s 4 (4). As to the statutory maximum see s 38 (1); and para 1005
   note 11 ante. At the date at which this volume states the law, the statutory maximum is £2,000.

1671. Endangering safety at aerodromes. It is an offence for any person by any
device, substance or weapon intentionally to commit at an aerodrome[1] serving
international civil aviation any act of violence[2] which causes or is likely to cause
death or serious personal injury and endangers or is likely to endanger the safe
operation of the aerodrome or the safety of persons at the aerodrome[3].

It is also an offence for any person by means of any device, substance or weapon
unlawfully[4] and intentionally to destroy or seriously damage property used for the
provision of any facilities at an aerodrome serving international civil aviation,
including any apparatus or facilities so used[5].

It is also an offence for any person by means of any device, substance or weapon
unlawfully and intentionally to destroy or seriously damage any aircraft which is at
an aerodrome serving international civil aviation but is not in service[6]. However,
no offence is committed if the aircraft is used in military[7], customs or police service
unless the act is committed in the United Kingdom or by a United Kingdom
national[8].

It is also an offence for any person by means of any device, substance or weapon
unlawfully and intentionally to disrupt the services of an aerodrome serving
international civil aviation[9].

All these offences may be committed in the United Kingdom or elsewhere and
whatever the nationality of the offender[10].

1 'Aerodrome' has the same meaning as in the Civil Aviation Act 1982 s 105 (1) (see para 1102 ante):
   Aviation and Maritime Security Act 1990 s 1 (9).
2 Ie an act done in the United Kingdom which constitutes the offence of murder, attempted murder,
   manslaughter, culpable homicide or assault, or an offence under the Offences Against the Person
   Act 1861 ss 18, 20–23, 28 or 29, or under the Explosive Substances Act 1883 s 2, or an act done
   elsewhere which would constitute such offence had it been done in the United Kingdom: Aviation
   and Maritime Security Act 1990 s 1 (9). See CRIMINAL LAW.
3 Ibid s 1 (1).
4 In relation to an act done outside the United Kingdom this means so that it would have been an
   offence under English law if committed in England: ibid s 1 (9).
5 Ibid s 1 (2) (a) (i).
6 Ibid s 1 (2) (a) (ii). An aircraft is taken to be in service during the whole of the period which begins
   with the pre-flight preparation of the aircraft for a flight and ends 24 hours after the aircraft lands
   having completed that flight, and also at any other time while the aircraft is in flight (as to which see
   para 1666 note 1 ante): s 1 (6), applying the Aviation Security Act 1982 s 38 (3) (b).
7 'Military service' includes naval and air force service: ibid s 38 (1), applied by the Aviation and
   Maritime Security Act 1990 s 1 (9).
8 Ibid s 1 (4). 'United Kingdom national' has the same meaning as in the Aviation Security Act 1982
   s 38 (1) (see para 1666 note 7 ante): Aviation and Maritime Security Act 1990 s 1 (9).
9 Ibid s 1 (2) (b).
10 Ibid s 1 (3). In each case the maximum penalty is life imprisonment: s 1 (5).

1672. Extradition. Where no general extradition arrangements have been made between the United Kingdom and a state which is a party to a relevant international convention an Order in Council applying the Extradition Act 1989 may be made under that Act[1] as if the convention constituted general extradition arrangements with that state, but only in relation to specified offences[2]. The relevant conventions include conventions concerning crimes against aviation[3] and offences created to give effect to those conventions[4].

1 Extradition Act 1989 s 4. See generally EXTRADITION.
2 Ibid s 22.
3 Ie those examined in para 1664 ante.
4 Ie any offence committed on board an aircraft in flight (see para 1663 ante), offences under the Aviation Security Act 1982 ss 1, 2, 3, or 6 (see paras 1666–1669 ante) and the Aviation and Maritime Security Act 1990 s 1 (see para 1671 ante).

(3) POWERS OF AIRCRAFT COMMANDER

1673. Commander's powers as to offences. For the purposes of any proceedings before any court in the United Kingdom[1], if the commander[2] of an aircraft[3] in flight[4], wherever that aircraft may be, has reasonable grounds to believe in respect of any person on board the aircraft (1) that the person in question has done or is about to do any act on the aircraft while it is in flight which jeopardises or may jeopardise the safety of the aircraft or of persons or property on board the aircraft, or (2) that the person in question has done on the aircraft while in flight any act which in the opinion of the commander is a serious offence under the law[5] of the state of registration[6], the commander may take in respect of that person such reasonable measures, including restraint of his person, as may be necessary to protect the safety of the aircraft or of persons or property on board, to maintain good order and discipline on board the aircraft, or to enable the commander to disembark or deliver the person[7].

1 Civil Aviation Act 1982 s 94 (1).
2 'Commander' in relation to an aircraft means the member of the crew designated as commander of that aircraft by the operator or, failing such a person, the person who is for the time being the pilot in command of the aircraft, and 'pilot in command' means the person who for the time being is in charge of the piloting of the aircraft without being under the direction of any other pilot in the aircraft: ibid s 94 (7). For the meaning of 'operator' see para 1663 note 1 ante.
3 For the meaning of 'aircraft' see para 1660 note 1 ante.
4 For the purposes of the commander's powers the period during which an aircraft is in flight is deemed to include, in addition to the period mentioned in para 1661 note 2 ante, any period from the moment when all external doors, if any, of the aircraft are closed following embarkation for a flight until the moment when any such door is opened for disembarkation after that flight, and, if the aircraft makes a forced landing, any period thereafter until the time when competent authorities of the country in which the forced landing took place take over the responsibility for the aircraft and for the persons and property on board the aircraft: ibid s 94 (8). If the forced landing takes place in the United Kingdom, this means the time when a constable arrives at the place of landing: s 94 (8). References to a country or its territorial limits include references to any territorial waters of that country: s 106.
5 The law must not be a law of a political nature or based on racial or religious discrimination: ibid s 94 (2) (b).
6 For the purposes of ibid s 94 (2) (b) any British-controlled aircraft (as defined in para 1663 note 1 ante) is deemed to be registered in the United Kingdom, whether or not it is in fact so registered and whether or not it is in fact registered in some other country: s 94 (2) in fine.

7 Ibid s 94 (2).

1674. Restraint of offenders. Any member of the crew and any other person on board the aircraft may, at the request or with the authority of the aircraft commander[1], and any crew member must if so required by the commander, render assistance in restraining any person whom the commander is so entitled to restrain[2]. Any member of the crew or any other person on board the aircraft may also, while the aircraft is in flight[3] and without the commander's authority, take, with respect to any person on board the aircraft, any measures which the commander would have power to take[4] and which the person acting has reasonable grounds to believe are immediately necessary to protect the safety of the aircraft or of persons or property on board[5].

1 For the meaning of 'commander' see para 1673 note 2 ante.
2 Civil Aviation Act 1982 s 94 (3).
3 For the meaning of 'in flight' for this purpose see ibid s 94 (8); and para 1673 note 4 ante.
4 See para 1673 ante.
5 Civil Aviation Act 1982 s 94 (3).

1675. Duty to terminate restraint. Any restraint imposed on any person on board an aircraft[1] must end when the aircraft first thereafter ceases to be in flight[2] unless, before landing or as soon as is reasonably practicable after landing, the aircraft commander[3] causes the competent authorities of the country of landing to be notified that a person on board the aircraft is under restraint and the reasons for it[4].

Subject to such notification the restraint may then be extended for any period, including the period of any further flight, between the time of this first landing and the first occasion thereafter on which the commander is able with any requisite consent of the appropriate authorities to disembark[5] or deliver[6] the person under restraint; or if the person under restraint agrees to continue his journey under restraint on board that aircraft[7].

1 See para 1674 ante.
2 As to when an aircraft ceases to be in flight for this purpose see para 1673 note 4 ante.
3 For the meaning of 'commander' see para 1673 note 2 ante.
4 Civil Aviation Act 1982 s 94 (4).
5 See para 1676 post.
6 See para 1677 post
7 Civil Aviation Act 1982 s 94 (4).

1676. Commander's powers to disembark offenders. The aircraft commander[1] may, if he has in the case of any person on board the aircraft, reasonable grounds to believe that the person in question has done or was about to do acts, while the aircraft was in flight, which might have jeopardised or did jeopardise either the safety of the aircraft or of persons or property on board, or good order and discipline on board, and also has reasonable grounds to believe that it is necessary to do so in order to protect the safety of the aircraft or of persons or property on board, or good order and discipline on board, disembark that person in any country in which the aircraft may be[2].

If the aircraft commander disembarks a person from a British-controlled aircraft[3] in any country, or from any other aircraft in the United Kingdom, he must

report the fact of and the reasons for that disembarkation to an appropriate
authority in the country of disembarkation and to the appropriate diplomatic or
consular office of the country of nationality of that person[4].

1 For the meaning of 'commander' see para 1673 note 2 ante.
2 Civil Aviation Act 1982 s 94 (5) (a).
3 For the meaning of 'British-controlled aircraft' see para 1663 note 1 ante.
4 Civil Aviation Act 1982 s 94 (6) (a). If the commander fails without reasonable cause to comply with
   this provision, he will be liable on summary conviction to a fine not exceeding level 3 on the standard
   scale: s 94 (6) (amended by virtue of the Criminal Justice Act 1982 ss 38, 46). As to the standard scale
   see para 1044 note 6 ante. At the date at which this volume states the law, level 3 on that scale is at
   £400.

1677. Commander's powers to deliver up offenders. An aircraft commander's[1] power to deliver up a person extends to any person who the commander
has reasonable grounds to believe has done on the aircraft while in flight any act
which in the commander's opinion is a serious offence under the law of the country
in which the aircraft is registered[2]. The commander may deliver the person
concerned in the United Kingdom to a constable or immigration officer, or, in any
other convention country[3], to an officer of that country having functions corresponding to the functions in the United Kingdom either of a constable or of an
immigration officer[4].

If he intends to deliver up such a person in the United Kingdom, the commander
must, before or as soon as reasonably practicable after landing, give notification of
his intention and the reasons for it to a constable or immigration officer[5]. If the
commander of the aircraft intends to deliver up the person concerned, in the case of
a British-controlled aircraft[6], in a convention country other than the United
Kingdom, the commander must notify, in the manner above mentioned, an officer
of that country having functions corresponding to the functions in the United
Kingdom either of a constable or of an immigration officer[7]. Whether the delivery
is to be effected in the United Kingdom or in another convention country, the
commander must also notify the appropriate diplomatic or consular office of the
country of nationality of that person[8].

1 For the meaning of 'commander' see para 1673 note 2 ante.
2 Civil Aviation Act 1982 s 94 (5) (b).
3 'Convention country' means a country in which the Tokyo Convention is for the time being in
   force: Civil Aviation Act 1982 s 105 (1). See para 1664 ante.
4 Ibid s 94 (5) (b).
5 Ibid s 94 (6) (b).
6 For the meaning of 'British-controlled aircraft' see para 1663 note 1 ante.
7 Civil Aviation Act 1982 s 94 (6) (b). As to failure to do so see note 8 infra.
8 Ibid s 94 (6) (a) (ii), (b) (ii). Any aircraft commander who without reasonable cause fails to comply
   with these requirements is liable on summary conviction to a fine not exceeding level 3 on the
   standard scale: s 94 (6) (amended by virtue of the Criminal Justice Act 1982 ss 38, 46). As to the
   standard scale see para 1044 note 6 ante. At the date at which this volume states the law, level 3 on
   that scale is at £400.

(4) CIVIL LIABILITIES GENERALLY

1678. Classification of liabilities. The civil liabilities of owners and operators
of aircraft fall broadly into two categories: (1) the liabilities of the owner or

operator, as carrier, to persons who are, or whose goods are, carried in the aircraft[1]; and (2) those liabilities of the owner or operator which arise independently of the carriage of persons or goods in the aircraft. The second category includes all liabilities for damage caused to persons or property not being carried in the aircraft, whether such persons or property are in the air, in another aircraft, or are on the surface of the ground or water[2].

1 The liabilities of carriers by air are dealt with in paras 1528–1650 ante.
2 These liabilities are dealt with in paras 1679–1689 post.

1679. Collisions. Statutory provisions regulate the liability of the owner or operator of an aircraft which, while taking off, in flight or landing, collides with another aircraft which is on the surface and is not taking off or landing, or with any other type of vehicle or vessel on the surface[1]. The provisions do not, however, cover collisions between aircraft in the air (except in so far as the collision causes damage to persons or property on the surface[2]), between aircraft on the surface when neither is taking off or landing, or between an aircraft on the surface which is not taking off or landing and any other type of vehicle or vessel on the surface[3].

Where the statutory provisions do not apply, the liabilities of the parties to the collision are governed by the ordinary rules of negligence[4].

1 See paras 1683–1689 post.
2 See para 1685 post.
3 The statutory provisions and their scope, and the meaning of 'in flight, taking off or landing', are considered in para 1685 post. As to collisions between aircraft which are both in flight, taking off or landing, and one or both of which are on the surface see para 1685 note 5 post.
4 See generally NEGLIGENCE; and *Blankley v Godley* [1952] 1 All ER 436n (collision at aerodrome between aircraft on ground and stationary motor car); see also para 1682 post (breach of statutory rules and regulations as evidence of negligence). Where, in a collision, damage is caused to passengers or cargo carried in one of the aircraft and the collision is caused entirely by the fault of that aircraft, the liability of the owner or operator to the passengers or owners of the cargo will in most cases be governed by the carriage by air rules, and may be limited; but where the other aircraft is in any degree at fault, the passengers or owners of the cargo will be able to recover unlimited damages from the owner or operator of that aircraft.

1680. Accidents occurring on the surface at aerodromes. Accidents occurring on the surface of the ground at aerodromes, other than collisions between aircraft or between aircraft and other types of vehicle[1], may, according to the circumstances, be governed by statutory provisions or by common law rules. The carriage by air rules cover accidents to passengers which take place in the course of any of the operations of embarking or disembarking[2], and they cover damage to cargo which occurs during the 'carriage by air' as that phrase is defined[3]. Statutory provisions also apply where damage is done to persons or property on the surface by an aircraft in flight, taking off or landing[4]. In cases not governed by statutory provisions, liabilities are normally governed by the ordinary rules of negligence[5].

1 See para 1679 note 4 ante.
2 See para 1559 ante.
3 See para 1579 ante.

4 This liability and the meaning of 'in flight, taking off or landing' are considered in para 1685 post.
5 See generally NEGLIGENCE; and see *Waring v East Anglian Flying Services Ltd* [1951] WN 55; cf *Olsen v Corry and Gravesend Aviation Ltd* [1936] 3 All ER 241.

1681. Breach of statutory rules and regulations. Where the liability of the owner or operator of an aircraft is to be decided by the common law rules of negligence[1], a failure on his part, or on the part of any person for whose negligence he is vicariously responsible, to comply with any of the statutory rules and regulations applicable in the circumstances of the case may be relevant as being evidence of negligence[2]. Thus, in the case of collisions particularly[3], a breach of the Rules of the Air Regulations 1990[4] will afford evidence of negligence, if there is a sufficient causal connection between the breach and the collision. Similarly, in the case of all accidents, those requirements of the Air Navigation Order 1989[5] and of the regulations made under it[6] which are designed to promote the safety of flying[7] will often be regarded as indicating the standard of care which owners and operators of aircraft ought to meet, and failure to comply with any such requirement where compliance might have averted the accident will be strong evidence of negligence[8].

1 See para 1678 ante.
2 As to breaches of statutory duty which of themselves give rise to a cause of action see para 1682 post; and TORT. As to vicarious liability see NEGLIGENCE.
3 As to the classes of collision where liability is governed by negligence see para 1679 ante.
4 SI 1990/2241; the Regulations contain (in Section VII) detailed aerodrome traffic rules: see paras 1213–1216 ante.
5 SI 1989/2004 (amended by SI 1990/2154 and SI 1991/1726).
6 Ie the Air Navigation (General) Regulations 1981, SI 1981/57 (amended by SI 1985/528), which have effect as if made under the Air Navigation Order 1989.
7 Eg the provisions as to the precautionary action to be taken before flight (see para 1426 et seq ante), as to weight and performance requirements (see paras 1430, 1431 ante), as to loading (see para 1432 et seq ante), as to the training of crews (see para 1436 ante), as to operations manuals (see paras 1438, 1439 ante), and as to minimum weather conditions (see paras 1440–1445 ante).
8 Cf *Blamires v Lancashire and Yorkshire Rly Co* (1873) LR 8 Exch 283; *Gorris v Scott* (1874) LR 9 Exch 125 at 130–131 per Pollock B; *Phillips v Britannia Hygienic Laundry Co Ltd* [1923] 1 KB 539 at 548–549 per McCardie J; affd [1923] 2 KB 832, CA.

1682. Actionable breach of statutory duty. In some cases the failure by the owner or operator of an aircraft, or by some person for whom he is vicariously responsible, to comply with a statutory duty imposed on him may of itself give a right of action to a person who has suffered damage by reason of that failure[1]. Whether such a right of action arises depends in each case upon the true construction of the statutory provision in question[2]. In a few cases a breach of the statutory rules and regulations of the class referred to in the preceding paragraph has been held to give a civil right of action to an injured person[3].

1 Cf *Lochgelly Iron and Coal Ltd v M'Mullan* [1934] AC 1, HL; *Monk v Warbey* [1935] 1 KB 75, CA; *London Passenger Transport Board v Upson* [1949] AC 155, [1949] 1 All ER 60, HL; *Solomons v R Gertzenstein Ltd* [1954] 2 QB 243, [1954] 2 All ER 625, CA. See generally TORT.
2 See generally TORT. It is only where the provision was enacted for the benefit of a particular class of persons, of whom the plaintiff is a member, that such a right of action may arise; and, if a penalty is imposed for breach of the provision, that is prima facie the only remedy, though the general rule is subject to exceptions; see eg *Cutler v Wandsworth Stadium Ltd* [1949] AC 398 at 407–408, [1949] 1 All ER 544 at 548, HL, per Lord Simonds.
3 *Hesketh v Liverpool Corpn* [1940] 4 All ER 429 (breach by aerodrome proprietor of statutory requirements as to lighting and obstructions at aerodromes gave right of action to injured pilot);

Dominion Air Lines Ltd v Strand [1933] NZLR 1 (breach of a New Zealand provision requiring the pilot of a passenger-carrying aircraft to hold a special class of licence). Cf, to the contrary, *Rockland Airways v Miller* (1959) 19 DLR (2d) 683. As to breach of statutory rules and regulations being evidence of negligence see para 1681 ante.

(5) DAMAGE TO THIRD PARTIES ON THE SURFACE

1683. International conventions. In 1933 a convention[1] was signed at Rome for the purpose of regulating in a uniform manner liability for damage caused by aircraft to third parties on the surface. The convention had two primary objects. The first was to bring about uniformity in private international law, particularly in specifying the circumstances in which the liability of aircraft operators arose. The second was to provide for a compulsory system of third party legal liability insurance. The convention has not been ratified by the United Kingdom.

In 1952 a further convention[2] was drawn up to supersede and improve the 1933 Rome Convention. Although there is little doubt that the 1952 convention is an improvement on that of 1933 it has not yet been ratified by the United Kingdom. One probable reason is that the limitation of liability figures are too low.

An amending protocol to the 1952 convention was signed in Montreal in 1978. Among other provisions, it greatly increased the limits of liability, and expressed them in terms of special drawing rights. The protocol is not yet in force.

1 Cmd 5056. See further para 1012 ante. Although the United Kingdom has not ratified the 1933 Rome Convention it was at one time intended to give effect to it. The necessary enabling powers were enacted in the Civil Aviation Act 1949, but the relevant sections have all been repealed.
2 Cmd 8886. See further para 1012 ante.

1684. Exclusion of liability for trespass and nuisance. No action lies in respect of trespass[1] or in respect of nuisance[2] by reason only of the flight of an aircraft over any property[3] at a height above the ground which, having regard to wind, weather and all the circumstances of the case[4] is reasonable[5], or by reason only of the ordinary incidents of such flight[6], so long as the provisions of any Air Navigation Order[7] and specified provisions of the Civil Aviation Act 1982[8] are duly complied with[9]. The protection given is thus lost if the aircraft flies below a reasonable height, or if, in any respect, the provisions of, for example, the Air Navigation Order 1989[10], have not been complied with in relation to the aircraft.

1 As to trespass see generally TRESPASS. For trespass to airspace see especially *Lord Bernstein of Leigh v Skyviews and General Ltd* [1978] QB 479, [1977] 2 All ER 902.
2 As to nuisance see generally NUISANCE; and *Steel-Maitland v British Airways Board* 1981 SLT 110.
3 The flight must be over, and not merely in the vicinity of, a particular property. See however *Roedean School Ltd v Cornwall Aviation Co Ltd* (1926) Times, 3 July.
4 These include, it seems, the circumstance that the aircraft is landing or taking off.
5 For statutory provisions as to the heights which aircraft must maintain see paras 1475–1493 ante.
6 'Ordinary incidents of flight' will cover eg noise and vibration arising from the flight. If, however, vibration caused 'material damage', liability would arise under the Civil Aviation Act 1982 s 76 (2): see para 1685 post.
7 This will include the Air Navigation Order 1989, SI 1989/2004, the Air Navigation (General) Regulations 1981, SI 1981/57, the Rules of the Air Regulations 1990, SI 1990/2241, the Air Navigation (Aircraft and Aircraft Engine Emissions) Order 1986, SI 1986/599, the Air Navigation (Aeroplane and Aeroplane Engine Emission of Unburned Hydrocarbons) Order 1988, SI 1988/1994, and the Air Navigation (Noise Certification) Order 1990, SI 1990/1514.
8 Ie the Civil Aviation Act 1982 ss 62 (control of aviation in times of war or national emergency) and 81 (dangerous flying).

9 Ibid s 76 (1). This provision applies to Crown aircraft: Civil Aviation (Crown Aircraft) Order 1970, SI 1970/289, art 2.
10 SI 1989/2004 (amended by SI 1990/2154 and SI 1991/1726).

1685. Statutory liability for material damage to persons or property. Where material[1] loss or damage[2] is caused[3] to any person or property on land or water by, or by a person in, or an article[4] or person falling from, an aircraft while in flight, taking off or landing[5], then unless the loss or damage was caused or contributed to by the negligence of the person by whom it was suffered[6], damages are recoverable in respect of the loss or damage without proof of negligence or intention or other cause of action, as if the loss or damage had been caused by the wilful act, neglect or default of the owner[7] of the aircraft[8].

Where, however, material loss or damage is thus caused and the circumstances are such that damages are recoverable in respect of that loss or damage by virtue only of the foregoing provisions, and a legal liability is created in some person other than the owner[9] to pay damages in respect of the loss or damage, the owner is entitled to be indemnified by that other person against any claim in respect of that loss or damage[10].

1 The term 'material' appears to be synonymous with 'physical'; the scope of recovery for the loss or damage would seem to depend on the general law as to damages in torts; see generally DAMAGES; NEGLIGENCE.
2 'Loss or damage' includes, in relation to persons, loss of life and personal injury: Civil Aviation Act 1982 s 105 (1).
3 See *Greenfield v Law* [1955] 2 Lloyd's Rep 696; cf *Southgate v Commonwealth of Australia* (1987) 13 NSWLR 188.
4 See *Weedair (NZ) Ltd v Walker* [1961] NZLR 153 (NZ CA), where it was held under the similarly worded New Zealand statute that 'article' includes a chemical liquid.
5 It seems that 'taking off' starts when taxiing ends and power is applied for take-off (see *Blankley v Godley* [1952] 1 All ER 436n), and that landing ends when the aircraft reaches the end of its landing run and begins to taxi.
6 As to contributory negligence see generally NEGLIGENCE; and the Law Reform (Contributory Negligence) Act 1945 which will, it is thought, apply. The burden is on the owner of the aircraft which is in flight, taking off or landing to show that the damage was caused or contributed to by the person suffering the injury: cf *Cubitt and Terry v Gower* (1933) 77 Sol Jo 732.
7 As to cases where the responsibility shifts from the owner see para 1686 post.
8 Civil Aviation Act 1982 s 76 (2). This provision applies in relation to all surface damage caused by Crown aircraft: Civil Aviation (Crown Aircraft) Order 1970, SI 1970/289, art 2.
9 As to cases where the responsibility shifts from the owner see para 1686 post.
10 Civil Aviation Act 1982 s 76 (3).

1686. Liability of owner. The liability imposed by the foregoing provisions is placed upon the owner of the aircraft; but where the aircraft concerned has been bona fide demised, let or hired out for any period exceeding 14 days to any other person by the owner, and no pilot, commander, navigator or operative member of the crew of the aircraft is in the owner's employment, the foregoing provisions have effect as if for references to the owner there were substituted references to the person to whom the aircraft has thus been demised, let or hired out[1]. Unless these conditions are satisfied, however, the statutory liability falls upon the owner, who is thus made liable where the aircraft is lent by him to another or even used by another without his knowledge or consent; but the owner will normally have a right of indemnity against the person actually responsible for the damage[2].

1 Civil Aviation Act 1982 s 76 (4).
2 See ibid s 76 (3); and para 1685 ante.

1687. Noise and vibration. No action lies in respect of nuisance arising specifically out of the noise and vibration caused by an aircraft in flight when the circumstances of the flight are reasonable[1]. Further, no action lies in respect of nuisance by reason only of noise and vibration caused by an aircraft on any of certain types of aerodrome[2] as long as the provisions of the Air Navigation Order 1989[3] are duly complied with[4].

1 See the Civil Aviation Act 1982 s 76 (1); and para 1684 ante.
2 Ie government aerodromes, aerodromes owned or managed by the Civil Aviation Authority, licensed aerodromes and aerodromes at which the manufacture, repair or maintenance of aircraft is professionally carried out: see the Air Navigation Order 1989, SI 1989/2004, art 83; the Air Navigation (General) Regulations 1981, SI 1981/57, reg 12; and para 1185 ante.
3 SI 1989/2004 (amended by SI 1990/2154).
4 Civil Aviation Act 1982 s 77 (2).

1688. Relevance of common law rights. The enactment[1] which excludes all rights of action in respect of trespass or nuisance arising by reason only of the flight of an aircraft over any property or the ordinary incidents of such flight, only has effect if the flight is carried out at a reasonable height above the ground and if no relevant statutory provision is contravened in respect of the aircraft. The provision[2] which imposes a statutory liability for surface damage on the owner of the aircraft does nothing to take away rights of action which may exist against persons other than the owner or operator.

Thus in various circumstances it may be necessary to inquire what rights and liabilities exist at common law in respect of the flight of aircraft or in respect of damage caused to persons or property on the surface.

1 Civil Aviation Act 1982 s 76 (1); see para 1684 ante.
2 Ibid s 76 (2); see para 1685 ante.

1689–1800. Trespass and nuisance. At common law, the entry by an aircraft into the airspace above a person's land is an actionable trespass if it is at such a height as to affect his rights; the owner of the land has rights in the airspace only to such height as is necessary for the ordinary use and enjoyment of the land and the structures upon it[1].

Such an entry may give rise to a right of action for nuisance; but since no action lies in respect of nuisance without proof of damage, it is thought that the flight of aircraft over or in the vicinity of a person's land is only actionable if it causes, by noise or vibration for example, a substantial interference with the ordinary enjoyment of that land[2]. Subject to provisions relating to aerodromes, there is no right to land in any place as against the owner of the land or other persons interested in it[3].

1 *Lord Bernstein of Leigh v Skyviews and General Ltd* [1978] QB 479, [1977] 2 All ER 902; *Didow v Alberta Power Ltd* [1988] 5 WWR 606 (Alberta CA). See TRESPASS.
2 See NUISANCE.
3 See generally TRESPASS.

BAILIFF

See COPYHOLDS; COUNTY COURTS; SHERIFFS AND BAILIFFS

BAILMENT

1. INTRODUCTION

(1) MEANING AND CLASSIFICATION

1801. Meaning of 'bailment'. A bailment, traditionally defined, is a delivery of personal chattels on trust, usually on a contract, express or implied, that the trust shall be duly executed, and the chattels redelivered in either their original or an altered form, as soon as the time or use for, or condition on, which they were bailed shall have elapsed or been performed[1]. Under modern law, a bailment arises whenever one person (the bailee) is voluntarily in possession of goods belonging to another person (the bailor)[2]. The legal relationship of bailor and bailee can exist independently of any contract, and is created by the voluntary taking into custody of goods which are the property of another, as in cases of sub-bailment or of bailment by finding[3]. The element common to all types of bailment is the imposition of an obligation, because the taking of possession in the circumstances involves an assumption of responsibility for the safe keeping of the goods[4]. An action against a bailee can be regarded as an action on its own, sui generis, arising out of the possession had by the bailee of the goods[5].

A bailment is distinguishable from a sale[6], which is effected wherever chattels are delivered on a contract for a money consideration called the price, and not for the return of the identical chattels in their original or an altered form[7]. The relationship of bailor and bailee is also to be distinguished from the relationship of licensor and licensee which, in the absence of special contractual provisions, carries no active obligation on the part of the licensor towards the licensee in relation to the chattel subject to the licence[8].

To constitute a bailment (which derives its name from the old French word *bailler*, to deliver or put into the hands of), the actual or constructive possession of a specific chattel must be vacated by its owner or possessor (the bailor), or his agent duly authorised for that purpose, in favour of another person (the bailee)[9] in order ıat the latter may keep the same or perform some act in connection therewith, for ᵣhich such actual or constructive possession of the chattel is necessary, thereafter ᵣturning the identical subject matter in its original or an altered form[10].

Thus a bailment may arise by attornment involving a constructive delivery of ᵢossession, as where, for example, a warehouseman holding goods as agent for an ᵣwner agreed to hold them for another person pursuant to the owner's instruc-ᵢons[11]. There can be a bailment by an owner without his ever having taken ᵢossession of the chattel concerned, so long as the title to it or the right to possess it as passed to him[12].

ᴵ See Bac Abr Bailment; see also 2 Bl Com 452; Jones on Bailments (4th Edn) 1, 117; Story on Bailments (9th Edn) s 2; 2 Kent's Com, Pt V, s 559; 1 Bell's Com lib 2, Pt 3, c 2, s 4, art 2. This definition was approved and adopted in *Re S Davis & Co Ltd* [1945] Ch 402. The use of the word 'trust' in this definition does not signify that bailments are a form of trust in the literal sense, but rather that, in the ordinary case, the goods are entrusted to the bailee. For a comparison of the relationship of bailor and bailee with that of master and servant, see *Fowler v Lock* (1872) LR 7 CP 272; on appeal (1874) LR 9 CP 751n; *Venables v Smith* (1877) 2 QBD 279; *Gates v R Bill & Son* [1902] 2 KB 38, CA; and cf *Hewitt v Bonvin* [1940] 1 KB 188, CA. See further EMPLOYMENT, where the subject is fully discussed.

₂ *Compania Portorafti Commerciale SA v Ultramar Panama Inc, The Captain Gregos (No 2)* [1990] 2 Lloyd's Rep 395 at 405, CA, per Bingham LJ. A possessor who is unaware that he is in possession of goods belonging to another is not a bailee, but he may owe to the owner a duty to take reasonable care to identify the owner's interest before destroying the goods: *A VX Ltd v EGM Solders Ltd* (1982) Times, 7 July ('unconscious' bailees held liable for destroying goods which they erroneously believed to be their property).

₃ See *Morris v C W Martin & Sons Ltd* [1966] 1 QB 716 at 731–732, [1965] 2 All ER 725 at 734–735, CA, per Diplock LJ; *Fairline Shipping Corpn Ltd v Adamson* [1975] QB 180 at 189, [1974] 2 All ER 967 at 975 per Kerr J; *Parastatidis v Kotaridis* [1978] VR 449 at 454–455 per Harris J; *Punch v Savoy's Jewellers Ltd* (1986) 26 DLR (4th) 546 at 551 per Cory JA; *Compania Portorafti Commerciale SA v Ultramar Panama Inc, The Captain Gregos (No 2)* [1990] 2 Lloyd's Rep 395 at 405, CA, per Bingham LJ. As to bailment by finding see para 1811 post; as to sub-bailment see para 1841 post.

ᵢ *Gilchrist Watt and Sanderson Pty Ltd v York Products Pty Ltd* [1970] 3 All ER 825 at 831, [1970] 1 WLR 1262 at 1268, PC, per Lord Pearson. See also *Global Dress Co Ltd v W H Boase & Co Ltd* [1966] 2 Lloyd's Rep 72 at 76, CA; *Learoyd Bros & Co and Huddersfield Fine Worsteds Ltd v Pope & Sons (Dock Carriers) Ltd* [1966] 2 Lloyd's Rep 142 at 147–148; *Moukataff v British Overseas Airways Corpn* [1967] 1 Lloyd's Rep 396 at 416; *Lee Cooper Ltd v C H Jeakins & Sons Ltd* [1967] 2 QB 1, [1965] 1 All ER 280; *Chesworth v Farrar* [1967] 1 QB 407 at 415–416, [1966] 2 All ER 107 at 112; and see para 1841 post.

₅ See *Building and Civil Engineering Holidays Scheme Management Ltd v Post Office* [1966] 1 QB 247 at 261, [1965] 1 All ER 163 at 167, CA, per Lord Denning MR; *Singer (UK) Ltd v Tees and Hartlepool Port Authority* [1988] 2 Lloyd's Rep 164 at 167–168 per Steyn J.

₆ See SALE OF GOODS. Where goods are delivered to a buyer under a contract of sale which contains a reservation of title clause, the relationship may concurrently amount to one of bailment: *Clough Mill Ltd v Martin* [1984] 3 All ER 982 at 987, [1985] 1 WLR 111 at 116, CA, per Goff LJ; cf *Borden (UK) Ltd v Scottish Timber Products Ltd* [1981] Ch 25, [1979] 3 All ER 961, CA. As to transactions between brewers and mineral water manufacturers and their customers concerning bottles which amount to bailments and not sales, see *Cantrell and Cochrane Ltd v Neeson* [1926] NI 107, CA; and *Barlow & Co v Hanslip* [1926] NI 113n (an English decision). See also *William Leitch & Co Ltd v Leydon, A G Barr & Co Ltd v Macgeoghegan* [1931] AC 90, HL.

₇ *South Australian Insurance Co v Randell* (1869) LR 3 PC 101 at 108, 113, approving 2 Kent's Com (11th Edn), s 589.

₈ *Ashby v Tolhurst* [1937] 2 KB 242 at 249, [1937] 2 All ER 837 at 840, CA, per Greene MR (held no delivery of possession; only a licence to leave car on parking ground); *Tinsley v Dudley* [1951] 2 KB 18 at 26, [1951] 1 All ER 252 at 256–257, CA, per Evershed MR (parking of vehicles by invitation or permission on private ground: no transfer of possession or custody); see also *BRS (Contracts) Ltd v Colney Motor Engineering Co Ltd* (1958) Times, 27 November, CA; *BG Transport Service Ltd v Marston Motor Co Ltd* [1970] 1 Lloyd's Rep 371 (both vehicle parking cases: no bailment); *Fred Chappell Ltd v National Car Parks Ltd* (1987) Times, 22 May (retention of keys by vehicle owner, and no barrier at car park: no bailment). A caravan site owner is not ordinarily a bailee of the caravans, but if he undertakes winter storage he may become a bailee then: *Halbauer v Brighton Corpn* [1954] 2

All ER 707, [1954] 1 WLR 1161, CA, applied in *Hinks v Fleet* [1987] BTLC 289, CA; but see *Wilme and Gladwin Pty Co v WAL Building Supplies Pty Ltd* (1955) 55 SR (NSW) 442 (NSW FC) (plainti rented storage bay in building; for access he had to communicate with defendant, who had the on key but who never handled the plaintiff's goods: held no bailment).

9 As to delivery, there must be a transfer of the exclusive right of possession: see *Midland Silicones Ltd Scruttons Ltd* [1959] 2 QB 171 at 189, [1959] 2 All ER 289 at 296; affd [1961] 1 QB 106 at 119, [1960] All ER 737 at 740, CA; sub nom *Scruttons Ltd v Midland Silicones Ltd* [1962] AC 446 at 470, [1962] All ER 1 at 8, HL (no bailment). Placing a coat in an unattended anteroom at a hotel may in particul. circumstances amount to delivery of possession: *Samuel v Westminster Wine Co Ltd* (1959) Times, May: see 6 Court Forms (2nd Edn) (1989 Issue) 240, Form 12. See also *Shorter's Parking Station Ltd Johnson* [1963] NZLR 135, [1963] CLY 178 (NZ CA), and *Mendelsohn v Normand Ltd* [1970] 1 Q 177, [1969] 2 All ER 1215, CA (both vehicle parking cases in which cars were left in garaɡ attendant's custody: held to be bailment in each case). Cases may occur in which there is a transfer possession intended by both parties to be a bailment, though obtained by the transferee by decei and then perhaps there is a contract of bailment (though voidable by the bailor), for there is a re consent by him (though induced by fraud) and the taking would not be trespassory and would n therefore amount to theft. If, however, one party means only to give a bailment and the other par accepts the chattel, meaning not to hold it on a bailment but to appropriate it contrary to the know intention of the bailor, there is no concurrence of intention and no contract; there is only an outwar appearance of consent on the bailor's part to the physical delivery of the chattel, and the possessic therefore does not pass by contract but by wrong. In such a case the taking of the chattel by th pretended bailee is trespassory and will support an indictment for theft: see *Lake v Simmons* [192 AC 487, HL, distinguished in *John Rigby (Haulage) Ltd v Reliance Marine Insurance Co Ltd* [1956] QB 468, [1956] 3 All ER 1, CA. See also the Theft Act 1968 ss 1–6, 15; and CRIMINAL LAW.

10 *South Australian Insurance Co v Randell* (1869) LR 3 PC 101. Cf *Borden (UK) Ltd v Scottish Timb Products Ltd* [1981] Ch 25, [1979] 3 All ER 961, CA; *Clough Mill Ltd v Martin* [1984] 3 All ER 982 987, [1985] 1 WLR 111 at 116, CA, per Goff LJ (bailment may arise although bailee empowered t intermix goods or dispose of them to third parties).

11 See *Dublin City Distillery Ltd v Doherty* [1914] AC 823 at 847, HL, per Lord Atkinson; and se para 1882 post.

12 *Belvoir Finance Co Ltd v Stapleton* [1971] 1 QB 210 at 217, [1970] 3 All ER 664 at 667, CA (plainti finance company obtained title to car under executed illegal contract of sale and, without takin delivery of it, hired it out to a company which converted it: hiring company held to be bailees *Transcontainer Express Ltd v Custodian Security Ltd* [1988] 1 Lloyd's Rep 128 at 135, CA, per Slade l (where the point was not decided); *Edwards v Newland & Co (E Burchett Ltd, third party)* [1950] 2 K 534, [1950] 1 All ER 1072, CA; *Johnson Matthey Ltd v Constantine Terminals Ltd and Internation. Express Co Ltd* [1976] 2 Lloyd's Rep 215.

1802. Classification. The legal concept of bailment as creating a relationshi which gives rise to legal duties owed on each side is derived from Roman law[1]. I the leading case of *Coggs v Bernard*[2] Holt CJ divided bailment into six classes, whic. Sir William Jones[3] rearranged into five classes, as follows:

(1) the gratuitous deposit[4] of a chattel with the bailee, who is simply to keep i for the bailor;

(2) the delivery[5] of a chattel to the bailee, who is to do something withou reward for the bailee to or with the chattel;

(3) the gratuitous loan[6] of a chattel by the bailor to the bailee for the bailee to us

(4) the pawn or pledge[7] of a chattel by the bailor to the bailee, who is to hold it a a security for a loan[8] or debt or the fulfilment of an obligation; and

(5) the hire[9] of a chattel or services by the bailor to the bailee for reward.

Bailments may also be classified as being either gratuitous or for reward: thus th first three classes above mentioned, being without recompense, are designate gratuitous bailments; the others are bailments for reward, or for valuable consider ation. Of the three kinds of gratuitous bailments, it will be noticed that the first tw are wholly for the benefit of the bailor, and the third wholly for the benefit of th bailee. This classification is the one adopted in this title, which deals only with th general law of bailment and not with particular forms of bailment, for which reference should be made to other titles[10].

In modern times much importance has become attached to the contract of hire purchase, which has in it not only the element of bailment, but also the element of sale[11]. This type of contract is considered separately in this work[12].

1 See *Morris v C W Martin & Sons Ltd* [1966] 1 QB 716 at 731, [1965] 2 All ER 725 at 734, CA, per Diplock LJ. The works of such foreign jurists as Pothier and Domat have in the past been cited, together with the law as found in the Digest and Institutes of Justinian: Inst lib 3, tit 14, 24.
2 (1703) 2 Ld Raym 909.
3 See Jones on Bailment (1st Edn) (1781) 35–36. Story considered that bailment might be rearranged in three classes: (1) in which the trust is exclusively for the bailor's or a third person's benefit; (2) in which the trust is exclusively for the bailee's benefit; and (3) in which the trust is for the benefit of both parties or of both or one of them and a third party: Story on Bailments (9th Edn) (1878), s 3. Story in his treatise nevertheless adhered to Jones's classification; so did Chancellor Kent: 2 Kent's Com, Pt V, s 559. For further discussion of the various classifications of bailment see Palmer on Bailment (1979) Chapter 2.
4 Ie *depositum*. See further paras 1806–1819 post.
5 Ie *mandatum*. See further paras 1820–1828 post.
6 Ie *commodatum*. See further paras 1829–1837 post.
7 Ie *pignus*, sometimes called *vadium*: see para 1881 post.
8 Where interest is payable on the loan in respect of which the chattel is held as security by the bailee, he can aptly be described as a bailee for mutual advantage: see *Canadian Imperial Bank of Commerce v Doucette* [1969] CLY 149, 70 DLR (2d) 657 (PEI SC in banco) (bank in possession of machinery by seizure under statutory lien and claim).
9 Ie *locatio conductio*. This is sometimes divided into four sub-classes: (i) the hiring of a chattel for use (*locatio rei*) (see paras 1851–1863 post); (ii) the hiring of work or labour on or with regard to a chattel (*locatio operis faciendi*) (see paras 1863–1880 post); (iii) the hiring of custody, ie of services in and about the keeping of the chattel (*locatio custodiae*) (see paras 1838–1849 post); and (iv) the hire of the carriage of chattels (*locatio operis mercium vehendarum*) (see CARRIERS).
10 See the list of cross-references on p 830 ante.
11 See para 1852 post. As to sale see SALE OF GOODS.
12 See HIRE PURCHASE

1803. Degree of care and diligence. Of the various rights and duties of bailors and bailees, that most discussed is the degree of care and diligence required of the bailee in each kind of bailment. That degree has, from the time of the Roman Empire until fairly recent times, been held to vary according to the benefits derived from the bailment by the bailor and the bailee respectively[1]. Thus, an ordinary degree of care and skill was traditionally required where both benefited from the transaction[2]; slighter diligence, perhaps, where the benefit was wholly that of the bailor (as in the first two classes above[3]); and greater diligence where the benefit accrued only to the bailee (as in the third class[3]). More recently, however, it has been recognised that the common law duty of every bailee is to take reasonable care of his bailor's goods, and not to convert them[4]. The standard of care required is therefore the standard demanded by the circumstances of each particular case[5]. To try to put a bailment into a watertight compartment, such as gratuitous bailment or bailment for reward, can be misleading[6]. It must be remembered, however, that bailment is frequently a contract, and the parties may always vary the incidents by the terms of the contract.

1 *Giblin v McMullen* (1868) LR 2 PC 317.
2 Ie a bailment for mutual advantage: see para 1802 note 3 ante.
3 See para 1802 ante.
4 *Morris v C W Martin & Sons Ltd* [1966] 1 QB 716 at 726, 732, 738, [1965] 2 All ER 725 at 731, 735, 738, CA.

5 *Houghland v R R Low (Luxury Coaches) Ltd* [1962] 1 QB 694 at 698, [1962] 2 All ER 159 at 161, CA. If
you confide a casket of jewels to the custody of a yokel, you cannot expect him to take the same care
of it that a banker would. Jones on Bailment (4th Edn) (1833) 100 cites an illustration from Muslim
law in which a man with an eye disorder consulted a farrier, who used one of his own medicines. The
man lost his sight and sued for damages, but the judge said, 'No action lies for, if the complainant
had not himself been an ass, he would never have employed a farrier'. See also para 1806 note 10 and
paras 1815, 1839 post.

6 *Houghland v R R Low (Luxury Coaches) Ltd* [1962] 1 QB 694 at 698, [1962] 2 All ER 159 at 161, CA

(2) JOINT BAILORS AND JOINT BAILEES

1804. Joint bailors. Where chattels belonging to co-owners are delivered to a
bailee to hold on behalf of all, it is implied, unless expressly stipulated to the
contrary, that he shall deliver up possession only upon the demand of all the
co-owners[1]. He is, therefore, justified in refusing to redeliver the chattels on the
demand of one or some of them only, and an action will not lie against him for such
a refusal[2]. But if, in such a case, he delivers up the chattels to one of the co-owners
upon his sole request, no action will lie against him for so doing unless all the
bailors join for that purpose; and as the person to whom they were actually
redelivered cannot join with his co-owners in maintaining an action for a breach
occasioned by his own act, no action will lie against the bailee[3]. As, however, the
bailee would occupy a position equivalent to that of a trustee of the chattels for all
the co-owners, he would be held liable in equity to those who were injured by his
breach of trust[4]. Two co-owners, having made a joint demand, may bring separate
actions[5].

1 *Broadbent v Ledward* (1839) 11 Ad & El 209.
2 *Atwood v Ernest* (1853) 13 CB 881; *May v Harvey* (1811) 13 East 197; *Nathan v Buckland* (1818) 2
Moore CP 153. But it is otherwise if one co-owner has a special property in the entire chattel (*Nyberg
v Handelaar* [1892] 2 QB 202, CA), or if, though belonging to co-owners, the chattel is delivered to
the bailee by one only to hold on his behalf (*May v Harvey* supra), in which case the bailee would be
estopped from denying the bailor's title: see para 1882 post. *Broadbent v Ledward* (1839) 11 Ad & El
209, turned upon a question of pleading only, and the observation of Lord Denman CJ at 212, that if
any inconvenient consequence arises to the defendant from detaining the property of joint owners, it
might have been avoided by giving it up to any of them, is a dictum only. If it means that, in general,
a bailee, entrusted by co-owners with property to hold on behalf of all, may lawfully deliver it to
one, without the authority or even against the wish of the others, it cannot, it is submitted, be
regarded as law.
3 *Brandon v Scott* (1857) 7 E & B 234.
4 *Brandon v Scott* (1857) 7 E & B 234 at 237 per Lord Campbell CJ. See also *Harper v Godsell* (1870) LR 5
QB 422.
5 *Bleaden v Hancock* (1829) 4 C & P 152.

1805. Joint bailees. Where a chattel is bailed to two or more bailees, each is
responsible for the acts and defaults of his co-bailees done or made within the scope
of their authority[1]. Probably, however, a joint bailee is not responsible if the act or
default is not negligence in the performance of the bailment, but something wholly
outside it[2].

1 *Davey v Chamberlain* (1803) 4 Esp 229; *Coupé Co v Maddick* [1891] 2 QB 413 at 415 per Cave J; Story
on Bailments (9th Edn) (1878), s 116.
2 Story on Bailments (9th Edn), s 116. This would seem to follow upon principle from the analogous
cases of a bailee's responsibility for his servants. See paras 1842, 1861, 1891 post; and see *Morris v
C W Martin & Sons Ltd* [1966] 1 QB 716, [1965] 2 All ER 725, CA.

2. GRATUITOUS BAILMENT

(1) DEPOSIT

(i) Meaning and Categories of Deposit

1806. Meaning of 'deposit'. Bailment by deposit[1] may be defined as a bailment of a chattel, to be kept for the bailor gratuitously[2], and returned upon demand[3]. This definition is sufficient for most purposes, and is complete, if it is understood that a return to the bailor covers delivery over to his nominee, for in some cases the primary object of the bailment may be that the bailee delivers over the chattel upon demand to a third party, and not to the actual bailor himself. This kind of bailment must always relate to a specific chattel[4].

As the bailee is to receive no reward for his services, there can never be an executory contract of deposit, for there can be no action upon an unsupported agreement[5], and until there is actual delivery and acceptance of the subject matter of the trust, there is no obligation on the bailee's part to carry out his promise[6]. As soon, however, as the bailee actually accepts[7] the chattel, he becomes in some degree responsible for it[8] whilst it remains in his possession or under his control, and is also bound, upon demand[9], to redeliver it to the true owner or his nominee, unless he has good excuse in law for not doing so[10].

1 Ie *depositum*: see para 1802 ante.
2 A bailment may be a bailment for reward even though the consideration does not flow from the bailor. Thus, if a member of a tenant's family deposits baggage with the landlord in the baggage room of the building containing the tenant's flat, the bailment is not gratuitous: *Andrews v Home Flats Ltd* [1945] 2 All ER 698, CA; cf *Chapman (or Oliver) v Saddler & Co* [1929] AC 584 at 596, HL (business operation in which bailor and bailee both relied for safety on the care of the bailor); and see para 1838 post.
3 2 Bl Com 453. For pleadings see 6 Court Forms (2nd Edn) (1989 Issue) 234–236, Forms 3–5. See also para 1883 post.
4 Pothier's Contrat de Dépôt, s 2.
5 Ie the maxim *ex nudo pacto non oritur actio* applies. See *Parastitidis v Kotaridis* [1978] VR 449 at 455 per Harris J (obiter).
6 Pothier's Contrat de Dépôt, s 7.
7 See *Blount v The War Office* [1953] 1 All ER 1071, [1953] 1 WLR 736 (acceptance of goods although locked in strong room of requisitioned building).
8 See *Houghland v R R Low (Luxury Coaches) Ltd* [1962] 1 QB 694, [1962] 2 All ER 159, CA; and para 1803 ante.
9 For the circumstances under which demand and refusal before the issue of a writ are or are not necessary to found an action see para 1885 post.
10 *Coggs v Bernard* (1703) 2 Ld Raym 909; *Phipps v New Claridge's Hotel Ltd* (1905) 22 TLR 49 (plaintiff handed over dog to one of defendant's servants, and as the dog could not be found when wanted, the defendant was liable); *Ultzen v Nicols* [1894] 1 QB 92 (where diner at restaurant handed his coat to a waiter, and it was gone when sought for): see also *Kahler v Midland Bank Ltd* [1950] AC 24, [1949] 2 All ER 621, HL (delivery by bailee to true owner would have been illegal by the proper law of the contract of bailment between bailor and bailee). The same rule appears to apply to all kinds of bailment. If the chattels bailed are not forthcoming, or are damaged, the onus is in the first place upon the bailee to show circumstances negativing negligence on his part: *Port Swettenham Authority v T W W v & Co (M) Sdn Bhd* [1979] AC 580, [1978] 3 All ER 337, PC; *British Road Services Ltd v Arthur V Crutchley & Co Ltd (Factory Guards Ltd, third parties)* [1968] 1 All ER 811, [1968] 1 Lloyd's Rep 271, CA; *Joseph Travers & Sons Ltd v Cooper* [1915] 1 KB 73, CA; *Houghland v R R Low (Luxury Coaches) Ltd* [1962] 1 QB 694, [1962] 2 All ER 159, CA; cf *Thomas v High* [1960] SR (NSW) 401 (NSW FC). See *Wiehe v Dennis Bros* (1913) 29 TLR 250 (pony left in possession of vendor); *Williams v Curzon Syndicate Ltd* (1919) 35 TLR 475, CA (goods deposited at club and stolen by porter who had been engaged without sufficient inquiry into his antecedents); *Copland v Brogan* 1916 SC 277 (gratuitous

carriage of bag containing money); cf *Brook's Wharf and Bull Wharf Ltd v Goodman Bros* [1937] 1 KB 534 at 538–539, [1936] 3 All ER 696 at 701–702, CA; *Gutter v Tait* (1947) 177 LT 1, CA (bailee robbed partly owing to his own lack of care); *Ballet v Mingay* [1943] KB 281, [1943] 1 All ER 143, CA (failure of bailee who had parted with goods to prove that his parting with them was within purview of contract); and see para 1843 note 3 post. But he need not establish the precise cause of the loss: *Bullen v Swan Electric Engraving Co* (1907) 23 TLR 258, CA; *Phipps v New Claridge's Hotel Ltd* supra; see also *Brook's Wharf and Bull Wharf Ltd v Goodman Bros* supra; and para 1843 notes 4, 5 post. Cf *Woods v Duncan* [1946] AC 401, [1946] 1 All ER 420n, HL; and cf paras 1815, 1826, 1830 post. As to the onus of proof in the case of bailment for reward see para 1843 post.

1807. Necessary deposit. A necessary deposit is one which is made under peculiar stress of circumstances, such as fire, flood, shipwreck, civil riot, or other unforeseen disaster. If, under such conditions, an owner of a chattel entrusts it to the care of a bystander or neighbour, and that person accepts it, it has been suggested that the confidence of the owner in the recipient, and the acceptance by him, constitute an obligation which can be satisfied only by a very strict measure of care on the part of the bailee; but it is conceived that according to our law his duties are merely those of any ordinary depositary[1]. Consequently the owner would probably recover damages only in the event of the depositary's being guilty of negligence or bad faith whilst the chattel was in his custody[2].

1   Jones on Bailments (4th Edn) 48; Story on Bailments (9th Edn), s 83.
2   Story on Bailments (9th Edn), s 83.

1808. Deposit under mistake. If a man who is mentally incapable of appreciating what he is doing, or who is under a mistake as to the identity of the person with whom he is dealing, entrusts another with a chattel, the recipient becomes a bailee[1].

1   *R v Reeves* (1859) 5 Jur NS 716, where a man who was lying on the ground partially tipsy, permitted an acquaintance to take his watch out of his pocket on the supposition that the acquaintance was actuated by a friendly motive; held: the evidence was sufficient to convict the person of the statutory offence of larceny as a bailee, ie now the offence of theft: see the Theft Act 1968 ss 1–6; and CRIMINAL LAW.

1809. Accidental deposit. An accidental deposit is made where a chattel, through circumstances over which neither the owner nor the recipient has any immediate control, is deposited on the land or premises of another. Examples are timber carried by the tide in a navigable river and left at low water on the towing path[1], fruit dropped on a neighbour's garden, or a tree which has fallen on the field of an adjacent proprietor. In such cases, so long as the involuntary depositary does no overt act to the chattel thus deposited on his land, he incurs no responsibility to the true owner in respect of it. But if he interferes with it an implied bailment is created, with all its obligations and responsibilities, and if he not only interferes with it, but uses it for his own purposes, this user amounts to a conversion, especially if the misuse is intentional[2].

1   *Nicholson v Chapman* (1793) 2 Hy Bl 254 at 257 per Eyre CJ: a person who voluntarily retrieves timber deposited on a river bank has no lien for his expenses in retrieving it, and is liable in conversion if he does not deliver it up to the owner on demand. But it is doubtful whether the finder would succeed in an action for his expenses on a quantum meruit: see para 1811 post; and cf *Lampleigh v Brathwait* (1615) Hob 105; see also CONTRACT. Cf *Binstead v Buck* (1776) 2 Wm Bl 1117.
2   *Mulgrave v Ogden* (1591) Cro Eliz 219; *Isaack v Clark* (1615) 2 Bulst 306. See also *Mills v Brooker* [1919] 1 KB 555 (fruit from lopped branch of overhanging tree).

1810. Involuntary deposit. Where a chattel is sent, without request or arrangement, by one person to another who does not hold himself out as willing to receive it, the person to whom it is sent is under no liability to the sender for its safe custody or protection[1], but must not use it or otherwise convert it to his own use[2]. Where unsolicited goods have been sent to a recipient with a view to his acquiring them, the recipient may, in certain circumstances, if he has no reasonable cause to believe that the goods were sent with a view to their being acquired for the purpose of a trade or business and has neither agreed to acquire nor agreed to return them, deal with them as if they were an unconditional gift to him[3].

Conversely, it has been suggested that where a man without previous request from the owner offers to take charge of a chattel, such an offer constitutes an inducement to the bailor to part with the possession of the chattel, and binds the bailee to exercise special care in its custody[4], but English law does not appear to recognise this refinement[5].

1   *Howard v Harris* (1884) 1 Cab & El 253 (plaintiff author, being asked by the defendant, the lessee of a theatre, to send him a synopsis of his play, sent the whole manuscript, which the defendant lost; held: no duty of any kind was cast on the defendant by sending him something he had not asked for: see per Williams J at 254). This decision accords with that in *Lethbridge v Phillips* (1819) 2 Stark 544 (where a picture was, without defendant's knowledge or request, sent to defendant's house, and was there injured). Cf *Neuwith v Over Darwen Industrial Co-operative Society* (1894) 63 LJQB 290. A slight assumption of control, however, may make the person a depositary: see *Newman v Bourne and Hollingworth* (1915) 31 TLR 209. Even so, if without negligence and acting reasonably he does something to the goods, for example, delivers them to a person falsely representing himself to be the owner, which results in the loss of the property, he will not be liable: *Elvin and Powell Ltd v Plummer, Roddis Ltd* (1933) 50 TLR 158.
2   This seems to follow on principle; compare the cases cited in para 1809 note 2 ante and the analogous principles governing the buyer's acceptance of goods not in accordance with the contract, as to which see *Grimoldby v Wells* (1875) LR 10 CP 391; *Harnor v Groves* (1855) 15 CB 667; *Chapman v Morton* (1843) 11 M & W 534, now embodied in the Sale of Goods Act 1979 s 35.
3   See the Unsolicited Goods and Services Act 1971 s 1; and SALE OF GOODS.
4   Jones on Bailments (4th Edn) 47, 121, following Pothier and the Roman lawyers.
5   Story on Bailments (9th Edn), s 82.

(ii) Finding of Chattels

1811. Bailment by finding. Where a lost chattel is found in a public place[1], the finder[2] is under no obligation to take charge of it at all. However, an occupier of land may owe an obligation to search for chattels which are lost upon his land, and to take them into custody[4]. If, moreover, the finder actually takes a lost chattel into his custody, he constitutes himself a depositary, and assumes the obligations of a depositary to the true owner[5], including the obligations to take reasonable steps to locate the owner and acquaint him with the finding and the present whereabouts of the chattel[6], to exercise due care for the safety of the chattel[7] until its return to the owner and to return it to him on demand[8]. Further, the finder cannot claim a lien on the chattel for any expense to which he may have been put in keeping or preserving it[9]. Unless the true owner has intentionally abandoned the chattel[10], his title to it is not lost and he may recover the chattel, provided that his right of action has not become barred by lapse of time, from any one in whose hands it may be found[11], unless it was sold in market overt[12]. The possession of the finder, however, is rightful and continues rightful until the owner demands the return of the chattel, and by taking the chattel into his custody he does no wrong to the true owner, unless he dishonestly appropriates it at any time with the intention of permanently depriving the owner of it, in which case the taking may be a trespass[1] and the finder is guilty of theft[14].

1 For provisions for the disposal of articles left in public conveyances, etc see AVIATION para 1242 ante RAILWAYS; ROAD TRAFFIC. Cf the Police (Property) Act 1897; and POLICE. For provisions as to the disposal of abandoned vehicles see the Road Traffic Regulation Act 1984 s 101; and ROAD TRAFFIC No provision, however, is made for the common case of property being found in the street and taken to the police; presumably the finder in taking it to the police is fully discharging his duty and will not be liable to the owner whatever the police may do: see *Hollins v Fowler* (1875) LR 7 HL 757 a 766 per Blackburn J. Cf YB 27 Hen 8, fo 13, pl 35: 'If a man comes into possession by a bailment then he is answerable by virtue of the bailment and if he bails the goods over or they are taken from his possession, still he is answerable to the bailor by virtue of the bailment. But otherwise if a man comes by goods by finding, for he is only answerable by reason of his possession and if, without wrongful act, he is out of possession before he who has the right has brought his action he is no answerable.' As to chattels found on private property see para 1814 post.

2 To call the finder a bailee would not be etymologically accurate in all cases, because the word 'bailee' is derived from the French *bailler*, to deliver or hand over, and there is no delivery or handing over to the finder: see *Gilchrist Watt and Sanderson Pty Ltd v York Products Pty Ltd* [1970] 3 All ER 825 at 831 [1970] 1 WLR 1262 at 1268, PC, per Lord Pearson. In the English courts the word 'bailment' has however, acquired a meaning wide enough to include cases of 'bailment by finding' and cases o sub-bailment (as to which see para 1841 post) where there is no contractual relationship between bailor and bailee or sub-bailee respectively: see *Gilchrist Watt and Sanderson Pty Ltd v York Products Pty Ltd* supra at 832 and 1270 respectively per Lord Pearson; *Morris v C W Martin & Sons Ltd* [1966] 1 QB 716 at 732, [1965] 2 All ER 725 at 734, CA, per Diplock LJ; *Southland Hospital Board v Perkins Estate* [1986] 1 NZLR 373 at 375 per Cook J (obiter); *Compania Portorafti Commerciale SA v Ultramar Panama Inc, The Captain Gregos (No 2)* [1990] 2 Lloyd's Rep 395 at 405, CA, per Bingham LJ.

3 *Kowal v Ellis* (1977) 76 DLR (3d) 546 at 547 per O'Sullivan JA.

4 *Parker v British Airways Board* [1982] QB 1004 at 1018, [1982] 1 All ER 834 at 843, CA, per Donaldson LJ (obiter).

5 *Isaack v Clark* (1615) 2 Bulst 306 at 312 per Coke CJ; *Newman v Bourne and Hollingworth* (1915) 3 TLR 209 (master held liable for servant's lack of care); *Parker v British Airways Board* [1982] QB 1004 at 1018, [1982] 1 All ER 834 at 843, CA, per Donaldson LJ (obiter). Cf Story on Bailments (9th Edn) ss 85–87, criticising the view expressed in Bac Abr Bailment, D.

6 *Parker v British Airways Board* [1982] QB 1004 at 1018, [1982] 1 All ER 834 at 843, CA, per Donaldson LJ (obiter).

7 As in ordinary bailment the obligation arises because in the circumstances the taking of possession involves an assumption of responsibility for the chattel's safe keeping: see *Gilchrist Watt and Sanderson Pty Ltd v York Products Pty Ltd* [1970] 3 All ER 825, [1970] 1 WLR 1262, PC; and para 1801 note 4 ante.

8 See para 1885 post. For a pleading see 6 Court Forms (2nd Edn) (1989 Issue) 236, Form 6.

9 *Binstead v Buck* (1776) 2 Wm Bl 1117. It seems that he has no claim for compensation in any form: see para 1809 note 1 ante; *Kowal v Ellis* (1977) 76 DLR (3d) 546 at 547–548 per O'Sullivan JA. But c *China Pacific SA v Food Corpn of India* [1982] AC 939, [1981] 3 All ER 688, HL.

10 'If one is possessed of a jewel, and casts it into the sea or a public highway, this is such an express dereliction, that a property will be vested in the first fortunate finder that will seize it to his own use But ... if he loses or drops it by accident, it cannot be collected from thence that he designed to qui the possession, and therefore in such case the property still remains in the loser, who may claim it again of the finder': 2 Bl Com 9.

11 *Clayton v Le Roy* [1911] 2 KB 1031 at 1048, CA, per Fletcher Moulton LJ. The observations in this and other cases, such as *Miller v Dell* [1891] 1 QB 468, CA, must be read subject to the Limitation Act 1980 ss 3, 32; see further para 1887 post; and LIMITATION OF ACTIONS.

12 As to sales in market overt see the Sale of Goods Act 1979 s 22; and SALE OF GOODS.

13 *Merry v Green* (1841) 7 M & W 623, where a person purchased, at a public auction, a bureau, in a secret drawer of which he later found money, which he appropriated to his own use. At the time of the sale neither the buyer nor the seller knew that the bureau contained anything, and Parke B said, at 631, that, though there was a delivery of the bureau, and a lawful property in it thereby vested in the finder, there was no delivery so as to give a lawful possession of the money. It was therefore a simple case of finding, and the property in the money remained in the seller. See also para 1812 post.

14 See the Theft Act 1968 ss 1–6; and CRIMINAL LAW. Where a finder comes into possession of a chattel as a result of his trespassing upon another's land, the finder may acquire no rights in the chattel as against the occupier, even where the occupier had no possession of the chattel immediately prior to

the trespass: *Parker v British Airways Board* [1982] QB 1004 at 1009, [1982] 1 All ER 834 at 837, CA, per Donaldson LJ (obiter).

1812. Finding by bailee or purchaser. If a bailee entrusted with a chattel for a specific purpose, such as its repair or alteration, finds concealed in it some property, that property belongs to the owner of the chattel and not to the bailee, and if the bailee commits some act in regard to property not warranted by the purpose for which the chattel was delivered to him, that unwarranted act amounts to a conversion at least and may amount to theft[1].

So, if a person purchases a chattel, such as a bureau, and subsequently finds concealed in it some article the existence of which was unknown to both buyer and seller at the time of the purchase, the property in that article will, apart from special circumstances such as the proved intention of the parties to sell and buy the chattel and its contents, known and unknown, remain in the seller[2] and will not pass to the buyer, who will become a mere depositary of the article, and may be guilty of theft if he appropriates it to himself though, as regards criminal liability, an important factor in determining the question is the honest belief of the purchaser as to what was to be conveyed to him at the time of the purchase[3].

1 *Cartwright v Green* (1803) 8 Ves 405 at 409 per Lord Eldon. See also the Theft Act 1968 ss 2, 3; and CRIMINAL LAW.
2 This statement was approved in *Thomas v Greenslade* (1954) Times, 6 November. See also para 1811 note 13 ante.
3 See the Theft Act 1968 s 2.

1813. Finder's rights against third parties. Subject to what is said in the next paragraph, as against everyone save the true owner or the finder's master or principal[1], the property in a chattel found vests in the finder on his taking possession of it[2], and thereafter he has all the rights which belong to a bailee by virtue of his possession[3]. Accordingly he can generally maintain an action against any person (except the true owner, or his agent), who may dispossess him of it, either by taking it out of his possession or by converting it to his own use after receiving it from him, and recover the full value of the article if he sues in trover[4]. The wrongdoer cannot defend himself by showing that the real title was in some third person[5] unless he invokes the statutory machinery whereby a defendant in an action for wrongful interference with goods can show that someone other than the claimant has a better title to the goods[6]. If the value cannot be established without the production of the article, and the wrongdoer fails to produce it, it may be presumed against him that the article was of the finest quality of its kind and its value may be assessed on that basis[7] in accordance with the principle that all things are presumed against a wrongdoer[8].

1 A person who, as a servant or agent, finds a thing finds it for his master or principal: *South Staffordshire Water Co v Sharman* [1896] 2 QB 44, DC, as explained in *Hannah v Peel* [1945] KB 509 at 519, [1945] 2 All ER 288 at 293; *Parker v British Airways Board* [1982] QB 1004 at 1017, [1982] 1 All ER 834 at 843, CA, per Donaldson LJ (obiter).
2 However, chattels found in the sea, whether jetsam (sunk under water), flotsam (afloat on the surface of the water), or ligan (sunk under water but tied to a buoy), or chattels cast ashore by shipwreck, belong to the Crown if the true owner fails to appear, unless the right to them has been granted to a subject: 1 Bl Com 290–292. The same principle applies to the finding of whales or sturgeon (which are royal fish), whether in the sea or cast ashore: 1 Bl Com 290. See further CONSTITUTIONAL LAW.

3 See para 1889 post.

4 *Jeffries v Great Western Rly Co* (1856) 5 E & B 802 at 807 per Crompton J; *Armory v Delamirie* (1722) 1 Stra 505; and see notes thereon in 1 Smith LC (13th Edn) 393. As to the right to sue in trover, which is the form of action for conversion, see TORT vol 45 para 1416 et seq. It is possible that a finder who assumes possession of the chattel by virtue of an act of trespass against an occupier on whose land the goods were situated at the time of the trespass obtains no title against that occupier, irrespective of whether the occupier had a prior possession: *Parker v British Airways Board* [1982] QB 1004 at 1009–1010, 1017, [1982] 1 All ER 834 at 837, 843, CA, per Donaldson LJ (obiter).

5 *Jeffries v Great Western Rly Co* (1856) 5 E & B 802 at 805 per Lord Campbell CJ. But see paras 1885, 1888, 1889 post.

6 Torts (Interference with Goods) Act 1977 s 8; see TORT vol 45 paras 1477, 1510.

7 *Mortimer v Cradock* (1843) 12 LJCP 166 at 167 per Tindal CJ; *Armory v Delamirie* (1722) 1 Stra 505.

8 Ie *omnia praesumuntur contra spoliatorem*: this embodies the grounds of the decision in *Armory v Delamirie* (1722) 1 Stra 505; *Indian Oil Corpn Ltd v Greenstone Shipping SA, The Ypatianna* [1988] QB 345, [1987] 3 All ER 893. As to cases where the maxim shifts the onus of proof see *Williamson v Rover Cycle Co* [1901] 2 IR 189 at 202; affd [1901] 2 IR 615.

1814. Chattels found on private property. So far as relates to chattels, other than treasure-trove[1], waifs[2] and estrays[3], found on private property, the possession of land carries with it, in general, possession of everything which is attached to or under that land and, in the absence of a better title elsewhere, the right to possess it[4]. Consequently, if a chattel is found on land by some person other than the owner of the land, that owner, though previously unaware of its existence, and not the finder is, except as against the owner of the chattel, entitled to it[5].

The difficulty arises where the chattel is lying unattached on the surface of the land. If the property on which it is found is an inn, the innkeeper may be entitled to it, for he is said to enjoy a special property in the goods of his guests[6]. If the landowner's servant or agent finds it in the course of his employment or agency, the landowner is entitled to it; the landowner may also be entitled when the finder has committed a trespass[7]. But a landowner does not necessarily possess a thing which is lying unattached on the surface of his land even though the thing is not possessed by someone else[8]. To establish possession in such circumstances, the landowner must demonstrate a manifest intention to exercise exclusive control over anything which might be on the premises[9]. Thus, where an airline passenger found a bracelet on the floor of an executive lounge at Heathrow Airport, the passenger and not the Airways Board was held entitled to possession[10]; where a customer found on the floor of a shop a packet of banknotes accidentally dropped by a stranger who could not be traced, the finder, not the shopkeeper, was held entitled to possession[11]; and where a soldier found a brooch in a house which had been requisitioned from the owner, who had never occupied the house himself, the finder, not the owner of the house, was held entitled to possession of the brooch[12].

1 Ie gold or silver of unknown ownership found concealed in a private place: see CONSTITUTIONAL LAW; CORONERS.

2 Ie goods stolen and thrown away by the thief in his flight: see CONSTITUTIONAL LAW.

3 Ie animals of unknown ownership found wandering in a manor or lordship: see CONSTITUTIONAL LAW.

4 *Parker v British Airways Board* [1982] QB 1004, [1982] 1 All ER 834, CA; *South Staffordshire Water Co v Sharman* [1896] 2 QB 44 at 46, DC, quoting with approval Pollock and Wright's Possession in the Common Law 41; and see *Hannah v Peel* [1945] KB 509 at 520, [1945] 2 All ER 288 at 293–294; *Re Cohen, National Provincial Bank Ltd v Katz* [1953] Ch 88, [1953] 1 All ER 378.

5 *South Staffordshire Water Co v Sharman* [1896] 2 QB 44, DC. Where the property on which the chattels are found is in the occupation of a lessee, they belong to the lessor, not the lessee, if they were there when the lease was granted, unless the terms of the lease are wide enough to cover them: *Elwes*

v Brigg Gas Co (1886) 33 ChD 562. But if they were not then on the property they would seem to belong to the lessee on the principle laid down in *South Staffordshire Water Co v Sharman* supra. See also *London Corpn v Appleyard* [1963] 2 All ER 834, [1963] 1 WLR 982 (lessee entitled as against finder, but lessor entitled as against lessee under special provision in lease).

6 *Bridges v Hawkesworth* (1851) 21 LJQB 75 at 76 per Patteson J. As to innkeepers see INNS.

7 *Hannah v Peel* [1945] KB 509 at 519–520, [1945] 2 All ER 288 at 293–294; and see paras 1811, 1813 ante. Cf *Hibbert v McKiernan* [1948] 2 KB 142, [1948] 1 All ER 860, DC (where a man trespassed on the property of a golf club and took ball which he found on the links and was held guilty of larceny).

8 *Parker v British Airways Board* [1982] QB 1004 at 1009, [1982] 1 All ER 834 at 837, CA, per Donaldson LJ (obiter); *Hannah v Peel* [1945] KB 509 at 520, [1945] 2 All ER 288 at 294; *Kowal v Ellis* (1977) 76 DLR (3d) 546.

9 *Parker v British Airways Board* [1982] QB 1004, [1982] 1 All ER 834, CA; *Kowal v Ellis* (1977) 76 DLR (3d) 546.

10 See note 9 supra.

11 *Bridges v Hawkesworth* (1851) 21 LJQB 75. This case has been much discussed by distinguished commentators, some of whom have supported it for reasons which differ from each other and from the reasons given by the court which decided it, while one at least has suggested that it was wrongly decided; see *Hannah v Peel* [1945] KB 509 at 515–517, [1945] 2 All ER 288 at 291–292. But the decision in *Bridges v Hawkesworth* supra was upheld and explained in *Parker v British Airways Board* [1982] QB 1004, [1982] 1 All ER 834, CA.

12 *Hannah v Peel* [1945] KB 509, [1945] 2 All ER 288. See further PERSONAL PROPERTY.

(iii) Bailee's Obligations

1815. Measure of diligence. In order that an action may be maintained in the case of a gratuitous deposit the defendant must have been guilty of either fraud[1], breach of orders, or negligence[2]. In negligence the standard of care required of a gratuitous bailee is that demanded by the circumstances of the particular case[3]: thus the measure of diligence demanded of a gratuitous depository is as a rule that degree of diligence which men of common prudence generally exercise about their own affairs[4], but if the bailee is notoriously dissipated, negligent or imprudent, and the bailor was aware of the fact, a presumption might perhaps be raised that the bailor expected of him only such amount of care as the bailee was in the habit of bestowing on his own chattels of a similar nature[5]. The fact that the bailee keeps chattels deposited with him in the same manner as he keeps his own may be, but is not necessarily, sufficient to exempt a gratuitous bailee from liability[6].

The amount of diligence which is required may also be affected by the particular locality in which the bailment is effected. Thus in agricultural districts it may be usual to leave barns, in which horses and other cattle are kept, unlocked at night; but in cities a corresponding practice would be deemed a great want of caution[7].

In each case it has to be decided whether, having regard to any exempting conditions[8] and all the circumstances of the particular case[9], including the nature, portability, value and character of the chattel, there has been a breach of duty on the bailee's part to justify a finding of negligence[10]. The fact that the chattel was lost or injured whilst in the bailee's possession raises prima facie a presumption against him[11], but he may rebut it by proving that he was not to blame for the loss or injury, even if he is unable to show how it happened[12].

Except by special agreement, a gratuitous depositary is not liable to his bailor for the misfeasances of third parties whereby the chattel bailed is damaged or stolen, unless it can be shown that he was guilty of negligence of a sufficiently culpable kind in its control or custody, or of fraud[13].

The bailee must return the chattel bailed to the bailor on demand[14].

1 *Moore v Mourgue* (1776) 2 Cowp 479 at 480 per Lord Mansfield CJ.

2 The term 'gross negligence' adds nothing and has been disapproved: see *Houghland v R R Low (Luxury Coaches) Ltd* [1962] 1 QB 694 at 697–698, [1962] 2 All ER 159 at 160–161, CA; and see para 1803 ante.

3 *Houghland v R R Low (Luxury Coaches) Ltd* [1962] 1 QB 694 at 698, [1962] 2 All ER 159 at 161, CA, per Ormerod LJ. The views expressed in older cases that the standard of care was to be adjudged according to rules peculiar to bailment are not now consistent with the modern law of negligence and these cases must now be read in the light of *Houghland v R R Low (Luxury Coaches) Ltd* supra and later authority: see note 4 infra. As to the degree of care and diligence required in different kinds of bailment see para 1803 ante.

4 *China Pacific SA v Food Corpn of India, The Winson* [1982] AC 939 at 960, [1981] 3 All ER 688 at 694, HL, per Lord Diplock; *Port Swettenham Authority v T W Wu & Co (M) Sdn Bhd* [1979] AC 580 at 589, [1978] 3 All ER 337 at 339, PC; see also *Giblin v McMullen* (1868) LR 2 PC 317; *Bullen v Swan Electric Engraving Co* (1907) 23 TLR 258, CA; *Blount v The War Office* [1953] 1 All ER 1071, [1953] 1 WLR 736; and para 1817 post. In several modern authorities, the duty is simply stated as one of reasonable care in all the circumstances: *Garlick v W & H Rycroft Ltd* [1982] CA Transcript 277, CA; *Mitchell v Ealing London Borough Council* [1978] QB 1 at 6, [1978] 2 All ER 779 at 781 per O'Connor J; and see *James Buchanan & Co Ltd v Hay's Transport Services Ltd and Duncan Barbour & Sons Ltd* [1972] 2 Lloyd's Rep 535; *Hedley Byrne & Co Ltd v Heller & Partners Ltd* [1964] AC 465 at 526, [1963] 2 All ER 575 at 608, HL, per Lord Devlin.

5 *The William* (1806) 6 Ch Rob 316. See also *Coggs v Bernard* (1703) 2 Ld Raym 909 at 914 per Holt CJ.

6 *Coggs v Bernard* (1703) 2 Ld Raym 909 at 914 per Holt CJ; *Giblin v McMullen* (1868) LR 2 PC 317 at 339 per Lord Chelmsford. Cf *Doorman v Jenkins* (1834) 2 Ad & El 256, where the defendant coffeehouse keeper accepted from the plaintiff the deposit of a sum with which to take up a bill which would be presented there for payment, and placed it with money of his own to a larger amount in a cash-box which he kept in the taproom, whence it was stolen on a day on which the room was open to the public while the rest of the house was closed. Lord Denman CJ at 258 said that it did not follow from the defendant's having lost his own money at the same time as the plaintiff's that he had taken such care of the plaintiff's money as a reasonable man would ordinarily take of his own. Lord Denman's direction was approved in *Giblin v McMullen* supra at 339. See also *Nelson v Macintosh* (1816) 1 Stark 237; *Dartnall v Howard and Gibbs* (1825) 4 B & C 345.

7 Story on Bailments (9th Edn), s 13.

8 See paras 1816, 1840 post.

9 *Houghland v R R Low (Luxury Coaches) Ltd* [1962] 1 QB 694, [1962] 2 All ER 159, CA.

10 *Giblin v McMullen* (1868) LR 2 PC 317. See also *Ryder v Wombwell* (1868) LR 4 Exch 32 at 38–39.

11 *Houghland v R R Low (Luxury Coaches) Ltd* [1962] 1 QB 694, [1962] 2 All ER 159, CA.

12 The onus is always on the bailee, whether a bailee for reward or a gratuitous bailee, to prove that the loss of goods bailed to him was not caused by his negligence: *Port Swettenham Authority v T W Wu & C (M) Sdn Bhd* [1979] AC 580, [1978] 3 All ER 337, PC; *Mitchell v Ealing London Borough Council* [1979] QB 1, [1978] 2 All ER 779. See *Wiehe v Dennis Bros* (1913) 29 TLR 250; *Ludgate v Lovett* [1969] 2 All ER 1275 at 1277, [1969] 1 WLR 1016 at 1019, CA, per Harman LJ; *Walsh v Holst & Co Ltd* [1958] 3 All ER 33 at 37, [1958] 1 WLR 800 at 805, CA, per Hodson LJ. See also para 1806 note 10 ante and para 1843 post.

13 *Coggs v Bernard* (1703) 2 Ld Raym 909 at 913; *Nelson v Macintosh* (1816) 1 Stark 237 at 238; *Giblin v McMullen* (1869) LR 2 PC 317; Jones on Bailments (4th Edn) 46–47.

14 See *Cranch v White* (1835) 1 Bing NC 414 at 420; *Wetherman v London and Liverpool Bank of Commerce Ltd* (1914) 31 TLR 20; *United States of America and Republic of France v Dollfus Mieg et Cie SA and Bank of England* [1952] AC 582 at 611, [1952] 1 All ER 572 at 585, HL; and para 1885 post.

1816. Liability limited or enlarged by special agreement. A gratuitous bailee may, by special agreement, limit or exclude his liability for any loss of, or damage to, the chattel[1]. His liability then depends upon the terms of the agreement[2], subject to any statutory controls imposed upon the disclaimer[3]. It is immaterial for this purpose whether the special agreement is oral or in writing[4].

Although the relationship of depositor and depositary is not, because of the lack of consideration moving from the depositor, contractual[5], it appears that the depositary can also enlarge his liability to the depositor by special agreement[6]. Consequently, if the bailee, in assuming possession of the chattel, expressly undertakes to keep it safely, he enlarges the measure of his responsibility, and by virtue of his special agreement may even make himself an insurer of it[7]. Similarly, a gratuitous bailee who undertakes to return the goods only to a particular person, or only upon particular conditions, will be answerable for the breach of that special undertaking[8]. Again, it appears immaterial for this purpose whether the special agreement is oral or in writing[9]. Yet such a bailee's responsibility is limited in some respects, for though his undertaking to keep the chattel safely binds him to keep it safely against all parties and to answer for accidents or theft[10], he will not be liable in the case of casualties happening by an act of God, or by the Queen's enemies[11].

Where a gratuitous bailee by way of deposit undertakes to redeliver the goods to the bailor at a particular time or place, and fails to discharge that undertaking, the bailee becomes an insurer of the goods and is strictly liable for any subsequent loss or damage[12]. However, the making of a second appointment with the bailor may cause the bailee's responsibility for the goods to revert to a duty of reasonable care[13]. This will not, however, relieve the bailee from his strict responsibility for misadventures occurring to the goods before the making of that second appointment[14]. Further, where the goods are damaged or lost at some time after the bailee's failure to meet the original appointment, and the bailee has since made a second appointment, the burden rests on the bailee to show that the misadventure occurred after the making of the second appointment and thus after his responsibility has reverted to that of an ordinary bailee[15].

1 *Brown v National Bank of Australasia* (1890) 16 VLR 475; Palmer on Bailment (1979) 321–322.
2 *Trefftz v Canelli* (1872) LR 4 PC 277 at 281; *Kettle v Bromsall* (1738) Willes 118 at 121; *Orchard v Connaught Club* (1930) 46 TLR 214. See also *Kay v Shuman* (1954) Times, 22 June; and see para 1840 note 1 post. It may be argued that this special agreement constitutes a contract, the depositor's consideration being his relieving the depositary from the normal duty of reasonable care owed by an unrewarded bailee; sed quaere.
3 The exclusion or restriction of liability for negligence is now subject to the provisions of the Unfair Contract Terms Act 1977; see CONTRACT.
4 *Coggs v Bernard* (1703) 2 Ld Raym 909 at 915.
5 *Morris v C W Martin & Sons Ltd* [1966] 1 QB 716 at 731–732, [1965] 2 All ER 725 at 734–735, CA, per Diplock LJ (obiter); *Thomas v High* (1960) SR NSW 401; *Parastatidis v Kotaridis* [1978] VR 449 at 454–455 per Harris J (obiter); but cf *New Zealand Shipping Co Ltd v A M Satterthwaite & Co Ltd* [1975] AC 154 at 167, [1974] 1 All ER 1015 at 1019, PC, per Lord Wilberforce.
6 *Kettle v Bromsall* (1738) Willes 118.
7 *Kettle v Bromsall* (1738) Willes 118.
8 *Trefftz v Canelli* (1872) LR 4 PC 277 at 281; but cf *Parastatidis v Kotaridis* [1978] VR 449.
9 *Coggs v Bernard* (1703) 2 Ld Raym 909 at 915.
10 *Kettle v Bromsall* (1738) Willes 118.
11 *Coggs v Bernard* (1703) 2 Ld Raym 909 at 918.
12 *Mitchell v Ealing London Borough Council* [1979] QB 1, [1978] 2 All ER 779.
13 *Mitchell v Ealing London Borough Council* [1979] QB 1 at 9, [1978] 2 All ER 779 at 784.
14 See note 13 supra.
15 See note 13 supra.

1817. Deposits with bankers or traders. Where a customer leaves valuables with his bankers[1] for safe custody, or allows a printer or any other trader to retain his plates or chattels upon which the trader may have worked, it is not always easy to say whether the bailment is gratuitous[2] or one for reward to the bailee[3]. Even if no specific charge for keeping is made, it may well be that the custodian indirectly obtains some consideration for the service, either in being allowed to continue to keep the customer's account[4], or in the prospect of future work[5]. On balance, it seems that such depositaries should be characterised as bailees for reward[6].

1 In *Giblin v McMullen* (1868) LR 2 PC 317, bankers with whom the plaintiff's testator had deposited for safe custody a box (of which he kept the key) containing debentures were found to be gratuitous bailees, whereas in *Re United Service Co, Johnston's Claim* (1870) 6 Ch App 212, bankers were held to be bailees for reward. See also BANKING vol 3 (1) (Reissue) para 206.

2 Ie *depositum*: see para 1802 ante.

3 Ie *locatio custodiae*: see para 1802 ante.

4 *Port Swettenham Authority v T W Wu & Co (M) Sdn Bhd* [1979] AC 580 at 589, [1978] 3 All ER 337 at 340, PC, per Lord Salmon (obiter); see also *Kahler v Midland Bank Ltd* [1948] 1 All ER 811 at 819–820, CA, per Scott LJ; on appeal, without reference to this point, [1950] AC 24, [1949] 2 All ER 621, HL.

5 *Bullen v Swan Electric Engraving Co* (1906) 22 TLR 275 at 277 per Walton J; affd (1907) 23 TLR 258, CA. See also PRESS.

6 Palmer on Bailment (1979) Chapter 8. Cf *Bullen v Swan Electric Engraving Co* (1906) 22 TLR 275 at 277 per Walton J; affd (1907) 23 TLR 258, CA; and see *Mitchell v Davis* (1920) 37 TLR 68.

1818. Use of chattel precluded. The bailee is precluded from using the bailed chattel for his own personal advantage in any manner whatsoever without the bailor's consent, express or implied, unless such use is necessary for its preservation[1]. Apart from such necessary use, if the bailee applies the chattel to any purpose other than that of bare custody he becomes responsible for any loss or damage resulting from his breach of good faith[2], except where the cause of the loss or damage is independent of his acts and is inherent in the chattel itself[3]. The bailee's act in doing something inconsistent with the terms of the contract terminates his status as a bailee, and causes the possessory title to revert to the bailor, entitling him to maintain an action of trover[4].

This rules applies a fortiori when the bailee's unwarranted action results in either the destruction or permanent alteration in character of the thing bailed[5].

If the chattel deposited is contained in a sealed or locked receptacle, the depositary has no right to open it, and it is a breach of the confidential relation on which this contract is based if he does so unnecessarily[6]; and it may be negligence to omit to take steps to see that the receptacle is not opened[7].

1 Bac Abr Bailment, A. See also *Re Tidd, Tidd v Overell* [1893] 3 Ch 154, where money was handed to be taken care of, but with the intention that the bailee might use it. North J held, at 156, that it was not a loan, but as a trust for safe custody.

2 Pothier's Contrat de Dépôt, ss 34, 35; Palmer on Bailment (1979) Chapter 9.

3 *Lilley v Doubleday* (1881) 7 QBD 510 at 511 per Grove J (a case of bailment for reward). See further *Mitchell v Ealing London Borough Council* [1979] QB 1, [1978] 2 All ER 779, applying *Shaw & Co v Symmons & Sons Ltd* [1917] 1 KB 799 (failure to return bailed goods at the appointed time).

4 *Fenn v Bittleston* (1851) 7 Exch 152; *Plasycoed Collieries Co Ltd v Partridge, Jones & Co Ltd* [1912] 2 KB 345 at 351 per Hamilton J, *R v Price* (1913) 9 Cr App Rep 15, CCA. The statement in the text was approved, as applying generally to bailments, in *North Central Wagon and Finance Co Ltd v Graham* [1950] 2 KB 7 at 15, [1950] 1 All ER 780 at 784, CA, per Cohen LJ; and see *Alexander v Railway Executive* [1951] 2 KB 882 at 887, [1951] 2 All ER 442 at 445 per Devlin J; *Reliance Car Facilities Ltd v Roding Motors* [1952] 2 QB 844 at 851, [1952] 1 All ER 1355 at 1358, CA, per Hodson LJ; *Union Transport Finance Ltd v British Car Auctions Ltd* [1978] 2 All ER 385, CA.

5 *Wilkinson v Verity* (1871) LR 6 CP 206.

6 Pothier's Contrat de Dépôt, s 38. See also *R v Robson* (1861) Le & Ca 93.

7 See *Blount v The War Office* [1953] 1 All ER 1071, [1953] 1 WLR 736.

1819. Consequence of breach of duty. If a bailee deals with the chattels entrusted to him in a way not authorised by the bailor, he takes upon himself the risk of so doing.

If, therefore, the bailee without necessity, and without the bailor's permission, fails to keep the chattel entrusted to him in the place where he has undertaken to keep it, that is to say, in the absence of express agreement, in the place where he himself usually keeps his own chattels of a similar description, he becomes by reason of his breach of duty an insurer of the chattel, and is liable to the bailor for any loss or damage caused[1], unless he can show that the loss or damage did not arise out of his breach of duty, but must have taken place as inevitably at the one place as at the other[2]. Similarly, a bailee by way of deposit who undertakes to redeliver the goods to the bailor at a particular time, and fails to do so, becomes thereafter an insurer of the goods[3]. The bailee's promise would appear to be enforceable irrespective of the absence of contract. If the bailee without necessity, and without the bailor's express or implied permission, sells the chattel, an action for conversion will lie against him[4].

A bailee is not free to divest himself of responsibility and substitute that of another without the bailor's consent[5].

1 Pothier's Contrat de Dépôt, s 38; Palmer on Bailment (1979) 322–324; cf *Mytton v Cock* (1738) 2 Stra 1099; *Ronnenburg v Falkland Islands Co* (1864) 17 CBNS 1; *Mitchell v Ealing London Borough Council* [1979] QB 1, [1978] 2 All ER 779 (delay in redelivery).
2 *Lilley v Doubleday* (1881) 7 QBD 510 at 511 per Grove J; *Davis v Garrett* (1830) 6 Bing 716 at 724 per Tindal CJ (cases of bailment for reward). Cf *Coldman v Hill* [1919] 1 KB 443, CA; see paras 1825, 1832 post.
3 *Mitchell v Ealing London Borough Council* [1979] QB 1, [1978] 2 All ER 779 (local authority, in possession of former tenant's goods as gratuitous bailee, made appointment for redelivery but failed to keep it; local authority held strictly liable for subsequent theft, notwithstanding reasonable care in custody of the goods). See further *Shaw & Co v Symmons & Sons Ltd* [1917] 1 KB 799, a case of bailment for reward, on which O'Connor J relied in *Mitchell v Ealing London Borough Council* supra. See further para 1818 ante.
4 *Sachs v Miklos* [1948] 2 KB 23 at 36, [1948] 1 All ER 67 at 68, CA; *Munro v Willmott* [1949] 1 KB 295, [1948] 2 All ER 983. As to agency of necessity see generally AGENCY vol 1 (2) (Reissue) para 28.
5 See *Blount v The War Office* [1953] 1 All ER 1071, [1953] 1 WLR 736.

(2) MANDATE

1820. Meaning of 'mandate'. Mandate[1] is another species of bailment gratuitously undertaken by the bailee. It may be defined as a bailment of a specific chattel[2] in regard to which the bailee engages to do some act without reward[3]. It has much in common with deposit[4], but whereas in the case of deposit the principal object of the contract is to provide for the safe custody of the thing, and any service or labour, such as feeding an animal or preserving a perishable article, is merely accessory, in the case of mandate the safe custody of the chattel deposited is ancillary to an undertaking by the bailee to do some act to it, or to perform some service in connection with it[5]. In this sense, therefore, it may be said that the great distinction between mandate and deposit is that the former lies in feasance and the latter in custody[6].

Formerly, in this form of bailment, the bailer's confidence in the capacity, skill and honour of the bailee duly to perform the task or employment undertaken by him, and not merely or chiefly the bailee's promise to safeguard the chattel while in his charge, has been held to constitute the consideration moving the bailor to deliver it into his custody[7]. Under modern law, however, it now seems preferable to recognise that the transaction of mandate (in common with that of deposit)[8] does not give rise to a contract[9].

An executory transaction of mandate creates no legal obligation, for a person undertaking to perform a voluntary act is not liable if he merely refuses or neglects to perform it[10], and the agreement remains executory at any rate until delivery of the chattel is accepted.

1 Ie *mandatum*: see para 1802 ante.
2 Money may be regarded as a chattel in this context, whether entrusted to the mandatary in the form of cash or obtained by him by means of a cheque or other negotiable instrument, or as the proceeds of the sale of property which he was authorised to sell on the mandator's behalf. Even where the identical coins need not be used, the mandator may be entitled to treat the equivalent of the sum entrusted to the mandatary as his property, and not merely as a debt due to him, if it is not used or laid out in accordance with the contract. Similarly, the mandator may claim as his own or obtain a charge upon any property purchased with the money in whole or in part, even if it is not the property which ought to have been purchased, and he may follow it if it is lent or given away by the mandatary: see *Taylor v Plumer* (1815) 3 M & S 562; *Re Strachan, ex p Cooke* (1876) 4 ChD 123, CA; *Re Hallett's Estate, Knatchbull v Hallett* (1880) 13 ChD 696, CA; *Sinclair v Brougham* [1914] AC 398, HL; *Banque Belge Pour L'Etranger v Hambrouck* [1921] 1 KB 321, CA.
3 Story on Bailments (9th Edn), s 137; Palmer on Bailment (1979) 327. See also Heineccius, Pandects, par 3, lib 17, s 230.
4 See paras 1806–1819 ante.
5 *Coggs v Bernard* (1703) 2 Ld Raym 909 at 918.
6 Jones on Bailments (4th Edn) 53. This distinction is criticised by Story on Bailments (9th Edn), s 140; see further Palmer on Bailment (1979) 329.
7 *Coggs v Bernard* (1703) 2 Ld Raym 909 at 919; *Banbury v Bank of Montreal* [1918] AC 626 at 657, PC; and see Story on Bailments (9th Edn), s 140; Pothier's Contrat de Mandat, c 1.
8 See para 1806 ante.
9 Palmer on Bailment (1979) 339.
10 *Skelton v London and North Western Rly Co* (1867) LR 2 CP 631 at 636 per Willes J; *Elsee v Gatward* (1793) 5 Term Rep 143 at 148 per Lord Kenyon CJ; *Balfe v West* (1853) 13 CB 466, and the American case *Thorne v Deas*, therein cited at 470; and see *Coggs v Bernard* (1703) 2 Ld Raym 909 at 919. See also NEGLIGENCE.

1821. Extent of bailee's obligations. The bailee, or mandatary, when he has entered upon the execution of the task which he has undertaken, is bound, in common with all others who render a gratuitous service[1], apart from special contract, to act prudently and honourably and to exercise reasonable care and diligence[2]. This imposes upon him the duty to use such care and diligence as persons ordinarily use in their own affairs and such skill as he possesses[3]. In addition, if, because the bailee holds himself out as possessing a professional or other special skill, the bailor entrusts him with the performance of a task which requires the exercise of such skill, he must use it[4].

The public profession of an art is a representation that the person professing it possesses the necessary skill and ability. When, therefore, a skilled worker or artist is employed, he warrants impliedly that he is possessed of sufficient skill to perform the task that he undertakes, even if the undertaking be without reward[5].

1 *Wilkinson v Coverdale* (1793) 1 Esp 74; *Dartnall v Howard and Gibbs* (1825) 4 B & C 345; *Gladwell v Steggall* (1839) 5 Bing NC 733; *Harris v Perry & Co* [1903] 2 KB 219, CA; *Karavias v Callinicos* [1917] WN 323, CA; *Pratt v Patrick* [1924] 1 KB 488.
2 *Houghland v R R Low (Luxury Coaches) Ltd* [1962] 1 QB 694, [1962] 2 All ER 159, CA; *Remme v Wall* (1978) 29 NSR (2d) 39; and see *Copland v Brogan* 1916 SC 277. Earlier expressions of the mandatary's duty in terms of gross negligence would now appear discredited: Palmer on Bailment (1979) 330–339.
3 *Beauchamp v Powley* (1831) 1 Mood & R 38; *Beal v South Devon Rly Co* (1864) 3 H & C 337 at 342 per Crompton J; *Shiells v Blackburne* (1789) 1 Hy Bl 159.
4 *Shiells and Thorne v Blackburne* (1789) 1 Hy Bl 159 at 162 per Heath J. See *Bourne v Diggles* (1814) 2 Chit 311; *O'Hanlon v Murray* (1860) 12 ICLR 161; and *Wilson v Brett* (1843) 11 M & W 113, where a skilled horseman gratuitously riding a horse to show it to a purchaser on its owner's behalf was held liable for injuring it by riding it on improper ground.

5 *Harmer v Cornelius* (1858) 5 CBNS 236; *Shiells and Thorne v Blackburne* (1789) 1 Hy Bl 158. Cf para 1869 post.

1822. Bailee's liability. The bailee's failure to discharge his obligations, referred to in the previous paragraph, renders him liable to be sued for negligence if it causes damage to the bailor. In addition, as in the case of a depositary, he is responsible to the bailor for the loss of or any damage to the chattel entrusted to him arising out of any breach of duty on his part in respect of its safe custody[1].

Moreover, the acceptance of the bailment of the chattel by the bailee may consitute a sufficient entering upon the task or service undertaken to make him liable to the bailor if he neglects to carry out his promise, and damage is thereby directly caused to the bailor, even if the neglect amounts only to nonfeasance[2]. There is uncertainty as to the juridical basis of this obligation. Older authorities held that where the bailor's only obligation was to hand over the chattel, his doing so constituted performance of his part of the agreement and was the consideration for the bailee's promise to carry out the particular act or perform the service concerned[3]. Under modern law, however, a contractual analysis seems inappropriate. Nor can it be maintained that the bailee's failure to perform constitutes (otherwise than in the most exceptional cases) the tort of negligence[4]. On balance, the duty to perform is preferably regarded as an incident peculiar to the bailment relation[5].

It is possible that, owing to the gratuitous nature of the undertaking, the bailee may relieve himself of responsibility by returning the chattel to the bailor at any such time as will enable the undertaking to be performed otherwise[6].

1 See para 1815 ante.
2 *Wilkinson v Coverdale* (1793) 1 Esp 74; *Streeter v Horlock* (1822) 1 Bing 34; *Oriental Bank Corpn v The Queen* (1867) 6 SCR (NSW) 122 at 125 per Faucett J; *Pilcher v Leyland Motors Ltd* [1932] NZLR 449 at 464–467 per Ostler J; *Roufos v Brewster and Brewster* [1971] 2 SASR 218 at 223–224 per Bray CJ; but cf *Heaton v Richards* (1881) 2 NSWLR 73; *Parastatidis v Kotaridis* [1978] VR 449 at 454–455 per Harris J. See further Story on Bailments (9th Edn), s 171 (a)–(c). If, for instance, a bailee undertakes gratuitously to present a bill of exchange for payment and gives all the necessary notices of dishonour on behalf of the holder and receives the bill for him, and then does nothing, and the acceptor is made bankrupt and the holder loses all his remedies against the drawer and indorsers owing to the non-presentment of the bill on the due date, it would appear that the bailee would be liable. And see *Chapman v Morley* (1891) 7 TLR 257.
3 Story on Bailments (9th Edn), s 171 (a)–(c). See *Shillibeer v Glyn* (1836) 2 M & W 143; and cf *Whitehead v Greetham* (1825) 2 Bing 464, Ex Ch.
4 *General Accident Fire and Life Assurance Corpn Ltd v Tanter, The Zephyr* [1985] 2 Lloyd's Rep 529 at 538–539, CA, per Mustill LJ; *Argy Trading Development Co Ltd v Lapid Developments Ltd* [1977] 3 All ER 785, [1977] 1 WLR 444.
5 Palmer on Bailment (1979) 340.
6 Story on Bailments (9th Edn), s 164.

1823. When bailee is excused from liability. If a contract of mandate is contained in a written instrument which is expressed in ambiguous terms, and the bailee is in fact misled and adopts one interpretation when the bailor intended him to follow the other, then the bailor will be bound, and the bailee will be exonerated[1].

In the case of impossible undertakings the bailee is not liable, unless the bailee should have been aware of the impossibility when giving the undertaking and can be treated as having undertaken to perform in any event. But the impossibility must, in any case, be absolute and not relative; mere difficulty in execution or the violation of trade custom is not sufficient ground for excusing non-performance when once the task is entered upon[2].

An agreement of mandate for the performance of an immoral or illegal act cannot be enforced, as no court will enforce an illegal contract or transaction or allow itself to be made the instrument of enforcing obligations alleged to arise out of a contract or transaction which is illegal. It is immaterial whether or not the defendant has pleaded the illegality[3].

1 Story on Agency (9th Edn), s 74. See *Ireland v Livingston* (1872) LR 5 HL 395; cf *European Asian Bank AG v The Punjab and Sind Bank (No 2)* [1983] 2 All ER 508, [1983] 1 WLR 642, CA.
2 *Tufnell v Constable* (1838) 7 Ad & El 798. As to the discharge of contracts on the ground of impossibility or frustration see CONTRACT.
3 *Scott v Brown, Doering, McNab & Co, Slaughter and May v Brown, Doering, McNab & Co* [1892] 2 QB 724 at 728, CA, per Lindley LJ, citing *Holman v Johnson* (1775) 1 Cowp 341. See further CONTRACT.

1824. Bailee's duty to account. A bailee who, under a mandate, receives money or chattels on account of his principal is bound to account for them[1]. If he deposits them in his own name, with other chattels of his own of the same kind, in the hands of a third party, he is liable to his principal for any loss or damage to them during the existence of the deposit, even if his principal was aware of his course of procedure but did not assent to it[1].

When the return of the bailed chattel constitutes part of the bailee's obligation, he must restore not only the chattel itself, but also all increments, profits and earnings immediately derived from it[2]. If, however, the mandate is to put out money at interest, the specific coins delivered to the bailee need not be returned; he is bound to return their equivalent in value, with interest[3].

The bailee is also liable to account to the bailor for any secret profits which he may have received in respect of the conduct or management of the business which he has undertaken gratuitously to perform[4].

1 *Massey v Banner* (1820) 4 Madd 413.
2 Pothier's Contrat de Mandat, ss 58–60. Thus if animals are to be restored, their young also belong to the bailor, and if a vehicle has been delivered to be let for hire, the bailee must account for the hire earned, as well as for the vehicle: Story on Bailments (9th Edn), s 194.
3 Pothier's Contrat de Mandat, s 59. Compare the case of *mutuum*, which is discussed in para 1834 post.
4 See *Kimber v Barber* (1872) 8 Ch App 56, CA; and AGENCY vol 1 (2) (Reissue) para 105 et seq.

1825. Misuse of bailed chattel. When under a mandate a bailee does some act to the bailed chattel unauthorised by the agreement made between himself and the bailor, he becomes responsible for any subsequent loss or damage which may be caused to the chattel by his unwarranted act[1].

1 *Nelson v Macintosh* (1816) 1 Stark 237; *Miles v Cattle* (1830) 4 Moo & P 630; Palmer on Bailment (1979) 342. Cf paras 1819 ante, 1832 post.

1826. Duty to return chattel. As a general rule, a bailee under a mandate is bound to redeliver to his principal the chattel entrusted to him upon the fulfilment of the purpose for which he received it; but if it has been destroyed or damaged without any default on his part, in the absence of special agreement or some positive rule of law he will be exempt from any claim for damage or non-delivery[1].

1 Story on Bailments (9th Edn), s 25.

1827. Delegation by bailee. As a general rule there is no power of delegation in the contract of mandate; the legal presumption is that the undertaking is personal to the bailee and may not be handed over by him to another[1]. But where in the ordinary course of business the custody would naturally devolve upon, or the acts be performed by, some servant or agent of the bailee, delegation is permissible[2]. In such a case the bailee is not liable if, without any negligence on his delegate's part, any loss or damage happens to the chattel during the period of delegation[3].

1 *Bringloe v Morrice* (1676) 1 Mod Rep 210; Palmer on Bailment (1979) 342. Cf *Edwards v Newland & Co (E Burchett Ltd, third parties)* [1950] 2 KB 534, [1950] 1 All ER 1072, CA; and para 1839 post.
2 *Lord Camoys v Scurr* (1840) 9 C & P 383 at 386 per Coleridge J, where the bailee, having received a mare to try, was held entitled to put a competent person on the mare to try her. See also AGENCY vol 1 (2) (Reissue) para 63 et seq.
3 *Lord Camoys v Scurr* (1840) 9 C & P 383.

1828. Reimbursement of bailee. As a general rule, a bailee under a mandate is entitled to his actual disbursements and out-of-pocket expenses in connection with the service he gives, as otherwise a gratuitous act would become a burden[1]. It seems, however, that this entitlement may be displaced by the particular circumstances of the mandate[2]. A mandatary who, in discharge of his duty of care, takes measures to protect the bailed goods from exceptional hazards may be entitled to recover the cost of their preservation[3].

1 Story on Bailments (9th Edn), s 154; Pothier's Contrat de Mandat, ss 68–78. Cf para 1831 post.
2 Palmer on Bailment (1979) 346–347.
3 *China Pacific SA v Food Corpn of India, The Winson* [1982] AC 939, [1981] 3 All ER 688, HL; and see AGENCY.

(3) GRATUITOUS LOAN FOR USE

1829. Nature of gratuitous loan for use. In deposit[1] and mandate[2] the bailor has all the advantages of the bailment. In gratuitous loan for use[3] the reverse is the case. This is a bailment where a chattel is lent by its owner to the bailee for the express purpose of conferring a benefit upon the bailee, without any corresponding advantage to its owner.

By English law this agreement is confined to goods, chattels or personal property, and does not, as under the Roman civil law, extend to real estate[4]. The loan of the use of real estate or chattels real is no more than a licence beneficially to occupy a tenement or other hereditament belonging to the licensor for a particular or indeterminate period[5]. Consequently there can be no bailment of a structure affixed to real property.

1 Ie *depositum:* see paras 1802, 1806–1819 ante.
2 Ie *mandatum:* see paras 1802, 1820–1828 ante.
3 Ie *commodatum:* see para 1802 ante.
4 Story on Bailments (9th Edn), s 223.
5 *Williams v Jones* (1865) 3 H & C 602.

1830. Borrower's obligations. The lender must be taken to lend for the purpose of a beneficial use by the borrower. The borrower, therefore, is not responsible for reasonable wear and tear[1]. Older authority holds that, as the borrower alone receives benefit from the agreement, he is liable for the slightest degree of negligence; and he is bound to exercise the utmost degree of care in regard to the bailed chattel[2] and anything accessory to it[3]. Under modern law, however, the borrower's responsibility is likely to be regarded as one of reasonable care and diligence in all the circumstances of the case[4].

What is proper diligence, and what constitutes neglect, in a borrower in his custody of the chattel lent depends upon the circumstances of each particular case, the nature of the chattel lent and the character and occupation of the borrower[5].

As a general rule the borrower is not liable if, without any default on his part, the performance of his agreement becomes an absolute impossibility; nor is he liable for loss or injury arising from a third person's wrongful act which could not be reasonably foreseen or prevented, or from the results of external and irresistible violence[6].

The borrower's liability, however, is qualified where a special agreement is substituted for the obligation imposed by the common law, and possibly also, though this has been denied, where there has been an offer of the chattel by the lender to the borrower[7].

The borrower is liable if he detains the chattel from its owner after demand, or after the agreed time for its return has expired. In that event, he becomes liable as an insurer[8].

1 *Blakemore v Bristol and Exeter Rly Co* (1858) 8 E & B 1035 at 1051 per Coleridge J; *Pomfret v Ricroft* (1669) 1 Saund 321 at 323. See also *Moorhouse v Angus & Robertson (No 1) Pty Ltd* [1981] 1 NSWLR 701 at 708 per Samuels JA (NSW CA). For a defence pleading wear and tear see 6 Court Forms (2nd Edn) (1989 Issue) 244–245, Form 19.
2 *Coggs v Bernard* (1703) 2 Ld Raym 909 at 915 per Holt CJ. See also *Vaughan v Menlove* (1837) 3 Bing NC 468 at 475 per Tindal CJ; Jones on Bailments (4th Edn) 64–65. This view of the measure of the borrower's responsibility is also taken by Pothier, who says that it is not sufficient for the borrower to exert the same ordinary care which fathers of families are accustomed to use about their own affairs, but that he ought to exert all possible care, such as the most careful persons apply to their own affairs, and that he is liable, not only for a slight fault, but also for the slightest fault: Pothier's Prêt à Usage, s 48.

This superlative degree of carefulness (the exactissima diligentia of the Roman law) has, however, been doubted by some jurists, one of whom states that the person to whom the thing is lent is not obliged to answer for any uncontrollable force, or for the loss or damage of the thing which happens by any fortuitous case, provided the accident does not intervene through his fault or neglect, for it is necessary that he should take the same care of the thing as every prudent man would take of his own goods, since this contract is entered into for his sake: Ayliffe's New Pandect of Roman Civil Law, book 4, tit 16, p 517.
3 Jones on Bailments (4th Edn) 66.
4 *Walker v Watson* [1974] 2 NZLR 175; *Fairley & Stevens (1966) Ltd v Goldsworthy* (1973) 34 DLR (3d) 554 at 562, 568 per Dubinsky J (obiter); Palmer on Bailment (1979) 368–371.
5 Wherever a hirer is responsible (as to which see para 1858 post), a fortiori a borrower is, and he may be responsible where a hirer is not, seeing that greater diligence is required of him.
6 Pothier's Prêt à Usage, ss 38–55, 56. See also note 2 supra. Consequently, if the borrower's house is destroyed by fire and, owing to his exertions in saving his own chattels, he is unable to save the chattel he has borrowed, it is extremely doubtful whether he must compensate the owner for its destruction merely because he preferred his own property to that which had been lent to him for his benefit: Pothier's Prêt à Usage, s 56. Pothier, basing himself upon the Roman law, takes the view that he must compensate the owner, and Sir William Jones accedes to this doctrine (Jones on Bailments (4th Edn) 69), but it is very doubtful if it is law in England. Cf Story on Bailments (9th Edn), s 345 et seq. A borrower, however, is usually liable to the lender for any loss or damage, if he borrowed the chattel from its owner merely for the purpose of saving his own chattels from risk of damage or destruction. But he may be exempt if he can prove that he had previously disclosed to its

owner that his object in borrowing it was to enable him to avoid hazarding his own property: Jones on Bailments (4th Edn) 70.
7 Pothier's Prêt à Usage, s 52. Cf para 1810 text and notes 4, 5 ante.
8 Jones on Bailments (4th Edn) 70. Cf *Mitchell v Ealing London Borough Council* [1979] QB 1, [1978] 2 All ER 779 (deposit); *Shaw & Co v Symmons & Sons* [1917] 1 KB 799 (bailment for reward). As to improper use see para 1833 post.

1831. Borrower's expenses. If in his use of what is lent the borrower is put to any ordinary expense, such as filling a car with petrol, he must, in the absence of any agreement to the contrary, bear the expense himself, for it is he who derives advantage from the use[1].

Extraordinary expenses incurred by the borrower in the preservation of the chattel lent, whether arising from inherent defect, or viciousness peculiar to the chattel itself, or from circumstances altogether beyond his control, such as the tortious acts of third parties, may be recoverable from the lender if, in incurring those expenses, the borrower was performing his duty of care. It is doubtful, however, whether the borrower has a lien on the chattel for the amount of such charges if paid by him[2].

1 *Handford v Palmer* (1820) 2 Brod & Bing 359; 1 Domat, book 1, tit 5, s 3, art 4.
2 The French jurists (Pothier's Prêt à Usage, ss 81–83; 1 Domat, book 1, tit 5, s 3, art 4) say that the lender must pay such expenses; cf Story on Bailments (9th Edn), ss 273, 274; and para 1828 ante. See also *China Pacific SA v Food Corpn of India, The Winson* [1982] AC 939, [1981] 3 All ER 688, HL.

1832. Lender's obligations. If the lender is aware of any defect in the chattel which is not apparent and renders it unfit for the purpose for which it is lent, and fails to communicate the fact to the borrower, who in consequence is injured, the borrower can recover damages against the lender for the injuries so caused[1]. So also, if the chattel lent has been put on one side and not used for years, and is then lent without any intimation to the borrower of this fact and, in consequence of its being out of repair, injury is caused to the borrower, he can recover in an action against the lender[2]. In order to fix the lender with liability, the use must be of a kind contemplated by him at the time of lending, or subsequently authorised by him[3].

It is uncertain whether the lender is liable for defects in the chattel of which he was unaware, but of which he should reasonably have been aware, when he delivered the chattel to the borrower. Older authority holds that the lender is not liable for injuries occasioned by such defects[4]. Under modern law, however, it would appear that the lender owes a duty of reasonable care to warn the borrower of any defect in the chattel of which the lender should reasonably have been aware[5].

The lender is not liable to third parties for damage caused by the negligent use of the chattel by the bailee[6].

1 *Blakemore v Bristol and Exeter Rly Co* (1858) 8 E & B 1035 at 1051 per Coleridge J; *Coughlin v Gillison* [1899] 1 QB 145 at 147, CA, per A L Smith LJ; *MacCarthy v Young* (1861) 6 H & N 329. The bailor may indeed be liable to a third party who is injured by reason of the bailee's user of the defective chattel; see *Blacker v Lake and Elliot Ltd* (1912) 106 LT 533, DC; and NEGLIGENCE. Cf *Pivovaroff v Chernabaef* [1978] 21 SASR 1 (warning given by bailor).
2 *Coughlin v Gillison* [1899] 1 QB 145 at 148, CA, per Rigby LJ.
3 *Blakemore v Bristol and Exeter Rly Co* (1858) 8 E & B 1035.
4 *MacCarthy v Young* (1861) 6 H & N 329; *Coughlin v Gillison* [1899] 1 QB 145, CA. Cf *Longmeid v Holliday* (1851) 6 Exch 761 at 767–768 per Parke B. The same rule applies to gifts: *Gautret v Egerton* (1867) LR 2 CP 371 at 375 per Willes J. The operations of lending and giving are known to the law, and the rule relating to them must be strictly confined to the special relations thereby created: see

M'Alister (or Donoghue) v Stevenson [1932] AC 562 at 591, HL, per Lord Atkin (where in the phrase 'letting or giving', 'letting' is obviously a slip for 'lending'). Different considerations, therefore, apply to the case of a master providing things to be used by his servants for his business; see *Baker v James* [1921] 2 KB 674, and, for a somewhat exceptional extension of this principle, *Chapman (or Oliver) v Saddler & Co* [1929] AC 584, HL, distinguishing *Caledonian Rly Co v Mulholland* [1898] AC 216, HL. It is, however, artificial to regard the relationship of gratuitous bailment as obtaining in the situation of the common interchange of tools and machinery between employers and workpeople: the user there is not gratuitous because each has an interest in the mutual prosecution of the common work, and in this situation the ordinary law of negligence applies, the issues being whether the danger was reasonably foreseeable if no precautions were taken, and whether the defendant was under a duty to take reasonable precautions to guard against the risk: see *Griffiths v Arch Engineering Co (Newport) Ltd* [1968] 3 All ER 217 at 220 per Chapman J. See also EMPLOYMENT; NEGLIGENCE. As to the liability of an employer whose employee suffers personal injuries because of a defect in equipment provided by the employer, where the defect is attributable wholly or partly to the fault of a third party, see the Employer's Liability (Defective Equipment) Act 1969 s 1; and EMPLOYMENT.

5 See *Griffiths v Arch Engineering Co (Newport) Ltd* [1968] 3 All ER 217; *Wheeler v Copas* [1981] 3 All ER 405; *Campbell v O'Donnell* [1967] IR 226; *Pivovaroff v Chernabaeff* (1978) 21 SASR 1 (in none of which did the question fall to be decided); Palmer on Bailment (1979) 349–363.

6 *Hewitt v Bonvin* [1940] 1 KB 188, CA. The bailor will be excused from liability only if the bailee is a person of ordinary discretion. To place a chattel in the hands of a child or other person incapable of appreciating its dangerous propensities, whether by way of gift, loan or otherwise, is an act of negligence and raises different questions: see *Dixon v Bell* (1816) 5 M & S 198; and NEGLIGENCE.

1833. Use of chattel lent. The borrower must use the chattel only for the particular purpose for which it was lent to him, and if he uses it for any materially different purpose he becomes liable as an insurer[1].

Generally speaking, the permission accorded by the owner of a chattel to a borrower to use it is purely personal, and cannot, except by the owner's express consent, be extended to a third party[2]. The reason for this limitation is obvious. The chattel is lent by the owner to a person with whose capacity and honesty he is presumably familiar. Should the borrower therefore license a third party to use it, the bailment is thereby determined, and the borrower becomes responsible for any accident that may happen[3].

When, however, the actual use by a third party is necessary for the reasonable enjoyment of the chattel lent, the mere fact of its being lent for use implies a limited power of delegation in the borrower[4]. Thus the loan of a traction engine, a threshing machine, or some other piece of machinery, must, in the majority of cases, of necessity imply both superintendence and use by some person other than the actual and responsible borrower[5].

1 Bac Abr Bailment C; Pothier's Prêt à Usage, s 21. See also *Coggs v Bernard* (1703) 2 Ld Raym 909 at 915 per Holt CJ: 'if a man should lend another a horse to go westward or for a month, if the bailee go northward or keep the horse above a month, if any accident happen to the horse in the northern journey, or after the expiration of the month, the bailee will be chargeable'. Cf *Wilson v Shepherd* 1913 SC 300 (defender, at request of bailee of aerated water bottles belonging to pursuer, put paraffin into them). Cf para 1825 ante. The French rule is the same (Code Civil, art 1881).

2 Story on Bailments (9th Edn), s 234.

3 *Bringloe v Morrice* (1676) 1 Mod Rep 210; cf *Ballett v Mingay* [1943] KB 281, [1943] 1 All ER 143, CA; and see *Gwilliam v Twist* [1895] 2 QB 84, CA.

4 Story on Bailments (9th Edn), s 234: if A lends his horse to B to make a certain ride, B alone may ride him, but that if he lends his horses and carriage to B for a month the use of them by B's family may be fairly presumed to be contemplated by A.

5 See *Lord Camoys v Scurr* (1840) 9 C & P 383, where the defendant was held entitled to put up a groom to ride a mare lent to the defendant for trial.

(4) GRATUITOUS QUASI-BAILMENT

1834. Nature of gratuitous quasi-bailment. Gratuitous quasi-bailment, or *mutuum*, is the loan of something which is not to be returned in specie, but which is to be replaced by something similar and equivalent[1]. The contract of *mutuum* differs from that of gratuitous loan for use, or *commodatum*[2], in that in the latter a bare possession of the chattel lent, as distinguished from the property in it, vests in the borrower, the general property in it still remaining in the lender; whereas in *mutuum* that property in the chattel passes from the lender to the borrower.

Mutuum is confined to chattels which are intended to be consumed and which are capable of being estimated by number, weight, or measure, such as money, corn, or wine[3]. A familiar example is a housewife borrowing a packet of sugar from a neighbour.

The essence of the transaction in the case of such loans is not that the borrower should return to the lender the identical chattels lent, for such specific return would ordinarily render the loan valueless, but that upon demand or at a fixed date the lender should receive from the borrower an equivalent quantity of goods of similar quality. Thus, if money is advanced, its value in money must be returned, and if corn, wine or sugar is lent, then similar corn, wine or sugar of an equivalent amount must be returned; and enhancement in the commercial value of the commodity lent will not justify the borrower in tendering a less quantity than he actually received[4].

It is not, however, a transaction of *mutuum* if a bargain is made by which an equivalent value of wine is to be returned for oil, or meat for corn. Such an exchange constitutes a contract of barter, and therefore comes within a different category of transaction altogether[5].

1 Justin Inst lib 3, tit 14; *Parastatidis v Kotaridis* [1978] VR 449 at 456 per Harris J, where the text was approved. Cf *Coleman v Harvey* [1989] 1 NZLR 723 at 725 per Cooke P (NZ CA).
2 See para 1829 ante.
3 1 Domat, boot 1, tit 6, s 1; Story on Bailments (9th Edn), ss 283, 284.
4 1 Domat, book 1, tit 6, s 1, art 9.
5 1 Domat, book 1, tit 6, s 1, art 10; Jones on Bailments (4th Edn) 64, 102. As to barter see SALE OF GOODS.

1835. Duty to return chattel. As a necessary consequence of the absolute transfer of the property in, as well as the custody of, the chattel lent, the borrower is not, by reason of its accidental loss or destruction, released from his obligation to return to the owner its equivalent in kind upon demand, for it is the borrower's property, and the rule is that the risk passes with the property in the chattel[1].

An actual demand is, however, a condition precedent to an action for the non-delivery of the equivalent; just as where a man deposits money in the hands of another, to be kept for his use, the possession of the bailee is deemed the possession of the owner until an application and refusal, or other denial of the right. For the purposes of the Limitation Act 1980, time runs against the bailor from the date of such demand only[2].

1 Ie *ejus est periculum, cujus est dominium:* Story on Bailments (9th Edn), s 283; St Germain's Doctor and Student, ed by Murchall (1815), 2nd dial chap xxxviii.
2 *Re Tidd, Tidd v Overell* [1893] 3 Ch 154 at 156 per North J, approving 2 Pothier's Law of Obligations, ed Evans, 126; and see *South Australian Insurance Co v Randell* (1869) LR 3 PC 101; and generally LIMITATION OF ACTIONS. See also para 1887 post.

1836. Pro-mutuum. Whenever a person, acting under misapprehension as to an existing fact or state of facts, delivers to another a chattel which cannot be restored in specie, there arises the quasi-contract of *pro-mutuum*, which imposes upon the recipient the obligation to restore its equivalent. *Pro-mutuum* differs from *mutuum*[1] in that this obligation is imposed by law, whereas in *mutuum* it arises out of the voluntary agreement between the lender and the borrower; it resembles *mutuum* in that the subject matter to which it relates must always consist of money or fungibles, that is, chattels which, owing to their being consumed in the using, cannot be restored in specie.

The liability only arises out of an actual delivery of such chattels by one person to another, and the repayment of the obligation in chattels answering to the generic description of those advanced will always satisfy it. Thus if one man owes another twenty bushels of wheat, and by a mistake as to the amount of his indebtedness, pays to his creditor thirty bushels in satisfaction of the supposed liability, the recipient is a bailee to his former debtor of the ten bushels so overpaid, and, as such, is bound to account to him for the surplus. A similar liability arises if a man discharges a debt twice over, or pays the debt of another under a mistaken assumption of fact as to his liability[2]; the general rule in such cases is that where money is paid to another under a mistake of fact, an action will lie to recover it[3]. As, however, the original cause of the obligation is the payer's mistake, the recipient is, as a rule, bound only to repay to him the actual amount overpaid, without interest[4]. A demand is a condition precedent to an action[5].

1 See para 1834 ante.
2 Pothier's Contrat de Prêt de Consommation, ss 132–134. See also *Cox v Prentice* (1815) 3 M & S 344; *Newall v Tomlinson* (1871) LR 6 CP 405; *Milnes v Duncan* (1827) 6 B & C 671.
3 *Kelly v Solari* (1841) 9 M & W 54 at 58 per Parke B. See MISTAKE vol 32 paras 63–100.
4 Pothier's Contrat de Prêt de Consommation, s 138.
5 *Kelly v Solari* (1841) 9 M & W 54. See para 1885 post.

1837. Intermixture of chattels. Where the chattels of two persons are intermixed by agreement[1], so that the several portions can no longer be distinguished, the proprietors have an interest in common in proportion to the respective shares[2].

If a bailee, without his bailor's consent, intermixes his own chattels with those belonging to his bailor, and the intermixed goods are of substantially the same nature and quality and cannot in practice be separated, the mixture will be generally held in common in such proportion as each party contributed to the combination[3]. This general rule applies where the intermixture results from an act of God or the act of an unauthorised third party[4] as well as from the inadvertence or wilful conduct of a bailee[5]. However, any cost attendant upon the separation into shares must be borne by the bailee[6]. Moreover a proprietor who, by wilfully intermixing his chattels with those of another, has destroyed the evidence by which the innocent proprietor could show how much he has lost must suffer from the resulting uncertainty[7]. In such a case, there is a presumption of utmost value in favour of the innocent proprietor, and he will be awarded the largest proportion of the whole that is consistent with the evidence[8]. If there is a complete absence of evidence as to the quantity of the innocent proprietor's goods which has been contributed to the mixture, the whole belongs to him[9].

If there is a diversity in quality in the intermixed substances the whole should be divided and a greater allowance made to the owner whose substance is better or finer than that of the other[10].

1 See Justin Inst lib 2, tit 1, s 28.
2 2 Bl Com 405; *Sandeman & Sons v Tyzack and Branfoot SS Co Ltd* [1913] AC 680 at 694–695, HL, per
   Lord Moulton; *Coleman v Harvey* [1989] 1 NZLR 723 (NZ CA) (where the text was approved). The
   doctrine of following trust money is considered in EQUITY.
3 *Indian Oil Corpn Ltd v Greenstone Shipping SA (Panama), The Ypatianna* [1988] QB 345, [1987] 3 All
   ER 893.
4 See *Spence v Union Marine Insurance Co Ltd* (1868) LR 3 CP 427, where the doctrine was applied to
   goods belonging to different owners on board ship, which had become indistinguishable owing to
   the obliteration of identification marks; and *Gill and Duffus (Liverpool) Ltd v Scruttons Ltd* [1953] 2 All
   ER 977, [1953] 1 WLR 1407, where bags of chestnuts in the hold of a ship, which were consigned to
   different merchants, burst on the voyage. As to the limits of the applicability of this doctrine to such
   cases, see *Sandeman & Sons v Tyzack and Branfoot SS Co Ltd* [1913] AC 680, HL. The dictum of Lord
   Russell of Killowen in *Smurthwaite v Hannay* [1894] AC 494 at 505, HL, must be read in the light of
   the latter case. See further SHIPPING; see also Mackeldey's Modern Civil Law (special part), Book 1,
   s 270.
5 *Indian Oil Corpn Ltd v Greenstone Shipping SA (Panama), The Ypatianna* [1988] QB 345, [1987] 3 All
   ER 893; and see *Coleman v Harvey* [1989] 1 NZLR 723 (NZ CA), especially at 726–727 per Cooke P.
   Formerly, it was thought that a bailee who wilfully intermixed his goods with those of another
   proprietor could not claim ownership of any part of the combined corpus, which belonged in its
   entirety to the innocent proprietor: see *Lupton v White* (1808) 15 Ves 432 at 440 per Lord Eldon; 2 Bl
   Com 405; *Colwill v Reeves* (1811) 2 Camp 575 at 576 per Lord Ellenborough: if a man puts corn into
   my bag, in which there is before some corn, the whole is mine, because it is impossible to distinguish
   what was mine from what was his; but it is impossible that articles of furniture can be blended
   together so as to create the same difficulty. But see *Sandeman & Sons v Tyzack and Branfoot SS Co Ltd*
   [1913] AC 680 at 695, HL, per Lord Moulton.
6 *Buckley v Gross* (1863) 2 B & S 566 at 575 per Blackburn J; *Jones v Moore* (1841) 4 Y & C Ex 351.
7 *Indian Oil Corpn Ltd v Greenstone Shipping SA (Panama), The Ypatianna* [1988] QB 345, [1987] 3 All
   ER 893, applying *Armory v Delamirie* (1722) 1 Stra 505.
8 *Indian Oil Corpn Ltd v Greenstone Shipping SA (Panama), The Ypatianna* [1988] QB 345, [1987] 3 All
   ER 893; *Armory v Delamirie* (1722) 1 Stra 505.
9 *Indian Oil Corpn Ltd v Greenstone Shipping SA (Panama), The Ypatianna* [1988] QB 345 at 370–371,
   [1987] 3 All ER 893 at 907–908 per Staughton J.
10 Ayliffe's New Pandect of Roman Civil Law, Book 3, tit 3, p 292.

3. BAILMENT FOR VALUABLE CONSIDERATION

(1) HIRE OF CUSTODY

(i) Nature of the Contract; Bailee's Obligations

1838. Hire of custody distinguished from deposit. The hire of custody[1] is a
contract analogous to that of deposit[2].

The two contracts, however, differ materially in that whilst in deposit there is no
reciprocity of advantage, all the benefit being conferred on the bailor, in the
contract of hire of custody there is a mutual advantage to both the owner of the
chattel and the person who undertakes to keep it safely for reward[3].

The contract of custody for reward, which is consensual[4] and need not be
evidenced by writing, necessitates for its inception the concurrence of the following conditions: (1) the subject matter must be a chattel; (2) the possession of the
chattel must be capable of transfer from one party to the other and must actually be
transferred[5]; (3) the custody of the chattel must be the object of the transfer of
possession; and (4) the transfer of the custody must be temporary and not permanent[6].

Given these conditions, the custodian's obligation for hire commences as soon as by any overt act he evidences an intention of exercising responsibility over the chattel entrusted to him, for instance, by applying a crane to raise goods into a warehouse[7].

1 Ie _locatio custodiae:_ see para 1802 note 9 ante.
2 Ie _depositum:_ see paras 1802, 1806–1819 ante. The liability of an innkeeper (ie the proprietor of a hotel within the meaning of the Hotel Proprietors Act 1956) differs from that of an ordinary bailee and is governed by s 2: see INNS.
3 Story on Bailments (9th Edn), s 442. The reward need not be money; it may be money's worth, and there need not be a specific reward for the custody if there is a reward for services which in fact cover the custody; see _Martin v LCC_ [1947] KB 628, [1947] 1 All ER 783 (hospital taking charge of patient's property); _Andrews v Home Flats Ltd_ [1945] 2 All ER 698, CA (landlords of block of flats providing a room for baggage).
4 _Buxton v Baughan_ (1834) 6 C & P 674.
5 _Ashby v Tolhurst_ [1937] 2 KB 242, [1937] 2 All ER 837, CA (car placed in car park on payment of a fee for which a receipt, called a 'car park ticket', was given: no contract of bailment, but mere licence); _Tinsley v Dudley_ [1951] 2 KB 18, [1951] 1 All ER 252, CA (customer's motorcycle stolen from yard of public house, which was not an inn: licensee held not liable as motorcle had not been delivered into his possession and he was unaware that it had been brought onto his premises; there was therefore no bailment). See also the other cases cited in para 1801 note 8 ante.
6 Pothier's Contrat de Louage, s 6 (mutatis mutandis).
7 _Thomas v Day_ (1803) 3 Esp 262. See also _Chapman v Great Western Rly Co_ (1880) 5 QBD 278; _Cailiff v Danvers_ (1792) Peake 144; _Mitchell v Lancashire and Yorkshire Rly Co_ (1875) LR 10 QB 256. See also _Re Webb_ (1818) 8 Taunt 443; _Bourne v Gatliffe_ (1841) 3 Man & G 643; _Cairns v Robins_ (1841) 8 M & W 258; _Heugh v London and North Western Rly Co_ (1870) LR 5 Exch 51; _Great Western Rly Co v Crouch_ (1858) 3 H & N 183; and CARRIERS.

1839. Care and diligence. A custodian for reward[1] must exercise reasonable care for the safety of the article entrusted to him[2]. The standard of care and diligence imposed on the custodian is that demanded by the circumstances of the particular case[3]. The precautions required of him may therefore be more exacting than those required of a gratuitous depositary[4].

On demand he must return the chattel to the bailor or deliver it in accordance with his instructions[5]; if he fails to do so, or if he misdelivers, the owner, if he has the right to immediate possession, or if there has been conversion or damage to the chattel, may bring an action direct against the wrongdoer[6].

The custodian is therefore bound to take reasonable care to see that the place in which the chattel is kept[7], and the tackle used in connection with it[8], are fit and proper for the purpose, to see that the chattel is in proper custody[9], to protect it against unexpected danger should that arise[10], to recover it if it is stolen[11], and to safeguard the bailor's interest against adverse claims[12]. If the chattel is injured through his negligence, he will not be excused on the ground that it has been subsequently destroyed by inevitable mischance[13].

Apart from special contract, the bailee is not an insurer[14] and therefore, in the absence of negligence on his part, he is not liable for the loss of or damage to the chattel due to some accident[15], fire[16], the acts of third parties, or the unauthorised acts of his servants acting outside the scope of their employment[17]. But if he entrusts the duty to take care of the chattel to a servant or agent, he is answerable for the manner in which that servant or agent carries out his duty[18].

The custodian must deal with the chattel in the manner authorised by the bailor[19]; he may not without authority hand it over to a third party for storage[20]. If he deals with it in a manner not authorised, he takes upon himself the risk of so doing, and may be precluded from relying upon stipulations inserted in the contract in his favour[21]. He will also be liable for any loss or damage, except such as arises from causes which he shows to be independent of his acts or inherent in the chattel itself[22].

The obligation to take due care exists independently of contract. An action based on breach of the obligation can be founded on bailment or on tort[23].

1 Among such custodians are included auctioneers, agisters of cattle, warehousemen, forwarding merchants and wharfingers: Story on Bailments (9th Edn), s 442. See also *Scarborough v Cosgrove* [1905] 2 KB 805, CA; *Paterson v Norris* (1914) 30 TLR 393 (boarding-house keepers); *Olley v Marlborough Court Ltd* [1949] 1 KB 532, [1949] 1 All ER 127, CA (proprietor of hotel which is not an inn); *Martin v LCC* [1947] KB 628, [1947] 1 All ER 783 (hospital managers). As to dock and harbour authorities see SHIPPING.

2 *Port Swettenham Authority v T W Wu & Co (M) Sdn Bhd* [1979] AC 580, [1978] 3 All ER 337, PC; *Coldman v Hill* [1919] 1 KB 443, CA; *British Road Services Ltd v Arthur V Crutchley & Co Ltd (Factory Guards Ltd, third parties)* [1968] 1 All ER 811, [1968] 1 Lloyd's Rep 271, CA; *Lockspeiser Aircraft Ltd v Brooklands Aircraft Co Ltd* (1990) Times, 7 March.

3 *Houghland v R R Low (Luxury Coaches) Ltd* [1962] 1 QB 694 at 698, [1962] 2 All ER 159 at 161, CA. See also para 1803 ante.

4 *Port Swettenham Authority v T W Wu & Co (M) Sdn Bhd* [1979] AC 580 at 589, [1978] 3 All ER 337 at 339, PC; *Garlick v W & H Rycroft Ltd* [1982] CAT 277. See para 1815 ante; and *Samuel v Westminster Wine Co Ltd* (1959) Times, 16 May. For a claim see 6 Court Forms (2nd Edn) (1989 Issue) 240, Form 12. See also *Coggs v Bernard* (1703) 2 Ld Raym 909 at 914, 916 per Holt CJ, and *Morris v C W Martin & Sons Ltd* [1966] 1 QB 716 at 725–726, [1965] 2 All ER 725 at 731, CA, per Lord Denning MR; *James Buchanan & Co Ltd v Hay's Transport Services Ltd and Duncan Barbour & Son Ltd* [1972] 2 Lloyd's Rep 535. See Jones on Bailments (4th Edn) 86, 87; *Dean v Keate* (1811) 3 Camp 4; and see the note to that case at 3 Camp 5.

5 *Hooper v London and North Western Rly Co* (1880) 50 LJQB 103 at 105, DC; *Alexander v Railway Executive* [1951] 2 KB 882 at 884–885, [1951] 2 All ER 442 at 444. For a claim see 6 Court Forms (2nd Edn) (1989 Issue) 233, 239, Forms 2, 11. A delivery order is a mere authority to a buyer to receive possession of goods; by itself it spells no promise of delivery: *Alicia Hosiery Ltd v Brown Shipley & Co Ltd* [1970] 1 QB 195 at 198, [1969] 2 All ER 504 at 510. For the meaning of delivery see SALE OF GOODS vol 41 para 757.

6 *Manders v Williams* (1849) 4 Exch 339 at 314; *Kahler v Midland Bank Ltd* [1950] AC 24, [1949] 2 All ER 621, HL. See further para 1888 post.

7 *Searle v Laverick* (1874) LR 9 QB 122; *Brabant v King* [1895] AC 632, PC; *Turner v Stallibrass* [1898] 1 QB 56, CA; *Martin v LCC* [1947] KB 628, [1947] 1 All ER 783; *British Road Services Ltd v Arthur V Crutchley & Co Ltd (Factory Guards Ltd, third parties)* [1968] 1 All ER 811, [1968] 1 Lloyd's Rep 271, CA. Cf *Marfell v South Wales Rly Co* (1860) 8 CBNS 525 at 537 per Byles J. See *Saunders (Mayfair) Furs Ltd v Chas Wm Davies Ltd* (1965) 109 Sol Jo 922.

8 *Thomas v Day* (1803) 4 Esp 262.

9 *Quiggin v Duff* (1836) 1 M & W 174 at 180 per Lord Abinger CB. Cf *Re United Service Co, Johnston's Claim* (1870) 6 Ch App 212. It is not sufficient for the bailee merely to institute a safe security system if he fails on a given occasion to operate that system with reasonable diligence and care: *Spriggs v Sotheby Parke Bernet & Co* [1986] 1 Lloyd's Rep 487, CA; *Port Swettenham Authority v T W Wu & Co (M) Sdn Bhd* [1979] AC 580, [1978] 3 All ER 337, PC; *Global Dress Co Ltd v W H Boase & Co Ltd* [1966] 2 Lloyd's Rep 72, CA; Palmer on Bailment (1979) Chapter 13.

10 *Brabant v King* [1895] AC 632, PC: see at 640 per Lord Watson. See also *Liverpool Grain Storage and Transit Co Ltd v Charlton and Bagshaw* (1918) 146 LT Jo 20, HL. But if the bailee provides a reasonably fit place for storing the chattels he is not responsible if that place proves defective under exceptional and unlooked-for stress: *Searle v Laverick* (1874) LR 9 QB 122; *Broadwater v Blot* (1817) Holt NP 547; *Edwards v Newland & Co (E Burchett Ltd, third parties)* [1950] 2 KB 534 at 540, [1950] 1 All ER 1072 at 1080, CA, per Somervell LJ (premises damaged by enemy action).

11 The duty to seek to recover the stolen chattel exists even though the theft occurred without default on the part of the bailee: *Coldman v Hill* [1919] 1 KB 443, CA.

12 *Ranson v Platt* [1911] 2 KB 291, CA. See para 1882 post.

13 Story on Bailments (9th Edn), s 450 (a).

14 *Coggs v Bernard* (1703) 2 Ld Raym 909 at 918 per Holt CJ: 'He is only to do the best he can. And if he be robbed it is a good account. If he receives money and keeps it locked up with reasonable care he shall not be answerable for it though it be stolen'. See also *Liver Alkali Co v Johnson* (1874) LR 9 Exch 338, Ex Ch; *Consolidated Tea and Lands Co v Oliver's Wharf* [1910] 2 KB 395.

15 *Searle v Laverick* (1874) LR 9 QB 122 (building collapsing).
16 *Garside v Trent and Mersey Navigation Proprietors* (1792) 4 Term Rep 581; *Chapman v Great Western Rly Co* (1880) 5 QBD 278; *Turner v Civil Service Supply Association* [1926] 1 KB 50; *Fagan v Green and Edwards Ltd* [1926] 1 KB 102; *Watkins v Cottell* [1916] 1 KB 10; *F & C Clarke Ltd and Pickwick Foods Ltd v Redburn Wharves Ltd* [1974] 1 Lloyd's Rep 52.
17 *Finucane v Small* (1795) 1 Esp 315 (theft); *Mintz v Silverton* (1920) 36 TLR 399 (theft by servant, there being no negligence in selecting the servant); contrast *Williams v Curzon Syndicate Ltd* (1919) 35 TLR 475, CA; and *Nahhas v Pier House (Cheyne Walk) Management Ltd* (1984) 270 Estates Gazette 328; *Sanderson v Collins* [1904] 1 KB 628, CA (servant took out carriage for his own purpose, without his master's knowledge); *Central Motors (Glasgow) Ltd v Cessnock Garage and Motor Co* 1925 SC 796 (night watchman of garage took out car for his own purpose, the master having delegated to him the duty of keeping the car safely); *Aitchison v Page Motors Ltd* (1935) 154 LT 128 (manager of garage, with authority to do so, collected customer's car from manufacturer's works, and used it for his own purposes).
18 *Port Swettenham Authority v T W Wu & Co (M) Sdn Bhd* [1979] AC 580, [1978] 3 All ER 337, PC; *Morris v C W Martin & Sons Ltd* [1966] 1 QB 716 at 728, 736, 741, [1956] 2 All ER 725 at 732, 737, 740, CA (sub-bailee liable for his servant's theft). See *Adams (Durham) Ltd and Day v Trust Houses Ltd* [1960] 1 Lloyd's Rep 380 at 386 (unauthorised driving of car by servant), and *British Road Services Ltd v Arthur V Crutchley & Co Ltd (Factory Guards Ltd, third parties)* [1968] 1 All ER 811 at 820, 824, CA (negligence of independent contractor).
19 *Streeter v Horlock* (1822) 1 Bing 34 at 36; *Lilley v Doubleday* (1881) 7 QBD 510 at 511 per Grove J.
20 *Edwards v Newland & Co (E Burchett Ltd, third parties)* [1950] 2 KB 534, [1950] 1 All ER 1072, CA.
21 *Gibaud v Great Eastern Rly Co* [1921] 2 KB 426 at 431, CA, per Lord Sterndale MR, and at 435 per Scrutton LJ; *London and North Western Rly Co v Neilson* [1922] 2 AC 263 at 273–274, HL, per Lord Atkinson; *Buerger v Cunard SS Co* [1925] 2 KB 646 at 663, CA, per Atkin LJ; affd sub nom *Cunard SS Co v Buerger* [1927] AC 1, HL; *Alexander v Railway Executive* [1951] 2 KB 882, [1951] 2 All ER 442 (allowing an unauthorised person to have access to goods deposited in a railway parcels office); *Garnham, Harris and Elton Ltd v Alfred W Ellis (Transport) Ltd* [1967] 2 All ER 940, [1967] 1 WLR 940 (unauthorised sub-bailment).
22 *Davis v Garrett* (1830) 6 Bing 716 at 724 per Tindal CJ; *James Morrison & Co Ltd v Shaw, Savill and Albion Co Ltd* [1916] 2 KB 783 at 795–796, CA, per Swinfen Eady LJ, and at 800 per Phillimore LJ; *Lilley v Doubleday* (1881) 7 QBD 510 (where the defendant contracted to warehouse certain goods for the plaintiff at a particular place but, contrary to the terms of his agreement, he warehoused part of them at another place where, without any negligence on his part, they were destroyed); *Edwards v Newland & Co (E Burchett Ltd, third parties)* [1950] 2 KB 534, [1950] 1 All ER 1072, CA, where the defendants, who had undertaken to store furniture, subcontracted for the storage with a third party without the bailor's knowledge. Cf *Shaw & Co v Symmons & Sons* [1917] 1 KB 799 (goods destroyed by fire when detained in breach of contract); and see also paras 1819, 1824, 1833 ante.
23 *Jackson v Mayfair Window Cleaning Co Ltd* [1952] 1 All ER 215 at 218. See also *Chesworth v Farrar* [1967] 1 QB 407, [1966] 2 All ER 107. See further the Torts (Interference with Goods) Act 1977 s 2 (2); and TORT. See also para 1887 post; and PRACTICE AND PROCEDURE.

1840. Limitation of bailee's liability. The bailee may limit or relieve himself from his common law liability[1] by special conditions in the contract[2]; but in cases of ambiguity these will be strictly construed[3]. They will be held not to exempt him from responsibility for losses due to his negligence unless the words used are clear and adequate for the purpose[4].

The burden is on the bailee to prove[5] that the loss or damage to the chattel occurred without any neglect, default or misconduct on his part or on the part of any servant to whom he may have delegated his duty[6], or that it occurred by negligence of a kind from liability for which he is exempted[7]. The more destructive or restrictive of rights an exempting condition is, the clearer must be the indication, by some sufficiently prominent or explicit notice, that the bailor is to be bound by it[8].

The construction of exemption clauses in cases of misdelivery may give rise to special difficulty[9]. Very carefully chosen words are required to protect a bailee from liability for misdelivery[10]. Unauthorised delivery ordinarily goes to the root of the relationship of bailor and bailee and may not be excused under the terms of a general exemption clause[11]. The question depends ultimately, however, upon the language of the clause. If it is clear and specific enough to apply to the particular breach (however severe) the bailee will be protected. There is no rule of law which prevents an exclusion or limitation clause from being given effect, irrespective of its language, simply by virtue of the severity of the breach or its consequences[12].

Where conditions are relied on the custodian must show that the bailor knew or should reasonably have known of them and can thus be taken to have assented to them; the mere fact that they are the custodian's usual terms will not be sufficient[13]. Moreover, a bailee may deprive himself of the right to rely on a contractual exemption by going outside the purview of the contract[14] or by innocent misrepresentation[15].

1 The exclusion and restriction of liability for negligence and breach of contract is now subject to the provisions of the Unfair Contract Terms Act 1977; see CONTRACT.

2 *Van Toll v South Eastern Rly Co* (1862) 12 CBNS 76 at 84 per Erle CJ; *Harris v Great Western Rly Co* (1876) 1 QBD 515, approved in *Gibaud v Great Eastern Rly Co* [1921] 2 KB 426, CA; *Joseph Travers & Sons Ltd v Cooper* [1915] 1 KB 73, CA; *Barton v Ruislip Dog Sanatorium Ltd* (1917) 33 TLR 458; *Reynolds v Boston Deep Sea Fishing and Ice Co Ltd* (1922) 38 TLR 429, CA; *Rutter v Palmer* [1922] 2 KB 87, CA; *Orchard v Connaught Club Ltd* (1930) 46 TLR 214; *H M F Humphrey Ltd v Baxter, Hoare & Co Ltd* (1933) 149 LT 603 (buyer of goods stored in warehouse bound by conditions of contract made between warehouseman and seller); *British Traders and Shippers Ltd v Ubique Transport and Motor Engineering Co (London) Ltd and Port of London Authority* [1952] 2 Lloyd's Rep 236 (where the bailees were held not to be relieved from liability); *Hollier v Rambler Motors (A M C) Ltd* [1972] 2 QB 71, [1972] 1 All ER 399, CA; *Spriggs v Sotheby Parke Bernet & Co* [1986] 1 Lloyd's Rep 487, CA. Cf *Calico Printers' Association Ltd v Barclays Bank* (1931) 145 LT 51, CA. See also note 11 infra; *L Harris (Harella) Ltd v Continental Express Ltd and Burn Transit Ltd* [1961] 1 Lloyd's Rep 251. As to whether a sub-bailee can rely on an exempting condition made between the bailor and the bailee see *Morris v C W Martin & Sons Ltd* [1966] 1 QB 716 at 729, 731, 741, [1965] 2 All ER 725 at 733, 734, 740, CA; *Singer Co (UK) Ltd v Tees and Hartlepool Port Authority* [1988] 2 Lloyd's Rep 164; and see para 1841 post. As to the exclusion or limitation of liability for goods deposited at railway left luggage offices see the British Railways Board Passenger Conditions of Carriage, June 1988, Condition 57 (maximum liability for items deposited at one time, £500, in respect of loss, delay or damage). As to the incorporation and construction of conditions see *Richardson, Spence & Co and Lord Gough SS Co v Rowntree* [1899] AC 217, HL; *Parker v South Eastern Rly Co, Gabell v South Eastern Rly Co* (1877) 2 CPD 416; *Lyons & Co v Houghton* [1915] 1 KB 489 at 502, DC, per Atkin J.

3 This is on the general principle that a person wishing to exempt himself from his legal liabilities must do so in express and unambiguous terms; see *Price & Co v Union Lighterage Co* [1903] 1 KB 750; affd [1904] 1 KB 412, CA; *Rutter v Palmer* [1922] 2 KB 87 at 94, CA; *Producer Meats (North Island) Ltd v Thomas Borthwick & Sons (Australia) Ltd* [1964] 1 NZLR 700, [1965] 1 Lloyd's Rep 130 (NZ CA), where the words used were held to be inadequate to exempt the respondents from negligence). But the courts should not manufacture ambiguity, and should endeavour to give effect to commercial contracts in accordance with their ordinary, common-sense meaning: *Photo Production Ltd v Securicor Transport Ltd* [1980] AC 827 at 851, [1980] 1 All ER 556 at 568, HL, per Lord Diplock.

4 *Canada SS Lines Ltd v R* [1952] AC 192 at 207–208, [1952] 1 All ER 305 at 309, PC; *Olley v Marlborough Court Ltd* [1949] 1 KB 532, [1949] 1 All ER 127, CA; *Aldersade v Hendon Laundry Ltd* [1945] KB 189, [1945] 1 All ER 244, CA; *Gillespie Bros & Co Ltd v Roy Bowles Transport Ltd* [1973] QB 400, [1973] 1 All ER 193; *Lamport & Holt Lines Ltd v Coubro & Scrutton (M & I) Ltd and Coubro & Scrutton (Riggers and Shipwrights) Ltd, The Raphael* [1982] 2 Lloyd's Rep 42, CA; and see CONTRACT. Cf also *Chapelton v Barry UDC* [1940] 1 KB 532, [1940] 1 All ER 356, CA. See also the text to note 7 infra.

5 Ie provided that the case against him has not been pleaded solely in negligence: see *J Spurling Ltd v Bradshaw* [1956] 2 All ER 121 at 125, [1956] 1 WLR 461 at 466, CA, per Denning LJ. See para 1843 note 3 post.

6 *Morris v C W Martin & Sons Ltd* [1966] 1 QB 716 at 726, [1965] 2 All ER 725 at 731, CA, per Lord Denning MR; *Port Swettenham Authority v T W Wu & Co (M) Sdn Bhd* [1979] AC 580, 3 All ER 337, PC. For claims see 6 Court Forms (2nd Edn) (1989 Issue) 242, 244–245, Forms 15, 19, 20.

7 *Woolmer v Delmer Price Ltd* [1955] 1 QB 291, [1955] 1 All ER 377 (unexplained loss); approved in *Levison v Patent Steam Carpet Cleaning Co Ltd* [1978] QB 69, [1977] 3 All ER 498, CA. See also *Aktieselskabet de Danske Sukkerfabrikker v Bajamar Compania Naviera SA, The Torenia* [1983] 2 Lloyd's Rep 210.

8 *Thornton v Shoe Lane Parking Ltd* [1971] 2 QB 163, [1971] 1 All ER 686, CA. See also *Mendelssohn v Normand Ltd* [1970] 1 QB 177, [1969] 2 All ER 1215, CA; *Metaalhandel J A Magnus BV v Ardfields Transport Ltd and Eastfell Ltd (t/a Jones Transport)* [1988] 1 Lloyd's Rep 197.

9 *Sydney City Council v West* [1966] CLY 536, [1966] ALT 538 (Aust HC), where it was held by a majority of three to two that the bailee was not exempted from negligent misdelivery. Three judges considered that exemption could have been achieved by adequate wording, and the two judges in the minority considered that it had been. Two of the judges in the majority held that unauthorised delivery, being not a mere act of negligence in relation to some act authorised by the bailment contract, precluded the bailee from relying on the exemption clause. See also *Hollins v J Davy Ltd* [1963] 1 QB 844, [1963] 1 All ER 370.

10 *Ashby v Tolhurst* [1937] 2 KB 242 at 258, [1937] 2 All ER 837 at 847, CA, per Scott LJ. See *Hollins v J Davy Ltd* [1963] 1 QB 844, [1963] 1 All ER 370, where the words were held to be sufficient to exempt the bailee from liability for innocent misdelivery.

11 *Sze Hai Tong Bank Ltd v Rambler Cycle Co Ltd* [1959] AC 576 at 587–588, [1959] 3 All ER 182 at 185, PC, per Lord Denning.

12 *Photo Production Ltd v Securicor Transport Ltd* [1980] AC 827, [1980] 1 All ER 556, HL; *Ailsa Craig Fishing Co Ltd v Malvern Fishing Co Ltd* [1983] 1 All ER 101, [1983] 1 WLR 964, HL; *George Mitchell (Chesterhall) Ltd v Finney Lock Seeds Ltd* [1983] 2 AC 803, [1983] 2 All ER 737, HL. See also the Unfair Contract Terms Act 1977 s 9 (1); and CONTRACT.

13 *Walker v Jackson* (1842) 10 M & M 161 at 170; *Long v District Messenger and Theatre Ticket Co* (1916) 32 TLR 596. See also *Victoria Fur Traders Ltd v Roadline (UK) Ltd and British Airways Board* [1981] 1 Lloyd's Rep 570, DC (standard terms of bailee not known to owners and not incorporated into contract with owners' agent); *Metaalhandel JA Magnus BV v Ardfields Transport Ltd and Eastfell Ltd (t/a Jones Transport)* [1988] 1 Lloyd's Rep 197.

14 *Martin v N Negin Ltd* (1945) 172 LT 275, CA.

15 *Curtis v Chemical Cleaning and Dyeing Co* [1951] 1 KB 805, [1951] 1 All ER 631, CA.

1841. Sub-bailment. A sub-bailee is a person to whom the actual possession of goods is transferred by someone who is not himself the owner of goods, but has a present right to possession of them as bailee of the owner[1]. When the sub-bailee accepts possession of the goods he thereby assumes the obligations of a bailee towards the original bailor[2]. The nature of these obligations will, as in the case of an ordinary bailment, vary according to the circumstances in which and the purposes for which the goods are delivered[3]. Thus, if the sub-bailment is for reward, the sub-bailee will owe to the bailor all the duties of a bailee for reward[4]. The bailor has a right of action against the sub-bailee for breach of any of his duties either if the bailor has the right to immediate possession of the goods or if they are permanently injured or lost[5]. The sub-bailee also owes, concurrently, the same duties to the original bailee[6], whose obligations to the bailor are not extinguished by the sub-bailment[7]. The relationship between the bailor and the sub-bailee exists independently of any contract between them, or of any attornment[8].

The bailor is bound by any exclusion or limitation clause[9] contained in the sub-bailment, irrespective of any contract between him and the sub-bailee, if he has expressly or impliedly consented to the making of the sub-bailment on such terms[10]. The bailor may also be bound by any exclusion or limitation clause contained in the sub-bailment, to the imposition of which he has not expressly or impliedly consented, if the exclusion or limitation clause represents an essential part of the sub-bailee's consideration for entering into the sub-bailment, at least if the duty which the bailor seeks to enforce against the sub-bailee would not have arisen but for the fact of the sub-bailment[11].

1 *China-Pacific SA v Food Corpn of India, The Winson* [1982] AC 939 at 959, [1981] 3 All ER 688 at 693, HL, per Lord Diplock. Under a sub-bailment, the original bailee remains responsible for the goods as a bailee and retains a right to the possession of the goods when the sub-bailment expires: cf *Transcontainer Express Ltd v Custodian Security Ltd* [1988] 1 Lloyd's Rep 128, CA, where the intermediate carriers failed to adduce evidence of any right to resume possession of the goods from the sub-carriers. Contrast the substitutional bailment, whereunder the original bailee withdraws from the bailment relationship once he has conferred possession upon the incoming bailee, and the incoming bailee takes his place as the direct bailee of the bailor. This variety of bailment is illustrated by the position of ship-owners once the cargo is off-loaded on to salvage vessels provided by a salvor to carry the cargo to a place of safety: *China Pacific SA v Food Corpn of India* supra. There is a third variety of extended bailment, sometimes known as the quasi-bailment, whereunder the intermediate party does not personally obtain possession of the goods before engaging the ultimate bailee to take possession: see *Metaalhandel JA Magnus BV v Ardfields Transport Ltd and Eastfell Ltd (t/a Jones Transport)* [1988] 1 Lloyd's Rep 197. See also Palmer on Bailment (1979) Chapter 20; [1983] Current Legal Problems 93.
2 *Morris v C W Martin & Sons Ltd* [1966] 1 QB 716, [1965] 2 All ER 725, CA; *Gilchrist Watt and Sanderson Pty Ltd v York Products Pty Ltd* [1970] 3 All ER 825, [1970] 1 WLR 1262, PC; *China Pacific SA v Food Corpn of India, The Winson* [1982] AC 939 at 957–959, [1981] 3 All ER 688 at 692–693, HL, per Lord Diplock: 'A person who holds possession of goods as sub-bailee of an original direct bailee also owes some duty of care towards the owner'. In most cases, it would appear that the sub-bailee's lack of knowledge as to the identity of the original bailor does not affect his obligations towards him: *Balsamo v Medici* [1984] 2 All ER 304 at 310–311, [1984] 1 WLR 951 at 959 per Walton J.
3 *Morris v C W Martin & Sons Ltd* [1966] 1 QB 716 at 731, [1965] 2 All ER 725 at 734, CA, per Diplock LJ.
4 *Morris v C W Martin & Sons Ltd* [1966] 1 QB 716 at 729, [1965] 2 All ER 725 at 733, CA, per Lord Denning MR. As to the nature of such duties see para 1839 ante. See also *James Buchanan & Co Ltd v Hay's Transport Services Ltd and Duncan Barbour & Son Ltd* [1972] 2 Lloyd's Rep 535 (gratuitous sub-bailee).
5 See *Kahler v Midland Bank Ltd* [1950] AC 24, [1949] 2 All ER 621, HL; *Morris v C W Martin & Sons Ltd* [1966] 1 QB 716 at 728–729, [1965] 2 All ER 725 at 733, CA, per Lord Denning MR; *Moukataff v British Overseas Airways Corpn* [1967] 1 Lloyd's Rep 396 at 415 per Browne J.
6 See Pollock and Wright on Possession 169, and *The Winkfield* [1902] P 42, CA, cited in *Morris v C W Martin & Sons Ltd* [1966] 1 QB 716 at 728–729, [1965] 2 All ER 725 at 732–733, CA, per Lord Denning MR.
7 *Gilchrist Watt and Sanderson Pty Ltd v York Products Pty Ltd* [1970] 3 All ER 825 at 829, [1970] 1 WLR 1262 at 1267, PC; Palmer on Bailment (1979) 829–834. See further *Metaalhandel JA Magnus BV v Ardfields Transport Ltd and Eastfell Ltd (t/a Jones Transport)* [1988] 1 Lloyd's Rep 197 (intermediate party under quasi-bailment held liable for defaults of ultimate bailee). The position will be otherwise under a substitutional bailment, where the original bailee withdraws from the relationship and the incoming bailee takes his place as the direct bailee of the original owner: see note 1 supra.
8 *Gilchrist Watt and Sanderson Pty Ltd v York Products Ltd* [1970] 3 All ER 825, [1970] 1 WLR 1262, PC. Cf *Compania Portorafti Commerciale v Ultramar Panama Inc, The Captain Gregos (No 2)* [1990] 2 Lloyd's Rep 395 at 404–406, CA, per Bingham LJ.
9 The principle appears to be confined to terms which purport to exclude or restrict the liability of the sub-bailee: see *The Forum Craftsman* [1985] 1 Lloyd's Rep 291, CA.
10 *Singer Co (UK) Ltd v Tees and Hartlepool Port Authority* [1988] 2 Lloyd's Rep 164, following *Morris v C W Martin & Sons Ltd* [1966] 1 QB 716 at 729–730, [1965] 2 All ER 725 at 733, CA, per Lord Denning MR (obiter); *Hispanica de Petroleos SA v Vencedora Oceanic Navegacion SA, The Kapetan Markos NL (No 2)* [1987] 2 Lloyd's Rep 321 at 336, CA, per Nicholls LJ, and at 340 per Dillon LJ. But the owner against whom this defence is invoked must have bailed the goods to the original bailee before the original bailee bailed them to the defendant; unless the defendant subsequently attorns to the new owner (as to which see para 1884 post), the defendant cannot invoke the defence against someone who becomes the owner of the goods after the goods have been bailed to the defendant: *Compania Portorafti Commerciale SA v Ultramar Panama Inc, The Captain Gregos (No 2)* [1990] 2 Lloyd's Rep 395, CA. In *Singer Co (UK) Ltd v Tees and Hartlepool Port Authority* supra at 168, Steyn J left open the question whether a mere ostensible authority in the original bailee to sub-bail the goods on certain exculpatory terms would suffice to enable the sub-bailee to invoke those terms in an action against him by the sub-bailee. But cf note 11 infra.
11 *Johnson Matthey & Co Ltd v Constantine Terminals Ltd* [1976] 2 Lloyd's Rep 215. The validity of this principle was left open in *Singer Co (UK) Ltd v Tees and Hartlepool Port Authority* [1988] 2 Lloyd's Rep 164 at 168 per Steyn J, but the principle appears to have been approved in *Compania Portorafti*

Commerciale SA v Ultramar Panama Inc, The Captain Gregos (No 2) [1990] 2 Lloyd's Rep 395, CA. But note the qualification stated in note 10 supra which would appear to apply equally to the principle here under discussion. See further *Swiss Bank Corpn v Brinks-MAT Ltd* [1986] 2 Lloyd's Rep 79 at 98 per Bingham J. And see Palmer on Bailment (1979) 1000–1006.

1842. Acts of employees. The custodian bailee is responsible to the owner of the chattel entrusted to him both for the negligence of his agents or employees[1], and for their acts of fraud or other wrongful acts[2], provided that those acts were committed in the course of their employment[3]. Although such a custodian usually incurs no responsibility where an act of fraud or negligence is committed by a servant or agent not in the course of his employment or outside the scope of his authority[4], the custodian may be liable if he was negligent in engaging the servant whose act occasioned the loss[5].

1 *Randelson v Murray* (1838) 8 Ad & El 109. This includes the negligence of the bailor's servants if placed under the bailee's control: *A H Bull & Co v West African Shipping Agency and Lighterage Co* [1927] AC 686, PC; *G W Leggott & Son v C H Normanton & Son* (1928) 98 LJKB 145; *L Harris (Harella) Ltd v Continental Express Ltd and Burn Transit Ltd* [1961] 1 Lloyd's Rep 251; contrast *Société Maritime Française v Shanghai Dock and Engineering Co Ltd* [1921] 2 AC 417n, PC.

2 *Barwick v English Joint Stock Bank* (1867) LR 2 Exch 259 at 265; *Mackay v Commercial Bank of New Brunswick* (1874) LR 5 PC 394; *Dyer v Munday* [1895] 1 QB 742, CA; *Lloyd v Grace, Smith & Co* [1912] AC 716, HL; *Central Motors (Glasgow) Ltd v Cessnock Garage and Motor Co* 1925 SC 796; *Aitchison v Page Motors Ltd* (1935) 154 LT 128; *Adams (Durham) Ltd and Day v Trust Houses Ltd* [1960] 1 Lloyd's Rep 380; *W Carsen & Co Ltd v Eastern Canada Stevedoring Co* [1962] 2 Lloyd's Rep 209 (Ont CA). Cf para 1859 post.

3 *Port Swettenham Authority v T W Wu & Co (M) Sdn Bhd* [1979] AC 580, [1978] 3 All ER 337, PC; *Morris v C W Martin & Sons Ltd* [1966] 1 QB 716, [1965] 2 All ER 725, CA; and see *United Africa Co Ltd v Sako Owoade* [1955] AC 130, [1957] 3 All ER 216, PC; *Rustenburg Platinum Mines Ltd v South African Airways* [1979] 1 Lloyd's Rep 19, CA (obiter). It is commonly stated that the employee must be one to whom the bailee has entrusted the goods: *Port Swettenham Authority v T W Wu & Co (M) Sdn Bhd* supra; *Morris v C W Martin & Sons Ltd* supra; *Swiss Bank Corpn v Brinks-MAT Ltd* [1986] 2 Lloyd's Rep 79. See also the cases cited in note 2 supra.

4 Cf *Swiss Bank Corpn v Brinks-MAT Ltd* [1986] 2 Lloyd's Rep 79; and see *Irving v Post Office* [1987] IRLR 289, CA; *Heasmans v Clarity Cleaning Co Ltd* [1987] ICR 949, CA. See also para 1839 note 17 ante. It is to be observed that the Lord President in *Central Motors (Glasgow) Ltd v Cessnock Garage and Motor Co* 1925 SC 796 reserved for consideration the general question whether the misconduct of the custodian's servant can ever be a defence to the custodian in view of *Lloyd v Grace, Smith & Co* [1912] AC 716, HL. See further *Armagas Ltd v Mundogas SA, The Ocean Frost* [1986] AC 717, [1986] 2 All ER 385, HL. See also AGENCY; EMPLOYMENT.

5 *Williams v Curzon Syndicate Ltd* (1919) 35 TLR 475, CA. See also *Adams (Durham) Ltd and Day v Trust Houses Ltd* [1960] 1 Lloyd's Rep 380; *Nahhas v Pier House (Cheyne Walk) Management Ltd* (1984) 270 Estates Gazette 328.

1843. Onus of proof. When a chattel entrusted to a custodian is lost, injured or destroyed, the onus of proof[1] is on the custodian to show that the injury did not happen in consequence of any neglect on the part of himself, or on the part of his servants acting within the course of their employment[2], to use such care and diligence as a prudent or careful man would exercise in relation to the property[3]. If he succeeds in showing this, he is not bound to show how or when the loss or damage occurred[4]. If a custodian declines either to produce the chattel entrusted to him when required to do so by the owner, or to explain how it has disappeared, the refusal amounts prima facie to evidence of breach of duty on his part, and throws n him the onus of showing that he exercised due care in the custody of the chattel nd in the selection of the servants employed by him in the warehousing[5].

1 See also para 1840 text and notes 4–6 ante. The onus may shift; see *Brazier v Whelan* (1960) Times, 21 July (custody of racehorse which died from disease).

2 The onus extends to requiring the custodian to prove that the chattel was not stolen or otherwise maltreated by any servant of his to whom he had entrusted the chattel, or to whom he had delegated the whole or any part of his duty of care: see para 1861 post.

3 *Mackenzie v Cox* (1840) 9 C & P 632; *Reeve v Palmer* (1858) 5 CBNS 84; *Phipps v New Claridge's Hotel Ltd* (1905) 22 TLR 49; *Brook's Wharf and Bull Wharf Ltd v Goodman Bros* [1937] 1 KB 534 at 538–539, [1936] 3 All ER 696 at 701–702, CA; *Gutter v Tait* (1947) 177 LT 1, CA; *Edwards v Newland & Co (E Burchett Ltd, third parties)* [1950] 2 KB 534, [1950] 1 All ER 1072, CA; *British Traders and Shippers Ltd v Ubique Transport and Motor Engineering Co (London) Ltd and Port of London Authority* [1952] 2 Lloyd's Rep 236 at 256; *W L R Traders (London) Ltd v British and Northern Shipping Agency Ltd and I Leftley Ltd* [1955] 1 Lloyd's Rep 554; *British Road Services Ltd v Arthur V Crutchley & Co Ltd (Factory Guards Ltd, third parties)* [1968] 1 All ER 811, [1968] 1 Lloyd's Rep 271, CA; *Transmotors v Robertson, Buckley & Co* [1970] 1 Lloyd's Rep 224 (failure to discharge onus); *Morris v C W Martin & Sons Ltd* [1966] 1 QB 716, [1965] 2 All ER 725, CA; *Port Swettenham Authority v T W Wu & Co (M) Sdn Bhd* [1979] AC 580, [1978] 3 All ER 337, PC; *Lockspeiser Aircraft Ltd v Brooklands Aircraft Co Ltd* (1990) Times, 7 March; *Fankhauser v Mark Dykes Pty Ltd* [1960] VR 376 (Vict FC); *Hobbs v Petersham Transport Co Pty Ltd* (1971) 45 ALJR 356 (Aust HC); and see para 1806 note 10 ante. As to misdelivery see *Becker v Lavender Ltd* (1946) 62 TLR 504; and cf *Alexander v Railway Executive* [1951] 2 KB 882, [1951] 2 All ER 442. If the bailee or his servants are guilty of negligence, and it is doubtful whether the negligence caused the loss or injury, the onus is on him to prove that it did not: *Joseph Travers & Sons Ltd v Cooper* [1915] 1 KB 73, CA; *Coldman v Hill* [1919] 1 KB 443, CA. Similarly, if he relies on an exemption he must prove that the facts bring him within it: *Levison v Patent Steam Carpet Cleaning Co Ltd* [1978] QB 69, [1977] 3 All ER 498, CA; *London and North Western Rly Co v J P Ashton & Co* [1920] AC 84, HL; cf para 1815 ante. If the time of the loss is material to the question whether the bailee is liable, the bailee must prove when the loss occurred: *Re S Davis & Co Ltd* [1935] Ch 402 (liability of liquidator); *Mitchell v Ealing London Borough Council* [1979] QB 1, [1978] 2 All ER 779 (gratuitous bailment).

4 *Bullen v Swan Electric Engraving Co* (1907) 23 TLR 258, CA; *Brook's Wharf and Bull Wharf Ltd v Goodman Bros* [1937] 1 KB 534 at 539, [1936] 3 All ER 696 at 702, CA. See also paras 1806 note 10, 1815 note 10 ante.

5 *Platt v Hibbard* (1827) 7 Cowen 497 at 500 per Walworth J (a US case). Contrast *H C Smith Ltd v Great Western Rly Co* [1922] 1 AC 178, HL (refusal to account for loss did not amount to proof of 'wilful misconduct' of defendants' servants within an exception to a clause exempting the defendants from liability).

1844. Insurance. Apart from special contract or negligence, a custodian is not responsible to the owner of the chattel entrusted to him in case of its destruction by fire[1], but if he insures it he has such an insurable interest in it that, as against the insurers, he is entitled to recover its full value[2]. A custodian who recovers insurance money occupies the position of a trustee to the owner of the chattel covered by the insurance for its value, less his agreed or reasonable charges for warehousing; and after demand by the owner and refusal by the custodian to account for the proceeds, an action will lie against him at the suit of the owner for money had and received[3].

A custodian will be bound by an express undertaking to insure the goods and will be liable for loss suffered by the bailor in consequence of the custodian's failure to do so[4]. In the absence of such an express undertaking, however, it would appear that (otherwise, perhaps, than in exceptional cases[5]) none will be implied[6].

1 *Sidaways v Todd* (1818) 2 Stark 400 at 401 per Abbott J; *Maving v Todd* (1815) 4 Camp 225. See also the cases cited in para 1839 note 16 ante.

2 *Waters and Steel v Monarch Fire and Life Assurance Co* (1856) 5 E & B 870. See also *Hepburn v A Tomlinson (Hauliers) Ltd* [1966] AC 451, [1966] 1 All ER 418, HL; and *Re Routledge, ex p Bateman*

(1856) 8 De GM & G 263. The chattels destroyed must be covered by the terms of the policy: *North British and Mercantile Insurance Co v Moffatt* (1871) LR 7 CP 25. See further INSURANCE.

3 *Sidaways v Todd* (1818) 2 Stark 400.

4 *Lockspeiser Aircraft Ltd v Brooklands Aircraft Co Ltd* (1990) Times, 7 March.

5 *Eastman Chemical International AG v NMT Trading Ltd and Eagle Transport Ltd* [1972] 2 Lloyd's Rep 25 (carriage).

6 *Koromvokis v Gregsons Auctioneers Pty Ltd* (20 November 1986, unreported), CA.

1845. Work to be done on chattels. The obligations of the custodian in the ordinary course of business are frequently varied and enhanced by the addition of a contract on his part to perform some act in connection with the chattels[1]. This additional undertaking raises a series of obligations between the owner of the chattel and the bailee which are collateral to the bare obligation of safe custody. In such cases a further undertaking on the bailee's part will be implied to exercise capacity, care and fidelity in the conduct of the particular employment for which it was entrusted to him, for when a person undertakes for reward to perform any work he must be considered as bound to use a degree of diligence adequate to the performance of it[2].

1 See eg *Bevan v Waters* (1828) 3 C & P 520; and *Forth v Simpson* (1849) 13 QB 680 (both cases of training horses); *Curling v Wood* (1847) 16 M & W 628, Ex Ch (mooring a ship); *Reynolds v Boston Deep Sea Fishing and Ice Co Ltd* (1922) 38 TLR 429, CA (negligence in placing ship on slipway for repairs). See further SHIPPING.

2 Jones on Bailments (4th Edn) 98–99; and see para 1868 et seq post.

1846. Measure of damages. In an action against a custodian for negligence, the measure of damages recoverable is generally the actual value of the lost chattel[1]. However, the plaintiff may be able to recover any consequential damage flowing from the negligence which is not too remote in law, which may include damages for loss of use of the chattel[2], or profits lost from the destruction of it[3]. Damages for inconvenience or loss of enjoyment may also be awarded in certain circumstances[4]. In cases of deliberate wrongdoing towards the chattel, aggravated and exemplary damages may also be awarded[5].

There is no implied undertaking on the part of a mere custodian to be answerable for consequential damages, and the simple deposit of chattels with him in the ordinary course of business raises no such notice by implication[6].

1 This is subject to any contractual terms which may govern the dealings between the parties.

2 *Davis v Oswell* (1837) 7 C & P 804; *Mediana (Owners) v Comet (Owners, Master and Crew), The Mediana* [1900] AC 113, HL; *Brandeis Goldschmidt & Co Ltd v Western Transport Ltd* [1981] QB 864, [1982] 1 All ER 28, CA.

3 *Bodley v Reynolds* (1846) 8 QB 779; *France v Gaudet* (1871) LR 6 QB 199, Ex Ch; *The Arpad* [1934] P 189, CA. See also *Strand Electric and Engineering Co Ltd v Brisford Entertainments Ltd* [1952] 2 QB 246, [1952] 1 All ER 796, CA.

4 See para 1886 post.

5 See para 1886 post.

6 *Anderson v North Eastern Rly Co* (1861) 4 LT 216; *Building & Civil Engineering Holiday Scheme Management Ltd v Post Office* [1966] 1 QB 247, [1965] 1 All ER 163, CA. As to the measure of damages recoverable by a bailor against a bailee see further *Strand Electric and Engineering Co Ltd v Brisford Entertainments Ltd* [1952] 2 QB 246 at 253–254, [1952] 1 All ER 796 at 800–801, CA, per

Denning LJ; *Lockspeiser Aircraft Ltd v Brooklands Aircraft Co Ltd* (1990) Times, 7 March; and para 1886 post. Compare the liability of a common carrier, who may be liable for loss of market or other consequential damage: *Simpson v London and North Western Rly Co* (1876) 1 QBD 274; see CARRIERS.

1847. Liability to distress. Generally, the owner of goods who has given them o another for custody, is protected from those goods being distrained for payment of rent in respect of the premises where the goods are stored[1].

At common law, chattels delivered to a person exercising a public trade to be carried, wrought, worked up or managed in the way of the trade are privileged from distress for rent due from the person in whose custody they are[2]. Under the Law of Distress Amendment Act 1908, protection is given to the goods of strangers who have no interest in the land[3]. The Act allows such a bailor to recover the goods from the distraining landlord, or to recover their value[4].

Statute governs the levying of distress upon livestock agisted on an agricultural holding[5], and machinery and breeding stock upon such a holding which are not the property of the tenant are privileged from distress[6].

1 See DISTRESS; and the Law of Distress Amendment Act 1908.
2 See DISTRESS. Examples of trades whose custodianship of goods has allowed privilege from distress to be claimed under this rule are warehousemen and wharfingers (*Miles v Furber* (1873) LR 8 QB 77; *Thompson v Mashiter* (1823) 1 Bing 283); factors or agents for sale (*Gilman v Elton* (1821) 3 Brod & Bing 75; *Findon v M'Laren* (1845) 6 QB 891); auctioneers, if on their own premises (*Williams v Holmes* (1853) 8 Exch 861) but otherwise not (*Lyons v Elliot* (1876) 1 QBD 210); and tradesmen who have to work on the goods (*Simpson v Hartopp* (1744) Willes 512; *Muspratt v Gregory* (1838) 3 M & W 677). Agisters and livery stable-keepers were probably on the same footing as warehousemen (*Parsons v Gingell* (1847) 4 CB 545, deciding against the privilege, being disapproved in *Miles v Furber* supra).
3 Subject to certain exceptions: see the Law of Distress Amendment Act 1908 s 4 (amended by the Consumer Credit Act 1974 s 192 (3) (b), Sch 5 Pt I, and the Agricultural Holdings Act 1986 s 100, Sch 14 para 4).
4 See the Law of Distress Amendment Act 1908 ss 1, 2.
5 For the meaning of 'agricultural holding' see the Agricultural Holdings Act 1986 s 1; AGRICULTURE vol 1 (2) (Reissue) para 301.
6 Ibid s 18. The Law of Distress Amendment Act 1908 does not apply to livestock within the Agricultural Holdings Act 1986 s 18: Law of Distress Amendment Act 1908 s 4 (1) (as amended: see note 3 supra). See further AGRICULTURE vol 1 (2) (Reissue) para 334. As to agistment generally see ANIMALS.

(ii) Bailee's Lien

1848. When bailee's lien is available. As a general rule a custodian for reward has, in the absence of some special agreement[1], no lien[2] for his charges upon the chattel entrusted to him for safe custody alone[3], though, unless the terms of the contract exclude it[4], he acquires a lien if, with the owner's consent, he expends labour and skill upon it for its improvement[5]. Nevertheless, by implication of law, wharfingers[6], packers[7], and possibly warehousemen[8], have a general lien[9] for their charges upon the chattels of their bailors, but in the case of wharfingers this implication may be rebutted in any particular district by local usage[10]. This general lien takes precedence of claims by the Crown[11], and the costs of defending it may be added to the security[12].

A general lien is presumed in the case of factors, bankers and stockbrokers, in the absence of a special contract[13], which is always construed strictly against the claimant[14]; consequently such bailees may retain chattels or securities deposited

with them, not only as security for the particular loan in respect of which they wer(
so deposited, but also for a general balance of accounts[15]. A similar rule prevails, a:
part of the law merchant, in certain other trades, although in all such cases th(
custom establishing the existence of a general lien must be proved strictly[16].

In the absence of a particular trade custom[17], a specific lien on a particular chatte]
cannot be enlarged so as to include a general balance of account[18]. If in such a case,
after the bailor demands the particular chattel and tenders the specific amount du(
on it, the bailee refuses to re-deliver, not only is his lien gone[19], but he is also liabl(
to the true owner in an action of trover for the tort of conversion[20]. The mer(
demand by the bailee of a sum exceeding that which is really due to him does not
usually dispense with the necessity of tender by the bailor of the amount actually
due, especially if the bailee particularises his demand and claims to hold the chatte]
for the correct sum to which he is entitled, as well as for the excessive one[21].

A bailee who keeps a chattel to enforce his lien on it cannot charge for keeping
it[22].

The British Railways Board has the right to retain possession of any articles
deposited with it as left luggage against payment of any charges due for their
deposit, and if the stated period for reclaiming them has elapsed, the board may sell
the articles and apply the proceeds of sale towards the unpaid charges and the
expense of arranging the sale[23]. At common law a railway authority has been held
to have a lien on all chattels deposited with it for safe custody[24] for the amount of its
reasonable charges. This lien applies not only against the person who actually
deposited the chattel, but also against its true owner, or a third party, even though
they may not have had privity with the original contracting parties[25].

A lien is exercisable against a bailor owner of a chattel in respect of work done to
it by an artificer at the bailee's instance provided that the work is reasonably
incidental to the bailee's reasonable use of the chattel, and that the owner has not
expressly excluded the bailee's authority to have the work done[26].

1 For an example of a special agreement see *Jowitt & Sons v Union Cold Storage Co* [1913] 3 KB 1.
   Contrast *United States Steel Products Co v Great Western Rly Co* [1916] 1 AC 189, HL.
2 See *Rushforth v Hadfield* (1806) 7 East 224 (common carrier). See also *Majeau Coastal Carrying Co Pty
   Ltd v Coastal Rutile Ltd* (1973) 1 ALR 1 (Aust HC); and para 1877 post.
3 *Judson v Etheridge* (1833) 1 Cr & M 743; *Jackson v Cummins* (1839) 5 M & W 342; *Smith v Dearlove*
   (1848) 6 CB 132. Cf *Orchard v Rackstraw* (1850) 9 CB 698 (no lien by livery stable-keeper for money
   paid to veterinary surgeon at owner's request for attendance on horse).
4 *Forth v Simpson* (1849) 13 QB 680; *Hatton v Car Maintenance Co* [1915] 1 Ch 621. And see *Borden (UK)
   Ltd v Scottish Timber Products Ltd* [1981] Ch 25, [1979] 3 All ER 961, CA (title retention clause;
   ineffective).
5 *Bevan v Waters* (1828) 3 C & P 520; *Scarfe v Morgan* (1838) 4 M & W 270. No lien attaches if the work is
   merely to maintain the chattel in its former condition; *Hatton v Car Maintenance Co* [1915] 1 Ch 621;
   Re Southern Livestock Producers Ltd [1963] 3 All ER 801, [1964] 1 WLR 24. As to workman's lien see
   para 1877 post.
6 *Bock v Gorrissen* (1860) 2 De G F & J 434 at 443 per Lord Campbell LC; *Spears v Hartly* (1800) 3 Esp 81.
7 *Re Witt, ex p Shubrook* (1876) 2 Ch D 489, CA. Cf *K Chellaram & Sons (London) Ltd v Butlers
   Warehousing and Distribution Ltd* [1978] 2 Lloyd's Rep 412, CA (consolidators of goods: no lien).
8 *R v Humphery* (1825) M'Cle & Yo 173; but see *Leuckhart v Cooper* (1836) 3 Bing NC 99. See also *Re
   Catford, ex p Carr v Ford* (1894) 71 LT 584; *Hill & Sons v London Central Markets Cold Storage Co Ltd*
   (1910) 102 LT 715. 'Warehouseman', 'wharfinger', 'warehouse' and 'wharf' are defined in the
   Merchant Shipping Act 1894 s 492. For the statutory lien of a warehouseman or wharfinger where
   goods have been placed in his custody under Part VII of that Act (ss 492–501) see s 499; and SHIPPING.
9 For the distinction between a general lien and a particular lien see LIEN.
10 *Holderness v Collinson* (1827) 7 B & C 212. See further SHIPPING. As to usages generally see CUSTOM
   AND USAGE.

1 *R v Humphery* (1825) M'Cle & Yo 173; a decision which seems to have turned on its special facts: *K Chellaram & Sons (London) Ltd v Butlers Warehousing and Distribution Ltd* [1978] 2 Lloyd's Rep 412 at 415, CA, per Megaw LJ.
2 *Moet v Pickering* (1878) 8 ChD 372 at 376, CA, per Cotton LJ.
3 *Bock v Gorrissen* (1860) 2 De G F & J 434. See AGENCY; BANKING; STOCK EXCHANGE.
4 *Kinnear v Midland Rly Co* (1868) 19 LT 387.
5 *Re London and Globe Finance Corpn* [1902] 2 Ch 416; *Jones v Peppercorne* (1858) John 430.
6 *Re Spotten & Co* (1877) 11 IR Eq 412. For cases where liquidation or bankruptcy avoids a general lien by contract, see *Re Bushell, ex p Great Western Rly Co* (1882) 22 ChD 470, CA; *Wiltshire Iron Co v Great Western Rly Co* (1871) LR 6 QB 776; cf *George Barker (Transport) Ltd v Eynon* [1974] 1 All ER 900, [1974]1 WLR 462, CA; and see generally LIEN.
7 *Re Spotten & Co* (1877) 11 IR Eq 412; *Bock v Gorrissen* (1860) 2 De G F & J 434; *Leuckhart v Cooper* (1836) 3 Bing NC 99.
8 *Jones v Tarleton* (1842) 9 M & W 675.
9 *Dirks v Richards* (1842) 4 Man & G 574; but see *Scarfe v Morgan* (1838) 4 M & W 270.
10 *The Norway* (1865) 3 Moo PCCNS 245 at 265.
11 *Scarfe v Morgan* (1838) 4 M & W 270, an instructive case on liens. See also *Albermarle Supply Co v Hind & Co* [1928] 1 KB 307 at 318–319, CA, per Scrutton LJ.
12 *Somes v British Empire Shipping Co* (1860) 8 HL Cas 338; and see *Delantera Amadora SA v Bristol Channel Shiprepairers Ltd and Swansea Dry Dock Co, The Katingaki* [1976] 2 Lloyd's Rep 372; *Rashtriya Chemicals and Fertilisers Ltd v Huddart Parker Industries Ltd, The Boral Gas* [1988] 1 Lloyd's Rep 342. Aliter, perhaps where the bailee's retention of the chattel is predominantly for the benefit of the bailor: *China Pacific SA v Food Corpn of India, The Winson* [1982] AC 939 at 962–963, [1981] 3 All ER 688 at 696, HL, per Lord Diplock, and at 964, 697 per Lord Simon of Glaisdale.
13 See British Railways Board Passenger Conditions of Carriage, June 1988, Condition 61.
14 *Van Toll v South Eastern Rly Co* (1862) 12 CBNS 76; *Pratt v South Eastern Rly Co* [1897] 1 QB 718, DC; *Roche v Cork, Blackrock and Passage Rly Co* (1889) 24 LR Ir 250; *Anderson v North Eastern Rly Co* (1861) 4 LT 216.
15 *Singer Manufacturing Co v London and South Western Rly Co* [1894] 1 QB 833 at 836, DC, per Mathew J, and at 837 per Collins J. In that case Collins J also based the lien upon the bailee's implied authority. In *Pennington v Reliance Motor Works Ltd* [1923] 1 KB 127 at 129, McCardie J expressed the view that the true ratio in *Singer Manufacturing Co v London and South Western Rly Co* supra was implied authority; but in *Cassils & Co and Sassoon & Co v Holden Wood Bleaching Co* (1914) 84 LJKB 834 at 840–841, CA, Buckley LJ was of opinion that a common law lien apart from contract exists in favour of a carrier or innkeeper and that *Singer Manufacturing Co v London and South Western Rly Co* supra was rightly decided on this ground as well as on the ground of implied authority. Cf *K Chellaram & Sons (London) Ltd v Butlers Warehousing and Distribution Ltd* [1978] 2 Lloyd's Rep 412, CA; *Robins & Co v Gray* [1895] 2 QB 501, CA (innkeeper).
16 *Tappenden v Artus* [1964] 2 QB 185, [1963] 3 All ER 213, CA (repairs to car to make it roadworthy).

1849. Loss of lien. The bailee's lien[1] is lost if the bailee loses possession of the chattel[2], or if he does anything amounting to a waiver[3], or if the identity of the chattel is lost by intermixture or confusion with other chattels of a similar nature belonging to a different owner[4]. The bailee's assertion of a right to retain the chattel otherwise than by way of lien may operate as a waiver of the lien[5].

As a general rule, a right of lien confers no right to sell the chattel[6] unless that right is expressly conferred by statute[7], and sale without right causes loss of the lien[8].

1 See para 1848 ante.
2 *Hutton v Bragg* (1816) 7 Taunt 14; *Pennington v Reliance Motor Works Ltd* [1923] 1 KB 127. Cf *Sweet v Pym* (1800) 1 East 4; *Dicas v Stockley* (1836) 7 C & P 587; *Barratt v Gough-Thomas* [1951] Ch 242, [1950] 2 All ER 1048, CA (solicitor); contrast *North Western Bank Ltd v John Poynter, Son and Macdonalds* [1895] AC 56, HL; *Albermarle Supply Co v Hind & Co* [1928] 1 KB 307, CA. See further LIEN.
3 *Mulliner v Florence* (1878) 3 QBD 484, CA, where the bailee sold the goods and thereby lost his lien; *Hill & Sons v London Central Markets Cold Storage Co* (1910) 102 LT 715.
4 *Grant v Humphery* (1862) 3 F & F 162.

5 *White v Gainer* (1824) 2 Bing 23 at 24 per Best CJ; *Weeks v Goode* (1859) 6 CBNS 367; *Boardman v S.* (1808) 1 Camp 410n; *Dirks v Richards* (1842) 4 Man & G 574.
6 *Pothonier and Hodgson v Dawson* (1816) Holt NP 383 at 385 per Gibbs CJ; *Smart v Sandars* (1848) 5 C 895; *Thames Iron Works Co v Patent Derrick Co* (1860) 1 John & H 93; *Bolwell Fibreglass Pty Ltd v Fole* [1984] VR 97 (Vict SC).
7 Eg the statutory right of a bailee to dispose of uncollected goods; see para 1880 post.
8 Cf *Mulliner v Florence* (1878) 3 QBD 484, CA, where an innkeeper was held not have a right to sell h. guest's horses over which he had a lien. The law on this point was altered by the Innkeepers A. 1878; see INNS. Some liens can be enforced by sale by means of an action asking for such relie (Story's Commentaries on Equity Jurisprudence (3rd English Edn), s 1217). For the statutory powe of a bailee to sell uncollected goods see para 1880 post. The provisions of the Reserve and Auxiliar Forces (Protection of Civil Interests) Act 1951, which restrict the exercise of certain remedies i relation to persons called up or volunteering for service in the armed forces, do not affect any right o power of a person to sell goods in his custody as a bailee if it is a right or power arising by reason c default in the payment of a debt: s 2 (2) proviso (iv).

(2) HIRE OF CHATTELS

(i) Nature of the Contract

1850. Hire of chattels. Hire[1] is a class of bailment. It is a contract by which the hirer obtains the right to use the chattel hired in return for the payment to the owner of the price of the hiring[2]. The general property in the chattel is not changed but remains in the owner[3], although upon delivery the hirer becomes legally possessed of the chattel hired[4], so that if it is lent for a time certain, even the true owner is debarred during that time from resuming possession against the hirer's will and, should he do so, becomes liable in damages for the wrongful seizure[5].

The contract must not be based on an immoral or illegal consideration, nor mus' it conduce to immorality or illegality[6].

Statutory control is exercised over certain types of hiring[7]. Further, it is ar offence to let on hire, or offer to let on hire, a motor cyclist's protective helme' which is not of a prescribed or authorised type[8], and to hire, offer for hire or expose or have in one's possession for hire a flick knife or gravity knife[9].

Certain terms are implied by statute into contracts for the hire of goods[10]. In the Supply of Goods and Services Act 1982 a 'contract for the hire of goods' means a contract, other than an excepted contract, under which one person bails or agrees to bail goods to another by way of hire[11]. An excepted contract is either (1) a hire-purchase agreement[12], or (2) a contract under which goods are, or are to be, bailed in exchange for trading stamps on their redemption[13]. 'Goods' include all personal chattels, including emblements, industrial growing crops, and things attached to or forming part of the land which are agreed to be severed before the bailment concerned, other than things in action and money[14]. For these purposes a contract is a contract for the hire of goods whether or not services are provided or to be provided under the contract, and, subject to other provisions[15], whatever is the nature of the consideration for the bailment or agreement to bail by way of hire[16].

Where a right, duty or liability would arise under a contract for the hire of goods by implication of law, it may, subject to other provisions[17], be negatived or varied by express agreement, or by the course of dealing between the parties, or by such usage as binds both parties to the contract[18]. An express condition or warranty does not negative a condition or warranty implied by the statute unless inconsistent with it[19].

Nothing in the statute prejudices the operation of any other enactment or rule of law whereby any condition or warranty, other than one relating to quality or fitness, is to be implied into a contract for the hire of goods[20].

1 Ie *locatio conductio rei*: see para 1802 text and note 9 ante.

2 Jones on Bailments (4th Edn) 86; Pothier's Contrat de Louage, s 1; 1 Dormat, book 1, tit 4, s 1, art 1. Cf *General Motors Acceptance Corpn (UK) Ltd v IRC* [1987] STC 122, CA (cars supplied by finance company to dealers on sale or return; held not let on hire for the purposes of the Finance Act 1976 Sch 5 para 29 (2) (c) (repealed)). For agreements to hire goods see 12 Forms & Precedents (5th Edn) 150–179, 41–47.

3 As to the nature of the hirer's interest see *Australian Guarantee Corpn Ltd v Ross* [1983] 2 VR 319 at 329–330 per Marks J (Vic Sup Ct, FC); Palmer on Bailment (1979) Chapter 19; Story on Bailments (9th Edn), s 370a. Where the contract of hire is specifically enforceable the hirer may have an equitable interest in the chattel: *Bristol Airport plc v Powdrill* [1990] Ch 744 at 759, [1990] 2 All ER 493 at 502, CA, per Browne-Wilkinson V-C (obiter).

4 As to the right to terminate a written contract for breach of an oral promise made at the time it was entered into see *Quickmaid Rental Services Ltd v Reece Ltd (t/a Forge Service Station)* (1970) 114 Sol Jo 372.

5 Supply of Goods and Services Act 1982 s 7; see para 1853 post. See also Bac Abr Bailment C; *Lee v Atkinson and Brooks* (1609) Yelv 172; *Turner v Hardcastle* (1862) 11 CBNS 683. The measure of damages is the hirer's interest in the chattel: cf *Brierly v Kendall* (1852) 17 QB 937; *Chinery v Viall* (1860) 5 H & N 288; *Johnson (Assignee of Cumming) v Stear* (1863) 15 CBNS 330; *Halliday v Holgate* (1868) LR 3 Exch 299 at 301. In such a case the bailor may also be guilty of theft: *Rose v Matt* [1951] 1 KB 810, [1951] 1 All ER 362, DC.

6 The maxim *ex turpi causa non oritur actio* applies to this as to any other contract: *Pearce v Brooks* (1866) LR 1 Exch 213 at 217 per Pollock CB; see generally CONTRACT.

7 See para 1851 post.

8 Road Traffic Act 1988 s 17 (2), (5) (amended as from a day to be appointed by the Road Traffic (Consequential Provisions) Act 1988 s 4, Sch 2 Pt III para 31). The offence is punishable on summary conviction by a fine not exceeding level 3 on the standard scale: Road Traffic Offenders Act 1988 s 9, Sch 2 Pt I. See ROAD TRAFFIC.

In any enactment contained in an Act passed either before or after the Criminal Justice Act 1982 'the standard scale' has the meaning given by s 37; s 75 (a). A standard scale of fines for summary offences was introduced by the Criminal Justice Act 1982 s 37 (1), to avoid the need, in times of high inflation, for frequent amendment of primary legislation. Where any enactment contained in an Act passed either before or after that Act provides (1) that a person convicted of a summary offence is liable on conviction to a fine or a maximum fine by reference to a specified level on the standard scale, or (2) confers power by subordinate instrument to make a person liable on conviction of a summary offence, whether or not created by the instrument, to a fine or a maximum fine by reference to a specified level on the standard scale, it is to be construed as referring to the standard scale for which s 37 provides as that scale has effect from time to time by virtue either of that section or of an order under the Magistrates' Courts Act 1980 s 143: Criminal Justice Act 1982 s 37 (3). In relation to Acts passed before the Criminal Justice Act 1982, this provision applies where references to the standard scale are substituted by s 46 as read with s 38 or s 40. At the date at which this volume states the law, the standard scale is as follows, in relation to offences committed after 1 May 1984: level 1, £50; level 2, £100; level 3, £400; level 4, £1,000; level 5, £2,000: s 37 (2) (amended by the Criminal Penalties etc (Increase) Order 1984, SI 1984/447, art 2 (4), Sch 4). As from a day to be appointed, the levels are increased to £200, £500, £1,000, £2,500 and £5,000 respectively: Criminal Justice Act 1991 s 17 (1).

9 Restriction of Offensive Weapons Act 1959 s 1 (1) (amended by the Restriction of Offensive Weapons Act 1961 s 1 and the Criminal Justice Act 1988 s 46 (2), (3)). The penalty on summary conviction of this offence is a fine not exceeding level 5 on the standard scale or imprisonment for a term not exceeding six months, or both: 1959 Act s 1 (1) (as so amended). As to the standard scale see note 8 supra.

10 Supply of Goods and Services Act 1982 ss 7–10; para 1853 et seq post. Note also the definition of a consumer hire agreement in the Consumer Credit Act 1974 s 15 (amended by the Consumer Credit (Increase of Monetary Limits) Order 1983, SI 1983/1878). For the effect of the 1974 Act on contracts of hire see HIRE PURCHASE.

11 Supply of Goods and Services Act 1982 s 6 (2).

12 Ibid s 6 (2) (a). 'Hire-purchase agreement' has the same meaning as in the Consumer Credit Act 1974 (see s 189 (1)): Supply of Goods and Services Act 1982 s 18 (1); see generally HIRE PURCHASE.

13 Ibid s 6 (2) (b). 'Trading stamps' and 'redemption' have the same meanings as in the Trading Stamp Act 1964: Supply of Goods and Services Act 1982 s 18 (1). For those definitions see the Trading Stamps Act 1964 s 10 (1) (definition of 'trading stamp' substituted by the Consumer Credit Act 197 s 192 (3) (a), Sch 4 Pt I para 26).
14 Supply of Goods and Services Act 1982 s 18 (1).
15 Ie ibid s 6 (2).
16 Ibid s 6 (3).
17 Ie ibid s 11 (2) (see text and note 19 infra) and the Unfair Contract Terms Act 1977 (see in particula s 7).
18 Supply of Goods and Services Act 1982 s 11 (1).
19 Ibid s 11 (2).
20 Ibid s 11 (3).

1851. Control of hiring. The Secretary of State for Trade and Industry may by order[1] provide for imposing, in respect of the disposal, acquisition or possession o articles of any description under agreements for letting on hire, such prohibitions or restrictions as appear to him to be required for restricting excessive credit[2].

It is an offence to hire, offer or agree to hire, expose or possess for hire[3] any consumer goods[4] which fail to comply with the general safety requirement contained in Part II of the Consumer Protection Act 1987[5]. The Secretary of State may make regulations ('safety regulations') for the purpose of ensuring compliance with the general safety requirement[6]. The regulations may prohibit the hiring or offering to hire or agreeing to hire any goods, or possessing any goods for hire, and contravention of the regulations is an offence[7].

A dealer who lets a television set on hire, arranges for a set to be so let by another dealer, or holds himself out as willing to engage in those activities, must register himself with the Secretary of State for Trade and Industry[8], and must notify the Secretary of State and keep a record each time he lets a set or arranges for another dealer to let one[9].

1 At the date at which this volume states the law, no such order was in force, earlier orders under this power having been revoked.
2 Emergency Laws (Re-enactments and Repeals) Act 1964 s 1 (1) (amended by the Consumer Credit Act 1974 s 192 (3) (a), Sch 4 Pt I para 23 (1), and by virtue of the Secretary of State for Trade and Industry Order 1970, SI 1970/1537). The statute confers concurrent powers on the Board of Trade, which were transferred to the Secretary of State by the 1970 Order. See further HIRE PURCHASE vol 22 para 11.
3 Consumer Protection Act 1987 ss 10 (1), 46 (1). The penalty on summary conviction is a fine not exceeding level 5 on the standard scale, or imprisonment for a term not exceeding six months, or both: s 10 (6). As to the standard scale see para 1850 note 8 ante. At the date at which this volume states the law, level 5 on that scale is at £2,000. See generally SALE OF GOODS vol 41 para 661 et seq.
4 'Consumer goods' means any goods ordinarily intended for private use or consumption, not being (1) growing crops or things comprised in land by virtue of being attached to it; (2) water, food, feeding stuff or fertiliser; (3) gas which has been, is or is to be, supplied by an authorised person; (4) aircraft (other than hang-gliders) or motor vehicles; (5) controlled drugs or licensed medicinal products; or (6) tobacco: ibid s 10 (7).
5 Ibid s 10 (1); as to the general safety requirement see s 10 (2), (3). This provides, in effect, that all goods must be reasonably safe having regard to all the circumstances, including those listed in s 10 (2). Part II of the Act comprises ss 12–16.
6 Ibid s 11. The Secretary of State may also issue prohibition notices and notices to warn: s 13. For a full list of regulations made or having effect under the Act see SALE OF GOODS vol 41 para 659.
7 Ibid s 12. By s 46 (1) 'supply' expressly includes 'hire'.
8 Wireless Telegraphy Act 1967 ss 1 (2), 6 (1) (s 1 (2) amended by virtue of the Post Office Act 1969 s 1 and the Ministry of Posts and Telecommunications (Dissolution) Order 1974, SI 1974/691); Post Office Act 1969 s 3 (1).
9 Wireless Telegraphy Act 1967 s 2 (1) (as amended: see note 8 supra); Post Office Act 1969 s 3 (1). See further TELECOMMUNICATIONS.

1852. Nature of hire purchase. This contract of hire purchase or, more accurately, the contract of hire with an option of purchase, is one under which the owner of a chattel lets it out on hire and undertakes to sell it to, or that it shall become the property of, the hirer, conditionally on his making a certain number of payments[1]. It is a modern development in commercial life, and some rules with regard to bailments which were laid down before hire purchase contracts were contemplated cannot logically be applied to them. Hire purchase contains not only the element of bailment but also the element of sale[2]. It is therefore treated in a separate title in this work[3].

1 *Helby v Matthews* [1895] AC 471, HL; *Re Davis & Co, ex p Rawlings* (1888) 22 QBD 193, CA.
2 *Karflex Ltd v Poole* [1933] 2 KB 251 at 263–264 per Goddard J.
3 See HIRE PURCHASE.

(ii) Owner's Obligations

1853. Right to hire goods and quiet enjoyment. In a contract for the hire of goods[1] there is an implied condition on the part of the bailor[2] that in the case of a bailment he has the right to transfer possession of the goods by way of hire, and in the case of an agreement to bail that he will have such a right at the time of the bailment[3]. In such a contract there is also an implied warranty that the bailee[4] will enjoy quiet possession of the goods for the period of the bailment except so far as the possession may be disturbed by the owner or other person entitled to the benefit of any charge or encumbrance disclosed or known to the bailee before the contract is made[5]. These provisions do not affect the right of the bailor to repossess the goods under an express or implied term of the contract[6].

1 For the meaning of 'contract for the hire of goods' see the Supply of Goods and Services Act 1982 s 6; para 1850 ante.
2 'Bailor', in relation to a contract for the hire of goods, means (depending on the context) a person who bails the goods under the contract, or a person who agrees to do so, or a person to whom the duties under the contract of either of those persons have passed: ibid s 18 (1).
3 Ibid s 7 (1). Cf SALE OF GOODS vol 41 para 687.
4 'Bailee', in relation to a contract for the hire of goods, means (depending on the context) a person to whom the goods are bailed under the contract, or a person to whom the goods are bailed under the contract, or a person to whom they are to be so bailed, or a person to whom the rights under the contract of either of those persons have passed: ibid s 18 (1).
5 Ibid s 7 (2). And see *Lee v Atkinson and Brooks* (1609) Yelv 172; *Warman v Southern Counties Car Finance Corpn Ltd* [1949] 2 KB 576, [1949] 1 All ER 711. Cf *European and Australian Royal Mail Co Ltd v Royal Mail Steam Packet Co* (1861) 30 LJCP 247. As to exclusion of these terms see the Supply of Goods and Services Act 1982 s 11; para 1850 ante; the Unfair Contract Terms Act 1977 s 7; and CONTRACT.
6 Supply of Goods and Services Act 1982 s 7 (3). As to whether the hirer may be entitled to equitable relief from forfeiture see EQUITY vol 16 paras 1447–1451.

1854. Correspondence with description. Where, under a contract for the hire of goods[1], the bailor[2] bails or agrees to bail the goods by description[3], there is an implied condition that the goods will correspond with the description[4]. If under the contract the bailor bails or agrees to bail goods by reference to a sample as well as a description it is not sufficient that the bulk of the goods corresponds with the sample if the goods do not also correspond with the description[5].
Provision is made for exclusion of these terms[6].

1 For the meaning of 'contract for the hire of goods' see the Supply of Goods and Services Act 1982 s 6; para 1850 ante.
2 For the meaning of 'bailor' see ibid s 18 (1); para 1853 note 2 ante.
3 Ibid s 8 (1). A contract is not prevented from being by description by reason only that, being exposed for supply, the goods are selected by the bailee: s 8 (4).
4 Ibid s 8 (2).
5 Ibid s 8 (3).
6 See ibid s 11; para 1850 ante; the Unfair Contract Terms Act 1977 (see in particular s 7); and CONTRACT.

1855. Fitness and merchantable quality. Except as otherwise provided[1] and subject to the provisions of any other enactment, there is no implied condition or warranty about the quality or fitness for any particular purpose of goods bailed under a contract for the hire of goods[2].

Where, under such a contract, the bailor[3] bails goods in the course of a business[4], there is an implied condition that the goods supplied under the contract are of merchantable quality[5]. There is, however, no such condition as regards defects specifically drawn to the bailee's attention before the contract is made, or, if the bailee[6] examines the goods before the contract is made, as regards defects which that examination ought to reveal[7].

The following provision applies where, under a contract for the hire of goods, the bailor bails goods in the course of a business[8] and the bailee, expressly or by implication, makes known to the bailor in the course of negotiations conducted by him in relation to the making of the contract, or to a credit-broker[9] in the course of negotiations conducted by that broker in relation to goods sold by him to the bailor before forming the subject matter of the contract, any particular purpose for which the goods are being bailed[10]. In that case there is an implied condition that the goods supplied under the contract are reasonably fit for that purpose, whether or not that is a purpose for which such goods are commonly supplied[11]. This provision does not apply, however, where the circumstances show that the bailee does not rely, or that it is unreasonable for him to rely, on the skill or judgment of the bailor or person by whom the antecedent negotiations are conducted[12].

An implied condition or warranty about quality or fitness for a particular purpose may be annexed by usage to a contract for the hire of goods[13].

The above provisions apply to a bailment by a person who in the course of a business is acting as agent for another as they apply to a bailment by a principal in the course of a business, except where that other is not bailing in the course of a business and either the bailee knows that fact or reasonable steps are taken to bring it to the bailee's notice before the contract concerned is made[14].

Provision is made for the exclusion of these terms[15].

1 Ie by the Supply of Goods and Services Act 1982 ss 9 (see text and notes infra), 10 (see para 1856 post).
2 Ibid s 9 (1). For the meaning of 'contract for the hire of goods' see s 6; para 1850 ante.
3 For the meaning of 'bailor' see ibid s 18 (1); para 1853 note 2 ante.
4 'Business' includes a profession and the activities of any government department or local or public authority: ibid s 18 (1).
5 Ibid s 9 (2). Goods of any kind are of merchantable quality if they are as fit for the purpose or purposes for which goods of that kind are commonly supplied as it is reasonable to expect having regard to any description applied to them, the consideration for the bailment, if relevant, and all other relevant circumstances: s 9 (9).
6 For the meaning of 'bailee' see ibid s 18 (1); para 1853 note 4 ante.
7 Ibid s 9 (3).
8 See note 4 supra.

9 'Credit-broker' means a person acting in the course of a business of credit brokerage carried on by him: Supply of Goods and Services Act 1982 s 18 (1). 'Credit-brokerage' means the effecting of introductions (a) of individuals desiring to obtain credit to persons carrying on any business so far as it relates to the provision of credit; or (b) of individuals desiring to obtain goods on hire to persons carrying on a business which comprises or relates to the bailment of goods under a contract for the hire of goods; or (c) of individuals desiring to obtain credit, or to obtain goods on hire, to other credit-brokers: s 18 (1).
10 Ibid s 9 (4).
11 Ibid s 9 (5). At common law, it has been held that, in the case of a hiring of a specific motor vehicle, the lessor's obligation to provide a vehicle which is reasonably fit for its purpose is not a continuing obligation but need be satisfied only at the commencement of the hiring: *UCB Leasing Ltd v Holton* [1987] RTR 362, CA (but cf at 375 per Balcombe LJ: position may be otherwise in relation to the hiring of a single item of unspecific domestic equipment such as a gas stove). See also SALE OF GOODS.
12 Supply of Goods and Services Act 1982 s 9 (6).
13 Ibid s 9 (7). See also SALE OF GOODS vol 41 paras 691–696.
14 Ibid s 9 (8).
15 See ibid s 11; para 1850 ante; the Unfair Contract Terms Act 1977 s 7; and CONTRACT.

1856. Sample. Where, under a contract for the hire of goods[1], the bailor[2] bails or agrees to bail the goods by reference to a sample[3] there is an implied condition (1) that the bulk will correspond with the sample in quality[4]; and (2) that the bailee[5] will have a reasonable opportunity of comparing the bulk with the sample[6]; and (3) that the goods will be free from any defect, rendering them unmerchantable, which would not be apparent on reasonable examination of the sample[7].

Provision is made for the exclusion of these terms[8].

1 For the meaning of 'contract for the hire of goods' see the Supply of Goods and Services Act 1982 s 6; para 1850 ante.
2 For the meaning of 'bailor' see ibid s 18 (1); para 1853 note 2 ante.
3 For this purpose, a bailor bails or agrees to bail goods by reference to a sample where there is an express or implied term to that effect in the contract concerned: ibid s 10 (4).
4 Ibid s 10 (2) (a).
5 For the meaning of 'bailee' see ibid s 18 (1); para 1853 note 4 ante.
6 Ibid s 10 (2) (b).
7 Ibid s 10 (2) (c). 'Unmerchantable' is to be construed in accordance with ibid s 9 (9); para 1855 ante. And see SALE OF GOODS vol 41 para 694.
8 See ibid s 11; para 1850 ante; the Unfair Contract Terms Act 1977 s 7; and CONTRACT.

1857. Repair of chattel. Where the owner has agreed with the hirer to keep the chattel lent in proper repair[1], the owner is entitled to resume possession of it for the limited purpose of executing repairs[2]. It is said that the hirer, if actually inconvenienced thereby, is entitled to an allowance or reduction from the rent for the period during which he has been deprived of the use of the chattel[3], but this probably depends on the nature of the thing itself and the inferences to be drawn from the terms of the contract and the surrounding circumstances.

An owner's liability to repair may be discharged by a party to whom he assigns the chattel[4].

1 This may be implied from the nature of the contract: *Sutton v Temple* (1843) 12 M & W 52 at 60, where Lord Abinger said that if a carriage be let for hire, and it break down on the journey, the letter of it is liable, and not the party who hired it. But in general the owner owes no duty in the absence of express contract to service and maintain the chattel during the period of the hiring: *Hadley v Droitwich Construction Co Ltd (Joseph Pugsley & Sons Ltd, third party)* [1967] 3 All ER 911, [1968] 1 WLR 37, CA. The cost of feeding a hired horse falls on the hirer unless it is otherwise agreed (Story on Bailments (9th Edn), s 393), and so does the cost of filling a hired car with petrol.

2 Story on Bailments (9th Edn), s 385.
3 Pothier's Contrat de Louage, s 77; 1 Domat, book 1, tit 4, s 3, art 7.
4 *British Waggon Co v Lea & Co* (1880) 5 QBD 149, DC (distinguishing *Robson v Drummond* (1831) 2 B & Ad 303). As to the assignment of contracts see further CONTRACT.

(iii) Hirer's Obligations

1858. Payment of rent. The hirer must pay at the agreed time the rent agreed upon for the use of the chattel hired[1] and a failure to do so is a breach of contract which entitles the owner to sue for damages and may, in an appropriate case, entitle the owner to bring the bailment to an end and retake possession of the chattel. A persistent failure to pay rent, which evinces an intention no longer to be bound by the contract, will generally be construed as a repudiation of the bailment entitling the owner to retake possession of the chattel and to claim loss of bargain damages[2]. But a failure to pay a single instalment on the due date will not normally amount to a repudiation by the hirer and will not entitle the owner to recover the chattel, unless the contract expressly states that failure to pay a single instalment on the due date will entitle the owner to terminate the contract and recover the chattel[3]. A contractual provision which provides that a failure to pay an instalment on the due date will entitle the owner to retake possession of the chattel will terminate the primary obligations of the parties remaining unperformed but it does not affect the hirer's secondary obligation to pay damages and therefore the measure of damages recoverable is limited to the recovery of the instalments due and unpaid at the date of termination[4]. Where, however, the contract provides that punctual payment of rent is of the essence of the contract then the damages recoverable are not confined to the arrears of rent as at the date of termination but extend to the loss of future instalments (discounted so as to give their present value), the costs of repossession and interest on these sums less the increased value to the owner of the right to earlier repossession of the chattel than would have been the case if the lease had run its course[5]. Stipulation for payment of a greater sum may fall foul of the penalty clause rule[6], unless the sum payable is simply the acceleration of an existing liability or a present debt[7] or the sum is payable on an event which is not a breach of contract[8], in which cases the penalty clause rule is inapplicable. A clause which is held to be a penalty clause is not struck out of the contract but the clause will not be enforced beyond the actual loss of the party seeking to rely upon it[9] and the clause cannot be relied upon as evidence of an intention that the owner be entitled to loss of bargain damages in the event of a breach[10]. If the owner sells the chattel before the end of the period of hire, this operates as a rescission of the contract and so the owner cannot recover the rent in accordance with the contract but is relegated to an ordinary action for damages[11].

If the owner of a chattel hired for a fixed term assigns his interest in the chattel to a third party, the hirer, upon notice in writing of the assignment[12], becomes liable to pay future instalments of rent to the third party[13], unless it can be inferred that the hirer contracted by reference to the owner's personal qualifications, in which case the contract cannot be enforced against the hirer after the owner has assigned his interest in the chattel[14].

1 For forms of pleading see 6 Court Forms (2nd Edn) (1989 Issue) 253, 255, 256, Forms 34, 41, 42.
2 *Interoffice Telephones Ltd v Robert Freeman Co Ltd* [1958] 1 QB 190, [1957] 3 All ER 479, CA; *Yeoman Credit Ltd v Waragowski* [1961] 3 All ER 145, [1961] 1 WLR 1124, CA; *Overstone Ltd v Shipway* [1962] 1 All ER 52, [1962] 1 WLR 117, CA; *Yeoman Credit Ltd v McLean* [1962] 1 WLR 131, 105 Sol Jo 990.

3 *Bowmakers Ltd v Barnet Instruments Ltd* [1945] KB 65, [1944] 2 All ER 579, CA.
4 *Financings Ltd v Baldock* [1963] 2 QB 104, [1963] 1 All ER 443, CA; *Brady v St Margaret's Trust Ltd* [1963] 2 QB 494, [1963] 2 All ER 275, CA; *Charterhouse Credit Co Ltd v Tolly* [1963] 2 QB 683, [1963] 2 All ER 432, CA; *Anglo Auto Finance Co Ltd v James* [1963] 3 All ER 566, [1963] 1 WLR 1042, CA; *United Dominions Trust (Commercial) Ltd v Ennis* [1968] 1 QB 54, [1967] 2 All ER 345, CA; *Eshun v Moorgate Mercantile Co Ltd* [1971] 2 All ER 402, [1971] 1 WLR 722, CA.
5 *Lombard North Central plc v Butterworth* [1987] QB 527, [1987] 1 All ER 267, CA; cf *UCB Leasing Ltd v Holtom* [1987] RTR 362, [1988] TLR 97, CA.
6 *Dunlop Pneumatic Tyre Co Ltd v New Garage & Motor Co Ltd* [1915] AC 79, HL; *O'Dea v Allstates Leasing System (WA) Pty Ltd* (1983) 57 ALJR 172 (Aust HC).
7 *Protector Endowment Loan and Annuity Co v Grice* (1880) 5 QBD 592, CA; *Wallingford v Mutual Society and Official Liquidator* (1880) 5 App Cas 685, HL; *O'Dea v Allstates Leasing System (WA) Pty Ltd* (1983) 57 ALJR 172 (Aust HC); *Oresundsuarvet Aktiebolag v Lemos, The Angelic Star* [1988] 1 Lloyd's Rep 122, CA.
8 *Alder v Moore* [1961] 2 QB 57, [1961] 1 All ER 1, CA; *Export Credit Guarantee Department v Universal Oil Products Co* [1983] 2 All ER 205, [1983] 1 WLR 399, HL; *Associated Distributors Ltd v Hall* [1938] 2 KB 83, [1938] 1 All ER 511, CA; *Re Apex Supply Co Ltd* [1942] Ch 108, [1941] 3 All ER 473; *Campbell Discount Co Ltd v Bridge* [1962] AC 600, [1962] 1 All ER 385, HL.
9 *Jobson v Johnson* [1989] 1 All ER 621, [1989] 1 WLR 1026, CA.
10 *AMEV-UDC Finance Ltd v Austin* (1986) 60 ALJR 741 (Aust HC).
11 *Wright v Melville* (1828) 3 C & P 542.
12 For notice of assignment of owner's rights under a hire-purchase agreement see 12 Forms & Precedents (5th Edn) 230, Form 78.
13 *British Waggon Co and Parkgate Waggon Co v Lea & Co* (1880) 5 QBD 149, DC.
14 *Robson v Drummond* (1831) 2 B & Ad 303 (explained in *British Waggon Co and Parkgate Waggon Co v Lea & Co* (1880) 5 QBD 149, DC: cf *Jackson v Swarbrick* [1870] WN 133. As to the assignment of contracts see further CONTRACT. As to whether such an assignment constitutes a bill of sale see *Re Davis & Co, ex p Rawlings* (1888) 22 QBD 193, CA; and BILLS OF SALE.

1859. Care of chattel. The hirer is, as a general rule, under an obligation to take reasonable care only of the chattel hired, and is not liable for loss or injury happening to it, unless caused by his negligence, or that of his servants[1]. His liability may be extended or diminished by the terms of a special contract, which will be construed with reference to the age and condition of the particular chattel at the time of the hiring[2] and the circumstances of the injury[3].

Apart from special contract, the hirer is not responsible for fair wear and tear[4]; nor is he under any obligation to do any repairs or incur expenses[5] except such as are naturally incidental to the due performance of his obligation to take reasonable care[6]. If he should exceed his duty and execute repairs for which he is not responsible, it is doubtful whether he has any right to claim to be reimbursed by the owner, even though the repairs are necessary and the expenditure reasonable, and therefore it is advisable for him not to execute them without first consulting the owner[7].

A term of the contract between the parties that the hirer shall keep the chattel from injury amounts, by implication, to an authority from the owner to the hirer to do all acts necessary for preserving the thing hired, and, as against the owner, a third party can acquire a lien on the chattel for the cost of repairing it at the hirer's request[8].

The hirer must not use the chattel hired for any purpose other than that for which it was hired; thus, a horse hired as a hack and not for hunting or driving must be used as a hack only, and the hirer will be responsible in case of damage arising from its use for any other purpose[9].

1 *British Crane Hire Corpn Ltd v Ipswich Plant Hire Ltd* [1975] QB 303, [1974] 1 All ER 1059, CA (negligent to order mobile crane to manoeuvre over marshy ground without protection of navi-

mats); *Sanderson v Collins* [1904] 1 KB 628, CA; *Bray v Mayne* (1818) Gow 1; *Handford v Palmer* (1820) 2 Brod & Bing 359; *Dean v Keate* (1811) 3 Camp 4, where the hirer of a horse prescribed for it himself when it fell sick instead of calling in a veterinary surgeon; *Ludgate v Lovett* [1969] 2 All ER 1275, [1969] 1 WLR 1016, CA. The fact that the chattel is injured whilst in the hirer's possession raises a prima facie presumption against him; see *Dollar v Greenfield* (1905) Times, 19 May, HL, per Lord Halsbury LC; *Fawcett v Smethurst* (1914) 84 LJKB 473, and the cases cited in para 1843 note 3 ante, the principle of which would seem to apply here. For an earlier decision to the contrary see *Cooper v Barton* (1810) 3 Camp 5n. For pleadings on a claim for damage during hire, see 6 Court Forms (2nd Edn) (1989 Issue) 257, 263, Froms 44, 54.

2 *Vendair (London) Ltd v Giro Aviation Co Ltd* [1961] 1 Lloyd's Rep 283 (hirers undertaking to return aircraft in 'condition equivalent to when supplied'; hirers liable for fair wear and tear and not merely for deterioration caused by breach of duty of reasonable care); *Schroder v Ward* (1863) 13 CBNS 410; *Brice & Sons v Christiani and Nielsen* (1928) 44 TLR 335; *Moons Motors Ltd v Kiuan Wou* [1952] 2 Lloyd's Rep 80, CA (contract for hire of car making hirer responsible for repairing damage by accident and stating that a policy of insurance was in force in relation to the use of the car, although no policy was in fact in force covering damage by accident: owner not entitled to recover from hirer in respect of damage caused by collision).

3 *British Crane Hire Corpn Ltd v Ipswich Plant Hire Ltd* [1975] QB 303, [1974] 1 All ER 1059, CA (trade usage; printed conditions incorporated into oral contract). See further *Ritchie's Car Hire Ltd v Bailey* (1958) 108 L Jo 348 (car hirer not liable for accident unless due to his act or default; to avoid a cat he hit a tree: held, inevitable accident).

4 See *Pomfret v Ricroft* (1669) 1 Wms Saund 321; *Blakemore v Bristol and Exeter Rly Co* (1858) 8 E & B 1035. These are cases of gratuitous loan, but the principle seems to apply here. See further *Moorhouse v Angus and Robertson (No 2) Pty Ltd* [1981] 1 NSWLR 700 at 708 per Samuels JA (obiter) (NSW CA).

5 *Sutton v Temple* (1843) 12 M & W 52 at 60 per Lord Abinger CB; *Hyman v Nye* (1881) 6 QBD 685. For a case of special contract excluding such repairs see *Reading v Menham* (1832) 1 Mood & R 234.

6 Eg feeding a hired horse: see Story on Bailments (9th Edn), s 393. The same would presumably apply to putting oil into a hired car.

7 Story on Bailments (9th Edn), s 392. As to the lien exercisable by a repairer against a bailor see para 1848 text to note 26 ante.

8 *Keene v Thomas* [1905] 1 KB 136. See para 1878 post.

9 *Burnard v Haggis* (1863) 14 CBNS 45. For pleadings on a claim for wrongful use see 6 Court Forms (2nd Edn) (1989 Issue) 258–259, 265, Forms 46, 59.

1860. Return of chattel. The hirer must return the hired chattel at the expiration of the agreed term[1]. This obligation applies notwithstanding the fact that the task of returning the chattel has become more difficult or costly as a result of some unexpected event occurring independently of the hirer's negligence[2]. But if the performance of his contract to return the chattel becomes impossible because it has perished, this impossibility excuses the hirer provided it did not arise from the fault of the hirer or from some risk which he had taken upon himself[3]. The hirer's common law duty to return the chattel can, of course, be diminished or enlarged by special contract[4].

1 *British Crane Hire Corpn Ltd v Ipswich Plant Hire Ltd* [1975] QB 303, [1974] 1 All ER 1059, CA (which turned on the wording of a special contract); *Mills v Graham* (1804) 1 Bos & PNR 140 at 145 per Mansfield CJ. See also *Ballett v Mingay* [1943] KB 281, [1943] 1 All ER 143, CA, where a minor bailee parted with possession of the goods to a third party who lost them, and the minor was held liable in detinue in the absence of any proof by him that, in parting with the goods, he had not stepped outside the bailment altogether. The last two cases, and *Burnard v Haggis* (1863) 14 CBNS 45, cited in para 1859 note 9 ante, were cases of minor hirers, who cannot be sued upon the contract of bailment unless the thing hired is a necessary, but may be sued upon independent torts committed in relation to the bailed chattel. As to the liability of minors generally see INFANTS, CHILDREN AND YOUNG PERSONS.

2 *British Crane Hire Corpn Ltd v Ipswich Plant Hire Ltd* [1975] QB 303 at 311–312, [1974] 1 All ER 1059 at 1063, CA, per Lord Denning MR, and at 313, 1064 per Sir Eric Sachs.

3 *British Crane Hire Corpn Ltd v Ipswich Plant Hire Ltd* [1975] QB 303, [1974] 1 All ER 1059, CA; *Taylor v Caldwell* (1863) 3 B & S 826 at 838 per Blackburn J. It would seem that the bailee cannot escape his

obligation to return the goods merely by proving that they were destroyed and asserting that the obligation has thus been frustrated; rather he must go further and establish positively that the destruction occurred independently of his default and fell outside his control. In *Jacksons (Edinburgh) Ltd v Constructors John Brown Ltd* 1965 SLT 37, the hired chattel was damaged by fire. In order to exculpate themselves the hirers had only to prove that the fire was accidental, ie that it was not caused by their deliberate act or negligence. See further *Port Swettenham Authority v T W Wu & Co (M) Sdn Bhd* [1979] AC 580 at 590, [1978] 3 All ER 337 at 340, PC, per Lord Salmon: '... The onus is always upon the bailee... to prove that the loss of any goods bailed to him was not caused by any fault of his or of any of his servants or agents to whom he entrusted the goods for safekeeping'; *Aktieselskabet de Danske Sukkerfabrikker v Bajamar Compania Naviera SA, The Torenia* [1983] 2 Lloyd's Rep 210 at 216 per Hobhouse J: '... it does not suffice for the bailee to prove that the goods have been lost or destroyed while in his possession; he must go further and prove that he is protected from liability by some common law or contractual defence'. Neither of the two foregoing authorities involved a bailment by way of hire; rather, they involved bailments for custody and carriage respectively. But it would seem that a similar principle is applicable to contracts of hire. Cf *Joseph Constantine SS Line Ltd v Imperial Smelting Corpn Ltd, The Kingswood* [1942] AC 154, [1941] 2 All ER 165, HL; *J Lauritzen AS v Wijsmuller BV, The Super Servant Two* [1990] 1 Lloyd's Rep 1, CA. As to the effect of impossibility of performance on contracts see generally CONTRACT.

4 *British Crane Hire Corpn Ltd v Ipswich Plant Hire Ltd* [1957] QB 303, [1974] 1 All ER 1059, CA.

1861. Liability for sevant's misconduct. The negligence of the hirer's servant is, if committed within the scope of the servant's employment, the negligence of the master[1]. The master is therefore liable for any want of care towards the hired chattel shown by the servant in the course of his employment[2]. Such liability may arise even though the servant acts in a manner which the master has forbidden, or would not have authorised had he known of the act[3].

The master is also liable where the servant commits a deliberate wrong to the chattel, such as damage or theft, if the master has entrusted the chattel to the servant and has delegated any part of his duty of care to him[4]. In that case, the servant commits the wrong in the course of his employment[5]. But where the master has not entrusted the chattel to the servant and has not delegated any part of his duty of care to the servant, the wrong is not committed in the course of the servant's employment and the master is not liable[6].

1 *Smith v Stages* [1989] AC 928, [1989] 1 All ER 833, HL (not a case of bailment); and see generally AGENCY; and EMPLOYMENT.
2 *British Crane Hire Corpn Ltd v Ipswich Plant Hire Ltd* [1975] QB 303, [1974] 1 All ER 1059, CA (instruction to take mobile crane over marshy ground without navimats). And see *Dollar v Greenfield* (1905) *Times*, 19 May (horse bolting from stable). Cf *Arbon v Fussell* (1862) 3 F & F 152 (negligent entrustment of management of chattel to incompetent servant).
3 *Smith v Stages* [1989] AC 928, [1989] 1 All ER 833, HL; *Limpus v London General Omnibus Co* (1862) 1 H & C 526; and see EMPLOYMENT.
4 *Morris v C W Martin & Sons Ltd* [1966] 1 QB 716, [1965] 2 All ER 725, CA (sub-bailment for work and labour); *Sanderson v Collins* [1904] 1 KB 628, CA, distinguishing *Coupé Co v Maddick* [1891] 2 QB 413; para 1842 ante. And see Palmer on Bailment (1979) 475–494, 750. The onus of negativing such conduct is, in common with the general onus of negativing negligence by the servant, on the hirer: *Port Swettenham Authority v T W Wu & Co (M) Sdn Bhd* [1979] AC 580, [1978] 3 All ER 337, PC (custody); *Transmotors Ltd v Robertson, Buckley & Co Ltd* [1970] 1 Lloyd's Rep 224 (carriage); Palmer on Bailment (1979) 471–472.
5 *Morris v C W Martin & Sons Ltd* [1966] 1 QB 716 at 738–739, [1965] 2 All ER 725 at 739, CA, per Salmon LJ.
6 Cf *Leesh River Tea Co Ltd v British India Steam Navigation Co Ltd, The Chyebassa* [1967] 2 QB 250, [1966] 3 All ER 593, CA.

1862. Measure of damage. A bailor is entitled to recover damages from the bailee if the chattel is damaged or destroyed by the negligence or breach of contract of the bailee[1]. In the event of damage to a chattel, the bailor is entitled to recover the cost of repair plus a sum representing the permanent diminution in value of the chattel[2]. The bailor may also claim damages for loss of use of the property during any necessary period of repair or recovery[3]. In certain circumstances it may be possible to claim loss of profits from damage to a profit-earning chattel[4].

If a chattel is destroyed, then the bailor can recover the value of the goods at the time of their destruction, together with any consequential damages which are not too remote in law[5].

1 Subject to any exclusion clauses in the contract of bailment. See DAMAGES.
2 See *Hughes v Quentin* (1838) 8 C & P 703, where the bailee's injury of an animal led to liability for the farrier's bill for keep and treatment, and the difference between the animal's original and subsequent value.
3 This is often quantified in terms of the cost of hiring an alternative: see *Davis v Oswell* (1837) 7 C & P 804, where the plaintiff was obliged to hire other horses; *Mediana (Owners) v Comet (Owners, Master and Crew), The Mediana* [1900] AC 113 at 117, HL; *Brandeis Goldschmidt & Co Ltd v Western Transport Ltd* [1981] QB 864, [1982] 1 All ER 28, CA; *Hillesden Securities Ltd v Ryjack Ltd* [1983] 2 All ER 184, [1983] 1 WLR 959.
4 This has been said to depend on the knowledge of the bailee of the profit-making capacity of the chattel: see *Bodley v Reynolds* (1846) 8 QB 779 and cf *France v Gaudet* (1871) LR 6 QB 199 Ex Ch; *The Arpad* [1934] P 189, CA; *Strand Electric and Engineering Co Ltd v Brisford Entertainments Ltd* [1952] 2 QB 246, [1952] 1 All ER 796, CA. See DAMAGES vol 12 paras 1164, 1165.
5 See DAMAGES; and TORT vol 45 para 1454 et seq.

(3) HIRE OF WORK AND LABOUR

(i) Nature of the Contract; Owner's Obligations

1863. Nature of contract. Hire of work and labour[1] is a class of bailment based on a contract in which one of the two contracting parties undertakes to do something to a chattel, for example, to carry it or repair it, in consideration of a reward to be given to him[2]. It is essential to constitute a valid contract of this description that there should be some work to be performed in connection with a specified chattel, and that a reward should be agreed to be given in return for the labour[3].

The distinction between this contract and that of sale lies in the fact that the work and labour results in nothing which can properly be deemed the subject of a sale, inasmuch as the chattel upon which the work is performed, or the materials out of which the chattel delivered to the hirer is made, are already the property of the hirer, and do not, as in the case of sale, become his property by virtue of the contract[4]. The contract is none the less one of work and labour where, though the principal materials belong to the hirer, the workman furnishes accessories or ornaments, as in the case of a tailor who is employed to make up the hirer's cloth, and who supplies his own buttons and thread[5]. If proceedings are brought to recover payment for work done and materials supplied for the purposes of the work, the value of the materials should be expressly claimed[6].

Certain terms are implied by statute[7] into contracts for the supply of a service[8].

In the statute, a 'contract for the supply of a service' means a contract under which a person ('the supplier') agrees to carry out a service[9]. A contract of service or apprenticeship is not a contract for the supply of a service[10]. A contract is a contract for the supply of a service whether or not goods are also transferred or to be transferred, or bailed or to be bailed by way of hire, under the contract, and whatever is the nature of the consideration for which the service is to be carried out[11].

1 Ie *locatio operis faciendi*: see para 1802 note 9 ante.
2 Jones on Bailments (4th Edn) 90–91; Palmer on Bailment (1979) Chapter 14. For a claim for loss to goods entrusted to repairers see 6 Court Forms (2nd Edn) (1989 Issue) 240, Form 13. As to carriers see CARRIERS.
3 It does not appear that the consideration need be monetary in order to constitute a contract for the hire of work and labour: cf Pothier's Contrat de Louage, ss 397–402; *Keys v Harwood* (1846) 2 CB 905. Any term in a commercial contract which requires a person to use only union labour or only non-union labour, or to recognise a certain union or unions in fulfilling a contract, is void: Employment Act 1982 ss 12, 13; see further TRADE AND LABOUR.
4 Cf *Lee v Griffin* (1861) 1 B & S 272 at 277 per Blackburn J; and see para 1801 ante. A contract, however, is not necessarily one of sale even where the workman supplies the materials, if the substance of the contract is that skill and labour have to be exercised and the materials are merely auxiliary: see *Grafton v Armitage* (1845) 2 CB 336 (explaining *Atkinson v Bell* (1828) 8 B & C 277); *Clay v Yates* (1856) 1 H & N 73; *Robinson v Graves* [1935] 1 KB 579, CA. Contrast *J Marcel (Furriers) Ltd v Tapper* [1953] 1 All ER 15, [1953] 1 WLR 49; and see further SALE OF GOODS.
5 Story on Bailments (9th Edn), s 423. Cf the cases cited in note 4 supra. Where materials are used in engineering or building operations to construct or erect engines or buildings, the contract will normally be one for work and labour: *Clark v Bulmer* (1843) 11 M & W 243; *Tripp v Armitage* (1839) 4 M & W 687; *Chanter v Dickinson* (1843) 5 Mann & G 253.
6 *Heath v Feeland* (1836) 1 M & W 543; cf *Cotterell v Apsey* (1815) 6 Taunt 322 (contract to build house, supplying labour and materials; value of materials not recoverable as goods sold, though original contract superseded as result of deviation).
7 Supply of Goods and Services Act 1982 Pt II (ss 12–16).
8 Ibid ss 13 (para 1869 post), 14 (para 1868 post), 15 (para 1864 post). The Secretary of State may by order made by statutory instrument, subject to annulment in pursuance of a resolution of either House of Parliament, provide that one or more of ss 13–15 is or are not to apply to services of a description specified in the order; and such an order may make different provision for different circumstances: s 12 (4), (5). See the Supply of Services (Exclusion of Implied Terms) Orders 1982, 1983, 1985, SI 1982/1771, SI 1983/902, SI 1985/1; para 1869 post.
9 Supply of Goods and Services Act 1982 s 12 (1).
10 Ibid s 12 (2).
11 Ibid s 12 (3). Where a right, duty or liability would arise under a contract for the supply of a service by virtue of Pt II, it may, subject to s 16 (2) and the Unfair Contract Terms Act 1977 (see in particular s 3) be negatived or varied by express agreement, or by the course of dealing between the parties, or by such usage as binds both parties to the contract: Supply of Goods and Services Act 1982 s 16 (1). An express term does not negative a term implied by Pt II unless inconsistent with it: s 16 (2). Nothing in Pt II prejudices (a) any rule of law which imposes on the supplier a duty stricter than that imposed by s 13 (see para 1869 post) or (b) subject to head (a) above any rule of law whereby a term not inconsistent with Pt II is to be implied into a contract for the supply of a service: s 16 (3). Part II has effect subject to any other enactment which defines or restricts the rights, duties or liabilities arising in connection with a service of any description: s 16 (4).

1864. Obligation to remunerate and pay for materials. The hirer of labour must, at the time or times and in the manner appointed, pay the workman the agreed price. Where, under a contract for the supply of a service, the consideration for the service is not determined by the contract, left to be determined in a manner agreed by the contract or determined by the course of dealing between the parties, there is an implied term that the party contracting with the supplier will pay a reasonable charge[1]. What is a reasonable charge is a question of fact[2].

The acceptance of services does not, however, in all cases necessarily imply that such services are to be remunerated. In general, remuneration cannot be successfully claimed for services voluntarily performed without request[3]. In general, whether or not work and labour is to be remunerated depends upon the contract under which the work was done[4], but employment of a man whose trade it is to do the work in question prima facie implies a contract by the employer to pay him a fair and reasonable price for his work[5]. A person called in to do work of a class which he holds himself out as qualified to do, which will be useful only if effective, and which he is left to do in his own way, can recover nothing if it proves ineffective and the employer gets no benefit from it[6]. A workman's right of action for the agreed remuneration for work completed does not arise until the work is done and the employer has had a reasonable opportunity of ascertaining whether it has been properly done[7].

Where one person is employed by another to do work, the workman can prima facie look for his remuneration only to the actual employer[8], unless it is known to both parties that the work is for the benefit of a third party for whom the employer is acting merely as agent[9].

The hirer must also pay for all materials employed by the workman in the manufacture, alteration or repair of the chattel which is the subject of the contract, provided they are necessary for the completion of the work, and were either specifically or impliedly ordered[10].

1 Supply of Goods and Services Act 1982 s 15 (1). As to the definition of a contract for the supply of a service see s 12; para 1863 ante. The statutory term corresponds with the obligation implied at common law: see *Jewry v Busk* (1814) 5 Taunt 302; *Brown v Nairne* (1839) 9 C & P 204; cf *Cannon v Miles* [1974] 2 Lloyd's Rep 129, CA. If it can be established that a particular rate of remuneration is customary for a particular employment, that rate is accepted as just and reasonable: *Brown v Nairne* supra at 205; and see eg *Price v Hong Kong Tea Co* (1861) 2 F & F 466; *A-G v Drapers' Co* (1869) LR 9 Eq 69; *Debenham v King's College, Cambridge* (1884) Cab & El 438; *Faraday v Tamworth Union* (1916) 86 LJ Ch 436; and AGENCY; AUCTION; BUILDING CONTRACTS; VALUERS. If there is no trade usage, the court may take into account any bargaining between the parties: *Scarisbrick v Parkinson* (1869) 20 LT 175; *Way v Latilla* [1937] 3 All ER 759, HL. As to evidence of usage see CUSTOM AND USAGE.
2 Supply of Goods and Services Act 1982 s 15 (2).
3 Cf *Taylor v Laird* (1856) 25 LJ Ex 329 at 332 per Pollock CB: 'Suppose I clean your property without your knowledge, have I then a claim on you for payment? One cleans another's shoes; what can the other do but put them on? Is that evidence of a contract to pay for the cleaning?'.
4 For examples of the principle see *Reeve v Reeve* (1858) 1 F & F 280; *Taylor v Brewer* (1813) 1 M & S 290; *Moffatt v Laurie* (1855) 15 CB 583; *Ex p Metcalfe* (1856) 6 E & B 287; *Hingeston v Kelly* (1849) 18 LJ Ex 360; and AGENCY; BUILDING CONTRACTS; EMPLOYMENT.
5 See AGENCY vol 1 (2) (Reissue) para 115.
6 *Farnsworth v Garrard* (1807) 1 Camp 38 at 39 per Lord Ellenborough: 'If there has been no beneficial service there shall be no pay, but if some benefit has been derived, though not to the extent expected, this shall go to the amount of the plaintiff's demand; ... the claim shall be co-extensive with the benefit'. Cf *Duncan v Blundell* (1820) 3 Stark 6 at 7 per Bayley J; *Pearce v Tucker* (1862) 3 F & F 136. See also para 1869 post.
7 *Hughes v Lenny* (1839) 5 M & W 183.
8 *Meriel v Wymondsold* (1661) Hard 205. See also the cases cited in para 1871 note 5 post.
9 *Chidley v Norris* (1862) 3 F & F 228. But the immediate employer is liable if he leads the person employed to believe that he, and not the third party, will pay for the work: *Chidley v Norris* supra. See also AGENCY vol 1 (2) (Reissue) para 168 et seq.
10 Story on Bailments (9th Edn), s 425; *Wilmot v Smith* (1828) 3 C & P 453.

1865. Payment where work not completed. The issue of whether payment may be demanded prior to completion of the work will depend as a matter of construction upon whether the contract consists of an entire obligation (sometimes called a 'lump sum' contract) or divisible obligations[1].

Where a man is employed to do work under a divisible contract, there is an express or implied agreement that payments will be made in proportion to the work performed[2], unless a trade custom to the contrary can be proved[3]. Where the work is not completed, whether through the fault of the workman[4] or otherwise[5], in the absence of an express or implied agreement to complete it, the hirer may nevertheless have to pay for the work actually done and for the materials provided[6].

A man who undertakes to do specified work in connection with a chattel for an agreed sum to be paid on completion (a lump sum contract), but who fails substantially to complete the work, is not entitled to recover the price agreed upon, nor even the actual value of the work he has done on a quantum meruit basis[7], unless the failure to complete it is due to the hirer's default or the parties can be held to have entered into a new contract, or the failure to perform is due to impossibility or frustration[8].

However, where a man engages to do work for a lump sum payable on completion and the work is substantially performed, the hirer cannot, as a rule, repudiate liability on the ground that the work is in some respects not in accordance with the specification if the breach does not go to the root of the contract; in such a case he is liable to pay the agreed price, less a deduction based on the cost of making good the defects or omissions proved[9]. Even if in such a case the parties have made entire performance a condition precedent to payment, a hirer who takes the benefit of the work done waives the condition and must pay the agreed price subject to appropriate deductions[10].

If the employer refuses to perform or renders himself incapable of performing his part of the contract or by his own acts prevents the full performance of the contract by the workman, the workman may rescind the contract and sue upon a quantum meruit[11]; or he may sue for damages for breach of contract[12]. Where a person sues upon a quantum meruit he must be prepared to show what the work was worth[13].

If a new contract is made to pay for the work actually done, the workman is entitled to recover the price agreed upon less a deduction, the measure of the deduction being generally the sum which it would take to alter or complete the work so as to make it correspond with the specification[14].

Where a contract has become impossible of performance or has been frustrated, the parties' rights and liabilities under it are governed by statute[15].

Where the hirer is under no obligation to pay for the work done, he incurs no additional obligation by reason of the fact that the workman has incorporated his own materials with those of the hirer[16].

1 See CONTRACT vol 9 para 473. Notice, however, that in most sizeable modern contracts the contractual terms will provide for payment by instalments, thus generally rendering this distinction irrelevant.

2 *Roberts v Havelock* (1832) 3 B & Ad 404; *The Tergeste* [1903] P 26; cf *Rosenthal & Sons Ltd v Esmail* [1965] 2 All ER 860, [1965] 1 WLR 1117, HL.

3 *Gillett v Mawman* (1808) 1 Taunt 137. See CUSTOM AND USAGE.

4 *Roberts v Havelock* (1832) 3 B & Ad 404.

5 *Menetone v Athawes* (1764) 3 Burr 1592.

6 *Appleby v Myers* (1867) LT 2 CP 651 at 660 per Blackburn J.

7 *Sinclair v Bowles* (1829) 9 B & C 92. Cf *Sumpter v Hedges* [1898] 1 QB 673, CA (building contract; followed in *Wheeler v Stratton* (1911) 105 LT 786, DC, and *Small & Sons Ltd v Middlesex Real Estates Ltd* [1921] WN 245); *Munro v Butt* (1858) 8 E & B 738; *Ellis v Hamlen* (1810) 3 Taunt 52; *Gillett v Mawman* (1808) 1 Taunt 137; *Adlard v Booth* (1835) 7 C & P 108 (explained in *Appleby v Myers* (1867) LR 2 CP 651 at 652 per Blackburn J); *Cutter v Powell* (1795) 6 Term Rep 320; *Bates v Hudson* (1825) 6 Dow & Ry KB 3; *Hulle v Heightman* (1802) 2 East 145; *Vigers v Cook* [1919] 2 KB 475, CA; *Crosthwaite v Gardner* (1852) 18 QB 640; *Bolton v Mahadeva* [1972] 2 All ER 1322, [1972] 1 WLR 1009, CA. See BUILDING CONTRACTS; CONTRACT; EMPLOYMENT.

8 *Hoenig v Isaacs* [1952] 2 All ER 176 at 181–182, CA, per Denning LJ; *Appleby v Myers* (1867) LR 2 CP 651 at 661 per Blackburn J.

9 *Hoenig v Isaacs* [1952] 2 All ER 176, CA, applying *Mondel v Steel* (1841) 8 M & W 858, and *H Dakin & Co Ltd v Lee* [1916] 1 KB 566, CA; *Bolton v Mahadeva* [1972] 2 All ER 1322, [1972] 1 WLR 1009, CA. As to the effect of negligence or lack of skill on the workman's part see further para 1869 post.
10 *Hoenig v Isaacs* [1952] 2 All ER 176 at 181, CA, per Denning LJ.
11 See eg *Planchè v Colburn* (1831) 8 Bing 14; *Kewley v Stokes* (1846) 2 Car & Kir 435; *Prickett v Badger* (1856) 1 CBNS 296; *Burn v Miller* (1813) 4 Taunt 745; *Craven-Ellis v Canons Ltd* [1936] 2 KB 403 at 410–411, [1936] 2 All ER 1066 at 1072–1073, CA, per Greer LJ. See further AGENCY; BUILDING CONTRACTS; CONTRACT.
12 See AGENCY; BUILDING CONTRACTS.
13 *Basten v Butler* (1806) 7 East 479.
14 *Thornton v Place* (1832) 1 Mood & R 218 at 219 per Parke J; *Ranger v Great Western Rly Co* (1854) 5 HL Cas 72.
15 See the Law Reform (Frustrated Contracts) Act 1943; and CONTRACT.
16 *Sinclair v Bowles* (1829) 9 B & C 92.

1866. Extras. If a workman without any order or request does more work than was originally stipulated for in the contract, and the hirer did not acquiesce in the change, although the extra work is essential to the proper performance of the contract, the hirer, in the absence of bad faith or concealment[1], is not bound to pay more than the sum originally agreed upon by him[2]. So if a workman, employed to do specified work on a chattel for an agreed sum, instead of doing the specified work does different, even if better, work, he can recover from the hirer neither the agreed sum under the special contract, nor the value of the work done on a quantum meruit basis, unless the hirer has sanctioned or acquiesced in the change. The mere fact that the hirer has received the chattel on which the work has been done and has sold it at an enhanced price does not amount to acquiescence[3].

But extra work which, during the course of the work, has been ordered or assented to by the hirer, must be paid for on a quantum meruit basis. In such a case, the contract is binding so far as it can be traced, and the quantum meruit applies to the remainder[4].

1 Story on Bailments (9th Edn), s 425.
2 *Brown v Lord Rollo* (1832) 10 Sh 667, Ct of Sess; *Wilmot v Smith* (1828) 3 C & P 453. See generally CONTRACT; BUILDING CONTRACTS.
3 *Forman & Co Pty Ltd v The Liddesdale* [1900] AC 190, PC. Cf *Munro v Butt* (1858) 8 E & B 738; and para 1864 note 3 ante.
4 *Napier v Lang* (1834) 12 Sh 523, Ct of Sess; *Shipton v Casson* (1826) 5 B & C 378.

1867. Hirer must not obstruct workman. The hirer must afford the workman every reasonable facility for entering upon and completing the contract which he has undertaken to perform[1]. If, after the contract has been entered upon, the hirer wilfully obstructs the workman and thereby retards him in his employment, or intervenes without just cause so as to prevent its completion, he is liable to the workman for the loss actually caused by his interference[2]. A similar duty and liability in case of default is imposed upon the hirer, if it is one of the terms of the bargain that he will supply the workman with the necessary materials for the employment undertaken[3].

1 *Wells v Army and Navy Co-operative Society Ltd* (1902) 86 LT 764; *Prickett v Badger* (1856) 1 CBNS 296; *Green v Lucas* (1875) 33 LT 584, CA; *Russell v Viscount Sa da Bandeira* (1862) 13 CBNS 149; *Courtnay v Waterford and Central Ireland Rly Co* (1878) 4 LR Ir 11.
2 *Mackay v Dick* (1881) 6 App Cas 251, HL. See also *Lilley v Barnsley* (1844) 2 Mood & R 548. The workman can claim damages for breach of contract, or under a quantum meruit claim to recover a reasonable remuneration for his partial performance: *Planchè v Colburn* (1831) 8 Bing 14.
3 Pothier's Contrat de Louage, s 410.

(ii) Workman's Obligations

1868. Obligation to do the work. The first obligation of the workman is to perform his undertaking[1]. If the workman agrees to perform work which will put the hirer's goods in a certain condition, and the hirer relies on the workman's skill and judgment, the workman owes an absolute obligation to put the goods into that condition and his failure to do so constitutes a total failure of consideration[2]. The workman will be relieved of the duty to perform, however, if the performance is rendered impossible by the hirer's act[3] or by circumstances beyond the workman's control, as where the chattel upon which the work is to be performed is accidentally destroyed by fire[4]. However, the fact that the work was, by its nature, impossible to perform will not relieve the workman from liability for failure to perform where the hirer has relied on his skill and judgment[5]. The workman is responsible if the impossibility should have been foreseen by him, and if the hirer has acted in good faith in relying on his ability to perform the work[6]. Where no time for performance is fixed, the undertaking must be performed within a reasonable time[7]. Where, under a contract for the supply of a service[8] by a supplier acting in the course of a business[9], the time for the service to be carried out is not fixed by the contract, left to be fixed in a manner agreed by the contract or determined by the course of dealing between the parties, there is an implied term that the supplier will carry out the service within a reasonable time[10]. What is a reasonable time is a question of fact[11]. If by his own act the workman incapacitates himself from performing his contract, he forthwith becomes liable for the breach[12].

1 *Alderslade v Hendon Laundry Ltd* [1945] KB 189 at 193, [1945] 1 All ER 244 at 246, CA, per Lord Greene MR. And see Story on Bailments (9th Edn), s 428.
2 *G K Serigraphics v Dispro Ltd* [1980] CA Transcript 916, CA.
3 See eg *Holme v Guppy* (1838) 3 M & W 387; and see generally CONTRACT.
4 *Menetone v Athawes* (1764) 3 Burr 1592. See also *Appleby v Myers* (1867) LR 2 CP 651. As to the discharge of contracts on the ground of impossibility of performance or frustration, and for statutory provisions as to the effect of frustration, see CONTRACT.
5 *Duncan v Blundell* (1820) 3 Stark 6 at 7 per Bayley J; *Pearce v Tucker* (1862) 3 F & F 136.
6 *Combe v Simmonds* (1853) 1 WR 289; *Pearce v Tucker* (1862) 3 F & F 136.
7 See eg *Wigginton v Dodd* (1862) 2 F & F 844; and see generally CONTRACT.
8 See the Supply of Goods and Services Act 1982 s 12; and para 1863 ante.
9 For the meaning of 'business' see ibid s 18 (1); and para 1855 note 4 ante.
10 Ibid s 14 (1).
11 Ibid s 14 (2). As to the exclusion of implied terms see ibid s 16; para 1863 ante; and the Unfair Contract Terms Act 1977. See CONTRACT.
12 See eg *Planchè v Colburn* (1831) 8 Bing 14; and see generally CONTRACT.

1869. Obligation to exercise skill. In a contract for the supply of a service[1] where the supplier is acting in the course of a business[2], there is an implied term that the supplier will carry out the service with reasonable care and skill[3]. This provision is in conformity with the general rule of common law that all workmen undertake to use the skills appropriate to their particular crafts[4]. The acceptance by a person of work of a class which he holds himself out as qualified to do amounts to a warranty on his part that he possesses the requisite skill and ability to do that work[5]. Where there is neither a general nor a particular representation of skill and ability, a workman incurs no responsibility in respect of his want of either. If, for instance, a man should employ a general labourer to clean or mend his watch, the employer would probably be held to have incurred all risks himself[6]. Moreover,

the public profession of an art or craft amounts only to a representation that the
artificer or craftsman is reasonably competent to carry out any work of the class he
professes to do, and does not make him an insurer; he contracts only to display
sufficient skill and knowledge of his calling to perform all ordinary duties connected with it[7].

When through negligence or lack of skill the workman fails to perform in a
workmanlike manner the work he has undertaken, he may forfeit in whole or part
his claim to remuneration[8], and, in addition, he may become liable to the hirer for
the loss sustained in consequence of his breach of duty[9]; but acceptance by the hirer
of the labour after a slight and unimportant breach of the contract may amount to a
waiver of the breach[10].

Where the contract is a contract for work and materials, and the hirer makes
known the purpose for which the materials are intended and that he relies on the
workman's skill and judgment, there is implied at common law a warranty that the
materials are fit for the purpose. The workman is accordingly liable for damage
resulting from unfitness of the materials, even though they may have been supplied
by a third party[11]. In a contract for work and materials there is also, at common
law, irrespective of the hirer's reliance on the workman's skill and judgment, an
implied warranty that the materials are of good or merchantable quality[12]. These
warranties have now been substantially superseded by statute[13].

1 For the meaning of 'contract for the supply of a service' see the Supply of Goods and Services Act
   1982 s 12; and para 1863 ante.
2 For the meaning of 'business' see ibid s 18 (1); and para 1855 note 4 ante.
3 Ibid s 13. As to exclusion of implied terms see s 16, para 1863 ante and the Unfair Contract Terms
   Act 1977. In exercise of his power under the 1982 Act s 12 (4) (see para 1863 ante), the Secretary of
   State has provided by order that s 13 is not to apply to the following services: (i) the services of an
   advocate in court or before any tribunal, inquiry or arbitrator and in carrying out preliminary work
   directly affecting the conduct of the hearing; (ii) the services rendered to a company by a director of
   the company in his capacity as such (Supply of Services (Exclusion of Implied Terms) Order 1982, SI
   1982/1771); (iii) the services rendered to a building society by a director in his capacity as such; (iv)
   the services rendered to an industrial or provident society by any member of the committee of
   management or other directing body in his capacity as such (Supply of Services (Exclusion of
   Implied Terms) Order 1983, SI 1983/902); (v) the services rendered by an arbitrator, including an
   umpire, in his capacity as such (Supply of Services (Exclusion of Implied Terms) Order 1985, SI
   1985/1).
4 Ie *spondet peritiam artis*; and see *Smith v Eric S Bush, Harris v Wyre Forest District Council* [1990] 1 AC
   831 at 843, [1989] 2 All ER 514 at 519–520, HL, per Lord Templeman.
5 *Duncan v Blundell* (1820) 3 Stark 6; *Harmer v Cornelius* (1858) 5 CBNS 236 at 246 per Willes J; 1 Bell's
   Com, Book 3, part 1, c 3, s 2, tit Skill; *Coggs v Bernard* (1703) 2 Ld Raym 909. Compare para 1821
   notes 1–3 ante (gratuitous bailment); and see also the cases cited in para 1868 note 6 ante; and
   NEGLIGENCE.
6 Jones on Bailments (4th Edn) 100; *Harmer v Cornelius* (1858) 5 CBNS 236 at 246 per Willes J.
7 *Smith v Eric S Bush, Harris v Wyre Forest District Council* [1990] 1 AC 831 at 843, [1989] 2 All ER 514 at
   519–520, HL, per Lord Templeman; *Lanphier v Phipos* (1838) 8 C & P 475 at 479 per Tindal CJ.
8 Cf *Cousins v Paddon* (1835) 2 Cr M & R 547; *Bracey v Carter* (1840) 12 Ad & El 373; *Shaw v Arden*
   (1832) 9 Bing 287; *Moneypenny v Hartland* (1824) 1 C & P 352; *Pardow v Webb* (1842) Car & M 531; and
   see further para 1865 ante. See also AGENCY; BUILDING CONTRACTS.
9 *Combe v Simmonds* (1853) 1 WR 289; Story on Bailments (9th Edn), s 431; cf *Seare v Frentice* (1807) 8
   East 348; and see NEGLIGENCE.
10 *Lucas v Godwin* (1837) 3 Bing NC 737; *Hoenig v Isaacs* [1952] 2 All ER 176, CA.
11 *G H Myers & Co v Brent Cross Service Co* [1934] 1 KB 46, DC; *Stewart v Reavell's Garage* [1952] 2 QB
   545, [1952] 1 All ER 1191 (applying principles laid down in relation to the sale of goods); cf *Cammell
   Laird & Co Ltd v Manganese Bronze and Brass Co Ltd* [1934] AC 402, HL; *Samuels v Davis* [1943] KB
   526, [1943] 2 All ER 3, CA; *Dodd and Dodd v Wilson and McWilliam* [1946] 2 All ER 691 (implied
   condition of fitness of toxoid used by veterinary surgeons); *Watson v Buckley, Osborne, Garrett & Co
   Ltd and Wyrovoys Products Ltd* [1940] 1 All ER 174; *Holmes v Ashford* [1950] 2 All ER 76, CA; *Ingham v*

Emes [1955] 2 QB 366, [1955] 2 All ER 740, CA; *Young and Marten Ltd v McManus Childs Ltd* [1969] 1 AC 454, [1968] 2 All ER 1169, HL (roof tiling); *Gloucestershire County Council v Richardson* [1969] 1 AC 480, [1968] 2 All ER 1181, HL (concrete columns for construction project). As to implied terms in the fulfilment of contracts see CONTRACT; and as to implied conditions of fitness on the sale of goods see SALE OF GOODS.

12 See the cases cited in note 11 supra.
13 See para 1872 et seq post.

1870. Obligation to exercise care. As the workman is entitled to a reward, either by express agreement or by implication, he is obliged not only to perform his work with reasonable care and skill, but also to take ordinary care of the chattel entrusted to him[1], and to restore it to the hirer at the expiration of the period for which it was entrusted to him. If, therefore, he detains it beyond the proper period, he is guilty of a breach of duty, the measure of damages for which is prima facie the sum which would have been earned in the ordinary course of employment of the chattel during the period of its detention[2]; the workman is liable as an insurer if it becomes lost or destroyed[3]. Where, however, it is lost or injured whilst properly in the workman's custody, he will be responsible for the full amount of the damage sustained, unless he can show[4] that the loss or injury is not attributable to any want of reasonable care on his part[5].

The workman is liable for any loss of the chattel arising from the unauthorised act of his servant, providing that the servant was acting within the scope of his employment[6].

1 Jones on Bailments (4th Edn) 91; *Leck v Maestaer* (1807) 1 Camp 138; *Clarke v Earnshaw* (1818) Gow 30; *Becker v Lavender Ltd* (1946) 62 TLR 504 (misdelivery); *Sinclair v Juner* 1952 SC 35; *Spriggs v Sotheby Parke Bernet & Co* [1986] 1 Lloyd's Rep 487, CA.
2 *Re Trent and Humber Co, ex p Cambrian Steam Packet Co* (1868) 4 Ch App 112 at 117 per Lord Cairns LC.
3 *Shaw & Co v Symmons & Sons* [1917] 1 KB 799.
4 See para 1843 note 3 ante and para 1859 note 1 ante.
5 *Leck v Maestaer* (1807) 1 Camp 138; *Clarke v Earnshaw* (1818) Gow 30. Cf *Gillett v Mawman* (1808) 1 Taunt 137; *Wilson v Powis* (1826) 11 Moore CP 543; *Jobson v Palmer* [1893] 1 Ch 71; *Bullen v Swan Electric Engraving Co* (1907) 23 TLR 258, CA; *Morison, Pollexfen and Blair v Walton* (1909), cited [1915] 1 KB at 90, HL; *Joseph Travers & Sons Ltd v Cooper* [1915] 1 KB 73, CA; *Cowan v Blackwill Motor Caravan Conversions Ltd* [1978] RTR 421, CA; *Idnani v Elisha* [1979] RTR 488, CA (motor repairers); *Spriggs v Sotheby Parke Bernet & Co* [1986] 1 Lloyd's Rep 487, CA (auctioneer in possession of diamond); *Lockspeiser Aircraft Ltd v Brooklands Aircraft Co Ltd* (1990) Times, 7 March (aircraft). Cf *Sinclair v Juner* 1952 SC 35. The liability continues after the work is done until the original relationship is expressly altered (*Mitchell v Davis* (1920) 37 TLR 68); or until the bailor has, by committing a repudiatory breach of his implied obligation to collect the goods within a reasonable time, forfeited the right to sue for breach of the bailee's duty of reasonable care (*Pedrick v Morning Star Motors Ltd* (14 February 1979, unreported), CA; *Ridyard v Roberts* (16 May 1980, unreported), CA). For a form of defence see 6 Court Forms (2nd Edn) (1989 Issue) 245, Form 20.
6 *Morris v C W Martin & Sons Ltd* [1966] 1 QB 716, [1965] 2 All ER 725, CA; and see the cases cited in para 1839 note 17 ante.

1871. Delegation. In general, the workman's obligation to perform the work is personal to him. The hirer is presumed to have engaged the workman on the strength of his personal skill and reputation. The workman cannot, therefore, delegate the work to a third party and is prohibited from conferring possession on a third party for that purpose[1]. This general rule applies irrespective of whether the contract expressly obliges the workman to perform in person or not and irrespective of whether the hirer has proved that he relied on the workman's personal skill and reputation in entrusting the work to him[2]. A workman who delegates in breach of the general rule does so at his peril[3]. He becomes strictly liable for the safety of the goods as an insurer[4]. Further, the third party to whom the work is delegated in breach of the general rule cannot bring an action in contract to recover the cost of his services from the hirer, because there is no privity of contract between the hirer and himself[5].

The general rule may be displaced by the express terms of the contract, or by a course of dealing between the parties[6], or by the particular circumstances of the case. In some cases the nature of the work will be such that permission to delegate or sub-contract can be inferred[7]. In others, the workman may be entitled to delegate non-specialist aspects of the work, such as the return carriage of the goods to the hirer when the work is completed[8]. But the workman remains liable for any default which his delegate or subcontractor commits during the period of his possession of the goods[9].

If the hirer, after receiving notice that the contract has been transferred to a third party, allows the assignee to proceed with the work, there may be a novation of the contract, and the assignee is entitled to sue the employer for the value of the work done by him[10]. Whether there is a novation depends upon the circumstances of the case.

The right of a workman to receive payment for his work, as distinct from the liability to perform the work, may be assigned in the same manner as any other debt[11].

1 *Davies v Collins* [1945] 1 All ER 247, CA; *Martin v N Negin Ltd* (1945) 172 LT 275, CA (dry-cleaning; but in both cases the court relied on the express terms of the contract); *Edwards v Newland & Co (E Burchett Ltd, third parties)* [1950] 2 KB 534, [1950] 1 All ER 1072, CA (warehousing); *Garnham, Harris & Elton Ltd v Alfred W Ellis (Transport) Ltd* [1967] 2 All ER 940, [1967] 1 WLR 940 (carriage; but goods exceptionally valuable and sub-carriers negligently selected); *Hobbs v Petersham Transport Co Pty Ltd, Petersham Transport Co Pty Ltd v ASEA Electric (Australia) Pty Ltd* (1971) 45 ALJR 356 at 362 per Windeyer J (Aust HC) (carriage); *Cassils & Co and Sassoon & Co v Holden Wood Bleaching Co Ltd* (1914) 84 LJKB 834 at 839–840, CA, per Buckley LJ, at 843–844 per Phillimore LJ, and at 845–846 per Pickford LJ (bleaching); *Morgan v Maurer & Son* (1964) 30 Ir Jur Rep 31 (repair of watch). Cf the Supply of Goods and Services Act 1982 s 13; para 1869 ante; and see AGENCY; CONTRACT.
2 *Edwards v Newland & Co (E Burchett Ltd, third parties)* [1950] 2 KB 534, [1950] 1 All ER 1072, CA.
3 See the cases cited in note 1 supra; and para 1839 ante.
4 For qualifications on the workman's liability as an insurer see paras 1869, 1870 ante.
5 *Schmaling v Thomlinson* (1815) 6 Taunt 147; and see *Cull v Backhouse* (1793) 6 Taunt 148n, note (a). See AGENCY.
6 *Kreiger v Bell* [1943] SASR 153 at 172 per Mayo J (S Aust SC) (repair of truck).
7 *Edwards v Newland & Co (E Burchett Ltd, third parties)* [1950] 2 KB 534 at 539, [1950] 1 All ER 1072 at 1076, CA, per Somervell LJ, and at 542, 1081 per Denning LJ; *Robson v Drummond* (1831) 2 B & Ad 303; *British Waggon Co and Parkgate Waggon Co v Lea & Co* (1880) 5 QBD 149.
8 *Punch v Savoy Jewellers Ltd* (1986) 26 DLR (4th) 546 (Ont CA) (repair of brooch; method of return carriage failed to take account of value of brooch; bailee liable).
9 *Genn v Winkel* (1912) 28 TLR 483, CA; Palmer on Bailment (1979) 517; and see *British Road Services Ltd v Arthur V Crutchley & Co Ltd (Factory Guards Ltd, third parties)* [1968] 1 All ER 811, [1968] 1 Lloyd's Rep 271, CA (warehouseman entitled to delegate security of warehouse to carefully selected firm of security guards, but remained answerable for defaults of latter).
10 *Aspinall v London and North Western Rly Co* (1853) 11 Hare 325; *Oldfield v Lowe* (1829) 9 B & C 73. As to the assignor's rights against the assignee see *Humphreys v Jones* (1850) 5 Exch 952.
11 *Russell & Co Ltd v Austin Fryers* (1909) 25 TLR 414. As to the assignment of rights under contracts see generally CHOSES IN ACTION; CONTRACT.

1872. Liability for materials supplied by workman. Certain terms are implied by statute into contracts for the transfer of goods[1]. In the statute, a 'contract for the transfer of goods' means a contract under which one person transfers or agrees to transfer to another the property in goods, other than an excepted contract[2]. An excepted contract means any of the following: (1) a contract for the sale of goods[3]; (2) a hire purchase agreement[4]; (3) a contract under which the property in goods is, or is to be, transferred in exchange for trading stamps on their redemption[5]; (4) a transfer or agreement to transfer which is made by deed and for which there is no consideration other than the presumed consideration imported by the deed[6]; (5) a contract intended to operate by way of mortgage, pledge, charge or other security[7].

For the purposes of the statute, a contract is a contract for the transfer of goods whether or not services are also provided or to be provided under the contract, and, subject to other provision[8], whatever is the nature of the consideration for the transfer or agreement to transfer[9].

A contract for work and materials[10] is a contract for the transfer of goods unless otherwise excepted. Thus, where a bailee for work and labour agrees, in addition to performing work upon the bailor's goods, to supply materials which are to be added to or intermixed with the bailor's goods, this is a contract for the transfer of goods unless it is an excepted contract within one of the categories described above.

Where a right, duty or liability would arise under a contract for the transfer of goods by implication of law, it may, subject to other provisions[11], be negatived or varied by express agreement, or by the course of dealing between the parties, or by such usage as binds both parties to the contract[12]. An express condition or warranty does not negative a condition or warranty implied by relevant provisions of the statute[13] into a contract for the transfer of goods, unless inconsistent with it[14].

1 Supply of Goods and Services Act 1982 Pt I (ss 1–5).
2 Ibid s 1 (1).
3 Ibid s 1 (2) (a). As to the meaning of 'goods' see s 18 (1); para 1850 ante. 'Transferee', in relation to a contract for the transfer of goods, means (depending on the context) a person to whom the property in the goods is transferred under the contract, or a person to whom the property is to be so transferred, or a person to whom the rights under the contract of either of those persons have passed: s 18 (1). 'Transferor', in relation to a contract for the transfer of goods, means (depending on the context) a person who transfers the property in goods under the contract, or a person who agrees to do so, or a person to whom the duties under the contract of either of those persons have passed: s 18 (1).
4 Ibid s 1 (2) (b). As to the meaning of 'hire purchase agreement' see s 18 (1); para 1850 note 12 ante.
5 Ibid s 1 (2) (c). As to the meanings of 'trading stamps' and 'redemption' see s 18 (1); para 1850 note 13 ante.
6 Ibid s 1 (2) (d).
7 Ibid s 1 (2) (e).
8 Ie ibid s 1 (2); text and notes 3–7 supra.
9 Ibid s 1 (3).
10 See para 1863 ante.
11 Ie the Supply of Goods and Services Act 1982 s 11 (2); see text and note 14 infra and the Unfair Contract Terms Act 1977 (see in particular s 7); and see CONTRACT.
12 Supply of Goods and Services Act 1982 s 11 (1).
13 Ie, in relation to a contract for the transfer of goods, ibid ss 1–5.
14 Ibid s 11 (2). Nothing in the preceding provisions of the statute (ie, in relation to a contract for the transfer of goods, ss 1–5) prejudices the operation of any other enactment or rule of law whereby any condition or warranty (other than one in relation to quality or fitness) is to be implied in a contract for the transfer of goods: s 11 (3).

1873. Right to transfer goods. In a contract for the transfer of goods[1], except as otherwise provided[2], there is an implied condition on the part of the transferor[3] that in the case of a transfer of the property in the goods he has a right to transfer the property and in the case of an agreement to transfer the property in the goods that he will have such a right at the time when the property is to be transferred[4]. In such a contract, except as otherwise provided[5], there is also an implied warranty that the goods are free, and will remain free until the time when the property is to be transferred, from any charge or encumbrance not disclosed or known to the transferee[6] when the contract is made[7]. In such a contract, except as otherwise provided[8], there is also an implied warranty that the transferee will enjoy quiet possession of the goods, except so far as it may be disturbed by the owner or other person entitled to the benefit of any charge or encumbrance disclosed or known to the transferee when the contract is made[9].

In a contract for the transfer of goods, in the case of which there appears from the contract or is to be inferred from its circumstances an intention that the transferor should transfer only such title as he or a third person may have[10], there is an implied warranty that all charges or encumbrances known to the transferor and not known to the transferee have been disclosed to the transferee before the contract is made[11]. In such a contract, there is also an implied warranty that the transferee's quiet possession of the goods will not be disturbed by any of the following: (1) the transferor[12]; (2) in a case where the parties intend that the transferor should transfer only such title as a third person may have, that person[13]; or (3) anyone claiming through or under the transferor or through or under that third person, otherwise than under a charge or encumbrance disclosed or known to the transferee before the contract is made[14].

Provision is made for the exclusion or restriction of liability for breach of the foregoing terms[15].

1　For the meaning of 'contract for the transfer of goods' see the Supply of Goods and Services Act 1982 s 1; para 1872 ante.
2　Ie by ibid s 2 (3)–(5); see text and notes 10–14 infra.
3　For the meaning of 'transferor' see ibid s 18 (1); para 1872 note 3 ante.
4　Ibid s 2 (1). Cf SALE OF GOODS vol 41 paras 744–747.
5　Ie by ibid s 2 (3)–(5); see text and notes 10–14 infra.
6　For the meaning of 'transferee' see ibid s 18 (1); para 1872 note 3 ante.
7　Ibid s 2 (2) (a). Cf SALE OF GOODS vol 41 para 687.
8　Ie by ibid s 2 (3)–(5); see text and notes 10–14 infra.
9　Ibid s 2 (2) (b). Cf SALE OF GOODS vol 41 para 687.
10　See ibid s 2 (3).
11　Ibid s 2 (4).
12　See ibid s 2 (5) (a).
13　See ibid s 2 (5) (b).
14　See ibid s 2 (5) (c).
15　Ibid s 11 (1), (2); para 1872 text and notes 11–14 ante; and the Unfair Contract Terms Act 1977 (see in particular s 7); and CONTRACT.

1874. Correspondence with description. Where, under a contract for the transfer of goods[1], the transferor[2] transfers or agrees to transfer the property by description[3] there is an implied condition that the goods will correspond with the description[4]. If the transferor transfers or agrees to transfer the property by sample as well as by description it is not sufficient that the bulk of the goods corresponds with the sample if the goods do not also correspond with the description[5].

Provision is made for exclusion of these terms[6].

1　For the meaning of 'contract for the transfer of goods' see the Supply of Goods and Services Act 1972 s 2; para 1872 ante.

2 For the meaning of 'transferor' see ibid s 18 (1); para 1872 note 3 ante.
3 Ibid s 3 (1). A contract is not prevented from being by description by reason only that, being exposed for supply, the goods are selected by the transferee: s 3 (4). For the meaning of 'transferee' see s 18 (1); para 1872 note 3 ante.
4 Ibid s 3 (2).
5 Ibid s 3 (3).
6 See ibid s 11; para 1872 ante; the Unfair Contract Terms Act 1977 (see in particular s 7); and CONTRACT.

1875. Fitness and merchantable quality. Except as otherwise provided[1], and subject to the provisions of any other enactment, there is no implied condition or warranty about the quality or fitness for any particular purpose of goods supplied under a contract for the transfer of goods[2].

Where, under such a contract, the transferor[3] transfers the property in goods in the course of a business[4], there is an implied condition that the goods supplied under the contract are of merchantable quality[5]. There is, however, no such condition as regards defects specifically drawn to the transferee's attention before the contract is made, or, if the transferee[6] examines the goods before the contract is made, as regards defects which that examination ought to reveal[7].

The following provision applies where, under a contract for the transfer of goods, the transferor transfers the property in goods in the course of a business[8] and the transferee, expressly or by implication, makes known to the transferor, or, where the consideration or part of the consideration for the transfer is a sum payable by instalments and the goods were previously sold by a credit-broker[9] to the transferor, to that credit-broker, any particular purpose for which the goods are being acquired[10]. In that case there is an implied condition that the goods supplied under the contract are reasonably fit for that purpose, whether or not that is a purpose for which such goods are commonly supplied[11]. This provision does not apply, however, where the circumstances show that the transferee does not rely, or that it is unreasonable for him to rely, on the skill or judgment of the transferor or credit-broker[12].

An implied condition or warranty about quality or fitness for a particular purpose may be annexed by usage to a contract for the transfer of goods[13].

The above provisions apply to a transfer by a person who in the course of a business is acting as agent for another as they apply to a transfer by a principal in the course of a business, except where that other is not transferring in the course of a business and either the transferee knows that fact or reasonable steps are taken to bring it to the transferee's notice before the contract concerned is made[14].

Provision is made for the exclusion of these terms[15].

1 Ie by the Supply of Goods and Services Act 1982 ss 4 (see text and notes infra), 5 (see para 1876 post).
2 Ibid s 4 (1). For the meaning of 'contract for the transfer of goods' see s 2; para 1872 ante. And see para 1869 ante.
3 For the meaning of 'transferor' see ibid s 18 (1); para 1872 note 3 ante.
4 'Business' includes a profession and the activities of any government department or local or public authority: ibid s 18 (1).
5 Ibid s 4 (2). Goods of any kind are of merchantable quality if they are as fit for the purpose or purposes for which goods of that kind are commonly supplied as it is reasonable to expect having regard to any description applied to them, the price (if relevant) and all the other relevant circumstances: s 4 (9).
6 For the meaning of 'transferee' see ibid s 18 (1); para 1872 note 3 ante.
7 Ibid s 4 (3).

8 See note 4 supra.
9 'Credit-broker' means a person acting in the course of a business of credit brokerage carried on by
   him: Supply of Goods and Services Act 1982 s 18 (1). 'Credit-brokerage' means the effecting of
   introductions (a) of individuals desiring to obtain credit to persons carrying on any business so far as
   it relates to the provision of credit; or (b) of individuals desiring to obtain goods on hire to persons
   carrying on a business which comprises or relates to the bailment of goods under a contract for the
   hire of goods (as to which see para 1850 ante); or (c) of individuals desiring to obtain credit, or to
   obtain goods on hire, to other credit-brokers: s 18 (1).
10 Ibid s 4 (4).
11 Ibid s 4 (5).
12 Ibid s 4 (6).
13 Ibid s 4 (7). See also SALE OF GOODS vol 41 paras 691–696.
14 Ibid s 4 (8).
15 See ibid s 11; para 1872 ante; the Unfair Contract Terms Act 1977 s 7; and CONTRACT.

1876. Sample. Where, under a contract for the transfer of goods[1], the transferor[2]
transfers or agrees to transfer the property in the goods by reference to a sample[3]
there is an implied condition that the bulk will correspond with the sample in
quality[4]. In such a contract, there is also an implied condition that the transferee[5]
will have a reasonable opportunity of comparing the bulk with the sample[6]; and an
implied condition that the goods will be free from any defect, rendering them
unmerchantable, which would not be apparent on reasonable examination of the
sample[7].

Provision is made for the exclusion of these terms[8].

1 For the meaning of 'contract for the transfer of goods' see the Supply of Goods and Services Act 1982
   s 1; para 1872 ante.
2 For the meaning of 'transferor' see ibid s 18 (1); para 1872 note 3 ante.
3 For this purpose, a transferor transfers or agrees to transfer goods by reference to a sample where
   there is an express or implied term to that effect in the contract concerned: s 5 (4).
4 Ibid s 5 (2) (a).
5 For the meaning of 'transferee' see ibid s 18 (1); para 1872 note 3 ante.
6 Ibid s 5 (2) (b).
7 Ibid s 5 (2) (c). 'Unmerchantable' is to be construed in accordance with s 4 (9). Cf para 1855 note 9
   ante and see SALE OF GOODS vol 41 para 694.
8 See ibid s 11; para 1872 text and notes 11–14 ante; the Unfair Contract Terms Act 1977 s 7; and
   CONTRACT.

(iii) Lien

1877. Workman's lien. Everyone to whom a chattel is delivered in order that he
may, for reward, do work upon it, and who does work upon the chattel which
improves it[1], has at common law a lien on the chattel for the amount of the
remuneration due to him for the work done, and therefore is not bound to restore it
until his remuneration is paid[2], unless that lien is excluded by express agreement or
is otherwise inconsistent with the express or implied terms of the contract[3]. But if a
chattel is bailed to a workman for the sole purpose of his working with it, and not
upon it, no lien attaches[4].

This lien applies, apart from agreement, only to the sum actually due to the
workman for materials and labour expended by him in connection with the repair
or alteration of the chattel, and does not extend to charges for warehousing[5]. Nor
will the fact that the owner of the chattel is aware that an additional charge will be
made for each day during which his property is detained in the valid exercise of the

lien suffice to render him liable for such charges. Thus the owner of a ship who knew that he must pay for dock room while the vessel was being repaired was held to have made no implied promise to pay any additional charge for the period during which his vessel was detained as security for the shipwright's charges, although he had received notice that such charges would be made[6].

Should the owner sell the chattel bailed, the workman's lien prima facie attaches only for the amount of the debt due to him at the time when he has notice of the sale, and not for any after-accruing debt[7].

1 See *Hatton v Car Maintenance Co Ltd* [1915] 1 Ch 621 (agreement by defendants for three years to maintain plaintiff's car, supplying all petrol and other things necessary for the running of the car and a driver: held to give no lien). And see *Re Southern Livestock Producers Ltd* [1963] 3 All ER 801, [1964] 1 WLR 24.

2 *Re Matthews, ex p Ockenden* (1754) 1 Atk 235; *Franklin v Hosier* (1821) 4 B & Ald 341; *Hollis v Claridge* (1813) 4 Taunt 807; *Scarfe v Morgan* (1838) 4 M & W 270; *Blake v Nicholson* (1814) 3 M & S 167; *Chase v Westmore* (1816) 5 M & S 180; Story on Bailments (9th Edn), s 440; Palmer on Bailment (1979) 543–552. See also para 1848 text to note 26 ante. See further LIEN.

3 *Raitt v Mitchell* (1815) 4 Camp 146; *Chase v Westmore* (1816) 5 M & S 180 at 186 per Lord Ellenborough CJ; *Scarfe v Morgan* (1838) 4 M & W 270 at 283 per Parke B; *Forth v Simpson* (1849) 13 QB 680; *Wilson v Lombank Ltd* [1963] 1 All ER 740, [1963] 1 WLR 1294; and contrast *Re Westlake, ex p Willoughby* (1881) 16 ChD 604.

4 *Steadman v Hockley* (1846) 15 M & W 553 at 556 per Pollock CB; *Bleaden v Hancock* (1829) 4 C & P 152; *Welsh Development Agency (Holdings) Ltd v Modern Injection Mouldings Ltd* (6 March 1986, unreported).

5 *Somes v British Empire Shipping Co* (1860) 8 HL Cas 338; *Bruce v Everson* (1883) Cab & El 18; *Hartley v Hitchcock* (1816) 1 Stark 408; and see para 1848 ante. The position may be otherwise where the workman retains possession of the goods predominantly for the benefit of the hirer: see *China Pacific SA v Food Corpn of India, The Winson* [1982] AC 939 at 962–963, [1981] 3 All ER 688 at 696, HL, per Lord Diplock, and at 964, 697 per Lord Simon of Glaisdale (where the point was left open).

6 *Somes v British Empire Shipping Co* (1860) 8 HL Cas 338; and see para 1848 ante.

7 *Barry v Longmore* (1840) 4 Per & Dav 344.

1878. Lien of third parties. When a bailee of goods delivers them to a third party to do work upon them, and the circumstances[1] are such as to support the implication that he had the owner's authority to do so, as when he expressly agrees with his bailor to keep the chattel bailed from injury, and this term in the agreement necessarily implies its repair by a third party, or a trade custom in that behalf can be proved, the third party who does the work on the bailee's order has an effective lien on the chattel against the owner, although there may have been no privity of contract between the owner and himself[2]. It seems that a lien will also attach against the owner in favour of a third party to whom the bailee has delivered goods, even in the absence of authority from the owner to the bailee to do so, if the third party was under a common law obligation to receive the goods, as for example where he is a carrier or an innkeeper[3]. Where, however, the third party is not under such an obligation, he will have no lien in the absence of an implied (or, possibly, an ostensible[4]) authority on the bailee's part to deliver the goods to him[5].

1 Such circumstances commonly arise where a car is let under a hire purchase agreement. The hirer has a right to pass it to a third party for repair: see *Bowmaker Ltd v Wycombe Motors Ltd* [1946] KB 505 at 509, [1946] 2 All ER 113 at 115; para 1848 text to note 26 ante; and *Tappenden v Artus* [1964] 2 QB 185, [1963] 3 All ER 213, CA (implied authority for repairs necessary to make car roadworthy).

2 *Keene v Thomas* [1905] 1 KB 136; *Green v All Motors Ltd* [1917] 1 KB 625, CA; *Albermarle Supply Co v Hind & Co* [1928] 1 KB 307, CA, where it was further held that the lien attached although it was stipulated that the bailee should have no right to create a lien in respect of the repairs to the chattel by a third party, the third party having no notice of this limitation on the bailee's authority; *Cassils & Co*

and Sassoon & Co v Holden Wood Bleaching Co (1914) 84 LJKB 834, CA, where the third party failed to prove the authority of the owner; and see *K Chellaram & Sons (London) Ltd v Butlers Warehousing and Distribution Ltd* [1978] 2 Lloyd's Rep 412, CA (bailee container shipping line delivered goods to third party for purposes of packing into containers).

3 *Singer Manufacturing Co v London and South Western Rly Co* [1894] 1 QB 833 at 837, DC, per Collins J, who based the lien, inter alia, upon a railway company's obligation to give reasonable facilities for the receipt and safe custody of baggage. But see *Pennington v Reliance Motor Works Ltd* [1923] 1 KB 127 at 129 per McCardie J; and see para 1848 ante.

4 *Tappenden v Artus* [1964] 2 QB 185 at 195–196, [1963] 3 All ER 213 at 216, CA, per Diplock LJ (obiter).

5 *Hiscox v Greenwood* (1802) 4 Esp 174; *Buxton v Baughan* (1834) 6 C & P 674; *Cassils & Co and Sassoon & Co v Holden Wood Bleaching Co* (1914) 84 LJKB 834, CA; *Pennington v Reliance Motor Works Ltd* [1923] 1 KB 127; *Bowmaker Ltd v Wycombe Motors Ltd* [1946] KB 505, [1946] 2 All ER 113 (bailee's authority under hire purchase agreement terminated by termination of the agreement).

1879. Loss of lien. The lien is lost by a relinquishment of possession on the part of the workman[1], or by any act or agreement amounting to waiver[2].

1 *Jacobs v Latour* (1828) 5 Bing 130; *Hartley v Hitchcock* (1816) 1 Stark 408; *Legg v Evans* (1840) 6 M & W 36 at 42 per Parke B; *Sweet v Pym* (1800) 1 East 4; *Pennington v Reliance Motor Works Ltd* [1923] 1 KB 127; *Hatton v Car Maintenance Co Ltd* [1915] 1 Ch 621. Contrast *Albermarle Supply Co v Hind & Co* [1928] 1 KB 307, CA.

2 *White v Gainer* (1824) 2 Bing 23. As to the position where the bailor countermands the work before its completion see *Lilley v Barnsley* (1844) 1 Car & Kir 344; *Green v All Motors Ltd* [1917] 1 KB 625 at 633–634, CA, per Scrutton LJ; cf *Bolwell Fibreglass Pty Ltd v Foley* [1984] VR 97 (Vict SC).

(iv) Disposal of Uncollected Goods

1880. Power to sell uncollected goods. There is provision[1] for sale by the bailee of goods in his possession or under his control where (1) the bailor is in breach of an obligation to take delivery of them[2] or, if the terms of the bailment so provide, to give directions for their delivery; or (2) the bailee could impose such an obligation[3] by giving notice to the bailor but is unable to trace or communicate with him; or (3) the bailee can reasonably expect to be relieved of any duty to safeguard the goods on giving notice to the bailor, but is unable to trace or communicate with him[4].

The bailee's power can be exercised only if he has either given notice to the bailor of his intention to sell the goods[5] or he has failed to trace or communicate with him with a view to giving such notice after having taken reasonable steps for the purpose[6], and if he is reasonably satisfied that the bailor owns the goods[7]. The bailee is then liable to account to the bailor for any proceeds of sale less any costs incurred[8]. Such a sale gives a good title to the purchaser as against the bailor[9] but where the bailor is not in fact the owner, does not give good title against the owner or a person claiming under him[10].

Where a bailee of goods to which these provisions apply satisfies the court that he is entitled to sell the goods, or would be had he given notice[11], the court may authorise the sale subject to any conditions, authorise the bailee to deduct from the proceeds any costs of sale and any amount due to him from the bailor and direct the payment of the net proceeds into court to be held for the bailor[12].

1 The following provisions do not apply where the goods were bailed before the commencement of the Torts (Interference with Goods) Act 1977: s 12 (9); *Anderson and Anderson v Earlanger* [1980] CLY 133.

2   For examples of cases where such an obligation was held to have been broken see *Pedrick v Morning Star Motors Ltd* (14 February 1979, unreported), CA; *Ridyard v Roberts* (16 May 1980, unreported), CA.

3   The bailee under any sort of bailment can impose an obligation on the bailor to collect goods by issuing written notice where those goods have been accepted for repair or other treatment, for valuation or appraisal or where they have been put in the bailee's custody and his obligation as custodian is over: Torts (Interference with Goods) Act 1977 s 12 (2), Sch 1 Pt I paras 2–5.

     The notice must (1) specify the bailee's name and address, and particulars of the goods and the address at which they are held; (2) state that the goods are ready or will be ready at the termination of the contract; and (3) specify the amount, if any, due to the bailee in respect of the goods before the giving of the notice: Sch 1 Pt I para 1 (3).

     The notice must be issued after the repair, valuation or appraisal has been carried out, or after the ending of the obligation to act as custodian (or at the same time as any notice terminating the obligation as custodian): Sch 1 Pt I paras 2–4. As to the form and delivery of the notice see Sch 1 Pt I para 1 (2).

4   Ibid s 12 (1). The provisions of s 12 and Sch 1 have effect subject to the terms of the bailment: s 12 (8). For the purposes of the relevant provisions, 'bailor' and 'bailee' include their respective successors in title: s 12 (7) (a). References to what is payable, paid or due to the bailee in respect of the goods include references to what would be payable by the bailor to the bailee as a condition of delivery of the goods at the relevant time: s 12 (7) (b).

5   Ibid s 12 (3) (a). Notice of intention to sell must be written, sent by registered letter or recorded delivery service and specify the name and address of the bailee, give sufficient particulars of the goods and the address or place where they are held, specify the date on or after which the bailee proposes to sell the goods, and specify the amount if any due to the bailee in respect of the goods before the giving of the notice: Sch 1 Pt II para 6 (1), (4). The interval between the giving of notice and proposed sale must be long enough to allow the bailor a reasonable opportunity of taking delivery of the goods and, if any amount is due to the bailee in respect of the goods, the interval must be at least three months: Sch 1 Pt II para 6 (2), (3).

     The bailee may not give notice or exercise his right to sell the goods pursuant to such a notice if he has notice that the bailor is questioning or refusing to pay all or some of the sum the bailee claims is due in respect of the goods because of a dispute concerning those goods: Sch 1 Pt II para 7.

6   Ibid s 12 (3) (b).

7   Ibid s 12 (3).

8   Ibid s 12 (5). The account must be taken on the footing that the bailee has adopted the best method of sale reasonably available in the circumstances: s 12 (5) (a). Where s 12 (3) (a) applies (see text and note 5 supra), any sum payable to the bailee in respect of goods which accrued before notice of intention to sell was given, is deductible from the proceeds of sale: s 12 (5) (b).

9   Ibid s 12 (6).

10   Ibid s 12 (4).

11   Ie notice under ibid Sch 1 (see text and notes 1–5 supra).

12   Ibid s 13 (1). A decision of the court is conclusive, subject to any right of appeal, of the bailee's entitlement to sell the goods, as against the bailor, and gives the purchaser good title against the bailor: s 13 (2). The county court has jurisdiction provided that the value of the goods does not exceed the county court limit: s 13 (3); see COUNTY COURTS.

(4) PLEDGE

1881. Nature of pledge. The remaining class of bailment for valuable consideration is pledge[1], whereby a chattel is delivered to a bailee to be held by him as security for a debt or other engagement[2]. The subject of pledge is separately treated at length in another part of this work[3].

1   Ie *pignus,* or *vadium*: see para 1802 ante.

2   *Coggs v Bernard* (1703) 2 Ld Raym 909 at 913 per Holt CJ; Jones on Bailments (4th Edn) 36; Story on Bailments (9th Edn), s 286.

3   See PLEDGES AND PAWNS.

4. CONSIDERATIONS COMMON TO ALL CLASSES OF BAILMENT

(1) ESTOPPEL OF BAILEE

1882. Estoppel of bailee. At common law[1], a bailee is estopped from setting up against his bailor's demand for a redelivery of the chattel bailed the right or title of a third person to the property in it[2].

This estoppel ceases, however, when the bailment on which it is founded is determined by what is equivalent to an eviction by title paramount[3]; and the bailee is thereby discharged from all liability to the bailor, unless there is a special contract, or the bailee is in some way to blame for the eviction[4]. It is not enough that the bailee has become aware of the title of a third person, or that an adverse claim has been made upon him[5]. Unless he has been actually evicted he can set up the title of a third person only where he does so on behalf and on the express authority of that third person[6].

Interrogatories may not be administered by a bailee to his bailor for the purpose of showing that the bailor has parted with his title in the chattel to a third person, unless the bailee justifies his detention of it by setting up the title of such third person with his consent[7].

The estoppel appears to have been abolished by statute. The defendant in an action for wrongful interference with goods[8] is entitled to show, in accordance with rules of court[9], that a third person has a better right than the plaintiff as respects all or any part of the interest claimed by the plaintiff, or in right of which he sues[10]. The bailee's estoppel may be preserved, however, where the bailor sues otherwise than in tort[11].

1 The common law rule is substantially abrogated by statute: see the Torts (Interference with Goods) Act 1977 s 8; and text and notes 8–10 infra.
2 *Biddle v Bond* (1865) 6 B & S 225; *Bettely v Reed* (1843) 4 QB 511; *Re Sadler, ex p Davies* (1881) 19 ChD 86, CA; *Leese v Martin* (1873) LR 17 Eq 224; *China Pacific SA v Food Corpn of India, The Winson* [1982] AC 939 at 959, [1981] 3 All ER 688 at 694, HL, per Lord Diplock; *Redler Grain Silos Ltd v BICC Ltd* [1982] 1 Lloyd's Rep 435 at 438, CA, per Kerr LJ, and at 440 per Stephenson LJ. See further ESTOPPEL. This rule does not apply to hire purchase: *Karflex Ltd v Poole* [1933] 2 KB 251; see HIRE PURCHASE.
3 *Biddle v Bond* (1865) 6 B & S 225 at 234 per Blackburn J.
4 *Ross v Edwards & Co* (1895) 73 LT 100, PC.
5 *Bettely v Reed* (1843) 4 QB 511 at 517 per Lord Denman CJ; *Leese v Martin* (1873) LR 17 Eq 224.
6 *Rogers, Sons & Co v Lambert & Co* [1891] 1 QB 318 at 325, CA, per Lord Esher MR. See also *Thorne v Tilbury* (1858) 3 H & N 534 where, at 539, Bramwell B and, at 540, Watson B express the opinion that the bailee may show that the bailor's title has expired since the bailment. This opinion is adopted by Lopes LJ in *Rogers, Sons & Co v Lambert & Co* supra at 328. Cf *Webb v Ireland and A-G* [1988] IR 353 (SC, Ireland) (bailee acquiring title from third party). Where a plaintiff failed to recover property from a bailee because she did not establish a gift to herself from a predecessor in title, the bailee was precluded, in proceedings by the personal representatives of the predecessor in title, from asserting against them that the property belonged to the former plaintiff: *Re Savoy Estate Ltd, Remnant v Savoy Estate Ltd* [1949] Ch 622, [1949] 2 All ER 286, CA.
7 *Rogers, Sons & Co v Lambert & Co* [1891] 1 QB 318, CA. Cf *Webb v Ireland and A-G* [1988] IR 353 (SC, Ireland).
8 Ie trespass to goods, conversion (formerly called trover), negligence so far as it results in damage to goods or an interest in goods, and any other tort so far as it results in damage to goods or an interest in goods: see the Torts (Interference with Goods) Act 1977 s 8 (1). As to the scope of the Act see TORT vol 45 para 1419.
9 See TORT vol 45 para 1477.
10 Torts (Interference with Goods) Act 1977 s 8 (1), which also states that any rule of law to the contrary (sometimes called jus tertii) is abolished.

1 See TORT vol 45 para 1477.

883. Interpleader. If a third person claims the chattel and threatens the bailee with proceedings, and the bailor nevertheless insists on his title, the bailee may interplead[1].

A bailee who forbears to interplead makes himself a party to a possibly wrongful detention by retaining the chattel for the bailor, and he must then stand or fall by the bailor's title[2]. Conversely, if he allows the third person to obtain the chattel, he may be liable to the bailor[3].

1 As to interpleader see RSC Ord 17, CCR Ord 33; and INTERPLEADER. Where there are competing claims made to goods held by a bailee, a bailee may interplead or he may invoke the procedure set out in the Torts (Interference with Goods) Act 1977 s 8 and given effect by RSC Ord 15 r 10A. See the discussion on this in *Redler Grain Silos Ltd v BICC* [1982] 1 Lloyd's Rep 435 at 438, CA, per Kerr LJ and at 440 per Stephenson LJ. As to the 1977 Act s 8 see TORT vol 45 para 1477.
2 *Wilson v Anderton* (1830) 1 B & Ad 450 at 456 per Lord Tenterden CJ.
3 *Ranson v Platt* [1911] 2 KB 291, CA.

884. Attornment. At common law, where a bailee in possession of goods attorns to a person other than his original bailor, he becomes the bailee of that person[1]. It would appear that he holds the goods as the attornee's bailee on the same terms as those on which he held them for the original bailor[2]. Subject to those terms, the attornee can recover damages from the bailee for any tort which the bailee commits against the chattel after his attornment[3].

At common law[4], the bailee who attorns is estopped from denying the attornee's title[5]. He cannot impugn the attornee's title by pleading that a superior title resides in a third party[6]. The rule applies even though the chattel comes into the bailee's possession after he has agreed to attorn; although an attornment made by a person out of possession has no immediate effect, it applies when he obtains possession[7].

As a general rule, to perfect an attornment, the goods must be specific, or there must be a specific appropriation so as to make them specific[8]. But on a sale of goods, where the seller has acknowledged the buyer's right to dispose of goods remaining in the seller's possession, the seller cannot subsequently defeat the right of a third person claiming under the buyer on the ground that, by reason of the want of any specific appropriation, no property has passed to the buyer and thus to that person[9]. Similarly, where the bailee of a seller attorns to a buyer in respect of a specified portion of an undivided parcel, he is estopped from denying the buyer's claim to the portion, notwithstanding that it has not been specifically appropriated from the parcel[10].

The common law rule that a bailee is estopped from pleading the jus tertii has been substantially abrogated by statute[11]. The defendant in an action for wrongful interference with goods[12] is entitled to show, in accordance with rules of court[13], that a third person has a better right than the plaintiff as respects all or any part of the interest claimed by the plaintiff, or in right of which he sues[14]. The bailee's estoppel may survive, however, where the attornee elects to sue otherwise than in tort[15].

1 *Hawes v Watson* (1824) 2 B & C 540; *Gosling v Birnie* (1831) 7 Bing 399; *Henderson & Co v Williams* [1895] 1 QB 521 at 529, CA, per Lord Halsbury; Palmer on Bailment (1979) Chapter 21.
2 *Leigh & Sillavan v Aliakmon Shipping Co Ltd, The Aliakmon* [1986] AC 785 at 812, [1986] 2 All ER 145 at 151, HL, per Lord Brandon of Oakbrook (obiter); *Compania Portorafti Commerciale SA v Ultramar*

Panama Inc, The Captain Gregos (No 2) [1990] 2 Lloyd's Rep 395 at 404–405, CA, per Bingham L (obiter); *H M F Humphrey Ltd v Baxter, Hoare & Co Ltd* (1933) 149 LT 603; *Britain & Overseas Tradin (Bristles) Ltd v Brooks Wharf and Bull Wharf Ltd* [1967] 2 Lloyd's Rep 51 at 60 per Widgery J (obiter); *Cremer v General Carriers Ltd* [1974] 1 All ER 1, [1974] 1 WLR 341.

3 *Henderson & Co v Williams* [1895] 1 QB 521 at 530, CA, per Lord Halsbury (in a case of conversion damages are prima facie to be estimated at the market value of the goods at the date of conversion)

4 The common law rule has been substantially abrogated by statute; see the Torts (Interference wit Goods) Act 1977 s 8 (1); text and notes 11–15 infra.

5 See the cases cited in note 1 supra.

6 See generally, as to the right to plead jus tertii, paras 1882 ante, 1889 post; and TORT vol 45 para 1477

7 *Holl v Griffin* (1833) 10 Bing 246 at 248 per Tindal CJ; *Maynegrain Pty Ltd v Compafina Bank* [1982] NSWLR 141 at 146 per Hope JA (NSW CA); revsd on another ground (1984) 58 ALJR 389, PC.

8 *Unwin v Adams* (1858) 1 F & F 312; *Tanner v Scovell* (1845) 14 M & W 28; *Laurie and Morewood v Dudi & Sons* [1926] 1 KB 223, CA.

9 *Woodley v Coventry* (1863) 2 H & C 164; cf *Ant Jurgens Margarine Fabrieken v Louis Dreyfus & Co* [1914 3 KB 40.

10 *Maynegrain Pty Ltd v Compafina Bank* [1982] 2 NSWLR 141 (NSW CA); revsd on another groun (1984) 58 ALJR 389, PC. Cf *Re London Wine Co (Shippers) Ltd* [1986] PCC 121.

11 Torts (Interference with Goods) Act 1977 s 8 (1); see para 1889 post and TORT vol 45 para 1477.

12 Ie trespass to goods, conversion (formerly called trover), negligence so far as it results in damage t goods or to an interest in goods, and any other tort so far as it results in damage to goods or to a interest in goods: see ibid s 1. As to the scope of the Act see TORT vol 45 para 1419.

13 Power to make rules is conferred by ibid s 8 (2). This power is without prejudice to any other powe of making rules of court: s 8 (3); see TORT vol 45 para 1477.

14 Ibid s 8 (1); see para 1889 post; and TORT vol 45 para 1477.

15 Ibid s 8 (1); see para 1889 post; and TORT vol 45 para 1477.

(2) ACTIONS; DAMAGES

1885. Demand. Subject to certain exceptions, in an action for wrongful detention of goods, it is necessary to show that a demand has been made for the goods[1] On the occasions when such a demand must be made, the action will lie after th bailee has wrongfully refused or failed to comply with the demand[2]. The baile cannot justify or excuse his failure to comply with the demand merely by proving that the chattel is no longer in his control or custody, or in that of anyone ove whom he can exercise control, if he parted with it without just cause[3] or negli gently lost it or allowed it to be destroyed[4]; but he is excused if he can show that hi failure to return the chattel arises from its loss or destruction, before the demand fo its return, without any default on his part[5]. If the chattel is lost or destroyed while i is wrongfully detained by him after the demand for its return, he is liable as an insurer[6].

Where, before any demand has been made, the bailee has done an act amounting to conversion of the chattel, a demand is not necessary in order to entitle the bailo to sue him[7].

1 See TORT vol 45 paras 1430, 1431; and see *Baldwin v Cole* (1704) 6 Mod Rep 212; *M'Combie v Davies* (1805) 6 East 538; *Alexander v Southey* (1821) 5 B & Ald 247 at 250 per Best J; *Jones v Dowle* (1841) 9 M & W 19; *Burroughes v Bayne* (1860) 5 H & N 296; *Pillot v Wilkinson* (1863) 2 H & C 72 (affd (1864) 3 H & C 345, Ex Ch). See also *Belsize Motor Supply Co v Cox* [1914] 1 KB 244; *Lord Churchill v Whetnall, Lord Aberconway v Whetnall* (1918) 87 LJCh 524; *Alicia Hosiery Ltd v Brown Shipley & Co Ltd* [1970] 1 QB 195, [1969] 2 All ER 504; *Howard E Perry & Co Ltd v British Railways Board* [1980] 2 All ER 579, [1980] 1 WLR 1375; *Finlayson v Taylor* (1983) 133 NLJ 720.

2 *Clayton v Le Roy* [1911] 2 KB 1031, CA, expecially at 1052 per Farwell LJ; *Miller v Dell* [1891] 1 QB 468, CA, where the action was detinue or conversion and the cause of action was held to accrue from the date of demand for documents of title fraudulently taken from the plaintiff and deposited with the defendant's predecessor in title.

3 See para 1840 ante.
4 See the Torts (Interference with Goods) Act 1977 s 2 (2); *Jones v Dowle* (1841) 9 M & W 19 at 20 per Parke B; *Reeve v Palmer* (1858) 5 CBNS 84; *Genn v Winkel* (1912) 107 LT 434 at 437, CA, per Fletcher Moulton LJ; *Lockspeiser Aircraft Ltd v Brooklands Aircraft Co Ltd* (1990) Times, 7 March. It appears that in such a case time runs against the bailor's right of action from the date when the bailee parted with possession; see para 1887 post. See also paras 1840, 1843 ante.
5 *Taylor v Caldwell* (1863) 3 B & S 826 at 838 per Blackburn J. As to the onus of proof see paras 1806, 1843 ante. See also para 1860 ante; and *Jacksons (Edinburgh) Ltd v Constructors John Brown Ltd* 1965 SLT 37.
6 *Shaw & Co v Symmons & Sons* [1917] 1 KB 799.
7 See eg *Grainger v Hill* (1838) 4 Bing NC 212; and see para 1818 ante.

1886. Measure of damages. The measure of damages in conversion is normally the value of the goods at the time of the conversion[1], together with any consequential damage flowing from the conversion which is not too remote to be recoverable in law[2].

Recoverable consequential damages may include aggravated damages[3], exemplary damages[4], and damages for inconvenience or loss of enjoyment[5] in addition to consequential monetary losses[6]. If the goods have been restored to their owner after a conversion the owner must give credit for their value and his damages must accordingly be reduced by that amount[7].

In an action for wrongful detention of goods the measure of loss is generally considered to be the same as that for conversion[8].

The measure of damages is subject to an allowance for any increase in the value of the goods due to expenditure or work on them by the defendant[9].

The plaintiff may be entitled to additional damages if the goods have risen in market value between the conversion and judgment, subject to the usual rules of mitigation[10].

The measure of damages in proceedings by a bailee against a third party in respect of the destruction of, or damage to, the chattel bailed is discussed later[11].

1 *Mercer v Jones* (1813) 3 Camp 477; *Reid v Fairbanks* (1853) 13 CB 692; *France v Gaudet* (1871) LR 6 QB 199 at 204, Ex Ch; *Solloway v McLaughlin* [1938] AC 247, [1937] 4 All ER 328, PC; *B B M B Finance (Hong Kong) Ltd v Eda Holdings Ltd* [1990] 1 WLR 409, PC; *Chubb Cash Ltd v John Crilley & Son (a firm)* [1983] 2 All ER 294, [1983] 1 WLR 599, CA, where it was held that the price reached at a subsequent sale of the converted chattel at a public auction was prima facie good evidence of its value at the date of the auction and, on the facts, good evidence of its value at the time of the earlier conversion. See generally TORT vol 45 para 1454. As to what constitutes market value see TORT vol 45 para 1460.
2 *General and Finance Facilities Ltd v Cooks Cars (Romford) Ltd* [1963] 2 All ER 314, [1963] 1 WLR 644, CA. See also *Douglas Valley Finance Co Ltd v S Hughes (Hirers) Ltd* [1969] 1 QB 738, [1966] 3 All ER 214. See further TORT vol 45 para 1454. This measure of damages is subject to an allowance for any increase in the value of goods due to expenditure or work on them by the defendant: Torts (Interference with Goods) Act 1977 s 6.
3 *Mafo v Adams* [1970] 1 QB 548 at 558, [1969] 3 All ER 1404 at 1410, CA, per Widgery LJ. See DAMAGES vol 12 para 1189.
4 *Cook v Saroukos* (1989) 97 FLR 33 (Aust FC); *Egan v State Transport Authority* (1982) 31 SASR 481 (SAust SC) (action in detinue by contractor for wrongful seizure of plant). As to the circumstances in which exemplary damages are available see *Rookes v Barnard* [1964] AC 1129, [1964] 1 All ER 367, HL; *Cassell & Co Ltd v Broome* [1972] AC 1027, [1972] 1 All ER 801, HL.
5 *Harris v Lombard New Zealand Ltd* [1974] 2 NZLR 161 at 169–170; *Millar v Candy* (1981) 58 FLR 145 (Aust); and DAMAGES vol 12 para 1165 note 6.
6 *Strand Electric and Engineering Co Ltd v Brisford Entertainments Ltd* [1952] 2 QB 246, [1952] 1 All ER 796, CA; and see para 1862 ante.
7 *Brandeis Goldschmidt & Co Ltd v Western Transport Ltd* [1981] QB 864 at 873, [1982] 1 All ER 28 at 34, CA, per Brandon LJ.

8 For the contrary argument, that the valuation to be taken is that at the time of judgment (as in the old action of detinue) see TORT vol 45 para 1454 note 3. This is unlikely to have any significance in view of the rule which allows the plaintiff to claim additional damages in conversion if there has been a rise in the market value between the date of the conversion and the date of the judgment (see TORT vol 45 para 1455).

9 See the Torts (Interference with Goods) Act 1977 s 6. See also TORT vol 45 para 1456.

10 *Greening v Wilkinson* (1825) 1 C & P 625; *Johnson v Hook* (1883) 31 WR 812; *Sachs v Miklos* [1948] 2 KB 23, [1948] 1 All ER 67, CA; *Aitken v Gardiner and Watson* [1956] OR 589, 4 DLR (2d) 119 (Can); and see TORT vol 45 para 1455.

11 See para 1889 post.

1887. Limitation of actions. An action under the Torts (Interference with Goods) Act 1977 must be brought within six years of the cause of action accruing[1]. An action in negligence is also subject to the six year limitation period from the accrual of the cause of action, except in the case of personal injuries where, in general, a three year time limit from the accrual of the cause of action, or the date of knowledge (if later), applies[2].

In the case of a conversion, the limitation period begins to run from the date of the conversion, and, subject to fraud by the defendant[3], this is so even where the owner does not become aware of the conversion until later[4]. In a case of conversion by wrongful detention alone, time runs from the refusal of a lawful demand for the return of the goods in question[5] or their equivalent.

In the case of successive conversions or detentions, time normally runs from the accrual of the cause of action in respect of the original conversion or detention[6].

Special provisions apply to the limitation of actions for damages brought under Part I of the Consumer Protection Act 1987[7].

1 Limitation Act 1980 s 2. An action may also, where appropriate, be brought in contract where there is also a six year limitation period (s 5), but the accrual of the cause of action in contract is rarely later than the accrual of the cause of action in tort. See generally LIMITATION OF ACTIONS vol 28 paras 609–616 (special periods of limitation), paras 657, 680 (general periods of limitation), para 684 (title deeds), and paras 833, 835 (property converted by a trustee). As to pleading cf LIMITATION OF ACTIONS vol 28 paras 647–656; PLEADING vol 36 para 48.

2 Limitation Act 1980 ss 11–13 (s 11A added, and s 12 amended by the Consumer Protection Act 1987 s 6 (6), Sch 1). See also the 1980 Act s 14 (as so amended) (relating to date of knowledge) and s 33 (as so amended) (discretion to extend time limit).

3 See ibid s 32 (amended by the Consumer Protection Act 1987 Sch 1 para 5); and cf LIMITATION OF ACTIONS vol 28 para 682.

4 *Granger v George* (1826) 5 B & C 149; *R B Policies at Lloyd's v Butler* [1950] 1 KB 76, [1949] 2 All ER 226. However, the limitation period may not run where the goods have been stolen from the plaintiff; see the Limitation Act 1980 s 4; and LIMITATION OF ACTIONS.

5 *Philpott v Kelley* (1835) 3 Ad & El 106; *Miller v Dell* [1891] 1 QB 468, CA. It appears that a demand and refusal is still required under the Torts (Interference with Goods) Act 1977 s 2 (2) because the section assumes that the bailee's default would formerly have given rise to an action in detinue, and such an action had to be prefaced by a demand.

6 See the Limitation Act 1980 s 3 (1); and cf LIMITATION OF ACTIONS vol 28 para 681. See also s 4, which provides a special time limit for goods which are converted by theft; and see LIMITATION OF ACTIONS.

7 See the Limitation Act 1980 s 11A (as added: see note 2 supra); and SALE OF GOODS. The Consumer Protection Act 1987 Pt I comprises ss 1–9.

(3) RIGHTS AND OBLIGATIONS AS REGARDS THIRD PERSONS

1888. Bailor's right to sue. Where there has been a sub-bailment[1] the owner has concurrent rights with the bailee against the sub-bailee; and if the owner has consented to the sub-bailment he will be bound by the terms of the sub-bailment contract².

Where under a contract of bailment the owner of a chattel has deprived himself of his right to its use or possession for a time, as in the case of hiring for reward or of pledge, he cannot during that time bring an action for the conversion³ of the chattel⁴ unless the act of conversion adversely affects his reversionary interest or his absolute property in it, such as by destroying the chattel or permanently injuring it⁵.

Where the bailee is merely a bailee during pleasure, as is the case in any gratuitous bailment⁶, or under any contract of carriage where the terms of carriage do not specifically deal with this question⁷, the bailor may, by reason of his property, sue for the conversion of the chattel a third party who wrongfully takes it out of the bailee's possession, for the property draws to itself the right of possession as an end has in fact been put to the bailment⁸.

As the bailor can at any moment demand the return of the object bailed, he may be said to have possession throughout the continuance of the bailment, for he has the right to immediate possession and by reason of this right can exercise those possessory remedies which are available to the possessor; the person having the right to immediate possession is frequently referred to in English law as being the possessor⁹.

Further, where the bailee, by a wrongful dealing with the chattel, has determined the bailment, all third persons, however innocent, who purport in any way to deal with the property in the chattel¹⁰ are guilty of conversion and liable to the bailor¹¹, unless protected by the law relating to sales in market overt¹² or by the Factors Act 1889¹³.

1 See para 1841 ante.
2 *Singer Co (UK) Ltd v Tees and Hartlepool Port Authority* [1988] 2 Lloyd's Rep 164; and see para 1841 ante.
3 *Gordon v Harper* (1796) 7 Term Rep 9. Still less can he maintain an action of trespass.
4 *Bradley v Copley* (1845) 1 CB 685 at 697 per Tindal CJ. For the same reason the purchaser of goods retained by the vendor in exercise of his lien cannot maintain trover. See TORT.
5 *Mears v London and South Western Rly Co* (1862) 11 CBNS 850; *Hall v Pickard* (1812) 3 Camp 187; *Meux v Great Eastern Rly Co* [1895] 2 QB 387, CA. The third person cannot defend himself by pleading that the injury was due to the joint negligence of himself and the bailee: *Wellwood v King Ltd* [1921] 2 IR 274, CA. The owner, however, must prove damage to his interest: *Tancred v Allgood* (1859) 4 H & N 438.
6 *Nicolls v Bastard* (1835) 2 Cr M & R 659; *Manders v Williams* (1849) 4 Exch 339. The owner may, perhaps, even maintain trespass.
7 *Gordon v Harper* (1796) 7 Term Rep 9 at 12 per Grove J. But the terms of the contract of carriage will often provide otherwise and will, if so, deprive the bailment of its character as a bailment at will: *Transcontainer Express Ltd v Custodian Security Ltd* [1988] 1 Lloyd's Rep 128 at 134–135, CA, per Slade LJ.
8 'No proposition can be more clear than that either the bailor or the bailee of a chattel may maintain an action in respect of it against a wrongdoer, the latter by virtue of his possession, the former by reason of his property': *Manders v Williams* (1849) 4 Exch 339 at 344 per Parke B. An action by one, however, is a bar to an action by the other: *Nicolls v Bastard* (1835) 2 Cr M & R 659 at 660 per Parke B.
9 See *United States of America and Republic of France v Dollfus Mieg et Cie SA and Bank of England* [1952] AC 582 at 605, 611, [1952] 1 All ER 572 at 581, 585, HL, per Earl Jowitt and Lord Porter, respectively. But cf *Transcontainer Express Ltd v Custodian Security Ltd* [1988] 1 Lloyd's Rep 128, CA.
10 *Barker v Furlong* [1891] 2 Ch 172. See *Wilson v Lombank Ltd* [1963] 1 All ER 740, [1963] 1 WLR 1294.
11 *Cooper v Willomatt* (1845) 1 CB 672; *Bryant v Wardell* (1848) 2 Exch 479; *Fenn v Bittleston* (1851) 7 Exch 152 at 159; *Loeschman v Machin* (1818) 2 Stark 311; *Consolidated Co v Curtis & Son* [1892] 1 QB 495; *North Central Wagon and Finance Co Ltd v Graham* [1950] 2 KB 7, [1950] 1 All ER 780, CA. See also *Union Transport Finance Ltd v British Car Auctions Ltd* [1978] 2 All ER 385, applying *North Central Wagon and Finance Co Ltd v Graham* supra, in which the statement in para 1818 text and note 4 ante

was approved as applying generally to bailments. See also *Chubb Cash Ltd v John Crilley & Son (a firm)* [1983] 2 All ER 294, CA. It is not certain whether a premature sale or sub-pledge by a pledgee determines the bailment within the meaning of the rule: see *Johnson (Assignee of Cumming) v Stear* (1863) 15 CBNS 330; *Donald v Suckling* (1866) LR 1 QB 585; *Halliday v Holgate* (1868) LR 3 Exch 299; and PLEDGES AND PAWNS. But if the holder of a lien wrongfully parts with the goods the bailment is determined: *Scott v Newington* (1833) 1 Mood & R 252; *Donald v Suckling* supra at 604 per Mellor J: *Mulliner v Florence* (1878) 3 QBD 484, CA.

12 See eg *Bishopsgate Motor Finance Corpn Ltd v Transport Brakes Ltd* [1949] 1 KB 322, [1949] 1 All ER 37, CA (sale in market overt by vendor in possession under hire purchase agreement; purchaser protected). As to sale in market overt see MARKETS AND FAIRS.

13 See the Factors Act 1889 s 2; and AGENCY vol 1 (2) (Reissue) paras 12, 160.

1889. Bailee's right to sue. In accordance with the general principle of law that possession gives title as against a stranger[1], the bailee of a chattel under any species of bailment may at common law sue for the tort of trespass or conversion or maintain an action for damages for the destruction of, or injury to, the chattel against the wrongdoer in all cases in which an absolute owner of a chattel may do so, and may recover in each case the same damages as he could if he were the absolute owner[2]. Thus in proceedings by a bailee against a third party in respect of the destruction of, or damage to, the chattel bailed[3], the bailee may at common law recover the full value of the chattel in respect of its destruction or the full cost of repairing any damage to it, and in addition any further damage which he may personally sustain by reason of his being deprived of its use while it is being repaired[4].

The fact that the bailee is under no responsibility to the bailor for the loss of or damage to the goods resulting from the act of the tortfeasor does not at common law avoid his right of action against him; for the common law rule that the wrongdoer cannot set up against the person in possession the jus tertii, unless he is claiming under it, is absolute, and the relation between the bailor and the bailee is immaterial[5].

The common law rule that a wrongdoer cannot plead the jus tertii in defence to an action by a bailee has now been substantially abrogated by statute[6]. The defendant in action for wrongful interference with goods[7] is entitled to show, in accordance with rules of court[8], that a third person has a better right than the plaintiff as regards all or any part of the interest claimed by the plaintiff, or in right of which he sues[9]. This provision therefore displaces the bailee's former entitlement to recover full damages from a third party wrongdoer, except where the wrongdoer elects not to plead the jus tertii, or there is an exception to the operation of the provision[10], or (perhaps) where the bailee sues otherwise than in tort[11].

A bailee who is not merely a bailee during pleasure may sue the bailor for the tort of conversion if the bailor wrongfully deprives him of the chattel[12].

1 This principle has been substantially abrogated by statute: see the Torts (Interference with Goods) Act 1977 s 8; and text and notes 6–11 infra.

2 *Burton v Hughes* (1824) 2 Bing 173 at 175 per Best CJ; *Rooth v Wilson* (1817) 1 B & Ald 59; *Croft v Alison* (1821) 4 B & Ald 590; *Raynor v Childs* (1862) 2 F & F 775; *Sutton v Buck* (1810) 2 Taunt 302; *The Winkfield* [1902] P 42, CA (where the cases are reviewed); *The Okehampton* [1913] P 173, CA. See also para 1813 ante. As to the measure of damages see paras 1846, 1886 ante.

3 For the bailor's right to bring such proceedings see para 1888 ante.

4 As to the measure of damages where the chattel is being used other than for profit see *The Greta Holme* [1897] AC 596; *Mersey Docks and Harbour Board v Marpessa (Owners)* [1907] AC 241, HL. In Admiralty cases the bailee can recover interest from the date of damage: *The Rosalind* (1920) 90 LJP 126. The court has a general power to award interest on damages: see the Supreme Court Act 1981 s 35A (added by the Administration of Justice Act 1982 s 15 (1), Sch 1 Pt I); and DAMAGES.

5 *The Winkfield* [1902] P 42, CA, overruling *Claridge v South Staffordshire Tramway Co* [1892] 1 QB 422; *Worthington v Tipperary County Council* [1920] 2 IR 233, CA. But see para 1890 note 2 post.
6 See the Torts (Interference with Goods) Act 1977 s 8 (1); TORT vol 45 para 1477.
7 Ie trespass to goods, conversion (formerly called trover), negligence so far as it results in damage to goods or to an interest in goods, and any other tort so far as it results in damage to goods or to an interest in goods: see ibid s 1 (1). As to the scope of the 1977 Act see TORT vol 45 para 1419.
8 Power to make rules is conferred by ibid s 8 (2). This power is without prejudice to any other power of making rules of court: s 8 (3).
9 See ibid s 8 (1), which also states that any rule of law to the contrary (sometimes called jus tertii) is abolished.
10 See TORT vol 45 para 1477 note 4.
11 Cf TORT vol 45 para 1477.
12 *Roberts v Wyatt* (1810) 2 Taunt 268; cf *Graig v Shedden* (1859) 1 F & F 553; *Sands v Shedden* (1850) 1 F & F 556; and see para 1850 note 5 ante.

1890. Bailee's duty to account to bailor. As between himself and the bailor, the bailee must account to the bailor for everything that he may recover from a third person beyond his own interest[1], and must therefore pay over to him any sum which he has recovered as representing the value of the chattel, its permanent deterioration, or the cost of repairing it if he has not himself repaired it. If the bailee sues, therefore, he ought in general to claim and be awarded the full damages, for then no further action can be brought by the bailor[2].

1 *Eastern Construction Co Ltd v National Trust Co Ltd and Schmidt* [1914] AC 197 at 210, PC; *The Joannis Vatis* [1922] P 92, CA; and see paras 1884, 1889 note 5 ante; and TORT vol 45 para 1477.
2 *Eastern Construction Co Ltd v National Trust Co Ltd and Schmidt* [1914] AC 197, PC; *Worthington v Tipperary County Council* [1920] 2 IR 233, CA, per O'Connor MR; and see para 1888 note 8 ante; Palmer on Bailment (1979) Chapter 4. If, however, the bailor has, before action, transferred to the wrongdoer the ownership of the goods, the bailee cannot recover more than the value of his own interest, and the wrongdoer in relying on such a transfer is not setting up a jus tertii but a jus sui: *Eastern Construction Co Ltd v National Trust Co Ltd and Schmidt* supra.

1891. Liability of bailee and bailor to third persons. At common law, the bailee alone is responsible to third parties for any injury which they may sustain by reason of his negligence or other wrongful act in the control or management of the chattel, for he is not the agent of the bailor in this connection[1].

On the other hand, if the owner of a chattel, though he places it at the disposal of someone else, retains control over it by himself or his servants, so that there is no bailment, he remains responsible to third parties for any injury or damage caused by negligence in its management[2] or by the dangerous qualities of the chattel itself; but in this latter case his liability is not dependent upon his retaining a measure of control and extends to any person he knows or ought to have contemplated might use it[3].

Whether there is a bailment or not is a question which must depend upon the particular circumstances of the case[4].

In other respects the question of liability to third parties is determined by general principles. The bailee is liable for the acts of his servants acting within the scope of their employment, but not for their unauthorised acts when acting outside the scope of their employment[5].

1 *Smith v Bailey* [1891] 2 QB 403, CA; *Gibson v O'Keeney* [1928] NI 66, CA; *Britt v Galmoye and Nevill* (1928) 44 TLR 294; *Hewitt v Bonvin* [1940] 1 KB 188, CA; *Everett's Blinds Ltd v Thomas Ballinger Ltd* [1965] NZLR 266, [1965] CLY 168 (NZ CA). Cf *Wellwood v King Ltd* [1921] 2 IR 274, CA; and EMPLOYMENT. As to the bailor's liability under the Consumer Protection Act 1987 Pt II (ss 10–19) see

SALE OF GOODS. Under the London Hackney Carriages Act 1843 the proprietor of a cab is liable for the negligence of the driver, even though the driver is not his servant but only a bailee: see *Venables v Smith* (1877) 2 QBD 279; *Smith v General Motor Cab Ltd* [1911] AC 188, HL, and cases there cited by Lord Atkinson at 192; and see ROAD TRAFFIC.

2 *Reichardt v Shard* (1914) 31 TLR 24, CA; *Samson v Aitchison* [1912] AC 844, PC; *Pratt v Patrick* [1924] 1 KB 488; *Ormrod v Crosville Motor Services Ltd (Murphie, third party)* [1953] 1 All ER 711; and see EMPLOYMENT.

3 *White v Steadman* [1913] 3 KB 340 at 347; *Griffiths v Arch Engineering (Newport) Ltd* [1968] 3 All ER 217. The bailor may have a defence to an action by the third party in respect of the defective condition of the chattel if he has given the bailee a sufficient warning about that condition: *Pivovaroff v Chernabaeff* (1978) 21 SASR 1 (S Aust SC, FC); and see *Lexmead (Basingstoke) Ltd v Lewis* [1982] AC 225, sub nom *Lambert v Lewis* [1981] 1 All ER 1185, HL; *Hurley v Dyke* [1979] RTR 265, HL. Cf *Hadley v Droitwich Construction Co Ltd* [1967] 3 All ER 911, [1968] 1 WLR 37, CA.

4 To prove a bailment, the owner must show that he had let out the chattel to a hirer and that the hirer or his agent had control over it to the exclusion of all interference with the working or management either by the owner or his agents: *Smith v Bailey* [1891] 2 QB 403, CA; *Nicholson v Harrison* (1856) 27 LTOS 56. And see para 1801 ante; Palmer on Bailment (1979) Chapter 7.

5 See eg the cases cited in para 1842 notes 1–4 ante. Generally as to liability for a servant's acts see AGENCY; EMPLOYMENT. As to liability where a servant is hired by one employer from another see *Mersey Docks and Harbour Board v Coggins and Griffith (Liverpool) Ltd* [1947] AC 1, [1946] 2 All ER 345, HL; and EMPLOYMENT.

(4) WAR DAMAGE

1892. Modification of liability in respect of war loss or damage. Certain obligations of a bailor or bailee, whether imposed by the provisions (express or implied) of a contract or by any enactment, rule of law or custom, are deemed not to extend to loss or damage by war[1]. The obligations in respect of which this exception applies are obligations to insure against loss of or damage to the goods[2]; to repair damage to the goods; to replace the goods in the event of loss; to restore the goods or deliver them up in good repair, notwithstanding such loss or damage; to continue to pay for the hire of the goods; and to pay damages or compensation for any loss of or damage to the goods[3].

A bailee is not, however, relieved from any liability for loss of or damage to goods occurring while they are being kept or transported in a manner or at a place which is contrary to the terms of any contract relating to their custody or transport[4] unless he satisfies the court that he had reasonable grounds for believing that the goods were less likely to be lost or damaged while being so kept or transported than while being kept or transported in accordance with the terms of the contract[5]. Nor is a bailee or bailor relieved of any contractual liability which is expressly related to war by the terms of the contract[6], other than, in the case of a bailee, a liability imposed by (1) a hire purchase agreement or a conditional sale agreement within the meaning of the Consumer Credit Act 1974 being (in either case) a consumer credit agreement defined by that act, or (2) a consumer hire agreement as defined by that Act[7].

1 Liability for War Damage (Miscellaneous Provisions) Act 1939 s 1 (1). For this purpose 'loss by war' and 'damage by war' mean respectively loss (including destruction) and damage caused by or in repelling enemy action, or by measures taken to avoid the spreading of the consequences of damage caused by or in repelling enemy action: s 8 (2). The onus is on the party seeking to avoid liability to establish that the loss or damage was loss or damage by war: *Re S Davis & Co Ltd* [1945] Ch 402 at 407 (goods stored in premises which were damaged by enemy action); cf *Edwards v Newland & Co (E Burchett Ltd, third parties)* [1950] 2 KB 534, [1950] 1 All ER 1072, CA (goods entrusted by bailee to third party without bailor's knowledge; third party's premises damaged by bomb; goods subsequently lost: bailee in breach of contract and liable for loss).

2 As to insurance schemes in respect of war damage to ships and aircraft cargoes under the Marine and Aviation Insurance (War Risks) Act 1952, see WAR.
3 Liability for War Damage (Miscellaneous Provisions) Act 1939 s 1 (1).
4 As to the general liability of a bailee who deals with the goods entrusted to him in an unauthorised manner see paras 1819, 1825, 1833, 1839 ante.
5 Liability for War Damage (Miscellaneous Provisions) Act 1939 s 1 (2).
6 Ibid s 1 (3).
7 Ibid s 1 (3) proviso (amended by the Consumer Credit Act 1974 s 192 (3) (a), Sch 4 Pt I para 9). See HIRE PURCHASE.

INDEX

Allotments and Smallholdings

References are to paragraph numbers; superior figures refer to notes

allotment (agricultural)—*continued*
  possession, recovery of, 39
  privately owned, 2
  provision of—
    common pasture and grazing, 33
    duties, 8
    planning permission, 9
  public purposes, for, 70
  reasonable rent, 38n[1]
  regulation of letting, 37
  rent for use of, 38
  representations by residents requiring, 8
  rules as to letting, 37
  sale or exchange of surplus land, 36
  schoolrooms, use of, 85
  size limits, 1
  sub-letting restriction, 37
  surplus land, 36
  tenancies—
    co-operatives or associations, 37, 84
    determination—
      allotment garden, 44
      applicable provisions, 43
      changes in employment status, restrictions, 43
      compensation. *See* tenant's compensation *infra*
      compulsory rights order, where, 43
      grounds, 43
      notice of, 43n[7]
    eligibility of tenants, 37n[3]
    field garden allotments, 66
    hens and rabbits, keeping of, 41
    model rules, 37n[2]
    recovery of rent and possession, 39
    rent, 38
    sub-letting, 37
    unlet allotments, 42
  tenant's compensation—
    agricultural holdings, 58
    allotment garden. *See under* allotment garden
    allotments not more than 2 acres, 59
    council lettings, 60
    councils or associations as tenants, 62
    entitlement, 46, 47
    market garden, as, 60
    presumption as to letting, 47
  transfer of land for use as, 10
  unlet, 42
  unoccupied land, use of, 10, 31
  vesting of fuel and other allotments, 71
  wardens, 63
allotment garden—
  meaning, 1
  compensation—
    adjustment, 53
    assessment and recovery, 55
    deterioration, for, 50
    Duchy land, 56
    government land, 56
    payment and receipts, 78
    royal parks, 56
    tenant, to. *See* tenant's compensation *infra*
  contributions to losses, 77
  counter-notice on determination of tenancy, 45
  deterioration, compensation for, 50
  determination of tenancy—
    applicable provisions, 43, 44
    compensation. *See* tenant's compensation *infra*

allotment garden—*continued*
  determination of tenancy—*continued*
    counter-notice procedure, 45
    excluded land, 44
    methods, 44
  duty to provide, 8
  growing crops, right to remove, 48n[5]
  landlord: meaning, 44n[2]
  landlord's compensation for deterioration, 50
  losses, government contributions to, 77
  New Forest land, lease of, 34
  notice to quit, 44
  re-entry powers, 44
  removal of improvements by tenant, 54
  resumption of possession, 45
  tenant's compensation—
    adjustment, 53
    assessment and recovery, 55
    compensation paid to outgoing tenant, 52, 54
    councils or association as tenants, 61
    disturbance, 49
    entitlement, 46, 47
    improvements, for, 48
    mortgagee, by, 51
    occupied land, 57
    payments and receipts, 78
    presumption as to letting, 47
allotment society—
  meaning, 82
  grants and allowances to, 83
  letting or sale to, powers, 37
  promotion of, 82
  schoolroom, use of, 85
allowance to allotment society, 83
annual report as to smallholdings, 119, 128
appropriation—
  allotments, land for, 29, 30
  common land, for allotments, 29, 30
  cottage holdings land, 131
  field garden allotments, 29, 68
  fuel allotments, 29, 72
  open space, for allotments, 29, 30
  town or village green, restriction, 30
auction of cottage holdings land, 138
borrowing for allotments purposes, 75
building, allotment, permitted on, 35
Charity Commissioners schemes as to fuel or field garden allotments, 73
Command Papers—
  Cmnd 4166 (allotments), 1n[9], 2n[3], 38n[1]
  Cmnd 7599 (Northfield Committee), 87n[1]
common (land), appropriation for allotments, 29, 30
compensation—
  allotment tenancies, as to. *See under* allotment (agricultural); allotment garden
  compulsory acquisition of land for allotments, 17
  compulsory hiring order, under, determination of, 21
  cottage holdings improvements, for, 139
compulsory acquisition—
  allotments, land for, 17
  field garden allotments, 68
  fuel allotments, of, 72
  smallholdings, for, restriction, 94
compulsory hiring of land for allotments. *See under* allotment (agricultural)
compulsory rights order, allotment tenancy determined by, 43

References are to paragraph numbers; superior figures refer to notes

References are to paragraph numbers; superior figures refer to notes

smallholding—*continued*
  reorganisation—*continued*
    proposals, 89
    review, 89
    subsequent reviews and proposals, 91
  sale under earlier legislation, 106
  size limits, 102
  Small Holdings and Allotments Acts 1908 to 1931 . .
    4n³
  smallholdings code, 5
  smallholdings estate: meaning, 89n³
  smallholdings land: meaning, 116n¹⁰
  succession on death, 110
  surplus land held by minister, 96
  system of, 5
  tenants, selection of, 103
  upper limit, 102
  working capital: meaning, 113n²
  year: meaning, 101n³
smallholdings authority—
  meaning, 117
  accounts, 120
  annual report, 87n¹, 119
  capital grant increases, 115
  dealings with land, powers, 95
  default powers of ministers, 125
  duties generally, 87
  equipment and improvements, powers, 111
  guarantees by, 113

smallholdings authority—*continued*
  letting of land. *See under* smallholding
  loans and guarantees by, 113
  losses, government contributions towards, 116
  management powers, 98
  plans and records, 118
  promotion of smallholdings societies, 121
  reorganisation plans. *See under* smallholding
  smallholding provided by: meaning, 113n³
smallholdings society—
  meaning, 121
  promotion of, 121
stone, gravel etc, allotment of land to highway authority
  for, 70
tenancy—
  allotment, of. *See under* allotment (agricultural)
  cottage holding, 135
  field garden allotments, 66
  smallholding. *See* smallholding (letting)
theft from allotment, 40
tools, power to provide for allotment tenants, 76
town or village green, restriction on appropriation for
  allotments, 30
unoccupied land, entry for use as allotments, 31
valuation of land compulsorily hired for allotments, 21
vesting of fuel and other allotments, 71
woodland, restriction on compulsory acquisition for
  allotments, 24

Animals

abandonment of animal, 416
acquisition of land under animal health provisions, 539
advertisement of rewards for stolen animals, 232
agent's warranty on sale of animals, 221
agistment—
  meaning, 214
  distress for rent, 480
  liability of agister, 215
  nature of contract, 214
  rights of agister, 216
agricultural land—
  meaning, 384n²
  dog worrying livestock on, 384
agricultural tenant's game rights. *See under* game rights
aircraft cleansing and disinfection under animal health
  provisions, 490
animal—
  meaning. *See* WORDS AND PHRASES
  agistment. *See* agistment
  Animal Procedures Committee, 447
  baiting, offences, 414
  bees. *See* bees
  boarding establishment. *See* animal boarding estab-
    lishment
  breeding and supply establishments, 435
  captive: meaning, 405n⁹
  carriage of—
    prevention of suffering, 413, 501
    prohibitions, 501
    statutory provisions, 501
  carriers' duties, 501
  classification, 201

animal—*continued*
  contractual restrictions on keeping, 217
  cruelty. *See* cruelty to animals
  dangerous—
    dog. *See under* dog
    strict liability for damage, 467
    wild animals, 396, 397
  destruction—
    animal health provisions. *See* animal health (slaugh-
      ter)
    carcases washed ashore, 540
    cruelty, on account of, 410, 463
    fighting dogs, 374n²⁵
    rabies control, 493
  disease. *See* animal health; rabies
  dog. *See* dog
  domestic—
    meaning, 202, 405n⁹
    absolute property in, 203
    shooting, civil liability, 238
    theft of, 229
  endangered species. *See* endangered species
  fighting—
    dogs, 374
    offences generally, 414
    films involving cruelty, 456
  game. *See* game; game rights
  health. *See* animal health
  highway trespass, liability, 474
  horse. *See* horse
  import and export—
    control generally, 247

common land—
  meaning, 474n[4]
  animals straying onto highway from, 474
compensation—
  false statements to obtain, 515
  fighting dogs, destruction of, 374
  game, damage by, 261
  killing or damaging animal, 237
  seizure of things to prevent spread of disease, 509
  slaughter—
    entitlement and valuation, 508
    export quarantine stations, 505
    false statements, 515
    insurance set-off, 508
    poultry, 522
    rabid animals, 493
    rate of compensation, 508n[1]
    withholding of compensation, 508
confidential information as to animal experiments, protection of, 450
Countryside Council for Wales, deer, licences, as to, 323n[12]
criminal proceedings—
  animal experiments, as to, 451
  animal health offences, 513
  badger setts, interference with, 357
  badgers, protection of, 357
  birds, protection of, 348
  Deer Act 1991, offences under, 331
  fighting dogs, as to, 374
  performing animals, as to, 454
  poaching—
    daytime, 272
    night, 278
    procedure, 283–285
  riding establishments, as to, 395
  wild animals, offences as to, 363
crossbow prohibition for protection of birds, 338
cruelty to animals—
  abandonment, 416
  animal: meaning, 405n[9]
  Animal Procedures Committee, 447
  appeals, 464
  application of legislation, 405
  arrest powers, 459
  badgers, 354
  baiting, 414
  breach of disqualification order, 462
  captive birds, 457
  carriage of animals, 413, 501
  causing or procuring, 408
  cockfighting instruments, possession of, 458
  court's powers, 405
  cruelty: meaning, 407
  decoy sound recordings, 457
  deprivation of ownership for, 462
  destruction of diseased or injured animals, 410
  destruction order, 463
  disqualification orders, 462
  docking and nicking of horses, 422
  dogs, 368
  driver or conductor of vehicle, production of, 460
  excepted operations, 417
  exceptions not constituting cruelty, 419
  experiments—
    medicinal tests, 453
    scientific. *See* scientific procedures *infra*
  farriery, 423
  fighting, 414
  films involving, 456

cruelty to animals—*continued*
  gassing, 425n[6]
  haulage by dogs, 421
  ill-treatment amounting to, 412
  injurious drugs or substances, 415
  intention, 407
  knackers' yards, 411
  legislation, 405n[1]
  liberation of captive birds for shooting, 457
  livestock, 424
  medicinal tests, 453
  myxomatosis, spreading of, 426
  omissions to alleviate suffering, 409
  operations, 417
  owner permitting, liability, 420
  penalties, 461
  poison or injurious drugs, 415
  poisoned grain and bait, 425
  poultry, protection of, 524
  procuring, 408
  protection of animals and birds generally, 406
  public exhibition—
    films, 456
    horses and bulls, 455
    performing animal. *See* performing animal
    scientific procedures, 444
  scientific procedures—
    admissibility of evidence as to code of practice, 452
    Animal Procedures Committee, 447
    breeding and supply establishments, 435
    codes of practice, 448, 452
    conditions—
      designation certificates, 438
      licences, in, 437
    confidential information, 450
    consultation, 436
    criminal proceedings, 451
    designation certificates, 434, 435, 438
    establishments, 434
    false statements, 449
    guidance, 448
    inspectors, 446
    killing of animals, 443
    living animal: meaning, 429n[1]
    neuromuscular blocking agents, 445
    personal licence, 432
    place: meaning, 432n[2]
    project licence, 433
    protected animals, 429
    protection of living animals, 429
    public displays, prohibition of, 444
    regulated procedures, 430
    representation as to licences etc, 440
    re-use of protected animals, 442
    search powers, 451
    suspension of licences or certificates, 441
    time limit for proceedings, 451
    unlicensed, prohibition, 431
    variation and revocation of licences etc, 439
  slaughterhouses, 411
  spring traps, 427, 428
  statutory offences generally, 405
  tethering, 418
  traps for rabbits etc, 427, 428
  unnecessary abuse, 407
  wild birds, 342
damage—
  animal, by. *See* animal (injury by, liability)
  animal, to. *See* animal (killing or injuring)
decoy sound recordings of animals in distress, 457

References are to paragraph numbers; superior figures refer to notes

References are to paragraph numbers; superior figures refer to notes

References are to paragraph numbers; superior figures refer to notes

References are to paragraph numbers; superior figures refer to notes

References are to paragraph numbers; superior figures refer to notes

Arbitration

References are to paragraph numbers; superior figures refer to notes

References are to paragraph numbers; superior figures refer to notes

References are to paragraph numbers; superior figures refer to notes

Auction

References are to paragraph numbers; superior figures refer to notes

auctioneer—*continued*
  credit or set-off, restrictions, 909
  delegation, 911
  distress, privilege from, 931
  duties to vendor—
    description of property, 916
    fiduciary—
      account, 922
      bidding for purchaser, 919
      list of, 918
      purchase by auctioneer, 920
      secret profit, 921
    goods, as to, 917
    skill and knowledge, 915
  excise licence requirements, 904
  expenses, recovery of, 923n[23]
  fiduciary duties to vendor. *See under* duties to vendor
    supra
  form of contract with vendor, 905
  fraud by, liability to purchaser, 952
  indemnity, right to, 925
  intermeddling, 928
  interpleader, 932
  joinder as defendant by purchaser, 951
  liabilities to purchaser—
    bailee, as, 953
    breach of warranty of authority, 952
    contract, on, 950
    defendant, auctioneer joined as, 951
    deposit, 948
    fraud, 952
    misrepresentation, 954
    specific performance or rescission, 951
  liability to third parties—
    conversion, 926
    duty of care, 927
    intermeddling, 928
    racial discrimination, 929
  licensing requirements, 904
  lien—
    deposit, exercise against, 948
    rights generally, 924
  limited partnerships, 902
  misdescription of goods, 956
  misrepresentation by, 910, 954
  money advanced on bill of sale, 904
  name and address, display of, 939
  negligence—
    loss of right to commission, 923n[17]
    vendor's right to damages, 915
  nuisance, 927n[2]
  oral statements by, 941
  partnerships, 902
  private treaty sales after reserve not reached, 907
  purchase by, 920
  purchaser—
    meaning, 935
    liabilities to. *See* liabilities to purchaser *supra*
    rights against, 955
  qualifications, 903
  racial discrimination by, 929
  redelivery of goods on demand, 917
  remuneration, 923
  revocation of authority, 913
  rights against purchaser—
    auctioneer suing in own name, 955
    set-off between vendor and purchaser, 955

auctioneer—*continued*
  rights against third parties—
    interpleader, 932
    possession of goods, 930
    privilege from distress, 931
  rights against vendor—
    expenses, recovery of, 923n[23]
    indemnity, 925
    lien, 924
    remuneration, 923
  secret profit, 921
  set-off between vendor and purchaser, effect of, 955
  stakeholder, deposit held as, 909, 948
  termination of authority, 912
  third parties. *See* liability to third parties; rights against
    third parties *supra*
  unauthorised representations, 910
  undisclosed principal, liability to purchaser, 950
  vendor—
    agency, 906
    authority. *See* authority *supra*
    avoidance of contract where bidding agreement, 946
    bidding by, 940
    duties to. *See* duties to vendor *supra*
    form of contract with, 905
    loss of deposit, liability, 949
    rights against. *See* rights against vendor *supra*
    withdrawal of authority, 913
  See also auction
authority of auctioneer. *See under* auctioneer
bailee, auctioneer's duties as, 917, 953
bill of exchange given by auctioneer partner, 902n[3]
cattle—
  meaning, 938n[2,6]
  auction, control provisions, 938
code of practice at auctions, 904
commission, auctioneer's. *See under* auctioneer
conditions of sale at auction, 935
conspiracy as to mock auction, 942
consumer safety, auctioneer's liability, 958
contract, signature by auctioneer, 914
conversion of property by auctioneer. *See under* auctioneer
criminal conviction, prohibition from auction on account of, 945
criminal offences by auctioneer. *See under* auction
dealer—
  meaning (auction), 944n[5]
  bidding agreements, 944
  convicted persons prohibition, 945
  purchasing on joint account, 944
delegation by auctioneer, 911
deposit as to auction sales. *See under* auction
distress, goods on auctioneer's premises, 931
endangered species, auction of, 960
excise licence as to auction sales, 904
exclusion clauses as to auction sales, 935
expenses, auctioneer's right to recover, 923n[23]
export licence, goods sold at auction, 904
firearm, auction provisions, 961
firearms certificate, auctioneer's exemption, 904
fraud—
  auctioneer's liability to purchaser, 952
  bidding at auction, 944
hallmarking offences by auctioneer, 957
indemnity of auctioneer, 925

References are to paragraph numbers; superior figures refer to notes

Aviation

References are to paragraph numbers; superior figures refer to notes

References are to paragraph numbers; superior figures refer to notes

aircraft—*continued*
  detention—
    customs and excise officer, by, 1226n³
    infringement of patents etc, 1339
    powers, 1339
    unpaid air navigation services charges, 1380
    unpaid airport charges, 1183
  disembarkation of offenders, 1676
  display authorisation, 1429
  distress, urgency etc signals, 1486
  documents—
    meaning, 1183n¹⁰
    breach of conditions in, 1424
    CAA's power to vary etc, 1422
    detention where unpaid airport charges, 1183
    ministerial power to vary etc, 1423
    offences, 1425
    penalties for flying without, 1416n³,¹⁰
    preservation and delivery, 1409
    prohibition of flight without, 1415
    records to be kept, 1417
    UK registered aircraft, to be carried on, 1416
  dropping of articles from, 1467
  drunkenness on, 1457
  embarkation cards for non-British citizens, 1229
  emergency instructions for passengers, 1312
  endangering safety of, 1668, 1669
  engine emissions. *See* aircraft engine emissions certificate
  equipment—
    emergency use, 1312
    inspection for airworthiness, 1313
    installation and storage, 1312
    navigation, 1317
    radio. *See* radio equipment *infra*
    statutory provisions, 1312
  excepted areas as to disease control, 1230
  exits and doors, obstruction of, 1427
  firearms and explosives, prohibition, 1670
  flight—
    meaning, 1091n³
    See also flight
  flight data recorders, 1414
  foreign—
    accident investigation, 1508, 1509
    aerodrome operating minima, 1444
    restriction of access to, 1005
  foreign countries, flights over, 1472
  heavier than air, examples, 1269
  hijacking, 1666
  hire purchase generally, 1332
  hovercraft as, 1270n³
  imported, Multilateral Agreement as to airworthiness, 1017n⁵
  infestation and fumigation, 1231
  inspection for aviation security, 1258
  instrument landing system, 1321n¹⁵
  Isle of Man, extension of Air Navigation Order, 1265
  landing approach in bad weather, 1445
  landing cards for non-British citizens, 1229
  lifejackets etc, provisions as to, 1312
  light, flight after repair etc 1330n⁴
  lighter than air, examples, 1269
  log books, statutory provisions, 1315
  low flying. *See* flight (minimum height)
  maintenance—
    radio equipment, 1320
    See also overhaul and repair *infra*

aircraft—*continued*
  maintenance review certificate. *See* maintenance review certificate
  manufacturer's liability, 1275
  marking of exits, 1314n⁴
  military. *See* military aircraft
  minimum flying height. *See under* flight
  minimum navigation performance, 1317
  modification. *See* overhaul and repair *infra*
  mortgage—
    discharge of, 1334
    inspection of register, 1334
    priority, 1335
    priority notice, 1334
    registration, 1334
    statutory provisions, 1334
  movement limitation, 1197
  movement on land. *See* aerodrome (traffic rules)
  movement on water. *See* sea collision rules *infra*
  nationality and registration, 1267
  noise and vibration. *See under* aerodrome
  noise certificate—
    meaning, 1305n¹
    aircraft required to have, 1306
    exemptions, 1305
    issue of, 1307
    necessity for, 1305
    offences, 1311
    prevention of flight without, 1310
    revocation etc, 1309
    validity, 1308
  non-power driven, examples, 1269
  operator—
    meaning, 1091n¹, 1340
    accident notification, 1510
    air navigation services charges, 1378
    breach of statutory duty, 1681, 1682
    certificates, 1341, 1342
    charterer as, 1336
    civil liability. *See under* civil aviation
    fatigue of crew, duties, 1367
    loading instructions, 1432
    noise and vibration, duties, 1186
    production of documents, 1419
    public transport. *See under* public transport aircraft
    search of aircraft, directions as to, 1246
  overhaul and repair—
    certificate of release to service, 1325n²
    consultation on standards, 1328
    contractual obligations, 1324
    installation of equipment after, 1329
    issue and preservation of certificates, 1331
    liability to third parties, 1325
    lien for repairs, 1326
    light aircraft, 1330n⁴
    negligence, 1325
    prohibition of flights, 1330
    regulations as to, 1327
  owner—
    breach of statutory duty, 1681, 1682
    civil liability. *See under* civil aviation
    liability where passenger refused entry to UK, 1229
    third party damage on surface, liability, 1686
  parachuting from, 1468
  permissions etc, Secretary of State's powers to vary etc, 1423

References are to paragraph numbers; superior figures refer to notes

References are to paragraph numbers; superior figures refer to notes

Bailment

References are to paragraph numbers; superior figures refer to notes

References are to paragraph numbers; superior figures refer to notes

Words and Phrases

Words in parentheses indicate the context in which the word or phrase is used

References are to paragraph numbers; superior figures refer to notes

References are to paragraph numbers; superior figures refer to notes

References are to paragraph numbers; superior figures refer to notes

place—
  (animal experiments), 432n[2]
  destination, of (aircraft), 1545n[6]
  infected, 496
planning decision, 1116n[4]
pledge, 1881
pleuro-pneumonia (animals), 507n[5]
pony—
  (export), 506n[9]
  registered, 506n[20]
poor allotment, 64
poultry (animal health), 517
poundbreach, 481
precision approach, 1441n[7]
premises, specified (endangered species), 244n[4]
prescribed area (protection of birds), 344n[4]
principal council (airport), 1042n[2]
principal place of business (carrier), 1545n[3]
private, flight, 1274
procedure, regulated (animal experiments), 430
proposed smallholding, 102n[17]
protected animal (scientific procedures), 429
public airport company, 1111
public place (fighting dog), 374n[10]
public transport aircraft, 1272
puffer (auction), 940n[4]
purchaser (auction), 935
purpose, industrial, 44n[11]
qualification—
  (veterinary surgeon), 542n[2]
  Commonwealth, 542n[2]
  foreign, 542n[2]
  recognised European, 553n[1]
quilt (bees), 529n[6]
rabbit hole, 428n[3]
rabies virus, 494n[4]
railway company (animal health), 501n[27]
range, runway visual, 1441n[6]
rateable occupation, 31n[2]
rating (personal licence), 1068n[1]
reasoned award, 708
recklessness (criminal damage), 234n[8]
recognised European qualification (veterinary surgery), 553n[1]
registered—
  baggage, 1562n[1]
  pony, 506n[20]
regulated procedure (animal experiments), 430
relevant—
  activities (airport), 1162n[8]
  authorities (civil aviation), 1127n[3]
  constable (aerodrome), 1239n[8]
  event (endangered species), 244n[5]
  overseas territory (aviation), 1080n[13], 1344n[13]
remedy-barring clause, 652n[6]
rental value (unoccupied land), 31n[21]
reportable—
  accident, 1504
  occurrence (aircraft), 1496
reputed manor, 294n[1]
restricted zone (aerodrome), 1245n[4]
retail trade or business, 933n[3]
reward (air transport), 1092n[6], 1533n[2]
riding establishment, 393
right or interest in property, 236n[4]
road traffic enactments, 1241n[1]
rotorcraft, 1269

ruminating animal, 503n[1]
runway visual range, 1441n[6]
safety signal, 1486n[8-10]
sanitary airport, 1107
scheduled international air service, 1004n[1]
scientific authority (endangered species), 242n[2]
Scott v Avery clause, 635n[1]
seaplane, 1217n[2]
season, close, 290
serious injury (air accident), 1504n[4]
service—
  air traffic control, 1394n[1]
  contract for the supply of, 1863
  ordinary (agriculture), 260n[8]
services, air navigation, 1371n[2]
sheep, 405n[9]
shop—
  (auction), 933n[3]
  pet, 398n[1]
signal—
  distress, 1486n[1-3]
  marshalling, 1213n[5]
  safety, 1486n[8-10]
simulated instrument flight, 1474n[1]
small aircraft, 1264n[13]
Small Holdings and Allotments Acts 1908 to 1931. . 4n[2]
smallholding—
  (generally), 4
  creation of new, 89n[11]
  existing, 4
  proposed, 102n[17]
  provided by a smallholdings authority, 113n[3]
smallholdings authority, 117
smallholdings estate, 89n[3]
smallholdings land, 116n[10]
smallholdings society, 121
snare, 289n[2]
society—
  (Agricultural Land (Utilisation) Act 1931), 82n[1]
  allotment, 82
  smallholdings, 121
special VFR clearance, 1406n[12]
special VFR flight, 1398n[8]
species—
  dangerous, 467
  endangered, 241n[1]
specified improvements (cottage holding), 139n[1]
specified premises (endangered species), 244n[4]
springes, 308n[8]
staff, operating (aircraft), 1438n[4]
stamps, trading, 1850n[13]
standard scale (criminal penalties), 1044n[6]
state aircraft, 1003n[2]
station, aeronautical radio, 1435n[4]
statutory undertaker (civil aviation), 1144
step in proceedings, 627
stop for non-traffic purposes, 1004n[2]
stores (aircraft), 1221n[3]
sub-bailee, 1841
surgery, veterinary, 541
take-off (aircraft), 1685n[5]
taking (game), 290n[1]
territory of a state, 1003n[1]
time, flight, 1367n[9]
town or village green, 474n[6]
trading stamps, 1850n[13]
train (performing animal), 454n[2]

References are to paragraph numbers; superior figures refer to notes

ORDER NO: P	55976
DATE:	03/01/2006
SUPPLIER:	Steidl

t.p.s:	240 x 200mm up
Extent:	160pp
	3/3 text and illustrations
Paper:	170gsm Pheonix Xantur
Binding:	10 x 16pps
cloth:	
endpapers:	140gsm plain laid paper
PLC:	5/0 130gsm woodfree gloss art, matt laminate one side only